70 YEARS at the MOVIES

70 YEARS at the MOVIES

From Silent Films to Today's Screen Hits

Edited by Ann Lloyd
Consultant Editor David Robinson

CRESCENT BOOKS
New York

Macdonald Orbis
© 1982 Orbis Publishing Limited
Reassignment of copyright © 1988
Macdonald & Co (Publishers) Ltd

A member of Maxwell Pergamon
Publishing Corporation plc

This 1988 edition published by
Crescent Books, distributed by
Crown Publishers Inc.,
225 Park Avenue South,
New York, New York 10003,
by arrangement with Macdonald & Co.
(Publishers) Ltd, London & Sydney.

ISBN 0-517-66213-2

Typeset by Servis Filmsetting Ltd
Printed and bound in Yugoslavia
by Mladinska Knjiga
h g f e d c b a

Editor
Ann Lloyd
Consultant Editor
David Robinson
Senior Sub Editors
Martyn Auty, Graham Fuller, Dan Millar
Research Consultant
Arnold Desser
Picture Researchers
Dave Kent, Liz Heasman
Research
Sally Hibbin, Paul Taylor, Julian Petley
Designers
Ray Kirkpatrick, Richard Burgess, Wayne
Léal, Clair Lidzey
Indexer
Alexandra Corrin

Abbreviations used in text
add: additional; **adv:** advertising; **anim:**
animation; **art dir:** art direction; **ass:**
assistant; **assoc:** associate; **chor:**
choreography; **col:** colour process; **comm:**
commentary; **cont:** continuity; **co-ord:** co-
ordination; **cost:** costume; **dec:** decoration;
des: design; **dial:** dialogue; **dial dir:** dialogue
direction; **dir:** direction; **doc:** documentary;
ed: film editing; **eng:** engineer; **ep:** episode;
exec: executive; **loc:** location; **lyr:** lyrics;
man: management; **mus:** music; **narr:**
narration; **photo:** photography; **prod:**
production; **prod co:** production company;
prod sup: production supervision; **rec:**
recording; **rel:** released; **r/t:** running time;
sc: scenario/screenplay/script; **sd:** sound; **sp
eff:** special effects; **sup:** supervision; **sync:**
synchronization; **sys:** system. Standard
abbreviations for countries are used. Most
are self-evident but note: A = Austria;
AUS = Australia; GER = Germany and West
Germany after 1945; E.GER = East
Germany.

CONTRIBUTORS

Gilbert Adair
Lindsay Anderson
Roy Armes
Martyn Auty

Geoff Brown

James Cameron-Wilson
Charlotte Chandler
Peter Cowie

Richard Dyer

Barry Edson
Phil Edwards
Lotte H. Eisner
Derek Elley
Allen Eyles
Olivier Eyquem

Joel Finler
Graham Fuller

Alan Lovell

Derek Malcolm
Roger Manvell
Colin McArthur
Rakesh Mathur
Tom Milne
Don Minifie
Ivor Montague
Sheridan Morley

David Overbey

Chris Peachment
Julian Petley
Jim Pines
Derek Prouse
Tim Pulleine

Jeffrey Richards
David Robinson

Dennis Gifford

Phil Hardy
Ray Harryhausen
Nina Hibbin
Sally Hibbin
Peter Howden

Steve Jenkins
Ian Johns

Michael Kerbel
George Robert Kimball
Gunter Knorr
John Kobal
Karol Kulik

John Francis Lane
Antonin Liehm
Jack Lodge

Jonothan Rosenbaum
Richard Roud

Barry Salt
Richard Schickel
Colin Schindler
Adrian Sibley
Brian Sibley
Neil Sinyard
David Stratton
Philip Strick
Martin Sutton

John Russell Taylor
Bertrand Tavernier
Richard Taylor
David Thomson
Adrian Turner

Marc Wanamaker
Sheila Whitaker
David Will
Ken Wlaschin
Stephen Woolley

The publishers would especially like to thank
James Cameron-Wilson, Sally Hibbin, Don
Minifie, Arnold Desser, Dave Kent – and David
Robinson

CONTENTS

INTRODUCTION

In ten decades, movies have generated an awful lot of history. Defying continuing portents of the cinema's demise, films of every kind and in every language continue to pour out at the rate of tens of thousands annually. It is many years since any one person could hope to study even a fraction of the output of films, from every country of the world. Likewise, no single volume can hope to record the whole history of the film. This book sets out to review the story of the cinema as it has appeared to several generations of the audiences of the English-speaking world. It does not aim (even if such a thing were possible) to provide a comprehensive account of all the cinema industries of every part of the world. The central core of the book is essentially the story of the English-language cinema. The films of other countries have their place mainly to the extent to which they were influential on the whole general development of film art, or – like the Italian neo-realists and the French *nouvelle vague* – achieved international theatrical distribution. Even within such limits as these, of course, it is hard today for one historian to be equally competent in all periods and areas and aspects of cinema. It is for this reason that the book is the collaboration of many specialist writers, each with his own historical viewpoint.

The first section of the book deals with the origins of the cinema and the silent period. This was the most truly international era: the silent film had developed the first true universal language and created a new art of great subtlety and sophistication, which was rendered extinct, practically overnight, by the coming of sound in the late Twenties.

Even though, with sound, the cinema lost its universal language, motion pictures retain a unique quality of international communication. This comes largely from the imperialistic dominance of the American cinema. In the Twenties Hollywood built up a huge motion-picture industry. Owing its prosperity to a vast home audience, and its incomparable technical and artistic achievements to the facilities afforded by that prosperity, the Hollywood film was to retain an enviable domination of the film market in most countries of the world.

The history related in this book will show world cinema punctuated by a series of landmarks and watersheds, of which the first was the sound revolution. By the end of the Thirties, the new medium had been triumphantly mastered, along with new technical refinements, such as colour, and new styles specifically suited to the film's new possibilities, like the musical. A decade after sound came World War II, as traumatic to the cinema as it was to every other aspect of life for so large a part of the world. In the combatant countries – who included, as it happened, the world's major film producers – the film was mobilized either to tasks of propaganda or of providing escape from the psychological pressures of war.

The end of the War found both the world and the cinema much altered. The Italian cinema, impoverished but spiritually renewed, achieved a world market and exerted far-reaching effects upon film makers' perception of reality, with its 'neo-realist' style. The political division of Europe saw the birth or revival of purposeful film industries in the Eastern Socialist countries, though the first euphoria was soon to be dashed by the oppressions of the Cold War, Stalinist early Fifties.

For Hollywood, the golden age that had endured for a quarter of a century was nearing its end. The vast audience that had so reliably supported the movies was soon to be lured away by television; and changed post-war social patterns were breaking the regular week-in, week-out cinema-going habits of audiences in America and Britain too. Anti-trust legislation dismantled the old monopolistic film empires on which the studio system, that had given production methods a stream-lined assurance, depended. Perhaps worst of all, the era of Cold War paranoia, with the witch-hunts of Senator McCarthy and the House Un-American Activities Committee, robbed Hollywood of many of its finest talents, and sapped morale, with fear and panic. The turn of the Fifties was a dispiriting era for the cinema, as for the world at large.

By the mid-Fifties, Hollywood was fighting a vigorous rear-guard action, trying to define and emphasize those specific qualities in cinema that could not be emulated by television's small screen. The immediate manifestations were the gimmickry of CinemaScope, VistaVision, Cinerama, 3-D and a host of other technical novelties; but alongside this was a real sense of a re-examination of the purposes and potential of the commercial cinema.

The turn of the Sixties saw a fundamental renewal. It is never possible to assign precise causes to such a generalized revolution as occurred at this time; though part of the explanation was chronological: the generation which had learned their craft in the silent years and dominated the industry throughout the war and post-war period, had reached the period of superannuation; while a new generation who had grown up during the Thirties and Forties, when the cinema was at its most potent as a popular cultural force, were ready and eager to take over. The appellation of *nouvelle vague* – new wave – properly belongs to the extensive generation of radical, innovative, remarkable young film-makers that emerged in France in the early Sixties; but practically every country, West and East (where the end of the Stalin period had brought new relaxation and optimism) had its new wave – for example the talented group who came out of the 'Free Cinema' movement to revitalize British film.

Meanwhile too, the audience was changing. In the English-speaking countries, at least, the cinema-going public was now dominated by the very young, whose allegiance to the cinema was confirmed in the period of exceptional political concern among the young, which culminated in the turbulent year of 1968.

In the succeeding decade Hollywood was to be dominated by a new generation of directors: artists like Francis Coppola, Steven Spielberg, John Carpenter. These were mostly people who had come up not through the traditional routes from within the industry, but were the products of the university film schools. They brought to American commercial film-making a refreshingly new and wider cultural experience, and an awareness of the changed audience.

Elsewhere in the world, a characteristic of the last two decades has been the phenomenon of sudden eruptions – the emergence or renaissance of the cinema, temporary or prolonged, in different national film industries. Greece and Spain and Argentina enjoyed sudden cinematic resurgences after throwing off dictatorships; Sweden, Switzerland and Australia as the apparent result of intelligent government support; Germany and Italy as the outcome of enlightened collaboration between the former rivals of film and television. The British cinema owes its apparent renaissance, and its new standing in the international cinema of the Eighties, almost entirely to the continuity of support given to film productions by Channel 4 Television.

Even though the economics of film-making constantly become more difficult, as inflation escalates production costs while the video boom continues to diminish the audience, in terms of morale the late Eighties are optimistic. In particular, political developments in the Socialist East have permitted a new outspokenness which is already showing results in the work of new, or newly emancipated film makers, notably in Hungary, Poland and the Soviet Union itself.

The cinema moves into its second century, just before the start of the Third Millenium. The majority of those of us who wrote or will read this history might still be around to see how well equipped it will prove itself in coping with the tasks of that challenging, exciting new age.

DAVID ROBINSON

THE LIVING IMAGE

In the cinema's long pre-history, shadows danced, projected pictures
jerked into activity and scientists strove to capture the fleeting gestures of movement

Motion pictures were not so much an invention as an evolution, the confluence and culmination of a number of separate lines of research that stretched back decades, and even centuries. Men seemed always to be groping towards the kind of optical entertainment of which the cinema was to be the apogee. Myths, folklore and fiction frequently explored the theme of magic glasses in which the world may be viewed in microcosm. Long before the cinema, audiences marvelled at the shadow show and the vague images of the first magic lanterns.

The second half of the eighteenth century, however, witnessed a quite new passion for optical entertainments which was to continue practically unabated till the advent of the cinematograph, and which may be associated with the growth of popular illustrated publications as printing became cheaper.

The shadow show enjoyed an enormous vogue throughout Europe. In the 1780s a painter and theatrical designer from Alsace, Philippe-Jacques de Loutherbourg, delighted London with a show which he called the Eidophusikon. This was a theatre of effects, in which miniature scenes were animated by the cunning deployment of light and shadow.

Later in the 1780s a Scottish portrait painter,

To please the eye with novelty was the universal aim of showmen and artists – and even toy-makers

Robert Barker, took out a patent for his 'Panorama'; and Barker's vast landscape paintings, viewed on the inside of a great cylindrical building, deceived the eye with a thrillingly real *trompe-l'oeil* effect. Such works and their successors, often topical in their choice of theme and subject, were to delight London audiences for nearly seventy years. Meanwhile the public flocked eagerly to the display of realistic paintings of exceptional size, such as the 19-year-old Robert Ker Porter's opportunistically topical depiction of a famous military engagement in India, *The Storming of Seringhapatam*, which was the rage of London in 1799.

The high point of this era of the painting as show was the Diorama, launched in Paris in 1822 by Louis Jacques Mandé Daguerre – whose work on photography, 17 years later, was to make another significant contribution to the evolution of the movies. The Diorama, which was re-created in London in 1823, consisted of huge paintings in which subtle effects of lighting and transformations were produced by the ingenious management of shutters and blinds controlling the light thrown from before and behind on the part-transparent image.

The names of the Panorama and Diorama were in time borrowed to describe a different method of bringing pictures to life. In Moving Panoramas

and Dioramas, a long, continuous painting was passed through a proscenium opening, to give the impression of a constantly changing landscape – an effect anticipating the 'panoramic' (or 'pan') shot in the modern cinema.

Of all optical entertainments, the magic lantern was the most venerable and the most durable. The magic lantern – whose basic form still survives in the modern slide projector – embodies the same essential principles as every moving-picture projector: a powerful light source, concentrated by a condenser and passed through a transparent image to project an enlarged impression of that image, in all its colour and detail, on a white screen.

The magic lantern was first described by the Jesuit scientist Athanasius Kircher in 1671; but it was certainly known before that. Throughout the late seventeenth and eighteenth centuries, everywhere in Europe and beyond, itinerant showmen travelled with their lanterns to delight, astound and terrify their simple audiences. It was the *magic* lantern, and audiences thrilled to the supernatural and horrific effects that anticipated the twentieth-century preoccupation with horror films.

In the 1790s a Belgian showman, Etienne Robertson, scored a great and lasting success in Paris with his Phantasmagoria: the interior of his theatre was decorated as a Gothic chapel, and ghosts, witches and demons were projected on to the screen. Mounting the lantern on a wheeled carriage behind the translucent screen and adjusting the lens to maintain focus, Robertson made his fearsome images seem to grow or diminish, to startling effect.

Robertson's discoveries were exploited in London

Above: the first illustration of the magic lantern, in Athanasius Kircher's Ars Magna Lucis et Umbrae, *second edition, published in 1671. Below: an English triple or 'triunial' magic lantern, c.1890, about three feet high. By projecting from the three lenses on to the same screen, elaborate effects of superimposition could be created if the projectionist were skilful enough*

Above: Reynaud's Praxinoscope used a turning battery of mirrors in a rotating drum to reflect the phases of movement, giving a clear, bright image. Top left and right: a magic-lantern slide designed to produce the illusion of movement when projected on the screen; the techniques of the shadow show are borrowed – the articulated figures are cut out of thin brass and operated by levers. Above right: Plateau's Phenakistiscope, 1833. The spectator spun the disc in front of a mirror, viewing the reflected images through the slots. Right and centre right: a magic-lantern show in the home, c.1830, shown in a 'dioramic' print which produces a realistic lighting effect when illuminated from behind

by another showman, Niemiec Philipstahl. Rival lanternists developed other refinements, such as Henry Langdon Childe's effects of dissolving or superimposing images projected from two separate lanterns.

The magic lantern reached the height of sophistication in England in the late nineteenth century. English opticians developed magic lanterns, gleaming with the splendour of brass and polished mahogany, of such technical complexity that they required teams of people to operate them and whole libraries of explanatory literature as guides to their proper management.

From an early stage, showmen tried to give their audiences the extra thrill of movement on the screen. A slide pushed through the projector could give a persuasive impression of a procession of figures moving across the picture. Ingenious arrangements of levers and ratchets to manipulate or rotate circular glasses could produce mechanical movements in the pictures on the slides. Eyes could be made to roll, limbs to change position, fish to swim around a tank.

In the 1860s and 1870s, a more sophisticated and perfect means of producing the illusion of movement suggested itself. In the first third of the nineteenth century, physicists, including Michael

Faraday and Peter Mark Roget, had been studying a phenomenon already observed since classical times, persistence of vision. The retina of the eye appears to retain an impression for a fraction of a second after the image producing that impression has been removed. One easy illustration of this is the effect produced if a point of light – a pocket torch, for instance – is rapidly revolved in the dark, whereupon the eye receives the illusion of a continuous circle of light.

In 1833, quite independently of each other, two physicists – Joseph Plateau in Brussels and Simon Stampfer in Vienna – developed a toy to demonstrate this principle. Around the circumference of a disc were drawn a dozen little pictures representing successive phases of a continuing action. Slots were cut out between the pictures. When the disc was revolved rapidly, facing into a mirror, and the reflection was viewed through the slots as they passed before the eyes, the effect presented to the eyes was not a series of pictures but a single image in movement.

The device was quickly popularized as an instructive toy, the Phenakistiscope, and in time refined and varied. The Zoetrope, which came into vogue in the 1860s, replaced the system of disc and mirror by a hollow, open-topped drum, pierced with slots along its edge, around the inside of which were placed strips of paper printed with the appropriate series of phase drawings. In 1877, the Frenchman Emile Reynaud replaced the slots – the equivalent of the shutter in a modern movie projector – by a prismatic arrangement of mirrors in the centre.

When, in the 1850s and 1860s, the rotating disc of the Phenakistiscope was adapted to the magic lantern, flickering motion pictures could be cast

Far left: a Zoetrope manufactured in London by H.G. Clarke, c.1860. Left: the single moving image in the Zoetrope that the viewer saw by looking through the slots as the drum revolved. Below: the camera obscura, *from a mid-19th-century engraving. The viewers in the darkened chamber saw an image of the outside scenery projected, through an arrangement of lens and mirror, onto a table-screen*

onto a screen. In 1892, Reynaud's Théâtre Optique adapted the principles of the Praxinoscope, Reynaud's own invention, to project on to the screen what were virtually the first cartoon films.

One element was still missing. All these early moving-picture devices required the painstaking *drawing* of the images to be animated. But in 1839, with the perfection of Daguerre's Daguerreotype process in France and Henry Fox Talbot's Calotype (later Talbotype) in England, photography became a practical technique.

In the very early days of photography, Plateau suggested that the Daguerreotype and the Phenakistiscope could be combined; and in the 1860s and 1870s, there were a number of patents for the use of photographs in Zoetropes or similar devices. Henry R. Heyl's Phasmatrope, for instance, demonstrated in Philadelphia in 1870, gave movement to series of photographs obtained by a painful process of positioning models for each successive phase of action. The problem that thwarted all these early attempts was how to take a series of photographs in a succession rapid enough to capture the individual phases of the action as they actually took place.

The problem was eventually to be solved by a number of scientists and photographers who initially had no particular interest in creating moving pictures, but simply sought means to analyse human and animal movement for the purposes of scientific study. Eadweard Muybridge, an English photographer who spent most of his active life in the United States, arrived in 1878 at a brilliant solution with a battery of cameras which were triggered – at first mechanically, eventually electrically – as a moving person or animal passed before them. Muybridge added to this considerable achievement when in 1879 he reconstructed the movements by projecting a disc of drawings,

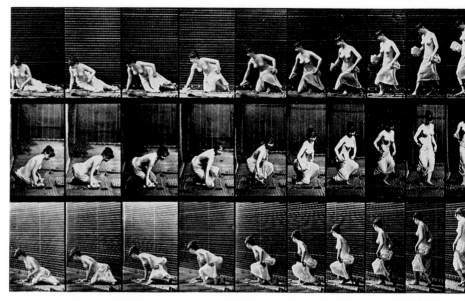

Above: a woman sitting down, photographed synchronously from three points of view by Muybridge at the University of Pennsylvania, c.1887–88. Below: Marey's photographic gun, 1882, could record phases of movement on a rotating photographic plate – the flight of a heron, for example (bottom)

closely based on the photographic images, in series to create an animated picture on the screen. The picture could be slowed down to show the details of motion. This development of the projecting Phenakistiscope was known as the Zoopraxiscope.

In Europe, Muybridge met Etienne Marey, a physiologist who had long experimented with graphic methods of recording animal and bird movement, and contemporaneously with Muybridge was applying photography to his work. Marey noted the example of the astronomer Jules Janssen, who in 1874 had succeeded in recording the passage of the planet Venus across the face of the

Animal locomotion was a challenge to science and a tricky puzzle to test the photographer's art

sun by means of a 'photographic revolver'. Shaped like a gun, this ingenious camera used a single circular plate, which revolved each time the shutter was opened, to expose one small area of its sensitized surface.

On much the same lines, Marey by 1882 had contrived a photographic gun (*fusil photographique*) which was capable of taking 12 individual photographs in one second. In 1885 in the USA, George Eastman perfected his paper roll film, which became very popular for still photography when he brought out a Kodak camera to use it in 1888. This development gave a new direction to Marey's experiments, and brought the motion-picture camera a considerable step nearer. Marey's Chronophotographe of 1888 used a continuous strip of paper film to record a sequence of individual photographs. When Eastman's celluloid roll film appeared in 1889, he promptly began to use that. In 1893, he suggested the construction of a projector to show the individual images he had recorded as a continuous action.

Marey's own assistant, Georges Demenÿ, in 1892 patented his Phonoscope, which used a sophisticated form of the Phenakistiscope to project a living photographic portrait on the screen. By this time, a great many other inventors, rich and poor, scientists and dabblers, visionaries and realists, had recognized the possibilities of a camera that would analyse movement and a projector that would reconstitute it on a screen.

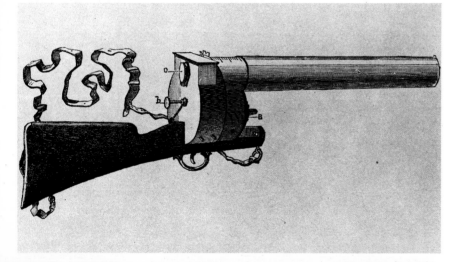

Seeing is believing
Special effects in the early years

By 1896 Méliès was making the first of his trick films. By 1899 G.A. Smith was using a primitive montage technique. By 1900 reverse-motion printing had been achieved. So even by the end of the nineteenth century the technical skills were being learned and applied, and some have remained almost unchanged to this day

Although the programme of Lumière films that made up the first public film show in 1895 included the first fictional work, *L'Arroseur Arrosé* (Watering the Gardener), Louis Lumière and his company did not develop that side of film-making further, but concentrated on the production of actuality films. The workers at the Edison company who were making films for the Edison Kinetoscope peep-show machine, also neglected attempts at narrative in favour of recording music-hall acts and other pre-existing documentary material filmed outdoors. Nevertheless, the first Edison products did include one significant staged item. *The Execution of Mary, Queen of Scots*, made in 1895.

In this film the illusion of the Queen's head being struck off is created by stopping the camera before the axe falls and substituting a dummy for the actress kneeling at the block, then restarting the camera and continuing the action of decapitation. The two separate parts were later spliced together to give what would appear to be one continuous shot – were it not for the slight changes in position of some of the by-standing actors while the camera was stopped and the substitution made. Since many of the Edison Kinetoscope films were used for ordinary projection by the first cinema exhibitors in Europe and elsewhere, it seems quite likely that *The Execution of Mary, Queen of Scots* gave Georges Méliès the clue as to how to carry out his cinematic conjuring tricks when he took up film-making a year later.

Méliès' magical movies

Méliès, who had abandoned his father's shoe factory in 1888 for the staging of miniature spectacles of conjuring and illusionism in the Théâtre Robert-Houdin which he had bought in Paris, acquired a projector from Robert W. Paul in London after seeing the first Lumière show. He had a camera built to the same mechanical design as the projector, and began producing films that were direct imitations of the first films made by Lumière and R.W. Paul. Up to this point everybody's films had been restricted in length to the 65 or 80 feet strips in which Eastman Kodak and other manufac-

turers produced the film, but Méliès' *Sauvetage en Rivière* (1896, Rescue on the River) – an imitation of R.W. Paul's earlier *Up the River* (1896) – was made up of two parts, sold separately, each 65 feet long.

Towards the end of 1896, Méliès made the first of the trick films that created his fame. This was *Escamotage d'une Dame chez Robert-Houdin* (The Vanishing Lady), and it used the same device as *The Execution of Mary, Queen of Scots* but in the service of a magical effect. In it a woman was changed into a skeleton and back again by stopping the camera and substituting one for the other. It is even questionable

whether Méliès was the first to use double exposure and photography against a black background, since G.A. Smith was also using these techniques at the same time in England, though it is certain that the Frenchman did the most striking things with them. In late 1898 he made *Un Homme de Tête* (The Four Troublesome Heads) in which the combination of the two devices allowed disconnected parts of the body to move round the set. After that date these methods, in combination with the 'stop-camera' effect, were his basis for large numbers of increasingly elaborate illusions.

Since trick films turned out to be merely a

Right: poster for Méliès' magic show at the Théâtre Robert-Houdin

Above: La Lune à un Mètre *(left to right), in which the astronomer falls asleep at work, dreams of a man-eating moon and an elusive goddess, and wakes a different man!*

passing fashion in the long view of history, Georges Méliès' most important contribution is that he led the way to making longer films made up of many shots. The earliest example of this was *La Lune à un Mètre* (1898, The Astronomer's Dream), closely based on one of the miniature fantastic shows that he had previously staged in his theatre. As such it indicates how not only *his* films, but also those of other film-makers of the early years were frequently indebted to the stage for their subjects.

La Lune à un Mètre was made up of three scenes, representing, first, 'The Observatory' in which an aged astronomer looks at the moon through a telescope and then falls asleep; next, 'The Moon at One Metre' in which the moon descends from the sky and swallows him up; and, lasfly, 'Phoebe' in which he meets the goddess of the moon. The second sequence and the beginning of the third were intended to be understood as the dream of the astronomer who wakes up in the middle of the final scene

when the goddess he is chasing vanishes by a stop-camera trick effect.

This was the first of a long line of films made over the next couple of decades that used the device of a dream story turning back to reality at the crucial moment, but the most important thing about *La Lune à un Mètre* was that the whole idea was not immediately apparent from the film itself. This was because there were only small changes made in the decor between one shot and the next, so that there was no way for the viewer immediately to realize the difference between what took place when the astronomer was awake and asleep. Since films in those days were nearly always shown with an accompanying commentary by the showman who projected them (just like the earlier lantern slide shows), this was not such a great handicap, but Méliès must have felt that the way he had treated the matter was not ideal, for in his next long fantasy film he joined all the scenes by dissolves, just as was the practice in slide shows.

He continued to put dissolves between all the shots in all his films ever afterwards – even when the action moved straight from one shot to the next without a time-lapse. *La Lune à un Mètre* was still not a very long film, being only

three times the standard 65 feet (195 feet or 3 minutes running time), but in 1899 Georges Méliès moved on to films that lasted about 10 minutes and were made up of many scenes. The most important of these was *L'Affaire Dreyfus* (1899, The Dreyfus Affair), which restaged the recent events surrounding the trial of Captain Dreyfus in front of sets made of painted canvas.

Méliès had begun making 'reconstructed actuality' films as early as 1897, but those depicted unconnected events in the war between Greece and Turkey in single scenes that were sold separately. Although all the action in *L'Affaire Dreyfus* was still isolated incidents with no scene directly leading to another, it was sold as one film. Moreover, in one respect some of the staging looked forward to future developments. For the most part the actors were far from the camera and miming broadly – as was always the case at that time – but in showing an attack on Dreyfus' lawyer in the street, the framing and the way the passers-by move into the picture recall the look of actuality shots of street scenes. And when a brawl develops between pro- and anti-Dreyfus journalists in a courtroom, the action moves up close to the camera and past it in the way that was shortly to become standard for handling violent behaviour. It may be that these features were accidental rather than intentional, for Méliès himself did not develop them, but continued with his pantomime-like stagings of fantasy and his trick films.

Thrills of speed

One special style of actuality filming had a minor part to play in the evolution of the standard form of cinema that is now all too familiar. Of the large numbers of actuality films that already filled the producers' catalogues by 1898, most merely duplicated the kind of exotic and picturesque subjects – Spanish scenes, the pyramids of Egypt – that appeared on the cards of the stereoscopic viewers lying in a thousand front parlours. Yet there *was* one purely filmic variety of the travelogue shot. This was the 'phantom ride', which was produced by fixing a film camera on the front of a railway engine running along a suitable stretch of track. All

Left: the courtroom fight from L'Affaire Dreyfus. *Opposite page, far right: an early use of the inset shot – the children are asleep as Santa Claus makes his call*

the film-makers were producing these from 1898 onwards, but G.A. Smith – one of the many Englishmen with photographic businesses who turned to motion pictures – found a novel use for them.

In 1899 he made a film called *The Kiss in the Tunnel*, which was in essence a one-line joke of the kind that appeared in that other major source of early film content, the cartoons or comic strips of the pre-cinema period. The scene G.A. Smith shot showed the interior of a railway compartment with a single man and woman sitting on opposite seats. Nothing but blackness is visible through the windows of the compartment. Then the man stands up, takes off his hat and kisses the lady, who, after a token show of resistance, returns the embrace.

Although this was all there was to the film as it was sold, the maker's instruction to buyers was to splice a 'phantom ride' taken from a train entering and leaving a tunnel onto the beginning and end of the scene, and this is indeed the form in which the film exists

Left: The Kiss in the Tunnel (*top to bottom*) *using the 'phantom ride' technique to amuse the audience of the day: train enters tunnel; man kisses girl; train leaves tunnel*

today. Thus the complete *The Kiss in the Tunnel* contained a continuous action – both seen and implied – stretching across the cuts between the three shots, and when the film was restaged and sold under the same title by Bamforth and Company of Holmfirth, Yorkshire in 1900, this point became even more obvious. In this version the kissing scene was preceded and concluded by shots taken from the sides of the tracks, which actually showed the train itself entering and leaving the tunnel. This kind of copying with interesting variations was extremely common in the first decade of the movies, and formed the main pattern for the evolution and development of film form.

Shooting with sophistication

It was G.A. Smith who also invented the technique of breaking down a sequence into more than one shot or, to look at it another way, of making cuts within a scene, keeping continuity of action across them. He first did this in *Grandma's Reading Glass* (1900), showing a little boy playing with the large magnifying glass which his grandmother (who is also present in the scene) uses to read with. As the child looks at a newspaper, a bird in a cage, his grandmother's eye and so on, there is a cut to a

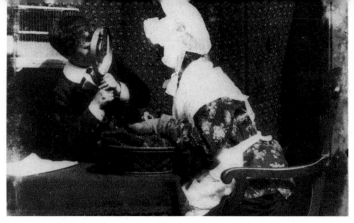

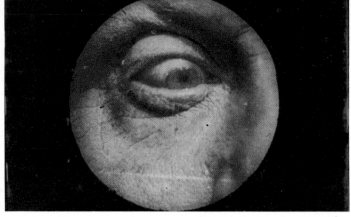

Above: on looking through Grandma's Reading Glass . . . *he sees grandma (right). Below right: the castle collapses at a touch but then re-forms in* The House That Jack Built

big close-up of each of the objects framed in a circular black vignette mask before the camera moves back to the more distant shot of the boy as he turns to look at something else.

Other innovations by G.A. Smith in these first years included the use of a second scene (inset within the main scene) to show what one of the characters was dreaming or thinking about, as in his *Santa Claus* of 1898. Here, two little children who have just been put to sleep on Christmas Eve have a dream of Santa on the rooftop climbing down into the chimney, and this dream is shown within a circular vignette in the top corner of the picture of their bedroom. This device was yet another taken over from the narratives of lantern slide shows, where it was used in the same way for the same purpose, and from that point onwards it became standard practice in films.

An even better example of Smith's technical mastery is given by *The House That Jack Built* (1901). The use of reverse motion in the cinema had existed from the outset, when it was achieved by the simple expedient of cranking the film backwards through the projector after it had been cranked through forwards. The Lumière film *Démolition d'un Mur* (1895, Demolition of a Wall) had always been a favourite for this treatment, and audiences had been fascinated to see the fallen wall rebuild itself. Smith decided to make a miniature version of the effect in permanent form, and he did it the hard way. In *The House That Jack Built* a little girl builds a castle of toy building blocks,

Below: in Smith's Let Me Dream Again *(1900, left to right) the changes of scene appear to follow without a break as the husband dreams of happier times*

and then a boy who is watching knocks them over. After a title announcing 'Reversed', the action appears in reversed motion, with the blocks flying up to reconstruct the original building. The scene was produced by making a print backwards one frame at a time from the original negative of the forwards action in a special projection-printer that Smith had constructed. In the very beginning (as is still mostly the case) positive prints were made from the negative by running them together in contact through a printer with light shining straight through. However, in a projection- or optical-printer the negative and the positive

stock are separated, and the image from the negative is focused by a lens onto the positive, so permitting the two films to be run in opposite directions if desired. A small number of comedy films were conceived around reverse-motion printing by other English filmmakers over the next few years, and it has since remained part of the arsenal of purely filmic effects used for comedy purposes.

So, with all these developments, the cinema was already by 1900 taking on a life and shape of its own, independently of the older art forms, and a number of its major features were already in place and working.

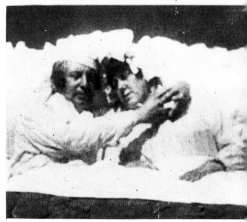

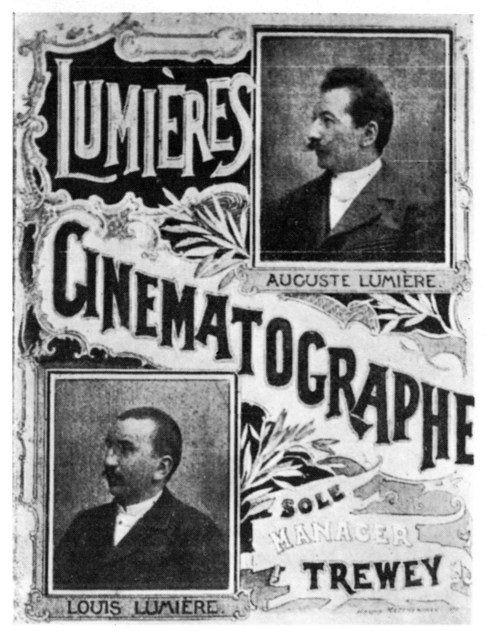

Left: the English poster for the Cinématographe. Scenes from the show (above): the workers leaving the factory (top) in the programme's opening film La Sortie des Usines; *Auguste and his wife feeding their already well-fed daughter (centre); an unsuspecting onlooker (bottom) about to be covered in dust after the demolition of a wall*

Auguste and Louis Lumière were born into the world of pictures; static pictures taken by their father, who was a photographer and manufacturer of photographic equipment. Edison's Kinetoscope inspired them to go one better and create the Cinématographe. Thus it was more by accident than design that Louis Lumière became known as the 'father of cinema'

'Oh, I never go to the cinema', admitted Louis Lumière in 1930; 'If I had known what it would come to, I would never have invented it'. Perhaps the latter was rather a sweeping statement, for the controversy over who was actually the first to perfect practicable moving-picture apparatus still continues. However, in one respect the Lumière brothers – Louis and Auguste, who always worked as a team – have an incontrovertible claim: on December 28, 1895 they presented the world's first show of projected moving pictures to a paying public.

Louis Lumière (1864–1948) conquered the practical problems of constructing a camera and projector in the course of a sleepless night during the winter of 1894; and on February 23, 1895 Louis and Auguste (1862–1954) took out a patent for their Cinématographe. As constructed by the skilled French optician Jules Carpentier, the Cinématographe was an exemplary apparatus – compact, light, highly efficient, and combining the functions of camera, projector and optical printer.

A patently obvious success
Ten months passed between the patent and the first public showing, and during this time (according to the French historian Georges Sadoul) Louis Lumière shot some hundred one-minute films. Meanwhile, the brothers were also trying out their invention on learned societies, starting on March 22, 1895 with the Society for the Encouragement of National Industry. The following month there was a demonstration for the Congress of Learned Societies of France and the Provinces, and in June the Congress of French Photographic Societies took place on the Lumières' home territory of Lyon; the brothers delighted the Congress by filming its most distinguished

members as they chatted and as they disembarked after a boat trip. These shows were followed by others in Paris and Brussels, and enthusiastic articles about the Lumières' work began to appear in the scientific press. It is hard to know whether or not these private showings were a deliberate advance campaign for the public launching of the Cinématographe, or whether the unanimously favourable reception eventually encouraged the Lumières to exploit the Cinématographe as a commercial, public entertainment.

Towards the end of the year Antoine Lumière, Louis and Auguste's father, began seeking a suitable place to house the show. The historian Jacques Deslandes says that among other sites considered was a photographer's studio over the Théâtre Robert-Houdin, which was run by the future film-maker Georges Méliès. Discussions with the Parisian waxwork show Musée Grévin came to nothing, perhaps because it was still running Emile Reynaud's Pantomimes Lumineuses. There were also negotiations with the Folies Bergère.

Finally, however, the Lumières settled on the Salon Indien of the Grand Café, Boulevard des Capucines. The Grand Café was situated on

the street level of the great Second Empire Grand Hotel; the Salon Indien was a room in the basement beneath. As the name implies, it had been extravagantly decorated in oriental style, but the proprietors of the Café seemed to have found no satisfactory use for it and were happy to let it to the Lumières for 30 francs a day. (Cautiously, but somewhat unwisely, they declined a counter-offer of 20 per cent of the receipts, which by the middle of January 1896 sometimes reached 2,500 francs a day).

The Lumières borrowed 100 gilt cane chairs from the Café, installed a house manager, Clément Maurice, and a projectionist, and on December 28 opened the doors to the public. The first advertising poster – a jolly affair looking as if the artist A. Brispot might have dashed it off at rather short notice – shows a moustachio'd policeman marshalling the enthusiastic hordes who press to the doors; though the first day of exhibition hardly justified this optimistic picture. The busy crowds were clearly too preoccupied with their New Year preparations to puzzle out the meaning of this bizarre new word, 'Cinématographe', and first-day admissions only numbered 35. However, by the second day word of the new marvel had evidently spread and queues stretched down the boulevard.

It seems likely that the programme was varied from day to day, since the Lumières already had an extensive stock of films to service the standard programme, but the opening picture seems to have remained constant: *La Sortie des Usines* (1895, Leaving the Factory) was probably the first film they had shot and was, as a tribute to their industrial success, a

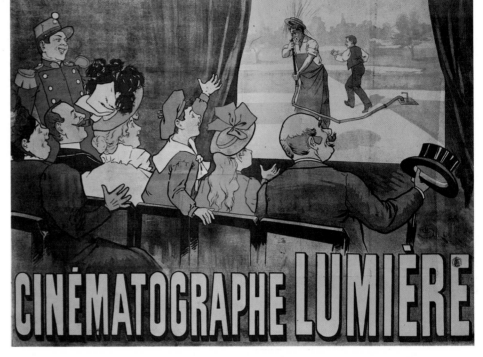

highly appropriate subject. The gates of the Lumière factory open; workers pour out – many of the men on bicycles, the women in long summer dresses and large hats. The last to leave is a little dog; and the gates close.

Like the rest of the following programme, this first film was technically faultless and composed with the visual sense of an

Below left: members of the Congress of French Photographic Societies leaving a pleasure boat. Below: Arrivée d'un Train en Gare should have been a horror film judging by the audience reaction. Below right: Antoine Lumière making merry with friends. Below, far right: Madame Lumière and two children watching a rowing boat about to dock

Left: a colourful poster depicting the delight of an audience on seeing L'Arroseur Arrosé, *the first of many Lumière gag films, in which (above, far left to far right) the gardener hoses the garden; a boy sneaks up and steps on the hose, thereby stopping the water flow; a puzzled gardener looks down the nozzle; the boy takes his foot away, resulting in a soaking for the gardener; the punishment is seen to fit the crime*

accomplished Victorian photographer. Above all, the films were the Lumières' own home movies. They provided a faithful picture, sure to charm and flatter the public of the boulevards, of French middle-class life at the end of the nineteenth century – a time when few people could have foreseen the events that were soon to destroy the illusion of unending security, prosperity and peace.

Happy families
In one film Auguste Lumière and his wife feed breakfast to their baby daughter who sits, dumpling-like, between them; in another film the same child is fascinated by a bowl of goldfish; elsewhere old Father Lumière plays cards and drinks a glass of beer with two cronies; a gentleman bathes in the sea; Madame Lumière and two children stand on a landing stage watching the arrival of a small boat. There are scenes of the public square in Lyon and of soldiers exercising. The smoke effects in a film about two blacksmiths, and the clouds of dust raised by the demolition of a wall, were particularly popular with audiences.

There were two films that dominated the

show and which for years were indispensable to every Lumière projection. *Arrivée d'un Train en Gare* (1895, The Arrival of a Train at the Station) is filmed looking up the platform so that the rails stretch obliquely into the distance. The express steams forward and passes the camera on the left; alighting passengers approach the camera and, again, pass it, this time to the right. The audience of the day is said to have bounded from their seats in shock at the approach of the train. Today the astonishing thing is the beauty and variety of composition achieved in a mere 50 feet of film. Louis Lumière was a highly accomplished photographer, sensitive to lighting and framing, and in addition the Cinématographe permitted a slow exposure rate with a consequently impressive depth of focus.

L'Arroseur Arrosé (1895, Watering the Gardener) earned its deserved success, and lasting fame, as the world's first film comedy. The gag is simple enough, though in 1895 it brought the house down and inspired the Lumières to feature it on a new poster. A naughty boy steals up on the gardener and treads on his hose. When the man peers into the nozzle to discover the cause of the trouble, the boy releases his foot, so spraying the poor man with water. The gardener administers a just boxing of the ears. Georges Sadoul points out that this was probably the first example of a film adaptation: the gag was inspired by a popular comic strip of the 1880s, which seems also to have been the source for later jokes.

Energetic exploitation
Perhaps because they had little confidence in

the future of the cinema, the Lumières were energetic in its short-term exploitation. Their strategy was to equip projectionist-cameramen with machines and film, and despatch them to conquer new territories. Once at their destinations they would present the Lumière spectacle in theatres and music halls and at the same time film the local scenery to add to the range and exoticism of the repertoire. As their English representative the Lumières selected 'Professor' Lucien Trewey, who as a juggler and hand-shadow performer had often appeared in London's music halls. Trewey negotiated with the Empire Theatre of Varieties, Leicester Square for a fee of £300 a week. He opened there on March 9, 1896. The programme consisted of ten films, billed by English titles as:

'Dinner Hour at the Factory Gate of M. Lumière at Lyons; Tea Time; The Blacksmith at Work; A Game at Ecarté; The Arrival of the Paris Express; Children at Play; A Practical Joke on the Gardener; Trewey's Serpentine Ribbon; Place des Cordeliers (Lyon); Bathing in the Mediterranean.' Soon Trewey had added a scene of the Empire with its advertisements for the Cinématographe.

It is difficult to re-create the first impact of these films. Audiences marvelled at the limitless detail and were astounded that every figure moved, that even the leaves on the trees were given motion. The Lumières' mirror image of their world enchanted the people of the late nineteenth century, and instilled a taste that would make the movies – for all Louis Lumière's later reservations – the art of the twentieth century.

GENEALOGY OF THE CINEMA

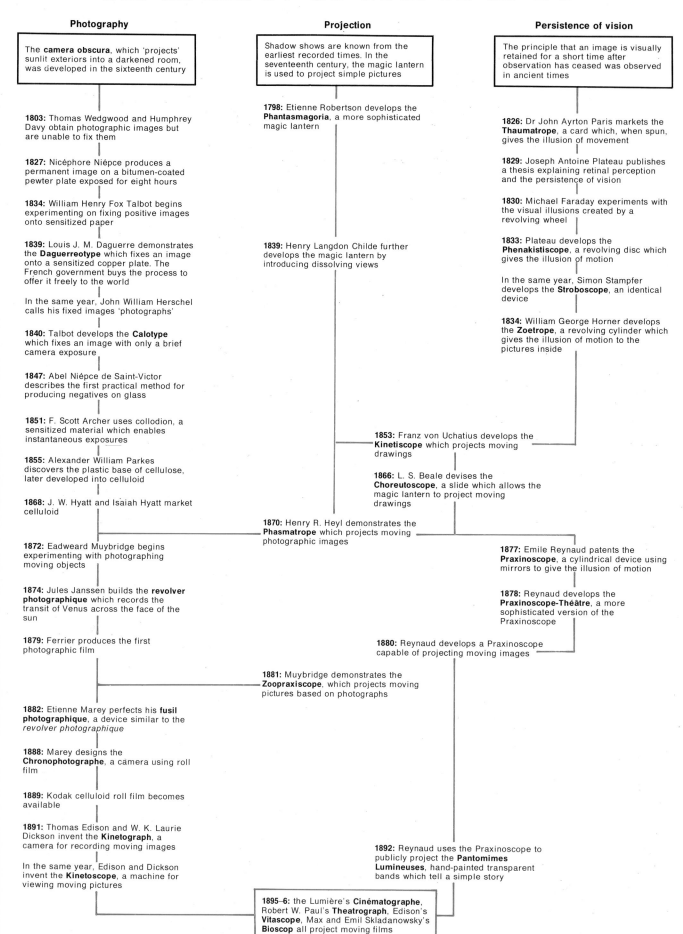

Photography

The **camera obscura**, which 'projects' sunlit exteriors into a darkened room, was developed in the sixteenth century

1803: Thomas Wedgwood and Humphrey Davy obtain photographic images but are unable to fix them

1827: Nicéphore Niépce produces a permanent image on a bitumen-coated pewter plate exposed for eight hours

1834: William Henry Fox Talbot begins experimenting on fixing positive images onto sensitized paper

1839: Louis J. M. Daguerre demonstrates the **Daguerreotype** which fixes an image onto a sensitized copper plate. The French government buys the process to offer it freely to the world

In the same year, John William Herschel calls his fixed images 'photographs'

1840: Talbot develops the **Calotype** which fixes an image with only a brief camera exposure

1847: Abel Niépce de Saint-Victor describes the first practical method for producing negatives on glass

1851: F. Scott Archer uses collodion, a sensitized material which enables instantaneous exposures

1855: Alexander William Parkes discovers the plastic base of cellulose, later developed into celluloid

1868: J. W. Hyatt and Isaiah Hyatt market celluloid

1872: Eadweard Muybridge begins experimenting with photographing moving objects

1874: Jules Janssen builds the **revolver photographique** which records the transit of Venus across the face of the sun

1879: Ferrier produces the first photographic film

1882: Etienne Marey perfects his **fusil photographique**, a device similar to the *revolver photographique*

1888: Marey designs the **Chronophotographe**, a camera using roll film

1889: Kodak celluloid roll film becomes available

1891: Thomas Edison and W. K. Laurie Dickson invent the **Kinetograph**, a camera for recording moving images

In the same year, Edison and Dickson invent the **Kinetoscope**, a machine for viewing moving pictures

Projection

Shadow shows are known from the earliest recorded times. In the seventeenth century, the magic lantern is used to project simple pictures

1798: Etienne Robertson develops the **Phantasmagoria**, a more sophisticated magic lantern

1839: Henry Langdon Childe further develops the magic lantern by introducing dissolving views

1853: Franz von Uchatius develops the **Kinetiscope** which projects moving drawings

1866: L. S. Beale devises the **Choreutoscope**, a slide which allows the magic lantern to project moving drawings

1870: Henry R. Heyl demonstrates the **Phasmatrope** which projects moving photographic images

1881: Muybridge demonstrates the **Zoopraxiscope**, which projects moving pictures based on photographs

1895–6: the Lumière's **Cinématographe**, Robert W. Paul's **Theatrograph**, Edison's **Vitascope**, Max and Emil Skladanowsky's **Bioscop** all project moving films

Persistence of vision

The principle that an image is visually retained for a short time after observation has ceased was observed in ancient times

1826: Dr John Ayrton Paris markets the **Thaumatrope**, a card which, when spun, gives the illusion of movement

1829: Joseph Antoine Plateau publishes a thesis explaining retinal perception and the persistence of vision

1830: Michael Faraday experiments with the visual illusions created by a revolving wheel

1833: Plateau develops the **Phenakistiscope**, a revolving disc which gives the illusion of motion

In the same year, Simon Stampfer develops the **Stroboscope**, an identical device

1834: William George Horner develops the **Zoetrope**, a revolving cylinder which gives the illusion of motion to the pictures inside

1877: Emile Reynaud patents the **Praxinoscope**, a cylindrical device using mirrors to give the illusion of motion

1878: Reynaud develops the **Praxinoscope-Théâtre**, a more sophisticated version of the Praxinoscope

1880: Reynaud develops a Praxinoscope capable of projecting moving images

1892: Reynaud uses the Praxinoscope to publicly project the **Pantomimes Lumineuses**, hand-painted transparent bands which tell a simple story

Hollywood Dawn

Into the Californian land of sunshine and orange groves came an invading horde of itinerant showbiz folk who created their own movie worlds in vacant lots and empty stores. Soon they built up a great new industry and the name of Hollywood, a suburb of Los Angeles, was known around the world

A Kansas couple, Harvey and Daeida Wilcox, came to Los Angeles in 1883 and opened a real-estate office. Three years later, they owned a 120-acre tract that was subdivided and advertised for sale under the name 'Hollywood'. In 1903 the residents voted for incorporation into the city of Los Angeles. The geographic area of Hollywood was determined to be from Normandie west to Fairfax Avenue and from the Santa Monica Mountains south to Fountain Avenue. This area, annexed to Los Angeles in 1910, was to become the focus of film production in the United States, and its name 'Hollywood' covered film-making in all studios in the various outlying Los Angeles areas.

Los Angeles itself was far from an urban metropolis at the turn of the century. Most of its 100,000 residents were concentrated in the districts surrounding the downtown commercial hub. To the west lay great stretches of bean fields, orange groves and empty land all the way to the ocean. Entertainment was centred in the downtown area, paralleling the mostly dry Los Angeles River. The exhibitor Thomas Tally was among the first to show motion pictures in Los Angeles in 1896, and in 1902 he opened his Electric Theatre, installing 200 fixed seats and charging the high price of ten cents for admission. He showed *The Capture of the Biddle Brothers* and *New York in a Blizzard* (both 1902), made in the east by Thomas Edison's company.

First on the scene

Colonel William Selig of the Chicago-based Selig Polyscope Company sent his director Francis Boggs to the West Coast early in 1907 to photograph coastal locations for *The Count of Monte Cristo* (1907). In 1908 Boggs rented a lot on Olive Street in downtown Los Angeles, where he made the first dramatic film shot completely in California: *The Heart of a Race Tout* (1909), starring Thomas Santschi and Jean Ward. Location scenes were shot at the old Santa Anita Race Track, which was about to be closed down.

In August 1908 Colonel Selig began construction of a completely equipped studio in Edendale, where *In the Power of the Sultan* (1909) was made with Hobart Bosworth and Stella Adams. Selig expanded his holdings in 1910 by enlarging both this and a second studio, complete with zoo, in what is now the Lincoln Park area. The second studio was particularly used for jungle pictures, which were very popular. When Selig pulled out, the zoo was donated to the city of Los Angeles and renamed the Luna Park Zoo. He sold his Edendale studio in 1916 to William Fox. Fox also moved into the old Dixon studio at Sunset and Western Avenue, where he continued to produce while he was constructing the Fox Movietone Studio in 1927, and for years thereafter. The new ultra-modern complex bordered on Pico Boulevard on the south and on Santa Monica Boulevard on the north; 20th Century-Fox has continued to make important pictures there to the present day.

Edendale in 1909 was the choice also of another early film pioneer, the New York Motion Picture Company (NYMPC), which sent a unit of actors called the Bison Company to California. They located themselves near Colonel Selig in a converted grocery store and

Top: Hollywood in 1905, looking south across Hollywood Boulevard. Above: Sunset Boulevard, a main artery of Hollywood, as a crowded thoroughfare in recent times

began shooting as soon as Indians and cowboys could be hired. If their unlicensed camera was threatened by an agent from the Motion Picture Patents Company, they would go into the mountains at Big Bear Lake and make Indian pictures. When the NYMPC brought Mack Sennett from New York to work at the Edendale studio, he improved the property by building one of the first enclosed concrete stages in the area for his two-reelers. The NYMPC also leased acreage in the Santa Ynez

21

Canyon, where Sunset Boulevard meets the ocean, and a young director brought from New York, Thomas Ince, took the Bison Company there. At 'Inceville' pictures were made with the resident village of Indians, who had previously been with a touring Wild West show.

One of the oldest studios in East Hollywood was the Lubin Manufacturing Company frame building at the corner of Sunset Boulevard and Hoover Street, established in 1912. It was later briefly occupied by Essanay, the Chicago-based company of George K. Spoor and Broncho Billy Anderson. They stayed long enough to make 21 Westerns before taking their unit back to their studio at Niles in northern California. Then, from 1913 to 1917, the studio housed Kalem, which had another West Coast studio in Glendale. Others who followed on the premises through the years included Monogram, Allied Artists and KCET, the Public Broadcasting television station, which bought the property in 1970.

Wild and free

Vitagraph, operating in Flatbush, Brooklyn, as early as 1907, came to Santa Monica in 1911, and in 1913 built a large plant in East Hollywood. Among its West Coast stars were Norma Talmadge, Anita Stewart, Lillian Walker and the comedian Larry Semon. The Santa Monica studio acquired an annex, described in *The Moving Picture World* of July 10, 1915 as:

'. . . a ranch up in the mountains near the studio . . . wild and free from civilization . . . which is used for big outdoors sets and Western frontier scenes.'

In 1919 Vitagraph absorbed the defunct Kalem's scenario properties, the first phase of the liquidation of the Kalem assets. By 1920 Vitagraph was very active in production on both coasts, and the East Hollywood studio had '. . . grown to enormous dimensions, with an extensive back lot, with sets, and street scenes of all genres'. Hundreds of actors and production people were on the payroll, earning from $100 to as high as $5000 a week in the case of some stars. Larry Semon headed the Vitagraph basketball team, and one of the team members was comedy actor, stunt man and later producer Joe Rock. Mr Rock recalls: 'When I worked at the Vitagraph western studio in 1916, I was paid at the front-gate pay window in gold coin every week.'

The *Motion Picture News* of January 1, 1921

Above: the famous old sign on Mount Lee became derelict in the Thirties and was eventually replaced by a new one in 1979.
Below left: Selig's first temporary studio in Los

Angeles, next to a Chinese laundry, 1908.
Below: David Horsley, president of Nestor, with the principals of the Desperate Desmond series of serials in 1911

22

reported that Vitagraph was making a prison-life picture *Three Sevens* (1921), starring Antonio Moreno and directed by Chester Bennett:

'The exteriors were taken at Florence, Arizona, where the Governor of the State permitted 300 convicts to be turned loose outside the walls in a daring escape for the picture . . . a train-robbery scene was filmed at Newhall, near the San Fernando Valley and an excellent prison set was constructed at the studio to match the interior of the Arizona penitentiary where it was impossible to light the corridors sufficiently for photographing.'

Vitagraph was sold on April 20, 1925 to Warner Brothers for $735,000, including the copyrights of its scenarios, which enabled Warners to remake the Vitagraph hits for years to come.

The American Mutoscope and Biograph Company sent its most prolific director, D.W. Griffith, to California for three seasons in 1910, 1911 and 1912. Griffith was not limited to his studio in downtown Los Angeles. He travelled with his cameramen Arthur Marvin and Billy Bitzer, as well as his acting and production unit, to actual locations of places mentioned in poems, stories and books that had been dramatized for the screen.

Griffith left Biograph in 1913 to join the Mutual Film Corporation, an independent company not licensed by the Motion Picture Patents Company. Mutual took over the Kinemacolor Studio located in East Hollywood at the intersection of Sunset and Hollywood Boulevards. This was later to become known as the Griffith Fine Arts Studio. It was here that the controversial picture *Birth of a Nation* (1915) was planned and edited, and its interior scenes shot. The film was premiered in Los Angeles under the title of the book on which it was based, Thomas Dixon's *The Clansman*. To counteract the widespread turmoil over the 'White Supremacy' aspect of this film, Griffith went on to make his monumental epic *Intolerance* (1916). His huge Babylonian sets, several storeys high, stood for years afterwards before they were dismantled.

Negative impressions

The first studio in Hollywood itself was a converted tavern and grocery store on the north-west corner of Sunset and Gower. David and William Horsley, owners and operators of the Centaur Film Company in Bayonne, New Jersey, came to the West Coast in 1911 and

Below left: the East Hollywood studio of the Philadelphia-based Lubin Company in 1912. Below right: Elmo Lincoln and Louise Lorraine, stars of the Tarzan series, at the studio of the

National Film Company in 1919. Insert above: a picture-postcard view of Universal City, the studio that is incorporated as a township and is a major tourist attraction

23

December 1913 and that year released the first feature-length Western made in Hollywood itself, *The Squaw Man*. Lasky joined forces with Adolph Zukor's Famous Players Company in 1916 to form the Famous Players-Lasky Corporation, which expanded the Lasky studio. Lasky and Zukor took over the Paramount distribution company and formed the Paramount Pictures Corporation, a major producing company to this day. By 1926 they had outgrown their premises and acquired the United studio at Melrose and Van Ness Avenue, which they proceeded to enlarge and equip with the most up-to-date inventions in

Top left: Rex Ingram directs The Four Horsemen of the Apocalypse *in 1921. Above: parade in downtown Los Angeles to publicize John Ford's epic* The Iron Horse *(1924). Right: John Travolta keeps up a Hollywood tradition by immortalizing his footprints outside Grauman's Chinese Theatre. Below: gunfight at the Universal corral today to entertain the tourists. Bottom left: Desi Arnaz warming up the studio audience for television's* I Love Lucy *show in the Fifties*

continued to produce as the Nestor Film Company. The film historian Kevin Brownlow quotes the cameraman Charles Rosher's description of conditions there:

'Although we had a developing room, we had no printing machinery. The picture was cut directly from the negative, and we thought nothing of running original negative through the projector. Scratches and abrasions were mere details.'

Across the street from Nestor, on the southwest corner of Sunset and Gower, the first West Coast studio of the Universal Film Manufacturing Company was set up in 1912. Carl Laemmle, president of Universal, planned a much larger complex across the hills from Hollywood, in an isolated valley, and he began to build there in spite of the lack of roads and the great distance from downtown Los Angeles, where the film-processing laboratories were located. Universal was the first studio to provide space for the public to watch a movie being made – special tours still take many thousands through the studio every day.

The Jesse Lasky Feature Play Company was established at Selma and Vine Streets in

movies. The old Lasky studio at Selma and Vine was abandoned in 1927 to make way for a miniature golf course. In later years, NBC built its radio studios there.

The small Oz Studio in Hollywood, at the corner of Gower and Santa Monica Boulevard, produced the Wizard of Oz series, based on L. Frank Baum's famous children's stories. The National Film Company, headed by Edgar Rice Burroughs, who wrote the Tarzan novels, was the next tenant, occupying this studio from 1915 and making the world-renowned Tarzan film series starring Elmo Lincoln.

William H. Clune, a successful Los Angeles film exhibitor, went into the film-production business in April 1915, and took over a studio from Fiction Pictures on Melrose Avenue. The Clune Studio started production on large feature films, the first of which was a 12-reel version of the story of *Ramona*, the Indian maiden, released in 1917. (D.W. Griffith had previously filmed the same subject in California as early as 1910.) Sets were built across the street, including a representation of the Santa Barbara Mission; a Mexican village; and the 'Moreno Homestead' with mansion and grounds. A small pueblo street was constructed in the eucalyptus grove adjoining the studio grounds. Archbishop Gillow came from Mexico in October 1915 to visit the *Ramona* sets, and was shown around by the director Donald Crisp. In February 1921 Douglas Fairbanks moved into the Clune Studio with his production company to make *The Three Musketeers*, transforming Clune's back-lot into a French-village. A succession of film-producing companies used the Clune Studio through the years, and in 1980 it was renamed Raleigh Studios.

Metro Pictures was a New York-based company that rented its first Hollywood studio in 1916 and the following year was housed in the Mutual 'Lone Star' studio used by Charles Chaplin for one year to make a dozen of his most famous two-reel comedies. By 1918 the company had moved all its eastern production to the Hollywood studio and proceeded to make noteworthy movies such as *The Four Horsemen of the Apocalypse* (dir. Rex Ingram, 1921), the Buster Keaton comedies and films with Mae Murray. Metro employed film favourites such as Alla Nazimova, Bert Lytell, Harold Lockwood, Renée Adorée, Ramon Novarro, the Dolly Sisters and Rudolph Valentino. Jackie Coogan, the child actor who had become famous working with Chaplin, signed with Metro in July 1923. Directors at Metro included Rex Ingram, who made *Scaramouche* (1923), and also Reginald Barker, Victor Schertzinger, Edward Sloman and Fred Niblo.

Charles and Sydney Chaplin acquired in 1917 an estate on the south-east corner of Sunset Boulevard and La Brea Avenue in Hollywood. They and their mother lived in the ten-room colonial-type residence, which could double as a set for filming. The land behind the house was developed into the Chaplin Studio, which was finished by March 1918. It consisted of six English Tudor-style bungalows with dressing rooms, storage facilities and two large stages, one open and one closed. The head cinematographer was Roland (Rollie) Totheroh, and the stock company in the main comprised actors from Chaplin's Essanay and Mutual days. Chaplin hired four-year-old Jackie Coogan and later starred him in *The Kid* (1921), which was considered a masterpiece

and added to Chaplin's world-wide fame. He continued to work at this studio until 1942, the year in which he reissued *The Gold Rush* (1925) with an added soundtrack. The plant was leased to Monogram Pictures in 1944 and thereafter to a number of others, until 1951 when Chaplin returned to begin work on *Limelight* (1952), his last American film. The plant reverted to a rental studio again until the end of 1966, when the music-recording company A & M Records moved into it. Chaplin's footprints are in concrete in front of Sound Stage 3, which is now the entrance to the recording studio.

Loving Lucy

On December 4, 1920, the *Motion Picture News* noted that:

'The new Robertson-Cole studios, which have been in course of construction since last summer at the corner of Gower and Melrose Streets, Hollywood, will be informally opened within the next few days . . . The studio proper covers a little over sixteen acres of ground . . . [having] eight huge stages . . .'

The company began on the East Coast as a releasing agency, which joined forces with Mutual and the Affiliated Distributing Corporation to distribute the Tarzan films and others. The producer and director Hunt Stromberg worked in the Hollywood studios, and in 1922 Robertson-Cole shared studio facilities with the adjoining United Studios. That year the company name was changed to the Film Booking Office (FBO). The East Coast giant Radio Corporation of America took over FBO in 1929 and, in an amalgamation with the Keith-Albee-Orpheum cinema circuit, built an even more modern studio on the premises, known as Radio-Keith-Orpheum (RKO). In the Fifties and Sixties the Desilu Company acquired this RKO plant as well as the RKO plant in Culver City, and made the *I Love Lucy* television series there. After about fifteen years of Desilu ownership, the entire complex was incorporated into Paramount, which was adjacent to it.

The Triangle Film Corporation, founded in 1915, offering financial backing and studio space to its three prolific producers, operated the Fine Arts Studio for D.W. Griffith, the studio at Edendale for Mack Sennett, and the studio at Santa Ynez for Thomas Ince. By October 1915 plans were in the works for Ince to begin construction on a projected studio in newly-founded Culver City, midway between the city of Los Angeles and the ocean, on land made available by developer Harry Culver. After a series of mergers, this studio became the home of Metro-Goldwyn-Mayer in the Twenties.

Meanwhile, in 1919, Ince built a colonial-style studio on Washington Boulevard in Culver City, and produced films there until his early death in 1924. This studio was then occupied by Cecil B. DeMille; Pathé; RKO; David O. Selznick, who made *Gone With the Wind* (1939) there and built the 'Tara Mansion' which stood for decades; Desilu; the Culver City Studio; and most recently, in 1980, Laird International Studios.

A great number of these old film factories have disappeared and their product with them. But their history survives and is becoming of greater interest to a new generation. Many film studios operate in Hollywood today, the present built on the past.

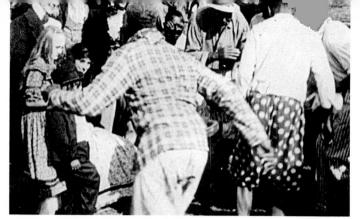

Directed by D. W. Griffith, 1915
Prod co: Epoch. **prod:** Harry E. Aitken, D. W. Griffith. **sc:** D. W. Griffith, Frank E. Woods, Thomas Dixon Jr, from the novel *The Clansman* by Thomas Dixon Jr. **photo:** G. W. Bitzer. **ass photo:** Karl Brown. **ed:** D. W. Griffith, James Smith. **cost:** Robert Godstein. **mus:** Joseph Carl Breil, D. W. Griffith. **ass dir:** George Siegmann, Raoul Walsh, W. S. Van Dyke, Erich von Stroheim, Jack Conway. **length:** originally 13,058 feet (approx. 180 minutes) censored to 12,500 feet (approx. 165 minutes). Original title: *The Clansman*.
Cast: Henry B. Walthall (*Benjamin Cameron*), Violet Wilkey (*Flora Cameron as a child*), Mae Marsh (*Flora Cameron*), Miriam Cooper (*Margaret Cameron*), Josephine Bonapart Crowell (*Mrs Cameron*), Spottiswood Aitken (*Dr Cameron*), André Beranger (*Wade Cameron*), Maxfield Stanley (*Duke Cameron*), Lillian Gish (*Elsie Stoneman*), Ralph Lewis (*the Hon. Austin Stoneman*), Elmer Clifton (*Phil Stoneman*), Robert Harron (*Ted Stoneman; black-face spy*), Mary Alden (*Lydia Brown*), Sam de Grasse (*Senator Charles Sumner*), George Siegmann (*Silas Lynch*), Walter Long (*Gus*), Elmo Lincoln (*'White-arm' Joe; slave auctioneer; Confederate officer*), Wallace Reid (*Jeff*), Joseph Henabery (*Abraham Lincoln*), Alberta Lee (*Mrs Lincoln*), Donald Crisp (*General U.S. Grant*), Howard Gaye (*General Robert E. Lee*), William Freeman (*the mooning sentry*), Olga Grey (*Laura Keene*), Raoul Walsh (*John Wilkes Booth*), Tom Wilson (*Stoneman's negro servant*), Eugene Pallette (*Union soldier*), Madame Sul-te-Wan (*negro woman*), William de Vaull (*Jake*), Jennie Lee (*Dixie*), Erich von Stroheim (*man who falls from roof*).

The Birth of a Nation, D. W. Griffith's cinematic masterpiece, provokes controversy even to this day: it enjoys the uneasy honour of being both a technically innovative film as well as one of the most explicitly racist pictures ever made. It has been rightly venerated for its artistic achievements, and just as rightly condemned for its reactionary content.

The Birth of a Nation was one of the first films to establish the convention of story-telling in the cinema with now familiar techniques, such as use of parallel action in a chase sequence, and to exploit the full potential of close-ups and fades. Other, less-lasting devices like the iris-shot (whereby the film image is vignetted at the corners) were also used to good effect. It was the first of the 'big' pictures, complete with vast panoramic shots as carefully composed as epic paintings and splendidly staged battle scenes, all of which are intermingled with scenes of plantation life and coy romance.

The film deals with a prickly period in American history – the Civil War and the period of Reconstruction in the South, from which many Americans were still recovering when Griffith made the film. He himself was a Southerner, raised on the values and traditions of the Old South, though his depiction of that experience is laid out in

epic proportions and succeeds in blurring sectional interests and antipathies. He does this by inter-weaving the lives of two families, the Stonemans and Camerons, re-spectively representing North and South, whose contrasting lives are eventually reconciled in the common interest of white sup-remacy or, as one of the film's intertitles puts it, 'in defence of their Aryan birthright'.

Such anti-black sentiments were not uncommon during the silent era, although most films tended to place emphasis on the traditional and relatively gentler image of de-voted black servility, or use the black man for comic relief. Griffith's film follows the same pattern, but with greater force and with the emotive stress placed on the image of blacks as villains. These stereo-types play against the equally stereotyped whites in the film – men are aristocratic and paternalis-tic, women frail and vulnerable – but they do not express the inter-ests of the blacks (played by whites in black-face) in the way that the white stereotypes express the interests of the whites.

The Birth of a Nation is one of few silent films to exploit the sexual stereotype of the black male in order to reinforce the doctrine of white supremacy. It achieves this through the use of the much-dreaded 'brute' figure – personified

here by the renegade Gus, who not only betrays his former masters by joining the black revolt, but also commits the unspeakable crime of lusting after and causing the suicide of one of the Cameron daughters. This motif is duplicated in the character and actions of Silas Lynch, the mulatto leader of his people. The sexual racism that these characters exemplify plays a crucial part in the film's thematic development; and it comes to a head in the film's last-minute rescue finale which justifies the actions of the Ku Klux Klan, cap-tioned by Griffith as 'the saviour of white civilization'.

Race feeling ran high wherever the film was shown, resulting in rioting in Boston and other cities.

While the publicity this generated undoubtedly increased box-office receipts, Griffith himself was strongly attacked in the liberal and black press for his blatant racism and romanticizing of the murderous Ku Klux Klan (whose membership trebled within months of the film's release). Cinemas were picketed, and the newly-formed National As-sociation for the Advancement of Coloured People (NAACP) man-aged to get the film banned in a number of states.

Today, at least in America, *The Birth of a Nation* is restricted lar-gely to cinema 'club' showings, and to video-cassette. But the spectre of the film's original impact lingers, and it incurs the same wrath.

GIVING BIRTH...

D.W. Griffith welded together the techniques evolved by earlier pioneers and single-handedly created the art of screen narrative

On December 31, 1913, D.W. Griffith announced his departure from the American Biograph Company with whom he had worked since 1908. In an advertisement in *The New York Dramatic Mirror*, he summarized his achievements during the Biograph years, claiming that he had 'revolutionised motion picture drama' and 'founded the modern technique of the art'. To Griffith, on the strength of his own declarations, are normally credited the first uses of such devices as the close-up and the long-shot, the flashback (or, as he termed it, the 'switchback'), the fade-in and fade-out, the use of the iris lens to pick out details of action, the use of titles, the concept of editing for parallel action and 'dramatic continuity', the atmospheric use of lighting, and the encouragement of 'restraint in expression' in screen acting.

Some of these claims, particularly where restrained acting was concerned, were to find more substantial justification in the post-Biograph years. By 1920, Griffith could reasonably be said to have pioneered the expressionist use of colour tinting, the concept of widescreen cinema, and the commissioning of original musical scores. He had also sent a camera up in a balloon, and directed at least two of the greatest films the cinema would ever know. But there was no doubt, even at the time, that Griffith left both Biograph and film history the richer for a five-and-a-half-year output unequalled by any other film-maker in any other era.

That output, as has since been clarified, was not quite the one-man, technical revolution Griffith suggested. In the process of copyright registration, American motion-picture producers during 1894 to 1912 printed the individual frames of their work as photographs on paper for preservation by the Library of Congress. Thanks to these 'paper prints', and to the research into them by archivist Kemp Niver in the late Forties, it has become possible for Griffith's Biograph films to be studied in a more informative light.

What has emerged is at first sight contradictory to the Griffith claims; instead, Edwin S. Porter (for the Edison Company) and G.W. 'Billy' Bitzer (for Biograph) are amply illustrated as authentic pioneers. Porter's *The Great Train Robbery* (1903) has long been established as a primitive example of parallel storytelling, and ends up (or starts, according to taste) with the medium close-up, in colour, of a bandit shooting at the camera and thus at the audience. But Porter's other Edison productions, from the turn of the century, are also alive with dissolves, close-ups and camera movements. The effects are far from sophisticated – but they are there. Similarly, in such dramas as *Moonshiners* (1904) Bitzer pans fluently, if not particularly smoothly, around the countryside, while in *The Black Hand* (1906) he can be seen making use of titles, a two-shot, and a close-up. In both technique and subject (as with, for instance, *A Kentucky Feud*, 1905) he clearly marks out the territory that was subsequently to be assigned to Griffith. This indebtedness to the first film-makers is further re-

inforced by the irony that Griffith was directed by, among others, Porter in *Rescued From an Eagle's Nest*, when as an aspiring actor he first worked at Biograph in 1907, and by Bitzer in *The Sculptor's Nightmare*, made in 1908, by which time he had officially joined the company. (Bitzer subsequently worked as Griffith's cinematographer for the next 16 years.)

What Griffith brought significantly to the screen, then, was not a collection of technical tricks, but the skill to use them effectively to enhance his stories. It was a skill derived partly from the theatre – his first love – and partly from his family background, with its 'scholarly atmosphere'. But most crucially, the skill grew inevitably from the experience of maintaining an output of around nine films a month throughout his stay with Biograph. In the startlingly prolific context of nearly five hundred productions in five-and-a-half years, Griffith was given

Above: though the Indians butcher the whites in The Battle of Elderbush Gulch *(originally* The Battle at Elderbush Gulch*), Griffith makes it clear that the settlers are to blame. Below: Griffith (right) and his cameraman Billy Bitzer. Bottom: in* Man's Genesis, *the fight between 'Brute-force' and 'Weak-hands' is won by the latter, inventor of the axe*

the unique opportunity – and had the responsive personality – to make every conceivable experiment in film-making at a time when the rules were few, the audience vast and enthusiastic, and the future unlimited.

Born on January 22, 1875 on a farm in Crestwood, Kentucky, Llewelyn Wark Griffith came of excellent Southern stock. His father had been a colonel in the Confederate army, and his domestic life seems to have been ordered along firmly ethical and devout (but not ardently militaristic) lines. 'My parents always directed our studies and our thoughts towards the noble, the great in literature', he later said, and from the age of six he was determined to become 'a great literary man'.

Numerous early jobs included being a salesman for the *Encyclopaedia Britannica*, a hop-picker, a newspaper reporter and drama critic in Louisville, and an actor under the stage name of Lawrence

Griffith in stock and touring companies. He wrote a
play, *The Fool and the Girl*, which was produced in
Washington and Baltimore in 1907 without much
success. Taken by a friend to his first picture show,
he found it 'silly, tiresome, inexcusable; any man
who enjoys such a thing should be shot at sunrise'.
But it led him to offer film stories to the Edison and
Biograph studios in New York, and it was only a
short step to finding employment as a bit-player for
the cameras, along with his wife Linda Arvidson.

Mrs Griffith has described in her autobiography
(*When the Movies Were Young*, published in 1925)
how the Biograph Company, originally created to
make the peepshow devices called Mutoscopes in
rivalry to Edison's Kinetoscopes, were by 1908
desperately searching for good material. At the
suggestion of Billy Bitzer's camera assistant, Arthur
Marvin (who happened to be the general manager's
brother), the studio offered a story by staff-writer
Stanner Taylor (later to write many of Griffith's
one-reelers) to the reluctant Lawrence Griffith –
only when established did he become known as
'David' or 'D.W.' – on the assurance that he could
have his acting job back if the project did not work
out. Photographed by Marvin, *The Adventures of
Dollie* (1908) starred Linda Arvidson and Arthur
Johnson, a young stage actor with no film
experience whom Griffith picked for his suitable
appearance. It was shot in a week, premiered in
New York on July 14, 1908 and judged successful
enough for Griffith to be granted a one-year contract which, with royalties, raised his salary from
practically nothing to $500 a month. Apart from
brief appearances when, in a crisis, there was
nobody else to fill the walk-on roles, he never did go
back to acting.

The torrent of films that poured from Biograph
for the next few years has survived remarkably
intact and has been carefully charted by, among
other film critics, Robert Henderson (in his book
D.W. Griffith: The Years at Biograph) and Edward
Wagenknecht and Anthony Slide (in *The Films of
D.W. Griffith*), although not too many film historians have had the stamina to voyage across the
full flood of Griffith's early output. His one-reelers
ventured into all conceivable territories long before
they were defined (and later *confined*) as separate
genres – in fact, the argument could be made that
Griffith was the inventor of everything but fantasy
cinema, which was pioneered by Georges Méliès
and Thomas Edison, and the epic spectaculars,
which he left to Italian film-makers until he could
afford to outclass them.

His were among the first – if not *the* first –
slapstick comedies (with *The Curtain Pole* in 1909
setting the scene for the Keystone antics of his
Biograph colleague Mack Sennett), suspense thrillers, Westerns, gangster stories, social-realism

dramas and romantic melodramas. He made costume films, adventure stories and war films, together with some adaptations, not always acknowledged, from such writers as Alfred Lord Tennyson, Leo
Tolstoy, Guy de Maupassant, James Fenimore
Cooper, and O. Henry. The variety of titles is
astonishing in any month picked at random from
the Biograph list: October 1908, for example, saw
the release of *The Devil*, *The Zulu's Heart*, *Father Gets
in the Game*, *The Barbarian Ingomar*, *The Vaquero's
Vow*, *The Planter's Wife*, *Romance of a Jewess*, *The Call
of the Wild* and *Concealing a Burglar*.

Today, just a handful of the Biograph works have
a lasting reputation, though many more deserve
attention. Among those most frequently reconsi-
dered are *Pippa Passes*, which achieved the distinction of being the first film to be reviewed by the *New
York Times* (on October 10, 1909); the Mary Pickford
classic *The Lonely Villa* (1909), a suspense story of a
family imprisoned in their own home by a mar-
auder with a gun; *The Lonedale Operator* (1911), in
which the camera was mounted on a locomotive to
observe the struggle between the heroine (Blanche
Sweet) and a railroad gang; and *Man's Genesis*
(1912), a Stone Age parable in which an early
screen dinosaur wobbled across the landscape.

If the one-reelers had anything in common (other

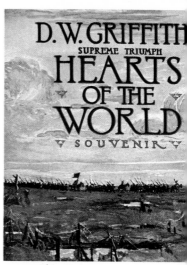

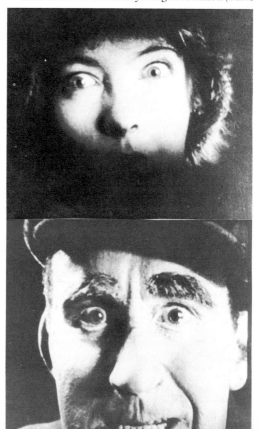

Far left: Griffith's screen debut as an actor in Rescued From an Eagle's Nest. *Left: scene from* Intolerance, *Griffith's epic portrayal of hypocrisy through the ages. Below: fragments of* Hearts of the World *(1918), a love story set during World War I, were actually shot at the Front. Bottom left: exemplary close-ups of a girl (Lillian Gish) and her brutal father (Donald Crisp) in* Broken Blossoms. *Bottom centre: Lillian and Dorothy Gish (blind girl in street) as the sundered sisters in* Orphans of the Storm. *Bottom right: Lillian Gish and Richard Barthelmess in* Way Down East

than the 'AB' logo that featured in all the backgrounds to protect copyright), not surprisingly it was a sense of speed. They could be made on any inspiration, even the slender basis of a change in the weather; the unit would make up a story on the spot to unfold against the background of a recent snowfall, or to take advantage of a vista of autumn trees. And since there was not time to show insignificant detail, Griffith used titles more creatively than had previously been tried, in the place of cumbersome or irrelevant action, pushing his stories headlong from climax to climax. Marriages were made, broken and mended in ten minutes, wars fought and lost in the space of a single shot. His stories, springing from this frantic schedule, frequently based themselves on a race against time, and the need to show widely separate events interacting with each other led him to the

Griffith had a vision of movies as 'the greatest spiritual force the world has ever known'

logical solution of cross-cutting.

Despite the misgivings of the studio bosses, the obstinate vitality of Griffith's editing style never seemed to upset the one-reeler audiences.

'I borrowed the idea from Charles Dickens. Novelists think nothing of leaving one set of characters in the midst of affairs and going back to deal with earlier events in which another set of characters is involved. I found that the picture could carry, not merely two, but three or four simultaneous threads of action – all without confusing the spectator.'

As Griffith's experience grew, so did his ambition. His stories were increasingly complex, his cast ever larger, his budgets less comfortable to Biograph. His later one-reelers, straying occasionally into two reels despite his producers' certainty that no audiences would tolerate such lengths, looked more and more like sketches and episodes from far grander projects. *The Battle* (1911) can now be seen as a rehearsal for *The Birth of a Nation* (1915), *The Musketeers of Pig Alley* (1912) for the modern story in *Intolerance* (1916), while *A Feud in the Kentucky Hills* (1912) anticipates both *The Massacre* (1913) and *The Battle at Elderbush Gulch* (1914), brilliant

and spectacular films which in turn were preparing for the sophisticated performances and magnificent photography of the later epics.

The parting of the ways came with *Judith of Bethulia* (1913), which Griffith made as a four-reeler at such casual expense, and in the teeth of such Biograph opposition, that there was no alternative but to fire him. As he left, he took his team with him – the teenagers who had matured to stardom in the same era that movie fandom had come into being as a direct response to the 'Biograph Girls', together with cameraman Bitzer, editor James Smith, and a score of designers and assistants. They moved to the Reliance-Majestic Company (distributing through Mutual) and between April and July 1914 they made the five-reel *The Battle of the Sexes* in five days for under $5000; the ill-fated (and ill-received) seven-reel melodrama *The Escape*; the six-reel, three-story *Home, Sweet Home*, which combined all the Griffith players in one film for the first time; and the six-reel oddity *The Avenging Conscience*, based on works by Edgar Allan Poe. None of these productions appears to have been successful, either dramatically or commercially. But it hardly mattered. Within six months, the Griffith team had created *The Birth of a Nation*, and the face of cinema was permanently changed.

Including the Reliance-Majestic productions, Griffith made 32 features after leaving Biograph. They were as disparate as his one-reelers had been, straying from the unargued (if controversial) classic status of *The Birth of a Nation*, *Intolerance*, *Broken Blossoms* (1919), and *Way Down East* (1920), to the ambitious but unsatisfying *Orphans of the Storm* (1921), *America* (1924) and *Abraham Lincoln* (1930), and to such largely peculiar and often plainly unattractive ventures as *Sally of the Sawdust*, *That Royle Girl* (both 1925) and the lavish *The Sorrows of Satan* (1926).

His final film, *The Struggle* (1931), a grim and obviously heartfelt warning of the perils of alcoholism, although vindicated by later critical re-evaluation, was a crushing commercial disaster, especially as it came within a year of his having won a 'best director' award for his first sound film, *Abraham Lincoln*. In the remaining 17 years of his life he made nothing further. Instead, he was avoided by the studios for whom he had almost single-handedly created the film industry, and he was forgotten by the public. When the D.W. Griffith Corporation went into bankruptcy and his films were auctioned, he picked up the rights to 21 of them for a mere $500.

'To us,' said Lillian Gish, his greatest star, 'Mr Griffith *was* the movie industry. It had been born in his head.' But the infant proved to be less respectful of past traditions than its creator, and as it grew his parental influence quickly lost its grip. Griffith's stories obsessively examined the theme of virtue under siege – he was repeatedly shutting his young lovers, his innocent heroines, his helpless children into traps from which they were usually (but certainly not always) rescued only at the last moment. With his affection for Dickensian romanticism, he held firmly and sentimentally to the view that entertainment and education were one, and that beauty and youth were their own justification – beauty not only of appearance but also of character and behaviour. If it was an approach that steadily lost headway against the accelerating cynicism of the times, it remained with Griffith himself as an undimmed faith. 'We are playing to the world', he would say jubilantly to his unit. 'We've gone beyond Babel, beyond words. We've found a universal language – a power that can make men brothers and end war forever. . . .'

After the triumph of *Shoulder Arms* (1918) Chaplin made *Sunnyside* (1919), which was a comparative failure. In 1919, with his marriage to Mildred Harris already showing signs of strain, he was at a crisis of self-doubt. He relates in his autobiography that he would go to his studio, day after day, along with his stock company of actors in the hope of inspiration that never came.

Just when he had despaired of finding a new idea, he went to the Orpheum music hall where Jack Coogan was appearing in his eccentric dancing act. Coogan's four-year-old son Jackie made a brief appearance along with him, and Chaplin was so engaged by the little boy's personality and way with an audience that he promptly began thinking up a scenario that would team the child and the Tramp. Jack Coogan had just signed a short-term contract with Fatty Arbuckle but the child was still free and Chaplin quickly hired him; as he recalls in his autobiography, the father's words were: 'Why, of course you can have the little punk.'

Jackie Coogan played Charlie's younger son in *A Day's Pleasure* (1919) as a preliminary to his major role in *The Kid*. Chaplin found the child a natural performer and quick learner:

'There were a few basic rules to learn in pantomime and Jackie very soon mastered them. He could apply emotion to the action and action to the emotion, and could repeat it time and again without losing the effect of spontaneity.'

The very real affection that grew up between Chaplin and Jackie is quite evident in *The Kid*. According to Chaplin, the poignant scene where Jackie cries real tears as the orphanage men are taking him away was achieved by the simple ruse of Jackie's father threatening that if he did not cry, he would be taken away from the studio to the real workhouse.

The film opened with a title: 'A picture with a smile – perhaps a tear.' Although previous Chaplin films had introduced sentiment and pathos, this was the first time in the history of film comedy that anyone had risked mingling a highly dramatic, near-tragic story with comedy and farce.

The film was also much longer – six reels, or 88 minutes at silent running speed – than any he had previously made. With his customary care (the one-minute scene of Charlie and Jackie's pancake breakfast is said to have taken two weeks and 50,000 feet of negative to achieve), his shooting schedule was long and costly. The sum of nearly $500,000 which he claimed to have invested was enormous for a comedy at that date.

It was completed under extreme difficulties. Mildred Harris was in the process of divorcing him by the time he was editing. Fearing that her lawyers might attempt to seize the film, Chaplin smuggled 500 reels of film to Salt Lake City, where the picture was cut in a hotel room, with only a small, elementary cutting machine on which to view the

This is the great picture upon which the famous comedian has worked a whole year.

6 reels of Joy.

Charles Chaplin IN "THE KID"

Written and directed by Charles Chaplin

A First National ⊕ Attraction

1

4

Directed by Charles Chaplin, 1921
Prod co: Charles Chaplin Productions, for First National. **prod:** Charles Chaplin. **assoc dir:** Charles (Chuck) Reisner. **sc:** Charles Chaplin. **photo:** Roland H. (Rollie) Totheroh. **length:** 5300 feet (approx. 88 minutes).
Cast: Charles Chaplin (*Tramp*), Edna Purviance (*mother*), Jackie Coogan (*boy*), Carl Miller (*artist-author*), Tom Wilson (*policeman*), Henry Bergman (*superintendent of the night shelter*), Chuck Reisner (*tough*), Lita Grey (*a flirtatious angel*), Phyllis Allen (*woman with the pram*), Nelly Bly Baker (*slum nurse*), Albert Austin (*man staying overnight in the shelter*), Jack Coogan (*pickpocket*).

material. Even when a preview was arranged at the local movie theatre, Chaplin had still not seen the finished picture on a screen. His inevitable apprehensions proved unfounded; from this very first screening, audiences responded wholeheartedly to the film, accepting totally the mixture of moods from high sentiment to low comedy.

Critics were not all so convinced. The playwright J. M. Barrie was among those who found the dream sequence out of place, which perhaps it is, though it is delightful with its slum angels (one of whom was, by chance, Chaplin's future wife, Lita Grey). Others were rather stuffy about 'vulgarities' such as Charlie's investigation of the foundling's sex, a joke about the child's dampness and the con-

sequent devising of toilet facilities. Today such endearingly truthful touches have ceased to shock. The sentimental elements are more alien to modern audiences; and when, almost half a century later, Chaplin reissued the film with new music of his own composition, he trimmed some shots that he felt would be unacceptable to a new public. He need hardly have worried. The film, his comic invention and Jackie Coogan's remarkable performance have lost none of their power – it is one of the most durable of all silent movies.

The Kid made Jackie Coogan a star and world-wide celebrity. His trip to Europe, when he was received by the Pope, monarchs and presidents, was a royal progress. He went on to a highly profitable

film career, playing such classic juvenile roles as the leads in *Peck's Bad Boy* (1921) and *Oliver Twist* (1922).

His beloved father, however, was killed in a road accident; and when, with adolescence and manhood, he found his star waning, his mother and stepfather withheld from him what was left of his earnings. Most of what remained was lost in lawsuits. This case had permanent results in the Californian legislation known as 'The Coogan Act' to secure half of the earnings of minors for their own future use. In later years Coogan, with no trace left of his cute baby looks, made occasional film appearances, and on television played the grotesque Uncle Fester in *The Addams Family*.

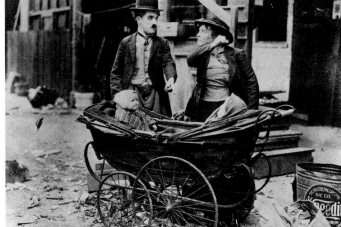

3

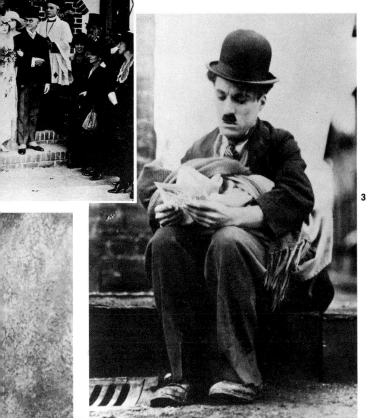

2

6

5

7

An unmarried mother (1) leaves her baby in an empty wedding limousine with a note asking the finder to care for the child. The car is stolen, and the thieves dump the baby in the slums where he is discovered by Charlie, a Tramp (2). Charlie's efforts to get rid of the child are all frustrated (3), and he is obliged to take him into his own garret room where he ingeniously devises a cradle, feeding bottles and other necessities.

Five years later (4) Charlie is a glazier; the boy precedes him around the street breaking windows. After a doctor has examined him (5), the child-care authorities try to take the little boy off to an orphanage (6); but Charlie manages to rescue him

from the truck that is carrying him away. Now fugitives (7), they pass the night in a doss-house among outcasts and thieves.

Meanwhile the mother, who has become a rich and famous singer, has by chance discovered the whereabouts of her long-lost and sought-after child. Learning of the reward she is offering, the superintendent of the doss-house snatches the child while Charlie is sleeping and carries him off to the police station.

Later Charlie, exhausted from seeking the child, dreams that the slums have been transformed into a paradise inhabited by angels and kindliness (8). He is awakened by a policeman – the mother has sent for Charlie to reunite him with the boy.

8

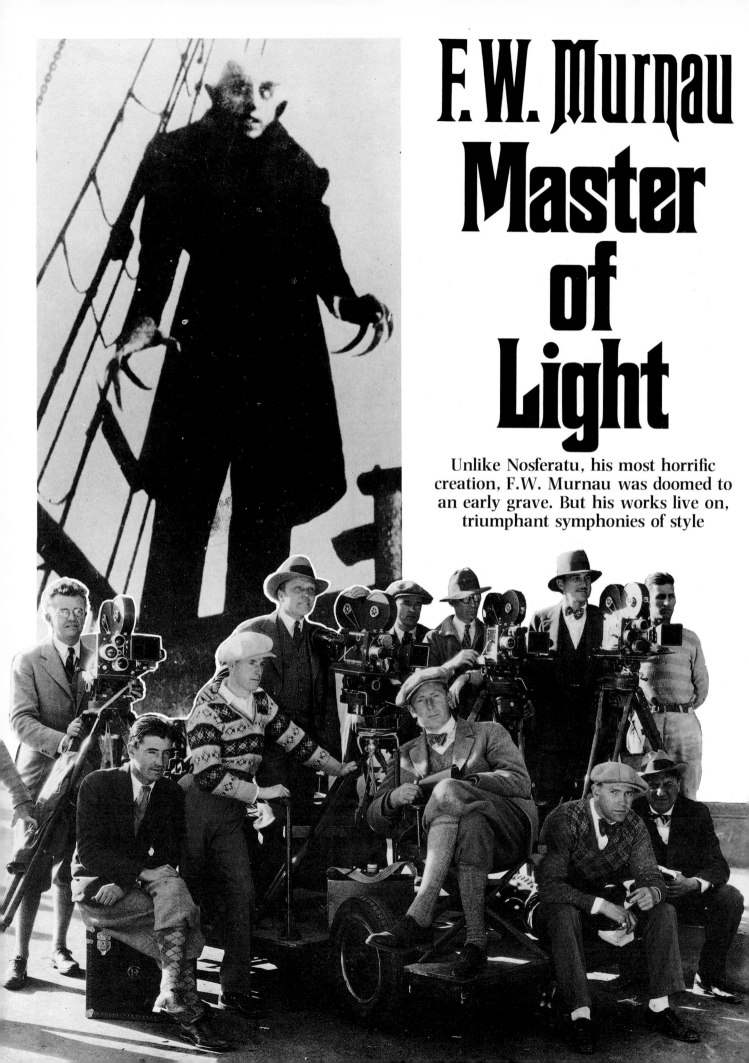

F.W. Murnau
Master of Light

Unlike Nosferatu, his most horrific creation, F.W. Murnau was doomed to an early grave. But his works live on, triumphant symphonies of style

Nothing appeals, of course, like a breath of scandal – especially Hollywood scandal – and rumours about the exact circumstances of the fatal car-crash on March 11, 1931, on the road from Los Angeles to Carmel, did not hesitate to paint the most lurid picture of orgiastic goings-on *en route*. In fact, all that seems to have happened was that F. W. Murnau, travelling in a chauffeur-driven Packard, eventually gave in to the pleadings of his young Filipino valet that he be allowed to take the wheel. Driving too fast and swerving to avoid a truck, the valet ran the car off the road. Most of its occupants were virtually unhurt, but Murnau suffered a fractured skull and died in hospital shortly afterwards. That, it appears, is the unexciting truth, but oddly enough the web of fantasy woven around the event has ensured that Murnau is known to many people who can never have seen any of his films.

They should, of course, know more. Murnau was far from a nobody back in his native Germany, and he may fairly be judged the most distinguished and talented of all the directors brought over to Hollywood in the Twenties with maximum publicity and the most elaborate red-carpet treatment. And Murnau's first Hollywood film, *Sunrise* (1927) has, in the last twenty years, been firmly reinstated in the 'Ten Best' lists of critics and film-historians throughout the world.

Left: Max Schreck as Nosferatu, the Vampire *– the new captain of a ship of death. Below left: Murnau (seated, centre) and the camera crew of* Sunrise. *Below: reflections and shadows highlight the downfall of the hotel doorman (Emil Jannings), forced to become a washroom attendant in* The Last Laugh

Sunrise is a staggering achievement – living proof that great European film-makers do not automatically sell their souls by going to Hollywood, or produce any less remarkable films than they were making back home in Germany, France, Sweden, Britain, or wherever. Murnau had in any case won the right to a degree of extravagance and perfectionism by directing some of the most famous and important films made in Germany in the silent era. Along with Fritz Lang and G. W. Pabst, he was at the forefront of the outstandingly creative German cinema of the early Twenties.

A master's missing links

It is difficult to trace the stages of his rise to fame and success in Germany, since only one of the nine films he made before his first masterpiece, *Nosferatu, eine Symphonie des Grauens* (1922, *Nosferatu, the Vampire*), survives anywhere near complete. After *Nosferatu, the Vampire*, the next three films are missing, or else, like *Phantom* (1922), are known only in newly unearthed fragments. So any picture of Murnau's early work has to be pieced together from contemporary accounts and more recent recollections.

He was born Friedrich Wilhelm Plumpe in Bielefeld in 1888, and as a young man was noted for his quiet and serious disposition. While studying art and literature at Heidelberg University, he took part in some student theatricals which impressed the great stage director Max Reinhardt, who offered Murnau what amounted to a six-year scholarship to study and work in his theatre in Berlin. Despite family opposition, Murnau accepted and acted in the company, as well as assisting Reinhardt as a director and closely observing him at

work, until the outbreak of World War I. During the war he served as a combat pilot, but his plane was forced down in neutral Switzerland and he was interned; he managed, however, to direct his own independent stage productions and worked with film for the first time, compiling propaganda materials for the German Embassy.

On his release he entered the film industry almost immediately, directing *Der Knabe in blau* (The Boy in Blue) in 1919. During the next two years he directed seven more films; these dealt with a wide variety of subject-matter, and were filmed in, as far as can be judged, a wide variety of styles. Then, at the end of 1921, he embarked on *Nosferatu, the Vampire*, his adaptation of Bram Stoker's novel *Dracula*. (The title had to be changed for reasons of copyright, but in fact Murnau's version is far closer to Stoker than Tod Browning's Hollywood talkie *Dracula*, 1931.) The film he made immediately before – *Schloss Vogelöd* (1921, Vogelöd Castle) – is usually said by historians who have not seen it to be a horror story anticipating *Nosferatu, the Vampire*, but in fact it is a very complicated melodrama ending with the deaths of several leading characters and containing two dream sequences, both treated rather comically.

With *Nosferatu, the Vampire*, Murnau demonstrated that he was one of the supreme masters at creating the dream-like mood of horror-fantasy in which so many classic German silents were bathed. He also showed that he had a most extraordinary visual sense, and though nothing is allowed to hold up the steady progress of the story, it is fixed on screen in images of unforgettable beauty and suggestive power.

He who laughs last . . .

Superficially, Murnau's next masterpiece, *Der letze Mann* (1925, The Last Laugh) could hardly be more different. *Nosferatu, the Vampire* is a perfect example of the dread-ridden German silent cinema – what the writer Lotte Eisner calls *The Haunted Screen* (the title of her book on German silent cinema). *The Last Laugh* seems to belong to the opposite tradition, that of the minutely realistic study of everyday life based on the small-scale theatrical production, called the *Kammerspiel*, which Reinhardt had developed alongside his famous spectacles. Yet Murnau's story of a resplendently uniformed

Below left: Conrad Veidt as the tormented doctor in Der Januskopf *(1920, Janus Head), Murnau's version of* Dr Jekyll and Mr Hyde. *Below: the conspirators and their victim (Harry Liedtke) in* Die Finanzen des Grossherzogs *(1924, The Grand Duke's Finances)*

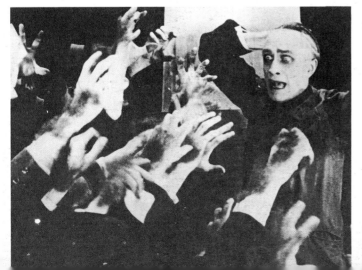

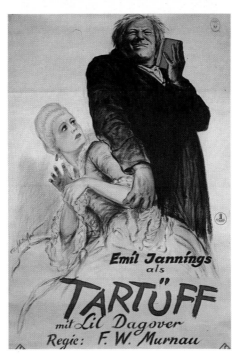

Above: Gösta Ekman as Faust *and Emil Jannings as the demon Mephisto. Above right: poster for* Tartuffe *showing Jannings in the title role of the hypocrite and Lil Dagover as the*

girl he lusts after. Below: George O'Brien as the peasant waiting on the edge of the swamp for his mistress in Sunrise *– the shot shows Murnau's eloquent use of space*

about a peasant wooing. He worked completely without interference, building giant sets, shooting and reshooting until he had got just the effect he desired. The result – *Sunrise* – is really a completely German film made in America with American stars (Janet Gaynor and George O'Brien). Visually stunning and atmospherically sublime, it is constructed in a European style: the story itself remains slight, though Murnau's treatment develops it like a symphony, reaching a crescendo with the storm on the lake in which the reunited husband and wife are nearly separated for ever. *Sunrise* was greeted with critical acclaim, and went on to win all kinds of awards. But the great American public did not buy it, and this relative failure overshadowed the progress of Murnau's two subsequent films for Fox.

The coming of sound did not help either, spreading uncertainty among the studios as to what they should do with the more expensive projects then in the works. Murnau's next film, a circus drama called *Four Devils* (1928), suffered from front-office interference designed to make it more general in its appeal. *Our Daily Bread* (1930) was begun with enormous ambition as a saga of the mid-Western grain lands, but got progressively cut down into a personal story of a city girl's problems with a hostile-seeming environment. Retitled *City Girl*, it was roughly re-edited with some talkie sequences (not by Murnau) to cash in on the new craze. Finally, though the silent version of the film contains some of the director's finest work, this was hardly noticed in the confusion of the talkies and his Hollywood career ended.

Paradise lost

He did, however, manage to make one more film: the privately financed and evidently non-commercial *Tabu* (1930), begun in collaboration with the documentary film-maker Robert Flaherty and intended as a semi-documentary, was filmed entirely in South Sea locations with a non-professional cast of Polynesians. Lacking the documentarist's ideals, Murnau insisted on making it into a rhapsody on the theme of fated young love, as elaborately structured as any of his studio pictures. The result was a perfect swansong for the director – a hymn to natural beauty, of people and of landscape, and a triumph of aesthetic cinema. But it did not open until a few days after his death, and what else he would have done – in America or Europe – remains one of the cinema's most intriguing fields of speculation.

doorman's fall from glory is realized in images just as haunting and atmospheric as those in which he clothed his vampire tales. And Emil Jannings' performance in the principal role – the one in which he first amazed international audiences with how much he could convey with his back to the camera – was also a potent factor in making the film the most universally noticed German feature of the year. It was, in fact, the immense American success of *The Last Laugh* which eventually brought both Jannings and Murnau to Hollywood.

Before he succumbed to the blandishments of the Hollywood producer William Fox, however, Murnau made two more films in Germany: both adaptations of theatrical classics, both with Jannings. *Tartüff* (1925, *Tartuffe*) was based on Molière's play, and *Faust* (1926) was based on Goethe's, and both opened in 1926.

Tartuffe is an ingenious attempt to adapt a stage work in terms of a stage performance, distanced by a framing device but retaining all the theatricality of Molière's original concept. *Faust*, on the other hand, seizes the opportunity to make the whole into a thoroughly 'cinematic' film. Such is Murnau's skill in using the basic syntax of the cinema to his own purposes that it is hard to say which film is the more successful or the more genuinely cinematic.

California sunrise . . .

Then came the red-carpet treatment in Hollywood. All the resources of the Fox studios were placed at Murnau's disposal. He was able to use a script by his favourite writer, Carl Mayer, an adaptation of *The Journey to Tilsit*. Hermann Sudermann's Lithuanian story

Filmography
1919 Der Knabe in blau/Der Todessmaragd. **'20** Satanas; Sehnsucht/Bajazzo; Der Bucklige und die Tänzerin; Der Januskopf/Schrecken; Abend – Nacht – Morgen; Der Gang in die Nacht (USA: Love's Mockery). **'21** Schloss Vogelöd. **'22** Nosferatu, eine Symphonie des Grauens (USA: Nosferatu, the Vampire) (German sound version: Die zwoelfte Stunde – Eine Nacht des Grauens, 1930); Marizza, genannt die Schmuggler-Madonna/Ein schönes Tier, das schöne Tier; Der Brennende Acker; Phantom. **'23** Die Austreibung. **'24** Die Finanzen des Grossherzogs. **'25** Der letzte Mann (USA/GB: The Last Laugh); Tartüff (USA: Tartuffe, the Hypocrite; GB: Tartuffe). **'26** Faust. *All remaining films USA:* **'27** Sunrise – A Song of Two Humans. **'28** Four Devils. **'30** City Girl/Our Daily Bread; Tabu (+co-prod; +co-sc).

Mack Sennett's comic touch

Mack Sennett gave up playing heavy-handed country bumpkins to concentrate on running his successful new company, Keystone. The name became a hallmark for pace-setting comedies that were turned out by the hundreds: best loved and best known are those featuring that immortal crew of crazy Kops, who perennially rush to the rescue – arms flailing, feet slithering as they concertina into each other, leaving mayhem in their wake

Mack Sennett was born Michael Sinnott on January 17, 1880 in Richmond, Quebec. When he was 17, his family, who were of Irish descent, moved to Connecticut, where the lad found a job in a local iron foundry. He grew into manhood endowed with not much else besides a good bass voice, a yearning for the theatre and an obstreperous determination which was later to serve him well.

When the great comedienne Marie Dressler visited Northampton – where the Sinnotts had settled in 1898 – Michael secured an introduction from a rising local lawyer, Calvin Coolidge (who was also to achieve future fame as

President of the United States). In her turn Miss Dressler gave the young man an introduction to the great theatrical impresario David Belasco. Impatiently Michael rushed off to New York, where Belasco unfeelingly told him that he would do better to look for an opening in burlesque rather than in legitimate theatre or grand opera. Michael was not too proud to take the advice, and, changing his name to Mack Sennett, he took a job as utility comic in Frank Sheridan's Burlesque Company. The next few years were spent between burlesque and work as a chorus boy and comic support in a number of Broadway musicals.

Two faces of Sennett: (top) as actor with Mabel Normand and Charlie Chaplin in The Fatal Mallet *(1914), and (above) as director on the set of* Stolen Magic *(1915)*

Perhaps because of the scarcity of theatre work, in 1908 or 1909 Sennett enrolled in the regular stock company at the Biograph studios. Linda Arvidson, the wife of D. W. Griffith, Biograph's leading director, recalls that he was ready and eager to play any part, as well as to muck in with the rest of the company in building sets, or in doing any other odd jobs about the place.

First steps

Sennett's first big chance as a film comedian came with *The Curtain Pole* (1909), directed by Griffith who had to turn his hand to anything from farce to classical tragedy. Sennett, who thought French characters essentially funnier than English – 'the French go all the way' – played Monsieur Dupont who, slightly elated by absinthe, carries a long curtain pole through a crowded market place, wreaking comic havoc.

Mrs Griffith, who was playing a customer in the market place, had special cause to remember Sennett's first starring role, which she describes in *When the Movies Were Young*:

'He succeeded very well, for before I had paid for my cabbage, something hit me and I was knocked not only flat but considerably out, and left genuinely unconscious in the center of the stage. While I was satisfied he should have them, I wasn't so keen just then about Mack Sennett's starring ventures. But he gave a classic and noble performance, albeit a hard-working one.'

Sennett writes in his autobiography that he assiduously studied Griffith's methods both on and off the set. Mrs Griffith recalled that:

'When work was over, Sennett would hang around the studio watching for the opportune moment when his director would leave. Mr Griffith often walked home wanting to get a bit of fresh air. This Sennett had discovered. So in front of the studio or at the corner of Broadway and 14th Street he'd pull off the "accidental" meeting. Then for twenty-three blocks he would have the boss all to himself and wholly at his mercy. Twenty-three blocks of uninterrupted conversation. "Well now, what do you really think about these moving pictures? What do you think there is in them? Do you think they are going to last? What's in them for the actor? What do you think of my chances?"

'To all of which Mr Griffith would reply: "Well, not much for the actor, if you're thinking of staying. The only thing is to become a director. I can't see that there's anything much for the actor as far as the future is concerned".'

Changing direction

Sennett also recalls these evening conversations; and his disappointment that Griffith did not share his feeling for the comic possibilities of policemen in movies. However, he took seriously the advice about directing. In 1910 Biograph introduced a new director, Frank Powell, to take charge of a second unit, which henceforth undertook all comedy production. When Powell fell ill, Sennett eagerly took over as director. There is some dispute about which is the first picture that he directed, since he may have worked for a while as assistant to Griffith or Powell rather than as a fully-fledged director. His directorial debut appears, however, to have been in October 1910 with *A Lucky Toothache* or *The Masher*, or in March

1911 with *Comrades*. What is certain is that from March 1911 until the summer of 1912 all Biograph comedies – numbering around one hundred titles, ranging from four-minute split-reels to one-reelers – were directed by Sennett.

It was wonderful training in the invention and direction of comedy; and Sennett admitted cheerfully to extensive theft of ideas from his admired French clowns. His favourite actor at Biograph was the plump Fred Mace, with whom Sennett played in a series of films about a couple of comic detectives. His favourite actress was, and was to remain, Mabel Normand. This beautiful, graceful and witty comedienne was barely fifteen when Sennett first encountered her at Biograph. It was the beginning of a stormy romance that outlasted Mabel's short life (she died in 1930 aged only 35): Sennett's love for her continued till his own death. It was an affair constantly interrupted and impeded by quarrels and reconciliations between two incorrigibly volatile personalities.

Key to success

Though they did not collect the reverential press coverage accorded to the Griffith dramas, the Biograph comedies captivated the public and made money. So Sennett was able to convince a couple of bookmakers, Kessel and Baumann, to whom he owed money, that their interests would be best served by setting him up in his own studio. Thus Keystone was born, and Sennett's backers were launched as moguls. The next years saw Sennett in whirl-wind activity. He quickly convinced Kessel and Baumann to let him move his operation to California, and took over the old Bison studios at Edendale. He established regular production of two split-reels each week then moved on to issue first two and then three one-reelers every week, with a monthly two-reel production. He

of curious and colourful characters; and – quite incidentally to Sennett's aims, which were simply to make money out of comedy – advanced movie art, giving a new freedom to the camera which had to develop the same agility as the funny-men themselves.

Sennett recruited his artists from burlesque, circus, vaudeville, from building sites and mental hospitals. At first he directed all the films himself, but as the Keystone output grew, to keep several units occupied at any one time, he recruited or created other directors, among them the comedians Mabel Normand, Fatty Arbuckle, Dell Henderson and Charles Parrott (alias Charlie Chase). The films were largely improvised; and a single prop (car, telephone, boat) or setting (a grocery store or a garage) was enough to inspire endless comic variations.

Law and disorder

Keystone comedy drew its inspiration from comic strips, French slapstick cinema, vaude-ville, pantomime; its techniques approached those of the old Italian *commedia dell'arte*; and yet it was different from all of these. The Keystone comedies remain a monument of twentieth-century popular art, transmuting

Left: Chester Conklin, nicknamed 'Fishface' because of his oversized moustache, was often the wide-eyed victim. Below: with the face and manner of a child, 'Fatty' Arbuckle nonetheless proved irresistible to the ladies in his many successful comedies

the reality of the life and times of the teens and twenties of the century into a comedy that is basic and universal. The Sennett shorts were uncompromisingly anarchic, celebrating an orgiastic destruction of goods and possessions, cars, houses and crockery. Authority and dignity were regularly brought low – most notably by the Keystone Kops, that supremely incompetent law-enforcement troupe who were forever falling out of windows, tumbling down stairs or flying off their skidding patrol wagons, heading – brakeless – for imminent, cliff-edge catastrophes.

Star-studded casts

The inhabitants of this world were larger and wilder and far more colourful than life. They might be fat or thin, giants or dwarfs, with oversize pants and undersized hats, entangled spectacles and uncontrollable moustaches. They were monstrous, wonderful caricatures of reality. After Normand and Mace, Sennett's long procession of stars was to include Ford Sterling, with his angry face and ludicrous goatee (generally the superintendent of the Kops); baby-faced Fatty Arbuckle; cross-eyed Ben Turpin, with his phenomenal Adam's apple; gangling Charlie Chase; walrus-moustached Billy Bevan; confused Chester Conklin and the gigantic Mack Swain. Later Keystone stars included Charles Murray, Slim Summerville, Sydney Chaplin (brother of Charles), Hank Mann, Edgar Kennedy, Harry McCoy, Cary Brooks, Don Barclay, Harry Booker, Francis Wilson and Billy Walsh. Two

took Mabel Normand, Fred Mace and the actor-director Henry 'Pathé' Lehrman from Biograph, and created new artists. He intro-duced the Keystone Kops, animal comedies and child comedies.

Sennett's Keystone developed a unique, sur-real style of visual comedy. It enriched the folk-lore of America and the world with a universe

Below: a comedy directed by Sennett for Biograph in 1912, the year he left to form Keystone. Below left: a gag typical of Keystone comedies, from Between Showers (1914) with Emma Clifton, Charlie Chaplin, Ford Sterling and Chester Conklin

Keystone Kops, Eddie Sutherland and Edward Cline, became distinguished comedy directors, as did two Keystone gag men, Malcolm St Clair and Frank Capra. As well as the divine Mabel, the Sennett troupe of funny women included Polly Moran, Minta Durfee, Alice Davenport, Phyllis Allen, Louise Fazenda and Alice Howell. Of the greatest comedy artists who passed through the Keystone studios, Harold Lloyd failed to make his mark under Sennett; while his major discovery, Charlie Chaplin, left him after only one year and 35 one- or two-reel pictures. (Sennett, fearful of wage escalation, would never pay well enough to retain his most successful stars for long.)

In July 1915 Sennett was one of the Big Three – the others were D. W. Griffith and Thomas Ince – who were formed into the Triangle company. Triangle-Keystone, without forfeiting any of its allegiance to slapstick and to the public, was able to enlarge its ambitions. At first – in line with the aspirations of his sister companies for the prestige of famous names – Sennett engaged major stage comedy stars of the time, Raymond Hitchcock, Eddie Foy, Weber and Fields, though the results were uneven; and Triangle-Keystone tended quite soon to revert to its own stars, more accustomed to the demands of the screen.

More important, Sennett was able to extend his comedy production and embark on two- and three-reelers. Production values were more elaborate; characterization was more developed. The old *commedia dell'arte* improvisation began to give way – with no appreciable loss of invention and freedom – to more careful scripting and pre-planning of production.

By 1917 however, the Triangle partnership was breaking up. In June of that year, Sennett succeeded in extricating himself from the contract, though the Keystone company remained part of the Triangle grouping. Without Sennett, its creator and guiding force, the unit finally foundered in 1919.

In the swim
Though he had lost the company and the name, Sennett still retained his studio at Edendale, and continued in full production, releasing his films as 'Sennett Comedies' through Paramount. It was apparently at this period that the Sennett Bathing Beauties were first consciously introduced. Ornamental as their presence was in the films themselves, the object of the Bathing Beauties was rather to secure publicity for Sennett productions in magazines and newspapers. Sennett discovered

Below and below left: called to the rescue, the patrol wagon roars off without its occupants. It swings round a corner and the Kops are spun round a pole – still hanging on

early on that while picture editors were unenthusiastic about printing photographs of bewhiskered or cross-eyed comics, a photograph of a line of pretty girls in chic bathing dresses (and Sennett commissioned couturiers to design swim-suits that revealed more of the feminine shape than the usual patterns then in mode) was irresistible.

A longer laugh
In this period, too, Sennett's productions took new directions. Ben Turpin's grotesque style inspired him to a whole series of parodies of current Hollywood hits, with names like *The Shriek of Araby* (1923) and *Three Foolish Weeks* (1924). Love perhaps inspired Sennett to feature production. To placate Mabel, who had demanded more challenging parts, Sennett created the Mabel Normand Feature Film Company, and starred her in a full-length film, *Mickey* (1918). Hollywood was sceptical about the idea of a feature-length comedy; and Sennett invested his own money in the project. He was wholly vindicated when the public took this modern Cinderella comedy to its hearts: the film is said to have grossed $16 million. Sennett was to star Mabel Normand, whose later life was shadowed by drugs and scandals but whose charm was unimpaired, in the subsequent features, *Molly O* (1921) and *Suzanna* (1922).

In 1921 Sennett established Mack Sennett Inc., and released his films through First National. In 1923 he made further organizational changes, and from then until 1929 distributed his films through Pathé Exchange. The Pathé period was notable mainly for the series of films made with Harry Langdon, perhaps the oddest of the great comedy stars with his character of a middle-aged baby or a demented Pierrot Lunaire. Frank Capra, who directed or wrote Langdon's best features,

Above left: the Kop and ubiquitious fat man were staple fare of Keystone. Above: Mack Sennett Comedies, formed in 1917, used far more sophisticated sets and costumes as here in The Shriek of Araby, *a parody exploiting Ben Turpin's ocular disability*

notably *Long Pants* (1927), was later to claim that it was he, as a gag-man with Sennett, who first perceived Langdon's potential and modelled his screen character. Though it is true that Langdon's later efforts as his own director were less than successful, Capra's version, which has been accepted by history, disserves Langdon. For more than twenty years he had been a vaudeville star, with a very clearly defined comic character; and even before Capra, his whole essence was evident in the Sennett two-reelers directed by Harry Edwards.

Times were changing. Sennett responded uncertainly to the new audiences who felt that they were too sophisticated for the old styles of slapstick two-reelers. He knew that sound was not his element, though in 1928 he made his first sound feature, *The Lion's Roar*, and in 1930 experimented with colour.

Industrial reorganizations meant that Sennett films in 1929 were distributed by the ominously named Educational Film Company. In 1932 Sennett was obliged to close his studios. In 1935 the economic problems of Paramount had repercussions which resulted in Sennett's considerable personal fortune being wiped out.

He moved back to Canada, where he worked for a while as an associate producer for Fox. Even by this time Sennett and the Keystone Kops had passed into Hollywood legend. But legend was of small benefit to Sennett. He died, still mourning his beloved Mabel, on November 5, 1960, in an old people's home in Hollywood.

Pretty girls have always drawn publicity – a startled bevy with Mack Swain (above) and two of Sennett's Bathing Beauties (inset)

Filmography

All shorts unless otherwise specified. **1908** *Films as actor:* 6 films including The Song of the Shirt; Mr Jones at the Ball; The Sculptor's Nightmare. **'09** 39 films including the Jones series; The Curtain Pole; A Sound Sleeper; What Drink Did; The Violin Maker of Cremona; The Lonely Villa; Her First Biscuits; Pippa Passes, or the Song of Conscience; The Little Teacher. **'10** 27 films including All on Account of the Milk; The Englishman and the Girl; An Arcadian Maid; A Lucky Toothache; The Masher; Effecting a Cure. **'11** 58 films including Priscilla's Engagement Kiss (+sup); Comrades (+dir); The Lonedale Operator (sc. only); Cupid's Joke (+dir); Misplaced Jealousy (+dir); The Country Lovers (+dir); The Manicure Lady (+dir); The Beautiful Voice (+dir); Taking His Medicine (dir. only). **'12** 71 films including Brave and Bold (dir. only); The Fatal Chocolate (+dir); A Voice From the Deep (dir. only); Those Hicksville Boys (+dir); Their First Kidnapping (+dir); When the Fire Bells Rang (dir. only); Katchem Kate (dir. only). *Films as producer and director:* Pedro's Dilemma (+act); At Coney Island (+act); Mabel's Lovers; The Duel (+act); Mabel's Strategem (prod. only). **'13** 128 films including the Mabel series; The Sleuth's Last Stand (+act); The Sleuth's at the Floral Parade (+act); A Wife Wanted (prod. only); Murphy's IOU; Cupid in the Dental Parlour (prod. only); The Darktown Belle; Barney Oldfield's Race for Life (+act); The Speed Queen; Peeping Pete (co-dir; +act); For Love of Mabel (prod. only); Love and Rubbish (prod. only); Cohen's Outing; The Firebugs; Baby Day; Fatty's Day Off (prod. only); Mabel's Dramatic Career (co-dir; +act); Schnitz the Tailor; Fatty at San Diego (prod. only); Love Sickness at Sea (+act); Fatty Joins the Force (prod. only); The Champion (prod. only). *As producer only:* **'14** 145 films

including the Mabel series and the Fatty series; Making a Living; Kid Auto Races at Venice; Mabel's Strange Predicament (+co-dir); Love and Gasoline; Between Showers; A Film Johnnie; Tango Tangles (+dir); His Favourite Pastime; Cruel, Cruel Love; The Star Boarder; Mabel at the Wheel (+act); Twenty Minutes of Love (+dir); Caught in a Cabaret; Caught in the Rain; The Fatal Mallet (+act); Mabel's Busy Day; Mabel's Married Life; Fatty and the Heiress; Laughing Gas; The Property Man; The Face on the Bar-room Floor; The Masquerader; His New Profession; The Rounders; Mabel's Last Prank (+dir; +act); Those Love Pangs; Dough and Dynamite; Gentlemen of Nerve; His Musical Career; His Trysting Place; Tillie's Punctured Romance (+dir) (feature); Getting Acquainted; His Prehistoric Past. **'15** 102 films including the Fatty and Mabel series, the Ambrose series and the Gussle series; Mabel's and Fatty's Wash Day; Ambrose's Sour Grapes; Miss Fatty's Seaside Lover; Gussle Tied to Trouble; Saved by Wireless; The Best of Enemies; Fatty and the Broadway Stars (+sc; +act); A Submarine Pirate (+sc). **'16** 67 films including A Modern Enoch Arden; A Movie Star; Bucking Society; The Surf Girl; The Fire Chief. **'17** 50 films including A Cream Puff Romance; Teddy at the Throttle; Roping Her Romeo; The Pullman Bride. **'18** 25 films including Sheriff Nell's Tussle; Mickey (feature). **'19** 25 films including Rip & Stitch, Tailors; East Lynne with Variations; Hearts and Flowers; No Mother to Guide Him; Yankee Doodle in Berlin/The Kaiser's Last Squeal (feature); Uncle Tom Without the Cabin; Salome vs Shenandoah. **'20** 22 films including The Star Boarder; Down on the Farm (feature); Married Life (feature); Love, Honour and Behave (feature). **'21** 16 films including A Small Town Idol (+sc) (feature); Molly O (+co-sc) (feature); Oh, Mabel Behave (+co-

dir; +act) (feature). **'22** 15 films including The Crossroads of New York (feature); Love and Doughnuts; Suzanna (+sc) (feature). **'23** 12 films including The Shriek of Araby (+sc) (feature); Where Is My Wandering Boy This Evening?; Nip and Tuck; The Extra Girl (+sc) (feature). **'24** 33 films including Picking Peaches; The Hollwood Kid (+sc; +act); The Lion and the Souse; Romeo and Juliet; The First 100 Years; East of the Water Plug (+sc); Lizzies of the Field; Three Foolish Weeks; Little Robinson Corkscrew; Riders of the Purple Cows; The Real Virginian; Galloping Bungalows; Love's Sweet Piffle; Feet of Mud; Bull and Sand. **'25** 42 films including The Sea Squaw; Boobs in the Woods (+sc); Water Wagons; He Who Gets Smacked; A Rainy Knight; Dangerous Curves Behind. **'26** 48 films including Whispering Whiskers; Gooseland; Spanking Breezes; Hooked at the Altar; Hoboken to Hollywood; A Harem Knight. **'27** 37 films including A Small Town Princess; His First Flame (feature). **'28** 32 films including A Finished Actor (+dir); The Good-Bye Kiss (+dir; +sc) (feature); The Lion's Roar (+dir; +sc) (feature). **'29** 36 films including Foolish Husbands; Caught in a Taxi. *Films as producer and director:* Midnight Daddies (feature). **'30** 23 films including Radio Kisses (+song); Hello Television (prod. only); Grandma's Girl. **'31** 33 films including A Poor Fish; One More Chance. *Films as producer only:* **'32** 32 films including Hypnotized (+dir; +sc) (feature). **'33** 21 films including Blue of the Night; A Fatal Glass of Beer; The Pharmacist; The Barber Shop. **'35** 5 films including Ye Olde Saw Mill (+dir; +co-sc). **'39** Hollywood Cavalcade (actor only). **'49** Down Memory Lane (appearance as self only).

The selected filmography above includes all of Sennett's major films.

The Cabinet of Dr Caligari

When it was released in Britain in 1922, *The Cabinet of Dr Caligari* was billed as 'Europe's greatest contribution to the motion picture art' and it remains one of the cinema's landmarks. But its making and its meaning continue to give rise to controversy, with the sometimes conflicting accounts left by the participants playing a significant part.

Evidently, Hans Janowitz and Carl Mayer, two young writers, devised a script in which they mingled their own memories of a notorious Hamburg sex murder and an unsympathetic army psychiatrist Carl encountered while on military service with several archetypal themes from German Romanticism. They apparently intended their story to be a modern pacifist parable, with Cesare as the symbol of the people and Caligari as the state, seemingly benign and respected but in fact ordering the people to kill (in wars). The meaning of the ending, in which Caligari is unmasked and overthrown, is therefore clearly anti-authoritarian.

Erich Pommer, head of the small Decla company, agreed to produce a film of the script and assigned Fritz Lang to direct. But when Lang's work on *Die Spinnen* (1919, *The Spiders*) went on longer than expected, the job fell to Robert Wiene, who, it was felt, was equipped to handle a story involving insanity because his own father, a once-famous actor, had gone mad towards the end of his life. Then either Pommer or Wiene or both insisted on adding a framing device to the script (a prologue and an epilogue), making the story a tale told by a madman. The result of this is to completely reverse the meaning of the original story and rob it of its subversive intent.

In his classic book, *From Caligari to Hitler*, Siegfried Kracauer elaborated the theory of the German cinema directly reflecting the mentality of the German people and foreshadowing the rise of the Nazis. In particular he saw Caligari as the first of a series of power-crazed tyrants in German films, to whom the other characters in the story situation submit without question. But this view is now regarded as too precise and mechanistic.

Equally untenable is the view advanced by scholars like Lotte Eisner that the Germans are somehow peculiarly obsessed with death, madness and twilight. Interestingly, although Hollywood in the Thirties produced horror films in the same style and on the same themes as Germany in the Twenties, no one suggests that the Americans are therefore peculiarly pessimistic or doom-laden. It seems more likely that the popularity of tales of horror in Weimar Germany and Depression America has the same cause – a turning to stylized horrors to escape the real horrors of depression and inflation.

What is incontrovertible is that *The Cabinet of Dr Caligari* is an Expressionist film. But to what extent? Expressionism was a movement in the arts beginning before World War I. It involved painters whose work was characterized by subjectivism, emotionalism and anti-naturalism. This is significant because Hermann Warm, Walter Reimann and Walter Röhrig, who designed *The Cabinet of Dr Caligari*, were themselves Expressionist artists. In literature, Expressionism embraced the themes of 'alienation, anti-authoritarianism, pacifism, salvation through love, and hostility to bourgeois society'. Some of these elements were certainly present in the original script but were negated by the framing device.

The visual style of the film was distinctly Expressionist – with painted backcloths, dominated by curves and cubes, deliberately distorted perspectives, and furniture unnaturally elongated. The effect was to disorientate the viewer, and it was enhanced further by the Expressionist style of acting – with Werner Krauss' top-hatted and bespectacled Caligari a shuffling, gesticulating, totally malign presence; and Conrad Veidt's somnambulist, a slender, hollow-eyed, ashen-faced, living corpse. There were only a few totally Expressionist films like *The Cabinet of Dr Caligari*, which drew themes, styles and visual motifs directly from the movement; but elements of Expressionism in art direction and the plastic, externalized acting style it fostered nevertheless became distinguishing features of the German cinema until the late Twenties.

Over the years considerable attention has been devoted to the political, psychological and artistic importance of *The Cabinet of Dr Caligari*, but only recently has its perhaps most obvious importance – as horror film – been more fully appreciated. For whatever else it was, the film also represented the latest manifestation of German Romanticism with a pedigree stretching back to the novelist E.T.A. Hoffman, the folklorists Jakob and Wilhelm Grimm, and the dramatist-poet Schiller. It is from these roots that the themes of death, tyranny, fate and disorder, and the subjects of haunted students, mad doctors, ghosts, mummies, vampires and somnambulists spring. *The Cabinet of Dr Caligari* was as much a product of this tradition as such contemporary horror classics as *Der Golem: wie er in die Welt Kam* (1920, *The Golem*), *Nosferatu, eine Symphonie des Grauens* (1922, *Nosferatu, the Vampire*), *Orlacs Hände* (1925, *The Hands of Orlac*) and *Der Student von Prag* (1926, *The Student of Prague*).

In the Romanticism of its content and the Expressionism of its form,

2

3

5

6

8

9

The Cabinet of Dr Caligari not only exercised a decisive influence on other German horror films, but also on the later Hollywood horror genre – where, for instance, in the films of Robert Florey, the students, fairground, mad doctor and killer ape of *Murders in the Rue Morgue* (1932) and the madman's fantasy of persecution in *The Beast With Five Fingers* (1946) are recognizably akin to the milieu of *The Cabinet of Dr Caligari*.

Seated on a bench in a lane, Francis tells his story to a companion (1) . . .

In the north German town of Holstenwall a travelling fair appears, and Francis persuades his friend Alan, a student, to visit it with him (2). Dr Caligari, one of the showmen, asks the town clerk to grant him the necessary

licence. The clerk mocks him and next day is found murdered.

Francis and Alan, now at the fair, go to see Caligari and his somnambulist Cesare (3). Cesare foretells Alan's future (4) – he will live until dawn. Next day, Alan is found killed in the same manner as the town clerk. Francis, suspecting Caligari, takes the doctor father of Jane, the girl he loves, to examine Cesare but the doctor can find nothing amiss. Francis, however, continues to watch Caligari, not knowing that he has replaced Cesare with a dummy, which now rests in the coffin where the somnambulist sleeps.

Sent to kill Jane, Cesare carries her off instead (5), chased by her family. Eventually he falls dead of exhaustion. The police discover the dummy in the coffin

(6), but Caligari escapes. Francis follows Caligari to the asylum and entering, discovers he is the Director (7).

Next night, Francis and three of the asylum staff search the Director's papers (8) and discover an account of an eighteenth-century Italian showman called Caligari who used his somnambulist Cesare to kill people. Francis confronts the Director with Cesare's corpse

and, raving, he is put in a strait-jacket.

Having finished his story, Francis returns to the courtyard of the asylum, where he, Cesare and Jane are inmates. The Director appears and Francis attacks him. Attendants overpower Francis (9) and the Director declares that now he has realized that Francis thinks he is Caligari, he can cure him of his madness.

Directed by Robert Wiene, 1919
Prod co: Decla-Bioscop. prod: Erich Pommer. assoc prod: Rudolf Meinert. sc: Carl Mayer, Hans Janowitz, from a story by Hans Janowitz. photo: Willy Hameister. art dir: Hermann Warm, Walter Röhrig, Walter Reimann. cost: Walter Reimann. length: 4682 ft (approx. 78 minutes). German title: *Das Kabinett des Dr Caligari*. Released in GB as *The Cabinet of Dr Caligari*. Cast: Werner Krauss (*Dr Caligari*), Conrad Veidt (*Cesare*), Friedrich Feher (*Francis*), Lil Dagover (*Jane*), Hans H. von Twardowski (*Alan*), Rudolf Lettinger (*Dr Olsen*), Rudolf Klein-Rogge (*captured murderer*).

Clara Bow

The 'It' Girl

Clara Bow was the 'It' girl – the star whose nickname survived after she, and the era that she had lit so brightly, had been long forgotten. She was an uninhibited, exuberant flapper, the embodiment of the Jazz Age and its pursuit of love and laughter

Had Clara Bow died at the peak of her popularity in the late Twenties her face would probably have remained as familiar as that of Jean Harlow and Marilyn Monroe, who both died young. The mention of her name would then have instantly conjured up that vibrant, tousle-haired prettiness which rushed from the screen with so much life to give. But if Clara Bow is remembered at all it is as the 'It' girl, the personification of sex appeal. 'It' was the term coined by the romantic novelist Elinor Glyn and defined, in the hit song by Sigmund Romberg, as 'That improper fraction, of vague attraction, that gets the action, somehow'. Asked to say who she thought had 'It', Madame Glyn mentioned Rex the Wonder Horse, the doorman at her hotel . . . and Clara Bow. She even wrote a script around it for Clara, and in *It!* (1927) the star played a sexy, rumbustious shop-girl who ends up marrying the boss of the department store where she works.

The 'It' girl did not die young. She lived on and faded away, to die at 58 in a Los Angeles sanatorium in 1965. But Clara Bow had packed more living, loving, tragedy and fame into her first twenty-five years than most people do in a lifetime.

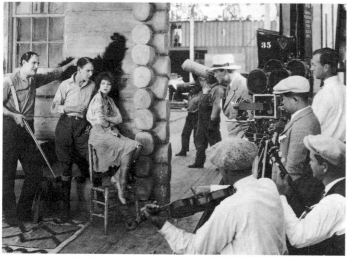

It is hard to see Clara Bow's films and not respond to the direct, simple, outgoing charm that had made her the idol of her generation. But while her on-screen image was one of great vitality and a compelling open-heartedness, underneath Clara was wracked by mistrust and nervous instabilities that were the result of a miserable childhood.

She was born on July 29, 1907, the third daughter – and the only one to survive birth – of Robert and Sarah Bow, a poor couple living in Brooklyn, New York. Her mother never recovered from losing her first two children and became increasingly ill. At five Clara watched her grandfather die from a stroke while swinging her in the makeshift swing he had built in the family's two-room apartment; at eight she held her young playmate in her arms as he died from burns.

Left: . . . butter wouldn't melt in her mouth. Below far left: all eyes on the star of Mantrap *– they belong to actors Ernest Torrence (left) and Percy Marmont, director Victor Fleming and cinematographer James Wong Howe. Below left: as* Rough House Rosie *(1927), with sparring partner Reed Howes*

But she wasn't without friends, most of them boys:

'When they played baseball in the evening in the streets, I was always chosen first and I pitched. I wasn't a pretty child at all . . . my eyes were too black and my hair was too red. When I was little, people always took me for a boy.'

The young Clara took solace in the movies and early on decided that she wanted to be a film actress. When she was 14 – and working as a telephone receptionist in a doctor's office – she entered a 'Fame and Fortune' contest run by some of the movie fan magazines. The winner got a silver trophy, an evening gown and a contract for a part in one film. Encouraged by her father, Clara had two pictures of herself taken at a cheap Brooklyn photographer's, sent them in and was one of 12 girls chosen for a screen test – in which she impressed the judges with her range of emotional expression. In November 1921 they announced that Clara was the winner. 'You are going straight to hell,' her mother said, 'I would rather see you dead.'

The small role she won as part of her prize was as a flirt in W. Christy Cabanne's *Beyond the Rainbow* (1922), starring Billie Dove. With no previous screen experience, Clara had to teach herself how to act as well as do her own makeup and provide her own wardrobe. When the film was released her five scenes had been cut out (when she became famous they were reinstated for the movie's reissue), and there was no work forthcoming. She was turned down by the studios for being too young, too little or too fat: 'Usually I was too fat.' But in 1922 she was sent for by the director Elmer Clifton who needed a small, tomboyish girl to play the second lead in *Down to the Sea in Ships*, and had spotted Clara's photograph in *Motion Picture* magazine. The night she got the part her mother came into her room with a

Left: in Clarence Badger's film Elinor Glyn expounds on 'It' to store-boss Cyrus (Moreno) – but Clara doesn't bother with words. Below left: as college flapper Cynthia in The Plastic Age, *with Gilbert Roland and Donald Keith. Below: in* Children of Divorce, *with Gary Cooper as the man she ensnares*

butcher's knife, threatening to kill her. While Clara was doing a bit in *The Enemies of Women* (1923), in which she played a flapper who dances on a table, she was home at nights nursing her mother:

'I remember thinking then that fun didn't seem to last very long, that something terrible always happened, and maybe it was the best to get *all* you could get out of it *when* you could.'

While the film was shooting, Clara 'used to be half-hysterical, but the director thought it was wonderful.' Her mother died in a mental hospital at this time and Clara said it was then that her childhood ended. She was 16.

After her first few film appearances audiences had begun to notice her and critics to single her out. She signed with the New York agent Maxine Alton who got her a successful test with former Paramount producer B. P. Schulberg at Preferred Pictures. Clara signed a three-month contract with Preferred at $50 a week, and went to Hollywood. The studio certainly got its money's worth out of her. It was nothing for Clara to shoot two or three movies at once, playing all sorts of parts in all sorts of pictures – nine in 1924, including Frank Lloyd's *Black Oxen*, in which she had a

---

'If I'm different, if I'm the "super-flapper" and "jazz-baby" of pictures, it's because I had to create a character for myself. They certainly didn't want me'

---

prototype flapper role; fifteen in 1925, including Ernst Lubitsch's *Kiss Me Again*, in which she was a lawyer's stenographer. She also fell in love – with Gilbert Roland, a young Mexican actor then also starting out on his career, whom she met on the set of *The Plastic Age* (1925). They were engaged but parted after 18 months. The affair was no secret. As public interest in Clara Bow registered with the press, they started to feed it with gossip. A rumour became a date, a date a romance, a romance an engagement – which would be broken so there could be further instalments. Clara, simple, open and spontaneous, saw nothing wrong in that, and continued to speak straight, hide little and set herself up to be hurt. She eventually discovered that her directness was rewarded with ridicule.

Meanwhile her career leapt ahead. Her zest for life, her immense capacity for understanding and love of excitement made people rush to see her films. When Schulberg rejoined Paramount he took Clara with him and her contract was bought up by Jesse L. Lasky for a reputed $25,000. No-one yet realized just how sensationally popular she was about to become. Her first film for Paramount, *Dancing Mothers* (1926), gave her third billing as the flapper-daughter of the heroine (Alice Joyce). Soon afterwards the colossal success of *Mantrap* (1926), directed by Victor Fleming, forced the studio to promote her to stardom, over Clara's own objections. Fleming, one of Hollywood's finest directors of women in action, brought out hitherto unknown depths and nuances in her performance as a wise-cracking city manicurist who catches a simple backwoodsman, goes up river with him as his wife, flirts with a lawyer on a hunting trip, only to go back to her lonely husband.

"IT'S THE SIGN OF 'THE HARD-BOILED MAIDENS' ~ NIFTY, WHAT?"

Above: in The Wild Party *Clara's nasal Brooklyn voice was heard for the first time; she played college girl Stella. Above right: in* Dancing Mothers *as the flapper whose man is stolen by her mother. Right: as the golden-hearted ambulance-driver Mary in* Wings

For a time Clara and the older Fleming were a romantic item. Then came her affair with Gary Cooper, whom she met on the set of *Children of Divorce* and who also appeared with her in *It!* and *Wings* (all 1927). Their romance made the headlines, but it fell victim to his jealousy and to her reluctance to settle down.

Increasingly salacious stories of her love life were exaggerated. She spoke of her three affairs up to that time:

'Is that so many romances for a girl of twenty-two? Yet just because I am Clara Bow and it is always printed, it sounds as though I were a regular flapper vamp.'

But the public preferred any news about her

'Being a sex symbol is a heavy load to carry, especially when one is tired, hurt and bewildered'

---

to none. She had become their idol – the wildest of flappers, the hottest of hot mamas, a woman dedicated to hedonism. *It!* made her their symbol and gave her a tag that she could not shake off. She was branded. Now her films became more lavish but her roles remained the same. Elinor Glyn was not alone in thinking that had Clara not retired from films:

'She would have become one of the greatest artists on the screen, particularly in tragic parts for which she had a far greater aptitude than for the comic scenes which I had to make her act in my films.'

Her directors – Victor Fleming, Clarence Badger, Frank Lloyd – thought the same, but Paramount knew that she would remain a gold-mine as long as they kept casting her as

the predatory 'It' girl. Towards this end screen-writers contrived as many situations as possible where Clara would have to strip down as far as was permissible. And as she played an ever steamier succession of virginal hoydens so her fame rose – much faster than her salary, which in 1929 was $2800 a week compared to the $10,000 less popular stars were drawing.

Clara made her talkie debut in *The Wild Party* (1929), which was a personal hit though the idea of sound scared her so much that she delivered her opening line – 'Hello everybody!' – with such force that she broke the light valve in the recording room. But she was not to stay in talkies for long. By now, private mistakes, scandals and studio pressures were beginning to effect her health. An alienation-of-affection

case brought against her by a Texan doctor's wife, the scandal of unpaid gambling debts and her on-again off-again romances with other stars all helped to tarnish her image and damage her popularity. The last straw came with a court case against her secretary, Daisy DeVoe, who had been pilfering Clara's money. Found guilty and sentenced to jail, DeVoe sold stories about her employer's supposed private life to a weekly tabloid, *The Coast Reporter*, to explain how she had been lured into her criminal actions by Clara's loose way of living. The ordeal shattered Clara and she had a nervous breakdown. She withdrew from *City Streets* (1931), which would have reteamed her with Gary Cooper, and was admitted to a sanatorium for rest.

Left: Clara as Bubbles in Red Hair *(1928), a girl who indignantly returns gifts of clothing to her admirers at a party – only to lose her coat. Above: the fiery Nasa finds true love with Moonglow (Gilbert Roland) in* Call Her Savage, *Clara's penultimate film*

Hoopla (1933), in which she played a hula dancer, Clara retired. She made the headlines again when she gave birth to two sons, in 1934 and 1938. But her health was wrecked (she was a chronic insomniac) and she spent more and more time in sanatoriums and mental homes. When her husband – who had been elected Lieutenant Governor of Nevada in 1954, and again in 1958 – died in 1962 they had been living apart for several years.

Shortly before she died, Clara Bow told a reporter about film stardom in the Twenties:

'We had individuality. We did as we pleased. We stayed up late. We dressed the way we wanted. Today, stars are sensible and end up with better health. But *we* had more fun.'

In June 1931, after work had been stopped on another of her films, Schulberg announced that her contract with Paramount had been cancelled at her request. Said Clara years later:

'The thing that burned me up was that the studio did nothing but scold me and threaten me all through the DeVoe trial . . . I had made them millions with what I and many critics thought were lousy pictures, but I received nothing but a salary, untrained leading men, and any old story they fished out of wastebaskets.'

In 1932 Clara married cowboy actor Rex Bell

and announced:

'I can live perfectly well on what Rex earns. . . . Until the right role turns up, I shall continue to turn down all offers. I won't ever play again the sort of stereotyped part I used to have to play. If all producers want me to do is register 'It' and show my underwear, they can keep their parts.'

She made her comeback for Fox, who reputedly offered her $125,000 for two films. In *Call Her Savage* (1932), opposite Gilbert Roland, she played a half-breed Texan wildcat who horse-whips men for laughing at her. After

Filmography
1922 Beyond the Rainbow; Down to the Sea in Ships. **'23** The Enemies of Women; The Daring Years; Maytime. **'24** Grit; Poisoned Paradise; Daughters of Pleasure; Wine; Empty Hearts; This Woman; Helen's Babies; Black Oxen; Black Lightning. **'25** Capital Punishment; The Adventurous Sex; My Lady's Lips; Eve's Lover; The Scarlet West; Lawful Cheaters; Parisian Love; Kiss Me Again; The Primrose Path; The Keeper of the Bees; Free to Love; The Best Bad Man; The Plastic Age; My Lady of Whims; The Ancient Mariner. **'26** The Shadow of the Law; Two Can Play; Dancing Mothers; Fascinating Youth; The Runaway; Mantrap; Kid Boots. **'27** It!; Children of Divorce; Rough House Rosie; Hula; Get Your Man; Wings. **'28** Red Hair; Ladies of the Mob; The Fleet's In; Three Week-Ends. **'29** The Wild Party; Dangerous Curves; The Saturday Night Kid. **'30** Paramount on Parade; True to the Navy; Love Among the Millionaires; Her Wedding. **'31** No Limit; Kick In. **'32** Call Her Savage. **'33** Hoopla.

No-one now will ever see Mauritz Stiller's last Swedish film, *The Atonement of Gösta Berling*, in its original form. A vast fresco of life in early nineteenth-century Sweden, drawn from a long and complex novel by Selma Lagerlöf, the film was released, as Stiller had planned, in two parts totalling some three hours. After Stiller's death in 1928, his script assistant, Ragnar Hyltén-Cavallius, cut the film by about half and added a musical score. In the Seventies, the Swedish Film Institute completed what restoration was possible, but even that version is some way short of the original.

The cutting of the film had of course been motivated by the desire to emphasize the part played by Greta Garbo, making her second film appearance. But as the film deals with the interlocking lives of three families, the Elisabeth Dohna character (played by Garbo) is in fact no more important than eight or ten others in the film. Thus the shortened version loses all balance.

The Atonement of Gösta Berling was the last great work of the golden period of Swedish silent film. Two directors, Stiller and Victor Sjöström, had given the period its shape and richness; Sjöström later went to America, followed by Stiller in 1925. *The Atonement of Gösta Berling* was a summation, an epitaph, of the period. The great virtue of the Swedish school had been the use it had made of natural landscape. This is aptly reflected in *The Atonement of Gösta Berling*, which is set in Värmland, on the Norwegian border, an area dominated by its great lakes. Not only in the famous pursuit by wolves at the climax, but throughout the film, Stiller uses the forests, the frozen lakes, the huge stillness of the region, as a complementary backdrop to his turbulent plot.

Stiller treated Selma Lagerlöf's novel, *Kavaljererna pä Ekeby*, in a cavalier fashion, excising scenes and adding others, and drastically altering the chronology. He had already incurred Lagerlöf's hostility by inserting a reindeer stampede as the climax of *Gunnar Hedes Saga* (1923, *Gunnar Hede's Saga*), and, inevitably, this time she had asked for the utmost fidelity. But Swedish Biograph had bought the film rights years before and, perhaps mercifully, there was nothing Lagerlöf could do. Stiller could proceed as he desired.

Contrary to popular belief, Stiller did not discover Greta Garbo. Needing two young girls for the roles of Elisabeth and Ebba, he asked Gustaf Molander, himself a distinguished director and at that time head of the dramatic school attached to Stockholm's Royal Dramatic Theatre, to send him his two best pupils. Molander sent Mona Mårtensson and Greta-Lovisa Gustafsson. Stiller engaged them both, and changed the latter's name to Garbo.

The Garbo of *The Atonement of Gösta Berling* was, in *Variety's*

GÖSTA BERLINGS SAGA

LARS HANSON

Greta Garbo

GERDA LUNDEQVIST

regi: MAURITZ STILLER

inimitable words, 'totally unlike the sleeky dame MGM experts made of her.' With luxuriant hair piled high above her head, eyebrows of their natural size, and fuller lips, she looks very young (she was only 18), very fresh and very lovely. Her acting is inevitably a little hesitant, owing far more to direction than was ever the case later, but Stiller and the experienced Lars Hanson, playing opposite her, see Garbo through, and her star quality shines out.

The best Swedish cinema of the time was justly famous for its development of a genuine cinematic style of acting. In *The Atonement of Gösta Berling*, the acting is in general restrained and subtle; Stiller never allows his players to be swamped by the elaborate interiors, the majestic landscapes, or the melodramatic artifices of the story.

Stiller's reputation had been made in comedy, of a refined and incisive kind; and his masterpiece in the genre, *Erotikon* (1920, *Bonds That Chafe*) was greatly admired by such directors as Ernst Lubitsch. The timing and exactitude of his comic style, however, carry over easily into the more melodramatic milieu of *The Atonement of Gösta Berling*.

Stiller was equally adept at great set-pieces. Of the two in *The Atonement of Gösta Berling*, the burning of the château of Ekeby is a masterpiece of scurrying confusion, while the chase over the frozen lake, superbly edited, has a taut excitement which quite obliterates its essential absurdity. Stiller was a complete film-maker. Writing his own scripts and editing his own films (like so many of his European colleagues), he could not fit into Hollywood's more sharply defined categories, and returned to Sweden disillusioned, to die in 1928 at the age of 45. The loving restoration of *The Atonement of Gösta Berling* was an overdue memorial.

1

The Countess Märtha Dohna engages Gösta Berling, an unfrocked priest, as tutor to her stepdaughter, Ebba, at her home in Borg (1). If Ebba marries a commoner she will be disinherited in favour of Märtha's son, Henrik. Märtha hopes that Berling, who is notoriously attractive to women, will marry Ebba. Ebba later overhears Märtha explaining her plot to Elisabeth (2), Henrik's wife. Now in love with Berling, Ebba becomes distressed. Berling,

ashamed, leaves to seek refuge with the Samzelius family, who keep open house for all kinds of spongers at their château of Ekeby (3). Ebba subsequently dies, heartbroken.

Elisabeth assures Berling of her friendship. During a gala at Ekeby, Berling is caught embracing Marianne Sinclair, whose father drives her from their house. Meanwhile, Major Samzelius learns that the previous owner of Ekeby, from whom he inherited the estate, had been a lover of his wife, Margareta. It transpires that the lover, a rich and generous man, had intended Ekeby for Margareta but bequeathed it to Major Samzelius in order not to betray the illicit love affair. Angered and shamed by this revelation, Major Samzelius promptly turns his wife out (4).

Later, Berling finds the destitute Marianne exhausted in the snow (5), and takes her back to Ekeby. Henrik is informed that, through a technical error, he and Elisabeth are not legally married. This offers a glimmer of hope for Elisabeth, who gazes from her window towards Ekeby (6), longing for Berling, whom she really loves.

Margareta returns to Ekeby and sets fire to the château, hoping to wipe out all trace of her sin. Berling rescues Marianne from the flames (7), but she dies. Seeing the fire, Elisabeth hurries to Ekeby, meets Berling, and is carried off by him across the frozen lakes. They confess their love for each other. Escaping from a wolf pack, they eventually return to Borg. Elisabeth then sends Berling away, to rebuild Ekeby and his own life. She also refuses to regularize her marriage with Henrik (8).

Later, Elisabeth, who is about to leave for Italy, is, with Margareta's help, reunited with Gösta Berling.

46

2

3

4

5

6

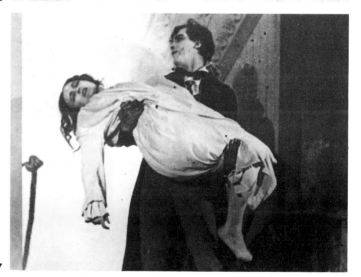

7

Directed by Mauritz Stiller, 1924
Prod co: Svensk Filmindustri. **sc:** Mauritz Stiller, Ragnar Hyltén-Cavallius, from the novel, *Kavaljererna pä Ekeby*, by Selma Lagerlöf. **photo:** Julius Jaenzon. **prod des:** Ragnar Bratten, Vilhelm Bryde. **cost:** Ingrid Günther. length: 8700 ft (approx. 145 minutes). Swedish title: *Gösta Berlings Saga*. Released in GB as *The Atonement of Gösta Berling*.
Cast: Lars Hanson (*Gösta Berling*), Gerda Lundeqvist (*Margareta Samzelius*), Hilda Forslund (*Margareta's mother*), Otto Ely-Lundberg (*Major Samzelius*), Sixten Malmerfeldt (*Melchior Sinclair*), Karin Swanström (*Gustava Sinclair*), Jenny Hasselqvist (*Marianne Sinclair*), Ellen Cederström (*Countess Märtha Dohna*), Mona Mårtensson (*Lady Ebba Dohna*), Torsten Hammaren (*Count Henrik Dohna*), Greta Garbo (*Elisabeth Dohna*), Sven Scholander (*Sintram*), Svend Kornbaeck (*Captain Kristian Bergh*), Hugo Rönnblad (*Beerencreutz*), Knut Lambert (*Rutger von Örneclov*), Oscar Bergström (*Julius*), Gaston Portefaix (*Major Anders Fuchs*), Albert Stahl (*Uncle Eberhard*), Anton de Verdier (*Cousin Kristoffer*), Axel Jacobsson (*Lilliencrona*), Jan de Meyere (*Löwenborg*), Edmund Hohendorf (*Kevenheuler*), A.T.H. Buch (*Ruster, a drummer*).

8

A Gentleman's Fate: the career of *John Gilbert*

Although the name of Rudolph Valentino remains a household name more than half a century after his death, the same cannot be said of the man who was his nearest rival, and successor, as the foremost romantic idol of the Twenties. John Gilbert, like Valentino, died tragically young, but unlike Valentino he did not die at the height of his fame, and unfortunately the sadness surrounding Gilbert's last years has tended to blot out the success that preceded them. Furthermore, the very distinction of the more significant films in which Gilbert appeared has tended to work against recognition of his own contribution to them: he may have been overlooked amid the attention paid to directors like Erich von Stroheim or King Vidor, and to his leading lady of several pictures, Greta Garbo. Be that as it may, John Gilbert is one of the cinema's neglected luminaries.

Gilbert, christened John Pringle, was born in Utah – and into show business – in 1897. His father ran a theatrical troupe in which his mother was a performer; after his parents separated he took his stepfather's surname. But it was to his own father that he turned when – after an education in California that was cut short by lack of parental funds – he became set on a show-business career. And, following some experience in repertory, it was through his father's contacts that he gained an introduction to Thomas H. Ince's Triangle studio in 1916. This led to his employment as a bit player at the less than princely salary of $15 a week. Gilbert later described himself as having always been 'movie struck'; it was on Hollywood, rather than Broadway, that his professional sights were set.

Right: Gilbert and Lillian Gish making their own kind of music in the silent La Bohème. *Below: the charming Prince Danilo (right) and* The Merry Widow *(Mae Murray) with a connoisseur of embroidery. Below right: Garbo and Gilbert provided the fire with the smoke in* Flesh and the Devil

John Gilbert was one of the best-known lovers on the silent screen. His great eyes could flash with passion and anger or soften to show pity and remorse. His screen presence was totally dominating, and audiences adored him. And then the fans deserted him, critics panned his films and the studios wouldn't give him work. With the advent of a wonderful new technical innovation – the coming of sound – his career was in ruins

If at first . . .

The first film in which he appeared was one of some note, *Hell's Hinges* (1916), now recognized as an early landmark in the Western genre, and a key work in the career of cowboy star William S. Hart. A sufficiently sharp-eyed spectator should spot Gilbert in several of the crowd scenes.

Advancement could be rapid in those pioneering days of the cinema, and within a year Gilbert – who for several years was billed as Jack, the name by which he was known to friends – had progressed to leading roles. The first of these was in *Princess of the Dark* (1917), and two years later he played opposite no less than Mary Pickford in *Heart o' the Hills*. However, despite this apparent success he evidently felt little confidence as a performer,

and his insecurity was increased by a brief and unhappy first marriage.

The figure responsible for brightening his professional horizon was the French-born director Maurice Tourneur. Tourneur became Gilbert's mentor, encouraging the screenwriting aspirations with which Gilbert sought to bolster his misgivings about acting. In rapid succession Gilbert contributed to several Tourneur films, starting with a prison drama *The White Circle* and continuing through *The Great Redeemer* and *Deep Waters* (all 1920) to *The Bait* (1921): Gilbert not only acted in the first three, but also served as Tourneur's unofficial assistant and occasional scriptwriter.

Gilbert was then hired by the millionaire Jules Brulatour – at a weekly salary of $1500, a considerable improvement on his earnings of

five years before – to direct films starring Brulatour's 'discovery', Hope Hampton. But without Tourneur, Gilbert's confidence evaporated and the only film he directed, *Love's Penalty* (1921), was a complete flop. Gilbert severed the connection with Brulatour and reluctantly returned to acting.

Trying and trying

From 1921 to 1924 he worked for the Fox studio in a variety of indifferent pictures. Studio boss William Fox apparently did not rate Gilbert highly, making the rather ridiculous objection that his nose was unphotogenically large and bulbous. In fact it was in an attempt to offset this alleged disability that Gilbert cultivated the pencil moustache, later to become one of his salient characteristics as a screen idol.

But if most of the Fox films were undistinguished, there was one exception, John Ford's *Cameo Kirby* (1923), a romantic melodrama about the Mississippi river boats of the nineteenth century. (Some of the footage later appeared in Ford's *Steamboat Round the Bend*, 1935.) It is perhaps in *Cameo Kirby* that Gilbert's screen persona first definitively appears. To the role of the Southern aristocrat of the title, reduced by circumstances to being a riverboat gambler, Gilbert brings both a brooding authority and a magnetic sense of refined sexuality. After the film's release Gilbert found himself on the threshold of professional triumph, although his domestic situation was rather less happy – his second marriage, to the actress Leatrice Joy, ended after barely two years, partly, it would seem, because of his dalliance with the Broadway star Laurette Taylor.

Success at last

In 1924, Irving Thalberg signed him up for MGM, and in his first film there, King Vidor's *His Hour* (1924), his playing of a dashing Russian nobleman amplified the romantic appeal he had displayed in *Cameo Kirby*. Over the next few years Gilbert appeared in a wide variety of notable movies: in particular he brought an outward dash and elegance, combined with an affecting suggestion of weakness and vulnerability, to the figure of Prince Danilo in Erich von Stroheim's *The Merry Widow* (1925). That same year he worked again for Vidor on *The Big Parade*. The director has admitted that Gilbert's casting was 'suggested' by the studio – Vidor had initially felt that an anonymous player would be more in keeping with the project – but has also been unstinting in his admiration for the unerring sensibility that the (clean-shaven) actor contributed to the role of a young American recruit in war-torn France.

Certainly *The Big Parade* proved that Gilbert's forte was not merely in glamorous costume roles, although his next two films were of that ilk. *Bardelys the Magnificent* (1926) saw him as a Fairbanks-style swashbuckler, whilst in a version (inevitably non-operatic) of *La Bohème* (1926), his leading lady was the ethereal Lillian Gish, whose painstakingly academic approach to her craft evidently clashed somewhat with his penchant for the spontaneous effect.

Heading for a fall

It was in the following year, however, that Gilbert was first teamed with his most celebrated co-star – Greta Garbo. Their first film together was *Flesh and the Devil* (1927).

Below: gathering the usual crowd as a sideshow barker in The Show *(1927). Below right: Gilbert in his last screen role, as a drunken writer in* The Captain Hates the Sea

Ironically, Gilbert was opposed to appearing with Garbo – presumably fearing that she would steal his thunder. However, the pairing proved inspired, and the intensity of romantic feeling in the film, which managed to defy the conventions of the time by including love scenes in a prone position, seems to have derived from a genuine attachment. According to the director Clarence Brown:

'They were in a blissful state of love . . . sometimes I felt I was intruding on the most private of emotions.'

Hollywood legend has it that Gilbert proposed to Garbo and even got her to the door of a Justice of the Peace; but whatever the real story, Garbo eluded him off screen. They made two further silent films together, *Love* (1927) and *A Woman of Affairs* (1928), but though their relationship may by this time have been purely professional, the on-camera chemistry was still highly effective.

Gilbert's last silent films showed his command of the screen undimmed, but with the advent of sound his career disintegrated. The traditional contention that Gilbert's high-pitched voice was his undoing scarcely withstands scrutiny: after all, MGM retained his costly services, and in 1933 again co-starred him with Garbo (apparently at the latter's bidding, after Laurence Olivier proved unsatisfactory to her) in *Queen Christina*. The soundtrack evidence from that film testifies that his voice in talkies was perfectly acceptable. Perhaps Gilbert's *style* of acting did not easily translate to the changed conventions of sound pictures, or perhaps the primitive sound recording of the earliest talkies undermined his self-confidence; in any event, the routine vehicles the studio subsequently

found for him can scarcely have helped.

Queen Christina was his last film at MGM. The next – his last film of all – was for Columbia. By this time his private life was in poor shape. There were two more brief marriages – to actresses Ina Claire (1930–32) and Virginia Bruce (1932–34), the latter his co-star in *Downstairs* (1932), scripted by himself – and Gilbert's drinking problem was worsening. Ironically, his last screen role was as an alcoholic trying to lay off the bottle in *The Captain Hates the Sea* (1934).

He died of a heart attack shortly after the

film was released. But despite all the glum attention that his decline and fall have compelled, in the long view of film history he should be remembered as the star of *The Merry Widow* and *Flesh and the Devil* – and as one of the silent screen's Great Lovers.

Below: although Gilbert minus 'tache was unpopular in The Big Parade, *it was again shown a blade for* Way for a Sailor *(1930). Right: Garbo and Gilbert in* Love – *a silent version of the Anna Karenina story*

Filmography

1916 Hell's Hinges; Bullets and Brown Eyes; The Apostle of Vengeance; The Phantom; The Eye of the Night; Shell 43. **'17** The Mother Instinct; The Devil Dodger; Golden Rule Kate; Doing Her Bit; Princess of the Dark; The Millionaire Vagrant; Happiness; Hater of Men. **'18** Nancy Comes Home; Sons of Men; Shackled; More Trouble; Wedlock; The Mask/The Mask of Riches; Three X Gordon; The Dawn of Understanding. **'19** The Red Viper; The White Heather; The Busher; Widow By Proxy; Heart o' the Hills; Should Women Tell? **'20** The White Circle (+co-sc); The Great Redeemer (+co-sc); Deep Waters (+co-sc); While Paris Sleeps (released 1923). **'21** The Bait/The Bait, or Human Bait (sc. only); The Servant In the House; Love's Penalty (dir; +sc. only); Shame; Ladies Must Live. **'22** Gleam o' Dawn; Arabian Love; Monte Cristo; The Yellow Stain; Honor First; Calvert's Valley; The Love Gambler; A California Romance. **'23** Truxton King; The Madness of Youth; Saint Elmo; The Exiles; Cameo Kirby. **'24** Just Off Broadway; The Wolf Man; A Man's Mate; The Lone Chance; Romance Ranch; His Hour; Married Flirts; He Who Gets Slapped; The Snob; The Wife of the Centaur. **'25** The Merry Widow; The Big Parade. **'26** La Bohème; Bardelys the Magnificent. **'27** Flesh and the Devil; The Show; Twelve Miles Out; Love; Man, Woman, and Sin. **'28** The Cossacks; Four Walls; Show People (as himself); The Masks of the Devil; A Woman of Affairs; Voices Across the Sea (short). **'29** Desert Nights; A Man's Man (as himself); The Hollywood Revue of 1929; His Glorious Night. **'30** Redemption; Way for a Sailor. **'31** Gentleman's Fate; The Phantom of Paris; West of Broadway. **'32** Downstairs (+co-sc). **'33** Fast Workers; Queen Christina. **'34** The Captain Hates the Sea.

After the great success of *Du Skal aere din Hustru* (1925, *Thou Shalt Honour Thy Wife*), its director Carl Theodor Dreyer was commissioned by the Société Générale de Films, which specialized in prestigious art films aimed at the international market, and whose products included Abel Gance's *Napoléon* (1927, *Napoleon*), Jean Epstein's *Finis Terrae* (1929, The End of the Land), and Maurice Tourneur's *L'Equipage* (1928, The Crew). Dreyer proposed three possible subjects: Marie Antoinette, Catherine de Médicis and Joan of Arc.

When Joan of Arc was finally selected it was decided to base the script partly on a recently published study by Joseph Delteil and partly on the original transcripts of the trial in Pierre Champion's 1921 edition. However, Dreyer and Delteil soon fell out and the director worked mainly from the transcripts, making Champion the film's historical advisor.

After some uncertainty the leading role went to Renée Falconetti, a theatrical actress, who was known, in 1927, for her roles in light, boulevard comedies. A surprising choice at first sight, perhaps, but Dreyer's defence of his decision provides the key to his whole conception of the film:

'Behind the make-up, behind the pose and that ravishing modern appearance, there was something. There was a soul behind that façade.'

The Passion of Joan of Arc is not a film about whether or not Joan was really inspired by visions. Nor is it particularly concerned with the religious and political whys and wherefores of the trial (in the way that George Bernard Shaw's play *Saint Joan* and Jean Anouilh's *L'Alouette* are, for example).

Dreyer is not concerned with historical accuracy or picturesque detail, but with psychological drama, or what Paul Schrader, previously a critic and now a film-maker, in his book *Transcendental Style* calls 'the spiritual progress of Joan's soul'. As Dreyer himself has said:

'I did not study the clothes of the time and things like that. The year of the event seemed as inessential to me as its distance from the present. I wanted to interpret a hymn to the triumph of the soul over life.'

For Dreyer the window into the soul is provided by the human face – 'everything human is expressed in the face', he once said, as 'the face is the mirror of the soul'. Hardly surprisingly, then, *The Passion of Joan of Arc* is a film in which intense close-ups of faces predominate. It is, as critic Tom Milne remarked, 'a symphony of faces'.

None of the cast wore makeup and the panchromatic film stock made their facial details stand out with extraordinary clarity, almost as if in etched relief. Indeed the effect is heightened by them being shot against what appear to be brilliant white walls – although, in fact, the interior sets were tinted yellow and the exteriors pink in order to achieve precisely this

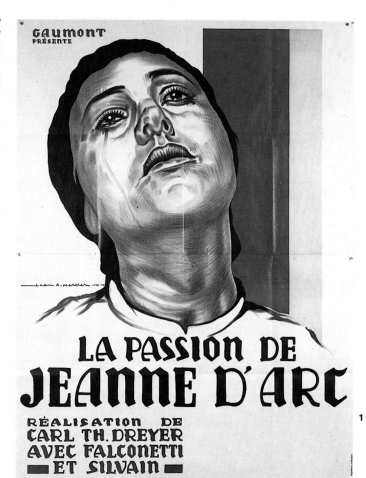

sense of brilliance.

Dreyer was concerned above all to penetrate beyond appearances, a desire he shared with many in the German silent cinema. Significantly, one of the art directors on the film was the renowned Hermann Warm, who co-designed Robert Wiene's expressionist classic *Das Kabinett des Dr Caligari* (1919, *The Cabinet of Dr Caligari*); whilst Dreyer's active, participatory camera style recalls F. W. Murnau's *Der Letzte Mann* (1925, *The Last Laugh*).

This creative use of outer appearances to express inner realities Dreyer called abstraction rather than Expressionism – which he defined as 'something that demands of the artist to abstract himself from reality in order to strengthen the spiritual content of his work'. By transcending the limitations of naturalism (which had come to dominate the film medium), Dreyer aimed at making a film that

was not merely visual, but spiritual.

Thus the close-ups of the demonic faces of Joan's inquisitors, the threatening low-angle shots, the intensely expressive quality of the architecture, the dramatic high-contrast lighting, the remarkable mobile camera – all these elements contribute to an expressive climate that leads the spectator to empathize intensely with Joan's inner state.

Like many of Dreyer's films, *The Passion of Joan of Arc* was a critical success and a financial failure. In the light of its box-office losses, allied with the losses from *Napoleon* and the various problems caused by the arrival of sound, the Société Générale de Films broke their contract with Dreyer for a further film – leaving the director free to make the independently-produced *Vampyr: Der Traum des Allan Gray* (*Vampyr: The Strange Adventures of David Gray*) in 1932.

Joan is brought before the judges (1); she refuses to recite the Lord's Prayer yet claims that God has sent her to save France. When questioned about her masculine attire she replies that when her mission is completed she will exchange it for a dress.

The judges – led by Bishop Cauchon (2) – continue to

Directed by Carl Theodor Dreyer, 1928
Prod co: Société Générale de Films. **sc:** Joseph Delteil, Carl Theodor Dreyer. **adap:** Carl Theodor Dreyer. **hist ad:** Pierre Champion. **photo:** Rudolph Maté. **set dec:** Hermann Warm, Jean Hugo. **cost:** Valentine Hugo. **ass dir:** Paul La Cour, Ralf Holm. **r/t:** 110 mins (commercial version, 86 mins). Original title: *La Passion et la Mort de Jeanne d'Arc*. Re-titled: *La Passion de Jeanne d'Arc*. Released in GB/USA as *The Passion of Joan of Arc*. Premiere, Copenhagen, 21 April 1928.
Cast: Renée Falconetti (*Joan of Arc*), Eugène Silvain (*Bishop Cauchon*), Maurice Schutz (*Nicolas Loyseleur*), Michel Simon (*Jean Lemaître*), Antonin Artaud (*Massieu*), Ravet (*Jean Beaupère*), André Berley (*Jean d'Estivet*), Jean d'Yd (*judge*), Jean Hemm, André Lurville, Jacques Arna, Alexandre Mihalesco, Robert Narlay, Henri Maillard, Jean Ayme, Léon Larive, Paul Jorge, Henri Gaultier.

The Passion of Joan of Arc

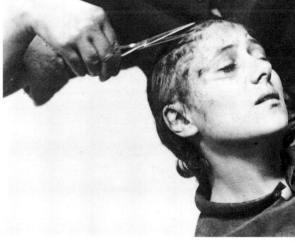

2

interrogate Joan, hoping to trap her in a blasphemy. Joan questions their right to judge her, however, and requests to be tried by the Pope himself. The judges dismiss the idea. Joan then tells them that she will be delivered from captivity soon, whereupon she is led out.

The judges decide to trick Joan into submission. They forge the King's signature and attach it to a letter of their own composition (3), recommending Joan to trust a priest they send to her cell.

Shortly after, the judges return to cross-examine Joan in her cell and succeed, through trickery, in extracting various 'blasphemous' statements out of her. Bishop Cauchon then gives orders to prepare the torture chamber. Though at first Joan refuses to sign an abjuration, the threat of the stake and her general state of physical and mental collapse (4) all finally force her to comply. Though saved from burning she is condemned to life-imprisonment.

While her hair is being shaved off (5), Joan regrets her action and makes a formal recantation. Preparing for death, Joan makes a confession to a young priest (6); then she is taken to the market-place where she is to be burnt at the stake (7). Meanwhile the crowd protests (8), accusing the judges of burning a saint, but they are ruthlessly suppressed.

4

5

7

8

Buster Keaton
The Great Stone Face

Keaton was the comic who greeted the hostile world without a flicker of emotion, and overcame its physical hazards with a series of breathtaking but coolly calculated stunts. His refusal – or inability – to register either elation or despair must have stemmed from a belief that triumph and tragedy inevitably follow each other, and that neither is worth getting excited about

He came to the Venice Film Festival in September 1965 when they presented Samuel Beckett's *Film*, directed by Alan Schneider and starring Buster Keaton. He came down the aisle as the audience applauded him after the morning press show, a tiny solemn figure in a precarious state of preservation, with the urbane Los Angeles theatre-owner Raymond Rohauer like a puppet-master at his elbow. On the big screen his face, only revealed at the end of Beckett's work, bore the imprint of a terrible despair; in the flesh, too, there was nothing reassuring about his frailty. What did he think of the film which, seemingly at odds with his life's work, was in no way a comedy? 'What I think it means is that a man can keep away from everybody, but he can't get away from himself.' Within five months, at the age of 70, Buster died.

As some consolation, it could be said that Keaton had been able to witness at least a part of the restoration of his true status in screen history, a process which has continued steadily since the Sixties thanks to Rohauer's tireless cataloguing of copyrights, resurrection of prints, and licensing of commercial reissues. Not that *The Navigator* (1924) and *The General* (1926) were unknown in Europe (the British Film Institute had maintained them in its library and programmed them at the National Film Theatre for years), but the full perspective of Keaton's creative genius had been

impossible to assess. It wasn't until a decade after his death that, for instance, *The Cameraman* (1928), narrowly rescued by MGM from negative decay, reappeared in Britain, and *Spite Marriage* (1929) was revived at the London Film Festival. Where Charles Chaplin has never been forgotten and Harold Lloyd has somehow never needed protection, Keaton had become thought of by the mid-Thirties as a mere pie-throwing extra from the Mack Sennett days. While he was seldom out of work, and apparently accepted his anonymity without rancour, his downfall followed the classic path (also trodden by Georges Méliès and D.W. Griffith among others) in being both ill-deserved and unavoidable.

Born in a trunk

Joseph Francis Keaton was born on October 4, 1895, the year in which cinema, too, was just beginning. His parents were members of the Mohawk Indian Medicine Company, a travelling vaudeville show, along with Harry Houdini, escapologist extraordinary, and were in Kansas when the baby arrived. Joe H. Keaton was Irish (although maybe with some Indian blood) and a former Wild West adventurer and journalist, whose stories lost nothing in the telling. With his tiny wife Myra, the pipe-smoking, card-playing, musical daughter of a travelling showman, he presented a knockabout acrobatic comedy act into

which their son was absorbed shortly after the baby crawled on stage one night to the delight of the audience.

Called 'Buster', according to the legend he repeated throughout his life, for having been picked up unhurt after falling down a flight of stairs at six months (the experience was referred to by Houdini as a 'buster', the stage slang for pratfall), the boy proved to be the making of 'The Three Keatons': he upstaged his parents by the simple process of being thrown about, walked on, and used as a punchbag. Dressed in the same grotesque wig and sideburns as his father, wearing the same dress suit, white waistcoat and spats, he was subjected to such violence that the Keatons were often challenged by legal authorities to prove that 'The Human Mop' was in fact undamaged by his treatment. A typical gag involved his being hit in the face with a broom, his response being several seconds of complete lack of expression before he said 'Ouch!'. From such ordeals,

Buster learned comic timing, physical endurance, and above all the discipline of 'freezing'
all emotional reaction.

As early as 1912, 'The Three Keatons' were
invited to appear on film, but Joe Keaton would
have nothing to do with the nickelodeons
which, in his eyes, were devaluing and destroying true theatrical entertainment. But
Buster had seen hundreds of films by the time
he was 21, and when the end came of the
Keaton family show (the result partly of his
father's hostility and drunkenness, partly of
the fact that, small as he was, Buster was
simply too big to be conveniently hurled
around), it was an easy step for him to move
into two-reelers. After a chance encounter
with Fatty Arbuckle in New York, he turned
down a Winter Garden Theatre engagement of
$250 a week in order to appear in movies at
$40 a week, beginning with *The Butcher Boy*
early in April 1917. This was also the first film
of Arbuckle's new Comicque Film Corporation.

Above left: teeing off in the earliest of The
Three Ages *(1923) – the others were Ancient
Rome and modern America. Top, from left to
right: the end of the road in* The Garage –
*Keaton's last film with Fatty Arbuckle; a
cinema projectionist dreams of love in*

Sherlock, Jr, *with Kathryn McGuire; umbrella
trouble in* Steamboat Bill, Jr. *Above: Keaton's*
Neighbors *(1920) were the girl he loves
(Virginia Fox) and her father (Joe Roberts).
Below: Friendless waits for Brown Eyes to
yield milk in* Go West *(1925)*

Above: a sailor takes up position in The Love Nest *(1923). Top right: a cyclone blows the front of a house on top of* Steamboat Bill, Jr – *fortunately a window is open; in performing the stunt, Keaton only allowed himself two inches to spare on either side. Above right: in* College *(1927) Keaton is a bookworm who tries to succeed at athletics to win a girl*

supervised by Joseph M. Schenck, and with the support and encouragement of both men Buster was immediately spellbound by both the technical and the creative side of film-making.

'One of the first things I did was tear a motion picture camera practically to pieces and found out the lenses and the splicing of film and how to get it on the projector – this fascinated me.'

After another five films – *A Reckless Romeo, The Rough House, His Wedding Night, Oh, Doctor!* and *Fatty at Coney Island* (all 1917) – the whole team moved to California. It took with it Keaton's family and one of the Talmadge sisters, Natalie. Very much in the shadow of her more famous sisters Norma and Constance, Natalie worked in a secretarial position at the studios where the Keatons met her. She became a special favourite of Myra's.

Accidents will happen

It was a foregone conclusion that Buster and Natalie would marry, not that there weren't many other girls in his life. As part of the Hollywood community, among a dazzling circle of friends including Chaplin, Douglas Fairbanks, W.S. Hart and Rudolph Valentino,

the private and habitually non-committal Buster found himself to be, like Arbuckle, very public property, his existence stage-managed for the benefit of the press. His marriage in 1921 gives the impression (as indeed do his two subsequent marriages, to Mae Scribbens in 1933 and to Eleanor Norris in 1940) of having occurred without his full comprehension, like the innumerable natural disasters in his films. With Natalie came the rest of the Talmadge family, who enlisted Louise Keaton (Buster's sister) as a stand-in for Norma, shared the Keaton residence (a huge Italian Villa was built for them all at Beverly Hills in 1925), and determined after the birth of their two sons that Natalie should have no more children. The divorce was not until 1932, a final blow when Keaton's fortunes were already in battered shape, but the marriage had finished years earlier. The Talmadges don't even rate a mention in Keaton's 1960 'autobiography', *My Wonderful World of Slapstick.*

Buster made six two-reelers with Arbuckle in California – *A Country Hero* (1917), in which Joe Keaton also appeared, *Out West, The Bell Boy, Moonshine, Good Night, Nurse!* and *The Cook* (all 1918). He was then drafted in mid-1918 and spent seven months entertaining the troops in France. During this time he caught an ear infection that rendered him partially deaf for the rest of his life. When he returned in 1919, it was to find Arbuckle preparing to move into feature production, though they completed three more two-reelers together – *Back Stage, The Hayseed* (both 1919), and *The Garage* (1920). Joseph Schenck then offered Buster his own company on a handshake deal,

and what was to be the golden era of Keaton comedy was under way, sadly and ironically aided by the collapse of Arbuckle's separate career following the scandal of 1921. From 1920 to 1923 Keaton made one feature (*The Saphead,* 1920) and 19 shorts, followed by 10 further features in the five years to 1928 when he changed producer.

If it was thanks to his brother-in-law (Schenck was married to Norma Talmadge) that Buster had no shares in his own company and finally made 'the biggest mistake of my life' by moving to MGM, it was also under Schenck's protection that he enjoyed in the last glorious years of silent cinema a seemingly limitless freedom to make whatever he liked, with no budgetary strings and no front-office interference. He was in peak condition as an athlete, he was inexhaustible on less than five hours sleep a night, he could drink copiously without side-effects, and if he needed a steam-engine or an ocean liner, they bought him one. But after this period never again would he have total control of his creativity, and never again would his films reflect the sheer uncluttered exuberance of his comic timing and his magical visual sense.

The hallmark of a Keaton comedy is the energy of its central character, all the animation that others display on their faces being expressed by Buster in a headlong ballet of acrobatics which he performed himself, in long-shot and without cuts. There is no trickery about the log-bouncing scene in *The General,* or Buster's high dive from the top of the ship in *The Navigator,* or the vaulting ease with which he skims down the riverboat decks in

Above: during a rail chase in The General, *Johnny sees a log blocking the line ahead. He struggles to the front of his engine with another log and at the vital moment throws it on to the obstacle, bouncing it clear . . .*

Steamboat Bill, Jr (1928) and all the way up again a moment later. In *Spite Marriage*, a single shot follows his desperate battle with the villain from one end of the luxury yacht to the other where, flung into the ocean, he is carried by the current back to the lifeboat trailing at the stern and hauls himself up over the side to resume the struggle. During his career, as he often reported in later years, he broke every bone in his body. In *The Paleface* (1921) he dropped 85 feet from a suspension bridge into a net, he was nearly drowned under a waterfall in *Our Hospitality* (1923), and during the train sequence in *Sherlock, Jr* (1924) he actually broke his neck yet continued stunting and

filming despite months of blinding headaches.

Where there's a will . . .

Nevertheless, it's not as a stuntman but as a unique tragi-comic personality that he survives as the most fascinating of the silent comedians. As if pursuing a redefinition of his private experience, his films illustrate the purgatorial struggles of an inconsequential reject, habitually bullied by a scornful father or disdainfully ignored by an unappreciative girl, who by sheer persistence and ingenuous courage (physical danger never seems to occur to him as a possibility) battles his way to social acceptability. In his tenacious war against the forces of evil, his endurance in restoring the rightness of things, and his enigmatic face that gives nothing away – no promises, no denials – he is one of the screen's great martyrs. Yet at the same time, he has an uncanny gift for adapting technology to provide unexpected

comforts; he uses a swordfish for protection, a boiler for a bedroom and a lobster-pot for an egg-holder in *The Navigator*, lazy tongs for a traffic indicator and a telephone for controlling a horse in *Cops* (1922), and can whip up a brisk asbestos suit in order to survive burning at the stake in *The Paleface*. As if in reward for his ingenuity, and for his obvious innocence, Providence is on his side, carrying him placidly off in an airborn canoe at the end of *The Balloonatic* (1923), or dropping the two-ton façade of a building over his body – he stands exactly where an empty window-frame drops over him – in that hair-raising shot from *Steamboat Bill, Jr* (even the cameraman, legend has it, couldn't bear to watch) leaving him dusty but unscathed.

At his best, Keaton's films found their least enthusiastic audience. While *The General* looks like a masterpiece today, it was a disaster when first released. Yet his MGM comedies of the early Thirties, *The Passionate Plumber, Speak Easily* (both 1932) and *What! No Beer?* (1933), uneasily teaming him with Jimmy Durante, and contemptuously regarded by Keaton himself, were huge moneyspinners. He took refuge from, and from a movie business becoming increasingly incomprehensible, in prolonged periods of alcoholism, and waited through 17 lacklustre years of mediocrity, bitparts, and gag-writing for other, lesser comedians, until, with *Sunset Boulevard* (1950) and *Limelight* (1952), the world began to notice him again. Then television provided a new home, and the final decade of his life afforded him a comfortable income from chat-shows, television commercials, and personal appearances at which, with a growing awareness, his audiences showed a genuine interest in the films that at first release had been taken so casually for granted. If the magnificent photography was now somewhat dimmed by chemical changes, Buster's own technical virtuosity still took the breath away. And as a symbol of the average man, struggling to find his place in a hostile society but unable to 'get away from himself', the great stone face speaks today with ever-increasing clarity.

Filmography

As actor only in shorts: **1917** The Butcher Boy; A Reckless Romeo; The Rough House; His Wedding Night; Oh, Doctor!; Fatty at Coney Island/Coney Island (GB: Coney Island); A Country Hero. **'18** Out West; The Bell Boy; Moonshine; Good Night, Nurse!; The Cook. **'19** Back Stage; The Hayseed. **'20** The Garage. *As co-director, co-scriptwriter and actor in shorts unless otherwise specified:* One Week; Convict 13; The Scarecrow; Neighbors; The Round Up (actor only); The Saphead (feature) (actor only). **'21** The Haunted House; Hard Luck; The High Sign; The Goat; The Playhouse; The Boat; The Paleface. **'22** Cops; My Wife's Relations; The Blacksmith; Screen Snapshots, No. 3 (guest); The Frozen North; Day Dreams; The Electric House. **'23** The Balloonatic; The Love Nest. *Features:* The Three Ages (co-dir; +act); Our Hospitality (co-dir; +act). **'24** Sherlock, Jr (co-dir; +act) (GB: Sherlock Junior); The Navigator (co-dir; +act). **'25** Seven Chances (dir; +act); Go West (dir; +act). **'26** Battling Butler (dir; +act); The General (co-dir; +co-sc; +act). *As actor only unless otherwise specified:* **'27** College. **'28** Steamboat Bill, Jr; The Cameraman (prod; +act). **'29** Spite Marriage; The Hollywood Revue of 1929 (guest) (GB: Hollywood Revue) (+guest in German version: Wir Schalten um auf Hollywood). **'30** Free and Easy/Easy Go (+Spanish version: Estrellados); Doughboys (prod; +act)

(GB: Forward March) (+actor only in German version: De Fronte, Marchen; and in Spanish version, title unknown). **'31** Parlor, Bedroom and Bath (prod; +act) (+actor only in French version: Buster se Marie; and in German version: Casanova Wider Willen); Sidewalks of New York (prod; +act); The Stolen Jools/ The Lost Jools/The Slippery Pearls (guest). **'32** The Passionate Plumber (prod; +act) (+actor only in French version: Le Plombier Amoureux); Speak Easily (prod; +act). **'33** What! No Beer? (feature) (actor only). *Shorts as actor only unless otherwise specified:* **'34** The Gold Ghost; Allez Oop; Le Roi des Champs Elysées (feature) (FR). **'35** The Invader/The Intruder/An Old Spanish Custom (feature) (GB); Palooka From Paducah; One Run Elmer; Hayseed Romance; Tars and Stripes; The E-Flat Man; The Timid Young Man. **'36** Three on a Limb; Grand Slam Opera (+co-sc); La Fiesta de Santa Barbara (guest); Blue Blazes; The Chemist; Mixed Magic. **'37** Jail Bait; Ditto; Love Nest on Wheels. **'38** Life in Sometown, USA (dir. only); Hollywood Handicap (dir. only); Streamlined Swing (dir. only). **'39** Pest From the West; Mooching Through Georgia; Hollywood Cavalcade (feature). **'40** Nothing But Pleasure; Pardon My Berth Marks; The Taming of the Snood; The Spook Speaks; The Villain Still Pursued Her (feature); Li'l Abner (feature); His Ex Marks the Spot. **'41** So You Won't Squawk; She's Oil Mine;

General Nuisance. *Features as actor only unless otherwise specified:* **'43** Forever and a Day. **'44** San Diego, I Love You. **'45** That's the Spirit; That Night With You. **'46** God's Country; El Moderno Barba Azul (MEX). **'49** The Loveable Cheat; In the Good Old Summertime; You're My Everything. **'50** Un Duel à Mort (+co-sc) (FR); Sunset Boulevard. **'52** Limelight; Ça c'Est du Cinema (compilation) (FR); L'Incantevole Nemica/Pattes de Velours (IT-FR); Paradise for Buster (short made for private showings only). **'56** Around the World in 80 Days. **'57** The Buster Keaton Story (tech. consultant only). **'60** The Adventures of Huckleberry Finn. **'62** Ten Girls Ago (unreleased) (CAN). **'63** Thirty Years of Fun (compilation); Its a Mad, Mad, Mad, Mad World; The Sound of Laughter (compilation). **'64** Pajama Party. **'65** Beach Blanket Bingo; Film/Project One; How to Stuff a Wild Bikini (GB: How to Fill a Wild Bikini); Sergeant Deadhead; The Big Chase (unreleased); The Rail Rodder/L'Homme du Rail (short) (CAN); Buster Keaton Rides Again/Buster Keaton (doc) (as himself). **'66** The Scribe (short) (CAN); A Funny Thing Happened On the Way to the Forum. **'67** Due Marine e un Generale (IT) (USA: War Italian Style). *Keaton was uncredited as gag-writer on:* **1938** Too Hot to Handle (+co-sc). **'40** Comrade X. **'44** Bathing Beauty. **'48** A Southern Yankee (GB: My Hero). **'49** Neptune's Daughter.

THE GOLDEN WEST

The silent Westerns carried on where real life left off, since the world they portrayed, although it still existed, was rapidly fading away in a glow of nostalgia

The Western is one of the finest creations of American culture, and the cowboy one of the great macho heroes of the world. Historically, the supreme era of the cowboy was short. It lasted from the end of the American Civil War in 1865 to the 1880s, when the cry was for beef to feed the hungry, growing nation. These were the days of the epic cattle drives up the famous trails like the Goodnight and the Chisholm, the days of the cattle empires, of the wide-open cow towns like Abilene and Dodge City, of range wars and murderous rivalries – the raw material of cowboy legend. But disastrous weather, bad management and the collapse of the beef market put an end to the boom; the arrival of homesteaders and the spread of barbed wire terminated the open range. Cowboys continued to exist and to ply their trade; but the old expansive, free-wheeling life had ended. Many cowboys moved on and the destination of some of them was Hollywood. By the Twenties, it was estimated that 500 a year came to Hollywood from ranches in Arizona and Colorado that were going broke.

The earliest Westerns therefore not only reconstructed the story and the life-style of the Old West – they overlapped with it and actually continued it. Real-life western characters appeared in films about their exploits: outlaws such as Al Jennings and Emmett Dalton and lawmen such as Bill Tilghman, last of the great western marshals. Tilghman made a number of films, actually interrupting the shooting of one of them to round up some bank robbers, thus mingling fantasy and reality with a vengeance. For the epic film *North of 36* (1924), the director Irvin Willat staged the first longhorn cattle drive for nearly thirty-five years, exactly replicating the conditions of the drives in the 1870s.

But for all the documentary-style realism of some of these Western reconstructions, the mass audience went to Westerns primarily for dashing heroes and plenty of action, preferably in impressive locations. So the films that the real-life cowboys helped to make in Hollywood gave worldwide currency to a romantic archetype which had been established even before the film industry came into being. The cowboy was seen as the embodiment of the virtues of the American frontier. These had been described by the historian Frederick Jackson Turner in 1893:

'That coarseness and strength combined with acuteness and inquisitiveness; that practical, inventive turn of mind, quick to find expedients; that masterful grasp of material things, lacking in the artistic but powerful to effect great ends; that restless, nervous energy; that dominant individualism working for good and for evil, and withal that buoyancy and exuberance which comes with freedom.'

These characteristics were blended with the essential elements of the chivalric gentleman of the Old World – courtesy, bravery and nobility – to create an ideal Westerner. This image was perfected by three men, all Easterners, all friends, all intoxicated by the heroic vision of the West and all destined to influence the Hollywood version of it. Owen Wister, a Philadelphian, made the cowboy the hero of his novel *The Virginian*, published in 1902. It was the first serious Western novel and gave the cowboy pride of place over the previously preferred heroes, the dime-novel favourites – the outlaw, the lawman, the pioneer, the trapper and the scout. Frederic Remington, a New Yorker, in his

Above: Prentiss Ingraham wrote the dime novels signed by Buffalo Bill as well as 200 stories about the popular Western hero. Below: The Covered Wagon. Opposite: Madge Bellamy and George O'Brien in Ford's epic The Iron Horse (1924)

paintings of cattle drives and round-ups, gunfights and hold-ups, recorded a West made up of swirls of action and colour, with manly cowboys at its centre. Theodore Roosevelt, aristocratic President, explorer and big-game hunter, preached in his life and in his books a militant Anglo-Saxonism of which the cowboy was the proud exemplar. The first epic Western film, *The Covered Wagon* (1923), was to be dedicated to his memory. The impact of the cowboy can be gauged from the fact that the terms 'Western film' and 'cowboy film' became interchangeable, although many Western films actually featured no cowboys as such.

Although the cowboy was being ennobled for the first time, the process was built on the tradition of the dime novels. From the 1860s onwards, as the West seized the imagination of America, a flood of cheap novels, written according to a few formulas, had poured from the presses, dramatizing and romanticizing the adventures of real and fictional Western heroes. Dime novels became one of the primary sources of film content, reinforced by stage melodramas with Western settings and the Wild West shows which popularized what became the great set-pieces of Western films – the stagecoach chase, the wagon-train attack and the cavalry charge.

One figure tapped all these sources of inspiration – Colonel William F. Cody, 'Buffalo Bill' himself. A real-life scout and buffalo hunter, he was taken up by the leading dime novelist, Ned Buntline, who started a long series of novels describing his fictional adventures. Cody took to the stage in 1872 in a rather bad melodrama called *The Scouts of the Plains* and, discovering that he lacked aptitude as an actor, launched his celebrated Wild West show in 1883. Towards the end of his life, he brought the wheel full circle by producing and starring in a film of his Western exploits, made in 1913 and known by various titles, including *The Adventures of Buffalo Bill*. His career is the perfect demonstration of how historical reality shaded into cinematic fiction.

It was inevitable that films would follow the lead of the stage and the printed page, and Westerns became a staple of the new entertainment medium

Above: Frederic Remington's 1899 painting Missing *depicts a cavalry trooper captured by hostile Indians and unlikely to survive for long, since Indians soon killed their prisoners. Top right: an encounter between Indian warriors in* The Way of a Mother *(1913), supervised by Thomas H. Ince. Right: G. M. Anderson as Broncho Billy (right) in a 1913 story of a tenderfoot who gets tired of being pushed around and becomes a crack shot. Far right: in* White Oak *(1921), William S. Hart plays Oak Miller, a gambler obsessed with visiting revenge on the man who deceived his sister; the villain is finally killed by an Indian chief whose daughter he has betrayed. Below right: Harry Carey as a good-hearted outlaw in Ford's* The Scarlet Drop *(1918)*

early on. The first recorded Western is a one-minute vignette entitled *Cripple Creek Bar Room*, produced in 1898. The first Western story film, *The Great Train Robbery*, followed in 1903. Directed by Edwin S. Porter, it was actually filmed in New Jersey but told a classic story of robbery, chase and retribution. It had enormous success at the box-office and was extensively imitated. One thing it did not have was a hero. But in the cast was an actor called Gilbert M. Anderson, who was soon ready to remedy this defect. Overcoming an initial tendency to fall off his horse, he saw the potential in the cowboy hero, launched a new company (Essanay) and took a film unit off first to Colorado and then to California, where he began producing one- and two-reel Westerns, many of them featuring Anderson himself as a sentimental tough guy called Broncho Billy. Anderson, who appeared in hundreds of Broncho Billy films between 1908 and 1916, thus became the first Western hero. Business problems kept him off the screen for over a year and when he

of his romanticism, plots that were sentimental, melodramatic and heavily moralistic. In his films he played a succession of ramrod-straight, grim-visaged badmen with names like Black Deering, Blaze Tracey and Draw Egan, who were underneath it all chivalric and sentimental and whose moral regeneration was a central theme of the stories. In *Hell's Hinges* (1916), he actually burns down a sinful town, in a sequence eerily prefiguring Clint Eastwood's *High Plains Drifter* (1973). Hart's horse Fritz became the first of a long line of star movie horses who became as well-known as their riders. But Hart's popularity waned and the piety, sentimentality and comparatively slow pace of his films came to seem increasingly old-fashioned with the rise of a very different sort of star – Tom Mix. Hart refused to change his style and after a final film, *Tumbleweeds* (1925), he retired. *Tumbleweeds* represents the triumphant summation of Hart's vision of the West and takes place symbolically against the background of the end of the open range and the arrival of the homesteaders. It also contains a stunningly executed and majestically shot set-piece, the Cherokee Strip land rush, which ranks with the best of its kind in the genre.

Where Hart had prided himself on the authenticity of his films, Tom Mix's films were pure fantasy. He has first entered films in mid-1909 as a stockman and supporting player in a rodeo picture, *Ranch Life in the Great Southwest* (1910), and from then until 1917 he worked for the Selig

Westerns drew for inspiration on dime novels, stage melodramas, rodeos and Wild West shows

company, turning out something like a hundred Westerns, one- and two-reelers, which he often wrote and directed as well as starring in. But in 1917 he moved to Fox and his career took off. The inspiration of his films was the circus and the Wild West show, where Hart's had been Victorian melodrama and photographic realism. Tom Mix's cowboy hero, flamboyantly costumed, involved himself in fast-moving, far-fetched stories, strong on stunts, action and comedy. Fleet of foot, keen of eye and effortlessly gallant, Tom Mix became the Doug Fairbanks of the sagebrush. He set the style and pattern for the Westerns of a host of rivals and imitators. Indeed from his own supporting casts emerged Buck Jones and George O'Brien, who were both to be promoted as Western stars by Fox.

Westerns received a tremendous boost in 1923 when Paramount released the first indisputable Western epic, *The Covered Wagon*. Based on Emerson Hough's novel, it began as a conventional programmer about a wagon boss falsely accused of a crime by his rival for the heroine's affections, but expanded to become the saga of wagons westward on the Oregon Trail in 1848. It exists now only in an incomplete print. Nevertheless it can be said that despite such assets as the grandeur of Karl Brown's photography, the documentary look imparted by eight weeks' location shooting to such large-scale action sequences as the wagon train's departure, the river crossing and a buffalo hunt, and the rich character comedy of Ernest Torrence and Tully Marshall as two old frontiersmen, it is a flawed film. The director James Cruze, whatever his strengths, was weak on action highlights and suspense, and the Indian attack on the wagon train and its rescue are clumsily mishandled.

But the film was a great box-office success, and it emboldened Fox to turn its new Western *The Iron*

returned he found that new idols had risen and his career faded.

The artistic possibilities in the Western became clear in the work of two of the cinema's great innovators – D. W. Griffith and Thomas H. Ince. Griffith in his years at Biograph brought his increasingly sophisticated technique and powerful visual sense to Westerns, imbuing such projects as *The Last Drop of Water* (1911), *The Massacre* (1913) and *The Battle at Elderbush Gulch* (1914) with truly epic qualities. Thomas H. Ince, the first producer to insist on fully detailed and comprehensive scripts for the guidance of the production team as well as the actors, and an organizational genius when it came to staging large-scale action, hired the Miller Brothers 101 Ranch Real Wild West Show, to provide him with a ready-made stock company of cowboys and Indians, longhorn cattle, stagecoaches and wagons. He turned out Westerns from his Inceville studios, one of the most successful of which was *Custer's Last Raid* (1912), directed by and starring Francis Ford (though Ince officially took the directorial credit). This film so impressed Carl Laemmle that he lured Ford away from Ince and set him to work at Universal, which was to become one of the major producers of Westerns. But Francis Ford was eventually to be eclipsed as a director by his younger brother John Ford and as an actor by Harry Carey and then Hoot Gibson, who both starred in many popular Westerns for Universal, some of them directed by the up-and-coming John (then known as Jack) Ford.

Ince, however, found a more-than-adequate replacement for Francis Ford in William S. Hart, who entered films in 1914 at the age of 44. Previously a stage actor, who had appeared not only in Shakespeare and *Ben-Hur* but also in such popular Western stage melodramas as *The Squaw Man* and *The Virginian*, Hart was an incurable romantic. He had been raised in the West, loved it and wanted to depict it realistically on the screen. First with Ince and later with Paramount, he succeeded in his aim, giving his films a gritty surface realism of austere, dusty townships and authentic cowboy costume and accoutrements. But with this went another side

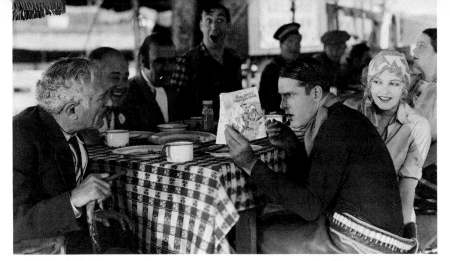

Above: a dime-novel-reading cowboy (Ken Maynard) acts as guide to a circus in The Wagon Show (1928) and becomes its star rider. Below: after an Indian attack, the train returns to the railhead in John Ford's The Iron Horse. Bottom: production shot of The Vanishing American, sympathetic to the Navajo Indians and filmed in authentic locations

packed Tom Mix model were what was required, and in his wake a posse of immortals galloped across the screen. These were the men in white hats riding white horses, the paladins of the prairies, the idols of the Saturday matinées.

MGM launched a group of historical Westerns starring the stalwart Colonel Tim McCoy, a former Indian agent who had handled the Indians used in the making of *The Covered Wagon*. At First National, Ken Maynard starred in rousing Western adventures, whose spectacular set-piece highlights were to be reused constantly as stock footage throughout the Thirties. At FBO, Fred Thomson, a former Presbyterian minister and Boy Scout leader, now forgotten but idolized in his day, rode and fought his way into the hearts of a legion of young admirers. From Paramount between 1921 and 1928 (and thereafter in the sound era) came an impressive series of adaptations of the novels of Zane Grey, arguably the most popular of Western writers. With classic plots and evocative titles like *The Thundering Herd*, *The Vanishing American* and *Wild Horse Mesa* (all 1925), they generally starred steely-eyed Jack Holt or rugged Richard Dix. They also benefited from being filmed, as the contract with Grey specifically demanded, on the actual locations of the stories.

By 1926, however, a glut of cheap Westerns took the edge off the public demand and the coming of sound apparently signalled their doom. Short on that essential commodity, dialogue, they were dubbed old-fashioned and over-romantic. The vogue was for bang-up-to-date films that could exploit the new medium, and Westerns were eclipsed by gangster films with their screeching cars and machine-gun battles and by musicals – 'all-talking, all-singing, all-dancing'. Production of Westerns was cut by as much as 75 per cent and in 1929 *Photoplay* magazine declared: 'Western novel and motion picture heroes have slunk away into the brush, never to return.'

Horse (1924) into an epic. So the familiar story of a young man seeking the murderer of his father burgeoned into a full-scale reconstruction of the building of the transcontinental railroad. In John Ford, Fox had a director who could combine visual sweep and exciting action sequences, rich comedy interludes and acutely-observed details of everyday life to counterpoint the epic theme. In George O'Brien, Ford found a wholly convincing Western star, virile, natural and likeable. The result was one of the great achievements of the silent cinema. Other epics followed, such as Irvin Willat's *North of 36* and James Cruze's *The Pony Express* (1925). But none of them achieved the success of *The Covered Wagon* and *The Iron Horse*, and it became clear that large-scale evocations of nationalistic sentiment were not entirely to the public's taste. Interestingly, after his magisterial land-rush epic *Three Bad Men* (1926), John Ford was not to make another Western until *Stagecoach* (1939).

Programme Westerns, however, flourished and production of them trebled in the year following *The Covered Wagon*. Films on the streamlined, action-

ON THE RED FRONT

The experimental ferment that followed the October Revolution of 1917 took the Soviet Union to the artistic forefront of world cinema during the Twenties

Lenin said: 'Of all the arts, for us the cinema is the most important.' What did he mean and to what extent were his hopes for the cinema realized in the Soviet Union during the silent film period?

First and foremost Lenin intended that the cinema should provide the new revolutionary regime with its most effective weapon of agitation, propaganda and education. The cinema had certain attractions for the Bolsheviks. By the time they seized power in October 1917, the cinema was already the most popular form of entertainment in the towns and cities – the idea of the cinema therefore did not have to be 'sold' to the urban population. In the countryside it was still very much a novelty, with all the advantages which that implied, if only the industry could organize itself to provide the necessary equipment and the appropriate films. That was, however, to prove in the event a big 'if'.

The silent film was particularly attractive to the new Soviet authorities. The population, more than two-thirds illiterate, spoke a wide variety of languages. Written communication could therefore be effective only in the long run as the educational level improved, whereas the Bolsheviks were anxious to develop quickly the class consciousness of the masses. The silent film was an overwhelmingly *visual* medium – at its best, indeed, a *purely visual* medium – and was accessible to all sections of the people, while the moving image cut more deeply into the popular memory than did the poster, also widely used at that time.

Of course the silent film had its limitations: the dependence on relatively few intertitles to clarify the narrative meant that silent film plots had to remain fairly simple; but in this context such simplicity was to prove an enormous advantage. Films were first used on the agit-trains that toured the country for purposes of agitation and propaganda during the Civil War of 1918–21. These agitational shorts (*agitki*) were simple and direct. Their dynamism and economy of style were to exercise a great effect on subsequent Soviet filmmaking, as indeed were the people involved with them. Several of the foremost directors cut their cinematic teeth on the agit-trains. These trains distributed material from the centre to the provinces and gathered other material in the provinces to be taken back to the centre and used in future journeys. The film material gathered by them provided the content of the earliest Soviet newsreels and documentaries and also the themes for an important genre of fictional feature films about the Civil War. In some ways the Civil War became for the Soviet cinema the equivalent of the Hollywood Western, a vehicle for mass entertainment laced with elements of historical and political legitimation of the society that produced it.

Vital parts of the Soviet cinema network – in production, distribution and exhibition – remained in private hands until the industry was nationalized in 1919. But the problems were only just beginning: many of the private entrepreneurs fled the country,

ОКТЯБРЬ

СТАРОЕ и НОВОЕ

taking their equipment, their talent and their expertise with them. The ravages of war, civil war and general neglect had left studios (or 'film factories', as they were called) and cinemas in tatters, while a ban by the Western powers on the export of film stock to the Soviet Union meant that the authorities had virtually no new materials to make their own films.

Before the Revolution Russia had produced none of its own film materials; all stock and equipment had been imported. The Western blockade therefore dealt a particularly heavy blow to the nascent Soviet film industry. Desperation led Lenin to approve a deal with a certain Jacques Cibrario, who promptly disappeared with the money he had been given but without providing the materials that had been paid for.

The disruption of war and civil war caused widespread starvation and epidemics. Hundreds of

Top: Eisenstein re-created the events of October, with Nikandrov as Lenin. Above: Marfa Lapkina as the peasant heroine of Eisenstein and Grigori Alexandrov's The Old and the New

thousands died and millions more suffered. Fuel was scarce and power supplies erratic. The Russian winters increased the toll. Clearly the Soviet cinema needed a massive injection of funds, but, equally clearly, the government had to concentrate its limited resources on the more immediate tasks of political survival. One positive step was taken: in 1919 the first State Film School was set up to train new cadres (groups of Party workers) of all sorts to people the cinema when times were better.

The advent of the New Economic Policy in 1921, with its limited return to private enterprise, provided temporary relief. The aim was to finance the restoration and development of the film industry from its own resources. Audiences were to be drawn to cinemas to see films that they were willing to pay to watch and the money that they paid was to be used to produce films that the authorities wanted them to view. Entertainment was to pay for propaganda.

Anatoli Lunacharsky who, as People's Commissar for Enlightenment, had overall responsibilty for the cinema, was the architect of this policy of pragmatism. He preferred that audiences should come voluntarily to the cinema and that the propaganda should be concentrated in the newsreel. He himself was the author of several screenplays for 'psychological salon dramas', some of which provided a vehicle for his actress-wife Natalya Rozenel.

But Soviet audiences wanted to see foreign and, above all, Hollywood films. Charlie Chaplin, Buster Keaton, Harold Lloyd and, especially, Mary Pickford and Douglas Fairbanks were the staple diet of the Soviet cinemagoer during the Twenties. When Pickford and Fairbanks visited the Soviet Union in 1926, they were mobbed by fans; a feature film *Potselui Meri Pikford* (1927, *The Kiss of Mary Pickford*), from an idea by Lunacharsky himself, was made around their visit; and their comments on Sergei M. Eisenstein's *Bronenosets Potemkin* (1925, *Battleship Potemkin*) as 'the greatest film ever made' were used to relaunch the film after its disastrous first run.

By 1928 the Soviet authorities felt able to turn their attention to the political tasks of the Soviet cinema and it was in that year that the box-office receipts from Soviet films exceeded those from imported films for the first time. The new regime was now secure, even if Stalin's imagination did not always allow him to admit it, and the task of rapid industrialization that lay at the heart of the First Five Year Plan (1928–32) meant that the cinema could no longer be left to its own devices. The 'industrial revolution' was to be accompanied by a 'cultural revolution' in which the cinema's vital

Top left: in The Extraordinary Adventures of Mr West in the Land of the Bolsheviks, *a hapless American tourist (Porfiri Podobed, bespectacled) is rescued from the 'Countess' (Alexandra Khokhlova), the 'Count' (Vsevolod Pudovkin) and an accomplice, who are showing him all the horrors he expects to find in the USSR. Centre top: an agit-train equipped to show and make films. Top right: poster for* Pokhozdeniya Oktyabriny (The Adventures of Oktyabrina), *a film of fantasy. Above right: Louise Poirier (Elena Kuzmina), a shopgirl, defending the Paris Commune of 1871 in* New Babylon. *Right: the pioneering documentarist Dziga Vertov. Above: Alexander Rodchenko's poster for Vertov's* Kino-Glaz *(1924, Kino-Eye)*

role was deemed to be the 'elevation of the cultural level of the masses'.

In March 1928 a Party Conference on Cinema outlined the tasks of the film industry and in 1929 a decree defined the responsibilities of the cadres of film workers. Despite reorganization of the industry in 1930, direct political control proved unexpectedly awkward to enforce. The attempt to impose it created its own troubles, and these were further complicated by the difficulties associated with the advent of sound and the refusal by many film-makers to recognize that sound was anything more than a passing novelty. Sound created problems in the West as well, but the by-now highly centralized organizational structure of the Soviet cinema turned those problems into nightmares.

Just as the political authorities had recognized the propaganda potential of the silent film, so a new generation of artists acclaimed the cinema as a new medium of artistic expression, as the new art form for the new epoch. Initially the political perspective merged with the artistic; but the political requirement of a medium of mass communication began to conflict with a need for artistic experiment, and the notion that here at last was an avant-garde which had the full support of the powers-that-be soon proved an illusion.

In addition to the functional attractions of the silent film, artists were drawn to the cinema as a relatively new medium untainted by a classical bourgeois tradition – unlike the theatre or literature, for instance – and with as yet untried but potentially limitless possibilities. For instance, the poet Vladimir Mayakovsky (1893–1930) tried his hand at writing three film scenarios in 1918. As the leading critic and scriptwriter Viktor Shklovsky (b. 1893) observed:

'Art forms "grow tired", burn themselves out, like flames. The change in forms is usually revolutionary. The cinema is the natural heir to the theatre and, possibly, literature.'

Others were more definite: 'The cinema is the new philosophy. . . the new international visual Esperanto of the future.' Since to many the new era was to be characterized by the modernization and industrialization of Russia, the mechanical base

of the cinema was also seized upon by theorists such as G.M. Boltyansky:

'The mechanical possibility of unending reproduction and distribution of the works of the cinema make it, as distinct from the other arts, the sole and exclusive *expression of the era of the new culture.*'

One of the leading exponents of the new art form was Lev Kuleshov (1899–1970), who has been described as the 'father of the Soviet cinema'. Like so many film directors Kuleshov came to the cinema after the Revolution and, like others too, he was astonishingly young – only 18 in October 1917. Since there was no film stock with which to make feature films, Kuleshov had to channel his energies into the establishment in 1921 of his own workshop at the new film school. Here Kuleshov and his students rehearsed films that would never be produced, the so-called 'films without film'. It was at this time that Kuleshov first developed the idea that the distinctive nature of cinema, its superiority to the theatre, lay in the principle of *montage* or editing. Experiments suggested to him that each film shot acquired meaning from its immediate context, from the shots that preceded and succeeded it on the screen and therefore in the perception of the audience. By altering the context, by placing the original shot in different sequences, the whole meaning could be transformed. This discovery, of crucial significance to the subsequent development of Soviet film theory, was to become known as the 'Kuleshov effect'.

Kuleshov acquired some experience of actual filming by travelling in the agit-trains and he used the material he collected for his agitational film *Na Krasnom Fronte* (1920, *On the Red Front*). His first fictional feature film was the remarkable satire *Neobychainye Priklyucheniya Mistera Vesta v Strane Bolshevikov* (1924, *The Extraordinary Adventures of Mr West in the Land of the Bolsheviks*), one of the most successful Soviet silent comedies. This was followed by the detective thriller *Luch Smerti* (1925, *The Death Ray*) and the more psychologically-orientated *Po Zakonu* (1926, *By the Law*), set in the Yukon during the Gold Rush. Kuleshov made three more silent films and in 1929 produced his major contribution to film theory, *Iskusstvo Kino* (The Art of the Cinema), a book still not translated in full into English.

Kuleshov's great importance goes beyond his own films, for he influenced almost every other Soviet film-maker, not only through his development of the idea of montage but also because of his attempts to encourage a new style of 'naturalistic' acting specific to cinema and in some ways resembling the stage and film director Vsevolod Meyerhold's experiments with bio-mechanics in training actors to use their bodies in the theatre. Kuleshov called his actor, who lacked the artificiality associated with conventional stage training, a *naturshchik* and explained:

'Individuality is exceptionally important in a *naturshchik.* . . . The actor can serve directors of all tendencies; the *naturshchik* only the director who has taught him and a small circle of like-minded people.'

Many of Kuleshov's ideas were taken up by a small group of very young film-makers in Petrograd (later Leningrad), who included Grigori Kozintsev and who called themselves FEKS or the Factory of the Eccentric Actor. Central to their ideas was the notion of 'impeded form': people and objects were to be portrayed in unfamiliar contexts, thus alienating the viewer in the sense, later used by the German playwright Bertolt Brecht, of forcing him to see things in a new light. Their most important films were: *Pokhozdeniya Oktyabriny* (1924, The Adventures of Oktyabrina), an anti-capitalist political

allegory; *Mishka Protiv Yudenicha* (1925, Mishka versus Yudenich), a children's comedy which, in possible homage to Kuleshov, was subtitled 'The Unprecedented Adventures of Mishka the Paper-Boy Among the White Guards'; *Chertovo Koleso* (1926, *The Devil's Wheel*), a story of gangsters in Petrograd during the Civil War; *Shinel* (1926, *The Cloak*), based on Gogol's story about a poor clerk; *Bratishka* (1927, Little Brother), a comedy about a truck; *Soyuz Velikogo Dela* (1927, *The Club of the Big Deed – SVD*), concerning the Decembrist revolt in 1825 in St Petersburg; and finally a film about the Paris Commune of 1871, *Novyi Vavilon* (1929, *New Babylon*), for which Shostakovich wrote a memorable score.

Far left: Vsevolod Pudovkin as The Living Corpse, *a drunkard who pretends to be dead so his wife can remarry. Below:* Earth *is a lyrical celebration of all that lives and dies. Below centre: Pudovkin's* Storm Over Asia *aroused protests for its satirical view of the British Occupation Forces in Mongolia. Bottom: Pavel Pol and Anna Sten in* The Girl With the Hatbox. *Bottom left: Alexandra Khokhlova, Vladimir Fogel and Sergei Komarov as three Yukon outcasts in* By the Law

One of Kuleshov's leading actors, and probably his most faithful pupil, was Vsevolod Pudovkin (1893–1953), who became an important director and retained in his own films much of the balance between actor's characterization and director's editing that Kuleshov preached. Pudovkin's first feature film was *Mat* (1926, *Mother*), about a woman who is led by the example of her son into political activism; this was followed by *Konyets Sankt-Peterburga* (1927, *The End of St Petersburg*), concerning World War I and the Revolution, and *Potomok Chingis-Khana* (1928, *Storm Over Asia*), a tale of the Civil War in Mongolia. Pudovkin's films, like those of Kuleshov, were among the most popular Soviet films of the Twenties. These directors employed and built upon the techniques developed by Hollywood with which audiences were familiar: their films had a clear plot and an individual hero and villain so that audiences found them accessible and were able to identify with the message that the director and his team were trying to convey.

In fact the bulk of Soviet films of this period tried to adapt American techniques to Soviet themes – the *Miss Mend* serial (1926) is a good example – and it was these Soviet films that Soviet audiences went to see rather than the works later acclaimed as masterpieces. Two of the leading figures of this popular cinema were Fyodor Otsep (1895–1949), who directed *Zhivoi Trup* (1929, *The Living Corpse*), based on Leo Tolstoy's play, and Boris Barnet, (1902–65), who directed *Devushka s Korobkoi* (1927, *The Girl With the Hatbox*) and *Dom na Trubnoi* (1928, *The House on Trubnaya Square*), two satirical comedies. Both men were disciples of Kuleshov.

In the world-famous masterpieces, as Party activists were quick to point out, form often seemed to

Eisenstein's movies shook the world of film but they generally flopped at the Soviet box-office

outweigh content, so that they were 'unintelligible to the millions'. The films of Sergei M. Eisenstein (1898–1948) fell into this category, though the accusation of 'unintelligibility' reflected more on the accusers than the accused. Eisenstein was by no means alone among Soviet artists in thinking that a revolutionary *society* needed a revolutionary *culture* that would instil a revolutionary *consciousness* into the masses. This culture had to find new forms untainted by a bourgeois past and Eisenstein felt that the cinema was the ideal vehicle for this.

His silent films, beginning with *Stachka* (1925, *Strike*), were essentially experiments to find appropriate new forms. Traditional individual characterizations were abandoned as bourgeois relics in favour of symbolic ciphers representative of the mass and played by ordinary people who had no training as actors. Eisenstein called this 'typage' and it was a highly stylized form of caricature. The characterization of the sailors and the middle-class people of Odessa in his film about the failed 1905 revolution, *Battleship Potemkin*, is a good example. These figures were brought together by editing in a manner that challenged conventional narrative conceptions. In what Eisenstein described as 'intellectual montage', objects and characters were juxtaposed in a way that deliberately jarred on the audience: images commented on one another, forcing audiences out of complacent preconceptions and into a new consciousness of reality. The sequences showing Alexander Kerensky, leader of the Provisional Government after the February revolution in 1917, in the Winter Palace in *Oktyabr*

(1927, *October*) are symptomatic. But the ironic analogy between Kerensky and the preening peacock on the tsar's clock was lost on contemporary audiences and confused them. Hence Eisenstein, though blazing a trail in terms of artistic theory and practice, failed to deliver the goods that the Party required and he fell into disgrace, though only temporarily, after the failure of his film on collectivization, *Staroye i Novoye* (1928, *The Old and the New*, sometimes known as *The General Line*).

There were of course many other directors active in the Soviet cinema. One of the most famous was the Ukrainian Alexander Dovzhenko (1894–1956), maker of *Zemlya* (1930, *Earth*), whose films evoked a pastoral folkloristic idyll. There was also an active film industry in Georgia, which produced such works as *Krasniye Diavolyata* (1923, *Little Red Devils*), *Moya Babushka* (1929, *My Grandmother*) and *Sol Svanetii* (1930, *Salt for Svanetia*).

Other artists went further in their search for forms appropriate to the revolutionary Soviet cinema by denouncing fictional feature films altogether. 'The film drama is the opium of the people. . . Long live life as it is!' wrote Dziga Vertov (1896–1954). He was the leading exponent of the inherent superiority of the documentary and newsreel format, the founder and leading member of the Cine-Eye group. He had begun working with film on one of the agit-trains during the Civil War and, while editing the *Kinonedelya* (Cine-Week) newsreels in 1918–19, made three documentary films from the material that he had collected. He went on to produce the series of *Kino-Pravda* (Cine-Truth) newsreels in 1922–25, the most famous of which is the *Leninskaya Kino-Pravda* (1925, Leninist Cine-Truth) depicting the reaction to Lenin's death in 1924 and initiating themes later developed in his sound films *Tri Pesni o Lenine* (1934, *Three Songs of Lenin*) and *Kolybelnaya* (1937, Lullaby). But the most important of Vertov's silent documentaries were *Shagai, Soviet* (1926, Stride, Soviet), *Shestaya Chast Mira* (1926, *A Sixth of the Earth*), *Odinadtsatyi* (1928, *The Eleventh Year*) and *Cheloviek s Kinoaparatom* (1929, *Man With a Movie Camera*), all depicting multifarious aspects of Soviet life with increasing virtuosity. In their manifestos the Cine-Eyes claimed to represent:

'. . . the art of organizing the necessary movements of objects in space and time into a rhythmic artistic whole, according to the characteristics of the whole and the internal rhythm of each object.'

They offered:

'Not a Pathé or a Gaumont newsreel (a newsreel of record), nor even a *Kino-Pravda* (a political newsreel), but a real Cine-Eye newsreel – a rapid survey of *visual* events interpreted by the film camera, pieces of *real* energy (as distinct from theatrical), brought by intervals to an accumulated whole by the great skill of montage.'

Through this montage the film-maker could organize 'life as it really is', improve upon it and 'see and show the world in the name of the world proletarian revolution'.

But by the end of the Twenties all this experimentation was giving way to the new orthodoxies of socialist realism. Soviet film directors initially wanted to use the new weapon of sound as an integral part of their concept of montage, with sound as counterpointing rather than merely illustrating the image; but the political situation had changed. Immersed in the world of collectivization and rapid industrialization, the Soviet cinema gradually adopted the tenets of socialist realism and attempted to 'describe not reality as it is but reality as it will be'. That became the clearly defined task of the Soviet cinema in the next decade.

Pandora's Box

G. W. Pabst's film *Pandora's Box* immortalized Louise Brooks. The American actress' portrayal of the doomed beauty, Lulu, with her startling helmet of black hair, is charged with alluring sensuality combined with a powerfully tragic sense of childlike innocence and vulnerability. Brooks personifies the joy and craving of sex; she is part predator, part supplicant – she both lures men to their death and attracts, like a magnet, her own lewd downfall.

Pandora's Box is based on the plays *Erdgeist* (Earth Spirit) and *Die Büchse der Pandora* (Pandora's Box) by Frank Wedekind, which were first performed in 1893 and 1905 respectively. The Lulu figure is an extension of the mythical Pand-ora, who, according to Greek mythology, was sent to earth with a box containing all the disorders of the world. In Pabst's film she is surrounded by admirers, though none more fervent than the proper if passionate Dr Peter Schön. Compelled by lust to marry Lulu, Schön himself becomes fatefully intwined in the zestful progress of the *femme fatale*. Lulu is sentenced to prison for Schön's murder, but she manages to escape to continue the good life with Schön's infatuated son, Alwa. Together they flee to England where Lulu, one fog-bound London evening, crosses the path of Jack the Ripper. Legend meets legend, each fulfilling the other's destiny.

Louise Brooks was under contract to Paramount in the autumn of

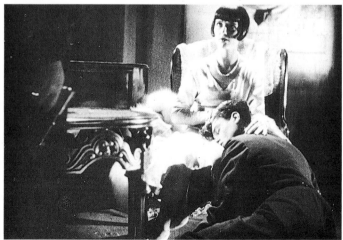

1

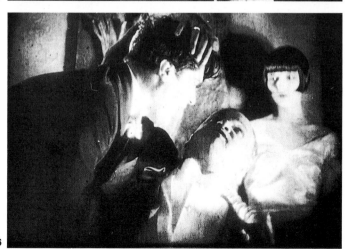

5

6

1928, when the request arrived from Berlin: could she appear in Mr Pabst's *Pandora's Box*? Marlene Dietrich, two years before *Der blaue Engel* (1930, *The Blue Angel*), had been considered and rejected as being 'too old and too obvious'. Although Brooks' career was by now beginning to languish, because of her inability to make the transition to sound, Pabst nevertheless hit at once on the dualism of the American's appeal. In contrast to her alluring beauty, Pabst placed Lulu in an environment of unutterable degeneracy, attended by the suave and prosperous Schön, his fawning son (played by Franz Lederer, subsequently to become a leading man in Hollywood), a brutish acrobat named Rodrigo Quast, and a sinister, perverse character called Schigolch, also known as Papa Brommer, who clings to Lulu's side like some faithful terrier through all the phases of her ruin.

The artificial gaiety of the opening scenes soon gives way to an almost stifling iconography of humiliation. At the wedding reception for Lulu and Schön, Lulu creates an embarrassing scene with her flirtatious dancing. Schön later discovers his wife in the bedroom embracing Schigolch. He loses his temper and threatens Schigolch with a gun. Schön's humiliation is further aggravated, when he discovers his son, Alwa, with his head on Lulu's lap. Schön reacts with appalling drama: 'Kill yourself!' he hisses at Lulu, thrusting the gun phallus-like towards her face; 'It is the only way to save both of us.' In a clumsy, yet also classical, struggle between the couple, the gun goes off, and Schön is mortally wounded. So the white satin of her wedding gown yields to the black veil of mourning and guilt, as Lulu stands in the court and hears sentence pronounced against her for manslaughter.

The symbols proliferate. A Cairo nightclub owner buys Lulu for 6,000 marks. The hefty trapeze artist, Quast, lurks within range, threatening to blackmail her and return her to Germany unless she joins his variety act. As he leers, a stuffed alligator on the wall behind him reflects his guile.

The epilogue, in London, carries the grace and inevitability of an operatic coda. Lulu's smile is so plangent, even in the bleakness of London's East End, that it beguiles the notorious murderer. She gazes at a candle as though rapt in some mysterious chapel of the mind, as though anticipating the significance of her death. Then the Ripper catches sight of the gleam of a bread-knife, and Pabst's close-up of his hand clasped urgently around Lulu's plump white arm has all the force of a violation.

Pandora's Box belongs as much to Pabst as to Louise Brooks. Her brilliance does not efface his talent, as Garbo's does many a journeyman director's. Pabst, after all, had seized and enhanced the gifts of Asta Nielsen, Brigitte Helm, Garbo herself. By opposing the American actress' beauty to the grotesqueries of Berlin high life, he created a rare dialectic, in which the characters are at the mercy of their images. Decadence has seldom appeared so enticing as in *Pandora's Box*.

Directed by G. W. Pabst, 1929
Prod co: Nero-Film. **prod:** George C. Horsetzky, Seymour Nebenzahl. **sc:** Ladislaus Vajda, from the plays *Erdgeist* and *Die Büchse der Pandora* by Frank Wedekind. **photo:** Günther Krampf. **ed:** Joseph R. Fliesler. **art dir:** Andrei Andreiev. **cost:** Gottlieb Hesch. **r/t:** 131 minutes cut to 120 minutes. German title: *Die Büchse der Pandora*. Released in USA/GB as *Pandora's Box*.
Cast: Louise Brooks (*Lulu*), Fritz Kortner (*Dr Peter Schön*), Franz Lederer (*Alwa Schön*), Carl Goetz (*Schigolch/Papa Brommer*), Alice Roberts (*Countess Anna Geschwitz*), Daisy D'Ora (*Marie de Zarniko*), Krafft-Raschig (*Rodrigo Quast*), Michael von Newlinsky (*Marquis Casti-Piani*), Siegfried Arno (*the stage director*), Gustav Diessl (*Jack the Ripper*).

to tell her he is going to get married. Schön discovers Brommer hiding, and leaves in disgust (2) when Lulu introduces Brommer as her first sugar-daddy.

Schön's son Alwa, who is infatuated with Lulu (3), is writing a musical revue in which she will star. Sometime later Schön, with his respectable fiancée, visits the theatre to see his son's show. Lulu gets upset and refuses to go onstage. While Schön comforts her, his fiancée walks in and catches them embracing. Schön decides to marry Lulu.

On their wedding night Lulu entertains her low-life friends to the dismay of her new husband. Schön enters their bedroom and sees Lulu embracing Brommer. Schön threatens him with a gun (4). The other guests hurriedly leave and Schön, already feeling betrayed, discovers Alwa with his head in Lulu's lap (5). Schön attempts to appease his honour by getting Lulu to kill herself but he is accidentally shot instead (6). She and Alwa flee the country. They are later forced to leave their refuge on a ship after Alwa has gambled away all his money and is caught cheating at cards (7). Lulu, Alwa and Brommer then escape to London where they are reduced to living off Lulu's earnings as a prostitute. But a killer is stalking the streets of the East End. On Christmas Eve Lulu brings a strange client back to her flat (8) . . .

Lulu is visited in her expensive flat by the shabby Papa Brommer, an old friend (1). He helps himself to her money and liquor and then asks her to dance for him. Lulu's lover, newspaper editor Dr Peter Schön, comes by

3

4

7

8

Charles Chaplin is the universal clown. His figure is recognized and his comedy instantly understood by hundreds of millions of people of every race, and his name and fame have endured since before World War I

It is no small part of Chaplin's magic and mystery that he rose to his unprecedented pinnacle of popularity from origins as humble and unpromising as might be imagined. He was born on April 16, 1889, according to his own account in East Lane, Walworth, London. Some uncertainty, though, has always surrounded the place of his birth: no birth certificate is recorded for him, and at various times publicity people attributed different locations to the event. Early in his film career, indeed, Chaplin fancifully claimed he had been born in Fontainebleau, France.

Certainly, however, he spent his earliest years in south London, in the Kennington district that was a favourite residential area for Victorian vaudeville performers. Charles Chaplin Senior was a music-hall ballad-singer whose portrait appears on a number of illustrated song sheets of the period. Until alcoholism – the occupational hazard of the music halls – overtook him, he seems to have been fairly successful, and the family was probably reasonably comfortably off at the time of Chaplin's birth. Within a year or so, however, his parents separated. His father died when young Charles was 12, and Mrs Chaplin, herself a not very successful music-hall singer, was left to bring up Charles and his older half-brother Sydney alone. According to Chaplin's own biography, they suffered periods of extreme poverty. When Mrs Chaplin eventually succumbed to the strains and declined into permanent mental breakdown, the two boys spent long periods in orphanages and institutions.

Chaplin's career as an entertainer seemed destined. He claimed that his first appearance before an audience was at five, when he stepped on stage at the Aldershot Canteen theatre to take over from his mother whose

voice suddenly failed her. At eight, he joined Jackson's Eight Lancashire Lads, one of the juvenile variety troupes then popular. He later obtained favourable press notices as a child actor in the legitimate theatre, and played the West End and lengthy provincial tours as Billy the Page Boy in *Sherlock Holmes*.

Meanwhile, Sydney Chaplin had become a star comedian with the Karno comedy companies. Fred Karno, a former acrobat, had created what he accurately called his 'Fun Factory' in Camberwell Road, London. Here he rehearsed and equipped the several sketch companies which for many years proved the English music-hall's richest school of comedy. Sydney Chaplin persuaded Karno to engage his brother for a sketch called 'The Football Match'. Within a couple of years Charlie had become a leading comedian, and the star of companies that Karno sent on American tours during 1910-11 and 1912-13.

It was on the second of these tours that he was offered a year's contract with Mack Sennett's Keystone film company. Hesitantly, persuaded largely by the $150 a week that doubled his salary with Karno, he joined Sennett in California. Chaplin was at first uneasy in the new medium. He was disturbed by the chaos of the Sennett studios, and the Sennett slapstick comedians found his more refined style of comedy too slow. Little love was lost between Chaplin and his first director, Henry Lehrman, and he resented, equally, taking direction from his young, lovely and volatile co-star comedienne Mabel Normand.

His first film, *Making a Living* (1914), in which he was dressed as a dubious dandy, was indifferent, though well received by the trade press of the time. For his second film, a five-minute improvisation shot during the event which gave it its title, *Kid Auto Races at Venice* (1914), however, he adopted the costume that was to become world-famous. According to legend, it was made up from various items borrowed from other Sennett comedians: Fatty Arbuckle's huge trousers; Charles Avery's tiny jacket; a derby hat belonging to Arbuckle's father-in-law; Ford Sterling's boots, so oversize that they had to be worn on the wrong feet; and Mack Swain's moustache, sharply pruned.

Charles Chaplin
y-two years
a King

Chaplin later wrote:

'I had no idea of the character. But the moment I was dressed, the clothes and the make-up made me feel the person he was. I began to know him, and by the time I walked on to the stage he was fully born.'

Over the next 22 years the character was to be refined and elaborated: the hero of *City*

Above left: Chaplin directs The Gold Rush. *Of the 87 films he was associated with, he directed 69 (5 jointly with Mabel Normand). Left: perhaps the most famous figure of the twentieth century, the Tramp took to the road in over 50 movies. Below: Charlie causes chaos at* The Rink – *with Edna Purviance, Eric Campbell and Albert Austin*

Lights (1931) or *Modern Times* (1936) is altogether more complex than the little Tramp of the first frantic Sennett slapstick shorts as he scurries on one leg around corners, clutching his hat to his head while being chased by Keystone Kops or angry, bewhiskered giants. But the general lines of the character – the range of emotions from callousness to high sentiment, and of his actions from nobility to larceny, the supremely human resilience and fallibility of his nature – were fairly soon defined.

Chaplin spent 1914 at Keystone, serving a valuable apprenticeship to his art, and making 35 films. From the twelfth of these, *Caught in a Cabaret*, he began to take a hand in the direction, and from the twentieth, *Laughing Gas*, he was permanently established as his own director. Seen today, these films are mostly primitive. The stock jokes involve intoxication, illicit flirtations, mallets, dentists, jealous husbands, cops, dough, dynamite, lakes to be fallen into, cars to crash, benches and boxing rings from which to fall. Already, however, in *The New Janitor* for example, Chaplin was trying out subtler skills as a storyteller and actor.

These skills were to be developed further and faster at Essanay, the company Chaplin joined in January 1915 in the first of a series of much-publicized changes of employer that would dramatically increase his earnings. Chaplin was at first unhappy in Essanay's Chicago studio, though he knocked out a lively little comedy about the film business, aptly titled *His*

New Job (1915). When he moved to the company's West Coast studio he took with him a new cameraman, Roland Totheroh, who was to work with him for over thirty years. At Niles, California, Chaplin began to build a company around himself, and his most important discovery was Edna Purviance, a beautiful stenographer with no screen experience. She was to remain his ideal leading lady for the next eight years. The warm and feminine quality of Edna's screen personality – in sharp contrast to the amusing madcap Mabel Normand – was probably partly responsible for the growing element of romantic yearning in Chaplin's work. This was most evident in two of Chaplin's earliest Essanay films, *The Tramp* and *The Bank* (both 1915). At the same time Chaplin was becoming more ambitious – he was taking more time over his films, and going on location. For *Shanghaied* (1915), he even blew up a small schooner to provide a dramatic climax. In his last film for Essanay, *Police* (1916), he first introduced touches of a social irony that anticipated *The Kid* (1921) and *The Pilgrim* (1923).

With Chaplin's next move, his salary soared to $10,000 a week, with extra bonuses. He spent 16 months over the 12 two-reelers he made at his Lone Star studio for Mutual release. They were polished gag structures, mostly inspired by a location or a situation, as their titles – *The Floorwalker*, *The Fireman*, *Behind the Screen*, *The Rink* (all 1916) and *The Cure* (1917) – suggest. Some of them are feats of virtuosity: *One a.m.* (1916) is virtually a solo

turn, with Charlie returning home inebriated to battle with a keyhole, a folding bed, a tigerskin rug and other domestic hazards; *The Pawn Shop* (1916) includes a long unbroken take of an autopsy on a customer's alarm clock. Other films, including *The Vagabond* (1916) and *The Immigrant* (1917), exploited Chaplin's developing gifts for drama and pathos.

A new distribution agreement with First National Distributors enabled Chaplin to fulfil his ambition of building his own studio, where he was to work for the next 24 years. His contract called for eight films to be made in eighteen months; instead, they took five years, and included at least three masterpieces. The first, *A Dog's Life* (1918), sharpened the henceforth ever-present element of social satire, drawing parallels between the existence of the Tramp and his faithful mongrel dog. Chaplin next boldly defied accusations of bad taste in making comedy out of life at the front in World War I; the men who best knew that life took *Shoulder Arms* (1918) to their hearts, and today Chaplin's comic metamorphosis of the war may give a more vivid sense of those days than a more solemn dramatic treatment. *Sunnyside* (1919) is an uncharacteristic and only modestly successful pastoral comedy. *A Day's Pleasure* (1919) is a delightful slice of humble life, the misadventures of a little man taking his Ford and family on an outing; one of the children in the film was played by Jackie Coogan, whose uncanny acting ability partly inspired Chaplin's next film, *The Kid*. Here, a melodrama about an unmarried mother and her abandoned child provides the motive for a rich comedy about the Tramp's unwilling adoption of the foundling and the odd comic-pathetic bond that grows between them. After finishing the film, Chaplin decided to make a

return visit to his homeland and to tour Europe. This was, perhaps, the peak of his career: few celebrities until this time had aroused the furore that attended every public appearance, or the adulation he received from the great men of the world.

The two films that he made on his return, *The Idle Class* (1921), a slapstick situation comedy with Chaplin in two roles, and *Pay Day* (1922), another slice-of-life comedy in which little Charlie is given a job, home and nagging wife, were only moderately successful; but with *The Pilgrim* his critical reputation soared again. This story of an escaped convict, who steals the clothes of a bathing priest and is mistaken for the new pastor of a little Midwest township, provided opportunities for nice irony at the expense of bigotry, hypocrisy and small-town manners.

Only when the First National contract was worked out was Chaplin free to make his first feature film for release by United Artists, the distribution organization he had formed in company with Douglas Fairbanks, Mary Pickford and D. W. Griffith four years before. *A Woman of Paris* (1923) was his first, long-contemplated attempt at serious drama. It was intended to launch the loyal Edna Purviance as a dramatic actress, and her elegant, restrained performance merited the chance, though her subsequent career was to be short-lived. Adolphe Menjou subtly partnered her and became a star. Chaplin himself appeared only in a walk-on part.

The film took the stuff of Victorian melodrama – the tragedy of a village girl turned courtesan and torn between an artist and a playboy – but applied to it an extremely sophisticated visual style, which was to influence the subsequent course of film comedy. To Chaplin's enduring chagrin, however, *A*

Woman of Paris, despite its enthusiastic press, proved a commercial failure, but he was to recover his losses and his confidence with two of his best comedy features, *The Gold Rush* (1925) and *The Circus* (1928).

From the Thirties onwards, Chaplin greatly slowed his output, taking not less than five years on each film. By the time he embarked on *City Lights*, sound pictures had arrived, and Chaplin had witnessed the downfall of other great silent comedians. He decided not to risk the voiceless character he had created or his vast international market by trying dialogue. *City Lights* is a silent movie with musical accompaniment. It is based on a series of comic variations built around an ironic melodrama about a blind girl and the sad little Tramp whose efforts give back the sight that enables her to see his pathetic reality. In *Modern Times*, which marked the last appearance of the Tramp, he risked a few moments of comic gibberish, though elsewhere retained his old mimetic comic style. With this film Chaplin first attracted the hostile and persistent line of criticism that charged the comedian with exceeding his 'proper' brief, and setting himself up as a philosopher. It was a criticism that inevitably attached no less to *The Great Dictator* (1940), a comic satire on totalitarianism. For all the anger underlying the laughter, Chaplin later said that had he known the truth about Hitler's concentration camps he would not have had the temerity to make the film.

A feeling for the dark and macabre had never been far absent from Chaplin's films, and it surfaced most strongly in *Monsieur Verdoux* (1947), the story of a French Bluebeard wife-killer between the wars. The philosophic contrast that Verdoux draws between his own kind of murder and the kind that is licensed by war was not popular in the Cold War years, and the character was made a weapon of that persecution that led to Chaplin's permanent exile from America in 1953.

Left: a fruitful union that produced 15 comedy classics. Far left: the Tramp dines with the drunk millionaire (Harry Myers) in City Lights. *Above, far left: Chaplin's film debut* Making a Living *as a bogus lord who charms the ladies (Minta Durfee, Alice Davenport). Above left: diagnosing the end for an alarm clock in* The Pawn Shop, *with Albert Austin. Below: Marie (Edna Purviance), her masseuse (Nelly Bly Baker) and a neurotic friend (Malvina Polo) in* A Woman of Paris. *Below left: the* Limelight *deserts an old clown – with Claire Bloom. Below right: keeping abreast of* A Countess From Hong Kong

Chaplin's last American film was a nostalgic tribute to his youth in the backstreets and variety theatres of London. Full of autobiographical references, *Limelight* (1952) tells of the friendship and mutual support of an old, failed, alcoholic comedian and a dancer struck with psychosomatic paralysis. Reversing the process, in Britain he made a film about America: *A King in New York* (1957) is a bitter and ferocious comedy about the paranoia and persecution of the McCarthy era. It is at its best where Chaplin relies upon pathos, casting his own son Michael as a Fifties parallel to *The Kid*, the child's mind and conscience brutalized by society as the Jackie Coogan character suffered in his body.

At 77 Chaplin made one last film. A pleasant romantic comedy, *A Countess From Hong Kong* (1967) might have been more successful and more kindly received if he had not made the mistake of using international stars – Marlon Brando and Sophia Loren – unsuited to his style of working. He never wholly retired, however. Almost until the end of his life he continued to work on the preparations of a film to be called *The Freak*. Having composed the music for his sound films, he continued to create new scores for reissues of his silent pictures. Barely a year before his death in 1977, Chaplin steeled himself to add music to *A Woman of Paris* for reissue, despite its painful memories. He had worked for more than eighty years; the 62 of those that he chose to spend in pictures established a record not likely to be beaten for a long time.

Filmography
Shorts unless otherwise specified: **1914** Making a Living (actor only); Kid Auto Races at Venice (actor only) (GB: Kid Auto Races); Mabel's Strange Predicament (actor only); Between Showers (actor only); A Film Johnnie (actor only); Tango Tangles (actor only); His Favourite Pastime (actor only); Cruel, Cruel Love (actor only); The Star Boarder (actor only); Mabel at the Wheel (actor only); Twenty Minutes of Love (sc;+act. only); Caught in a Cabaret (co-dir; +sc; +act); Caught in the Rain (+sc; +act); A Busy Day (+sc; +act); The Fatal Mallet (co-dir; +sc; +act); Her Friend the Bandit (co-dir; +co-sc; + act); The Knockout (sc; +act. only); Mabel's Busy Day (co-dir; +co-sc; +act); Mabel's Married Life (co-dir; +co-sc; +act); Laughing Gas (+sc; +act); The Property Man (+sc; +act); The Face on the Barroom Floor (+sc; +act); Recreation (+sc; +act); The Masquerader (+sc; +act); His New Profession (+sc; +act); The Rounders (+sc; +act); The New Janitor (+sc; +act); Those Love Pangs (+sc; +act); Dough and Dynamite (+sc; +act); Gentlemen of Nerve (+sc; +act); His Musical Career (+sc; +act); His Trysting Place (+sc; +act); Tillie's Punctured Romance (feature) (actor only); Getting Acquainted (+sc; +act); His Prehistoric Past (+sc; +act). '15 His New Job (+sc; +act); A Night Out (+sc; +act); The Champion (+sc; +act); In the Park (+sc; +act); A Jitney Elopement (+sc; +act); The Tramp (+sc; +act); By the Sea (+sc; +act); His Regeneration (guest app. only); Work (+sc; +act); A Woman (+sc; +act); The Bank (+sc; +act); Shanghaied (+sc; +act); A Night in the Show (+sc; +act). '16 Carmen/Charlie Chaplin's Burlesque on Carmen (short and feature versions) (+sc; +act); Police (+co-sc; +act); The Floorwalker (+prod; +co-sc; +act); The Fireman (+prod; +co-sc; +act); The Vagabond (+prod; +co-sc; +act); One a.m. (+prod; +sc; +act); The Count (+prod; +sc; +act); The Essanay-Chaplin Revue of 1916 (compilation); The Pawn Shop (+prod; +sc; +act); Behind the Screen (+prod; +sc; +act); The Rink (+prod; +sc; +act). '17 Easy Street (+prod; +sc; +act); The Cure (+prod; +sc; +act); The Immigrant (+prod; +sc; +act); The Adventurer (+prod; +sc; +act). '18 A Dog's Life (+prod; +sc; +act); Chase Me Charlie (compilation); Triple Trouble (co-dir; +co-sc; +act); Shoulder Arms (+prod; +sc; +act); The Bond (+sc; +act) (GB: Charles Chaplin in a Liberty Loan Appeal). '19 Sunnyside (+prod; +sc; +act); A Day's Pleasure (+prod; +sc; +act). *All remaining films features unless otherwise specified:* '21 The Kid (+prod; +sc; +act); The Nut (guest); The Idle Class (short) (+prod; +sc; +act). '22 Pay Day (short) (+prod; +sc; +act). '23 The Pilgrim (short) (+prod; +sc; +act); A Woman of Paris (+prod; +sc; +act; +mus. for 1976 reissue); Souls for Sale (guest); Hollywood (guest). '25 The Gold Rush (+prod; +sc; +act; +mus. for 1942 reissue). '26 A Woman of the Sea/The Sea Gull (add. dir; +prod; +co-sc) (unreleased). '28 The Circus (+prod; +sc; +act; + mus. for 1970 reissue); Show People (guest). '31 City Lights (+prod; +sc; +mus; +act). '36 Modern Times (+prod; +sc; +mus; +act). '40 The Great Dictator (+prod; +sc; +co-mus; +act). '47 Monsieur Verdoux (+prod; +sc; +mus; +narr; +act). '52 Limelight (+prod; +sc; +mus; +chor; +act). '57 A King in New York (+prod; +sc; +mus; +act) (GB). '59 The Chaplin Revue (compilation) (+prod; +sc; +mus; +narr). '67 A Countess From Hong Kong (+sc; +mus; +act) (GB).
Chaplin also appears in: 1915 Introducing Charlie Chaplin (short). '38 Charlie Chaplin Carnival; Charlie Chaplin Cavalcade; Charlie Chaplin Festival. '66-74 The Chaplin Documentary (unshown). '67 The Funniest Man in the World; Stimulantia *ep* Upptackten (*SWED*).

METROPOLIS

MANUSKRIPT:
THEA VON HARBOU

MUSIK:
GOTTFRIED HUPPERTZ

EIN FILM VON FRITZ LANG

JN DEN HAUPTROLLEN:
BRIGITTE HELM · GUSTAV FRÖHLICH,
ALFRED ABEL, RUDOLF KLEIN-ROGGE, THEODOR LOOS, FRITZ RASP, HEINRICH GEORGE
AN DER KAMERA · KARL FREUND, GÜNTHER RITTAU

UFA FILM IM VERLEIH DER PARUJAMET

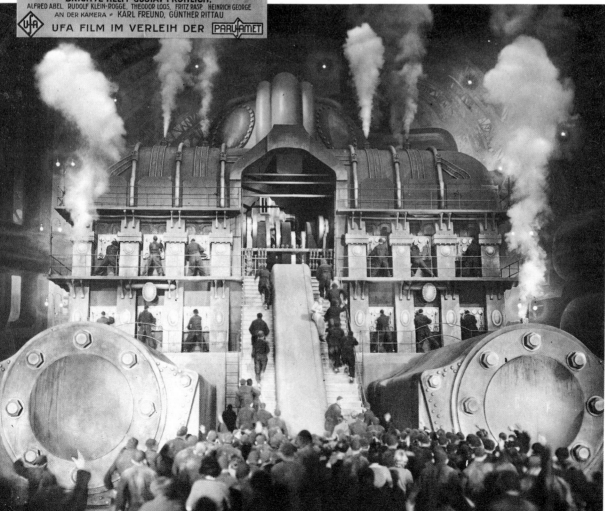

3

Directed by Fritz Lang, 1927
Prod co: Ufa. **prod:** Erich Pommer. **sc:** Fritz Lang, Thea von Harbou, from her own novel. **photo:** Karl Freund, Günther Rittau. **sp eff photo:** Eugen Schüfftan. **art dir:** Otto Hunte, Erich Kettelhut, Karl Vollbrecht. **sculpture:** Walter Schultze-Mittendorf. **cost:** Anne Willkomm. **r/t:** 120 minutes.
Cast: Alfred Abel (*John Fredersen*), Gustav Frölich (*Freder*), Brigitte Helm (*Maria*), Rudolf Klein-Rogge (*Rotwang*), Fritz Rasp (*Slim*), Theodor Loos (*Josaphat*), Erwin Biswanger (*No. 11811*), Heinrich George (*foreman*), Olaf Storm (*Jan*), Hanns Leo Reich (*Marinus*).

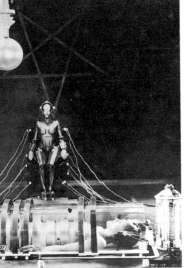

Fritz Lang quickly established himself at the forefront of German cinema. He had been an enthusiastic art student, but during World War I he became interested in the theatre and cinema, and began to write film scenarios in order to gain an entrée into the cinematic world. He began by writing scripts for the great serial specialist of the time, Joe May, and by 1919 had progressed to direction with *Der Halbblut* (The Half-Caste), a film made in only five days. From there he moved on to bigger things such as the two-part *Die Spinnen* (1919–20, *The Spiders*), but after preparing the script of a big two-part spectacle *Das Indische Grabmal* (1921, *The Hindu Tomb*), which he also intended to direct, he found himself baulked by Joe May and determined to work for himself from then on. The first major film he made after this decision was *Der Müde Tod* (1921, *Destiny*, which recounted three historical horror stories. It turned into a big international success, and Lang's future career seemed assured.

However, Lang was not one to sit back and take the easy option. Instead, he launched into three of the largest and most expensive productions to be made in Germany, or indeed anywhere else in the world at that time. First came the two-part story of an insane master-criminal *Dr Mabuse der Spieler* (1922, *Dr Mabuse, the Gambler*), then the even bigger *Die Nibelungen* (1924). The latter, also in two parts, required enormous sets and vast crowd scenes in order to evoke the stories of Siegfried and Kriemhild, characters from the set of German legends previously quarried by the composer Richard Wagner in his *Ring*-cycle music.

Scarcely had Lang finished with this vast project than he embarked on *Metropolis*, a vision of the future written, as had been the three previous films, by himself and his wife Thea von Harbou.

From the outset *Metropolis* was conceived as both a colossal

spectacle and as a film-with-a-message. The message, if any, has always been a subject for controversy – not surprisingly, for Lang's political attitudes during the Twenties were sufficiently far to the left for him to be rootedly anti-Nazi and later to get him into trouble with the Hollywood witch-hunters. In contrast, Thea von Harbou's politics were sufficiently to the right for her to stay on happily in Germany after Hitler's rise to power, and become one of the most successful screenwriters of the Third Reich. Thus, as a product of both minds *Metropolis* takes on no less than the whole problem of Capital versus Labour, postulates a gigantic slave community dominated by a small elite in the year 2000, imagines a slave revolt, and invents a solution to reconcile the warring elements.

Of course the 'solution' is, as Lang later ruefully admitted, monumentally naive and banal: simply that love conquers all, and that 'the intermediary between the hand and the brain is the heart' ('That's a fairytale – definitely' added Lang). But even if, on a political level, the idea is simplistic and sentimental, it has to be admitted that it effectively identifies the keystone in *Metropolis*' gigantic construction, for the structure is more emotional and visual than reasoning. The story as a whole is seen as a battle between light and dark, good and evil, rather than something so prosaic as management and labour. Indeed, in the view of the film's creators it was about magic and the dark ages as against the illumination of modern science. Taking this approach, it is possible to argue that all the good in the story comes from science, and all the bad from magic, especially in the person of the magician Rotwang. But as the magical element was minimized in the shooting, Rotwang comes over instead as just another mad scientist and the distinction becomes hopelessly blurred.

What does remain as impressive as ever is the mastery with which

In *Metropolis*, a giant city of the twenty-first century, everything is done by enormous machines run by an army of ant-like slave workers (1). They live in labyrinthine underground slums, while the minority ruling class lives above ground in the 'eternal gardens' (2). They are not conscious of being tyrants, but one day Freder, son of the city's Master John Fredersen, notices a beautiful young woman – Maria – with a clutch of hungry children at the gates of the gardens (3). Moved by her beauty, he sets out in pursuit of her, and discovers the squalor of Metropolis' hidden power centre (4).

In the subterranean tenements he finds Maria; she has been urging the restless workers to have patience and wait for salvation from 'the forgotten Christ'. Their meeting is discovered by Freder's father, who then instructs his principal scientist Rotwang to make a robot in the image of Maria in order for her to gain the worker's confidence in the rulers, and so put a stop to all revolutionary tendencies.

Rotwang kidnaps Maria and creates an android (5) with the idea of furthering his own designs – which are ultimately to displace Fredersen as Master and take power himself. The ensuing revolt (6), urged on by the false Maria who has gone beserk, is all too effective: the pumps stop turning and all the underground areas occupied by the workers are flooded. Freder and the real Maria – who has managed to escape – lead the worker children out of danger (7). The workers, realizing how they have been misled, burn the robot.

Seeing the collapse of all his plans, Rotwang goes mad. John Fredersen sees the error of his ways (8), and with the joining of Maria and Freder's hands in front of the cathedral, Capital and Labour are united – by love.

Lang stages his dramas. Evidently he had learnt, like most other directors in Germany at the time, an enormous amount from Max Reinhardt's stage spectacles: his management of the huge crowds of robot-like slaves – and of the rebellion when, spurred on by the false Maria, they go on a rampage of destruction – is as stunning as anything in that line before or since. True, the characters are dwarfed by their environment and reduced to stereotypes, but with so much else going on to interest and amaze, who is going to stop and argue? Certainly not the film's first audiences: even in America *Metropolis* was taken as a model of how to do things, and Lang was deluged with offers to come and make films of equal quality in Hollywood. But he refused. Why should he go when he had resources just as vast at his disposal in Germany, and far more freedom than he could ever hope for in America? Or so he thought in 1927.

Glorious Swanson

People always think that Gloria Swanson was Norma Desmond, the flamboyant, crazed heroine she plays in Billy Wilder's acid *Sunset Boulevard* (1950) – for, like Desmond, Swanson was a big movie star in the silent days. She was directed by Cecil B. DeMille and Erich von Stroheim, both of whom appear in *Sunset Boulevard* as figures from Norma Desmond's past. Moreover, the extract from *Queen Kelly* (1928) which illustrates how Stroheim used to direct Norma is in fact from the film in which Stroheim directed Swanson for her own production company. Thus the identification seems complete; except that Norma Desmond is living in the past and is quite out of touch with the modern world, while Swanson was truly-up-to-date until her death in 1983, a successful businesswoman in many areas, a busy actress on stage and screen, a world-famous proselyte for macrobiotic foods and a member of the international jet-set.

Second sunrise

However, it was undoubtedly *Sunset Boulevard* that made Swanson into a modern cult figure, and it contains her best performance, no doubt partly because it is overall the best film she has made in her long career. It is also the most spectacular and newsworthy comeback in the whole history of cinema, for in 1950 she had made only three films in the previous 17 years,

Gloria Swanson is a movie legend. She has survived the rigours of a superstar's life, she has made and lost fortunes, married and re-married, and has worked with the greatest names in Hollywood. She is witty, charming, elegant, intelligent and is one of the most sought-after characters from cinema's past

and had not had a hit since *The Trespasser* in 1929. Suddenly handed a role which most actresses should have given their eye-teeth for, she seized on it with such unsparing relish as to make it totally her own – and seemingly to disappear into it.

The real Gloria Swanson was no tragedy queen like Norma Desmond but a 'lightweight' and often a comedienne. She was also a famous clothes-horse, and when scenarists could think of nothing else for her to do, she could always be relied upon to take an audience's breath away by sweeping on to screen in yet another stunning confection.

Swanson was born in Chicago, according to her own account, on March 27, 1899 – although other sources suggest a year or two earlier. She was brought up mainly in Florida, where her father worked with the army, and returned to Chicago just long enough to be 'discovered' at the Essanay studio at the age of 15. She was tested by Chaplin for one of his pictures but was turned down as lacking in comedy sense – and also, perhaps, because she

was physically too similar in type, as can be seen from her stunning impersonation of him in *Sunset Boulevard*.

On her way to the Philippines to join her father in 1915, she and her mother stopped off in Los Angeles. She decided to try the studios there, and at once managed to get noticeable roles, several of them in films with Wallace Beery, whom she married in 1916. Most of her first Hollywood films were slapstick comedies for Mack Sennett; she often said later on that she was so determined to be a dramatic actress at that time that she always played dead straight, not realizing that the more genuine her emoting, the funnier the final effect. In 1917 she decided to move away from Sennett, and found herself employed at another studio, Triangle, starring in a series of dramas about marital misunderstandings and the mishaps of courting couples. They had titles like *Society for Sale*, *Everywoman's Husband*, *Shifting Sands* and *Wife or Country* (all 1918), and in most of them she starred opposite her boyish partner from Sennett days, Bobby Vernon. Although

she was playing drama she became restive of the restrictions at Triangle and was eager to take up an offer to star in a Cecil B. DeMille film, but Triangle prevented her on a contract technicality. In 1919 she was finally free to go over to Paramount and the first film she made for DeMille was *Don't Change Your Husband* (1919), one of his biggest successes.

Youthful old-timer

Thus at the age of 20 Gloria Swanson became an 'important star', with five years of film experience already behind her. 'Working for Mr DeMille', she recalls in her autobiography, *Swanson on Swanson*, 'was like playing house in the world's most expensive department store'. If this is taken to mean that there was a lot of getting elaborately dressed in Swanson-DeMille films, that is quite possible. for at this time DeMille was going through his period of specialization in 'mature', sophisticated society dramas. In *Don't Change Your Husband*, for instance, Swanson plays the wife who does, only to discover at the end that the first husband was better than the alternative, who proves to have a roving eye. In *For Better, for Worse* (1919) she is a woman who wrongly believes her sweetheart to be a coward, but experience showed otherwise. And both films had comfortingly happy endings.

But the best and most famous of the six films she made in a row for DeMille was *Male and Female* (1919), a free version of J. M. Barrie's *The Admirable Crichton* which gave scope for grand society goings-on at the beginning, drama in the shipwreck, comedy on the island and then a bitter-sweet conclusion back in Mayfair – plus a typical DeMille dream-scene set in ancient Babylon, with Swanson being sacrificed to the lions. This was one of the peaks of her career. Otherwise her roles became rather repetitious as she suffered in gorgeous gowns through *Why Change Your Wife?*, *Something to Think About* (both 1920), and finally *The Affairs of Anatol* (1921), where she had mainly to wait at home while vamps like Bebe Daniels had all the fun with tame cheetahs and the like.

Changing affairs

It was time for DeMille and Swanson to part company, and in *The Great Moment* (1921) she was handed on to Sam Wood, a director who was to guide her through a string of ten films.

Left: Gloria Swanson and Warwick Ward in Madame Sans-Gêne. Far left: the comedienne Swanson with Juanita Hansen in an early Mack Sennett movie. Above: in Queen Kelly as a madame in Africa – this final section of the film was cut out before release. Below right: Indiscreet (1931) included a scene that showed a silhouetted Swanson in the shower. Below left: in Why Change Your Wife? Swanson plays a wife who regrets her divorce

For this one, which was actually made before *The Affairs of Anatol*, she first received billing above the title, and had the story specially devised for her by Elinor Glyn, the great resident expert in high passion and higher society. In her later Sam Wood films she ranged from heavy suffering in *Under the Lash* (1921) through further problems in *Don't Tell Everything* (1921), and an extra-marital relationship opposite Rudolph Valentino in *Beyond the Rocks* (1922), to the light comedy of the French farce *Bluebeard's Eighth Wife* (1923). By this time she was the top star at Paramount, and her 1923 contract was almost

Below: Swanson's greatest triumph – Sunset Boulevard. Below left: during a visit to London in 1981. Left: Swanson as Sadie Thompson *the tough lady who gains the attentions of a reformer (Lionel Barrymore); he commits suicide when she leaves him*

without parallel in the powers it gave her to choose her own films. This she used to good effect in order to vary her roles constantly: *Zaza* (1923), a strong story of the French music-hall was followed by others such as *Manhandled* (1924), directed by Allan Dwan, in which she gives a brilliantly funny performance as a gum-chewing shop girl who finds out that society life is not all it is supposed to be, and *Wages of Virtue* (1924), in which she surpassed even her own previous extravaganzas by wearing a wedding dress alleged to have cost $100,000.

In 1925 she insisted on going to France to make *Madame Sans-Gêne* on the right locations under the direction of a real Frenchman, Léonce Perret, and returned with a real Marquis (de la Falaise de la Coudraye) as a husband. In her autobiography she gives a frightening account of her apparently triumphant return to America – after a near-fatal abortion in a Paris hospital – but the film was another career highpoint. After four more films she left Paramount to set up her own company (with the help of her then lover Joseph Kennedy), and began with *The Love of Sunya* (1927), which was something of a misfire, and *Queen Kelly* (1928), which was never properly finished due to Stroheim's extravagances and the inopportune arrival of sound. Two other pictures, however, were complete triumphs: she played a briefly reformed prostitute in the tropics in *Sadie Thompson* (1928), her last silent film, and in *The Trespasser* (1929) she wowed audiences by not only talking but singing too.

Comedy comebacks

After that her career went rapidly downhill through four wishy-washy comedies, the last of which, *A Perfect Understanding* (1933), was shot in Britain and co-starred a very young and inexperienced Laurence Olivier. There followed contracts with MGM and Columbia; ambitious projects were announced, but none was fulfilled, and the only film she did make, *Music in the Air* (1934) when on loan to Fox, was a flop. Her first official comeback, a comedy with Adolphe Menjou, *Father Takes a Wife* (1941) did not do much better. Finally in 1950 Billy Wilder, after thinking of Pola Negri, Mary Pickford, Mae Murray and various other silent movie stars, settled for her in *Sunset Boulevard*. She portrays an ex-movie queen, from the silent era, who is adamant that with the help of an out-of-work screenwriter (William Holden) she will make a dramatic comeback. But she becomes jealous of his girlfriend and eventually murders him. Even as she is being taken away by police she believes she is making a triumphant return to superstardom.

The rest is history. She then made only a few more films: a negligible farce, *Three for Bedroom C* (1952); a rather funnier parody costume epic, *Mio Figlio Nerone* (1956, *Nero's Weekend*), in which she was a redoubtable Agrippina to Alberto Sordi's Nero; a stint as one of the long-suffering airline passengers in *Airport 1975*; and *Killer Bees* (1974) for television and several stage appearances as well as numerous chat shows, discussing life and diet, her career and her book. She really did not have to do anything more: she was more than a star; she was a legend. Norma Desmond says defiantly in *Sunset Boulevard*, 'We had faces then!' Gloria Swanson always did.

Filmography
1915 The Fable of Elvira and Farina and the Meal Ticket; Sweedie Goes to College; The Romance of an American Duchess; The Broken Pledge (credited as Gloria Mae). **'16** A Dash of Courage; Hearts and Sparks; A Social Club; The Danger Girl; Love on Skates; Haystacks and Steeples; The Nick of Time Baby; Teddy at the Throttle. **'17** Baseball Madness; Dangers of a Bride; The Sultan's Wife; The Pullman Bride. **'18** Society For Sale; Her Decision; You Can't Believe Everything; Everywoman's Husband; Shifting Sands (reissued as: Her Wanton Destiny); Station Content; Secret Code; Wife or Country. **'19** Don't Change Your Husband; For Better, For Worse; Male and Female (GB: The Admirable Crichton). **'20** Why Change Your Wife?; Something to Think About. **'21** The Great Moment; The Affairs of Anatol (GB:

A Prodigal Knight); Under the Lash; Don't Tell Everything. **'22** Her Husband's Trademark; Beyond the Rocks; Her Gilded Cage; The Impossible Mrs Bellew; My American Wife. **'23** Prodigal Daughters; Bluebeard's Eighth Wife; Zaza; Hollywood (as herself). **'24** The Humming Bird; A Society Scandal; Manhandled; Her Love Story; Wages of Virtue. **'25** Madame Sans-Gêne; The Coast of Folly; Stage Struck. **'26** Untamed Lady; Fine Manners. **'27** The Love of Sunya. **'28** Sadie Thompson; Queen Kelly (unfinished). **'29** The Trespasser. **'30** What a Widow! **'31** Indiscreet; Tonight or Never. **'33** A Perfect Understanding (GB). **'34** Music in the Air. **'41** Father Takes a Wife. **'50** Sunset Boulevard. **'52** Three for Bedroom C. **'56** Mio Figlio Nerone (IT-FR) (USA: Nero's Mistress; GB: Nero's Weekend). **'74** Airport 1975.

THEY HAD FACES THEN

The great silent stars of Hollywood enjoyed an international fame and mass worship that the world had never known before

In 1919, three men sat down in the Palace of Versailles: they were playing a board game in which the pieces were the bloodied parts of Europe that had been fought over in the remorseless stalemate of World War I. The French Premier Georges Clémenceau, the British Prime Minister David Lloyd George and the American President Woodrow Wilson could have been forgiven for thinking that they were the most powerful and therefore the most important and best-known people alive. They were the figureheads of the new nation states. But they were not in pictures, and their political eminence was being surpassed by the new volatile celebrity of movie stars.

A couple of years later, Charlie Chaplin completed *The Kid* (1921) and struck this deal with First National: they would distribute the film in return for a payment of $1.5 million to Chaplin; once they had recouped that investment, Chaplin received 50 per cent of the net profits; and after five years the picture reverted to him. Chaplin decided he would take a trip to England and the rest of Europe. He would go by sea, on the *Olympic*:

'It had been ten years since I had left England, and on this very boat with the Karno Company; then we had travelled second class. I remember the steward taking us on a hurried tour through the first class, to give us a glimpse of how the other half lived. He had talked of the luxury of the private suites and their prohibitive price, and now I was occupying one of them, and was on my way to England. I had known London as a struggling young nondescript from Lambeth; now as a man celebrated and rich I would be seeing London as though for the first time.'

In London, wherever he went, Charlie was mobbed. In the space of Chaplin's lifetime, theatrical stardom had gone from being hailed and followed on a few city streets to being known all over the world. Although he and the picture business could only see box-office in 1921, stardom had a political dimension. Stardom was not simply the use of attractive personalities to sell motion pictures. It was the promotion of a supposedly desirable concept of personality that would rapidly take on ideological connotations. In proving the impact of new media, it established a new relationship between power and the masses. Henceforth, leaders would have to compete with movie stars. Adolf Hitler, Benito Mussolini and Franklin D. Roosevelt were faces and voices that penetrated every household. By the late Thirties, Chaplin had come to believe it was his duty to join with the great dictators in speaking to the public. Over forty years later, a second-rate star, Ronald Reagan, was given a fresh chance at inspiring the audience in the role of President of the United States.

More than anyone alive, Chaplin epitomized the dynamic of universal recognition. In 1921 (and for several years before and after), no other human image could have been identified by so many in the world. Charlie was the movies; his name and his sentimental resilience were synonymous with the

The World's Leading Moving Picture Magazine

PHOTOPLAY

July 25c

Hattie
of
Hollywood
by
SAMUEL MERWIN

Greatest Story of Movie Life Ever Written

jazzy but soft-hearted entertainment provided by the medium. Look and be transported; it had happened to Charlie himself, and the audiences knew that their own adoration had made the Tramp one of the richest men in the world.

Stardom may be the crucial communicative discovery of the movies. It also characterized the medium's grasp of story-telling. Ever since the days of Florence Lawrence, the 'Biograph Girl', film companies had appreciated how far audiences liked to see certain lovely and arousing personalities in film after film. A title could sell a picture, some indication of genre was helpful, but a picture of a star was most persuasive. So film companies began to assess possible stories as 'vehicles' for their stars. Whereas action had been the prevailing feature of very early films – a rush of business seen in long shot – stardom insisted on the close-up, and it brought the movies the reverie of introspection:

Rudolph Valentino (top) died on August 23, 1926. His New York lying-in-state and the funeral cortège a week later (centre) drew huge crowds. Pola Negri (above) was among the mourners and claimed they had planned to marry

Below: one Sunday in the summer
of 1926. friends dropped in at
Richard Barthelmess' place and
others at Constance Talmadge's.
They joined up at her Malibu
beach house. From left to right on
the fence are: Roscoe (Fatty)
Arbuckle, Mae Murray, Ward
Crane, Virginia Valli, Ronald
Colman, Bessie Love, Jack
Pickford, Rudolph Valentino and
Pola Negri. Scattered through the
middle row are: Louella O.
Parsons (columnist), Carmel
Myers, Alan Forrest, Bert Lytell,
Claire Windsor, Richard
Barthelmess, Constance Talmadge,
Beatrice Lillie, Josephine Lovett,
Julanne Johnston, Agnes Ayres,
John S. Robertson and Marshall
Neilan (director). The bottom row
includes: Antonio Moreno, Prince
David Mdivani, Charles Lane, Alf
Goulding, Marcel de Sano, Manuel
Reachi (Agnes Ayres' husband),
Harry d'Abbadie d'Arrast
(director), Natalie Talmadge
Keaton, Captain Alastair
MacIntosh (Constance Talmadge's
husband), Mrs Antonio Moreno
and Blanche Sweet. List from
Motion Picture, October 1926

'What is Little Mary thinking?' Stars were those loved by the camera, and capable of inspiring love in the anonymous masses when intense images of their yearning faces were projected in the dark but public places built for movies. Stardom is the force that invites the viewer's imagination to come up onto the screen. Tycoons and producers reckoned it was enough to get people into the theatres, but the greatest films involve that extra, fantastic journey.

This is a kind of sleep-walking, an indulgence in fantasy that can seem morbid, escapist or mad. In other words, stardom has an irrational undertone at odds with those modern disciplines of hard work, civic duty and common sense. There is the beginning of a widespread, often unconscious, feeling of shame that goes with star worship, and which demands the occasional fall and humiliation of some of these demi-gods. The ostensible leaders of society did not enjoy the competition of these movie ghosts, and thus the establishment was always ready to condemn stars and the frivolity that believed in them.

Granted that latent antagonism, it is surely very important in the history of stardom that Chaplin, Douglas Fairbanks and Mary Pickford could demonstrate that stars might be radiant public servants and happy examples, like royalty given the extra good luck of casting. They were the three greatest stars of the time, and they went on tours of America to promote the sale of Liberty Bonds in support of the war effort. It is said that they sold $3 million-worth. Chaplin was excused for not going

back to Britain to enlist, while Doug and Mary apparently fell in love in that open car that seemed to be forever flanked by cheering crowds who had the movies' faith in true love.

Of course, they were both married – Doug to Beth Sully, and Mary to the actor Owen Moore. They were both anxious about what the public would think of convenient divorces. Chaplin told them to live together, and get it out of their systems; but they had aspirations towards respectability and a deep longing to be both honest and popular, to be admired for themselves. It is the moment at which a star wants to be more than his or her screen roles. So they contrived their divorces, and in 1920 they married. The public rejoiced – this was like a movie romance come true. The nation's athletic hero and 'America's Sweetheart' made a dynasty of stereotypes, and a kind of royal household for the raw, insecure Hollywood community as they held court at Pickfair, the Beverly Hills property that Doug bought, developed and gave to Mary as a wedding present.

Once married, Doug and Mary went on a triumphal tour of Europe, to be greeted by immense crowds wanting to touch Mary and see Doug do some flamboyant jumps. They were a better couple than anyone knew – Doug a natural and inoffensive show-off, Mary a sweet face and a quick business brain. Before marrying, they had made a commercial pact, forming United Artists with Chaplin and D.W. Griffith. The festival of their honeymoon was not just a holiday. It was also a publicity gesture, all the more effective in that it was not cold-blooded – stars must always believe in their own story. The couple did weary of the lack of privacy. They went to Germany where they were less well known,

Above: Mary Astor was already a star in the Twenties, and this portrait of her by Ruth Harriet Louise shows why. Above right: Betty Blythe as The Queen of Sheba (1921), nearly topless in pre-Hays Office style. Far right: Doug and Mary as proud proprietors of their studios on Santa Monica Boulevard in February 1922. Right: a 1927 portrait by Marland Stone of Dolores Costello, newly a star

because of wartime banning of their films. But not being recognized hurt them more, and they quickly slipped back into the limelight – royal figures, but prisoners too.

Pickfair was a model for new success enjoying itself in the Twenties, a party for Hollywood celebrities, for writers, artists, sportsmen and the reject royalty of old Europe. But the Pickfair party was robust, good-natured and generally wholesome – Doug was romantic and Mary practical, but they were both conservatives at heart and already older than the fast set. Doug remained a star of the silent era, with *Robin Hood* (1922), *The Thief of Bagdad* (1924) and *The Black Pirate* (1927); but he was getting into his forties, a little stiffer than screen high-jinks ever suggested, and thoroughly rattled when the new career of his son, Douglas Fairbanks Jr, invaded his aura of swashbuckling sun-tan. Mary was ten years younger, but she made far fewer films after 1923 – in part because she felt trapped as an *ingénue*, and also because she spent more time worrying over United Artists. As for Chaplin, his work fell away to a trickle, as if celebrity added weight to his pondering.

The stardom of these three endured, but it had been won in the years 1914–20. A new generation of stars really marks the Twenties, typified by Rudolph Valentino and Gloria Swanson. Valentino had not much more than seven years in pictures. His stardom was defined by his premature, tragic death and by the feeling of fatality being allied to his erotic potency. He was sexy in a way that dated Doug and Mary. There was also an air of scandal and sleaziness to Valentino that matched the public's growing instinct that stars might be vulnerable, unhealthy and hiding guilty secrets.

Valentino only came to America in 1913. He worked as a gardener and a dancer, and he had quite a few small movie jobs before June Mathis, head of the script department at Metro, got him a lead part in *The Four Horsemen of the Apocalypse* (1921). Valentino would make another 13 films as a 'Latin lover', dark-eyed, soulful, brooding, exotic and with hints of masochism and violence adding to his romantic lustre. But here was a star whose public reputation exceeded the reality and perhaps daunted the man. Valentino lost one wife, allegedly

MOST VALUABLE PAIR OF SHOES IN THE WORLD!

CHARLIE CHAPLIN would not part with this pair of shoes for $1,000,000. He wears them again in— HIS NEW COMEDY "THE CIRCUS"

Above: Gloria Swanson with the MGM executive Irving Thalberg on St Valentine's Day, 1934. Her MGM contract was the kiss of death to her career – she made only one film (on loan to Fox). Her successful comeback was with Paramount in 1950. Top: based on the autobiography I, Mary MacLane, *this 1918 Essanay production starred and was written by Mary MacLane, who relived her experience of six lovers. Top right: despite having dined off a boot in* The Gold Rush *(1925), Chaplin had the pair intact for* The Circus *(1928)*

because he could not please her as fully as a laboratory-technician lover could. His second wife, Natacha Rambova, dominated him and sought to organize his career. They had separated before he died, in New York in 1926, aged 31, the victim of an ulcer and of press innuendo about gay inclinations.

More than a hundred thousand people came to the funeral parlour to see his humbled but fabled body. Pola Negri sent an arrangement of 4000 roses. Hollywood potentates such as Adolph Zukor and Joseph Schenck served as pallbearers. Huge crowds watched the cortège pass by. His last film, *The Son of the Sheik* (1926), had just opened, and its portrait of a romantic hero, filled with dark, morbid urges, became part of the Valentino legend that linked love and death, stardom and ruin.

Gloria Swanson had been a teenage bathing beauty for Mack Sennett, but it was only in 1918, under the guidance of Cecil B. DeMille, that she gained stardom. She was the new woman – sexy, shrewd, carefree and assertive – liberated from the Victorian codes that had previously dictated the hopes and fears of screen women. For Paramount, she made such films as *Male and Female* (1919), *Prodigal Daughters* (1923) and *Manhandled* (1924). Swanson was a fresh, home-grown heroine, much

Valentino and Swanson summed up modern sex-appeal in the Twenties

more vivacious and amusing than might be deduced from her comeback performance in *Sunset Boulevard* (1950).

Like several others, Swanson fought her studio and branched out on her own to star in and produce several films, including the ill-fated *Queen Kelly* (1928), in which she refused to be overawed by either her co-producer Joseph Kennedy or her director Erich von Stroheim. A few years after the coming of sound, she temporarily retired.

Sound would become the bluntest measure the studios had to control their stars; it was also a technical departure that made it far harder for independent stars to go it alone. The moguls had very mixed feelings about their properties: they needed them, and milked their fame, working them as hard as possible; but they envied their glory, their looks and their reckless living, especially if it required a studio cover-up.

The stars of the Twenties were not as free as Chaplin or Pickford. They were as vulnerable as all pretty people are to time and fickle taste – today, for instance, Lois Moran, Barbara La Marr and Carmel Myers are just vivid faces who each had her moment. Stars were owned by studios, and they were the test cases of the contract system. Some

were well looked after: Irving Thalberg appreciated and promoted Lon Chaney, the only great star of ugliness; and for a time Joseph Schenck gave Buster Keaton his greatest creative liberty. Others were treated badly: Lillian Gish was dismissed as out-of-date, and Louise Brooks was regarded as out-of-line. There were also the scandals that made the first great wave of Hollywood paranoia in the early Twenties. Fatty Arbuckle could never fully extricate himself from a Labor Day weekend party and the body that was left in the aftermath. Mabel Normand and Mary Miles Minter were both damaged beyond repair by their involvement with the murdered director William Desmond Taylor. The death of the actor Wallace Reid accelerated legends that many stars lived on booze and drugs.

These scandals reflect two new professions, inseparable from stardom. There is the newspaper gossip writer always looking for revelations about the stars – the trade that would include Hedda Hopper, Louella Parsons, *Confidential* and the *National Enquirer*. To ward off these reporters, the studios and the stars hired publicity people, press agents and managers to concoct, write and spread a more favourable legend. Neither side was especially fond of the truth, and so it is that the history of stardom is recorded in biased, sensational and mercenary printed materials – hand-outs and exposés, alike in their hysterical tone.

The stars had faces, to be sure, but they also had an army of necessary supporters – still photographers, doctors, agents, accountants, lawyers, confessors, makeup men, hairdressers, costumiers and astrologers. The studio system played on their vulnerability, just as it flattered and indulged them. It wanted their films, but it flinched from salary demands that recognized how much the pictures grossed. So it was that the men who spent their working days glorifying stars might abuse them in private, dumping them when fortune shifted and exploiting them personally. Love and dislike, glory and envy – the star's life soon became an ordeal.

But Hollywood made all of America dream of going west for its big opportunity. The studios imported actors and actresses from Europe: some were abandoned, some stayed to change the notion of stardom – Pola Negri, Greta Garbo, Marlene Dietrich, Ronald Colman. When sound became standard, so Hollywood cleaned house. One generation of stars yielded to another, trained in the theatre, able to play dialogue. The era of the face and the image gave way to the power of total screen presence. John Gilbert was replaced by Clark Gable. And the public absorbed every small gesture in these new people: Gable's grin and his insolent, redneck vitality became an ideal of uncomplicated American decency. The stars were advertisements for a way of life, front runners in the pursuit of happiness.

THE COMING OF SOUND

By the mid-Twenties the movies had been moving for thirty years; now the race was on to find the best way to make them talk and sing

Films were fully thirty years old before they learned to speak – a surprising fact when you consider that Thomas Edison had first put his mind to the idea of motion pictures as an extension of his talking machines in the 1880s. Edison went so far as to equip some of his Kinetoscope peepshow machines with phonographs, for which he coined the name 'Kinetophone', but he was unsuccessful in matching sound to picture precisely enough to make the image of a person on the screen appear to be actually speaking or singing.

Even so, films of the 'silent cinema' era were rarely exhibited in silence. Back in 1897 the Lumière brothers engaged a saxophone quartet to accompany the Cinématographe at their theatre in Paris. The composer Saint-Saëns was asked to write a special score for the prestigious film production *L'Assassinat du Duc de Guise* in 1908, and after that it became customary for any major feature-length film to have a specially composed or compiled musical accompaniment. Music, therefore, was an important branch of the silent film business. It provided employment not only for the composers and music publishers, but also for the musicians who played at each performance.

But music was not the only type of sound associated with silent films, as a writer of 1912, Frederick Talbot, observed in his *Moving Pictures: How They Are Made and Worked*:

'When a horse gallops, the sound of its feet striking the road is heard; the departure of a train is accompanied by a whistle and a puff as the engine gets under weigh; the breaking of waves upon a pebbly beach is reproduced by a roaring sound. Opinion appears to be divided as to the value of the practice.'

To provide sound effects cinema owners could equip themselves with special machines that made all kinds of noises, from bird song to cannon fire. The drawback to these live accompaniments was that they depended so much on the availability and skill of the people making the noises – whether musical performers or mere machine operators. Frederick Talbot recalled an effects boy who 'enjoyed the chance to make a noise and applied himself with a vigour of enthusiasm which overstepped the bounds of common sense'.

The elaborate musical accompaniments devised by Joseph Carl Breil for the films of D. W. Griffith, or the musical 'suggestions' supplied as a matter of course by distributors in the Twenties, were one thing when the film was performed at Picture Palaces but quite another when it arrived at some backwoods fleapit with only a derelict piano.

Machine-made sound effects added drama to silent movies – or unwanted hilarity if the operator missed his cue

From an early stage, it was clear that a truly satisfactory sound accompaniment must be recorded and reproduced mechanically. The means, it seemed, were already at hand. A decade or more before movies, Edison's phonograph and Berliner's disc-gramophone had made mechanical reproduction possible. In the early stages these had the disadvantage that even with huge trumpet-like horns for amplification, the volume of sound they could produce was limited: but by the early Twenties electrical recording and reproduction had overcome this problem. The more persistent difficulty was to make the sound fit the image exactly.

As early as the 1890s a Frenchman, Auguste Baron, had taken out patents for several systems of synchronizing phonograph and projector. By 1900 at least three competing sound film systems were on show at the Paris Exposition. The most successful of them was the Phono-Cinéma-Théâtre of Clément-Maurice Gratioulet and Henri Lioret (who had earlier patented a cylinder recording device called the Lioretographe). First shown at the Exposition on June 8, 1900, the Phono-Cinéma-Théâtre offered one-minute talking or singing movies of eminent theatrical celebrities.

Another Frenchman, Léon Gaumont, exhibited a device called the Chronophone, which succeeded in synchronizing projector and phonograph but required the projectionist to adjust the film speed

Top: souvenir programme from the Phono-Cinéma-Théâtre announcing 'talking' films of theatrical celebrities – among them Sarah Bernhardt – as early as 1900. Above: as silent movie audiences demanded more than mere musical accompaniments, cinema owners bent over backwards to satisfy the craze for more 'realistic' sound effects. Right: wiring up a phonograph to a film camera inside Edison's 'Black Maria' studio in the 1890s

constantly. Gaumont developed his apparatus in competition with other commercial imitators, and enjoyed considerable success in the course of the decade. In America such systems were exploited by the Actophone Company, Camerafilm, and Edison's Cinemaphonograph. In Germany Oscar Messter, in Sweden Paulsen and Magnussen and in Japan the Yoshizawa Company all developed sound film devices. In Britain Hepworth's Vivaphone Pictures had a host of competitors with names like Cinematophone, Filmophone and Replicaphone.

But supposing that, instead of trying to match a separate disc recording to the film, the sound and image could be recorded on the same strip of film? The idea was explored: attempts were made at cutting a needle groove along the edge of the film, but such ingenious efforts to marry phonograph-style recording to film projection were not practicable. Other experiments, however, had shown that sound waves could be converted into electrical impulses and registered on the celluloid itself; the sound *track* (a narrow band running down the edge of the film) was printed on to the film. As the film was projected the process was reversed: variations of light on the track were translated back into sound again.

Soon after World War I, the development of radio greatly assisted engineers researching into sound projection. As sound film systems were patented, it was the giant electrical and radio companies who bought up the patents and moved in on the potential sound-film market. Through the early Twenties the General Electric Company was concentrating on a sound-on-film system, while Western Electric and Bell Telephone still favoured a sophisticated method of synchronized disc reproduction.

By 1923 Lee De Forest, who had been working independently on a sound-on-film system since 1919, was ready to demonstrate his Phonofilms. His first public show of short films was presented in April at the Rivoli Theatre in New York; and in 1924 it went on tour with some 30 theatres specially wired to play it. The repertory included not only songs and turns by vaudeville artists, but also newsreel-style interviews with President Coolidge and other politicians, a dramatic short – *Love's Old Sweet Song* – and musical accompaniments to James Cruze's epic *The Covered Wagon* (1923) and Fritz Lang's *Siegfried* (1924).

Phonofilms were a moderate success, though by no means a revolution. When De Forest demonstrated his system to the moguls of the American cinema, they showed no serious interest. Perhaps the recession that gripped the film industry in the mid-Twenties influenced their better judgment: certainly public interest was falling off; seat prices were rising; quality of the product was declining, and audiences were becoming more discriminating. Above all the new excitement of radio posed a serious threat – a big broadcast could empty cinemas for an evening (much as television can today). Had the Hollywood tycoons taken up De Forest's Phonofilms sooner, however, they might have won back their huge audiences. As it was they went for stop-gap solutions: vaudeville turns, potted light operas between films, Saturday night lotteries – in short, novelty at any price.

On the other hand, the big companies were no doubt shrewd enough to foresee the threat that talking pictures posed to their vested interests, should they permanently catch on with audiences. And the companies were proved right: when talkies arrived, the great studios and their equipment became obsolete overnight, along with backlogs of silent films and bevies of former stars whose talents were better suited to mime than to vocalization.

One company – Warner Brothers – decided to take the plunge with the Vitaphone sound-on-disc system. In later years there was a popular belief that – with nothing to lose by the risk – they had grasped at Vitaphone in a desperate bid to stave off imminent bankruptcy. Recently, however, Professor J. Douglas Gomery and others have shown that at this time Warner Brothers were, in fact, pursuing a policy of dramatic expansion.

Radio gave the American public talking Presidents, wise-cracking comics and instant music. Unless the movies could go one better, radio might put them out of business

In 1924 the company had sufficiently impressed Waddill Catchings, investment banker with the Wall Street firm of Goldman Sachs, to secure substantial investment. Catchings was apparently struck by Warners' rigid cost accounting system; and, with Harry Warner's approval, he devised a master-plan for long-term growth, similar to an earlier plan whereby he had helped transform Woolworths from a regional business to a national corporation. Early in 1925, Catchings accepted Warners' offer of a seat on the board of directors, and devoted his energies to securing more capital.

Thus financed, Warners embarked on a programme of major prestige pictures, set about acquiring cinemas and distribution facilities, modernized their laboratories, and developed their publicity and exploitation methods. At the same time they started a radio station. The consequence of such enormous capital outlay was that Warner Brothers went heavily, but calculatedly, into the red in 1926. The 'near bankruptcy' myth is based mainly on a misreading of annual accounts which showed, but did not explain, an abrupt fall from a $1,102,000 profit to a $1,338,000 loss between March 1925 and the end of the next fiscal year.

No doubt it was this expansionist mood that made the Warners receptive to Western Electric who, since 1924, had consistently failed to interest the major producers in their sound-on-disc system

of synchronization. In later years, having survived all his brothers, the youngest Warner, Jack, was inclined to claim credit for introducing sound pictures. In fact, however, it seems to have been Sam Warner who was mainly responsible, having perhaps had contact with sound through dealing with the affairs of the company's radio station.

In June 1925 the Warners built a new sound stage at the old Vitagraph Studio in Brooklyn and began production of a series of synchronized shorts. On April 20, 1926, the company established the Vitaphone Corporation, to lease Western Electric's sound system along with the right to sub-license. Sam Warner began to plan the launching programme for Vitaphone; his expenditure of some $3

Left: an explanatory and perhaps idealized drawing of how the Chronophone entertained audiences. Top: Hepworth's was a workable sound-film system on the market from 1909 but the pictures did not sing and talk synchronously. Centre: Lee De Forest's trade ad summed up his achievement but it was the big companies who profited from his work. Above: songsheet from the historic film-with-music Don Juan

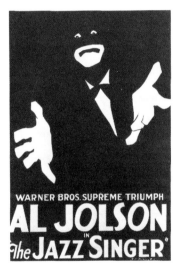

Above centre: not the first sound film but the one that started it all. Above: within a year talkies were shot on location

Lindbergh, Coolidge and Mussolini; and in October 1927 Fox introduced a regular Movietone newsreel.

Any doubt that the future of the film industry was bound up with sound was removed by the triumph of *The Jazz Singer*, which had its premiere on October 6, 1927. The public had already seen films that talked and sang. What seems to have caught their imagination in this sentimental melodrama about a cantor's son who becomes a jazz singer, was the naturalness of the brief dialogue scenes that Jolson improvised, and the fact that he addressed the audience directly.

Warners stole a march on the industry by plunging into sound. The other moguls waited to see if they would sink or swim

Sound films could no longer be ignored, and the major companies had no intention of ignoring them. After the *Don Juan* premiere Adolph Zukor's Famous Players Company had begun negotiations with Warners and Vitaphone, but these had broken down. In December 1926 Zukor formed a committee representing most of the major companies – Famous Players, Loew's, Producers Distributing Corporation, First National, United Artists and Universal – who agreed upon joint research and united action in the matter of sound pictures.

For the next 15 months the committee received reports from technical experts on the various systems available to them: Vitaphone could be subleased from Warners; Fox's Movietone also attracted their interest; Photophone, developed at General Electric, was on offer from RCA; and Western Electric, although marketing their disc system, were busy developing a sound-on-film system. But the choice was still fairly evenly balanced between sound-on-disc and sound-on-film. The priority was to settle upon a system that would make all equipment compatible, thus avoiding the kind of wrangling and litigation over patents that had beset the early days of movies.

While the other studios analyzed tests and deliberated, Warners and Fox gained a brief but considerable advantage. Not until May 1928 did the six companies enter into an agreement with Western Electric to adopt their sound-on-film system; a year later several of the smaller Hollywood companies followed suit and subscribed to this agreement. Accordingly, although Warner Brothers invested extensively in sound-on-disc productions from 1927 to 1929, the writing was on the wall for the Vitaphone system less than a year after *The Jazz Singer*'s premiere, and Warners would soon follow the other studios in adopting sound-on-film (though retaining the name Vitaphone).

1928 was a year of transition, for the changeover could not happen overnight. It took time to re-equip the studios, and for many months sound films continued to be released in alternative silent versions; at the same time sound effects and music were patched on to silent films to prolong their commercial life. Nevertheless, the silent cinema, with all the art and sophistication it had perfected over the last three decades, had instantly become archaic. Some 80 features with sound were made in the course of 1928.

Warners held on to their lead, maintaining a regular output of silent films with synchronized music and effects, along with a prolific production of Vitaphone shorts. Between April and June 1928 they released three part-talkies – silent films with sound sequences hastily added: Michael Curtiz's

million on it is hardly consistent with the idea of a bankrupt studio.

The culmination of this feverish activity came on August 6, 1926 with the great Vitaphone premiere of *Don Juan* – the first film with a fully synchronized score. (It is important to remember here that it was musical accompaniment and not talking pictures that appealed to the film moguls.) The supporting programme consisted of a series of rather classy musical shorts, preceded by a stodgy filmed speech of introduction by Will Hays, president of the Motion Picture Producers' Association.

Don Juan is a variation on the theme of the great philanderer conquered by true love; and as a swashbuckler it still retains a great deal of attraction today. The title role is played by John Barrymore, in the athletic style of Douglas Fairbanks; and the heroine is the young and exquisite Mary Astor. The film was scripted by Bess Meredyth, and directed by Alan Crosland.

The first Vitaphone programme amply justified Warners' faith and investment – it ran in New York for well over half a year – and henceforth the brothers were wholeheartedly committed to sound. They announced that all their future releases would be provided with Vitaphone accompaniments, and began the process of equipping major cinemas throughout the country for sound. On October 6, 1926 Warners presented a second Vitaphone programme with Sydney Chaplin in *The Better 'Ole*, and some new short films of vaudeville material in contrast to the prestige shorts shown at the Vitaphone premiere two months earlier.

Although most of the major companies were still watching and waiting, behind the scenes William Fox's film company had bought rights in a sound system so close to De Forest's Phonofilm that it became the subject of lengthy litigation. Fox combined in his system elements from Phonofilm and the German Tri-Ergon system (whose American rights he owned), and launched Fox Movietone with a programme of shorts on January 21, 1927. In May he presented a synchronized version of Frank Borzage's *Seventh Heaven*. The supporting programme included a dialogue short – Chic Sale's sketch *They're Coming To Get Me*. In June a new Movietone programme included sound film of

85

Tenderloin was a gangster story; *Glorious Betsy* was an Alan Crosland costume spectacle; and Lloyd Bacon's *The Lion and the Mouse*, a melodrama, with a leading performance by Lionel Barrymore which confirmed the growing belief that stage-trained actors were what the talkies needed.

On July 8, 1928 Warners released the first all-talkie, *Lights of New York*, a simple tale of two country lads who come to New York and get mixed up with bootleggers. Directed by Bryan Foy, the film ran only 57 minutes, and was from all accounts banal and crude, with the actors shackled to the microphone and nervously delivering their lines in a halting monotone. For all that, it proved a box-office success. Later in the year Warners repeated the triumph of *The Jazz Singer* with a new Al Jolson vehicle, *The Singing Fool*.

Fox's Movietone News provided a major sensation with an interview with Bernard Shaw, in which the 72-year-old celebrity cunningly used the talking film to project his well-managed and much-publicized personality. For the most part Fox concentrated on putting out silent features with synchronized scores and effects. Their 1927–1928 output included a group of pictures made by the studio's star directors, veterans of the silents who would become major figures of the sound era: John Ford (*Four Sons; Mother Machree*), Raoul Walsh (*The Red Dance; Me, Gangster*), Howard Hawks (*Fazil; The Air Circus*) and Frank Borzage (*Street Angel*). Movietone newsreels had indicated the possibilities of shooting sound in the open air; and Ford and Walsh, fearless action directors, took their recording equipment on location, Ford for a short subject, *Napoleon's Barber*, and Walsh for a feature, *In Old Arizona*. Despite rather a lot of wind and an overgrowth of sage brush to hide the microphones, *In Old Arizona* was the first truly successfuly talking action picture.

By the end of 1928 Movietone had been adopted by some major studios including MGM whose sound projects in this transitional year were tentative. Synchronized scores and sound effects were added to Harry Beaumont's jazz-era drama *Our Dancing Daughters* and to King Vidor's delightful comedy *Show People*, starring Marion Davies; otherwise the company experimented with two part-talkies, W.S. Van Dyke's *White Shadows in the South Seas* (which was virtually a silent film) and a crime melodrama *Alias Jimmy Valentine* (1929).

'Talkies, squeakies, moanies, songies, squawkies . . . Just give them ten years to develop and you're going to see the greatest artistic medium the world has known' D.W. Griffith

---

For release in 1928 Universal added sound to their prestige pictures of the previous year: Paul Leni's *The Man Who Laughs*, and Harry Pollard's *Uncle Tom's Cabin*; they also, somewhat unnecessarily, provided dialogue sequences for Paul Fejos's admirable *Lonesome*. The studio's first all-dialogue film, A.B. Heath's *Melody of Love*, was poorly received: the public was sufficiently accustomed to sound films to reject a hasty run-up.

Paramount had tried an experiment with sound early in 1927, when *Wings* had been provided with a synchronized score and sound effects. After opting for Movietone, the company embarked seriously on a sound programme in 1928. They also concentrated on equipping their major silent pictures, such as Ernst Lubitsch's *The Patriot*, William Wellman's *Beggars of Life* and von Stroheim's The

Wedding March, with music and sound effects. The first Paramount picture to be conceived as a sound film was a part-talkie, *Warming Up*, a baseball drama of which it was said that the crack of the bat and the roar of the crowd did not match particularly well with the pictures. Their first full talking picture was *Interference* (1929), with Clive Brook, whose stage experience served him well.

Coincidentally, Brook also starred in *The Perfect Crime* which was the first sound venture of RKO (Radio-Keith-Orpheum). This new studio was formed in 1928 through the amalgamation of Joseph Kennedy's distribution network (FBO), the Keith-Albee-Orpheum cinema chain, and Rockefeller's Radio Corporation of America (RCA). The merger enabled RCA to apply its own Photophone sound system to the studio's product and begin production of talkies.

It was also a year of reorganization. First National Pictures was absorbed by Warner Brothers, and put out eight features in the course of 1928. The first was a part-talkie, *Ladies' Night in a Turkish Bath*, but the most successful was George Fitzmaurice's *Lilac Time* with Colleen Moore and Gary Cooper, and a synchronized music score provided by the company's own Firnatone system.

The full creative possibilities of sound were revealed by a mouse. Walter E. Disney had boldly taken the decision to marry sound to an animated cartoon. Mortimer, later known as Mickey Mouse, starred in *Steamboat Willie* which opened at the Roxy Theatre on the same day as *The Singing Fool*. The ingenuity and fluency with which Disney used sound in *Steamboat Willie* and the early 'Silly Symphonies' was greatly admired in the early years of the sound film.

By the close of 1928 every significant American studio had talking pictures in production. It was timely. Between 1927 and 1930 box-office takings, which had been falling unnervingly, shot up by 50 per cent. The renewal of interest in the movies, mainly attributable to the novelty of sound, must go far towards explaining the ability of the film business to ride out the storms of the great Crash and Depression that hit the USA as the Twenties gave way to the Thirties. Hollywood had reason to be grateful to the timing of the Warner Brothers' initiative in sound films.

Top: talkies gave Joan Crawford her break into stardom as a Jazz Age flapper. Centre: Mickey Mouse talks – and the voice was Walt Disney's! Above: Clive Brook's classy English tones were heard for the first time in Paramount's debut talkie

THE STUDIO SYSTEM

Was the studio system an honest attempt to streamline Hollywood, or simply a mania for empire building by unscrupulous, power-mad movie moguls?

From the Thirties to the Fifties, American film production was utterly dominated by a handful of Hollywood film companies: Paramount, MGM, Warner Brothers, 20th Century-Fox and RKO Radio. Often referred to as the Big Five or the 'majors', they were not just production companies and international distributors of motion pictures but also owned massive cinema circuits, thus controlling the entire movie business from film-making through to exhibition.

In the second division of the studio league were two studios, Universal and Columbia, and a releasing company, United Artists. These companies differed from the majors in that they owned few or no cinemas. Without that measure of control they could not be guaranteed prime booking time for their films, but had to take what programme slots were left in the Big Five's cinemas or deal with independent exhibitors.

United Artists differed from all the others in one crucial respect: it was not a studio but a distribution company formed in 1919 by Mary Pickford, Douglas Fairbanks, Charlie Chaplin and D.W. Griffith in order to gain greater control over the marketing of their films.

Finally there was the group of minor studios, known collectively as 'Poverty Row', that specialized in B pictures. Of these only Republic and Monogram (later to become Allied Artists) lasted for any length of time or made much impression on film history. Their story is told in a future chapter.

The financing of motion pictures was based in New York. Wall Street had consolidated its hold on the big film companies during the financial crises of the late Twenties and early Thirties when the cost of equipping for sound and rapid acquisitions of theatres stretched the resources of most companies to snapping point. As the Depression set in, cinema audiences fell away by almost 50 per cent, and without the strong support of the East Coast finance houses some studios might well have gone under.

But it was on the West Coast that the flamboyant and legendary moguls who had built their dream factories in Hollywood created, through their individual enterprises, a superstructure that became known as the studio system. This system was an

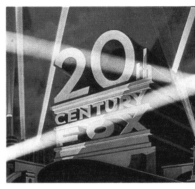

attempt to make films in the most efficient and orderly way possible. Studios not only had directors, actors, supporting players and writers on contract but also cameramen, art directors, special effects men, editors and composers, all of whom could be ordered about as it suited the studio, regardless of the wishes of the individual.

The few individuals who really mattered in this system were the old moguls and the young whizz-kids – MGM's Louis B. Mayer and Irving Thalberg, Warners' Jack L. Warner, Columbia's Harry Cohn and Darryl F. Zanuck at 20th Century-Fox.

At RKO the young David O. Selznick was appointed head of production in October 1931 and was promised a completely free hand to carry out the studio's merger with Pathé. But interference from one of RKO's backers soon caused Selznick to leave and join MGM. Even there, under the benevolent eye of his father-in-law, Louis B. Mayer, Selznick felt curbed and in 1935 he left to form an independent company. Later at RKO another production chief, Dore Schary, responsible for encouraging new talent like directors Robert Wise and Edward Dmytryk, was harried out of office by the studio's last owner, the eccentric millionaire Howard Hughes.

Universal's problems in the early Thirties stemmed largely from boss Carl Laemmle's practice of nepotism. As Universal's founder he gave his son the post of head of production for a twenty-first birthday present. Laemmle's faith in youth could be forgiven, for back in 1920 he had appointed the 20-year-old Irving Thalberg to run the studio but Thalberg had taken his estimable talent off to MGM and left Universal to the Laemmles. Carl Laemmle Jr initiated a memorable horror-film cycle with *Dracula* (1931) and *Frankenstein* (1931) but the company's output was not strong enough to withstand the ill winds of the Depression and both father and son were eventually forced out of office. At this time it was proved, in the words of a popular rhyme, that 'Carl Laemmle had such a large family', for over 70 relatives and dependents had found their way onto the studio payroll. Universal went through the next decade excessively dependent on the few major stars – Deanna Durbin, Abbott and Costello – it was lucky enough to discover.

More than anyone, Irving Thalberg at MGM refined the system of delegated responsibility that became a management blueprint for other studios. Louis B. Mayer handled the temperamental actors, looked for new talent, welcomed important guests, made big speeches; Thalberg, who abhorred publicity and declined any form of screen credit, chose the pictures and got them made.

He assigned each project to a supervisor (like Albert Lewin, Bernard Hyman, Hunt Stromberg or Lawrence Weingarten) who worked on the script with the writers and saw the film through production. Thalberg would keep an eye on the script but tended not to view the rushes during shooting. Believing, however, that 'Films aren't made, they're remade', he took a keen interest in audience pre-

Above: the signs of things to come – although a studio's films could often be recognized by visual style and subject matter. Left: David O. Selznick, founder of 20th Century Productions

Above: the 'second league' studios Universal and Columbia and the independent distribution company United Artists, were to find their way into the big league after World War II: Republic Pictures, despite defying their 'Poverty Row' status with an eagle trademark, eventually abandoned production in the late 50s

views, recutting and even reshooting sections of a film until audience reaction satisfied him.

After Thalberg's early death in 1936, Mayer reigned supreme over the studio until 1948, and encouraged a committee system of decision-making, rather than allowing a single-handed production chief to dominate the studio. MGM was extremely well-funded and certainly the richest studio for talent: it had a regular staff of some 20 directors, 75 writers and 250 players on the payroll, and an annual profit that went from $4 million (in a bad year!) to $10 million in a good year.

Under Mayer's paternalistic rule MGM was jokingly said to stand for Mayer's *Ganz-Mispochen*, Yiddish for 'Mayer's whole family' and members who got out of line were brought to heel politely but firmly. Mayer believed, for example, that stars should behave like royalty and once criticized a performer for eating with a minor employee in the studio dining room. He prided himself on 'clean pictures' for family viewing.

Warner Brothers' Darryl F. Zanuck had been a screenwriter before his promotion to production chief. It was Zanuck who launched the gangster and musical cycles that carried Warners to success past the initial boost provided by Vitaphone talkies. Zanuck and Jack Warner understood each other, but Harry's meanness eventually led to Zanuck's resignation and Hal B. Wallis took over. Wallis kept Warners in the money with his shrewd choice of supervisors, directors and writers.

Everyone under contract was kept ferociously busy at Warners: a director like Michael Curtiz was responsible for five or six features annually in the early Thirties; a leading actor like George Brent was in as many as seven films in the course of 1932.

Cooped up in their office, the Warners' writers expended more ingenuity in circumventing Jack Warner's tiresome regulations than they did on shaping their plots. When Jack forbade his scribes to make outside phone calls from their office in an attempt to make them more industrious, the entire department formed one mighty queue in front of his eyes at the single pay-phone on the lot.

Jack Warner's workhorse regime provoked some famous quarrels. Stars like Bette Davis and James Cagney protested at the films they were being forced to make. Miss Davis hoped to make better films in Britain but was defeated in the courts. Cagney managed to make two independent films but both Davis and Cagney returned to Warner Brothers with the satisfaction of being offered better parts.

Another criticism of the studio system voiced by actors was the practice of adding time spent on suspension to the original expiry date of a contract. Olivia de Havilland, for example, took Warners to court on this issue – she had been suspended six times on a seven-year contract for refusing to make particular films – she won the case but it kept her off the screen for over a year while it was settled.

At Paramount creativity was given a freer hand. Indeed the company went so far as to appoint a major established artist, the producer-director Ernst Lubitsch, to run the studio. Unfortunately this was not a happy move and he soon returned to directing. In the late Thirties certain directors, like William Wellman and Mark Sandrich, were permitted to produce their own films. The studio also gave some writers the chance to direct. Preston Sturges made *The Great McGinty* (1940) and Billy Wilder began with *The Major and the Minor* (1942).

How well the studio system worked for RKO depended largely on who was running the 'shop'. When George Schaefer was appointed head of production, he brought in Orson Welles and his Mercury Players and gave them unprecedented

freedom. The result was *Citizen Kane* (1940).

Schaefer's policy failed, however, to produce profits. His successor, Charles Koerner, was the production chief who put an end to Welles's activities at the studio. Welles may never have been comfortable within any studio format but he suffered particular harassment from a production manager at Columbia named Jack Fier during the shooting of *The Lady From Shanghai* (1947). Welles walked off the set in protest and hung up a huge sign for his fellow-workers: 'You Have Nothing To Fear But Fier Himself'. Fier retaliated with a sign 'All's Well That Ends Welles'.

At its most rigid the system resembled a military regime: writers were locked into their rooms, productions went to the wall at a whim and actors were left to languish on suspension

Columbia studios were run by the notoriously foul-mouthed Harry Cohn. In the Thirties his hottest property was the director, Frank Capra, whose *Lost Horizon* (1937) was one of a string of films that conferred profits and prestige upon the studio. The success of the film served to attract other major film directors like John Ford, Howard Hawks and George Stevens.

In the Thirties the studio was desperately short of big stars: Cohn had to borrow Clark Gable from MGM and Claudette Colbert from Paramount for Capra's *It Happened One Night* (1934), and Edward G. Robinson from Warners for Ford's *The Whole Town's Talking* (1935). Fortunately Columbia developed some stars of its own in the Forties and Fifties, notably Rita Hayworth and Jack Lemmon. Whatever was said about Harry Cohn, he had picture-making in his blood; it was his penny-pinching brother Jack who brought about Capra's exit from Columbia when he refused to allow the director to make *The Life of Chopin* in colour.

Darryl Zanuck's status after he left Warners was sufficient for the money-man Joe Schenck to finance a wholly new company, 20th Century Productions. In the first place they simply produced films, releasing them through United Artists but in 1935 when they merged with the ailing Fox Film Corporation, the new 20th Century-Fox company made its own movies in its own studio and took care of its own releasing.

Down on 'Poverty Row' two studios stood out from the rest: Monogram made itself known for series films like the Charlie Chan mysteries (from an original story bought from 20th Century-Fox) and the Dead End Kids (taken over from Warners). Republic, on the other hand, had flirtations with the big time thanks to a contract they had with John Wayne. Having loaned him out for *Stagecoach* (1939), which made him a major star, Republic toplined him in *The Dark Command* (1940), even though they had to borrow a director (Raoul Walsh from Warners) and co-star (Walter Pidgeon from MGM) to ensure first-feature quality.

Republic's powerful boss Herbert J. Yates also had Western stars Gene Autry and Roy Rogers on contract, but Wayne's films made the really big money until Yates backed out of a deal to let Wayne make his cherished project *The Alamo* in 1951 and lost the star's services for good. Yates further handicapped Republic by insisting that Vera Ralston, later to become Mrs Herbert J. Yates, starred in the company's pictures even though her

box-office appeal was dubious. Veteran studio director Joseph Kane recalled:

'Republic was a public corporation owned by the stockholders, but Yates did as he pleased and the stockholders had about as much say as a native in Timbuktu.'

In the late Forties the Big Five came under government pressure to break up their monopolistic control of the film industry into smaller units. At the same time more stars and directors sought independent projects to work on. In these circumstances, and faced with the challenge posed by television, it was inevitable that the monolithic studio system should begin to fall apart. Production declined and it was no longer feasible to have so many artists on contract expecting to be paid weekly; it was better to hire them when necessary.

Only Universal kept to traditional procedures, turning out formula films as vehicles for its new generation of stars: Rock Hudson, Tony Curtis, Jeff Chandler and, after she left Warners, Doris Day.

United Artists passed into new management in 1951 after its surviving founders, Chaplin and Mary Pickford, sold out their interests. In the changing climate of production, United Artists reaped rewards from a large number of independent producers who brought their projects to them for additional finance and guaranteed distribution. Otto Preminger, who produced and directed *The Man With the Golden Arm* (1956) described United Artists' post-war set-up:

'Only United Artists has a system of true independent production . . . They recognize that the independent has his own personality. After they agree on the basic property, ie projected film, and are consulted on the cast, they leave everything to the producer's discrimination.'

After World War II, when the ownership of cinema chains had been divorced from the production side of the business, the roster of Hollywood studios reflected the loss of economic advantage held by the Big Five. Columbia, Universal and United Artists now ranked alongside the others; all were on an equal footing for the upcoming battle with television.

The studio system was never so rigid as to justify the 'factory production line' label sometimes attributed to it, but it is important to recognize a consistency in the product of each studio.

While it is true that Warners specialized in topical, tightly edited, realistic pictures in the early Thirties, that MGM made classy comedies and

musicals, that Paramount encouraged a Continental sophistication (in their Thirties films) and that Universal went from horror movies in the Thirties to Technicolored adventure films in the Forties, every studio also made films that ran counter to its prevailing image.

When a studio is said to have possessed a certain visual style, this often refers to the 'look' of a film as determined by the laboratory processing favoured by each individual studio. An experienced film editor might tell at a glance which studio had made the film according to the graininess of the black and white or the tones of the colour.

An easier although less reliable guide to the studio origins of a particular film lay in the recurrence of particular stars in one studio's movies: Tyrone Power, for example, was identified with 20th Century-Fox, Alan Ladd with Paramount, Gable with MGM, and so on down the list of supporting players and technicians.

The studios looked after their own: MGM even maintained its own police force, medical teams and lawyers. In return they expected unswerving devotion and total dedication

What is certain is that the studio system encouraged high standards of technical excellence. Most independently made films of the Thirties and Forties looked tatty by comparison, lacking the strong casts and lavish settings that the big studios could always provide. Goldwyn and Selznick certainly spent money on a scale equivalent to that of the majors, if not in excess of it, but other independents were usually either short of cash or keen to spend as little money as possible to get adequate results.

The studio system offered 'the safety of a prison', said Bette Davis. But good films were made, nonetheless, and every company permitted the occasional experiment. Paramount, Columbia and Republic, for example, all indulged the offbeat notions of the writer-director Ben Hecht. Orson Welles, however fiercely single-minded, was more productive while the big studios were flourishing than he has been ever since.

Increasing freedom of subject matter has been the only real advance – and a mixed blessing at that – since the studio system faded away. Even by 1960 one of Hollywood's leading directors, John Huston, a man with a strongly independent streak, could look back with some regret on the passing of the old Hollywood: 'I'm not sure I wasn't better then. Some of the worst pictures I ever made I've made since I've had complete freedom!'

Top: Marion Davies and director Mervyn LeRoy are visited, on the set of Page Miss Glory, *by Jack Warner and Hal B. Wallis. Below left: Howard Hughes, eccentric multi-millionaire and independent producer, with Warners star, Bette Davis. Centre: Universal's founder, Carl Laemmle, and son in earlier, happier days, and (above) Laemmle's ex-employee, whizz-kid Irving Thalberg, with his mogul boss at MGM, Louis B. Mayer*

![ALL QUIET ON THE WESTERN FRONT]

Directed by Lewis Milestone, 1930
Prod co: Universal. **prod:** Carl Laemmle Jr. **sc:** Del Andrews, Maxwell Anderson, George Abbott, from the novel *Im Westen Nichts Neues* by Erich Maria Remarque. **dial:** Maxwell Anderson, George Abbott, C. Gardner Sullivan. **dial dir:** George Cukor. **titles:** Walter Anthony. **photo:** Arthur Edeson. **sp eff photo:** Frank H. Booth. **ed:** Edgar Adams, Milton Carruth, Maurice Pivar. **art dir:** Charles D. Hall, W. R. Schmitt. **sync/mus:** David Broekman. **rec sup:** C. Roy Hunter. **sd:** William W. Hedgecock. **sd sys:** Movietone. **ass dir:** Nate Watt. **r/t:** 138 minutes. New York premiere, 28 April 1930.
Cast: Lew Ayres (*Paul Baumer*), Louis Wolheim (*Katczinsky*), John Wray (*Himmelstoss*), George 'Slim' Summerville (*Tjaden*), Raymond Griffith (*Gerard Duval*), Russell Gleason (*Müller*), William Bakewell (*Albert*), Scott Kolk (*Leer*), Walter Rogers (*Bohm*), Ben Alexander (*Kemmerich*), Owen Davis Jr (*Peter*), Beryl Mercer (*Paul's mother* – sound version), ZaSu Pitts (*Paul's mother* – silent version), Edwin Maxwell (*Paul's father*), Harold Goodwin (*Detering*), Marion Clayton (*Paul's sister*), Richard Alexander (*Westhus*), G. Pat Collins (*Lieutenant Bertinck*), Yola D'Avril (*Suzanne*), Poupée Andriot, Renée Damonde (*French girls*), Arnold Lucy (*Kantorek*), William Irving (*Ginger*), Edmund Breese (*Herr Meyer*), Heinie Conklin (*Hammacher*), Bertha Mann (*Sister*), Bodil Rosing (*Wachter*), Joan Marsh (*poster girl*), Tom London (*orderly*), Vincent Barnett (*cook*), Fred Zinnemann (*man*).

Our bodies are earth and our thoughts are clay and we sleep and eat with death

Erich Maria Remarque wrote *Im Westen Nichts Neues* to free himself from his memory of the Great War and from 'my thoughts and those of my companions'. Like the leading character in the novel, the author was one of a class of 18-year-olds who enlisted in the infantry and suffered the brutalities of life in the trenches. The book was a best-seller. Soon after it appeared in the United States, the rights were snapped up by Carl Laemmle, head of Universal. Laemmle originally intended to use the story for a silent movie, and a silent version with synchronized music exists – running a reel longer than the complete talkie copy and with ZaSu Pitts in the role of Mrs Baumer instead of Beryl Mercer, who played the part in the sound film. (Perhaps Miss Mercer's stage experience was thought to fit her better for talkies.)

Lewis Milestone set himself uncompromisingly to reproduce the realism of the novel. It is arguable that no film – whether fiction or fact – has given so vivid an account of the physical actuality of World War I; and fragments of *All Quiet* have frequently turned up in later compilations, credited as documentary.

The battle scenes were shot on an area of almost 1000 acres on the Irvine Ranch, 69 miles south-east of Los Angeles. Over 5 miles of water

pipes were laid to provide the authentic water-logged appearance of the battlefields. And 2 miles of road were built for the operation of Universal's high new camera crane which was assigned to the picture. In all, 35 different sets were built for the film – those representing front-line France being destined for destruction during filming.

Unerringly, Milestone reconciled the realism of the setting with the deliberately lyrical style of the dialogue: 'Our bodies are earth and our thoughts are clay, and we sleep and eat with death'. He also blended the extreme stylization of some performances with the easy naturalism of Louis Wolheim (Katczinsky) and Slim Summerville (Tjaden).

Milestone used his facilities with incomparable flair. He brought all the fluidity of silent films to the camera – which freely tracked and panned and soared over the battlefields or the little German town from which the hero and his schoolboy friends march out to war – and to the editing. At the same time Milestone imaginatively explored the possibilities of sound, from the beginning where the bellicose harangues of the schoolteacher are drowned by the noise of a band outside, to the haunting echoes of the battlefield as the cry of 'Mind the wire' goes down the line.

At the outset of World War I a group of German boys leave their desks for the army, inspired by the marching soldiers in the streets (1) and by the uplifting rhetoric of their schoolmaster. Only one wavers but he too is eventually persuaded (2). Sent to the front, their illusions are shattered by the cynical stoicism of seasoned soldiers (3) and by their own first experiences under fire (4). They share the terror and exhaustion of constant fighting as well as the bewilderment of watching their schoolfriends die (5) on the battlefield.

The central character is Paul Baumer. His first experience of killing a man, face to face, is traumatic (6): in other circumstances the Frenchman could have been a friend and comrade rather than the enemy.

After being wounded, Paul is sent home on leave to find a world with which he now has little contact. False romantic ideas of war still persist in the school and among the belligerent old men in the beer cellars (7).

Almost with relief he returns to the front. A few old comrades are still alive in his unit but it is mostly filled with new recruits – as young and green as he was once, not so many months ago.

Some time later Paul is peering through the loophole of his trench (8) when he sees a butterfly. He reaches out to catch it (9). A French sniper takes aim. Paul's hand falls limp.

Across the corpse-strewn fields of France march columns of ghostly soldiers – accusation in their eyes (10).

1

2

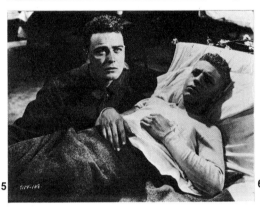

3

4

5

6

7

8

10

9

Marlene

Dietrich

'One sees what one wants to see',
said Josef von Sternberg, 'and I gave her nothing
that she did not already have.'

The Blue Angel

Josef von Sternberg described his first film with Dietrich as 'a celluloid monument to her'. It certainly made her a star.

The Blue Angel is the story of an elderly, respected school professor who becomes obsessed with a cabaret singer at the Blue Angel nightclub. Sacked from the school after being seduced by Lola-Lola, he marries her and becomes a clown in her travelling troupe. When it visits his old town he is painfully humiliated and, looking for solace, finds instead Lola with her new lover. Cast out, the pathetic figure wanders to his former classroom and dies there alone.

In Sternberg's cruellest study of sexual desire, Dietrich was teasingly provocative as the heartless Lola, stealing most of the scenes as she huskily sings 'Falling in Love Again' and 'I'm Naughty Little Lola', and bares her legs to Emil Jannings' professor. Heinrich Mann, author of the original novel, told Jannings during production that 'the success of this film will be found in the naked thighs of Miss Dietrich!'

'She makes reason totter on her throne' wrote the critic James Agate. Marlene Dietrich, who for so many years defied time, has also denied history. For more than two decades she included in her remarkable stage act some fragments of purely mythical autobiography that obliterated all that she had achieved before Josef von Sternberg made her an international star with *Der Blaue Engel*.

Dietrich has claimed that she was an unknown drama student when Sternberg 'discovered' her. She was, in fact, a veteran of 7 years and 17 films, not counting walk-on parts that date from as early as 1919.

Never the most modest of men, even Sternberg grew irritated with her insistence that he was her 'Svengali':

'She has never ceased to proclaim that I taught her everything. Among the many things I did not teach her was to be garrulous about me . . . I did not endow her with a personality that was not her own; one sees what one wants to see, and I gave her nothing that she did not already have. What I did was to dramatize her attributes and make them visible for all to see; though, as there were perhaps too many, I concealed some.'

The new angel

Maria Magdalene Dietrich was born in 1901, the daughter of an officer in the Royal Prussian Police. Abandoning a musical training in favour of the stage, she telescoped her names into 'Marlene' and in January 1922 had her first break with a small part in *Der Grosse Bariton* (The Great Baritone).

Her first credited film role is as a maid-servant, helping her mistress to escape, in the comic costume romance *So Sind die Männer* (1922, Men Are Like This). In Joe May's

Right: the myth takes shape in the silent Three Loves. *Left: a scene from* Shanghai Express *and an early incarnation of the myth.*

Tragödie der Liebe (1923, *Tragedy of Love*), a rambling four-part murder serial starring Emil Jannings, she plays the girlfriend of a lawyer.

She moved into supporting roles in films which included *Manon Lescaut* (1926), and *Cafe Electric* (1927), and was leading lady to the 'adventure king' Harry Piel in *Sein Grösster Bluff* (1927, His Greatest Bluff). Alexander Korda cast her as a coquette, enraged by the shopgirl heroine who borrows her gown in *Eine Dubarry von Heute* (1926, A Modern Dubarry). in *Ich Küsse Ihre Hand, Madame* (1929, *I Kiss Your Hand, Madame*) she has an unrewarding lead part in an operetta tale of thwarted love and mistaken identity. In Maurice Tourneur's *Das Schiff der Verlorenen Menschen* (1929, The Ship of Lost Souls), she is again in the lead, playing an aeronaut pursued by the woman-hungry crew of the ship that rescues her from a crash.

Fatal attractions

Die Frau, nach der Man Sich Sehnt (1929, *Three Loves*), directed by Kurt Bernhardt, showed a clear understanding of Dietrich's *femme fatale* quality and strange sexual aura.

She bewitches a young man on his honeymoon – travelling on the same train – and begs him to rescue her from her sinister companion, later revealed to be her lover. He abandons his bride to pursue this lovely creature, but she seems unable, or unwilling, to break from Karoff, her jealous lover who, it seems, has murdered her husband with her knowledge. She eventually dies at Karoff's hands. The decorative manner of this film remarkably anticipates the visual style of Sternberg: in a party scene, balloons and streamers fill the air to confuse and torment the characters; lighting is used to model the star's face; and in one memorable shot a shaft of light from an opening door gradually creeps up Dietrich's silk-clad legs, with startlingly sensuous effect.

It is apparent that somebody already recognized the mythical possibilities of Dietrich. The tempting conclusion is that it was the star herself, for it was she who approached the writers Walter Wassermann and Walter Schlee to give her a 'similar script' for her next film. They obliged with *Gefahren der Brautzeit* (1929, Dangers of the Engagement), in which a baron meets an unknown beauty (Dietrich) on

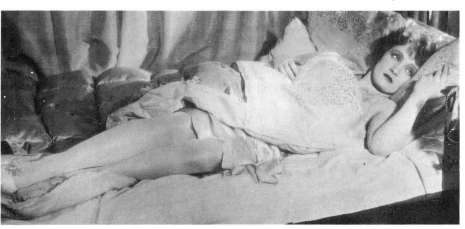

Above and above right: the mystique of Marlene Dietrich was never more powerful than in Morocco *and* Blonde Venus *(and below, with Cary Grant). Above, far right: not even a soaking in* Destry Rides Again *could impair her magic*

a train; the first glimpse of her, framed in a frosted carriage window, might well be from a Sternberg film. The train breaks down and the couple spend a night of love in a hotel. The next morning the lady has disappeared. Arriving at his destination the Baron meets his best friend, who introduces his fiancée – the unknown beauty. She later comes to the Baron's room to tell him their meeting must be forgotten; but they are surprised by her betrothed who shoots his friend in a fit of jealousy. The Baron pretends the injury is nothing and succeeds in reconciling the couple; he then dies alone, using his last strength to feign suicide. The film is almost a carbon copy of its predecessor, with the significant difference that here it is the man, not the *femme fatale*, who dies.

And along came Jo
Then Josef von Sternberg entered her life. According to him, he chose Dietrich for the part of Lola-Lola after seeing her on stage in *Zwei Krawatten* (Two Neckties). Only later did he see her screen-work which he described as:
'. . . an ordeal. If I had first seen her films . . . my reaction would have been the same as everyone else's. In them she was an awkward, unattractive woman, left to her own devices, and presented in an embarrassing exhibition of drivel.'

This is patently untrue, though perhaps Sternberg saw the wrong films. In *Die Frau, nach der Man Sich Sehnt* and *Gefahren der Brautzeit* the form of the mythical Marlene is evident, though still rough-hewn. Sternberg's role was to perfect it, and provide a wonderful visual framework for the image: 'What I did was to dramatize her attributes and make them visible for all to see'.

This extraordinary man was born Jonas Sternberg in Vienna in 1894. His early life seems to have been a struggle for survival and self-education, which permanently marked a sensitive but defiantly arrogant personality.

Emigrating to the United States as a child, he found his way into the cinema, worked his way up in various technical jobs, and in 1925 directed a low-budget, independently produced feature, *The Salvation Hunters*. It brought him work in Hollywood on successful silents like the gangster story, *Underworld* (1927), and *The Last Command* (1928), which earned Emil Jannings the first Best Actor Oscar.

As a result Jannings, having now returned to Germany, requested Sternberg as the director of his first all-talkie film – *Der Blaue Engel* (*The Blue Angel*). The film was a triumph and so was its leading lady – Dietrich.

The road to Morocco
Summoned by Paramount, she departed immediately after the film's premiere. She was preceded by Sternberg, who had persuaded the studio to sign her and was the obvious choice to direct her first American film.

Again Dietrich seems to have taken the initiative in selecting her vehicle. She is said to have given Sternberg a copy of the novel *Amy Jolly* to read on the boat. Later she cabled him that it was, after all, 'weak lemonade' but Sternberg proceeded to make *Morocco* (1930) from it. The story centres on a woman (Dietrich plays another cabaret artist) whose feelings are divided between loyalty to a wealthy socialite (Adolphe Menjou) and passion for a legionnaire (Gary Cooper) whom she eventually follows into the desert. Even today the sexual suggestions and ambivalences in Marlene's cabaret act can still raise eyebrows. In any event, *Morocco* consolidated the legend and securely launched her American career.

Paramount partners
In the next five years Dietrich and Sternberg worked together on five more films that, ultimately, were to elevate her into a screen goddess. In *Dishonored* (1931) she is a beautiful spy in the Mata Hari mould, dying with *sangfroid* in front of the firing squad. In *Shanghai Express* (1932) she is spellbindingly erotic as Shanghai Lily, the woman with a past, sacrificing herself to a Chinese rebel to save the man she loves. This is perhaps Sternberg's most perfect film; visual spectacle and narrative are totally integrated. In *Blonde Venus* (1932) she

is a woman who turns singer (and perhaps worse) to pay for the operations needed to save her husband's life. Perhaps the most startling sequence of *Blonde Venus* is the 'Hot Voodoo' number in the nightclub with its chorus of spear-carrying girls. In the midst of them Dietrich emerges, like a butterfly out of a chrysalis, from a huge and hairy gorilla suit, which she proceeds to remove before singing the song. In *The Scarlet Empress* (1934), a witty interpretation of history, she is a sensuous Catherine the Great. In *The Devil Is a Woman* (1935) she becomes a Spanish siren who enslaves a young political refugee and an older grandee. Here Sternberg's ability to decorate the *femme fatale* myth reached a peak, but the film's commercial failure (the Spanish government demanded its withdrawal) was the excuse for Paramount, alarmed by his extravagance and dogged independence, to end his contract. In any case, he had announced during filming that it would benefit neither Dietrich nor himself to stay together.

The parting of the ways

'I didn't leave Sternberg. *He* left *me*!' Dietrich told the *Sunday Times* nearly 30 years later. 'That's very important. In my life, he was the man I wanted to please most. He decided not to work with me any more and I was very unhappy about that.'

Dietrich's dependence and attachment to Sternberg were intense. Sternberg's wife had earlier sued her for alienation of affection and libel. Dietrich won the case but it sparked off a great deal of controversy and speculation about the exact nature of the union between the director and his protégée, and may have been a major cause of their separation.

Only once between *Der Blaue Engel* and *The Devil Is a Woman* had Dietrich worked under another director – Rouben Mamoulian in *Song of Songs* (1933). It was apparently an uneasy collaboration for director and star. Dietrich is said to have been in the habit of murmuring into the microphone before a take 'Where are you, Jo?' In later years she herself elaborated this story; her actual words, she told director Peter Bogdanovich (*Esquire*, January 1973) were 'Oh Jo – why hast thou forsaken me?'

For both director and star, the cycle of pictures they made together represented the summit of their achievement in the cinema. Sternberg had proved himself one of Hollywood's supreme artists, with Dietrich at the centre of the decadent, dreamlike world created by his lush, exotic style. He worked on only 9 more features in the remaining 18 years of his career, and of these, Korda's *I, Claudius* (1937) was abandoned and 3 were reworked by other directors. Only *The Shanghai Gesture* (1941) and *The Saga of Anatahan* (1953) can stand alongside the great Sternberg pictures of the Thirties.

Dietrich's career also suffered a decline. She made the kitschy *The Garden of Allah* (1936) with Richard Boleslavsky; a couple of frothy comedies, Frank Borzage's *Desire* (1936) and Ernst Lubitsch's *Angel* (1937); and in Britain, Jacques Feyder's beautiful but dull *Knight Without Armour* (1937). By this time she was ungallantly labelled 'box-office poison' and ranked at number 126 in the list of money-making stars. Shortly afterwards Paramount announced: 'Marlene Dietrich will be permitted to work elsewhere'.

Dietrich rides again

Her career revived dramatically in 1939 with George Marshall's tongue-in-cheek Western, *Destry Rides Again*, in which she plays Frenchy, a saloon singer in love with the mild-mannered sheriff (James Stewart). None of the many films that followed framed and deified her as carefully as the Sternberg pictures had done; but by this time it hardly seemed to matter. The myth was already complete, unchangeable and impregnable, and – whatever Sternberg may have contributed – it was clear that its conservation was mostly due to Dietrich herself.

We have the evidence of nearly everybody who worked with her that nothing she did was accidental or unconscious. Lee Garmes, Sternberg's cameraman, said, 'She had a great mechanical mind and knew the camera. She would always stop in the exact position that was right for her . . .' Harry Stradling, who filmed *The Garden of Allah*, confirmed:

'While each shot was being lined up she had a full-length mirror set up beside the camera and was able to see just how she would look on the screen. If she thought the light on her arms was too strong, or her shoulders were catching too much from a certain arc, she never hesitated to say so; and she was always right.'

Perhaps the surest proof of her great professionalism lay in the dramatic roles she played in her last pictures: the wife giving treacherous evidence in Billy Wilder's *Witness for the Prosecution* (1957); the tough madame in Orson Welles's *Touch of Evil* (1958); and the widow of a Nazi general in Stanley Kramer's *Judgement at Nuremberg* (1961). To be a star and a myth, she revealed, did not preclude intelligent and concentrated dramatic interpretation. Then in 1979, after a 16-year absence, she returned to the screen, playing another madame in David Hemmings's *Just A Gigolo*. Her career in motion pictures now spans over 60 years.

The eternal superstar

Yet the masterpiece of the myth was perhaps the Dietrich who emerged as a solo concert performer during and after World War II.

In 1953 she began the series of tours that were to take her around the world. Dietrich never disappointed her audiences. And every night the myth was brought to life on stage. In private she could be a loving mother and wife (Dietrich married Rudolf Sieber, one of Joe May's production assistants, in 1924), an industrious housekeeper, a practical and willing nurse, a determined trouper and a sensible traveller. On stage, however, the glamour of that solitary figure, sheathed in sequins and furs, never flickered; it defied all the inroads of time. And her performance was not just a magnificent illusion. When she sang 'Where Have All the Flowers Gone' and 'Lili Marlene', or touched the past with 'Falling in Love Again', she became a tragic actress – as well as a mythical figure encompassing a lifetime of all our history.

Quotations from: Fun in a Chinese Laundry *by Josef von Sternberg;* Marlene Dietrich *by Sheridan Morley;* All My Yesterdays *by Edward G. Robinson.*

Filmography

1922 So Sind die Männer/Napoleons Kleiner Brüder/Der Kleine Napoleon. '23 Tragödie der Liebe (USA/GB: Tragedy of Love); Der Mensch am Wege. '24 Der Sprung ins Leben/Die Roman eine Zirkuskindes. '25 Die Freudlose Gasse (USA: Streets of Sorrow, reissued with post-synchronized sound in 1937 as The Street of Sorrow; GB: The Joyless Street). '26 Manon Lescaut; Eine Dubarry von Heute; Kopf Hoch, Charly!; Madame Wünscht Keine Kinder; Der Juxbaron. '27 Sein Grösster Bluff/Er Oder Dich; Cafe Electric/Wenn ein Weib den Weg Verliert (A: Die Liebesbörse). '28 Prinzessin Olala; Die Glückliche Mutter (short: edited version of home movies made by her husband in mid-1920s, reputedly shown publicly). '29 Ich Küsse Ihre Hand, Madame (USA: I Kiss Your Hand, Madame); Die Frau, nach der Man Sich Sehnt (USA/GB: Three Loves); Das Schiff der Verlorenen Menschen; Gefahren der Brautzeit/Liebesnächte. '30 Der Blaue Engel (English-language version: The Blue Angel, USA/GB, 1931). *All remaining films USA unless specified:* '30 Morocco. '31 Dishonored. '32 Shanghai Express; Blonde Venus. '33 The Song of Songs. '34 The Scarlet Empress. '35 The Devil Is a Woman. '36 Desire; I Loved a Soldier (unfinished; refilmed without her as Hotel Imperial in 1939); The Garden of Allah. '37 Knight Without Armour (GB); Angel. '39 Destry Rides Again. '40 Seven Sinners; The Flame of New Orleans; Manpower. '42 The Lady Is Willing; The Spoilers; Pittsburgh. '43 Stage Door Canteen (publicity sketch not used in actual film). '44 Follow the Boys (guest); Kismet. '46 Martin Roumagnac (FR) (USA: The Room Upstairs). '47 Golden Earrings. '48 A Foreign Affair. '49 Jigsaw (guest); Stage Fright (GB). '51 No Highway (GB) (USA: No Highway in the Sky). '52 Rancho Notorious. '56 Around the World in 80 Days (guest); The Monte Carlo Story. '57 Witness for the Prosecution. '58 Touch of Evil (guest). '61 Judgement at Nuremberg. '62 The Black Fox (narr. only). '63 Paris When It Sizzles (guest). '79 Schöner Gigolo – Armer Gigolo (GER) (GB: Just a Gigolo).

Below: Dietrich as the madame in Just a Gigolo; *half a century after* The Blue Angel *and the allure of Lola-Lola lingers on*

M

It is astonishing that Fritz Lang's first sound film, *M*, should already have so completely mastered the new medium that it could not have been made with the same effect as a silent film. In the opening, a large shadow falls across a poster warning the public about the murderer, just as a little girl tosses her ball against it. We only hear a voice saying, 'What a nice ball you have. What is your name?'; and we feel the implied threat all the more for not actually seeing the man.

The scene switches to the girl's mother who is making lunch for her. She anxiously puts the absent child's meal back into the oven to keep it warm. In the next shot we see the unknown man for the first time, but only from behind, as he buys Elsie a balloon from a blind pedlar. He begins to whistle, off-key, a few bars of Grieg's *In the Hall of the Mountain King*. The whistled tune becomes a gruesome leitmotif indicating that the murderer is on the prowl.

Frau Beckmann, worried about her daughter, leans over the bannister of the stair-well and cries, 'Elsie!' The cry resounds through the block of flats and an empty loft. The murder is not shown. Instead Lang supplies a series of images – Frau Beckmann's cries echoing over shots of the empty building, Elsie's vacant place at table, Elsie's ball rolling from beneath a bush and her new balloon caught in telegraph wires – and leaves the audience to imagine the crime itself. The final shot of the sequence is of a paperseller who shouts out the latest headlines: a new murder!

Panic grows in the menaced town, and the police make random raids on the underworld. Gangsters cannot pursue their 'work' quietly, so they resolve to find the murderer. Two conferences about the murders are paralleled; that of the police authorities and that of the gangsters. Here Lang uses a startlingly new sound technique: the overlapping of sentences from one scene to the next. This emphasizes the parallel action while tightening and accelerating the drama. He does not neglect visual effect, but bathes the gangsters in shadows.

In contrast to the plodding investigations of the police, the gangsters organize the network of beggars to watch for the murderer. Ironically he is detected by the blind balloon seller who recognizes the whistling. The blind man tells a boy to follow the murderer, who has a little girl with him.

Directed by Fritz Lang, 1931
Prod co: Nero Film, A. G. Ver. Star Film GmbH. **prod:** Seymour Nebenzal. **sc:** Fritz Lang, Thea von Harbou, from an article by Egon Jacobson. **dial:** Thea von Harbou. **photo:** Fritz Arno Wagner, Gustav Rathje, Karl Vash. **sd ed:** Paul Falkenberg. **art dir:** Carl Vollbrecht, Emil Hasler. **backdrop photos:** Horst von Harbou. **mus:** excerpts from *Peer Gynt* by Edvard Grieg ('murderer's theme' whistled by Fritz Lang). **sd:** Adolf Jansen, **r/t:** 120 minutes. Berlin premiere, 11 May 1931.
Cast: Peter Lorre (*the murderer*), Otto Wernicke (*Inspector Karl Lohmann*), Gustav Gründgens (*Schraenker*), Theo Lingen (*Baurenfaenger*), Theodor Loos (*Commissioner Groeber*), Georg John (*peddler*), Ellen Widman (*Frau Beckmann*), Inge Landgut (*Elsie Beckmann*), Ernst Stahl-Nachbaur (*Chief of Police*), Paul Kemp (*pickpocket*), Franz Stein (*minister*), Rudolf Blümner (*defence lawyer*), Karl Platen (*watchman*), Gerhard Bienert (*police secretary*), Rosa Veletti (*owner of the Crocodile Club*), Hertha von Walter (*prostitute*), Fritz Odemar (*safe-breaker*), Fritz Gnass (*burglar*).

The murderer buys the child some oranges and pulls out his flick-knife – but only to peel one. Alarmed, the watching boy chalks an 'M' (for murderer) on his hand, jostles the murderer and manages to mark the man's back with a sign.

Realizing he has been spotted, the murderer panics and runs into the nearby courtyard of an office block. Two fire engines rush past ringing their bells, and by the time they have gone, the murderer has disappeared. The gangsters, alerted by the beggars, break into the building. Again, sound betrays the murderer: accidentally locked in an attic, he tries to hammer a nail into a makeshift key. The sound is heard by the hunters, who break in and seize him. Wrapped in a carpet, he is caried off for 'trial'.

Before a jury largely made up of criminals and prostitutes, the murderer screams out his confession:

'Who are you . . . all of you? . . . Criminals! Perhaps you're even proud of being able to break safes, to climb into buildings or cheat at cards . . . Things you could just as well keep your fingers off . . . But I . . . I can't help myself! I haven't any control over this evil thing that's inside me – the fire, the voices, the torment . . . I want to escape . . . but it's impossible.'

The police, meanwhile, have been told of the gangsters' activities and break into the 'courtroom' just as the mob is howling for the murderer's death. No silent film could have created the emotional climax of the murderer's confession with titles alone.

Although Lang's use of the underworld was influenced by Berthold Brecht's famous satirical play *Die Dreigroschenoper* (*The Threepenny Opera*), he based much of the screenplay on contemporary press reports. Lang also investigated police methods of detection and spoke to gangsters (even giving them parts in the film). He asked his set designer, Emil Hasler, for 'everyday' sketches for decor, and his cameraman, Fritz Arno Wagner, to adopt newsreel techniques when shooting.

This well-documented approach is typical of Lang's films, but does not obscure his genuine human concern. In an interview with Gero Gandert, Lang recalled:

'In *M*, I was not only interested in finding out why someone was driven to a crime as horrible as child murder, but also to discuss the pros and cons of capital punishment. But the film's message is *not* the conviction of the murderer but the warning to all mothers, "You should keep better watch over your children". This human message was felt particularly strongly by my wife at the time, Thea von Harbou.'

A shadow looms over Elsie Beckmann (1). Her name will soon figure on the list of the murderer's victims. As the townsfolk panic, an innocent man is seized by a mob (2). Unaware that every beggar in the city is on the watch for him, the murderer eyes yet another victim (3). He catches sight of the tell-tale 'M' chalked on his back by a boy who suspects him (4) and panics (5). He hides in an attic full of bric-a-brac (6), but is eventually caught by a vigilante force of gangsters and taken to an abandoned factory to be 'tried' by criminals (7). The gang boss confronts him with a picture of Elsie (8), and a blind balloon-seller also gives evidence against him (9). Finally he makes his confession (10).

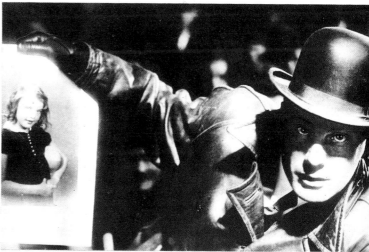

THE 4 MARX BROTHERS

How did four nice little boys called Julius, Adolph, Leonard and Herbert grow up into the Marx Brothers? Perhaps because they never really were nice little boys

Groucho Marx seldom ventured any comment on his own comic style. He felt that humour, like romance and sex, loses its magic if examined too closely: 'If you talk about those things, they go away.' When asked why he thought he was funny, he would answer simply, 'I'm a funny-looking jerk'. He did believe, however, that all great comedy is based on character.

People who had known the Marx Brothers before they became famous (when they were still Julius, Adolph, Leonard, Milton and Herbert), even before they entered show business, all agreed that the five brothers never had to create the characters they played so convincingly on stage, screen, and television – they already *were* those characters. A neighbour of the Marx family in New York City during the early 1900s remarked:

'They were wild youngsters with a talent for having fun. The place would be a shambles, especially if Mrs Marx left them alone. They would tear down the draperies. There was a woman across the way, a doctor's wife, who used to send over notes saying that she was going to call the police, which probably made them do it even more.'

The poor Marx Brothers

The Marx family was poor but, as Groucho said of his childhood:

'We didn't know it, so we were happy. At Christmas we didn't have a tree, just a branch, and we each hung up one of our black socks and got a half an orange each for Christmas. All our neighbours even had better garbage than we did. Harpo used to skate in Central Park with one ice skate he tied on. When my Aunt Hannah cooked the clam chowder, she used the same pot she used for the laundry, and there was plenty of starch in both.'

Although the Marx Brothers' theatrical characters were based on real people and actual experiences, their mannerisms and costumes were developed through trial and error during their years in vaudeville. For Groucho

this all began in 1905 when he joined a travelling troupe as a boy soprano. He got the job out of economic necessity:

'I became an actor because I had an uncle in show business who was making $200 a week, and I wasn't making anything, not even an occasional girl.'

Although the job didn't last long, and three times he found himself stranded on the road without money, Groucho persisted. Eventually he landed work with the Gus Edwards school act – his first professional encounter with stage comedy.

Donkey business

Three years later Minnie Marx gathered her sons (Groucho, Gummo, and later Harpo) to-

gether into a singing act called first *The Three Nightingales*, then *The Six Mascots*. She was their agent, and sometimes joined the act with her sister, Hannah. Sam Marx (known as 'Frenchie'), the father of the Marx Brothers, stayed at home with the cooking and housework, as well as a threadbare tailoring business. Apparently this pioneering role-sharing worked out perfectly: Sam was a superb cook while, in Groucho's words: 'Minnie couldn't make anything except my father.' But as an agent she was unsurpassed: 'Without her, we wouldn't have been anything,' Groucho often said. 'She was the most important woman in my life.'

As a singing act the Marx Brothers were condemned to second-rate or even third-rate vaudeville, and it was only by accident that they discovered how funny they could be. Groucho described the moment:

'We were playing a small town in Texas, a

Above: stowaways Harpo, Zeppo, Chico and Groucho about to create havoc aboard ship in Monkey Business. *Below: in* Room Service *it is a hotel that suffers their onslaught*

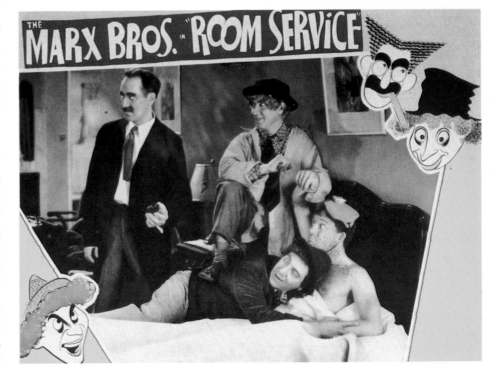

farming town. The farmers came in and tied up their horses beside the Pantages Theatre. We were doing a singing act, a mule runs away, and the whole audience left to catch the mule. Then they came back. By this time we were so angry we started making sarcastic remarks. Like, ''Nacogdoches is full of roaches'' and ''The jackass is the finest flower of Texass.'' Instead of getting mad, the audience laughs. This is the first time we ever did comedy like that.'

This incident happened in 1912 during a tour through Louisiana, Texas and Oklahoma.

School Marx
After their unexpected triumph they attempted comedy whenever it seemed appropriate, and in Denison, Texas, *The Six Mascots* were received so enthusiastically that they were invited to stay over, this time with a guarantee. Wishing to please an audience of teachers who were there for a conference, Groucho wrote a comedy sketch based on the Gus Edwards school act. Groucho became Herr Teacher, Harpo played the stupid boy, and the other members of the troupe, who included Gummo, became the standard school act characters of that day. This act was called *Fun in Hi Skule*, and much of what the Marx Brothers did afterwards was influenced by it. Most notable of all, Harpo donned his famous red wig (later to become blond for the films) and became himself; Groucho assumed a stern countenance and an air of unqualified authority; and Gummo played the juvenile straight-man role that Zeppo later inherited. Then Chico joined the act as the confidently ignorant 'Eye-talian'.

All of the Marx Brothers shows that followed *Fun in Hi Skule*, including the films and even Groucho's TV programme, owed a great deal to it. *You Bet Your Life* was the same routine but in modern dress, with Groucho still playing Herr Teacher. *Horse Feathers* is *Fun in Hi Skule* graduated to college and Hollywood. As the great white hunter in *Animal Crackers*, the prime minister in *Duck Soup*, or the bogus doctor in *A Day at the Races*, Groucho is still in many respects Herr Teacher, and his brothers play almost exactly the same roles as in *Fun in Hi Skule*.

Harpo loses his voice
It was their uncle (Minnie's brother), Al Shean – himself a big star in American vaudeville – who had helped to crystallize further each brother's stage personality. Groucho was allowed to talk incessantly, while Harpo became mute, and Chico played comic straight-man to both. According to Groucho, Al Shean felt that Harpo's voice did not match his whimsical appearance. Harpo was disappointed, but accepted Uncle Al's dictum. Thereafter Harpo talked professionally only once again during his entire career. A quarter of a century later, he spoke at the end of the stage tryouts for *Go West*. The brothers decided that this speech, whilst comically effective, departed from the innocent Harpo character, and it was omitted from the movie. In later life, after his retirement from films, Harpo would not accept any speaking engagements, and requested that his family never allow a recording of his voice to be played. He felt that to allow his voice to be heard by the public would be unfaithful and destructive to the character he had created. Groucho said the question he was most often asked was, 'Can Harpo talk?' His answer was

Above: A Day at the Races *marked a crucial point in the Marx Brothers' career as a team*

always, 'Of course not.'

By 1914, *Mr Green's Reception*, as *Fun in Hi Skule* was now called, had established the Marx Brothers as rising vaudeville stars. They were not yet, however, known by their famous 'O' names. This happened while they were touring Illinois in 1914. Another performer on the bill with them had a penchant for giving nicknames to his friends. Julius became Groucho because of his serious demeanour. Adolph became Harpo for the obvious reason. Leonard became Chico because of his passion for the chicks, as girls were then called. (Thus the correct pronunciation of his name is 'Chicko') Milton became Gummo because, as he later explained: 'I always had holes in my shoes, so I'd wear rubbers, or gumshoes, over them even when it wasn't raining, and I got called Gummo.' Herbert was only 13 and at home in Chicago when his brothers were being renamed, but he became Zeppo later. No one, especially Zeppo, is certain why. They continued to use their real names until 1924, but the 'new' names eventually took over.

He stoops to conquer
Harpo's devotion to the harp was not accidental. His grandmother had played, in the family's travelling magic show in Germany, on a wondrous instrument without strings. As a child Harpo would also 'play' on this harp which was stored in a closet in their New York apartment, and when he finally got a harp with real strings he taught himself to play, but

Below: Chico and Harpo lose their clothing, but not their ability to win out, in Horse Feathers. *Right: in the same film Harpo has already proved that he is a law unto himself*

in an unorthodox style that in later years amazed professional harpists.

Before they were established as stars, however, the Marx Brothers ran through a number of what were then called musical tabloids: several thinly plotted scenes, as sumptuously mounted as a tight budget and difficult physical conditions would allow, were held together by song, dance and comedy. In each of these shows the brothers enriched their comic characters and developed routines that would serve them – with variations – for decades. The sloping, stooping Groucho walk, for instance, happened by accident. 'I was just kidding around one day, and I started to walk funny. The audience liked it so I kept it in.'

After one failure, the Marx Brothers appeared in the successful *On the Mezzanine Floor*, which, along with *Home Again*, toured Great Britain in 1922. They opened at the Coliseum in London. At first, the audience did not understand the Marx Brothers' humour and responded by throwing pennies onto the stage. 'In those days,' Groucho recalled, 'it was the custom when the audiences didn't like an act – a pretty dangerous custom, too, since the English penny was as large as a silver dollar.' Groucho waded into the shower of coins and addressed the audience: 'We came all the way from America to entertain you, so you might at least throw some shillings.' His ad lib won over the audience, and their entire British tour was enormously successful.

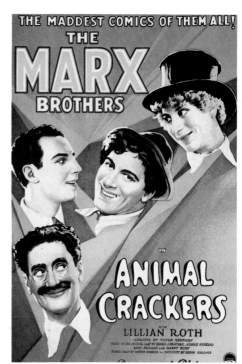

A night in New York

Back in the United States in 1923 they had serious difficulties with the United Booking Office, which controlled virtually all of vaudeville. Unable to get work they were forced to put on their own show. They were helped by a Pennsylvanian industrialist who owned a theatre in Philadelphia and the sets and props from several theatrical flops, and were thus able to put together *I'll Say She Is*, their most ambitious musical tabloid to date. Although Groucho always referred to this show as 'a real turkey,' it was a huge success in Philadelphia. After a tepid road trip, they came to Broadway. Fortunately, on the night they opened in 1924 a more important show postponed its premiere, and the most influential New York drama critics went to *I'll Say She Is* instead. Their rave reviews established the Marx Brothers as permanent superstars.

Two even bigger Broadway hits followed: *The Cocoanuts* in 1925 and *Animal Crackers* in 1928; both were later filmed in New York – in 1929 and 1930 respectively – almost exactly as they were presented on the stage.

After filming *Animal Crackers*, the Marx Brothers left for California, where they remained. Their first three Hollywood pictures were produced for Paramount by Herman J. Mankiewicz, writer of *Citizen Kane* (1940) and one of Hollywood's great non-conformists. (Assigned to write a Rin-Tin-Tin picture, he had the courageous police dog carry the baby *into* a burning building instead of out of it. He was never assigned to a Rin-Tin-Tin film again.) The Marx Brothers' pictures of this period – *Monkey Business* (1931), *Horse Feathers* (1932), and *Duck Soup* (1933) – all bear the imprint of their iconoclastic producer.

Under Thalberg's wing

The next two films, *A Night at the Opera* (1935) and *A Day at the Races* (1937), were produced by Irving Thalberg at MGM. Groucho credited Thalberg with saving their careers after *Duck Soup* had done poorly at the box office. Thalberg felt that the Marx Brothers were appealing only to a minority, and that they

Above: Chico and Harpo in the scene from At the Circus *where they attempt to rob the strong man's room, and (above right) in* Animal Crackers *the Marxes were let loose on high society*

were missing especially the female audience that so often decided which film the family attended. He found the Marx Brothers characters of the Paramount films 'unsympathetic' because they were not helping anyone. To remedy this, he reinforced the plots so that they could stand alone as romantic comedies, recast the Marx Brothers as helpful avuncular types rather than totally uninhibited anarchists, and added the kind of lavish production numbers that a major studio like MGM could afford. He also allowed the Marx Brothers to try out material for their next picture in front of audiences on a road tour; this was especially helpful, as the Marx Brothers had always depended heavily on the reaction of live audiences to their ad libs. Thalberg returned to the original successful formula of George S. Kaufman who, with Morrie Ryskind, had conceived and written *The Cocoanuts* and *Animal Crackers*; and at Groucho's behest, Kaufman and Ryskind were imported from the East Coast to write *A Night at the Opera*.

After *Duck Soup* Zeppo had quit the act and

Filmography

Groucho, Harpo, Chico and Zeppo: **1926** Humorisk (unreleased and no cast list); '**29** The Cocoanuts. '**30** Animal Crackers. '**31** Monkey Business. '**32** Horse Feathers. '**33** Duck Soup.
Groucho, Harpo and Chico: '**35** A Night at the Opera. '**37** A Day at the Races. '**38** Room Service. '**39** At the Circus. '**40** Go West. '**41** The Big Store. '**46** A Night in Casablanca. '**49** Love Happy. '**57** The Story of Mankind (separate appearances).
Harpo only: '**25** Too Many Kisses. '**36** La Fiesta de Santa Barbara (short). '**43** Stage Door Canteen. '**44** Hollywood Canteen. '**45** All-Star Bond Rally. *Groucho only*: '**37** The King and the Chorus Girl (co-sc. only). '**47** Copacabana. '**50** Mr Music. '**51** Double Dynamite. '**52** A Girl in Every Port.

started a talent agency. Zeppo had never been happy with his role as a straight-man. 'I always wanted to be a comedian, but I came along too late, and three comedians in the act was already enough.' Gummo, who had been out of show business since his discharge from the army in 1919 and never appeared in the films, joined Zeppo, and the two built their agency into one of the biggest in Hollywood. One of Zeppo's first deals for the Marx Brothers was buying the rights to the Broadway hit *Room Service* for their next picture in 1938.

Thalberg's premature death during the filming of *A Day at the Races* marked a crucial point in the Marx Brothers' career as a team. No longer did they have their champion at the biggest studio in Hollywood. Their next three pictures, *At the Circus* (1939), *Go West* (1940), and *The Big Store* (1941), were made for MGM on a production-line basis, and by 1942 they were ready to retire as a team, each brother going his own way professionally.

The laughter maker

Groucho, who had published *Beds* in 1930, continued to write, eventually writing five books. He had always aspired to being a writer, even before wanting to become an actor, and he was as proud of his literary output as of anything else he ever did. He was also proud of being able to make people laugh. 'It's a lot easier to make people cry than it is to make them laugh,' he said. Groucho also tried radio but was unsuccessful until *You Bet Your Life* in 1948. Although he was known as one of the screen's great talkers, the visual aspects of his comic style were important, too. 'The way he moved greatly enhanced his character,' Lee Strasberg noted. Studying the famous dialogues between Groucho and Chico, one immediately becomes aware of Groucho's sense of movement, even in a static scene. He is always in motion, yet what he does is so appropriate to what is being said that it heightens it while not being obtrusive. Director King Vidor noted that Groucho's reactions were always perfect, and that reacting is the most difficult aspect of film acting.

Final Marx

During their first 'retirement' Harpo and Chico continued to make personal appearances on stage, in concert, or at nightclubs, sometimes alone, sometimes together. Occasionally Chico would join Groucho on a radio broadcast, but by 1945 Chico, who was an inveterate gambler, was broke. To help Chico, the other brothers agreed to come out of retirement and made *A Night in Casablanca* in 1946. This film, which satirized *Casablanca* (1942), was successful but the team disbanded again immediately afterwards. However, a later reunion, *Love Happy* (1949), was not successful, and the team made only one more professional appearance, in a television special called *The Incredible Jewel Robbery* (1960). In neither of these last two productions does Groucho make more than a cameo appearance. At the time his own career was soaring with starring roles in major motion pictures and with his own successful TV quiz show, *You Bet Your Life*.

Chico died in 1961 (aged 74), Harpo in 1964 (aged 75), Gummo in 1977 (aged 80) and Groucho in 1977 just before his 87th birthday. Zeppo, who was born in 1901, lives in Palm Springs. He has not been associated with show business for years.

Others have tried this same kind of irreverent comedy, but none with the *élan* or style of the Marx Brothers. Groucho, Harpo, Chico, and Zeppo really *were* those zany characters they played on stage and screen.

As children, the Marx Brothers slept four in a bed, two at each end, and early developed the respect for each other's privacy and the close friendship that lasted throughout their lives. Groucho once said:

'We played every town in America and I think we were the only group that never fought. No act in vaudeville got along better than we did. There never was anyone like my brothers and me.' He was right.

Margaret Dumont

Margaret Dumont was a versatile actress who played a wide range of roles during her 60-year theatrical career, but she will always be remembered as the naive social climber who so confidently entrusted her rise in society to Groucho in seven Marx Brothers films.

Born Daisy Baker in 1889 in Atlanta, Georgia, she was brought up in the home of her godfather, Joel Chandler Harris, creator of Uncle Remus, Brer Rabbit, and Brer Fox. While still in her teens she became an actress, choosing as her stage name Daisy Dumont. She trained first for the opera, and then served her theatrical apprenticeship for two years as a show girl in the music halls of England and France, making her debut at the Casino de Paris. Reviewers commented on the 'tall, statuesque and beautiful' Daisy Dumont. She was playing in a musical, *The Summer Widowers*, when she met John Moller Jr, son of a wealthy businessman and a member of New York's socially prominent '400' families. They were married in 1910.

When her husband died, Margaret Dumont resumed her theatrical career; 'My husband's family didn't entirely approve of my return to the stage,' she used to say, and it was while she was acting the part of a social climber in *The Four Flusher* that Sam Harris, who was producing *The Cocoanuts* on stage, cast her as Mrs Potter which was to be the first of her many comic trysts with Groucho.

Morrie Ryskind, co-author of *The Cocoanuts* (1929), *Animal Crackers* (1930) and *A Night at the Opera* (1935), recalled that Margaret Dumont really was the character she played so successfully on stage and screen:

'She'd been a social lady, and her husband died, so she needed a job. Groucho would explain to her that something was funny, and she would walk out to the audience and ask them what was going on.'

Groucho described his favourite leading lady in the same way:

'I enjoyed all my romantic scenes with Margaret Dumont. She was a wonderful woman. She was the same offstage as she was on it – always the stuffy, dignified matron. She took everything seriously. She would say to me: "Julie, why are they laughing?"'

Actress Margaret O'Sullivan said that Margaret Dumont actually believed that *A Day at the Races* (1937) was a serious film:

'I used to get a lot of fun out of Margaret Dumont. She had no idea why *A Day at the Races* was funny or even that it was funny. When we started, she told me: "It's not going to be one of *those* things, I'm having a very *serious* part this time".'

But in fact Margaret Dumont herself was far from naive about her contribution to *A Day at the Races*, for which she won the Screen Actors Guild award in 1937:

'I'm a straight lady, the best in Hollywood. There is an art to playing the straight role. You must build up your man but never top him, never steal the laughs.'

She once expressed her own conception of her famous dignity:

'It isn't the gown or its fine material that makes a woman stylish or otherwise nowadays, but her carriage and the amount of clothing she has on beneath the gown.'

Besides the 7 Marx Brothers films, Margaret Dumont appeared in 36 others, including memorable performances in *Never Give a Sucker an Even Break* (1941) with W.C. Fields and *The Horn Blows at Midnight* (1945) with Jack Benny. In her last film, *What a Way to Go* (1964), she played Shirley MacLaine's shrewish mother so convincingly that few recognized her as the *grande dame* of the Marx Brothers comedies. She herself was happily resigned to being type-cast.

She died of a heart attack on March 6, 1965, at the age of 76. That inimitable quality which set her apart from all other actresses was perhaps best described by George Cukor, who directed her in *The Women*: 'Her elegance was so perfectly bogus.'

Below: Captain Spaulding woos Mrs Rittenhouse in Animal Crackers

Filmography

1917 A Tale of Two Cities. **'29** The Cocoanuts. **'30** Animal Crackers. **'31** The Girl Habit. **'33** Duck Soup. **'34** Fifteen Wives (GB: The Man With the Electric Voice); Kentucky Kernels (GB: Triple Trouble); Gridiron Flash (GB: Luck of the Game). **'35** A Night at the Opera; Orchids to You; Rendezvous. **'36** Song and Dance Man; Anything Goes. **'37** A Day at the Races; Life of the Party; Youth on Parole; High Flyers; Wise Girl. **'38** Dramatic School. **'39** The Women; At the Circus. **'41** The Big Store; For Beauty's Sake; Never Give a Sucker an Even Break (GB: What a Man). **'42** Born to Sing; Sing Your Worries Away; About Face; Rhythm Parade; Dancing Masters. **'44** Up in Arms; Seven Days Ashore; Bathing Beauty. **'45** The Horn Blows at Midnight; Sunset in Eldorado; Diamond Horseshoe. **'46** Little Giant (GB: On the Carpet); Susie Steps Out. **'52** Three for Bedroom C. **'53** Stop, You're Killing Me. **'56** Shake, Rattle and Rock. **'59** Auntie Mame (uncredited). **'62** Zotz! **'64** What a Way to Go!

ALFRED HITCHCOCK

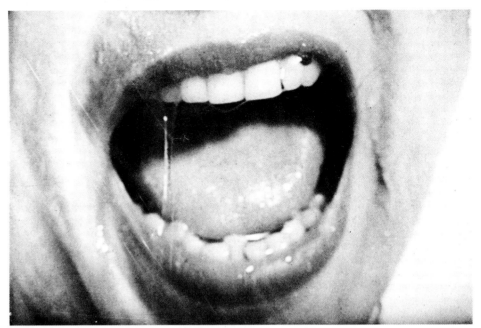

MOMENTS OF FEAR

A glimpse of the Master's world of terror

Hitchcock's creative genius expresses itself through a series of visual or aural effects – startling conjuring tricks calculated to make audiences gasp or giggle. In the course of his long career – he was born in 1899 and started working in films in 1919 – Hitchcock has created hundreds of these moments of virtuosity. He employs trick photography, bizarre settings, striking film and soundtrack editing, and telling single shots or whole sequences that have a fantastic or nightmarish reality of their own. Some of these devices are present in his earliest films, but their full impact was first visible in *The Lodger* (1926).

This silent film is built largely upon a succession of effects. A quick, impressionistic montage at the beginning shows London terrorized by an unknown Jack the Ripper-like murderer. The opening is followed by a series of 'virtuoso' set-piece scenes which made audiences, at that time not usually aware of the director's hand, realize that here was someone of importance behind the camera. *The Lodger*'s most famous device shows the anxiety of an ordinary suburban family disturbed by the endless pacing of their mysterious lodger upstairs. Hitchcock built a glass floor and filmed from below as the man paced across it – an effect that greatly impressed critics and public in 1926.

His next substantial success, *Blackmail* (1929), was begun as a silent movie, but by this time cinema audiences were eager to see talking films, so the producers decided to insert a few lines of dialogue into the last reel. This did not satisfy Hitchcock who secretly shot

additional scenes for the film in sound.

His gamble paid off: the producers were so encouraged by what he showed them that they allowed *Blackmail* to be reshot with sound. It was Britain's first all-talking film. Despite the addition of sound and dialogue, Hitchcock retained the silent film's freedom of movement and avoided the danger of making 'photographs of people talking'. It, too, had a show-piece scene which attracted particular attention. The heroine has, half-accidentally, stabbed a would-be seducer to death and returned home just in time to cover her absence. At breakfast the next morning a neighbour chatters about the murder – now reported in the papers: 'What a terrible way to kill a man. With a *knife* in his back. A *knife* is a terrible thing. A *knife* is so messy and dreadful . . .' The words run together so as to be almost indistinguishable, except for the word 'knife' stabbing out of its context again and again, as though audibly striking the guilt-ridden girl.

The effect is there to be noticed, and noticeable it is, perhaps at the expense of the rest of the film, since it is rather showy and self-conscious. Nevertheless, at the time it demonstrated to producers, the public and especially the unwilling critics – who looked askance at the new talkie medium – that sound, and even dialogue, could be used creatively. The talkie did not have to be merely a photographed stage play but had other, more exciting possibilities. *Blackmail* confirmed Hitchcock as the most important and talented British film-maker of his day.

In 1934, he began the great series of six suspense thrillers, made in four years, which carried his reputation round the world and finally took him to Hollywood in 1939. The first of them, *The Man Who Knew Too Much*, established his penchant for the brilliantly conceived effect as the basis of film-making. A family on holiday in St Moritz witness the murder of a secret agent who, before he dies, tells them of a plan to assassinate a foreign diplomat in London. Realizing this, the enemy spies kidnap the couple's daughter to ensure their silence. The couple have to thwart the villains' plans without police help.

Whereas in *The Lodger* and *Blackmail* the tricks had tended to stand out from the overall texture, *The Man Who Knew Too Much* was virtually a succession of memorable scenes and incidents which kept the audience totally at the director's mercy. This became Hitchcock's hallmark during the Thirties and still remains an important part of his style.

Not everyone approved – Graham Greene,

Right and far right: tennis star Guy Haines (Farley Granger) and suave, beguiling Bruno (Robert Walker) meet as Strangers on a Train. *Bruno tells Guy his plan for the perfect murder – two people exchange victims and so the crimes appear motiveless. A shocked Guy learns later that his wife has been murdered by Bruno – who wants his father murdered in return . . . at a society party, Bruno playfully demonstrates strangling to a guest. Barbara (Patricia Hitchcock), looking on, does not share his macabre sense of fun . . .*

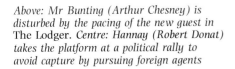

Above: Mr Bunting (Arthur Chesney) is disturbed by the pacing of the new guest in The Lodger. *Centre: Hannay (Robert Donat) takes the platform at a political rally to avoid capture by pursuing foreign agents*

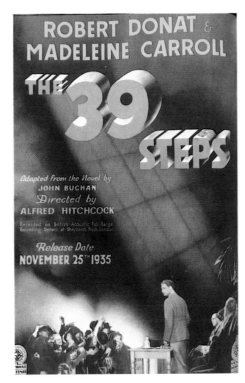

Above: the Suspicion *that her charming husband Johnny (Cary Grant) is a murderer haunts Lina (Joan Fontaine). She is paralyzed with fear when he brings her a bedtime glass of milk. Is it poisoned? Does he want to kill her too . . .?*

then influential film critic of the *Spectator*, wrote of *The Secret Agent* (1936):

'His films consist of a series of small "amusing" melodramatic situations: the murderer's button dropped on the baccarat board; the strangled organist's hands prolonging the notes in the empty church; the fugitives hiding in the bell-tower when the bell begins to swing. Very perfunctorily he builds up to these tricky situations (paying no attention on the way to inconsistencies, loose ends, psychological absurdities) and then drops them: they mean nothing: they lead to nothing.'

It is curious that Greene, of all people, should have been quite so unsympathetic to what Hitchcock was doing in these films, since it was so close to those stories of his own that he labelled 'entertainments'. Hitchcock was always first and foremost a popular entertainer, with no overt pretensions, leaving

others to find deeper meanings in his work. His way of involving his audience was to deploy his unique technical skills and extraordinary inventive faculties in the elaboration of telling incident through specific effect. There are many single shots in the British thrillers which everyone who has seen them remembers. There is, for instance, the famous shot near the end of *Young and Innocent* (1937) in which the camera travels slowly across a crowded ballroom during a *thé dansant*, moving closer and closer to the black-face band, then concentrating on the drummer and finally pausing in an arresting close-up of his eye twitching – the crucial identifying mark of the murderer.

But memorable though such isolated moments are, and though Hitchcock enjoyed devising them and making them work, the dramatic effects in his films are usually more far-reaching. There are whole sequences that use or exploit well-known conventions of suspense. Take, for example, the idea of there being 'safety in numbers'. In *The Thirty-Nine Steps* (1935), the hero, Hannay, hotly pursued by foreign agents, stumbles into a political meeting. Realizing that his only hope of escape

is to get up and speak, he delivers an absurd, off-the-cuff speech and makes himself so conspicuous that the villains are unable to do anything to him for fear of giving themselves away. Hitchcock liked this idea so well that he later used variations of it in the two American films which had similar chase formulas to *The Thirty-Nine Steps*, *Saboteur* (1942) and *North by Northwest* (1959).

Yet crowds and public places are not always havens from danger – they can also conceal it. The climactic scene of *The Man Who Knew Too Much* occurs at the Royal Albert Hall during the performance of a cantata; the sound of the assassin's bullet is planned to coincide with the clash of cymbals at the end of the piece. In *The Thirty-Nine Steps*, Mr Memory is murdered on stage in full view of the music-hall audience, while, in a superb sequence in *Foreign*

Above: in The Man Who Knew Too Much, *Dr McKenna (James Stewart) and his wife, Jo (Doris Day), witness the murder of a French agent. With his dying breath he tells McKenna of an assassination plot. The doctor soon discovers that he knows too much for his own – and his family's – good . . .*

Correspondent (1940), a diplomat, surrounded by umbrella-carrying crowds, is murdered during a downpour. His assassin, posing as a reporter, shoots him with a gun hidden in his camera.

Hitchcock arrived in Hollywood in 1939. He still continued to work primarily within the thriller genre, telling his stories in the same strongly graphic style and taking the same infinite pains to set up particular effects. Indeed, there were many critics who complained in the Forties that he became even more self-conscious in his use of gimmicks in order to disguise a lack of inspiration. However, some of his devices did transcend gimmickry even during this comparatively slack period: the idea of shooting, completely against the Hollywood convention of the time, all the exteriors of *Shadow of a Doubt* (1943) in the real-life town of Santa Rosa, instead of on a studio back-lot, paid handsome dividends in terms of authenticity and vivid local colour. Other devices, like employing Salvador Dali to devise the dream sequence in *Spellbound* (1945), were at least interesting failures.

Hitchcock's most powerful film of this period is *Notorious* (1946). This has one-shot effects in plenty, such as the alleged longest kiss in screen history, between Cary Grant and Ingrid Bergman, and the climactic shot in which the camera takes in a smart party from the top of the stairs and then gradually swoops down into extreme close-up of a vital key secretly held in Ingrid Bergman's hand as she stands at the door greeting guests; it also has a powerfully constructed screenplay by Ben Hecht from a story by Hitchcock himself. Devlin, played by Cary Grant, is an American agent given the task of discovering Nazi secrets in Rio de Janeiro. He offers Alicia Hubermann (Ingrid Bergman), whose father has earlier been sentenced for treason against the USA, a job as an undercover agent. This she accepts, hoping to expiate her father's crimes. The prime suspect is Alexander Sebastian (Claude Rains), who soon falls under Alicia's spell and desires to

marry her. She agrees, despite her feelings for Devlin, in order to find out more information. The organization's secrets are discovered, but Sebastian realizes Alicia's identity and plans to poison her. She is almost on the point of death when she is rescued by Devlin, who has grown to trust and love her. Sebastian is left to explain this situation to his irate confederates.

Despite the success of *Notorious*, Hitchcock's tendency to allow style to dominate content in his films was still criticized, and not until his second great period, which runs from *Strangers on a Train* (1951) to *Marnie* (1964) did he satisfy the most determined doubters.

Though these films still have surprising effects, such as the fairground strangling of *Strangers on a Train* portrayed solely as a series

of reflections in the victim's glasses which have fallen on the grass, these are normally integrated into the structure of the film. A whole film may be dominated by a single effect, such as *Rear Window* (1954) with its studied observation of everything outside from the point of

Below and bottom: in North by Northwest *a bad case of mistaken identity finds Roger Thornhill (Cary Grant) cornered in an auction room by would-be killers. His plan of escape is to create such an uproar that he has to be escorted out . . . Tracking down the villainous foreign agents to their hideout on Mt Rushmore, he is captured, but escapes at night with a beautiful double-agent, Eve (Eve Marie Saint). The climax is truly cliff-hanging . . .*

Left: As Melanie (Tippi Hedren) is collecting Cathy (Veronica Cartwright) from school, the children are attacked by The Birds. *She gets Cathy into her car but the birds swoop down, crashing against the windscreen . . .*

Above: in Family Plot, *George (Bruce Dern) and Blanche (Barbara Harris) are stranded on a lonely mountain road. Though Blanche is a medium, she fails to foresee peril when a car appears in pursuit of them . . .*

view of the temporarily crippled hero. But most of the later films have a new depth, a new disturbing charge of emotion. The feelings may sometimes be bizarre, as in *Vertigo* (1958) in which the hero morbidly tries to remake a girl he picks up into the image of his (as he supposes) dead love, or *Marnie*, where the hero perversely determines to rape a pathological liar and thief into normality; but there is no doubt about their strength and consistency. *North by Northwest* (1959) and *Psycho* (1960) are perhaps the best of these later films. The former is a sort of nostalgic harking-back to the world of the British thrillers, while *Psycho* is the most beamingly brutal, blackest of black comedies, a technical and dramatic *tour de force* which Hitchcock has never surpassed. Almost every scene is a set piece, until one ends by accepting its baroque texture as some kind of crazy standard. However often the spine-chilling murder in the shower is seen, it is impossible to be completely prepared, completely impervious to its terrors.

Hitchcock began his career with a young man's fascination with innovation. His sheer delight in putting all his goods in the shop window was in itself infectious. But from *Strangers on a Train* onwards Hitchcock proved himself a master of his medium, able to integrate his effects into the structure and content of the film instead of being carried away by them.

He wryly observed in *Film Review* in 1946:

'In the old days of melodrama they used to bring the sawmill in out of the blue – no excuse for it, it was just there when the heroine's neck needed cutting.

'We are more realistic now. It is an age of enlightenment and taste. We make the heroine the daughter of a lumberjack.'

Filmography

1922 Number Thirteen (unfinished). **'23** Always Tell Your Husband (short) (uncredited dir). **'25** The Pleasure Garden. **'26** The Mountain Eagle (USA: Fear o' God); The Lodger (+co-sc) (USA: The Case of Jonathan Drew). **'27** Downhill (USA: When Boys Leave Home); Easy Virtue; The Ring (+co-sc). **'28** The Farmer's Wife (+co-sc); Champagne (+co-sc); The Manxman. **'29** Blackmail (silent and sound versions) (+co-sc). **'30** Juno and the Paycock (+co-sc) (USA: The Shame of Mary Boyle); Elstree Calling (co-dir); Murder (+co-sc); An Elastic Affair (short); Mary/Sir John Grieft Ein! (GB-GER) (German version of Murder). **'31** The Skin Game (+co-sc). **'32** Rich and Strange (+co-sc) (USA: East of Shanghai); Number Seventeen (+co-sc); Lord Camber's Ladies (prod. only). **'33** Waltzes from Vienna (USA: Strauss's Great Waltz). **'34** The Man Who Knew Too Much. **'35** The Thirty-Nine Steps. **'36** The Secret Agent; Sabotage (USA: The Woman Alone/Hidden Power (reissue)). **'37** Young and Innocent (USA: The Girl Was Young). **'38** The Lady Vanishes. **'39** Jamaica Inn. *All remaining films USA unless specified:* **'40** Rebecca; Foreign Correspondent. **'41** Mr and Mrs Smith; Suspicion. **'42** Saboteur. **'43** Shadow of a Doubt. **'44** Lifeboat; Bon Voyage (GB) (short for war effort); Aventure Malagache (GB) (short for war effort). **'45** Concentration (doc. unfinished); Spellbound. **'46** Notorious. **'47** The Paradine Case. **'48** Rope (+prod). **'49** Under Capricorn (+prod) (GB); Stage Fright (+prod) (GB). **'51** Strangers on a Train (+prod). **'52** I Confess (+prod). **'54** Dial M for Murder (+prod); Rear Window (+prod). **'55** To Catch a Thief (+prod). **'56** The Trouble with Harry (+prod); The Man Who Knew Too Much (+prod). **'57** The Wrong Man (+prod). **'58** Vertigo (+prod). **'59** North by Northwest (+prod). **'60** Psycho (+prod). **'63** The Birds (+prod). **'64** Marnie (+prod). **'66** Torn Curtain (+prod). **'69** Topaz (+prod). **'72** Frenzy (+prod) (GB). **'76** Family Plot (+prod).

Alexander Korda
Director, producer and maker of stars

Korda was born Sándor Kellner on September 16, 1893, near Túrkeve, Hungary. He worked as a journalist and editor of a film magazine before directing his first film in 1914. Two younger brothers, Zoltán and Vincent, were later to work with him as director and art director respectively.

Korda's turbulent 25 years in Britain tend to overshadow his previous 17 years as a director in his native Hungary and later in Vienna, Berlin, Hollywood and Paris. Although he and Michael Curtiz dominated the early Hungarian film industry between 1917 and 1919, Korda was scarcely known outside his own country during that period.

When the communist regime of Béla Kun fell in 1919, Korda fled the country. He emigrated with his actress wife, Maria Corda, to Vienna where he directed four films. The first, an adaptation of Mark Twain's novel *The Prince and the Pauper*, was successfully released in America. The praise for its evocative recreation of British pageantry convinced Korda that foreign directors could effectively handle national subjects outside their own experience. In Berlin, from 1922–26, with films like *Das Unbekannte Morgen* (1923, *The Unknown Tomorrow*) he accommodated his own preference for light romantic subjects, adopting the Expressionist preoccupations with destiny and mysticism then fashionable in German cinema. Determined to make films that would attract Hollywood, Korda directed the lavish and sophisticated *Eine Dubarry von Heute* (*A Modern Dubarry*) in 1926. It earned him a contract with First National in Hollywood which he took up early in 1927.

During his four years in Hollywood (1927–30), however, Korda was typecast as a director of female stars or of films with Hungarian settings. The only notable film he made there, *The Private Life of Helen of Troy*

Alexander Korda remains one of the most remarkable and controversial figures in British film history. His charismatic personality combined ambition and great charm with a flair for showmanship that delighted his admirers as much as it infuriated his critics

(1927), was an impressively photographed version of the Greek legend, reshaped into a marital comedy, with the characters given contemporary speech and attitudes. This humanizing approach to history, though anticipated by Lubitsch's German costume pictures, became the model for Korda's later films.

Korda returned to Europe in 1930. At Paramount's French subsidiary at Joinville he made *Marius* (1931), the first of the trilogy of film adaptations from Marcel Pagnol's plays about Marseilles life.

In the autumn of 1931 Alexander Korda came to Britain to direct 'quota' pictures for Paramount's British subsidiary, but within a few months he had decided to form his own company, London Film Productions. The company's sixth production, *The Private Life of Henry VIII* (1933), achieved Korda's goal of successful competition in world markets. It captured the American box-office and earned ten times its cost in its first world run. Historical costume films were considered passé at the time, but Korda 'humanized' a well-known historical subject, turning it into a sex romp which owed much to the vitality of Charles Laughton's performance.

For the next seven years, Korda sought to build on *Henry*'s success, first with other 'private life' films (*The Rise of Catherine the Great* and *The Private Life of Don Juan* in 1934, both box-office failures) and then with a series of over 30 prestige films for which Korda mixed and matched the nationalities and talents he had collected to achieve an international production. Although none of the subsequent films equalled *Henry*'s profitability (as they all cost much more to make, they could hardly be expected to recoup proportionally as much), even a selective list shows how much the British film industry owed to this emigré Hungarian: *The Scarlet Pimpernel* (1934), *Things To Come* and *Rembrandt* (both 1936), *Fire Over England* and *Knight Without Armour* (both 1937), *The Drum* (1938), *The Four Feathers* (1939) and *The Thief of Bagdad* (1940).

All these films exhibited the Korda stamp in varying degrees, according to the amount of control he exerted as head of production. This stamp is best defined by a brief analysis of his strengths and weaknesses as a film director.

Although associated with all the 100 films which London Films produced between 1932 and 1956, he directed only 8 of them. The subjects he chose tended to fall into two categories: the satirical, high-society comedies: *Wedding Rehearsal* (1933), *The Girl from Maxim's* (1933) and *An Ideal Husband* (1947); and the 'private life' films (*The Private Life of Henry VIII*, *The Private Life of Don Juan*, *Rembrandt* and *That Hamilton Woman!* (1941).

The most outstanding quality common to all these films is their visual polish, which owes much to French cameraman Georges Périnal and to Korda's brother Vincent, London Films' head of art direction. These two men created impressive films that rivalled anything produced in Hollywood, both in grandeur of scope and sumptuousness of detail. Established actors and actresses were chosen for the lead parts, while Korda cast the supporting roles from his stable of young contract starlets. There is an urgency and vitality in the acting of the experienced players, but Korda sometimes seems unsure in the direction of his untrained actors (the new stars he loved to create), contenting himself with glamorizing them or treating them as part of the decor. Even though Korda considered the script stage the most important in the making of a film (he worked uncredited on many of the scripts of his and others' movies), the basic structure of his films is often too flimsy to support their load of over-elaborate detail. There is a tendency towards repetition of scenes and dialogue, and the dialogue itself is unconvincing and often depends heavily on rather childish metaphors. The films he directed and those he produced mostly share a nostalgic view of Britain and

Left: Alexander Korda. Top left: nymphs and satyrs sport together in The Private Life of Helen of Troy. *Top right and right:* The Four Feathers *and* The Drum *were action-packed 'British Empire' films directed by Zoltan Korda. Below:* Things to Come *was a bold attempt to forecast 100 years of Man's future*

proudly champion her past glories.

What Korda lacked as a film-maker, however, he made up for as a film impresario, combining a fertile imagination, always open to new ideas, with a journalist's understanding of publicity and promotion. But his special gift was his ability to manipulate finance and financiers, and it was this which was to be most exercised during the late Thirties.

The business of making internationally marketable films was an expensive one, and London Films required immense financial investment. This came from two sources: the American United Artists Company (in which Korda became a full partner in 1935) and the City of London's Prudential Assurance Company. The United Artists tie-up was a mixed blessing as UA owned no cinema chains itself and could not guarantee American distribution for Korda's films. Heavy investment by the Prudential became Korda's mainstay in the Thirties and led to the building of Denham studios. Opened in 1936, Denham was the most up-to-date studio in Europe, yet it was too

large for a single producer and, by the time it was fully operational, the investment boom in the film industry, caused by the success of *Henry VIII*, had given way to a slump. Korda was forced to add cheaper features to his production schedules and to accept independent producers as tenants to fill Denham's empty stages. Korda found himself losing control of Denham to the financiers (eventually to J. Arthur Rank). He was finally forced to become a tenant producer in the studio he had built just a few years before.

Having gone to Hollywood in 1940 to supervise the completion of *The Thief of Bagdad*, Korda stayed there to direct *That Hamilton Woman!* in which Nelson's efforts against the French became an open metaphor for Britain's current war with Germany. This film earned him a subpoena from isolationist American senators who charged him with making the American branch of his company a centre for pro-British propaganda. Although criticized by many in Britain for having 'deserted' to Hollywood, Korda did in fact make several transatlantic crossings during the war and it now seems clear that he was acting as a courier for Winston Churchill. In 1942 he was knighted by King George VI, the first film personality to be so honoured.

In the summer of 1943, Sir Alexander

Filmography

In Hungary: **1914** A becsapott újságíró: Tutyu és Totyo. **'15** Lyon Lea: A tiszti kardbojt. **'16** Fehér éjszakák/Fedora: A nagymama (+sc); Mesék az írógéprol (+sc); A kétszívu ferfi; Az egymillió fontos bankó (+sc); Ciklámen; Vergodo szívek: A nevoto Szaszkia; Mágnás Miska. **'17** Szent Péter esernyoje; A gólyakalifa; Mágia; Harrison és Barrison. **'18** Faun; Az aranyember; Mary Ann. **'19** Ave Caesar!; Feher rozsa; Yamata; Se ki, se be; A 111-es. *In Austria*: **'20** Seine Majestät das Bettelkind/Prinz und Bettelknabe (GB: The Prince and the Pauper). **'22** Herren der Meere; Eine Versunkene Welt; Samson und Delila, der Roman Einer Opernsängerin (+co-sc) (GB: Samson and Delilah). *In Germany*: **'23** Das Unbekannte Morgen (+prod; +co-sc) (GB: The Unknown Tomorrow). **'24** Jedermanns Frau (+sc); Tragödie im Hause Habsburg (+prod). **'25** Der Tänzer Meiner Frau (+co-sc) (GB: Dancing Mad). **'26** Madame Wünscht Keine Kinder (USA: Madame Wants No Children); Eine Dubarry von Heute (GB: A Modern Dubarry). *In USA*: The Stolen Bride; **'27** The Private Life of Helen of Troy. **'28** Yellow Lily; Night Watch. **'29** Love and the Devil; The Squall; Her Private Life. **'30** Lilies of the Field; Women Everywhere; The Princess and the Plumber. *In France/Britain/USA*: **'31** Die Männer um Lucie (FR); Rive Gauche (FR); Marius (FR); Zum Goldenen Anker (FR). **'32** Service for Ladies (+prod) (GB). **'33** Wedding Rehearsal (+prod) (GB); The Private Life of Henry VIII (+prod) (GB); The Girl from Maxim's (+co-prod) (FR). **'34** La Dame de Chez Maxim (French version of The Girl from Maxim's) (+co-prod) (FR); The Private Life of Don Juan (+prod) (GB). **'36** Rembrandt (+prod) (GB). **'41** That Hamilton Woman! (+prod) (USA) (GB: Lady Hamilton). **'45** Perfect Strangers (+prod) (GB) (USA: Vacation from Marriage). **'47** An Ideal Husband (+prod) (GB).

Of the 102 films with which Korda was associated as producer, executive producer or 'presenter' between 1933 and 1956, the most important include: **'34** The Rise of Catherine the Great (USA: Catherine the Great); The Scarlet Pimpernel. **'35** Sanders of the River (USA: Bosambo); The Ghost Goes West. **'36** Things To Come. **'37** The Man Who Could Work Miracles; Fire Over England; I, Claudius (unfinished); Elephant Boy; Knight Without Armour. **'38** The Drum (USA: Drums). **'39** The Four Feathers; The Spy in Black (USA: U-Boat 29); The Lion Has Wings. **'40** The Thief of Bagdad. **'41** Lydia. **'42** Jungle Book. **'48** Anna Karenina; The Fallen Idol. **'49** The Third Man. **'51** The Tales of Hoffman. **'52** Outcast of the Islands; Cry, the Beloved Country (USA: African Fury); The Sound Barrier (USA: Breaking the Sound Barrier). **'54** Hobson's Choice. **'55** A Kid for Two Farthings; Summer Madness; Storm Over the Nile. **'56** Richard III.

Korda returned to London and spent two frustrating years trying to set up the merged MGM-British/London Film Productions company from which he then resigned in late 1945 having completed only one film, *Perfect Strangers* (1945). Throughout 1946 he was busy resurrecting London Films as a separate company. Korda, tired of directing, was now the executive producer – an administrator and businessman. After 1947, his name ceased to appear on the film credits, and as the name disappeared, so did the old Korda style. His major triumph during his last years was in drawing a large number of independent British film-makers to his company and allowing them freedom to work without interference. Directors like Michael Powell and Emeric Pressburger, Carol Reed, David Lean, Anthony Asquith, Frank Launder and Sidney Gilliat and Laurence Olivier made some of their best films while working under the aegis of Korda's umbrella organization.

To obtain adequate distribution for these films, Korda gained control of British Lion in 1946, and rebuilt and refitted Shepperton Studios which became London Film's production base. During the 1948 financial crisis in the film industry, Korda's British Lion secured the first government loan to the film business through the newly created National Film Finance Corporation. By 1954 the NFFC loan, amounting to £3 million, had still not been repaid, and with the appointment of an official receiver for British Lion, the second Korda film empire collapsed. Even after this debacle, Korda was able to form new financial alliances which enabled him to continue producing films until his death in 1956.

Top left: Merle Oberon, the star Korda created and married. Top right: That Hamilton Woman!, *Winston Churchill's favourite film, caused a political storm in the USA. Below: Laurence Olivier in* Richard III, *one of the last and most prestigious films backed by Korda*

Korda was almost as famous for the films he did not make as for the ones he did – indeed, he received the honour of having an entire television documentary devoted to footage from a film, *I Claudius* (directed by Josef von Sternberg), which was abandoned after a month's shooting. He was more successful as a producer than as a director and his reputation for extravagance now seems deserved. Yet he demonstrated to the world 'that in spectacle and lavishness of production the British industry could legitimately hope to match the best that America could produce'.

Busby Berkeley:
the man who matched girls like pearls

If Ziegfeld had not used the film title *Glorifying the American Girl* in 1929, it would make an ideal description for the work of Busby Berkeley. Berkeley knew a very great deal about girls, even though at first he did not know much about dance. However, dance directors in the Twenties had a rather different job from those of today. Then, the dance director was more a stage manager who had picked up the rudiments of moving people around on stage, and less a trained dancer or experienced choreographer.

Although Busby Berkeley's background was appropriate for this kind of occupation – he was born in 1895 of an actress mother and a stage-director father – his parents determinedly turned him away from a stage career. But in the army during World War I, he discovered a talent for devising trick drills to display the skill and precision of as many as 1200 men. After the war he sought work in the theatre.

Before long he found himself playing comic leads in touring musicals, while earning a bit of extra money by turning his skill in patterned drilling to the fairly elementary demands of stage choreography at the time. His first Broadway show was called *Holka Polka*, performed in 1926; his first big hit was Rodgers and Hart's *A Connecticut Yankee* in 1927, followed by another Rodgers and Hart musical *Present Arms*. With no special musical or dance training, he was already getting favourable notices for his use of intricate jazz rhythms in his routines, which he improvised in rehearsal with the girls on stage in front of him.

His arrival in Hollywood seems to have been equally unpremeditated. Early in 1930, Sam Goldwyn persuaded him to make the journey westward to direct the dance numbers of *Whoopee!*, starring Eddie Cantor. It was still early days in the talkies, and musicals had not yet outgrown their first flush of popularity. As a musical specialist on Broadway, Berkeley was an obvious choice to direct film musicals.

Probably no one expected him to do anything more than recreate on film the kind of routine he had done on stage. But that was not his way. His first action (after insisting that he direct the camera as well as the dancers) was to dismiss three of the four cameras normally placed around the set, and use a single camera-eye which he treated as a dynamic participant in the action.

Berkeley seems to have appreciated instinctively that film space is completely fictional and may be rearranged at will from shot to shot without any necessity for literal continuity. Nevertheless, literal-minded critics objected to his filmed routines at first, saying that his scenes shot from immediately above the centre of a pattern of girls did not correspond to any natural human viewpoint. Later, when many of his biggest sequences were ostensibly set on a theatre stage, they objected that no real theatre could possibly accommodate them – and in any case no theatre audience could possibly see enough from a real auditorium to make sense of them.

All of which seems to have worried him not a jot. Berkeley firmly avoided theorization. And though it is unlikely that he would have wished to claim any kinship between his

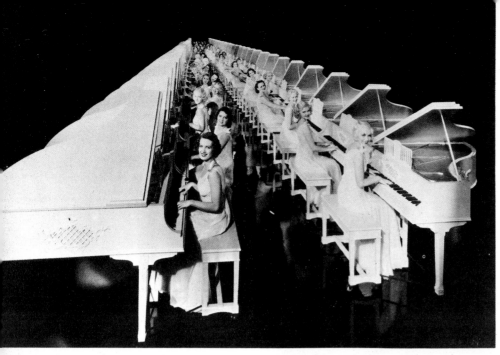

Above: the piano number from Gold Diggers of 1935. *Above right: slave girls in the 'No More Love' number from* Roman Scandals, *the first Hollywood musical to feature nude girls. Right: human harps in* Fashions of 1934

musical numbers and European avant-garde art, it is still tempting to see connections with the so-called 'Cubist' experiments of Léger, Man Ray and others during the Twenties. They sought to film people and objects in a manner that would transform them into abstract patterns. Berkeley's is also an abstract world, in which the pictures seldom tell a story but instead evoke a vague, diffused eroticism.

Berkeley's remarkable approach to the musical routine was first fully realized in *42nd Street*, made for Warner Brothers in 1933. By this time, the early talkie craze for musicals had passed and for a couple of years they had been regarded as box-office poison. Berkeley, almost single-handedly, re-established them with his unparalleled gift for spectacle. The title number of *42nd Street* was outstanding, as was the 'Shuffle Off to Buffalo' routine which showed a whole train of sleeping cars dividing and reconnecting on stage.

The style revealed in *42nd Street* was then ever more extravagantly exploited in *Gold Diggers of 1933*, *Footlight Parade* (both 1933), *Dames* (1934) and in many more Warner Brothers films throughout the Thirties – his great period. He directed several complete musicals and a handful of dramatic films, including *They Made Me a Criminal* (1939), but only in the conceiving and filming of dance numbers was his touch truly original.

In 1939 he moved to MGM and repeated the formula with decreasing success for another decade. The arrival of the integrated dramatic musical, following the success of *On the Town* (1949, dir. Gene Kelly, Stanley Donen), made his 'plums-in-the-pudding' approach to musical routines look old-fashioned, though he continued to work on the occasional speciality piece in other directors' films up to 1962.

Since his death in 1976 his reputation has rested on these 'plums'. It is difficult to describe Berkeley's art because many of his best sequences have no plot or narrative structure. However, there are some set pieces which do tell a story of sorts, like 'Lullaby of Broadway'

in *Gold Diggers of 1935* (1935), a hectic account of a 'Broadway baby's' dance-mad night and tragic dawn. It includes some of his most extraordinary effects. The opening shows the singer's face in close-up against a black background; the face revolves in camera and then, upside down, dissolves into an aerial view of Manhattan. The 'conventional' tap sequence in the middle is rendered fantastic by its sheer size (over 100 male and female dancers do a tightly choreographed routine in unison). Berkeley conveys the frenzy of it all by inventive use of camera angles.

'Pettin' in the Park', from *Gold Diggers of 1933* and 'Honeymoon Hotel' from *Footlight Parade* are examples of Berkeley's lighter side. Both show his (pre-Hays Code) gift for sexual double entendre and innuendo. 'Pettin' in the Park' is an illustration of eager boys and coquettishly uncooperative girls having some fun in a park until interrupted by a rainstorm. The girls strip off their wet clothes in provocative silhouette behind screens and emerge apparently more accessible. In fact they are actually armoured in tinfoil bras, and in the

final shot Billy Barty – Berkeley's favourite midget, playing as usual a sly, precocious child – offers Dick Powell a tin-opener. 'Honeymoon Hotel' mixes the pleasures and embarrassments of a honeymoon with suggestions that our hero and heroine are the only couple in the hotel who are actually married; again, Billy Barty intrudes in several of the tableaux as the youngest and most voyeuristic member of the newlyweds' accompanying family.

Though a case could be made out for some kind of serious political message on Berkeley's part in 'Remember My Forgotten Man', also from *Gold Diggers of 1933*, it is doubtful if he did more than stage (with imaginative play of marching shadows and a boldly expressionistic setting) another of the then fashionable Depression songs. His own deepest involvement seems to have been with the abstract researches of numbers like 'By a Waterfall' in *Footlight Parade*, 'I Only Have Eyes for You' in *Dames*, or 'The Words Are in My Heart in *Gold Diggers of 1935*. 'By a Waterfall' virtually beggars description: the notion behind it is a sort of midsummer night's dream, suggested

Above: the Berkeley girls form a gigantic jigsaw of Ruby Keeler's face in the dream number 'I Only Have Eyes for You' from Dames. *Right: a tableau from the water ballet in* Footlight Parade

Filmography

1930 Whoopee! (chor. only); **'31** Kiki (chor. only); Palmy Days (chor + actor only); Flying High* (GB: Happy Landing). **'32** Night World*; Bird of Paradise*; The Kid From Spain (chor. only). **'33** 42nd Street (chor. only); Gold Diggers of 1933 (chor + actor); She Had to Say Yes (co-dir. with George Amy); Footlight Parade (chor. only); Roman Scandals (chor. only). **'34** Fashions of 1934 (GB: Fashion Follies of 1934) (chor. only); Wonder Bar (chor. only); Twenty Million Sweethearts*; Dames (chor. only). **'35** A Trip Thru a Hollywood Studio (short) (actor only); Gold Diggers of 1935 (+ chor); Go Into Your Dance* (GB: Casino de Paree); In Caliente (chor. only); Bright Lights (GB: Funny Face); I Live for Love (GB: I Live for You); Stars over Broadway (co-chor. only). **'36** Stage Struck; Gold Diggers of 1937 (chor. only). **'37** The Go Getter; The Singing Marine (chor. only); Varsity Show (chor. only); Hollywood Hotel. **'38** Gold Diggers in Paris (GB: The Gay Imposters) (chor. only); Men Are Such Fools; Garden of the Moon; Comet Over Broadway. **'39** They Made Me a Criminal; Broadway Serenade (GB: Serenade) (chor. only); Babes in Arms; Fast and Furious. **'40** Forty Little Mothers; Strike Up the Band. **'41** Blonde Inspiration; Ziegfeld Girl (chor. only); Lady Be Good (chor. only); Babes on Broadway. **'42** Born to Sing (chor. only); Calling All Girls (short) (chor. only); For Me and My Gal (GB: For Me and My Girl). **'43** Three Cheers for the Girls (short) (chor. only); Girl Crazy (chor. only); The Gang's All Here (GB: The Girls He Left Behind). **'45** All Star Musical Revue (short) (co-dir. with Leroy Prinz). **'46** Cinderella Jones. **'48** Romance on the High Seas* (GB: It's Magic). **'49** Take Me Out to the Ball Game (GB: Everybody's Cheering). **'50** Two Weeks with Love (chor. only). **'51** Call Me Mister (chor. only); Two Tickets to Broadway (chor. only). **'52** Million Dollar Mermaid (GB: The One-Piece Bathing Suit) (chor. only). **'53** Small Town Girl (chor. only); Easy to Love (chor. only). **'54** Rose Marie (chor. only). **'62** Jumbo/Billy Rose's Jumbo (2nd unit dir. only). **'70** The Phynx (guest actor only).
* *Choreography attributed to Berkeley, but no screen credit given.*

by the image of falling water, with hundreds of gorgeous girls in and around it. With dream-like speed and arbitrariness the action moves from a moderately realistic stage setting to a succession of cascades thick with water nymphs, giant swimming pools in which the girls swim into intricate geometrical patterns (viewed from directly above), and a staggering finale with girls piled on a revolving fountain.

'I Only Have Eyes for You' is the ultimate hymn to the charms of Ruby Keeler, star of so many of Berkeley's films in the early Thirties. Again it is – explicitly this time – in the form of a dream, dreamed by Dick Powell on a subway train. A host of dancing girls, wearing Ruby Keeler masks and dressed to look like her, finally tilt, displaying a portrait of Ruby Keeler formed piecemeal by boards attached to their backs. 'The Words Are in My Heart' routine has 56 girls in white, each one sitting at a white grand piano while the whole ensemble gyrates smoothly in waltz time to make up a series of intricate patterns. It has always prompted spectators to ask 'How *did* he do it?' Here, the answer is simple: little men in black, unnoticeable (unless they are pointed out) were placed under each piano against the black reflecting floor, and it is their movements which dictate the movements of the pianos.

Not all of Berkeley's solutions were so simple. Often what we see has been run backwards in the camera, so that what appears to be a pattern forming with incredible speed is actually a pattern that is dissolving. But though there is often extreme technical ingenuity in his routines, in the way of camera movement and trickery, it is usually the inventiveness of the basic idea that is their most impressive feature. It is not surprising that a contemporary lobby display for the film *Fashions of 1934* (1934) gave enormous prominence to the statement: 'Pageant of Ostrich Plumes – Hall of Human Harps – Web of Dreams – Venus and Her Galley Slaves – and Other Spectacle Creations by . . . Busby Berkeley'. His inventive genius is still apparent in his later, simpler creations like 'I Gotta Hear That Beat' in *Small Town Girl* (1953), in which Ann Miller (who was not, needless to say, the small town girl in question) taps her way all over a fantastic set in which all we can see of a full orchestra is arms coming out of floor and walls holding and playing instruments. Berkeley's concepts are inconceivable in any medium other than film. He remains one of the cinema's great originals.

The story of Fred Astaire

One of the best stories of Hollywood in the early Thirties tells of Fred Astaire's first screen test at RKO. An executive's report on it read: 'Losing hair. Can't sing. Can dance a little.' Happily, David O. Selznick, head of production, took a cheerier view: 'I am still a little uncertain about the man, but I feel, in spite of his enormous ears and bad chin line, that his charm is so tremendous it comes through even in this wretched test.' Astaire was promptly loaned out to MGM for a brief appearance in one of the big production numbers of the Joan Crawford vehicle *Dancing Lady* (1933). In this humdrum way began one of the most spectacular careers in the Hollywood cinema, spanning nearly five decades.

Fred Astaire was certainly no overnight sensation. His real name was Frederick Austerlitz and he was born on May 10, 1899. At the age of four and a half he was enrolled, along with his six-year-old sister Adele, in a dance school by his ambitious mother. From then on it was show business every inch of the way. By 1917 Fred and Adele had featured roles in a Broadway musical; five shows later, in 1922, they starred in *The Bunch and Judy*. Four big shows followed – *Lady, Be Good!* and *Funny Face*, both written by the Gershwins, *Smiles*, by

Vincent Youmans, and *The Band Wagon* by Dietz and Schwartz – that brought the pair legendary status. Adele's retirement to get married in 1932 was the first real crisis in Fred's career: the team was great, but how would he make it on his own? The answer, in his next show, *Gay Divorce*, in which he starred with Clare Luce, proved to be: very nicely, thank you. But he was clearly ready for a real change, and offers from Hollywood seemed to provide it.

Shall we dance?

There still remained the problem of a partner. Though Fred usually had a speciality solo of some kind in his shows, the centre had always been the numbers he shared with his sister, who everyone agreed was his perfect complement in height, personality and technique. Someone had to be found for Fred's next film *Flying Down to Rio* (1933). Back at his own studio, RKO, he was only fifth on the bill below Dolores Del Rio (in very big letters) and (much smaller) Gene Raymond, Raul Roulien and Ginger Rogers.

Ginger Rogers was by no means a name to conjure with at this time. She had recently been put under contract by the same studio after singing and dancing in vaudeville and stage musicals. She had provided the romantic interest in a number of small movie comedies, and, on loan to Warner Brothers, had received tolerable reviews for her playing of hard-boiled chorus girls in *42nd Street* (1933) and *Gold Diggers of 1933* (1933). She was hard-working and resilient, but no-one thought she was a great dancer – or a great anything. But she *was* available, and thus easy to team with Astaire in a story which mainly concerned Dolores Del Rio trying to choose between the relative merits of Gene Raymond and Raul Roulien. Just as casually as that, one of the great romantic teams of the Thirties cinema came into being.

Against all expectation, the big success of the film was not its main romantic story but these two supporting players performing their one number together. Vincent Youmans' 'The Carioca'. At a time when Hollywood was quick to respond to audience reaction, the flood of letters and comments from ordinary movie-goers meant only one thing: Fred and Ginger

must be brought together as soon as possible in a film of their own. *The Gay Divorcee* (1934), a thorough reworking of Astaire's last stage success soon followed, and then in almost unbroken succession *Roberta* (1935), *Top Hat* (1935), *Follow the Fleet* (1936), *Swing Time* (1936), *Shall We Dance?* (1937), *Carefree* (1938) and *The Story of Vernon and Irene Castle* (1939). Throughout these years, the Astaire/Rogers films were RKO's most reliable box-office, performing the same bacon-saving function as the Mae West films did at Paramount and, a little later, Deanna Durbin films did at Universal. They also featured some amazing collaborators, especially on the musical side, with scores (often original scores) by Youmans, Cole Porter, Jerome Kern, the Gershwins and Irving Berlin – who, in particular, did much of his best work for *Top Hat*, *Follow the Fleet* and *Carefree*.

A fine romance, with no kisses

But the point was always Fred and Ginger. Though sentimental fans liked to fantasize real-life romances between their screen favourites – not always inaccurately, as in the case of Jeanette MacDonald and Nelson Eddy – Fred and Ginger's was a professional marriage of convenience. Socially they had little to do with each other outside the studio; but they worked perfectly together. It may be that a

Top: Fred, the epitome of elegance for his big solo number in Top Hat – in which the chorus become targets in a mock shooting-gallery. Below: Fred poses with his sister Adele – his stage partner until her retirement in 1932 – in a Twenties publicity shot

measure of antagonism is good in such a relationship – certainly many of their most famous romantic numbers show them at first pulling away from each other and then drawing together, as if in spite of themselves. Similarly the plots of their films nearly always consisted of variations on the formula: boy meets girl, boy hates girl (and vice versa) – but since they are really deeply attracted to each other (hence the superficial hostility) everything turns out right in the end.

Someone (supposedly Katharine Hepburn, the other big RKO star at the time) said that the secret of their success together was that he gave her class, and she gave him sex-appeal. Certainly her bright, brash exuberance contrasted very well with his elegant understatement and ironic charm. Though he was the creative one behind the scenes – he would spend weeks working out the films' dance routines, rehearsing himself, her and everybody else involved within an inch of their lives to get it all exactly right – she was a quick and eager study, able, when shown how, to be not only a perfect foil for him but a full partner with a positive contribution to make. The films are consequently memorable, not only for his speciality dance solos but also for two similar but distinguishable kinds of dance duet: the straight romantic, and the love-hate kind.

Dancing cheek to cheek

It takes two or three films for the pattern to become perfectly established; in *The Gay Divorcee* the normal relationship between the partners is not yet clear, though the film does have a typical romantic number, 'Night and Day', and a novelty dance to introduce 'The Con-

tinental', in which 'you kiss while dancing'. In *Roberta* it is nearly there, though the main romantic interest resides in Irene Dunne and Randolph Scott – at least Fred and Ginger have a 'togetherness' dance number to 'Smoke Gets in Your Eyes' and an 'antagonism-rivalry' number in 'I'll Be Hard to Handle'. By *Top Hat* it is all there: Astaire's showy solo dancing on sand in 'No Strings', and again in the title number, where he 'shoots' a whole chorus of white-tied look-alikes; a love-hate number in 'Isn't This a Lovely Day?' with the two of them marooned by a freak thunderstorm on a bandstand in the park; and a classic love-love number with them dancing unmistakably 'Cheek to Cheek'.

From that point on Astaire's routines read like a roll-call of brilliant moments in the

A matchless pairing of man about town with girl next door was the secret of Fred and Ginger's magic. A dance leads to a fine romance in Swing Time *(top left and below) and* Top Hat *(top right). In* Follow the Fleet *(above) Fred swaps a tailcoat for bell-bottoms*

Filmography
1931 Municipal Bandwagon (short). '33 Dancing Lady; Flying Down to Rio. '34 The Gay Divorcee (GB: The Gay Divorce). '35 Roberta (+co-chor); Top Hat. '36 Follow the Fleet; Swing Time. '37 A Damsel in Distress; Shall We Dance? '38 Carefree. '39 The Story of Vernon and Irene Castle. '40 Second Chorus; Broadway Melody of 1940. '41 You'll Never Get Rich. '42 You Were Never Lovelier; Holiday Inn. '43 The Sky's the Limit (+chor). '45 Yolanda and the Thief. '46 Ziegfeld Follies; Blue Skies. '48 Easter Parade. '49 The Barkleys of Broadway. '50 Let's Dance; Three Little Words. '51 Royal Wedding (GB: Wedding Bells). '52 Belle of New York. '53 The Band Wagon. '54 Daddy Long Legs (+co-chor). '57 Funny Face (+co-chor); Silk Stockings. '60 On the Beach. '61 The Pleasure of His Company. '62 The Notorious Landlady. '64 Paris When It Sizzles. '67 Finian's Rainbow. '69 The Midas Run (GB: A Run on Gold). '74 That's Entertainment!; The Towering Inferno. '76 That's Entertainment, Part 2; The Amazing Dobermans. '77 Un Taxi Mauve (FR-IT-E). '81 Ghost Story.

Ginger Alone

Although Ginger Rogers was a virtual nobody when she first teamed up with Fred Astaire, she had plenty of ambition and a driving show-business mother, so it was not surprising that her career diversified more rapidly and radically than that of her dance-obsessed partner. She was, in fact, one of the busiest stars on the RKO lot, appearing in all kinds of thoroughly unmemorable dramas and

Below: Ginger in her Oscar-winning role of Kitty Foyle. Opposite page right: her good looks, twinkling feet and comic gift were all displayed in Roxie Hart. *She plays a gold-digging chorus girl in the Twenties, who, as a publicity stunt, confesses to a murder she did not commit*

Hollywood musical. He taps a sailor chorus to death in 'I'd Rather Lead a Band' (*Follow the Fleet*), dances blackface with an enormous chorus on a mirrored floor the size of Central Park in 'Bojangles of Harlem' (*Swing Time*), slaps 'that bass' (*Shall We Dance?*) and performs the most astonishing feats of golfmanship while dancing to 'Since They Turned Loch Lomond into Swing' (*Carefree*). Fred and Ginger clown and tussle in 'I'm Putting All My Eggs in One Basket' (*Follow the Fleet*) and 'A

Fine Romance' (*Swing Time*) and dance on roller-skates in 'Let's Call the Whole Thing Off' (*Shall We Dance?*). They are all elegance and restraint, but their passion is unmistakable, in the wonderful miniature ballet (he saves her from suicide after a gambling disaster) to the tune of 'Let's Face the Music' (*Follow the Fleet*). The same mood characterizes the numbers 'Never Gonna Dance' (*Swing Time*) and 'Change Partners' (*Carefree*).

Everything they did seemed effortless – it

was meant to seem that way. It was a meeting of disparate but equally genuine star personalities, whose encounters had a continuing spice and savour that survived changes of fashion. Even today, so long after the partnership broke up, and many years since their only return match in *The Barkleys of Broadway* (1949), people still tend to think of Astaire and Rogers as an indivisible entity, and it is generally accepted that Ginger was the best of all his partners.

comedies and always losing out on the roles she really wanted – like Mary Queen of Scots – to Katharine Hepburn. Her best film without Astaire during this period actually co-starred her with Hepburn: they both played young hopefuls in *Stage Door* (1937) – Rogers the apparently tough one with a vulnerable side.

Her first film after the break with Astaire was a successful comedy, *Bachelor Mother* (1939), about a shop-girl who takes in an abandoned baby which people assume to be her own. In 1940 she was in an eccentric comedy drama by Gregory La Cava, *The Primrose Path*, in which she was a shanty-town girl bent on escaping her awful family. She always counted this among her favourite films, along with *Kitty Foyle* (1940), a tale of conflict

between love and money, for which, against unusually heavy competition, she won an Oscar. This was the high point of her career, though there was no immediate falling off, and the war years included three of her best comedies, *Tom, Dick and Harry* (1941), *Roxie Hart* (1942) and *The Major and the Minor* (1942), as well as her most lavish vehicle, an adaptation in colour of Gertrude Lawrence's Broadway success *Lady in the Dark* (1944).

In the decade after the war, she made quite a number of films, most memorably *The Barkleys of Broadway* (1949) – for which she was persuaded to renew her partnership with Astaire in place of an ailing Judy Garland – *Monkey Business* (1952), a comedy about rejuvenation with Cary Grant, *Forever Female*

(1953), in which she played an ageing gangster's moll. Later she appeared frequently on the stage, notably in *Mame* in 1969. She usually played vivacious working-girls – as a 'lady' she seemed rather self-consciously on her best behaviour. It was this quality which made Graham Greene say that she would have been an ideal choice as the eccentric Augusta in the film adapted from his hilarious book, *Travels With My Aunt* (1972). The part went to Maggie Smith: sadly, roles of this quality too seldom came Ginger's way.

Filmography
1929 Campus Sweethearts (short); A Night in a Dormitory (short); A Day of a Man of Affairs (short). '30 Young Man of Manhattan; Queen High; The Sap from Syracuse (GB: The Sap Abroad); Office Blues (short); Follow the Leader. '31 Honor Among Lovers; The Tip-Off (GB: Looking for Trouble); Suicide Fleet. '32 Carnival Boat; The Tenderfoot; Hollywood on Parade, No 1 (short); The Thirteenth Guest; Screen Snapshots (short); Hat Check Girl; You Said a Mouthful. '33 42nd Street; Broadway Bad (GB: Her Reputation); Hollywood on Parade, No 3 (short); Professional Sweetheart (GB: Imaginary Sweetheart); Gold Diggers of 1933; A Shriek in the Night; Don't Bet on Love; Sitting Pretty; Flying Down to Rio; Chance at Heaven. '34 Rafter Romance; Finishing School; 20 Million Sweethearts; Change of Heart; Upperworld; The Gay Divorcee (GB: The Gay Divorce); Romance in Manhattan. '35 Roberta; Star of Midnight; Top Hat; In Person. '36 Follow the Fleet; Swing Time. '37 Shall We Dance?; Stage Door; Holiday Greetings (short).

'38 Having Wonderful Time; Vivacious Lady; Carefree. '39 The Story of Vernon and Irene Castle; Bachelor Mother. '40 The Primrose Path; Lucky Partners; Kitty Foyle. '41 Tom, Dick and Harry. '42 Roxie Hart; Tales of Manhattan; The Major and the Minor; Once Upon a Honeymoon. '43 Tender Comrade; Show Business at War (short); Battle Stations (short). '44 Lady in the Dark; I'll Be Seeing You. '45 Weekend at the Waldorf. '46 Heartbeat; Magnificent Doll. '47 It Had to Be You. '49 The Barkleys of Broadway. '50 Perfect Strangers (GB: Too Dangerous to Love); Storm Warning. '51 The Groom Wore Spurs. '52 We're Not Married; Monkey Business; Dream Boat. '53 Forever Female. '54 Black Widow; Beautiful Stranger (USA: Twist of Fate) (GB). '55 Tight Spot. '56 The First Travelling Saleslady; Teenage Rebel. '57 Oh, Men! Oh, Women! '64 The Confession/Quick Let's Get Married/Seven Different Ways. '65 Harlow.
Note: it is estimated that she made about a dozen shorts between 1929 and 1931 and several wartime shorts.

Let's call the whole thing off
All the same, they broke up – mainly, it seems, because she wanted to branch out as a dramatic actress, but it is not impossible that he was also growing restive with the limitations of their collaboration. In 1937, he had made one film outside the partnership *A Damsel in Distress* (1937), with a non-dancing partner, Joan Fontaine, whom he had to dance around – a not very satisfactory solution. But when (after the patchy biographical film *The Story of*

Vernon and Irene Castle) Ginger departed, a world of partners and possibilities opened up for him. Eleanor Powell in *Broadway Melody of 1940* (1940) and Rita Hayworth in *You'll Never Get Rich* (1941) and *You Were Never Lovelier* (1942) showed that Astaire was not necessarily tied to one partner, but was even 'improved' by variety.

Astaire made one serious attempt to retire, in 1946, but he was lured back to replace Gene Kelly – his only serious rival as a dancing star in films – in *Easter Parade* (1948) opposite Judy Garland. He was part of the great heyday of colour musicals at MGM in the late Forties and early Fifties, appearing in some of the best, such as *Ziegfeld Follies* (1946), *Royal Wedding* (1951), *The Band Wagon* (1953) and *Silk*

Stockings (1957), as well as *Funny Face* (1957) at Paramount with Audrey Hepburn and Kay Thompson. As he got older he danced less in his films – partly also because the number of good musicals being made greatly diminished after 1960 – but he did several memorable television specials in which he sang and danced, and kept himself busy as an excellent comedian and more than competent straight actor, being Oscar-nominated for his part in the disaster movie *The Towering Inferno* (1974). He was even dangerous at the age of 77 in *That's Entertainment, Part 2* (1976). There was never anyone to touch him as a dancer; as a singer he was the only interpreter of many song classics, perhaps more of which he directly inspired than anyone else has ever done. And as an actor and a personality he could always charm the birds off the trees. He will be sorely missed long, long after his death in 1987. Call him irreplaceable.

Opposite page: Fred and Ginger dance to Kern's 'Lovely to Look at' in Roberta *(top left). Nanette Fabray and Jack Buchanan partner Fred for the hilarious 'Triplets' number from* The Band Wagon *(left). Astaire's first straight acting role was in* On the Beach *(1960) with Gregory Peck and Ava Gardner (right). This page: Fred was still dancing at the age of 69 in* Finian's Rainbow *(far left). He also waltzed (and escaped the flames) in* The Towering Inferno *(left)*

Change Partners and Dance

Fred Astaire and Ginger Rogers chose to go their separate ways in 1939 – she wished to further her career as a straight actress, he wanted to explore more fully the musical's potential.

Eleanor Powell (above centre), who could tap faster and kick higher than anyone else, was the first of his new partners, starring with him in Broadway Melody of 1940.

Rita Hayworth came from a family of professional dancers. Her youth, beauty and sheer vitality graced You'll Never Get Rich and You Were Never Lovelier (below).

In the mid-Forties, Fred made two films with Lucille Bremer – Ziegfeld Follies and Yolanda and the Thief (above left), which was supposed to make her a big star. But the partnership never quite worked and she soon retired.

Easter Parade provided Astaire with two partners – Ann Miller for the more classic

duos and Judy Garland for the comedy numbers, the highpoint of which was 'A Couple of Swells' (below right).

The next major sensation in Fred's career was Cyd Charisse – tall, statuesque, and in dance at least, smoulderingly sexy. Cyd and he were an explosive team, starring in The Band Wagon (above right) and Silk Stockings, Rouben Mamoulian's remake of Ninotchka.

Astaire's last two major partners, Leslie Caron in Daddy Long Legs (right) and Audrey Hepburn in Funny Face had both undergone ballet training. Their youth brought out a protective quality in Fred, and he provoked a special warmth in them.

Astaire has remained vague about who was his favourite partner: his stock answer is Gene Kelly, with whom he danced in Ziegfeld Follies and That's Entertainment Part 2.

Fred Astaire and Rita Hayworth—dancing and singing together!

ASTAIRE • HAYWORTH in "YOU WERE NEVER LOVELIER"

IMAGES OF FRANCE

Outside of Hollywood, the Thirties belonged to the French cinema, and the atmosphere of romantic fatalism created by France's famous directors seemed appropriate to the prevailing mood of the time

The structure of the film industry in France changed markedly with the arrival of sound in 1930. The extra costs of talkie production eliminated many of the smaller film companies, though others continued to proliferate throughout the decade, albeit undercapitalized and short-lived; in 1936 alone, for example, 175 new film companies were founded.

Financial considerations also led to the creation of two massive and vertically-integrated companies (embracing production, distribution and exhibition) formed out of the pioneering companies of Charles Pathé and Léon Gaumont. Both the resulting companies, however, withdrew from film production in the mid-Thirties, partly as a result of the illegal financial manipulations of Bernard Natan who had taken over the Pathé company in 1929.

From an output of some fifty feature films in 1929, French film production doubled by 1931 and more than tripled by 1933. But the native film industry never supplied any more than 25 per cent of the movies distributed annually in France. Moreover these were years of chaos and disorder in the industry: technical crews struggled with the limitations of unwieldy new sound-recording equipment; cinema owners required considerable capital to convert their buildings to sound; and producers contrived to add sound to projects conceived originally as silent films. For a while the cumbersome business of multi-language shooting occupied the studios until dubbing and subtitling enabled French films to be distributed abroad with ease. In retrospect it seems almost a miracle that the cinema survived at all.

Certainly in the confusion of the early years of the decade, much of the specifically French quality of the national film production was lost. France had a slow start in talkies since patent rights to the most successful sound systems were owned by American and German companies. The early Thirties had also seen the establishment of large-scale multi-language production in Paris, both on the part of the American Paramount company and the German Tobis company, operating from suburban studios at Joinville and Epinay respectively.

The upheavals of sound were followed, from the middle of the decade onwards, by further crises which reflected the contradictions of contemporary French society as much as the inherent problems of the film industry itself.

In this climate a sense of national identity was difficult to achieve and sustain even after the era of multi-language production had come to an end. Germany, in particular, was a major foreign influence. On the one hand co-productions with Ufa at the Neubabelsberg studios in Berlin continued to provide work for French directors, writers and actors throughout the decade. On the other hand, the advent of Hitler to power in 1933 caused a mass emigration to Paris of German producers, directors and technicians. Figures as important as Erich Pommer, Fritz Lang, Billy Wilder, Robert Siodmak, G.W. Pabst and Eugen Schüfftan worked, some of

them for several years, in the French film industry. It has been estimated that up to a third of French cinema in the Thirties was strongly shaped and influenced by emigrés like, for example, Max Ophuls who spent eight years in France during the decade.

In the new situation of sound-film production, many of the characteristic features of earlier French cinema were lost, in particular the visual experiment associated with the various avant-garde movements of the Twenties.

The interaction of film with Surrealism in France had reached a climax by 1930 with the premiere of Luis Buñuel's *L'Age d'Or* (*The Golden Age*), a masterly indictment of society which provoked riots when first shown in Paris. In the same year the Vicomte de Noailles financed Jean Cocteau's *Le Sang d'un Poète* (1930. *The Blood of a Poet*), but with the increased costs of sound-film production this kind of private patronage of independent film-making came to an end. *Le Sang d'un Poète* was Cocteau's first venture into film and though attacked and derided by the Surrealists on its first appearance, the film now stands as a major achievement and a statement of the personal vision which would be fully orchestrated in *Orphée* (1950, *Orpheus*) some twenty years later.

Sound meant that other key figures of French silent cinema, such as Abel Gance, Marcel l'Herbier and Jean Epstein were reduced to merely commercial film-making. Gance, for example, alternated remakes of some of his earlier successes – he made a sound version of his famous *Napoléon* in 1935 – with routine assignments which offered only rare opportunities to show his full talents. L'Herbier made a couple of lively thrillers, adapted from the novels of

Above left: if any one face typified the look of French cinema in the Thirties it was that of Jean Gabin; in this film he played a fugitive from the law. Top: Jean-Louis Barrault as Napoléon, and Jacqueline Delubac as Josephine, in Les Perles de la Couronne. *Above: Fernandel in his first serious role in Pagnol's* Regain

117

Above: Abel Gance's J'Accuse *was a 1937 sound version of his 1919 anti-war classic. Right: Jean Grémillon's* Gueule d'Amour *was a Hollywood-style romance with Gabin at the mercy of a* femme fatale. *Below: poster for* Marius. *Bottom: in* La Kermesse Héroïque *a Flanders town is occupied by Spanish troops who are first seduced and then routed by the townswomen. Bottom right: the delightfully nostalgic* Un Carnet de Bal *related a woman's search for the beaux of her youth*

Gaston Leroux, – *Le Mystère de la Chambre Jaune* (1930, The Mystery of the Yellow Room) and *Le Parfum de la Dame en Noir* (1931, The Perfume of the Lady in Black). Otherwise l'Herbier's output was restricted to dull historical spectacles, while Epstein's work of the Thirties was equally compromised by unsuitable scripts and financial restraints.

One thread of continuity is provided by the career of René Clair, the master of silent cinema whose writings of the late Twenties opposed the notion of sound (and particularly talking) films but who was one of the first in France to exploit the new form with wit and inventiveness.

The five Clair comedies released in the early Thirties create a distinctive universe where the entanglements of his characters are presented with good-humoured sympathy, and where good eventually triumphs over evil. His first sound film, the internationally successful *Sous les Toits de Paris* (1930, *Under the Roofs of Paris*) with its treatment of characters living on the fringes of society, is an early precursor of what was later to be called 'poetic realism'. Generally, however, Clair's comedies are much lighter and involve a great use of the interplay of dream and reality.

Clair is at his weakest when attempting abstract statements about society, as at the end of *A Nous la Liberté* (1931), or politics, which form the background of *Le Dernier Milliardaire* (1934, *The Last Millionaire*). But despite the reticence and restraint which characterizes all his work, Clair's films of the early Thirties remain genuinely moving and affectionate works.

He left for England in 1935 and was absent from

France for 12 years except for a brief period during 1939 when he began, but failed to complete, *Air Pur* (Pure Air).

Another great loss to the French film industry was that of Jean Vigo, who died in 1934 at the age of 29. Vigo was one of France's most talented and promising young film-makers, whose entire output amounted to two documentaries and two longer fictional works.

After a penetrating study of Nice, *A Propos de Nice* (1930), which blends documentary and surrealist elements, and a short film about a champion swimmer, *Taris* (1931), Vigo made the two films on which his reputation principally rests. Both were dogged by misfortune. The 47-minute *Zéro de Conduite* (1933, *Nought for Behaviour*) was banned by the French censor until 1945, and the feature-length *L'Atalante* (1934) was re-edited and redubbed by its producers while Vigo himself lay dying.

Through both films runs a unique vein of poetry. The world of childhood has seldom been so accurately captured as in *Zéro de Conduite* and the combination in *L'Atalante* of realistically detailed barge life with larger-than-life elements (such as the figure of the mate, brilliantly played by Michel Simon) is a splendid fusion of fantasy and reality.

The outstanding film-maker throughout the decade, however, is Jean Renoir – the son of the painter Auguste Renoir. Like Clair, he had worked extensively during the silent period but the Thirties, when he made some fifteen films, were the richest years of his career. His work is enormously varied and combines elements drawn from his father's Impressionist style and from the naturalism of the nineteenth-century novel or theatre.

Renoir's work during the early years of the decade is marked by his collaborations with the actor Michel Simon. The first film they made together was a farce called *On Purge Bébé* (1931, Purging Baby). Next they did two splendidly amoral tales designed to exploit the actor's remarkable talents: Simon excels as Legrand in *La Chienne* (1931, The Bitch), a timid cashier turned painter who murders his faithless mistress and allows her lover to be executed for the crime. He is equally impressive as Boudu, the tramp in *Boudu Sauvé des Eaux* (1932, *Boudu Saved From Drowning*) who rewards his rescuer by seducing both his wife and his mistress. The anarchism celebrated in the figure of the tramp links the Renoir film with Vigo's *L'Atalante* and to some extent with the mood at the end of Clair's *A Nous la Liberté*. It is a measure of Renoir's versatility that he could subsequently follow adaptations of Simenon – *La Nuit du Carrefour* (1932, Night at the Crossroads) and Flaubert's *Madame Bovary* (1934) – with *Toni* (1934) a sober study of migrant workers shot on location and in a style which anticipates some aspects of post-war Italian neo-realism.

In the great theoretical debate about sound, and particularly talking pictures, two highly successful French dramatists declared themselves opposed to

the traditional view of the primacy of the image. Sacha Guitry and Marcel Pagnol both initially turned to the cinema simply as a means of recording their own work written for the theatre. Both of them had plays adapted for the cinema by other directors in 1931 and then began to direct their own work for the screen a few years later. The results were paradoxical. Their best films, far from being stage-bound, show a freedom shared only by Renoir among their contemporaries.

Guitry was a prolific dramatist who wrote some hundred and thirty plays; most of his Thirties films are simple adaptations, but in his original work written for the screen he shows a freedom of construction, a light and playful style of performance and an inventive approach to the relationship of image and sound which would later be acknowledged as an influence by post-war directors like Alain Resnais. Among Guitry's notable films are: *Le Roman d'un Tricheur* (1936 Story of a Cheat), *Les Perles de la Couronne* (1937, Pearls of the Crown), *Remontons les Champs-Elysées* (1938, Let's Go Up the Champs-Elysées) and *Ils Etaient Neuf Célibataires* (1939, They Were Nine Bachelors).

The work of Pagnol, too, has its surprises. His first contact with the cinema was through his own adaptations of his famous Marseilles trilogy – *Marius* (1931), *Fanny* (1932), and *César* (1936, directed by Pagnol himself). He later made his own film adaptation of his play *Topaze* in 1936, which has subsequently been much filmed.

The success of these works in the tradition of filmed theatre allowed Pagnol to build his own studio and exercise total control over production, even to the extent of completely remaking films that displeased him, either through defects of sound, as in *Merlusse* (1935) or in *Cigalon* (1935).

Pagnol's major films of the Thirties, however, were all adapted not from his own plays, but from novels and stories by the popular author Jean Giono. *Angèle* (1934) and *Regain* (1937, *Harvest*) with Fernandel, and *La Femme du Boulanger* (1938, *The Baker's Wife*) with the great Raimu, were filmed away from the studios on location in Provence so as to make the most of the landscape. The construction and the direction of these films is characterized by a freedom that now strikes us as extremely modern and undated.

Less successful in the Thirties, despite his enormous talent, was the director Jean Grémillon who experienced difficulties in establishing himself in feature film production.

His first sound film, *La Petite Lise* (1930, Little Lise), was a box-office failure and from then on he was condemned to make films that were guaranteed commercial projects or, subsequently, to seek work abroad in Spain and Germany.

Working at the Ufa studios in Berlin, Grémillon made two films from scripts by Charles Spaak. Both *Gueule d'Amour* (1937) starring Jean Gabin and *L'Etrange Monsieur Victor* (1937, *The Strange Mr Victor*) with Raimu had considerable merits. It was,

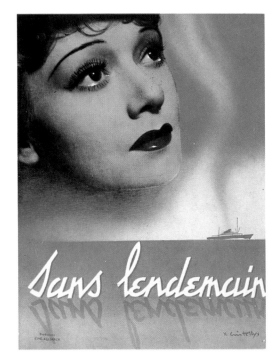

however, typical of Grémillon's ill-fortune that when, in 1939, he had the opportunity to direct the ideal couple of the period – Jean Gabin and Michèle Morgan – in Jacques Prévert's scenario *Remorques*, the plan to make the film was disrupted by the outbreak of World War II.

While Grémillon was forced to seek work abroad, the French studios were filled with refugees from Germany. Max Ophuls achieved some impressive melodramas that portrayed the misfortunes of beautiful women: *Divine* (1935), *La Tendre Ennemie* (1935, Tender Enemy), *Yoshiwara* (1937), and *Sans Lendemain* (1939, No Tomorrow).

What distinguished the French cinema of the Thirties artistically was its sheer literacy. The lead was given by Jacques Feyder, the Belgian-born director who returned from Hollywood to make three films that re-established his European reputation (first acquired during the silent era). The films were *Le Grand Jeu* (1933, *The Great Game*), *Pension Mimosas* (1934) and *La Kermesse Héroïque* (1935, *Carnival in Flanders*) and the team of technicians Feyder assembled to make them included the designer Lazare Meerson, the photographer Harry Stradling and a young assistant, Marcel Carné.

All three films starred Feyder's wife, Françoise Rosay, and were scripted by Charles Spaak, another Belgian who had earlier worked with Feyder on *Les Nouveaux Messieurs* (1928, The New Gentlemen). The writer's contribution, not only to the surface brilliance of the dialogue but also to the structural organization of the plot, was vital. It was to be the first of several writer-director collaborations that characterized the French cinema of the period.

Left: in Sans Lendemain *Edwige Feuillère played a typically tragic Max Ophuls heroine who makes desperate sacrifices to retain her lover and her small son. Above: the director Julien Duvivier. Below:* Le Parfum de la Dame en Noir: *the heroine is 'haunted' by her first husband, whom she believes dead. Below: Raimu at the centre of a typical peasant group in* La Femme du Boulanger. *Bottom left: scene from* Pépé-le-Moko, *an early film noir set in North Africa*

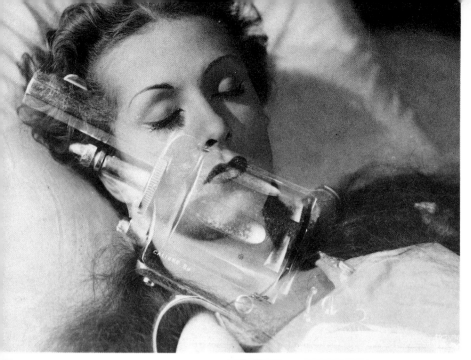

Above: surrealistic images found their way into mainstream cinema – here a dream sequence with Daniéle Darrieux in Anatole Litvak's Mayerling (1936). But the overtly surrealist films appeared earlier in the decade. Right: Le Sang d'un Poète was Jean Cocteau's first film; using trick shots and bizarre images like the 'animated' statue of the poet's muse, he explored the act of artistic creation. Below right and bottom: the dream-like imagery of Buñuel's L'Age d'Or; the first shot illustrates his anti-clerical sentiments and the second his erotic fetishism

Spaak himself went on to work with another veteran of silent cinema, Julien Duvivier. They made two films starring Jean Gabin: both *La Bandera* (1935) and *La Belle Equipe* (1936, The Fine Team) captured the confused aspirations of the period when the left-wing Popular Front government came to power in France.

Duvivier's other major script collaborator was the more superficial but nonetheless brilliantly witty writer Henri Jeanson. Together they worked on the gangster film *Pépé-le-Moko* (1936), a striking example of the romantic pessimism of the time, starring Jean Gabin and the nostalgic *Un Carnet de Bal* (1937, Christine) in which a woman seeks out all the men whose names appear on an old dance card to discover what fate has befallen them.

To return to the work of Jean Renoir in the latter half of the Thirties is to confirm him as the greatest director of the decade. He was, in every sense, the complete author of his films and was far less dependent than either Feyder or Duvivier on the quality of scripts written by others.

Many of his greatest films like *Une Partie de Campagne* (1936, A Day in the Country), *La Bête Humaine* (1938, Judas was a Woman) and *La Règle du Jeu* (1939, The Rules of the Game) were made from his own scripts. *Le Crime de Monsieur Lange* (1935, The Crime of Monsieur Lange), however, announces a new orientation for his work since it was made in collaboration with the poet and scriptwriter Jacques Prévert.

The two of them captured the essential socialist optimism of the Popular Front period and subsequently Renoir found himself caught up in political activity to the extent of making *La Vie Est à Nous* (1936, People of France), an explicit propaganda piece for the Communist Party.

The following year he made *La Grande Illusion* (1937, The Great Illusion), a passionate anti-war statement and a triumph of human observation, controlled rhetoric and total professionalism. At the end of the decade Renoir completed his masterpiece *La Règle du Jeu*, a perceptive dissection of a divided society which amounts to his personal statement on the eve of world war.

If the genius of Renoir is of a kind that defies classification and generalization, the talent of Marcel Carné, by contrast, is defined by a single period and style. Carné was the protégé of Feyder and had proved himself a brilliant organizer of artistic collaborators like the designer Alexandre Trauner and the composer Maurice Jaubert. Before he was 30, Carné had completed five star-studded features, four of them from scripts by Jacques Prévert.

After his debut with *Jenny* (1936), he made the striking comedy *Drôle de Drame* (1937, Bizarre, Bizarre), a comparatively rare example of Prévert's purely comic gifts. Carné and Prévert's two masterpieces *Quai des Brumes* (1938, Quay of Shadows) and *Le Jour se Lève* (1939, Daybreak) are both fatalistic pieces in which Jean Gabin loses all chance of happiness with the woman he loves after a confrontation with two personifications of evil, respectively portrayed by Michel Simon and Jules Berry. The combination of Prévert's anarchic poetry and Carné's technical prowess creates an unforgettable mixture that is echoed in the Carné-Jeanson collaboration *Hôtel du Nord* (1938).

The achievements of Clair and Vigo in the early Thirties and, later in the decade of Feyder, Duvivier, Renoir and Carné, together with their writers Spaak, Jeanson and Prévert, combine to make this a seminal period in the development of French cinema. Its influence extends not only to post-war France but also to Italian neo-realism.

Animating the Ape

Filming *King Kong* involved many ingenious trick effects. Ray Harryhausen, world-famous special-effects man, describes the film's technical innovations

In 1933 RKO presented *King Kong* as 'the Eighth Wonder of the World'. Of course audiences knew that he was not actually alive. Yet Kong, like his prehistoric companions, looked so amazingly lifelike that the public, for almost half a century, has credited him with a reality and personality of his own.

The illusion was basically achieved by the extensive use of the process of stop-motion animation. Successive still poses are photographed on motion picture, frame by frame. The process is similar to that of the animated cartoon, but unlike the cartoon the subject to be given movement is made in a full three-dimensional form; and this dimension gives an appearance of greater reality.

Over the years I have come to prefer the word 'Dynamation' for this process capable of giving the illusion of a living form to something which could in all probability not be found in nature, or photographed in the ordinary way. I have adopted this term because Charles Schneer, my associate for many years, and myself found so often that the word 'animation' was interpreted to mean the use of cartoon animation.

On screen King Kong appears 50 feet (15.24m) tall. In reality he stood a mere 18in (45cm) – a scale model. He was the creation of Willis J. O'Brien, a wizard at technical effects since 1914, who had devised the prehistoric creatures for *The Lost World* in 1925. The great ape's interior skeleton was constructed of steel, with complicated friction ball-and-socket joints. His flesh was of rubber; and his exterior was covered in clipped rabbit fur (which gave the animators some problems because it tended to show their finger-marks). The figure would hold in any position in which he was placed: to keep him upright, as his weight moved from foot to foot, required a baseboard with holes into which he could be firmly fixed and yet remain mobile.

For some close-up scenes – for instance where Fay Wray is held in the creature's hand, or actors are seen struggling as he grips them in his teeth – full-size animated sections of the beast were required. For the scene where the ape chews people, a huge model was constructed, and operated by motors and compressed air. It required 40 bear hides to cover it,

Top: Fay Wray as King Kong's victim. Above: the diminutive Kong – an 18-inch model worked and moved by hand – photographed against a painted backdrop of the jungle. Below: the sequence filmed above is back-projected onto a screen in front of which the actress Fay Wray is positioned (on a dummy tree branch), and the entire sequence is filmed by the camera (bottom left)

121

Above: Kong shaking people off a tree trunk. The ape model is worked by hand against a painted backdrop and the sequence is filmed through a painted glass plate edged with real foliage. The whole sequence is printed together with the matte shots (top left) of actors walking up a ramp

and four men to make it move convincingly. The eyebrows raised or lowered at will; the great 'twelve-inch' eyeballs rolled and blinked, and the jaws seemed to change expression as they clamped down on the unfortunate natives. Similarly, internally operated sections of arms and legs were built in full-size, all to maintain the impression of Kong's gargantuan appearance.

To combine these disparate elements, so different in scale, required some very elaborate mathematical work, and the use of the whole repertory of special photography as it was then known – though the work on *Kong* in itself developed the range of special effects. A usual method was to obscure a part of the camera lens with a painted glass while filming one element of the scene – perhaps the animated miniature. The 'blackout' would mean that a certain portion of each frame remained unexposed. The film could therefore be run back to the start; a different mask was placed over the lens to correspond to the material already shot; and the film was then exposed for a second time, to photograph the setting.

This technique is the basis of the 'matte' shot; and already in 1933 very much more sophisticated developments of the system were available, using colour filters. The principle was that an image photographed under orange-yellow light would pass through orange-dyed positive film and print as normal on the negative film. On the second exposure, blue light reflected from the scene's background would be blocked out by the image on the (orange-dyed) positive film and register as a negative image on the negative film. Through this technique, for example, figures could be made to interact with backgrounds in a way that could not have been filmed normally.

King Kong was one of the earliest – at RKO the first – films to use much back projection. This technique, employed extensively in the later Thirties and Forties, involved projecting a filmed background onto a large translucent screen, while the actors performed and were filmed in front of it. *King Kong* made use of a new form of cellulose back-projection screen which won its inventor, Sidney Saunders, an Academy Award. Previously sand-blasted glass screens had been employed, and apart from giving rather poor technical results, exposed actors and crew to grave peril from breakage.

Almost an inversion of this process was the projection of live-action shots of actors onto a tiny screen within a miniature model of the setting. This was used for the sequence in which we see Fay Wray dangled from the Empire State Building by Kong. Subsequently known as 'miniature projection' the technique was used again by Willis J. O'Brien in another gorilla movie, *Mighty Joe Young* (1949).

The spectacular jungle scenes were achieved by the use of paintings on three or four separated planes of fine plate glass. Miniature sets – trees made of paper and lacquer, thin copper, the twisted roots of old vines – were then sandwiched in between them. The technique was probably to an extent influenced by the work of early Victorian illustrators, in which the impression of depth is achieved by a dark foreground, a medium-toned middle ground and a pale, diffused background. The method produced an illusion of great depth in the fabulous, mystic jungles.

Thus it was that a team of twentieth-century necromancers employed all the magic of the painter, the model-maker, the camera, the laboratory, and the tricks of the animator – as well as intense patience – to achieve a work of magnificent scenic value and fantastic imagination that has stood the test of time. They had achieved a milestone in the creation of the grand illusion.   RAY HARRYHAUSEN

Above and right: in this scene of the ape on the rampage in New York, the illusion of perspective is achieved by matching a painted backdrop of the Hudson River shoreline to a glass painting of skyscrapers and in turn to the model of Kong. The model aircraft were moved on wires, and a doll replaced Miss Wray

CHAPAYEV

What Eisenstein's *The Battleship Potemkin* was in 1925 to Soviet silent cinema, *Chapayev* became 10 years later to the young Soviet talkie. *Potemkin* only required its titles to be translated to make a universal impact; *Chapayev*'s great quality is its characterization, but as this is necessarily heightened by dialogue, the film is a favourite chiefly in its own country.

Like *Potemkin*, *Chapayev* is based upon real events which are altered in detail but remain in essence. Its subject is the character and fate of a civil war hero, Chapayev, who successfully led partisans of the Red Army against Kolchak's White Army in Siberia for a period in 1918 and 1919, before falling in battle. Its main theme is the conflict between the personalities of the peasant Chapayev and the communist commissar assigned from headquarters to advise and help him. The film traces the growth of trust and affection between the two men after their initial clash.

The commissar himself, Dmitry Furmanov, who was transferred from the detachment before its final battle, wrote of his adventures in a popular novel, altering the names of most of the participants. The book was popular and in 1932 Furmanov's widow suggested it as a film. The Lenfilm studio liked the idea and turned the project over to two young novice directors, Sergei and Georgi Vasiliev.

The Vasilievs plunged into *Chapayev* with enthusiasm. The result was an extraordinary success – a film packed with wit, humour, and earthy dialogue. The clash of personalities is as tense and gripping as the clash of armies; the battles are spectacular, but depicted with clarity.

The impression given throughout is one of freshness and spontaneity. Yet it had been achieved only with infinite pains. More than two years were taken on scripting and shooting. Scenes were written, rewritten, and rewritten again.

Chapayev was chosen for the Revolution anniversary show in November 1934; it was the star again for the fifteenth anniversary of the 'official' birth of Soviet cinema in January 1935, and again one month later at an international film festival in Moscow. 'Public, industry and film-makers joined in its praise,' says Jay Leyda in his book *Kino*: 'it was known that the heads of Government and Army had endorsed it at earlier screenings in the Kremlin.' Why did everybody like it so much? Certainly not just because of the official approval.

Leyda calls it 'an easy film to love'. The characters are recognizable and believable. The heroes show fear as well as courage, weakness as well as strength, folly as well as wisdom; love and gaiety is mixed with sacrifice and suffering. And deep down, the kernel of the story is something that everyone knew was true and important – the need for trust between two good men.

Some wiseacres have seen in *Chapayev* an initial victory for the school of socialist realism over the experimental work of Eisenstein, the theorists of montage, and other innovators. But the facts of the case do not fit.

When *Chapayev* first appeared, Soviet artists were on the eve of a great and long-lasting ideological debate. At the first All-Union Congress of Soviet Writers in the summer of 1934, Maxim Gorky had formulated the idea of 'socialist realism'. He contrasted it with the 'critical realism' of nineteenth-century literature, which, he said, only exposed society's imperfections.

'Socialist realism' he lauded as creative: its chief characteristic was the development of people, to help them achieve wealth and love and life and turn the earth in its entirety into 'the magnificent dwelling-place of mankind united in one big family'.

In other words it is identified by its social and political function. It is not narrow, not a style. Tragedy is acceptable and even the fairy-tale may fit so long as the general tenor is true to human nature and society, and is not pessimistic but helps strengthen confidence and hope for the future. Eisenstein's experiment-laden *Battleship Potemkin* (1925) or *Alexander Nevsky* (1938) suit the definition just as well as the more 'realistic' *Chapayev*.

In later years the confrontation became bitter and the opposed terms 'socialist realism' and 'formalism' were used as weapons. 'Socialist realism' was an accolade without argument, 'formalism' was the ultimate in sin. Actually, of course, 'realism' is no synonym for 'naturalism', and 'formalism' does not mean 'experiment in form' – a sense in which it was often far too casually employed – but 'distortion of reality for the sake of formal experiment'. Whether in art, literature or music such phrases have been the ammunition of controversy in every period and clime – convenient for pundits to veil personal prejudices or whims of taste, for administrators to hide a motive or join a stream.

Chapayev, as I have said, fits into the principle of 'socialist realism'. But there never was any conflict between the theoretical school and those who liked *Chapayev*. The Vasilievs were actually favoured pupils of Einsenstein, who went out of his way to praise the film, greeting it as heralding a "third period" in Soviet film history, synthesizing the mass film of the first period with the individual, naturalist stage of the second (or sound) period'.

Quotations from: Kino, A History of the Russian and Soviet Film *by Jay Leyda.*

3

4

In the Russian Civil War of 1918–19 Chapayev (1) is leading a detachment of partisans against Kolchak's White Army. A workers' detachment arrives to augment his forces. At first the relationship between Chapayev and Furmanov, the new commissar sent with the reinforcements, is uneasy (2). Chapayev fears that his authority is being undermined. Furmanov does not ease the situation by arresting Chapayev's lieutenant for allowing looting, but Chapayev is reconciled when he finds peasant support is won over by the return of their livestock.

After explaining his tactics to his officers with the help of potatoes (3), he quells a mutiny, and then makes his final plans for the next encounter with the enemy.

The day of the battle arrives. Chapayev watches from a hilltop as the White Army officers' detachment advances in parade order, banners flying, drums beating, in a terrifying display. The partisans hold their fire, according to orders, but with morale shaken (4). When the battle is joined (5) the Whites are defeated.

Quiet days follow. Chapayev's machine-gunner Petka, and his sweetheart Anna, the worker

5

recruit he has trained as a second gunner, seize a moment to rest (6). But a surprise night attack goes against the partisans. Chapayev, wounded, is helped down a cliff (7) where the last survivors of his forces are massacred trying to swim the river. But Anna has alerted the main Red Army, who turn defeat into victory.

6

7

Directed by Sergei Vasiliev and Georgi Vasiliev, 1934
Prod co: Lenfilm (USSR). **sc:** Sergei Vasiliev and Georgi Vasiliev, based on a book by Dmitry Furmanov and the writings of Anna Furmanova. **photo:** Alexander Sigayev and A. Ksenofontov. **art dir:** Isaak Makhlis. **mus:** Gavril Popov, Moscow premiere, 7 November 1934.
Cast: Boris Babochkin (*Chapayev*), Boris Blinov (*Furmanov*), Varvara Myasnikova (*Anna*), Leonid Kmit (*Petka*), Illarian Pevtsov (*Colonel Borozdin*), Vyacheslav Volkov (*Yelan*), Nikolai Simonov (*Zhikharev*), Stepan Shkurat (*cossack*), Boris Chirkov (*peasant*).

In Glorious Technicolor

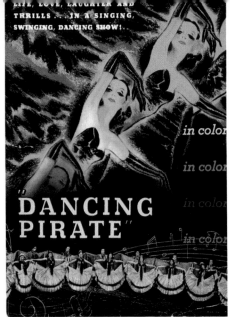

The full emergence of Technicolor as the pre-eminent name in colour film-making dates from 1932 with the development of the three-strip process. Where previously only two primary colours – red and green – had been possible, the third, blue, was now introduced. As a result 'natural' colours were possible for the first time.

Despite the increase in expense – filming in Technicolor added about fifty per cent to the negative cost – Hollywood was eager to experiment with the new medium. With varying degrees of success, every kind of film – costume pictures, musicals, Westerns, even screwball comedy – was seen by audiences for the first time 'In Glorious Technicolor'.

Disney paved the way with the animated film *Flowers and Trees* (1932). Then in 1935 Rouben Mamoulian, another film-maker always eager to try something new, completed the feature which is acknowledged as the first modern colour film – *Becky Sharp*. Mamoulian had definite theories concerning the aesthetic role of colour. In *Picturegoer Weekly* of July 13, 1935 he wrote:

'. . . there is a definite emotional content and meaning in colour and shades . . . the director of a colour picture must be acutely aware of, and take advantage of, the emotional implications of colours and use them to enhance the emotional in dramatic effectiveness of a scene or situation.'

Virtually the whole of *Becky Sharp* is confined to studio interiors, allowing Mamoulian and designer Robert Edmund Jones exceptional control over colour and mood. However, Mamoulian's anti-realistic, symbolic approach was misunderstood or was not entirely successful; *Becky Sharp* had little immediate influence on future colour productions.

The effectiveness of Technicolor in capturing the colours and textures of natural settings was first exploited in *The Trail of the Lonesome Pine* (1936). Critics were quick to praise the film's colour landscape photography. *Today's Cinema* of April 18, 1936 commented that 'the colouring of mountain, forest and lake is in many cases supremely beautiful'. The actors did not come off so well – the same review noted that they appeared 'flushed or unpleasantly anaemic . . . It seems impossible to produce the red that is correctly suggestive either of health, blood or fire; black too seems difficult . . . for most dark-haired players sport all the iridescence of the beetle's wing.'

The Trail of the Lonesome Pine was followed in 1936 by a diverse group of colour films which have been largely forgotten. These include the first three-strip Technicolor musical, *The Dancing Pirate* produced by Pioneer Pictures/RKO

(of which no prints appear to survive); *Ramona* from 20th Century-Fox, *The Garden of Allah* produced by David O. Selznick, and Warner Brothers' *God's Country and the Woman*. Thus each of the major studios (apart from MGM) had made an attempt to jump onto the colour bandwagon. However, *Ramona*, *The Garden of Allah* and *God's Country and the Woman* were all adapted from weak stories and failed at the box-office; *Garden of Allah*, in particular, was a financial disaster having cost over $2 million. Selznick was quick to redeem his reputation, with *A Star Is Born* and *Nothing Sacred* (both 1937, and both directed by William Wellman). *A Star Is Born* was nominated for seven Oscars and won two – for best original story (Wellman) and a special award for colour cinematography. In both films colour was used in a restrained and realistic way in keeping with their stories about contemporary life in America, providing a unique picture of what the world of the Thirties looked like in colour.

For most film companies 1937 was a boom year; the recession which followed in 1938 hit the industry hard. Despite this, the number of Technicolor films grew steadily throughout the late Thirties and early Forties. Perhaps the novelty value of colour was regarded as a means of fighting the slump – certainly the three aspiring majors, Fox, Paramount and Warners, saw colour as a means of competing in prestige with the top company MGM, where the attitude was, 'if our films make money in black and white, what do we need colour for?'

Warners first big prestige colour film was *The Adventures of Robin Hood* (1938) which cost over $1.5 million. The striking colour photography – with much of the picture filmed on location – was achieved by Sol Polito, Tony

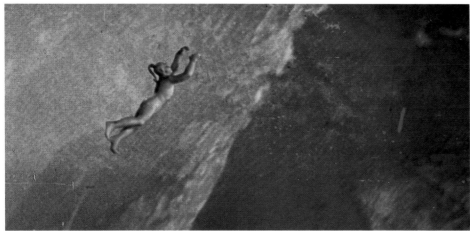

Opposite page: Technicolor exploded onto the screen in the mid-Thirties in many different kinds of films, including a Western, The Trail of the Lonesome Pine – the first colour film to be shot on location (left); a musical, The Dancing Pirate (top right); and a satirical comedy, A Star Is Born (right).
This page: by the Forties colour was used primarily for adventure and fantasy films. Three of the finest were The Adventures of Robin Hood (top left), The Thief of Bagdad (left) and The Wizard of Oz (above)

Gaudio and W. Howard Greene. The film strikes an ideal balance between intimate moments, spectacle and action sequences, and between a toned-down, restrained use of colour and the brighter, more lavish scenes featuring the costumes of Milo Anderson.

Despite all this, the reaction of film audiences at the time was disappointing; the picture hardly managed to recoup its substantial cost. A new incentive for filming in colour – with a new emphasis on musical fantasy – was supplied by the smash success of Disney's *Snow White and the Seven Dwarfs* (1937). In addition Selznick finally embarked on filming *Gone With the Wind* (released in 1939).

From the beginning of his work on the project, Selznick had been firmly committed to colour. He was particularly insistent that the film should not be confined to the kind of neutral and pastel shades favoured by the colour consultants assigned to the project by the Technicolor company. He commented:

'This picture in particular gives us the opportunity occasionally to throw a violent dab of colour at the audience to sharply make a dramatic point.'

The film's director, Victor Fleming, accomplished the remarkable feat of making the other most famous movie of 1939 – *The Wizard of Oz*, MGM's most expensive film up to that date. In view of its substantial cost the film was not a commercial success on its initial release, reinforcing MGM's prejudice against the added cost of Technicolor.

In marked contrast to MGM's reluctance, the producer Darryl Zanuck had, towards the end of 1938, embarked on a series of Technicolor pictures at 20th Century-Fox which continued into the Forties and averaged five or

six films per year. This represented the first substantial and lasting commitment to colour by any of the major studios and established the pattern of colour-filming for the Forties. Although he concentrated on musicals and Westerns, Zanuck nevertheless provided the opportunity for a number of important directors to express their individual styles in colour for the first time, including John Ford (*Drums Along the Mohawk*, 1939), Fritz Lang (*The Return of Frank James*, 1940), Ernst Lubitsch (*Heaven Can Wait*, 1943) and Busby Berkeley (*The Gang's All Here*, 1943).

Ford in particular made effective use of location filming with the emphasis on a tonal range of greens and browns, of heavily wooded forests and log cabins. The peace of the community is disrupted by the appearance of enemy redskins, with the striking image of home and crops on fire – the red and the orange flames outlined against a pale blue sky.

Wings of the Morning (1937), produced by 20th Century-Fox, was the first British Technicolor film. A story of horse-training and racing, it is memorable mainly for some outstanding photography of Irish locations. During the following years only a small number of British productions were filmed in colour. The one producer of note in this respect was Alexander Korda. His company was allied with the Technicolor corporation for the production of five features between 1938 and 1940. The most successful were *The Four Feathers* (1939) an action-packed tale of the British Empire, and *The Thief of Bagdad* (1940). Despite a strong cast, the real stars of *The Four Feathers* were the four cameramen who teamed with the art director Vincent Korda to give the film a stunning appearance – espe-

cially in the sequences filmed in Egypt and the Sudan, including a spectacular battle climax.

Korda was equally successful with *The Thief of Bagdad*, co-directed by Michael Powell, Ludwig Berger and Tim Whelan. The combination of cameraman Georges Périnal and Vincent Korda produced colour effects which matched the fantasy and spectacle of this story, inspired by *The Arabian Nights*. The film spawned a host of imitations in Hollywood during the early Forties. Inevitably the outbreak of war seriously affected British production of colour films – even *The Thief of Bagdad* had to be completed by Korda in the USA.

The preference for escapist entertainment during the war meant that colour films were predominantly musicals or other lightweight fare. Many of the leading directors of the Forties avoided colour entirely, including Capra, Cukor, Huston and Wyler, while Hawks, Sturges, Welles and Wilder directed only one minor colour film apiece. Even Ford, Lang, and cameraman James Wong Howe, all of whom had done some distinguished colour work during the late Thirties, returned to black and white.

The first substantial move into colour did not take place until the early and middle Fifties to counteract the effects of TV on movie audiences. There remained a widespread prejudice against colour for certain types of film – particularly gangster pictures and psychological dramas. Both from an artistic point of view and also from 'realistic' considerations – owing perhaps to the fact that documentaries were filmed in black and white – colour was frequently disparaged by critics. A typical comment was made by James Agee:

'Colour is very nice for costume pieces and musical comedies, and has a great aesthetic future in films, but it still gets fatally in the way of any serious imitation of reality.'

The contradictions inherent in this statement would not be realized for several years.

All About Bette

'What a fool I was to come to Hollywood where they only understand platinum blondes and where legs are more important than talent'

On December 3, 1930, Bette Davis arrived in Hollywood. Originally from Lowell, Massachusetts (she was born in 1903), she had studied drama at the John Murray Anderson school, acting in summer repertory. She had won a modest but growing reputation as a promising young actress in two Broadway plays – *Broken Dishes* and *Solid South* – and had come to the attention of Universal studios, who put her under contract.

It was hardly an auspicious time for someone like Davis to break into films; she was pretty enough, in an odd way, but hardly fitted any of the moulds by which either the studios or the public judged beauty. The fact that she was, or wanted to be, a serious actress was irrelevant, if not actually a handicap to success. When she got off the train, no-one from the studio was there to meet her. In fact, a representative *had* been at the station but later reported that he had seen 'no-one who looked like an actress.' When head of the studio Carl Laemmle saw the first film in which she was cast, *Bad Sister* (1931), he said, 'Can you picture some poor guy going through hell and high water in a picture and ending up with *her* at the fade-out?'

Five undistinguished films later, Universal dropped her contract. Just as she and her

mother were packing to return to New York and the theatre, George Arliss, then a leading star at Warner Brothers telephoned. A friend of his, Murray Kinnell, had worked with Davis in her fifth film *The Menace* (1932) and had thought she might be right for Arliss' upcoming *The Man Who Played God* (1932). In his autobiography, Arliss recalled:

'I did not expect anything but a nice little performance. But . . . the nice little part became a deep and vivid creation . . . I got from her a flash that illuminated mere words and inspired

them with passion and emotion. That is the kind of light that cannot be hidden under a bushel.'

Warners, however, either didn't see that light, or didn't care; she was put under contract, but given a series of roles in mediocre pictures which today have few, if any, redeeming qualities except Davis' presence.

She was, of course, noticed by critics and the public, and her reputation as a solid actress continued to grow. She was a convincing vixen in *Cabin in the Cotton* (1932), and man-

Above: even in publicity portraits Bette Davis avoided the glamorous extravagances of most other Hollywood actresses. Right: The Man Who Played God *provided her with a prestigious role as the fiancée of a concert pianist (George Arliss)*

aged to make even the most ludicrous Southern dialogue – 'Ah'd luv ta kiss yo, but ah jes washed mah hayuh' – sound believable. She fought with director Archie Mayo over the way she should play her mad scene in *Bordertown* (1935); she won, as she often did in battles with directors, and was proved right, as she often was in such cases, when the film was well received. Critics pointed to the subtlety of her portrayal of 'a fiery-souled, half-witted, love-crazed woman' (*Film Weekly*) in their reviews.

Davis has claimed that 'There wasn't one of my best pictures I didn't have to fight to get.' *Of Human Bondage* (1934), from the novel by Somerset Maugham, was one of the first. Director John Cromwell wanted her for the role of Mildred, a scheming waitress who ensnares a sensitive medical student, but Warners was reluctant to loan her to RKO for the film. Bette hounded Jack Warner every day for six months, and he finally gave in simply to be left in peace. She recalled in her autobiography *The Lonely Life*:

'My employers believed I would hang myself playing such an unpleasant heroine . . . I think they identified me with the character and felt we deserved each other.'

It is, seen now, perhaps not one of Davis' best performances; her Mildred is so constantly overwrought and nasty that one begins to wonder what even the obsessed student Philip Carey (Leslie Howard) could see in her. Put in historical perspective, however, the performance is both effective and courageous; at a time when 'movie star' meant glamour and sympathy, Davis had dared to look terrible and to be unsympathetic. All were surprised when

she was not even nominated for an Academy Award. When she won an Oscar for *Dangerous* (1935), she claimed it was given her because she had been overlooked the previous year.

In spite of the acclaim she received for *Of Human Bondage*, Warners threw her into five melodramas of variable quality before giving her the script of *Dangerous*. Davis says that she thought it 'maudlin and mawkish, with a pretense at quality', and that she had to work hard to make something of her role as an alcoholic actress bent on self-destruction. She is undoubtedly right about the screenplay, but she gives a performance of such intensity that one overlooks everything that is going on around her on screen.

Those critics who had begun to complain that she was fast developing a set of mannerisms and was playing too broadly for the screen were suprised at her tender and restrained Gaby in *The Petrified Forest* (1936). Yet, in spite of her obvious power at the box-office and her critical standing as a serious actress, Warners insisted that she make an empty comedy, *The Golden Arrow* (1936), and a flat and confused version of Dashiell Hammett's *The Maltese Falcon* called *Satan Met a Lady* (1936). Davis was understandably angry. To preserve her self-respect and her popularity, she wanted to make fewer films each year and to act only in those with scripts she thought intelligent. Warners reply was to cast her in something called *God's Country and the Woman* (made in 1936 with Beverley Roberts as the female lead), with the promise that if she made it she could have the part of Scarlett O'Hara in *Gone With the Wind* (1939). She refused and the studio put her on suspen-

Left: a role Davis fought to get – Mildred in Of Human Bondage, *co-starring Leslie Howard. Centre: Davis (with Miriam Hopkins) in* The Old Maid *– a study of repressed love. Top left:* Dark Victory *was one of her strongest melodramas; Humphrey Bogart played a minor part. Top: as the rich flirt Madge, she bewitched her father's employee Marvin (Richard Barthelmess) in* Cabin in the Cotton

sion for three months. She held out, refusing two other scripts offered her, with the comment 'If I continue to appear in mediocre pictures, I'll have no career worth fighting for'.

With the Davis–Warners feud at an impasse, Ludovico Toeplitz, who produced films in England, offered her a two-picture contract at £20,000 for each film, with script approval. She signed, but upon her arrival in London found herself under injunction from Warners. They claimed that she was contracted to work exclusively for that studio and was not allowed to make films for others. The entire film industry watched the ensuing court battle (which all actors applauded) as the outcome would determine how the studio system would work in the future. Davis lost her suit and was forced to return to Warners or to give up films until her long-term contract expired – but she

---

'I have never known the great actor who . . . didn't plan eventually to direct or produce. If he has no such dream, he is usually bitter, ungratified and eventually alcoholic'

---

did not lose out in the long run. Warners paid her legal fees and began to take her more seriously; the standard of her material temporarily rose.

Her first film upon her return to Hollywood was *Marked Woman* (1937), an above-average social-problem (prostitution) film which gave her a chance to show a wider range of emotion than usual. *Jezebel* (1938) began a long series of films specially tailored for Davis. They were for the most part what was then called 'women's pictures', melodramatic soap operas turning on romantic conflict and sacrifice. It would be a mistake, however, to dismiss them in the

light of the wider freedom of expression allowed in today's films. In the Thirties and Forties such films were taken seriously and accorded more than a little respect. The best of them attempted to illuminate areas of emotion, sexuality and human situation which could not be portrayed on the screen at that time in any other way. Those that Davis made were certainly among the best – she continuously fought for a certain level of intelligence in plot and dialogue, and insisted on as much realism as possible in her portrayals of disturbed or troubled women.

In *Jezebel* she was convincing as a wilful Southern belle who is made to suffer for her own strange peversity. In *Dark Victory* (1939) she alone lifted a maudlin tale of a woman slowly dying into an illuminating study of human understanding and sacrifice. In *Now*

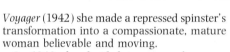

Voyager (1942) she made a repressed spinster's transformation into a compassionate, mature woman believable and moving.

In 1946 she decided to set up her own production company with the films thus made to be released through Warners. A single film came from her company – *A Stolen Life* (1946) in which she played twins, one good, one evil, both in love with the same man. She found she was uncomfortable in the role of producer: 'I never really *produced*,' she said, 'I simply meddled as usual. If that was producing, I had been a mogul for years.'

From 1946 onward, Davis seemed to have a problem finding suitable material, and her popularity began to slip. *Winter Meeting* (1948) is a talky film about a poetess meeting a naval

Left: Bette with William Dix in The Nanny, *one of her best later roles. Above left: Her performance as stage star Margo Channing (here with Celeste Holm and Hugh Marlowe) helped* All About Eve *achieve a record of 14 Academy Award nominations (it won six). Above: Davis in full regalia as* The Virgin Queen *– her second portryal of Elizabeth the First*

officer who wants to be a priest. *Beyond the Forest* (1949) was forced upon her by Warners in spite of her warning that 'I'm too old and too strong for that part'. The film was savaged by the critics and the public stayed away. Nonetheless, it is one of the most enjoyable bad movies ever made. ('There never was a woman like Rosa Moline, a twelve-o'clock girl in a nine-o'clock town.') Davis pulls out all the stops and turns in one of the finest Bette Davis caricatures ever seen. She asked for her release from the studio and got it, although Jack Warner was considering her for Blanche in *A Streetcar Named Desire* (later made in 1951).

She was completing a rather ordinary melodrama about divorce, *Payment on Demand* (1951) at RKO, when she was offered the part of ageing actress Margo Channing in *All About Eve* (1950). Davis later recalled:

'I can think of no project that from the outset was as rewarding from the first day to the last . . . It was a great script, had a great director, and a cast of professionals all with parts they liked . . . After the picture was released I told Joe [Mankiewicz, the director] he had resurrected me from the dead.'

Davis was never better in a role that allowed

'There was more good acting at Hollywood parties than ever appeared on the screen'

---

her to play an actress larger than life, and at the same time to reveal the self-pity and vulnerability beneath. But this upswing in her career was not maintained; throughout the decade she was cast in poor roles.

Still, as had happened with *All About Eve*, a film came along which once more revitalized her career: Robert Aldrich's *What Ever Happened to Baby Jane?* (1962). She obviously more than enjoyed playing 'Grand Guignol', and the film was overwhelmingly popular everywhere in the world. Perhaps the one unfortunate aspect of its success was that, in spite of minor

Left: Bette became one of the murderer's victims in the whodunnit Death on the Nile. *Above: as the crazy, former child star in* What Ever Happened to Baby Jane? *she slowly destroyed her crippled sister*

forays back into 'women's films' such as *Where Love Has Gone* (1964), she was offered and accepted a series of ghoulish roles in progressively worse movies.

However, in 1987, she and another veteran actress. Lillian Gish, took awards from the US Council of Film Organizations as Best Performers in Lindsay Anderson's *The Whales of August*, justification of her claim:

'I'll never make the mistake of saying I'm retired. You do that and you're finished. You just have to make sure you play older and older parts. Hell, I could do a million of those character roles. But I'm stubborn about playing the lead. I'd like to go out with my name above the title.'

She is still known as 'the finest actress of the American cinema'. There are those who have disputed that she acted at all, maintaining that all the characters she played were drowned by her own strong personality. It is a moot point, depending upon one's standards and definition of screen acting, although one could reply that she has played the widest range of roles in the widest range of mood of any actress ever to work in American films. Whatever the final judgment of her abilities as an actress, however, it cannot be denied that, whatever she does on the screen, it is impossible to take one's fascinated eyes off her.

Quotations from The Lonely Life, *by Bette Davis (New York, G.P. Putnam's Sons, 1962)*

Filmography

1931 Bad Sister; Seed; Waterloo Bridge; Way Back Home (GB: Old Greatheart). **'32** The Menace; Hell's House (reissued as: Juvenile Court); The Man Who Played God (GB: The Silent Voice); So Big; The Rich Are Always With Us; The Dark Horse; Cabin in the Cotton; Three on a Match. **'33** 20,000 Years in Sing Sing; Parachute Jumper; Ex-Lady; The Working Man; Bureau of Missing Persons. **'34** The Big Shakedown; Fashions of 1934 (GB: Fashion Follies of 1934; USA retitling for TV: Fashions); Jimmy the Gent; Fog Over Frisco; Of Human Bondage; Housewife. **'35** Bordertown; The Girl From 10th Avenue (GB: Men on Her Mind); Front Page Woman; Special Agent; Dangerous. **'36** The Petrified Forest; The Golden Arrow; Satan Met a Lady. **'37** Marked Woman; Kid Galahad (USA retitling for TV: The Battling Bellhop); That Certain Woman; It's Love I'm After. **'38** Jezebel; The Sisters. **'39** Dark Victory; Juarez; The Old Maid; The Private Lives of Elizabeth and Essex. **'40** All This and Heaven Too; The Letter. **'41** the Great Lie; Shining Victory (uncredited guest); The Bride Came COD; The Little Foxes; The Man Who Came to Dinner. **'42** In This Our Life; Now, Voyager. **'43** Watch on the Rhine; Thank Your Lucky Stars; Old Aquaintance. **'44** Mr Skeffington; Hollywood Canteen. **'45** The Corn is Green. **'46** A Stolen Life; Deception. **'48** Winter Meeting; June Bride. **'49** Beyond the Forest. **'50** All About Eve. **'51** Payment on Demand; Another Man's Poison (GB). **'52** Phone Call From a Stranger; The Star. **'55** The Virgin Queen. **'56** The Catered Affair (GB: Wedding Breakfast); Storm Center. **'59** John Paul Jones; The Scapegoat (GB). **'61** Pocketful of Miracles. **'62** What Ever Happened to Baby Jane? **'63** La Noia (IT). **'64** Dead Ringer (GB: Dead Image); Where Love Has Gone; Hush . . . Hush, Sweet Charlotte. **'65** The Nanny (GB). **'67** The Anniversary (GB). **'69** Connecting Rooms (GB). **'71** Bunny O'Hare. **'72** Lo Scopone Scientifico (IT) (USA: The Scientific Cardplayer). **'76** Burnt Offerings. **'78** Return From Witch Mountain; Death on the Nile (GB); The Children of Sanchez. **'80** The Watcher in the Woods. **'87** The Whales of August.

The Epic Entertainments of

Cecil B. De Mille

During the Thirties DeMille rescued his floundering career with grand re-creations of the power and debauchery of Ancient Rome and with Westerns that celebrated the American pioneering spirit

When sound first came to the movies, the career of Cecil B. DeMille, Hollywood's greatest showman, had reached an unprecedented crisis. From his first film, *The Squaw Man* (1913), he had unerringly mirrored changing fashions in public taste. During World War I he made contemporary war stories like *The Little American* (1917), which depicted the sinking of the *Lusitania*. Thereafter, in the changing moral climate of the early Twenties, he specialized in spicy marital dramas such as *The Affairs of Anatol* (1921), visions of opulence centring on the bathroom and bedroom. He

then undertook his most ambitious project to date, *The Ten Commandments* (1923), a block-busting epic costing $1.5 million.

Although he was a household name, De-Mille's professional position was far from secure. Arguments over the cost of *The Ten Commandments* initiated a widening rift be-tween DeMille and his business associates at Famous Players-Lasky – especially Adolph Zukor. DeMille left under a cloud to form his own company in 1925: However, despite the success of an epic life of Christ, *The King of Kings* (1927), many of his company's films failed at the box-office and his backers and partners lost confidence in him. As DeMille explained him-self in his autobiography:

'The trouble in 1928 was that I did not have

Above: DeMille's Cleopatra; *the star, Claudette Colbert, was one of his favourite leading ladies in the Thirties. Right: Cecil Blount DeMille in favourite directorial garb – riding boots, jodhpurs and open-necked shirt*

DeMille contracted to make three pictures with MGM. *Dynamite* (1929) was made in both silent and sound versions (he still was not convinced): *Madame Satan* (1930), a musical, was a box-office flop, and in something of a panic he attempted to repeat earlier successes with his third version of *The Squaw Man* (1931), but this, too, failed disastrously. At this time DeMille attempted to form an organization known as the Directors' Guild with Lewis Milestone, King Vidor and Frank Borzage. The Guild's aim was to place creative control of picture-making with the directors rather than the financiers. DeMille claimed:

' . . . the conditions under which motion pictures are now generally produced are not conducive to the best creative work, and must, if long continued, result in a deadly uniformity of ideas and methods, thus seriously retarding the highest commercial and artistic development of the craft.'

This move by DeMille highlights one of his fundamental contradictions: by forming the Guild he was attempting to gain for himself an artistic freedom from financial constraint which was impossible in such a highly capita-

enough 'picture money' to be completely independent and make only the kind of pictures I wanted to make.'

In 1928 he embarked upon *The Godless Girl*, a moral tale set in a girl's reform school. The shooting of this film is a typical example of DeMille's methods. His production team spent months researching reform schools and a realistic set was constructed on the lot. True to DeMille's passion for authenticity this set was to be burnt down at the end of the film with the actors (literally) escaping the flames – a procedure which was planned to the second. Despite the fine timing, when one wing of the set fell down on cue (pulled by special wires) two girls were trapped. They luckily managed to escape by climbing up a gable and down the other side.

DeMille was convinced that the success of *The Jazz Singer* (1927) was only temporary and that *The Godless Girl*, which he had shot silent, would be a hit, but his backers insisted that sound should be added. The quarrels that ensued finally prompted him to sign with MGM. On his departure a soundtrack was added to the film.

Top: Charles Laughton as the Emperor Nero, with Claudette Colbert and Fredric March, in The Sign of the Cross, *one of DeMille's finest epics. Above:* The Plainsman *marked DeMille's successful return to the Western. Below: the last spike is hammered in to complete the Western Union railroad in* Union Pacific

lized industry, yet as a fervent Republican, DeMille had absolutely no wish to change the industry's structure.

Louis B. Mayer, head of MGM, was, not surprisingly, unhappy about this move; his unhappiness was compounded by DeMille's box-office failures. After an extended trip to Russia and Europe, lack of money forced DeMille to mortgage his property and swallow his pride; he approached his first company (which had, in the meantime, become the Paramount Pictures Corporation) and Lasky and Bud Schulberg (the head of production on the West Coast) persuaded Zukor to let DeMille back into the fold. He was assigned to direct a Roman epic entitled *The Sign of the Cross* (1932) on a budget of only $650,000; he received a meagre salary of $450 per week. (In 1916 DeMille had been drawing a salary of $1000 per week plus a share of the profits.) DeMille was forced to adopt a more rigorous production operation: Nero's palace, far from being an authentic, life-size reproduction, was largely constructed in miniature with special flights of stairs and ramps of sufficient size for the cast to walk on. DeMille was not allowed to marshal thousands of extras as he had in the old days; instead, the cameraman used a prism lens which gave the effect of doubling the number of people in a crowd. However the Roman circus was genuinely full-size; it seated

133

7500 and had a vast arena. DeMille brought the picture in on budget (apparently stopping shooting in the middle of a take so as not to exceed it) and it was a box-office smash.

Clearly a great deal of this success was due to the film's sexual content, which included the attempts of Poppea (Claudette Colbert) to seduce Marcus Superbus (Fredric March) and his futile efforts to seduce a Christian girl called Mercia (Elissa Landi) in the course of which he forces her to attend an orgy with him. DeMille writes that William Hays, the industry's moral guardian, was very upset about a dance in the orgy scene and telephoned to ask him what he was going to do about it. 'Not a damn thing,' DeMille replied, and didn't. DeMille's insistence that 'I will always resist, as far as I am able, the claim of any individual or group to the right of censorship' is ironic in view of his support of Hays' appointment, which he defended on the grounds that some pictures were '... bad art as well as bad morals and bad taste'.

The film's success reinstated DeMille within the industry. After two pot-boiling films (*This Day and Age* in 1933 and *Four Frightened People* in 1934) he launched himself into another epic, *Cleopatra* (1934). This time DeMille's passion for authenticity was rampant – even Cleopatra's hairpins were museum copies – in addition to his pleasure in sexual symbolism and innuendo, which he justified on commercial grounds. A slave girl danced almost naked with and on a golden bull, and the film was a box-office if not a critical success. From then on, with the exception of *The Greatest Show on Earth* (1951), all DeMille's films were historical.

His position at Paramount was now assured, not only because of these successes but also because Ernst Lubitsch had become production director at the studio (both Lasky and Schulberg had long since departed) and he was a great admirer of DeMille's silent films. Lubitsch's presence was a godsend; although DeMille's next picture, *The Crusades* (1935), failed miserably, he was able to abandon the ancient world for a while to make *The Plainsman* (1936), based on the lives of Wild Bill Hickok and Calamity Jane – but *not* with any historical accuracy in terms of events. DeMille built sets covering six acres of the Paramount lot and was once again able to use as many extras as he wanted for the battle scenes. Reviewing the film, *Variety* weekly wrote: 'It's cowboys and Indians on a broad, sweeping scale: not a *Covered Wagon* but realistic enough.' Realistic or not, it was a financial

success, as was his later *Union Pacific* (1939) which dealt with the construction of the Western Union railroad. His researchers went through the company's records going back 70 years. In Utah he built a complete reproduction of the town of Cheyenne and imported by bus over a thousand Navajo and Cheyenne Indians. During shooting, DeMille was taken ill and after an emergency operation he directed from a stretcher, but large sections of the film had to be shot by Arthur Rossen and James Hogan. The film's enormous success led Paramount to grant him a four-year contract and virtual independence. His next two films, *North West Mounted Police* (1940) and *Reap the Wild Wind* (1942) were both hits, the latter breaking Paramount's record for grosses at the box-office previously held by DeMille's silent version of *The Ten Commandments*.

DeMille then became carried away with the idea of filming the story of a missionary and naval commander, Dr Corydon E. Wassell, who had run a Japanese blockade in order to rescue nine wounded sailors despite orders to abandon them. The subject especially appealed to DeMille, who practised what would today be described as something of a 'macho' lifestyle. Prior to his film career he had loved attending Pennsylvania Military College, where the regimen included daily Bible readings and cold baths; until his last years he went every day for a nude swim in his pool. The film he made, *The Story of Dr Wassell* (1944), was a success, but the critics, as DeMille admits, did not like it. In

Top left: Loxi Claiborne (Paulette Goddard) sights a ship running on the rocks in Reap the Wild Wind, *a seafaring drama set in Georgia in the 19th century. Right: Charlton Heston as Moses in DeMille's second version of* The Ten Commandments, *his last biblical epic. Below: Samson (Victor Mature) brings the house down on his Philistine captors at the climax of* Samson and Delilah

ploying some 12,000 extras and 15,000 animals for the Exodus scene alone. DeMille was, of course, well versed in the organization and control of huge productions. He habitually directed from a platform, with a megaphone, and in sequences with thousands of extras used to communicate his instructions to his assistant directors in amongst the action by radio telephone. The film's final cost was $13 million and by the end of 1959 it had grossed over $83 million and been seen by more than 98 million people.

DeMille's career is significant for his production of Biblical epics and other films on a grand scale. He acknowledged the influence of the silent Italian epics on his work, and his contribution to the genre was both formative and substantial. However the artistic value of his films, of which he himself was quite convinced, probably lies in his silent work, not simply because, despite his Christian beliefs, he undoubtedly began to serve Mammon in his later work, but also because his despotic professional personality blinded him to the possibilities of fine art on small budgets. The *New Yorker*'s review of *Samson and Delilah* read:

'It may be said of Cecil B. DeMille that since 1913, when he teamed up with Jesse Lasky to create *The Squaw Man*, he has never taken a step backward. He has never taken a step forward either, but somehow he has managed to survive in a chancy industry where practically everybody is incessantly going up, down, or sideways . . . '

This, sadly, probably sums up his career.

Below: DeMille's career was financially successful, but not until The Greatest Show on Earth *did a film of his win a Best Picture Oscar. Here, the circus manager (Charlton Heston), injured in a train crash, is tended by a murderer (James Stewart) who, to escape dectection, wears the makeup of a clown*

the *Nation* James Agee wrote:

' . . . Cecil DeMille's [film] is to be regretted beyond qualification. It whips the story, in every foot, into a nacreous foam of lies whose speciousness is only the more painful because Mr DeMille is so obviously free from any desire to alter the truth except for what he considers to be its own advantage.'

This is an interesting point with regard to DeMille's complex character. His devout Christian beliefs and adherence to the Episcopalian Church, his increasingly right-wing political opinions and his somewhat unusual sex life – he was a foot fetishist and openly maintained relationships with two mistresses (Jeanie MacPherson and Julia Faye) for many years – combined with his strict moral sense, inevitably produced violent contradictions in himself, his actions and his films.

DeMille's devotion to the American way of life led him to become passionately involved in the anti-communist movement that took hold in the USA after World War II. He was one of the first to name the respected left-wing writer John Howard Lawson as a leader of communist infiltration.

DeMille's career ended in grand style: *Samson and Delilah* (1949), *The Greatest Show on Earth* and *The Ten Commandments* (1956). The script of this film took three years to write and it was shot in Egypt after two years' preparation. It was a monumental production, em-

Children of the Night

'Listen to them...children of the night...what music they make.' Count Dracula on the baying wolves that prowl outside his castle grounds could equally well refer to the directors and stars who composed those incomparable masterpieces of the American cinema – the horror films of the Thirties

Horror movies are almost as old as the cinema itself. Primitive, heavily abridged versions of *Dr Jekyll and Mr Hyde* and *Frankenstein* were made in America in 1908 and 1910 respectively. Vampires appeared – in *The Vampire* – in 1911, and three years later Edgar Allan Poe's short stories, *The Tell-Tale Heart* and *The Pit and the Pendulum*, provided inspiration for D.W. Griffith's grisly *The Avenging Conscience*. But the first mature horror films came from the pre-war German cinema which, reviving the dark romantic spirit of E.T.A. Hoffmann's stories of the supernatural and demonic, laid the groundwork for its later Expressionist triumphs with early versions of *Der Student von Prag* (1913, The Student of Prague) and *Der Golem* (1914, The Golem).

Beauties, beasts and boffins

Then, in 1919, in Germany, Robert Wiene's *Das Kabinett des Dr Caligari* (The Cabinet of Dr Caligari) drew up what was to become virtually a blueprint for a specifically cinematic horror genre. Cesare, the somnambulist invoked by the evil Dr Caligari to murder those who sneer at his work, is sent to kill the pretty heroine in her bedroom. Instead, hesitating before her beauty, the black-garbed sleepwalker steals away with her over the rooftops into the night – trailing white draperies in a sequence of weird grace. All this takes place against a painted backdrop of tortured angles and shadows.

These three characters – the mad doctor, the monster he has created, and the girl they terrorize – were to become the key figures in Hollywood horror. The ghost-ridden *angst* of defeated, depressed Germany after World War I was, however, a far cry from the euphoria of America in the Twenties. *The*

Cabinet of Dr Caligari and the other great German Expressionist fantasies came to Hollywood's attention just as Broadway, the source of so much of its raw material, was revelling in a profitable vogue for spoof horrors.

Horror films made during the last years of the American silent cinema were condemned to play for laughs (Rex Ingram's *The Magician* of 1926, and Tod Browning's *The Unknown* of 1927 were rare exceptions). At the same time, the Expressionist lesson had clearly been learned: dramatic use of effects of light and shadows could be used to enhance tormented gestures and graceful movements, and a sense of the beauty in horror began to filter through the work of directors like Tod Browning, Roland West, Benjamin Christensen, and especially Paul Leni.

Leni had been an important director and art director in the early German cinema. The first Hollywood film he directed, *The Cat and the Canary* (1927), opens superbly with a hand brushing cobwebs from the screen to reveal the credit titles. Although the plot of this haunted-house movie tends to creak, the supernatural, as conjured up by Leni's camera, became a distinct, alarming possibility. After making only three more, equally atmospheric films, Leni died from blood poisoning in 1929.

The wages of fear

Universal earned its reputation as Hollywood's legendary home of horror with 3 films it made at the beginning of the Thirties. Tod Browning's *Dracula*, released on St Valentine's Day 1931, with Bela Lugosi repeating the role of the bloodsucking Transylvanian Count he had created on Broadway in 1927, soon emerged as the studio's leading contender for money-maker of the year; the gamble that sound would add a new dimension to terror had paid off handsomely. Then came *Frankenstein*, which was originally scheduled to be directed by Robert Florey, but was finally made by James Whale and starred Boris Karloff after Lugosi had refused to appear in a non-speaking

role as the Monster. Released in November 1931, it grossed twice as much at the box-office as *Dracula*. Lugosi and Florey emerged with their consolation prize for missing out on *Frankenstein* when they made *Murders in the Rue Morgue* (1932). It was another major success for Universal though less profitable.

Like *The Cabinet of Dr Caligari*, all three films featured white-robed maidens assailed by mad geniuses and monsters (even if *Dracula* combined the two latter roles into one). And all three had the same atmosphere of dark, fairy-tale magic. Although this special quality was later tapped by other film-makers – Cocteau, for example, in his superlative version of *La*

Above: Bela Lugosi's Hungarian background made him an ideal choice for the Transylvanian Count Dracula. Left: Fredric March as Mr Hyde, the only monster to win an Oscar. Right: Elsa Lanchester played Mary Shelley as well as Karloff's intended in The Bride of Frankenstein.

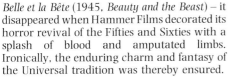

Belle et la Bête (1945, *Beauty and the Beast*) – it disappeared when Hammer Films decorated its horror revival of the Fifties and Sixties with a splash of blood and amputated limbs. Ironically, the enduring charm and fantasy of the Universal tradition was thereby ensured.

The beautiful and the damned

Soon mad geniuses were everywhere: busily hypnotizing heroines in *Svengali* (1931), fashioning murderous hands from synthetic flesh in *Doctor X* (1932), modelling human waxworks in *The Mystery of the Wax Museum* (1933), creating man-beasts in *Island of Lost Souls* (1933), and animating fiendish manikins

in *The Devil Doll* (1936). Meanwhile a bizarre assortment of beasts, from Frankenstein's Monster to King Kong himself, were impelled to pursue Beauty in a forlorn, foredoomed hope that they might turn out to be the long-awaited prince.

In addition to this fairy-tale element, another factor that contributed to the mythical status of horror films was their underlying appeal to post-Depression dissatisfaction with authority. Many of these films implied a desire to rise up against the authoritarian regimes that callously curtailed man's inalienable freedom to pursue happiness. Enclosed by a prologue and an epilogue in which the Doctor is shown to be

Above left: the complex plot of The Black Cat *had virtually nothing to do with Poe's short story. Above: Lugosi on the prowl in* Dracula, *which at least paid lip-service to Bram Stoker's original novel*

the sinisterly benevolent director of a lunatic asylum and all the other characters to be inmates, *The Cabinet of Dr Caligari* was the product of a similar mood of oppression in post-war Germany. It is governed, as the film's scriptwriters Carl Mayer and Hans Janowitz have observed, by Mayer's brushes with an army psychiatrist who diagnosed his rebellious attitude to authority as mental instability, and

by Janowitz's obsessive conviction that undetected and unrepentant murderers were roaming the streets by their thousand.

The legacy of all this as far as the horror genre is concerned, is that the films present, in microcosm, a world of dictatorial authority in which any straying from the norm is regarded as monstrous, intolerable behaviour to be rejected in disgust and ruthlessly exterminated. In *Frankenstein*, newly born from electrodes harnessing the elemental power of an electrical storm, Dr Frankenstein's creature ecstatically raises his face and hands to the warmth of the sun; it is only after encountering the implacable hostility and incomprehension of his fellow-beings in authority over him that he becomes a monster. In *King Kong* (1933), daring to aspire to love and beauty, Kong is hunted down and killed by outraged society. The monster in the great horror movies is the classic hero: Byronic, misbegotten, misjudged.

The quest for sanity

The few classic horror films that escape the madman-monster-maiden format also drew their power from this vision of the world as a lunatic asylum in which a tiny oasis of sanity and innocence must be fought for and preserved. It takes only a very small stretch of the imagination to see Count Zaroff (Leslie Banks), a hunter and disciple of De Sade who likes to titillate his jaded palate by pursuing human prey in *The Most Dangerous Game* (1932, also known as *The Hounds of Zaroff*), as a prototype Führer. In *Island of Lost Souls*, adapted from an H.G. Wells story, Dr Moreau (Charles Laughton) – like Zaroff, another megalomaniac figure – finally gets his comeuppance from the mutants he has sadistically crossbred; they rise against him in a peasant's revolt. *The Black Cat* (1934), set in a marble mansion built over the fort where thousands of men were betrayed and killed in World War I, concerns two men left morally dead by their experiences of war.

The Men Behind the Monsters

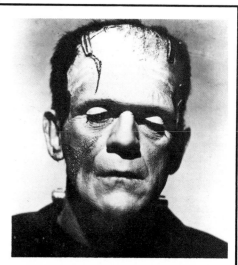

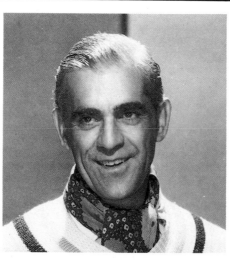

Lon Chaney was originally chosen for the lead role in *Dracula* (1931). When he died in August 1930, less than two months after the release of his first and only sound film, *The Unholy Three*, Bela Lugosi inherited the part – but not Chaney's mantle as the undisputed king of horror. That honour went to the Englishman Boris Karloff (1887–1969), an actor of intelligence, elegance, and a much greater range.

Lugosi (1882–1956), though very proud of his stage background in his native Hungary where he played in Shakespeare, Shaw, Wilde and Ibsen, was basically a ham, best remembered for the impressive, but somewhat absurd, oratory of his first two lines in *Dracula*: 'I am Dracula! I bid you welcome', and, referring to the wolves howling outside, 'Listen to them . . . children of the night . . . what music they make'. In *Frankenstein* (1931), Karloff hardly seems to be acting at all, but his eyes, huge pools of pain, and his dangling hands, uncertain whether to plead or to strangle, speak volumes. In contrast, Lugosi's only attempt at the Monster, in *Frankenstein Meets the Wolf Man* (1943), is risibly overplayed. But cast opposite Karloff for the first time in Edgar Ulmer's *The Black Cat* (1934), and for once in a sympathetic role, Lugosi gives what is probably his best performance. He is forced into restraint by Karloff and matches the master's subtleties.

Peter Lorre's chief assets for acting in horror films were his sinister baby face and whiningly caressing voice. He arrived in Hollywood a little late to partake in the first great days of horror, though he was memorable as Dr Gogol in *Mad Love* (1935). Lorre (1904–64) worked only occasionally at Universal and never with Whale or Browning. Condemned for most of the Thirties to appear in a series of routine thrillers and horrors, invariably providing their brightest moments, he came into his own in the Forties, perfecting the idiosyncratic brand of menace he had displayed earlier with Lang in Germany and Hitchcock in England.

Top: Boris Karloff – Frankenstein's Monster
Centre: Bela Lugosi – Count Dracula
Bottom: Peter Lorre – Dr Gogol

Now given over to devil worship, betrayer (Boris Karloff), and a surviving victim (Bela Lugosi), are locked in a duel over an innocent girl – ended when the arsenal concealed in the fort explodes. Weaving an almost abstract web of anguish out of its sense of all-pervasive evil, *The Black Cat* is surely one of the bleakest indictments of war and its spiritual aftermath to have emerged from any studio.

Tales from other crypts

Universal's success was not allowed to go unchallenged. *Svengali*, for instance, was a Warner Brothers film, the first of two in which John Barrymore confirmed the gift for outlandish characterization he had revealed in his *Dr Jekyll and Mr Hyde* of 1920. But Warners lacked directors like Whale and Browning who had a real flair for horror. Michael Curtiz, who directed the second Barrymore vehicle, *The Mad Genius* (1931), went on to make *Doctor X* and *The Mystery of the Wax Museum*; these films are workmanlike rather than inspired by the breath of dark poetry and Warners' challenge to Universal's supremacy faded away.

Other studios contributed occasional films. Paramount made *Island of Lost Souls* and Rouben Mamoulian's superb *Dr Jekyll and Mr Hyde* (1931), the only version to have really investigated the underlying sexuality in Stevenson's story. MGM terrified itself with its own daring in using real circus freaks – midgets, pinheads, a living torso, a half-man, a frog-man, an armless woman – in Tod Browning's widely banned *Freaks* (1932), but the studio did let Browning loose again, on *The*

Devil Doll. MGM finally retreated into respectability with a staid *Dr Jekyll and Mr Hyde* (1941) which, despite the implications of a dream sequence that has Spencer Tracy whipping Ingrid Bergman and Lana Turner harnessed to a chariot, was sexually whitewashed compared with the Mamoulian film. RKO, later to usurp Universal's leadership with Val

Above: in Frankenstein, *the poignant meeting of the Monster and the little girl is followed by the discovery of her death at his hands – and implications of far worse*

Lewton's excellent series of low-budget features celebrating the horrors that are sensed rather than seen, produced *The Most Dangerous Game* (1932) and the immortal *King Kong* (1933). But RKO also drowned their remake of *The Hunchback of Notre Dame* (1939) and star Charles Laughton (in the role which had made a star of Lon Chaney in Universal's marvellous 1923 original) in a deluge of spectacle.

Universal decline

Apart from Mr Hyde, Quasimodo was the only monster who did not belong to Universal in the Thirties. But although the studio retained the services of Dracula, Frankenstein's Monster, the Invisible Man, the Wolf Man, the Mummy, and the Phantom of the Opera, it never really discovered new directors to match Whale and Browning. Karl Freund, a great cameraman of the German Expressionist cinema, had been given a chance to direct, but *The Mummy* (1932) is excruciatingly dull – apart from the one eerie moment when Boris Karloff comes back to life. *Mad Love* (1935, MGM), the only other film Freund directed, is memorable chiefly for Peter Lorre's macabre performance as the mad, bald-headed, glassy-eyed Dr Gogol who gives Orlac new hands – those of a knife-murderer. Subsequently, with rare exceptions like Rowland V. Lee's stylishly architectural *Son of Frankenstein* (1939) and Robert Siodmak's spooky *Son of Dracula* (1943), Universal came to rely on studio workhorses and top cameramen who produced often enjoyable but pallid imitations of the characters and images created by Whale and Browning.

There was also the problem of scripts. In his autobiography, playwright and scriptwriter R.C. Sherriff recalls how he was hired to write the script of *The Invisible Man* (1933) for Whale. He asked Universal for a copy of H.G. Wells's novel but was instead given a stack of scripts which had been developed and rejected in turn – and in which the original character had been

James Whale

Born in Dudley in 1889, Whale was an Englishman whose career as a stage actor and producer brought him to New York in the late Twenties. He became a film director after directing dialogue on *Hell's Angels* (1930). Although he made only four horror films, they remain Universal's unmatched masterpieces. *Frankenstein* (1931), the first and best known, is also, for all its sombre visual beauty and archetypal quality, the least successful. Whale was most at home with comedy of manners in which he could express his yearning for gracious living and at the same time puncture it with malicious wit. It is possible that Whale, a working-class boy who made good, was compensating for his dubious upper-crust position in society. In his horror films the results are irresistible: the waspishly effeminate Horace Femm in *The Old Dark House* (1932), serenely observing the social niceties in a household that includes a mute, drunken giant of a butler, a killer with a knife, and a pyromaniac; the unseen hero of *The Invisible Man* (1933), gloating over his new-found power but lamenting that an invisible man must be hungry, naked, and spotlessly clean; the frizz-wigged, adder-tongued woman created for the Monster in *The Bride of Frankenstein* (1935), glancing at her intended mate and hissing with dismay. Without ever jeopardizing the grave beauty he found in horror, Whale was able to laugh long before the audience began.

Right: Claude Rains in The Invisible Man

Filmography
1929 The Love Doctor (dial.dir.only). '30 Hell's Angels (dial.dir.only); Journey's End (USA/ GB). '31 Waterloo Bridge; Frankenstein. '32 The Impatient Maiden; The Old Dark House. '33 The Invisible Man; The Kiss Before the Mirror; By Candlelight. '34 One More River (GB: Over the River). '35 The Bride of Frankenstein; Remember Last Night? '36 Show Boat. '37 The Road Back; The Great Garrick. '38 Sinners in Paradise; Port of Seven Seas; Wives Under Suspicion. '39 The Man in the Iron Mask; Green Hell. '41 They Dare Not Love. '49 ep Hello Out There (rest of film released as Face to Face, 1952).

Above: Universal's tortured lycanthrope was largely the creation of Lon Chaney Jr and had little to do with Endore's original werewolf

subjected to increasingly imaginative inflations so that he ended up as an invader from Mars. Sherriff quietly returned to the novel for a script from which Whale made a masterpiece. The inflations, needless to say, began to turn up in sequels. It is small wonder that, by the Forties, Universal's monsters had flitted to Poverty Row studios, became foils for comedy teams like the Bowery Boys or Abbott and Costello, or were packed in three or four to a film, hopefully to provide the requisite thrills. *House of Frankenstein* (1944), for example, brought together the Monster, Dracula and the Wolf Man.

Shadows of the originals

Both the lasting power and the severe limitations of the Universal tradition are perhaps most keenly indicated by the failure of that studio and its imitators to translate the major source novels of the horror film with any measure of adequacy. Mary Shelley's *Frankenstein*, for example, has an astonishing epic sweep, ending in a kind of frozen eternity with the Monster being endlessly pursued across icy arctic wastes by its despairing creator: an image that no one has ever faithfully committed to film. Bram Stoker's *Dracula* is invariably adulterated so badly that the character of Renfield, the Count's acolyte, and his education in bloodlust as he progresses from eating flies and spiders to birds, is always rendered meaningless. And Guy Endore's superb novel, *The Werewolf of Paris*, has never been filmed with any fidelity whatsoever. All the Wolf Man films ignore the novel's historical and religious account of the evolution of the werewolf, as well as Endore's ironic vision of how a werewolf's savagery pales into insignificance when compared to the barbarisms committed by man upon man during times of stress (here during the siege of Paris in 1870). Doubtless for copyright reasons, Universal created its own distinctly inferior Wolf Man myth – *The Werewolf of London* (1935), *The Wolf Man* (1941) – which has been slavishly followed ever since.

Nothing is more indicative of the way Universal and the horror movie ran out of creative steam than the emergence of Lon Chaney Jr as the all-purpose replacement for Boris Karloff in the early Forties. Even in his worst films, Karloff was an actor of rare quality: Chaney Jr was not – but by then the films, endlessly churning over old ground, did not ask him to be.

Tod Browning

More solemn than James Whale, Browning was interested in the freakish psychopathic nature of his characters rather than in their picturesque possibilities. Born in Louisville, Kentucky, in 1880, he ran away from school to become a circus performer and then entered films as an actor in 1913. He had already started to direct his own films when he assisted D.W. Griffith in *Intolerance* (1916).

Browning's best work was done during the Twenties in a string of films with Lon Chaney, who always tried to provide his monsters with a basis of psychological realism. The climax of their association was *The Unknown* (1927), in which Chaney, hiding out in a circus disguised as an armless knife-thrower, decides to have his arms amputated to remove the thumb-prints which would convict him of murder. Having thus escaped justice, he also happily congratulates himself that as the disturbed girl whom he desires (played by Joan Crawford) cannot bear to be held by a man, she will now be able to love him.

A horrifying and utterly convincing exercise in sado-masochism, *The Unknown* was surpassed in intensity only by *Freaks* (1932). This film is a nightmarish collision between normality and abnormality. Olga Baclanova plays a trapeze artiste who marries a dwarf for his money, planning to poison him with the aid of her strong-man lover. As a result she is subjected to hideous mutilation by the vengeful circus freaks – they turn her into a chicken. Browning presents the closed world of the freaks with immense sympathy and clearly shows the human emotions beneath their inhuman forms so that these misshapen men and women seem more 'normal' than the 'normal' characters. After disastrous premieres *Freaks* was banned in some States and eventually 'lost' in MGM's vaults. It was not seen in Britain for over 30 years.

Below: Browning surrounded by the circus freaks who starred in his and MGM's most controversial film.

In the rest of his sound films Browning was stylish but patchy. Magnificent moments, like Lugosi's first appearance on the steps of his castle in *Dracula* (1931), the concentrated eeriness in the misty churchyard at the beginning of *Mark of the Vampire* (1935), and the Lilliputian assassin in *The Devil Doll* (1936) methodically scaling a giant dressing table in search of a hat pin as her murder weapon, are followed by disastrous drops in temperature. Especially after *Freaks*, Browning was prevented by cinema conventions from probing the psychological motivations and scars he found interesting. He retired early and though his death was announced in 1944, he did not in fact die until 1962.

Filmography (films as director)
1915 The Lucky Transfer; The Slave Girl; An Image of the Past; The Highbinders; The Story of a Story; The Spell of the Poppy; The Electric Alarm; The Living Death; The Burned Hand; The Woman From Warren's; Little Marie. **'16** Puppets; Everybody's Doing It!; The Deadly Glass of Beer/The Fatal Glass of Beer. **'17** Jim Bludso (co-dir; +co-sc); A Love Sublime (co-dir); Hands Up! (co-dir); Peggy, the Will o' the Wisp; The Jury of Fate. **'18** The Eyes of Mystery; The Legion of Death; Revenge; Which Woman; The Deciding Kiss; The Brazen Beauty; Set Free (+sc). **'19** The Wicked Darling; The Exquisite Thief; The Unpainted Woman; A Petal on the Current; Bonnie, Bonnie Lassie (+co-sc). **'20** The Virgin of Stamboul (+co-sc). **'21** Outside the Law (+prod; +co-sc); No Woman Knows (+co-sc). **'22** The Wise Kid; The Man Under Cover; Under Two Flags (+co-adap). **'23** Drifting (+co-sc); The Day of Faith; White Tiger (+co-sc). **'24** The Dangerous Flirt (GB: A Dangerous Flirtation); Silk Stocking Sal. **'25** The Unholy Three (+prod); The Mystic; Dollar Down. **'26** The Black Bird; The Road to Mandalay. **'27** The Show (+prod); The Unknown; London After Midnight (+prod) (GB: The Hypnotist). **'28** The Big City (+prod); West of Zanzibar. **'29** Where East is East (+prod); The Thirteenth Chair (+prod). **'30** Outside the Law (+co-sc). **'31** Dracula; The Iron Man (+prod). **'32** Freaks (+prod). **'33** Fast Workers (+prod). **'35** Mark of the Vampire. **'36** The Devil Doll. **'39** Miracles for Sale.

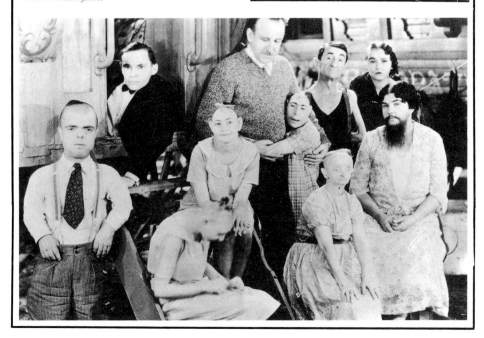

How John Ford's West was Won

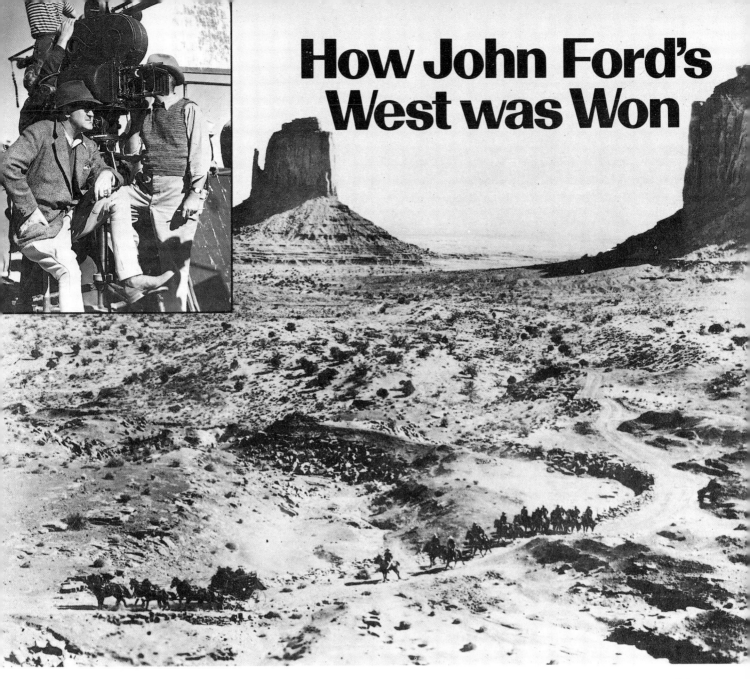

The heroes of John Ford's films are the frontiersmen, pioneers and peacemakers who dedicated themselves to the founding of the homes and communities that make up America. Ford's vision is a folk vision: a celebration of the ideals that sent wagon trains of settlers westwards in search of freedom and opportunity, but couched in the homeliest of terms – where a dance or a gathering round a graveside speaks volumes more than the dramatic battles and gunfights that were also waged in the winning of the West

Above: Stagecoach, in which John Ford (inset) first made use of the spectacular mesas of Monument Valley, Utah. The film itself was a landmark in the career of one of the most respected directors in world cinema. Ford (1895–1973) directed his first feature, Tornado, in 1917. Born Sean Aloysius O'Feeney, thirteenth child of Irish immigrant parents, in Maine, he had come to Hollywood after failing to get into naval college. He worked his way up as prop man, stunt man and actor

By the end of the Thirties John Ford already had a hundred films to his name. Whereas a lesser director would have probably burned himself out, the best years for Ford were still ahead. His 'golden age' spanned nearly three decades. It began in 1939 with two films, *Stagecoach* and *Young Mr Lincoln*, and encompassed along the way such milestones as *She Wore a Yellow Ribbon* (1949), *Wagonmaster* (1950) and *The Searchers* (1956). These films are packed with unforgettable sequences and images: the young Lincoln (Henry Fonda) climbing a hill in a storm; Nathan Brittles (John Wayne), the old cavalry captain in *She*

Wore a Yellow Ribbon, riding out of the fort for a final mission and furtively shielding his face from the sun, or Brittles going to his wife's grave in the evening to 'talk' to her. There is the moment when the showgirl Denver (Joanne Dru) flashes a mysterious look at the wagon-train leader Travis (Ben Johnson) in *Wagonmaster*; or when Ethan (Wayne) lifts up and cradles the niece (Natalie Wood) he has sought to kill in *The Searchers*, understanding in those few instants the uselessness of his hatred; or Frank Skeffington (Spencer Tracy) returning home alone after failing to be re-elected as the mayor in *The Last Hurrah* (1958). These

sublime moments in Ford's films reveal more than a thousand critical post-mortems that his art is above all meditative – one might even say symphonic.

The contemplative nature in Ford has rarely been understood. In France, for example, his Westerns have been promoted with pompous phrases like 'heroic charge', 'hellish pursuit' and 'fantastic journey' which suggest that the films somehow belong to the epic genre. Nothing is further from the essence of these fundamentally peaceful works of art. And although Voltaire's assertion that 'Epic authors had to choose a hero whose name alone

141

Above: Judge Billy Priest (Will Rogers) and other veterans of the Civil War evoke nostalgia for the Confederate States in Judge Priest *(1934). Ford remade the film as* The Sun Shines Bright *in 1953*

would impress itself on the reader' can be applied to certain Ford films like *Young Mr Lincoln* (a splendid evocation of the youth of the American president), it is certainly not applicable to most of his work, including the Westerns. In *My Darling Clementine* (1946), that legendary hero Wyatt Earp (Henry Fonda) is reduced to everyday dimensions; he has no exalted status.

A man's gotta do . . .

It is interesting to compare the socially minded motivation of the typical Ford hero with the personal motivation of the classic Western hero. The classic Western is chiefly built around a ruggedly individualistic vision of the world: Allan Dwan's *Silver Lode* (1954), with John Payne as a man trying to clear his name, and King Vidor's *Man Without a Star* (1955), with Kirk Douglas as a drifter motivated by revenge, are perhaps the most extreme examples of this. Strong feelings, often of physical or psychological violence, predominate; there is hatred, vengeance, rebellion and conquest. A cowboy is usually out to avenge his brother, his friend or his own honour; an outlaw tries to escape from his past; a gunfighter follows his will to kill; a man needs to prove he is not a coward or has to overcome the devil within himself. In short, the genre draws its dramatic force from a few powerful ideas: a confrontation, an opposition, a tearing away. From the films of Raoul Walsh to those of Delmer Daves, Western heroes pitch themselves into a battle by their own free choice. And it is a battle that will allow them to accomplish their purpose – but from which, if they survive, they will emerge permanently scarred. Even if there are no horseback chases or bloody shoot-outs, the dramaturgy of the classic Western is precisely structured and depends on a number of climactic moments.

With Ford, however, the essential motivation is looser, more attenuated, and rarely drawn around an individual emotion or a negative, destructive driving force like vengeance. What predominates at the heart of his Westerns are journeys and wanderings: the slow odyssey of a wagon train, the patrolling of a group of cavalrymen, the crossing of a desert by a stagecoach, or by a group of bandits on the run. Ultimately his films are all odysseys of groups – the stage passengers in *Stagecoach* (1939), farmers and their families escaping from the Oklahoma Dust Bowl in *The Grapes of Wrath* (1940), cavalrymen out on missions in *Fort Apache* (1948), *She Wore a Yellow Ribbon*, *Rio Grande* (1950) and *The Horse Soldiers* (1959), the Mormon settlers in *Wagonmaster*, Ethan and Martin Pawley (Jeffrey Hunter) searching for Debbie in *The Searchers*. Each group consists of several people who either belong to the same walk of life, or are brought together and bound by the same collective purpose. Ford is only interested in personal

problems in so far as they overlap those of society at large; whereas in Howard Hawks' Westerns, for example, adventure remains the right of the individual and only concerns society by chance or accident. In Hawks' *Rio Bravo* (1959) the sheriff (John Wayne) refuses the help offered to him; Ford's Wyatt Earp, however, accepts it immediately. It is a fundamental difference: the first sheriff seeks to fulfil himself through his duty, the second thinks primarily about helping those around him.

. . . what a man's gotta do

At the same time Ford frequently shows us the dissensions and disagreements that divide communities, and his heroes act only in relation to the environment they live in. It is that environment that provides their task – a duty to fulfil for the good of the community; any personal vendettas are usually subjugated to the communal cause. The notion of having a task or a mission takes precedence over all personal considerations. This is especially true of *Rio Grande* in which Captain Kirby Yorke (John Wayne) puts his duty as a soldier before his marriage and family; and in *The Sun Shines Bright* (1953), in which an old Southern judge (Charles Winninger) risks his reputation in

Most of Ford's films are about men working for a common cause and sharing the hardships incurred. Above: John Qualen, Ward Bond, Jack Pennick, John Wayne and Thomas Mitchell toil on the sea in The Long Voyage Home. *Below: Welsh miners enduring a pit disaster in* How Green Was My Valley, *with Walter Pidgeon and Oscar-winner Donald Crisp*

order to rescue a black boy from being lynched. In *My Darling Clementine* Wyatt Earp's vengeance on the Clantons for the killing of his brother is given much less importance than the dance in front of the church and the Shakespearian monologues of the travelling showman (Alan Mowbray). Earp is a supremely calm figure, not someone driven by a nameless hatred (as is the case of the Western heroes in the films of Anthony Mann).

Indeed, violence linked to the notion of a personal quest hardly exists at all in Ford's films. Killings, even woundings, are rare. Not a single Indian is seen to be killed or wounded in *She Wore a Yellow Ribbon*. In *Two Rode Together* (1961), Sheriff McCabe (James Stewart) fires only two revolver shots – the only gunshots in the film. Ford could never conceive a scene like the one in Anthony Mann's *The Man From Laramie* (1955) where Stewart's hand is maimed. Violence is never a goal in Ford's films or a means of self-fulfilment, but a duty or a last resort. When violence is inescapable, Ford

Above: in My Darling Clementine *Henry Fonda portrayed Wyatt Earp as a balanced, pensive peace-loving man. Right: a custodian of the West retires – John Wayne as Captain Brittles in* She Wore a Yellow Ribbon *with Harry Carey Jr, Joanne Dru and Victor McLaglen. Below: Travis (Ben Johnson) and Denver (Joanne Dru) in* Wagonmaster

evokes it briefly and objectively, without any indulgence or lyricism; the swift shoot-out at the OK Corral in *My Darling Clementine* and the killing off of the outlaws who threaten the settlers in *Wagonmaster* are good examples.

Even the adventures themselves are non-violent in the way they progress; they are unfolded for us in a rhythm that is at once casual yet majestic. In telling a story Ford takes his time and works like a painter, rather than a strategist or a theoretician.

The true Ford hero has no need to use violence to prove himself. He simply does it, carried along by the collective ideal that leaves no space in his mind for doubt. Perhaps Ford's real heroes are the communities themselves: the unknown soldiers bringing peace to the West; the pioneers who are crossing the country to build new states; the inhabitants of

a township whose chief aim is to establish a society of law and order – all those people who, whether consciously or not, have helped to build the United States and whose names and faces have been forgotten. And so it is their work that the films celebrate. This work may not be exalting; it is often thankless, seldom on a big scale, but it is stamped with a day-to-day heroism.

The homing instinct

Most of Ford's pictures are based on and perpetuate a theme that seems to haunt his last Western, *Cheyenne Autumn* (1964) – his elegy on the dispossessed Indians who seek to reclaim their ancestral lands – and that is the need not simply to build or see something through to its conclusion, but to arrive at the possession of a piece of land, a home or hearth, or perhaps simply a rocking-chair, which is exactly what is sought by Mose (Hank Worden) in *The Searchers*. There is also a need to fight against enemies and the elements to keep possessions in order to understand their complete value.

The story of Ford's films is a great saga of agrarian life: claiming or reclaiming, cultivating and enlarging territorial possessions.

Accordingly Ford's heroes take their character from the peasant, whatever their social origins. Heroes may be Irish peasants, farmers, Welsh miners, soldiers, whatever. In Ford's eyes the soldiers who run a territory in *She Wore a Yellow Ribbon* are involved in the same struggle as the Joad family in *The Grapes of Wrath*. And although the different communities in Ford's films are closed communities governed by their own rules, they are similar in that they share not only the struggles of life but its simple pleasures, too, like a dance, as in *Fort Apache* and *My Darling Clementine*.

The notion of possession accounts for Ford's passion for ceremonies. Celebrations, drunken festivities, dances, even funerals are the tangible proof of the need to affirm publicly the ownership of a place, especially since it could be taken away at any time – as Lars Jorgensen (John Qualen) remarks in *The Searchers*.

The same motivation underlies Ford's fondness for landscapes that are immutable, notably the desert and rocky outcrops of Monument Valley, his favourite location. It is almost as if the film-maker shares with his characters the desire to possess these vast terrains in order to gain a profound appreciation of stability.

Even that antithesis of the Ford hero, Ethan Edwards in *The Searchers*, who can find no place for himself in stable society, is concerned with its continuation. In this fragmented, poignant film – the only one of Ford's based on a notion of individualism – Ethan sets himself against the ordered life and is seemingly involved in a desperate struggle to remain a loner, a rebel. After a hopeless search for his niece that lasts ten years, Ethan finally understands the uselessness of his revolt. He cannot bring himself to kill the girl when he finds her, tainted though she may be by living with an

Indian 'buck' and therefore a threat to white society. Because he is so concerned to preserve the wholeness of the homestead, he does not realize that the people who made it what it was, and thus its very nature, have changed. There is no place for him and after returning Debbie to the community he disappears, leaving the new generation represented by Martin Pawley to take over.

Exiles and nomads

Ethan is just one of scores of exiles that struggle to preserve society in Ford's films. Others include Irish and European immigrants who dream of gaining some sort of new birthright in America. In *The Man Who Shot Liberty Valance* (1962), restaurant-owner Peter Ericson (John Qualen) actually leaps for joy on hearing the news that he has earned his American citizenship. Ford's universe is also peopled by rootless characters who wander aimlessly – like the sailors in *The Long Voyage Home* (1940). Among these exiles there is even a tribe of Indians: the Comanches of *The Searchers* are Indians who have no territory;

they are constantly on the move. There is also the immigrant prizefighter (John Wayne) returning to his home town after killing a man in the ring in *The Quiet Man* (1952), and families put on the road by the effects of the Dust Bowl to look for new work in *The Grapes of Wrath*.

Other characters are exiled in different ways: the crazed white children and women in *The Searchers* who are refused recognition by their kinsfolk as they have been defiled by Indians. There are also the soldiers for whom the bugle song of retreat in *She Wore a Yellow Ribbon* and *The Wings of Eagles* (1957), or disgrace in *Fort Apache*, sounds a little like exile.

In Ford's films it is not only characters that may be uprooted but entire nations and historical periods. The director has often returned to moments when a social class, or indeed a whole race – in *Cheyenne Autumn* the whole Indian community is oppressed and exiled – is on the brink of extinction. Cheyenne autumn, Welsh twilight – these are both situations from which men and women are forced away to find new means of survival. In *How Green Was My Valley* (1941), industrial strife disrupts the working community and the idyllic family life of the Morgans in the Welsh village where they live at the turn of the century. The youngest son, Huw (Roddy McDowall), whose childhood provides the basis of the story, must finally follow his brothers and move on to pastures new.

Ford portrays people trying to remain faithful to themselves, and to their way of thinking, even when threatened by great historical upheavals. In this respect he may be a spiritual relative of the great Soviet director Donskoi,

Above left: an inaptly titled Belgian poster for The Searchers; *the film is less concerned with Debbie and her 'imprisonment' by Indians than with Ethan, who is a 'prisoner' of his obsession with finding her. Right: the killing of Liberty (Lee Marvin) – but not by Stoddard (James Stewart) – in* The Man Who Shot Liberty Valance. *Below: John Wayne and William Holden in* The Horse Soldiers, *one of Ford's poetic tributes to the US Cavalry*

Filmography

As Jack Ford: **1914** Lucille Love – the Girl of Mystery (serial) (prop man; possible credits for act; stunts; ass. dir); Lucile/Lucille, the Waitress (series of four films: She Wins a Prize and Has Her Troubles; Exaggeration Gets Her Into All Kinds of Trouble; She Gets Mixed Up in a Regular 'Kid Kalamity'; Her Near Proposal) (credited as dir. in some sources); The Mysterious Rose (act. only). **'15** The Birth of a Nation (act. only); Three Bad Men and a Girl (act. only); The Hidden City (act. only); The Doorway of Destruction (act; +ass. dir); The Broken Coin (serial) (act; +ass. dir). **'16** The Lumber Yard Gang (act. only); Peg o' the Ring (serial) (act. only); Chicken-Hearted Jim (act. only); The Bandit's Wager (act. only). **'17** The Purple Mask (serial) (ass. dir); The Tornado (+act; +sc); The Trail of Hate (dir. copyrighted to Ford, no screen credit; +act; +sc); The Scrapper (+act; +sc); The Soul Herder (reissued as short 1922); Cheyenne's Pal; Straight Shooting (reissued as short Straight Shootin', 1925); The Secret Man; A Marked Man; Bucking Broadway. **'18** The Phantom Riders; Wild Women; Thieves' Gold; The Scarlet Drop (GB: Hillbilly); Delirium (co-dir); Hellbent (+co-sc); A Woman's Fool; Three Mounted Men. **'19** Roped; A Fight for Love; The Fighting Brothers; Bare Fists; By Indian Post; The Rustlers; Gun Law; The Gun Pusher (reissued as short 1924); Riders of Vengeance; The Last Outlaw; The Outcasts of Poker Flats; The Ace of the Saddle; The Rider of the Law; A Gun Fightin' Gentleman; untitled one-reel promotion film for personal appearance tour by actor Harry Carey. **'20** Marked Men; The Prince of Avenue 'A'; The Girl in No. 29; Hitchin'

whose films were usually set in a period of social change or revolution. Generally the protagonists do adapt and overcome the crises they face in Ford's films, but they are often required to make costly sacrifices. In *The Man Who Shot Liberty Valance*, Tom Doniphon (John Wayne) kills the outlaw Liberty (Lee Marvin) but makes it seem as though Ransom Stoddard (James Stewart) has done so. For this

Above: Indian women robbed of their homes in Cheyenne Autumn, *based on the real tragedy of the Cheyenne. It was Ford's last Western and the last of nine films he shot wholly or partially in Monument Valley*

noble act Doniphon sacrifices the personal glory of the deed and the girl he loves to Stoddard, lives a lonely life and dies alone.

Ford's desire to celebrate collective effort in his later films was tainted with the cynicism of advancing years, and there are hints of bitterness. Between the winning simplicity of *Drums Along the Mohawk* (1939) – Ford's tribute to the spirit of pioneer America on the eve of the Revolutionary War – and *She Wore a Yellow Ribbon*, there is a great difference in outlook. In the latter Nathan Brittles reconsiders his existence as a cavalry officer and begins to question it, and also doubts the validity of his current mission to subdue the Indians even though he continues to pursue it.

Monuments to America

Ford's heroes age with his work. The last shot of *The Man Who Shot Liberty Valance* is of the elderly Ransom Stoddard crying: doubt and uncertainty are bound up with sadness. Perhaps by the early Sixties, the time of *Liberty Valance*, *Cheyenne Autumn* and *Donovan's Reef* (1963) – a kind of melancholic, sometimes comic, reflection on the past, set in the mythical paradise of a Pacific island – Ford had become aware of his own uprootedness and of his own peculiar state of being an exile within American cinema. Perhaps he also realized that the nature of his work would ultimately remain as unchangeable as his own Monument Valley, but that everything around him was crumbling and disappearing. But when he ceased making pictures John Ford left behind him several of his own enduring monuments to the building of a country: a few massive rocks left in the middle of a vast desert.

Posts; Just Pals. '21 The Big Punch (+co-sc); The Freeze Out; The Wallop; Desperate Trails; Action; Sure Fire; Jackie. '22 Little Miss Smiles; Nero (uncredited add. dir); Silver Wings (prologue dir. only); The Village Blacksmith; The Face on the Barroom Floor (GB: The Love Image). '23 Three Jumps Ahead (+sc). As John Ford: '23 Cameo Kirby; North of Hudson Bay; Hoodman Blind. '24 The Iron Horse; Hearts of Oak. '25 The Fighting Heart (GB: Once to Every Man); Kentucky Pride; Lightnin'; Thank You. '26 The Shamrock Handicap; Three Bad Men (+sc); The Blue Eagle; What Price Glory (uncredited add. dir). '27 Upstream (GB: Footlight Glamour); Mother Machree (+sound version 1928). '28 Four Sons; Hangman's House; Napoleon's Barber; Riley the Cop. '29 Strong Boy; The Black Watch (GB: King of the Khyber Rifles) (silent scenes only); Salute; Men Without Women. '30 Born Reckless (silent scenes only); Up the River (silent scenes only; +uncredited sc). '31 Seas Beneath (silent scenes only); The Brat; Arrowsmith. '32 Air Mail; Flesh. '33 Pilgrimage; Doctor Bull. '34 The Lost Patrol; The World Moves On; Judge Priest. '35 The Whole Town's Talking (GB: Passport to Fame); The Informer; Steamboat Round the Bend. '36 The Prisoner of Shark Island; The Last Outlaw; Mary of Scotland; The Plough and the Stars. '37 Wee Willie Winkie; The Hurricane. '38 The Adventures of Marco Polo (uncredited add. dir); Four Men and a Prayer; Submarine Patrol. '39 Stagecoach (+prod); Young Mr Lincoln; Drums Along the Mohawk. '40 The Grapes of Wrath; The Long Voyage Home. '41 Tobacco Road; How Green Was My Valley. '42 Sex Hygiene (Army training short); The Battle of Midway (doc)

(+co-photo); Torpedo Squadron (private Army film not publicly shown); How to Operate Behind Enemy Lines (Office of Strategic Services training film for restricted showing). '43 December 7th (co-dir) (feature version for Navy; short for public); We Sail at Midnight (doc) (USA-GB: Ford possibly sup. dir. of American version). '45 They Were Expendable (+prod). '46 My Darling Clementine. '47 The Fugitive (+co-prod). '48 Fort Apache (+co-prod); Three Godfathers (+co-prod). '49 Mighty Joe Young (co-prod. only); She Wore a Yellow Ribbon (+co-prod). '50 When Willie Comes Marching Home; Wagonmaster (+co-prod); Rio Grande (+co-prod). '51 The Bullfighter and the Lady (uncredited ed. only); This Is Korea (doc) (+prod). '52 The Quiet Man (+co-prod); What Price Glory? '53 The Sun Shines Bright (+co-prod); Mogambo; Hondo (uncredited 2nd unit co-dir. only). '55 The Long Gray Line; The Red, White and Blue Line (short with footage from The Long Gray Line); Mister Roberts (some scenes only). '56 The Searchers. '57 The Wings of Eagles; The Rising of the Moon (Eire); The Growler Story (short). '58 Gideon's Day (USA: Gideon of Scotland Yard); The Last Hurrah (+prod). '59 Korea (doc) (+co-prod); The Horse Soldiers. '60 Sergeant Rutledge. '61 Two Rode Together. '62 The Man Who Shot Liberty Valance; How the West Was Won (ep. only). '63 Donovan's Reef (+prod); The Directors (short) (appearance as himself only). '64 Cheyenne Autumn. '65 Young Cassidy (some scenes only); Seven Women. '70 Chesty: a Tribute to a Legend (doc) (+interviewer) (shorter version reissued 1976). '71 Vietnam! Vietnam! (doc) (exec. prod. only).

Frank Capra's American Dream

'I would sing the songs of the working stiffs, of the short-changed Joes, the born poor, the afflicted. I would gamble with the long-shot players who light candles in the wind, and resent with the pushed-around because of race or birth. Above all, I would fight for their causes on the screens of the world.'

Frank Capra, when writing these words in 1971 about downtrodden workers ('the working stiffs') was not just repeating the flattering

Above, left to right: James Stewart and Jean Arthur in Mr Smith Goes to Washington; *Gary Cooper, with tuba, in* Mr Deeds Goes to Town, *and with Barbara Stanwyck in* Meet John Doe. *Tall, lean men of integrity, Stewart and Cooper perfectly conformed to Capra's idea of the populist hero. Left and below left: early Capra comedies included* The Strong Man, *with the childlike Harry Langdon, and* Platinum Blonde, *with Jean Harlow as a sexy 'society girl' seeking a husband*

comments critics had made about his films. While other successful Hollywood directors in the Thirties were content to coast along on the charms of stellar performances and glitteringly unreal plots, Capra made a clear stand for films with a recognizable basis in the world the audience lived in or, more accurately, the world they wanted to live in. These were films that – along with the romantic clinches, chases and slapstick – provided idealism.

A dream comes true

Capra himself was born poor and pushed-around, one of seven peasant children, in Sicily in 1897. By 1903 the bulk of the family had emigrated to Los Angeles, and Capra began his determined climb up the ladder of success in the fabled land of opportunity. The fable in his case proved spectacularly true: Capra even writes that he thought of his films as one way of saying 'Thanks' to America, its people and history. In the Twenties he became a gagman for Mack Sennett and directed two celebrated films – *The Strong Man* (1926) and *Long Pants* (1927) – starring the baby-faced comic Harry Langdon. Langdon's ego subsequently got the better of his talent and his career declined; Capra's ego and talent fortunately developed at the same rate. Once ensconced at Columbia – the Poverty Row studio ruled by Harry Cohn, a man of drive, independence, and scant tact – Capra's career shot upwards. He cannily leapt at subjects with 'headline' appeal – an airship's crash in the Antarctic in *Dirigible* (1931) a bank crisis in *American Madness* (1932).

In this last film Capra was warming to his theme and to his technique. In the chaos of the Depression the bank president, played by Walter Huston, appeals to the virtues of good neighbourliness against the vices of blind self-interest. Thus encouraged, his customers earnestly rush to return the money they had

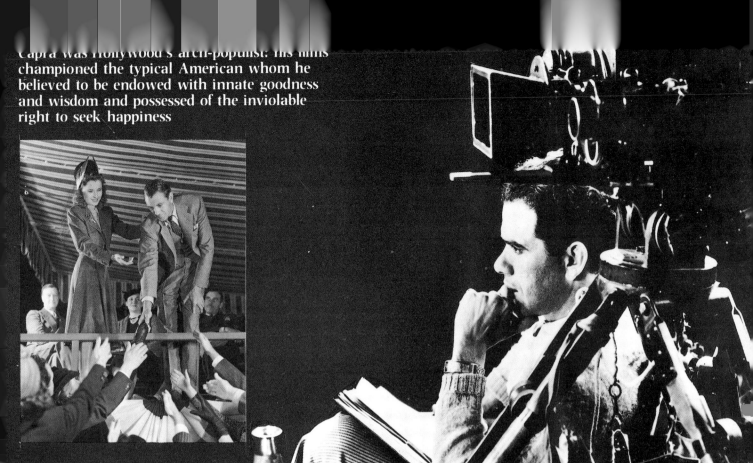

Capra was Hollywood's arch-populist: his films championed the typical American whom he believed to be endowed with innate goodness and wisdom and possessed of the inviolable right to seek happiness

previously rushed to take out. But everyone was rushing: beginning with this film Capra deliberately speeded up the dialogue, made speeches overlap, cut out all dawdling camera fades and character entrances. The dialogue itself was written by Robert Riskin, a former playwright who collaborated with Capra throughout the Thirties and had an acute ear for the twists and turns of everyday speech. He also shared many of Capra's own beliefs about the rights of America's ordinary citizens.

The delectable *It Happened One Night* (1934) provided another stepping-stone for Capra. He had long set his sights on the Oscars, Hollywood's ultimate accolade of success, and with this comedy he secured an armful for himself, his stars, and his writer. He also achieved a new spontaneity in his direction: scenes between Clark Gable, the snappy news-paperman, and Claudette Colbert, the run-away heiress he pursues first for a story and later for love, had an almost improvisational ease. And Capra had now departed decisively from the drawing-room setting of earlier comedies like *Platinum Blonde* (1931). The action takes place in a cross-country bus, along the highways, inside the motels. The haughty Colbert character can't but be humanized by the experience; even her father, played by Walter Connolly, proves to be a plutocrat with a heart of gold, allowing her to run away all over again with honest, down-to-earth Gable rather than marry a dull, wealthy aviator.

Good Deeds

Elements of the Gable character – his un-complicated decency, his fondness for homely pursuits like dunking doughnuts in coffee or giving piggybacks – reappear in bolder form with Gary Cooper's Longfellow Deeds in *Mr Deeds Goes to Town* (1936). Deeds is catapulted by an uncle's inheritance from small-town

peace in Mandrake Falls to New York turmoil. His simple habits – tuba-playing, writing greeting-card verses – provoke scorn and derision, while lawyers, creditors and opera committees jump on him for every penny. He finally puts his money to work for the country's impoverished farmers in a self-help scheme, giving them a cow, a horse, some seed and some land. The cream of New York society responds by declaring him insane; the sub-sequent courtroom trial provides a perfect setting for Capra and Riskin's brilliantly en-gineered debate on the values of American life.

Road to Utopia

Capra's next film, *Lost Horizon* (1937), may at first glance seem an unlikely venture. But this lavish fantasy, based on James Hilton's book, provided an opportunity for the director and writer to create an abstract version of the Utopia their Longfellow Deeds and other good citizens were working towards. The Utopia of Shangri-La is located in a Himalayan monas-tery, where all strife and all old age have been eradicated. But without strife, without Capra's usual endearing characters and rushing crowds (the benign lamas walk very slowly), the film's visual and dramatic interest sinks dangerously low.

Capra quickly worked himself back towards his top form with an adaptation of another popular success – Kaufman and Hart's play *You Can't Take It With You*, filmed in 1938. Typically, the adaptation strengthens the characters and the beliefs they espouse. An-thony P. Kirby (Edward Arnold), the man who wants to take as much of it with him as possible, is made more of a grasping, villainous ogre, while those for whom money and worldly goods mean nothing – the Vanderhof family and assorted guests (like the iceman who delivers ice and just stays) – are made less

whimsical, more forthright. And, as in *It Happened One Night*, the obstructive plutocrat is finally humanized, joining in the music-making at the Vanderhof's home-grown Shangri-La, joyfully playing 'Pollywolly-doodle' on a harmonica.

With *Mr Smith Goes to Washington* (1939) Capra returned to the proven formula of *Deeds*, but deployed it over a larger canvas. Now his unassuming all-American hero was tilting not just at snobbish, money-grabbing New York society – but at the whole government mach-ine in Washington DC. Jefferson Smith (James Stewart), pet-shop owner and Boy Scouts leader, is voted to the Senate on the strength of his gullibility (there is a pocket-lining deal coming up involving the construc-tion of a dam). His bird-calls cause as much laughter as Longfellow Deeds' poetry, yet he proves a sterner customer than his Party overlords anticipated. He proposes building a National Boys' Camp on land that would be flooded by the dam, and argues its merits – along with much else – in a filibuster speech lasting almost a day: a clear parallel with Deeds' courtroom trial.

Government of the people

Capra had pushed his concern for the rights of 'the working stiffs . . . the short-changed Joes' straight into the political arena with *Mr Smith*. Yet his own political position in his films was vague in the extreme – they would hardly have had such a wide success had it been otherwise. Their motivating beliefs were simple, naive even, but Capra's picture of America as a continent of small communities helping each other to prosperity and happiness held great attraction in the Thirties. This wasn't Roosevelt's vaunted New Deal, with its elab-orate network of Government bodies guiding, marshalling, even creating work. Rather it

Above: in A Hole in the Head *Sinatra plays a down-and-out Miami hotelier who tries to get his wealthy brother to bail him out. Capra was at his best when he sent his characters in search of less tangible goals, such as happiness; in the Shangri-La of* Lost Horizon *(above left) with John Howard, H.B. Warner and Jane Wyatt; in the communal life of small-town America in* You Can't Take It With You *(left) with James Stewart and Jean Arthur; in life itself in* It's a Wonderful Life *(below left) with Stewart, Thomas Mitchell and Donna Reed*

Filmography
1922 The Ballad of Fultah Fisher's Boarding House/Fultah Fisher's Boarding House (short). '24 The Wild Goose Chaser (short) (co-sc.). '25 The Marriage Circus (short) (co-sc. only); Plain Clothes (short) (co-sc. only); Super Hooper-Dyne Lizzies (short) (co-sc. only); Breaking the Ice (short) (co-sc. only); Good Morning, Nurse (short) (co-sc. only); Cupid's Boots (short) (co-sc. only); Lucky Stars (short) (co-sc. only); There He Goes (short) (co-sc. only). '26 Saturday Afternoon (short) (co-sc. only); His First Flame (co-sc. only); Tramp, Tramp, Tramp (co-sc; + un-credited dir. and prod); Fiddlesticks (short) (co-sc. only); Soldier Man (short) (co-sc. only); The Strong Man. '27 Long Pants; For the Love of Mike. '28 That Certain Thing; So This Is Love; The Swim Princess (short) (co-sc. only); The Matinee Idol; The Way of the Strong; Say It With Sables; The Burglar/Smith's Burglar (short) (co-sc. only); The Power of the Press; Hubby's Weekend Trip (short). '29 The Younger Generation; The Donovan Affair; Flight. '30 Ladies of Leisure; Rain or Shine. '31 Dirigible; The Miracle Woman; Platinum Blonde. '32 Forbidden; American Madness; The Bitter Tea of General Yen. '33 Lady for a Day. '34 It Happened One Night (+ prod); Broadway Bill (GB: Strictly Confidential). '36 Mr Deeds Goes to Town (+ prod). '37 Lost Horizon (+ prod). '38 You Can't Take It With You (+ prod). '39 Mr Smith Goes to Washington (+ prod). '40 The Cavalcade of Academy Awards (doc) (sup. only). '41 Meet John Doe (+ prod). '42 Divide and Conquer (doc*) (co-dir; + prod). '43 Prelude to War (doc*) (+ prod); The Battle of Britain (doc*) (prod. only); The Nazis Strike (doc*) (co-dir; + prod); Battle of Russia/Battle for Russia (doc*) (prod. only). '44 Arsenic and Old Lace (+ prod); Know Your Ally: Britain (doc) (prod. only); Tunisian Victory (doc) (co-dir; + prod); The Negro Soldier (doc) (prod. only); The Battle of China (doc*) (co-dir; + prod). '45 Know Your Enemy: Germany (doc) (prod. only); Two Down and One to Go! (doc) (+ prod); War Comes to America (doc*) (prod. only); Know Your Enemy: Japan (doc) (co-dir; + prod). '46 It's a Wonderful Life (+ co-sc; + prod). '48 State of the Union (GB: The World and His Wife) (+ prod). '50 Riding High (+ prod). '51 Here Comes the Groom (+ prod). '59 A Hole in the Head (+ prod). '61 Pocketful of Miracles (+ prod). '64 Rendezvous in Space/Reaching for the Stars (short).
* *Why We Fight war documentary series. Capra also worked as a gag writer on six films in 1924.*

from the top of City Hall (at Christmas-time) too!). Capra and Riskin found themselves in a quandary about the ending: their final choice, with Doe's supporters persuading him to carry on fighting for his ideals, fails to convince – though it is difficult to imagine what could bring this ambitious, garrulous, awkward film to a satisfactory conclusion.

Liberty's last fling

When Capra returned to feature films as an independent director-producer in 1946, after a notable career supervising the wartime documentary series *Why We Fight*, the hysteria that marred *Meet John Doe* had evaporated. But Capra's ideals were clearly no longer quite intact: George Bailey, the despairing, philanthropic hero of *It's a Wonderful Life* (1946), is brought to the point of suicide. And it takes divine intervention by an angel to save George (James Stewart) and show him what a grim, garish, materialistic town Bedford Falls would have become if he had never existed. For all its prolixities and whimsies, the film remains a stunning example of Capra's consummate technical skills and his unbounded love for small-town America. It is the last example, too, for after making the hectic *State of the Union* (1948) – with an election candidate involved in more political buccaneering – Capra's independent company Liberty Films was sold to Paramount, and Capra lost his liberty indeed.

Pushed into a tight corner, Capra responded with the kind of films he produced in the years before *Deeds* when he was still evolving his style and subject-matter. *Riding High* (1950), starring Bing Crosby and various horses, was a flaccid remake of his earlier film *Broadway Bill*

was an Old Deal, the deal of Abraham Lincoln, Thomas Jefferson and other statesmen (duly mentioned and revered in the scripts) whose lives and beliefs showed the strengths of the pioneer spirit and individual initiative untrammelled by faceless authorities interfering from on high.

As the decade came to a close, however, the threats to Capra's American dream became more perilous. As one critic has pointed out, even Capra couldn't stop Hitler's evil designs armed with a harmonica. And in *Meet John Doe* (1941) the ordinary man is almost defeated and duped out of existence. Long John Willoughby (Gary Cooper), a former baseball player, is publicized as an incarnation of the folk hero John Doe by a publisher and would-be President bent on fascist domination. When Willoughby learns he is just a puppet he decides to enact the suicide threat that sparked off the whole campaign – by falling to his death

(1934); *Here Comes the Groom* (1951) featured Crosby in another weak comedy romance – about a reporter who adopts war orphans.

After eight quiet years Capra returned – in Cinemascope and colour – with *A Hole in the Head* (1959), a rancid sentimental comedy with Frank Sinatra. But with *Pocketful of Miracles* (1961), a remake of another of his early films, *Lady for a Day* (1933), Capra rallied. The screen once again teemed with lovable, eccentric characters – mostly Broadway types rushing about to help Bette Davis' Apple Annie, the apple-seller whose daughter has been led to expect a society queen for a mother. It was Capra's last display of good neighbourliness in action. Following this he prepared a science-fiction subject, *Marooned* (1969), eventually directed by John Sturges. The title was sadly suitable, for Capra himself had become marooned in post-war Hollywood – a place where working stiffs and short-changed Joes wanted their songs sung in far more harsh and complex ways than Capra could possibly manage.

Leni Riefenstahl

The career of the director whose brilliant documentaries for Hitler demonstrated to the world the awesome power of Nazi Germany

In Germany in 1933 the new Nazi government embarked on wide-scale reorganization and a policy of assimilating all political, economic and cultural activities into the National Socialist state. Within the 'co-ordination' of the film industry, the new rulers paid particular attention to the documentary film. Entertainment films would continue to exert *indirect* political influence. But it was through documentary that film – a medium which Hitler and Goebbels considered most important – could be used to increase the impact of the Nazis' mass rallies and demonstrations of power. Direct and straightforward propaganda became the province of newsreels, shorts and full-length documentary films. In the latter category a peak of effectiveness was achieved by the work of one particular film artist: Leni Riefenstahl.

The mountain road

Riefenstahl was born in 1902. She came from a respectable middle-class Berlin family in which the fine arts were highly regarded. In her youth she was interested in the theatre, and was a student at the Academy of Art in Berlin; later she went to ballet school and attained some success as a dancer before an injury forced her to give up this career.

She was 23 when she entered films. Her first work was for Dr Arnold Fanck – the outstanding director of 'mountain films'. This curious genre, popular from the mid-Twenties on-

wards, incorporated wild mountain scenery into the action in such a way that it almost became the major protagonist. Fanck perfected his unique contribution to cinema in pictures like *Der Berg des Schicksals* (1924, The Mountain of Fortune) and *Der Heilige Berg* (1926, *The Holy Mountain*) and it was in the latter that the young Riefenstahl made her film debut playing the lead female role. She went on to make several more films for Fanck but was not content with her successes in front of the camera – she wanted to succeed as a director as well.

Light of experience

The 'mountain films', with their emphasis on natural laws, found favour with the Nazi politicians and could be used to promote National Socialist ideals. In 1931 Riefenstahl realized her ambition to direct when she made *Das Blaue Licht* (1932, *The Blue Light*), a 'mountain film' on which she was assisted by Fanck's experienced cameraman, Hans Schneeberger, and the Marxist film theoretician Béla Belász (whose contribution as scriptwriter was later conveniently forgotten by the Nazis). It was this film that attracted Hitler's attention and greatly impressed him. *The Blue Light* is the dramatization of a mountain legend: the light in question shines out from a crystal grotto in the mountains and only the wild and secretive Junta knows the way to it. But it is discovered by a painter who shares the secret with the superstitious villagers – and brings about the girl's death from a fall. As well as directing the film, Riefenstahl produced it and also took the star part of Junta.

Riefenstahl was pleased with the outcome of her first film as director. It was, as she had hoped, successful in creating an atmosphere – through montage and effects – that made the audience susceptible to the power of myth.

Above and above left: early acting performances by Leni Riefenstahl in The White Hell of Pitz Palu *and in her directorial debut* The Blue Light. *Top: filming* Triumph of the Will *and (left) at Nüremberg with Hitler*

She met Hitler shortly afterwards in 1932 and was personally commissioned by him to make a documentary film of the Nazi Party Rally at Nuremberg. There was little time to prepare the picture, *Der Sieg des Glaubens* (1933, *Victory of Faith*), which emerged as a kind of test-run for her next, and major, work – *Triumph des Willens* (1934, *Triumph of the Will*). The following year Walter Ruttmann, the highly respected documentary film-maker, worked briefly on a plan for a film of the 1934 Nuremberg Rally, but his intention to incorporate a history of the Nazi Party into the film did not fit in with the political climate that followed the purging of the SA (the Nazi storm troops) under Röhm in June 1934. Riefenstahl took on the project afresh. The result was *Triumph of the Will*, a documentary of perfect film craftsmanship and propaganda.

Triumph of technique

The first principle that the film follows is that its overall arrangement does not seek to impose any intellectual meaning on the political event as a whole. The film-maker herself seems silent in the face of things and refrains from any words of commentary. The images and sounds on the film appear to speak for themselves – though Riefenstahl's montage technique constantly suggests to the spectator an emotional commentary on the action. The film begins, however, with a title sequence (said to be the work of Walter Ruttmann) which expresses an unequivocally positive attitude towards the Nazi regime. The Party Rally, held 18 months after the rebirth of Germany, is Hitler's review of the faithful.

The second principle concerns the emphasis on atmosphere. Here, it is a matter of evoking atmosphere by means of the rhythm of the film, and Leni Riefenstahl has always made it clear that the word 'effect' is important to her work. She has arranged the film in such a way that it forcibly presents a series of highly charged images interspersed with quieter sequences. These highlights include the arrival of Hitler at the rally by aircraft, and his addresses to the SA, and SS (Hitler's bodyguard), the Hitler Youth and the Labour Service. The quieter sequences are typified by shots of early morning and life under canvas in the huge tent city, the pageant of national costume, and parts of the parades.

The key to the atmosphere and impact achieved in the film is the montage. Riefenstahl consistently intercuts the great and the small. Close-ups of the spectators, long shots of the event as a whole, and shots from the point of view of the Party leaders are constantly mixed together by the rapid editing.

Thus the illusion is created of the all-embracing presence of both the camera and the film audience. Through the film, therefore, the Party Rally can be experienced in a much stronger, more intense, but also more emotionally manipulative, manner than would have been possible at the event itself.

In conclusion, Leni Riefenstahl's ideal was visual harmony (enhanced by music). The result was the suggestion of unity of leader, army, Hitler Youth, SA, SS, and the people – an encouraging and uplifting ideal indeed for the Party still inwardly shaken by the murder of Ernst Röhm. Riefenstahl used the occasion of the Party Rally for a study in harmony; the Party used Riefenstahl for a filmically brilliant and politically effective lesson for the German cinemagoer. To argue that the camera merely photographs what is at hand is naive and denies the film artist's creative power. *Triumph of the Will* was a success artistically and commercially and covered its production costs twice over.

Spirit of the Olympics

The second high point of Leni Riefenstahl's directorial career came in 1936 when she made *Olympia*, the much-praised film of the Olympic Games in Berlin. The film is in two parts: *Fest der Völker* (Festival of the People) and *Fest der Schönheit* (Festival of Beauty). The Olympic idea, its origin in classical Greece and its resurrection in modern times, offered the sportswoman and aesthete Riefenstahl a richly attractive source of material. She utilized this material in a film that is far more than mere reportage of a sporting event and reveals her own cinematic ideals more directly than *Triumph of the Will*. In the prologue the director draws heavily on cinematic special effects,

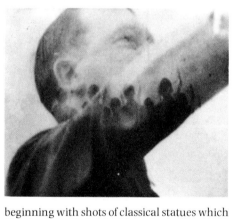

beginning with shots of classical statues which dissolve into shots of athletes in similar poses. From the outset Riefenstahl formulates her ideal visually: in men strength and competitiveness should be dominant, in women grace, charm and liveliness.

Fest der Völker concentrates on events in the Berlin Olympic Stadium, but quite differently from the way television covers sporting events today: the film is in no sense a detailed and comprehensive documentary analysis of a sports meeting, but rather, like *Triumph of the Will*, a dramatization of highlights. Here, how-

Left and above left: the ominous pomp, pageantry and power of the Nazis at the Nuremberg Rally as displayed in Triumph of the Will. *Above: a portentous superimposition of Hitler's salute over shots of Germany's soldiers on the march*

ever, there is no slackening of tempo.

Fest der Schönheit disregards the stresses and strains of the athletic feats and concentrates instead on emphasizing bodily aesthetics, on the grace of athletically trained bodies in motion, and, in the final analysis, pays homage to the same anti-intellectual cult as *Triumph of the Will*. The beauties of nature and the relaxed atmosphere of the Olympic village are also brought into play. Riefenstahl again achieves a sense of harmony and underlines it with an intense musical accompaniment. The piling on of aesthetic elements finally becomes tiresome, though the film does possess a certain charm.

Olympia was a great international success for Leni Riefenstahl. Compared with other documentary films of the time its craftsmanship was highly developed. It stood far above conventional newsreel reportage. The press,

national and foreign, generally received it positively. But the fame it brought Riefenstahl may have exceeded personal success in career terms. By the time the later footage was in preparation she was encountering opposition from the Propaganda Ministry under Goebbels who had never forgiven her for being appointed, without his authority, by Hitler. The film's coverage of the Negro athlete Jesse Owens outstripping the 'master race' on the track was too much for the authorities. It would have been better for Riefenstahl's career as a propagandist if she had left such 'embarrassing' scenes out of the film.

Out of favour

From that time she had no further opportunity to make her mark in the German cinema. As it was, her film company was responsible for a few short films (some of them

compiled from surplus material from the Olympic film) and was active during the war on unimportant documentaries. In 1940 Riefenstahl herself resumed work on her abandoned feature film *Tiefland* and this occupied her throughout the course of the war. Based on the opera by Eugene d'Albert and starring Leni Riefenstahl as a gypsy, it was not completed until 1953, and even then some of the footage was missing.

After the war Riefenstahl was blacklisted by the Allies for her propaganda work. She was arrested and spent time in prison camps before eventually clearing her name. Her critical reputation has always been overshadowed by her ostensible celebration of Nazism and as a result, this great film artist has directed no more pictures. She has, however, made a name for herself as one of the world's leading, and most respected, photographers.

Filmography
1926 Der Heilige Berg (actress only). (GB: The Holy Mountain). **'27** Der Grosse Sprung (actress only). **'29** Die Weisse Hölle vom Piz Palü (actress only) (USA/GB: The White Hell of Pitz Palu). **'30** Stürme über dem Montblanc (actress only) (USA: Storm Over Mont Blanc; GB: Avalanche). **'31** Der Weisse Rausch. **'32** Das Blaue Licht (+prod; +act) (GB: The Blue Light). **'33** SOS Eisberg (actress only); Der Sieg des Glaubens (doc). **'34** Triumph des Willens (doc) (USA/GB: Triumph of the Will). **'35** Tag der Freiheit – Unsere Wehrmacht (doc). **'36** Olympia (Pt 1: Fest der Völker; Pt 2: Fest der Schönheit) (doc) (+sc) (USA: The Olympic Games; GB: Berlin Olympiad). **'53** Tiefland (+sc;+act) (unfinished). **'56** Schwarze Fracht (doc. unfinished).

Above and left: the concept of the beauty, grace and strength of the ideal Aryan form was extolled by Riefenstahl through her images of gymnasts and athletes in Olympia, her documentary of the 1936 Olympic Games

151

Kings of the Underworld

The Twenties spawned gangsters in the gutters and ghettos of America's cities; the Thirties immortalized them on the screen

Gangster movies are about professional criminals for whom crime is a way of life. Films about gangsters were being made in the USA before World War I, and two fine examples – Josef von Sternberg's *Underworld* (1927) and Lewis Milestone's *The Racket* (1928) – were produced during a gangster cycle that preceded the talkies. But the golden age of the gangster movie is the Thirties, and its heyday lasted only three or four years, from shortly after the coming of sound until 1933.

In his autobiography, *Child of the Century*, screenwriter Ben Hecht (a former Chicago newspaperman, as many other screenwriters were) explained the thinking behind his *Underworld* screenplay, which set the pattern for many subsequent talking gangster films:

'The thing to do was to skip the heroes and heroines, to write a movie containing only villains and bawds. I would not have to tell any lies then. As a newspaperman I had learned that nice people – the audience – loved criminals, doted on reading about their love problems as well as their sadism. My movie, grounded on this simple truth, was produced with the title *Underworld*. It was the first

---

> I'm going to run the whole works. There's only one law – do it first, do it yourself and keep doing it.
> **Tony Camonte, Scarface**

---

gangster movie to bedazzle the movie fans and there were no lies in it – except for a half-dozen sentimental touches introduced by its director Joe von Sternberg.'

All that was needed to enhance this cynical recipe was to capture the noises of gangland on a soundtrack: the background jazz music of night-clubs and speakeasies; the mobsters' abrasive speech; the chatter of machine-guns and pistols; the ominous wail of police sirens; the roar of engines and the screech of tyres.

The gangster films of the years 1929–34 charted a world of nightclubs, flophouses, deserted streets, clandestine drinking-places, flashy apartments, crowded tenements, belowstreet cafés, gambling dens and police stations – a world that was both realistic and oddly abstract. Virtually all these films were shot on

Hollywood studio sets, and while Chicago or New York might be specified as the locale, the action seemed to be placed in a universal city rather than in any particular one.

From the 250 to 300 gangster films made in those years, only 3 have enduring reputations – Mervyn LeRoy's *Little Caesar* (1930), William Wellman's *The Public Enemy* (1931) and Howard Hawks's *Scarface* (1932). They were immediately recognized by contemporary critics as superior works, though each one was greeted by reviewers professing their weariness of gangster pictures. These films stood out not because they were new but for the definitive way they handled familiar material.

With chilly detachment these three films show the rise and fall of professional crooks from Catholic immigrant backgrounds. In each the main character was modelled on Al Capone, and all three turned a well-known stage actor into a movie star. Edward G. Robinson's Caesar Enrico Bandello (*Little Caesar*) and Paul Muni's Tony Camonte (*Scarface*) are Italians; James Cagney's Tom Powers (*The Public Enemy*) is Irish. All are short, strutting, violent men, driven by burning ambition,

Left: Rico (Edward G. Robinson) cornered in a back alley tries to shoot his way out in Little Caesar. *Right: Tony Camonte (Paul Muni) and his gang get tough in* Scarface

hungry for power and social acceptance. They shoot their way to the top of the criminal heap and are then destroyed – partly because conventional morality demands such an ending, but mainly through pride and a talent for self-destruction. Like all the gangsters of this era, they are denied domestic comforts. They desert loving mothers and are then torn between the blonde 'molls' they despise and the high-class, chaste brunettes they aspire to marry. They die alone, miserably and memorably – bullet-riddled Little Caesar asking 'Mother of Mercy – is this the end of Rico?', Tom Powers being delivered home dead and wrapped in a blanket, and Tony Camonte gunned down beneath a neon sign which ironically proclaims, 'The World Is Yours'.

Although the forewords and afterwords to these films point up a moral to the action – *Little Caesar* ends with the title 'Rico's career had been a skyrocket, starting in the gutter and ending there', *Scarface* was compelled by the authorities to carry the sub-title 'Shame of a Nation' – these movies are not moralizing tracts. We are not invited to see their central characters as psychopaths. Killings are frequent, but not dwelt upon sadistically. When Tom Powers bumps off his treacherous former mentor Putty Nose, for example, and then immediately starts thinking about a date with his mistress Gwen, we are confronted with an association of killing and sex that might well be interpreted as psychotic. However the scene's overall message is that murder is just a particularly ruthless way of conducting business – Powers is just 'settling debts'.

The gangster was a product of metropolitan alienation at a time when the USA was changing from being a rural agrarian society to becoming a predominantly urban, industrial one. For the audiences of the early Depression years, the gangster represented a number of things, both fearful and reassuring. His career was a parody of the American Dream, reflecting the way the Rockefellers, Goulds, Fisks and other so-called robber barons had made their fortunes. The gangster was also a social bandit driven into crime as the only way to advance in a society that denied him proper channels of expression. His life challenged and exposed a corrupt system.

The careers of these ethnic gangsters closely resemble those of the immigrant movie

Below: Underworld, *a silent picture, fired the public's imagination and anticipated the talkie gangster films of the Thirties*

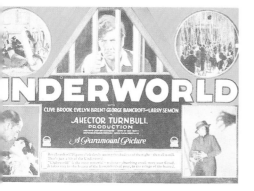

pioneers, men such as Jack Warner, Louis B. Mayer, Adolph Zukor and Harry Cohn. The movie moguls also fought their way up from the ghetto and were briefly outlaws themselves when resisting the viciously repressive Motion Picture Patents Company; it tried to put them out of business before World War I by the imposition of levies on cameras and projectors, and sanctions on their use. The studio bosses had spent the Twenties building commercial empires using methods only a little more honest (though much less violent) than the beer barons of Prohibition. The movie tycoons enjoyed the company of gangsters and mixed with them freely while pursuing their passion for gambling and horse-racing. The West Coast head of the Syndicate and creator of modern Las Vegas, Bugsy Siegel, was well known to many Hollywood personalities, and set up house in Beverly Hills, where, in 1947,

he was murdered. Among his Hollywood admirers were the writer-producer Mark Hellinger, responsible for *The Roaring Twenties* (1939), *Brute Force* (1947) and *The Naked City* (1948), who liked to dress like a gangster, and the actor George Raft, who in *Scarface* created the famous coin-tossing gesture that reflected so accurately the uncertainty of a gangster's life. Raft knew Capone and numerous hoods, and in the Sixties was denied entry to Britain by the Home Office on the grounds that he was a front man for Mafia gambling interests. More seriously the movie tsar Will H. Hays brought in hoodlums to settle strikes, and for a time in the Thirties and Forties, the Chicago branch of

Below: Tom Powers (James Cagney) watches helplessly as his boyhood pal and partner in crime Matt Doyle (Edward Woods) is gunned down by a rival gang in The Public Enemy

JAMES CAGNEY·PRISCILLA LANE

"THE ROARING TWENTIES"

A WARNER BROS. PICTURE

Left: Mark Hellinger, author of The Roaring Twenties, *described this tale of Prohibition as 'a memory of the past'. By 1939 the gangster had become a romantic anachronism*

criminals tended to make audiences condone unorthodox methods of law enforcement and turn current discontent not against society but against petty criminals.

William Keighley followed *G-Men* with a second trend-setting film, *Bullets or Ballots* (1936). This rehabilitated another gangland hero Edward G. Robinson by putting him on the right side of the law as an incorruptible New York cop. The film is important for two reasons. Firstly, in having Robinson infiltrate Barton MacLane's New York mob, it introduced the key figures of the undercover agent who was to play such a prominent part in crime pictures of the next two decades. Secondly, it laid particular stress on the real power behind the rackets being in the hands of conservatively dressed businessmen, who meet in tastefully appointed boardrooms and leave the messy job of killing people to underworld minions. This, too, was to become part of the pattern of American crime in both the movies and real-life.

G-Men was a conscious part of Hollywood's effort to change its image in the face of outside pressures from such organizations as the newly-formed Catholic Legion of Decency (to which Capone is said to have contributed) that demanded the cleaning up of the motion picture industry. In 1934 the Production Code, designed to protect public morals, became mandatory, and the essentially amoral character of the early gangster pictures could not be maintained. Equally, the coming of Roosevelt's New Deal policy, with its belief in the possibility of progress through social organization and reform, induced in Hollywood's producers and film-makers a greater sense of responsibility and optimism than they had shown in the earlier years of the decade.

Three important Broadway plays of 1935, helped the genre to diversify after its classic period. In Robert E. Sherwood's *The Petrified Forest*, Duke Mantee (played on stage and in Archie Mayo's 1936 film by Humphrey Bogart) is a Dillinger-type hoodlum who represents the final dying gasp of the 'free-enterprise' criminal system. In Maxwell Anderson's verse drama *Winterset* (filmed by Alfred Santell in 1936) the gangster Trock Estrella (Eduardo Ciannelli), a life-hating figure dying of cancer, is the link between the underworld and a crooked judiciary in a story concerning the

the Syndicate controlled the principal Hollywood union for non-specialist studio employees (IATSE – the International Alliance of Theatrical Stage Employees), including cameramen, sound recordists and projectionists.

While Hollywood churned out gangster pictures in the early Thirties, a new wave of crime was sweeping the middle-west of the USA resulting in an orgy of robberies, bank holdups and kidnappings. The perpetrators were not big-time urban crooks from the newly-arrived immigrant groups. They were disorganized criminals from the hills and farms of the mid-west and south-west, from Indiana, Missouri, and Texas – white Anglo-Saxon Protestant boys and girls with names like John Dillinger, Bonnie Parker and Clyde Barrows. They loved the movies and were much impressed by them. Dillinger, for instance, would vault bank counters in imitation of his hero Douglas Fairbanks, and was shot down outside

Below: in G-Men *Cagney is a young lawyer who joins the FBI to avenge the murder of his best friend. Below right: Duke Mantee (Humphrey Bogart) threatens his hostages (including Bette Davis and Leslie Howard) in* The Petrified Forest

Chicago's Biograph cinema in 1934 after seeing Clark Gable and William Powell in the gangster film *Manhattan Melodrama* (1934).

When he heard of Dillinger's death, Will H. Hays sent a telegram to his chief adjutant and enforcer of the Hays Office Code, Joe Breen, which read in part:

'No picture on the life or exploits of John Dillinger will be produced or exhibited by any member [of the Motion Picture Producers and Distributors Association of America] . . . This decision is based on the belief that the production, distribution or exhibition of such a picture could be detrimental to the best public interest. Advise all studio heads accordingly.'

The FBI, however, found posturing psychopaths like Dillinger and Baby Face Nelson easier to capture than big city criminals. J. Edgar Hoover made capital out of them to boost the Bureau's public image. He also enlisted the help of Hollywood, and the result was a series of films glorifying the FBI. The first was *G-Men* (dir. William Keighley, 1935); for this James Cagney crossed over from public enemy to public defender, playing a young lawyer recruited by the FBI. The basic scenario was similar, as was the quantity of violence. The glorification of investigators rather than

Above: Bogart and Robinson shoot it out to the death in Bullets or Ballots, one of the first films to show organized crime as a threat to the whole of American society. Above right: Wallace Beery as the leader of desperate convicts in The Big House

Below: Bogart in High Sierra, where he played Mad Dog Earle, a gangster with a soft heart, hoping to pull one last big job. Bottom: The Dead End Kids, watched by Father Connolly, are stunned by news of Rocky's cowardice in Angels with Dirty Faces

exposure of a frame-up. In Sidney Kingsley's *Dead End* (filmed in 1937 by William Wyler) the doomed criminal 'Baby Face' Martin, played by Humphrey Bogart, returns to the Manhattan slum that spawned him.

These three plays came to Hollywood wreathed in theatrical glory and cloaked in cultural respectability, for all three dramatists had recently won the Pulitzer Prize. They gave new impetus to the gangster movie during the next four years before it gave way to the private-eye picture, the war movie and the *film noir*. Tame as they may appear today, these earnest, carefully constructed works seemed hard-hitting, progressive pieces to most audiences at the time.

The old-style lone-wolf gangster was beginning to look something of an anachronism in an age of confident bureaucrats and burgeoning corporations. Edward G. Robinson played, somewhat prematurely, *The Last Gangster* (dir. Edward Ludwig, 1937), who after 10 years in jail finds himself bewildered by the new world of the late Thirties, and anxious to give up his former way of life. The opportunity is denied him. In *Brother Orchid* (dir. Lloyd Bacon, 1940) Robinson guys his old Warner Brothers roles in a rather sombre comedy as a hoodlum who seeks refuge in a monastery from would-be assassins. There he finds the 'class' that had eluded him outside. He helps his fellow monks reorganize their flower-growing business on profitable lines, and briefly slips out to fix the treacherous gangster, played by Humphrey Bogart, who double-crossed him.

The whole Thirties cycle came to an end the following year with Raoul Walsh's *High Sierra*. Adapted from a novel by W. R. Burnett, author of *Little Caesar*, the picture is tinged throughout with nostalgia – the crooked Big Mac (Donald MacBride) who springs Roy Earle (Humphrey Bogart) from jail for one last job observes sadly that 'All the A-1 guys are gone – dead or in Alcatraz'; a mob doctor looks back dreamily to the golden days when he removed bullets from fugitive gangsters in the Mid-west.

High Sierra was produced by Mark Hellinger, who had anticipated the enduring nostalgia for the Twenties with the original story for *The Roaring Twenties* (dir. Raoul Walsh, 1939), wherein the careers of three World War I friends were traced from the trenches of the Western Front to their post-war lives during the Prohibition: Bogart as a former saloon-keeper turned bootlegger, Cagney as a taxi-driver brought by economic circumstances into the underworld, and Jeffrey Lynn as

a struggling lawyer who joins a crime-busting squad. The movie is a kind of superficial social history, an affectionate re-creation of a free-wheeling decade, a digest of familiar gangster plots and imagery, and a slick study of the effect of environment on character.

This last theme was much affected by current ideas of social reform that saw slums as the high-schools of crime and prisons as its universities. *The Big House* (dir. George Hill,

1930) led to a series of films depicting prison life. *The Big House*, was an MGM picture, but it was at Warner Brothers that virtually every one of the studio's contract players 'did time' in such films. *20,000 Years in Sing Sing* (dir. Michael Curtiz, 1933) has Spencer Tracy behind bars; in *San Quentin* (dir. Lloyd Bacon, 1937), Bogart is locked up, Barton MacLane plays a sadistic turnkey, and Pat O'Brien is the reformist warden seconded from the army; and in *Each Dawn I Die* (dir. William Keighley, 1939) a crusading journalist, who has been framed for manslaughter, joins forces with 'honest' gangster George Raft against the corrupt politicos on the outside.

In the late Thirties, under the influence of the New Deal and in response to pressure from Federal agencies, films took on an increasingly sanguine tone about the possibility of steering potential criminals into constructive activities and rehabilitating the sinners. *Invisible Stripes* (dir. Lloyd Bacon, 1939), based on a novel by a former prison warden, is one of numerous pictures pleading for ex-convicts to be given the opportunity to 'go straight'. In this case George Raft and Humphrey Bogart are two newly released prisoners who return to crime, the former involuntarily, the latter by choice.

Left: Bonnie and Clyde try to escape a hail of bullets. Below: Eddie Bartlett (James Cagney) dies in the arms of Panama Smith (Gladys George) in The Roaring Twenties

The most optimistic string of movies involve the cinema's first gang of juvenile delinquents, The Dead End Kids, who came out of the play and film *Dead End*. In *Angels with Dirty Faces* (dir. Michael Curtiz, 1938) they were won away from an allegiance to hoodlum Rocky Sullivan (James Cagney) by Rocky's old school friend Father Connolly (Pat O'Brien). Sullivan, perhaps because of Father Connolly's persuasiveness, or maybe because he truly is 'yellow', goes screaming to the electric chair, so destroying his heroic image among the slum kids. In *Crime School* (dir. Lewis Seiler, 1938) they are reformed by a liberal Commissioner of Correction (Humphrey Bogart) after an insensitive reformatory superintendent's brutal methods had only served to confirm them in a life of crime. In *They Made Me a Criminal* (dir. Busby Berkeley, 1939), the Kids learn to walk the straight and narrow on an Arizona farm under the influence of an underworld fugitive from New York. They finally took their place on the side of law and order in the 1941 serial *Junior G-Men*.

The gangster film did not vanish with the war and the end of the Depression. It appeared sporadically throughout the Forties and Fifties, but it was not until *Bonnie and Clyde* (dir. Arthur Penn, 1967), *The St Valentine's Day Massacre* (dir. Roger Corman, 1967) and *The Godfather* (dir. Francis Coppola, 1972) that the genre was revived for yet another generation of film-goers.

Europe at war

When war broke out in 1939 the cinema was mobilized to provide vital footage from the front and morale-boosting propaganda for the home screens

When Archduke Ferdinand was assassinated at Sarajevo in June 1914, precipitating World War I, the movie industry was still in its infancy. Many pioneers were just getting into their stride, exploring the power of the medium and its potential hold over audiences. When Hitler invaded Poland in September 1939, precipitating World War II, a huge, profitable, world-wide industry had long been established with massive resources of equipment, manpower and 'star power'.

European governments had an unparalleled weapon at their command in the film medium. It was vastly popular with the public, it could easily disseminate war information, instruction and, if necessary, lies, through documentaries, newsreels or (most persuasively of all) in dramatic features. The cinema even served a valuable purpose by providing a few hours of escapist fun before audiences stepped out into their beleaguered, blitzed cities. There was no better way of keeping a controlling hand on national morale.

In a way the industry had long been preparing for war, though the bosses – their eyes glued to production schedules and box-office receipts – might not have realized it. Ever since Hitler took control in 1933, studios throughout Europe and America had absorbed directors, producers, cameramen, writers, composers, actors and actresses, all escaping from the threat of persecution under Nazi Germany's anti-Semitic laws.

Hitler himself had partly designed the 1934 Nuremberg rally as a cinema spectacle (duly filmed as *Triumph of the Will*). In place of Hollywood's all-talking, all-singing, all-dancing musicals, here was the Nazi equivalent – all-shouting, all-stomping, all-saluting. For Hitler knew that potent images and the emotional fury of his speeches had far more power to persuade than any rational argument.

The world watched Hitler's activities with unease and incomprehension. He had risen to power by marshalling nationalistic feelings of discontent with the 1918 defeat and the harsh terms of the Versailles treaty. He had rearmed the country and proclaimed the notion of *lebensraum* – the right of the German nation to have enough living space. And by the end of the Thirties Hitler was taking his first steps in this search for extra accommodation by

attacks, annexations and alliances.

Austria was invaded in March 1938. Sudetenland (on Czechoslovakia's borders) in October. Further east, Hitler formed an opportunistic non-aggression pact with Stalin. In the West, Britain's Prime Minister, Neville Chamberlain, naively joined the French in a policy of appeasement and met the Führer at Berchtesgaden and Munich in September 1938. On his return he waved at the newsreel cameramen a bit of paper which promised 'peace in our time'. Unfortunately it guaranteed nothing of the kind. Czechoslovakia fell to Hitler in March; with the invasion of Poland one year later, Britain and France entered the battle and the world war was on.

Britain's television service, only three years old and serving a tiny minority, was promptly shut down. Film-studio space was requisitioned for storing ammunition, greatcoats and all the paraphernalia of war. But the industry continued. Indeed, the experience of working with limited resources under pressure concentrated the minds of many film-makers. And the involvement of the entire country in the war effort – all classes, both sexes – made many old cinema genres and attitudes inadequate. No longer could studios rely upon laboured farces or thrillers featuring stereotypes of the elegant rich or the rude poor.

The transformation, however, did not occur overnight. Alexander Korda's *The Lion Has Wings* (dir. Michael Powell, Brian Desmond Hurst, Adrian Brunel), a hopeful salute to the fighting power of the RAF, was rushed into release in the autumn of 1939. The film was a mixture of newsreel footage, and mocked-up battles but was over-burdened by a quaintly genteel, fictional sub-plot.

Yet slowly the industry buckled to. The Ministry

Top: Douglass Montgomery (left) as an American fighter-pilot teams up with RAF aces David Tomlinson (centre) and Trevor Howard (right) in Anthony Asquith's Battle of Britain film The Way to the Stars. *Above: in Cavalcanti's* Went the Day Well? *a sleepy English village is invaded and occupied by Germans disguised as Royal Engineers, but eventually the British Army and the Home Guard come to the rescue. Left: the San Demetrio was a merchant ship carrying a precious cargo of oil from the USA to besieged Britain. Crippled by enemy fire, the ship limped home to port, a testament to the quiet heroism of the times*

A Great Adventure Story of the sea
SAN DEMETRIO
London
SOS

PRODUCED BY MICHAEL BALCON
WALTER FITZGERALD · MERVYN JOHNS · RALPH MICHAEL
ROBERT BEATTY · GORDON JACKSON · FREDERICK PIPER

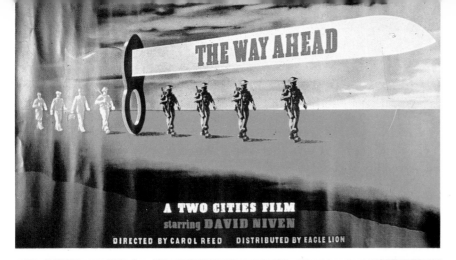

THE WAY AHEAD

A TWO CITIES FILM
starring DAVID NIVEN

DIRECTED BY CAROL REED   DISTRIBUTED BY EAGLE LION

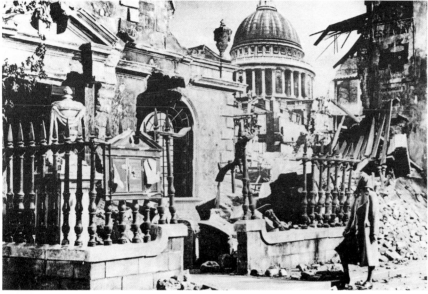

Top: David Niven had trained at Sandhurst in the Thirties and saw active service during the war before returning to films. This one, scripted by Eric Ambler and Peter Ustinov, was a great success and was used at Sandhurst as a training film. Above: The Bells Go Down *featured the work of the Auxiliary Fire Service during London's Blitz. Below:* The Gentle Sex *(1943), showing women's role in the war, was directed by Leslie Howard*

of Information, after many changes of personnel and unfortunate gestures like the slogan 'Your Courage, Your Cheerfulness, Your Resolution, will Bring Us Victory' (hardly the best way to bind a nation together), established a solid system of film distribution, sending out to cinemas short films on war topics every week. In addition, travelling projectionists showed films in those parts of the country where there were no proper cinemas.

Style and subject in these shorts varied tremendously. Most artistically polished were the poetic essays of Humphrey Jennings, who found in the war an ideal way of expressing his strong feelings for Britain's cultural heritage. Richard Massingham found a similar niche providing crisp, comic illustrations of wartime regulations, such as bathing in only five inches of water.

At the other end of the scale there were filmed lectures given by Ministry men seated behind desks and blinking nervously. These films were so embarrassing that cinema managers occasionally showed them with the curtains tactfully drawn. But it is clear that some of this huge output had considerable effect – particularly abroad, where America was uninvolved in the fighting until Japan attacked Pearl Harbor in December 1941.

Jennings' *London Can Take It* (devised for showing in Allied countries in 1940) filled out its Blitz images with a commentary by the American journalist Quentin Reynolds, full of praise for London's 'unconquerable spirit and courage'. Later, there was much direct film cooperation between the Allies, as each arm of the services prepared photographed accounts of their operations. In the war's last stages Carol Reed and the American Garson Kanin came

together to produce *The True Glory* (1945), a film charting Europe's liberation.

But the greatest changes in British cinema occurred in feature films. Previously the feature industry had been inhibited by American competition, and the presence of so many foreign moguls and visiting directors hardly promoted indigenous product. But with the war, the visitors returned home and rising talent, previously confined to scriptwriting or editing, eagerly moved into the director's chair – David Lean, Charles Frend, Frank Launder, Sidney Gilliat were among them.

All at once there were dramatic subjects to make feature films about: life at RAF and army bases in *The Way Ahead* (1944) and *The Way to the Stars* (1945); war service on the high seas in *In Which We Serve* (1942) and *San Demetrio, London* (1943); and in the munitions factories – *Millions Like Us* (1943). Here was an area where the Americans could not compete. The tone of the films – humorous, quietly heroic – was also unique.

British films found an audience and a popularity they had never enjoyed before. As the war went on escapist entertainment increased in volume and popularity. Traditional tosh was given a topical inflection in *Dangerous Moonlight* (1941), where a Polish concert pianist joined the RAF and played Richard Addinsell's popular 'Warsaw' Concerto.

As the bombs fell on her cities, Britain's cinemas kept open a vital channel of information about the war

Gainsborough studios produced period melodramas like *The Man in Grey* (1943), with ladies and gentlemen behaving amorally, dressed in wigs, masks and riding boots. On a far higher artistic level were the films of Michael Powell and his Hungarian collaborator Emeric Pressburger, who viewed the war through a complex maze of satire and fantasy in bold creations like *The Life and Death of Colonel Blimp* (1943), a film that was loathed by Churchill for its caricature of the army's upper crust. The same team also produced *A Canterbury Tale* (1944). And no world war, however devastating, could halt Gabriel Pascal's determination to film Shaw's *Caesar and Cleopatra* (1945), which began shooting at Denham six days after D-Day, despite the threat of flying bombs and the difficulties of securing nubile young ladies and white peacocks to flit by in the backgrounds.

While British cinema stumbled uncertainly into war production, Germany began with its propaganda machine in top working condition. Ever since Hitler secured control in 1933, his propaganda minister Josef Goebbels had organized the industry to fit Nazi requirements. Jews were banned immediately; a film censor office was established in 1934; film criticism (and all arts criticism) was abolished in 1936, thereafter newspapers could print only facts, not opinions. The independent studios, including the mighty Ufa, were absorbed by the government during 1937. By 1939 many of Germany's best film talents had emigrated; those that remained were regarded as part of the country's fighting forces.

Goebbels sensed how powerful a weapon film could be, but he had known for a long time that audiences resented hard-core propaganda in fictional, dramatic formats. Instead propaganda was channelled into newsreels, compiled or doctored from material shot at the fighting fronts and decked out with animated maps full of pulsating arrows that indicated German advances.

The newsreels were eventually lengthened to as much as forty minutes, and there are reports that cinema doors were carefully secured so that there was no possibility of escape. Special productions were concocted to lower the morale of countries about to be occupied: *Feuertaufe* (1940, Baptism of Fire), a film that glorified the Luftwaffe's conquest of Poland, was shown at the German Embassy in Oslo four days before the invasion of Norway in April 1940. The most notorious production of all, however was *Der Ewige Jude* (1940, The Eternal Jew), an illustrated lecture by Dr Fritz Hippler designed to fan the flames of anti-Semitism to inferno proportions.

Once the newsreels were over, audiences could settle down to suffer bombastic, shoddy epics glorifying various sections of the armed forces, or Veit Harlan's viciously anti-Semitic *Jud Süss* (1940, Jew Süss) – a key exhibit in the post-war trials. Other films aimed at influencing the all-important German youth included *Kadetten* (1941, Cadets) which told the story of young Prussians fighting in 1760 during the Seven Years' War. History, in fact, proved a boon for German film-makers who wanted to please their Nazi overlords without being rabidly propagandistic. German history was, after all, well-stocked with belligerently nationalistic heroes. Films about Frederick the Great of Prussia had long formed a separate genre and the actor Otto Gebühr did little else but play him.

Colonial activities in Africa proved a fruitful source of anti-British propaganda. *Ohm Krüger* (1941, Uncle Kruger), though one of the more impressive productions, offered a wickedly coarse caricature of Queen Victoria and blithely credited the British with inventing concentration camps.

Other films slanted the same way included *Titanic* (1943), where the ship hit the iceberg as a result of the sins of Jewish–English plutocracy, and two films by Goebbels' brother-in-law Max Kimmich, portraying British brutalities in Ireland: *Der Fuchs von Glenarvon* (1940, The Fox of Glenarvon) and *Mein Leben für Irland* (1941, My Life for Ireland).

Many other films were simply escapist entertainment with the odd twinge of propaganda. Goebbels spent much money developing Agfacolor so that German audiences would not lose out on colour films while the rest of the world was enjoying the early Technicolor movies.

In celebration of Ufa's twenty-fifth anniversary, Goebbels planned the highly elaborate fantasy film *Münchhausen* (1943) and studied Disney's feature cartoons and Korda's *The Thief of Bagdad* (1940), and almost produced something comparable. But his monumental undertaking was *Kolberg*, begun in 1943 and completed towards the end of 1944. Geared to the declining course of the war, the film shrewdly portrayed the citizens of Kolberg, besieged during the Napoleonic wars and heroically holding out against amazing odds. By the time the film was ready for release in early 1945, it had no value as propaganda for Germany was close to defeat.

Italy, Germany's ally in Europe, went about its film-making as it went about its fighting, with little of the manic fervour displayed by Goebbels. Most of the country's fascist tub-thumping had been performed in the late Thirties, when mammoth spectacles like *Scipione l'Africano* (1937) were mounted to reflect Italy's new image as an imperial, conquering power. Mussolini had ensured that the film industry was well equipped for the task. The vast Cinecittà film studios were built outside Rome and a film school (Centro Sperimentale di Cinematografia) was established. Mussolini's own son Vittorio pursued an active interest in the medium, securing his name on film credits and on the mast-head of a cinema magazine.

Many directors in the war avoided overt propaganda by retreating to unassuming romantic comedies and tales of provincial life. Some talents did manage to cut through the dross. Alessandro Blasetti's *Quattro Passi fra le Nuvole* (1942, Four Steps in the Clouds) focused sharply on the torments of daily life and had a script co-written by Cesare Zavattini, who was later associated with the director Vittorio De Sica and the neo-realist movement. In the same year, Visconti's *Ossessione* (1942, Obsession), a story of adultery and murder, exploded onto the screen with a kind of brute force unseen before in the Italian cinema.

Equally distinctive, though now largely forgotten, were the films of Francesco De Robertis. He was head of the Naval Ministry's film department and made features imbued with the spirit, and often the footage, of documentary, with non-professional players and location shooting.

La Nave Bianca (1941, The White Ship), for instance, began as a straight documentary about the brave work of a hospital ship. When the authorities wanted to boost the Italian entries at the 1941 Venice Film Festival, De Robertis obligingly built in a love story. Despite such compromises, his films had great impact, and his assistant, Roberto Rossellini (nominally the director of *La Nave Bianca*), followed this style in his own wartime films, *Un Pilota Ritorna* (1942, A Pilot Returns) and *L'Uomo della Croce* (1943, The Man of the Cross).

Looking back on the wartime period from the safe distance of 1960, De Sica observed that 'the war was a decisive experience for all of us. Each of us felt the wild urge to sweep away all the worn-out plots of the Italian cinema and to set up our cameras in the midst of real life.' With the studios under allied bombardment, there was also little alternative.

When Italy surrendered to the Allies and declared war on Germany, it only produced more turmoil, with facilities, equipment and talent scattered throughout the country. De Robertis went north, obstinately loyal to Mussolini who was now installed as puppet-head of the short-lived Salò

Top and above: two examples of the virulent anti-Semitic propaganda shown on German screens during the war: Veit Harlan's Jew Süss *was adapted from a novel while* Der Ewige Jude *purported to be a documentary. Left: the disastrous sinking of the* Titanic *was blamed on the Jews and the English. During the filming, the director Herbert Selpin complained about the interference of several Nazi naval advisers. He was arrested and later found murdered in his prison cell. Below: Ginette Leclerc in Clouzot's* Le Corbeau *made by the German-backed Continental studio in Paris*

REGIE: HERBERT SELPIN

SYBILLE SCHMITZ · HANS NIELSEN
KIRSTEN HEIBERG · E.F. FÜRBRINGER
KARL SCHÖNBÖCK · OTTO WERNICKE
CHARLOTTE THIELE · THEODOR LOOS
SEPP RIST · FRANZ SCHAFHEITLIN

OHM KRÜGER

Emil Jannings

Republic. Rossellini went south and helped establish the cinema branch of the Committee of National Liberation.

A few weeks before the Allies entered Rome in June 1944, his film *Roma, Città Aperta* (1945, *Rome, Open City*) went into production. It was a harsh, moving tale of a Resistance leader's betrayal. But the Italian cinema had already encountered its own kind of liberation.

The Soviet Union's path through the war was just as checkered as Italy's. After several years of mounting tension on its western borders with the dismembered parts of the old Austro–Hungarian Empire, Stalin concluded the non-aggression pact with Hitler in 1939. Feature films described the occupation of Poland, the invasion of Finland; items with anti-German leanings such as *Professor Mamlock* and *Alexander Nevsky* (both 1938) swiftly returned to the vaults. But they soon emerged after June 22, 1941, when Germany's shock invasion brought the pact to an end. Film studios were now uprooted from Moscow to safer surroundings. Various Soviet policies were modified and the customary anti-religious bias was abandoned. Suddenly the much-despised Tsarist generals received homage from the cinema for their part in the Napoleonic wars and other conflicts. There were also new forms of presenting films in the Soviet Union during the war. From August 1941 so-called 'Fighting Film Albums' appeared in cinemas every month; these were a mixture of short films that included miniature dramas, satiric japes and war-effort propaganda. Cameramen at the front maintained a constant stream of filmed dispatches which were edited into powerful documentaries. Alexander Dovzhenko supervised and wrote a moving

From 1940 French cinema was made to toe the Nazi line. When Hitler laid siege to Russia, the cinema became a weapon of resistance

commentary for *The Fight for Our Soviet Ukraine* (1943) that reflected his feelings for his homeland.

Soviet features tended to follow the usual propaganda pattern, spotlighting German atrocities or the heroic activities of the partisans. But as in other countries pure entertainment was never neglected, indeed its quantity increased as the war continued. One of the most popular films of 1944 was a musical entitled *At 6 pm After the War*.

The celebrated Soviet director Sergei Eisenstein spent most of the war engaged on *Ivan the Terrible* in Mosfilm's wartime headquarters at Alma-Ata in Kazakstan. By the end of December 1944, the first part of the projected trilogy was ready for release. The film was a ferocious and monumental excursion into Russia's medieval past, with Tsar Ivan bludgeoning his way from childhood to coronation. As a cinematic history lesson, the film was complex and unsettling for audiences.

For those countries occupied by the Germans – France, Denmark, the Low Countries, Norway – there were obviously fewer opportunities to fly their own flag. German films swamped the cinemas; German film censors controlled production. But the censor's limited powers of perception sometimes allowed carefully disguised anti-Nazi sentiments to slip by. When the Danish censor sat through *Kornet Er i Fare* (1944, The Grain Is in Danger) he obviously regarded it as just a boring short about the *sitophilus granariae*, an insect gnawing its way through a whole harvest of wheat. Audiences of a different persuasion realized the insect was also the Nazi

pest, gnawing its way through Europe.

France was under Nazi occupation from June 1940, though the official French government still existed at Vichy in an uneasy collaboration with the Germans. The main film studios in Paris were taken over by the German company Continental. A few films like *Les Inconnus Dans la Maison* (1942, *Strangers in the House*) betrayed German sympathies, but there was never any concerted effort to promote Nazi propaganda in the course of the film. Continental's output was noted instead for its imitation of Hollywood genre movies, since American films had been banned in France after 1942.

Many of the best French directors were then abroad – Renoir, Clair, Duvivier; those who remained took the obvious way out of their difficult situation by largely avoiding subjects with a topical edge. Simenon's crime stories, boulevard theatre comedies, Maupassant and Balzac all received uncontroversial adaptations. The bulk of film propaganda, in fact, originated from the Vichy government, whose need to foster some spirit of national pride generated a tepid trickle of features in praise of domestic life, hard work and *la patrie*.

Nevertheless, French cinema still managed to develop a special identity and a fighting spirit. New

directors as varied as Robert Bresson, Jacques Becker and Henri-Georges Clouzot embarked on their careers. Some strove to deal with France's problems allegorically: one of the period's most popular films was Jean Delannoy's *Pontcarral, Colonel d'Empire* (1942, Pontcarral, Colonel of the Empire), with its historical colonel fighting the enemy from his barricaded house at the time of the First Empire.

Equally pertinent was Clouzot's *Le Corbeau* (1943, *The Raven*), a thriller about poison-pen letters, produced by Continental. The movie was so bleak and negative in atmosphere that the director and the writer were accused of serving enemy propaganda through their analysis of a town (and, therefore, country) shaken by guilt and suspicion.

Les Visiteurs du Soir (1942, *The Devil's Own Envoy*) took the viewer back to the Middle Ages for a magical story of love conquering the wiles of the Devil, but there was no overt ideological thrust behind Marcel Carné's direction.

Other film-makers and writers (Jean Cocteau included) also luxuriated in fantasy and visual extravagance, though none could match the power and scope of Carné's *Les Enfants du Paradis* (*Children of Paradise*), a period panorama of Paris life begun during the Occupation in 1942 and released in 1945. In its length (three hours) and its lavishness, this film might almost be a symbol of the French film industry's determination not to be cowed by the war but to come up fighting. Most film industries did, all over Europe.

Top: Feuertaufe celebrated the role of the German air force in the conquest of Poland, offering heroic images of the 'master race' on the attack. Above: Ohm Krüger dealt a blow at the British, charging them with great brutality in the course of their imperialist adventures in Africa. Right: Les Visiteurs du Soir proved that the French cinema was able to continue its great tradition despite the restrictions imposed upon it by the German army of Occupation

Hollywood goes to war

The war had been a tricky subject for American films, but after Pearl Harbor Hollywood opened up with all guns blazing

To understand the way in which America rather tentatively entered World War II it is necessary to appreciate the horrifying spectacle of twelve million men unemployed in the bitter winter of 1932–33 and ten million as late as 1938. The shock to the American psyche was profound and would have long-term effects.

It was Herbert Hoover's contention that the Depression had originated in Europe and that the contagion had somehow been transported to America, possibly in the manner of Dracula coming ashore in Bremen. Since everybody was also aware that most of the European countries had defaulted on their war loans, the isolationist mood of the USA in general and Congress in particular remained essentially unbroken throughout the decade.

The isolationist senator Gerald P. Nye chaired the Congressional Committee which concluded that arms manufacturers, in an unholy alliance with the international bankers and businessmen, had been responsible for the entry of the United States into World War I. Consequently in August 1935 Congress passed the Pittman Neutrality Resolution prohibiting the export of munitions and the shipment of arms on American vessels to foreign belligerents.

America was hardly alone in its introspection. The assembled powers of the world were equally unwilling to act after Italy had invaded Abyssinia in 1935, when Hitler re-occupied the Rhineland in 1936, or when Italy and Germany both sent troops to fight with Franco in the Spanish Civil War.

After the Japanese invaded North China in 1937, Roosevelt made a notorious speech in Chicago in which he called for a 'quarantine' of those nations who were the aggressors (or, in other words, an international embargo against Japan, Italy and Germany) lest the 'disease' of war infect the Western Hemisphere. The allegory instantly outraged a vast spectrum of opinion, both official and unofficial, and thereafter the President kept his anti-fascist feelings to himself. Hollywood, which invariably luxuriated in the warmth of the majority opinion, looked on approvingly as all the political pressures were exerted on the side of caution.

When war eventually broke out in Europe, Roosevelt began 27 months of what he later termed 'walking on eggs'. Congress was immediately called into special session to push through a clause that permitted foreign powers to buy arms from the United States, provided the munitions were paid for in cash and transported on non-American vessels. This was designed to help Great Britain who, unfortunately, had neither the money nor the ships to conform to such requirements.

This was a difficult period for Hollywood. The studio heads read Dr Gallup's poll, which announced that although 84 per cent of all Americans wanted an Allied victory, 96 per cent of them felt that their country should stay out of the conflict. The contradiction almost paralysed the film industry.

In the summer of 1939 all the studios postponed their spy, refugee or anti-Nazi stories. Warner Brothers shelved *Boycott* and *Underground Road* (eventually released in 1941 as *Underground*); Fox held up production on *I Married a Nazi* and Walter Wanger dithered over his dramatization of Vincent Sheean's *Personal History*, which finally saw the light of day as *Foreign Correspondent* (1940). It was felt that a sudden declaration of war or conclusion of peace would ruin the market value of the stories. The events of early September gave the green light to production although there remained the nagging fear, intensified in the wake of the Phoney War in the West, that peace would break out and cause the pictures to be shelved yet again.

Warner Brothers, who had made the one explicitly anti-Nazi film of the pre-war period (1939, *Confessions of a Nazi Spy*), were unofficially told by the government not to make any more such pictures. In April 1940 the news filtered back to Hollywood that several Polish exhibitors who had shown *Confessions of a Nazi Spy* had been hanged in the foyers of their own cinemas.

Warners were thus happy to mute their anti-Nazism by making such films as *The Sea Hawk* (1940) in which Errol Flynn as a swashbuckling privateer rouses a somnolent England to inflict a crushing defeat on the Spanish Armada – a simple parallel with the Luftwaffe and the Battle of Britain.

When the Phoney War of 1939 gave way to the blitzkrieg of 1940, the struggle in America between the isolationists and the supporters of intervention increased in bitterness. Charles Lindbergh, the aviator hero of the Twenties, called passionately for

Left: support for Britain and her allies was evident in Hollywood before the USA joined the war. As well as this airborne adventure, 1941 also saw the release of A Yank in Libya, *a film with an equally contrived plot that had an American as hero of a British campaign. Above: cover from* The Saturday Evening Post *depicting the role of Hollywood in the war effort; films were shipped to all the fighting fronts and screened in improvised 'cinemas'. Below: British troops were also sustained on a diet of Hollywood cinema. Here ATC cadets attend a show of* I Wanted Wings, *an action movie about young flyers proving themselves in training*

total isolation and warned that American intervention would be a disaster in view of the invincibility of the German armed forces and the inevitability of German domination of Europe.

When President Roosevelt summarily dismissed his opinions, Lindbergh angrily resigned his Commission as a colonel in the Air Corps. Roosevelt ignored the petulant retaliation. In Charlotte, North Carolina, the residents of Lindbergh Drive renamed their street Avon Terrace.

Hitler's victories in the West were undoubtedly bad for Hollywood. In the Low Countries alone 1400 cinemas were immediately closed, representing a loss of $2.5 million in annual revenue to the American film companies. That, added to the losses previously sustained in parts of Scandinavia, Poland, Italy, Spain and the Balkans, meant that they had lost over a quarter of their annual revenue. By the end of 1940, the whole of Continental Europe was closed to US film imports apart from Sweden, Switzerland and Portugal.

Hollywood directly reflected the troubled anxieties of these confusing days. Chaplin's *The Great Dictator* (1940), though ostensibly a satire on Hitler, worked best when it was at its furthest remove from the political parallel and the film's mawkish descent into moral sentimentality in the closing sequence sat unhappily on the preceding farce.

MGM's *Escape* and *The Mortal Storm* (both 1940) doffed their caps in the direction of the horrors of Nazi Germany but they testified to Louis B. Mayer's insistence on avoiding overt condemnation of fascism for fear of political and economic reprisals.

Roosevelt's desperate anxiety to help Britain as she suffered the Blitz and the U-boat war in the Atlantic was tempered by the knowledge that he had decided in 1940 to run for President for an unprecedented third term of office. Only when he had defeated the Republican candidate, Wendell Willkie, could he afford to make sweeping demands of 'Lend-Lease', the Act of Congress which permitted complete and open aid to Britain, short of actual military involvement.

Roosevelt's increasing involvement in the war aided those Hollywood films which touched on the conflict, although most of them treated the issues lightly: there was the Bob Hope comedy *Caught in the Draft*, Abbot and Costello in *Buck Privates* and Tyrone Power and Betty Grable in *A Yank in the RAF* (all 1941). The more serious movies – Robert Taylor in *Flight Command* (1940), Errol Flynn in *Dive Bomber* (1941) and Ray Milland and William Holden in *I Wanted Wings* (1941) – were still far stronger on traditional Hollywood melodrama than ideological content.

It was, therefore, highly encouraging that the coveted place of 1941's top money-making picture was taken by the reflective Howard Hawks film *Sergeant York* (1941), which portrayed a World War I hero (an Oscar-winning performance by Gary Cooper) who overcame his pacifism when he realized that killing for one's country could be also construed as doing God's work. York's rapid elevation to the status of war hero seems to bear divine endorsement, and his decision to fight becomes, by implication, America's decision too.

The easiest way Hollywood could treat the war without offending the isolationists was to make films about Britain for whom sympathy was high in 1941. *That Hamilton Woman!* with Vivien Leigh and Laurence Olivier, was an instant success despite the limited budget on which Alexander Korda made it. The historical parallel of Britain triumphing over the threatened invasion of a foreign tyrant was particularly attractive to Winston Churchill, who took time off from conducting the war to cable Korda with 'helpful' suggestions.

Top right: Gary Cooper played Sergeant York, *the pacifist hick who takes up arms for his country in World War I. The film was a powerfully persuasive argument for American intervention in World War II. Right: it was hardly possible to forget Pearl Harbor, especially as Republic's first contribution to the war effort was released only two months after the event. Below: the film trade papers promoted new alliances (Britain, USA and USSR) through the old alliance between the film distributor and the exhibitors. Bottom: Bob Hope and Dave Willock in* Let's Face It. *Bob ended up a hero and so won a medal*

Despite the marked pro-Allied sentiments in the country at large, Congress still contained a small but significant group of die-hard isolationists. Hollywood was given conclusive evidence of this in October 1941, when Senators Nye and Clark introduced the Senate Resolution 152 which proposed the formation of a committee to investigate:

'. . . any propaganda disseminated by motion pictures . . . to influence public sentiment in the direction of participation by the United States in the . . . European war.'

Of the movies that had caused so much heart-searching in Hollywood during the previous two years, 17 were resurrected and paraded before a collection of unsympathetic politicians. Warner Brothers were condemned for making *Confessions of a Nazi Spy*, *Underground*, *Dive Bomber* and *Sergeant York*. MGM was accused of impure thoughts during the making of *Escape* and *The Mortal Storm* and Fox was keel-hauled for producing *I Married a Nazi* (eventually released as *The Man I Married* in 1941).

Hollywood resigned itself to facing the inevitable rebuke. Ironically it was saved by intervention of the Japanese air squadrons which, in the early morning of December 7, 1941, sank or badly damaged eight battleships and three light cruisers and killed 2400 Americans on the drowsy naval base at Pearl Harbor.

The Pearl Harbor disaster instantly resolved all doubts regarding America's entry into World War II. Hollywood 'enlisted' in a burst of patriotic enthusiasm and economic shrewdness. Paramount changed the title of their picture *Midnight Angel* to *Pacific Blackout* (1942) but it failed to rescue the truly awful nature of the film. David Selznick copyrighted the title *V for Victory* but never got round to using it and in March 1942 Republic Pictures emptied cinemas all over the country with a quickie entitled *Remember Pearl Harbor*.

More significant were the wartime regulations which the government imposed on Hollywood. In December 1941, only two days after Pearl Harbor, army officials moved into all the studios and commandeered the firearms used in any production which were then turned over to civil defence units. All studios were ordered onto a daylight shift of 8 am to 5 pm so that employees could get home before the blackout began and, as a result, night filming was temporarily halted. Most of these instinctive measures were only imposed in the early days of the war when it was still feared that the Japanese were preparing to invade along the vast, undefended coastline of California, but the moves were, at the same time, symptomatic of the government's new involvement in the affairs of the US film industry.

As early as May 1942, the trade paper *Variety* divulged that top-level discussions had resulted in a decision not to portray Hitler and Hirohito as personal symbols of German and Japanese evil. The American public was to be taught that the German and Japanese people were equally to blame for tolerating and cooperating with such leaders.

It was the US government that outlined for Hollywood the six basic patterns for pictures related to the war. The first was the issues of the war itself, into which category fell such diverse movies as *This Above All* (1942) and *Watch on the Rhine* (1943). The second was the nature of the enemy, as exemplified

Once America had entered the war, the Hollywood studios hurled everything into the fight – even star comics and crooners

in *Hitler's Children* (1943) and *This Land Is Mine* (1943). Third came the notion of 'United Nations and its Peoples' by which was meant everything from *Mrs Miniver* to *Mission to Moscow* (both 1942) and *Dragon Seed* (1944).

The fourth category focused on the pressing need for increased industrial production, and here the portrayals featured ordinary people engaged in factory work in films like *Wings for the Eagle* (1942) and *Swing Shift Maisie* (1943).

The last two categories were self-explanatory morale-boosting films about the home front and movies dealing with the fighting forces, a genre in which Hollywood had a long and successful record. Even films which were simply composed of military heroics invariably made obeisance to at least one of the categories mentioned.

No genre was excluded from the fight against fascism. The musical made a forceful entry with *Yankee Doodle Dandy* (1942), starring James Cagney as George M. Cohan, the author of the song 'Over There', the one universally acknowledged hit of World War I. Paramount's contribution included *Star Spangled Rhythm* (1943), which served as a passable excuse for a series of flag-waving and eyebrow-raising numbers. More bizarre than most war musicals was *When Johnny Comes Marching Home* (1943), which starred a heroic marine (played by the irrepressible Allan Jones from *A Night at the Opera*), the teenage wonder Gloria Jean and Phil Spitalny's all-girl orchestra.

Basil Rathbone returned to the attack as Sherlock

Holmes, chasing Nazi villains in contemporary London (where the head of the Nazi spy ring was, inevitably, Moriarty). Nazis also showed up in Maria Montez's temple (in *White Savage*, 1943) and even attacked a coonskin-clad Errol Flynn in the wilds of Canada in *Northern Pursuit* (1943). They also managed an appearance in the 1943 version of *The Desert Song*, where they signally failed to achieve either victory or a decent song.

The progress of the war itself seemed to follow the traditional narrative line laid down by Hollywood. America's initial experience was a series of desperate defeats. By New Year's Day 1942, the Japanese had made successful landings on Guam, Hong Kong, Borneo, Wake Island and the Philippines. General MacArthur was forced to retreat to the fatal Bataan peninsula from which he was removed while his troops died bravely and helplessly. The names of Bataan and Corregidor became synonymous with death and despair. On May 6, 1942, to prevent even more pointless slaughter, General Wainwright was compelled to surrender the rock with its 11,000 American defenders. It was the biggest capitulation in American history and its effect on the population was profound.

The American film industry had, therefore, to address itself to the unaccustomed atmosphere of military disaster. In an attempt to finish *Wake Island* (1942) on a rousing note, Paramount took the costly step of halting production just before shooting was due to take place on the closing sequences. In this way they hoped that the real military events would permit them a happy ending. They didn't. MGM's *Bataan* (1943) closes with the massacre of the American patrol whose fortunes we have been following, although the end caption points out that from such sacrifices sprang the victory of the Battle of Midway.

Victories in North Africa and Italy in 1943 were followed the next year by the successful invasion of France and, as military events foreshadowed ultimate victory, Hollywood's major problem became how to avoid making war movies which would be immediately outdated if the Germans surrendered before the editing was completed.

In the event it did not really matter. 1946 proved to be the most successful year in the history of the film industry. If the war had driven people into the cinemas to escape, peace sent them there to celebrate. All the major studios did their bit for the war effort, supplying propaganda and escapism in generous helpings. Spectacular profits were their reward. These were indeed the golden years of Hollywood. It was a time, so it was said, when even good pictures made money.

Above: the theme and closing hymn of Mrs Miniver *was 'There'll always be an England', but there was no mistaking MGM's all-purpose 'English' mansion as Walter Pidgeon and Greer Garson's home. Below: the last defender in* Bataan. *Bottom: James Cagney helps the RAF in* Captains of the Clouds *(1942)*

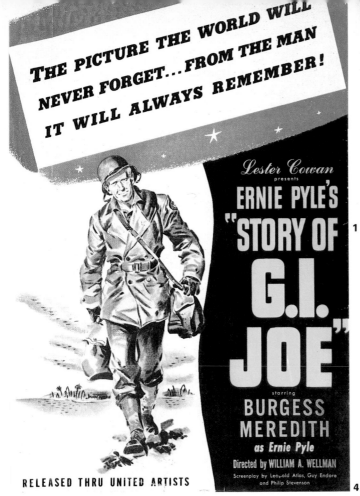

Directed by William Wellman, 1945

Prod co: Lester Cowan Productions/United Artists. **prod:** Lester Cowan. **assoc prod:** David Hall. **sc:** Leopold Atlas, Guy Endore, Philip Stevenson, from the book by Ernie Pyle. **photo:** Russell Metty. **ed:** Otho Lovering, Albrecht Joseph. **art dir:** James Sullivan, Edward G. Boyle. **mus:** Ann Ronell, Louis Applebaum. **mus dir:** Louis Forbes. **sd:** Frank McWhorter. **ass dir:** Robert Aldrich. **r/t:** 109 minutes. Re-released as *War Correspondent*.

Cast: Burgess Meredith (*Ernie Pyle*), Robert Mitchum (*Lt Walker*), Freddie Steele (*Sgt Warnicki*), Wally Cassell (*Pte Dondaro*), Jimmy Lloyd (*Pte Spencer*), Jack Reilly (*Pte Murphy*), Bill Murphy (*Pte Mew*), Tito Renaldo (*Lopez*), William Self (*'Gawky' Henderson*), Yolanda Lacca (*Amelia*), Dorothy Coonan (*Red*), 'and as themselves, combat veterans of the campaigns in Africa, Sicily and Italy'.

'Many things in the film move me to tears – and in none of them do I feel that I have been deceived, or cynically seduced or manipulated, as one usually has to feel about movies.'

So wrote James Agee in a rapturous review of *The Story of GI Joe* on its original release in 1945. And Sam Fuller, himself no mean chronicler of the brutalities of war in *Fixed Bayonets*, *The Steel Helmet* (both 1951) and *Merrill's Marauders* (1962), has commented that:

'Except for Wellman's *GI Joe*, with its feeling of death and mass murder, all war films are kind of adolescent, completely insincere.'

Today's viewers may feel a little less enthusiastic than Agee and Fuller. Vietnam brought into the open one of the rarely acknowledged facts about war: that not all officers are resourceful leaders, and that their tired and frightened men may be as likely to shoot them as to obey them. But *The Story of GI Joe*, devoting itself to the propo-

sition that Captain Walker is one of the good officers, careful and caring about the lives of his men, proceeds to demonstrate it with such quiet conviction that one feels a genuine sense of loss at his death. The closing sequence then shows Private Dondaro – last seen resentfully digging latrines as punishment for neglect of duty – weeping as he holds his dead captain's hand. Here, at least, we are being 'seduced or manipulated', not cynically but sentimentally.

In fairness to Agee, it must be remembered that in 1945, in the context of Hollywood's insistence on flag-waving and rampant heroism in all war movies, *The Story of GI Joe* came as a breath of honest, clean air with its infantryman's angle on war as a meaningless vista of mud, muddle and fatigue ending very probably in a wooden cross. And in fairness to the film itself, it should be added that the final sequence is its only serious lapse. Elsewhere, what Fuller de-

scribes as its feeling of death and mass murder comes over with an astonishing power, more effective than all the anti-war sentiments of *All Quiet on the Western Front* (1930) because the terrible carnage of war is implied, never stated.

The film's masterstroke is its use of the war correspondent Ernie Pyle as an intermediary between us and the action: his commentary supplies the emotional significance that the scenes themselves are not required to carry. Much of the film is therefore shot in documentary style, not imitating newsreel images so much as *interpreting* them while this documentary approach is barely marred by the character sketches and personal conflicts used by most war movies to ensure audience involvement.

In the film's exemplary opening sequence, for instance, we sense not so much fear as a terrible vulnerability as the men are told that they are going into the line and almost lose their talisman, a little dog. That night, vague characterizations – with nostalgia evoked by music from a radio ('This is Berlin bringing you the music of Artie Shaw') – begin to emerge with Dondaro expounding on his favourite topic of women, Murphy grieving that he is too tall to become a pilot, and so on. But by the time battle comes, after weary days of endless marching through rain and grey dawns, anonymity has taken over again; and as the shells scream, Pyle's voice speaks for all of them:

'This was their baptism of fire; it was chaos . . . each boy facing the worst moment of his life, alone.'

Thereafter, as one battle gives way to the next, the audience is chiefly aware that some faces have disappeared to be replaced by others, that familiar faces have suddenly become older and warier, that all are blanketed by an overwhelming fatigue and despair.

But Ernie Pyle is himself a participant in this drama as he wanders around with his typewriter, his next dispatch always in mind. Harassed by tiredness and the apprehension of death as he watches these men, he grows to love them and faces the almost impossible task of making sense of what is happening to them in the stories he writes for their families at home.

This explains the abrupt shift in manner with the bravura sequence in the Italian town; it begins with the snipers being cleared from the church (the last one, shot by Walker as Warnicki kneels to pray, clutches a bell-rope to toll an ironic knell as he falls), then continues with Warnicki finding a gramophone, Dondaro finding a complaisant Italian girl, and Murphy's marriage to an army nurse in a bombed church.

These scenes function as the random personal impressions out of which Pyle builds a meaningful basis for his tale of the terror of war. We hear the beginning of one of his dispatches after Murphy's death: 'He was just a plain Hoosier boy [a native of Indiana]; you couldn't imagine him ever killing anybody . . .' Sentimental, yes; but *The Story of GI Joe* cancels out all mawkishness by showing exactly why Pyle felt as he did about the GI who 'lives so miserably, dies so miserably'.

2

3

ERNIE PYLE

SOMEWHERE IN ITALY (BY WIRELESS)

I HAD LONG AGO COME TO THINK OF PRIVATE

"WINGLESS" MURPHY AS AN OLD, OLD FRIEND.

HE WAS JUST A PLAIN HOOSIER BOY.

YOU COULDN'T IMAGINE HIM EVER KILLING

5

6

7

8

War correspondent Ernie Pyle watches as Lt Walker, leading a company of untried GIs into action, allows them to take along a pet dog (1). After sharing their miseries and their baptism of fire, while recording it all in his dispatches (2), Pyle begins to look upon the boys as his special family. He is later parted from them but, after the North African and Sicilian campaigns, they are reunited in Italy.

Entering an enemy-held Italian town, Walker (now a captain) and Sgt Warnicki (3) clear German snipers from the bell-tower of a ruined church. Warnicki, whose wife has sent him a record of his child's voice, finds a gramophone in a shattered house (4) but it has no needle. In the bombed church,

Pyle gives away the bride when Murphy and an army nurse are married by the chaplain.

Finding their way blocked by a hilltop monastery held by the Germans, the frustrated GIs dig in. Murphy is killed and Pyle's moving story about him (5) wins him the Pulitzer Prize. At Christmas, Pyle insists his 'family' get turkey and whisky (6).

Warnicki at last gets to hear his son's voice but succumbs to battle fatigue and has to be put under restraint (7). Walker leads the rest of the company in a desperate assault on the monastery. As the exhausted survivors sit on the road they have cleared to Rome (8), mules bring the dead down from the hilltop. Walker is among them (9).

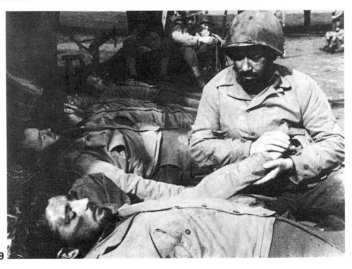

9

165

Howard Hawks rediscovered

Hawks was a much-neglected director until the French critics of the Fifties saluted his personal style of film-making and established him as one of Hollywood's great individual talents

Howard Hawks has created some of the most memorable moments in the history of the American cinema. The problem, however, is how do these moments hang together? Is there a shaping intelligence behind them, or are they merely the accidental benefits of Hollywood movie-making? Until recently the consensus of opinion favoured the latter view. Richard Griffith's remark in 1948, in *The Film Till Now*, that Hawks is 'a very good all-rounder', is representative of the attention paid to Hawks before the French film journal *Cahiers du Cinéma* championed him as *the* American *auteur*. And even after the first rumblings of the *politique des auteurs* (the theory of authorship, by which the creative and artistic credit for a film is attributed to its director) in the mid-

Above: Hawks, seated by the cameraman, directs Gary Cooper in Sergeant York *(1941), and (left) discusses the script of* Gentlemen Prefer Blondes *(1953) with Marilyn Monroe. He was born in Goshen, Indiana, in 1896, and after graduating in engineering from Cornell University in 1917 served in the Army Air Corps during World War I. He then worked as an aircraft builder and pilot and as a racing driver before entering movies in 1922. Although Hawks continued to write, direct and produce films until 1970, flying and driving remained his great passion – revealed in such pictures as* The Air Circus *(1928),* The Crowd Roars *(1931) and* Red Line 7000 *(1965). He died in 1977 – partly from blood poisoning contracted from injuries sustained motorcycling when he was 78 years old*

Fifties, in 1959 *Sight and Sound*, the leading organ of British film culture, had no qualms about not reviewing *Rio Bravo*, a film now acknowledged as one of the great Westerns.

Prior to the *auteur* theory, the mark of a film artist in the American cinema could be found in his choice of subject-matter, in his obvious artistic aspirations, or in his personal visual style. Clearly, by these criteria, Hawks was an unambitious director. In 53 years as a film-maker he was responsible for no major cinematic innovations and was happy to produce pictures that in their sober adherence to the conventions of Hollywood movie-making lack the personal touch of a Hitchcock or the artistry of a Chaplin. Certainly Hawks was a prolific genre director: *Scarface* (1931) is a gangster film; *Gentlemen Prefer Blondes* (1953), a musical; *Land of the Pharoahs* (1955), a biblical epic; *The Dawn Patrol* (1930) and *Air Force* (1943) are war films; *To Have and Have Not* (1944) and *The Big Sleep* (1946), thrillers; *Red River* (1948) and *Rio Bravo* (1959), Westerns; *Bringing Up Baby* (1938) and *Monkey Business* (1952), comedies; and *Only Angels Have Wings* (1939) and *Hatari!* (1962) are just two of his many adventure films.

The breadth of Hawks' films and their consistent commitment to action rather than reflection blinded early critics to the clear pattern of repetition and variation that binds the films together. It was precisely the attempt to trace such a pattern in such a diversity of films directed (and, in most cases, produced) by one man that led 'auteurist' critics to propose Hawks' work as the test case of their theories,

and revealed that behind the mask of Hollywood there lurked artists.

Turning from the ostensible subject-matter
of Hawks' films then, it is possible to discern
a clear pattern of themes running through
them: the group, male friendships, the nature
of professionalism, the threats women pose
men. Recurring motifs include the passing and
lighting of cigarettes for friends, communal
sing-songs, and bizarre sexual role-reversals.

Accordingly, rather than relating *Only
Angels Have Wings* to the spate of aviator
movies that appeared in the Thirties, *To Have
and Have Not* to Curtiz's *Casablanca* (1942), and
Rio Bravo to the development of the Western, it
is more useful to relate these Hawks films to
each other, or even, as Robin Wood has
suggested in his book *Howard Hawks*, to regard
them as a loose trilogy in which notions of
heroism and self-respect are interrogated.

Band of angels
Only Angels Have Wings is concerned with
the problems of a group of mail plane flyers.
From the start the group is hermetically sealed
off from the outside world by storms, giant
condors, mountains and highly dangerous
landing-strips – and the action takes place
almost entirely in the saloon-cum-office run by
Dutchie (Sig Ruman). Here the group is self-
sufficient with its members demanding and
acknowledging support for each other's actions, as instanced in the talking down of pilots
in bad weather, and details like Kid (Thomas
Mitchell) passing Geoff (Cary Grant) a cigarette
even before Geoff searches for one. Geoff is the
leader of the group, who flies when the
weather is too bad to send up his comrades.

Into the group comes Bonnie (Jean Arthur),
down on her luck but asking for help from no-
one. When one of the flyers, Joe (Noah Beery
Jr), attempts a landing in bad weather –
against Geoff's advice – to keep a dinner date
with her, he crashes and is killed. His feelings
for a woman have affected his judgment,
caused him to behave irresponsibly and let his

*Above right: Sergeant York, based on the diary
of a pacifist who eventually joined the army
and became America's greatest hero of World
War I. Released shortly before America joined
World War II, it made a powerful call to arms.
Below and below right: Hawks' films are full of
sing-songs – as in* Only Angels Have Wings
*with Jean Arthur and Cary Grant – and the
lighting of cigarettes – as in* To Have and
Have Not *with Humphrey Bogart and Lauren
Bacall – and similar gestures of friendship*

comrades down by breaching the professional
code that binds the flyers together and makes it
possible to keep the mail-run going in the face
of overwhelming odds. 'Who's Joe?' says Geoff
when Bonnie berates him for his callousness in
eating the steak that had been prepared for the
man who has just died, and goes on to sum Joe
up with the words, 'He just wasn't good
enough'. The sequence finally ends, however,
with the celebratory (and defiant) singing by
Geoff and Bonnie of 'The Peanut Vendor', a
communal act which has the double function
of initiating her into the group as a professional in her own right (she is a singer) and
confirming her acceptance of the rules of the
game of Hawks' group of flyers.

As the story develops, and Bonnie's love for
Geoff deepens, it becomes evident that although suspicious of emotional entanglements
– he has been fooled once before – he is, in fact,
'in love' with Kid, his assistant, as his breakdown after Kid's death testifies. At this point
the interlocking web of relationships becomes
even more complex. Kid's death is, on the one
hand, self-inflicted: his eyesight is failing and
he flies against Geoff's instructions; but as a
grounded flyer he has only a living death to
look forward to. At the same time his death is
caused by his taking on an important job
meant for a flyer whose abilities he distrusts.
The flyer, Bat McPherson (Richard Barthelmess), once baled out of a plane leaving a
friend of Kid's to die, and has since determined
to win back his self-respect by taking on the
most hazardous flights possible. This wash of
conflicting emotions and loyalties that Hawks

sees as life is only held in check by the sense of
what Robin Wood calls 'the constant shadow
of death', which in turn demands responsible
behaviour and self-respect if the group, or the
individual, is to survive.

Loners together
The pattern of relationships in *To Have and
Have Not* is similar – but with significant
differences. In *Only Angels Have Wings* the
group comprises a leader, his friend, the failed
professional who is seeking redemption, and
an intruder; in *To Have and Have Not* there is
the loner Harry Morgan (Humphrey Bogart),
Eddie (Walter Brennan) – 'who used to be
good' – as a drunken version of Kid, and Slim
(Lauren Bacall) as a far more assertive and
aggressive Bonnie figure. The equivalent of the
McPherson character is Paul de Bursac (Walter Molnar), a man who needs physical assistance from Morgan rather than moral support.
And in contrast to Geoff in *Only Angels Have
Wings*, who is desperately trying to secure a
mail-run contract for Dutchie, Morgan in *To
Have and Have Not* is working only for himself.
Despite the existence of a group, the characters
in *To Have and Have Not* are much more
independent and self-motivated than in the
earlier film.

Although the bar run by Crickett (Hoagy
Carmichael) in *To Have and Have Not* has a
communal function in a similar fashion to
Dutchie's, the dramatic thrust of the film is
provided by the Morgan–Slim relationship.
Bogart and Bacall fell in love while making *To
Have and Have Not* and their scenes reflect it –

Cary Grant (above), and Elsa Martinelli in Hatari! (below), learn what it is like to be hunted. Bottom: Cowpunchers Noah Beery Jr, Walter Brennan and Montgomery Clift enjoy a game of cards in Red River

especially the one where Slim instructs Morgan to whistle when he wants her ('You just put your lips together and blow') and then exits to the sound of his whistle of surprise. They give the movie a depth of emotion that is missing from the bite-on-the-bullet stoicism of Only Angels Have Wings.

In Rio Bravo Hawks heightened emotions by having a hero who is completely sexually embarrassed. Previously Hawks had restricted the sexual humiliation theme to the string of crazy comedies he made alongside his adventure films. Rio Bravo, though, is a bringing together of comedy and adventure in Hawks' work, a summation of two traditions his films had established.

In his adventure films, the hero is master of all he surveys; in the comedies he is the victim, both of society and of women – who only have marginal roles in the adventure films. The adventure films occupy a world, far from society's grasp, of hunters, fishermen, aviators and so on, who lead their lives struggling against natural hazards; survival depends on every member of the group being 'good enough', and they celebrate that survival through the ritual of sing-songs. Their reaction to death is to pass over the event as quickly as possible. 'We brought nothing into

the world and it's certain we'll take nothing out,' recites Tom Dunson (John Wayne) dryly over a grave in Red River. The emotional, romantic reactions of the characters in the adventure films are similarly muted; the women go through elaborate rituals of courtship (usually confiding their love not to the loved one but to his friend) in the course of which they prove themselves as tough as men.

The heroes of the adventure films are emotionally repressed and a current of homosexuality runs beneath the male friendships – in A Girl in Every Port (1928) which Hawks himself has described as 'a love story between two men', and erupting closest to the surface in The Big Sky (1952).

In the comedies the hero is perpetually humiliated, as often as not by a domineering woman. This humiliation takes two forms: in the regression to childhood – in Monkey Business where Barnaby (Cary Grant) and Edwina Fulton (Ginger Rogers) take a rejuvenating drug that turns them – emotionally – back into children, and in the reversal of normal sexual roles, the extreme case being I Was a Male War Bride (1949) in which Grant is, for most of the picture, dressed as a woman.

Hunt the man down

In the classic Hawks comedy, Bringing Up Baby, the woman is the hunter. Susan (Katharine Hepburn) sees David Huxley (Cary Grant), falls in love with him, pursues him and against all odds – he is engaged to be married – catches him. Bringing Up Baby draws a parallel with Hawks' adventure films, extended by the big-game-hunting metaphor that runs through it: Baby (Susan's pet leopard) and a wild leopard are both let loose and hunted during the course of the film. The timid David is constantly humiliated by Susan; at one point he has to dress in a monstrously feminine negligée in order to escape – and is then confronted by a decidedly masculine aunt. But forced to keep company with Susan, he is liberated from the stultifying world of zoological research. Fittingly, the film ends with Susan climbing up the huge scaffolding surrounding the dinosaur skeleton he is completing (in another comic inversion of the big-game-hunting adventure film David 'hunts' dead animals) and bringing down the whole edifice crashing to the floor – and with it David's past dull life.

Filmography
1917 The Little Princess (some scenes only, uncredited). '23 Quicksands (sc. only). '24 Tiger Love (sc. only). '25 The Dressmaker From Paris (sc. only). '26 The Road to Glory; Fig Leaves (+prod); Honesty – the Best Policy (sc. only). '27 The Cradle Snatchers; Paid to Love (+prod); Underworld (add. sc. only, uncredited). '28 A Girl in Every Port (+prod); Fazil (both sound and silent versions); The Air Circus (silent scenes only). '29 Trent's Last Case (both sound and silent versions; unreleased in USA). '30 The Dawn Patrol (+co-sc) (reissued as Flight Commander). '31 Scarface/Scarface, the Shame of a Nation (+co-prod); The Crowd Roars; Tiger Shark; Red Dust (add. sc. only, uncredited). '33 Today We Live (+prod). '34 Viva Villa! (some scenes, uncredited; +add. sc, uncredited); Twentieth Century (+prod). '35 Barbary Coast; Ceiling Zero (+co-prod). '36 Sutter's Gold (add. sc. only, uncredited); The Road to Glory (USA retitling for TV: Wooden Crosses/Zero Hour); Come and Get It (co-dir). '37 Captains Courageous (add. sc.

Rio Bravo, which on the surface is a Western adventure film, has been described by Hawks himself as a comedy, but it is by no means a high farce in the *Bringing Up Baby* tradition. Nevertheless, it is inflected at every stage by the tone of the comedies. For example, there is a strong element of parody, most explicit in Feathers' (Angie Dickinson) sophisticated education of Chance (John Wayne) through a process of sexual humiliation and taunting: thus the scene when she sees a pair of scarlet bloomers being held against him and declaims, 'Those things have great possibilities Sheriff, but not on you'.

Chance meeting

Though the characters of *Rio Bravo* can be traced back to the seminal roles of *Only Angels Have Wings* – Chance to Geoff, Stumpy (Walter Brennan) to Kid, Dude (Dean Martin) to McPherson and Feathers to Bonnie – the group is no longer a natural formation. It gathers around Chance but for reasons of loyalty rather than professionalism, and at one point, in the communal sing-song that takes place, Chance is even excluded, becoming merely an observer. More significantly, the fear of old age and failing powers, introduced with Kid in *Only Angels Have Wings*, is placed much closer to the centre of *Rio Bravo* in the form of Stumpy, Chance's anarchic, nagging deputy sheriff who performs the tasks of a wife, cleaning and feeding the inhabitants of the jail as they wait for attack from outside. Colorado (Rick Nelson), the young gunman, introduces a theme of youth-versus-age that dominates later Hawks films, notably *El Dorado* (1967) and *Rio Lobo* (1970), which with *Rio Bravo* make up another loose trilogy.

In *Rio Bravo* the squabbling group eventually grows into a kind of 'family' in which the stoical rules of conduct common to previous Hawksian groups are replaced by something closer to family ties. The final shoot-out – photographed like a firework display – becomes a celebration of new-found unity.

In *El Dorado* Hawks goes further, emphasizing the superiority of filial and family loyalties to any professional ethic. But if in *Rio Bravo* Chance is 'not good enough' to overcome his enemies on his own, in *El Dorado* Cole Thornton (Wayne again) isn't 'good enough' even with help. He only kills the professional gunman who opposes him (and who had ironically

acknowledged him with the courtesy that one professional pays another) by trickery. Thornton is even denied the moral authority that Chance possesses in *Rio Bravo*. When he brings the dead body of their son to the MacDonalds – the boy committed suicide when he failed to kill Thornton – there is no shot of Thornton speaking. We simply hear him accepting responsibility for the boy's death. Returning home, he is ambushed and wounded by Maudie (Charlene Holt), the dead boy's sister; her bullet represents the pangs of conscience Thornton has already given voice to, and the paralysis it causes him is an indication of his age. In contrast to Maudie and Mississippi (James Caan) who both exact personal revenge on their enemies, Thornton and the drunken sheriff, J.P. Harrah (Robert Mitchum), have their roots in Kid in *Only Angels Have Wings*. Logically, like Kid, they should have 'grounded' themselves; instead they wearily and farcically – as in the intensely physical (and comic) curing of Harrah's drunkenness with a stomach-turning antidote, compared with the spiritual curing of Dude's in *Rio Bravo* – wend their way through the action.

In *Rio Lobo*, the age of the Wayne character, Colonel McNally, is once again central to the film, though not in the exploitative fashion of

John Wayne leads his men into action in Rio Lobo *(above) and* El Dorado *(below)*

Henry Hathaway's *True Grit* (1969). Hawks gives his 'baby whale' (the fat, aged army officer played by Wayne) the dignity of a revenge quest, as McNally finally capitulates to filial feelings for the son he never had. But Hawks also undercuts this dignity with broad farce in the activities of the group, a group held together purely by the desire for several private revenges and divided equally carefully into young and old characters. The final break from the world of *Only Angels Have Wings*, however, is signalled by the surprisingly elegant, occasionally almost abstract, photography.

Hawks' world is a limited one, lacking, say, the richness and complexity of John Ford's. But his straightforward stories about the stresses and joys of men and women working together in groups, about the nature of friendship, love and professionalism, are stamped with the consistency and highly individual authorship of a great film artist. Howard Hawks has created a body of work that in its laconic optimism is as majestic as the towering mountains Geoff Carter and his foolhardy band of pilots must fly over in the deliciously titled *Only Angels Have Wings*.

only, uncredited). '38 Bringing Up Baby (+prod); Test Pilot (add. sc. only, uncredited). '39 Gunga Din (add. sc. only, uncredited); Only Angels Have Wings (+prod); Gone With the Wind (add. sc. only, uncredited). '40 His Girl Friday (+prod). '41 Sergeant York; Ball of Fire. '43 The Outlaw (some scenes only, uncredited); Air Force (+co-prod); Corvette K-225 (add. sc. uncredited;+prod;+sup). '44 To Have and Have Not (+prod). '46 The Big Sleep (+prod). '48 Red River (+prod); A Song Is Born (USA retitling for TV: That's Life). '49 I Was a Male War Bride (GB: You Can't Sleep Here). '51 The Thing (co-sc;+sup;+cast dir) (GB: The Thing From Another World). '52 The Big Sky (+prod); O. Henry's Full House *ep* The Ransom of the Red Chief (GB: Full House); Monkey Business. '53 Gentlemen Prefer Blondes. '55 Land of the Pharoahs (+prod). '59 Rio Bravo (+prod). '62 Hatari! (+prod). '64 Man's Favorite Sport (+prod). '65 Red Line 7000 (+co-sc;+prod). '67 El Dorado (+prod). '70 Rio Lobo (+prod).

Deadlier than the male

The *femme fatale* has always loomed large in the imagination of the tempted, tormented, lovelorn male, the creation of his own misgivings and inadequacies. He has projected her onto the screen as well, and in the Forties she found her rightful place in *film noir* – less as a tempest-tossed love goddess than as a sullen, heartless broad waiting in the dark to ensnare some faint-hearted fool with her slinky, seductive ways . . .

The *femme fatale* was always a fake. She lied, and made the husky, sincere whisper seem like a knife in the groin. But the men who created her lied too. Their bitter regrets about her duplicity, her corrupt loveliness and the need to send her to the electric chair were all a cover-up for the fact that they really wanted to live alone without thinking less of themselves.

She sauntered into innocent or weak lives, asking for a light but requiring the soul. She spread scent, languor, a mystically ultimate sophistication or depravity, her silky legs and the legend that some crime undertaken in the

Above left: Lola-Lola (Marlene Dietrich) lures the Professor (Emil Jannings) to his doom in The Blue Angel. *Above: Lulu (Louise Brooks) and one of her victims in* Pandora's Box. *Left: Rita Hayworth shows the dark, voluptuous side to her beauty*

dark would be as thrilling and as sweet as the unlimited, intricate experience she offered in herself. That vicious, velvet spiral was the innovation that made masochism a new pleasure in the male sexual fantasy. Despite a man's best efforts, the *femme fatale* was thinking of something else:

'But all of a sudden she looked at me, and I felt a chill creep straight up my back and into the roots of my hair. "Do you handle accident insurance?" '

She's not asking whether he's using a French letter; instead, there's a rich, stupid husband that they could remove. Taken from a James M. Cain novel, *Double Indemnity*, published in 1936, the she is Phyllis Nirdlinger, and he is Walter Huff. Those are depressive names. Moviegoers know them better as Phyllis Dietrichson and Walter Neff: the man edgier, more deft and alert than his literary counterpart; the woman (related to that most iconographic enchantress, Marlene) so authoritative that she carries off the role as a burnished blonde.

We know Phyllis better still as Barbara Stanwyck, the Glendale Medusa in Billy Wilder's 1944 film version of *Double Indemnity*, the epitome of the *film noir* dark lady – all sexual innuendo and glamorous dishonesty. She seems sticky, alive with heat, a collection of surfaces begging to be touched – most of all the anklet she wears and which Fred MacMurray as Neff imagines 'biting into her leg'. That cunning detail was invented for the film – by the screenwriters, Wilder and Raymond Chandler – and it is the perfect promise of pain in pleasure, of jewellery being a mark of slavery, of narcissism as flirtation.

Who thought of the anklet? Wilder probably. So many of his other films have narrators like Neff who improve upon the visuals by verbalizing their inner thoughts. Yet Chandler's contribution to the film is surely significant, for his private-eye novels are gloomy with the conviction that good-looking dames are dishonest. Then again, it is important to remember that Cain's original novel is far more pessimistic than the movie. Cain has the illicit lovers go free. But their stew of evil and guilt is so intense that they are about to act out a suicide pact as the book ends, if Walter can trust Phyllis to keep her word. He contemplates her – the woman who has wrecked all their lives with her murderous scheming:

'She smiled then, the sweetest, saddest smile you ever saw. I thought of . . . the three little children, Mrs Nirdlinger, Nirdlinger, and myself. It didn't seem possible that anybody that could be as nice as she was when she wanted to be could have done all those things.'

The language is sentimental, nearly maudlin, which may be why Cain adopted such tough attitudes: the hard-boiled style is so often the disguise for a soft centre. Similarly, the *femme fatale* is the creation of romantic dismay. She emerges from the rueful sense of the failure or impossibility of love. Thus she has her movie origins less in the quaint vamping of Theda Bara and other silent wantons, than in the romantic agony of Germany in the Twenties and in the Surrealists' awareness that love yearned for is purer than love enjoyed.

America in the Twenties hardly dreamed of dark women. The *femme fatale* needs sound, so that she may say very little; silent heroines have to act out their good intentions. The city woman in Murnau's *Sunrise* (1927) is one

Above: the devil in a black negligée – Hazel Brooks in Sleep, My Love. Above right: sultry Linda Darnell with Percy Kilbride and Dana Andrews in Fallen Angel. Right: ice-cold Veronica Lake's first film with Alan Ladd. Below: Lizabeth Scott, sulky and ruthless, with Humphrey Bogart in Dead Reckoning

example of allure; otherwise, Janet Gaynors flourished. And Louise Brooks had to go to Germany to make *Die Büchse der Pandora* (1929, *Pandora's Box*), a film in which the actress transcends the director G.W. Pabst's caution and reclaims the original author Frank Wedekind's fascinated anguish for the idea of an anti-social goddess of ecstatic chaos. Brooks may still be the greatest *femme fatale* because she is the least sinister or mannered. It is her compulsive vitality that is most danger-ous. Although the men in *Pandora's Box* are all her victims – prostrate, cowering or devastated by her energy – Brooks never makes Lulu two-faced. The film is *her* tragedy, for her stunning sensuality can only rest after self-destruction. By the Forties, the dark woman was so much more restrained, secretive and brooding: the big sleep hiding beneath her fur coat was so ominous a haven. But Lulu's preoccupation with life and the moment makes all the men

look feeble, stilted or malicious.

Only one year later, in Germany still but about to be transported to Hollywood, Marlene Dietrich's enigmatic smile understood all too well. Dietrich moved more slowly than any other actress, taunting the viewer to see the absurd, delirious fatalism, and covering her mischief with the pretence of helplessness. Clearly it is not her fault, Lola-Lola suggests in song at the end of *Der Blaue Engel* (1930, *The Blue Angel*), if the men who dote on her get hurt – men like the professor who, destroyed, creeps away to end the life she has exposed as bogus. But when Josef von Sternberg brought her to America, Dietrich altered. Weight and spontaneity fell away like worry. Sternberg willed a colder, more serene image and, in his own words, 'disguised her imperfections and led her to crystallize a pictorial aphrodisiac'. In terms of plot, some of her Paramount films could be called happy (or fulfilled), but their thematic consistency is the amusement that knows the thought of love and sex – the aphrodisiac image – is greater than the thing itself. Sternberg made love-letter movies that always end with a sighing 'alas' and Dietrich's face like a light burning in the memory.

Together they made the word *fatale* reson-ant: their best films – *Morocco* (1930), *The*

Scarlet Empress (1934), *The Devil Is a Woman* (1935) – are superbly taut constructions in which desire faces futility. There is less cruelty in them than there had been in Twenties films, and far less moroseness than there would be in Forties films, just the delicious realization (torture but bliss) that looking and dreaming are more romantic than embracing. No wonder the cinema's greatest surrealist, Luis Buñuel, remade *The Devil Is a Woman* more than forty years later as *Cet Obscur Objet du Désir* (1977, *That Obscure Object of Desire*), with the man's mixed feelings of lust and love manifested by two actresses in the central role.

'How can a man be so dumb . . . I've been waiting to laugh in your face ever since I met you. You're old and ugly and I'm sick of you – sick, sick, sick!'
Joan Bennett in Scarlet Street

Sternberg's Dietrich seemed too cynical, or too enlightened, for America in the Thirties. The great majority of movie women loyally aspired to the commercial code of romance. There were 'bad' women – Bette Davis, most notably – but they were ugly-pretty villain-esses who got their just deserts. Vivien Leigh's Scarlett O'Hara may have helped secure the place of conniving beauty, but it was only in the Forties that the Hollywood *femme fatale* came into her own as a deceitful beauty who lures men to their doom. Why was this? Was it the accumulated loss of confidence of the Thirties with the new male dilemma of being overseas, wondering what the women were doing at home, and dreaming of betrayals that would prove only to be suspicions? Or was it a reflection of deeper fissures in American sexual relations? This becomes a distinct possibility when you consider the chronic self-pity that beholds the *femme fatale*, and because the acts of treachery are the first signs of an indepen-dent woman coming onto the American screen. Jane Fonda as a latter-day *femme fatale* in *Klute* (1971) is an interesting example of the woman men cannot trust growing into some-one who controls her own destiny.

It is important to see how far the bitch had been defined in the Thirties in the work of writers like Cain, Chandler and Dashiell Ham-mett. Their misogynist distaste is actually more hostile than anything filmed. Indeed, they can hardly conceive of women as any-thing other than loyal doormats or snakes in the grass; Mary Astor as the scheming Brigid O'Shaughnessy in *The Maltese Falcon* (1941)

was too old and too stable for the part – as if Hollywood had not yet quite understood the fickleness of such women.

Ida Lupino had actually given a far better performance in *They Drive By Night* (1940) where she plays a woman of many moods and radiant falsehood. Lupino played good girls too – and she was seldom exotically glamorous – but she had no equal at taking on men.

So many actresses in the Forties responded to the low-key of *film noir* by adopting the same image. Veronica Lake also looked mysterious – in *This Gun for Hire, The Glass Key* (both 1942) and *The Blue Dahlia* (1946) – but there was nothing substantial behind the lock of hair. Ann Sheridan – in films like *They Drive By Night, Nora Prentiss* (1947) and *The Unfaithful* (1947) – often looked as if she had been slow-cured in cigarette smoke. Rita Hayworth was a crazy-eyed traitress for her baby-faced husband, Orson Welles, in his *The Lady From Shanghai* (1947), and was otherwise cast as

temptresses and reptiles. The stealthy apparition that was played by Joan Bennett in *The Woman in the Window* (1944) was a lovely throwback to the Germanic dread of a woman who will lead the settled bourgeois gentleman astray; surely Fritz Lang, who directed the film, appreciated her in this and *Scarlet Street* (1945), and Bennett herself enjoyed the lazy animal frivolity of the parts. She had the cutest pout until Gloria Grahame came along.

There are others, less well-known, but worth recalling: Jean Brooks in Mark Robson's *The Seventh Victim* (1943); Linda Darnell in Otto Preminger's *Fallen Angel* (1945); Lizabeth Scott in John Cromwell's *Dead Reckoning* (1946) – beguiling until she talks; Jane Greer in Jacques Tourneur's *Out of the Past* (1947); Hazel Brooks in Douglas Sirk's *Sleep, My Love* (1948); and maybe even Gloria Swanson in Wilder's *Sunset Boulevard* (1950), the ultimately grotesque distortion of female glamour.

And Lauren Bacall? Well, yes and no. Bacall

Above left: Ann Sheridan, who was known as 'the Oomph Girl', with Robert Alda in Nora Prentiss. *Above: the tarty, conniving 'Lazy Legs' (Joan Bennett) sneers at Chris Cross (Edward G. Robinson), the man she has led on and lived off in* Scarlet Street

in *To Have and Have Not* (1944) and *The Big Sleep* (1946) plays the *femme fatale*, but the framework of the films makes it clear that she is only pretending in order to be one of the boys. Howard Hawks and Humphrey Bogart never ask a moment of unkindness from her: they both recognize that she is a grown-up adolescent 'hiring out to be tough'. It is the cleverest compromise: the girl-next-door pretending to be the angel of death, sophistication without threat. Yet in both these two early Bacall films she was the invention of male dreams – just as the *femme fatale* was always a phantom that men invoked to justify their own fears.

They lived by night

The hero of the *film noir* was usually in a place where he knew he shouldn't be, perhaps lurking in the shadows of a dark street – the rain glistening, a harsh neon sign flashing – ready to keep an assignation with his intended victim, or maybe his own death. If he wasn't the dupe of some woman, of his own shady past, or just a guy entangled with fate, then he was probably a cold killer with a twisted smile . . .

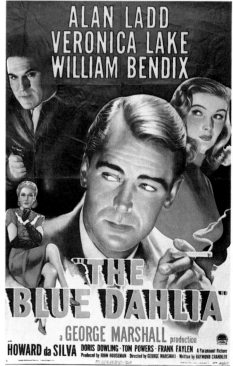

Above: in The Blue Dahlia *Ladd is a man suspected of his wife's murder and Lake is a woman who picks him up. Left: time runs out for Jeff (Robert Mitchum), trapped by his ex-girl (Jane Greer) and her gangster-lover (Kirk Douglas) in* Out of the Past

Above: Dana Andrews as the brutal cop who accidentally kills a murder suspect in Where the Sidewalk Ends. *Above right: Clifton Webb, as the suave murderer Cathcart, with William Bendix in* The Dark Corner. *Far right: Dan Duryea as the pimp in* Scarlet Street. *Below: Tommy Udo (Richard Widmark) and Nick Bianco (Victor Mature) in* Kiss of Death

In the introduction to their survey of the bad men of Hollywood movies, *The Heavies*, Elizabeth and Ian Cameron suggest that 'the Heavy's suitability for his part is more a matter of appearance than it is of good acting'. This is a good general rule, but like most rules it has its exceptions. Probably the most obvious one is Robert Mitchum, whose forceful presence on the screen is so dominating that it is hard to credit any director with complete control over the actor's performance.

A more interesting exception, however, is Clifton Webb. In his first two sound films, Otto Preminger's *Laura* (1944) and Henry Hathaway's *The Dark Corner* (1946), Webb turned in magisterial performances as fragile but deeply treacherous aesthetes; he then took on the anodyne role of Mr Belvedere, a dreary bachelor baby-sitter in the comedy *Sitting Pretty* (1948) and never really got the chance to be nasty again. Webb was a talented actor, but what made his first two appearances so menacing was not so much the parts themselves as the grim romanticism of the sweet-smelling but foul world of darkness and vio-

lence that was *film noir*, which made the roles possible in the first place. The context of *film noir* gave an extra twist to the mannered severity of Webb's performances.

Film noir can be seen as a movement that for the first time allowed the traditional heavies to act as well as 'be'. Dealing as it did with claustrophobia, paranoia, fear and despair, and finding its natural home in B rather than A features, *film noir* required – even demanded – ambiguous heroes and villains rather than the clean-cut dramatics of 'good guys versus bad guys'. If, historically, the bad guy has always been the best role, in the tainted world of *film noir* there were no good guys anyway, only bad and ambiguous guys.

Such roles allowed a number of actors to shine: Dana Andrews, Richard Conte, Dan Duryea, Farley Granger, Alan Ladd, Charles McGraw, Fred MacMurray, Victor Mature, Robert Mitchum, and Richard Widmark – to name but a few. Take Fred MacMurray, for example. Prior to Billy Wilder's *Double Indemnity* (1944), his jocular easy-going nature (later re-established when he played the

---

'I killed Dietrichson – me, Walter Neff – insurance salesman – 35 years old, no visible scars – till a while ago, that is. I killed him for money – and for a woman. It all began last May . . .'
Fred MacMurray in Double Indemnity

---

understanding father in a number of Disney pictures of the Sixties) had cast him as a bland, second-string male lead. *Double Indemnity* revealed the possibility of emptiness behind that bluff good-humour. The insurance salesman he plays is rapidly and willingly corrupted by the pitiless woman (Barbara Stanwyck) who seduces him into murdering her husband. Caught between the puritan rigidity of Edward G. Robinson as the father-figure claims-investigator and Stanwyck's cold temptress, MacMurray was the perfect fall guy. If it was Billy Wilder who caught the exact desultory quality of urban Californian life (just as Michael Curtiz did with *Mildred Pierce* in 1945), it was MacMurray's performance that gave the film its tragically fatalistic trajectory.

Farley Granger, who, unlike MacMurray, had no screen persona to be twisted out of skew but simply looked fallible enough to play the terse nice guy in Hitchcock's *Strangers on a Train* (1951), is fooled by an insane offer from the mad Bruno (Robert Walker) to exchange

murders. Both performances were to haunt their creators, but outside the confines of *film noir* the deranged personalities they projected had little substance.

If MacMurray and Granger drifted quickly in and out of the shadows of *film noir*, Dan Duryea and Dana Andrews regularly walked down the mean streets of Hollywood in the Forties. Duryea, with his striped suits and fancy neckties, light sneering voice and petty sadism (which was to flower into true psychosis in Westerns like Anthony Mann's *Winchester 73*, 1955), was the small-time hustler pimping his way to the top of the heap. He perfected the role of the smiling corrupter in films like Mann's *The Great Flamarion*, Fritz Lang's *Scarlet Street* (both 1945) and Robert Siodmak's low-key *Criss Cross* (1949).

If Duryea was essentially working-class, Dana Andrews' chiselled, aristocratic features – he had disconcertingly cold, piercing eyes and a sense of disillusionment to match – suggested he came from the better side of town. Looking like a nice guy, more often than not he turned out to be false – and an evil influence. For Preminger, he was a confidence trickster in *Fallen Angel* (1945), a philanderer in *Daisy Kenyon* (1947) and a detective on the make in *Where the Sidewalk Ends* (1950) – all roles which had their origins in the neurotic detective of *Laura*.

The contrast between the working-class and

aristocratic backgrounds of such villains was paralleled by the different styles of the out-and-out hoods who also populated *film noir*. Thus Charles McGraw and Victor Mature brought a sweaty, hulking viciousness to their roles, while Richard Conte and Alan Ladd offered a more austere and disdainful violence. McGraw is best remembered as the heavy who takes great delight in turning up the steam in a Turkish bath on a trapped Wallace Ford (playing the fall-guy role usually reserved for Elisha Cook Jr) in Mann's *T-Men* (1947). McGraw later graduated to Western heavies, but Victor Mature's gross, strong-man presence proved surprisingly adaptable beyond the confines of *film noir*. Nevertheless, in films like Hathaway's *Kiss of Death* (1947) and Siodmak's *Cry of the City* (1948), he gave his venal gangster and sanctimonious policeman a particularly appealing doomed innocence.

Between 1945 and 1955, Richard Conte played the Hispanic or Italian hood so often that in 1972 Francis Ford Coppola used him in *The Godfather* to give an added touch of mythical 'realism' to the film's Mafia backdrop. A smart dresser, Conte brought a determined stylishness to the criminals he played in films like Hathaway's *Call Northside 777* (1948). He was even more successful as the wealthy psychiatrist in Preminger's *Whirlpool* (1949), proving his wife's innocence and thereby sending the hypnotist (José Ferrer) to the chair for murder. But it was primarily as an upper-crust gangster that Conte made his way suavely through the Forties.

If Conte's characters were always men who ran or worked for 'the Organization', Alan Ladd, from the moment of his first appearance as the fragile killer of Frank Tuttle's *This Gun for Hire* (1942), was always a man alone. Though George Stevens' Western *Shane* (1953) provided Ladd with his best-known role as a loner, his gangster films provided his best moments. Even better than his performance as the amoral private detective in Stuart Heisler's *The Glass Key* (1942) was his ex-serviceman suspected of murder in George Marshall's *The*

Blue Dahlia (1946). Veronica Lake was his co-star in both.

The two actors who best call to mind *film noir* of the Forties, yet survived as stars, are Richard Widmark and Robert Mitchum. Widmark's film debut, in *Kiss of Death*, was one of the most dramatic ever. As Tommy Udo, his skin stretched taut over his skull, he giggled maniacally as he vented his sadism on those around him. With a slight shift of character, he mixed gruesome sentimentality with gross sadism in his finest role as the three-time loser in Sam Fuller's *Pick Up on South Street* (1953). He has proved his versatility with differing roles in films by such diverse directors as Ford, Siegel and Minnelli – and even played the hypochondriac victim in the elaborate Agatha Christie period piece, Sidney Lumet's *Murder on the Orient Express* (1974).

If, in the Forties, Widmark was an actor who was all flashes and sparks, Robert Mitchum was the deepest of Hollywood's actors. Laconic in the extreme, he was the brooding man of action who suggested he had not only an inner self but intelligence as well. And Mitchum has survived more bad films than most actors. A one-time heavy in Hopalong Cassidy films, he graduated early in the decade to tough-guy roles in grander Westerns and war films and then, in 1947, turned in superb performances in two of the most stunning *films noirs*. The first was Raoul Walsh's *Pursued*, the blackest ever 'psychological Western' with its great, looming close-ups and doomed revenge structure; the second was Jacques Tourneur's *Out of the Past*. The latter had Mitchum as a man caught between the past – represented by a gangster (Kirk Douglas) and their former mistress (Jane Greer) – and a hopeless future with his girl (Rhonda Fleming). Forced to return to the past to save his future, he is doomed from the start.

With the arrival of the Fifties, Mitchum extended his range until by the late Sixties he had become a major star. Yet ironically, as the Seventies closed and remakes became popular in Hollywood, Mitchum was called in to be the tough guy again, playing detective Philip Marlowe brilliantly in Dick Richards' *Farewell, My Lovely* (1975) then disastrously in Michael Winner's *The Big Sleep* (1978).

Like Duryea, Ladd, Widmark and the others, like the directors, writers and lighting cameramen who together assembled *film noir* from a myriad of influences, Mitchum took the opportunity in the Forties to explore the dark side of life to the hilt. The results were some outstanding films and performances.

Above left: Charles McGraw turns the heat on Wallace Ford in T-Men.
Above: the gangster (Richard Conte) gets the drop on the cop (Victor Mature) who used to be his pal in Cry of the City. *Below: anxious moments for Guy (Farley Granger) in Hitchcock's* Strangers on a Train

Lovely Rita

Woman of mystery or happy-go-lucky girl-next-door? Rita Hayworth somehow blended the attributes of both in her screen personality. The result was irresistible

In John Huston's madly haphazard but inspired *Beat the Devil* (1953), Humphrey Bogart is led off by Arabs to a seemingly certain death. When next seen, however, he is in cosy conversation with the local sheikh who smiles benignly and says, 'And so you really know the lovely Rita?' while behind him hang dozens of glittering photographs of the star. The joke would not have been half as amusing had it not been founded on fact. From the Gulf of Aden to Brooklyn (where she was born in 1918), Rita Hayworth was *the* love goddess of films, the incarnation of eroticism in the post-war years.

That image of the free-living, sleekly sophisticated, sexual animal – fully realized for the first time in *Gilda* (1946) – was, nonetheless, consciously created by Hayworth and various collaborators, and was almost a decade in the making. In spite of her apparent defiance of convention – her much publicized series of marriages, divorces and romances – Hayworth and her co-workers have often denied that the image has much connection with her real personality. This denial is summed up by her

Above: this publicity shot of Hayworth taken in the early Fifties bears out Orson Welles' comment that 'she was one of those whom the camera loved and rendered immortal'. Right: in her first A film – Only Angels Have Wings

most oft-quoted statement. In an attempt to explain the failure of several of her marriages she once said: 'They all married Gilda, but they woke up with me.'

The lovely señorita

Hayworth started her career as a rather dumpy 13-year-old, dancing with her then-famous father Eduardo under her real name, Margarita Carmen Cansino, in various nightclubs, primarily in Mexico. Trained by her father, she became an accomplished dancer, especially to Latin rhythms. Joseph Cotten once commented later that 'no matter how bad the rest of the film, when Rita started to dance it was like seeing one of nature's wonders in motion.'

She was discovered by Hollywood in 1933. Warner Brothers turned her down after a test because she was overweight and her hairline was too low, but Winfield Sheenan, head of production at Fox, signed her; he was impressed with the way she held herself and her grace of movement. As Rita Cansino she danced briefly in a club sequence in *Dante's Inferno* (1935) and appeared in four mediocre films. When Fox merged with 20th Century Films, the new head of production, Darryl F. Zanuck, replaced her in the title role of the Technicolor *Ramona* (1936) with Loretta Young, and then cancelled her contract.

Hayworth freelanced her way through the tepid *Meet Nero Wolfe* (1936) and four forgettable Westerns.

Those of her admirers who claim with hindsight to be able to perceive all Hayworth's later qualities in those early appearances do her a disservice by disregarding the years of hard work and professional craftsmanship which made her a star. In these first films she was adequate in parts that called for little. The profile was there, as was a certain exuberance, but not much more.

A head start

Her husband, Edward C. Judson, then took a hand in her career. He insisted that she take diction lessons, put her on a diet, changed her makeup and way of dressing, and sent her to an electrolysist to have her hairline raised, therby broadening her forehead. Harry Cohn, boss of Columbia studios, saw her and liked what he saw. He signed her at $250-a-week (to rise to $1750 over seven years), changed her name – in part to conceal her past film work – and put her in a dozen programmers to let her gain experience and to find out what might be made of her. She was ambitious, patient and anxious to learn. When a good part in a good film came along, she was ready for it.

She got her chance in Howard Hawks' *Only Angels Have Wings* (1939). She was cast as the second female lead, playing Richard Barthelmess' flighty but ultimately loyal wife. She was good enough to be noticed by audiences and critics, and at least held her own with Cary Grant and Jean Arthur, the film's two main stars. George Cukor, a director with a keen instinct for a talented actress, had tested Hayworth in 1938 for the female lead in *Holiday* (subsequently given to Katharine Hepburn), but had felt she was too inexperienced. He remembered her, however, and borrowed her from Columbia for MGM's *Susan and God* (1940), starring Joan Crawford. Her role was not large but it was glamorous. The public quickly responded. Columbia began to churn out publicity photographs to satisfy her growing following; Cohn was aware that he had found a star, but he was not sure quite what to do with her.

He tried her in two A films: *The Lady in*

Question, (1940), which was the first time Hayworth was directed by Charles Vidor who would later collaborate on three of her biggest hits, and *Angels Over Broadway* (1940). The reviews were good, including those for Hayworth, but neither film did much business. Two other studios then showed Cohn Hayworth's real possibilities.

Warner Brothers had planned *The Strawberry Blonde* (1941) for Ann Sheridan. When she refused to do it at the last moment, the studio looked for an available second-level star whose size and colouring (in spite of the film being shot in black and white) would fit the costumes designed for Sheridan. Hayworth, who dyed her black hair to its now famous red, was thus given the role of the sunny gold digger out to steal dentist James Cagney from nice Olivia de Havilland. The film was a smash, as was Hayworth. After a minor comedy at Warners she was then loaned to 20th Century-Fox to replace Carole Landis (who refused to dye her hair red or to play an unsympathetic part) in Mamoulian's Technicolor *Blood and Sand* (1941). As Dona Sol, the noblewoman-temptress who temporarily steals bullfighter Tyrone Power from Linda Darnell, Hayworth was ravishing to look at. The film, quite rightly, was not very popular, but Hayworth received a great deal of attention. Between 1941 and 1942, her face appeared on the front cover of 23 magazines.

Naughty but nice

Although she played an unfaithful wife in one episode of Ben Hecht's *Tales of Manhattan* (1942), it was the lighter side of her role in *The Strawberry Blonde* that was emphasized in five films over the next four years – during which she established herself as a major star. She managed to be beautiful and erotic, in a 'nice' way – a girl-next-door whom women could admire and not worry if their men admired her as well, for she was never a conscious threat. She also returned to her origins as a dancer, becoming connected in the mind of her public with musicals. Until the late Fifties, audiences would eagerly await her big

Top: a young dentist (Cagney) manages to get a date with the girl of his dreams in The Strawberry Blonde. *Above, far right: Hayworth (left) in the musical* Down to Earth. *Right: both she and her then husband Orson Welles look pleased with her new, short, blonde hair-do created for* The Lady From Shanghai.

number(s) no matter what kind of film she was appearing in. Unfortunately her singing voice was weak, so that her songs were always dubbed (a closely guarded secret during her Columbia days). *You'll Never Get Rich* (1941) and *You Were Never Lovelier* (1942) had everything that musicals of the time needed for success – except colour – including songs by Cole Porter (for the former) and Jerome Kern (for the latter), with Fred Astaire appearing in both.

The plot of *Cover Girl* (1944) is silly and clichéd (will girl dancer make it on talent or beauty, remain with the poor dancer who loves her or run off with a wealthy playboy?), but that hardly matters, even when the film is seen today. Never more beautiful in colour (cameraman Rudolph Maté worked with Hayworth on her next four films and remained her favourite), she was teamed with Gene Kelly and 'sang' and danced to songs by Kern and Ira Gershwin. The film was the biggest hit of Hayworth's career up to then.

Down to Earth (1947) was planned before the release of *Gilda* and put into production just 18 days before that film's release. In it she plays a goddess (Terpsichore, the muse of dancing) who comes down to earth to help a young stage producer (Larry Parks) succeed on Broadway. The film was lavishly shot in colour, Hayworth looked beautiful and the

box-offices did good business. But the film was overshadowed by *Gilda*, which had provided Hayworth with a new image more in keeping with the prevailing attitudes of post-war America. She had also discovered a new maturity as an actress. As the far-from-innocent *film noir* 'heroine' she was asked to do a good deal more than simply look beautiful and dance well. Although she would appear, from time to time, in less demanding roles in indifferent films, from *Gilda* until *The Money Trap* (1965), there is a seriousness of intent and achievement in Hayworth as an actress often overlooked by critics.

The thrill is gone

After *Gilda*, Hayworth's career slowly began to fade. She continued to have box-office hits for another seven years, but much of the excitement and erotic charge of *Gilda* was lacking. During those seven years, however, she made one of her finest films with her then husband Orson Welles, *The Lady From Shanghai* (1947). It was a financial failure when it was first released, partially because it was a

Welles film and not a Hayworth vehicle: her hair was cut and bleached; there were no dances (and just one, ironic, song); and her character did not even have the sympathetic qualities that Gilda had possessed. Yet, with *Gilda*, it is vintage Hayworth, and one of the finest films Hollywood made in the Forties. *The Lady From Shanghai* cuts through every romantic illusion and 'civilized' institution on which American society rests. The film was years ahead of its time, and Hayworth rightly regards it as one of the best things with which she has ever been associated.

Under a new Columbia contract (in which she stipulated that she must always be presented sympathetically on screen), she became a fun-loving, misunderstood Carmen in *The Loves of Carmen* (1948), beautiful (in colour) but unconvincing (especially with a wooden Glenn Ford as her Don José). She returned to the screen after an absence of four years (during which she married and separated from Aly Khan) in *Affair in Trinidad* (1952), a faded remake of *Gilda*. Entering the then popular biblical sweepstakes, she played a sympathetic, misunderstood *Salome* (1953) who dances to *save* John the Baptist. In the same year, obviously fighting a weight problem but full of a mature sexuality, she played *Miss Sadie Thompson* in colour and 3-D. The inferior and splashy *Salome* made money, the delightfully trashy *Miss Sadie Thompson* did not.

At odds with Cohn, she turned down a project entitled *Joseph and his Brethren*, but made *Fire Down Below* (1957) playing very much third string to Robert Mitchum and Jack Lemmon. After her role as an older woman who loses Frank Sinatra to Kim Novak in *Pal Joey* (1957), she left Columbia (although in 1959 she did an interesting Western, *They Came to Cordura*, for the studio).

Right: Hayworth freshens up in Pal Joey, *which marked the end of a distinguished musical career. Below: GIs drool and Hayworth looks cool in* Miss Sadie Thompson, *one of several versions of Somerset Maugham's* Rain. *Bottom: Hayworth and Gary Cooper in a tender moment from* They Came to Cordura

'Zip', her delightful tongue-in-cheek strip in *Pal Joey*, also marked the end of her musical days. She now turned to drama as an ageing actress (*Separate Tables*, 1958), a suffering wife on trial for murder (*The Story on Page One*, 1959), and a suffering mother (*Circus World*, 1964), and to comedy (*The Happy Thieves*, 1962). The first was popular and got good reviews; the rest were failures with the critics and the public (although Hayworth herself was not bad in any of them). The old romantic team of Hayworth and Glenn Ford worked well in *The Money Trap*; the director, Burt Kennedy, generated a good deal of excitement in their scenes together. In the film, a dishonest cop (Ford) visits his old flame (Hayworth) who has fallen on hard times. Still beautiful, Hayworth fills her brief scenes with pain and an undercurrent of still-smouldering eroticism. The film was a commercial failure; when it was released for TV, Hayworth's intelligent performance had been cut for time. That, unfortunately, is the print which re-entered theatrical distribution.

Rita Hayworth ended her career with half a

dozen low budget films in the USA, Italy and Spain. Two – *I Bastardi* (1968, *Sons of Satan*) and *Sur la Route de Salina* (1970, *Road to Salina*) – are of more than passing interest because of her fine performances of what are similar parts, a drunken ex-actress and a down-at-heel café proprietress. She considered various films in the Seventies, but most came to naught. In 1987 she died, as a result of Alzheimer's disease, yet to many she is, and always will be, the ultimate Love Goddess. A TV biopic of this name featured Lynda Carter (or Wonderwoman) as Hayworth. Ms Carter tried hard, but comparisons are odious, particularly to those of us who can brighten a dark winter night by rolling our memory projectors and glorying once again in 'the lovely Rita'.

Filmography
1926 untitled short on folk dancing. **'35** Cruz Diablo (extra) (MEX); promotional film for studio Spanish-language versions (short); Under the Pampas Moon; Charlie Chan in Egypt; Dante's Inferno; Paddy O'Day. **'36** Human Cargo; Meet Nero Wolfe; Rebellion. **'37** Trouble in Texas; Old Louisiana/Louisiana Girl (GB: Treason); Hit the Saddle. **'37** Criminals of the Air; Girls Can Play; The Game That Kills; Paid to Dance (USA retitling for TV: Hard To Hold); The Shadow (GB: The Circus Shadow.) **'38** Who Killed Gail Preston?; There's Always a Woman; Convicted (CAN); Juvenile Court; The Renegade Ranger (CAN). **'39** Homicide Bureau; The Lone Wolf Spy Hunt (GB: The Lone Wolf's Daughter); Special Inspector (CAN); Only Angels Have Wings. **'40** Music in My Heart; Blondie on a Budget; Susan and God (GB: The Gay Mrs Trexel); The Lady in Question; Angels Over Broadway. **'41** The Strawberry Blonde; Affectionately Yours; Blood and Sand; You'll Never Get Rich. **'42** My Gal Sal; Tales of Manhattan; You Were Never Lovelier. **'43** Show Business at War (short). **'44** Cover Girl. **'45** Tonight and Every Night. **'46** Gilda. **'47** Down to Earth; The Lady From Shanghai. **'48** The Loves of Carmen. **'51** Champagne Safari/Safari So Good (doc). **'52** Affair in Trinidad. **'53** Salome; Miss Sadie Thompson. **'57** Fire Down Below; Pal Joey. **'58** Separate Tables. **'59** They Came to Cordura; The Story on Page One. **'62** The Happy Thieves (GER-SP). **'64** Circus World (GB: The Magnificent Showman). **'65** The Money Trap. **'66** Danger Grows Wild (United Nations) (USA: The Poppy Is Also a Flower). **'67** L'Avventuriero (IT) (USA: The Adventurer; GB: The Rover). **'68** I Bastardi (GER-IT-FR) (USA/GB: Sons of Satan/The Cats). **'70** Sur la Route de Salina (FR-IT) (USA/GB: Road to Salina); The Naked Zoo. **'72** The Wrath of God **'76** Circle.

'Bogie'

Left: the quintessential Bogart 'look'. Top: the almost universally forgotten A Devil With Women *(1930), co-starring Mona Maris, was Bogart's second feature film. Shortly after making it, he vowed never to return to Hollywood. Above: the vampiric title role in* The Return of Dr X *(1939) was Bogart's only flirtation with the horror film*

The name perhaps means more things to more people than that of any other Hollywood hero. Bogart's ugly-handsome face, perpetual cigarette and rasping voice bespoke a man who was nobody's fool, a loner but never an outcast

Humphrey Bogart was born in New York on January 23, 1899. His father, Dr Belmont DeForest Bogart, was one of the city's most eminent surgeons. His mother, Maud Humphrey, was a magazine illustrator. After completing his studies at Trinity School, Bogart entered Phillips Acadamy in Andover, Massachusetts. Expelled for bad behaviour, he joined the US Marines in 1918 and served several months. On his return to civilian life, he was hired by the theatrical producer William A. Brady, who made him his road manager and encouraged him to try his hand at acting. His first appearances were somewhat unconvincing, but Bogart persevered and gradually learned to master the craft.

In 1929 he was spotted by a talent scout in *It's a Wise Child* and put under a year's contract by 20th Century-Fox. At this period he was just a young stage actor with no particular following; the studio, uncertain how best to use him, tried him out in an assortment of genres. The results were uneven and unpromising and Bogart, after being loaned out to Universal for a brief appearance in *Bad Sister* (1931) – as a man-about-town who leaves his young wife in the lurch – returned to Broadway, convinced that he was through with the cinema for good.

In December 1931, however, he signed a short-term contract with Columbia and left the stage to star in *Love Affair* (1932), a comedy directed by Thornton Freeland. He then moved to Warner Brothers where he made, for director Mervyn LeRoy, *Big City Blues* and *Three on a Match* (both 1932), the second of which provided him with his first gangster role. He then returned to the theatre.

The decisive turning-point in his hitherto erratic career came in 1935 with Robert E. Sherwood's play *The Petrified Forest*, in which, for more than seven months, he played the gangster Duke Mantee opposite Leslie Howard.

When asked to repeat his role on the screen the following year, Howard insisted on Bogart for his co-star. And so it was that, at the age of 37, Bogart finally gave up the theatre and began a profitable career as a supporting actor under the aegis of Warners, for which he would make almost all his films until 1948.

Plug ugly

He made an average of one film every two months for the studio, which filed him from the start under 'bad guys'. In four years he had completed an impressive number of gangster roles, supporting such established actors as Edward G. Robinson, James Cagney and George Raft. The parts he played – frequently double-crossers condemned to die an ignominious death – were most often used to set the main star off to advantage. These characters' backgrounds remained obscure and their psychology was extremely primitive. Several years had passed since *Little Caesar* (1930) and *The Public Enemy* (1931); the gangster was no longer seen as a romantic figure, he was just the flotsam of a sick society. Bogart, above all, played the kind of small-time loser who could always be outwitted by a strong adversary.

A few films, however, enabled him to escape from type-casting: *Isle of Fury* (1936), in which he was a reformed fugitive; *China Clipper* (1936), for which he donned the uniform of an ace pilot; and *Two Against the World* (1936), in which he played the manager of a radio station at odds with his unscrupulous employer. In *Marked Woman* (1937) he was a tough but kindly district attorney who succeeded in breaking up a gang of racketeers with the help of a nightclub hostess (Bette Davis); and in *Crime School* (1938), he was the liberal head of a prison, who established more humane relations between his staff and the troublesome young inmates.

These dissimilar roles, however, were not sufficient to modify the actor's predominant image, and it was not until Raoul Walsh's *They Drive by Night* (1940) that he was able to break out of the stereotype which had been imposed on him. Although his role was secondary to George Raft's, his playing of a truck-driver contending with the everyday problems of

Above left: as chief warden in Crime School *he had all kinds of problems with the Dead End Kids. Above right: in the gangster film* Brother Orchid *(1940) Bogart played his then usual role of a double-crosser. Right:* High Sierra *gave him the chance to show a human side. Below left: Bogart made a rare appearance in Western garb for* The Oklahoma Kid

travel fatigue and lack of money was concrete and recognizable. It reflected a realistic and documented context, and it embodied, however modestly, certain new attitudes to screen characterization.

In 1941, Bogart's luck suddenly changed for the better. He was given the lead in Walsh's *High Sierra* in place of George Raft (who had turned the part down). Although Ida Lupino had top billing (and gave one of her finest performances), it was Bogart, in the role of Roy Earle, an ageing and disillusioned gangster, who was the discovery of the film. For the first time he revealed a human dimension and depth which went beyond the requirements of the plot. Caught between loyalty to his old boss (who engineers his escape from prison for one last job) and the desire to start afresh with the young woman (Joan Leslie) whom he naively believes is in love with him, Roy is neither a hero nor a villain. He has a *history*, a past which weighs heavily on his present existence and offers him freedom only at the price of his own death.

The lone wolf

The Forties saw a radical change of direction in Bogart's career. As a result of the general anxiety caused by the war, the cinema gained in maturity, acquiring a new kind of gravity and urgency. *Film noir*, an eminently sceptical and ambiguous genre, came to the forefront and sought out heroes who would measure up to this increasingly troubled context. It was no longer an age for defying authority and not yet one for collective commitment. Neither gangster nor cop (but a little of both), the private eye asserted himself as one of the dominant heroic figures of the decade.

In 1941 this epitome of virile scepticism took on the features of Sam Spade. The character created in 1929 by the novelist Dashiell Hammett had already been twice adapted for the screen but without success; however the third version of *The Maltese Falcon*, which was more faithful than the others to Hammett's novel, hit the jackpot. Surrounded by a brilliant cast, Bogart perfectly illustrated the ethics of the private eye. Intransigent, totally independent, indifferent to the police yet wholly unself-serving, his Spade had absolute authenticity. The

Bogartian character had suddenly found its true physiognomy. He was, and would remain, a man who concealed his own needs behind a hard-bitten exterior, who rejected all higher principles and distrusted all abstract causes. He was a loner, who did not ask help from anyone.

Casablanca (1942) and *To Have and Have Not* (1944) both cast him in the midst of a cosmopolitan and divided world. In these films, fascists, Gaullists and refugees of every kind attempt to obtain his support but Bogart remains very much his own man. He acts solely according to his own inclinations: out of loyalty to a woman he has not forgotten (Ingrid Bergman in *Casablanca*) or to keep the love of the girl who has succeeded in winning his heart (Lauren Bacall in *To Have and Have Not*).

Cherchez la femme

Walsh had endowed Bogart with humanity in *High Sierra*; Huston gave him morality and the means to defend himself in *The Maltese Falcon*; Curtiz, in *Casablanca*, added to these a romantic dimension and a reason for living. At the beginning of the film, Rick, the hero, is shown to have taken refuge behind a mask of cynicism, in keeping with the unscrupulous political climate of wartime Casablanca. The unexpected arrival of the woman he has loved painfully reawakens his emotions, forcing him to renounce his pose of disinterested spectator. The film concludes with the need for commitment, one which concerned not only the hero but the whole of America. This moral framework reappears in *To Have and Have Not* in

Left: *Bogart meets Bacall in* To Have and Have Not. *Above left: with Ann Sheridan and George Raft in* They Drive by Night. *Above right: the moment in* Casablanca *when Bogart almost said 'Play it again, Sam' to Dooley Wilson. Right: in* Dead Reckoning *(1947) he finds that the trail of murder leads to the door – and the arms – of a femme fatale*

Carrolls. These off-beat performances had only a limited impact in comparison with *The Big Sleep* (1946), in which Bogart, once more working with Hawks and Bacall, played another mythical detective: Philip Marlowe.

Trouble is his business

Created by Raymond Chandler in the late Thirties, Marlowe was a more romantic character than Spade. More directly implicated in the action, more conscious of the values which he represented, he was engaged in a quest for 'hidden truth'. Without being a paragon of virtue he had a rigorous conception of honour. No other actor would catch as precisely as Bogart this character's blend of strength and derision, or his equivocal pleasure in venturing down the 'mean streets' and daily facing death.

As Bogart himself became a mythical figure, he would meet up with replicas of his former self. In *Key Largo* (1948) Bogart played, opposite Lauren Bacall, a role analogous to Leslie Howard's in *The Petrified Forest*, while Edward G. Robinson played a mean gangster reminiscent of Duke Mantee. There was the same kind of allusive interplay in *The Treasure of the Sierra Madre* (1948), in which John Huston offered Bogart one of the most unusual roles of his career: as an adventurer on the skids, who sets off in search of gold and meets a squalid death, a victim of his own greed. The casting of Bogart against type disconcerted audiences when the film was released but, little by little, the actor managed to make himself accepted in character roles.

The last seven years of his career saw him gradually abandon heroic parts. With the exception of *Beat the Devil* (1953), in which Huston attempted a parodic approach to Bogart's screen persona, the majority of his films were well-received, proving that the actor had established a lasting and authentic relationship with his fans.

As the producer at the head of his own company, Santana Pictures, Bogart made *Knock on Any Door* (1949), a socially conscious film which took a firm stand against capital punishment. Then, after two conventional action films, *Tokyo Joe* (1949) and *Chain Lightning* (1950), he played the part of a disenchanted

which the hero, Harry Morgan, is caught between the temptation of detachment and the need to struggle against fascism. But the motives for which Harry finally resolves upon action remain strictly personal. The director Howard Hawks, as was his custom, reduced plot and action to the minimum and emphasized the romantic banter of Bogart and Lauren Bacall. As their on-screen romance became genuine love, Hawks reworked entire sequences day after day to explore their remarkable chemistry. The narrative thus gives a marvellous impression of authenticity and intimacy, and the film remains one of the highlights of Bogart's career.

In 1945 Bogart, whose previous wives had been actresses Helen Menken, Mary Phillips and Mayo Methot, married Lauren Bacall, who was then 21 and would be his greatest partner. Since 1943 and the box-office triumph of *Casablanca*, Bogart had become one of the top ten Hollywood stars. The end of the war saw him return to *film noir*. In 1945 he twice played the role of a murderer: opposite Alexis Smith in *Conflict* and Barbara Stanwyck in *The Two Mrs*

Hollywood screenwriter who is subject to attacks of murderous violence in Nicholas Ray's *In a Lonely Place* (1950). In *The Enforcer* (1951) he was a district attorney up against Murder Inc. Shot in the semi-documentary style typical of Warners, it became a *film noir* classic, particularly remarkable for the complexity of its editing and its powerful scenes of violence. (Twenty years later it was discovered that the film's direction, credited to Bretaigne Windust, was the work of Raoul Walsh.)

After the fourth, last and most disappointing film for Santana, *Sirocco* (1951), Bogart worked with Huston on *The African Queen* (1951). Half comedy of character, half adventure movie, totally and unashamedly implausible, the whole film was constructed on the confrontation of two personalities. Bogart gave one of his most colourful performances as a grouchy alcoholic transformed into a hero by a frigid, devout spinster (Katharine Hepburn) in the throes of her first amorous stirrings. That year, the actor received an Oscar, a reward honouring 20 years of a richly successful career. Modestly Bogart declared: 'I've been around a

long time. Maybe the people like me.'

With *Deadline USA* (1952), a vibrant plea for the freedom of the press, Bogart, with the director Richard Brooks, returned to the democratic inspiration of *Key Largo* and *Knock on Any Door*. The following year, Brooks cast him in *Battle Circus* as a sceptical and gruff military doctor, overfond of women and alcohol. In *The Caine Mutiny* (1954), an ambitious Stanley Kramer production directed by Edward Dmytryk, Bogart took on the part of Captain Queeg, a neurotic, dictatorial officer forcibly removed from command by his subordinates. The film was an ambiguous reflection on power and responsibility, in which the actor created an unusual character role. In Billy Wilder's *Sabrina* (1954) he was the sarcastic heir of a rich family in love with his chauffeur's daughter (Audrey Hepburn). Made in the same year, Joseph L. Mankiewicz's *The Barefoot Contessa*, one of the most fascinating evocations of the world of Hollywood, definitively made Bogart an outsider, a witness. He plays a film director, Harry Dawes, who watches the dazzling rise to stardom of a Spanish dancer (Ava Gardner)

and her tragic involvement with an impotent aristocrat. The narrator and spectator of action in which he cannot intervene, Dawes is the voice of Mankiewicz himself, the director's disillusioned double who embodies the magic of a vanished Hollywood. The actor's creased, serene face and understated performance brought both an exceptional resonance and a poignant sense of authenticity to the subject.

The commercial failure of the film, which was considered too literary at the time, led Bogart to return to more conventional roles in films of less interest: in Curtiz's *We're No Angels* (1955) he was a comic convict in company with Aldo Ray and Peter Ustinov; in Dmytryk's *The Left Hand of God* (1955) a sham priest taking refuge in a Chinese mission-house to escape the tyrannical war-lord whose adviser he has been. In William Wyler's *The Desperate Hours* (1955), already ravaged by the illness of which he was to die, Bogart played his last gangster role.

The long goodbye

In 1956 Mark Robson's *The Harder They Fall* cast him once more as a journalist, this time denouncing the boxing racket. Similar in mood to *Deadline USA*, it ended his career, if not in glory, then on an appropriately high note.

Bogart's relatively slow start was rapidly compensated for by the depth and variety of his roles from 1941 onwards. If the war years stand out by virtue of *The Maltese Falcon*, *Casablanca* and *To Have and Have Not*, after the war he was much freer in his choice of roles and was equally brilliant in socio-political films, thrillers and comedies. His last films reveal an actor totally identifying with his roles, enriching them with his own maturity, his unique capacity for understatement and irony.

Humphrey Bogart died of cancer on January 14, 1957. During the Sixties his reputation never ceased to grow until it reached the proportions of a cult. He possessed elegance, courage and insolence, and knew how to efface himself when necessary. Aggressive, precise, economical, his acting was astonishingly modern. Bogart remains today linked with the best that the American cinema has had to offer.

Filmography

1930 Broadway's Like That/Ruth Etting in Broadway's Like That (short); Up the River; A Devil With Women. **'31** Body and Soul; Bad Sister; A Holy Terror. **'32** Love Affair; Big City Blues; Three on a Match. **'34** Midnight. **'36** The Petrified Forest; Bullets or Ballots; Two Against the World (USA retitling for TV: One Fatal Hour) (GB: The Case of Mrs Pembrook); China Clipper; Isle of Fury; The Great O'Malley. **'37** Black Legion; Marked Woman; Kid Galahad (USA retitling for TV: The Battling Bellhop); San Quentin; Dead End; Stand-In. **'38** Swing Your Lady; Men Are Such Fools; Crime School; Racket Busters; The Amazing Dr Clitterhouse; Angels With Dirty Faces. **'39** King of the Underworld; The Oklahoma Kid; You Can't Get Away With Murder; Dark Victory; The Roaring Twenties; The Return of Dr X; Invisible Stripes. **'40** Virginia City; It All Came True; Brother Orchid; They Drive by Night (GB: The Road to Frisco). **'41** High Sierra; The Wagons Roll at Night; The Maltese Falcon. **'42** All Through the Night; The Big Shot; Across the Pacific; Casablanca. **'43** Action in the North Atlantic; Thank Your Lucky Stars (guest); Sahara. **'44** Passage to Marseille; To Have and Have Not. **'45** Conflict; The Two Mrs Carrolls; Hollywood Victory Canteen (guest) (short). **'46** The Guys From Milwaukee (uncredited guest) (GB: Royal Flush); The Big Sleep. **'47** Dead Reckoning; Dark Passage; Always Together (uncredited guest). **'48** The Treasure of the Sierra Madre; Key Largo. **'49** Knock on Any Door; Tokyo Joe. **'50** Chain Lightning; In a Lonely Place. **'51** The Enforcer (GB: Murder Inc.); Sirocco; The African Queen. **'52** Deadline USA (GB: Deadline); Battle Circus; Beat the Devil (GB-IT). **'54** The Love Lottery (uncredited guest) (GB); The Caine Mutiny; A Star Is Born (voice only); Sabrina (GB: Sabrina Fair); The Barefoot Contessa. **'55** We're No Angels; The Left Hand of God; The Desperate Hours. **'56** The Harder They Fall.

Top left: an experienced prospector (Walter Huston) frowns grimly as his partner (Bogart) exhibits all the symptoms of gold fever in The Treasure of the Sierra Madre. *Below left: a 25-year gap in their ages did not prevent the marriage of Humphrey Bogart and Betty (Lauren) Bacall from being one of the happiest between two stars. Below: the cast of* The Caine Mutiny *(including Bogart, left, and Van Johnson, right) joke between takes*

The Third Man

Directed by Carol Reed, 1949
Prod co: (Alexander Korda, David O. Selznick for) London Films. **prod:** Carol Reed. **assoc prod:** Hugh Perceval. **sc:** Graham Greene. **photo:** Robert Krasker. **add photo:** John Wilcox, Stan Pavey. **ed:** Oswald Hafenrichter. **art dir:** Vincent Korda, Joseph Bato, John Hawkesworth. **mus:** Anton Karas. **sd:** John Cox. **ass dir:** Guy Hamilton. **r/t:** 104 mins.
Cast: Joseph Cotten (*Holly Martins*), Orson Welles (*Harry Lime*), Alida Valli (*Anna Schmidt*), Trevor Howard (*Major Calloway*), Paul Hoerbiger (*porter*), Ernst Deutsch (*Baron Kurtz*), Erich Ponto (*Dr Winkel*), Wilfred Hyde White (*Crabbit*), Bernard Lee (*Sergeant Paine*), Siegfried Breuer (*Popescu*), Geoffrey Keen (*British policeman*), Annie Rosar (*porter's wife*), Hedwig Bliebtrau (*Anna's 'Old Woman'*), Harbut Helbek (*Hansl*), Alexis Chesnakov (*Brodsky*), Paul Hardtmuth (*hall porter*).

Left: Carol Reed directs the chase scene in the sewers

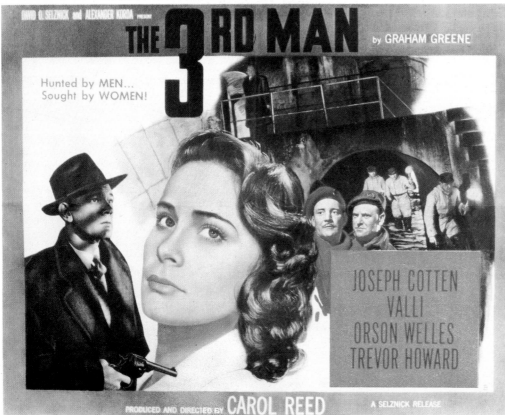

After they had completed *The Fallen Idol* (1948), director Carol Reed and writer Graham Greene dined with Alexander Korda, who was anxious for them to work on a new film together. Although they agreed on a setting – post-war Vienna – they were stuck for a story until Greene produced an old envelope on which years before he had written a single sentence:

'I had paid my last farewell to Harry a week ago, when his coffin was lowered into the frozen February ground, so it was with incredulity that I saw him pass by, without a sign of recognition, among the host of strangers in the Strand.'

This became the basis of Reed's *The Third Man*, a film that was to take the Grand Prix at the Cannes Film Festival and earn him a third successive British Film Academy Award for Best Picture.

Greene drafted the story as a novel and then, working closely with Reed, turned it into a screenplay. Although it is in many ways a classic Greene tale, with its themes of guilt and disillusionment, corruption and betrayal, Greene himself has been quick to accord to Reed credit for many of the film's memorable qualities. It was Reed who insisted on the bleakly uncompromising ending where Anna, as she leaves Harry's funeral, walks not into Holly's arms in the conventional final clinch, but passed him, staring impassively ahead. It was Reed who discovered the zither-player, Anton Karas, whose 'Harry Lime theme' gave the film a special haunting quality. It was Reed who prevailed on a reluctant Orson Welles to play the comparatively small but pivotal part of Harry Lime. Welles became so enthusiastic about the film that he contributed to the script a much-quoted justification of Harry's criminal activities:

'In Italy for thirty years under the Borgias they had warfare, terror, murder, bloodshed. They produced Michelangelo, Leonardo da Vinci and the Renaissance. In Switzerland they had brotherly love, five hundred years of democracy and peace. And what did that produce – the cuckoo clock. So long, Holly.'

It was, of course, also Carol Reed who gave remarkable visual life to Greene's brilliantly wrought script, a perfect marriage of word and image, sound and symbol. Holly's odyssey in search of a truth that is to destroy his oldest friend, the girl they both love and, in a sense, Holly himself, is conducted against the background of post-war Vienna, unforgettably evoked by Robert Krasker's powerful chiaroscuro photography which won him a deserved Oscar. The vast, echoing, empty baroque buildings that serve as military headquarters and decaying lodging houses are a melancholy reminder of the Old Vienna, the city of Strauss waltzes and Hapsburg elegance, plunged, in the aftermath of war, into a nightmare world of political intrigue, racketeering and murder. The shadowed, narrow streets and the jagged bomb-sites are the haunt of black marketeers, vividly portrayed inhabitants of a dislocated society. There is a powerful symbolism, too, in the places where Harry makes his appearances: a giant ferris wheel from which he looks down contemptuously at the scuttling mortals, and the Viennese sewers where, after a breathtaking and sharply edited final chase, he is cornered, rat-like, and dispatched.

The angled shooting, atmospheric locations, and sombre shadow-play eloquently convey the pervading aura of tension, mystery and corruption. It is an aura enhanced rather than dissipated by flashes of black humour, such as the sequence in which Holly, bustled by strangers into a car and believing himself kidnapped, discovers he is being taken to address a cultural gathering, the members of which think he is a famous novelist.

The cast is superlative, with the four stars outstanding: Joseph Cotten as decent, dogged, simple, faithful Holly; Alida Valli as the wonderfully enigmatic Anna; Trevor Howard as the shrewd, determined, quietly spoken military policeman Calloway; and Orson Welles as the fascinating Harry Lime. *The Third Man* was one of the peaks of post-war British filmmaking and remains a flawlessly crafted, timelessly perfect work of art.

Holly Martins, a writer of hack Westerns, arrives in Vienna to look for his friend Harry Lime, only to be told that Harry has been killed in a street accident. Holly attends the funeral (1) and is questioned by military policeman Major Calloway (2), who tells him that Harry was a racketeer selling penicillin so diluted that it caused the deaths of sick children.

Holly sets out to find the truth and visits Harry's girlfriend, actress Anna Schmidt (3), who suggests that Harry's death may not have been accidental. An elderly porter reports seeing a mysterious third man at the scene of the accident (4); next day the porter is found dead. Holly is chased by two thugs but escapes. Leaving Anna's apartment, he sees Harry in the shadows (5) and realizes he is 'the third man'. Harry's coffin is exhumed and found to contain the body of a police informer.

Harry arranges to meet Holly and offers to buy his silence (6). But when Calloway arrests Anna (7) (who has a forged passport) and plans to deport her behind the Iron Curtain, Holly, who is in love with her, betrays Harry to the police in return for her release. A chase through the sewers underneath the city (8), ends with Holly shooting Harry dead. Anna attends the funeral and then walks away past Holly without speaking to him (9).

The discreet charm

of Alec Guinness

During the 1979 British Academy Film and Television Arts awards, Sir Alec Guinness, coming forward to collect the Best Actor prize for his brilliant portrayal of secret service man George Smiley in the BBC's *Tinker, Tailor, Soldier, Spy*, seemed daunted at the prospect of addressing the audience and the TV cameras. When, shy and diffident, he eventually stepped up to the microphone, his hurried thank-you suggested all the embarrassment of a schoolboy at a prize-giving, not the charismatic ease

of a much-fêted star acknowledging another tribute to his genius. But then Alec Guinness is a supreme example of the actor who hides behind the mask of his characters and who prefers to let his performances speak for him. Consequently he is an unknown quantity. Very few critics have penetrated the makeup; the nearest that biographer Kenneth Tynan came was when he described Guinness as 'a master of anonymity . . . the whole presence of the man is guarded and evasive'. Guinness himself has remarked, 'I was always rather embarrassed with me personally, and I was glad to go into a thin cardboard disguise.'

He was born in London in 1914 and educated at private schools in the South. At 18 he took a job as a copy-writer in an advertising agency, but the stage beckoned and in 1934 he won a scholarship to the Fay Compton Acting

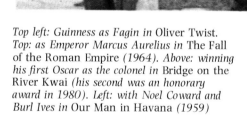

Top left: Guinness as Fagin in Oliver Twist. *Top: as Emperor Marcus Aurelius in* The Fall of the Roman Empire *(1964). Above: winning his first Oscar as the colonel in* Bridge on the River Kwai *(his second was an honorary award in 1980). Left: with Noel Coward and Burl Ives in* Our Man in Havana *(1959)*

School. John Gielgud saw him, was impressed, and gave him his first break as Osric in *Hamlet*; by 1938 Guinness had the lead in the Old Vic's modern dress version of the play. He joined the Royal Navy in 1941 and quickly became an officer.

After the war he returned to the stage and in 1946 began his film career as Herbert Pocket in David Lean's *Great Expectations*. It was a character well known to him – he had played Pocket in his own stage adaptation of Dickens' novel in 1940. Lean next cast him as Fagin in *Oliver Twist* (1948). If the revered *Kind Hearts and Coronets* (1949), which followed, was to establish Guinness as the screen's most perceptive and refined interpreter of English idiosyncracy, his Fagin first revealed him as a

(1972, *Brother Sun, Sister Moon*). Guinness was himself received into the Roman Catholic Church in the mid-Fifties.

He was reunited with Lean in 1957 and won the Best Actor Oscar for *The Bridge on the River Kwai*. Guinness has probably never been more intense, more fierce: his Colonel Nicholson, leader of British POWs held by the Japanese, is a fanatic, a figure of iron will perverted by blind pride: the skill and endurance of his men in building a bridge for the enemy means much more to him than the need to win the war.

Like many actors of his generation, Sir Alec (he was knighted in 1959) tended to play supporting cameo roles from the Sixties onward. He was Oscar-nominated as the old wizard in *Star Wars* (1977), but his reunion with David Lean in *A Passage to India* (1984) was disappointing. It is happier to record that in his finest role of the Eighties, as the sad old patriarch in *Little Dorrit* (1987), he was aptly reunited with Charles Dickens.

Filmography

1934 Evensong (extra). **'46** Great Expectations. **'48** Oliver Twist. **'49** Kind Hearts and Coronets; A Run for Your Money. **'50** Last Holiday; The Mudlark. **'51** The Lavender Hill Mob; The Man in the White Suit. **'52** The Card (USA: The Promoter). **'53** Malta Story; The Captain's Paradise. **'54** Father Brown (USA: The Detective); The Stratford Adventure (doc; as himself) (CAN). **'55** To Paris With Love; The Prisoner; The Ladykillers; Rowlandson's England (doc; narr. only). **'56** The Swan (USA). **'57** The Bridge on the River Kwai; Barnacle Bill (USA: All at Sea). **'58** The Horse's Mouth (+sc). **'59** The Scapegoat; Our Man in Havana. **'60** Tunes of Glory. **'61** A Majority of One (USA). **'62** HMS Defiant (USA: Damn the Defiant!); Lawrence of Arabia. **'64** The Fall of the Roman Empire (USA). **'65** Hotel Paradiso; Situation Hopeless, but Not Serious (USA-GER); Doctor Zhivago (USA). **'66** The Quiller Memorandum. **'67** The Comedians (GB-GER-FR). **'70** Cromwell; Scrooge. **'72** Fratello Sole, Sorella Luna (GB: Brother Sun, Sister Moon) (IT-GB). **'73** Hitler: the Last Ten Days (GB-IT). **'76** Murder by Death (USA). **'77** Star Wars (USA). **'80** The Empire Strikes Back; Little Lord Fauntleroy; Raise the Titanic! (USA). **'83** Return of the Jedi (USA); Lovesick (USA). **'84** A Passage to India. **'87** Little Dorrit. **'88** Handful of Dust.

Top and top right: two outstanding performances for Ealing in 1951 – as Henry Holland in The Lavender Hill Mob, *with Stanley Holloway, and as Sidney Stratton in* The Man in the White Suit. *Above right: as Yevgraf in* Doctor Zhivago *(1965). Right: as the space-guru in* Star Wars *(1977)*

master of disguise. An extraordinary study in nervous, jealous avarice masquerading as avuncular warmth, the fumbling, hook-nosed old Jew – sketched straight from Cruikshank's illustrations – his beard matted and his heavy-lidded eyes sparked with cunning, repels and demands sympathy at the same time. Guinness' remarkable performance was regarded as anti-Semitic in 1948 and the American release of *Oliver Twist* was long delayed.

The Ealing comedies and more stage-work occupied Guinness for the next few years and he became a major star. He was the detective-priest in *Father Brown* (1954), and a cardinal held captive in *The Prisoner* (1955); perhaps the logical conclusion to this sequence was his Pope Innocent III in *Fratello Sole, Sorella Luna*

Few films make effective reading when their words are divorced from their images. And if one is found that does, the tendency is immediately to assume that there must be something wrong with it. Certainly *Kind Hearts and Coronets* has often posed this kind of a problem: it allows such weight to the spoken word that it has often been thought of as literary and uncinematic. And yet, at this distance of time from its first appearance in 1949, it stands out as the least faded, most indubitably alive of all the British films of its era. And, perhaps because cinema criticism is now a lot less hidebound by simplistic theories of what is or is not 'cinematic' than it once was, it would probably not occur to anyone seeing the film for the first time to query its 'summit meeting' of words and images or worry about how it could somehow be made to fit into a world-view shaped by neo-realism.

The corollary of this is that today's audience would not realize how exceptional the film was in its time; but part of Robert Hamer's stated principle in making it was that it should be 'a film not noticeably similar to any previously made in the English language'. Hamer had

been a film editor, then a writer, then – as one of Michael Balcon's bright young men at Ealing – a director, making his debut with an episode in the composite picture *Dead of Night* (1945). He had followed it with a couple of solo features, *Pink String and Sealing Wax* (1945), a period murder story, and *It Always Rains on Sunday* (1947), a downbeat study of working-class life which he also wrote; the elegance of the first and the social perceptiveness of the second retrospectively provide a hint of what was to come. No-one, however, could have guessed what Hamer was up to when he discovered and began to adapt the little-known Edwardian novel, *Israel Rank* – a rather self-consciously decadent piece written by Roy Horniman (a follower of Oscar Wilde) – having decided that it had the makings of a film comedy.

In adapting it Hamer remained true to the period of the story and to the allegiance to Wilde. Otherwise, only the basic plot of the novel was retained: the plight of a young man whose mother has married beneath her and been cast out by her family, and his determination to get revenge and repair his spoilt fortunes by murdering his way through a

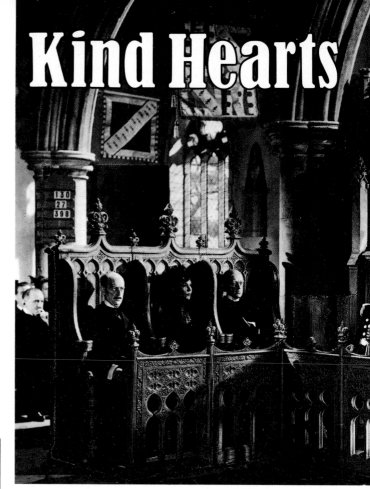

Kind Hearts

1

When the younger daughter of the Duke of Chalfont runs off with a penniless Italian singer her family disowns her. She tells her son Louis about his grand forbears but, denied any aid from her family, he has to work in a draper's shop. Stung by the family's refusal to recognize kinship with his mother – even when she dies – he determines to get his own back and to impress his suburban girlfriend Sibella (1)

by disposing of all who stand between him and the family title.

First, he murders his most obnoxious cousin (2) during a dirty weekend at Henley, and then blows up another cousin, an amateur photographer (3). A cleric uncle is poisoned (4); a suffragette aunt it shot down in her balloon (5); a soldier uncle is booby-trapped while recounting his most famous campaign (6); and a sailor uncle goes down

2

3

4

7

8

9

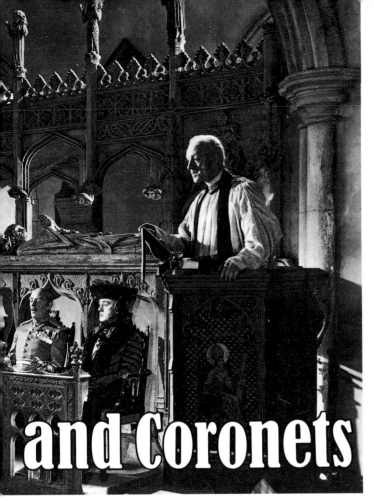

and Coronets

Directed by Robert Hamer, 1949
Prod co: Ealing. **prod:** Michael Balcon. **assoc prod:** Michael Relph. **sc:** Robert Hamer, John Dighton, from the novel *Israel Rank* by Roy Horniman. **photo:** Douglas Slocombe, Jeff Seaholme. **sp eff:** Sydney Pearson, Geoffrey Dickinson. **ed:** Peter Tanner. **art dir:** William Kellner. **mus:** Ernest Irving, extract from Mozart's *Don Giovanni* played by The Philharmonic Orchestra, conducted by Ernest Irving. **cost:** Anthony Mendleson. **sd:** Stephen Dalby, John Mitchell. **ass dir:** Norman Priggen. **r/t:** 106 minutes.
Cast: Dennis Price (*Louis Mazzini*), Valerie Hobson (*Edith d'Ascoyne*), Joan Greenwood (*Sibella*), Alec Guinness (*Ethelred, Duke of Chalfont*; *Lord Ascoyne d'Ascoyne*; *The Reverend Lord Henry d'Ascoyne*; *General Lord Rufus d'Ascoyne*; *Admiral Lord Horatio d'Ascoyne*; *Ascoyne d'Ascoyne*; *Henry d'Ascoyne*; *Lady Agatha d'Ascoyne*), Audrey Fildes (*Mama*), Miles Malleson (*hangman*), Clive Morton (*prison governor*), John Penrose (*Lionel*), Cecil Ramage (*Crown Counsel*), Hugh Griffith (*Lord High Steward*), John Salew (*Mr Perkins*), Eric Messiter (*Burgoyne*), Lyn Evans (*farmer*), Barbara Leake (*schoolmistress*), Peggy Ann Clifford (*Maud*), Anne Valery (*girl in the punt*), Arthur Lowe (*reporter*).

with his ship after a collision at sea (7). This makes Louis heir apparent to the Chalfont title, and the accepted fiancé of Edith (the photographer cousin's widow).

Just as Louis is achieving his goal by shooting the present duke (8) – whereupon the last remaining uncle expires on hearing he has succeeded to the dukedom – Sibella's husband dies in suspicious circumstances and he is charged with the one

Above: two down, six to go – the funeral service for the second d'Ascoyne cousin

murder he didn't do. Sibella agrees to get him acquitted if he will dispose of Edith and make her the next duchess (9). All goes according to plan, but there is still the problem of Louis' compromising memoirs (10) which he has absent-mindedly left in his prison cell on being freed (11) . . .

whole family of unspeakable relatives on his way to a dukedom. In the novel this involves a lot of Nietzschean attitudinizing on the part of the self-styled superman hero; in the film it is all distilled into an exquisitely subversive comedy of manners, decorated with a constant sparkle of verbal wit such as Wilde himself would not have disowned.

But that is not all. The film's visual wit perfectly complements the verbal. If the tone is established primarily by the dialogue and by the ruthless Louis' voice-over commentary on the action, it is still true that the best effects are produced by a knowing counterpoint of word and image. A typical example of this is when Louis' tea-time conversation with his cousin's chilly wife (soon to be his) is accompanied by the gradual appearance of a column of smoke indicating that something nasty has happened to his cousin in the woodshed. Elsewhere Hamer's precise selection of what details to show us in the behaviour of his characters lets the audience know just how to read every move in this cool but by no means unemotional game.

The performances are, of course,

superb. Dennis Price as the dandyish, but under it all slightly demonic, Louis was never better, and neither were Joan Greenwood and Valerie Hobson, perfectly cast as the two contrasting women in his life. Alec Guinness' extraordinary feat, playing eight members of the d'Ascoyne family, has been much remarked on, but the most remarkable thing about it is that it is virtually unnoticeable. So exactly is each member of the family portrayed that, while seeing the film, the spectator is aware only of the diversity and believability, not of the one actor who achieves it. But, first and foremost, the film is the personal creation of Robert Hamer, as close to a genuine *auteur* film as the British cinema has ever come.

Though some of Hamer's later films were enjoyable – notably *Father Brown* (1954), which reunited him with Guinness and Greenwood – he never had another comparable chance to express his elegant, uncomfortable wit in the context of a generally conservative British cinema. A pity – but at least Hamer's *Kind Hearts and Coronets* remains a masterpiece of its kind, and unique.

5

6

10

11

David Lean

In Search of New Horizons

Lean's fascination with the effect of natural environment on character and motivation has led him to the wildest parts of the globe – a restless quest that is reflected in the powerful, contradictory emotions that sway his protagonists

David Lean is at once the most prestigious and most mysterious British film director; he is also perhaps the least understood, having an unenviable reputation among the most influential British and American critics. Lean's films, especially his later ones, attract huge audiences and win Academy Awards, yet the majority of commentators dismiss him as a brilliant technician without a personality, squandering needlessly inflated budgets on calculatedly tasteful spectacles. Rarely interviewed, Lean is widely regarded as remote and outmoded.

Lean has not been a prolific director but has preferred to be highly selective and to control every aspect of his productions; his perfectionist techniques have become legendary. His last three films have brought him much personal wealth, enabling him jealously to guard his privacy and leaving him free to travel extensively to research new projects. He is an intensely likeable man, very distinguished-looking, disarmingly modest about his own achievements and generous and perceptive in his praise of other people's.

A terrible beauty

By the mid-Eighties Lean had been forced to abandon his long-standing dream to re-make *Mutiny on the Bounty* (eventually directed by the New Zealander Roger Donaldson). Instead, in 1984 he directed *A Passage to India* – another 'spectacular' tale. Both stories have themes concerned with the obligation on an individual to obey the dictates of a rigid discipline, but expose the disintegration of that obligation when the individual is confronted with the terrible beauty of an exciting new environment – be it ocean or continent – and the desperate

struggle for sanity and survival in it.

These are important keys to the meaning of Lean's work which, since his breakthrough film *Brief Encounter* (1945), has dealt obsessively with the conflict between discipline and individualism, between a peculiarly British emotional reticence and Romantic excess. The widely contrasting locales of his later films – the jungle in *The Bridge on the River Kwai*

(1957), the desert in *Lawrence of Arabia* (1962), the icy wastes of *Doctor Zhivago* (1965), the wild Irish coastline in *Ryan's Daughter* (1970) – are no mere pictorial backdrops. Lean's characters are shaped by their social and physical environments and are constantly in conflict with them. They are placed in necessarily alien, inhospitable and challenging landscapes that offer a source of escape and self-discovery.

Lean's heroes and heroines are compulsive fantasists and fanatics, whether they be found in suburban railway stations, in decaying

Above: David Lean behind the camera. Above left: Lawrence (Peter O'Toole) leads his Bedouin allies into battle in Lawrence of Arabia.
Below: Pip (Anthony Wager) encounters Miss Havisham (Martita Hunt) in Lean's fine adaptation of Dickens' Great Expectations

Victorian mansions, designing supersonic aircraft, on holiday in Venice, building bridges in Burma, forging myths from the sands of Arabia, or dreaming of escape from an Irish village torn apart by racial hatred and religion.

Running parallel to these assertive and tragic characters are the precisely delineated societies founded on class barriers, discipline, traditional values and moral complacency, all of which are challenged yet remain indomitable. Lean's is a deeply pessimistic vision, as evidenced by the fates of his characters: Laura, in *Brief Encounter*, renouncing love for drab security; Pip finding disillusionment in *Great Expectations* (1946); Mary, in *The Passionate Friends* (1949), driven, like Laura, to near-suicide and then a living death; *Madeleine* (1950) ostracized and condemned by the courts to spiritual limbo; Ridgefield, in *The*

Sound Barrier (1952), sacrificing a son for an obsession; Jane, in *Summer Madness* (1955), slipping back to her grey life; Nicholson, in *The Bridge on the River Kwai*, realizing, at the moment of his death, that the very quality that made him such a good leader – his iron fixedness of purpose – has made him a traitor to his country; Lawrence, in *Lawrence of Arabia*, destroyed by his own legend; Lara and Zhivago, in *Doctor Zhivago*, frozen into anonymity; Rosy Ryan, ostracized and damned, with a suicide and several shattered lives resting on her conscience. The few happy endings are equivocal, undermined by the compromises which make such endings possible.

Lean's films are pessimistic, but never grim. He is first and foremost a master story-teller, an entertainer with a fine sense of drama and humour, an ironist – a poet and imagist, as his frequent collaborator the playwright and screenwriter Robert Bolt has called him.

Lean was born on March 25, 1908, in Croydon, Surrey, the son of a comfortably-off accountant whose strict Quaker principles led him to regard film-going as a sinful waste of time and money. But when Lean went to a boarding school at Reading he spent hours at the local cinemas and took up photography. After briefly following his father into accountancy, he was encouraged by his mother and an aunt to take a job as a teaboy and general dogsbody at Gainsborough studios. This was in 1927, so Lean witnessed at first hand the arrival of talking pictures. He minutely observed how films were made (Anthony Asquith was one of the directors he studied) and quickly realized the importance of editing and how ability in that department might lead to direction.

By 1930 he had left Gainsborough to become

Above: Henry Hobson (Charles Laughton) wakes with a king-size hangover in Hobson's Choice – *a rare excursion into comedy for Lean, and his last black-and-white film. Below: Lean's Oscar for* The Bridge on the River Kwai *was the first won by a British director*

assistant editor of British Movietone News, then its editor, and in 1934 he joined Paramount-British where he cut 'quota quickies'. Lean's talents were recognized by the Hungarian emigré director Paul Czinner who invited Lean to cut *Escape Me Never* (1935). This success led to further prestigious assignments – Asquith's *Pygmalion* (1938), Gabriel Pascal's *Major Barbara* (1941), Michael Powell and Emeric Pressburger's *One of Our Aircraft Is Missing* (1941) among them – which earned Lean respect within the industry and a range of technical experience that was to form the backbone of his work as a director.

Utterly English

Lean's next big break came from Noel Coward who wanted someone to help him direct *In Which We Serve* (1942), which Coward had written and would star in. Coward sought Britain's most skilful editor and Lean found himself directing virtually the entire film since Coward apparently soon tired of the chore. Coward acted as producer and screenwriter in three further collaborations with Lean. *This Happy Breed* (1944) gave Lean his first solo director's credit and *Blithe Spirit* (1945) allowed him to experiment with comedy; but it was the third, *Brief Encounter*, that enabled Lean to impose his own essentially cinematic style and thematic emphases over Noel Coward's story. One of the British cinema's enduring masterpieces, it is open to a variety of interpretations, but is immaculate in its detail and depiction of a certain strata of British society.

Great Expectations and *Oliver Twist* (1948) both furthered Lean's reputation as a director and remain the best adaptations of English literature ever filmed. It is difficult to choose between the two, but if *Great Expectations* is the more profound work, echoing Dickens' growing maturity and brilliantly evoking the darkness surrounding the characters in its combination of fairly-tale and social realism, *Oliver Twist* is the more ambitious, with some vivid characterizations – particularly Alec Guin-

finally, to justify a meaningless life in enforced exile. His moment of self-revelation comes when he attempts to foil an Allied raid on his beloved bridge, resulting in the deaths of several of the commandos taking part. His cry 'What have I done?' is a tragic epitaph.

Lawrence of Arabia, scripted by Robert Bolt, is perhaps Lean's greatest film. Far from being an objective analysis of Lawrence the film projects his *legend*, his contradictions and tortured soul as a subjective Homeric adventure. The film is arranged as a continuous mirage, showing Lawrence's self-delusion as an almost biblical hero – if not a god – who achieves the impossible and has power over life and death. Rich in characterization and social observation, it also united Lean with cameraman Freddie Young, whose 70mm compositions and colour texturing are astonishing.

Epics of passion

Lean, Bolt and Young turned *Doctor Zhivago* into MGM's biggest hit since *Gone With the Wind* (1939), which it closely resembles in its love story engulfed by the tide of history (this time the Russian Revolution). *Doctor Zhivago* might lack the neurotic qualities that characterize Lean's best work but it still leaves cinemas awash with tears.

The pantheist imagery of Lean's work was most fully realized in *Ryan's Daughter*, an ambitious and prohibitively expensive film mostly shot on location on the awesome west coast of Ireland and which was approximately three years in the making. Bolt's original screenplay reworks Hardyesque formulas into a story about romantic excess and moral cowardice, set during the Troubles of 1916 and complete with overbearing priest, village idiot, crippled war hero and sexless schoolteacher. It is Lean's most extreme film, for his admirers a masterpiece and for his detractors the last straw.

A Passage to India (1984) also had its critics. Yet the film is not only visually ravishing, it unites a preoccupation of the source author, E.M. Forster, 60 years earlier, with one of Lean's own – the fate bestowed by an uncomprehending society on the individual who attempts to be different.

Above: Judy Davis as Adela Quested, a young girl at the centre of controversy in A Passage to India. *Below: Sarah Miles as the romantic dreamer Rosy Ryan in* Ryan's Daughter

ness' Fagin – and some stunningly executed sequences, such as the climax with Sikes on the roof which utilizes both Russian montage theories and German Expressionism.

Based on H.G. Wells' novel, *The Passionate Friends* re-examines some of the themes found in *Brief Encounter*. The film starred Trevor Howard and Lean's actress wife Ann Todd (they divorced in 1957). *Madeleine* is a visually striking Victorian melodrama in which Ann Todd plays an upper-middle-class girl who is accused of poisoning her former lover, a destitute Frenchman. Madeleine is tried for murder but the case against her is 'unproven'. It is a bleak, unresolved story that contains Lean's most elaborate attempt to examine the hypocrisies of 'polite' society.

These early films were produced by Cineguild, a company founded by Lean, producer Anthony Charles Havelock-Allan and cameraman Ronald Neame. In 1952, Cineguild was disbanded and Lean went to Alexander Korda's ailing London Films to make *The Sound Barrier*, written by Terence Rattigan and starring Ralph Richardson as a typical Lean hero driven by an obsession (designing a supersonic plane) which consumes both his family and his humanity. After *Hobson's Choice* (1954), a delightful Victorian comedy with the incomparable Charles Laughton as a drunken bootmaker whose chauvinism is successfully challenged by his eldest daughter, and *Summer Madness*, another return to *Brief Encounter* territory with Katharine Hepburn as an

American schoolmarm frightened by romance in a gloriously visualized Venice, Lean teamed up with producer Sam Spiegel to make *The Bridge on the River Kwai*.

One of the key British films of the Fifties, this film uses the basic framework of the 'war is futile' genre for an exemplary study of military codes and conduct. While confined in a remote Japanese POW camp, Lean's extraordinary hero Colonel Nicholson builds a bridge to boost morale among his dejected troops, to show the enemy what British soldiers are made of and,

Filmography
1934 Java Head (ed. only). '35 Escape Me Never (ed. only). '36 Ball at Savoy (ed. only); As You Like It (ed. only). '37 The Wife of General Ling (ed. only). '38 Pygmalion (ed. only). '39 Spies of the Air (ed. only); French Without Tears (ed. only). '41 Major Barbara (some scenes only, uncredited; +ed); 49th Parallel (ed. only) (USA: The Invaders); One of Our Aircraft Is Missing (ed. only). '42 In Which We Serve (co-dir. only). '44 This Happy Breed (+co-sc). '45 Blithe Spirit (+co-sc); Brief Encounter (+co-sc). '46 Great Expectations (+co-sc). '48 Oliver Twist (+co-sc). '49 The Passionate Friends (+co-sc) (USA: One Woman's Story). '50 Madeleine (USA: The Strange Case of Madeleine). '52 The Sound Barrier (+prod) (USA: Breaking the Sound Barrier/Star Bound). '54 Hobson's Choice (+prod; +co-sc). '55 Summer Madness (+co-sc) (USA/GB) (USA: Summertime). '57 The Bridge on the River Kwai. '62 Lawrence of Arabia. '65 The Greatest Story Ever Told (some scenes only, uncredited) (USA). '65 Doctor Zhivago (USA). '70 Ryan's Daughter. '79 Lost and Found – The Story of Cook's Anchor (co-dir; co-prod; +narr. only) (NZ) (doc). '84 A Passage to India.

Rank and film

The late Forties were years of success and optimism for the British cinema: two moguls, Korda and Rank, fought for the rich rewards offered by the American market

The British film industry entered the post-war period in a spirit of optimism. Annual attendances at British cinemas in 1946 climbed to 1635 million, a figure which was to be an all-time high. The statistic is all the more remarkable since, out of 5000 cinemas, as many as 230 remained closed owing to bomb damage and, because the limited supply of building materials was reserved for more essential uses, no new cinemas could be built.

It was not until April 1949 that cinemas were allowed to switch on their front-of-house display lighting once again. But despite a certain dinginess, the cinema was still an attractive escape from the austerity of post-war Britain with its fuel crises, rationing and various other shortages.

The major cinema circuits – Odeon and Gaumont (both controlled by J. Arthur Rank), and the rival ABC (Associated British Cinemas) – were prevented from further expanding their share of the market by the Board of Trade. It was a time for smaller companies like Granada, Southan Morris and Star to expand by taking over independent cinemas. The biggest single growth, however, occurred in Sol Sheckman's Essoldo circuit which more than tripled in size between the end of the war and the end of the decade.

The traditional low esteem accorded to home-produced films by British audiences had vanished. J. Arthur Rank, an established producer in the late Thirties, was encouraged by the popularity of such pictures as *Madonna of the Seven Moons* (1944) and *A Place of One's Own* (1945) and embarked on a great crusade to put British films on an equal footing with Hollywood product throughout the world. There were new markets to be won in the formerly occupied countries, long deprived of Hollywood and British films, and Rank's salesmen were there, trying to earn money vital to Britain's post-war economy.

Rank also had his eye on the lucrative North American market. In 1944, he bought a half-interest in the circuit of 80 Odeon cinemas in Canada, and a year later he was contemplating building a new Odeon to seat 2500 people in New York's Times Square.

Rank was the largest shareholder in Universal pictures and set up a new company in partnership with them to distribute eight Rank pictures a year in North America. These films were block-booked with new Hollywood films to make a package acceptable to the American circuits. But the US government had for some time been opposed to the system of block-booking and Rank was forced to change his plans. He eventually persuaded the five major American circuits to book British pictures on their own merits.

Britain could not afford to let all the money earned by Hollywood films in the UK leave the country – unless British films could earn more money in the USA to help redress the balance. At the same time the British market was vital to the American studios. In 1946, for example, it was worth $87 million and provided 60 per cent of their

foreign income. The American circuits were controlled by the big Hollywood companies who realized that they would have to play their fair share of British films in order to keep their side of the bargain. Expensive and prestigious Rank productions like *Henry V* (1944) and *Caesar and Cleopatra* (1945), as well as the more modestly budgeted *The Seventh Veil* (1945), were already making inroads into the American market.

In 1946, six British pictures shared 11 Academy Award nominations. Among the Oscar winners were Laurence Olivier, with a special award for *Henry V*, Clemence Dane for the story of *Perfect Strangers* (1945) and Muriel and Sydney Box for their original screenplay for *The Seventh Veil*. Success in America continued into 1947 when Rank's production of *Great Expectations* (1946) played at the mighty Radio City Music Hall in New York, and *Odd Man Out* (1947) appeared at another important Broadway cinema. The following year *Hamlet* (1948) won the Oscar for Best Picture and Best Actor, marking further triumphs for Olivier. *The Red Shoes* (1948) was also nominated for Best Picture. Hollywood smarted under charges that it was losing its artistic initiative.

Rank built up his British studio on Hollywood lines. He established an animation unit with David Hand, a recruit from Disney; he started a two-reel documentary series *This Modern Age* to rival the *March of Time*; he founded the 'charm school' at his Highbury studios to develop new talent.

As an exhibitor, Rank extended his empire. By the end of 1947, he had an interest in 725 overseas cinemas with more than a hundred in five countries – New Zealand, Canada, South Africa, Italy and Australia – and strong representation in Eire, Ceylon, Holland, Egypt, Jamaica and Singapore. In Britain, his two cinema circuits formed the prime outlet for the Hollywood majors (except Warners and MGM who had distribution ties with the ABC circuit) and at the same time Rank was programming British cinemas with his own films.

ABC had no overseas cinemas and were, therefore, a smaller concern than Rank. Furthermore

Top left: J. Arthur Rank and some of the starlets from his Highbury 'charm school'; among them are Sally Gray and Jean Kent. Top: trade ad celebrating Rank's reception in the USA as a film salesman. Centre: the man with the gong; Rank's trade mark. Above: another famous British logo, the Gainsborough Lady

Above: post-war realism characterized Robert Hamer's It Always Rains on Sunday. *The film was set in London's East End, amid the street markets and railway yards, and told the story of an escaped prisoner who is sheltered by his former girlfriend (now married) but is rounded up and recaptured – all in the space of a Sunday. Above right: Robert Donat as the QC who defends a young naval cadet accused of stealing a postal order in* The Winslow Boy. *Above centre: Ann Todd and James Mason in* The Seventh Veil *as the young concert pianist and her jealous, embittered guardian. Below: David Lean's* Oliver Twist *was remarkable for its detailed evocation of the squalor of Dickensian London and for the performances of Alec Guinness and Robert Newton*

they were substantially owned by Warner Brothers and had no-one of J. Arthur Rank's drive and zeal at the helm.

The only potential opposition to Rank's dominance of the British film industry was Alexander Korda, but he did not have the benefit of a cinema circuit. During 1943–45, Korda worked in association with MGM but he only produced one picture, *Perfect Strangers* and the chance to curb Rank's power was lost. MGM called off their deal with Korda; he re-established London Films and took over Shepperton studios.

Korda never became a prolific producer on the scale of J. Arthur Rank. In 1948, he was in severe financial difficulties following losses on two very expensive pictures, *An Ideal Husband* (1947) and a new version of *Anna Karenina* (1948). His extravagant spending on *Bonnie Prince Charlie* (1948), filmed over nine months, only made matters worse.

Fortunately, productions like *Mine Own Executioner* (1947) and *The Winslow Boy* (1948) were more economically filmed and Korda's company made some profit from distributing several of the upper-class romances that Herbert Wilcox pro-

duced and directed starring his wife Anna Neagle and Michael Wilding. These films – *The Courtneys of Curzon Street* (1947), *Spring in Park Lane* (1948) and *Maytime in Mayfair* (1949) – reflected Wilcox's opinion that audiences were sick of 'gloomy horrors' and 'wanted films about nice people'.

Associated British had some successes with the Boulting Brothers' production of *Brighton Rock* (1947) and *My Brother Jonathan* (1948). The first of these was adapted from Graham Greene's crime thriller and starred Richard Attenborough as the teenage gangster Pinky; and the second film had Michael Denison playing an ambitious young doctor in a northern industrial town.

Most of the notable British films of the late Forties were backed, produced or released by Rank

Rank also backed the independent producers' company Cineguild, formed in 1942 by David Lean, Ronald Neame, Anthony Havelock-Allan and Noel Coward. It was this team that produced *This Happy Breed* (1944), *Blithe Spirit* and *Brief Encounter* (both 1945). David Lean directed all three films and went on to make his two celebrated adaptations from Dickens, *Great Expectations* and *Oliver Twist* (1948), under the Cineguild banner.

Gainsborough, the production company of the Gaumont empire, specialized in costume melodramas about gypsies, bandits and brutality featuring such stars as Margaret Lockwood, James Mason and Stewart Granger. Despised by the critics, films like *They Were Sisters* and *The Wicked Lady* (both 1945) and *Caravan* (1946) were adored by the public. Thereafter, Gainsborough appeared to lose its popularity and eventually the company ran into financial losses with *Christopher Columbus* (1949), a tedious historical drama starring Fredric March as the intrepid explorer.

Michael Powell and Emeric Pressburger, one of the most prolific production teams of the period, formed their own company, The Archers, which was also backed by Rank, and it was Rank that released their idiosyncratic, widely discussed films: *I Know Where I'm Going* (1945), *A Matter of Life and Death* (1946), *Black Narcissus* (1947) and *The Red Shoes* (1948). Frank Launder and Sidney Gilliat's Individual Pictures company (also linked to Rank)

ROBERT NEWTON, ALEC GUINNESS
KAY WALSH
FRANCIS L. SULLIVAN
with HENRY STEVENSON
"OLIVER TWIST"
and introducing
JOHN HOWARD DAVIES as "Oliver Twist"

made a number of accomplished films that brought credit to the parent company: *The Rake's Progress* (1945), *I See a Dark Stranger* (1946) and *The Blue Lagoon* (1949). The latter film was handicapped by interference on the part of Rank who insisted that it be shot in the studio rather than on location, thus forcing the film beyond its budget.

One of the fiercest critics of Rank's monopoly was Michael Balcon, the production chief and head of Ealing Studios, but even he was obliged to turn to Rank for distribution from 1944 onwards. The immediate post-war period was not a notable time for Ealing despite the critical successes of *Dead of Night* and *Pink String and Sealing Wax* (both 1945) and the acclaim given to *Hue and Cry* and *It Always Rains on Sunday* (both 1947). But in 1949 the company brought out *Passport to Pimlico*, *Whisky Galore!* and *Kind Hearts and Coronets* in rapid succession. The era of Ealing comedy had truly arrived at last.

Rank was making headway as an independent businessman selling his films in the USA when the British government intervened and placed a 75 per cent *ad valorem* tax on American films imported after August 1947. The result of this measure was twofold: Hollywood stopped sending new films to Britain, and American circuits were no longer disposed to show British films. Overseas sales, like those that Rank was pursuing, became harder to achieve. In Britain, cinemas were soon reduced to playing reissues of old films and to extending the runs of new British films. By the spring of 1948 the film business was in a bad way.

Rank's response to the crisis was to launch a crash programme of production at a cost of over £9 million, drawing on the spare funds of his highly profitable Odeon circuit for the first time. But the new Rank pictures spread the available talent too thinly and the quality of these films was not high enough to guarantee profits. At the same time, the Chancellor of the Exchequer, Sir Stafford Cripps, arranged for the original import tax on Hollywood films to be repealed in May 1948 in exchange for an agreement on the part of the Americans to limit the amount of earnings removed from the country to an annual figure of $17 million. The remainder of this revenue was to be reinvested in British film production. Hollywood, not surprisingly, un-leashed a backlog of 265 pictures and the new British films were swamped under the competition.

Once again the government tried to take re-medial steps. It raised the quota of British features to be shown in cinemas throughout the land from 20 to 45 per cent. The new figure made impossible demands on the British film industry even though Rank kept up production in an attempt to fulfil the quota. Hollywood was once again handicapped as the various studios scrambled for the limited play-ing time the new British law left them.

In the summer of 1949, Rank's £86 million empire had a £16.25 million overdraft and had lost £3.35 million in production, resulting in an overall year's trading loss of £750,000. J. Arthur Rank ordered savage cut-backs. No future Rank film was to cost over £150,000 – a far cry from the half-million spent on the two Olivier/Shakespeare films. Rank stopped making cartoons, terminated *This Modern Age*, closed the studios at Highbury (and the 'charm school'), Islington and Shepherds Bush and cut back on production activity at Denham. Pine-wood was to be the main base for Rank production but the economies had forced many film-makers away, most of them joining up with Korda, a popular and cultured figure with whom artists felt at home.

Investment in production was no longer the

Above left: James Mason carries off Margaret Lockwood in The Wicked Lady. *This historical romance, about a noblewoman who teams up with a highwayman, was typical of the 'Gainsborough Gothic' style. Above:* London Belongs to Me *(1948) was made at Pinewood by Launder and Gilliat for Individual Pictures. Launder said, 'It was well acted and well directed but its overall drawback to my mind was too many characters in too many stories, and not enough stars.' Nevertheless it helped Richard Attenborough on his way, providing him with another working-class role, and Alastair Sim had fun with the part of the fake medium. Below: the fanciful allegory* A Matter of Life and Death *told how a young airman was judged in a celestial court.*

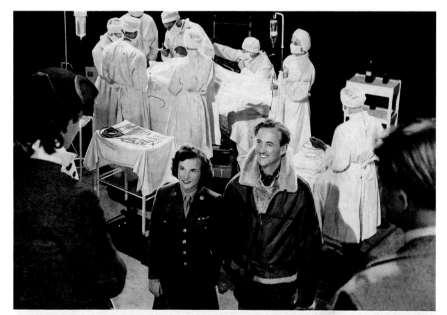

193

Above: setting up a shot (involving interiors and exteriors) for Whisky Galore! *on location in the Outer Hebrides. Above right: one of several adaptations from the novels of Graham Greene in the Forties, the Boulting Brothers' version of* Brighton Rock *was, for its time, an unusually violent film. Above, far right: publicity picture of Anna Neagle and Michael Wilding, who together made half a dozen films; in* Piccadilly Incident *(1946) they were wartime lovers, then came* The Courtneys of Curzon Street, Spring in Park Lane, Derby Day *(1952) and* Maytime in Mayfair. *Below: Neagle and Wilding's penultimate film together in 1951*

attractive gamble it had been to financiers in the Thirties. Instead the government of the day created the National Film Finance Corporation which began in October 1948 with £5 million to loan to producers who proposed safe-looking projects for films. Rank made no attempt to borrow NFFC money, not wanting to increase his organization's debts, but Korda seized the opportunity and borrowed £3 million for a variety of productions.

The money gave Korda a new lease of life. He engaged Carol Reed to make *The Fallen Idol* (1948) and *The Third Man* (1949). The latter film was partly financed by the Hollywood producer David O. Selznick who supplied Joseph Cotten and Alida Valli from his roster of stars. Selznick also collaborated with Korda on Powell and Pressburger's *Gone to Earth* (1950), a melodrama set in the Shropshire countryside with spectacular hunting scenes. This film prompted an argument between Korda and Selznick over the quality of the close-ups of Jennifer

Jones and Selznick had the scenes featuring Jones re-shot in the United States before releasing the film as *The Wild Heart*.

In contrast to Ealing's eccentric style, the Neagle–Wilding films offered an image of elegance

Associated British responded to Rank's cut-back with the announcement of a major production programme in association with Warner Brothers. One of the products of this collaboration was *The Hasty Heart* (1949) starring Richard Todd. The film was directed by Vincent Sherman from a script by Ranald MacDougall and co-starred Patricia Neal; all three were Warners stalwarts from Hollywood. Associated British also drew on Hollywood talent for their lavish, American-style musical *Happy-Go-Lovely* (1951): the film was directed by H. Bruce Humberstone and starred David Niven, Vera-Ellen and Cesar Romero.

Other Hollywood companies were actively involved in British production, using up some of the frozen assets created by governmental restrictions. 20th Century-Fox made *Escape* (1948) and *Britannia Mews* (1949), a period romance written by Ring Lardner Jr. In 1949, MGM filmed *Edward My Son* and the Cold War thriller *Conspirator*, starring Robert Taylor and Elizabeth Taylor, as well as establishing its own studio at Borehamwood.

At the end of the decade, the British film industry was badly battered. The high hopes of the post-war revival were dashed. In 1949, the government set up the British Production Fund which has always been known as the Eady Plan after Sir William Eady who devised the scheme. Briefly, the fund was the product of a levy on the price of cinema admission which would be returned to producers in direct proportion to the performance of their films at the box-office. The Eady levy placed a premium on financial success and British film producers felt it keenly. In the same year as the Eady Plan was introduced, the government reduced the quota of British films exhibitors were obliged to play to 40 per cent. This move may have eased the pressure on British production but the industry would never again enjoy the financial stability of the mid-Forties.

Home on the range

The great Western revival in the Forties reflected America's renewed interest in her history at a time when the war encouraged a spirit of national unity

The successful revival of the Western in 1939 may be ascribed to the mood of the times. War, for the Americans, was on the distant horizon. Europe was dominated by dictators, and alien doctrines were abroad. It was a time when men's minds turned to the nature of 'Americanism' and in particular to the nation's history and its values. It is significant that the Western, celebrating the heroic period of American expansion and highlighting its distinctive qualities of democracy, determination and self-reliance, now eclipsed the distinctly un-American swashbuckler. The latter genre, with its gentlemen heroes adventuring in the aristocratic and hierarchic world of Old Europe (a continent the Americans were currently inclined to mistrust), seemed suddenly anachronistic.

Warner Brothers, the home of swashbuckling films, put Errol Flynn, the erstwhile star of *Captain Blood* (1935) and *The Adventures of Robin Hood* (1938), into a series of expensive, lavish and vigorously staged Westerns in the wake of his success in *Dodge City* (1939). The following year Flynn was seen in *Virginia City* and *Santa Fe Trail* and went on to make other Westerns later in the decade – *They Died With Their Boots On* (1942) and *San Antonio* (1945).

In a hilarious piece of miscasting, Warners even put James Cagney and Humphrey Bogart into a Western romp called *The Oklahoma Kid* (1939). Cecil B. DeMille, the re-creator of the spectacle and grandeur of the Ancient World, had already contributed to the Western genre in the Thirties with *The Plainsman* (1936) and *Union Pacific* (1939). He followed these films with a tribute to the Canadian lawmen in *North West Mounted Police* (1940) and an epic celebration of America's own colonial past in *Unconquered* (1947).

During the war years, all the Hollywood studios contributed to the Western boom. 20th Century-Fox specialized in grand historical epics. They produced *Brigham Young* (1940), dealing with the Mormon trek to Utah in the 1840s, *Western Union* (1941), showing the creation of the telegraph system across the West, and *Buffalo Bill* (1944), a heavily fictionalized account of the career of the frontier scout, buffalo hunter and showman.

The creation by pioneers of the great new western states was celebrated in Columbia's *Arizona* (1940) and *Texas* (1941), MGM's *Wyoming* (1940), Republic's *In Old Oklahoma* (1943) and *Dakota* (1945) and Paramount's *California* (1946). The Texan leader Sam Houston and the frontier scout Kit Carson, two of the most famous heroes of the West, were the subjects of handsome and exciting epics from smaller studios: Republic's *Man of Conquest* (1939) and Monogram's *Kit Carson* (1940).

Other colourful characters of the West flooded onto the screen. Many of them were glamorized outlaws committed to 'truth, justice and the American way' and were pitted against the villains of monopolistic corporations, railroad companies, banks and big business. Among the nineteenth-century bad men canonized on celluloid in the

twentieth century were Billy the Kid in *Billy the Kid* (1941) and *The Outlaw* (1943), Belle Starr in a 1941 film of the same name, the Daltons in *When the Daltons Rode* (1940), the Youngers in *Badmen of Missouri* (1941) and Quantrill's Raiders in *Dark Command* (1940).

The re-establishment of the Western as a cinema staple is demonstrated by the eagerness with which film comedians took the trail West to satirize the conventions of the genre. Among the comic cowboys were the Marx Brothers in *Go West* (1940) and Abbott and Costello in *Ride 'Em Cowboy* (1942). One of the best and most enduring of these films is *The Paleface* (1948), which teamed Bob Hope, in his familiar comic persona of the cowardly, lecherous braggart, and Jane Russell, guying the sultry, sexy, siren image she had created in *The Outlaw*.

During the Forties – and after the war in particular – certain trends began to be discerned, which were to flower in the Fifties when Westerns took on a new sharp edge and intensity. The themes of social significance, sexuality, violence and psychoanalysis testify to a process of maturing on the part of both the industry and the audiences. The move towards more demanding, more complex and more controversial Westerns was to find its full expression in the Fifties.

One of the earliest and most celebrated examples of the socially significant Western, however, was William Wellman's *The Ox-Bow Incident* (1943), a powerful and sombre indictment of lynch law. The obvious artificiality of the studio-shot landscapes emphasized the stark nature of the film's message, and a strong cast, headed by Henry Fonda, vividly portrayed the nature and effects of mob rule.

Equally controversial, but for a different reason, was Howard Hughes' production of *The Outlaw*. The film was designed to launch the career of his newest discovery, Jane Russell, and Hughes devoted much footage to advertising Miss Russell's breasts, which the judge who banned the film in Maryland described as hanging over the picture 'like a thunderstorm spread over a landscape'. After problems with the film censors and the Catholic Legion of Decency, Hughes withdrew the film following its premiere in 1943. He then shrewdly created a full-scale pub-

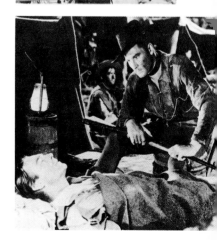

Top: in Texas two Civil War veterans go into cattle farming. Centre: poster from Fritz Lang's Western Union. *Above: Errol Flynn and Randolph Scott in* Virginia City

Top: in Go West, *the Marx Brothers began the film in some semblance of Western costume but soon abandoned it for their more familiar garb. Above: Jack Benny and his manservant, Rochester, in the comedy Western* Buck Benny Rides Again *(1939). Below: the controversial poster for the first openly sexy Western,* The Outlaw

licity campaign to exploit the situation and whip up popular interest in the film. Photographs of Jane Russell in a tight-fitting blouse made her a national sex-symbol long before the film went into release.

The Outlaw finally came out, slightly cut, in 1946 and grossed $3 million in the USA alone. In fact it is a poor film, clumsy, ponderous and slow-moving, the action centring on an all-male triangle, with Pat Garrett pursuing Billy the Kid because he is jealous of Billy's relationship with Doc Holliday. The three men are far more interested in each other and in the prize horse Little Red than in Rio (Jane Russell), the smouldering Mexican girl whose strictly peripheral role is mainly concerned with cooking meals and indulging in a couple of rather suggestive romps with Billy.

Nevertheless *The Outlaw*'s reputation ensured that sex had entered the Western for good. This was confirmed by the success of *Duel in the Sun* (1946), which dealt with the amatory adventures of the half-breed Pearl Chavez (Jennifer Jones), another hot-blooded figure in the tradition of Rio. The film was suffused with a sweaty eroticism and one critic irreverently dubbed it 'Lust in the Dust'.

David O. Selznick sought to repeat the scale and success of *Gone With the Wind* (1939) in *Duel in the Sun* which was directed in the main by King Vidor. Shot in bold Technicolor, this was a Texan *Gotterdämerung* ('Twilight of the Gods'), a veritably Wagnerian Western, full of lurid, blood-red sunsets, breakneck horseback chases, wild dances and intense love-making, punctuated by flashes of lightning and the pealing of bells. The screen constantly

erupted into large-scale action sequences, as wild horses were rounded up, cattlemen confronted the cavalry and a train was derailed. This torrent of activity counterpointed the violent love affair of Pearl Chavez, the spitting, scowling, sneering, tousled, tigerish, half-breed (Jennifer Jones) and Lewt McCanless (Gregory Peck), all-male, all bad, cigarette insolently drooping from the corner of his lips, hat perched jauntily on the back of his head, his whole being oozing an irresistible animal magnetism. Their relationship climaxes in true operatic style with a shoot-out at Squaw's Head Rock, which ends with both mortally wounded, crawling across the sun-baked rocks with bloodied hands to die in each other's arms.

Ritualized violence had always been a key ingredient in Westerns. In the main it was seen as exciting but essentially harmless fun. One of the best examples of this was the prolonged fist fight between hero and villain that was the highlight of the gold-rush Western *The Spoilers* (1942) with John Wayne and Randolph Scott as the protagonists. In the late Forties, however, critics began to voice their concern that violence was becoming much more realistic and brutal. Films like André de Toth's *Ramrod* (1947) were singled out for criticism on this count. The increasingly prevalent use of Technicolor for Westerns further highlighted blood and bruises, although the experience of war had conditioned audiences to accept a greater degree of screen violence.

During the war, public interest in psychology and psychoanalysis had grown and the cinema was quick to capitalize on the phenomenon. The theories of Freud came to the West in Raoul Walsh's

---

World War II may have conditioned audiences to more violence but the critics protested at the blood and gore in new Technicolor Westerns

---

moodily impressive *Pursued* (1947) with its hero (Robert Mitchum) dogged by a half-forgotten childhood trauma that is revealed in a complex series of flashbacks. After this, Western heroes could never again be simple, uncomplicated men in white hats riding white horses.

The early Forties saw two classic expositions of the traditional themes of the Western. William Wyler's *The Westerner* (1940) was a slow-moving but beautifully photographed tale that depicted the resistance of decent, hard-working homesteaders to the ruthlessly organized might of the cattlemen. The film offered powerful contrasts between the peaceful, communal celebrations of the settlers (a service of thanksgiving among the cornfields, a cheerful hoedown) and the eruptions of savage violence among the cowboys (trampling down the crops, carousing in the town and beating up their opponents). In the last resort it was a film of character rather than action, exploring the love-hate relationship between Cole Harden, personified by Gary Cooper as the soul of integrity, and Walter Brennan's cunning, hard-drinking old reprobate Judge Roy Bean, dispensing summary justice from a saloon and worshipping the beauty of the actress Lillie Langtry. The relationship ends inevitably but satisfyingly with a final shoot-out on the stage of a theatre where Lillie Langtry is due to appear.

The romance, excitement and glory of war was the subject of Raoul Walsh's sprawling and enthralling US cavalry movie *They Died With Their Boots On*. The film followed the flamboyant career of General Custer from West Point Academy through

JANE RUSSELL MEAN...MOODY...MAGNIFICENT!

HOWARD HUGHES' DARING PRODUCTION

THE OUTLAW

ACTION! THRILLS!! SENSATIONS!!!
PRIMITIVE LOVE!!!!

JACK BUETEL
THOMAS MITCHELL
WALTER HUSTON

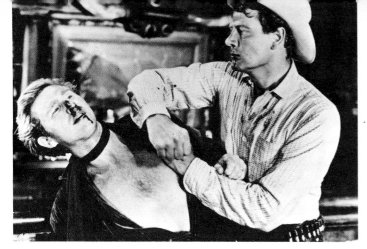

the Civil War to the Western Frontier and his death at the battle of Little Big Horn. In true Hollywood style, this final disaster was turned into an act of heroic self-sacrifice, with Custer knowingly and deliberately sacrificing himself and his troops to protect the main army column from massacre.

Errol Flynn was perfectly cast as the long-haired American general, a swashbuckling paladin of the plains, with a boyish enthusiasm for fighting, a hunger for glory, a delight in gaudy uniforms, a respect for his enemies and a chivalrous devotion to his wife Libby (Olivia de Havilland).

Howard Hawks' *Red River* (1948) provided a prototype hero for the next decade in John Wayne's tough, relentless, revenge-seeking cattle-rancher, Tom Dunson. This is a classic Hawksian film, with its emphasis on professionalism, male cameraderie and dangerous, exciting work on the fringes of civilized society. It re-creates the rigours of the cattle drive – complete with stampede, river crossing and Indian attacks. There are moments of sheer poetry, too, like the start of the drive: mist, dust, dawn, a 180° pan across the waiting herd, and then Dunson yells, 'Take 'em to Missouri, Matt' and Matt's wild yahoo is taken up by each of the drovers in turn in a rapid succession of close-ups as the great herd starts to move.

At the heart of the film is the relationship between Tom Dunson and his adopted son Matthew Garth (Montgomery Clift). When Tom's obsessive desire to get to Missouri leads to rebellion among the drovers, Matt takes over and Dunson pursues him, consumed with bitterness and seeking revenge. The final gunfight between them, however, is frustrated by the quintessential, self-possessed Hawksian heroine (Joanne Dru), who tells them that they really love each other and are not going to kill each other. They accept her logic and are reconciled at the last moment.

John Ford returned from wartime service to begin one of the most richly productive phases of his long career. In *My Darling Clementine* (1946), he took the historical facts of the confrontation between the Earps and the Clantons at the OK Corral and reworked them into a very personal and characteristically complex statement about the bringing of civilization to the West. The Clantons – brutal, lawless and anarchic, ruled with a bullwhip by a tyrannical old patriarch (Walter Brennan) – represent the unacceptable face of the Old West. They are destroyed by the Earps, whose family solidarity and mutual affection is placed at the service of the nascent community. The values of this community are demonstrated in the justly famous sequence in which the decent citizens of Tombstone hold a celebratory square dance in their half-built church, beneath the fluttering flags of the United States. The imagery represents a potent blending of religion, patriotism and community spirit, the cement of the society the Earps are helping to build. Shot, lit and

staged with an austere and strictly ritualized formality, the film undercuts its style with flurries of bustling action and comic interludes like that of the visit of a travelling theatrical troupe.

The same sense of community, allied to a powerful feeling for tradition and the unifying concept of service to the nation, provides the links in Ford's cavalry trilogy: *Fort Apache* (1948), *She Wore a Yellow Ribbon* (1949) and *Rio Grande* (1950). The values of the idealized society which Ford saw embodied in the US cavalry are succinctly encapsulated in the fluttering yellow ribbon, crossed sabres and lusty singing voices of the soldiers, seen and heard behind the credits of *She Wore a Yellow Ribbon*. They are affirmations of its continuity (the ribbon – a symbol of a cavalry sweetheart and hence of the family tradition of service), its role (crossed sabres – an emblem for the maintenance of peace and order), and its community spirit (male voices singing in unison 'The Girl I Left Behind'). It was these values that attracted Ford to the concept of the cavalry at a time when the USA had emerged from World War II to face new problems and rapid social change.

In *The Man Who Shot Liberty Valance* (1962) Ford uses the quotation 'When the legend becomes fact, print the legend'. But in *Fort Apache* Ford is at pains to show the truth behind the legend – in this case, Custer's last stand – at the same time as showing how the legend is born and endorsing the need for heroes and legends in the process of fortifying national memory. Ford lovingly re-creates the rituals of cavalry life – the parades and patrols, regimental balls and dinner parties – and thrillingly stages the battles, charges and Indian attacks as a background to the story of an embittered martinet, Colonel Thursday (Henry Fonda), a thinly disguised Custer figure whose ambition and stubbornness lead the regiment to disaster.

The virtues and strengths of the cavalry are fully embodied by Captain Nathan Brittles (John Wayne) the hero of *She Wore a Yellow Ribbon*. Tough, sentimental, dedicated and professional, he has grown old in the army and given his all to it. The film deals with his last mission – to avert an Indian uprising – before he retires. The mellow autumnal Technicolor in which the film is shot reflects this sense of a career's twilight. If we can see Shakespeare in Prospero breaking his wand and retiring to the country after *The Tempest*, then perhaps it is permissible to see John Ford in the character of Nathan Brittles, the hard-nosed, old professional whose life is his work and whose work is his life. Ford is so devoted to the character of Brittles that he sidesteps the clearly implied tragic ending to recall Brittles from his retirement and have him appointed chief of scouts for the army. *She Wore a Yellow Ribbon* is quintessential Ford and a mature middle-period masterwork that ranks with Hollywood's finest.

Top left: the new violence of Forties Westerns, as meted out by Joel McCrea to Lloyd Bridges in Ramrod. *Top: the opening up of the West in* Brigham Young. *Above: John Wayne and Montgomery Clift in Howard Hawks'* Red River

The Enchanted Realms of Walt Disney

For decades the release of each new, full-length animated film by Walt Disney has been an eagerly awaited event. Children have thrilled at seeing their favourite characters given the breath of life by his studio's artists, and adults rejoiced at being able to re-experience a child-like sense of wonder and delight

For over fifty years the name of Walt Disney has been synonymous with the production of animated feature films. Even when the Disney empire diversified into other, more lucrative, forms of entertainment, its continuing success was largely due to the consistent popularity of Mickey Mouse and the characters created in the animated features.

The secret of Disney's genius was his skill as a story editor, choosing tales that were ageless or had a period setting, and which could, therefore, be systematically reissued to each new generation of moviegoers. This formula was established with the ambitious *Snow White and the Seven Dwarfs* (1937). Those critics who had dubbed the film 'Disney's folly' were finally forced to concede that his version of this well-loved story, told with music, humour, romance, pathos, suspense and no small amount of excitement and terror was a huge success – albeit, at a cost of $1,700,000, an expensive one.

The wooden hero

It was thus with confidence that in 1938 Disney launched his artists on several new projects of which the first to see completion was *Pinocchio* (1940). *Snow White and the Seven Dwarfs* had been Disney's greatest personal achievement, but *Pinocchio* remains his greatest film.

Costing $2.5 million, the film is a masterpiece of animation, containing stunning setpieces such as the opening multi-plane camera shot of Gepetto's village by starlight, the underwater sequences and the climactic whale chase, all of which proved that Disney's work could no longer be adequately described by the word 'cartoon'. *Pinocchio*'s pictorial richness, imaginative camera angles and fast-moving storyline were enhanced by such superb characterizations as Stromboli, the volcanic puppet-master, and the foxy Dickensian villain J. Worthington Foulfellow. The film also had an exceptional musical score, highlighted by the Oscar-winning song 'When You Wish Upon a Star' sung by Jiminy Cricket, whose moralistic role as Pinocchio's 'official conscience' helps the film to avoid undue sentimentality. The song, with its promise of dreams coming true, became the touchstone of Disney's screen philosophy.

Brilliant and banal

The year 1940 also saw the premiere of *Fantasia*, a film made possible by the skills developed while working on *Snow White and the Seven Dwarfs* and *Pinocchio*, but which came to a public quite unprepared for any-

thing other than another fairy-tale.

Fantasia grew out of Disney's search for a starring vehicle for Mickey Mouse. Paul Dukas' 'The Sorcerer's Apprentice' was chosen as a musical pantomime for Mickey, and in 1938, Disney invited conductor Leopold Stokowski to record the music.

This collaboration developed into the notion of 'The Concert Feature', as *Fantasia* was first called, for which Disney's artists would animate an entire programme of classical music. The musicologist Deems Taylor was enlisted as an advisor and remained to provide the film's linking narration. Perhaps the selection of compositions was too diverse, perhaps the differing approaches of the various sequence directors is too perceptible – whatever the reason, the film is a patchwork of the brilliant and the banal.

Fantasia contains sequences of exquisite animation (the flowers, fairies and dancing mushrooms of the 'Nutcracker Suite' and the terrors of the prehistoric pageant illustrating Stravinsky's 'The Rite of Spring'); and splendidly conceived passages of humour (Mickey's sorcery and the 'Dance of the Hours' ballet choreographed for ostriches, hippopotami and alligators). But *Fantasia* also contains items of pretentious trivia (the abstract accompaniment to Bach's Toccata and Fugue in D Minor); arch-sentimentality (the pseudo-religious 'Ave Maria', which serves as a gauche postscript to the fearful grotesqueries of Mussorgsky's 'Night on Bald Mountain'); and blatant tastelessness (the Hollywood kitsch with which Disney polluted Beethoven's pastoral landscape).

Fantasia remains a brave experiment, and a clear development of the use of music in the early Silly Symphonies, but Disney's uneasiness in the 'highbrow' atmosphere of the concert hall is reflected in the completed film.

Studio strike

Financial pressures caused Disney to abandon the sophisticated sound system (Fantasound) which he had developed for the film. Cut from 126 to 82 minutes, *Fantasia* went on general release in the USA with a Western. The press were divided over the picture and the public were confused by it. Plans to re-release the film with a varied repertoire never materialized, and it remained in its emasculated form until

1956, when most of the deleted footage was reinstated and, becoming a cult movie, it at last began to show a profit on the original investment of $2,280,000.

Fantasia was a financial failure at a time when Disney could least afford one. The war in Europe was curtailing overseas markets and had already affected the earning potential of *Pinocchio*. In addition, Disney's other major project, *Bambi* (1942) (in production since 1937), was costing vast sums of money.

Disney made economies and quickly put two less ambitious films into production. The first of these, *The Reluctant Dragon* (1941), combined live-action footage (featuring Robert Benchley on a tour of the studio) with three short cartoons. The second was the fully animated *Dumbo* (1941).

However, by this time financial uncertainties about the studio's future had led its huge work-force to become more discontented with labour relations in the studio. Disney refused to sign with either of the leading cartoonists' unions and a bitter strike ensued that was only finally resolved in his absence. Nelson Rockefeller, who was co-ordinator of Inter-American Affairs, asked Disney to make a goodwill tour of South America as part of the government's Good Neighbor policy. Disney agreed, on the understanding that he be allowed to gather film material while he was there, and that the movies that resulted would be underwritten by the government.

The tour was a success and a financial bonus to the studio. It also took Disney out of the centre of controversy so that others could settle the strike. However, the studio's unique creative atmosphere was irreparably damaged by the dispute.

Flights of fancy

By the time Disney returned from South America, *Dumbo* had been completed. In many ways, it is Disney's most satisfying feature. Running for just 64 minutes, the film tells a simple story dramatically and with great poignancy – and at a cost of only $700,000. The only extraneous sequence is that in which Dumbo has alcoholic hallucinations of pink elephants, and that is pardonable because of its sheer inventiveness.

There are many appealing qualities about *Dumbo*: the circus-poster colourings, the in-

Opposite page: the Prince finds his way to the castle blocked by a dragon in Sleeping Beauty. *Above left: Walt Disney. Above: Mlle Upanova and an alligator chorus in the 'Dance of the Hours' ballet from* Fantasia. *Below: The Three Caballeros was geared to the Latin American market. Bottom: as well as Bambi, the poster shows two of the film's most famous creations, Flower the skunk and Thumper the rabbit*

Above left: Lady and the Tramp*'s urban setting made the film unusually realistic. Top left: Alice tries to reach the key to the door of* Wonderland in Alice in Wonderland. *Top right: Dick Van Dyke and Julie Andrews in an animated landscape in* Mary Poppins. *Above right: Kaa the snake eyes Mowglie in* The Jungle Book

genious score of funny songs and wistful ballads and the animation set-pieces, such as the raising of the big top by night in torrential rain and the circus train's journey across an animated map of the USA. The film's memorable cast includes Dumbo's champion, the spunky little Brooklyn tough-guy, Timothy Mouse, the negroid crow quintet who teach Dumbo to fly, the bitchy female elephants and the addled Mr Stork who is responsible for the baby Dumbo's delivery. At the centre of this group is the pathetic silent hero himself.

Released a year later, *Bambi* was a very different movie, being as naturalistic as *Dumbo* was stylized. *Dumbo* has the frenzied pace of the circus-ring, but *Bambi* has a hauntingly lyrical rhythm; and, whereas Dumbo's triumph over adversity is lightly handled, the same moral in *Bambi* is heavily underlined.

Although the animals in *Bambi* were modelled on life studies, they were sufficiently 'Disneyfied' to make them appear uncomfortable residents in the film's beautiful forest settings. The stock cartoon gags used from time to time are intrusive and the animal's childish voices only proved how right the studio had been to keep Dumbo dumb.

There are, nevertheless, moments of animation in *Bambi* which remain unsurpassed; in particular, the battle of the stags (impressively shot in dramatic browns and purples), and the terrifyingly vivid forest-fire sequence. However, American audiences of 1942, now fighting the war they had once hoped would pass them by, found little in the sequestered glades of Bambi's forest with which to identify.

Makeshift movies

The studio survived the war years by making propaganda and training films for the government, although Disney's standards of professionalism often led him to subsidize the official budgets. The most significant of these movies was *Victory Through Air Power* (1943), which had animated sequences of great potency, as when the American Eagle battles with a grotesque Japanese octopus to free the world from its tentacled grasp.

The material gathered on Disney's South American tour was made into two features: *Saludos Amigos* (1943) and *The Three Caballeros* (1945). The first of these films, running for just 43 minutes, scarcely merits feature status, although it contains some remarkable sequences, particularly the concluding 'Acquarela do Brazil' ('Watercolour of Brazil'), in which an animated paint brush creates a lush jungle background against which a Brazilian parrot, José Carioca, teaches Donald Duck how to dance the samba. This episode heralded even wilder flights of surreal fancy in *The Three Caballeros* which combined real and animated characters. It was this technique which was later to be used in several other features, including *Song of the South* (1946), *Mary Poppins* (1964), and *Pete's Dragon* (1978).

The compilation format used in the South American movies, was employed to construct a number of so-called features which contained anything from two to ten short subjects. These films, sometimes linked with live action, are a random rag-bag, in which even the best sequences are hardly masterpieces. Among the highlights are 'Peter and the Wolf' and 'The Whale Who Wanted to Sing at the Met', from *Make Mine Music* (1946); 'Mickey and the Beanstalk', from *Fun and Fancy Free* (1947) and 'Johnny Appleseed' and 'Little Toot', from *Melody Time* (1948).

A new era

This inconsistent, unstatisfying period concluded with the patchy *Ichabod and Mr Toad* (1949). *Cinderella* (1950) marked the beginning

Above left: Captain Hook and his henchman Smee prepare to place a bomb in Peter's underground home in Peter Pan. *Above: Pongo, Missus and their puppies watch TV in* 101 Dalmatians. *Left: alligators Brutus and Nero carry Penny and her teddy-bear off in* The Rescuers; *Bernard and Bianca the mice and their two friends look on helplessly*

of a new era. This was the first animated feature since *Bambi*, and tried hard to re-create the brilliance of the studio's earlier films without quite capturing their graphic quality of line. *Cinderella* is a graceful film, but its heroine lacks the sympathetic qualities of Snow White, and much of the film's success is due to the mouse characters, Jac and Gus, and their running battle with Lucifer the cat.

Alice in Wonderland followed in 1951, and, despite the critics unanimous disapproval, is still the screen's most satisfying interpretation of Lewis Carroll's book. True, the crazy characters are constantly upstaging one another, and the pace is a shade too frenetic, but the comic invention never flags and there is much fine animation, especially in the 'March of the Cards' sequence and the Daliesque nightmare of the finale.

Increasingly in this period we find Disney making concessions to meet what he supposed were the narrow expectations and limitations of his audiences. In *Alice in Wonderland*, he failed to grasp the implicit seriousness of Lewis Carroll's humour and abandoned most of the disturbing elements in the story. Similarly in *Peter Pan* (1953) Disney shows no understanding of the story's sinister and emotional depths or the tragedy that is implicit in Peter's perennial youth. Disney's Peter has charm and bravado but lacks the self-sacrificing heroism

of the original, while the whimpering buffoonery of the film's Captain Hook has nothing of the genuine malevolence of J.M. Barrie's black-hearted Old Etonian.

Changing directions

The increased production of live-action movies and the studio's diversification into television and the amusement-park business contributed to a slowing up of Disney's output of animated films. His next feature, *Lady and the Tramp* (1955), was the first to use CinemaScope; Disney filled the wider screen with a picturesque conception of America at the turn of the century, with its opulent 'gingerbread' architecture and its seedy tenements. The canine characterizations are believable and endearing and the film has much adult appeal, not least because of Peggy Lee's 'bluesy' songs and her sophisticated vocal performance as Peg, the 'Dietrich' of the dog pound.

Sleeping Beauty in 1959 marked the end of another era at the Disney studios, being the last feature to have its characters inked onto the cels by hand – a costly process replaced, in *101 Dalmatians* (1961), by the freer, but less stylish, method of using Xeroxed drawings.

Sleeping Beauty cost an astronomical $6 million and was a financial disaster. It was poorly received by the critics, perhaps because the storyline seemed too close to *Snow White*

and the Seven Dwarfs. But its neglect is undeserved; the wicked fairy Maleficent is the embodiment of evil, the ornate settings are full of gothic horror and the final battle between the Prince and the dragon is a *tour de force*.

The transition from traditional fables and established classics to contemporary stories like *101 Dalmatians* (also the first feature in which songs were of minimal importance) was the most surprising development in the studio's history. However the studio failed to follow up the success of this film with its next movie *The Sword and the Stone* (1963), having to wait until *The Jungle Book* (1967) for its next triumph which Disney, who died on December 15, 1966, was never to witness.

Jungle jive

Released 30 years after the premiere of *Snow White and the Seven Dwarfs*, *The Jungle Book* was the last animated film to be personally produced by Disney. He gave the stories by Rudyard Kipling a decidedly up-beat treatment, and his cast of finely delineated characters jive and swing through rich jungle landscapes. Much of the film's strength was derived from the use of the voice-actor's personalities as character models – particularly George Sanders' sneering Shere Khan, the tiger.

This proved so successful that it became adopted as a standard feature of the studio's post-Disney productions, *The Aristocats* (1970) and *Robin Hood* (1973), presumably in the hope of strengthening stories which show a singular lack of imagination and originality. *Robin Hood* also has the dubious distinction of being technically the worst animated film the studio has ever made, with much of its animation plundered wholesale from earlier films.

Not until *The Rescuers* (1977), did the Disney studio produce a movie which re-established its supremacy of line. Possessing a plot which balances drama with humour and sentiment, it is a film that is worthy of the name of the dream-merchant who 40 years before had laboured at building a folly that became a gateway to a realm of enchantment. Indeed, more recent studio fare, such as *The Fox and The Hound* and *The Black Cauldron*, have been eclipsed by re-releases of 'the classics'.

On with the show

By the end of the Thirties musicals had lost their popularity. Band singers, skaters, even swimmers were recruited to bolster their appeal

When the Fred Astaire–Ginger Rogers team broke up in 1939 after *The Story of Vernon and Irene Castle*, it was the end of an era. Gone were the suave elegance and deco chic of the Thirties and gone was the musical based on the romantic tussles of a dancing team – for although people kept looking for a new partner for Fred Astaire, he never found one for more than two films together.

There had been another type of Thirties musical which was based on romantic teamwork – for instance, the well-upholstered operettas which had Jeanette MacDonald and Nelson Eddy trilling at each other in all kinds of fancy period rig-outs. But this couple's days were also numbered: the inseparables were increasingly separated and the end came when in 1942 they tried to go modern with an ill-fated version of the Rodgers and Hart stage show *I Married an Angel*.

Obviously tastes were making that noticeable, if not exactly definable, shift which seems to occur at the end of every decade. Musicals, apparently, were particularly vulnerable to this change. In the early Thirties they had hit an unexpected slump and had been labelled 'box-office poison' until in 1933 the genre was revitalized with the *Gold Diggers of 1933* and *42nd Street* – both of which had a new super-spectacular formula, courtesy of Busby Berkeley. Now, once again, all the sure-fire formulas seemed to have worn out their efficacy: even Berkeley had left his old home at Warner Brothers to try his luck at MGM and elsewhere. No-one knew for sure what might be found to make musicals attractive to the public again – if, indeed, anything could be found.

In a spirit of try-anything-once, film-makers hit on two new gimmicks – youth and the popular classics. Of course, if the two could be combined in one package that would be even better. As luck would have it, just such a combination was waiting in the wings – Deanna Durbin. She was pretty, wholesome and hardly more than a child, but with a true adult coloratura soprano.

Her voice may not have been of operatic quality but it was more than good enough for the odd classical selection and songs like Tosti's 'Goodbye' and 'Ave Maria'. She had made her first appearance in an MGM young-talent short, *Every Sunday* (1936), alongside another singing hopeful, Judy Garland. According to a possibly apocryphal story, someone misunderstood Louis B. Mayer's instructions to 'fire the plump one' and let her go while putting Garland under contract. She was snapped up by Joe Pasternak at Universal and put into a cheery comedy with music – *Three Smart Girls* (1937) – a low-budget film which made millions and saved the company from bankruptcy.

From then on she received the full star treatment. Her next film, *One Hundred Men and a Girl* (1937), places her in the realms of highbrow music as she attempts to persuade Leopold Stokowski to conduct an orchestra of out-of-work musicians.

Later films like *Mad About Music* and *That Certain Age* (both 1938) kept closely to variations on the same winning recipe. Although the film-makers

congratulated themselves loudly on their boldness in bringing 'great music' to a mass audience, it was not so much a desperate enterprise but rather seeing clearly which way the wind was blowing. The supposed battle between jazz and the classics had already been dramatized, rather cursorily, by Fred Astaire who was torn between ballet and tap in *Shall We Dance?* (1937), by the Romeo and Juliet ballet in *The Goldwyn Follies* (1938), and in *On Your Toes* (1939). There were also dozens of teenage musicals in which the swots wore bow ties and prated about Bach and Beethoven, only to be taken down a peg or two by their more enlightened hepcat fellows. As the Forties wore on, the schism was most frequently healed by embarrassing scenes in which Jose Iturbi played boogie-woogie, or Wagnerian singers showed that they were good guys at heart by, in the idiom of the day, 'cutting a rug'.

The high-school musical which provided a favourite location for 'jazzing the classics' flourished both at MGM, in the early days of Mickey Rooney and Judy Garland – *Babes in Arms* (1939) and its successors – and, in much humbler circumstances, at Universal. There Donald O'Connor and Peggy Ryan, who were hep, and Gloria Jean, who was not, appeared variously combined in any number of B films about co-eds, young army recruits and the like; all three were in *When Johnny Comes Marching Home*, *Mr Big* (both 1943) and *Follow the Boys* (1944). Meanwhile the other studios developed their own specialities. It was politic to have at least one musical star under contract, and so singers and dancers of all kinds (not to mention skaters, swimmers and various exotics) were under constant scrutiny in the hope that they might prove suitable film-star material.

Top left: Deanna Durbin played in One Hundred Men and a Girl *with Leopold Stokowski. The mixture of girlish charm and fine orchestration set a pattern for other musicals. Top:* Naughty Marietta *(1935) was the first film of the popular duo Jeanette MacDonald and Nelson Eddy. Above: Judy Garland and Deanna Durbin in an MGM test short* Every Sunday. *Joe Pasternak of Universal, after viewing the short, signed up Durbin for* Three Smart Girls

Below: Betty Hutton in Here Come the Waves *tried a new image when she played twins, one of whom was quiet and refined. Centre: Eleanor Powell dubbed 'The World's Greatest Tap Dancer', in* Rosalie. *Bottom: the sisters in* Tin Pan Alley *(1940) were Alice Faye and Betty Grable. Bottom right: Astaire and Hayworth's first film together*

Even MGM, which tended to be a law unto itself, had – as well as its fading singing duo, MacDonald and Eddy, and its teenage threats, Garland and Rooney – its own big dancing star, Eleanor Powell. She was an extraordinary, stainless-steel-clad lady who was no great shakes as an actress but, once she started on her machine-gun taps, was so magnetic that she could manage single-handed to hold the audiences' attention through such otherwise tiresome and patchy vehicles as the *Broadway Melodies* of 1936 and 1938 and *Rosalie* (1937). In *Broadway Melody* of 1940, for about the only time in her career, she was given a partner of equal standing, Fred Astaire, and some of the splendid Cole Porter numbers (particularly a long version of 'Begin the Beguine' which goes through many phases) represent a height of sheer style and technique rarely matched in the Hollywood musical. As things turned out, this proved to be the high point of her career: within three years she was reduced to playing second fiddle to Red Skelton, the company's new comic sensation, and she retired gracefully in 1944.

Other kinds of dancers were equally sought after. Vera Zorina, a ballet star, was introduced to the screen in *The Goldwyn Follies*. She went on to star in the film version of *On Your Toes*, which she had played on the stage in London, and then appeared sporadically in films like Paramount's spectacular *Star Spangled Rhythm* (1943) and *Follow the Boys* before retiring from dancing at the end of the war. On the masculine side there were attempts to build up Buddy Ebsen, a gangly junior later to know belated fame as the leading Beverly Hillbilly, and Ray Bolger, of the rubber face and legs that went on forever. Buddy Ebsen partnered ladies as various as Judy Garland, Eleanor Powell and Shirley Temple, but never really made it on his own; Ray Bolger remained one of the biggest stars on Broadway, but his unromantic appearance was against him as a leading man in films, and his finest screen moment was, heavily disguised, as the Scarecrow in *The Wizard of Oz* (1939).

These players tended to wander from studio to studio. The more fortunate stars were under contract to just one which took the trouble to care for them and build their careers, to select the right vehicles for their talents, to mix a little new material with the old in order to test the market and generally protect the studio's investment. The division of roles in a studio was carefully worked out. At Paramount, for instance, Bing Crosby was the reigning king of musicals, Bob Hope was the leading comedy star and sang a little, and there were four principal girls who divided most of the plum feminine roles at the studio between them. Paulette Goddard got the fiery dramatic roles, Dorothy Lamour was exotic in a sarong, Veronica Lake was the resident siren and Betty Hutton was the hard-sell musical comedienne. Their areas were clearly defined and no-one stepped on anyone else's toes: they could all, from time to time, let their hair down (or put it up, according to the fashion of the moment) to play in comedy or even musical roles – though only Betty Hutton specialized in the genre with occasional assistance from the former band singer Dorothy Lamour.

Many aspirants to screen stardom during the Thirties and Forties originally sang with bands – including Bing Crosby. Paramount had snapped him up in 1932, after he had become an instant sensation with his own radio show, and kept him for 24 years (although he was occasionally loaned out to other companies). With his lazy charm and seemingly effortless crooning, he was the constant

The new musical attractions ranged from Carmen Miranda's exotic hats to Betty Hutton's biting humour

factor in Paramount musicals. He was never teamed with any particular leading lady for long, apart from the series of seven 'Road' films, starting with *Road to Singapore* (1940), in which he and Bob Hope were regularly rivals for the affections of Dorothy Lamour. Otherwise, Mary Martin was nearest to a romantic partner in *Rhythm on the River* (1940) and *The Birth of the Blues* (1941) when Paramount were trying to transform her from a Broadway to a Hollywood star – without success.

Curiously enough Crosby was only once teamed with Paramount's female musical star, Betty Hutton (or perhaps one should say twice, since in *Here Come the Waves*, 1944, she played twins – one was quiet and refined and the other her usual raucous self). Perhaps Paramount feared that Crosby's relaxed, easy style would not blend with the Hutton oversell, and indeed it was a lot easier and more satisfactory to team her with Eddie Bracken in *The Fleet's In* (1942), *Star Spangled Rhythm*, and *The Miracle of Morgan's Creek* (1943) or with Sonny Tufts in *Cross My Heart* (1945) since they offered no competition and did not have to be protected from her onslaughts.

In her frenzied, but rather pathetic, determination to shout down all opposition – not least from any of the mere men who attracted her attention – Betty Hutton was a specifically Forties kind of star who was born of the years when all the real male stars were likely to be off to war and women had to keep the home fires burning as well as the machines turning. The war and then the post-war situation created other new kinds of stars. The great government drive towards Pan-American friendship and the Good Neighbor policy encouraged producers to

FAYE GRABLE
TIN PAN ALLEY

FRED ASTAIRE ☆ RITA HAYWORTH

Songs by COLE PORTER

YOU'LL NEVER GET RICH

look for a suitably Pan-American star to decorate films with titles like *Down Argentine Way* (1940), *That Night in Rio* and *Weekend in Havana* (both 1941). They found Carmen Miranda (who was in fact born in Portugal but nobody quibbled) – the Brazilian Bombshell. She belonged to another class of Forties star – those who could do only one thing but did that very well – the speciality star. As far as anyone could tell, all she was ever able to do was her characteristic hip-wagging, finger-twisting, pseudo-Latin number (usually written for her by old Hollywood stalwarts like Harry Warren) and wear her notorious tutti-frutti hats. The art of the film-maker consisted mainly of finding plausible ways to trundle her on and off screen between her big numbers.

Carmen Miranda was the most famous – or notorious – speciality star, but not the biggest. For that honour it was a close competition between skating Sonja Henie and swimming Esther Williams. Sonja Henie prettily skated her way to music through nearly a dozen films at 20th Century-Fox from *One in a Million* (1936) to *The Countess of Monte Cristo* (1948) and retired from the screen to make a fortune promoting ice shows. Esther Williams, MGM's home-grown mermaid, began in *Bathing Beauty* (1944) and was a regular in ever more exotic and elaborate watergoing romances until *Jupiter's Darling* (1955); she also retired with a fortune. Where Carmen Miranda was an incidental attraction, never called upon to provide more than semi-comic relief, Williams and Henie were undoubtedly stars, with whole big-budget films built around them. But then it was the era, above all, of the star musical.

After the eclipse of the Busby Berkeley-style spectacle (which was considered unpatriotic in wartime), everybody went instead for the fast, simple formula of picking a star and then selling him or her for all they were worth. Warners no longer had any tame musical stars, but then Warners did not make many musicals in the Forties. They produced only a handful of dramas with music which were quite frequently based on the life of a popular composer like George M. Cohan (*Yankee Doodle Dandy*, 1942), George Gershwin (*Rhapsody in Blue*, 1945) or Cole Porter (*Night and Day*, 1946). This continued until 1948 when they discovered yet another band singer called Doris Day and made her into a star with her first movie – *Romance on the High Seas*.

Columbia had Rita Hayworth and, since she was about all they had, they had to make her go a long way. Unfortunately she could not sing – or nobody could spare the time to coach her. But she could dance and, in between weightier assignments, she proved, in *You'll Never Get Rich* (1941) and *You Were Never Lovelier* (1942), to be one of the best partners Fred Astaire ever had and worked surprisingly well with Gene Kelly in *Cover Girl* (1944).

The best that RKO could come up with as a musical substitute for Astaire and Rogers was Anna Neagle, who was in Hollywood under contract at the beginning of the war in Europe and made such innocuous, undistinguished musicals as *Irene* (1940), *No, No, Nanette* and *Sunny* (both 1941).

Of the major independents, David Selznick had bigger things to do than bother his head with such frivolity, but Samuel Goldwyn discovered a musical comic in 1943 and unleashed Danny Kaye on the waiting world in *Up in Arms* (1944) and a succession of other tiresome, semi-musical vehicles.

But the big studio for musical stars and star musicals during the Forties was 20th Century-Fox. They had something for just about every taste. At the beginning of the decade there was still Shirley Temple, and there was Sonja Henie skating and very soon there was Carmen Miranda doing whatever she always did. Then when the studio went in for band singers the whole band would come along; two big Glenn Miller films – *Sun Valley Serenade* (1941) and *Orchestra Wives* (1942) – were made at that studio.

There were also the serious musical stars. Chief among them were Betty Grable and Alice Faye – both were blondes, both were Forces' sweethearts, but they were otherwise very different in style. Betty Grable had worked her way up from the chorus and did a bit of everything sufficiently, if nothing very well. She had bounce and good humour and rather short, pudgy legs which were regarded as the epitome of feminine allure. It was, perhaps, her very ordinariness that made her the great wartime pin-up – soldiers felt that, given the right breaks, the girl-next-door back home could probably do just as well, and they enjoyed Grable for being a trier. Alice Faye had been a band singer and, with her quivering bee-stung lips and throaty mezzo, was perfect for being soulful and singing songs like 'You'll Never Know' and 'No Love, No Nothing'.

Like goddesses of dissimilar races, they were usually kept apart, each in her own particular sphere, but it was a fair guess that one or other of them would be in any major 20th Century-Fox musical. The men who played opposite them – Don Ameche, John Payne, even Dan Dailey – were neither here nor there; they were merely moral support for the duration of the film. The films which surrounded them were brash and vulgar, conceived in the glaring tints of saturated Technicolor and made no grand claim to be works of art. They were, one might say, primitive Hollywood at its best, and as such they retain their vitality even today (so long as the stars retain theirs) when many more pretentious offerings have long since irretrievably faded.

Art, of course, is something else again. But for that one has to look elsewhere: to that special area of MGM where Arthur Freed and his team were up to something new and exciting and completely different.

Top left: Sonja Henie, seen here in My Lucky Star *(1938), was the world figure-skating champion before turning to films. Top: Donald O'Connor, Peggy Ryan and Gloria Jean in the high-school musical* When Johnny Comes Marching Home. *Centre: Esther Williams in* Jupiter's Darling. *Above: England's Anna Neagle made* No, No, Nanette *in Hollywood*

Metro-Goldwyn-Musical

Arthur Freed's production unit at MGM created a new kind of musical where action, song and dance were carefully interwoven into a flowing story

'More stars than there are in the heavens' was the proud boast of MGM. When you consider the number of the very greatest stars, from Greta Garbo to Mickey Rooney, who were under contract to the company at the end of the Thirties, such an image does not seem too extravagant. But even if the stars were extraordinary, what the studio did with them was not necessarily quite so remarkable. The same patterns applied at MGM as elsewhere; the same cycles of popularity were observed; stars were built in the same way, and faded (or were broken) in the same way. There, as anywhere else, stars were sometimes brought into a film in order to enliven poor material. Even so, however wonderful stars may be on the screen, they cannot exist in a vacuum: they have to have the right (or at least reasonable) circumstances in which to display themselves.

MGM were seldom innovative in these respects. In musicals, as in other films, the studio tended to employ directors because they were good company men rather than because of their ability. It encased its stars in safe, well-upholstered vehicles which did not diminish them but which rarely spectacularly enhanced them and which often depended on the stars for vitality and appeal. It was entirely unexpected, therefore, that in the early Forties MGM should, in the one area of the musical, produce something very different from anything that had been seen on the screen since the early days of the sound film. There were, however, no signs of this change appearing at the end of the Thirties when MGM began to acquire the stars who were going to shine most brightly in their new kind of musical.

Mickey Rooney and Judy Garland were the first to appear. Rooney, who came from a show-business background, was in silent films (once as a midget), juvenile shorts and many features before arriving at MGM where, in 1937, he made the film that was to change his life. *A Family Affair* was the first of the seemingly unending series of small-town comedy-dramas featuring Andy Hardy and his family. Rooney was not specifically a musical star but he could do something of everything and his career continued to flourish as long as he could credibly play teenagers – which, since he was very small, was well into his twenties.

Judy Garland was virtually born in a trunk, like the heroine of one of her most famous numbers from *A Star Is Born* (1954); she had been performing almost as long as she could walk, originally as one of the singing Gumm Sisters and then by herself. She was not a pretty-pretty child, like Shirley Temple or Deanna Durbin, (allegedly Louis B. Mayer used to call her affectionately 'my little hunchback') but she had personality plus, a rich and vibrant singing voice which she knew how to use and, above all, youth. This made her perfect for the fashionable high-school musicals and, after her test with Deanna Durbin in a musical short, *Every Sunday* (1936), she eased her way into the movies by playing everybody's younger sister until the winning combination occurred when she was put

together with Mickey Rooney in *Thoroughbreds Don't Cry* (1937) and *Love Finds Andy Hardy* (1938). Even so, she had to make it on her own in *The Wizard of Oz* (1939) before she and Rooney became a major musical team in *Babes in Arms* (1939).

After this they made three more big musicals together – *Strike Up the Band* (1940), *Babes on Broadway* (1941) and *Girl Crazy* (1943). They also made a couple more Andy Hardy films which

Above: the spectacular 'Broadway Rhythm Ballet' was the climax of the film within the film Singin' in the Rain. Arthur Freed, Stanley Donen and Gene Kelly collaborated on this musical about the early days of sound film. Below: Judy Garland and Mickey Rooney in Strike Up the Band

Above: Judy Garland in the classic 'Born in a Trunk' routine from A Star Is Born. *The number was added after George Cukor had finished shooting and became a regular spot in Garland's later stage shows. Below: Ann Miller displays her dexterity and precision as a tap dancer in* Small Town Girl *(1953)*

usually featured the efforts of a group of talented youngsters to put on their own show ('Gee, there's that old big barn down the road . . .') and which ended in musical fireworks from the practised hand of Busby Berkeley who was briefly under contract to MGM at this period.

These musicals were very much the traditional kind, but the shape of things to come had already been hinted at in *The Wizard of Oz*. Although it is difficult to establish responsibility for the film – in the case of a famous victory everybody rushes in to claim that he alone achieved it – it seems certain that a very important part of its success was due to the work of its uncredited associate producer, Arthur Freed. Freed had been around MGM since 1929 when he had come to Hollywood to write the songs (with composer Nacio Herb Brown) for *The Broadway Melody* (1929). Their evergreen songs, including 'You Are My Lucky Star', 'Singin' in the Rain', 'You Were Meant for Me' and 'I've Got a Feeling You're Fooling' were featured in many MGM films of the decade. By 1939 Freed was being groomed as a producer. He bought the book of *The Wizard of Oz* for the studio and oversaw the whole musical side of it. He also pressed for the casting of Judy Garland when the studio wanted to borrow Shirley Temple. The resulting film closely corresponded to his ideal of a musical as a story told in speech, song and dance in natural progression from

one sequence to another.

The Wizard of Oz was a fantasy and therefore something of a special case in the musicals' tradition. There had been an unofficial 'rule' that the public would not accept performers in films bursting into song or dance without any rational justification. But it had been broken so often with impunity that, by the end of the Thirties, no-one really believed in it any more. Its legacy still persisted in the enormous number of putting-on-a-show musicals. These were felt to take the sting out of the exotic and irrational side of the musical by placing the major numbers in a rehearsal room or on a stage (however inconceivable this might be in theatrical terms). Even then, if the principals sometimes behaved a bit oddly by everyday standards, well, show-people were like that. This meant that rather than being smoothly integrated into the story part of the film, the numbers were isolated interludes which had little functional relationship with the rest of the film and were quite often directed by someone else anyway. Those who made costume operettas (like the Jeanette MacDonald–

Gene Kelly, Fred Astaire and Judy Garland graced the screen with their song and dance routines to give the MGM musicals their unique flavour

Nelson Eddy films) or out-and-out fantasies had more freedom in this respect, but few film-makers had the special talents required to utilize it fully.

This was why Arthur Freed was so important. The first films he produced himself, *Babes in Arms* and *Strike Up the Band*, were traditional, youthful, putting-on-a-show stories. However, he was plotting at the same time as he was planning. In 1940 he brought a very successful New York stage-designer and director, Vincente Minnelli, to Hollywood just to have him hang around for a while, observe the film-making process and help out directing odd sequences for films. This slow lead-in brought results when, in 1943, Minnelli directed his first film for Freed – a version of the successful black musical *Cabin in the Sky*. This film, like *The Wizard of Oz*, was a fantasy but Minnelli directed it with unique ease and fluidity, slipping comfortably between dramatic scenes and musical numbers. Each musical interlude took the plot forward and the numbers seemed to arise naturally out of what had gone before, as either a sort of crystallization of emotion or excitement, or a pause for reflection. For once, there was nothing arbitrary about the introduction of the musical element as it was incorporated into the very texture of the film.

There were still a few more films to come from Arthur Freed's unit (now virtually an independent company within MGM) which more or less followed the traditional line in musical films. These films unobtrusively introduced the elements which were to become important in the new kind of musical at MGM. Judy Garland was being developed into an adult performer from film to film; in 1942 she had been given her first really grown-up role and a new leading man, Gene Kelly, in *For Me and My Gal*. Kelly had been discovered in the original Broadway production of the brightly cynical 1940 Rodgers and Hart musical *Pal Joey*. Freed signed him up and, although he was employed primarily as an actor-dancer, he was also being prepared for other things. He was allowed, almost from the start, to stage and choreograph his own numbers in films, usually in collaboration with his colleague from *Pal Joey*, Stanley Donen.

Another star who was to prove hardly less important in the MGM constellation, Fred Astaire, had also been introduced into Freed's films. His first important film after leaving Ginger Rogers and RKO – *Broadway Melody of 1940* (1940) – had been made for MGM, but not for Freed. Very soon afterwards he was set to work on Freed's giant wartime spectacular *Ziegfeld Follies* (1946), creating two of the biggest numbers 'Limehouse Blues' and 'This Heart of Mine' for it with a new dancing partner Freed was grooming for stardom – Lucille Bremer.

Long before *Ziegfeld Follies* was finished, (it took two years to make) the film appeared which, more than any other, established the new kind of musical with the moviegoing audience: *Meet Me in St Louis* (1944). Directed by Vincente Minnelli, this was the prime example of cinematic, American nostalgia: it was a simple story of a year in the life of an ordinary mid-Western family – the year leading up to the St Louis International Exposition of 1904. It had that rarest of all qualities in films – genuine charm – and it starred Judy Garland who was soon to become Minnelli's wife. In it she sings one of her theme-

tunes, 'The Trolley Song', and demonstrates an unexpected maturity as an actress – a natural comic with the power to break your heart if she wanted to.

In the next five years the Freed unit turned out classic musicals in an almost unending stream. Judy Garland was kept busy in *The Harvey Girls* (1946), *The Pirate* and *Easter Parade* (both 1948), all of which are among her best films, as well as making memorable guest appearances in the composer-biographies of Jerome Kern – *Till the Clouds Roll By* (1946) – and Rodgers and Hart – *Words and Music* (1948). Gene Kelly in *The Pirate* was perfectly matched against Garland and had some of his most intricate and stylish routines to a superb original Cole Porter score. Then, in *Take Me Out to the Ball Game* (1949), he was allowed, in collaboration with Donen and supervised by Busby Berkeley, to try his hand at writing and directing his own vehicle.

Fred Astaire starred in an ambitious, if none too successful, musical fantasy *Yolanda and the Thief* (1945) – co-starring Lucille Bremer and directed by

Minnelli – then shortly afterwards announced his retirement. In 1948, however, he was lured out of it by Freed to replace the ailing Gene Kelly in *Easter Parade* opposite Judy Garland. This was such a success for both the stars that the formula was immediately repeated in *The Barkleys of Broadway* (1949). But this time Judy Garland was ill and Freed brought back Ginger Rogers to replace her – she was dancing with Fred Astaire again after a ten-year gap.

Freed encouraged people talented in other spheres to bring their skills to the cinema. He found new directors – like ex-dancer-choreographer Charles Walters who made *Good News* (1947) and *Easter Parade*, and ex-jazz musician George Sidney who made *The Harvey Girls* and *Annie Get Your Gun* (1950). He also brought back Rouben Mamoulian who had once been famous as the director of *Applause* (1929) and *Love Me Tonight* (1932) to make *Summer Holiday* (1947). This was a new musical adaptation of Eugene O'Neill's *Ah, Wilderness!* which failed to revive Mickey Rooney's flagging career.

But the really exceptional thing about the Freed unit was the high standard of its work in all departments: the musical arrangements were done by people like Conrad Salinger, Lennie Hatton and Adolph Deutsch; special numbers by Roger Edens and Kay Thompson; choreography by Robert Alton and Eugene Loring; design by Jack Martin Smith, Merrill Pye and Randall Duell; scripts by Betty Comden and Adolph Green, and so on.

It is worth noting that most of the musicals made between *Cabin in the Sky* and *Take Me Out to the Ball Game* were still either period pieces or biographical pictures with show-business backgrounds and putting-on-a-show stories, where the musical numbers could as a rule be rationalized if anybody thought to question them. The next stage in the evolution of the musical came when Kelly and Donen were given a free rein to create *On the Town* (1949) – a contemporary, urban musical which would closely integrate song, dance and story. It was adapted from a successful Broadway show about three sailors on shore leave in New York, but for the screen it was almost completely rewritten and featured extensive location shooting on the street where, if they thought about it, nobody could seriously suppose that it ever really happened. The film gave Kelly one of his definitive roles as the wise-guy hero and Frank Sinatra was perfectly cast as his blushing sidekick and Ann Miller, for long a regular in MGM musicals, as the man-eating anthro-

Top left: Vincente Minnelli and Gene Kelly were two of the people who contributed to the fame of the Forties MGM musicals. Top: Eddie 'Rochester' Anderson is accompanied by Lena Horne in Cabin in the Sky – *the first all-black musical and Minnelli's directorial debut. Above: The* Band Wagon, *a satire about life on Broadway, stars Fred Astaire as a musical-comedy dancer trying to make a comeback. Left, top: Gene Kelly and Frank Sinatra in* Take Me Out to the Ball Game. *Left, below: Fred Astaire in* The Barkleys of Broadway

was brash energy, those involved in *The Band Wagon* (1953) – Minnelli, Astaire, Jack Buchanan and Cyd Charisse – favoured elegance and style. It was romantic, funny and nostalgic and was the putting-on-a-show musical to end all putting-on-a-show musicals. It told much of the uncomfortable truth about show-business as well as sending the audience out with the rousing reflection that 'That's Entertainment'.

This was pretty well the end of the great days of musicals at MGM, Kelly and Donen tried a strangely downbeat subject – the disenchantments of post-war life for the returning veteran – for their third directorial collaboration, *It's Always Fair Weather* (1955), before going their separate ways. Minnelli was less at home with the folksiness of *Brigadoon* (1954) and the broadness of *Kismet* (1955) and it is a matter of opinion whether he recovered his old form with *Gigi*. Mamoulian made one more musical, *Silk Stockings* (1957) with Fred Astaire and Cyd Char-

Above: in Ziegfeld Follies *Lucille Ball tames her 'panthers' in the 'Bring on the Beautiful Girls' sequence. Above right: Barbra Streisand* On a Clear Day You Can See Forever, *one of Minnelli's later musicals*

pologist ready to tap anyone into submission. The large cast worked more as a team than as so many stars in their settings.

The film was enormously popular and sparked off many other musicals in modern surroundings including Kelly's next big success, *An American in Paris* (1951), which he choreographed while Minnelli directed. Although it can be accused of pretentiousness and trying to be too knowing about French Impressionism and modern ballet, it contains some of the most exciting and imaginative sequences in the history of the American musical – including the long and controversial ballet sequence at the end. It also introduced Leslie Caron to the screen. She came from the Roland Petit Ballet and was to become an important star as the heroine of *Gigi* (1958) – the film which next to *An American in Paris* earned Freed the largest number of Oscars and plaudits.

Kelly and Donen as a directing team had another hit with *Singin' in the Rain* (1952) which is a compendium of songs by Freed and Nacio Herb Brown attached to a story about the coming of sound to Hollywood. It has good claim to be the best musical ever made. It certainly allows Kelly his finest few minutes in his solo routine during a torrential downpour against the background music of the title number. The film also makes the most of Donald O'Connor – a dancer and comic who seldom got the right chances – and gave Debbie Reynolds her first substantial chance.

Almost simultaneously another musical, often regarded as the best ever, was in the works. Whereas the forte of the Kelly–Donen musicals

The heyday of the musical was over, but new stars like Barbra Streisand carried on the tradition and familiar faces made welcome comebacks

isse, but it was generally felt, a little unfairly perhaps, to fade in comparison with its non-musical original *Ninotchka* (1939). After Minnelli's charming but minor film *Bells Are Ringing* (1960), Arthur Freed retired from musicals production.

It was not exactly the end of musicals in Hollywood. There were still the super-productions based closely on Broadway hits, to be made at regular intervals. Minnelli directed one – *On a Clear Day You Can See Forever* (1970) – and Kelly directed another – *Hello, Dolly!* (1969) – both starring the new wonder of the age, Barbra Streisand. After he left MGM, Stanley Donen directed one more wonderful musical *Funny Face* (1957) – which reunited most of the old MGM production team and brought together Fred Astaire and Audrey Hepburn with the music of George Gershwin.

When Gene Kelly and Fred Astaire were brought together as the singing-dancing compères of *That's Entertainment, Part 2* (1976), the second of MGM's musical anthologies which were tributes to its own past, Fred Astaire was already 77 and Gene Kelly 64, and there was no doubt that their point of view was entirely retrospective. But then, what marvellous wonders they had to remember.

Realism, Italian-style

After the false rhetoric of the Fascist regime had been exposed, Italian film-makers went in search of the truth and found it in everyday life

When the great Italian director Roberto Rossellini was asked to define neo-realism, he said:

'For me it is above all a moral position from which to look at the world. It then became an aesthetic position, but at the beginning it was moral.'

To understand both the moral and aesthetic position which informed neo-realism, as well as the forces which helped destroy it, it is necessary to begin with the economic, political, and social context in which it was born.

There were, of course, harbingers of a 'new realism' before Rossellini's *Roma, Città Aperta*

(1945, *Rome, Open City*). But when that film burst upon the international cinema scene in the immediate post-war years, neo-realism proper can be said to have begun. *Rome, Open City* was a direct product of the 'War of Liberation' taking place in Italy in 1945.

During 1943 and 1944, Italy had been torn apart. Mussolini's government had fallen, the new Badoglio government had surrendered to the invading Allied armies in the South while the Germans had occupied the North; anti-fascist Italians of every political and religious persuasion had been involved in the fighting to liberate their country and had been united by the struggle against fascism.

To film-makers and all other artists of the period it was clear that if the lies and empty rhetoric of the Mussolini government had brought Italy to agony, then a confrontation with reality, an encounter with 'truth' would save Italy. In terms of the cinema this meant the rejection of what had gone before, for although there were few blatant propaganda films made under the Fascist regime, the films that were produced in Italy during the war years had

little to do with Italian reality.

Some long-term benefits emerged from the Fascist government's control of the film industry. The huge studio complex of Cinecittà had been built and the Italian film school, Centro Sperimentale di Cinematografia, had already trained many important Italian film-makers. Not every film made under the Fascist regime was poor but none of them came close to touching the social reality of Italy; for the most part, they were slick, glossy, vacuous melodramas made entirely in the studios and featuring upper-middle-class characters. Collectively they were known as 'white telephone' films, a nickname that has come to typify film production in Italy under the Fascists.

Inspired by the 'War of Liberation', film-makers rejected the old cinema and its conventions. Their belief in showing 'things as they are' was placed in the service of the construction of a new Italy. In this way the moral and aesthetic principles of neo-realism were united. The manner and style of the new cinema was to be as much a statement as its subject-matter.

The theory of neo-realism was formulated in part from basic assumptions about the nature of cinema and its function in society, and in part from the early films of the movement. Theory and practice rarely coincided in one film and many were only superficially neo-realist films. Some astute Italian critics decried the use of neo-realist mannerisms to disguise purely commercial ventures (usually exploitative sexual melodramas) and the forcing of material which cried out for a different treatment into a neo-realist style.

Cesare Zavattini, the writer of Vittorio De Sica's major films, and a director himself in the Fifties, formulated the theory of neo-realism; cinema's task was no longer simply to 'entertain' in the usual sense of the word, but to confront audiences with

Above: Massimo Girotti in Visconti's Ossessione. *A stranger in a remote rural district, he finds casual work with a couple who run a roadhouse, seduces the wife and plots with her to murder the husband. Left: the hurried burial of a partisan in Rossellini's six-part film* Paisà, *about the resistance and liberation of Italy in 1944–45. Below: production shot from De Sica's* The Children Are Watching Us (1943), *not strictly a neo-realist film but one that anticipates the style, notably through its use of exterior shots and urban settings*

Above: a starkly realistic scene from La Terra Trema, *filmed several years before the term 'kitchen sink' was used to describe realist drama. The actors were non-professionals and the details of life in the Sicilian fishing community were totally authentic. Right: father and son (Lamberto Maggiorani and Enzo Staiola) walk the rain-soaked streets in* Bicycle Thieves. *Below right:* Sperduti nel Buio (Lost in Darkness), *a melodrama filmed in the slums of Naples, provides evidence of a realist style in Italian cinema as early as 1914. With its scrupulous attention to detail, its cracked walls and worn steps and its use of natural light, this film influenced several generations of Italian film-makers*

their own reality, to analyse that reality, and to unite audiences through a shared confrontation with reality. The most disheartening thing for the neo-realist film-makers must have been that this basic goal was not achieved, simply because Italian audiences remained indifferent or hostile to the films, preferring instead pure escapism. They had no desire to confront on the screen the depressing reality of their everyday lives.

If cinema was to present things 'as they are', it meant that fiction, particularly that derived from novels and plays, would have to be replaced by looser, rather 'open ended' narratives, based on real experience familiar to the film-makers or, perhaps,

found in newspapers. Zavattini cited the example of a woman buying a pair of shoes to show how simple such narratives could be and how social problems – poverty, unemployment, poor housing – could be illustrated within a fiction film.

Although most of the problems presented in neo-realist films were susceptible to political solution, the neo-realists never presented a clear political programme. Their party affiliations were, after all, quite diverse: a number of writers and directors were Marxists but just as many were Christian Democrats, or held various other political ideas.

The theorists, especially Zavattini, insisted that there was a natural affinity between the cinema and 'reality', despite the fact that a camera will record whatever is in front of the lens and that the processed film will then (depending upon the skill of the film-maker) convince a spectator of the 'reality' of what he is seeing. But it was never quite so simple and Zavattini frequently made it clear that, for him, the entire question remained ambiguous, that cinematic 'realism' was merely a convention, and that the neo-realist method was only one possible approach to cinema.

Inevitably audiences become accustomed to cinematic conventions, even those as initially 'shocking' as open-air shooting on real streets with non-professional actors. In *Rome, Open City* real locations were used for almost the entire film but no-one has complained (and very few people even knew) that the priest's room, the Gestapo headquarters and one apartment were constructed entirely in a studio and therefore broke the rules of authenticity. Similarly the theoretical principle that roles be played by 'real people' – which was partly an over-reaction to the artificiality of movie stars – became a convention in itself.

In De Sica's *Umberto D* (1951), the non-actor playing the role of the unemployed government official was in real life an elderly professor. He was highly praised for the 'reality' of his performance, but it was a performance; the professor had nothing in common with the character except age.

The only neo-realist film which followed the theory by having the entire cast made up of non-professionals was Visconti's *La Terra Trema* (1948,

Pure neo-realism lasted only for a few short years, although the style was soon absorbed into Italian popular cinema

The Earth Trembles). In that film, however Visconti rehearsed his village fishermen over and over again until they delivered the performances he wanted. They were effective, not so much because they were fishermen, but rather because they had been formed into good actors.

For some critics and film-makers, 'reality' meant 'social reality' and in particular the representation of the conditions of the poor and unemployed. Later, when directors like Rossellini and Visconti moved away from the working classes, they were denounced as 'betrayers of neo-realism', as if the middle classes were not a part of 'social reality'.

Social criticism was hardly lacking in neo-realist films, but it was rarely their major thrust. In De Sica's *Ladri di Biciclette* (1948, *Bicycle Thieves*) the camera pans along rows of pawned sheets while the protagonist attempts to pawn those belonging to his wife. Throughout the film we are made aware of the thousands of people like him, all seeking work. Yet the problem of unemployment is never analysed. Instead the story takes a dramatic turn as the protagonist steals a bicycle and is thus criminalized by his poverty. He is subsequently humiliated and finally 'redeemed'. At the end of the film we are moved by the man's plight, but we are no closer to an understanding of his social reality.

Visconti's *La Terra Trema* comes closest to being the perfect neo-realist film: it achieves a clear understanding of how the fishermen are exploited and of how this 'social reality' works to oppress people generally. Ironically, while the theory of neo-realism was fulfilled by *La Terra Trema*, Visconti violated one of Zavattini's fundamental tenets by basing the film on a novel, *I Malavoglia*, by the nineteenth-century writer Giovanni Verga, who is often mentioned by critics and film historians as one of the possible sources of Italian neo-realism.

Most of the arguments and polemics surrounding neo-realism had already been rehearsed in the nineteenth century. At that time the literary movements of the *verismo* novelists concerned themselves primarily with the lower classes and their problems. One of the stated goals of the verist writers was the social education of their readers. Such work, however, rarely reached the class which might have drawn benefit from it.

Most verist novelists, like the neo-realist directors, sought to increase their popularity by recounting routine shop-girl fantasies, cloaked in the mantle of realism. But a small core of film-makers remained faithful to the principles of neo-realism; among them were Giuseppe De Santis, who made *Caccia Tragica* (1947, *Tragic Pursuit*), a tale of robbery at a collective farm and *Roma Ore Undici* (1952, *Rome, Eleven O'Clock*), a memorable film of a real-life incident in which a staircase collapsed under the weight of two hundred girls who had all applied for the same job.

In tracing the origins of Italian neo-realism, 'realist' film styles can be detected in the early Italian cinema: even the historical spectaculars which gave Italian cinema its international reputation contain a vividly realistic streak.

The American cinema may also be evidenced as an antecedent of Italian neo-realism: it is clear, for example, that everyone working in Italian cinema of the Forties was familiar with such 'realist' classics as Vidor's *The Crowd* (1928) and Stroheim's

Greed (1924). Also influential was the so-called 'poetic realism' of Jean Renoir and his fellow film-makers in France during the Thirties. Visconti's own training as an assistant on *Toni* (1934) and his close study of Renoir's films is echoed in films like *Ossessione* (1942, *Obsession*) and *La Terra Trema*.

The 'War of Liberation' may have temporarily united Italians of diverse political beliefs and provided an inspiration for the neo-realists but the honeymoon was short-lived. After the liberation, anti-communist propaganda took root in Italy.

Although the social criticism of neo-realist cinema was essentially mild and non-Marxist, the films did illuminate problems in Italy that remained unsolved. In the immediate post-war climate, 'anti-fascist' had come to mean much the same thing as 'communist' and the government did not take too kindly to the image of the country that the neo-realist film-makers were projecting. For its part, the Church claimed that such films were unsympathetic to the clergy and even blasphemous.

Some neo-realist films had great success at the box-office, but for the most part they depended on foreign receipts to cover the costs of even the small budgets involved. The huge popularity of American films all but destroyed whatever financial basis the domestic market had for Italian films, neo-realist or otherwise. Gradually the producers, too, became hostile to the neo-realist style.

When the government appointed Giulio Andreotti as the head of Direzione Generale dello Spettacolo (an agency for overseeing the performing arts), he was given wide-ranging powers over the cinema. Andreotti controlled bank loans: he restricted them to 'suitable' films and vetoed loans on films which were 'infected with the spirit of neo-realism'. His powers went even further: Andreotti could, and often did, ban public screenings of films that he decided were 'not in the best interests of Italy'. Even more harmful were the bans on the exportation of films that maligned Italy. And it was these moves as much as anything else that brought about the demise of the neo-realist movement – but the seeds of Italian realism were safely sown.

The immediate inheritance of the neo-realist movement was to be evidenced in the Fifties, the decade that also saw the break up of the original core of directors – Rossellini, Visconti, De Sica and the young Antonioni. As their careers diverged and the political realities of Italy in the Fifties went through several changes, the Italian cinema gradually shed its mantle of neo-realism.

Top: in Riso Amaro (1948, Bitter Rice) *Silvana Mangano and Vittorio Gassman try to steal the rice crop from a small valley in the North of Italy. The film portrayed the painful labour of rice-growing with a documentary zeal, but its success at the box-office, both at home and abroad, was probably due to its erotic content (below left). Above:* Stromboli, *made in 1949, is a transitional film that bears the vestiges of the documentary style so beloved of the neo-realists, but also indicates the shift in Italian cinema towards the use of international stars in sensational dramas set against a background of rural poverty*

Directed by Vittorio De Sica, 1948
Prod co: Produzione De Sica (PDS). **prod:** Vittorio De Sica. **prod man:** Umberto Scarpelli. **sc:** De Sica, Oreste Bianco, Suso Cecchi d'Amico, Adolfo Franci, Gherardo Gherardi, Gerardo Guerrieri, adapted by Cesare Zavattini, from the novel by Luigi Bartolini. **photo:** Carlo Montuori. **ass photo:** Mario Montuori. **ed:** Eraldo da Roma. **art dir:** Antonio Traverso. **mus:** Alessandro Cicognini. **mus dir:** Willy Ferrero. **ass dir:** Gerardo Guerrieri. **r/t:** 90 minutes. Italian title: *Ladri di Biciclette*. Released in USA as *Bicycle Thief*, in GB as *Bicycle Thieves*.
Cast: Lamberto Maggiorani (*Antonio Ricci*), Enzo Staiola (*Bruno Ricci*), Lianella Carell (*Maria Ricci*), Vittorio Antonucci (*the thief*), Elena Altieri, Gino Saltamerenda, Giulio Chiari, Michele Sakara, Carlo Jachino, Nando Bruno, Fausto Guerzoni, Umberto Spadaro, Massimo Randisi.

With *Bicycle Thieves*, Vittorio De Sica came very close to perfecting the kind of realist film to which he hoped to dedicate himself as a director. His previous film, *Sciuscià* (1946, *Shoeshine*) had shown him freeing himself from the theatrical influences that had shaped his earlier work, and had also established the importance of the contribution that writer Cesare Zavattini could make to his films. It was Zavattini who adapted *Bicycle Thieves* from the novel by Luigi Bartolini. 'I had liked Bartolini's book,' said Zavattini in 1980. 'I thought it would make the basis for a good film. I think it was an inspired film idea, even if it was completely different from the book which was based on the author's own experience. Later, when the film came out, Bartolini

made a bit of a fuss, prompted by someone in the bourgeois press who hated the film. But Bartolini was quite aware of what we were going to do to his story when we paid him for the title.'

De Sica had to go the rounds of the producers trying to raise money to make *Bicycle Thieves*. He acted out all the parts for them to try and catch their interest, but no-one would back his picture. He went to France, where *Shoeshine* had been very successful, but the French producers said they'd be delighted to buy the film – after they had seen it. In London De Sica met the director-producer Gabriel Pascal who kept him locked up in his country home for a weekend to prevent him from going to Korda with the film, but then Pascal only offered £5000. In

the end De Sica found three Italian businessmen who were prepared to finance him.

In order to capture the kind of 'reality' that he and Zavattini felt was essential to the telling of the story, De Sica insisted on using only non-professional actors. He had even turned down a generous offer from David O. Selznick who was prepared to finance the film if Cary Grant played the central role of the bill-sticker.

To find the right non-professional for the main part, however, was not easy. In the end De Sica used a workman, Lamberto Maggiorani, who had brought his child to be auditioned for the part of the bill-stickers' ten-year-old son.

If in *Shoeshine* De Sica could still lapse into sentimentality, particularly in the ending, in *Bicycle Thieves* he showed restraint and a firm grip of film narrative. The subject-matter is grim and De Sica lets the bare facts dictate the style of the film. He avoids sentimentality even in the fade-out with the father and son – reunited after the humiliating scene in front of the stadium – walking off into the distance with a Chaplinesque resignation to life's pitfalls.

The Rome of *Bicycle Thieves* is not that of Mussolini's heroics, or of the German Occupation, or of Hollywood's many 'Roman Holidays' to come. Though the workman's bike is stolen in a street in the centre of the city, only a stone's throw from the Spanish Steps, the Rome that De Sica shows is that of the embankments by the sluggish and muddy Tiber, the flea markets

in the rain, the ugly suburban houses. It is a harsh setting and a sad story but De Sica enlivens it often with characteristic touches of humorous observation – the scene, for example, in the restaurant when Bruno tries to manage a knife and fork and is looked down on by the well-behaved middle-class boy; the caricatures of the fortune-teller and her clients, the charity helpers in the church, and the rowdy women protecting the thief in the brothel. Despite the intensity of Zavattini's political commitment and his own social conscience, De Sica was still able to make a film that, although a powerful cry of despair, never lapses into a shout of propaganda. It was clearly the work of an artist who had mastered a medium that for so long had only given him the chance to show his professional competence. De Sica commented on the film:

'What is so important about a bike in the Rome of 1948 where so many bikes are stolen every day? Yet for a worker who loses his means of support a stolen bike is a very tragic circumstance. Why should we, filmmakers, go in search of extraordinary adventures when we are confronted in our daily lives with facts that cause genuine anguish? Our literature has already explored this modern dimension that puts an emphasis on the smallest details of everyday life which are often dismissed as commonplace. The cinema has at its disposal the film camera which is the best medium for capturing this world. That's what I think this much-debated question of the new realism is all about.'

Antonio Ricci is an unemployed workman in his thirties, married with two children. He is offered a job as a bill-sticker on condition that he has his own bicycle. Ricci does have a bike but it is in a pawn shop. He has to pawn the family bed linen to get it out (1). Ricci goes to work the next day, but while he is sticking up a poster of Rita Hayworth (2) his bike is stolen (3). Many bikes are stolen every day in Rome and the police suggest he looks for the thief himself. Ricci, accompanied by his ten-year-old son Bruno, first searches the flea markets (4) where stolen bikes and parts are on sale. They see the thief talking to an old man whom they follow into an almshouse (5), but he slips away from them. Ricci takes

Bruno to eat in a smart restaurant in order to forget their problems for a while (6).

When Ricci sees the thief again he follows him into a brothel (7), but the young man denies the charge. In the street the crowd turns on Ricci and the thief has an epileptic fit. Nobody can prove anything. In despair, Ricci and Bruno sit outside the football stadium and listen to the crowd roaring inside. Ricci sends Bruno away and on an impulse steals an unguarded bike (8). He is caught immediately but the owner doesn't bring charges. Bruno has watched his father's humiliation They walk away – at first separated, but then together as Bruno offers his hand in comfort and solidarity (9).

5

6

8

9

Cinema of the Rising Sun

Against all odds, the Japanese film industry made a dynamic recovery in the years after the war. Its commercial progress was matched by the new cultural and artistic trends set by directors like Ozu, Kurosawa and Mizoguchi, who were making bold attempts to reflect contemporary attitudes in their films

The dropping of the atomic bombs on Hiroshima and Nagasaki in August 1945 brought an already weakened Japan to its knees. Within a few days the American occupying forces under the leadership of General Mac-Arthur had accepted Japan's surrender and commenced the process of 'democratizing' what the Allies regarded as an essentially feudal state. This entailed breaking down all the old feudal allegiances in commerce, politics and society in general, and the establishing of equal rights for all. The changes in the structure and operation of industry that were forced on the defeated country affected virtually every aspect of life. The cinema did not escape the upheavals.

Japan had tended to depict its long tradition of a highly structured, feudalistic society very firmly in its films. Prior to the war many films had been made which roused and reinforced the people's loyalty to the Emperor and the ideals of the nation. During the war such movies had become more overtly propagandist, and it was these to which the new American censors turned their attention. Of the 554 films from the war years, 225 were judged to be feudal or anti-democratic and were ordered to be destroyed. The Occupation forces not only censored completed films, but also kept a watchful eye on new scripts. Kon Ichikawa's puppet film *Musume Dojiji* (1946, *Girl at the Dojo Temple*) was burned simply because he had not submitted the script for approval.

At the start of the war all Japanese film companies had been amalgamated, but afterwards they were allowed to start up production as independent studios again. Censorship control was handed to the Civil Information and Education Section (CI & E) of MacArthur's Supreme Command Allied Forces in the Pacific (SCAP) in March 1946. Japanese films were subject to its rulings for the next four years but, freed from this yoke, production exploded in the Fifties and Sixties. Another reason for this boom was the physical rebuilding of the industry, especially the cinemas. In October 1945 there were only 845 cinemas in operation; more than half of the pre-war cinemas had been destroyed in the bombing, although the majority of the studios had miraculously escaped damage. By January of 1946 the number had increased to 1137 cinemas; this rate of building continued so that by 1957 it had reached the astonishing total of 6000.

There were, however, negative and destructive influences at work, including the search by the CI & E for war criminals. The task of naming these was given to the Japanese Motion Picture and Drama Employees Union; but the Americans, failing to realize that this union was largely communist-controlled, thereby unleashed a wave of political revenge rather than justice, and many who were banned from the industry had to fight for twenty years or more for reinstatement.

Meanwhile, the democratization process (which gave workers the initiative to seek greater powers), coupled with a colossal, crippling tax on the box-office returns, caused

Left: poster from Hiroshi Inagaki's Musashi Miyamoto *(1954–55,* Samurai*), a three-part colour remake of his 1941 version. The earlier film was one of the better-quality Japanese films to survive the post-war censorship purge by the American occupying forces*

terrible strife in the studios and strikes resulted. Toho, the company that gained a virtual monopoly after the war, suffered a spectacular 'work-in' in 1948 which was eventually broken by two thousand police supported by a cavalry company, seven armoured cars and three planes from the US Eighth Army. Few films were produced during this period and it was not until 1949 that a balanced pattern emerged with five major companies carving up the market between them; these were Toho, Toei, Shochiku, Daiei and Shin Toho. Toho, for example, became the main distributors for period films. Daiei had previously specialized in military films, so obviously, in the post-war climate, had to seek new material; the choice of films full of sex and violence may not have made them readily exportable, but their product was sufficiently popular at home to allow the company to rebuild its finances. Shochiku survived on domestic comedies, but in the Fifties these lost favour with audiences and the studio suffered a few lean years until it developed its enormously popular *yazuka*, or gangster films. With these new trends, Japanese film production expanded from 67 films in 1946 to the staggering total of 547 in 1960, by which time 18 companies were in business (the five majors plus a series of small independent companies).

After the war, all the precepts by which the Japanese had lived were being questioned, and writers, artists and film-makers had to cope with new ideas imposed by the West. Some indulged in recrimination; some, like Yasujiro Ozu, retreated to the conservatism of what might be called an essentially Japanese view of life; while others, like Akira Kurosawa, sought to find a balance between old and new values. Despite the problems they faced, some of the greatest talents in Japanese – and world – cinema worked throughout this period and prepared the ground for the glories of the Fifties and Sixties.

Whereas before and during the war the predominant mode of thought in Japan was of group identity (nation, family or company), the post-war turmoil generated what was for the Japanese an unfamiliar concept: that each person had to work out his or her own future. Film-makers started to examine the new ideo-

logies, and the radical importance of this can only be fully appreciated in realizing the strength of the traditionalist views of parental power in Japan, of the obedience of children and the veneration of the family as a unit, and especially the great extent to which pre-war cinema had upheld these beliefs.

Ozu acknowledged the fragmentation of the traditional group ethic in *Nagaya Shinsi Roku* (1947, *Record of a Tenement Gentleman*) in which a boy, roaming the streets amongst physical and moral disorder, seeks and finds his father. The failure of the family to provide the virtues of stability are exemplified in the boy's rejection of his father and the foster mother's 'un-Japanese' reaction to the loss of the boy (in setting up a home for war orphans she moves outside the accepted family support structure). Yet at the same time the family group remains the only hope there is for stability and order. *Kaze No Naka No Mendori* (*A Hen in the Wind*), made the following year, is a melodramatic story of a mother, awaiting the return of her husband from the war, who is compelled to become a prostitute to support her sick child. It was not until 1949 with *Banshun* (*Late Spring*) that Ozu returned to the narrative style that he had begun to develop before the war. His best films have little or no story but examine a quality that has been

Above left: the filming of Kurosawa's crime story Stray Dog. *Above: a father (Chishu Ryu) prepares to give away his daughter (Setsuko Hara) in Ozu's* Late Spring. *Below left: prostitutes in* Women of the Night. *Below right: a political prisoner in* My Love Has Been Burning. *Both films were typical studies of women by Mizoguchi.*

termed *mono-no-aware* – an acceptance of things as they are. This view of life is not fatalistic but depends rather on a calm belief in a world that changes slowly around one. At the end of *Late Spring*, a daughter has gone to be married and her father is left alone, resigned but content. The quiet, controlled style of this and other Ozu films was to become better known in the West after the success of *Tokyo Monogatari* (1953, *Tokyo Story*).

Daisuke Ito had previously specialized in the period film, but after the war he became one of the first directors to expose the resurgence of the gangster in urban life in his film *Oshó* (1947, *The Chess King*). Tadoshi Imai, who had shown his support for Japanese Imperialism in such films as *Boro No Kesshitai* (1943, *Suicide Troops of the Watch Tower*), turned against the feudal code with *Minshu No Teki* (1946, *An Enemy of the People*), a call for communist-based political action. A more humanistic approach was evident in his later film, *Aoi*

Above: Ito's The Chess King. *Above right: Imai's* Blue Mountains, *which explored the generation gap in post-war Japan. Below: Kinoshita's* Broken Drum, *which traced the breakdown of parental authority. Below right: Toshiro Mifune in* Drunken Angel

Sammyaku (1949, *Blue Mountains*), which examined teenage love and parental authority. The popularity of this particular film may have resided in its attack on the rigid views of the parents – a stance unthinkable before the war – and thereby on the basis of the family. Keisuke Kinoshita's *Yabure-Daiko* (*Broken Drum*), made the same year, showed the futility of a father trying to hold a family together with feudal authority. Kinoshita had attacked traditional family values two years earlier with *Kekkon* (1947, *Marriage*), showing that a girl can make up her own mind to marry the man of her choice.

Part of the search for new ideas – some of which bordered on the anarchic – led to the reconsideration of the woman's place in Japanese society. Directors such as Kenji Mizoguchi had long been concerned with the plight of women, but few had dared to make honest exposés of their subservient position. The new post-war freedom encouraged the fight for women's liberation. Mizoguchi in *Joyu Sumako No Koi* (1947, *The Loves of Actress Sumako*), and Teinosuke Kinugasa, in *Joyu* (1947, *The Actress*) both celebrated the heroic figure of Sumako Matsui, an actress who had earlier struck a major blow for the emancipation of women by playing Ibsen heroines in the newly formed *Shingeki* theatre. This had been the first entry of social drama into a traditional theatre dominated by *onnagatu*, male actors playing female roles.

Already famous before the war for his studies of women in such films as *Naniwa Ereji* (1936, *Naniwa Elegy*), *Gion No Shimai* (1936, *Sisters of the Gion*) and *Zangiku Monogatari* (1939, *The Story of the Last Chrysanthemums*),

Mizoguchi had avoided the worst excesses of nationalism during the war by setting his stories back in history and making them intensely personal. During the immediate post-war years he made *Josei No Shori* (1946, *Women's Victory*), a long-promised film about women fighting for and gaining professional posts with the law courts, and *Waga Koi Wa Moeru* (1949, *My Love Has Been Burning*), dealing with the part played by women in active politics. The competence and strength of women is a subject that threads its way through many of Mizoguchi's films, particularly those with a modern setting.

Even his *Utamaro O Meguro Gonin No Onna* (1946, *Five Women Around Utamaro*), the story of a famous artist set in feudal times, deals with the way in which women are exploited, and his most famous film of this period, *Yoru No Onnatachi* (1948, *Women of the Night*), is an unsentimental portrayal of the life of post-war prostitutes – a film largely instrumental in changing the laws governing prostitution.

Kurosawa, after an apprenticeship with Kajiro Yamamoto, directed his first film, *Sugata Sanshiro* (1943, *Sanshiro Sugata – The Judo Story*), during the most nationalistic period. Immediately after the war he made a series of films each of which concentrated on an individual having to work out a course of action for him or herself. There is much of the humanist in Kurosawa, but there is also something essentially feudal. In his early films the *sensei-deshi*, or master-pupil, relationship on which many, but not all, of his later films were to pivot is clearly discernible. Perhaps Kurosawa's greatest gift, supporting his great narrative strength, is his psychological insight into character. It is rare to find clearly defined 'good' or 'bad' people in his films.

Waga Seishin Ni Kuinashi (1946, *No Regrets for Our Youth*) looked back to the political turmoil that had preceded the war and centred on a young woman who, when her illusions of people are shattered and the man she loves dies in prison, chooses to live the life of a peasant

with the man's parents. The villagers turn out to be as harsh and unjust as those people she had known in politics, yet she makes a conscious choice to stay and carry out what she sees as her duty.

The conflict between will and honour or duty, the key to much Japanese literature, is turned by Kurosawa, in his films, into a modern, self-determined driving force. *Yoidore Tenshi* (1948, *Drunken Angel*) tells the story of a gangster (the first starring role for Toshiro Mifune) befriended by an alcoholic doctor who tries to cure him of his tuberculosis; the action centres round a festering pond that symbolizes the rotting heart of the lower depths of society. At the end the gangster is killed and, although little seems to have changed, along the way the story gives several lessons in humanity by showing how, though morally tarnished, people still help each other. *Shizukanaru Ketto* (1949, *The Quiet Duel*) is about a doctor (Mifune) who, during an operation, becomes infected with syphilis from a patient. From this point his own life has to be reassessed as he turns away from the woman he loves and tracks down the infected man. It is a flawed film, however, lacking the psychological strength evident in his next film, *Nora Inu* (1949, *Stray Dog*). This is based on a true story of a detective (Mifune again) whose gun is stolen. With his section chief (Takashi Shimura), he follows a chain of clues deeper and deeper into the criminal underworld. The thief is not seen until the end of the film, yet it is the relationship between the three characters that opens up aspects of human will and perseverance. After a fight in a paddy field the detective eventually captures the thief but, by this time, they are all so covered with mud that 'good' and 'bad' are indistinguishable. This fine film, with its questions about who is really on the side of law and justice, was a precursor to *Rashomon* (1950), the film with which Kurosawa entered a new decade and thrust the Japanese cinema before a worldwide public once more.

Preston Sturges:

A pretty girl is better than a plain one
A leg is better than an arm
A bedroom is better than a living room
An arrival is better than a departure
A birth is better than a death
A chase is better than a chat
A dog is better than a landscape
A kitten is better than a dog
A baby is better than a kitten
A kiss is better than a baby
A pratfall is better than anything

Preston Sturges' Golden Rules for Successful Comedy

Comedy with a kick

'I make no claim to any artistic ambition, I am merely a story-teller . . . and success is judged only by how many persons see your pictures.'

Preston Sturges, one of the giants of screen comedy, was 'different'. He was the screen-writer who dispensed with collaborators and then with directors, pioneering the idea that the scribes could sometimes successfully direct their own work. For five hectic years, Sturges had the satisfaction of delighting audiences and critics with a succession of films he wrote and directed himself, including *The Great McGinty* (1940), *The Lady Eve*, *The Palm Beach Story* (both 1941) and *Hail the Conquering Hero* (1944).

After this frantic display of creative energy during the early Forties, Sturges seemed to have burnt himself out; although he kept on working, further success largely eluded him. Nevertheless, Sturges' achievements were as remarkable as those of Woody Allen today; like Allen, and despite his hankering for popular success, Sturges expressed an intensely personal vision of life.

Born in 1898, Sturges came from an unconventional background, shunted – at six-

Right: Henry Fonda, Barbara Stanwyck and Preston Sturges pose for a production shot during the filming of The Lady Eve, *the romantic farce which helped to launch Sturges as a writer and director*

monthly intervals – between a mother in Paris and a stepfather in Chicago. The mother claimed to have dosed the infant with champagne to cure a bronchial ailment that threatened his life. Being the closest friend of Isadora Duncan, she also dosed him with excessive helpings of art and music. By contrast, his stepfather taught him to ride a bicycle and showed him the business world.

Sturges went to work as manager of one of his mother's beauty salons, created a kiss-proof lipstick and then set out to be a freelance inventor without much financial success. While in hospital in 1927, recovering from appendicitis, he turned his thoughts towards playwriting. *Strictly Dishonorable* was a runaway success on Broadway in 1929; Hollywood snapped up this romantic comedy for filming in 1931 and Sturges was hired to write dialogue for the early sound pictures being shot in New York.

Meanwhile, he continued writing in his own time and sold one of his screenplays to an enthusiastic Jesse Lasky in Hollywood. It was filmed at Fox and called *The Power and the Glory* (1933). It displayed the typical Sturges preoccupation with success in its story of a

railroad magnate's phenomenal career rising from humble beginnings to despairing suicide and was daringly constructed in non-chronological flashbacks.

Then came the screenplays of such comedies as *Easy Living* (1937), in which a discarded mink coat sets off a train of events that causes Wall Street to crash – then rise again for the happy ending – and *Remember the Night* (1940), both directed by Mitchell Leisen.

However, Sturges felt that he could do a better job of shooting his scripts and persuaded Paramount to let him direct *The Great McGinty* on a small budget, if he sold the studio his screenplay for a mere ten dollars. The comedy – a cynical study of American political chicanery in which a corrupt governor, played by Brian Donlevy, attempts to reform under the influence of a good woman and has to flee the country – was a big hit and won Sturges an Oscar in 1941. Like *The Great McGinty*, *The Lady Eve* was the story of a man, this time played by Henry Fonda, who is putty in the hands of a determined woman.

In *Sullivan's Travels* (1941), Sturges made an extraordinary justification for screen comedy in telling the story of a young and successful

JOEL McCREA ★ VERONICA LAKE

SULLIVAN'S TRAVELS

ROBERT WARWICK · WILLIAM DEMAREST
MARGARET HAYES · PORTER HALL
FRANKLIN PANGBORN · ERIC BLORE

Top left: Jimmy Conlin, Brian Donlevy and Dewey Robinson in The Great McGinty. *Top right: Ellen Drew and Dick Powell in* Christmas in July *(1948). Above: Joel McCrea as Sullivan researches the hobo life for his film in* Sullivan's Travels *and (above right) in more familiar surroundings. Far right: Joel McCrea as Morton tests his anaesthetic in* The Great Moment. *Below:* Mad Wednesday *with Harold Lloyd and Jimmy Conlin*

Hollywood director, much like Sturges himself, who is tempted to make a serious picture about poverty, goes off to do some research as a hobo and discovers that the people need his gift for humour: 'Laughter is all some people have.'

Two uncomfortably hard-hitting satires won Sturges Oscar nominations for best screenplays. *The Miracle of Morgan's Creek* (1943) and *Hail the Conquering Hero*. Both starred Eddie Bracken as a nervous small-town figure, mistakenly acclaimed as the father of quintuplets in one and as a war hero in the

other. The former film had a delayed release owing to censorship problems; a pregnant heroine is about to bear illegitimate offspring as a result of an in-haste marriage that is not properly recorded. The latter film managed to make Bracken's Woodrow Truesmith a sympathetic character even though he masqueraded as a war hero. Unfit for military service, owing to hayfever, Truesmith is unable to emulate his father's heroic effort in World War I. He is concerned at disappointing his mother and so agrees to the masquerade suggested by real marine heroes – and duly squirms with embarrassment at the consequences.

The Great Moment was also released in 1944, and is the biography of the nineteenth-century dentist W.T.G. Morton, who may have discovered anaesthetics. Sturges relieved a rather grim and downbeat story with 'injections' of slapstick comedy and arranged it to end on an uplifting note when the dentist (Joel McCrea) reveals his discovery to end someone's immediate pain instead of patenting it for personal benefit. As in *The Great McGinty*, the noble gesture ends in personal ruin. Filmed in 1943, then shelved for a year, *The Great Moment* was the one commercial flop of Sturges' golden years from 1940 to 1944.

All his films during this period were an extraordinary blend of sophistication and slapstick, of verbal and visual humour. The subsidiary roles were taken by a gallant band of largely unsung supporting actors, who made richly idiosyncratic contributions to the proceedings. William Demarest had substantial roles in all of them, and portly Robert Greig, prissy Franklin Pangborn, jittery, sparrow-like

Jimmy Conlin, burly Dewey Robinson, ostrich-necked Torben Meyer, monotoned Harry Hayden, and blowzy Esther Howard were among the ageing players who made up the unofficial Preston Sturges stock company. Many of them appeared together in *The Palm Beach Story* as the Ale and Quail Club, a sporting bunch of millionaires who adopt the film's heroine as a mascot and shoot up their carriage on a train in a bout of drunken revelry.

Preston Sturges parodied the American success story. He celebrated the unpredictability of fate and the sudden reversals of fortune that mocked the ethic of hard work rewarded. His leading men were usually innocents, ill-equipped to deal with life but sticking their necks out, inviting the confusion and chaos that descends upon them. Sturges' heroes succeed when they least expect or deserve it. Norval Jones (Eddie Bracken) has 'greatness thrust upon him' in *The Miracle of Morgan's*

Filmography
1930 The Big Pond (co-dial only); Fast and Loose (dial only). **'33** The Power and the Glory (GB: Power and Glory) (sc only). **'34** Thirty Day Princess (co-sc); We Live Again (co-sc); Imitation of Life (adapt uncredited). **'35** The Good Fairy (sc); Diamond Jim (co-sc); The Gay Deception (song lyrics only). **'36** Next Time We Love (GB: Next Time We Live) (adapt uncredited); One Rainy Afternoon (song lyrics only). **'37** Hotel Haywire (sc); Easy Living (sc). **'38** Port of Seven Seas (sc); If I Were King (sc). **'39** Never Say Die (co-sc). **'40** Remember the Night (sc); The Great McGinty (GB: Down Went McGinty) (+sc); Christmas in July (+sc). **'41** The Lady Eve (+sc);

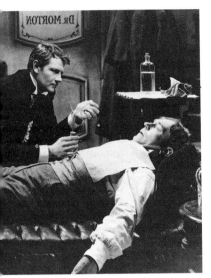

Creek when he receives the credit for fathering the quintuplets.

Unfortunately, Sturges' own career was to take as big a dip as that of any of his heroes. He left Paramount in 1944 to join up with Howard Hughes, expecting more artistic freedom and a bigger income from a share in the profits. However, their first production, *The Sin of Harold Diddlebock* (1946), was stalled by the post-war shortage of film stock and then by the whim of Hughes, who withdrew it for re-editing and finally re-released it as *Mad Wednesday* in 1950.

A come-back picture for Harold Lloyd, *Mad Wednesday* re-introduced the cliff-hanger 'thrill comedy' for which Lloyd was famous, showing the exhilarating result of a meek clerk's spending spree after he is fired from his job of 20 years. In one memorable moment, a veteran bartender accepts the challenge of providing the teetotal Diddlebock with his first drink. 'Sir, you arouse the artist in me,' he

declares – yet another example of how people are stimulated by the activity that Sturges' plots generate.

However, the partnership with Hughes did not live up to Sturges' expectations and they broke up. In 1948 Sturges was hired at a phenomenal salary by 20th Century-Fox. Unfortunately he failed to earn his keep. *Unfaithfully Yours* (1948) was a dazzlingly imaginative, complex comedy about an irascible musician who devises various solutions to the apparent infidelity of his young wife as he conducts a concert. When he tries to put them into effect, he finds that what seems simple in the mind's eye is fraught with difficulties in practice. It was a box-office failure.

Sturges finished his Hollywood career with another flop. *The Beautiful Blonde From Bashful Bend* (1949) starred one of 20th Century-Fox's hottest stars, Betty Grable, and was a very expensive Western satire that came out as a crude hillbilly farce. The old skill with actors remained, but suddenly in this one film Sturges' sense of style and timing, his visual and verbal ingenuity, mysteriously collapsed.

He returned to the theatre and later went to live in France where he shot his last film – an efficiently-made but impersonal bilingual – *The Diary of Major Thompson/Les Carnets du Major Thompson* (1955). Back in New York, he negotiated a huge advance to write his memoirs, piquantly entitled *The Events Leading Up to My Death*; the last chapter came ahead of schedule when Sturges died in mid-manuscript – he was only 60.

Preston Sturges was more than just a writer: his films were technically adventurous – as illustrated by the long takes in many of them –

Top left: Claudette Colbert as the mascot of the Ale and Quail Club in The Palm Beach Story. *Top right: Porter Hall, Betty Hutton and Eddie Bracken in* The Miracle of Morgan's Creek. *Above left: Bracken again as a nervous, reluctant hero. Above: Betty Grable as* The Beautiful Blonde From Bashful Bend. *Below:* Les Carnets du Major Thompson *starred Jack Buchanan and Noel-Noel but had none of Sturges' old flair*

and he knew and loved the medium, frequently paying homage to other great directors. The projection-room scene of *Sullivan's Travels* draws on *Citizen Kane* (1940) just as Welles' film drew on the earlier *The Power and the Glory*.

William Wyler wrote this of him in 1975:
'I never could make a good film without a good writer – but neither could Preston Sturges. Only he had one with him all the time. He was a true *auteur*, the compleat creator of his own films.'

Sullivan's Travels (+sc); The Palm Beach Story (+sc). '42 Star Spangled Rhythm (as himself). '43 The Miracle of Morgan's Creek (+sc). '44 The Great Moment (+sc); Hail the Conquering Hero (+sc). '46 The Sin of Harold Diddlebock (re-issued as Mad Wednesday, 1950) (+sc). '47 I'll Be Yours (sc. basis). '48 Unfaithfully Yours (+prod;+sc). '49 The Beautiful Blonde From Bashful Bend (+prod;+sc). '51 Vendetta (add dir;+sc). '55 Les Carnets du Major Thompson (USA: The French, They Are a Funny Race; GB: The Diary of Major Thompson) (FR) (+sc). '56 The Birds and the Bees (sc. basis). '58 Paris Holiday (act only); Rock-a-bye Baby (sc. basis).

John Huston: Teller of Tall Tales

After forty years as a director, during which only a handful of his films have been acclaimed as masterpieces, Huston was till recently reckoned as little more than a story-teller. But opinion is warming, and posterity may well find Huston the most inventive director of his generation

One of John Huston's most engaging character creations was Huston himself: the tall, craggily handsome, elegantly loping, irresistibly charming man with an insatiable zest for life – for horses, women, booze, gambling, adventure, work, reading, art, the Irish, and for almost everything else in the world.

It must be confessed that Huston's incorrigible love for a character and his seductive gift as a story-teller may have slightly obscured the record of his early life; and pleasant tales like that of the grandfather who won and lost townships at poker seem to have only flimsy foundations.

The clear facts are that Huston was born on August 5, 1906, in Nevada, Missouri, and christened John Marcellus. His father Walter Huston (1884–1950) moved from engineering to vaudeville and by the Twenties became a distinguished stage actor. With the coming of sound, the elder Huston drifted, inevitably, to

Hollywood. John's parents separated when he was still a child and he divided his boyhood between his father's theatrical lodgings and the hardly less erratic life of his mother, a newspaper-woman with a passion for travel and horses which she passed on to her son. As a child he was delicate; he once told the critic James Agee that he had cured himself – and at the same time acquired his life-long delight in adventure – by breaking out of a sanatorium nightly to plunge into an icy stream and shoot a waterfall.

In his teens he was a boxing champion. At 20 he made the first of several marriages. On account of his horsemanship he briefly held a commission in the Mexican army. He wrote a book which retold the story of *Frankie and Johnny* and is said to be a mature and accomplished work; this led to the publication of several of Huston's short stories in major magazines. Still restless, he lived as a café sketch artist in Paris, moved in the fringes of the Bohemian set in London, acted a bit, edited a New York magazine and finally arrived in Hollywood, where he married for the second time, in 1931.

Thanks to the influence of his father, who had so risen in the ranks of Hollywood actors as to have played the title role in D.W. Griffith's *Abraham Lincoln* (1930), Huston was taken on as a writer at Warners. His first assignment was to work on the script of *A House Divided* (1932) directed by William Wyler, who was only four years his senior but whom he came

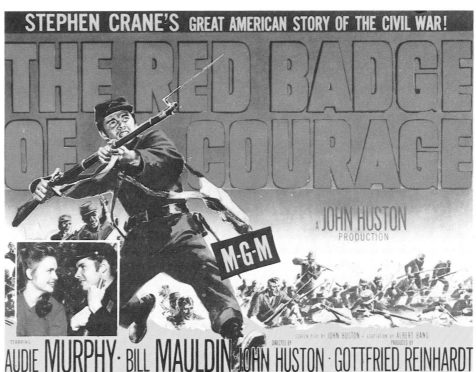

Far left: Huston the actor as Noah in The Bible – In the Beginning. *Above left: the 1948 classic* The Treasure of the Sierra Madre *in which Huston's father Walter (far left) teamed up with Bogart. Above: another of Bogart's roles was in* Key Largo, *Huston's last film for Warners. Left: Bogart and Katharine Hepburn on board* The African Queen. *Right:* The Red Badge of Courage *launched Audie Murphy's brief career. Below: Captain Ahab (Gregory Peck) loses his battle with the white whale in* Moby Dick

to regard as his master. The list of scripts on which Huston worked at Warners was impressive: Robert Florey's *Murders in the Rue Morgue* (1932), Wyler's *Jezebel* and Anatole Litvak's *The Amazing Dr Clitterhouse* (both 1938), William Dieterle's *Juarez* (1939) and *Dr Ehrlich's Magic Bullet* (1940), Raoul Walsh's *High Sierra* and Howard Hawks' *Sergeant York* (both 1941). Henry Blanke, who produced several Huston films, remembered him on his arrival in Hollywood as 'just a drunken boy; hopelessly immature. You'd see him at every party . . . with a monkey on his shoulder. Charming. Very talented, but without an ounce of discipline in his make-up.'

By 1941, however, Huston had clearly convinced Warners that he was mature enough to be trusted with direction. Jack Warner told him that if he could make a screenplay out of Dashiell Hammett's *The Maltese Falcon* – already filmed twice before – he would let him direct it. Huston's version of the story is that as a first step he and the writer Allen Rivkin began simply breaking the novel into separate scenes and dialogue, but eventually left the task to Huston's secretary. This mechanical breakdown fell into the hands of Jack Warner, who pronounced it 'great' and told Huston to go ahead. Huston undoubtedly likes to give the impression that his work has been the result of this kind of 'accident' and chance and gag; but it seems a tallish story – particularly since on other occasions, more recently in *Wise Blood* (1979), Huston has avoided reworking to an unrecognizable degree the work of famous authors, but has chosen novels from which he can cleanly extract his scripts.

More convincing is Huston's account of the advice of his producer Henry Blanke: 'Shoot each scene as if it is the most important one in the picture. Make every shot count. Nothing can be overlooked, no detail overlooked.' The advice was evidently followed; the casting was perfect and Huston's first feature film remains, after 40 years, a classic.

Huston's succeeding films did not sustain the first promise. *In This Our Life* (1942) was a Bette Davis vehicle hurried out in the wake of the success of *Jezebel* and *The Little Foxes* (1941). *Across the Pacific* (1942) was a spy comedy-thriller reassembling most of the team from *The Maltese Falcon* to no great effect. Huston was then called to war service and made three short films for the army – *Report From the Aleutians* (1943), *San Pietro* (1945) and *Let There Be Light* (1946). The last, which dealt with mentally affected war veterans, was never shown; but it did provide Huston with valuable material and inspiration when he came to make *Freud* (1962) 16 years later.

He returned to Warners to make another classic in 1948. *The Treasure of the Sierra Madre*, based on a novel by the mysterious writer B. Traven, had a theme which recalled *The Maltese Falcon* story and recurred throughout Huston's later work – a group of people in passionate, even murderous, quest for some object which will in the end prove only an illusion. Humphrey Bogart was teamed with Walter Huston in his most memorable performance. Huston's last assignment for Warners was *Key Largo* (1948), which had a fine cast (Bogart, Lauren Bacall, Edward G. Robinson and Lionel Barrymore) but remained an essentially stagebound adaptation of a pre-war play by Maxwell Anderson.

Huston's next film, *We Were Strangers* (1949), was less than successful, although a good deal of vitality remains in its story of Cuban revolutionaries tunneling, for slightly obscure reasons, through a graveyard. At MGM Huston enjoyed some success and won Oscar nominations for *The Asphalt Jungle* (1950), a taut story of urban crime filmed in the hard realistic style of the period. MGM, despite Louis B. Mayer's reservations, next permitted Huston to direct a favourite novel – Stephen Crane's *The Red Badge of Courage* (1951). Lillian Ross's book *Picture*, a day-by-day account of the making of the film, tells how it fell victim to studio politics in the days of MGM's decline, eventually emerging in a heavily cut 69-minute version. Still, much of the quality survives in the portrait of a boy's reactions to war and in the performance of Audie Murphy, a World War II veteran who was launched by the film into short-lived stardom.

The African Queen (1951), scripted by Agee from C.S. Forester's novel – with Bogart as the boozy riverboat captain and Katharine Hepburn as the starchy missionary who becomes his unlikely ally against the German army in Africa – was to be one of Huston's most successful films. It was also the first of several times that cast and crew suffered from his delight in adventure. He insisted on filming in

Above: The Asphalt Jungle – *which included Marilyn Monroe and Louis Calhern – won Oscar nominations. Above right: Richard Burton confronts Sue Lyon in the film of Tennessee Williams' play* The Night of the Iguana. *Far right:* The Misfits *was to be the last film for Clark Gable – here enjoying the company of Monroe*

the Congo, despite the heat, insects and disease which afflicted the unit – though not, apparently, the director. Errol Flynn, Trevor Howard and the unit of *The Roots of Heaven* (1958) were later to suffer even more in Chad.

Established as a major Hollywood director, from this point Huston seemed to lose clear direction and cohesion. Despite his feelings for art, the next film *Moulin Rouge* (1952) – with José Ferrer stumbling about on his knees in impersonation of the stunted Toulouse Lautrec – was a conventional Hollywood biopic. *Beat the Devil* (1953) – evidently seeking to retrieve the lost times of *The Maltese Falcon*, with Bogart, Peter Lorre and Robert Morley as a latter day Sydney Greenstreet – had the sort of slackness that has sometimes seemed symptomatic of Huston's tendency to see a film as a personal party. *Moby Dick* (1956), despite Huston's subsequent loyal defence of Gregory Peck's wooden performance, was a pale shadow of Herman Melville's novel. The bold experiments with colour, made in collaboration with the English cameraman Ossie Morris, were to be developed later in *Reflections in a Golden Eye*.

Huston's next major achievement was *The Misfits* (1961), which emerged from a stormy and much publicized production period as a

sad, elegaic drama of doomed people – a divorcee and three men hunting mustang in Nevada. Perhaps only Huston could have survived the constant attention of the press and nursed his ailing cast through Arthur Miller's script. There was Marilyn Monroe, suffering from acute personality disorders and drug dependence; Montgomery Clift in a comparable condition; and Clark Gable who was to die from a heart attack almost immediately after shooting was completed.

Huston also directed Clift in the actor's last major film role, *Freud* (1962), which failed to gain critical or commercial success. *The List of Adrian Messenger* (1963) was a gimmicky thriller; but Huston's adaptation of Tennesse Williams' *The Night of the Iguana* (1964) had at least a picturesque cast (Richard Burton, Ava Gardner and Deborah Kerr) and a good deal of vitality. Thereafter Huston lent himself to two costly commercial follies: Dino De Laurentiis' production of *The Bible – In the Beginning* (1966) and the James Bond film *Casino Royale* (1967), on which he was one of five directors.

Just when it seemed he was no longer an artist to be taken seriously, however, Huston returned to the peak of form with the haunting *Reflections in a Golden Eye* (1967), in which he won memorable and complementary performances from Elizabeth Taylor, Marlon Brando, Brian Keith and Julie Harris. Of the two failures that followed, *A Walk With Love and Death* (1969) had at least ambition to commend it – which *Sinful Davey* (1969), a prankish period comedy, did not. *The Kremlin Letter* (1970) was a comedy-thriller in the style of the period.

Then in 1972 came the second of the intermittent masterpieces which have marked

the latest period of Huston's career. The virile, elegaic *Fat City* (with marvellous performances by Stacy Keach, Jeff Bridges and Susan Tyrell) is a very personal reminiscence of Huston's youthful period in the world of professional boxing. Huston remained curiously erratic, following up the film with the too easy-going *The Life and Times of Judge Roy Bean* (1972) – for once a writer, in this case John Milius, complained that Huston had betrayed his script – and an indifferent thriller, *The Mackintosh Man* (1973).

Huston nevertheless responded to a chance to film a long-cherished project – *The Man Who Would Be King* (1975). Rudyard Kipling had been his favourite boyhood reading; he had planned to film the book several times before – intending it, in turn, for Walter Huston, for Gable and Bogart, for Sinatra, for Richard Burton and Peter O'Toole. The parts of the two English soldiers in India who briefly become rulers of a lost kingdom were finally played (after Paul Newman had turned down one of the roles) by Sean Connery and Michael Caine.

At the age of 74 Huston was to emerge as the director of a new and majestic work – *Wise Blood* (1979) – adapted from Flannery O'Connor's novel about the Southern 'Bible Belt' and with a script that follows its original almost as loyally as the scenario for *The Maltese Falcon*, made four decades before.

Huston, who began his career as a writer, has retained a deep respect for the script. His best films have been taken from writers of the first rank and adapted with sincere appreciation and understanding of the originals. After Huston had filmed *A Walk With Love and Death*, its author Hans Koningsberger commented:

'Real books are seldom seen circulating in the movie world; its dealings are with the story outlines . . . Huston wanted to film a novel; not the movements of the people in a story, but the idea of the book.' Koningsberger found, indeed, that Huston's critical analysis put the book and its author to strenuous tests.

Journalists around a Huston set were always annoyed because there was really nothing of Huston's direction to see. Huston tended to stand on the edge of the crowd and appear to leave things to the first assistant and the cameraman. 'I see my role', he said at the time of *The Mackintosh Man*, 'as that of the innocent bystander.' The fact is that his creative contribution to the performances starts early. 'The trick', he told Karel Reisz who interviewed him on the set of *The African Queen* and remarked how he simply left Hepburn and Bogart to get on with their performances on their own, 'is in the casting'. Whether dealing with a major star like Hepburn or comparatively unknown faces like Audie Murphy in *The Red Badge of Courage* or Brad Dourif in *Wise Blood*, with major roles or one-line supports, the very confrontation of the actor's personality and the part was a creative action. Marilyn Monroe who played a small role at the start of her

career in *The Asphalt Jungle* and made her last screen appearance in *The Misfits*, said with characteristic perception: 'John watches for the reality of a scene, then leaves it alone.'

Part of this skill was no doubt due to his massive, affectionate curiosity about people and his delight in eccentrics – whether in real life or in fiction. And this quality is one aspect of his dominating gift as a story-teller. Like Hitchcock, his own curiosity infects the spectator, forcing him into a hunger to know more about each character, a compulsion to know what happens next – the true purpose of suspense.

When James Agee wrote a *Life* profile of Huston – 'Undirectable Director' – in 1950, he had few reserves: 'The most inventive director of his generation. Huston has done more to extend, invigorate and purify the essential idiom of American movies, the truly visual telling of tales, than anyone since the prime of D.W. Griffith.'

'To put it conservatively,' he wrote elsewhere in the article, 'there is nobody under 50 at work in movies, here or abroad, who can excel Huston in talent, inventiveness, intransigence, achievement or promise.'

Agee was perhaps too close to his subject – he was shortly to start work with Huston on *The African Queen* (1951); but later, critical opinion shifted against him. *Victory* (1981), a POW escape story, using professional footballers, was a sorry kid's-comic adventure, and the lavish musical *Annie* (1982), though competent, showed none of his earlier fire.

But in the mid-Eighties Huston seemed to gain a second wind. *Under the Volcano* (1984) was a brave effort to depict a useless man (Albert Finney) dying with a sense of dignity, and *Prizzi's Honor* (1985), an ebony-black comedy about a hit-man (Jack Nicholson) trying to ingratiate himself with the Mafia, and find true love, was a huge success with critics and public alike, reaffirming his story-telling skills. His last film *The Dead* (1987) is a perfectly realized 'chamber' film, although most prophetic in its anticipation of his own demise, and the perfect epitaph in its longing for better times, as well as being a fine story well told.

Filmography

1928 The Shakedown (extra only). '**29** Hell's Heroes (extra only). '**30** The Storm (extra only). '**32** A House Divided (dial. only); Law and Order (dial. only); Murders in the Rue Morgue (dial. only). '**35** Death Drives Through (co-sc. only) (GB). '**38** Jezebel (co-sc. only); The Amazing Dr Clitterhouse (co-sc. only). '**39** Juarez (co-sc.). '**40** Dr Ehrlich's Magic Bullet/The Story of Dr Ehrlich's Magic Bullet (co-sc. only). '**41** High Sierra (co-sc. only); Sergeant York (co-sc. only); The Maltese Falcon (+sc). '**42** In This Our Life; Across the Pacific (some scenes only). '**43** Report From the Aleutians (doc) (+sc). '**45** San Pietro/The Battle of San Pietro (doc) (+sc; +narr; +co-photo); Three Strangers (co-sc. only). '**46** Let There Be Light (doc) (+co-sc; +co-photo) (restricted Service showings only). '**48** The Treasure of the Sierra Madre (+sc; +act); Key Largo (+co-sc). '**49** We Were Strangers (+co-sc; +act). '**50** The Asphalt Jungle (+co-sc). '**51** The Red Badge of Courage (+co-sc); The African Queen (+co-sc). '**52** Moulin Rouge (+prod; +sc). '**53** Beat the Devil (+co-sc) (GB-IT). '**56** Moby Dick (+co-prod; +co-sc). '**57** Heaven Knows, Mr Allison (+co-sc). '**58** The Barbarian and the Geisha; The Roots of Heaven. '**60** The Unforgiven. '**61** The Misfits. '**62** Freud (+co-sc; +narr) (GB: Freud – The Secret Passion). '**63** The List of Adrian Messenger (+act); The Cardinal (actor only). '**64** The Night of the Iguana (+prod; +co-sc). '**66** La Bibbia (+act; +narr) (IT) (USA/GB: The Bible – In the Beginning). '**67** Casino Royale (co-dir; +act) (GB); Reflections in a Golden Eye; The Life and Times of John Huston, Esq. (doc: appearance as himself only). '**68** Candy (actor only). '**69** Sinful Davey (GB); A Walk With Love and Death (+act); De Sade (actor only) (USA-GER). '**70** The Kremlin Letter (+co-sc; +act); Myra Breckinridge (actor only); Bridge in the Jungle (actor only) (USA-MEX). '**71** La Spina Dorsale del Diavolo (actor only) (YUG-IT-USA) (USA/GB: The Deserter; retitling for TV: The Devil's Backbone); Man in the Wilderness (actor only) (USA-SP). '**72** Fat City; The Life and Times of Judge Roy Bean (+act). '**73** Battle for the Planet of the Apes (actor only); The Mackintosh Man (GB). '**74** Chinatown (actor only). '**75** Breakout (actor only); The Wind and the Lion (actor only); The Man Who Would be King (+co-sc) (GB). '**76** Hollywood on Trial (doc; narr. only). '**77** Tentacoli (actor only) (IT-USA) (USA: Tentacles); Angela (actor only) (CAN). '**79** Wise Blood (+act) (USA–GER); Jaguar Lives (actor only); The Visitor (actor only); Winter Kills (actor only). '**80** Phobia (CAN); Agee (doc, as himself only); Head On (actor only). '**81** Victory (GB: Escape to Victory). '**82** Annie; Cannery Row (voice only). '**83** Lovesick (actor only); A Minor Miracle (GB: Young Giants) (actor only). '**84** Under the Volcano; Notes From Under the Volcano (doc, as self only); Observations From Under the Volcano (doc, as self only). '**85** Prizzi's Honor. '**87** The Dead.

From left to right: Marlon Brando and Elizabeth Taylor in an intimate scene from Reflections in A Golden Eye; *Brad Dourif (right) and Harry Dean Stanton in* Wise Blood, *and Anthony Andrews and Jacqueline Bisset enjoying the fiesta in* Under the Volcano

On the Road

A producer's intuition and a fair slice of luck brought together the Forties' most famous comedy team, Bob Hope, Bing Crosby and Dorothy Lamour. Hope and Crosby's wisecracking charm and musical abilities plus Lamour's exotic glamour proved an unbeatable combination in a hugely popular series – the Road films

Left: in Road to Rio *Hope and Crosby play a couple of musicians who try to save the beautiful Lucia De Andrade (Lamour) from the hypnotic influence of her evil aunt. Above:* Road to Zanzibar *found the team on safari in darkest Africa and allowed them to make fun of every Hollywood jungle epic ever made*

'After *The Cat and the Canary* (1939), Paramount told me to hit the road,' jokes Bob Hope in his book, *The Road to Hollywood*. The seven films in the Road series were strictly Fortiesstyle fun pictures, even if the last two, *Road to Bali* (1952) and *The Road to Hong Kong* (1962), were made in later decades. To Road addicts, it is the first five that count: the rest are usually seen as sentimental journeys or slightly desperate cash-ins.

The story of the Road films began on the golf course – a popular area of sparetime activity for many of the show-biz fraternity. Bob Hope, comedian, and Bing Crosby, crooner, were good golfing buddies, and had been such since they met on a vaudeville bill at the Capitol on Broadway in 1932. Seven years later they met professionally again on the Paramount lot, both under contract to the studio – Hope for comedies and Crosby for musicals. The fateful day came when the boys made up a foursome on the links with the producer Harlan Thompson and the director Victor Schertzinger. They had so much fun that Schertzinger said to Thompson, 'What a team those boys would make in pictures'. Thompson agreed enthusiastically; once the non-golfing Dorothy (Dotty) Lamour, sarong girl from a string of South Sea Island epics, was added, a perfect team had been created.

Paramount handed the trio *Road to Singapore* (1940), an old script by Harry Hervey that had already been doctored twice – once for George Burns and Gracie Allen, and once for Jack Oakie and Fred MacMurray. Whether or not Hervey ever recognized the Hope-Crosby-Lamour version, the trio lifted a medium-budget picture into the $1.5 million profit class. This led the studio to call for sequel after sequel, until a classic comedy series

had been developed – the most successful of its kind in cinema history.

The affectionate rivalry between Hope and Crosby, which had already begun on their respective radio programmes, carried over into the films. They cracked gags about their contrasting ages, their waistlines, their hairlines and their vocal abilities; Hope joked about Crosby's outstanding ears, Crosby about Hope's 'ski-snoot' nose; Hope called Crosby 'Dad', and Crosby called Bob 'Junior'. Their screen rivalry expressed itself most fully for Lamour's sultry charms. Their radio personas also played an important part in the pictures, as Paramount's publicity proves – 'The Dean of the Kraft Music Hall meets the Top Man of the Pepsodent Show!' The wisecracking gag and insult formulas pioneered on the airwaves came fresh to the moviegoing millions, especially to the British, for whom the snappiest radio comedian was Tommy Handley.

Hope actually brought his radio writers to work on *Road to Singapore* without telling the director, Schertzinger. He and Crosby would stroll onto the set to start a scene and reel off a stream of freshly-minted gags, much to the director's surprise. Although first takes were invariably ruined by the technicians' laughter, Schertzinger was smart enough to realize that in *Road to Singapore* he was capturing on film all the spontaneity of a live performance.

'When Bing and Bob meet – those Torrid Tropics sure Get Hot!' quipped the ads, continuing 'They put the Sing in Singapore!'; the team certainly did, with five songs (two of which were by Schertzinger). Crosby's 'Too Romantic' made the hit parade; Hope had fun with 'Captain Custard', an off-beat ditty about a cinema commissionaire; and Lamour crooned 'Kaigoon'. However, the best song,

'Sweet Potato Piper', featured all three in a jazzy novelty number that set audiences' toes tapping.

Two other ingredients of *Road to Singapore* that became perennial favourites were the 'Patty-cake, patty-cake, baker's man' routine with which the boys confused antagonists before socking their way out of tight corners, and the brief appearance of 'Professor' Jerry Colonna, a pop-eyed, walrus-whiskered refugee from Hope's radio show.

Road to Zanzibar (1941) was next season's follow-up, and funnier by far. It was originally named *Find Colonel Fawcett*, but the studio decided that the success of the first film was too good to miss and quickly changed the title. Hope plays Fearless Frazier the Living Bullet, while Crosby plays Chuck, his con man manager. Dorothy Lamour was cast as Donna Latour, saved from the slave trade after the boys 'patty-cake' the baddies. But not before more songs have been sung and Hope has wrestled a gorilla.

Road to Morocco (1942) was promoted as 'The Greatest Road Show of 'Em All!' – and for once the fans agreed with the publicity. Crosby ('He's a Pasha with the accent on the Pash') and Hope ('He's a Wolf in Sheik's Clothing') meet Lamour ('The Queen of Araby') in 'A Harem-Scarem Riot of Song and Laughter!'. Yet even this high-pressured oversell failed to describe adequately the wild and wacky goings-on once Crosby and Hope, 'like Webster's dictionary, were Morocco-bound'. As Mabel the Talking Camel aptly remarked (courtesy of Paramount's 'Speaking of Animals' shorts): 'This is the screwiest picture I ever was in!'

There were more animals sharing the screen in *Road to Utopia* (1944), a period piece set during the Alaskan gold-rush. Hope cuddles up to a grizzly bear, believing it to be Lamour: 'Dear, you've been working too hard', he says, patting a paw. The boys, playing washed-up vaudevillians, sing 'Put It There, Pal', one of their best double-act ditties, while the urbane humourist Robert Benchley wanders in and out of the proceedings, trying to make sense of the story. One of Hope's best-remembered gags occurs in this film: 'Gimme a lemonade', he snarls at the barman, 'In a dirty glass!'

Road to Rio (1947), the fifth and last of the Forties Road films, saw a return to a strong plot-line and a consequent lessening of spontaneity. As Scat Sweeney and Hot-lips Barton the boys perform another splendid number, 'Apalachicola, Florida'. 'America's most Gleesome Threesome', as the publicity called them, played opposite two other trios, the Andrews Sisters, who sang 'You Don't Have to Know the Language', and the Three Weire Brothers, fiddle-playing zanies from the cabaret circuit. These acrobatic eccentrics, usually confined to straight filmings of their regular routine, were here worked into the plot with hilarious results.

The Fifties were well under way before Paramount broke the news that Hope, Crosby and Lamour were 'paving a New Love-happy Road for you – Rocked with Laughter, Bumpy with Songs, Curved with Girls and Splashed with Colour!'. As the ads proudly revealed, *Road to Bali* (1952) was the first Road film to be made in Technicolor. Hope and Crosby (whom Hope called 'a collapsible Como') were hoofing the boards once more, this time as Harold Gridley and Gene Cochran, singing 'Hoot-Mon' in Hollywood Scottish, Lamour played Princess Lalah MacTavish and the animal opposition took the form of a giant squid, evidently left over from Cecil B. DeMille's

Reap the Wild Wind (1942). For once, Hope nearly got the girl, even if she was not Lamour but Jane Russell in an unbilled guest spot. Humphrey Bogart also made a brief, uncredited appearance, looking for his boat, *The African Queen.*

In the late Fifties, at the height of the sci-fi boom, Paramount announced *The Road to the Moon.* It was never made, but some of the script was used in *The Road to Hong Kong* (1962). This final outing was filmed in England and featured an ageing trio trying desperately to recapture their youthful spirits. At first Lamour was not going to be cast, but in the end sentiment, and sense, prevailed – although her part was reduced to rather long-range walk-ons; the younger Joan Collins took over her third-line billing. Even the addition of a string of guest stars (Peter Sellers, doing his famous Indian doctor impression, plus Frank Sinatra, Dean Martin, David Niven, Zsa Zsa Gabor, Dave King and the ever-popular Jerry Colonna) failed to lure back the fans. Perhaps, feeling as old as the 'Roadsters' now looked, they preferred to stay home, watching re-runs of the other Road films on TV. For, in their prime, there was never such good company as Paramount's 'Road' company – Bing, Bob and Dotty.

Above left: Road to Bali *was the only Road film made in colour. Above:* Hope and Lamour *in the Alaskan wilderness of* Road to Utopia. *Below left: the boys try to escape the cruel Mullay Kasim (Anthony Quinn) in* Road to Morocco. *Below: Joan Collins provided the love interest in* The Road to Hong Kong

Picking up the pieces

In the aftermath of World War II, film industries in Europe and the Far East were resurrected and played a vital role in building new societies

On September 3, 1943, four years to the day after the outbreak of hostilities between Britain and Germany, Italy unconditionally surrendered to the Allied powers. On May 7, 1945, General Jodl signed the document of Germany's surrender. Alone of the Axis powers, Japan fought on a few weeks more. On August 6, 1945, a United States B-29 bomber dropped an atom bomb on the city of Hiroshima, and less than a month later Japan finally surrendered. The war, in which 15 million military personnel and countless civilians had perished, was over. Out of the wreckage of the old, a new world had to be built, and the men who made the movies were everywhere conscious of their role in this reconstruction.

The Liberation found the French cinema at a complete standstill. German preparations for the Allied advances had paralysed the life of Paris, closing all the city's cinemas and halting film production. Nevertheless, despite chronic shortages of equipment and energy, production did recover and rose in 1946 to 96 films – not far short of pre-war levels – though, in most cases, post-war budgets were smaller.

In the following year, however, an agreement with the Americans to relax pre-war quota controls on the importation of Hollywood films caused French film production to plummet sharply. Imported films, dubbed into French, dominated the market and handicapped home-made product for 12 months until the quota was re-established. The subsequent recovery of the cinema industry was assisted by the introduction of two government measures: the Loi d'Aide à l'Industrie Cinématographique (1949) and the Loi de Développement de l'Industrie Cinématographique in 1953.

If the French cinema's economic situation was shaky, its prestige still rated highly. A series of notable films of the Occupation period, including Marcel Carné's *Les Visiteurs du Soir* (1942, *The Devil's Own Envoy*) and *Les Enfants du Paradis* (1945, *Children of Paradise*) and Robert Bresson's *Les Anges du Péché* (1943, *Angels of Sin*) were all revealed after the Liberation to worldwide acclaim.

Of the pre-war masters, Jacques Feyder was dead and Jean Renoir had stayed in America. Only René Clair resumed work in France and made *Le Silence Est d'Or* (1947, *Man About Town*), an attractive and mature reflection on old age. Claude Autant-Lara rose to fame with a series of literary adaptations – the exquisite *Le Diable au Corps* (1947, *Devil in the Flesh*), from a novel by Raymond Radiguet, about a youth's first love, and *Occupe-toi d'Amélie* (1949, *Keep an Eye on Amelia*) from a play by Feydeau.

Jean Cocteau, whose wartime film *L'Eternel Retour* (1943, *Love Eternal*) had been wrongly suspected of purveying 'German mysticism', pursued his own idiosyncratic way with the magical *La Belle et la Bête* (1946, *Beauty and the Beast*) and *Les Parents Terribles* (1948), adapted from his own play.

René Clément's *La Bataille du Rail* (1945, *The Battle of the Railway Workers*), one of the first French films released after the war, portrayed

railway workers fighting for the Resistance and suggested, through its spare shooting style, that French films might have developed a neo-realist movement similar to that of Italian cinema in the post-war years. Clément himself followed this film with another war subject in the realist mode, but *Les Maudits* (1947, The Accursed) did not find favour with audiences and Clément's example was not followed by other film-makers.

French directors seemed, in fact, more inclined to take up where they had left off, resuming the fatalistic style of pre-war films like *Quai des Brumes* (1938, *Quay of Shadows*) and *Le Jour se Lève* (1939, *Daybreak*). Carné made *Les Portes de la Nuit* (1946, *Gates of the Night*), a drama set in the wartime black market. Clément added to the melancholic mood with *Au Delà des Grilles* (1949, *Beyond the Gates*), and several other films echoed the 'noir' atmosphere – doomed lovers playing out their lives in gloomy surroundings; these included: Duvivier's *Panique* (1946, *Panic*) and Clouzot's *Quai des Orfèvres* (1947, *Jenny Lamour*).

Of the French directors who came to the fore in the immediate post-war years, the most notable was Jacques Becker. His first success was a light-hearted, unsentimental film, *Antoine et Antoinette* (1946), about a lost lottery ticket. This was followed by *Rendez-vous de Juillet* (1949, *Rendezvous in July*), in which Becker examined post-war youth through the interwoven stories of several young actresses. *Edouard et Caroline* (1951) portrayed a Parisian, bourgeois marriage and confirmed Becker's reputation as an expert maker of everyday comedies.

The documentary film-maker Georges Rouquier

Top left: Quai des Orfèvres *(the Paris police HQ), an atmospheric thriller in which a music-hall artist is accused of a crime passionnel, starred Louis Jouvet as a police inspector in one of his most celebrated roles. Top:* Panique *contained an outstanding performance by Michel Simon as an aged eccentric pursued by a suspicious community. Above:* Farrebique, *a highly acclaimed story that traces the fortunes of a rural family through the four seasons of the farming year*

226

Top: Jean Marais and Josette Day in Cocteau's La Belle et la Bête, *a surrealistic fantasy based on the age-old fairy-tale. Above:* Le Blé en Herbe *(1954, Ripening Seed) dealt with the awkwardness and hesitancy of young love. Top right: the story of the artist Utamaro and his unique art of body-painting is told in Mizoguchi's* Five Women Around Utamaro. *Above right: Denjiro Okochi in Kurosawa's* They Who Tread on the Tiger's Tail. *The title is taken from a proverb: 'From the mouth of a serpent, they had a narrow escape. No less hard way, they went, than walking on a tiger's tail'*

made a single feature-length, dramatized documentary, *Farrebique* (1947), about the life of a farming family in the Massif Central. The film owed much to the style of the American documentarist Robert Flaherty, and the same tendency was perceptible in the post-war work of Roger Leenhardt – *Les Dernières Vacances* (1947, Last Holidays) and Louis Daquin, whose outstanding film *Le Point du Jour* (1948, First Light) dealt with the lives of the miners of northern France.

However progressive these films may have been, the popular fare was bourgeois comedy in which stars like Fernandel, Bourvil and Noël-Noël were consistently popular. Alongside such traditional offerings, the debut of Jacques Tati in *Jour de Fête* (1949, Day of the Fair) – combining the influences of Chaplin, neo-realism and French rustic comedy – was a singular and welcome innovation.

The end of the war found Japan, the last Axis enemy, in a desperate situation. Most cinemas were closed, and though the studios had remained theoretically open, the shortage of materials and equipment was acute. The whole country was placed under the regulations of the Supreme Command Allied Forces in the Pacific (SCAP) whose officers drafted and implemented the rules about what films should and should not be made.

Existing films about militarism, feudal loyalty, ritual suicide and the oppression of women were placed on the banned list. As to new projects, uplifting, recommended subjects included the peaceful organization of trade unions, respect for individual rights and the emancipation of women. The latter category provided the pretext for Mizoguchi's *Utamaro O Meguro Gonin No Onna* (1946, *Five Women Around Utamaro*). Meanwhile

the SCAP authorities industriously burned negatives and prints of some 225 forbidden films, which included works by outstanding directors like Kinoshita, Ichikawa and Kurosawa. Many prominent people in the industry were condemned as war criminals and removed from their posts as a result of SCAP investigations. Industrial troubles and strikes further undermined the structure of the Japanese film industry in the late Forties, most seriously affecting the giant company Toho.

Under the Occupation, subjects and styles of film-making changed radically. The period film practically disappeared, though old chivalric stories were often updated as modern gangster films, to which SCAP registered no objections. The much-favoured films about the new, emancipated woman resulted in some major works like Mizoguchi's *Joyu Sumako No Koi* (1947, *The Loves of Actress Sumako*) and Kinugasa's *Joyu* (1947, *The Actress*). Kurosawa's *Tora-no-o* (1945, *They Who Tread on the Tiger's Tail*) had the distinction of being banned both before and after the defeat of Japan. But Japan's recent past was examined in the same director's *Waga Seishun Ni Kuinashi* (1946, *No Regrets for Our Youth*).

Other major directors analysed post-war society, its problems and its victims: Mizoguchi in *Yoru No Onnatachi* (1948, *Women of the Night*) and Ozu in *Kaze No Naka No Mendori* (1948, *A Hen in the Wind*).

The Occupation brought one incidental but novel revolution to the Japanese cinema – the kiss. By the late Forties it had become an essential, sensational ingredient of any film with box-office ambitions. But even despite such dramatic Western innovations, the full revelation and flowering of post-war Japanese cinema was delayed until *Rashomon* (1950) brought Japan to the attention of the moviegoers abroad.

Germany was defeated, destroyed, demoralized and artificially divided into zones under the control of the British, American, French and Soviet conquerors. By the end of the war the number of operative cinemas had dwindled to a fraction. But, as the occupying powers realized, the value of cinema in the rehabilitation of a defeated people, they set about reopening movie houses and promoting production.

In the American zone the entertainment permitted to the Germans was strictly limited to Hollywood escapism. There was little reminder or re-examination of the recent war. Production, too, was closely supervised by the military government, which was rigorous in excluding suspected ex-Nazis.

In 1947 production was licensed at the Geiselgasteig Studios in Munich and at the old Templehof Studios in Berlin. Apart from some footage shot for

227

Hollywood films like *Berlin Express* and *A Foreign Affair* (both 1948) and a notable success with Robert Stemmle's *Berliner Ballade* (1948, *The Ballad of Berlin*), a satire on post-war Germany, no truly distinguished films emerged from the Berlin studios in this period.

The British Control Commission was more relaxed about the film entertainment permitted the defeated people. Old German films were allowed, if they were thought to be clean of Nazi content. Foreign films, too, were re-introduced after their long wartime absence and were shown in both subtitled and dubbed versions; among them were British war pictures like *The Foreman Went to France* (1942) and *San Demetrio, London* (1943).

A number of German productions dealt frankly with recent history and contemporary problems. Wolfgang Liebeneiner, who had been an active director during the war years, portrayed a young woman's gradual disillusionment with Hitler in *Liebe '47* (1947, *Love '47*): she falls in love with a man suffering from war wounds and her faith in humanity is restored. Rudolph Jugert's *Film Ohne Titel* (1947, *Film Without a Title*) adopted a humorous approach by posing the question of how to make a comedy for German audiences who were suffering the tribulations of the post-war period. On the other hand, Arthur Brauner's *Morituri* (1946, *Those About to Die*) confronted the reality of the death camps.

Although these films used plenty of location footage and adopted a straightforward shooting style, they were never part of the mainstream of neo-realism. One German film, however, can be properly termed neo-realist: Rossellini's *Germania, Anno Zero* (1947, *Germany, Year Zero*), a grim and desolate description of a young boy's degradation in the social conditions of the defeated land.

The Eastern zone, under Soviet control, began with considerable advantages. The newly formed Defa (Deutsches Film Aktiengesellschaft) inherited

Above: the legacy of the Nazi regime was shown in *Stronger Than Night*, a film that revealed how communists were interned in concentration camps. Left: Robert Stemmle's *The Ballad of Berlin* made post-war German society and the occupying forces objects of satire. Gert Frobe played 'Otto Nobody', a 'little man' picking his way through the black marketeers, the rationing and the rubble of Berlin. Below: cold-war politics prompted a succession of anti-American films; the Soviet *Meeting on the Elbe* was typical of such propaganda

German film-makers – whether in the East or the West – seemed more preoccupied with the legacy of the war than with plans for peacetime

the old Ufa organization, the Neubabelsburg and Johannistal Studios and the Agfa laboratories along with the Agfacolor process. Everything received full state backing. In the immediate post-war years some of the best and most progressive German directors were attracted to work for Defa. Wolfgang Staudte's *Die Mörder Sind Unter Uns* (1946, *The Murderers Are Among Us*) examined varying attitudes to former war criminals and was perhaps the best of the group of films set in the ruins of Berlin that earned the generic name *Trümmerfilme* ('rubble films'). Other notable examples were Gerhard Lamprecht's *Irgendwo in Berlin* (1946, *Anywhere in Berlin*), a film about the plight of children in the aftermath of defeat, and Kurt Maetzig's *Ehe im Schatten* (1947, *Marriage in the Shadows*), based on the story of the famous actor Gottschalk who, together with his Jewish wife, committed suicide in Nazi Germany.

Slatan Dudow, who had directed *Kühle Wampe* (1932, *Whither Germany?*), from a Brecht scenario, before fleeing from Nazi Germany, returned to make *Unser Tägliche Brot* (1949, *Our Daily Bread*), a somewhat schematic film about socialist reconstruction. Dudow was later to direct a striking feature, *Stärker als die Nacht* (1954, *Stronger Than Night*) about Nazi oppression of communists.

Defa was now headed by the Moscow-trained Sepp Schwab. Bureaucracy took root and the best of

Above: Polish Resistance fighters defend their ground in Border Street, a re-creation of the Warsaw ghetto uprising of 1943. Below: Adám Szirtes in The Soil Beneath Your Feet, a man with marital problems. Below right: Somewhere in Europe, about a band of homeless Hungarian children who wander from town to town amid the rubble of post-war Hungary

film was suppressed (it finally emerged more than a decade later). The intended third part was finally abandoned. Eisenstein never worked again and died, at the age of 50, in 1948.

The films that did meet with approval were, for the most part, historical fabrications. Highly favoured, of course, were those that deified Stalin, like Mikhail Chiaureli's appalling The Vow (1946), The Fall of Berlin (1949) and The Unforgettable Year of 1919 (1951). Other films, like Abraham Room's Court of Honour and Mikhail Romm's The Russian Question (both 1948), Alexandrov's Meeting on the Elbe (1949) and Chiaureli's Secret Mission (1950) attacked the American character and US imperialist aims, as well as 'cosmopolitanism' in general.

Under Zhdanov's control Soviet film production dropped gradually until 1952 when only five feature films appeared in the year. The preference was more and more for apparently 'safe' subjects and this explains the seemingly endless output of idealized historical biographies, direct records of stage productions (favoured by Stalin, who liked the theatre but had become increasingly paranoid about appearing in public), children's films and technical novelties like a version of Robinson Crusoe (1946) made in 3-D.

The Polish cinema was nationalized in November 1945, with Aleksander Ford, a notable pre-war director, as head of the new organization called Film Polski. The first post-war Polish feature, Leonard Bucskowski's Forbidden Songs, did not appear until 1947 but fast became a great hit at the box-office. The film popularized folk ballads that had been banned under the Nazis and is still one of the most successful films ever made in Poland.

Bucskowski followed it with a contemporary story of post-war reconstruction, Skarb (1948, The Treasure). This film, starring Danuta Szaflarska who had appeared in Forbidden Songs, dealt in a gently humorous manner with the acute housing shortage in post-war Poland. Aleksander Ford, himself a Jew, made Ulica Granicza (1948, Border Street) about the solidarity of Jews and Poles which culminated in the Warsaw ghetto uprising of 1943.

Wanda Jakubowska drew on her own recent memories of Auschwitz for Ostatni Etap (1948, The Last Stage). This small group of films was a remarkable start of a new-born industry, but in 1949 the Polish Workers Party assumed power and a congress of film-makers at Wisla laid down the new, strict dogmas of socialist realism: interest in imaginative and stylistic devices was condemned along with the portrayal of introspective characters; instead 'the positive hero of the new Poland' was to be made the subject of films that dealt with everyday life in the new socialist state.

the directors, who had provided a brief renascence in East Germany, crossed to the West: Arthur Maria Rabenalt, Gerhard Lamprecht, Erich Engel and finally – after completing three more films for Defa – the gifted Staudte. Even after the death of Stalin in 1953, the revival of East German cinema was to be slow and reluctant.

The developments in East Germany, paralleled throughout the whole of socialist Europe, were primarily the result of the strengthening influence of the Soviet Union. In the USSR the ending of the war brought a renewal of the grim repressions that had marked Stalin's domination in the Thirties. A. A. Zhdanov, a prominent member of the Politburo, had become Stalin's mouthpiece and led the campaign to bring art and artists into order, making them serve the precise and immediate needs of the Party. A Resolution of the Central Committee in September 1946 condemned the second part of Leonid Lukov's film A Great Life (1946) for its realistic treatment of the people of the Donbas coal basin during the war. What was now officially required was an idealized image of Soviet history.

Other films came under attack: Kosintsev and Trauberg's Plain People (1945) was alleged to have dealt too frankly with the war, and V.I. Pudovkin suffered criticism for his historical biography of Admiral Nakhimov (1946). Eisenstein, too, was a victim of the prevalent ideology. In the second part of Ivan the Terrible (1946) his portrait of the Tsar as an iron ruler surrounded by a secret army was evidently too close to being a likeness of Stalin. The

In Hungary the path of cinema history, from euphoria to reconstruction and from reconstruction to disillusion, was very much the same, if more complex. Production had continued in Budapest during the war, though by 1945 it had fallen to only three films a year. After the war the great film theorist Béla Balász returned from a quarter of a century of exile to teach at the newly founded Academy of Dramatic and Film Art. The classic Soviet films were shown in Hungary for the first time and film-makers also had the chance to see large numbers of Hollywood films. But from 1947 film production permits were granted only to the leading political parties. Two outstanding films resulted from this period: István Szöt's *Enek a Búzamezökröl* (1947, *Song of the Cornfields*) and Géza Radványi's *Valahol Europában* (1947, *Somewhere in Europe*). The latter was scripted by Béla Balász and told the story of a group of delinquent war orphans through a touching, idealistic fantasy that owed much to the Soviet film *The Road to Life* (1931).

In March 1948 the Hungarian film industry was

In the post-war period, the film industries of Eastern Europe revived, but the films' subject-matter was often dull and dogmatic

nationalized and the first films produced by the state were auspicious: Frigyes Bán's *Talpalatnyi Föld* (1948, *The Soil Beneath Your Feet*) Imre Jeney's *Egy Asszony Elmdul* (1949, *A Woman Makes a New Start*) and Felix Mariassy's *Szabóné* (1949, *Anna Szabó*) which dealt compassionately with problems of adjustment to the new socialist world.

Soon, however, Hungarian film-makers, too, found their work forced into the schematic moulds of socialist realism. The script, which had to be approved in advance, became paramount. Béla Balász was removed from his post at the Academy. Pudovkin was sent from Moscow as an adviser on film affairs and Hungary moved into the most sterile period of her long film history.

No other Eastern European cinema began the post-war period with greater optimism than that of Czechoslovakia. A well-established film industry had survived the war and was nationalized in August 1945. A body of expert and experienced directors was assembled, among them Otakar Vávra, a specialist in historical and literary subjects. Jiří Weiss returned from London, where he had worked with the Crown Film Unit, and made his first feature film *Uloupená Hranice* (1947, *Stolen Frontier*). The Czech cinema was given a great moral boost when Karel Steklý's *Siréna* (1946, *The Strike*) won the Golden Lion at the first post-war Venice Film Festival.

Similar patterns evolved in the Romanian cinema (nationalized in 1948 but barely past the stage of primitive comedy and socialist morality films) and the Bulgarian film industry, though in 1948 the celebrated Soviet director Sergei Vasiliev was loaned to the Bulgarians to make *Geroite na Shipka*, (*Heroes of the Shipka*) about the liberation of Bulgaria from Turkish rule in the nineteenth century.

In post-war Yugoslavia it had been necessary to create a national cinema from scratch – rather as the state itself had been established. The separate republics that made up Yugoslavia had their own languages and their own cultural character. In the summer of 1945 a state film enterprise was established. Promising young people were sent abroad to film schools and film centres were established in Belgrade and in the major cities of the six republics.

The first productions of this newly-formed in-

dustry were documentaries, but in 1947 a feature film *Slavica* (dir. Vjekoslav Afrić) was released. The film dealt with the partisans' struggles against the Nazis and this theme has remained a dominant preoccupation of Yugoslav cinema. Similar partisan films from the same period included Radoš Novaković's *Decak Mita* (1948, *The Boy Mita*) and Vojislav Nanović's *Besmrtna Mladost* (1948, *Immortal Youth*). Despite the break with the Soviet Union in 1948, Yugoslavia itself evolved a dogma of socialist realism, though here it was defined as 'national' realism. Whatever the name, the image of Eastern European cinema in the late Forties was one conditioned by the political situation – namely the Cold War.

Top: a dramatic scene from Stolen Frontier, *a post-war Czech account of the German occupation of the Sudetenland. Above: the wives of striking steel workers in the Czech film* Siréna; *the film was based on a novel by the popular author Marie Majerova. The end of the war saw the start of a feature-film industry in Yugoslavia; the aspirations of the new country were often expressed in films about youth;* The Boy Mita *by Radoš Novaković (below) was typical of this trend*

Epic entertainment

To win back audiences Hollywood encouraged its technicians to extend the dimensions of the cinema screen, and producers exploited the new technology with bigger-than-life themes

In the face of declining audiences and the threat posed by television, the film industry sought to make the big-screen film as different as possible from the tiny image on the tube in the corner of America's living rooms.

TV in the early Fifties had two clear drawbacks: it was in black and white and the moving pictures it showed were on a small scale. By contrast the cinema offered scope, depth and colour. When the double-bill of Ann Sheridan in *Take Me to Town* and Jeff Chandler in *East of Sumatra* (both 1953) went into release the main line of promotion was:

'Only your cinema can give you an all-Technicolor, 2-picture programme like this!'

Most crucial among these economic measures to win back cinemagoers were the various technical experiments and processes designed to change the shape of the screen to a much wider, panoramic format beyond the reach of television. Cinema returned to the wide-screen experiments of the Twenties. In the Cinerama process, three 35mm cameras were used to shoot a scene and three projectors beamed the final films side by side on a huge curving screen that took up almost all the audience's field of vision. *This Is Cinerama* (1952) was the spectacular launching film for the new process, premiered on September 30, 1952, in New York. This two-hour travelogue also featured stereophonic sound from speakers positioned behind the screen and around the auditorium; sequences like the famous rollercoaster ride seemed frighteningly real. But it was such rapid-motion scenes that came off best in Cinerama, and it did have some distinct disadvantages. The exact matching up of the three images was not always easy to achieve; sometimes the images overlapped and occasionally the colour seemed inconsistent from one image to the next. Cinerama was also a costly system to install and only a few cinemas in big cities around the world were converted for it.

A film version of the Broadway musical *Paint Your Wagon* was planned to be shot in Cinerama,

but the production was shelved and the process was most frequently used for travelogues. Eventually most of the movie theatres equipped for Cinerama switched to a single-projector system when the more workable 70mm gauge became available and did the same job of filling the enormous screens.

Late in 1952, 20th Century-Fox decided to take up CinemaScope. This process had been evolved from Henri Chrétien's experiments of the Twenties and Thirties and its advantage in the Fifties was that it provided a means of bringing wide-screen pictures to ordinary cinemas.

Films are always shown in one of several available 'aspect ratios' (the ratio of width to height); the standard or 'Academy' ratio was – and still is – 1.33 : 1 (roughly four units broad for every three units high) but in the early Fifties many so-called panoramic screens had been erected to present films in a broader 1.66 : 1 ratio. It wasn't always fair on the films. George Stevens' *Shane* (1953), for example, was not photographed with the newly fashionable ratio in mind and looked uncomfortable on a panoramic screen with the top and bottom of its images cropped off. CinemaScope, however, was an altogether different ratio (2.55 : 1), and the first film to be screened in this new size was *The Robe* (1953), a biblical epic about the aftermath of the crucifixion. The film was shot by 20th Century-Fox's leading cameraman Leon Shamroy in both a CinemaScope and standard version so that the picture could be given its big-screen spectacular presentations and also released in conventional 16mm prints for use in schools. Like most experimental techniques, CinemaScope was a gamble and the only other studios to attempt it were MGM and Walt Disney, but the public response to *The Robe* convinced the studios that CinemaScope had a future, and by 1954 the demand for big-screen pictures was so great that Warners even halted the shooting of *A Star Is Born* (1954) after three weeks and re-started it in the CinemaScope process.

Paramount presents

HELL'S ISLAND
Tropic inferno of love, hate and adventure! Starring

JOHN PAYNE · MARY MURPHY
COLOR BY **TECHNICOLOR**

with FRANCIS L. SULLIVAN · EDUARDO NORIEGA · ARNOLD MOSS
Written for the Screen by MAXWELL SHANE · From a story by Jack Leonard and Martin M. Goldsmith
Directed by PHIL KARLSON · Produced by William H. Pine and William C. Thomas

Above: Phil Karlson's melodramatic thriller was made in VistaVision; the new clarity of definition obtained by this process was advertised in the following terms: '. . . it brings this beautiful girl within reach of [the audience's] arms . . . her full-dimension allure so real, they'll share their emotions with her!' Below: the advertisements for House of Wax conveyed, imaginatively, the thrill of 3-D cinema. Below left: the most memorable moment from the documentary This Is Cinerama – *the ride on the rollercoaster*

"The most astounding development in Cinema history since sound"
—DAILY MIRROR

WARNER BROS. BRING YOU THE FIRST FEATURE PRODUCED BY A MAJOR STUDIO IN 3D!

NATURAL VISION **3 DIMENSION** WARNERCOLOR **"HOUSE OF WAX"**

VINCENT PRICE · FRANK LOVEJOY · PHYLLIS KIRK

How Natural Vision Functions

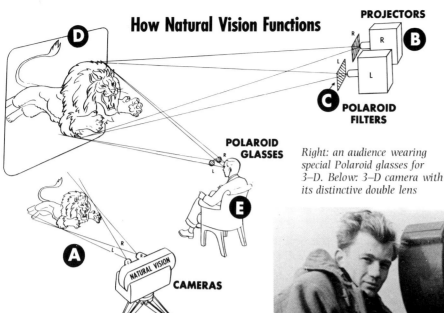

Right: an audience wearing special Polaroid glasses for 3–D. Below: 3–D camera with its distinctive double lens

Above: 3-D images are filmed by a special, Natural Vision camera (A) from two different points of view, as they are seen in nature. Each lens, focusing on an object almost as precisely as does the human eye, provides a separate and complete two-dimensional picture. In the cinema two separate pictures from two (conventional) projectors (B) are superimposed on the screen. Right and left images pass through Polaroid light filters (C). The two images are superimposed as one on a reflective screen (D). The images are reflected back to the viewer who is equipped with Polaroid spectacles

Since 20th Century-Fox held the rights to Cinema-Scope and leased its use to other film producers, some studios preferred to adopt the other systems that suddenly appeared on the market. RKO took up SuperScope – first used on the independently made, United Artists release *Vera Cruz* (1954) – and later renamed it RKO-Scope for the studio's own use. Republic opted for a process closely modelled on the French Cinépanoramique system called Naturama. Warners dabbled with their own version called WarnerScope but on the whole they preferred the effects achieved with CinemaScope. Around this time the term 'Scope came into usage to cover all wide-screen processes of differing makes both in the USA and abroad.

The biggest challenge to CinemaScope's dominance of the wide-screen game was VistaVision, a system developed for Paramount which used a larger negative area to achieve better definition of the image. VistaVision films could be shown in a variety of ratios from the old-fashioned 1.33 : 1 to 2 : 1. The usual aspect ratio for VistaVision was 1.85 : 1. Careful composition on the part of the cinematographers ensured that no important detail was cut off at the top and bottom of the image as tended to happen with Academy ratio prints shown in the wide-screen format. *White Christmas* (1954) was the first film to be shot in this process and the principle was quite simple: the negative was made on 70mm film stock and then reduced to 35mm for distribution; the scaling down by half of the image size vastly improved the definition. In the long run, however, VistaVision proved too expensive and fell into disuse. Marlon Brando's visually arresting Western *One-Eyed Jacks* (1961) was perhaps the final demonstration of the process at its best.

It became clear that one way of broadening the

picture was to use wider film stock. The Todd-AO process used 65 mm film along with a special camera (developed by American Optical for the producer Mike Todd) and was chiefly responsible for the visual splendour of *Oklahoma!* (1955) and *Around the World in 80 Days* (1956). Fox came up with CinemaScope 55, a process that depended on the use of 55mm film for shooting, from which would be struck the standard 35mm prints for distribution. Technicolor developed a system called Technirama which involved the use of a 70mm negative for the filming thus providing sharper, better defined images when the 35mm release prints were made from it. *The Big Country* (1958) and *Spartacus* (1960) both owed their exceptional focus and visual clarity to this method.

The same impetus that led to this proliferation of wide-screen systems also encouraged movie technicians to re-investigate the early experiments with 3-D pictures. Once again there was nothing new about the idea of 3-D motion pictures but the notion of making them widely available to the viewing public was a challenge that the rise of television made more acute.

It was an independent film called *Bwana Devil* (1952), shot in Ansco Color and filmed in the new Natural Vision 3-D process, that captured Hollywood's interest in the possibilities of 3-D. *Bwana Devil* promised 'A Lion in Your Lap' and exploited its crude jungle story to good effect by literally throwing everything at the audience.

The big studios quickly took up 3-D, and Warner Brothers enjoyed a huge success with *House of Wax* (1953). In the wake of this hit nearly twenty 3-D features were released in 1953. It must be admitted that 3-D was very effective as a means of enhancing films with spacious settings – the deserts of *Inferno* and *Hondo* (both 1953), the South Seas of *Miss Sadie Thompson* (1953) or the valley over which a cable-car is suspended for the tense climax of *Second Chance* (1953).

All too often, however, 3-D was used as a gimmick. Audiences were assailed by a great variety of objects. Sensational moments of bullets,

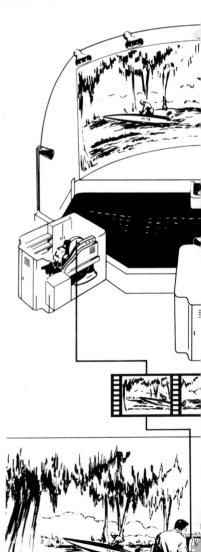

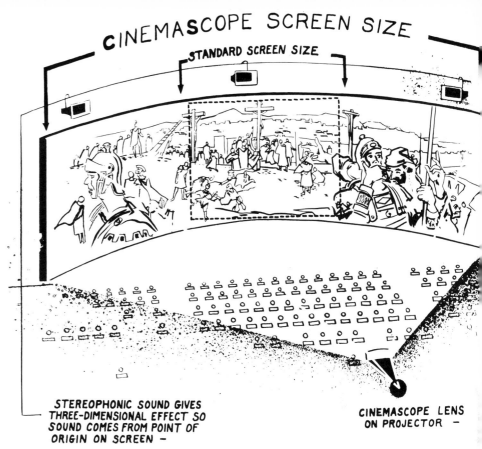

Below: Cinerama was another attempt to create an impression of three-dimensional reality – but without glasses. Three lenses were used to photograph different sections of the same scene and three separate projectors threw these images onto a 90 foot curved screen. The heart of the illusion lies not so much in the wide expanse of the screen as in its curved shape. The 3-D effect obtained from Cinerama is due to the optical phenomenon of peripheral vision: what we see out of the corners of our eyes is crucial in giving three-dimensional perception. Working from this principle, Fred Waller, Cinerama's inventor, sought to exploit peripheral vision to create in audiences the sensation of being in the middle of the action. Right: CinemaScope was a technical innovation made possible by the introduction of a special anamorphic lens. The word means simply 'changing the shape'. Using this lens on the movie camera, cinematographers could film a scene approximately two and a half times as wide as it was high and the image was then squeezed onto ordinary 35mm negative film. A similar anamorphic lens on the projector swelled the scene out to its original shape. Both Cinerama and CinemaScope aimed to complete the illusion of 'being there' with stereophonic sound. CinemaScope had four tracks (three behind the screen and one for the auditorium) printed on to 35mm film; Cinerama used a separate film just for sound

STEREOPHONIC SOUND GIVES THREE-DIMENSIONAL EFFECT SO SOUND COMES FROM POINT OF ORIGIN ON SCREEN –

CINEMASCOPE LENS ON PROJECTOR –

arrows, boulders and bodies coming 'from' the screen frequently distracted viewers from the story-line – the gimmick sometimes became the sole *raison d'être* of the film.

Finally, as well as earning a reputation for being somewhat contrived for the sake of their effects, 3-D films also suffered from the major disadvantage that the audience had to wear special spectacles to see them. Screens had to be specially treated and occasionally the synchronization lapsed between the two projectors operating to give the 3-D image. By the mid-Fifties, audiences were gripped in the excitement of CinemaScope which offered both depth and breadth, and did not require glasses.
ALLEN EYLES

There was little in the technology of wide-screen presentation that had not been perfected in the Twenties, but in the Fifties it was seen as a panacea for the industry's ills

It would be wrong to claim that spectacle was a specific creation of Fifties cinema; rather, that during the decade the form had greater reason to indulge its latent tendencies in that direction. The threat from television was naturally a prime motivation in the revival of the genre, but Hollywood had for some years been seeking a way to maintain audiences and support the gigantic structures of the studio system.

Making films bigger, longer and more colourful than ever was a way of providing a complete entertainment in contrast to TV's instant but small-scale attractions. What was required was the technology that would enable film-makers to expand the size of the projected image and to improve sound and colour quality to go with it. Many of the technical innovations of the Fifties had been briefly pioneered in the Twenties, but in view of falling attendances throughout the film trade,

there was now an urgent need to redevelop wide-screen processes and experiment seriously with film of a wider gauge.

The various wide-screen processes that were perfected and used in the Fifties caused directors and cameramen more than a few problems. The new oblong shape imposed its own personality on the screen and the broader space had to be satisfactorily filled. The letter-box shape of CinemaScope was perfect for two-shots, rolling landscapes and casts of thousands but could be less accommodating for single close-ups, intimate moments, or anything of vertical stature.

It was not until the Sixties, when new through-the-lens viewfinders were perfected, that the director could be sure what the final framing would look like in elaborate compositions. In the early days of the application of wide-screen processes, cinemas were reluctant to re-equip for the new system. As a consequence, most audiences saw the films in an ordinary 35mm format. When CinemaScope and the other wide-screen systems began to be more universally appreciated, there was a sudden demand for new visual stylists with a fresh eye for composition.

When 20th Century-Fox released *The Robe*, it was clear that the director, Henry Koster, failed to exploit the potential offered by the 2.55:1 aspect ratio, although Delmer Daves, who directed the concurrently-shot sequel *Demetrius and the Gladiators* (1954), showed greater flexibility and was later to become one of the top artists in the medium of CinemaScope. Fritz Lang's *Moonfleet* (1955) shows how he had surmounted some of the problems of the new screen size by the atmospheric use of light and shadow to break down the screen's rigid rectangular shape.

Other directors found different solutions. Stanley Donen masked off portions of the CinemaScope screen in *It's Always Fair Weather* (1955) and the VistaVision screen in *Funny Face* (1957), so that different scenes would appear on the screen simultaneously. Joshua Logan played with colour filters and hazy iris effects in *South Pacific* (1958). In *Bad*

Day at Black Rock (1955) the director John Sturges used the emptiness of the desert locations to emphasize the social isolation of the stranger (Spencer Tracy), and in *To Catch a Thief* (1955) Hitchcock subtly exploited the new technology by positioning his actors throughout the visual field, and in one shot treating viewers to a visual joke – a huge close-up of a cigarette being stubbed out in a fried egg.

The wide screen was put to a variety of uses, but there was one genre with which it became particularly associated: the epic. Just as silent cinema had sought to present bigger and better spectacle through historical epic films. So the cinema of the Fifties turned to ancient history for inspiration to find subject-matter which would do proper justice to the elaborate filming techniques recently perfected.

The impetus came from Italy where the development of neo-realism gave way to demands for a new, grander look to Italian films. The flamboyance of the historical epic fitted the bill. Alessandro Blasetti's *Fabiola* (1949) was made on a lavish scale and recalled the silent cinema epics of the poet Gabriele D'Annunzio. The film's success was one of many nails in the coffin of neo-realism.

As the Italian cinema developed its native epic genre (which French critics would later term *peplum*), Hollywood companies set up massive productions in Europe and brought large casts and crews to Italy and Spain. Mervyn LeRoy's successful remake of *Quo Vadis* (1951) provided the definitive impetus for a spate of costume pictures.

There was a world of difference between the Italian *peplum* and the Hollywood epic. The first was made quickly and cheaply and the second was shot on a grand scale over a long period with a seemingly limitless budget. *Quo Vadis, Knights of the Round Table* (1953), *Helen of Troy* (1955), *Alexander the Great* (1956), *The Vikings* (1958) and *Ben-Hur* (1959) all exploited European facilities such as the easier tax rates, the relative cheapness of labour and the opportunity to release the once frozen capital that Hollywood companies had amassed in Europe.

At the end of the decade an American producer named Samuel Bronston expanded on these principles by convincing several business cartels, with money tied up in Spain, to invest their capital in a series of historical pictures which he would then sell on a world-wide basis. The first film in this programme was *King of Kings* (1961) which required a financial subsidy from MGM, but Bronston went on to finance *El Cid* (1961), *55 Days at Peking* (1963), *The Fall of the Roman Empire* (1964) and *Circus World* (1964) by pre-selling the distribution rights throughout the world.

With the increased budgets came intensified pressures: these expensive films simply had to

Far left, top: a publicity shot from Helen of Troy attesting to the relationship between screen size and subject matter. Far left: Peter Ustinov as the Emperor Nero in Mervyn LeRoy's Quo Vadis. Far left, below: the building of the pyramids in Howard Hawks' Land of the Pharaohs. Above: a monument to spectacle, design and art direction – the Forum Romanum in The Fall of the Roman Empire Left: Robert Taylor as Vinicius, making his triumphant entry into Rome in Quo Vadis. Below: The slaying of the tiger in the Circus Maximus in Demetrius and the Gladiators; the shot reveals the powerful framing of close-up action in CinemaScope

succeed; production could not be allowed to begin until the sale of distribution rights was well under way. The climactic period of the American historical epic was inaugurated right at the end of the Fifties with the appearance of *Ben-Hur*, William Wyler's triumphant blend of spectacle and psychological drama which will probably never be surpassed.

The first few years of the Sixties were rich in masterpieces which explored different facets of epic form in the cinema: Nicholas Ray's *King of Kings*, Stanley Kubrick's *Spartacus*, Anthony Mann's *El Cid*, Richard Fleischer's *Barabbas* (1962) and, finally, Joseph L. Mankiewicz's *Cleopatra* (1963). Soon, however, social as well as financial pressures were to take their toll on the epic. It was the age of media interest in youth and protest, of moral revaluation and political change beside which the film epic, with all its accumulated grossness of scale and budget, seemed slow and outmoded. And also, quite simply, after a decade of success, the genre needed a rest.

In the pursuit of epic dramatizations, the Hollywood companies plundered the talents of Europe's film industries. Generally the producers opted for a kind of modified realism but occasionally they permitted themselves moments of sheer stylization. Designers such as Veniero Colasanti, John Moore, Mario Chiari, Edward Carfagno, Alexander Golitzen, John de Cuir and André Andrejew provided dramatic settings to the action which often ranked as artworks in their own right: the frontier fort and *Forum Romanum* of *The Fall of the Roman Empire*, the stadium at Antioch in *Ben-Hur*, the Sicilian sulphur mines in *Barabbas*, the temple of Jerusalem in *King of Kings*.

Such handicraft would be nothing, however, without cameramen of great talent to register it. It is often forgotten how much of a debt is owed to such cinematographers as Leon Shamroy, Robert Krasker, Russell Metty and Robert Surtees, as well as the Italians Aldo Tonti and Giuseppe Rotunno, to name a few who did fine work in this field. Equally the emotional effect created by composers of epic music like Miklós Rózsa, Frank Waxman, Alex North and Alfred Newman should never be underestimated in discussion of the epic genre. Their music often supplies that essential accompaniment which both binds and annotates the drama itself. Would *Ben-Hur* possess half its grandeur or emotional undertow, or *King of Kings* its simple majesty, without Rózsa's thematic commentary? Would *The Silver Chalice* (1955) realize its stylized piety without Waxman's finely detailed score, or *Spartacus* its incipient brutality without Alex North's music?

Thematically the historical epic film is dominated by the message of personal and political freedom. In American cinema this notion frequently emerged in the form of Christianity or Zionism triumphant. The

Italian *peplum* was less dogmatically concerned with religion and more inclined to explore areas of (pre-Christian) history in which the Hollywood film-makers showed little interest. The American epics invariably championed a cosy, middle-American life-style and showed an inordinate fascination with the grosser parallels between twentieth-century America and Ancient Rome.

The huge mass of Christian homilies which form the bulk of Hollywood's output are generally dramatized in the form of pious martyrs vs callous Romans, with appropriate Judaic interpolations. Howard Hawks' *Land of the Pharoahs* (1955) – Warner Brothers' response to 20th Century-Fox's CinemaScope showpiece *The Egyptian* (1954) – is interesting for the way in which the central pyramid is personified as the 'hero' of the drama, shaping destinies and delivering its suffering builders from their torment. Both *The Vikings* and *Solomon and Sheba* (1959) make play with their Christian vs pagan themes but the latter film (undoubtedly the better of the two) settles for a glib final conversion of the wicked queen (played by Gina Lollobrigida in a commanding performance of

electrifying sexuality).

When dealing directly with the story of Christ, the epic cycle produced two fascinatingly opposed portraits: *King of Kings* conceals a complex re-structuring of the main biblical characters and a specifically Zionist ideology beneath its colourful, Sunday-school appearance, while *The Greatest Story Ever Told* (1965) is structured like a majestic symphony with Christ as the prime mover and central focus in a devout, almost funereal atmosphere.

Curiously, for the greatest works in this genre one must look to those stories in which the central protagonist functions as a mixture of the Christ-figure and pragmatic hero. *Barabbas* evokes *film noir* in its portrait of a man moving towards a destiny only half-perceived and from which he originally appeared to escape. *El Cid* presents an intense portrait of a medieval proto-Christ who is, at the same time, a knight redeemer. Finally, king of them all, is *Ben-Hur* where the protagonist progresses from nobility through oblivion to final redemption. It is a film, that stands as a testament to the entire epic genre.

Above: Jean Simmons, Jay Robinson and Richard Burton in 20th Century-Fox's The Robe; *an epic tale of the struggles of early Christians, this was the first film to be released in CinemaScope. Below right: the sermon on the mount from Nicholas Ray's* King of Kings *in which Jeffrey Hunter played Christ. Below, far right: Gina Lollobrigida as the Queen of Sheba in* Solomon and Sheba. *Her leading man was originally Tyrone Power but when Power died during filming in Spain, the role was given to Yul Brynner*

Space invaders

Cold War paranoia made its mark on the cinema in a variety of ways, most spectacular of which was the science-fiction boom of the Fifties with its topical theme of being taken over by aliens

Left: the classical science-fiction landscape of dunes and mountain ranges in Forbidden Planet *was given a new visual appeal through George Folsey's mellow, CinemaScope photography. The plot was a free adaptation of Shakespeare's* The Tempest. *Below: the rocket ship designed to carry a select group of humans away from their planet which is on a collision course with the planet Bellus. The designer George Pal won an Oscar for his apocalyptic special effects*

To look back at the science-fiction cinema of the Fifties from a 30-year vantage point is to identify, with some surprise, a golden decade. It's not that the films were masterpieces. Far from it. In technical ingenuity, not one of them could match ten minutes of *The Empire Strikes Back* (1980). In dramatic values, they alternated between the steely gaze (signifying incredulity, determination or lust) and the dropped jaw (defeat), with a tremulous grin occasionally permitted for the end credits. In story-line they were, by the dozen, what has since become recognized as first-generation schlock – a term which appropriately evokes the sound of rotting garbage hitting the bottom of a bucket.

They deserve their reputation. As bad films go, Fifties schlock movies achieved magnificent depths, plumbing the all-time low at the end of the decade. This was the era of *Invasion of the Saucer-Men, The Brain from Planet Arous, I Was a Teenage Frankenstein* (all 1957), *The Astounding She Creature, The She Demons, Colossus of New York* (all 1958), *Teenage Zombies*, and *Plan 9 From Outer Space* (both 1959). The last film is arguably the worst ever, but the foregoing titles give a fair indication of the artistic standards in question.

The title role in *The Astounding She Creature* (also known as *The Astonishing She Monster* and *The Mysterious Invader*) was played by Shirley Kilpatrick under the direction of Ron Ashcroft. A silent wayfarer from the skies, she wandered the Sierra Madre in lurex pyjamas, creating a ripple in the

WHEN WORLDS COLLIDE

PRODUCED BY GEORGE PAL
MAKER OF *'DESTINATION MOON'*
DIRECTED BY RUDOLPH MATÉ
COLOR BY Technicolor
A PARAMOUNT PICTURE

advised by rocketeer Hermann Oberth, the film proclaimed its authenticity in every detail. It even avoided the extremes of Heinlein's original (in which Nazis are discovered plotting away on the moon), by translating his precocious schoolboy astronauts into average American adults, all courage and good humour, such as would capture a hill in Korea or carry the flag into space with equal resourcefulness.

Destination Moon showed firmly that space-flight opened a new frontier, offering fun, sacrifice, and fresh subjects for the amateur photographer, plus a place in the history books and a long-distance call from the White House. The film also observed that the Moon offered strategic advantages and that if the Americans didn't get there first some other nation would.

It wasn't a message to be ignored. Since 1947, the torrent of UFO reports had led to keen speculation about the Moon as a base for flying saucers. If the Earth was under surveillance, it was time to repay the interest. If national security was also at stake, nothing could be permitted to stand in the way of

Above: Roger Corman's Attack of the Crab Monsters, *a quintessential piece of schlock science fiction: a group of scientists are studying marine life on a remote island, when suddenly . . . Right: in* The Alligator People *Bruce Bennett plays a disabled man who takes a special serum and turns into an alligator to the surprise of his friends and family. Below right: a distinctly paranoid fable,* Invaders From Mars, *showed aliens taking control of their victims' minds. Below: a scientist transplants his son's brain into a giant robot who goes on the rampage in New York*

camera lens and snarling radioactively at other members of the cast. The She Demons, on the other hand, were an all-girl dance ensemble on a nuclear testing-site where they were caged by Nazis whose leader conducted facial transplants. Hard to beat, that one.

Notable monstrosities were to follow. With the approach of the Sixties, however, the mood changed and the zestful innocence of schlock was overshadowed by darker complexities. Before considering these, we should return to the start of the golden decade, launched as it was by the film that changed the face of science-fiction cinema, *Destination Moon* (1950). George Pal's production was pure technology, the giant leap for mankind, prestaged as simple, stirring prophecy. The fantasies of the Forties had tended to be macabre and gloomy, even vaguely unhealthy like *The Beast With Five Fingers* (1946) or the equally creepy *House of Darkness* (1948). And while Superman, Captain Video and Batman marked the return of good, old-fashioned heroism in the movie serials of 1948 onwards, their comic-book image trivialized them.

There was nothing trivial, however, about *Destination Moon*, with its majestic space-flight and super-spectacular lunar surface. It made science fiction on the screen respectable, even if the magazines persisted in disguising themselves as lurid nonsense. Derived from a Robert Heinlein story, designed by the space-artist Chesley Bonestell,

EDWARD L. ALPERSON
presents

INVADERS FROM MAR

Photographed in COLOR

STARRING HELENA CARTER · ARTHUR FRANZ · JIMMY HUNT
with LEIF ERICKSON · HILLARY BROOKE · MORRIS ANKRUM · MAX WAGNER · BILL PHIPPS · MILBURN STONE · JANINE PERREAU
AN EDWARD L. ALPERSON PRODUCTION · Released by 20th Century-Fox
PRODUCTION DESIGNED AND DIRECTED BY   SCREENPLAY BY   ASSOCIATE PRODUCER   MUSIC BY
WILLIAM CAMERON MENZIES · RICHARD BLAKE · EDWARD L. ALPERSON, JR. · RAOUL KRAUS

PARAMOUNT PRESENTS
THE COLOSSUS OF NEW YORK

STARRING
JOHN BARAGREY
MALA POWERS
OTTO KRUGER
ROBERT HUTTON
ROSS MARTIN

PRODUCED BY
WILLIAM ALLAND
DIRECTED BY
EUGENE LOURIE
SCREENPLAY BY
THELMA SCHNEE
BASED ON A STORY BY WILLIS GOLDBECK

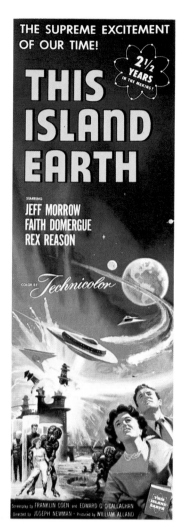

Above: an allegory of the human race torn apart by nuclear war: the story of This Island Earth *was actually set on the planet 'ietaluna where superintellectuals had enslaved a race of gruesome mutants. Below: women exile the men and rule the planet Venus until the Queen decides 'vimmen cannot live vizout men'. Below right: more powerful images of female dominance in* Attack of the Fifty-Foot Woman

the space programme, which thus merged conveniently with the American Dream.

Thanks to *Destination Moon*, the 'good guys' were the riders to the stars; thanks to the Cold War and the McCarthy hearings, the political leanings of the 'bad guys' were seldom in question. They were either leftovers from the last war or instigators of the next. In the films immediately following *Destination Moon* they made their treachery felt in a remarkable variety of ways.

The three classic science-fiction films of 1951 were *The Thing, The Day the Earth Stood Still* and *When Worlds Collide*, and they demonstrate how quickly the film-makers and their public recognized that a simple moonshot would do little to restore domestic security. The ending to *The Thing*, with its famous warning 'Watch the skies!', illustrated that teamwork and wisecracks can burn one bloodthirsty alien but there are plenty more available, ready to propagate their seed-pods at the drop of a severed hand. And if they don't arrive as chilly foreign agents, they'll turn up as Michael Rennie accompanied by his giant robot, ready to burn *us* to a crisp by way of chastisement. Mankind must learn its lesson, or God will surely intervene once more; the gospel according to Philip Wylie's script for *When Worlds Collide* shows a new Ark leaving for a Technicolor Eden.

God retreated from the struggle very early in the Fifties, having appeared in William Wellman's *The Next Voice You Hear* (1950) and in *Red Planet Mars* (1952), although the divine presence was invoked from time to time – most notably in *War of the Worlds* (1953), where the Martian desecration of a church is promptly followed by the invaders' deaths. God's part is taken over by the figure of the scientist, wandering uneasily in a borderland between exile and acceptance as a consequence of having brought one hideous war to an end by inventing the weapon that could start another.

From 1953 (when *Quatermass* began on British TV), screen eccentrics settled down in earnest to the task of pumping hypodermics and spraying noxious fumes, their experiments unleashing a menagerie of destructive mutants. For the rest of the decade, cinema audiences had a choice of being taken over by *Invaders From Mars, It Came From Outer Space* (both 1953), *Invasion of the Body Snatchers* (1956), *Invisible Invaders* (1959); squashed flat or otherwise intruded upon by *The Beast from 20,000 Fathoms* (1953), *Them!* (1954), *Gojira* (1954, *Godzilla*), *Tarantula* (1955), *The Monolith Monsters* (1957); confronted by the surgically unspeakable, as in *Donovan's Brain, The Magnetic Monster* (both 1953),

The Fly (1958), *The Alligator People* (1959); or being driven back from space in a nasty condition as, for example, the protagonists of *The Quatermass Experiment* (1955), *The Brain Eaters* (1958), *The First Man Into Space* and *The Hideous Sun-Demon* (both 1959).

Although Byron Haskin's 1955 epic *Conquest of Space* sought to restore some charisma to the solar system, it seems that the new age heralded by *Destination Moon* was quickly taken over by fear and cynicism. The dominant image of the rocket, a symbol that could be directed either upwards to explore fresh mysteries, or downwards to punish the unrepentant, was habitually taking the latter course. Not until Kubrick's *2001: A Space Odyssey* (1968) did it seem that man could return to the stars with an easier conscience.

The second half of the Fifties saw the world brought to an end with increasing frequency – most depressingly with *The World, the Flesh and the Devil* (1959), and *On the Beach* (1960) and most intriguingly with *The Last Woman on Earth* (1960) and *Rocket Attack USA* (1961). The Cuban missile crisis was just around the corner, and for students of science fiction it would be no great surprise.

The most consistent message of the period, as we now look back on it, was one of helplessness. William Cameron Menzies' film *Invaders From Mars* was an early example: a melancholy account of a small boy's discovery that his parents have been taken over by aliens. The takeover theme returned in the mid-Fifties with *The Quatermass Experiment, 1984* (1956) – two very different sides of the same coin – *Invasion of the Body Snatchers* and Roger Corman's trilogy of compulsion: *It Conquered the World, Not of This Earth* and *Attack of the Crab Monsters* (all 1956).

Each film shows society being eaten away from within. In dramatic terms, a few individuals gradually become aware of the developing cancer and make futile attempts to arrest its progress, often sacrificing themselves in the process. In *Attack of the Crab Monsters*, the struggle actually takes place on an island where malignant forces gain in power by absorbing the intellect of their victims. The culprit, as usual, is the all-purpose potency of radioactivity, the ultimate scientific obscenity which mocks the ageing process by accelerating it.

More complex fears are exposed by the films dealing with changes in size. *The Incredible Shrinking Man* (1957) was an almost Orwellian exercise in paranoia that was promptly echoed by *Amazing Colossal Man* (1957); *Attack of the Puppet People* and the near-legendary *Attack of the Fifty-Foot Woman*

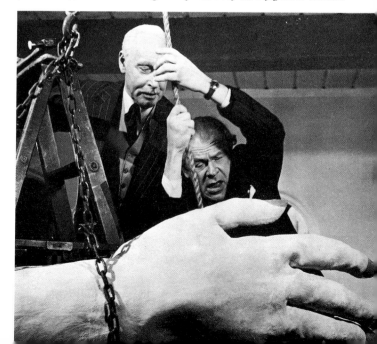

Above: urban destruction in War of the Worlds. *Below: a typical alien from* Invasion of the Hell Creatures. *Bottom: in far-off Sumeria, deep under ground lived* The Mole People, *a race of slaves*

bitterly into the twentieth century to demonstrate that the perpetual struggle between nations was a meaningless waste of planetary resources and a neglect of the magical powers that science could reveal to men. Ultimately, the vessel *Nautilus* may have achieved more influence than all the Cape Kennedy launchings, but the scorn expressed by Jules Verne's hero remains valid today.

In Joseph Newman's *This Island Earth* (1955), the fragility of our own planet is demonstrated through the story of a bright young scientist recruited to save the distant world of Metaluna from destruction by interplanetary warfare. Quite how he will achieve this when his hosts (who have much larger foreheads) have failed, is perhaps unclear but our hero and heroine (played by Jeff Morrow and Faith Domergue) did their best to make themselves useful while homicidal mutants patrolled the corridors and meteors bombarded Metaluna from neighbouring Zahgon. Lacking the focal character that, for example, Verne's Nemo would have provided. *This Island Earth* is too bland to inflict any bruises, but what it does offer is distinctly discouraging: the greater the science, the mightier the destruction.

With *Forbidden Planet* (1956), the triptych is completed. Jules Verne's Nemo character becomes Shakespeare's Prospero, alias Morbius, a castaway on Altair-4. This planet contains, in mile upon mile of storage chambers, the accumulated knowledge of the Krell race, long since disappeared. Again mankind is offered scientific wealth that could bring, if anyone is interested, the key to the universe. Again mankind proves incapable of looking further than his immediate hungers, and Morbius is unable to prevent himself from using the Krell power simply to attack his fellow creatures. It wasn't a lesson to take too seriously at the time. The hit of the film was Robby the Robot, not the star, Walter Pidgeon, and while critics made passing allusions to *The Tempest*, it was overlooked that Shakespeare's play had also dealt with disenchantment and the collapse of a once-stable system.

Viewing *Forbidden Planet* in context, however, it looks above all like the first 'inner space' story, cancelling the cheery optimism of *Destination Moon* with one elegant, anarchic sweep and opening the way for a spate of brash, trashy, truthful parables. Other contemporary allegories included *Fiend Without a Face* (1958), where brain power became a form of lethal parasite, and *Queen of Outer Space* (1958) in which the costumes and props of *Forbidden Planet* were used once again, though here to parody the whole idea of anyone or anything being brighter than a terrestrial. Together these films shook science fiction every which way, like a cinematic kaleidoscope.

At the end of the golden decade, comedy entered the genre. Jerry Lewis paid a *Visit to a Small Planet* (1960) and Fred MacMurray played *The Absent-Minded Professor* (1961) in Disney's fantasy film. A more serious tone was struck in *The Time Machine* (1960) where the scriptwriter David Duncan and the director George Pal dispensed with H.G. Wells' evolutionary background and patched together an amiable love story between Rod Taylor and Yvette Mimieux. Just over the horizon were Joseph Losey's *The Damned* (1962) a merciless tale of omnipotent children and Val Guest's *The Day the Earth Caught Fire* (1961) a contemptuous account of how nuclear testing knocks the world off its axis and sends it careering towards the sun. After Antonioni's *L'Eclisse* (1962, *The Eclipse*) and Stanley Kubrick's *Dr Strangelove, or How I Learned to Stop Worrying and Love the Bomb* (1964) – two contrasting accounts of nuclear paranoia – it looked more and more as if the future, should we survive to enjoy it, would be rather less than fun.

(both 1958). Since the days of *King Kong* (1933), it had been apparent that a solitary anthropoid could capture an audience's affection, but in the era of schlock – typified by the cheapest possible special effects – the idea tended to be unsupported by visual clarity and precision.

The Fifty-Foot Woman is no exception; she is either revealed merely as a papier-mâché hand or she is glimpsed transparently drifting about on another piece of celluloid (thanks to the rather crude matte-work), in a charmingly styled two-piece. What makes her predicament strikingly memorable is precisely that there is no incentive at all to see it in other than metaphorical terms. A wife is driven to distraction by her unfaithful husband and her passion destroys them both. The science-fiction aspect is almost irrelevant except that it serves to heighten, so to speak, the struggle between the characters. But what spectacular melodrama it makes!

The three greatest science-fiction films of the decade date from the mid-Fifties. They had widely different origins, but were alike in the care with which they were produced and their special effects were excitingly successful. Coincidentally, they illustrate the same theme of disenchantment. In Disney's *20,000 Leagues Under the Sea* (1954) Jules Verne's volatile recluse, Captain Nemo, cruised

FROM A LOST AGE... **HORROR** CRAWLS FROM THE DEPTHS OF THE EARTH!

The **MOLE** **PEOPLE**

JOHN AGAR · CYNTHIA PATRICK
STARRING
WITH **HUGH BEAUMONT · NESTOR PAIVA · ALAN NAPIER**
Directed by **VIRGIL VOGEL** · Written by **LASZLO GOROG** · Produced by **WILLIAM ALLAND** · A UNIVERSAL-INTERNATIONAL PICTURE

Above: Farley Granger and Cathy O'Donnell in
Ray's directorial debut, They Live by Night.
Left: hands on hips, Ray directs Ava Gardner
and Martin Miller in 55 Days at Peking, the
film that ended his Hollywood career

Nicholas Ray
The Lost Romantic

'If it was all in the script . . . why make the movie?' The words of
the director Nicholas Ray enshrine his belief in the purity and power
of the cinematic image, a belief he was able to translate into
stunning effect with his mastery of colour, composition and
performance – vibrantly displayed in his poetic but downcast views
of America. But Ray's is a tragic story. Forced for many years to
compromise his vision and cater to the bland expectations of Fifties
audiences, he finally decided it was better to leave Hollywood and
film-making behind and became a lonely wanderer in exile, a rebel
without a career, bitterly consigned to an artistic wilderness

Nicholas Ray was always a problem. His career
is central to that most difficult of critical
conundrums: how great an artist can a director working in the commercial Hollywood
system be? Not at all, according to one history
of world cinema published in Britain in 1964,
which contains just two fleeting references to
him. In complete contrast, French critics analysed and eulogized. 'The cinema *is* Nicholas
Ray', said Jean-Luc Godard. Although the
divergence of opinion on Ray has narrowed
over the years, there is a special irony in the

director's own dictum that 'There is no formula for success. But there is a formula for
failure; and that is trying to please everyone'.

Ray was born in Wisconsin in 1911. He
studied architecture under Frank Lloyd
Wright at Chicago University, but chose to
become a stage actor and occasionally a
director, and at the same time a travelling
student of American folklore. Diverse though
these four interests might appear, they are
combined in the movies he directed – all which
bear the indelible stamp of one personality.

Knocking on the Hollywood door

While acting on Broadway in the Thirties, Ray
met the producer John Houseman and the
director Elia Kazan. He worked with Houseman on radio propaganda programmes during
World War II, and when Kazan went to
Hollywood in 1945 to make *A Tree Grows in
Brooklyn*, Ray accompanied him as an assistant. It was Houseman's television production
of the classic suspense thriller *Sorry Wrong
Number*, which Ray directed in 1946 (and
which virtually established TV drama in the
USA), that brought both men to the attention
of Dore Schary, head of production at RKO.
The result was *They Live by Night* (1948),
produced by Houseman (who already had
several film credits to his name) and directed
by Ray.

They Live by Night immediately established a
framework of reference points to which Ray's
later movies inevitably return. Based on
Edward Anderson's novel *Thieves Like Us* (and
remade under that title by Robert Altman in
1974), the movie is the story of the doomed
love affair between Bowie Bowers (Farley
Granger) and Keechie (Cathy O'Donnell).
Bowie is the first of Ray's 'outsiders' – solitary,
anguished characters at war with society and
themselves. He is an escaped convict – wrongly
jailed for murder – who believes quite
genuinely that the proceeds of bank robberies
can hire him the best lawyer to clear his name.
As the title suggests, the world into which the
two central characters escape is one of darkness, pessimism and loneliness; yet there they
find the love and freedom that has been denied
them in the daylight world. Seven years later,
in Ray's most famous movie, *Rebel Without a
Cause* (1955), the three teenagers played by
James Dean, Natalie Wood and Sal Mineo
would share similar moments of peace and
tenderness in a deserted mansion which for a
brief time becomes their own little universe.

In lonely places

This pessimistic, lonely and doomed existence
is depicted again and again in Ray's movies,
whether it is the harsh, transient world of the
professional rodeo circuit in *The Lusty Men*
(1952), or one of the last outposts of unspoiled,
primitive society like the Eskimo settlement
threatened by an encroaching 'civilization' in

Ombre Bianche (1959, *The Savage Innocents*).

'I'm a stranger here myself', says Johnny (Sterling Hayden) in *Johnny Guitar* (1954) to explain his diffidence as he watches a bank robbery in progress, and it is an attitude that is at the heart of Ray's world. It suggests both an inner peace of mind, a world of dreams, a means of escape from an unacceptable world outside, and the root of a conflict when that outside world advances threateningly on such a mind. Of these conflicts were the best Ray movies made.

The least interesting of his early movies contain few of these complexities. *A Woman's Secret* (1949), *Born to Be Bad* (1950) and *Flying Leathernecks* (1951) were all to Ray reluctant chores handed out by RKO studio boss Howard Hughes. They were, by Ray's standards, simple movies: two 'women's pictures', with Gloria Grahame (who briefly became Ray's wife) as Susan in *A Woman's Secret*, and Joan Fontaine as Christabel in *Born to Be Bad* – both scheming their way to success by ruthlessly using everyone around them; and a traditional war movie with John Wayne as a marine hammering friend and foe in the national cause.

Of greater interest was *Knock on Any Door* (1949), made for and starring Humphrey Bogart. The huge commercial success of this film helped Ray's career immensely. Its case history of a young hoodlum on trial for the murder of a policeman looks forward to the starting point of *Rebel Without a Cause*. Its polemical condemnation of society, which is deemed as much responsible for the crime as the accused boy, recalls Ray's own involvement in Elia Kazan's radical theatre-workshop groups in the mid-Thirties. Another major ingredient of *Knock on Any Door*, and a recurring interest of Ray's, is the theme of the latent violence in man – a trait that is often only brought to the surface by its opposite, love. Both Ray's best movies of the early Fifties, *In a Lonely Place* (1950) and *On Dangerous Ground* (1951), are depictions of this theme.

On one level, *On Dangerous Ground* is an exciting thriller, the story of a sadistic cop (Robert Ryan) and his relationship with a blind girl (Ida Lupino) who is the sister of a hunted

killer. On another, it is a return to the dark world of *They Live by Night*, but in an urban environment. *In a Lonely Place* has a Hollywood setting with a scriptwriter (Humphrey Bogart) suspected of murder and saved only by the alibi given by his next-door neighbour (Gloria Grahame). The relationship that develops between these two characters provides the basis for Ray's most forceful portrait of an outwardly strong and intelligent man destroyed by his own inner melancholy and his inability to communicate except through terrible fits of violence.

Above: In a Lonely Place *starred Humphrey Bogart as a Hollywood scriptwriter driven by rumour and suspicion to the brink of murdering the girl (Gloria Grahame) he loves. Right: John Wayne as a fighter pilot in* Flying Leathernecks. *Below right: James Mason as the drug addict in* Bigger Than Life. *Below left: the death of a rodeo rider in* The Lusty Men, *with Susan Hayward*

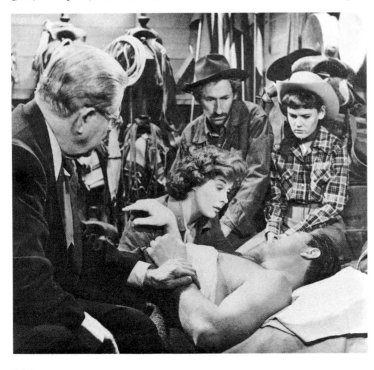

Above: saloon-keeper Vienna (Joan Crawford) faces a lynching at the hands of the mob whipped up by cattle boss Emma Small (Mercedes McCambridge) in Johnny Guitar. *Below right: Curt Jurgens in the war film* Bitter Victory

Violence, types of and uses

Ray constantly explored this expressive side of violence in his Fifties films. *Johnny Guitar*, possibly the most bizarre Western ever made, concentrates on the psychological and sexual tensions in the relationship between the two main female characters, Vienna (Joan Crawford) and Emma (Mercedes McCambridge), and ends in a savage gunfight between them. Violent outbursts punctuate *Rebel Without a Cause* as Jim Stark (James Dean) is transformed from social misfit to a self-determining adult through the death of the unhappy and unloved Plato (Sal Mineo). In *Bigger Than Life* (1956), the drug cortisone is the metaphor for the change of character in Ed Avery (James Mason) from underpaid teacher (a man forced to work as a taxi-driver after school to maintain his family's standards of living) to virtual madman. Initially he takes the drug to relieve the pain of a fatal nervous disease, but discovers that it offers a freedom that he has never before experienced. His abuse of it leads to paranoid delusions of grandeur and a state of insanity which almost destroys his life and family. Captain Leith (Richard Burton) in *Bitter Victory* (1957) uses the horrors of a World War II desert campaign to satisfy his own masochism. And do these characters add up to a portrait of their creator? They do, admitted Ray in a 1974 interview, 'but it is the role of the poet – and every artist hopes to be a poet – to expose himself. It's the only way he communicates'.

It is also difficult not to see Ray the rebel, the loner and the fighter, as the sheriff played by James Cagney in *Run for Cover* (1955), embarking on a law-and-order campaign based on humanity rather than lynching; or identifying with the misfit outlaw band of *The True Story of Jesse James* (1957); the drunken-teacher-turned-wildlife-preserver (Christopher Plummer) in turn-of-the-century Florida in *Wind Across the Everglades* (1958); the two outsiders

of *Party Girl* (1958) – the crooked lawyer trying to go straight (Robert Taylor) and the prostitute who falls in love with him (Cyd Charisse). Another side of Ray can be seen in the anthropological and ecological issues raised by *The Savage Innocents* as Inuk the Eskimo (Anthony Quinn) confronts a scathing portrait of the white man's civilization and rejects it.

Epic farewells

Hollywood and Nicholas Ray rejected each other in 1963 after two big-screen epics, *King of Kings* (1961) displayed more interest in the traitor Judas Iscariot than in Christ, and there were no miracles. Finally, Ray made 55 *Days at Peking* (1963), the story of the Boxer rebellion in China in 1900 starring Charlton Heston, Ava Gardner and David Niven. Like all Ray's movies, it contains some fine performances (including one by the director himself in a cameo role). Indeed, Ray drew some of the finest performances in their careers from such diverse stars as Robert Mitchum, James Mason, James Dean, Joan Crawford and Richard Burton. He embedded these performances in his films with a unique visual style which

even mastered that most cumbersome of screen ratios, CinemaScope. Ray attributed this success to his early architectural training. His work is littered with extraordinary compositions, both of form and colour, which are not just masterly demonstrations of craftsmanship but counterpoints to the actions, emotions and psyches of his characters. Even his worst film, *Hot Blood* (1956), comes alive with some frenetic musical sequences.

The End

Ray spent the last 16 years of his life outside the commercial Hollywood system. He taught film studies at New York State University and made, as a joint project with his students, *We Can't Go Home Again* (1973), a semi-documentary collage of images in which he played a teacher with a death-wish. His health, never good, declined over the years and his only other piece of film-making was a sad segment of an omnibus 'sexploitation' movie, *Dreams of Thirteen* (1974). His final feature-film appearance was as an army general in Miloš Forman's 1979 film adaptation of the stage success *Hair*, but a more satisfying farewell image was his role in *Das Amerikanische Freund* (1977, *The American Friend*). It was directed by Wim Wenders, who later recorded the last few months of Ray's life – he died in June 1979 – in *Lightning Over Water* (1980).

In *The American Friend*, an adaptation of Patricia Highsmith's novel *Ripley's Game*, Ray plays an artist whom the world believes to be dead. The real-life parallel is obvious. To him goes the honour of the movie's closing shot as he turns away from the camera and walks into the distance. Twenty years earlier it was Ray who walked into the final shot of *Rebel Without a Cause*, stopping briefly to admire a flowerbed. At the end of *The American Friend* he walks forcefully on and the scene goes dark. It is a moment of which Nick Ray, for all his pessimism always a great Romantic, must surely have approved.

Filmography
1945 A Tree Grows in Brooklyn (ass. dir. only). '48 They Live by Night (+ co-sc). '49 A Woman's Secret; Knock on Any Door; Roseanna McCoy (add. dir. uncredited). '50 Born to Be Bad; In a Lonely Place. '51 Flying Leathernecks; The Racket (add. dir. uncredited); On Dangerous Ground. '52 Macao (add. dir. uncredited); The Lusty Men; Androcles and the Lion (add. dir. uncredited). '54 Johnny Guitar (+ assoc. prod). '55 Run for Cover; Rebel Without a Cause (+ co-sc). '56 Hot Blood; Bigger Than Life. '57 The True Story of Jesse James; Bitter Victory (+ co-sc). '58 Wind Across the Everglades; Party Girl. '59 Ombre Bianche (GB: The Savage Innocents) (IT-FR-GB). '61 King of Kings. '63 55 Days at Peking (+ act). '64 Circus World (co-sc. only) (GB: The Magnificent Showman). '65 The Doctor and the Devils (GB-YUG) (unfinished). '73 I'm a Stranger Here Myself (doc) (appearance as himself only). '73 We Can't Go Home Again (+ act). '74 Dreams of Thirteen *ep* The Janitor (+ sc; + act) (GER-NETH). '75 James Dean, the First American Teenager (doc) (appearance as himself only) (GB). '77 Das Amerikanische Freund (actor only) (GER-FR) (USA/GB: The American Friend). '79 Hair (actor only). '80 Lightning Over Water/Nick's Movie (co-dir; + appearance as himself).

Edward G. Robinson

Robinson as Rico down on his luck in Little Caesar *(left), as a scientist in* Dr Ehrlich's Magic Bullet *(above), a framed businessman in* Blackmail *(1939, above right) and a jaded lawyer in* Illegal *(1955, far right)*

Edward G. Robinson, describing the opening of one of his earlier speeches while entertaining the troops during World War II, wrote in his autobiography:

'I began by saying: "I am happy to be here, the most privileged moment of my life, to see the men who are defeating Hitler." . . . I could sense the audience despising me . . . and to stop the buzz of their boos and Bronx cheers, I ad-libbed, "Pipe down, you mugs, or I'll let you have it. Whaddya hear from the mob?" There was an instant burst of high laughter and applause.'

Throughout his book Robinson returns obsessively to a fact that he found incomprehensible; people knew him and wanted to see him primarily as Rico, the title figure in his famous 1930 film *Little Caesar*. The reasons why he found this so surprising have partly to do with

cultural attitudes as to what is important in art – in particular the debate about whether High Art is to be preferred to Popular Art – but in Robinson's case the reasons go deeper. They relate to the time and place in which he was born and raised.

Born Emanuel Goldenberg on December 12, 1893 in Bucharest, Romania, Robinson's family background was based on Jewish discipline and middle-class values. At that time the Jews were denied civil rights in Romania and were subjected to periodic persecution, an important factor in the emigration of the family to the United States in the early years of the century. The moral tone of the Goldenberg family was akin to a certain brand of Protestantism which stressed morality and hard work. However, the Goldenberg family was slightly unorthodox, having a European predisposition

Above left: with Claudette Colbert in The Hole in the Wall *(1929), one of Robinson's earliest gangster roles. Above:* East is West *(1930) featured Lupe Velez and Robinson as an unlikely Chinese pair*

to a highly romantic conception of art.

These elements would have, of themselves, inclined the young Robinson to be hostile to the cinema as a mass art – which was indeed to be the case – but they were reinforced by his choice of career as a theatre actor. During the Twenties Robinson rose to become a considerable figure on the Broadway stage, appearing in a whole range of classic and modern plays and deciding early on that because of his appearance his future was as a character actor rather than as a leading man.

It is often assumed that *Little Caesar* was

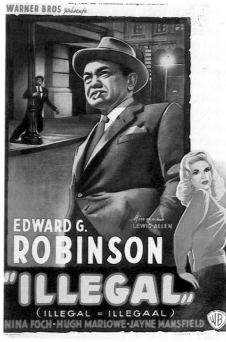

A Master of his Art

Above: in danger of being typecast, Robinson played a corrupt gangster figure in Barbary Coast *(1935). Above right: a scornful Kitty (Joan Bennett) makes use of her besotted admirer (Robinson) in* Scarlet Street

Robinson's first picture but his stage reputation ensured that he had received offers to go to Hollywood from the early Twenties. The handful of movies he made before *Little Caesar* confirmed for him his intuitive dislike of the medium. Characteristically, while appearing in a theatrical production of *Peer Gynt* he stole off to see himself in his first film, the silent *The Bright Shawl* (1923) – in which he played a Spanish aristocrat – and was appalled.

Little Caesar is regarded as the first of the classic gangster movies and Rico, the Italian immigrant whose rise and fall the film charts,

the first of the classic gangster 'heroes' – even to the extent of his lying dead in the street at the end of the film. Robinson never understood its success and his remarks on the film sought to make analogies with Greek tragedy as a way of explaining its popularity:

'He (Rico) is a man who defies society, and in the end is mowed down by the gods and society, and doesn't even know what happened . . . the picture has sustained itself throughout these years because it was constructed as a Greek tragedy.'

His upbringing and training made it impossible for him to appreciate the virtues of pace, simplicity, action and contemporaneity.

The paradox is that Robinson became a complete master of the art of screen acting while at the same time regarding most of his film work as beneath contempt. Understand-

ably he was to play in several gangster films as a contract player with Warner Brothers during the Thirties, but he always aspired to roles which approximated more to his conception of 'good theatre'.

He always regarded his finest role as that of Paul Ehrlich – the man who discovered a cure for syphilis – in *Dr Ehrlich's Magic Bullet* (1940) perhaps because of the manifest seriousness of the project. It is significant that the aggressive, lower-class hoodlums he played in the Thirties tended to give way, in the mid-Forties, to articulate bourgeois figures as in *Double Indemnity* (1944), in which he played a shrewd insurance investigator, *Woman in the Window* (1944), which featured him as a psychology professor, *Scarlet Street* (1945), in which he was a clerk who finds in painting an escape from the oppression of the *petit-bourgeois*

milieu in which he lives and works, and *All My Sons* (1948), in which he played a man selling defective airplane parts to the government.

At the same time Robinson seems to have had an odd blindness and lack of sympathy for *Scarlet Street*, given its critical importance as a major film by Fritz Lang and the closeness of its theme – a Sunday painter who produces masterpieces – to an important dimension of his own life. In the debate about High Art or Popular Art Robinson was firmly on the side of High Art. He had built up a renowned collection

of Impressionist pictures and was a considerable painter in his own right, as well as being a confidant of the most illustrious musical figures in America.

If his European background inclined him to an elitist and rather conservative view of art, it predisposed him to an egalitarian and progressive view of politics. Throughout the Thirties and early Forties he lent his name, time and money to a number of progressive causes, a fact which was to cost him dearly during the infamous anti-communist witch-hunts of the late Forties and early Fifties. Though not remotely a communist himself, Robinson's affinity with democratic ideals got him blacklisted for a time.

This and his own early commitment to 'character' roles, meant that his later career was as a supporting actor of great eminence, range and distinction. The more 'theatrical' side of his persona was perhaps best shown in his playing of the temperamental film director in *Two Weeks in Another Town* (1962) and the 'cinematic' side in his role as ace poker player in *The Cincinnati Kid* (1965). There was more than some truth in his final remark to Steve McQueen in the latter: 'As long as I'm around, you're second best; you may as well learn to live with it.'

Above left: The Kid (Steve McQueen) and The Man (Robinson), rivals at the poker table in The Cincinatti Kid. *Below: Robinson as an accomplice in the theft of a statue from St Peter's, Rome, in* Operazione San Pietro *(1968, Operation St Peter's). Below right: with Raquel Welch on the set of* The Biggest Bundle of Them All *(1967)*

Filmography

1923 The Bright Shawl. '29 The Hole in the Wall. '30 Night Ride; A Lady to Love; Outside the Law; East is West; The Widow from Chicago; Little Caesar. '31 Smart Money; Five Star Final. '32 The Stolen Jools (short) (GB: The Slippery Pearls); The Hatchet Man (GB: The Honourable Mr Wong); Two Seconds; Tiger Shark; Silver Dollar. '33 The Little Giant; I Loved a Woman; Dark Hazard. '34 The Man With Two Faces. '35 The Whole Town's Talking (GB: Passport to Fame); A Day at Santa Anita (short) (guest); Barbary Coast. '36 Bullets or Ballots. '37 Thunder in the City (GB: Kid Galahad; The Last Gangster. '38 A Slight Case of Murder; The Amazing Dr Clitterhouse; I Am the Law. '39 Confessions of a Nazi Spy; Blackmail. '40 Dr Ehrlich's Magic Bullet (GB: The Story of Dr Ehrlich's Magic Bullet); Brother Orchid; A Dispatch From Reuters (GB: This Man Reuter); Manpower. '41 The Sea Wolf; Unholy Partners. '42 Moscow Strikes Back (doc) (narr only); Tales of Manhattan; Larceny Inc. '43 The Red Cross at War (doc) (narr only); Projection of America (doc) (on-screen narr only); Destroyer; Flesh and Fantasy; Screen Snapshots, Series 22, No 4 (short) (compere only). '44 Tampico; Screen Snapshots, Series 23, No 9 (short) (guest); Double Indemnity; Mr Winkle Goes to War (GB: Arms and the Woman); The Woman in the Window. '45 Our Vines Have Tender Grapes; Journey Together (GB); Scarlet Street. '46 The Stranger. '47 The Red House. '48 All My Sons; Where Do You Get Off? (short) (narr only); Key Largo; Night Has a Thousand Eyes. '49 House of Strangers; It's a Great Feeling (guest). '50 My Daughter Joy (GB) (USA: Operation X); Screen Snapshots (short). '52 Actors and Sin *ep* Actor's Blood. '53 Vice Squad (GB: The Girl in Room 17); Big Leaguer; The Glass Web. '54 Black Tuesday; The Violent Men (GB: Rough Company). '55 Tight Spot; A Bullet for Joey; Illegal; Hell on Frisco Bay. '56 Nightmare; The Ten Commandments. '57 The Heart of Show Business (doc) (co-narr only). '59 A Hole in the Head; Israel (doc) (narr only). '60 Seven Thieves; Pepe (guest). '61 My Geisha. '62 Two Weeks in Another Town. '63 Sammy Going South (GB) (USA: A Boy Ten Feet Tall); The Prize. '64 Good Neighbour Sam; Robin and the Seven Hoods (guest); The Outrage; Cheyenne Autumn. '65 The Cincinnati Kid; Who Has Seen the Wind? (United Nations). '67 Le Blonde de Pekin (FR-IT-GER) (USA: Peking Blonde); The Biggest Bundle of Them All (USA-IT); Ad Ogni Costa (IT-SP-GER) (USA/GB: Grand Slam). '68 Never a Dull Moment; Operazione San Pietro (IT-FR-GER); Uno Scacco tutto Matto (IT-SP). '69 Mackenna's Gold. '70 Song of Norway. '72 Neither by Day or Night (USA-IS); Soylent Green.

The concrete jungle

Images of violence and conspiracy dominated the gangster movies of the Fifties, together with a certain nostalgia for the good old days of crime – Prohibition-style

Film critics quite often write about the cinema in terms of the excellence of particular films or the careers of particular directors. Ordinary cinemagoers (including off-duty critics), however, tend to talk about the cinema in terms of the stars and the types of film they like (such as Westerns, musicals, horror movies and so on). It may be that ordinary cinemagoers are closer to the way the cinema actually works as a social process, an essentially industrial/commercial process in which pleasures are produced, marketed and consumed.

To talk about the excellence of particular films is to concentrate on only one aspect of the process, the film as object or individual product, a unique experience labelled by a particular title (*Casablanca*, *Charley Varrick* or *Quadrophenia*, for example). To talk about the careers of particular directors (Nicholas Ray, Don Siegel, Walter Hill) is to suggest that the cinema works primarily through expressing the personality and interests of particular film-makers, a notion that even the most casual cinemagoer knows to be generally false, though the media now tend to push this viewpoint, once largely confined to specialist criticism.

When talking about stars and types (or genres) of film, it is very difficult not to talk also about all the stages of the cinema process, a more inclusive and accurate kind of examination. In particular, such discussion includes consideration of the audience, what it does with the films it sees. The audience once had, and to some extent still has, a habit of cinema-going and this affects how particular films are understood and interpreted. At the very least, it can be said that the audience brings to any individual film its experience of other films.

Since the primary purpose of popular cinema is to deliver a set of particular satisfactions to audiences, there is a sense in which all popular films do the

same thing in much the same way. They employ a form of narrative in which one form of stability is shattered by intrusive forces and a new form of stability established at the outcome. The conclusion usually has a strong sense of narrative closure, of having the ends neatly tied up. Within this movement, in itself highly satisfying, the more static satisfactions of the cinema, the opportunity to gaze on particular stars and events, are delivered.

There is, however, a certain tension at the core of the process of recurrent cinema-going. On the one hand, certain *known* satisfactions require to be delivered; on the other hand, the experience is expected to be sufficiently different from previous ones to avoid boredom. This tension between repetition and innovation is central to the way the cinema's genres work and goes a long way towards explaining the process of development and renewal in the genres. A question it will not answer, though, is why particular genres first emerge and then re-emerge at particular historical moments. Such explanations would be very complex, involving discussion of the economic demands of production companies and the ideological and aesthetic needs of film-makers and audiences in particular eras.

As Hollywood entered the Fifties, it inherited a very rich and varied tradition in the crime film. The ensemble of features associated with the classic gangster movie of the Thirties was still in evidence: a particular kind of narrative form (itself a variant of the order/instability/new-order form) which charts the rise and fall of a gangster; an iconography of figures dressed in a particular way, moving through the familiar milieux and engaging in special activities; and set pieces of spectacle, often involving guns or cars. This had been overlaid with and interpenetrated by the qualities of the thriller: a different variant of the order/instability/new-order

Above left: Bugsy Siegel, gangster and friend of several film producers, was shot dead at his Beverly Hills home on June 20, 1947. The real-life photograph is more bloody and horrific than most movies of the period but would not have been unusual in crime magazines of that time. Above: Marilyn Maxwell and Broderick Crawford in New York Confidential, *the story of a big crime-boss who comes to a violent end. Newspaper headlines often feature in gangster movies, both to speed up the narrative and to represent public opinion, the straight world, in the crooks' environment*

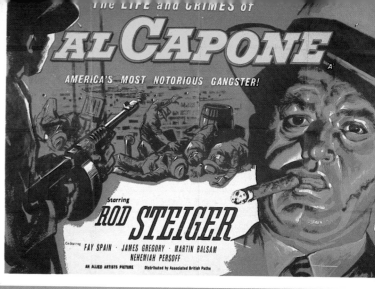

narrative form whereby a mystery is solved; forms of lighting derived primarily from the German Expressionist cinema; a different range of figures such as the private eye, the *femme fatale* and the intellectual, sophisticated, Europeanized and often psychologically perverse villain; and an overall awareness of human alienation and cruelty. Overlaid upon both of these major forms were the passion for location shooting, the use of documentary origins of stories and the emphasis on the intricate workings of particular technologies which characterized crime films of the late Forties.

The crucial process of renewal and transformation within the genre can be indicated by comparing the way the elements are handled from one era to another. Thus in *The Public Enemy* (1931) the energy and dynamism of the James Cagney figure are presented as laudable ambition gone wrong and his mother is portrayed as a source of traditional values, while in *White Heat* (1949), Cody Jarrett (James Cagney) is presented as psychotic and his mother as a monstrous harpy goading her son to greater excesses. While the satisfactions delivered by the crime movie (and any other popular form) at any moment invariably involve the following-through of variants on the classical narrative forms

and the opportunity to gaze at stars and spectacle, the crime movies of any era take their subject-matter from what is actually happening, or has recently happened, in American crime. This is one way a genre might be renewed and transformed. Thus after the repeal of the Volstead Act in 1933 which brought an end to Prohibition, labour racketeering occupied a great deal of the attention of organized crime, as in *Racket Busters* (1938), until 1943, when gambling moved to the fore, as in *Force of Evil* (1949).

In the Fifties the gangster movie produced three new strains, one of which took its impulse directly from the reality of American crime at the time. In this first strain there are two characteristic images: one is of a figure, very often a racketeer, testifying, amid considerable media coverage, before a Senate sub-committee; the other is of a group of elderly, sober-suited men sitting around a boardroom table and voting on whether an erstwhile colleague should be murdered. The real events to which both these images relate are the hearings and conclusions of the Senate Special Committee to Investigate Crime in Interstate Commerce, usually called the Kefauver Committee after its chairman. It was the findings of this committee which gave rise to the

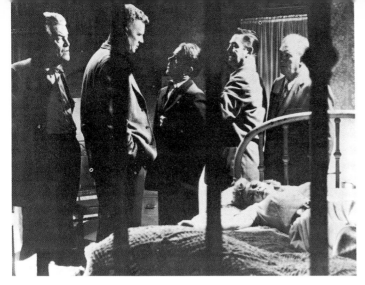

Top far left: John Dall and Peggy Cummins as a couple of young robbers in Joseph H. Lewis' Gun Crazy *(1949). Top left: Richard Wilson's re-creation of Twenties Chicago,* Al Capone. *Far left: another period piece from Richard Wilson, again expertly photographed by Lucien Ballard,* Pay or Die! *was set in New York's Little Italy in 1906. Left: Roger Corman's* Bloody Mama *recounted the violent lives and deaths of Ma Barker (Shelley Winters) and her four sons in the Thirties. Bottom left: Richard Conte as one of* The Brothers Rico *in Phil Karlson's version of a Simenon novel. Above: Jay C. Flippen, Sterling Hayden, Elisha Cook Jnr, Ted de Corsia, Joe Sawyer and (on the bed) Marie Windsor in Stanley Kubrick's* The Killing. *Above right: My Gun Is Quick was based on Mickey Spillane's novel. Below: Roger Corman's* The St Valentine's Day Massacre *was a convincingly detailed retelling of Al Capone's most famous crime*

cycle of gangster movies in which 'the Syndicate' (sometimes city-wide, sometimes nation-wide) figured.

In many respects *The Enforcer* (1951) is *the* transitional crime film between the Forties and the Fifties. Dealing with the activities of 'Murder Incorporated', it has some of the features of the so-called 'semi-documentary' film of the Forties but sounds the note which was to dominate the Fifties, the existence of an all-embracing crime conspiracy modelled on legitimate business activity. This cycle includes *Hoodlum Empire* (1952), *New York Confidential* (1955), *The Brothers Rico* (1957) and *Underworld USA* (1960). This motif, more than any other, should have provided the means of offering explanations of crime in terms of social structure rather than personal disposition; but the form of the classical narrative movie, with its emphasis on individual characters, is not well suited to posing questions and explanations in other than personal terms. Similarly, the issues of politics in American movies are displaced on to the terrain of personal action and morality. The Syndicate is usually defeated in this cycle of movies, but almost always through the action of one man motivated by vengeance.

The two central recurring scenes of this cycle are of testimony and conspiracy; there is often a sense, in these movies, of the power of the Syndicate stretching into every area of the characters' lives, as

in *The Brothers Rico*. It is interesting to speculate on the extent to which these images of testimony and conspiracy involving crime were providing the terrain on to which was displaced other kinds of testimony and conspiracy which were quite literally unspeakable in the Hollywood films of the Fifties – those associated with the McCarthy hearings and the aftermath of blacklisting.

The second strain which appeared in the Fifties indicated that Hollywood was beginning to have a conscious sense of its own history. This strain consisted of a series of films set in the Prohibition and Depression periods, the time of the early gangster movies. Very often they took the form of a biography of a notorious criminal. This cycle includes *Baby Face Nelson* (1957), *The Bonnie Parker Story*, *Machine Gun Kelly* (both 1958), *Al Capone* (1959) and continues into the Sixties with *The Rise and Fall of Legs Diamond*, *Pay or Die!* (both 1960), *Portrait of a Mobster* (1961), *Bonnie and Clyde*, *The St. Valentine's Day Massacre* (both 1967) and *Bloody Mama* (1970). The sense that these films offer of Hollywood consciously raking over its own history was pointed up by their stylized, balletic quality and the use of music designed to evoke the Twenties and Thirties.

The third strain which came to the fore in the Fifties had its origins to some extent in the Forties. Films such as *Criss Cross* (1949) and *White Heat* involved carefully prepared robberies which

In the Fifties, gangster movies and thrillers became more conscious of style and history

remained a secondary element in these films. *The Asphalt Jungle* (1950) was unique in American cinema for the attention it gave to the preparation for and execution of the robbery. The form which it initiated – the 'caper' movie – is in many respects a celebration of the narrative process of cinema itself. Within this form, a group of disparate individuals comes together to pull off a robbery. The cycle includes *The Killing* (1956), *Odds Against Tomorrow* (1959), *Seven Thieves* and *Ocean's Eleven* (both 1960).

One of the strangest elements in the transition from the Forties to the Fifties in Hollywood was the virtual disappearance of the thriller and *film noir*. Hollywood cinema of the Fifties is generally bright and colourful; even its bleakest films, such as *The Big Heat* (1953), appear bathed in light by comparison with Forties films. The thriller did survive to a limited extent into the Fifties. But virtuous heroes

Above: in The Wrong Man, *Mrs Balestrero (Vera Miles) has struck her husband, Manny (Henry Fonda), resenting the collapse of family life since his wrongful arrest. Maxwell Anderson's book and Hitchcock's film were based on a real-life case of mistaken identity. Below right: a poster for* Strangers on a Train, *based on Patricia Highsmith's first novel, shows Hitchcock's use of his own popular humorous image. Bruno (Robert Walker) does indeed strangle the unwanted wife of a tennis player (Farley Granger) to whom he has proposed a swopping of murders*

like Sam Spade in *The Maltese Falcon* (1941) and Philip Marlowe in *Murder, My Sweet* (1944), *The Big Sleep, The Lady in the Lake* (both 1946) and *The Brasher Doubloon* (1947) gave way to the considerably less virtuous Mike Hammer of the Mickey Spillane adaptations which characterize the decade – *I, The Jury* (1953), *Kiss Me Deadly* (1955) and *My Gun Is Quick* (1957). The change is partly indicated in the casting. While Bogart has a certain toughness, it does not altogether conceal his humour and vulnerability. These qualities are hardly evident in the screen persona of Ralph Meeker in *Kiss Me Deadly*.

If the thriller and *film noir* were largely missing from Fifties Hollywood, their spirit lived on. Nowhere was this more apparent than in the realization of particular acts of violence in the Fifties. In the classic gangster movie of the Thirties, violence tended to be swift, unritualized, unmarked by specific cinematic effects (such as close-ups) and usually executed by firearms. Violence in the thriller and *film noir* of the Forties involved beating, crushing, burning, cutting, disfigurement, pushing from high buildings and poisoning. This more tactile sense of violence is evident, primarily in the Fifties gangster movie and thriller, but also in other Fifties genres such as the Western and the war movie. An example which excited much comment at the time was the shooting of James Stewart's gun hand in *The Man From Laramie* (1955). Among the most disturbing acts of violence in the Fifties gangster movie are those enacted (actually or potentially) on women, such as the disfigurement suffered by Debbie (Gloria Grahame) in *The Big Heat* and the threat of acid to the face of Vicki (Cyd Charisse) in *Party Girl* (1958).

The increasingly disturbing violence of American cinema in the Fifties is perhaps an indication of the sense of unease which underlay the apparent stability of Eisenhower's America. Critics have revealed the presence of a similar sense of unease in the displacement of the nuclear threat into fantasies about mutated monsters in the same period and in the stresses and strains lying just underneath the surface of the family melodrama.

Unease is a key word when discussing a very special variant of the crime film in the Fifties, that type of film in which the focus is less on an account of organized crime or on the solving of a mystery than on the mechanics of suspense.

This type of film is particularly associated with the name of Alfred Hitchcock, for whom the Fifties was a particularly prolific decade. The pattern of the classical Hollywood narrative whereby initial stability is undermined is writ large in Hitchcock's work in the sense that the central figures of his films very often inhabit the most mundane worlds – a tennis player in *Strangers on a Train* (1951), a priest in *I Confess* (1952), a temporarily incapacitated news-photographer in *Rear Window* (1954), an advertising man in *North by Northwest* (1959) – which collapse under their feet, tumbling them into the most nightmarish situations. As critics have demonstrated, these nightmares do not have a *social* basis; they are not concerned with the characters' relations with the outside world. Rather, they are concerned with the fragility of the characters' own personality and identity and with the horrors which may lie in the depths of their own psyches. Thus the priest of *I Confess*, the tennis player of *Strangers on a Train* and the ad-man of *North by Northwest* effectively take on the appearance of guilty men; the policeman of *Vertigo* (1958) becomes a necrophiliac and the temporary invalid of *Rear Window*, a voyeur.

But the bleakest film in Hitchcock's Fifties canon and the film which perhaps best conveys the underlying unease of Fifties America is *The Wrong Man* (1957), in which an unassuming bass player (Henry Fonda) is wrongly identified as an armed robber. Slowly and deliberately, the judicial process locks him into this role, his family disintegrates under the experience and his wife retreats into madness.

It may be that highly stylized genres like the gangster movie, the thriller and the suspense movie offer a better guide retrospectively to the mood of a particular society at a given time than more overtly social films. Certainly they tend to have lasted better when seen again nowadays.

Olivier's Heights

Laurence Olivier's towering achievements in the theatre have overshadowed his work in the cinema. Yet whether in his own daring adaptations from Shakespeare, or in his many superbly realized romantic and character roles, Olivier time and again proved his great talents on film

Spencer Tracy once called Olivier 'the greatest screen actor of them all', a tribute that is particularly remarkable in that it comes from the one actor who could legitimately lay claim to the title. Yet because Olivier has always considered himself first and foremost a stage actor (a consideration for which he was rewarded with the first peerage ever given to an actor), critics have been inclined to regard his screen career as of secondary importance.

It comes, therefore, as something of a surprise to realize that his film list includes nearly sixty productions. The list is dominated by his three major Shakespeare adaptations – *Henry V* (1944), *Hamlet* (1948) and *Richard III* (1956) – but his screen work began as far back as 1930, in which year he played in a 'quota quickie' called *Too Many Crooks*.

His career can be divided into four phases. First, in the Thirties, came his films as a romantic juvenile lead: there are roughly fifteen of these, leading up to William Wyler's *Wuthering Heights* (1939) which was the first production to give Olivier any real respect for the cinema. Until then it had been on his own admission a place to make money in between the stage appearances that were his *raison d'être* as an actor. After some early and best-forgotten comedies, such as *The Temporary Widow* (1930) and *Potiphar's Wife* (1931), he had been ignominiously sacked by Greta Garbo from *Queen Christina* in 1933, thereby confirming his own belief that he was not cut out to be a film star.

Despite one early attempt at screen Shakespeare (as Orlando in Paul Czinner's *As You Like*

It, 1936, opposite the enchantingly miscast Elisabeth Bergner) the Thirties were not a very happy time for Olivier; although his prestige as a stage actor continued to grow, he was generally only ever considered for film roles that Leslie Howard or Ronald Colman were unwilling or unable to accept. Not until the meeting with Wyler did he find a director who could teach him the basic techniques of film acting. Until then, 'stagey' is the word that best describes much of his screen work, even in such acknowledged successes as *Fire Over England* (1937), the first of the three films he made with his future second wife Vivien Leigh.

But then came Wyler and *Wuthering Heights*, though again Olivier only got to play Heathcliff after Ronald Colman proved unavailable and Robert Newton had done a poor test for the role. Olivier's acting won him the first of nine Oscar nominations.

'Looking back', he said later, 'I was snobbish about films until *Wuthering Heights* . . . then, gradually, I came to see that film was a different medium and that if one treated it as such and tried to learn it humbly, with an open mind, one could work in it. I saw that it could use the best that was going; it was Wyler who

Left: Olivier, sporting a medieval haircut, studies the script of Henry V, *which he directed and starred in. Above: Henry at the siege of Harfleur*

gave me the simple thought – "if you do it right, you can do anything". And if he hadn't said that I'd never have done *Henry V* five years later.'

In the meantime came *Rebecca*, *Pride and Prejudice* (both 1940) and *That Hamilton Woman!* (1941) as well as one or two guest appearances for the war effort in Britain. There is little doubt that had Olivier stayed in Hollywood he could have become another of the screen's great romantic Englishmen. But, as he was once quoted as saying, somewhat uncharitably. 'I don't wish to become just another film star like dear Cary'; if he were going to act in front of a camera again, it would be on his own terms and those terms were now Shakespearean.

Rooted in an English classical tradition (Olivier was born, the son of a clergyman, in Dorking on May 22, 1907) he began to look upon the filming – and therefore the popularizing – of Shakespeare as something of a personal crusade. He initially hoped to involve Vivien Leigh (whom he had married in the USA in 1940 after divorcing his first wife, the

Above: Olivier with Mina Burnett in his first film, Too Many Crooks. *Below: Olivier's*

every word and gesture bespoke malevolence in his portrayal of Richard III

actress Jill Esmond) in his plans. Their acting partnership had established them both at the head of their profession, though there was always to be some doubt about her strength in his company on stage. On the screen, however, they were sadly never to work together again after *That Hamilton Woman!*; Leigh's triumph as Scarlett O'Hara in *Gone With the Wind* (1939) led the owner of her contract, David O. Selznick, to refuse to allow her to appear in 'insignificant' roles. When compared to Scarlett, even Ophelia was deemed 'insignificant'.

For this reason Olivier was unable to cast Leigh as Princess Katherine in his first attempt to film Shakespeare, *Henry V*. In addition he was unable to obtain the services of Wyler as director; this setback led him to take on the

mantle of director as well as the lead role. Indeed, as film historian Roger Manvell has noted, the film might never have been made at all had it not been for a volatile Italian lawyer called Filippo del Giudice, who had earlier persuaded Noel Coward to make *In Which We Serve* (1942) and was now looking for another patriotic classic to coincide with the D-Day landings in Normandy.

Working to a budget of £300,000 (which was only exceeded by one-third) Olivier cut

Shakespeare's text by about one-quarter, adding to it only a spectacular Agincourt battle sequence (shot in Ireland) and the death of Falstaff, which he lifted from the end of *Henry IV Part II* to serve as a kind of soundtrack-flashback to explain the old man's disgrace. The decision to start and end the film within the confines of Shakespeare's Globe Theatre, and to cast the celebrated music-hall comedian George Robey as Falstaff was an indication of considerable courage in a producer-director making his first film.

Though the print cost of *Henry V* was not to be recovered for several years, its critical success encouraged Olivier to make *Hamlet*. He had doubts about his suitability for the lead, commenting that his style of acting was 'more

suited to stronger character roles rather than the lyrical, poetic Hamlet'. These feelings were echoed by some critics, although James Agee thought that 'a man who can do what Olivier does for Shakespeare (and for those who treasure or will yet learn to treasure Shakespeare) is certainly among the more valuable men of his time'. The film won a total of four Oscars.

Richard III, the last of Olivier's major Shakespeare films, and his own personal favourite,

was made in 1956 for Alexander Korda. This had been one of Olivier's greatest stage successes, but he again only took on the direction after a more experienced man (in this case Carol Reed) had declined the challenge. The film opened to considerable critical acclaim on both sides of the Atlantic. In the USA, following an unprecedented deal with American TV, the film was first shown by NBC, who interrupted it for three General Motors ads, one for a car battery 'more powerful than all the horses in *King Richard*'.

Sadly, however, none of the Shakespeare films had done well enough at the box-office to encourage production companies to provide Olivier with the money to make an adaptation of *Macbeth*.

The two final periods of his film-making career can best be divided into the films in which he played sizeable parts and those in which he guest-starred. In the former group are nineteen post-war films, of which only five were original, modern-dress screenplays: Peter Glenville's *Term of Trial* (1962), Otto Preminger's *Bunny Lake Is Missing* (1965), Joseph Mankiewicz's *Sleuth* (1973), John Schlesinger's *Marathon Man* (1976) and Franklin Schaffner's *The Boys From Brazil* (1978). This statistic may help to explain why Olivier is still thought of in primarily stage terms though many years have elapsed since his last theatrical appearance.

Carrie (1952) reunited Olivier with Wyler, who had originally wanted 'dear Cary' for the role. Nonetheless, Olivier's performance, as a man inadvertently destroyed by the woman he loves, indicated the kind of screen actor Olivier could still be if he chose to put his mind to it. Of his subsequent features *The Entertainer*, which he made for Tony Richardson in 1960, represents Olivier at his absolute non-Shakespearian best. The part of Archie Rice, a down-at-heel pier comic, was one that he had first created on stage three years earlier. At that time the notion of Britain's leading classical actor allying himself with the playwright John Osborne, a well-known 'angry young man', caused considerable press disquiet. However Olivier had recognized that in *The Entertainer* Osborne had created one of the great roles of all time:

'You see this face? It can split open with warmth and humanity. It can sing, and tell the worst, unfunniest stories in the world to a great mob of dead, drab erks and it doesn't matter, it doesn't matter because – look at my eyes. I'm dead behind these eyes, dead, just like the whole inert shoddy lot out there.'

Olivier's performance in this film remains convincing proof of his greatness on camera. Another fine role was in *Term of Trial* (1962), as a schoolmaster tempted by Sarah Miles. There followed some film versions of famous National Theatre productions, such as *Othello* (1965), *The Dance of Death* (1969) and *Three Sisters* (1970) – all of which hovered, in Dilys Powell's phrase, 'on the very margin of cinema'. He then made a return to major screen roles as a player of macabre practical jokes in *Sleuth*, the two-handed thriller with Michael Caine (who said that acting with him was like acting with God), a sadistic Nazi dentist in *Marathon Man*, and an Austrian Jew on the track of a Nazi war criminal in *The Boys From Brazil*.

On the guest-starring front his performance as the Mahdi in *Khartoum* (1966) was perhaps

Below left: A student (Dustin Hoffman) falls victim to the tender mercies of Olivier's Nazi dentist in Marathon Man. Left: Michael Caine and Olivier confront each other in a scene from Sleuth. Above: Olivier and his second wife Vivien Leigh

of Shakespeare and Chekov, Olivier has little trouble probing the nooks and crannies of Harold Robbins', observed *Newsweek* on his appearance in *The Betsy* (1978). And, indeed, how many other actors could have gone from the Bard to Harold Robbins with such grace?

The critic Kenneth Tynan wrote, 'Olivier pole-vaults across the gulf between good and great acting in a single animal leap', while another critic commented, 'Olivier resembles a panther – just when you know where he is and that you've got him cornered he springs out at you from some totally different direction.' And that also sums up the story of his screen career.

Filmography

1930 Too Many Crooks; The Temporary Widow (GB–GER). **'31** Potiphar's Wife (USA: Her Strange Desire); Friends and Lovers (USA); The Yellow Ticket (USA). **'32** Westward Passage (USA). **'33** Perfect Understanding; No Funny Business. **'35** Moscow Nights (USA: I Stand Condemned). **'36** As You Like It. **'37** Fire Over England; 21 Days (USA: 21 Days Together). **'38** The Divorce of Lady X. **'39** Q Planes (USA: Clouds Over Europe); Wuthering Heights (USA). **'40** Rebecca (USA); Conquest of the Air; Pride and Prejudice (USA). **'41** Words for Battle (narr. only) (short); That Hamilton Woman! (USA) (GB: Lady Hamilton); 49th Parallel (USA: The Invaders). **'43** The Demi-Paradise (USA: Adventure for Two). **'44** Henry V (+dir; +prod; +co-sc). **'48** Hamlet (+dir; +prod). **'51** The Magic Box. **'52** Carrie (USA). **'53** A Queen Is Crowned (narr. only) (doc); The Beggar's Opera. **'56** Richard III (+dir; +prod). **'57** The Prince and the Showgirl (+dir; +co-prod). **'59** The Devil's Disciple. **'60** The Entertainer; Spartacus (USA). **'61** The Power and the Glory (USA). **'62** Term of Trial. **'63** Uncle Vanya. **'65** Bunny Lake Is Missing; Othello. **'66** Khartoum. **'68** Romeo and Juliet (narr. only) (GB-IT); The Shoes of the Fishermen (USA). **'69** Oh! What a Lovely War; The Dance of Death; Battle of Britain; David Copperfield. **'70** Three Sisters (+dir). **'71** Nicholas and Alexandra. **'72** Lady Caroline Lamb (GB-IT). **'73** Sleuth. **'75** Love Among the Ruins* (USA). **'76** Marathon Man (USA); The Seven-Per-Cent Solution (USA). **'77** A Bridge Too Far. **'78** The Betsy (USA); The Boys From Brazil (USA). **'79** A Little Romance (USA-FR); Dracula (USA). **'80** Inchon; The Jazz Singer; **'81** Clash of the Titans. **'83** The Jigsaw Man. **'84** The Bountry, **'85** Wild Geese II.
* shot as TV film but shown cinemas

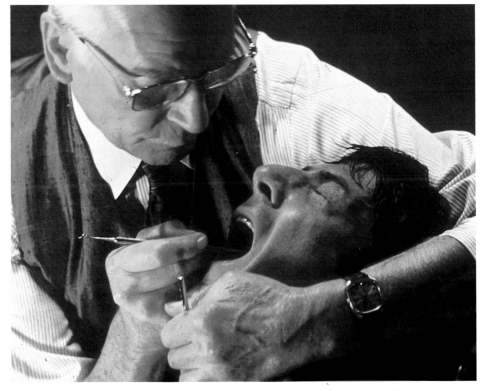

a deliberate reminder of his then-current stage Othello, also very gutteral and way over the top, and here as in *Spartacus* (1960), in which he plays a homosexual Roman general, it seems fair to assume that for Olivier, epic acting means overacting. His other guest-starring work has been only occasionally distinguished (Richard Attenborough got a remarkable performance out of him as the old Dutch doctor in *A Bridge Too Far*, 1977).

After this, Olivier told his interviewers that his later screen roles had been taken considerably more for his then still-young offsprings' bank balance than for acting kudos. 'As long as I can stand,' he said, 'I'll go on doing my job',

and this was after a decade of ill-health brought on by three crippling afflictions. Joan Plowright – his third wife, and mother of his youngest three children (there is an elder son by Jill Esmond) – once said she somehow could never visualize Olivier in an orchard working on his memoirs.

It must be admitted that several of these later roles could never qualify as quintessential screen art. Funny foreigners tended to proliferate – the roguish French con-man in *A Little Romance*, a geriatric Van Helsing in *Dracula* and Rudolph Hess in the awful *Wild Geese II*. Yet these should not be allowed to overshadow his greatest roles. 'Having plumbed the depths

The Wilder side of life

'They say Wilder is out of touch with his times. Frankly I regard it as a compliment. Who the hell wants to be in touch with these times?'   Billy Wilder in 1976

In Mitchell Leisen's *Hold Back the Dawn* (1941), a gigolo, played by Charles Boyer, has fled war-torn Europe and waits impatiently at the Mexican border for an entry-visa so he can get into the USA. He and the other refugees gaze longingly at the checkpoint, which consists of a wire fence, an immigration office and, beyond that, an extraordinary archway of welcome and promise with the legend 'The United States' emblazoned across it. The archway resembles nothing less than a cinema marquee on Sunset Boulevard.

Hold Back the Dawn was written by Charles Brackett and Billy Wilder and was one of several films of the period designed to influence American opinion about the war in Europe. It is the most overtly biographical of Wilder's films. Wilder was part of the artistic and intellectual exodus from Europe in the early Thirties, and for film-makers like Fritz Lang, Max Ophuls, Otto Preminger, Robert Siodmak and Wilder, America *was* Hollywood, as the *Hold Back the Dawn* set amusingly suggests. Appropriately, at the end of the film, the gigolo sells his story to Paramount Pictures.

The Europeans on the run from Hitler were to exert a profound influence on the American cinema, just as earlier emigrés like Ernst Lubitsch and Victor Sjöström did in the Twenties. Their cultural heritage and recent traumatic experience brought a visual exoticism, a sophistication and wit, a sourness and a pessimism lacking in the more homespun,

Below: Don Taylor and William Holden as POWs in Stalag 17. *Below right: the romantic comedy* Love in the Afternoon *starred Gary Cooper as a playboy and Audrey Hepburn as the young girl who beguiles him*

optimistic visions of native American directors like Howard Hawks and King Vidor. The European sensibility permeated all genres and Wilder's contribution – his unrivalled series of satires, thrillers and romances – was to be as significant as any.

Not just a gigolo
He was born Samuel Wilder in 1906 in Sucha, Austria (now part of Poland), into a fairly rich Jewish family. After completing his studies in Vienna, Wilder entered journalism and scored a few notable coups, interviewing Freud, Richard Strauss and Arthur Schnitzler. He moved to Berlin in 1926 where he gained a reputation as a crime reporter who specialized in daring exposés. He also claims to have been a gigolo, entertaining well-to-do ladies at the Adlon Hotel. Berlin was then the world's cultural centre and its expression of decadence; the German cinema, based at the Ufa studios, was technically and stylistically more advanced than any other. Apart from *Menschen am Sonntag* (1929, *People on Sunday*), made as a kind of challenge to the glossy Ufa style, Wilder's early films as a scenarist were mainly zestful comedies and light romances which, despite their limitations, contain glimmers of the Wilder to come – particularly in their Viennese humour, the play with deception and mistaken identity, and the lure of America and Hollywood.

Wilder packed his bags for Paris the day after the Reichstag fire in February 1933. (Many of his relations who stayed behind were to perish in concentration camps.) He had a rough time in Paris – though it would later be the setting for some of his most enchanting films – but was able to direct his first feature

there, the recently rediscovered *Mauvaise Graine* (1933), a freewheeling comedy-drama about car thieves. The film ends as the hero and heroine are about to set sail for America. Wilder's own departure soon followed, his route taking him via Mexico.

Within five years of arriving in Hollywood, Wilder had attained a position of some eminence. His scripts with Brackett, notably *Bluebeard's Eighth Wife* (1938), *Midnight*, *Ninotchka* (both 1939), *Hold Back the Dawn* and *Ball of Fire* (1941), were models of their kind and made the pair the highest-paid writers in the industry. (Their partnership was dissolved in 1950 and since 1957 Wilder's collaborator has been I.A.L. Diamond.) Wilder's first four features as a director in America – *The Major and the Minor* (1942), *Five Graves to Cairo* (1943), *Double Indemnity* (1944) and *The Lost Weekend* (1945) – demonstrated his versatility and were all critical and commercial successes. Wilder also

Above: Billy Wilder and Marilyn Monroe arrive at the press reception for Some Like It Hot. *Above right: in the film Monroe was Sugar Kane, a tipsy band-singer involved with a musician (Tony Curtis) and his buddy who dress in drag to escape from gangsters*

promoted himself effectively, and rapidly became one of Hollywood's most celebrated wits, his picturesque insults and wisecracks entering folklore and forming the basis of three hagiographies.

Despite the occasional dispute at Paramount, the 'Europe in Exile' studio where he worked from 1937 to 1954, Wilder could do no wrong. He provided intelligence and entertainment in equal measure. Sadly, Wilder's position today is very different from that of, say, the early Sixties when he collected three personal Oscars for *The Apartment* (1960) and could name his own price. His most recent film,

Fedora (1978), was financed with German tax-shelter money and only received limited distribution. The archway to Hollywood was no longer welcoming, Universal terminated his contract after *The Front Page* (1974), and Wilder found himself behind the wire again, making his film in Europe. But *Fedora* is Wilder's testament, arguably the greatest film of his entire career.

Memories of old Europe
It is important to stress Wilder's background for it appears in his films in the fundamental structural opposition between Europe and America. Inevitably, Wilder's feelings about both are deeply ambivalent and this accounts for much of the tension in his work.

His evocations of Europe are tinged with melancholy, the humour being a safeguard against emotional indulgence, as in the pre-Occupation Paris of *Ninotchka*, the re-creation of Lubitschean Vienna in *The Emperor Waltz* (1948), the devastation of Berlin in *A Foreign Affair* (1948) and that city's East-West partition in *One, Two, Three* (1961). In Wilder's Parisian films the tone is always romantic and in the Berlin films the tone is astringent; both are nostalgic.

Nearly half of Wilder's output is set in some expressive European location and in using places with autobiographical associations – Vienna, Berlin, Paris – Wilder is obviously lending a certain authenticity to his films. But a closer examination reveals that he is exploring a geography more psychical than physical that has less to do with place than moral values. Paris, for instance, rarely registers as a location in the filmic sense – Wilder prefers to set his scenes in hotel rooms and, for *Irma La Douce* (1963), rebuilt Les Halles in Hollywood – but it is intensely felt as a spiritual influence. Europe, in the romances at least, functions as a place of rehabilitation, educating New Worlders in a manner reminiscent of Henry James.

Time and time again Wilder despatches Americans to Europe where they undergo a process of humanization. The purest example of this is *Avanti!* (1972), in which a harassed

Filmography
1929 Der Teufelsreporter (sc. only); Menschen am Sonntag (co-sc. only) (USA: People on Sunday). '**31** Der Mann, der Seinen Mörder Sucht (sc. only) (USA: Looking for His Murderer); Ihre Hoheit Befiehlt (co-sc. only) (co-sc. only on French version: Son Altesse Ordonne/Princesse à Vos Ordres, 1931; and USA version: Adorable, 1933); Der Falsche Ehemann (co-sc. only); Emil und die Detektive (sc. only) (USA/GB: Emil and the Detectives). '**32** Es war Einmal ein Waltzer (sc. only) (USA: Blonde Dream) (co-sc. only on British version: Happy Ever After, 1932; and French version: Un Blond Rêve, 1932); Scampolo, ein Kind der Strasse (co-sc. only) (GER-A); Das Blaue von Himmel (co-sc. only). '**33** Madame Wünscht Keine Kinder (co-sc. only) (GER-A); Was Frauen Traümen (co-sc. only) (USA: What Women Dream) (co-sc. only on USA version: One Exciting Adventure, 1935); Mauvaise Graine (co-dir; +co-sc) (FR). *All remaining films USA unless specified:* '**35** Music in the Air (co-sc. only); Lottery Lover (co-sc. only). '**37** Champagne Waltz (co-sc. only). '**38** Bluebeard's Eighth Wife (co-sc. only). '**39** Midnight (co-sc. only); What a Life (co-sc. only); Ninotchka (co-sc. only). '**40** Arise My Love (co-sc. only); Rhythm on the River (co-sc. only). '**41** Hold Back the Dawn (co-sc. only); Ball of Fire (co-sc. only). '**42** The Major and the Minor (+co-sc). '**43** Five Graves to Cairo (+co-sc). '**44** Double Indemnity (+co-sc). '**45** The Lost Weekend (+co-sc). '**48** The Emperor Waltz (+co-sc); A Foreign Affair (+co-sc). '**50** Sunset Boulevard (+co-sc). '**51** Ace in the Hole (+prod; +co-sc) (GB: The Big Carnival). '**53** Stalag 17 (+prod; +co-sc). '**54** Sabrina (+prod; +co-sc) (GB: Sabrina Fair). '**55** The Seven Year Itch (+prod; +co-sc). '**57** The Spirit of St Louis (+co-sc); Love in the Afternoon (+prod; +co-sc); Witness for the Prosecution (+co-sc). '**59** Some Like It Hot (+prod; +co-sc). '**60** The Apartment (+prod; +co-sc). '**61** One, Two, Three (+prod; +co-sc). '**63** Irma La Douce (+prod; +co-sc). '**64** Kiss Me, Stupid (+prod; +co-sc). '**66** The Fortune Cookie (+prod; +co-sc) (GB: Meet Whiplash Willie). '**70** The Private Life of Sherlock Holmes (+prod; +co-sc) (GB). '**72** Avanti! (+prod; +co-sc). '**74** The Front Page (+co-sc). '**78** Fedora (+prod; +co-sc) (GER). '**82** Buddy, Buddy (+sc; +co-prod).

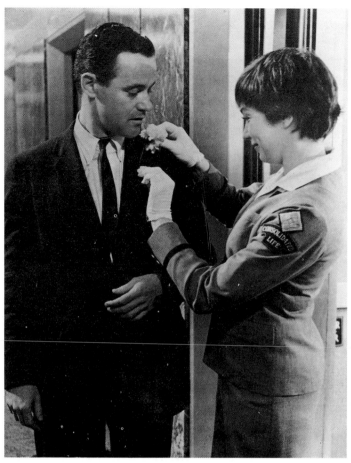

Baltimore executive (Jack Lemmon) goes to Italy to reclaim his father's corpse. Because of bureaucratic complications he is delayed and consequently discovers a potential for life he never knew existed. This may sound trite or overly schematic on the page but in the context of a long career and as performed by Lemmon, Wilder's regular and most brilliant interpreter, *Avanti!* becomes a deeply moving personal pilgrimage and a masterpiece of discreet exegesis. This strand of Wilder's career, which also includes the underrated *Sabrina* (1954) and *Love in the Afternoon* (1957), in which the all-American personas of Humphrey Bogart and Gary Cooper are reconstituted in the light of European experience, contains some of Wilder's most elegant and characteristic work, demonstrating his high regard for Lubitsch. However, it is the more caustic side of Wilder, the Stroheim side, which has received more general critical acclaim.

It is significant that in *A Foreign Affair* and *One, Two, Three* the occupying American forces – GIs in the former, Pepsi Cola in the latter – signally fail to impose their set of values on the Europeans. The transformation process never works in reverse. When they are denied access to Europe and its life-enhancing potential, Wilder's Americans are the victims of paranoia, motivated by greed and sexual enslavement, and either wind up dead or, just as

Above: Shirley MacLaine as the French whore who captivates the gendarme (Jack Lemmon) in Irma La Douce. *Above right: Lemmon, as an aspiring executive, and MacLaine, as the elevator girl sleeping with his boss, in* The Apartment. *Right: Wilder's courtroom drama starred Dietrich as a treacherous wife*

disconcertingly, renouncing secure material values at the call of personal, moral principles. Wilder's heroes have to choose between money and happiness and the mark of the hero's maturity (and Wilder's esteem) is in his choosing of the humanist rather than the materialist option. Films in this group include *Double Indemnity*, a classic *film noir* co-scripted with Raymond Chandler, *Ace in the Hole* (1951), *Stalag 17* (1953), which uses a German POW camp as a microcosm of the civilian rat-race, *The Apartment*, *Kiss Me, Stupid* (1964) and *The Fortune Cookie* (1966).

Playing his ace

Wilder's tendency in these films is to sympathize with the individual rather than the group but he stops short of actually endorsing his hero's attitudes or actions. A character like Chuck Tatum (Kirk Douglas) in *Ace in the Hole* will enliven a sterile community but the cost in personal and moral terms is unaccountably high. Tatum is a 'yellow' journalist who prolongs one man's suffering in order to whip-up human interest. The site of this modern morality play is a remote desert area, as arid as its inhabitants, and immediately the crowds

arrive seeking some kind of vicarious excitement. Although Tatum investigates the story (and dies for his trouble), Wilder's hatred is reserved for the mob, perhaps even for his own audience and, indeed, *Ace in the Hole* played to empty cinemas and upset Wilder's relations with Paramount.

Love American-style
Similarly, an important Wilder film like *Kiss Me, Stupid* presented such a bleak picture of middle-America that Wilder was the victim of a sustained press campaign against him. Only *The Apartment* received wide acclaim, its devastating critique of the American success ethic seemingly diluted by the growing love between its victims, C.C. Baxter (Jack Lemmon) and Fran Kubelik (Shirley MacLaine). Yet · *The Apartment* is not a glossy comedy but a disturbing portrait of urban loneliness and at the end Baxter and Miss Kubelik are homeless and jobless. It is not exactly the happiest ending in movies.

But if these films are variously virulent hate-letters addressed to America, Wilder has also written two love-letters as well, unequivocal tributes to American innocence and exuberance but both significantly 'distanced' by being set in the Twenties: *The Spirit of St Louis* (1957), an almost Fordian biography of Lindbergh, and the classic comedy *Some Like It Hot* (1959).

Some Like It Hot is probably Wilder's best-loved film and its daring plot contrivance – Lemmon and Tony Curtis play Jerry and Joe, two musicians who disguise themselves as girls after they witness the St Valentine's Day Massacre and have to escape – lies at the heart of Wilder's preoccupation with role-playing and transformation. There are outrageous impersonations in *The Major and the Minor* (Ginger Rogers as a 12-year-old), *Witness for the Prosecution* (1957, Marlene Dietrich as a cockney tart) and *Irma La Douce* (Lemmon as an elderly English Lord) but the point is not the effectiveness of the disguise but its very transparency. The comical identity crises of characters like Jerry, when his female self takes over in *Some Like It Hot*, are lighter versions of the torments of characters like Fedora, Norma Desmond in *Sunset Boulevard* (1950) and Sherlock Holmes in *The Private Life of Sherlock Holmes* (1970). This last is perhaps Wilder's most deeply moving study of the psychological split between private lives and public personas.

Some like it Hollywood
There is a cinematic allusiveness in all of Wilder's films (*Ace in the Hole*, for example, can be approached as an allegory concerning Hollywood methodology; *Kiss Me, Stupid* is certainly that) which is expressed through various homages and the use of specific performers. James Cagney in *One, Two, Three*, applying gangster methods to international trade; William Holden and Jack Lemmon playing virtually the same roles in successive films; Marilyn Monroe in *Some Like It Hot* playing herself in all but name; appearances by real-life directors like Cecil B. DeMille and Erich von

Stroheim – these devices all reveal an acute awareness of Hollywood mythology. This allusiveness is most intensely realized in *Sunset Boulevard* and *Fedora*, two explorations of Hollywood image-making that have as many intriguing points of confluence as divergence. *Fedora* is a rich summation, the poignancy of the occasion oddly transcended by the exalted expression. A film of constantly shifting moods and perspectives, *Fedora* – in which a washed-up film producer attempts to lure an elderly star out of retirement – casts a nostalgic eye over the old Hollywood and a rueful eye over the

new. Its very defiance of modishness – its concern for narrative and character – makes it one of the most beautiful of modern films.

Wilder's wittily sardonic views of the American Dream gone sour, of Europe, Hollywood, and of manners and morals in general do not lose their sharpness – or their poignancy – with the passing of time. Norma Desmond, talking of silent pictures in *Sunset Boulevard*, says, 'Still wonderful, isn't it?' Thirty years later the same words apply equally well to Billy Wilder's humanism and classicism – and to *Fedora* in particular.

Above right: Avanti! cast Lemmon and Juliet Mills as strangers who go to Italy to collect the bodies of their respective (and recently deceased) father and mother, who had been lovers; they then embark on an affair of their own. Right: William Holden as the ageing film producer Barry Detweiler in Fedora

The Blonde Gentlemen Prefer

The trials and tribulations and the incendiary mixture of wide-eyed innocence and sumptuous sexiness have often obscured the fact that Marilyn Monroe was a supreme talent, 'as near genius as any actress I ever knew' said Joshua Logan who directed her in *Bus Stop*. There was certainly no-one else like her . . .

Hollywood's great stars seldom seem to have been the products of happy homes and stable childhoods. Chaplin's father walked out on the family when his son was one year old, and Fairbanks' when Douglas was four. Mary Pickford's father died when she was four, Valentino's when he was eleven, Garbo's when she was thirteen. Marilyn Monroe was never even certain who her father was: he may have been a mechanic called Mortensen or a film-laboratory employee called Gifford, or a Mr Baker who was the father of her elder brother and sister. For safety's sake, early publicity gave it out that whoever he was he had been killed in a car crash shortly after the birth of his daughter.

Like Chaplin again, Marilyn was committed to an orphanage after her mother retreated into madness. In her case the legacy of mental instability was more terrifying: her maternal grandfather and grandmother – a fanatical disciple of the evangelist Aimee Semple Mac-Pherson, in whose temple Marilyn was baptised Norma Jeane Mortensen – ended their lives in mental institutions.

Unlike the other great stars, however, Norma Jean (the final 'e' only appears on her birth certificate) was a child of the movie capital. She was born, on June 1, 1926, in the Los Angeles General Hospital. Her room in the

Los Angeles Orphan home is said to have looked directly onto the neon sign over RKO studios, and Marilyn later told interviewers that one of the most wonderful memories of her childhood was a Christmas party given by RKO for the orphan children, when she was nine. None of her biographies or interviews reveal at what age this apparently lonely, shy and introverted girl conceived the determination to become a movie star; but that determination must have been single-minded and steely to survive the inevitable years of disappointment and frustration that she was to experience after her first arrival at 20th Century-Fox.

At the time World War II ended she was working in an aircraft factory, testing parachutes, when a photographer taking official propaganda pictures spotted her potential and introduced her to an agent, Emmeline Snively. By 1946 she was launched as a pin-up and cover girl, and a smart publicity stunt secured a test at Fox. Ben Lyon, the actor, who was then the studio's talent scout, advised her to change her name: Monroe was her grandmother's married name; Marilyn was Lyon's suggestion – a tribute to an earlier star, Marilyn Miller. She was signed by Fox for a year and went through the familiar processing of potential starlets: she was photographed; given

a couple of small parts – one of which, in *Scudda Hoo! Scudda Hay!* (1948) was entirely cut out – but the studio did not renew her contract.

By this time, however, Marilyn seems already to have been actively organizing her career. She kept up her classes at the Actors'

Laboratory where she had been enrolled by Fox; acquired the first of the personal drama coaches who were later to try the patience of her directors; and made good use of the admirers, advisers, patrons and protectors – the most significant of them was the agent Johnny Hyde, thirty years her senior – whom she readily attracted. She won a featured role in a Columbia musical, *Ladies of the Chorus* (1948), was chased by Groucho Marx in *Love Happy* (1949), and received her first small but favourable critical attention for the role of a crooked lawyer's girl in *The Asphalt Jungle* (1950). Its director John Huston – who some 11 years later was to guide her patiently and painfully through her last completed film, *The Misfits* (1961) – told her, 'You know, Marilyn, you're going to be a good actress'.

She had already had half a dozen small parts when she walked through *All About Eve*

had advised the film business, 'Don't fool yourself. This girl is a coming star'. Much later, on Laurence Olivier's *The Prince and the Show-girl* (1957), there appears to have been a touching mutual admiration and affection between Marilyn and the veteran Dame Sybil Thorndike.

The three years between *Niagara* and *Bus Stop* (1956) were the peak of her professional career, a period comparatively untroubled by the personal problems that were eventually to dog her. A keen judge of material – her intelligent rejection of scripts often caused friction with the studio – she regretted Otto Preminger's *River of No Return* (1954) as a miscalculation, a crude exploitation of her sexual attractions.

It is almost inconceivable now that so many of Marilyn's contemporaries were sceptical about her technical achievements and about her ambitions to be a serious artist – her touchingly demanding literary pursuits and her work with Lee and Paula Strasberg at the Actors' Studio in New York. Her performances in *Gentlemen Prefer Blondes* and *How to Marry a Millionaire* show a refined and precious comic talent; in the latter she plays an acutely myopic beauty forever crashing into walls when, from vanity, she discards her enormous spectacles. In *There's No Business Like Show Business* (1954), developing her endearing, funny, baby singing voice, she parodies the conventions of the stage musical star. In *The Seven Year Itch* (1955) she proves an altogether equal comedy partner to old hand Tom Ewell and outstrips the director Billy Wilder with the subtlety of her comic effects. The climax of this period of her career, however, is reached in Joshua

Above left: Marilyn Monroe – 'a beautiful profile all the way down' – with Yves Montand (in tails) in Let's Make Love. *Top: Marilyn's look and Groucho's leer in* Love Happy. *Above and below: dramatic roles in* The Asphalt Jungle *and* Don't Bother to Knock. *Right: as Lorelei Lee in* Gentlemen Prefer Blondes, *with Jane Russell*

(1950), leaving behind one of the first authentic 'Monroisms'. As Miss Caswell, a starlet, she arrives at a party on the arm of stage critic Addison DeWitt (George Sanders) who suavely introduces her to Margo Channing (Bette Davis), 'You know Miss Caswell, of course?' 'No', Margo mercilessly snaps back. 'That', smiles Miss Caswell guilelessly, 'is because we

never met.' Marilyn became well known for such deceptively artless and worryingly enigmatic ripostes.

The public had already noticed her, and her parts became bigger and more significant. In 1952 Fox made the mistake of casting her in a dramatic role – as a psychopathic girl in *Don't Bother to Knock*. The notices and the box-office returns were bad, but in retrospect it is a creditable performance, with moments of intuition and intensity which may well have been stirred by the parallels to her own childhood.

The three Marilyn Monroe films that were released in 1953 – *Niagara*, *Gentlemen Prefer Blondes* and *How to Marry a Millionaire* – definitively established her as a star and a new sex image for the age. *Niagara*, Henry Hathaway's tongue-in-cheek handling of a torrid melodrama of passion, teamed Marilyn's own natural splendours with the Niagara falls – and introduced 'The Walk' with a 70-foot shot of Marilyn undulating away from the camera in uncomfortable high heels across cobble-stones. Her unique ambulation was a celebration of her sensuous physique, a positive percussion and choreography of limbs, buttocks and the thighs that seem to have an extra curve (she always gave out her *upper* and *lower* hip measurement). In *Gentlemen Prefer Blondes* she was teamed with Jane Russell, and in *How to Marry a Millionaire* with Betty Grable and Lauren Bacall. It was no doubt Monroe's presence that made both films major box-office hits; but she always seemed to work well with other actresses of character and intelligence and to inspire their liking. Working with her on *Clash by Night* (1952), Barbara Stanwyck

Above: Marilyn as a saloon singer in River of No Return. *Right: as gold-digger Pola with Mr Denmark (David Wayne) disproving that men never make passes at girls who wear glasses in* How to Marry a Millionaire

Logan's *Bus Stop*, with a comic performance of flair and charm and pathos that transcends the stage-bound screenplay.

Already Marilyn was regarded as a 'difficult' actress. Her attendances on the set became more and more erratic. For a while she abandoned Hollywood for New York and her mentor, Lee Strasberg. At this time too she acquired Paula Strasberg, his wife, as a new

---

'I want to be an artist . . . not an erotic freak. I don't want to be sold to the public as a celluloid aphrodisiacal'

---

drama coach to replace Natasha Lytess. First married at 16, Marilyn later became the wife of the baseball star Joe Di Maggio in 1954, but the marriage foundered after a year. A third marriage to the playwright Arthur Miller and her appearance alongside Olivier in *The Prince and the Showgirl*, her only British film, seemed the culmination of her cultural ambitions.

Her private life had begun to darken, however. Already there was the horrifying dependence on drugs, and prolonged periods in mental clinics. The unpunctuality and absenteeism which had first seemed a caprice were revealed as symptoms of sickness. She

became hard to work with. She is charming and funny in Billy Wilder's *Some Like It Hot* (1959), but her co-star Tony Curtis said, 'Kissing Marilyn Monroe was like kissing Hitler'. Curtis wears women's clothing for most of the film and Marilyn serenely retorted to his ungallant remark, 'He only said that because I had prettier dresses than he did'.

Let's Make Love (1960) was the most insignificant film of her later career, despite George Cukor's direction and the lift to her morale provided by her affair with co-star Yves Montand. Finally she struggled through *The Misfits*. Her marriage to Arthur Miller – who

had scripted the film and had clearly based the character of Roslyn on his wife – was breaking up. She was sick, frequently quite incapacitated by narcotics, and repeatedly hospitalized. Still Marilyn's performance is one of the finest of her career: she seemed only to gain in depth and insight. Some of her most touching scenes are those when Roslyn expresses her horror at the inhumanity of the men to the mustangs they are catching: Marilyn always revealed an extreme and even neurotic empathy with animals and children.

She began work, again with Cukor, on *Something's Got to Give* in 1962. But she

appeared on the set only 12 times in the first month of shooting. Fox fired her and sued for compensation. Seven weeks later, on August

---

'Talent is developed in privacy . . . but everybody is always tugging at you. They'd all like sort of a chunk of you. They'd kind of like to take pieces out of you'

5, she died from a drug overdose. She was 36. The few brief sequences that she had shot for *Something's Got to Give* showed a new and metamorphosed Marilyn. There was little trace of the round-faced pin-up of the early days in this woman of breathtaking grace, beauty, luminosity and awful fragility. In a series of costume tests she walks and walks again (and by this time she no longer undulates, but floats); and the hieratic, ritual magic of the rushes is haunting and unforgettable.

Marilyn belonged to the last years of the studio system and the last real generation of stars. Her contemporaries included Grace Kelly, Audrey Hepburn, Marlon Brando, James Dean, Kim Novak and the grown-up Elizabeth Taylor. She hated being a sex symbol ('I thought symbols were something you clash'); yet she was one of the most potent embodiments of sexuality the screen has ever known. It seemed to emanate from her own exultation and fascination with her physique and sexuality. 'I'm very certainly a woman and I enjoy it,' she said. She was said to wear her dresses two sizes too small so that she was always conscious, from their clinging, of every part of her body. She liked to look at herself in mirrors. When she moves or stands or sits, she gives the impression that she is unconsciously feeling and testing and *enjoying* every limb and nerve. The nude bathing scene filmed for *Something's Got to Give* survives, an act of solitary devotion.

With the sexuality, however, there went a refined comic technique. We can never know to what extent it was instinctive and to what extent developed by her very intense and serious studies in the studios and with her drama coaches. Certainly there is nothing accidental about her management of the cabaret scene in *Bus Stop* as she struggles through 'That Old Black Magic', and there is something almost mystical about her ability to

Above left: as the bruised, bewitching Sugar in Some Like It Hot. *Above: the serene beauty of Marilyn Monroe – caught in a relaxed mood while filming* The Misfits

shift mood from low-comedy to the heart-touching pathos of which she was uniquely capable.

'I'm not interested in money,' she told a somewhat surprised early producer, 'I just want to be wonderful'. That ambition she achieved, triumphantly.

Filmography

1947 Dangerous Years. **'48** Ladies of the Chorus. **'49** Love Happy. **'50** A Ticket to Tomahawk; The Asphalt Jungle; The Fireball; All About Eve; Right Cross. **'51** Home Town Story; As Young As You Feel; Love Nest; Let's Make It Legal. **'52** Clash by Night; We're Not Married; Don't Bother to Knock; Monkey Business; O. Henry's Full House *ep* The Cop and the Anthem (GB: Full House). **'53** Niagara; Gentlemen Prefer Blondes; How to Marry a Millionaire. **'54** River of No Return; There's No Business Like Show Business. **'55** The Seven Year Itch. **'56** Bus Stop. **'57** The Prince and the Showgirl (GB). **'59** Some Like It Hot. **'60** Let's Make Love. **'61** The Misfits. **'62** Something's Got to Give (unfinished).

A little light relief

As the Fifties progressed, the movies showed American life becoming more secure, cosy and domestic. Hollywood comedies endorsed the image

The Fifties may have been the decade which began with the Cold War and ended with the Campaign for Nuclear Disarmament, but it was also the era of Jayne Mansfield, the hula-hoop craze and rock'n'roll. Just as in the Thirties people found relief from the external worries of the Depression and the rise of fascism in the elegant abstractions of Astaire-Rogers musicals and in screwball comedies, so in the Fifties the dark clouds had to have a silver lining of some kind.

In the magical sanctuary of the cinema you could have been forgiven for supposing that the most important issue in the world was whether Doris Day would succeed, despite all the fairly gentlemanly stratagems of her leading men, in preserving her virginity until wedding bells at the final fade-out. The star system was still functioning unshakably, or so it seemed, and it was hard to tell, watching Marilyn Monroe's progress from a one-gag scene in The Marx Brothers' *Love Happy* (1949) to superstardom in *Gentlemen Prefer Blondes* (1953), that we were seeing the last act of the star-making machine which had been so carefully built up over the years in the Hollywood dream factory.

In the Fifties nearly all the great stars of the talkies were still alive and working. It was only at the end of the decade, with the deaths, in rapid succession, of Humphrey Bogart, Tyrone Power, Errol Flynn, Clark Gable and Gary Cooper, that filmgoers realized how frail and mortal the gods of the screen were.

For the moment, however, the worst menace was the new toy, television. Film-makers – real film-makers who made movies exclusively for cinemas – could still afford to wax satirical about television, or simply dismiss it as beneath notice. Likewise, movie stars steered clear – with one or two spectacular exceptions. Lucille Ball, for instance, who had been a star of fairly modest stature around Hollywood for a decade or so, but then went on to television in a family situation-comedy series, *I Love Lucy*, with her real-life husband Desi Arnaz, instantly found fame and success far greater than anything she had ever dreamed of in the movies. When she went back to the cinema, it was on her own terms, as a visiting celebrity. This she did most notably in *The Long Long Trailer* (1953), in which Vincente Minnelli gave polish and sparkle to what was basically an extended *I Love Lucy* episode, and *The Facts of Life* (1960), in which she co-starred with Bob Hope, in a comic variation on *Brief Encounter* (1945).

Bob Hope was rather a different matter. He was a veteran from the Thirties and had been big in films throughout the Forties. He entered the Fifties with his star lustre more or less intact. Like Lucy, he did not shun television – or indeed anything which would keep him busy and before the public. But his films of the Fifties came to seem more and more like sequels to his earlier successes such as *Son of Paleface* and *Road to Bali* (both 1952), or films in which his special gift for quick-fire, stand-up comedian gags was less suited to the more relaxed comic style of Hollywood in the Fifties. With the solitary

exceptions of *That Certain Feeling* (1956) and *The Facts of Life*, he seemed to have difficulty playing a character instead of merely playing Bob Hope. Even in such lightweight biographies as *The Seven Little Foys* (1955) and *Beau James* (1957), the ostensible subjects (the vaudevillian Eddie Foy and the famous Mayor of New York, Jimmy Walker) were fed through Hope's gag machine to come out disconcertingly more like the usual screen Hope than anyone else.

Things fared better for the other important survivor from wartime comedy, Danny Kaye. After the lavish musical biography, *Hans Christian Anderson* (1952), he separated from Sam Goldwyn, the producer who had made him what he was. But Kaye managed to keep his own brand of zany, frenetic comedy going in films like *Knock on Wood* (1954), *The Court Jester* (1956) – perhaps the best of all his films – and *Merry Andrew* (1958). He even did surprisingly well, when he succumbed to the alleged ambition of all comics to play Hamlet, by taking the straight role in *Me and the Colonel* (1958) and leaving most of the comedy to Curt Jurgens. But then, love him or hate him, Danny Kaye was always in a class of his own and likely to be less affected than most by changing fashions in comedy.

It was characteristic of the Fifties that Danny Kaye could peacefully co-exist with the biggest new challengers in comedy, Dean Martin and Jerry Lewis. They were to the Fifties what Laurel and Hardy had been to the Thirties and Abbott and Costello to the Forties. Martin and Lewis somehow brought to perfection a sort of lowest common denominator in comedy, and so built their popularity up from a solid base of mass appreciation on the part of unsophisticated audiences. In the case of Laurel and Hardy, the duo eventually became the idols of the intelligentsia as well as the idiots' delight and the same thing happened to Martin and Lewis as a result of their critical acclaim in France. But Anglo-Saxon film critics of the Fifties, when they were not moralizing about the overstressed sexuality of Elvis Presley and the dangers of his effect on the young, were quite likely to be tut-tutting about Jerry Lewis' spastic humour and claiming that his moronic screen persona made cruel fun of the afflicted.

Despite such admonitions, the films Martin and Lewis made together between *My Friend Irma* (1949) and *Hollywood or Bust* (1956) were among the most reliable box-office champions of their day, and after the team split up each individually went on to become a major star in his own right.

Comedy in the Fifties tended to be pretty unsophisticated as, for example, in the endless encounters between Donald O'Connor and Francis the Talking Mule. But even glossy comedy had a heart of pure candy-floss. This was certainly true of the comedies and lightweight dramas to which Doris Day graduated when she gave up musicals towards the end of the decade. Though some of them, like *Pillow Talk* (1959) and *That Touch of Mink* (1962), might seem to feature mildly risqué situations, it

Top: Bob Hope and a cast of juveniles in The Seven Little Foys, *a comedy about a father who raises his seven children as vaudeville performers. Above: Bob Hope and Jimmy 'Schnozzle' Durante do a soft-shoe shuffle in* Beau James *the story of a man who becomes mayor of New York but is compromised by his love for an actress*

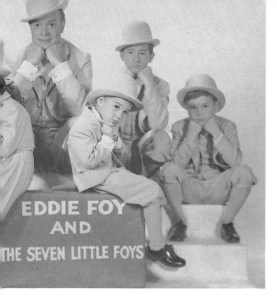

EDDIE FOY
AND
THE SEVEN LITTLE FOYS

was from the outset a foregone conclusion that the heroine's virtue, faintly endangered though it may have been, was going to remain impregnable. Besides, audiences could comfort themselves with the knowledge that Miss Day, now nearing forty, seemed old enough to look after herself – hence the famous comment 'I knew Doris Day before she was a virgin'. The rather jolly, absurd thrillers like *Julie* (1956) and *Midnight Lace* (1960) similarly eschewed any real sense of menace, especially when, as with the latter film, drenched in soapy colour thanks to the production values unique to Ross Hunter's Universal-International house style.

Not all comedy during the Fifties was quite so toothless. There was a little cycle all on its own which harked back in a fresh way to the splendours of the Thirties. In collaboration with the husband-and-wife team Garson Kanin and Ruth Gordon (who worked as writers, either separately or together), George Cukor made a series of sparklingly witty and sometimes surprisingly tender comedies with Spencer Tracy and Katharine Hepburn and a distinctive new discovery – the zany comedienne Judy Holliday.

The three-way partnership between Tracy, Hepburn and Holliday began with *Adam's Rib* (1949), a battle between rival lawyers who just happen to be married to each other. Tracy and Hepburn were then teamed (without Judy Holliday) as athlete and trainer in *Pat and Mike* (1952). Tracy then played the unwilling father of *The Actress* (1953) and Judy Holliday portrayed several variations of her lovable kooky character who turns out to be somehow wiser than the rationalists around her in *Born Yesterday* (1950), *The Marrying Kind* (1952) and *It Should Happen to You* (1954). Indeed Judy Holliday made a career from such roles throughout the decade, with other writers and directors, in films like *Phffft* (1954), *The Solid Gold Cadillac*, *Full of Life* (both 1956) and the last Minnelli musical made at MGM, *Bells Are Ringing* (1960).

What these films have in common with the less sophisticated variety during the Fifties is that they are all star vehicles, and take their tone and pace very largely from the established screen personality of the star or stars in question. Spencer Tracy and Katharine Hepburn, for example, extended their sparring screen partnership in *The Desk Set* (1957). They also preserved their individual, slightly spiky personalities which had made and kept them famous by exploiting these comic personae outside of the celebrated partnership. Tracy appeared alone in *Father of the Bride* (1950) and its sequel *Father's Little Dividend* (1951), while Hepburn starred with Bob Hope in a pale imitation of *Ninotchka* (1939) called *The Iron Petticoat* (1956).

And the newest stars were not forgotten. Once Marilyn Monroe had arrived as a superstar in Hawks' gloriously garish musical *Gentlemen Prefer Blondes*, her energies were most happily channelled into comedy rather than drama, and in Billy Wilder she found a director who knew how to display her qualities to perfection. *The Seven Year Itch* (1955) and *Some Like It Hot* (1959) captured unforgettably – and hilariously – her innocent sexuality and her air of being the totally unconscious *agent provocateur* of all the male preenings, palpitations and jockeyings for position which went on around her.

With *Sabrina* (1954) and *Love in the Afternoon* (1957) Billy Wilder also created ideal vehicles for the very different charms of another brand-new star, Audrey Hepburn, and made the definitive transition from his image as a hard-hitting scourge of the world's follies to that of Hollywood's most brilliant comedy director, a role he was to revel in throughout the Sixties.

Not that he had so much competition. By the end of the Fifties, his were just about the only comedies not suffering from terminal softening of the brain. The musical too, which entered the decade at some kind of peak, left it a faded, overblown remnant. In 1949 Gene Kelly and Stanley Donen had made their debut as directors with *On the Town*, which boldly took its singing and dancing stars out on the streets of New York and blended song, dance and drama more inextricably than ever before into one unquestionable whole. It was the cue for a series of triumphs. In 1951 Kelly worked with Minnelli on *An American in Paris*, and in 1952 Kelly and Donen were back together again for *Singin' in the Rain*, which remains for many the finest flower of the genre. But it had ample competition for the title, notably from Minnelli's 1953 offering *The Band Wagon*. Judy Garland achieved some sort of apotheosis in *A Star is Born* (1954) but great musical stars were few and far between in the Fifties. Gene Kelly danced in films like *Invitation to the Dance* (1956), *Brigadoon* (1954), *It's Always Fair Weather* (1955), his final collaboration with Donen, and *Les Girls* (1957), which included Cole Porter's last original score for the screen.

More astonishing still, Fred Astaire, who had announced his definitive retirement in 1946, considering himself too old at 47 to go on dancing, reversed his decision and continued to dance and delight right through the decade.

The high points of the Fifties for him were *The Band Wagon* and *Silk Stockings* (1957), in both of which he partnered the statuesque Cyd Charisse. There were also two May-September matings, first with the elfin Leslie Caron in *Daddy Long Legs* (1954) and then with the ineffable Audrey Hepburn in *Funny Face* (1957).

Most of the musical partnerships of the Forties and early Fifties broke up towards the end of the decade. Stanley Donen went on to direct two more musicals at Warners, *The Pajama Game* (1957) and *Damn Yankees* (1958) before transferring his allegiance to dramatic films. Gene Kelly went on to direct non-musical films too. Many of the musicals that were made in the latter half of the Fifties were safe, faithful transcriptions of recent Broadway successes: *Oklahoma!* (1955), *The King and I* (1956) and *South Pacific* (1958). Original creations for the screen like *Seven Brides for Seven Brothers* (1954) and *Gigi* (1958) were, by and large, considered too risky in a Hollywood reeling at the onslaught television had made on its public. Never mind the quality, look at the size, might be the motto of Hollywood in the Sixties, and in comedy and the musical the small, sophisticated pleasures which had illuminated so many films of the Fifties had been brushed aside for ever.

Above: Bob Hope and Lucille Ball in The Facts of Life, *a wry comedy about a couple who spend an illicit weekend together away from their respective spouses and confront the familiar domestic situations once again. Top: Bob Fosse and Gwen Verdon in the smash-hit musical* Damn Yankees *– yet another Fifties film that revolved around a marriage break-up*

The gentle anarchy of

Left: the familiar outline could only belong to Jacques Tati. Above: as Monsieur Hulot, Tati surveys the aftermath of his helpful intentions while his dazed victims examine themselves for damage in Traffic

Jacques Tati, real name Tatischeff, was born at Le Pecq in France on October 9, 1908. His father, of Russian descent, ran a picture-framing business and when the boy wasn't helping in the shop he was developing a passion for sport. It was in the staging of 'action-replays' for the amusement of his friends that Tati discovered his talent for mimicry. His sporting mimes – in which he would portray the referee, both teams, and the entire crowd – became so accomplished that sport gave way to the music-hall as a prospective career and by his early twenties he was well established as a mime comedian. In pre-war Paris he was in great demand, working with Piaf, finding an ardent fan in Colette, and even achieving some bookings outside France, notably in Berlin.

As early as 1931, Tati experimented with film, creating an extended version of his tennis sketch – later to be expanded further in *Les Vacances de Monsieur Hulot* (1953, *Monsieur Hulot's Holiday*). Written, directed and acted by himself, *Oscar, Champion de Tennis* (1932, Oscar, the Tennis Champion) was of poor technical quality and attracted little attention, but it helped Tati to shape the awkward, amiable figure who was to become François the postman in *Jour de Fête* (1949, Day of the Fair) and

then Hulot. For his second film Tati enlisted the help of two professionals, Charles Barrois and René Clément, to direct him in *On Demande Une Brute* (1934, They Want a Beast); the 'brute' was Tati, a timid husband driven by a series of misunderstandings to pose as a champion in a wrestling match. Then came *Gai Dimanche* (1935, Happy Sunday), directed by Jacques Berr, starring Tati and the clown Rhum. Again the story of a misfit, it showed the brisk deterioration of what was intended as an idyllic picnic being beset by gastronomic, mechanical and rustic upsets, culminating in a stampede. With *Soigne ton Gauche* (1936, Guard Your Left), directed by René Clément, and *Retour à la Terre* (1938, Return to the Land), entirely produced by Tati, further hints of *Jour de Fête* can be spotted in his use of the countryside, of children, and even of a meddling postman. Technically, however, the films were poor and roughly edited.

The war then interrupted Tati's career for six years, but after the French surrender he found himself in Sainte-Sévère-sur-Indre, the village that gave him the setting for *Jour de Fête*. In 1945, Tati started putting all the pieces together – in collaboration with Henri Marquet – and the result was the one-reeler *L'École des Facteurs* (1947, School for Postmen), part-

financed by rather uncharacteristic Tati appearances in two Autant-Lara films, *Sylvie et la Fantôme* (1945, *Sylvie and the Ghost*) and *Le Diable au Corps* (1947, *Devil in the Flesh*). For four years, Tati built up his film, testing different gag sequences on different preview audiences, until in 1949 *Jour de Fête* won the prize for best scenario in Venice and in 1950 the Grand Prix du Cinéma at Cannes.

More of the same was immediately requested by would-be financiers, to the extent that *L'École des Facteurs*, even though only a first draft, was separately promoted and won its own prize in 1949. But Tati was not interested in fresh postman stories; he was preoccupied with what he termed a twentieth-century Everyman, a figure affording him more scope because he would fit – or rather, *not* fit – into a wider range of settings. The filmed result – after financial problems, painstaking preparation, and several years – was *Monsieur Hulot's Holiday*, which became an instant world-wide favourite.

Once again using an authentic background, that of St. Marc-sur-Mer in Brittany, the film satirized the universal holiday-maker and introduced the frightening and endearing character of Hulot, who charged into the peculiarly brittle fabric of seaside society with all the gusto and misapprehension of a three-year-old. Despite his air of desperate improvisation, Hulot's mishaps were meticulously planned before Tati even arrived at the location, and it was another three months before he started shooting. So much comic detail was inserted that at times the film appears not to be about Hulot at all and this, surprisingly, is just what Tati was after. A French interviewer at the time reported:

'Ideally, Tati would like a film of the adventures of Hulot in which Hulot himself did not appear. His presence would be apparent simply from the more or less catastrophic upheavals left in his wake.'

It was not an approach that would find many sympathizers, and Hulot has remained

Filmography
1932 Oscar, Champion de Tennis (short) (+sc; +actor). '34 On Demande Une Brute (short) (co-sc +actor only). '35 Gai Dimanche (short) (co-sc +actor only). '36 Soigne ton Gauche (short) (sc. +actor only). '45 Sylvie et le Fantome (USA: Sylvie and the Phantom; GB: Sylvie and the Ghost) (act. only). '47 L'Ecole des Facteurs (short) (+sc; +dial; +act); Le Diable au Corps (USA: The Devil in the Flesh) (act only). '49 Jour de Fête (USA: Day of the Fair) (+co-sc; +co-dial; +act). '53 Les Vacances de Monsieur Hulot (Monsieur Hulot's Holiday) (+co-sc; +co-dial; +act). '58 Mon Oncle (My Uncle) (+co-sc; +co-dial +act) (FR-IT). '68 Playtime (+sc; +act). '70 Trafic (Traffic) (+co-sc; +act) (FR-IT). '74 Parade (+sc; +act) (made for FR TV).

Jacques Tati

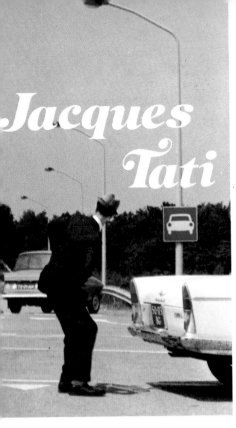

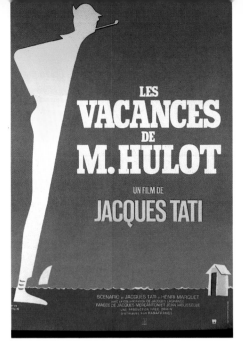

Left and above: the film that established Tati's Hulot character. Below: Hulot regards his sister's new kitchen (left) in Mon Oncle and the modern glass office-blocks of Playtime (right) with equal suspicion

on view in all Tati's subsequent work, He has echoes of many screen clowns, primarily in his embarrassment at the problem of what to do with himself in a world patently ill-suited, not only to his physical awkwardness, but also to his inner remoteness. Hulot works twice as hard as anybody else at the task of integration – the tennis match in *Monsieur Hulot's Holiday* and the garden party in *Mon Oncle* (1958, My Uncle) show him at his most frenzied in the battle to keep up appearances – but a certain jauntiness in the angle of pipe and umbrella, a natty style of hat, and a private choreography of walk in which he seems to choose his own confident road along invisible stepping-stones, imply that secretly he does not care too desperately that the world is hell-bent on progress. He is a gentle anarchist, too polite and affectionate to shake the nonsense out of his contemporaries; if they cannot be contented, at least he can find his own kind of peace in isolation.

In *Mon Oncle* – which appeared after nine months of shooting and a year of cutting and dubbing – Hulot often seems withdrawn, a hermit in his own cosy part of town, although his struggle to be a part of everything continues. Tati explained:

'The film conducts a defence of the individual, I don't like to be regimented, I don't like mechanization. I believe in the old quarter,

the tranquil corner, rather than in highways, roads, aerodromes and all the organization in modern life. People aren't at their best with geometrical lines all round them'.

Mon Oncle proceeded to show people *not* at their best in a quietly biased, irresistibly sentimental comparison between the old and the new and the widening gulf between them. Winner of the Special Jury Prize at Cannes in 1958, the film was celebrated by the *Cahiers du Cinéma* critics such as Godard and Truffaut, who were to bring about a stylistic revolution in their films the following year – putting across their own disquiet more forcefully. For all that, however, *Mon Oncle* more clearly defined the views of the 'old-school' such as Renoir and Clair. Hulot the charming recluse was the model for a decade of drop-outs, but his unswerving kindness and imperturbable good manners were an archaic and quixotic armour in the era of computerized dehumanization that called for the rude brutality of Godard's comic-book detective Lemmy Caution to defend such concepts as poetry and love.

When *Playtime* appeared a long time later in 1968, after Tati had spent three years constructing it with a massive £1 million budget, it had nothing to add. An anaemic Hulot wanders around the glass boxes of the modern Paris, an aimless ghost in a procession of repetitive and only mildly amusing incongruities. Like Antonioni, Tati strengthened his anti-urban argument by making the architecture a dominating force, but went a stage further by building his own studio city, spotless and soulless, like a maze enclosing experimental mice. And like the holiday-makers of

Monsieur Hulot's Holiday, the mice are recognizable 'types' – the American tourists, the German salesmen, the little old ladies who need someone to mend a simple electric lamp but find that such expertise is not available in today's sophistication, the fussing married couple, the waiters who never get round to serving anybody. Hulot strikes up a tentative friendship with an American girl and gives her a present to take back home; it is a small bunch of flowers, but they are plastic. Intentional or not, it makes a melancholy symbol for the film as a whole; precise, well-meant, a spectacular piece of craftsmanship but not much of a substitute for reality.

With *Trafic* (1970 *Traffic*), Tati was on happier ground. Hulot is a driver in a convoy of new cars *en route* from Paris to an international motor show in Amsterdam. More prominent as a character than in *Playtime*, but still a model of detachment, he has come to terms with progress to the extent that he tends to have the solution to such problems as breakdowns, traffic-jams, and car crashes, offering good sense while his contemporaries swarm about in counterproductive distraction. Tati satirizes all the less lethal driving habits, stringing together an amiable line of sight-gags – like a squashed shape under a car-wheel that could be either dead dog or discarded jacket – which have an edge to them that is discreetly blunted to avoid the shedding of blood.

Jacques Tati died in 1982. But the discretion and gentle humour of Monsieur Hulot live on, as a calming – an essential – antidote to a frenzied world.

A DELUGE OF *Delight* — SPLASHED WITH SONG HITS!

METRO-GOLDWYN-MAYER
presents

Singin' in the Rain

IN COLOUR BY
TECHNICOLOR®

Starring

GENE KELLY · Donald O'CONNOR
Debbie REYNOLDS · Cyd CHARISSE

1

2

6

7

10

If there is one image which sums up the MGM musical, it is this: Gene Kelly, walking home in euphoric mood, is caught in a particularly heavy fall of Californian dew. But does he care? No, not a bit of it. On along the empty street, past the glamorous shop windows he dances, twirling under a water spout, tap-dancing in the gutter, finally stamping around with child-like delight and abandon in a giant puddle which covers half the road. When a mystified and vaguely hostile policeman comes up to find out just what is going on, Kelly has a simple answer: 'Just singin', and dancin', in the rain.'

The convention of the musical as a never-never land, where normal rules of life were for the moment suspended and invisible orchestras would accompany ordinary people as they expressed their ordinary emotions in an extraordinary way, found its complete justification in the integrated musicals of producer Arthur Freed. *Singin' in the Rain* is the finest hour of this school of film-making. It does, it is true, contain elements of the old 'putting on a show' musical formula (or in this case a film), but hardly any of its numbers are tied down to a stuffily rational context. Even the ambitious 'Broadway Melody' sequence is presented as a fantasy in the minds of its creators which they are trying to put over to their reluctant boss – and which he stubbornly fails to visualize.

In *Singin' in the Rain*, as in all the best musicals, the characters' behaviour has its own logic: song and dance are kept in reserve for the moments of irrepressible high spirits, passionate romance and the like, those moments when we might all feel like bursting into song or whirling away into dance if only we knew how, if only we were not worried what passers-by might think, if only we had the MGM orchestra and chorus to hand.

The title number is the climax of the film, but it is also the simplest. At the other end of the scale is the big 'Broadway Melody' number, which

Above right: a publicity shot of the film's opening scene

tells a show-business rags-to-riches story in miniature with a multiplicity of sets, costumes and extras. As a sizzling addition to the proceedings, Cyd Charisse features as the hero's dream woman.

The film's story manages to comprehend both these extremes. The script by Betty Comden and Adolph Green (both of whom had already worked with directors Gene Kelly and Stanley Donen on their first great success, *On the Town*, 1949) is probably the funniest and sharpest ever invented for a film musical. The image that it offers of Hollywood at the coming of sound has the ring of truth, for all its comic exaggeration. Who can forget the picture of the nitwit silent-movie queen Lina Lamont wrestling with round vowels as she bleats 'I caaan't stan'm' in response to her voice coach's patient tuition? Or the opening sequence in which her opposite number, romantic idol Don Lockwood reminisces for the listening public about his rise to the top, with 'dignity, dignity, always dignity', while the scenes of dancing for pennies and tatty burlesque which flash before us belie every word he says? Or the unstoppable *élan* with which Don and his two fellow conspirators, once they hit on the perfect solution to their dilemma (make the disastrous costume movie into a musical), burst into 'Good Morning' and gyrate and tap all over Don's beautiful, baronial, Hollywood home?

However, it is invidious to pick out any single treasure in *Singin' in the Rain* without mentioning all the rest. None of its stars were ever shown to better advantage and the formidable MGM machine never worked more smoothly or to greater effect, down to the last detail of design and orchestration. Whatever happened to the Hollywood musical in later years, *Singin' in the Rain* survives as irrefutable testimony to the wonderful way they were.

Directed by Gene Kelly and Stanley Donen, 1952
Prod co: MGM. **prod:** Arthur Freed. **sc:** Betty Comden, Adolph Green. **photo:** Harold Rosson. **col:** Technicolor. **ed:** Adrienne Fazan. **art dir:** Cedric Gibbons, Randall Duell. **mus dir:** Lennie Hayton. **mus:** Nacio Herb Brown. **lyr:** Arthur Freed. **r/t:** 103 minutes.
Cast: Gene Kelly (*Don Lockwood*), Donald O'Connor (*Cosmo Brown*), Debbie Reynolds (*Kathy Selden*), Jean Hagen (*Lina Lamont*), Millard Mitchell (*R. F. Simpson*), Rita Moreno (*Zelda Zanders*), Douglas Fowley (*Roscoe Dexter*), Cyd Charisse (*dancer*), Madge Blake (*Dora Bailey*), King Donovan (*Rod*), Kathleen Freeman (*Phoebe Dinsmore*), Bobby Watson (*diction coach*), Tommy Farrell (*Sid Phillips*).

Hollywood, 1927. Don Lockwood and Lina Lamont, famous stars of the silent screen, arrive at the premiere of their latest romantic swashbuckler (1). Don entertains the radio public with a conveniently laundered account of his rise from vaudeville (2) to stardom opposite Lina. On his way to a party after the film, Don is mobbed by fans and seeks refuge in the car of an aspiring actress, Kathy Selden (3). She piques Don by making 'superior' remarks about the movie business.

At the party, where Don's producer, R. F. Simpson, demonstrates talking pictures (4), a huge cake is brought in. Out of it pops none other than Kathy herself. Don makes fun of her; she throws a pie at him, hitting Lina by mistake, and vanishes.

Don looks in vain for Kathy, but his friend, Cosmo Brown, cheers him up with a song about the entertainer's lot (5).

Following the tremendous success of *The Jazz Singer*, Simpson orders the instant conversion of Don and Lina's new film, *The Duelling Cavalier*, to sound. Don has no real trouble with this, but Lina's squeaky Brooklyn accent and inability to speak into the microphone drive the director to distraction (6). While making the movie, Don encounters Kathy, who has a bit part in a musical being made at the studio; he makes his peace with her and declares his love (7). On the way home, Don sings and dances with joy during a cloudburst (8).

The premiere of *The Duelling Cavalier* is a hilarious disaster. That night, Don, Kathy and Cosmo come up with the idea that matters can be retrieved if the film is quickly turned into a musical and Lina's voice replaced by Kathy's (9). Don and Cosmo tell Simpson their adventurous plans, which concern the story of a young dancer's success on Broadway (10) and his involvement with an exotic nightclub queen (11). Simpson does not share the boys' enthusiasm but agrees to make *The Duelling Cavalier* into a musical.

Lina discovers that her voice has been dubbed by Kathy, whom she jealously regards as the breaker of her (non-existent) romance with Don. By a clause in her contract she seems able to confine Kathy to being for ever her voice in films. But when Lina decides to 'sing' following the triumphant premiere of the revamped movie, Don and Cosmo reveal to the audience that Lina's vocal talents really belong to Kathy. Kathy becomes a star in her own right, and she and Don live happily ever after (12).

4

5

8

9

12

267

A Rebel Named Brando

When Marlon Brando went to Hollywood his challenging style of acting became the controversial symbol of new hopes for American culture. Since the Fifties, he has brought to the screen a range of memorable characters – from Stanley Kowalski to Superman's father

Nowadays, one approaches a performance by Marlon Brando with a certain trepidation. Will he have bothered to learn his lines, or will he, as is his recent want, pin bits and pieces of the script to the set, so that the problem of memorization will not, as he claims, interfere with the process of creation? Will he be merely overweight, or will he be completely grossed out – as he was in *Apocalypse Now* (1979)? Will he focus his full concentration on the role, or will he content himself with what amounts to self-parody?

It seemed for a short time in the early Seventies, after *The Godfather* (1972) and *Ultimo Tango a Parigi* (1972, *Last Tango in Paris*), that he had not merely returned to form, but attained a new one – an ability to literally act his age – and that such tense questions might finally be rendered moot. Ah, foolish optimism! How could we have forgotten that the very basis of his screen character, the source of its fascination, lies in his childishly erratic, entirely anarchical nature. Brando would not be Brando if you could count on him. From the beginning we have attended his work not in search of seamless technical perfection, but as we do a thrill act at a carnival. We go to see him dive down into the depths of himself, to see if he will surface with some new pearls of existential awareness or a heap of rusting mannerism or, more likely, a

couple of the former mixed with a lot of the latter. If you cannot stand the sometimes instantaneous alternations between exasperation and exhilaration which he thus induces, then you have no business at a Brando film – which is, of course, a position many have adopted.

About the deepest sources of his wild ways one can only speculate. But about one of the matters that has driven him crazy, right from the start of his career, there can be no doubt. That is his unsought position as a hero of a special modern sort, a *cultural* hero, burdened with the large, if ill-defined, hopes of at least two generations for the renewal of American acting, and through it, of the American theatre, American films, perhaps even of American culture. It was not a role he sought! It was, indeed, a role he fought. And yet, somehow, it settled upon him.

Brando's Method
Brando, a high-school dropout, came more or less accidentally to acting, and he enjoyed an early success in it before developing a sense of vocation. He was thus forced to confront the personal and public demands of his profession without an aesthetic or a sense of cultural tradition. This gap was filled by the 'Method', that American variation on Stanislavky's theories, which was very much in the air in

New York when Brando was breaking into the theatre. Emerging from small parts into the unforgettable glory of his Stanley in *A Streetcar Named Desire*, he was seen as the personification of 'Method' principles (though, in truth, he had passed only briefly through its cathedral, the Actors' Studio). And since his own instinctive method – a search through memory for psychological truth, a rejection of classic manner and technique, squared with the 'Method', ('You have to upset yourself! Unless you do you cannot act'), the role of leader in a generational revolt was imposed upon him. American provincialism was to be shaken off; English acting standards would no longer go unchallenged.

Many in the older generation were appalled, but if you were young and cared about the mystery of acting, then Brando's singularity – there really never had been anyone quite like him – exercized a powerful symbolic hold on your imagination. Indeed, some part of you became his forever. And when he went out to Hollywood, hope mingled with fear over what would result. Would he revolutionize the place, or succumb to it. In the event, he remained . . . himself. That is to say, volatile and difficult, brilliant and indifferent. But there was no gainsaying the impact of his work in those first films, which were widely variable in their overall quality: the crippled war veteran in *The Men* (1950), the brutal Stanley Kowalski in *A Streetcar Named Desire* (1951), the Mexican revolutionary in *Viva Zapata!* (1952), the motorbike rebel in *The Wild One* (1953) and the ex-boxer in *On the Waterfront* (1954) – in these pictures he gave us moments which had never been seen on the screen before. For young

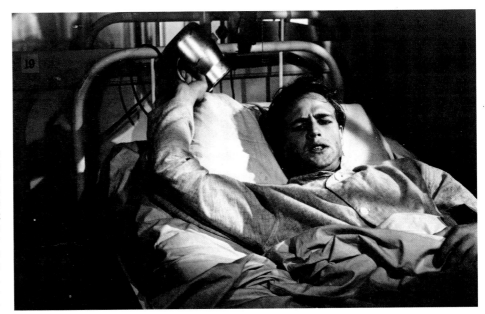

people his sullen, inarticulate rebelliousness won them to him forever. Even when he was playing brutes and dummies you sensed his vulnerability, his tentativeness, and, even, his underlying sweetness and sense of comedy. He was the first movie star who showed, right there on the screen, the truth behind the image – the insecurity and the nagging, peculiarly American fear that acting may not be suitable work for a grown-up heterosexual male. He was exploring what no-one else had explored.

In his first great role, that of Stanley Kowalski in *A Streetcar Named Desire*, people identified Brando with the image he played. Few heard him when he said:

'Kowalski was always right, and never afraid . . . He never wondered, he never doubted. His ego was very secure. And he had that kind of brutal aggressiveness I hate . . . I'm afraid of it. I detest the character.'

Stanley was crass, calculating and materialist – a type who was a factor in every aspect of American life in this century. The power of Brando's performance derives from his hatred and fear of the character, though manifestly there is something of Brando's own egotism and rudeness in Stanley too.

Winds of change

Brando found Hollywood – a town always full of Kowalskis – in a state of transition. The reliable mass market was slipping away to television; the factory system, ruled by a handful of industry 'pioneers', was losing its sovereignty to stars and directors who were, with the help of powerful agencies, creating their own packages. Brando had a long-term contract with Fox, but he fought the studio constantly and, unlike the older generation of stars, had the option to make independent films, so he could not be disciplined by suspensions or blacklisting. In addition he did not dress like a star, could not be coerced into interviews or publicity gimmicks he found demeaning. 'The only thing an actor owes his public is not to bore them' he declared.

The men who ruled Hollywood, quite rightly, distrusted Brando. They might talk about his manner and style (or lack of it) but deep down, they knew he was on to them, was parodying them on the screen. Still, through *On the Waterfront* an uneasy truce was maintained between Brando and Hollywood, if only because until that picture was finished – and they rewarded him with an Oscar – he stuck close to the type they had decided was correct for him and which was easily saleable – brooding, capable of brutality, yet gropingly sensitive and rebelious. Indeed, Terry Malloy, the ex-boxer, betrayed by his brother in *On the Waterfront*, seemed to many at the time a painfully accurate projection of Brando's own mood. When he says 'I could have been a contender . . . instead of a bum', some took this as an admission that the great roles were not for him. Others saw it as a generational

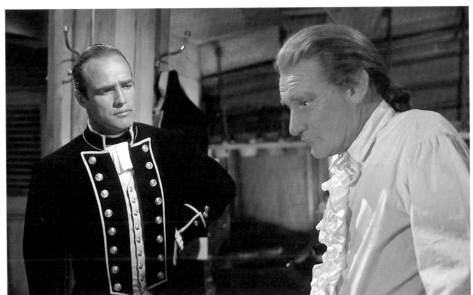

Above: Brando brought new depth – and an English accent – to Fletcher Christian, the officer who confronts Captain Bligh (Trevor Howard) in Mutiny on the Bounty. *Left:* One Eyed Jacks *shows up the images of male strength and violence used in Westerns*

lament, a declaration of betrayal not merely by an institution, but by the whole society in which humane, liberal values now seemed inadequate to a monstrously complex age.

Nevertheless, he won an Academy Award for *On the Waterfront* and continued to maintain himself as his contemporaries hoped he would – an inner-directed man in an other-directed world. There was, however, one big change in him. He no longer wanted to play roles that were projections of himself or even of his earlier image. In Terry Malloy he had achieved a kind of apotheosis; he now wanted to prove he could submerge self in characters. He undertook a staggering variety of roles from 1954 onwards: a Damon Runyon gambler in *Guys and Dolls* (1955); Napoleon in *Desiree* (1954); Sakini, the Japanese interpreter in *The Teahouse of the August Moon* (1956); the Southern soldier fighting his own racial prejudice in *Sayonara* (1957); the German soldier undergoing self-induced de-Nazification in *The Young Lions* (1958); the vengeful good-bad man in *One Eyed Jacks* (1961) and Fletcher Christian in *Mutiny on the Bounty* (1962).

Some of these pictures were successful at the box-office; some were not. There was a steady muttering about his waste of himself in subjects that, for the most part, were drawn from the less exalted ranges of popular fiction. In fact, he was playing a higher risk game than the critics knew, for his price was now something like a million dollars a picture in return for which he was supposed, by his presence, to guarantee a profit. What other actor would have risked that status in roles which were deliberately off-type and which caused him to use weird makeups and strange accents?

Gillo Pontecorvo, who directed him in *Queimada!* (1969, *Burn!*), declared, 'I never saw an actor before who was so afraid of the camera.' His hatred of publicity, his desire to hide-out in roles was based, in part, on simple shyness. Moreover, the kind of acting he was now doing demanded less of him emotionally, if more of him technically. As he said:

'There comes a time in one's life when you don't want to do it anymore. You know a scene is coming where you'll have to cry and scream and all those things, and it's always bothering you, always eating away at you . . . and you just can't walk through it . . . it would be disrespectful not to try to do your best.'

So he settled for imitations of life, which was not only easy for him, but fun. Acting at this level, he has been heard to say, is 'a perfectly reasonable way to make your living. You're not stealing money, and you're entertaining people'.

Other pressures came from the financial expectations of the industry. Directing *One Eyed Jacks*, he went way over budget, perhaps because he thought directing was a way of making an artistic statement without exposing so much of himself. The result was a lovely and violent film but still, to most people, just another Western.

Mutiny on 'Mutiny'

He might have escaped that set-back unscathed had he not followed it with *Mutiny on the Bounty*. There was a certain logic in the casting – Brando, the famous rebel, playing Fletcher Christian, the famous rebel. The trouble was that Brando insisted on playing Christian, not as a he-man of principle, as Clark Gable had, but as a foppish idler, with homosexual overtones, a character whose previously dormant sense of class difference, the basis of order in the British navy, turns torpid under Tahiti's tropical skies. It was not at all what the producers had in mind for a multi-million-dollar film on which MGM was depending for survival.

They claimed it was Brando's temperament that cost them an extra $10 million, but he was, in fact, taking the rap for all kinds of mismanagement, which included sending cast and crew off to shoot in the rainy season without a finished script in hand. Of course, Brando was angry and of course he turned as mutinous as Christian himself had.

What got lost in the resulting controversy was the fact that Brando's Christian was one of his finest sustained performances, a daring attempt to blend the humorous with the heroic, a projection of a modern, ironic sensibility backward into history. There was no-

thing cool or held back in this characterization; Brando took it right up to the hot edge of farce. If he was out of key with the rest of the players and the square-rigged plot, he actually did what a star is supposed to do, hold our interest in a big dumb remake – while risking comparison with the remembered performance of a beloved actor in a beloved role.

After *Mutiny on the Bounty*, came the deluge – poor parts, not a few of which he walked out on. In some of these films one can see the germ of the idea that attracted Brando: the chance to confront comedy directly in *Bedtime Story* (1964) and *A Countess From Hong Kong* (1967); the opportunity to make social comments he considered worthy in *The Ugly American* (1963), *The Chase* (1966) and *Queimada!*; even roles that matched his gift, despite their flawed context, notably that of the repressed homosexual army officer in *Reflections in a Golden Eye* (1967).

There are in these films isolated moments where Brando shines through. There is the scene in *Sayonara*, for example, when he confesses to his commanding general (and would-be father-in-law) that he is throwing

Top: in The Chase, *Bubber Reeves (Robert Redford) is arrested by the sheriff (Brando) but is shot – like Lee Harvey Oswald – before he can be tried. Directed by Arthur Penn,* The Chase *is a highly political film of bigotry and violence in the Deep South. Above: Brando plays a disillusioned English adventurer in* Queimada! *– a film about slavery and the colonization of the Caribbean*

over his fiancée for a Japanese girl. He conveys his anguish over this decision by picking up a cushion and concentrating on it the entire time they talk – a perfectly observed banal gesture. In *Reflections in a Golden Eye*, there is the scene when he thinks Robert Forster is coming to pay a homosexual call on him and he absurdly pats down his hair and smiles vainly to himself. Then there is *The Nightcomers* (1971) in which he hides out behind an Irish brogue and spends a lot of time indulging a bondage fetish with the governess, when, in the midst of it, he tells the children a long tall story and suddenly he's alive and playful and inventive, giving himself pleasure and making us share in it.

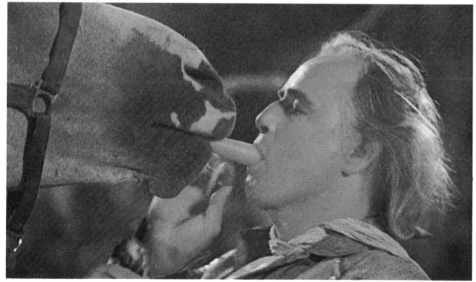

Left: light relief from Brando and Maria Schneider as the couple who share a frenentic sexual relationship in Last Tango In Paris. Below left: in The Missouri Breaks (1976), Brando is a lawman – a typical John Wayne character – who, in this scene, shares a carrot with his horse before declaring his undying love for her. Above: the deranged Major Kurtz from Apocalypse Now

nities. There is also in him something of the youthful, public Brando – self-romanticizing, self-pitying, yet self-satirizing too. All Brando's character Paul does in the film is have a restorative affair with a much younger woman. In the last sequences he is restored to a handsomeness that can be termed nothing less than beauty, a vitality, even a romantic energy, that is both miraculous and moving.

In the brilliant monologue at his dead wife's bier, perhaps the single greatest aria of his career, it all comes together, talent and technique, to express the violent ambivalence of his relationship with not merely this woman, but with himself and the world at large.

It was Brando's art, not director Bertolucci's, that made the highly melodramatic ending – in which, for no good reason, the star must die – a triumph. Brando removes the sting of death by the simple act of removing his chewing gum from his mouth and placing it neatly under the railing of the terrace where he takes his final fall – the tiny, perfect bit of actor's business, neatly undercutting the director's strain for a big finish.

Perhaps only a young director, cognizant of what Brando has meant to his generation, a director who self-consiously stripped from his work all intellectual and artistic traditions other than that of the cinema, could give his age's great *movie* actor this unprecedented opportunity for self-portraiture.

But it was *The Godfather* that provided the long-awaited proof that he could still do most of it as an actor. He went after the part; even submitted to the indignity of a test. The result was a sustained characterization that depended for its success on more than a raspy voice and a clever old man's makeup. There were in his very movements, the hints of mortality that men in their forties begin to feel no matter· how youthfully they maintain their spirits. His manner epitomized all the old men of power who had leaned across their desks to bend the young actor to their will – their wile and strength sheathed in reasonableness, commands presented in the guise of offers it *is*

hard to refuse. It was the culmination of his second career as a character man.

What one really wondered, though, was whether he had it in him to go all the way down the well again, come out from behind the masks and show again the primitiveness and power of his youth. That, quite simply, is what he did in *Last Tango in Paris*. Brando was playing physically what he is psychologically, an expatriate from his native land. Moreover, he was playing a man passing through the 'male menopause'. Yet in his sexual brutality there is something of Stanley Kowalski, and, like Terry Malloy, he is a one-time boxer, vulnerable in his mourning for lost opportu-

Filmography
1950 The Men. '51 A Streetcar Named Desire. '52 Viva Zapata! '53 Julius Caesar; The Wild One. '54 On the Waterfront; Desiree. '55 Guys and Dolls. '56 The Teahouse of the August Moon. '57 Sayonara. '58 The Young Lions. '60 The Fugitive Kind. '61 One Eyed Jacks (+prod; +dir). '62 Mutiny on the Bounty. '63 The Ugly American. '64 Bedtime Story. '65 Morituri (GB: The Saboteur – Code Name 'Morituri'). '66 The Chase; The Appaloosa (GB: Southwest to Sonora). '67 A Countess From Hong Kong (GB); Reflections in a Golden Eye. '68 Candy (USA-FR-IT); The Night of the Following Day. '69 Queimada! (USA: Burn!) (IT-FR). '71 The Nightcomers (GB). '72 The Godfather; Ultimo Tango a Parigi (USA/GB: Last Tango in Paris) (IT-FR). '76 The Missouri Breaks. '78 Superman, the Movie (GB). '79 Apocalypse Now. '80 The Formula. '82 Jericho.

JAMES
DEAN

NATALIE
WOOD

SAL
MINEO

in Warner Bros.

"REBEL
WITHOUT
A CAUSE"

CINEMASCOPE
and WARNERCOLOR

...and they both come
from 'good' families!

Directed by Nicholas Ray, 1955
Prod co: Warner Bros. **prod:** David Weisbart. **sc:** Stewart Stern, Irving Shulman, from a story by Nicholas Ray. **photo:** Ernest Haller. **ed:** William Zeigler. **art dir:** Malcolm Bart. **mus dir:** Leonard Rosenman. **r/t:** 111 minutes.
Cast: James Dean (*Jim*), Natalie Wood (*Judy*), Jim Backus (*Jim's father*), Ann Doran (*Jim's mother*), Rochelle Hudson (*Judy's mother*), William Hopper (*Judy's father*), Sal Mineo (*Plato*), Corey Allen (*Buzz*), Dennis Hopper (*Goon*), Edward Platt (*Ray*), Steffi Sidney (*Mil*), Marietta Canty (*maid*), Ian Wolfe (*lecturer*), Frank Mazzola (*Crunch*).

When *Rebel Without a Cause* was premiered in Britain, in January 1956, the British critics considered it well-made, but some reviewers sustained severe moral outrage. *The Spectator* said:
'Its solemnity is rather irritating, seeing that a few good spanks would settle a lot of its problems.'
The *Daily Sketch* critic praised Nicholas Ray's direction but warned: 'That kind of brilliance in this kind of picture can be dangerous.'
Rebel Without a Cause is, of course, a 'problem picture' in the honourable Warner's tradition and can trace its ancestry back through the Dead End Kids' movies and *Angels With Dirty Faces* (1938) to the founding principles of 'social conscience' drama. In the wake of location-shot thrillers like *Gun Crazy* (1949) and alongside con-

temporary 'teenpix' – B movies like *Five Against the House* (1955) – *Rebel Without a Cause* looks even more like the 'realist' romance it is. But Nicholas Ray and screenwriter Stewart Stern made determined efforts to accommodate a documentary feel within the parameters of the high-gloss, A-feature production values required at Warners.
Ray and Stern spent weeks interviewing youth leaders and juvenile officers. They sat in on juvenile court sessions and spoke with criminologists including one who had been the chief psychiatrist at the Nuremberg trials. They did their homework.
The scenario, as Eric Rohmer observed in the French magazine of film theory *Cahiers du Cinéma* in 1955, falls neatly into the five acts of classical tragedy: exposition, with the conflict between the parents

and the children clearly stated; act two, in which Jim befriends Plato and is taunted by Buzz; act three, which includes the 'chicken run' with its fatal climax; act four, where Jim and Judy enjoy a transitory peace and share their love with Plato; and the final tragic act whose full impact is engraved on Jim's anguished face. As befits Aristotle's rules, the action is all but contained within 24 hours.
With that kind of narrative compression, the film could have emerged as hysterical melodrama, but even in the emotionally climactic scene of the domestic quarrel, the audience is never allowed to assume a dispassionate, 'objective' perspective. 'We are all involved!' as Jim exclaims. Ray's direction is in control: his camera spins upright out of a brilliant inverted shot from Jim's viewpoint. He then forces the action of the argument across the room and back against the stairs for greater dramatic effect and intercuts low-angle, high-angle and obliquely distorted shots to disrupt the perspective that the viewer normally considers his or her privilege. It is a bravura piece of direction in a film whose *mise-en-scène* is elsewhere distinguished by set-pieces, like the 'chicken run' and the final planetarium scenes – both of which are staged under the artificial, theatrical lighting of a circle of car headlights.
The real director of *Rebel Without a Cause*, however, may be James Dean, in the sense that the film critic David Thomson describes him 'redirecting the picture by virtue of sheer presence'. If the complex experience of reading a film can be premised on the *look* constantly exchanged between the

viewer and the on-screen protagonists, then *direction* may be construed as the control and orientation of that look. The unique qualities of James Dean as an actor, especially in the intuitive relationship he shared with Nicholas Ray, permit the 'lingering' of the look (Dean's characteristic pauses) and provoke the disorientation of the look (his restlessness in the CinemaScope frame). In short, Dean tells us where to look and what to notice.
In the scene where Jim meets Judy outside her house at night, we anticipate the confirmation of the love between them and, therefore, might expect a progression from individual close-ups, to two-shot, to embrace. Instead, shooting in medium close-up, Ray shows Jim, agitated, lolling or rolling over, dominating the central and left areas of the vast CinemaScope image; while Judy remains almost motionless right of frame. The framing, like everything else in the film, privileges Dean, confirming his dominance and suggesting that Ray was taking advantage of this opportunity to play Dean as his *alter ego* and extend the art of directing through performance so that Dean can be seen as acting out Ray's romantic fantasy. To quote David Thomson again:
'Arguably only Nicholas Ray could have given Dean a part that guessed at the looming alienation in America.'
Dean and Ray were two loners from Middle America, down there in the comfortable (studio-set) suburban homes, who fled to the wide-open spaces of a mansion in the hills and an observatory that showed moving pictures of the heavens.

2

3

WARNER BROS. Present
JAMES DEAN
IN
"REBEL without a CAUSE"
COLOUR BY WARNERCOLOR   ALSO STARRING SAL MINEO
with NATALIE WOOD   Cert X

5

6

7

8

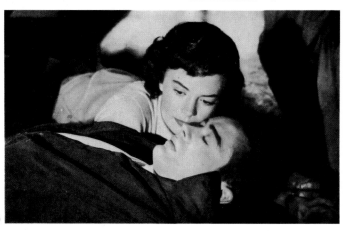

9

Jim, the adolescent son of middle-class parents recently moved to California, is run in for drunkeness by the police (1). He sobers up and has a sympathetic hearing from the juvenile-offenders officer (2).

The following day, Jim's first day at his new high school, he meets Judy and her gang of rowdy friends. In the course of a school visit to the local planetarium, Jim becomes friendly with Plato, an unbalanced, orphaned kid seeking affection. Outside the planetarium Jim is taunted into a fight with Buzz (3), the leader of the pack and Judy's boyfriend. They agree to meet later that evening for a 'chicken run' – an endurance test in which each will drive an old car to the cliff edge and leap clear at the last possible moment.

Seeking, but failing to get, advice from his father, Jim joins Buzz at the rendezvous (4). They line up (5), Judy signals the start of the race and the cars head for the cliff-edge. Buzz's sleeve catches in the doorhandle

causing him to go over the edge with the car. Jim consoles Judy and drives her home.

Jim feels he must go to the police but his parents object: a violent quarrel ensues (6). However, Jim goes to the police station and is seen by Buzz's gang-mates (7). They swear to get even with him.

Picking up Judy on the way, Jim drives to a large deserted house in the hills where they are joined by Plato (8). Jim and Judy declare their love (9). Buzz's gang follow them there and beat up Plato who nevertheless manages to shoot one of them. The police arrive and chase Plato to the planetarium.

Jim finally persuades the frightened Plato to give himself up but, at the crucial moment, shots are fired from the police cordon and Plato falls down. An anguished Jim zips up the jacket on his friend's body and escorts Judy from the scene.

Right: setting up the final scene in which Plato is lured from the planetarium to his death

The Noble Art of Akira Kurosawa

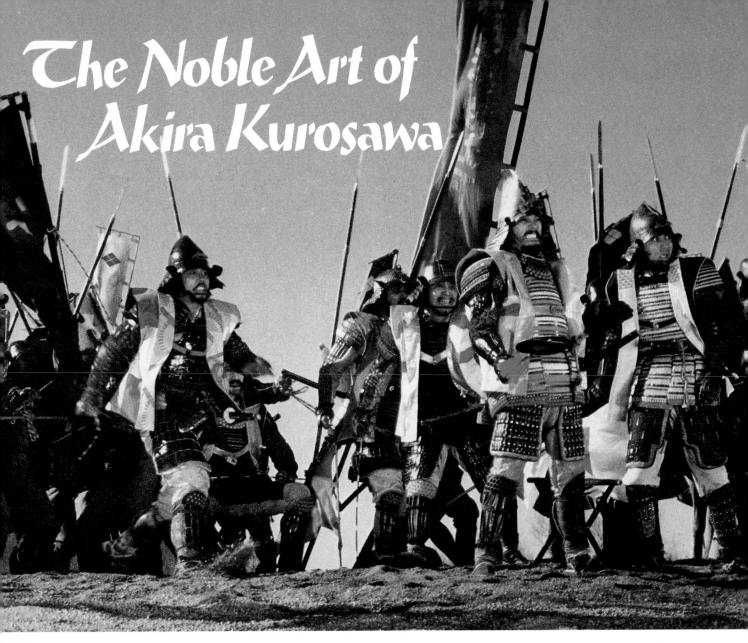

The films of Kurosawa first opened Western eyes to the imaginative power and beauty of Japanese cinema. Best known for his enthralling, epic studies of the samurai warrior, he has also investigated modern themes, displaying a deep compassion for the human condition

The impact of Akira Kurosawa's *Rashomon* (1950) on the 1951 Venice Film Festival was nothing short of shattering, and only the Japanese were surprised when it won the Golden Lion. Daiei, the company that produced the film, had been reluctant to submit it, certain that it would meet with incomprehension, even ridicule. But *Rashomon* triumphed and opened Western eyes to other great names of Japanese cinema such as Mizoguchi, Ozu, Gosho and Ichikawa; it seems incredible that an industry which had had its beginnings at the turn of the twentieth century should have remained until then virtually unknown in the West.

Japanese critics had never rated *Rashomon* highly, declaring that it lacked the social

Above: a poor thief (Tatsuya Nakadai), posing as his clan's chief, leads his men in battle in Kagemusha. *Left: Akira Kurosawa on location during the making of that film*

commitment of Kurosawa's earlier films and ignoring its basic theme of the subjective nature of truth. It deals with four separate accounts of a rape and murder. A samurai and his wife are travelling through a bandit's territory. A gust of wind blows the lady's veil aside revealing her beauty to the bandit who is inflamed at the sight. He rapes the lady and murders the samurai, a coward who abjectly begs to be spared. Or does he? The samurai's own version of the event, told through a medium in the courtroom where the case is investigated, claims that he killed himself according to the samurai code, unable to live with dishonour. The bandit's version insists that the lady was compliant; she, of course denies this. The complications mount, compounded by a fourth witness, a woodcutter, who tells his version to a priest as they shelter under the rain-lashed, ruined Rashomon Gate, a symbol of the demoralized, anarchic nature of Japan in the eighth century.

Above: Sugata Sanshiro *(1943, Judo Saga).*
Kurosawa's first feature. Above right: a violent
scene from the gangland drama Drunken
Angel. *Above, far right: poster for* Living.
Below right: a dishonoured woman (Machiko
Kyo) asks her husband (Masayuki Mori) to
kill her in Rashomon. *Below: Denjiro Okochi*
in They Who Tread on the Tiger's Tail

Many key aspects of Kurosawa's genius
emerge from *Rashomon*: his masterly control of
a complex narrative; his direction of his actors;
and the film's dazzling use of light and shade.
No one could forget the bandit's race through
the glinting forest, or the rape scene when the
camera makes a 360° revolution around the
tree tops to suggest an orgasm (a device that
was subsequently much imitated). It was
abundantly clear that henceforward Kurosawa must be numbered among the world's
truly great film-makers.

Kurosawa was born in Tokyo in 1910. He
initially wished to become a painter, but
decided that his talents did not lie in that area.
He became instead the assistant to the director
Kajiro Yamamoto (also collaborating on his
scripts) before becoming a director in his own
right. The acclaim won by *Rashomon* afforded
Western access to Kurosawa's earlier work, in
particular *Tora-no-o* (1945, *They Who Tread on
the Tiger's Tail*). Though much less successful

in the West than *Rashomon*, this film was a
fascinating, hour-long version of a Noh play. It
was not released until seven years after its
completion because the American occupying
authorities condidered it too feudalistic – a
doubtful judgement, as a character inserted by
Kurosawa and played by a famous comedian,
Kenichi Enomoto, makes mock of the traditional values ritualistically observed by the rest
of the cast.

Another key early work was *Yoidore Tenshi*
(1948, *Drunken Angel*), a great success in Japan
and Kurosawa's first film with Toshiro Mifune,
who was to become the director's favourite
actor. This tale of a tubercular ex-gangster
(Mifune) whose spiritual redemption is fought
for by a doctor working in the slums, clearly
prefigures Kurosawa's later studies of close
relationships between two men.

It is certain that the foreign success of
Rashomon gave Kurosawa greater artistic freedom; the immediate result of this was *Ikiru*
(1952, *Living*), which must rank among his
finest works. The main character is a late
middle-aged bureaucrat (superbly played by
Takashi Shimura) who learns that he is suffering from terminal cancer; this causes him to
take stock of his life, which he realizes has
been sterile and empty. He overhears a conversation which brings home to him that his
family cares only for his money; he also

discovers that in his professional life he has
been little more than a cog in the bureaucratic
wheel. When he happens upon a filed, ignored
request from slum-dwellers for a patch of
wasteland to be turned into a children's playground, he determines to bring this to fulfilment as a belated justification for his life. He
dies, a lone figure, on a swing in the playground he has helped to create. In his last
months he had forged a pleasurable relationship with a young girl from his office; this he
foregoes, sacrificing everything to what becomes an obsession. The film's message is that
one cannot afford to leave this life unfulfilled or
with bitter misgivings – a belief implicit in Zen
and Indian Buddhism.

The latter half of *Living* deals with the old
man's funeral rites. His office associates, his
son and daughter-in-law and the suppliants
for the playground gather together to appraise
his life. Only one speaks of him with any
genuine sympathy or understanding, while
credit for the playground goes to everyone
except its real instigator.

Two years later, Kurosawa made his
greatest world success, *Shichinin No Samurai*
(1954, *Seven Samurai*). He has always claimed
that John Ford was one of his inspirations and
Seven Samurai does have affinities with the
Western. Each of the samurai is impeccably
characterized, and Mifune as a jokey braggart,

a would-be samurai and a hanger-on to the sternly dedicated band of warriors, reveals an unsuspected gift for comedy. The underlying moral of the film is that only in unity lies strength. The peasants who employ the samurai to deliver them from oppression are saved but at the end of the titanic struggle, a samurai observes: 'They have won but we have lost', indicating that they, unlike the peasants, are rootless, migratory, lost in time, heading for extinction.

In 1957 Kurosawa filmed two adaptations from foreign sources: *Kumonosu-Jo* (*Throne of Blood*), based on Shakespeare's *Macbeth*, and *Donzoko* (*The Lower Depths*), from Gorky's play. In *Throne of Blood*, for the first and only time, the director allowed Mifune to be overshadowed: splendid though Mifune is, it is the subtle, deadly performance by Isuzu Yamada as his wife that haunts the imagination. As she glides through the sleeping castle directing their murderous activities with only the sinister swish-swish of her kimono on the soundtrack she becomes the very incarnation of evil.

For *The Lower Depths* Kurosawa employed a new multi-camera technique. He rehearsed his cast and crew for six weeks with full makeup.

Above: Yuzo Kayama and Toshiro Mifune in Red Beard. *Right: poster for* Throne of Blood, *starring Mifune and Isuzu Yamada. Below: Mifune as a samurai warrior in the action-packed adventure* The Hidden Fortress

costumes and lighting. The result was an unusually closely-knit acting ensemble which perfectly served this series of vignettes set in the latter days of the Tokugara period of Japanese history (1601–1868). Death loses its sting when life is hardly worth living and yet the strange little dance executed by the band of wretched characters at a final drinking party is buoyant until news of another suicide is brought. A character looks straight into the camera and remarks: 'What a pity! Just when the party was getting going.' And thus, curtly, unsentimentally (and true to the spirit of Gorky's play) the film ends. There are no star roles, but once more Mifune and Yamada are outstanding, the former as a thief, the latter as a fiendish virago of a landlady.

Having plumbed the depths of human depravity, treachery and greed in *Throne of Blood* and *The Lower Depths*, Kurosawa made three period films over the next five years which dealt with the less lethal, even the comic aspects of evil. The first was *Kakushi Toride No San Akunin* (1958, *The Hidden Fortress*), a kind of action-packed fairy-tale. The other two were *Yojimbo* (1961) and *Tsubaki Sanjuro* (1961, *Sanjuro*). All three starred Mifune, his formidable presence and athletic prowess still undiminished. Underlying the comic approach to the traditional violence however, was a thread of something akin to desperation; a suggestion that the human condition was so irretrievably base that the only thing to do was to poke fun at it.

Yojimbo ridiculed feudal values, while in *Sanjuro*, Mifune (as a samurai) makes a group of young apprentice samurai aware that real life cannot be encompassed by their rigid codes of honour and traditional obligations. There is also in these two films an element of what one might call today 'high camp', as exemplified in the scene from *Sanjuro* where messages are transmitted to fellow-fighters by an arrangement of lotus flowers drifting down a stream through enemy lines.

In *Akahige* (1965, *Red Beard*) Kurosawa plunged once again into deeper waters. The film traces the growth of a strong emotional relationship between Red Beard, a doctor (Mifune) and his young disciple (Yuzo Kayama). The doctor convinces the young man that only by dedicating himself wholly to the service of the needy can his life become meaningful. Yet the final implications have a bleak edge. In *Living* Kurosawa hinted that even a last-minute bid to redeem an egotistical life could bring spiritual salvation and a serene acceptance of death. *Red Beard* implies that although the old feudalistic concepts are patently valueless, no other, more humane doctrines have been evolved to take their place. Therefore people live in a state of flux, if not desperation. Although this beautiful film is once more set in late-Tokugawa Japan, it is evident that the film's forebodings have their reference to the social evils of today.

By the early Seventies Kurosawa's career had hit the doldrums. In 1970 he made his first colour film *Dodesukaden* (*Dodeskaden*) the title of which is onomatopoeic, evoking the sound of a train running along the tracks. It dealt with low life in a large city and is a stylized variant on *The Lower Depths*. A proposal that he would co-direct the American account of the Japanese attack on Pearl Harbor, *Tora! Tora! Tora!* (1970) aborted in disagreeable circumstances. In addition, the Japanese film industry was at a low ebb; finance for anything but routine subjects was well-nigh impossible to find. These factors may well have contributed to the depression that led him to attempt suicide. Happily Kurosawa rallied and found new inspiration in the USSR.

The Soviet-sponsored story he embarked on, *Dersu Uzala* (1975), is set in the nineteenth century and once more explores a relationship between two men, this time from vastly different cultural backgrounds, that changes both their lives. The eponymous hero is a hunter whose life is inextricably linked with his surroundings; he is at one with nature. Dersu is hired by Arseniev, the leader of an expedition to survey the wastes of Siberia. The guide reveals the ways of nature to the party; Arseniev thus discovers through Dersu the true meaning of life. When Dersu's eyesight begins to fail, diminishing his hunting prowess, Arseniev takes him back to live with his family in Moscow – an environment in which Dersu is pitifully out of place. Dersu decides to return to his beloved wilderness, but is killed on the outskirts of the city by a thief who covets the gun that Arseniev had given Dersu to help him survive in the wild.

True purity of spirit, the film attests, can only be attained in the world today by those who have remained outside the mainstream of modern life and who remain close to nature. Kurosawa worked mainly with Russian technicians on this project, the chief exception being a Japanese cameraman, Asakadzu Nakai, with a rare talent for capturing the beauty of the desolate landscapes.

When Kurosawa succeeded in setting up *Kagemusha* (1980, Shadow Warrior) ten years had elapsed since he had worked in his own country. The directors Francis Ford Coppola and George Lucas helped to persuade 20th Century-Fox to invest in the production. Set in the latter part of the sixteenth century, the film concerns a poor thief who is spared on account of his resemblance to a powerful warlord. When this leader is wounded in battle and dies, the thief is ordered to impersonate him to keep the warlord's clan together and keep its enemies at bay. He grows more and more accustomed to the role of clan leader, but is exposed when he is unable to ride the warlord's horse. Thrown out, he watches helplessly as his clan is overwhelmed by enemy forces.

Above: the ritual ceremony of the family is one of the beautiful, stylish sequences of Ran. *Below: a close relationship develops between Dorsu (Maksum Munzuk) and Arseniev (Yuri Solomin) as they cope with life in the wilderness in Dersu Uzala*

Kagemusha, budgeted at $6.5 million was the most expensive Japanese film ever made. At the Cannes Film Festival in 1980, where the film shared the Grand Prix with Bob Fosse's *All That Jazz* (1979), some critics found the battle scenes magnificent but protracted. This was not surprising as, in the rush to make the film available for the Festival, Kurosawa had left himself no time to trim these scenes as he had envisaged. For years he has favoured a multi-camera technique of shooting which, while ensuring the spontaneity that he feels may become lost in repeated takes, naturally calls for a longer period than usual in the cutting room.

In 1985, an original Kurosawa screenplay saw the light of day as a Russian-directed, American-set thriller – *Runaway Train*. But that same year also gave us *Ran*, a masterly reworking of *King Lear*, visually spectacular in its sweeping battle scenes but subtly deceptive in its closing 'pessimism' – and a compassionate regard for human weakness. Now in his seventies, Kurosawa is still making masterworks.

Filmography
1943 Sugata Sanshiro (+sc) (USA/GB: Judo Saga). **'44** Ichiban Utsukushiku (+sc) (USA: The Most Beautiful). **'45** Zoku Sugata Sanshiro (+sc) (USA/GB: Judo Saga, Part II); Tora-no-o/Tora no o o Fumu Otokotachi (+sc) (USA; The Men Who Tread on the Tiger's Tail; GB: They Who Tread on the Tiger's Tail). **'46** Asu O Tsukuru Hitobito (co-dir. only) (USA: Those Who Make Tomorrow); Waga Seishun Ni Kui Nashi (+co-sc) (USA/GB: No Regrets for Our Youth). **'47** Subarashiki Nichiyobi (+co-sc) (USA: One Wonderful Sunday; GB: Wonderful Sunday). **'48** Yoidore Tenshi (+co-sc) (USA/GB: Drunken Angel). **'49** Shizukanaru Ketto (+co-sc) (USA/GB: The Quiet Duel); Nora Inu (+co-sc) (USA: Stray Dog). **'50** Skyandaru (+co-sc) (USA: Scandal); Rashomon (+co-sc). **'51** Hakuchi (+co-sc) (USA/GB: The Idiot). **'52** Ikiru (+co-sc) (USA/GB: Living). **'54** Shichinin No Samurai (+co-sc) (USA/GB: Seven Samurai). **'55** Ikimono No Kiroku (+co-sc) (USA: I Live in Fear). **'57** Kumonosu-Jo (+co-sc) (USA/GB: Throne of Blood); Donzoko (+co-sc) (USA/GB: The Lower Depths). **'58** Kakushi Toride No San Akunin (+co-sc) (USA/GB: The Hidden Fortress). **'60** Warui Yatsu Hodo Yoku Nemuru (+co-sc) (USA: The Bad Sleep Well). **'61** Yojimbo (+co-sc); Tsubaki Sanjuro (+co-sc) (USA/GB: Sanjuro). **'63** Tengoku To Jigoku (+co-sc) (USA/GB: High and Low). **'65** Akahige (+co-sc) (USA/GB: Red Beard). **'70** Dodesukaden (+co-sc) (USA: Dodeskaden). **'75** Dersu Uzala (+sc) (USSR-JAP). **'80** Kagemusha (+co-c). **'85** Ran; A.K. (as self in doc.); Runaway Train (orig. sc).

Satyajit Ray-Visions of India

More than any other director, Satyajit Ray has articulated and interpreted the Indian way of life. His films explore the forces that govern and quicken the hearts and minds of his people and form a rich and varied contribution to world cinema

Satyajit Ray is universally regarded as India's foremost film-maker, in addition to being a notable artist, journalist, composer and novelist. His background and middle-class orientation are the two most important factors behind his talent for perceiving the reality around him and rendering it with simplicity. He comes from an extremely gifted family. His father (who died when Ray was three) was a writer and artist, while Ray's grandfather was a prominent author of children's books. Ray paid homage to his grandfather by basing two films, *Goopy Gyne Bagha Byne* (1968, *The Adventures of Goopy and Bagha*) and *Hirok Rajar Deshe* (1980, *The Kingdom of Diamonds*) on one of his novels. In addition, Ray's mother had a tremendous influence on his life; he tried to capture this relationship in *Aparajito* (1956, *The Unvanquished*) in his depiction of the adolescent Apu and his mother Sarbojaya.

After gaining a degree in science and economics at Calcutta University, Ray joined Shantiniketan, an educational institution founded by the Nobel Prize-winning author Rabindranath Tagore. The main emphasis in Shantiniketan (the name literally means 'house of peace') is to bring pupils close to nature and offer them freedom to create in tranquil surroundings. Ray's experience there helped to make him keenly aware of the value of form,

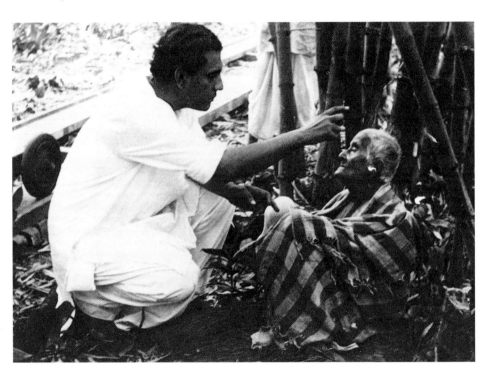

rhythm and movement.

Sometime before he left Shantiniketan in 1942, Ray had come across the film theories of Rudolf Arnheim and Paul Rotha. These writers made Ray aware of cinema as an art form, and he resolved to become a film-maker. In order to train himself (there were no film schools in India at that time), Ray invented his own way of writing screenplays. Whenever it was announced that a Bengali film based on a famous Bengali literary work had begun shooting, Ray would write his own treatment. When that film was released, he would compare his treatment with the finished work.

Top left: Aparna Das Gupta as Pagli, the wayward young bride of Samapti, *the final part of* Teen Kanya. *Top: Ray sets up a shot for* The Chess Players. *Above: Ray with the actress Chunibala Devi, who at the age of 80 agreed to take part in* Pather Panchali

In 1948, while Ray was working as a commercial artist for an advertising company, he and his friends formed the Calcutta Film Society. This gave him a chance to view many of the world's finest films and to meet various celebrities, in particular Jean Renoir. Renoir came to India in 1950 to make *The River* (1951)

and was to be an early influence on Ray's work.

Ray became increasingly determined to make a film himself and decided to adapt for the screen a novel by Bibhutibhushan Bandapaddhaya called *Pather Panchali* (which Ray had been asked to illustrate some years earlier). Ray did not want to lose the security of his job, so he became a part-time film-maker, devoting Sundays and holidays to shooting *Pather Panchali*. He pawned his wife's jewellery and sold his precious books and records in order to buy raw stock and hire a camera.

Ray would have been unable to afford to finish the film without the help of a friend of his mother-in-law, who persuaded the Bengali government to provide financial assistance. *Pather Panchali* (*Song of the Little Road*), completed in 1955, was shown at the Cannes Film Festival the following year and won worldwide acclaim. Its success resulted in Ray receiving many offers to make films abroad; yet, though he speaks excellent English, he has said that he feels incapable of making films in any language other than his own, Bengali.

An exception to his standard practice was *Shatranj Ke Khilari* (1977, *The Chess Players*), which he made in Hindi-Urdu. The film is based on a short story by the most prominent Hindi author, Munshi Premchand, and concerns two chess players who are so obsessed with their game that they are totally unaware of the important political developments taking shape around them. Ray interwove Premchand's story with details of the annexation of the state of Oudh by the British in 1856, a major factor behind the Indian Mutiny of the following year. Ray commented:

'Though the story and the history could be kept separate, since they were linked both thematically and temporally, the film ended up as one piece about the annexation. This was one of the most peaceful historical events – not a single shot was fired and Wajid Ali Shah, the last king of Awadh [Oudh], who was more interested in various art forms than battles, gave up his throne without any recourse to action.'

This film was a big challenge to Ray because

the language used in that period was a very ornate, highly Persianized Urdu, replete with difficult idioms. It was necessary to keep the flavour of the period without making the language incomprehensible to his audience. In addition, there had to be a difference between the language spoken in Wajid Ali Shah's court and the more everyday speech used by the chess-playing Nawabs (noblemen) and their acquaintances. At that time, too, the women used a different style of Urdu, which had certain peculiar idioms and forms of address; then there were the house servants and the village boy of the closing scenes who spoke the dialect used in the villages around Lucknow.

Shama Zaidi, who assisted Ray on his Urdu script, recalled:

'In his Bengali films, he makes almost no changes in the dialogues once he has written them but in this film he kept making minor changes – sometimes just before the shooting started. Even the English portions were rewritten in this manner.'

Ray employed the best professional actors available in *The Chess Players*. Probably because he was working in a new language and because it was an historical film, he preferred to work with actors and actresses with whose work he was already familiar. He has said that in Bengali he is able to work with inexperienced actors because he can instruct them about each gesture and intonation by demonstrating what he wants; not being as fluent in Hindu, he could only direct the actors of *The Chess Players* by suggestion.

Indian politics are glimpsed in Ray's films though he does not make direct political comments in his work. In *Jana Aranya* (1975, *The Middle-Man*), Somnath Bannerjee (Pradip Mukherjee) walks through the Calcutta streets, past walls painted with the slogans of the Naxilites (an extremist wing of the Indian Communist Party which had started a futile terrorist campaign in an attempt to abolish the

Above: Apu (Soumitra Chatterjee) teaches Aparna (Sharmila Tagore) to read in The World of Apu *(1959). Below: Soumitra Chatterjee and Madhabi Mukherjee in* Charulata

bourgeoisie and economic disparities). Ray's camera pans over these walls with Pradip in the foreground.

Pratidwandi (1970, *The Adversary*) was close to the political climate of India in the late Sixties. But here, Ray concentrates on the pursuit of security (the perennial problem of an Indian youth) undertaken by the hero, Siddhartha; the uncompromising political activism of Siddhartha's brother is kept in the background. In *Ashani Sanket* (1973, *Distant Thunder*) a man-made famine (brought about by the requisition of food for military requirements), leads to the death of five million people. Only the events leading up to the calamity are shown. The film's last, lingering shot of starving villagers makes no comments but raises questions about the human values and priorities of civilization. These themes are also explored in *Seemabadha* (1971, *Company Limited*), in which a young married couple struggles to adjust to the competitive business ethics of the Western capitalist system.

Ray spoke of his predominantly humanist concerns in an interview about *Hirok Rajar Deshe* (*The Kingdom of Diamonds*):

'I hope . . . *Hirok Rajar Deshe* makes my commitment to moral values clear to all. In this picture, I am telling a story which may be a continuation of the characters in *Goopy Gyne Bagha Byne*. There is a King Dictator and a crazy scientist who has invented a brain-washing machine – he has abolished education and only discipline and obedience are being fed into people's brains. The revolt is led by the school teacher with Goopy's and Bagha's help, so that the people are freed at last from the tyranny of the King Dictator and the mad scientist.'

'The moral values to which I am committed will be clear in this film. There are haves and have-nots, there is good and bad. My films and I are all for the have-nots and the good . . .'

Speaking of the issues raised in some of his other films, Ray said:

'*Devi* (1960, *The Goddess*) was against superstition and dogmatism. *Jalsaghar* (1958, *The Music Room*) tried to show the inevitability of the old being replaced by a new (not necessarily better) system. But my commitment is not to a particular political system because it may begin as good but become bad because of the personalities of its leaders. I am certainly not interested in power politics.'

The portrayal of women in Ray's work differs from film to film; sometimes they are one step ahead of men and sometimes they are subservient to them. In *The Goddess*, Dayamoyee (Sharmila Tagore), deified as the result of a vision seen by her father-in-law,

Above: a young wife (Shabana Azmi) tries to convince her husband (Sanjeev Kumar) that there is more to life than chess in The Chess Players. *Below: a scene from* The Adventures of Goopy and Bagha

eventually rebels against being an object of worship. In *Kanchenjunga* (1962) Ray's first film about contemporary society, the women assert themselves and their independence in a so-called man's world. In *Mahanagar* (1963, *The Big City*), Arati Majumdar (Madhabi Mukherji) not only fights against the conventions of making women home-bound but also becomes the financial supporter of her family.

Ray has strong feelings about children. He has not only made four films for children, but has also created much of his fiction and illustrative work for the young. He was a champion of The Year of the Child in 1979, and headed the jury of the Bombay International Film Festival for Children.

The references to children in Ray's 'adult' movies are at times indulgent. In *Samapti* (*The Conclusion*), the final episode of *Teen Kanya* (1961, *Two Daughters*), the tomboyish Pagli, constantly plays with her pet squirrel even when she is married and expected to behave in a responsible manner. Later, when she has acquired a measure of worldly wisdom, having separated from her husband, a young friend brings the dead squirrel to her. She tells him to cremate it; its death symbolizes the death of her childhood.

Ray uses the term 'artless simplicity' to describe his style. Though he has made a number of films in colour, he believes that colour can never be realistic as it has a tendency to make things look attractive whatever the context. Ray operates the camera himself and leaves the technical aspects of shooting to his cameraman – a post usually held by Subrata Mitra. Ray knows how much to take in a shot and where to cut while he is filming, although he is open to improvisations by the actors which might add extra depth to the finished film. The dialogue tends to be strictly functional, though in *Charulata* (1964, *The Lonely Wife*), which he considers his best

film, he resorted to dialogue in order to probe the psychology of his characters.

Despite his popularity in the West, Ray remains adamant in his determination to retain his national identity.

The world of Satyajit Ray's films is India in miniature, with all its paradoxes and baffling complexities.

Filmography
1955 Pather Panchali (+sc) (USA: Song of the Little Road). '**56** Aparajito (+sc) (USA/GB: The Unvanquished). '**57** Paras Pather (+sc) (USA/GB: The Philosopher's Stone). '**58** Jalsaghar (+sc) (USA/GB: The Music Room). '**59** Apur Sansar (+sc) (USA/GB: The World of Apu). '**60** Devi (+sc) (USA/GB: The Goddess). '**61** Rabindranath Tagore (+sc;+comm) (doc); Teen Kanya (+sc;+mus) (USA/GB: Two Daughters; one *ep* was cut from the original print). '**62** Kanchenjunga (+sc;+mus); Abhijan (+sc; +mus) (USA: Expedition). '**63** Mahanagar (+sc; +mus) (USA/GB: The Big City). '**64** Charulata (+sc;+mus) (USA: The Lonely Wife). '**65** Two (+sc;+mus) (short); Shakespeare Wallah (mus. only); Kapurush-o-Mahapurush (+sc; +mus) (USA: The Coward and the Saint; GB: The Coward and the Holy Man). '**66** Nayak (+sc;+mus) (USA/GB: The Hero). '**67** Chiriakhana (+sc;+mus). '**68** Goopy Gyne Bagha Byne (+sc;+mus) (USA/GB: The Adventures of Goopy and Bagha). '**69** Aranyer Din-Ratri (+sc;+mus) (USA/GB: Days and Nights in the Forest). '**70** Pratidwandi (+sc;+mus) (USA/GB: The Adversary). '**71** Seemabadha (+sc;+mus) (USA/GB: Company Limited); Sikkim (+sc;+mus) (doc). '**73** Ashani Sanket (+sc;+mus) (USA/GB: Distant Thunder); The Inner Eye (+sc) (short). '**75** Sonar Kella (+sc;+mus) (USA/GB: The Golden Fortress); Jana Aranya (+sc;+mus) (USA: The Masses' Music; GB: The Middle-Man). '**77** Shatranj Ke Khilari (+sc;+mus) (USA/GB: The Chess Players) (made in Urdu and English language versions); Bala (+sc;+mus) (short). '**79** Joi Babs Felunath (+sc;+mus) (USA/GB: The Elephant God). '**80** Hirok Rajar Deshe (+sc;+mus) (GB: The Kingdom of Diamonds). '**81** Sadgati (USA: Deliverance). '**82** Ghare Baire (USA/GB: Home and the World).

The Intimate Dramas of Ingmar Bergman

'What matters most in life is being able to contact another human being.' This remark by Ingmar Bergman explains his devotion to cinema, perhaps the most powerful means of communication. It also crystallizes the plight of his characters in their bitter struggles for understanding and love

Above: in this scene from Persona, *Alma (Bibi Andersson, left), nurse to a neurotic actress, Elizabet (Liv Ullmann) dreams that her charge has come to her room*

Since the mid-Forties, Ernst Ingmar Bergman has been making feature films at an average rate of one a year. If sheer output were the sole criterion, he would fully have earned his celebrity status alongside such prolific grand masters of celluloid as Hitchcock, Ford, Buñuel and Renoir.

Uniquely, however, Bergman's work reflects no apparent interest in commercial success, no urge to appeal to a wider audience. When Hollywood names have been thrust upon him as part of the production price – Elliott Gould in *Beröringen* (1971, *The Touch*) for example, or David Carradine and James Whitmore in *Das Schlangenei* (1977, *The Serpent's Egg*) – they have been absorbed almost without trace into Bergman's world. It is as though throughout his career he has been making one continuous film, personal and autobiographical, a diary of dreams, damnations and desires.

Such introspection is seldom accessible or entertaining to anyone but its author, but Bergman's genius has been to render from privacy a miraculously public text. His sense of

the dramatic, his command of his players, his mesmeric story-telling, all have been combined to display for us an anguish in which we can all share, an anguish resulting from the special complexities of survival in contemporary Western society. No other film-maker has so obsessively, so intelligently or so openly analysed what it has been like to live on this planet since World War II.

Bergman was born on 14 July, 1918 in the Swedish university city of Uppsala where, as he has since recalled, a number of influences came to bear upon him so vividly that they have recurred throughout his work. The bells of Uppsala Cathedral, the heavy furniture in his grandmother's flat which 'in my fantasy, conversed in a never-ending whisper', the nursery blind which, when lowered, somehow unleashed a horde of menacing shadows – these recollection continue to echo in Bergman's mind. Fifty years later, for example, they are combined to create the hallucinatory atmosphere of *Ansikte mot Ansikte* (1975, *Face to Face*), in which a woman (Liv Ullmann), visit-

ing her grandparents, sleeps fitfully among the shadows, cries and whispers of her nursery room. More crucially, *Face to Face* also restages a particular trauma from Bergman's childhood, the severe punishment administered on occasion by his father: the boy would be locked in a cupboard containing, it was asserted, a creature that would bite off his toes. Not surprisingly, the characters in Bergman's films have often been subjected to confinement, sudden outbursts of violence, and almost casual torture.

According to Bergman, his parents were 'sealed in iron casks of duty', his mother running a meticulous household for his father, a Lutheran pastor who was chaplain to the Royal Swedish court. The severity of this upbringing, leading to an inevitable conflict between love and rejection, between faith and doubt, richly and fortuitously provided for Bergman what were to be both the message and the method of his career. He remembered:

'If one is born and brought up in a vicarage one gets an early picture of behind-the-scenes of life and death. Father performed funerals, marriages, baptisms, gave advice and prepared sermons. The devil was an early acquaintance

behind it, that we are both victims and instigators, but in the era of the television newsreel it is not an easy truth to share.

'I have worked it out that if I see a film which has a running time of one hour, I sit through 27 minutes of complete darkness. When I show a film I am guilty of deceit. I am using an apparatus which is constructed to take advantage of a certain human weakness, an apparatus with which I can sway my audience in a highly emotional manner – to laugh, scream with fright, smile, believe in fairy stories, become indignant, be shocked, be charmed, be carried away or perhaps yawn with boredom. Thus I am either an imposter or, in the case where the audience is willing to be taken in, a conjurer.'

Bergman's harsh opinion of himself and his work, again a legacy from his Lutheran upbringing, finds illustration in the perpetual doubts and confusions of his chosen characters. Best conveyed by the haggard features of Max Von Sydow, the burden of guilt has also been carried in recent films by Erland Josephson; its opposite, the burden of cold, absolute certainty, has been borne most often in Bergman's work by Gunnar Björnstrand.

Above: the girls of the remand home in Hamnstad *(1948,* Port of Call*), a Bergman film that dealt with social as well as personal issues. Right: Harriet Andersson and Åke Grönburg as a pair of ill-matched lovers in* Sawdust and Tinsel

and in the child's mind there was the need to personify him. This was how the magic lantern came in. It consisted of a little metal box with a carbide lamp (I can still remember the smell of the hot metal) and coloured glass slides – Red Riding Hood and the Wolf and all the others. And the Wolf was the devil, without horns but with a tail and a gaping red mouth, strangely real but yet inapprehensible, a picture of wickedness and temptation on the flowered wall of the nursery.'

Presented with a toy projector when he was ten, Bergman's fascination with images grew:

'This little rickety cinematograph was my first conjuring set. It was strange. The toy was simply a mechanical one and there were always the same little men doing the same thing. I have often wondered what fascinated me so about it, and what still does in exactly the same way. It will suddenly come over me in the studio or in the dimness of the cutting room, as I look at the little frame in front of me, the film running through my fingers . . .'

The spell cast both by the cinematic gadget and by the experiences it could produce is integral to Bergman's work; repeatedly his characters have paused in their remorse to gaze at unexpected dramas, microcosms of their own plight, flickering before them. In *Fängelse* (1949, *Prison*), Birger Malmsten and Doris Svedlund find an old projector in the attic and watch a fragment of silent slapstick directed by Bergman in the style of Méliès and featuring, as Méliès' comedies so often did, a demonic visitation. In *Summarlek* (1951, *Summer Interlude*), another doomed couple watches, during their brief idyll, an animated film. In *Ansiktet* (1958, *The Face*), a tormented illusionist and a dying actor contemplate images thrown by a smoking magic lantern, even mingling with them at one point. And in *Persona* (1966), which briefly resurrects the

silent film from *Prison*, the whole artifice of film itself is analysed, from the flaring carbons providing illumination to the fragile sprocket-holes, until it finally falls apart in the despairing director's hands.

In later films, the small screen has logically become that of the television set, although other images confronting Bergman's spectators include enlarged photographs, in *En Passion* (1969, *A Passion*), slides, in *Herbstsonate* (1978, *Autumn Sonata*), and even, in *Vargtimmen* (1968, *Hour of the Wolf*), a tiny model theatre with magically living performers. But the charm has gone, and when his characters stare at the light-shows today it is not to lose themselves but horrifyingly to find something they would prefer to have avoided. In *The Serpent's Egg*, the whirring projector shows stages in the decline and collapse of victims of Nazi experiments with drugs – terrible and violent episodes that are studied with urbane pride by the scientist responsible. Bergman is once again repeating his point that we are all in front of the projector as well as

The key film in the confrontation between conjurer and analyst is *The Face*, in which Von Sydow plays a melancholy travelling showman who may or may not have genuine magical powers and is dissected by the merciless Björnstrand, scalpel in hand. The film came hard on the heels of the two masterpieces, *Det Sjunde Inseglet* (1957, *The Seventh Seal*) and *Smultronstället* (1957, *Wild Strawberries*), which had suddenly established Bergman's international reputation, and it was seen as an ironic comment on the many critics who sought to interpret Bergman's signs and meanings with excessive zeal.

Since *The Face* there have been a number of harrassed illusionists in Bergman's films: the painter in *Hour of the Wolf*, the violinist in *Skammen* (1968, *Shame*), the forger in *A Passion* – all played by Von Sydow. All have been savaged by their environment, their ultimate fate uncertain; in the case of *A Passion*, the central figure is actually pulled apart by the celluloid itself, processed so that his shape is no more than a mass of colour dots on the screen.

Bottom: Bergman chats with Bibi Andersson and Victor Sjöström, the stars of Wild Strawberries. Bottom left: the first appearance of Death (Bengt Ekerot) in The Seventh Seal. Below left: Gunnar Björnstrand and Harriet Andersson in Through a Glass, Darkly. Left: Kvinnodröm (1955, Journey Into Autumn), featuring Eva Dahlbeck as a fashion photographer and Harriet Andersson as a model. Above: Dahlbeck and Björnstrand in A Lesson in Love, a rare Bergman comedy

It is an ending which reaffirms Bergman's apology; he is using deceit to portray deception, yet the inexplicable magic remains.

The question of the artist's place in society is one of Bergman's most familiar themes. It can be traced from the broken-hearted ballet-dancer in *Summer Interlude* to the unemployed tightrope-walker in *The Serpent's Egg*, with some particularly emphatic outbursts represented by *För att inte Tala om Alla Dessa Kvinnor* (1964, *Now About These Women*) and *Riten* (1969, *The Rite*). In such films as *Persona* (dealing with a mute stage actress), and *The Shame* (musicians) and *Autumn Sonata* (concert pianist), the art-in-society debate can, however, be seen as part of a more general discussion about the predicament of the average human being in a collapsing environment. Again *The Face* provides a reference point, in the despairing words of the actor:

'I have prayed one prayer in my life: use me. Make use of me. But the Lord never understood how strong and devoted a servant I would have been, so I went unused . . .'

The sense of helplessness refers back to the film by which Bergman is perhaps best known, *The Seventh Seal*, and forward to perhaps his most disregarded film, *Nattvardsgästerna* (1962, *Winter Light*), and again it is linked with his childhood. The search for God – or some acceptable equivalent – haunted the Bergman career up to the point at which, with the trilogy of *Såsom i en Spegel* (1961, *Through a Glass, Darkly*), *Winter Light* and *Tystnaden* (1963, *The Silence*), he appeared to exorcise it. If God insisted on remaining silent, to pursue Him was at worst to risk insanity (Harriet Andersson in *Through a Glass, Darkly* claims to see God as a giant spider) and at best futile (the priest in *Winter Light* is unable to deflect one of his parishoners from suicide). Although hints of both can be found in the later films, particularly in *Viskningar och Rop* (1972, *Cries and Whispers*), with its central character on the brink of death, and in the despondent priest in *The Serpent's Egg*, from *The Silence* onwards Bergman begins to favour a different kind of comfort.

Left: inner suffering in a tranquil setting is conveyed by this close-up of Ingrid Thulin in The Silence. *Above left: Björnstrand and Max Von Sydow in* The Face. *Above: the demonic inhabitants of the castle as they appear to the artist in* Hour of the Wolf

At the time he escaped from the parental tyranny in 1937, to study literature and art at the University of Stockholm, the only panacea he could find for the pain of agnosticism was the theatre. His first public success was with a stage production of *Macbeth* in 1940, and for two years he was assistant director at the Royal Dramatic Theatre, writing and producing plays. Although Svensk Filmindustri tempted him into screen play-writing in 1942, and then into film direction. Bergman's theatrical work has continued ever since, in startling parallel to his cinema career. His earliest films demonstrated more of a theatrical energy than a cinematic awarness, but by 1947 this had begun to take shape. *Musik i Mörker* (1947, *Night Is My Future*), although written by somebody else, clearly anticipates Bergman's later work not only in its cast (which includes Birger Malmsten, Naima Wifstrand and Gunnar Björnstrand) but also in such assertions as 'Pain and suffering are part of God's design'. With his first original piece for the

screen, *Prison*, his agnostic irony was at its most poisonous: 'Life is only a cruel, meaningless journey from birth to death', stated the film, illustrating its theme with the wrist-slashed suicide of a defeated girl. The Devil rules the world, churches are his allies and God is his own invention.

Fortunately the darkness begins to lift almost immediately, and by the time of *Summer Interlude*, a fine, delicate, complex elegy of a film, Bergman's affection for over-statement has been tempered with subtlety. For the ballet-dancer, the stage is the only compensation for the lover she has lost after one perfect (and very Swedish) summer, but in the course of the film she shows signs of being resurrected from beneath the mask of greasepaint. Himself divorced in 1950, Bergman seemed able to study the processes of love and marriage with a more varied perspective from this point onwards – affectionately in *Sommaren Med Monika* (1953, *Summer With Monika*), sensitively in *Gycklarnas Afton* (1953,

Sawdust and Tinsel), humorously in *En Lektion i Kärlek* (1954, *A Lesson in Love*) and with elegant and memorable irony in *Sommarnattens Leende* (1955, *Smiles of a Summer Night*), which marks the end of the cycle.

The Seventh Seal and *Wild Strawberries* were two journeys through the wasteland that led Bergman's restlessness to a temporary haven. In both films, the only certainty is death, in both the only compensation is the family unit, in both the only unknown is God's ultimate purpose, if any. In *The Seventh Seal*, the knight, trying to discover something of value in the plague-swept country he is about to leave, realizes that the clown's family, eating wild strawberries in the afternoon sun, has found the only available peace of mind. In *Wild Strawberries*, the aged professor, pursuing a solution to his 'death-in-life' problem on a pilgrimage through the territory he knew as a young man, discovers in the evocation of the family birthday party and in the memory of his parents beside a lake in summer the love that slipped so long ago out of his own marriage and left it empty. Marriage alone is hell; marriage as a trinity (with definite holy connections) is salvation.

Bergman was unable to see it quite so simply in his later films in which, more realistically and more courageously, he was prepared to tackle more elusive matters. The signpost was *The Silence*, with its despairing illumination of the obstacles confronting *any* kind of communication between generations, between sexes or between nations. The political events of the Sixties and Seventies increasingly touched upon in his work even it was centred on his island home of Fårö, have seemed to support his argument – culminating in his own flight from the Swedish tax authorities into a cathartic exile. But in *Cries and Whispers, Scener ur ett Äktenskap* (1973, *Scenes From a*

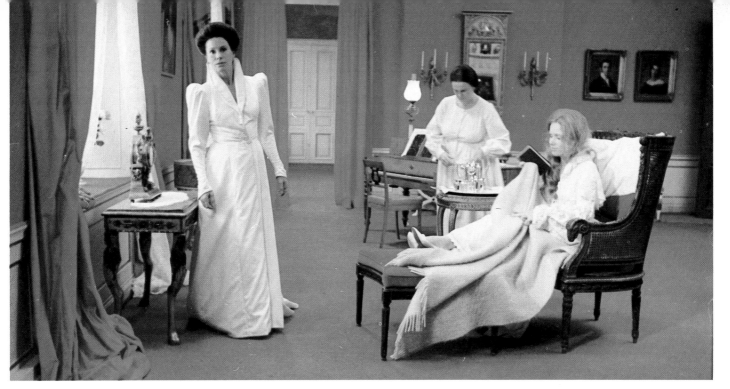

Marriage), Face to Face and (if perhaps less convincingly) *Autumn Sonata*, he has found the same small crust of comfort. The priest expresses it in *The Serpent's Egg*:

'We live far away from God, so far away that no doubt He doesn't hear us when we pray to Him for help. So we must help each other. We must give each other the forgiveness that a remote God denies us.'

Bergman has not, of course, prepared us for too sympathetic a hearing to the words of his clergymen, but it is intriguing that this viewpoint is consistent with Bergman's own enthusiasm for his work – an enthusiasm which serves also to explain it:

'There is something about the work itself that you get very dependent upon. You are part of a group. If you are a relatively inhibited, shy and timid person like me who has difficulty establishing deeper relations, it's wonderful to live in the collective world of film-making. I think it's an outgrowth of an enormous need for contact. I have a need to influence other people, to touch other people both physically and mentally, to communicate with them.'

Below left: Elliott Gould and Bibi Andersson in The Touch, *an English-language film. Above: though* Cries and Whispers *was set in the late 19th century, Bergman avoided period 'prettiness', using colour symbolically to suggest the characters' troubled states of mind. Right: Liv Ullmann in a nightmare sequence from* Face to Face, *in which she is terrified by the apparition of her dead grandmother*

Wonder and teamwork combined in his award-laden *Fanny and Alexander* (1981), a visually sumptuous period family saga with supernatural overtones and a huge cast. It is the apotheosis of Bergman's career – a magical, optimistic reply to those critics who have accused him of being doom-laden.

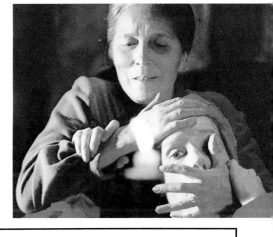

Filmography
1944 Hets (sc;+ass. dir. only) (USA: Torment; GB: Frenzy). **'46** Kris (+sc) (USA/GB: Crisis); Det Regnar på Vår Kärlek (+co-sc) (USA: It Rains on Our Love; GB: The Man With an Umbrella). **'47** Kvinna Utan Ansikte (sc. only) (USA/GB: The Woman Without a Face); Skepp till Indialand (+sc) (USA: The Land of Desire/A Ship to India; GB: Frustration); Musik i Mörker (USA/GB: Night Is My Future). **'48** Hamnstad (+sc) (USA/GB: Port of Call); Eva (co-sc. only). **'49** Fängelse (+sc) (USA: Prison/The Devil's Wanton); Törst (USA: Three Strange Loves; GB: Thirst). **'50** Till Glädje (+sc) (USA/GB: To Joy); Sånt Händer inte Här (USA: This Can't Happen Here; GB: High Tension). **'51** Sommarlek (+co-sc) (USA: Illicit Interlude; GB: Summer Interlude); Frånskild (co-sc. only) (USA/GB: Divorced). **'52** Kvinnors Väntan (+sc) (USA: Secrets of Woman; GB: Waiting Women). **'53** Sommaren Med Monika (+co-sc) (USA: Monika; GB: Summer With Monika); Gycklarnas Afton (+sc) (USA: The Naked Night: GB: Sawdust and Tinsel). **'54** En Lektion i Kärlek (+sc) (USA/GB: A Lesson in Love). **'55** Kvinnodröm (+sc) (USA: Dreams; GB: Journey Into Autumn); Sommarnattens Leende (+sc) (USA/GB: Smiles of a Summer Night). **'56** Sista Paret Ut (co-sc. only) (USA: The Last Couple; GB: Last Pair Out). **'57** Det Sjunde Inseglet (+sc) (USA/GB: The Seventh Seal); Smultronstället (+sc) (USA/GB: Wild Strawberries). **'58** Nära Livet (+co-sc) (USA: Brink of Life; GB: So Close to Life); Ansiktet (+sc) (USA: The Magician; GB: The Face. **'60** Jungfrukällan (+sc) (USA/GB: The Virgin Spring); Djävulens Öga (+sc) (USA/GB: The Devil's Eye). **'61** Såsom i en Spegel (+sc) (USA/GB: Through a Glass, Darkly); Lustgården (co-sc. only under pseudonym) (USA: The Pleasure Garden). **'62** Nattvardsgästerna (+sc) (USA/GB: Winter Light). **'63** Tystnaden (+sc) (USA/GB: The Silence). **'64** För att inte Tala om Alla Dessa Kvinnor (+co-sc. under pseudonym) (USA: All These Women; GB: Now About These Women). **'66** Persona (+sc). **'67** Stimulantia ep Daniel (+sc; +photo). **'68** Vargtimmen (+sc) (USA/GB: Hour of the Wolf); Skammen (+sc) (USA: The Shame; GB: Shame). **'69** Riten/Ritorna (+sc) (USA: The Ritual; GB: The Rite)(shot as TV film but shown in cinemas); En Passion (+sc) (USA: The Passion of Anna; GB: A Passion) (GB retitling for TV: LI82 – A Passion). **'70** Fårödokument (+sc) (doc) (USA/GB: The Farö Document). **'71** Beröringen (+sc) (USA-SWED) (USA/GB: The Touch). **'72** Viskningar och Rop (+sc) (USA/GB: Cries and Whispers). **'73** Scener ur ett Äktenskap (+sc) (USA/GB: Scenes From a Marriage)*; Trollflötjen (+sc) (USA/GB: The Magic Flute). **'75** Ansikte mot Ansikte (+sc;+co-prod) (USA/GB: Face to Face)*. **'77** Das Schlangenei (+sc) (GER-USA) (USA/GB: The Serpent's Egg); Paradistorg (prod. only) (USA/GB: Summer Paradise). **'78** Herbstsonate (+sc, uncredited) (GER) (USA/GB: Autumn Sonata). **'80** From the Life of the Marionettes (GER). **'81** Fanny och Alexander*. **'86** Notes on Fanny and Alexander (doc.).

Sweat, lust and dreams

The Italian popular cinema of the Fifties ranged from the lust of *Bitter Rice* by way of the blood-soaked fantasies of pirate films to the belly-laughs of Totò's comedy series

The years 1951–60 were the most exciting ever for Italian film-makers; they were the years of a remarkable and sustained dominance of European film culture by a group of writers and directors whose work astonished the world. Rossellini, Visconti, Fellini, De Sica, Antonioni and the unjustly neglected Pietro Germi destroyed the complacent image of the Italian cinema which had flourished under Mussolini. Their mastery of the medium was immediate, their talent acknowledged both at home and abroad, and their output prolific.

The neo-realist films of Rossellini and others had made immediate impact on critics and film-makers everywhere, and their influence on all Italian directors of the Fifties, excepting the historical genres, was considerable – especially in the matters of choice of subject and locations. The major effect of neo-realism on Italian cinema had been to broaden the scope of the industry, and to admit to its preoccupations the activities of the lower strata of Italian society. These were the influences which shaped the professional activities of many directors and writers thereafter.

The outstanding visual feature of neo-realism was the rawness of the image. The plots were simple or melodramatic, the dialogue functional or contrived, only some of the actors non-professionals. All the directors and writers whose work was initially neo-realist in style became full and confident users of the professional studios and equipment as they became available. The look of early neo-realism therefore was largely determined by economic constraints. The interest in the social and personal problems of real people – partly a reaction against the glossy fantasies of the Italian fascist cinema – was certainly sincere; but no Italian director in 1945 could afford to make *Quo Vadis* anyway.

By 1952, films such as Renato Castellani's *Sotto il Sole di Roma* (1948, *Under the Roman Sun*) and *Due Solde di Speranza* (1952, *Two Pennyworth of Hope*), Luciano Emmer's *Domenica d'Agosto* (1950, *Sunday in August*) and also Pietro Germi's work had led to the coining of a new phrase to describe a branching-out from neo-realism to *neorealismo rosa*, or realism through rose-tinted spectacles.

The films of Pietro Germi, whatever their ostensible backgrounds, were invariably preoccupied with questions of personal honour and commitment to codes of behaviour. Although he had never been to Sicily before making *In Nome della Legge* (1949, *In the Name of the Law*), he frequently returned to the island, with its brooding ambience of fearful independence, its tribal suspicions and its perverse moralities. Marcello Mastroianni's restlessly comic wife-murderer in *Divorzio all' Italiana* (1961, *Divorce – Italian Style*) is a prisoner of the same society as Sarò Urzi's honest carabiniere of *In the Name of the Law* and the tragic heroine of *Sedotta e Abandonata* (1964, *Seduced and Abandoned*), a Sicilian girl (Stefania Sandrelli) whose life is ruined because of the rigid code of honour which prevails in the mafioso-riddled island.

The protagonists of *Il Ferroviere* (1956, *Man of Iron*) and *L'Uomo di Paglia* (1958, *Man of Straw*) are faced with problems of choice, of betrayal of family or social obligations. In each case the strong paterfamilias is ultimately destroyed by the pressure of doubt or renunciation of previously accepted codes of behaviour. Even in the frothy costume comedy of *La Presidentessa* (1953, *The Lady President*), the plot involves the age-old double standard of wife and mistress and 'never the twain shall meet'. In *Un Maledetto Imbroglio* (1959, *A Sordid Affair*), the police investigator's constantly renewed touchstone of reality amid the deceit and violence of his daily routine is the camaraderie and mutual trust of his colleagues.

Artists like Germi, Rossellini, Visconti and the later neo-realists did not work in isolation but the masterpieces of great directors are rarely the first choice of the cinema-going public. Most of these film-makers were recognized by Italians as their finest directors and writers, but the comedies and melodramas of Mario Monicelli, Dino Risi and Raffaello Matarazzo were usually better attended.

The largest studios, at Cinecittà, had resumed production in 1947, with a programme of five films. In the ten years from 1950, total Italian film production rose to an average of 140 films per year. Box-office admissions reached 819 million in 1955, compared with 662 million in 1950 and 745 million

Below left: Pietro Germi, as the adulterous Man of Straw, *breaks with his girl (Franca Bettoja), who then commits suicide, forcing him to confess to his wife. Below: Gina Lollobrigida in King Vidor's lavish epic,* Solomon and Sheba *(1959). Bottom: Anna Maria Pierangeli (also known as Pier Angeli) is menaced by Robert Alda, Alan's dad, in Steno's* I Moschettieri del Mare *(1962, The Musketeers of the Sea)*

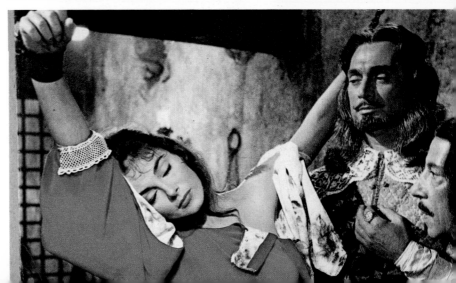

Top left: a French poster for the third of the Don Camillo series, Don Camillo e l'Onorevole Peppone *(1955), distributed in Britain as* Don Camillo's Last Round. *Top right: in* La Nave delle Donne Maledette *(1953, Women's Prison Ship), Mai Britt loves and suffers as an innocent convict whose cousin (Kerima) plots against her. Above: Gina Lollobrigida and Vittorio De Sica became an immensely popular team in the 'Bread, Love and . . .' films. Right: Totò plays the tutor in safe-cracking to an incompetent gang led by Vittorio Gassman in* Persons Unknown, *a prize-winner at the Locarno Film Festival in 1959*

in 1960 (falling to 319 million in 1978).

Much of the production activity reflected the peculiar and perennial preoccupation with the *peplum* and historical adventure film. The direct Hollywood involvement, from *Quo Vadis* (1951), directed by Mervyn LeRoy, through to *Ulisse* (1954, *Ulysses*), *Attila Flagello di Dio* (1965, *Attila the Hun*) and Robert Wise's *Helen of Troy* (1955), complemented and encouraged local initiatives.

Although more public and critical attention has been paid to the historical-mythological *peplum* films, the cape-and-sword melodramas were not entirely devoid of interest. They lacked the budgets and the lightness of touch of their Hollywood cousins, but often their disturbing mixture of juvenile plot development and blatant sadism was exemplary of a recurrent theme in Italian popular culture. Two films directed by Mario Soldati and starring Mai Britt, a would-be Garbo who never reached the heights, are clear examples: *Jolanda, la Figlia del Corsaro Nero* (1952, Yolanda, Daughter of the Black Pirate) and its simultaneously shot sequel, *I Tre Corsari* (1953, *The Three Pirates*). Bloody revenge, flogging, transvestism and torture embellish the threadbare plots of these swashbuckling

Sex and violence, preferably combined, were a sure-fire formula for commercial success

melodramas. The later so-called 'spaghetti' Westerns and increasingly perverse comic books, or *fumetti*, of the late Sixties and the Seventies amply illustrate developments of these themes.

Film series, in Italy as elsewhere, usually degenerated in quality as each succeeding film reworked the material of the original. Occasionally, a subsequent film in a series could equal the first. Both Julien Duvivier's *Il Piccolo Mondo di Don Camillo* (1952, *The Little World of Don Camillo*) and his *Il Ritorno di Don Camillo* (1953, *The Return of Don Camillo*) were exceedingly funny and faithful to Giovanni Guareschi's tales of unholy discord between the wily priest (Fernandel) and the communist mayor, Peppone (Gino Cervi), of a small village in the Po Valley. Later Don Camillo films, however, increasingly caricatured the pair, becoming unfunnier in the process, and failed to repeat the international success of the originals.

The 'Bread, Love and . . .' films, which also had wide distribution abroad, began with two directed by Luigi Comencini, *Pane, Amore e Fantasia* (1954, *Bread, Love and Dreams*) and *Pane, Amore e Gelosia* (1954, *Bread, Love and Jealousy*), both featuring Vittorio De Sica and Gina Lollobrigida at their most appealing. But it was the third in the series, Dino Risi's *Pane, Amore e . . .* (1955, *Scandal in Sorrento*) which achieved the greatest critical and public success.

The Totò films were the most enduring series: low-budget comedies which were rarely exported but were churned out by the dozen from 1948 to 1964. Totò (Antonio de Curtis Gagliardi Ducas Comnuno di Bisanzio) was a phenomenon. Between 1951 and 1960 he appeared in 48 films, most of which carried his name in the title and were opportunistically linked to some current film success or public event. In spirit they were a throwback to the Mack Sennett/Ben Turpin satires of the Twenties. The titles told all, and the quality of the material was rarely equal to the star's considerable talents: *Totò le Moko, Totò Sceicco* (Totò the Sheik) and *Totò Tarzan* (all 1950); *Totò Terzo Uomo* (1951, Totò the Third Man); *Totò al'Inferno* (1955, Totò in Hell); *Totò nella*

Luna (1958, Totò on the Moon) and so on. Totò was beloved by the crowds in the same way the British adore their comedians, with great tolerance of weak material. An admixture of Max Linder, Keaton and Chaplin, he combined lower class gentility with sly anti-authoritarianism, presented with an economical inventiveness of gesture and ingenious facial manipulation.

His Pulcinello face and slightly demonic dapperness were seen to brilliant effect in Mario Monicelli's superb caper-movie satire, *I Soliti Ignoti* (1958, *Persons Unknown*). He played an elder statesman of safe-cracking, tutoring a gang of resolutely incompetent thieves in the finer arts of larceny. While Totò's contribution was masterly, the whole film was a triumph of ensemble playing. Vittorio Gassman and Marcello Mastroianni were particularly effective.

Gassman never equalled the lightness of touch and comic sureness that he showed in the Monicelli and Risi films. Prior to *Persons Unknown* he had been known as a rather heavy dramatic actor, particulary in his Hollywood films of the early Fifties. After his success as the decidedly unintelligent would-be mastermind in that film, he largely concentrated on comedy. The results were variable, and he tended to ham. Nevertheless, he became a great favourite with the public, and in later years he expanded his range with considerable success.

Marcello Mastroianni took longer to gain the high regard his performances deserved. Constantly in demand, he served a steady apprenticeship, from his debut in Riccardo Freda's *I Miserabili* (1948, Les Misérables) and by 1960 had appeared in some fifty films. He had always seemed deliberately to avoid an easy choice of roles, and although his greatest successes came in the Sixties he had already made *Cronache di Poveri Amanti* (1954, Chronicles of Poor Lovers) for Lizzani and Visconti's *Le Notti Bianche* (1957, *White Nights*) when *Persons Unknown* and Monicelli's *La Grande Guerra* (1959, *The Great War*) confirmed him as one of the country's outstanding comic actors. He varied his performances and subjects as much as possible, and at the end of the Fifties was heading for the international stardom which came with *La Dolce Vita* (1959, The Sweet Life), Bolognini's *Il Bell'Antonio* (1960, Handsome Antonio), Antonioni's *La Notte* (1961, *The Night*) and *Divorce – Italian Style*.

Italian stars shone most nights in as many film appearances as health and strength would permit

Italians were very loyal to their stars, who rewarded them by appearing in as many films each year as their doctors would allow. Ugo Tognazzi, whose comic appeal remained resolutely local during 30 years of effort, starred in 12 films in 1959 alone, while the incredible Vittorio De Sica – in between directing six features of his own – appeared in 65 films between 1951 and 1960.

Alberto Sordi is a magnificent screen actor, and of late has turned to directing with some success. His recent work has renewed the respect of those who must have become wearied by the succession of Sixties and Seventies comedies and light dramas which atrophied the image of the star of Fellini's *Lo Sceicco Bianco* (1952, The White Sheik) and *I Vitelloni* (1953, The Spivs) and of Rosi's *I Magliari* (1959, The Swindlers). These three films alone, with their subtle change-ringing of the same basic character gave some indication of the flexibility and depth of his screen persona. The dangerous gangster of *I*

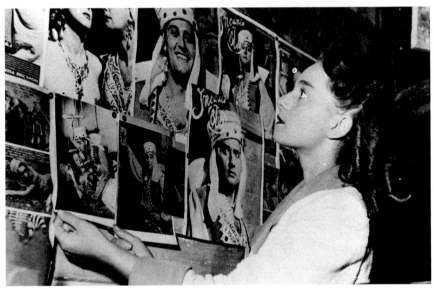

Top: Marcello Mastroianni has established himself since the Fifties as the versatile and ever-reliable star of many films, including La Notte, *the second of Antonioni's 'trilogy'. Above: Brunella Bovo, as a star-struck girl, feasts her eyes on images of her hero,* The White Sheik, *played by Alberto Sordi. Left: knee-deep in the Vercelli marshes of northern Italy, Silvana Mangano became a star in* Bitter Rice, *which managed to be both neo-realist and yet very popular at home and abroad*

Above: Francesco Rosi's Salvatore Giuliano *reconstructs the life and death of the notorious Sicilian bandit, mysteriously killed in 1950. Right: an unusual publicity shot of Sophia Loren in* Due Notti con Cleopatra *(1953, Two Nights With Cleopatra), in which she plays a dual role, as Cleopatra and her look-alike maid who rescues her lover from execution after he has spent one night each with the false and the real Cleopatra. Below:* Amore in Città *(1953, Love in the City) was the first and only edition of a magazine film,* Lo Spettatore *(The Spectator). Carlo Lizzani's episode,* L'Amore Che Si Paga, *(Bought Love), examined prostitution in Rome*

Magliari is recognisably brother under the skin to the vainglorious photo-comic hero of *The White Sheik*.

Few Italian actresses of this period were esteemed by overseas critics, although the world's press took keen interest in the physical attributes of many Italian leading ladies. Giulietta Masina and Anna Magnani were respected and admired for the consistent intensity and brilliance of their performances; but Silvana Mangano's effective work in De Santis' *Riso Amaro* (1948, *Bitter Rice*) was overshadowed by the publicity attendant on her physical presence: the famous thighs-in-the-paddy-fields shot boosted the film's earnings but adversely affected her career as a dramatic actress for many years.

Gina Lollobrigida and Sophia Loren were both international cleavage celebrities well in advance of their acceptance as fine actresses. Each of them survived this early publicity and subsequent Hollywood careers in banal material to earn overdue recognition of their genuine talent.

Film production companies in Italy rarely specialized in particular genres, and individual producers were far more adventurous than their British and American counterparts. Carlo Ponti and Dino De Laurentiis formed Ponti-De Laurentiis Productions in 1950, and in the seven years they were together they worked on projects as diverse as Totò films, Rossellini's *Europa '51* (1951), *Jolanda, La Figlia del Corsaro Nero, Le Notti di Cabiria* (1957, *Nights of Cabiria*), Germi's *Man of Iron* and epic Hollywood co-productions such as King Vidor's *War and Peace* (1956).

Carlo Ponti's earlier involvements had included neo-realist films by Germi, Alberto Lattuada and Luigi Zampa; and after the break-up of Ponti-De Laurentiis he continued with great success to produce a wide variety of films, often starring his wife, Sophia Loren. De Laurentiis was the more ambitious of the duo. After a number of un-remarkable low-budget features, he had achieved great success with *Bitter Rice*, and worked steadily to increase his international affiliations. Today the De Laurentiis organization is the largest in Europe.

Old and new producers responded to the excitement of the booming Fifties. Angelo Rizzoli started in films in 1934, but had been inactive for many years when, in 1950, he produced Rossellini's *Francesco, Giullare di Dio* (*Flowers of St. Francis*). For the rest of the decade he was very active indeed, often setting up French co-productions, including René Clair's *Les Belles de Nuit* (1952, *Beauties of the Night*) and *Les Grandes Manoeuvres* (1955, *The Grand Maneuver*) as well as the first two Don Camillo films. He entered the Sixties on a high note with Fellini's *La Dolce Vita*.

Franco Cristaldi was only 30 when he produced his first three films in 1954. His early films were routine romantic dramas but did reasonably well at the box-office. Following greater success with Steno's *Mio Figlio Nerone* (1956, *Nero's Weekend*), starring Alberto Sordi and Vittorio De Sica, he showed himself willing to take chances by producing Visconti's *White Nights*. He backed Francesco Rosi's first two features as director, *La Sfida* (1958, *Defiance*) and *I Magliari*, and was later to finance the same director's politically sensitive examination of the myth of the Sicilian bandit, *Salvatore Giuliano* (1961). He also produced the two best Italian comedies in *Persons Unknown* and *Divorce – Italian Style*.

The Fifties were years of enthusiasm and manic energy; geniuses and hacks rubbed shoulders in a crowded, jostling film factory. An industry which had been virtually wiped out in 1944 was back and booming.

Tall, dark and terribly handsome

Cary Grant

With his good looks, casual air, wit and extraordinary accent, Cary Grant appeared to be the epitome of an English gentleman. However, there was mystery and amusement behind his smile and he was equally capable of being a playboy, a male chauvinist or a calculating villain

There have been enough nice guys in movies for it to be clear that Cary Grant is more than handsome, gracious and pleasing. Yet it is easy now that he's gone (he died in 1986) to accept the notion of Grant as the epitome of classy likeability. Everyone still feels affection for him. He was never vain or crass; his life seemed tidy and rational. There were four divorces, but no woman walked away raging at his impossibility. Instead, they seemed a little wistful that a dream had not quite worked out, and insistent about his decency.

Even at eighty, he remained trim, dashing

Top left: Blonde Venus *gave Grant his opening, opposite Marlene Dietrich, as a romantic lead. Above: a debonair portrait taken by John Miehle in 1945. Left: playing the clown as a man who falls for his fiancée's sister (Katherine Hepburn) in* Holiday

and attractive. He doted on his daughter, the Los Angeles Dodgers and his business interests with Fabergé. He was modest and retiring, laughing a lot and believing in excellence. In 1979, when Marlon Brando was unable to present a special Oscar to Laurence Olivier, Grant had no qualms about being second choice, and glowed with the honour and pleasure of the occasion. That was grace, for the Academy had never given him a Best Actor Oscar, although he was awarded a special Oscar in 1970 for 'sheer brilliance'.

Grant may well remain the best actor the

screen has ever had, but that could not be said if he was merely a romantic lead beyond compare. He certainly had those attributes – no-one else in the movies looked so good and so intelligent at the same time. He came over from the screen as nothing short of beautiful, but there was always a mocking smile or impatience behind his eyes that knew being beautiful was a little silly. You could never expect narcissism or vanity once you heard him speak. Grant could handle quick, complex, witty dialogue in the way of someone who enjoyed the language as much as Cole Porter or Dorothy Parker. Remember his delight when Grace Kelly offers him a leg or a breast at the picnic in *To Catch a Thief* (1955).

Only Fred Astaire ever moved as well as Grant – no wonder, for Grant had been an acrobat, a stilt-walker and a dancer for ten years before he got into pictures – but Grant

KATHARINE
HEPBURN *Sylvia Scarlett*

CARY GRANT
MARTHA SCOTT
THE HOWARDS
OF VIRGINIA

Produced and Directed by **FRANK LLOYD**
A COLUMBIA PICTURE

Above left: despite poor billing, Grant stole the show with his portrayal of a swindler. Above: in this drama he plays a man opposing his wife's family during the American Revolution. Left: in His Girl Friday, *with Rosalind Russell as his ex-wife*

moved with more dramatic eloquence while Astaire cherished the purity of movement. Grant could look as elegant as Astaire, but he could manage to look clumsy without actually sacrificing balance or style.

Still, his movements had the same undertone as his looks. Grant is always a little restless on screen and beneath the grace and élan there is a twinge of anxiety. With his accent caught between English and American his tone is uncertain whether to stay cool or let nerviness show. This is more than a perfect dance partner. This is the image of excellence hoping that hidden problems will stay out of sight.

The shadow of a smile

Grant's strength as a screen actor is in giving us a sense of the doubt and dismay that lies behind being 'Cary Grant'. Good looks do not relieve a man of every choice between good and its alternatives. That is why he seems to smile with some inner understanding, and why he is occasionally bitter or malign.

'He smiled understandingly – much more than understandingly. It was one of those rare smiles with a quality of eternal reassurance in

it . . . It faced . . . the whole eternal world for an instant, and then concentrated on *you* with an irresistible prejudice in your favour. It understood you just so far as you wanted to be understood, believed in you as you would like to believe in yourself, and assured you that it had precisely the impression of you that, at your best, you hoped to convey.'

Is that a Hollywood figure of the Thirties on first meeting Grant? No, it is Scott Fitzgerald (through Nick Carraway) describing Jay Gatsby – apparently the ideal host at Long Island parties – a mid-Western kid who had been a gangster and who kept a list of instructions for himself that included 'Practise elocution, poise and how to attain it'.

Gatsby was the essential fake in Americana, the rough become smooth, but never himself convinced by the change. Grant was not a fake, but his quality was ambiguous and intriguing because of a similar transformation.

Destination Hollywood

The immaculate man of the world would seem as smart as Cole Porter's songs and as dry as martinis, but there was a hint of roughneck and a history of enormous social journey.

Grant was to marry Barbara Hutton, one of the wealthiest women in the world, but he supported a mother in England who had entered a lunatic asylum when he was 12.

He was born in Bristol in 1904 and christened Archibald Alexander Leach. It was 1920 before he went to America and he had already spent five years working as part of a travelling company of acrobats and comics. He was brought up on patter, somersaults and pratfalls, and he did the same thing in American vaudeville without much recognition. However, by the late Twenties Grant began to get parts on the stage in musical comedy and was 28 when Hollywood, in the person of the producer B.P. Schulberg, thought to give him a chance.

For several years he was not much more than a romantic escort for leading ladies at Paramount, but in his second picture – *Blonde Venus* (1932) – he was very confident and restrained, opposite Marlene Dietrich, as the shady lover. Mae West was another screen goddess who knew how appreciatively he could look at a woman – Grant was always an actor who listened and watched so intently on screen that he was credited with a degree of intelligence and sensitivity that might not exist in the script. He played with West in *She Done Him Wrong* (1933), as an undercover agent investigating white-slave traffic, and in the same year *I'm No Angel*, as the playboy pursued by the vamp, effortlessly catching her risqué association of sex and humour.

By way of a change he was the Mock Turtle in *Alice in Wonderland* (1933), but he then had to do his duty in a run of undistinguished romances. Rescue came in a form that reminded him of his past. He played a charming cockney swindler in George Cukor's *Sylvia Scarlett* (1936). It was also his first movie with Katharine Hepburn, a team usually wittier and more romantically interesting than her celebrated association with Spencer Tracy.

The late Thirties saw Grant coming into his own, principally in comedy, and always playing men amused by the passing scene.

291

Above: Tracy Lord (Katharine Hepburn) re-marries her ex-husband (Grant) with the reporter (James Stewart) as best man in The Philadelphia Story. *Above right: Grant and Ann Sheridan as newly-weds in* I Was a Male War Bride. *Right: in* To Catch a Thief *as the cat-burglar who comes out of retirement in order to catch his imitator*

However, few of his roles are clear-cut. For instance, the stories in both *The Awful Truth* (1937) and *The Philadelphia Story* (1940) concern themes of divorced couples still in love and allowed Grant to add depths of feeling and melancholy to the comedy. As the ex-husband in *The Philadelphia Story* he is unashamed of his own errors, rakishness and irresponsibility, but still certain that pride and superiority are to be the downfall of Katharine Hepburn's Tracy Lord. These films could not be such searching character studies without Grant's convincing references to the off-screen plot so vital to the central characters' relationship.

Equally in *Bringing Up Baby* (1938), he makes the humanizing of his short-sighted professor as touching as the melting of Garbo's Ninotchka. How generously he allows Hepburn to be the force of the film but how richly he develops his stooge character to the point where the overly sane man is beginning to be liberated by the screwball woman. Further evidence of Grant's skill is apparent in *Holiday* (1938). This film – about an easy-going man who falls in love with his fiancée's sister, a girl much repressed by her surroundings – would not be so good a comedy about snobbery and integrity if it were not for Grant's sensitive use of humour; never for a moment did Grant's comic style suggest that comedy concerned less than the marrow of existence.

Therefore, when a joke is made the audience is aware of the serious man who sometimes needs to laugh at awful and frightening things. That is the essence of his humane toughness in *Only Angels Have Wings* (1939), the Howard Hawks film in which Grant is the leader of a group of pilots who ferry mail in South America. He worked for Hawks again in *His Girl Friday* (1940), a comedy so rapid that it is easy to miss the conniving and ruthlessness in Grant's part. For the first time there was something formidable in his authority and fatalistic attitude. *His Girl Friday* is yet another version of the plot whereby a man regains his ex-wife, played by Rosalind Russell. However in this case it is less easy to believe in a surviving love than in the challenge of conquest. In all these love stories Grant established the idea of an aloof, rather lonely man who could never put all his faith in lasting love.

From Hitch to Hawks
Certainly Alfred Hitchcock noticed the heartless gaiety of *His Girl Friday* and decided to cast Grant in *Suspicion* (1941). Nervousness softened the ending of the film, but Hitchcock had intended it as a black comedy about a wife who is being poisoned by the charming husband she adores. The film dropped that sinister line in favour of the theme of misunderstanding, but for most of the time Grant's debonair smile is masking murderous thoughts – and how well it works on screen. Five years later Hitchcock again explored the darker side of Grant in *Notorious* (1946) – the story of a man who coldly uses a woman (Ingrid Bergman) even though he loves her.

The Forties saw Grant in a lot of praiseworthy movies, although most were less striking than his work for Hawks and Hitchcock. One of his few completely dramatic roles was as

Filmography

1931 Singapore Sue (short). **'32** This Is the Night; Sinners in the Sun; Merrily We Go to Hell (GB: Merrily We Go to . . .); The Devil and the Deep; Blonde Venus; Hot Saturday; Madame Butterfly. **'33** She Done Him Wrong; Woman Accused; The Eagle and the Hawk; Gambling Ship; I'm No Angel; Alice in Wonderland. **'34** Thirty-Day Princess; Born to Be Bad; Kiss and Make Up; Ladies Should Listen. **'35** Enter Madame; Wings in the Dark; The Last Outpost. **'36** Sylvia Scarlett; Big Brown Eyes; Suzy; Private Party on Catalina Island (short); Wedding Present; The Amazing Quest of Ernest Bliss (GB) (USA: Romance and Riches) (retitling for TV: Amazing Adventure). **'37** When You're in Love; Topper; Toast of New York; The Awful Truth. **'38** Bringing Up Baby; Holiday (GB: Free to Live/Unconventional Linda). **'39** Gunga Din; Only Angels Have Wings; In Name Only. **'40** His Girl Friday; My Favorite Wife; The Howards of Virginia; The Philadelphia Story. **'41** Penny Serenade; Suspicion. **'42** Talk of the Town; Once Upon a Honeymoon. **'43** Mr Lucky; Destination Tokyo. **'44** Once Upon a Time; None But the Lonely Heart; Arsenic and Old Lace; Road to Victory (short). **'46** Night and Day; Without Reservations (uncredited guest); Notorious. **'47** The Bachelor and the Bobby Soxer (GB: Bachelor Knight); The Bishop's Wife. **'48** Mr Blandings Builds His Dream House; Every Girl Should Be Married. **'49** I Was a Male War Bride (GB: You Can't Sleep Here). **'50** Crisis. **'51** People Will Talk. **'52** Room for One More; Monkey Business. **'53** Dream Wife. **'55** To Catch a Thief. **'57** The Pride and the Passion; An Affair to Remember; Kiss Them for Me. **'58** Indiscreet; Houseboat. **'59** North by Northwest; Operation Petticoat (+prod co). **'60** The Grass Is Greener (+prod co). **'62** That Touch of Mink (+prod co). **'63** Charade. **'64** Father Goose (+prod co). **'66** Walk, Don't Run (+prod co). **'70** Elvis: That's the Way It Is (guest).

a revolutionary fighter in *The Howards of Virginia* (1940), set at the time of the American Revolution, and he was good in two George Stevens films – *Penny Serenade* (1941), a story of marital break-up, and *Talk of the Town* (1942), with Grant as an alleged murderer on the run. He played another cockney drifter in *None But*

Left: as a scientist with 'higher' things in mind Grant is unmoved by the attributes of his secretary (Marilyn Monroe) in Monkey Business. *Below left: the problems of flat-sharing and cocktail-mixing are examined by an industrialist (Grant) in* Walk, Don't Run *(1966). Below: the undercover agent gets his man in* Charade *(1963)*

the Lonely Heart (1944) and Cole Porter in *Night and Day* (1946). However, many of his romantic comedies had lost the sharp edge apparent in his pictures ten years earlier.

It was Howard Hawks who gave him new life in *I Was a Male War Bride* (1949), one of the most brilliant American sex comedies, and successful because of the glee with which Grant approached playing in drag. Three years later in *Monkey Business* (1952) – with Hawks, Ginger Rogers, Marilyn Monroe and the ploy of a rejuvenating drug – Grant was again able to free the boyish energy that was usually kept under wraps.

With the Fifties he let his hair go grey and worked a little less, but there was no difficulty in seeing him as a match for younger women. In *To Catch a Thief* he was very sympathetic support for Grace Kelly and fully at ease in the sophisticated adventure.

His last great fling came in 1959 when he played Roger Thornhill in Hitchcock's *North by Northwest*. In a cornfield pursued by an airplane, in a small train compartment with Eva Marie Saint, at an art auction, on the run, creeping into an occupied hospital room, waking the young woman patient, hushing her screams and being briefly tempted to stay, Grant was at his very best. And he knew all along that Thornhill was a flippant, spoiled baby cad being taught to grow up. *North by Northwest* is a comedy and an adventure, but it is, nevertheless, also a moral tale.

In that year, too, Grant must have known that he had passed into fond folklore when he saw the delicious and very respectful impersonation of him provided by Tony Curtis in *Some Like it Hot*.

Directed by William Wyler, 1959

Prod co: MGM. **prod:** Sam Zimbalist. **sc:** Karl Tunberg from *A Tale of Christ* by General Lew Wallace. **photo:** (Technicolor, Camera 65): Robert L. Surtees. **sp photo eff:** A. Arnold Gillespie, Lee Le Blanc, Rober R. Hoag. **ed:** Ralph E. Winters, John D. Dunning. **art dir:** William A. Horning, Edward Carfagno. **set dir:** Hugh Hunt. **mus:** Miklós Rózsa. **cost:** Elizabeth Haffenden. **sd:** Franklin Milton. **2nd unit dir:** Andrew Marton, Yakima Canutt, Mario Soldati. **2nd unit photo:** Piero Portulupi. **3rd unit dir:** Richard Thorpe. **3rd unit photo:** Harold E. Wellman. **r/t:** 217 mins. World premiere, State Theatre New York, 18 November 1959.
Cast: Charlton Heston (*Judah Ben-Hur*), Stephen Boyd (*Messala*), Haya Harareet (*Esther*), Jack Hawkins (*Quintus Arrius*), Hugh Griffith (*Sheikh Ilderim*), Martha Scott (*Miriam*), Cathy O'Donnell (*Tirzah*), Frank Thring (*Pontius Pilate*), Sam Jaffe (*Simonides*), Finlay Currie (*Balthazar*), Terence Longdon (*Drusus*), George Relph (*Tiberius*), Adi Berber (*Malluch*), Laurence Payne (*Joseph*), André Morell (*Sextus*), Marina Berti (*Flavia*), Claude Heater (*Christ*), John Le Mesurier (*doctor*), Stella Vitelleschi (*Amrah*), Jose Greci (*Mary*), John Horsley (*Spintho*), Richard Coleman (*Metallus*), Duncan Lamont (*Marius*), Ralph Truman (*aide to Tiberius*), Robert Brown (*chief-of-rowers*).

With its current worldwide gross exceeding $80 million and its still unbeaten 11 Academy Awards, *Ben-Hur* is one of the most successful films of all time. It is the Hollywood epic *par excellence*.

Made at Cinecittà Studios in Rome for $15 million, *Ben-Hur* was then the most expensive film ever made. MGM had previously filmed the story in 1925. It was a production beset by difficulties that, owing to its massive cost, failed to show a profit but which was a milestone in cinema history. The 1959 film was a make-or-break venture for MGM and they entrusted it to the fastidious William Wyler, who had worked briefly on the silent version.

If some of the film's spectacle is betrayed by unconvincing model and matte shots, the chariot race (co-directed by Andrew Marton and the ace stuntman Yakima Canutt) is deservedly celebrated as the most thrilling action sequence ever filmed. Early in the film, Ben Hur gives Messala a white horse as a token of their friendship, but from that moment Messala becomes the film's electrifying villain, casting a dark shadow over the whole story. The race is the great symbolic ritual of the narrative as Judah Ben-Hur's white horses run neck-and-neck with Messala's blacks.

It is a tribute to Wyler's narrative skill and to the intense performances by Charlton Heston, as Judah Ben-Hur, and Stephen Boyd, as Messala, that the race does not render the final hour an anti-climax. Despite the towering sets and thronging extras we never lose sight of the human drama. Judah might win the race but, as the dying Messala says, 'the race goes on'. At this point, Judah's victory seems as elusive as ever.

The novel, by General Lew Wallace and first published in 1880, exists within the branch of Victorian fiction which presents the reader with a daunting fresco of characters

and sub-plots resolved only by dramatic coincidences. The film's literate and often poetic screenplay – credited to Karl Tunberg, but co-written with the playwright Christopher Fry and the novelist Gore Vidal – eliminates Wallace's padding but retains the Victorian elements of melodrama and divine intervention.

'There are many paths of God, my son', says Balthazar to Judah, 'I hope yours will not be too difficult.' In fact, Judah's path is extremely difficult, involving the moral and physical challenges all classical heroes must endure. Judah's destiny is to become a believer at the Crucifixion and the cross itself becomes a compelling structural motif. Most obviously there is the cross-beam into which Judah and Messala throw their javelins – less obviously there are the three nails in the wall at which Judah prays before the race – and the paths of the characters within each stage of the story repeat the pattern.

After the race Esther snaps to Judah, 'It's as though you have become Messala!' and to underline the point Judah is subsequently seen resisting his destiny by ignoring the Sermon on the Mount, claiming he has 'business with Rome'. The imagery here, with Judah and Jesus occupying the same frame but with an immense distance between them, is epical in the purest sense.

At another point Balthazar mistakes Judah for Jesus and indeed, one can interpret Judah, Messala and Jesus as facets of a single character: Judah's life is saved by Messala, then by Jesus; Judah takes Messala's life and Jesus dies to 'save us all'. In another way the Roman Quintus Arrius and the Wise Man Balthazar are basically the same character, both searching – from pagan and Christian perspectives – for divine guidance and both adopting Judah as their son.

All the characters and episodes are linked in this way and by Wyler's extensive use of water to signify purification. This culminates in the moment when the blood from the cross is gradually dispersed by the rain, heralding a new beginning.

The subtleties of such details are unusual for a film on this scale, as are the varieties of mood and emotion. On the one hand there are sweeping dramatic moments – the race, the prolonged argument between Judah and Messala, the uplifting sequence when Judah is given water by Jesus and later when the scene is reversed on the road to Calvary. On the other hand there are moments of extraordinary warmth and intimacy – the tentative love scene between Esther and Judah, and Balthazar gazing into the night sky ablaze with stars, wondering what became of the child he saw born in Bethlehem. Therefore, even though the spectacular chariot race made *Ben-Hur* famous, it is nonetheless highly valued for a multitude of other reasons.

294

2

3

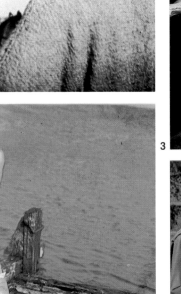

5

6

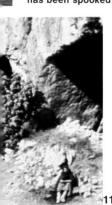

8

9

In Jerusalem the newly appointed Roman Tribune Messala meets his childhood friend Judah Ben-Hur, a Jewish aristocrat, and asks his help in eliminating rebellion (1). Judah refuses and his friendship with Messala suddenly ends. When the Roman Governor is injured in a fall after his horse has been spooked by a tile which falls from Judah's roof, Messala declaims Judah as a rebel and imprisons his mother and sister. In chains and dying of thirst, Judah is given water by a carpenter's son (2). Condemned to the galleys (3). Judah saves the life of the Roman Consul Quintus Arrius during a sea battle (4–5). The grateful Quintus Arrius takes Judah to Rome and adopts him as his son (6).

Returning to Jerusalem after seven years, Judah arrives at his old home, now neglected and overgrown, and is reunited with Esther, whom he loves, and her father, steward to the House of Hur. In a chariot race (7) Judah takes revenge on Messala (8) who, on his death-bed (9), tells Judah to look for his mother and sister in the Valley of the Lepers (10). Esther persuades Judah to take them to Jesus of Nazareth. They arrive at his trial. Recognising the Nazarene (11), Judah attends the Crucifixion and returning home he finds his mother and sister cured (12).

11

12

High noon in the West

The Western took on a new lease of life in the Fifties, using many varieties of colour film and a wider range of themes, including the good Indian

---

The early history of the Western is largely associated with B pictures and programmers, aside from the relatively small number of prestige productions like *The Covered Wagon* (1923), John Ford's *The Iron Horse* (1924) and *Cimarron* (1931). An upgrading of the genre during 1939–41 proved short-lived as the war film took over, while many leading male stars were lost to the armed services. But a genuine revival began to develop during the immediate post-war period with prestige productions from David O. Selznick (*Duel in the Sun*, 1946) and Howard Hawks (*Red River*, 1948), and a notable series of Westerns directed by John Ford including *My Darling Clementine* (1946) and *She Wore a Yellow Ribbon* (1949). And by the early Fifties the Western was flourishing as it never had before.

High-quality Westerns, mainly in Technicolor, were produced by all the major studios alongside the last of the cheapie programmers in black and white (soon to be killed off by television), while Westerns from the small independent companies like Republic, Monogram and United Artists often exploited the new, cheap, two-colour processes like Cinecolor and Trucolor. There were still 'serious' pictures in black and white like *The Gunfighter* (1950) and *High Noon* (1952). A new respect for the Indian was a feature of 20th Century-Fox's *Broken Arrow* (1950) and MGM's *Across the Wide Missouri* (1951). The more traditional action film also continued to flourish, as represented by the Audie Murphy cycle of Westerns from Universal. The contribution of veteran directors like Ford and Hawks was matched by experienced men like Anthony Mann, Delmer Daves and John Sturges, who had begun their careers during the Forties, along with a group of younger directors coming to maturity, including Robert Aldrich, Budd Boetticher and Nicholas Ray.

Perhaps more than any other genre, the Western during the early and mid-Fifties reflected that this was a period of transition. The political uncertainties of the post-war years – the Cold War, the Korean War and the election of Eisenhower in 1952, the first Republican President for 20 years – contributed to a new American preoccupation with the national past and a reaffirmation of traditional virtues and values, suggesting a need for old-fashioned escapist Westerns newly bedecked in colour, CinemaScope and 3-D. Yet the film audience was more sophisticated than before and demanded a greater complexity and maturity in Western themes and characterization.

The decline of the old studio system coincided with a greater emphasis on location filming of major features in colour making use of authentic settings; the B feature was virtually abandoned. And many leading directors chose a Western for their first venture into colour, including Delmer Daves' *Broken Arrow*, Anthony Mann's *Bend of the River* (1952) followed by *The Naked Spur* (1953) – both starring James Stewart; Don Siegel's *Duel at Silver Creek* (1952, starring Audie Murphy) and George Stevens' *Shane* (1953). Sets and costumes

were generally less expensive than for other types of period picture, while the colourful landscapes and settings were conveniently close to Hollywood.

As for the cheaper colour processes like Trucolor and Cinecolor, outdoor subjects like Westerns were almost a necessity, for their limitations were more apparent when filming interiors with artificial lighting – not surprisingly, the best ever film in Republic's Trucolor process was Nicholas Ray's Western *Johnny Guitar* (1954), starring Joan Crawford. A Western was often used for the 'trial run' in introducing various new colour processes and other technical innovations. For example, MGM's first production in Ansco colour was *The Wild North* (1951), followed by John Sturges' first colour film, *Escape From Fort Bravo* (1953), also shot in a 3-D version.

Similarly, the first films in the new Warnercolor (a version of Eastman Colour) in 1952 were mainly Westerns. And Pathecolor, yet another version of Eastman Colour, was introduced in 1953–4. The first group of 3-D pictures in 1953 included Westerns such as Raoul Walsh's *Gun Fury* and John Farrow's *Hondo* starring John Wayne. The musical Western *Oklahoma!* (1955) was the first production in the new Todd-AO (65 mm) process as well as the first venture into colour by Fred Zinnemann, who had directed the best-known black-and-white Western of the Fifties, *High Noon*. James Stewart starred in the first Technirama production, *Night Passage*, in 1957; and Westerns also proved ideally suited for filming in the other new processes like Cinema-Scope and VistaVision.

Many of the top male stars who were first discovered and developed by the major studios during the peak years of the Thirties and early Forties had reached an age and maturity by the Fifties which could best be exploited within the Western format. Established Western stars such as John Wayne, Gary Cooper and Randolph Scott appeared in many of their best roles. James Stewart suddenly emerged as a major Western star, after

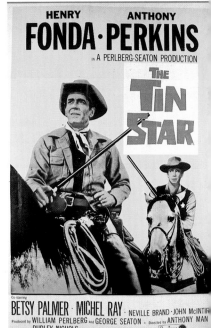

Top: Jay C. Flippen, Claire Trevor and Kirk Douglas in King Vidor's Man Without a Star *(1955). Douglas gives an aggressive performance as a rugged saddletramp reluctant to recognize that the Old West is dying and that barbed-wire has come to the range to stay forever. Above: in* The Tin Star, *a veteran former lawman (Henry Fonda) tutors an inexperienced sheriff (Anthony Perkins). Opposite: Alan Ladd in the classic Western* Shane

Above: Jessica Drummond (Barbara Stanwyck), ruler of 40 gun-wielding cowboys, and Griff Bonnell (Barry Sullivan) as the frustrated lovers in Forty Guns; *a number of critics have rightly remarked on the close connection between sex and violence in this film. Above right: 3.10 to Yuma starred Van Heflin as an Arizona lawman trying against considerable opposition to catch an afternoon train for the state penitentiary with his prisoner (Glenn Ford). Below: in* Westward the Women, *150 would-be brides trek from Chicago to California by wagon train in search of husbands; here one of these hopeful ladies (Hope Emerson) is slugged by another*

appearing in only one previous Western, *Destry Rides Again* (1939). Alan Ladd and James Cagney, previously identified with the gangster or thriller genre, made their mark: Alan Ladd's Shane provided one of the archetypal Western heroes of the decade, and the triumphant revival of Cagney's career began with an off-beat Western, Nicholas Ray's *Run for Cover* (1955). Veteran character actors like Walter Brennan and Andy Devine were much in demand, along with a new generation of 'heavies' including Dan Duryea, Richard Boone and Jack Elam. Young, up-and-coming actors were often teamed with older established stars, for example, Jeffrey Hunter with John Wayne in *The Searchers* and with Robert Ryan in *The Proud Ones*, both in 1956, or Anthony Perkins with Henry Fonda in Anthony Mann's *The Tin Star* (1957).

Leading female stars also took to the saddle. Marlene Dietrich totally dominated Fritz Lang's *Rancho Notorious* (1952) although, according to Lang, she was not happy playing an older woman. Jean Arthur made a notable screen comeback as the homesteader's wife in *Shane*. Joan Crawford gave a suitably larger-than-life performance as the tough owner of a gambling saloon in *Johnny Guitar*. But for toughness and self-reliance no-one could rival Barbara Stanwyck, who emerged as a leading Western star during the mid-Fifties in such pictures as *Cattle Queen of Montana* (1954), *The Violent Men* (1955), *The Maverick Queen* (1956) – Republic's first film in the new 'Scope-like anamorphic 'Naturama' – and, most impressive of all, as the ruthless ranch boss of *Forty Guns* (1957), Sam Fuller's much underrated Western, appropriately filmed in black-and-white CinemaScope.

In the landmark year of 1950 there was a major upgrading of the Western genre. John Ford directed *Rio Grande* (the last of his cavalry trilogy) and *Wagonmaster*. This superb tribute to the pioneers who travelled west in wagon trains drew on Ford's stock company of favourite actors, including Ward Bond, Jane Darwell, Russell Simpson, Ben Johnson and Harry Carey Jr.

Another veteran director, Henry King, produced an unexpected bonus from his collaboration with Gregory Peck, sandwiched between the prestige productions of *Twelve O'Clock High* (1949) and *David and Bathsheba* (1951). The theme of the gunslinger unable to live down his past has often been dealt with since, but never more effectively than in *The Gunfighter*, from 20th Century-Fox. Along with

Broken Arrow, it represented a natural extension of Darryl Zanuck's emphasis on the problem picture during the late Forties, which was here combined with his special interest in Americana.

The year 1950 also marked the debut of a number of new Western stars, and directors such as Anthony Mann and Delmer Daves. Mann directed his first three Westerns in 1950: *The Furies*, at Paramount, starring Barbara Stanwyck and Walter Huston; *Winchester '73*, at Universal, with James Stewart in his first mature Western role; and, at MGM, *Devil's Doorway*, in which Robert Taylor played an Indian fighting for the rights of his people. In Delmer Daves' *Broken Arrow*, Stewart played an Indian-scout who falls in love with and marries an Indian girl; Jeff Chandler played Cochise in this first modern Western to portray the Indians with human stature and dignity. William Wellman's

---

Shane was the box-office front-runner, but Mann's Westerns outdrew all opponents with the critics, especially in France

---

Across the Wide Missouri (1951), with Clark Gable, presented an intelligent treatment of the theme of a white trapper and his Indian wife which, although released in a badly shortened version, did well at the box-office.

However, the claim for a new respectability for the Western was firmly established in 1952 with the phenomenal success of *High Noon*. Its director, Fred Zinnemann, said:

'From the time Stanley Kramer and Carl Foreman told me the outline of the story, I saw this film *not* as a comment on the American Western hero, but as an enormously important contemporary theme which happened to take place in a Western setting.'

The tightly constructed script provided Gary Cooper with one of the best roles of his career (and his second Oscar).

The revival of Westerns by 1952 was reflected in their prominence among the top hits of that year. *High Noon* was closely followed in the box-office stakes by *Son of Paleface*, with Bob Hope, and Anthony Mann's *Bend of the River*, which marked a further advance in his collaboration with James Stewart, Raoul Walsh's *Distant Drums*, again with

Gary Cooper, and three pictures from MGM – William Wellman's *Westward the Women, Lone Star* with Gable, and *The Wild North* – all recorded distributors' rentals of over $2 million. But *Shane*, with rentals of over $8 million the following year, was the biggest Western hit of the decade. The fine cast was headed by Alan Ladd, Jean Arthur, Van Heflin and Brandon de Wilde, with Jack Palance as the villainous hired gun brought in to intimidate the homesteaders. The director, George Stevens, was ably supported by A.B. Guthrie's fine script and the Oscar-winning Technicolor camerawork of Loyal Griggs.

Among the many Westerns filmed in the new processes, Robert Aldrich had a big hit in 1954 with *Vera Cruz*, one of the first films in SuperScope. And although Anthony Mann proved in *The Far Country* (1954) that it was still possible to get excellent results from the old format, he finally made the transition to CinemaScope with *The Man From Laramie* (1955), the last of his films with Stewart; all of his subsequent Westerns were in 'Scope. Similarly, John Ford's masterpiece, *The Searchers* (1956), benefitted from the superior photographic quality of VistaVision. The picture presents a harsher, more

bitter and sophisticated view of the West than is found in his earlier films.

The black-and-white picture made a temporary comeback during the late Fifties with Delmer Daves' *3.10 to Yuma* (1957) and Arthur Penn's *The Left-Handed Gun* (1958) starring Paul Newman. Both films presented sophisticated and realistic treatments of traditional themes – the lone lawman bringing an outlaw to justice, the story of Billy the Kid – with a modern emphasis on character and relationships on a small scale. The moments of violence develop naturally out of the intensity of personal conflict. Appropriately enough, *The Left-Handed Gun* was in the true Warners tradition of hard-hitting black-and-white pictures featuring a tough hero who dies a violent death in the final reel.

Warners was also responsible for one outstanding Western which brought the decade to a close, Howard Hawks' *Rio Bravo* (1959). Reflecting Hawks' dislike of *High Noon*, the picture may appear conventional on the surface; yet the characters and relationships are observed with great insight and wit while retaining the kind of vitality and spontaneity found in Hawks' earlier pictures:

'I determined to go back and try to get a little of the spirit we used to make pictures with. In *Rio Bravo* I imagine there are almost as many laughs as if we had started out to make a comedy.'

Hawks neatly built on the juxtaposition of old, established Westerners like John Wayne and Walter Brennan with a newer generation represented by Dean Martin and Angie Dickinson. And if the Wayne-Dickinson relationship, a mature man trying to cope with an independent-minded, tough-talking girl, recalls the Bogart-Bacall films of the Forties, this is not surprising, since Hawks was collaborating with two of his favourite scriptwriters from this period, Leigh Brackett and Jules Furthman.

Unfortunately, as the decade drew to a close those qualities developed by directors such as Daves, Boetticher and Hawks during the late Fifties were largely forgotten, and the studios increasingly turned to the overblown, blockbuster Western in the tradition of William Wyler's *The Big Country* (1958). The Sixties began rather unpromisingly with *The Alamo, The Magnificent Seven* – based on *Seven Samurai* – and a disappointing remake of *Cimmaron* (all 1960). These were followed by the scrappy *How the West Was Won* (1962), the first story picture in Cinerama.

Above left: Jack Palance as a hired gunfighter about to kill one of the settlers in Shane. Above: a showgirl (Sophia Loren) in a touring theatrical troupe joins the gentlemen for a round of poker in George Cukor's Heller in Pink Tights (1960). Below, far left: in Broken Arrow Jeff Chandler played Cochise for the first but not the last time. Below left: the sheriff (John Wayne) makes his evening patrol in Rio Bravo. Below: Glenn Ford and Shirley MacLaine star in George Marshall's The Sheepman (1958), a delightful send-up of the archetypal range-war between sheepmen and cattlemen

THE MIRISCH COMPANY Presents

JACK LEMMON
SHIRLEY MacLAINE
FRED MacMURRAY

He lent his flat for love- of his job!

A BILLY WILDER PRODUCTION

"The Apartment" (A)

starring ray walston AND edie adams

Written by BILLY WILDER and I. A. L. DIAMOND · Directed by BILLY WILDER · FILMED IN PANAVISION · UNITED ARTISTS

At his greatest, the director Billy Wilder resembles nothing so much as an expert tightrope walker. After the initial apprehension, the technique is even more impressive and breath-taking than the risk.

On the face of it, *The Apartment* offers a daunting challenge even to Wilder's exquisite sense of balance. The material is essentially a mordant vision of office politics, where pimping rates more highly than probity in the race for promotion. It is a stinging vision of the kind of dehumanization necessary for advancement in a coldly competitive modern society where materialism overwhelms values.

But the harshness of the social message is cunningly disguised by Wilder until the appropriate moment. Like a great bridge-player, he withholds his trump card until it can be used for its most devastating effect. Because of the hero's opening friendly narration and because of Jack Lemmon's astute and winning performance as the humble clerk, C. C. Baxter, a sympathy is forged between hero and audience before the squalor of his situation is fully revealed. This is appropriate because the hero himself becomes embroiled in the situation before he fully appreciates its implications.

Also it is the humour of the situation that Wilder chooses to unfold first. Various confusions are deftly

1

2

5

6

Directed by Billy Wilder, 1960
Prod co: Mirisch Company. **prod:** Billy Wilder. **sc:** Billy Wilder, I. A. L. Diamond. **photo** (Panavision)**:** Joseph LaShelle. **ed:** Daniel Mandell. **art dir:** Alexander Trauner. **mus:** Adolph Deutsch. **r/t:** 120 minutes.
Cast: Jack Lemmon (*C. C. 'Bud' Baxter*), Shirley MacLaine (*Fran Kubelik*), Fred MacMurray (*Jeff D. Sheldrake*), Ray Walston (*Joe Dobisch*), David Lewis (*Al Kirkeby*), Jack Kruschen (*Dr Dreyfuss*), Joan Shawlee (*Sylvia*), Edie Adams (*Miss Olsen*), Hope Holiday (*Margie MacDougall*), Johnny Seven (*Karl Matuschka*), Naomi Stevens (*Mrs Dreyfuss*), Joyce Jameson (*beautiful blonde*).

exploited for comic effect. Characters misread the evidence of their own eyes, leaping to wildly improbable and salacious deductions from innocent encounters. Running jokes, such as the neighbour's wilful misunderstanding of Baxter's own sexual proclivities, accumulate increasingly manic mileage as the mistake is perpetuated.

Baxter's timetable for his apartment is so complicated that, when he catches cold and needs the apartment himself for a night, he has to spend an entire morning on the office's internal phone rearranging the schedule of adultery. Baxter's bizarre situation leads to a parody of domestic life with ordinary routines such as eating, shaving and even sleeping interrupted by the clamours of impatient clients. He begins to take on the demeanour of a sad clown, simultaneously trying to juggle his home arrangements and respond to the

intimidating whip of his gratified but menacingly insistent superiors.

Wilder succeeds in taking his basic situation all the way from humour through sadness to near-tragedy, the latter quality reflected in Shirley MacLaine's deeply moving performance as the elevator operator unhappily involved in an affair with her boss. From an initial comic statement of his theme, Wilder begins to weave the most complex and dramatic counterpoint. The revels of a Christmas party shriek discordantly against shattering personal revelations. Baxter has to face the music when his discovery of an attempted suicide in his bedroom abruptly terminates his party with a casual pick-up. Tragedy is suddenly a mere room away from fun and laughter.

The finale is distinctly bitter-sweet, largely because of the ruthless logic with which Baxter's daw-

ning humanity is inexorably linked to his social fall. He might righteously renounce his job, and Fran the girl he loves, might run out on her lover and rejoin Baxter in the apartment – but Wilder takes care to present these actions as impulsive gestures more than weighty resolutions. However one applauds Baxter's moral stand and Fran's emotional decision, it is clear they are running away from a harsh reality that must overtake them sooner or later. Part of the poignancy of the last scene is the contrast between their personal happiness and their social precariousness. They might have opted out of the rat race but the denuded, gloomy apartment at the end of the film is Wilder's stark visual reminder of what this might involve.

If the film is nevertheless more moving and exhilarating than depressing, and well worth its five Oscars, the reason for this is that it contains practically all the elements that one values in Wilder as a master film-maker: his honesty as a social commentator; his skill with actors; the intelligence and care with which he structures and executes his material. Above all, there is his incomparable blend of wit and morality, whereby the absurdity of human folly is observed with a generosity of spirit that inspires humour more than hatred, compassion more than contempt. 'If you

want to tell people the truth,' said George Bernard Shaw, 'you'd better make them laugh – or they'll kill you.' With *The Apartment*, Wilder has never seemed more fully alive.

Manhattan insurance clerk, C. C. Baxter (1), lends a friend his apartment key. Soon his superiors are borrowing the key for their extramarital affairs in return for glowing reports about Baxter to the company boss, Sheldrake, who also asks to borrow the key.

Baxter loves the firm's elevator operator, Fran Kubelik (2). But at the office party (3), he unhappily discovers that Sheldrake has been entertaining her in his apartment. Fran is similarly distressed to learn about Sheldrake's previous affairs. After arguing with Sheldrake in Baxter's apartment (4), she attempts suicide. Baxter finds her (5) and revives her with the help of his neighbour, Dr Dreyfuss (6).

Caring for Fran over Christmas (7), Baxter becomes more devoted than ever, though on hearing that Sheldrake is getting divorced Fran returns to him. Sheldrake rewards Baxter with promotion but, now sickened by his situation, Baxter resigns (8). Fran learns this from Sheldrake and she responds by rushing back to rejoin Baxter.

3

4

7

8

British 'New Wave'

The British 'New Wave' drew on literary sources and the documentary tradition to bring new life to the stagnant waters of British feature-film production

When *Room at the Top* hit the screen in 1959, it signalled the beginning of one of the most exhilarating bursts of creativity in the history of British cinema. During the following five or six years new film-makers with fresh ideas brought to the screen a sense of immediacy and social awareness that had people queuing again after nearly a decade of decline.

These dynamic film developments sprang from the political and social agitation of the period. British imperialism had been dealt a severe body blow by the failure of the 1956 Suez venture in alliance with France against Egypt. Thousands of young people had gathered in London's Trafalgar Square to demand the withdrawal of British troops from Egypt. Thousands more were flocking to join the annual anti-nuclear Aldermaston marches in order to campaign for unilateral nuclear disarmament.

It was a time of protest and demonstrations. Ideas were in the melting pot. Young people were no longer accepting that their elders were necessarily their betters, and in the process of re-examining basic principles they were gaining a new sense of collective identity, which in turn was transforming books, plays and popular entertainment.

Singers like Tommy Steele, Cliff Richard and Lonnie Donegan were spurning traditional showbiz glamour in favour of a jeans-and-T-shirt image. Authors ultimately as different as John Braine, Alan Sillitoe and Stan Barstow were all writing grittily from working-class and lower-middle-class experience. On the London stage, the 'kitchen sink' era had begun. At the Royal Court Theatre, John Osborne had created the concept of the 'angry young man' and Arnold Wesker was facing West End audiences with East End problems. Joan Littlewood, creator of Stratford Theatre Royal and Theatre Workshop, was bringing a whole new generation of playwrights, actors and actresses into being, to express the questing, socially critical spirit of the times.

Things moved more slowly in the film industry, which is notoriously reluctant to risk its money on anything new. The measures it was taking to counter the catastrophic drop in cinema attendances, caused largely by the upsurge of TV, were mainly commercially opportunist and gimmicky, and this only succeeded in driving more people back home to watch TV.

The first hint of change in feature production came from a modest suspense drama, *The Man Upstairs* (1958), tautly directed by Don Chaffey for ACT Films (the production company of the film technicians' union). Set in a London boarding house, it touched upon many of the vital issues of the day and challenged conventional, cosy attitudes to class relationships and the role of the police. It was a straw in the wind. But it was completely overshadowed by the smash-hit success of *Room at the Top*, released early the next year.

Directed by Jack Clayton, and based on the John Braine best seller – a key book in the new-style

literature – *Room at the Top* was, in fact, a transitional film. Its starry cast, its steamy sex scenes and its depiction of life at the top belonged to the past. But its Northern setting and its candid exploration of the social barriers, corruption and palm-greasing of class-divided Britain signposted the future. Its enormous popularity at home and abroad brought fresh confidence to the film industry and helped to shake some of its more entrenched notions of what draws people to the cinema.

Meanwhile, back at the National Film Theatre, a group of youngish, independent film-makers, including Karel Reisz, Tony Richardson, Lindsay Anderson and cameraman Walter Lassally, were showing each other and young audiences the documentary films they had made with small grants from the British Film Institute or at their own expense, in a series of programmes they called *Free Cinema*.

The stated aim of the group was, by adopting far more personalized styles, to break away from the approach to documentary film-making established by John Grierson in the Thirties. Most of their films were free-flowing observations of work and play among young working-class people; and in retrospect they are more striking for their continuity with the Grierson tradition than for their rejection of it. Anderson looked at a Margate amusement arcade in *O Dreamland* (1953); at life in a school for deaf children in *Thursday's Children*, which won an Oscar in 1954; and at the people of Covent Garden market in *Every Day Except Christmas* (1957). Richardson's *Momma Don't Allow* (1955) observed young people at a jazz club; Reisz's *We Are the Lambeth Boys* (1959) was about a South London youth club.

The 'personalized' view was sometimes patronizing or snobbish. The standard of the films was

Top: the success of John Osborne's Look Back in Anger *at the Royal Court Theatre in 1956 started a fresh movement in British drama. The film version retained the play's claustrophobic force, despite location filming in Romford market. Above: the* Free Cinema *documentarists had to eke out a living in television, advertising and the theatre while awaiting the chance to make feature films*

Top: the subject of school obviously inspires Lindsay Anderson; Thursday's Children *(co-directed by Guy Brenton) is a fine documentary in which deaf children are taught to speak by various ingenious methods, including feeling the vibrations of sound in a balloon. Top right:* Saturday Night and Sunday Morning *had the best press of any 'New Wave' film; as the Sixties went on, pop music dominated the media more than new films. Above: Joan Littlewood, best known for her lively work in the theatre, directed only one film,* Sparrows Can't Sing, *which starred Barbara Windsor, James Booth and George Sewell as an East End love-triangle*

uneven; but the best of them had a freshness and sense of urgency which was a taste of things to come. They stimulated discussion in the pages of the serious film journals; Lindsay Anderson argued for the recognition of the relationship between art and society in his much-discussed article, 'Stand Up! Stand Up!', published in *Sight and Sound*, Autumn 1956. The enthusiasm generated by the group in its search for contemporary styles to match contemporary attitudes helped to open up new possibilities for feature production.

First to the starting post was Tony Richardson, who had produced John Osborne's plays on the stage, and joined with him to form Woodfall Films with a view to adapting them for the screen. Neither *Look Back in Anger* (1959), with Richard Burton as Jimmy Porter, the original 'angry young man', nor *The Entertainer* (1960) with Laurence Olivier as the has-been stand-up comic, was as successful as they had been on the stage, largely, perhaps, because Osborne had been addressing himself to middle-class theatre audiences.

It was not until Woodfall linked up with a working-class writer, Alan Sillitoe, that it was able to launch the cinematic equivalent of the theatre's 'kitchen sink' revolution, with the screen version of Sillitoe's best seller, *Saturday Night and Sunday Morning* (1960), directed by Karel Reisz.

Despite the ripples made by *Room at the Top*, Woodfall had a long and difficult struggle to raise the finance for a film with a factory worker as 'hero'. Few believed that it could succeed. In the event, it beat all former box-office records for a British film and proved that there need be no contradiction between artistic integrity and commercial success. The ripples then grew into a floodtide; and for the next few years British cinema rode on the crest of the 'New Wave' which, for a time, freed a section of it from Hollywood financial and cultural domination.

The new film-makers, like the pioneers of the 'Grierson school' before them, rejected studio sets in favour of location shooting in the back streets, waterways and working-class homes of industrial cities. The black-and-white photography, mainly with natural lighting, gave rise to the 'grainy realism' which was the typical visual style, and the influence of recently developed TV techniques helped achieve a sense of immediacy.

The star system was abandoned, and leading roles were taken by new or up-and-coming players (Albert Finney, for example, was virtually unknown outside London theatre circles before *Saturday Night and Sunday Morning*). Many had been trained at Theatre Workshop. The characters they played were close to life, complex – like real people rather than standard 'heroes' and 'heroines'; the contemporary mood of social protest was expressed less through what they said on the screen than through the close relationship that was depicted between their frustrations and rebelliousness and the specific context of their environment.

Most of the films were based on books and plays by authors with personal experience of working-class life in the provinces (very few of the films were made from original scripts). This contrasted with the rather condescending view of working-class life that had been adopted in earlier feature films. For the first time, typical cinema audiences were able to feel a strong sense of identity with what was happening on the screen.

Over-reliance on novels and plays made the new start precarious and unlikely to last the course

Woodfall Films, with the backing of the British Lion subsidiary, Bryanston Films, continued to lead the field. Tony Richardson brought Shelagh Delaney's Theatre Royal play, *A Taste of Honey*, to the screen (1961), with Rita Tushingham as the pregnant schoolgirl and Murray Melvin (from Theatre Workshop) as the lonely homosexual with whom she shares a brief spell of contented domesticity. Richardson followed it with *The Loneliness of the Long-Distance Runner* (1962), based on Alan Sillitoe's remarkable short story, with Tom Courtenay as the young delinquent in Borstal who demonstrates which side he is on by deliberately losing the race that, if won, would have brought great prestige to the Borstal authorities. Much underrated by critics at the time, it has proved to be among the most enduring films of the period. Both these films gained much from Walter Lassally's brilliant camerawork.

It was not until 1963 that Lindsay Anderson made his first feature film, *This Sporting Life*, based on a David Storey novel. At one level, it explored a miserably stormy relationship of two lovers (Richard Harris and Rachel Roberts); at another, it exposed the corruption and commercialism of Rugby League as a business. It was highly acclaimed by most critics; but its fragmented flashback structure and rather heavily emphatic symbolism – a departure from typical 'New Wave' directness – operated against commercial success; it was six years before Anderson was able to make his second

and more successful feature film, *If . . .* (1968).

Woodfall also launched Desmond Davis as a director; his two films based on Edna O'Brien stories – *The Girl With Green Eyes* (1964) and *I Was Happy Here* (1966) – were late contributions to the no-longer-new trend.

One of the key directors of the period was John Schlesinger who, after gaining attention with his Waterloo Station documentary, *Terminus* (1961), teamed up with the Italian producer Joseph Janni to make *A Kind of Loving* (1962), in which he explored the effect of upper-working-class puritanism – and the housing shortage – on the uncertain relationship between a young couple, played by Alan Bates and June Ritchie. His second feature film was *Billy Liar* (1963) with Tom Courtenay as a young office worker who lives in a fantasy world and Julie Christie, in a small but important role, as the girl who helps him to face reality.

The young Canadian director, Sidney Furie, probed deeply into current social issues among working-class youngsters in *The Boys* (1962) and *The Leather Boys* (1963). He injected a crisp, contemporary style into British musicals with *The Young Ones* (1961) and *Wonderful Life* (1964), both featuring Cliff Richard. The 'pop' scene was also the launching pad for Richard Lester, who captured the changing spirit of the times in *It's Trad, Dad!* (1962) and in the first of his two films with the Beatles, *A Hard Day's Night* (1964).

Among the screen versions of the key stage plays of the period were a poor adaptation of Brendan Behan's *The Quare Fellow* (1962) and a good,

straightforward version of Wesker's *The Kitchen* (1961), directed by James Hill for ACT Films. Joan Littlewood herself, whose Theatre Workshop at Stratford was supplying so many new faces and new ideas for the screen, made a brief but lively excursion into cinema with the perky and resilient cockney comedy, *Sparrows Can't Sing* (1963), adapted from the Theatre Royal play by Stephen Lewis – another much underrated film.

In 1963, over a third of the films generally released dealt with aspects of contemporary life in Britain. It was a vintage year for the 'New Wave' – but it spelled the beginning of the end. Ironically, it was Woodfall Films, prime mover in freeing British cinema from Hollywood domination, which unwittingly handed it back.

The 'New Wave' films had not been costly. But Tony Richardson needed a bigger budget for *Tom Jones* (scripted by John Osborne from Henry Fielding's classic novel) which was to be shot in colour, with expensive costumes. When British Lion declined to take the risk, United Artists stepped in. Despite its period setting, the film's racy, rumbustious spirit and strong social comment – together with Albert Finney's roistering central performance – hit the contemporary mood. It was a fabulous success – and it opened the floodgates for American capital to pour into British production. The 'New Wave', with its regional nuances and its lack of star value and glamour, was an early victim of the Americanization process. British cinema lost much of its native character and again became part of transatlantic movie culture.

Top left: Tom Courtenay's bony, melancholy face was his fortune in The Loneliness of the Long-Distance Runner, *which set him on the path to stardom. Top: a girl (Rita Tushingham) about to become an unmarried mother tries to develop some maternal feelings with the dubious help of a plastic doll, while her flat-mate (Murray Melvin) looks on uneasily in* A Taste of Honey. *Above: Rita Tushingham plays a young girl in love with an older man (Peter Finch) in* The Girl With Green Eyes. *Left: a little boy feels lost in* Terminus. *The film's director, John Schlesinger, had previously worked mainly in TV documentary, notably for the arts programme,* Monitor

THE FRENCH NOUVELLE VAGUE

After knocking for years, young French directors finally broke down the door and entered film production with an unprecedented energy and enthusiasm

The talking-point of 1959 in the film world was the sudden emergence of the French *nouvelle vague* ('new wave'). It was an astonishing burst of creative activity which saw forty young directors given the opportunity to make their first films over the next year. It seemed to herald new approaches and techniques that would revolutionize the industry.

It was all, of course, a misunderstanding – or, at least, an exaggeration. A famous publicity photograph purports to show the '*nouvelle vague*' at the Cannes Film Festival of 1959. This was the year in which François Truffaut, banned from attending as a critic because he had savagely derided the standard of the French entries in his magazine column, returned as a film-maker to take the Best Direction prize with *Les Quatre Cents Coups* (1959, *The 400 Blows*). Since the 'young Turks' of criticism had proved their point by making successful films – so the industry's reasoning ran – let them have their heads and hope that some of them will bring in the money.

The photograph shows, sitting on the steps of the *Palais du Festival* at Cannes, a group of young film-makers, namely: François Truffaut, Raymond Vogel, Louis Félix, Edmond Séchan, Edouard Molinaro, Jacques Baratier, Jean Valère, François Reichenbach, Robert Hossein, Jean-Daniel Pollet, Roger Vadim, Marcel Camus, Claude Chabrol, Jacques Doniol-Valcroze, Jean-Luc Godard and Jacques Rozier.

If many of these are not exactly household names today – well, that was the way the *nouvelle vague* went. Some of these directors were not noticeably talented. Some, like Vadim and Molinaro, were even then making films indistinguishable from the commercial norm, except that the directors came from a younger generation. Even this last categorization did not always apply. Marcel Camus won the Festival's *Grand Prix* with *Orfeu Negro* (1958, *Black Orpheus*), a slice of picturesque exoticism that could have been made at any time during the past ten

years but which earned him the accolade of '*nouvelle vague*'. He was 47 at the time.

Nevertheless, there *was* a *nouvelle vague*, given a tenuous identity and unity only because the sudden influx of new directors was the result of inexorably critical pressure that had been brought to bear on the French film industry over a number of years; and because when the dam of tradition and box-office caution finally gave way, the most talented newcomers – Godard, Truffaut, Chabrol, Jacques Rivette and Eric Rohmer – also happened to be critics collaborating on *Cahiers du Cinéma*, the magazine which had articulated and applied most of that pressure.

The first rumblings of discontent were given influential expression in 1948 by Alexandre Astruc in an article called 'The Birth of a New Avant-Garde: *Le Caméra Stylo*', which fulminated against the assembly-line method of producing films which the French industry had inherited from Hollywood, and where front-office interference ensured that maverick films were tailored to fit tried-and-trusted formulas:

'Our sensibilities have been in danger of getting blunted by those everyday films which, year in year out, show their tired and conventional faces to the world.'

The great film-makers, Astruc argued, directors such as Renoir, Welles and Bresson, were using the camera much as a writer uses a pen (*stylo*), to make a personal statement or to describe a personal vision. When Astruc came to illustrate his arguments by making films such as *Le Rideau Cramoisi* (1953, *The Crimson Curtain*), *Les Mauvaises Rencontres* (1955, Bad Encounters) and *Une Vie* (1958, *One Life*) the results were stiff and glacially correct, intelligent but fatally tinged with the aura of artiness that invariably used to infect Hollywood Movies on the rare occasions when they aimed at 'art'.

But the seed had been sown. In the early Fifties *Cahiers du Cinéma* took Astruc's argument a stage further in a series of close critical analyses of the

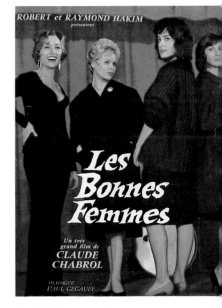

Top left: the nouvelle vague *directors at Cannes, 1959; from front left, the rows consist of (first) Truffaut, Vogel, Félix, Séchan; (second) Molinaro, Baratier, Valère; (third) Reichenbach, Hossein, Pollet, Vadim, Camus; (fourth) Chabrol, Doniol-Valcroze, Godard, Rozier. Top right: a carnival scene in Rio de Janeiro from* Orfeu Negro *Above: four shop girls are disappointed in their dreams of a better life; left to right: Ginette (Stéphane Audran), Rita (Lucile Saint-Simon), Jane (Bernadette Lafont) and Jacqueline (Clotilde Joano)*

Above: André Bazin, who died in 1958 at 40, helped to found Cahiers du Cinéma *and encouraged the younger critics who were to become the principal film-makers of the* nouvelle vague

Above: Jack Nicholson plays an introspective night-time disc jockey in Bob Rafelson's The King of Marvin Gardens. *His outgoing, ambitious brother lives in a fantasy world on the fringes of crime and is finally shot dead by one of the women he lives with. The unusual Atlantic City locations and the feeling of an unpredictably off-beat genre movie recall the sense of discovery in the early* nouvelle vague *films. The title comes from the game of* Monopoly *(American version)*

work of outstanding film-makers such as Hitchcock and Hawks who had worked exclusively within the major studio system, mostly in Hollywood itself. Similar articles and reviews drew attention to Samuel Fuller, Robert Aldrich, Don Siegel and Jacques Tourneur who had higherto been neglected as mere studio journeymen. All these critiques amounted to a demonstration of how a creative personality could surface even if the script was uncongenial to the director or had to be shaped to fit box-office preconceptions.

These ideas were formulated as what later came to be known as the 'auteur theory', after a cautionary article by the critic André Bazin, 'La Politique des Auteurs', published in 1957. *Cahiers du Cinéma*'s concepts were unique in the history of the cinema's avant-garde movements in that they accepted the realities of the film industry and the need to keep an eye on the box-office. Even so, the argument ran, a true film-maker could shape characters, situations and attitudes in order to impose a distinctive personal style. He should infiltrate his personal preoccupations and, if necessary, transform alien material into his own.

The early films of the *Cahiers du Cinéma* critics are not immediately recognizable as 'Art' – in the sense that a Henry James novel, as opposed to a pulp thriller by David Goodis or Cornell Woolrich, is considered to be 'Art'. Truffaut started his career in feature films with a down-to-earth tale of a delinquent boy, *The 400 Blows*, and then moved into gangster territory with *Tirez sur le Pianiste* (1960, *Shoot the Pianist*) based on a David Goodis thriller. Godard began with *A Bout de Souffle* (1960, *Breathless*), a casually joky gangster story, continued with *Le Petit Soldat* (1960, The Little Soldier), an exploration of political conscience so pragmatic that it was banned as unacceptable to either Right or Left, and then proceeded in *Une Femme Est une Femme* (1961, *A Woman Is a Woman*) to dismantle the mystique of the Hollywood musical with a destructive curiosity that left the pieces lying around like a disembowelled clock. Chabrol might have been guilty of headily abstract theological speculations in his first feature, *Le Beau Serge* (1958, *Handsome Serge*), but he was careful to anchor them in an

earthily detailed portrait of village life and, what is more, to avoid ever making the same mistake again.

Shoot the Pianist, with its mercurially shifting moods and ambiguity as to whether it means to make the audience laugh or cry, is of course far from Hollywood's gangster conventions. It is as much part of Truffaut's personal world as *Breathless* is idiosyncratically Godard's. At first glance, Godard seems to be playing the genre game with absolute fidelity. His hero Michel Poiccard (Jean-Paul Belmondo) pays a small-time thug's tribute of imitation to Humphrey Bogart; there is raw and

Pretending to make genre movies, young directors ditched the over-literary 'tradition of quality'

contrasty photography, with casual bursts of violent action – all dedicated 'to Monogram Pictures', Hollywood's Poverty Row home of the cheap action flick.

At second glance, the unorthodox three-part structure of the film dominates. Sandwiched between the swift, staccato beginning and ending, the elaborately sinuous sequence of Michel Poiccard's lengthy bedroom conversations with his girl (Jean Seberg), who will eventually betray him to the police, suggests that this man, apparently living only for the moment, *may* perhaps be shyly envisaging a future for himself. Even in this film which delivers the pleasures of action to its audience,

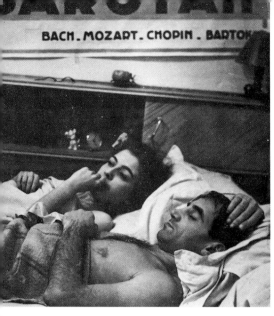

Godard has managed to subvert the genre conventions by inserting a time of reflection, a long moment when thought is more to the fore than violence.

In the early days of the *nouvelle vague*, each new film was a major event, eagerly awaited by anyone who cared about cinema, and excitedly scanned for conceptual innovations and technical audacities. But these were all too quickly transformed into the newly current clichés of film-making when industry hacks gratefully adopted them as ready-made sales packaging for conventional films.

Now the dust has settled and audiences barely notice – to cite the most obvious example – the jump-cuts once hailed with critical jubilation as the most radical new departure offered by *Breathless*. As a number of older film-makers somewhat tetchily pointed out at the time, there was nothing new about jump-cutting: the technique had been familiar in Hollywood for years, and little or no critical excitement had been noticeable when, six years before Godard and *Breathless*, Kurosawa used it every bit as systematically in *Shichinin No Samurai* (1954, *Seven Samurai*).

But where Kurosawa used the jump-cut in its traditional role as a purely technical means towards an end – speeding up the action, keeping things constantly on the move – Godard lent it an additional, metaphorical dimension. In *Breathless* the jump-cutting does indeed keep the film racing along in amiable pastiche of the Monogram B movies; but, acquiring an undertone of insolence through being identified with Belmondo's raffishly but ineffectually Bogartian Michel Poiccard, the technique *also* implies a parody-appraisal of the

Hollywood thriller genre as a whole.

Looking back, it is apparent now that the *nouvelle vague* films – Godard's in particular – generated so much electricity because they comprised a critique of both the cinema's past and its present, rejecting what was worthless in film history, sifting out what remained valid, raising signposts for future exploration. As Godard remarked in an interview in 1962:

'Criticism taught us to admire both Rouch and Eisenstein. From it we learned not to deny one aspect of the cinema in favour of another. From it we also learned to make films from a certain perspective, and to know that if something has already been done there is no point in doing it again. A young author writing today knows that Molière and Shakespeare exist. We were the first directors to know that Griffith exists. Even Carné, Delluc and René Clair, when they made their first films, had no real critical or historical background. Even Renoir had very little; but then of course *he* had genius.'

Some may feel that the *nouvelle vague* played itself out well before the Eighties; Truffaut died in 1984 and both Chabrol and Rhomer began to confine their talents to thrillers and conversation pieces – although still fruitfully harvesting their own idiosyncratic fields. Rivette's name probably means little to the current filmgoing generation. Godard – carried on being Godard. But they have their heirs in such as Jean-Luc Bidou and Jean-Jacques Beneix. And there is no denying their influence, albeit perhaps subconscious, on many excellent American films that followed, from *Badlands* and *Night Moves* through *Mean Streets*, *The Conversation* and *The King of Marvin Gardens*.

Top left: in bed with Léna (Marie Dubois), a waitress from the bar where he plays piano, Charlie (Charles Aznavour) recalls his earlier life as a concert pianist, Edouard Saroyan, a career cut short by his wife's suicide, in Shoot the Pianist. *Top right: Truffaut's first feature led to a whole series of autobiographical films about Antoine Doinel (Jean-Pierre Léaud). Above far left: Truffaut also wrote the original story for* Breathless *as an early draft for the same series, to be about the boy grown up after reform school and the army. But Godard's Michel (Jean-Paul Belmondo) and Patricia (Jean Seberg) are his own characters though he followed Truffaut's plotline quite closely. Above left: shooting a scene near Geneva for* Le Petit Soldat; *in the car, Bruno Forestier (Michel Subor) is making a first, unsuccessful attempt to assassinate a Swiss radio commentator sympathetic to the cause of Algerian independence. Above: stalemate between lovers Emile (Jean-Claude Brialy) and Angéla (Anna Karina) in* Une Femme Est une Femme; *in which she wants a baby, but he doesn't*

LAST YEAR IN MARIENBAD

What really happened 'last year in Marienbad'? Rarely has critical speculation over a film's content been so active. It was reported that not even the director, Alain Resnais, and the writer, Alain Robbe-Grillet, were in complete agreement. Resnais claimed that an encounter had occurred the previous year while Robbe-Grillet declared that one sometimes had the impression that the whole episode was a figment of the narrator's imagination. But perhaps this much-publicized divergence of views was a calculated ploy, a hint to the spectator as to how the film should be approached – that is, with no preconceived idea. One eminent French critic, Jacques Brunius, declared unequivocally after several viewings that it was the greatest film ever made; others dismissed it as a pretentious art-movie spoof. One thing is certain: a true appreciation of the film calls for the audience's complete surrender to its unique form and mood.

The first voice to be heard is that of the narrator, faintly and then more clearly, as the camera examines the furnishings of a vast, baroque hotel with its endless, empty corridors, numbered rooms, ornate ceilings and glittering mirrors. The voice intones: 'Once again I walk, once again, along these corridors, across these salons, these galleries, in this edifice from another century . . .' In one of the great salons an audience sits motionless, watching a play. 'And now,' says the on-stage actress, 'I am yours'. The curtain falls. The play's conclusion prefigures the final surrender of the film's heroine.

Gradually, through snatches of overheard conversations, shots of curiously posed single figures or static groups, the film establishes its disturbing world, which might be dream or stylized reality. The three central characters start to reveal their identities: the melancholy woman who is staying in the hotel with a gaunt-faced man who may, or may not, be her husband and an insinuating stranger, the narrator, who claims that the woman agreed a year ago to meet him again now.

She denies all knowledge of him or previous acquaintanceship but the stranger relentlessly pursues his detailed tactic of persuasion. Does she not recall the time when, while walking through the garden, she slipped and broke off the heel of her shoe? Later on, when they are walking together, she stumbles and grabs his arm for support. This is seen in long-shot and it is uncertain whether she actually breaks the heel. Is this the scene that, according to his claim, happened in the past, or a re-enactment, or history repeating itself? In this delicate fusion between past and present nothing can ever be quite certain.

Several questions suggest themselves. Is this strange château, set in its formal gardens, an exclusive nursing home and is the stranger perhaps the woman's psychoanalyst, striving to make her recall a past emotional experience which she has unconsciously blocked from her memory? And her clothes, quintessential expression of outré Parisian chic by Chanel . . . do they provide a clue? It seems that in general a white dress is worn for scenes in the past and black for the present – but not quite consistently. What about the

shadowy figure of the man who 'may be her husband' ... husband? lover? brother? He is frequently seen playing a pre-ordained match-stick game which he invariably wins. Usually it is the stranger whom he defeats.

At one point, when the stranger seems almost on the verge of forcing the woman to admit the reality of the past events he describes and has left the couple alone, she turns to her 'husband' and begs him, with a hint of desperation, not to leave her. His reply is reasoned and cool: 'But it is you who are leaving me – you know that!' When his prediction proves true, she departs with no sense of joy or fulfilment; she seems rather to have left her haven for an unknown destination. In this contest of wills and persuasion she appears to be the victim of an inexorable fate, possibly leading to her death or some kind of oblivion.

The eternal fascination of *Last Year in Marienbad* is that each time the spectator feels sure of having grasped the key to its sphinx-like riddle, it presents another aspect to disprove his theory. Though not completely convincing, the theory of the recurrent dream is worth considering. The obsessive nature of such dreams still allows for some

measure of improvisation of the events to suit the dreamer's fancy; they can incorporate acceptance and rejection of particular elements – even adjusted replays.

When, for example, the woman asks the stranger to leave her alone, he leans against a balustrade which crumbles under the pressure. There is a quick cutaway. This must surely be a moment of fantasy and when the balustrade is next seen it ought to be intact. But it is still broken! Does this reflect the dreamer's unshakeable conviction that the event actually occurred? Is it not more likely to be the woman's wish-fulfilment, a persistent longing to rid herself of the importunate stranger. On reflection, the second explanation is more plausible. But with everything in this enigmatic film it is a matter of 'I think so'; never 'I know for sure'.

On further inspection, *Last Year in Marienbad*, with its subtle clues, its intricate juggling with past and present, its depiction of a reality that might be dream or of a dream with a hallucinatory hint of reality, takes on the aspect of a masterly detective story. The figures – for they are figures rather than personages – are moved through their

exquisitely controlled paces by a director who demonstrates the precision of a master chess player. Its enclosed world has the mesmeric

quality of a superior fairy-tale with, like many of the most haunting fairy-tales, a touch of veiled menace.

Directed by Alain Resnais, 1961

Prod co: Terra-Film/Société Nouvelle des Films Cormoran/Précitel/Como-Films/Les Films Tamara/Cinetel/Silver Films (Paris)/Cineriz (Rome). **prod:** Pierre Courau (Précitel), Raymond Froment (Terra-Film). **sc:** Alain Robbe-Grillet. **photo:** Sacha Vierny (Dyaliscope). **ed:** Henri Colpi, Jasmine Chasney. **art dir:** Jacques Saulnier. **mus:** Francis Seyrig. **cost:** Chanel, Bernard Evein. **sd:** Guy Villette. **r/t:** 94 minutes. World premiere: Venice Film Festival, 29 August 1961. Released in the USA and GB as *Last Year in Marienbad*.
Cast: Delphine Seyrig (*A*), Giorgio Albertazzi (*X*), Sacha Pitoëff (*M*), Françoise Bertin, Luce Garcia-Ville, Héléna Kornel, Françoise Spira, Karin Toeche-Mittler, Pierre Barbaud, Wilhelm Von Deek, Jean Lanier, Gérard Lorin, Davide Montemuri, Gilles Quéant, Gabriel Werner.

A vast, grandiose hotel, set in formal grounds, is sparsely peopled with guests standing around in statuesque poses (1) or watching an obscure drama (2) or playing an apparently simple game (3). The hotel provides the setting for a strange encounter: a beautiful woman, A, staying there with M, who is possibly her husband (4), is approached by a man, X (5). He claims that they had had a close relationship here the previous year, when they had

arranged to meet again a year thence with the intention of going away together (6). She denies all knowledge of this (7). But he assails her with such persuasive detail (8) of their shared experience that her resistance crumbles and he prevails upon her to leave with him. She sits rigidly in her bedroom awaiting the stroke of midnight before joining him at the appointed rendezvous outside, from which she can see the hotel she is leaving forever (9).

Directed by François Truffaut, 1962
Prod co: Les Films du Carrosse/SEDIF. **prod man:** Marcel Berbert. **sc:** François Truffaut, Jean Gruault, from the novel by Henri-Pierre Roché. **photo** (Franscope): Raoul Coutard. **ed:** Claudine Bouché. **cost:** Fred Capel. **mus:** Georges Delerue. **song:** Boris Bassiak. **ass dir:** Georges Pellegrin, Robert Bober. **narr:** Michel Subor. **r/t:** 105 minutes. Paris premiere, 27 January 1962. Released in USA and GB as *Jules and Jim*.
Cast: Jeanne Moreau (*Catherine*), Oskar Werner (*Jules*), Henri Serre (*Jim*), Vanna Urbino (*Gilberte*), Boris Bassiak (*Albert*), Sabine Haudepin (*Sabine*), Marie Dubois (*Thérèse*), Jean-Louis Richard (*first customer in the café*), Michel Varesano (*second customer in the café*), Pierre Fabre (*drunkard in café*), Danielle Bassiak (*Albert's friend*), Bernard Largemains (*Merlin*), Elen Bober (*Mathilde*), Kate Noëlle (*Birgitta*), Anny Nielsen (*Lucy*), Christiane Wagner (*Helga*).

Based on a little-known autobiographical novel written by Henry-Pierre Roché when in his seventies, *Jules et Jim* was François Truffaut's third film and is still the one by which he is most affectionately known. Endlessly inventive and unquenchably high-spirited, it is one of those rare films which, after no more than a single viewing, inspire virtually total recall. Even its soundtrack continues to possess a naggingly memorable life of its own, thanks to Jeanne Moreau's breathy giggle, Oskar Werner's softly accented French and, not least, Georges Delerue's haunting theme music, which over the years has become almost the signature tune of the *nouvelle vague*.

Most astonishing of all, however, is the masterly ease with which, in this tale of an intermittently felicitous *ménage à trois*, Truffaut modulates between comedy (or rather, gaiety), drama and, ultimately, tradegy, while deploying a battery of perilously modish devices – jump cuts, freeze frames, nostalgic iris shots. His numerous imitators have managed only to hitch these techniques to the kind of broad comic romp of which Tony Richardson's *Tom Jones* (1963) might be the prototype. Though the triangle formed by Jules, Jim and the flighty, elusive Catherine is, in its restlessly shifting sympathies, anything but eternal and too often overcast to be considered unreservedly idyllic, none of the film's more sombre elements ever succeeds in snuffing out its youthful exuberance. For an example of how subtly it functions, one need look no further than Catherine herself, in Jeanne Moreau's enchanting and somehow 'definitive' performance. Rarely has the cinema invested one of its classic *femmes fatales* with such generous helpings of humour, charm and tenderness. Yet *fatale* she unquestionably is: figuratively, by the cavalier treatment which she metes out to her pair of suitors, capriciously switching her amorous attentions from one to the other and back again, even ditching both of them for the more immediately gratifying stimulation of an affair with a casual pick-up; and literally, at the end, when she nonchalantly drives Jim and herself headlong into the Seine. It is, above all, Catherine's mercurial femininity which has allowed the film to wear so much better than those sweatily explicit dramas of uncensored passion made during the same period (for instance, Jack Clayton's *Room at the Top*, 1959). Sex here is fun, at least on occasion. If the three protagonists fail to arrive at a workable 'design for living' no moral condemnation is implied by Truffaut: less unconventional relationships prove equally doomed.

Prior to their relationship with Catherine, the two Bohemian young men are so bewitched by the placidly mysterious features of a Greek goddess on a lantern slide that they promptly set off for the Adriatic to catch a glimpse of the original sculpture. Catherine, too, is an 'ideal' woman (the most perfectly realized, perhaps, in Truffaut's extensive gallery of portraits), all things to both men, separately or together – and the tragedy of the final suicide is not only her own and Jim's death, but the inconsolable solitude of Jules.

The balance between tragedy and comedy, so miraculously maintained throughout, derives also from the fact that, as the characters never physically age (though at the end Moreau sports granny glasses, the face behind them is just as radiantly, mischievously beautiful), it is from outside that the passage of time comes abruptly and cruelly to impinge on their intimate universe.

World War I, evoked in newsreel footage that is startlingly stretched out to the full dimensions of the CinemaScope screen, causes the two friends to fear that one might kill the other (his name notwithstanding, Jules is German).

Then, suddenly, it is already 1933, as in a cinema the trio watch more newsreel footage of bookburning in Nazi Germany. And the advancing years are more benignly telegraphed by the ubiquitous Picasso paintings, passing through several stages of the artist's evolution. From the very beginning, however, the film has ominously hinted at the impermanence of their happiness: Catherine's first whimsical leap into the Seine; her ritualized burning of letters from past lovers ('old flames'), which almost results in her self-immolation; and the spectre of jealousy in a Rhineland chalet, a striking crane shot encapsulating both a nervously pacing Jim downstairs and Catherine and Jules romping ecstatically in the upstairs bedroom.

Of all the *nouvelle vague* directors, it was Francois Truffaut who carried on the tradition of French lyricism out of Vigo and Renoir despite once being its most vitriolic critic: in *Jules et Jim* his feeling for the countryside, sensuously captured by Raoul Coutard's ravishing black-and-white photography, is worthy – as is the whole film – of Renoir's *Une Partie de Campagne* (1936, A Day in the Country). And if Godard was without question the more revolutionary figure, it is surprisingly hard to imagine the course of contemporary cinema bereft of Truffaut's inimitable (though often imitated) delicacy and charm.

Below: Truffaut discusses a point with Jeanne Moreau who gives a moving performance as the capricious Catherine

1

2

3

4

In pre-World War I Paris, two young men, the German Jules and Frenchman Jim, form an indestructible friendship (1). The situation changes however when Catherine, a beautiful but volatile young woman, enters their lives (2) and begins an affair with the diffident Jules (3).

They marry and, with their small daughter (4), settle in Germany; when war breaks out soon after, the once inseparable friends find themselves conscripted on opposite sides. After the war Jim, now a successful journalist in Paris, pays the couple a visit, during which he is deceived into believing that they are idyllically happy (5). But Jules sadly confesses in a letter that he is unable to hold on to Catherine and even encourages his friend, in a desperate attempt to keep his wife, to sleep with her (6).

Jim, no less defeated by her capricious moods and casual infidelity, soon returns to Paris and the passively loyal girlfriend, Gilberte, whom he had left behind. Several years pass. Jules and Catherine settle in Paris and the friends seem, on the surface, to have resumed their earlier relationship (7). But Jim, having recovered his independence, refuses to see it swallowed up once more in what he knows to be an unworkable situation. Whereupon the ever-inscrutable Catherine invites him into her car and drives them both into the Seine. Jules is left alone (8).

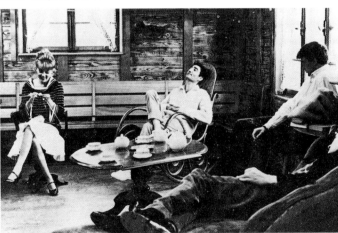

5

6

7

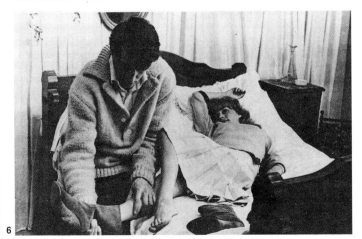

8

Jean-Luc Godard

Whatever is thought of his films, it cannot be denied that Jean-Luc Godard is the most important director of the last twenty years. This is shown by the enormous influence his films have had on other film-makers all over the world, and although the films of Alain Resnais, François Truffaut, Eric Rohmer or Jacques Rivette may be preferred, no-one has revolutionized cinematic ideas as much as Godard.

He burst onto the international film scene in 1960 with his first feature *A Bout de Souffle*. Unfortunately the English title – *Breathless* – is a mistranslation, for '*a bout de souffle*' means 'out of breath', whereas 'breathless' has a more romantic, less despairing tone. But in another sense his film career had begun almost ten years earlier with his film criticism which first appeared in the short-lived *La Gazette du Cinéma*, and later in *Cahiers du Cinéma*. Born in

Is Godard brilliant or are his films impenetrably obscure and boring? Have audiences yet to catch up with his vision as they had to do with the work of cinema's other great innovators Eisenstein and Welles? One thing is certain – no other post-war director has inspired such confusion of admiration and scorn or has had such effect on the making, viewing and understanding of movies

Paris in 1930, Godard was first educated in Switzerland and went on to the Sorbonne to study ethnology. It was during his university days that he discovered his passion for cinema and, like Louis Delluc, his Twenties predecessor, he began his film career by writing about it.

Once upon a time

From the very beginning he considered himself a storyteller rather than an essayist, 'I write essays in the form of novels or novels in the

form of essays. Instead of writing criticism, I now film it' he wrote, and it is true that conventional narrative – the backbone of most cinema – has never been the most important element in his films. Godard believes that the distinguishing feature of modern art is that it 'never tells a story'. Of course in his earlier films he felt the need for some sort of fictional support:

'I don't really like telling a story . . . I prefer to use a kind of tapestry, a background on which I can embroider my own ideas. But I do

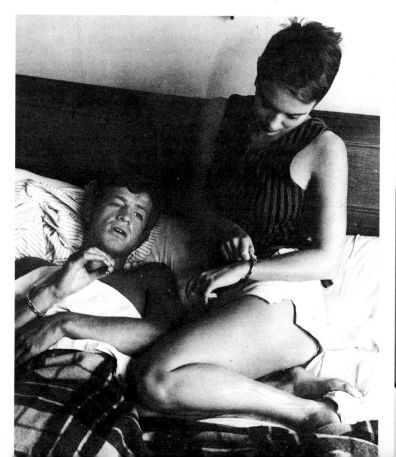

Two or three things we know about him

generally need a story. A conventional one serves as well, perhaps even best.'

As a story, *Breathless* is not much different from any of the American thriller novels he was later to adapt – D. Hitchen's *Fools Gold* for *Bande à Part* (1964, *The Outsiders*), and Lionel White's *Obsession* for *Pierrot le Fou* (1965, Pierrot the Fool). Even when he adapted literary works of a higher level – Moravia's *A Ghost at Noon* in *Le Mépris* (1963, *Contempt*) – he always transformed the original material with a massive injection of documentary material.

'You can either start with fiction or with documentary. But whichever you start with, you will inevitably find the other'. Eventually documentary was to gain the upper hand.

It is often said that Godard's career can be split into two – his films before and after 1968. With the advantage of hindsight, however, it

Above: Godard at London's National Film Theatre in 1980. Far left: a car-thief turned killer (Jean-Paul Belmondo) is finally given away to the police by his girlfriend (Jean Seberg) in Breathless. *Left: a young scriptwriter's marriage breaks up when his wife is attracted to the producer. Below: Raoul (Sady Rebbot) with Nana (Anna Karina), the prostitute in* Vivre Sa Vie. *Below right: Karina showing her emotional range as a woman desperate for a baby in* Une Femme Est une Femme *(1961, A Woman Is a Woman).*

seems as if the break was less violent than had been thought. His films before *La Chinoise, ou Plutot à la Chinoise* (1967, The Chinese Girl), in which a group of students sets up a Marxist cell during their holidays, were less overtly political than those which followed, and yet *Vivre Sa Vie* (1962, It's My Life) was in fact already as much a study of prostitution as the story of its heroine Nana; *Le Petit Soldat* (1960, The Little Soldier) was the first French film to attempt to deal with the Algerian war – and it was banned by the French government until 1963 as a result. Even the more intimate films – *Une Femme Mariée* (1964, *A Married Woman*), or *Contempt* – could be called studies in micropolitics, the politics of the couple, the politics of sex. And a film like *Deux ou Trois Choses Que Je Sais d'Elle* (1967, *Two or Three Things I Know About Her*) was in many ways a sociological essay.

The main difference between Godard and most of his contemporaries was that he was not only interested in the social content of his films, he was even more concerned by the way in which they were made. The nub of Godard's pre-occupation as a film-maker was that he didn't merely put forward political or social ideas, he was after the destruction of those forms that accept the *status quo*. The only way to attack the dominant ideology, according to Godard, was to attack the forms in art that, perhaps unknowingly, proceed from it. It was not sufficient merely to make a political

film, it was even more important to make a film politically.

The art of life

All Godard's films – even *Masculin-Féminin* (1966) which on the surface looks as casually put together as a TV film – reveal a very complex formal substructure under scrutiny. At the same time as being insistent on 'realism' – direct sound, filming on location – Godard was equally concerned in taking these pieces of direct reality and abstracting them. He takes a moment of real life, a moment in time, and transforms it into art through his editing. Most of his films are broken up into sections, tableaux, or chapters, just as individual sequences are often like mosaics, with each shot contributing a tiny tessera that goes to make up the complete picture. Godard is fascinated with the possibility of capturing reality on film, and then (and only then) doing something with it.

But if there was not such a total break between his films of the Sixties and those of the Seventies, it is true that in the Seventies – or even as early as *Un Film Comme les Autres* (1969, A Film Like the Others) – Godard gave up both stories and stars. He deliberately attempted to make unpopular films, and succeeded. As he explained at the time, 'The only way to be an intellectual revolutionary was to give up being an intellectual.' He did not want his films to be liked, he did not want them to be consumer objects, he did not want them to be

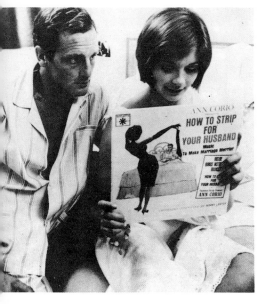

Above: a lesson in lust – Bernard Noël and Macha Méril in Une Femme Mariée. *Above right: despite a basic plot,* Masculin-Féminin *is a study of 'the younger generation'. Above, far right: inspired by a newspaper report, this film charts the day of a housewife whoring for pocket-money. Below: the apartment of the Marxist students in* La Chinoise. *Below right: a couple (Jean Yanne and Mireille Darc) have difficulty removing 'Romeo' (Jean-Pierre Léaud) from the phone-booth in* Weekend

accepted by the middle-classes. He set out to disturb, to frustrate, even to test the patience of his audience. But in so doing he successfully suppressed most of his talents as a film-maker. Although he was not a storyteller, his earlier films allowed his talent for the lyrical full rein; and although he often cast his stars against the grain – eking out extraordinary performances, such as Mireille Darc's in *Weekend* (1967) – they did contribute a great deal to his films.

In his post-1968 period of total ascetism, he

masochistically would not allow himself to do what he could do best. The critic Vincent Canby wrote of *Vladimir et Rosa* (1971) that it looked weak and under-nourished, like someone who has given his salary to The Cause, and must subsist on fish and chips. This is, metaphorically, exactly what Godard had done. If proof be needed, compare *Tout Va Bien* (1972, All Goes Well) with others of the period: there, the presence of Jane Fonda and Yves Montand again allowed him to display his talent for

Filmography
1950 Quadrille (short) (prod; + act. only). '51 Présentation, ou Charlotte et son Steack (short) (actor only). '54 Opération Béton (short) (+ prod; + sc; + ed) (SWITZ). '55 Une Femme Coquette (short) (+ prod; + sc; + photo; + ed; + act) (SWITZ). '56 Le Coup du Berger (short) (actor only). '57 Tous les Garçons s'Appelent Patrick/Charlotte et Veronique (short) (GB: All Boys Are Called Patrick); Le Sonate à Kreuzer (short) (prod. only). '58 Charlotte et son Jules (short) (+ sc; + ed; + voice); Une Histoire d'Eau (short) (co-dir; + co-sc; + narr). '59 Le Signe du Lion (actor only) (GB: The Sign of Leo). '60 Le Petit Soldat (+ sc; + act) (released in 1963); A Bout de Souffle (+ sc; + act) (USA/GB: Breathless); Paris Nous Appartient (actor only) (USA/GB: Paris Belongs To Us). '61 Une Femme Est une Femme (+ sc; + lyr) (USA/GB: A Woman Is a Woman); Cléo de 5 à 7 (actor only) (FR-IT) (GB: Cleo From 5 to 7); Les Fiancés du Pont Macdonald (short) (actor only). '62 Les Sept Péchés Capitaux ep La Paresse (+ sc) (FR-IT) (USA: The Seven Capital

Sins ep Sloth); Le Soleil dans l'Oeil (actor only); Vivre Sa Vie (+ sc; + voice) (USA: My Life To Live; GB: It's My Life). '63 RoGoPaG/Laviamoci Il Cervello ep Le Nouveau Monde (+ sc; + act) (IT-FR); Les Carabiniers (+ co-sc) (FR-IT) (GB: The Soldiers); Shéhérazade (actor only); Le Mépris (+ sc; + act) (FR-IT) (USA/GB: Contempt); The Directors (doc. short) (appearance as himself only) (USA); Petit Jour (doc. short) (appearance as himself only). '64 Bande à Part (+ sc; + narr) (USA: Band of Outsiders; GB: The Outsiders); Statues (doc. short) (co-comm; + voice only); Paparazzi (doc. short) (appearance as himself only); Témoinage sur Bardot-Godard (doc. short) (appearance as himself only); Begegnung Mit Fritz Lang (doc. short) (appearance as himself only); Les Plus Belles Escroqueries du Monde ep Le Grand Escroc (+ sc; + narr; + act) (subsequently cut from film) (FR-IT-JAP-NETH); Une Femme Mariée (+ sc) (USA: The Married Woman; GB: A Married Woman); Reportage sur Orly (short). '65 Paris Vu Par . . . ep Montparnasse-Levallois (+ sc); Alphaville, une Étrange

Aventure de Lemmy Caution (+ sc) (FR-IT); Pierrot le Fou (+ sc) (FR-IT). '66 Masculin-Féminin (+ sc) (FR-SWED); L'Espion (actor only) (FR-GER) (GB: The Defector); Made in USA (+ sc; + voice). '67 Deux ou Trois Choses Que Je Sais d'Elle (+ sc; + narr) (USA/GB: Two Or Three Things I Know About Her); Le Plus Vieux Métier du Monde ep L'An 2000 (+ sc) (subsequently shown separately); La Chinoise, ou Plutot à la Chinoise (+ sc); Loin du Vietnam (co-dir; + co-sc; + co-narr; + appearance as himself) (USA/GB: Far From Vietnam); ep L'Amore/Andata e Ritorno dei Figli Prodighi (+ sc) (IT-FR) (USA/GB: Love and Anger) (shown separately; part of complete film: Amore e Rabbia/Vangelo 70, 1968); Weekend (+ sc) (FR-IT). '68 Cinétracts (anonymous co-dir); One Plus One/Sympathy for the Devil (+ sc; + voice) (GB). '69 Le Gai Savoir (+ sc) (FR-GER); Un Film Comme les Autres (+ sc; + voice); British Sounds (GB) (USA: See You at Mao)*; Voices (doc) (appearance as himself only) (GB). '70 Pravda (FR-CZ); Le Vent d'Est (FR-IT-GER); Lotte in Italia (IT). '71 1

directing actors. Although the film was austerely made, his genius for the staggering image, and his unique sense of sound and editing were very much in evidence. And he went back to fiction – although only as a support – with a large injection of documentary material. It was precisely the dialectics between reality and fiction that made *Tout Va Bien* a more successful film than his other films at that time.

Paris belongs to 'them'

Tout Va Bien was not the commercial success Godard had hoped for and he abandoned Paris and the world of commercial film-making, retiring to Grenoble to set up his own company Sonimage, making films for cassette and television. The films made in Grenoble were interesting in many ways, particularly *Ici et Ailleurs* (1976, Here and Elsewhere), in which he tries to explain why he could never finish his 1971 pro-Palestinian film *Jusqu'à la Victoire*. However, the Grenoble films were not seen by many people and Godard concentrated on television. He had made two films for television in 1969 – *British Sounds* for Britain's London Weekend Television, and *Le Gai Savoir* for the French radio and television company ORTF – but neither was ever shown on the small screen. This time he was more successful, for *Sur et Sous la Communication (Six Fois Deux)* (1978, On and Under Communication, Six Times Two) did get shown on French television – but only late at night and at the height of summer when most people were on vacation.

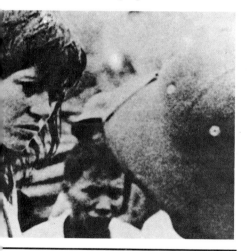

After one more attempt, Godard returned to feature-film making with *Sauve Qui Peut (La Vie)* (1980, *Slow Motion*) and the film achieved a greater success and wider audiences than any of his films since *Weekend*.

However, *Slow Motion* is not a masterpiece in the sense of being a perfectly balanced work of art. On the one hand it is an encapsulation of all his previous work, both of his Sixties' feature films and his Seventies' documentary essays, and on the other it is like all Godard's best films, an attempt to deal differently with familiar themes. If it is less perfect than *Two or Three Things I Know About Her*, that is because it is striking out on radically new lines and because Godard's sensibility matches the confusion of the world as it enters the Eighties. The hero of the film is actually called Paul Godard; he is a man at the end of his tether, and the film is a pessimistic and fragmentary reflection of the chaotic late Seventies, a collision course with catastrophe.

Many elements from Godard's earlier films reappear in *Slow Motion*. There is a parody of the end of *Vivre Sa Vie* in the scene where the prostitute (Isabelle Huppert) is not killed, but spanked by her pimp. The fragmentation of a film like *Made in USA* (1966) is surpassed in this new film, for Godard uses stop-motion technique to fragment even the simplest of movements. Probably inspired by the Instant Replay of television sportscasts, as well as by the early pre-cinema experiments of the Frenchman Étienne-Jules Marey, and the Anglo-American Eadweard Muybridge, he breaks down movement into its constituent steps, just as in earlier films he had broken sequences into brief shots.

Bewitched, bothered and bewildered

The main thematic difference between *Slow Motion* and its predecessors of the Sixties is that it is the story of three women and one man, whereas the earlier films usually dealt with one woman and two men (*Vivre Sa Vie, Contempt, Une Femme Mariée*). This change is particularly significant in *Slow Motion*: Godard is able to split the 'eternal feminine' into three because in a sense *all* the characters are

Left: this news photograph of Jane Fonda in Vietnam received stiff critical analysis in Godard's A Letter to Jane (1973). Below: the young prostitute (Isabelle Huppert) and a client discuss her life in Slow Motion

Godard himself. The fact that he calls his hero Paul Godard should not fool the audience, for there is as much of Godard in the three women as in the man. The prostitute represents that side of Godard which feels as if he has often had to 'sell' himself to make the films he wants to; Isabella Rimbaud, the girl who decides to leave town for the simple life in the country, is an image of Godard's flight first from Paris to Grenoble, and then to the Swiss countryside where he now lives; and Paul's ex-wife and their daughter Cecile would seem to represent all the women who have left Godard – Anna Karina, Anne Wiazemsky. They were not only his wives or mistresses, they were his stars.

Anne-Marie Mieville, Godard's present companion, is not an actress but she has contributed to his films over the past seven years. On the soundtrack of *Ici et Ailleurs* she intervenes to criticize things Godard says, and she is credited as co-scriptwriter on *Slow Motion*. Perhaps the fact that she is not an actress, or that Godard has not tried to put her in front of the camera, has obliged him to deal with several women in this film.

In spite of the fact that *Slow Motion* is an accurately chaotic reflection of the times in which it was made, it is also a highly accomplished work of art. A first viewing is perplexing or disorientating, but a second look reveals that for all its portrayal of chaos, it is a beautifully organized film. It is no accident that the credits read *composed* by Godard rather than *directed* by Godard. Music may be the title of only one of the four sections of the film (the others are The Imaginary, Fear, and Commerce), but the whole film is a musical composition with each section bearing a tempo marking (largo, allegro, etc) and all the themes coming together at the end.

Tales of the unexpected

To critics and viewers of the Eighties, Godard's once-famous 'unpredictability' has perhaps become all too predictable. *Prénom Carmen* (1984) and *King Lear* (1987) bear little resemblance to Bizet and Shakespeare, and *Hail Mary* (1985), updating the Nativity with low-life participants, outraged the Papacy. But these should not be allowed to diminish the fact that Godard's early films, like them or hate them, were instrumental in galvanizing the slow motion of cinema's liberation from its hitherto narrative restrictions.

P.M./One Parallel Movie (+sc) (USA) (incorporating footage from unfinished film: 1 A.M./One American Movie); Vladimir et Rosa (+act) (GER-USA) (USA/GB: Vladimir and Rosa); Two American Audiences (doc. short) (appearance as himself only) (USA). '72 Tout Va Bien (co-dir; +co-sc); La Longue Marche de Jean-Luc Godard (doc) (appearance as himself only) (BELG). '73 A Letter to Jane, or Investigation About a Still (co-dir; +co-prod; +co-sc; +narr). '75 Numéro Deux (+co-prod; +co-sc; +appearance as himself). '76 Ici et Ailleurs (co-dir; +co-sc) (incorporating footage from unfinished film: Jusqu'à la Victoire, 1971). '78 Comment ça Va (co-dir; +co-sc); Sur et Sous la Communication (Six Fois Deux) (co-dir; +co-sc)*; Der Kleine Godard (appearance as himself only) (GER) (GB: Junior Godard). '80 France/Tour/Détour/Deux/Enfants (co-dir; +co-sc)*; Sauve Qui Peut (La Vie) (co-dir; +co-sc) (FR-SWITZ) (USA: Every Man for Himself; GB: Slow Motion) '80 Passion; Comment Ca Va? (short). '84 Prénom Carmen (+act); '85 Je Vous Salue, Marie (USA/GB: Hail Mary) (FR-SWED); Detective. '87 Aria (ep dir) (GB); King Lear (+act).

File on Fonda

'I want to be responsible, positive, constructive. And I want to be the best actress I can be. I am a political animal, I am a woman who is personally engaged, and I am an actress. It has taken me some time to reconcile the two positions.'

Jane Fonda

It is hardly a new phenomenon for the children of famous show-business personalities to follow them into careers in the entertainment world. However, as Liza Minnelli once commented:

'Of course your parents' names open doors, but at 8.30 when the curtain goes up, it's you out there, not them. Without something of your own, those same doors can shut fast.'

The truth of that can be seen in the fact that Henry Fonda's name opened doors for both of his children, but while daughter Jane became an important international star with a reputation as a serious actress, her brother Peter's career, after an auspicious beginning, simply petered out.

Born in 1937 (her mother was Frances Brokaw), Jane went with her father to the East Coast when, in 1948, he went to New York to star in the Broadway production of *Mister Roberts*. She lived with her grandmother in nearby Connecticut, and then studied at Vassar, where she did a little acting in University productions. In the early Fifties her father cast her in his summer stock productions of the plays *The Country Girl* and *The Male Animal*. She was so dissatisfied with her own performances that she gave up acting to study

painting (in Paris) and piano (in New York). Feeling she was even less gifted at those two disciplines, she returned to enrol at Lee Strasberg's Actors Studio, supporting herself by modelling. Then the Fonda name began to open doors.

Joshua Logan – an old friend of her father – cast her in the college comedy *Tall Story* (1960) as a newly married cheer-leader, and in the ill-fated Broadway show *There Was a Little Girl*.

The reviews of both were negative, and her personal notices were, at best, mixed. After another Broadway failure – *The Fun Couple* – she returned to movies. Critical opinion remained unsure as she moved through a mostly mediocre series of films, playing a prostitute in *Walk on the Wild Side*, a naive wife in *The Chapman Report*, a naive bride in *Period of Adjustment* (all 1962), and an adultress in *In the Cool of the Day* (1963). While the satirical magazine *Harvard Lampoon* named her 'the year's worst actress', both critics and audiences were beginning to notice that she had

Top: the two faces of baby Jane – as space-age seductress Barbarella *with David Hemmings (left), and with husband-to-be Tom Hayden (right) on a troublesome visit to Britain in 1972 to promote their anti-Vietnam War campaign. Below:* In the Cool of the Day *Murray Logan (Peter Finch) has an affair with a colleague's wife (Fonda)*

something; that magnetic quality which makes an actress watchable, no matter how awful the vehicle. She was also obviously sincere, intelligent, and attempting to make something worthwhile out of even the trashiest dialogue and situations. The fact that she was sexy and oddly beautiful kept her career going in spite of the less than magnificent box-office results.

It is impossible to guess what might have happened to that career – and her life – had she then not been called to France to appear in René Clément's *Les Félins* (1964, *The Love Cage*), in which (not surprisingly) her cool sexuality failed to strike sparks from Alain Delon's own glacial eroticism. But her temporary role as an international sex symbol – 'the American Bardot' – had begun. Immediately after the Clément film, she went to work in Roger Vadim's *La Ronde* (1964, *Circle of Love*). When asked later why she married her lover – the director who 'created' Bardot and was known for his elegant sex films – she said it was because he was charming, dashing, romantic and represented a kind of world that was

very foreign to her.

Over the next five years, she returned to the United States to work but she lived in France. Vadim and Fonda had a daughter (Vanessa) and made four films together, in all of which she moved through titillating situations in various stages of undress. The most commercially successful of them was *Barbarella* (1968), based on a comic strip, and emphasizing even more than usual Vadim's cinematic conception of woman as sexual object and plaything. That particular image was, in reality, one which Fonda herself was less and less comfortable with.

Although she has since turned her back on the work done before *They Shoot Horses, Don't They?* (1969) – referring to that part of her output as 'when I wasn't very good' – she has never said even the least negative thing about ex-husband Vadim, with whom she has remained friendly. She now sees her experience in France as valuable: in 1968 France exploded politically, and more than a few people were politicized for the first time in their lives. Jane Fonda was one of them.

Above: Dove Linkhorn (Laurence Harvey) meets lost love Kitty Twist (Fonda) working in a brothel in Walk on the Wild Side. *Left: as a prostitute again in* Klute. *Below left: Jane at home with father Henry, husband Vadim and daughter Vanessa. Below:* They Shoot Horses, Don't They? *is a painful portrayal of the dance marathons of the Depression; Gloria (Fonda) and Robert (Michael Sarrazin) battle on*

By 1970 she was often called Hanoi Jane, and was as well known for her political activities as for her screen performances. She explained that she came from a bourgeois, liberal background – her father was a Roosevelt and Stevenson Democrat – and she, like her family, had donated money to various liberal causes and had signed petitions without actually engaging in politics on a personal level. It was the atrocities and misleading reports concerning Vietnam that led her to become interested – and active – in various causes, including the rights of American Indians and blacks and, most importantly, ending the war in Vietnam.

Whereas she won well-deserved awards for her performance as the threatened prostitute in *Klute* (1971), it was about the same time that the press and government crucified her as a 'traitor' and worse. She became active in the Free The Army movement, touring American Army bases with a revue in an attempt to get soldiers to refuse to fight in Vietnam. Neither of the two films which resulted from those tours – *F.T.A.* (1972) and *Steelyard Blues* (1973) – received wide distribution. She also returned to France briefly to appear in Jean-Luc Godard's *Tout Va Bien* (1972, All Goes Well), a forthrightly political film concerning, among other things, a strike in a factory. Fonda was not entirely pleased with either the film or with Godard as a director – a compliment he returned in the short *A Letter to Jane, or Investigation About a Still* (1973), which features a still photograph of her. This was an analysis of what he saw as Fonda's superficial

Left: Fonda continued her anti-war protest on film with Donald Sutherland in Steelyard Blues. *Below left: in* Coming Home, *Jon Voight plays a crippled veteran. Below: with James Caan in* Comes a Horseman *(1978)*

and 'radical chic' approach to the war and revolution.

Since then, Fonda admits that her one error during the period of her first politicization and the anti-war movement was that she was shrill – preaching rather than talking to audiences – and that there was the chance that she alienated many who then refused to listen to her. She has noted that people now tell her she has become more human, although she has not become any less political. She works actively with her politician husband, Tom Hayden, for the political organization they founded – the California Campaign for Economic Democracy. At least half of her films now have something of a political message: the war and returning Vietnam veterans in *Coming Home* (1978), the dangers of nuclear power plants in *The China Syndrome* (1979), the lives of 'repression' lived by office secretaries in *9 to 5* (1980). Yet, there is, now, a difference:

'I chose to do *Fun With Dick and Jane* (1977)

No longer the sexy nymphet, Jane Fonda's screen image is maturing. She plays a TV reporter in The China Syndrome *(top), and reaches for the hair of the dog from the night before in* The Morning After *(above)*

because I thought the time had come to do a comedy, a film which would be commercial, a film in which I was pretty. It showed I was a good actress and that I was commercial. I think that *The China Syndrome* had a social and commercial impact that was very strong. It is an example of a fusion of two kinds of film. We wanted to have a film which said something we wanted to say, but we wanted to attract the widest possible audience to say it to. It functions as a suspense film, but it is also about something important in the daily lives of those who see it. Let's not exaggerate, of course. No film can support a mass movement. Films can have a certain effect, but they represent only a small step in a certain direction. I think I now

understand how to say things and still have a large number of people listen. In the new film we wanted to say something about the condition of secretaries, but *9 to 5* is first of all a very funny comedy.'

Recently, Fonda has accepted a new challenge – how to grow old gracefully. While her Jane Fonda Workout business has become a household word for fitness and energy, in films she has left her youth behind. *Agnes of God* (1985) saw her cast as a chain-smoking psychiatrist, called to a convent to investigate a baby's bizarre death. In Sidney Lumet's *The Morning After* (1986), she plays a lush who can barely remember whose bed she wakes up in. Clearly locating herself as a woman in mid-life crisis, she proved she had come a long way since the sex symbol of her youth.

Quotations are taken from an interview by Henri Béhar, part of which was published in the May 1979 issue of Premiere.

Filmography
1960 Tall Story. '62 Walk on the Wild Side; The Chapman Report; Period of Adjustment. '63 In the Cool of the Day; Jane (doc) (appearance as herself only); Sunday in New York. '64 Les Félins (FR) (USA: The Joy House; GB: The Love Cage); La Ronde (FR-IT) (USA: Circle of Love). '65 Cat Ballou. '66 The Chase; La Curée (FR-IT) (USA/GB: The Game Is Over); Any Wednesday (GB: Bachelor Girl Apartment). '67 Hurry Sundown; Barefoot in the Park. '68 Histoires Extraordinaires *ep* Metzengerstein only (FR-IT) (USA: Spirits of the Dead; GB: Tales of Mystery); Barbarella (FR-IT). '69 They Shoot Horses, Don't They? '71 Klute. '72 Tout Va Bien; F.T.A. (+co-prod; +co-sc). '73 Steelyard Blues (re-released in USA as: Final Crash); A Doll's House (GB-FR). '74 Jane Fonda on Vietnam (doc. short) (NOR) (appearance as herself only); Vietnam Journey; Introduction to the Enemy (doc) (+co-dir; +appearance as herself). '76 The Blue Bird (USA-USSR). '77 Fun With Dick and Jane; Julia. '78 Coming Home; Comes a Horseman; California Suite. '79 The China Syndrome; The Electric Horseman. '80 9 to 5; No Nukes (appearance as self only). '81 On Golden Pond. '82 Rollover. '85 Agnes of God. '86 The Morning After. '88 Old Gringo.

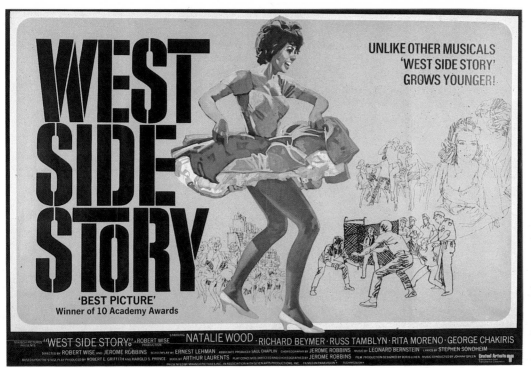

WEST SIDE STORY

UNLIKE OTHER MUSICALS 'WEST SIDE STORY' GROWS YOUNGER!

'BEST PICTURE'
Winner of 10 Academy Awards

WEST SIDE STORY — ROBERT WISE PRODUCTION — NATALIE WOOD · RICHARD BEYMER · RUSS TAMBLYN · RITA MORENO · GEORGE CHAKIRIS
DIRECTED BY ROBERT WISE AND JEROME ROBBINS SCREENPLAY BY ERNEST LEHMAN ASSOCIATE PRODUCER SAUL CHAPLIN CHOREOGRAPHY BY JEROME ROBBINS MUSIC BY LEONARD BERNSTEIN LYRICS BY STEPHEN SONDHEIM
BASED UPON THE STAGE PLAY PRODUCED BY ROBERT E. GRIFFITH AND HAROLD S. PRINCE BOOK BY ARTHUR LAURENTS PLAY CONCEIVED, DIRECTED AND CHOREOGRAPHED BY JEROME ROBBINS FILM PRODUCTION DESIGNED BY BORIS LEVEN MUSIC CONDUCTED BY JOHNNY GREEN United Artists

Directed by Robert Wise, Jerome Robbins, 1961
Prod co: Mirisch/Seven Arts. **prod:** Robert Wise. **assoc prod:** Saul Chaplin. **sc:** Ernest Lehman, based on the stage production by Robert E. Griffith, Harold S. Prince, from the book by Arthur Laurents. **photo** (Technicolor, Panavision 70): Daniel L. Fapp. **sp eff:** Linwood Dunn. **ed:** Thomas Stanford, Marshall M. Borden. **art dir:** Boris Leven, M. Zuberano. **titles:** Saul Bass. **cost:** Irene Sharaff. **mus:** Leonard Bernstein. **mus dir:** Johnny Green. **mus arr:** Sid Ramin. **mus ed:** Richard Carruth. **lyr:** Stephen Sondheim. **chor:** Jerome Robbins. **sd:** Gilbert D. Marchant. **sd rec:** Murray Spivack, Fred Lau, Vinton Vernon. **prod man:** Allen K. Wood. **ass dir:** Robert E. Relyea. **r/t:** 152 minutes.
Cast: Natalie Wood (*Maria*), Richard Beymer (*Tony*), George Chakiris (*Bernardo*), Russ Tamblyn (*Riff*), Rita Moreno (*Anita*), Tony Mordente (*Action*), Tucker Smith (*Ice*), Simon Oakland (*Lieutenant Schrank*), William Bramley (*Officer Krupke*), Ned Glass (*Doc*), José De Vega (*Chino*), Sue Oakes (*Anybody's*), John Astin (*Glad Hand*), Penny Santon (*Madam Lucia*), Jay Norman (*Pepe*), Gus Trikonis (*Indio*), Robert Thompson (*Luis*), Eliot Field (*Baby John*), Larry Roquemore (*Rocco*), David Winters (*A-Rab*).

West Side Story begins even before the house-lights go down in the cinema. A long, low whistle fills the auditorium; the whistle is repeated; the lights go down and the film starts with a breathtaking aerial shot of Manhattan – a geometric display of crossing lines. Then the camera plunges to the streets below: a gang of youths walking along the road, clicking their fingers, keeping 'cool'; suddenly they freeze and move into a dance sequence. It is a daring and visually exciting opening to a film.

But more than that, these first few minutes establish a number of key elements: its location – the tenements and streets of Manhattan; its content – the rivalry between two gangs (one of white youths, one of Puerto Rican immigrants); and its form – a highly stylized musical. The opening prepares the audience for what is to follow.

West Side Story was conceived and developed for the stage by Jerome Robbins, who also choreographed and directed several of the dance routines. One of his early stage ballet hits was the choreography for Leonard Bernstein's *Fancy Free* which later became the Broadway success *On the Town*. The film of *On the Town* (1949) had broken with tradition by attempting to integrate fully song, dance and dialogue into one continuous narrative, rejecting the often contrived excuses for breaking into song that had been a feature of previous musicals. However, it is relatively easy to do this when the plot of the film is nothing more than three sailors going ashore for 24 hours' leave, meeting three girls and returning to their ship.

West Side Story is a more difficult proposition. Loosely based on Shakespeare's *Romeo and Juliet*, it transposes the rivalry between the Capulet and Montague families to the tensions between racial groupings in New York, thus becoming one of the first musicals to deal with serious, contemporary issues – racialism and juvenile delinquency. The vigour and vitality of *West Side Story* owe a lot to its departure from the facile plots of *On the Town* or *Pal Joey* (1957) or the fantasy lives of *Seven Brides for Seven Brothers* (1954).

It presented Robbins and Robert Wise with the difficulty of how to carve out a modern style of presentation suitable for important problems. *West Side Story* found its style both by not trying to carry the plot forward in song and dance sequences – as *On the Town* did – and also by abandoning the hoedown set pieces of *Oklahoma!* (1955). Instead, the songs, at their best, add something more to the narrative, informing the audience about the atmosphere and details of the lives. The opening shots do this by economically establishing the territorial basis of the gangs' control. Later in the film, the aggressive and lively roof-top sequence 'America' is a hard-hitting proclamation of the disillusionment of immigrants with American society. On the other hand, the love song 'Maria' and the dance-hall routine, where the gangs challenge each other, are firmly part of the old tradition.

Of the criticisms ranged against the film, one concerns its combination of naturalism through location shooting and the obvious stylization of studio work. Whereas the beginning was actually danced on the streets of New York, the 'rumble' takes place in a studio-constructed set. And the choice of Natalie Wood as Maria – she had to have her singing voice dubbed and had difficulty looking Puerto Rican – has also been questioned as giving the film an unreal texture. But *West Side Story* does not aim to be realistic: it is a modern parable of what *could* happen in a racially divided society.

With its combination of innovatory and traditional elements, this was very much a transitional musical. Bob Fosse took the techniques of *West Side Story* further when he brought serious issues to *Sweet Charity* (1969), and combined them with biting satire in *Cabaret* (1972). Robert Wise went on to

direct his biggest success, another big-budget musical – *The Sound of Music* (1965). It needed other directors to see that there was a valuable exuberance and youthfulness that could be exploited to provide the material for even more exuberant and youth-orientated rock musicals of the next decade.

On New York's West Side two gangs control the streets – the Jets (white teenagers) (1) and the

1

4

8

Sharks (Puerto Rican immigrants) (2). Riff, the leader of the Jets, tries to persuade Tony, who founded the gang but has since drifted away, to go to the local dance.

Maria, the sister of Bernardo who leads the Sharks, is excited about her first dance. She goes with Chino, Bernardo and his girlfriend Anita. When they arrive, the two gangs display their rivalry through the dances they perform (3). Tony enters and sees Maria:

they are both entranced (4). When he asks her to dance, Bernardo warns her that Tony is a member of the rival gang. Riff uses the incident as an excuse to propose a 'rumble'.

Tony visits Maria on the fire-escape outside her room (5) and they realize that, despite the difficulties, they love each other. Returning to Doc's shop (where he works) Tony finds a war council in session. He persuades them to have a fair fist fight

between representatives from each side.

Telling Bernardo that she will be working late (6), Maria stays at the dress-shop until Tony arrives. She persuades him to try and stop the fight, but when he gets to the 'rumble' his offer of friendship is misunderstood. Bernardo kills Riff (7), and Tony kills Bernardo. When the police turn up, the gangs scatter (8).

Learning of her brother's death, Maria decides to stand by Tony,

and begs Anita to take a message to him. Anita goes to Doc's but is insulted by the Jets; she then lies when she tells them that Chino has killed Maria in anger.

Desolate, Tony roams the streets calling for Chino to come and get him. He sees Maria too late: he has already been spotted by Chino who shoots him. Both gangs appear, and Maria, crying, accuses them all of Tony's death (9). They take Tony's body off, for once united in tragedy (10).

2

3

5

6

7

9

10

When *The Graduate* was released in 1967, it became something of a cult film with the 18–25 age group. It represented a breakthrough for Hollywood with these young people – students and others went to see it again and again. Its popularity far outstripped the original expectations of its makers. There was even a 26-page article, assessing its merits, in the *New York Times*.

The year 1968 was to be a time of unrest around the world, particularly among students and other youth. In America that unrest eventually crystallized into opposition to the Vietnam War, but in 1967 the issue was not yet clearly focused – there was only a general dissatisfaction with the *status quo*. The anarchic mood of *The Graduate* perfectly matched the feelings of the time. It combined humour with satire on social and sexual customs, complemented by the music of Simon and Garfunkel.

Benjamin, the slightly unprepossessing hero of the film, is fresh out of college and uncertain whether to go on to graduate school. An innocent in a sophisticated society, he is seen by his elders as a means to fulfil their own ambitions, while he himself is trying to search out an honest and sincere way to live his life. Only Elaine Robinson, the daughter of his father's business partner and apparently the only other young person in his environment, is able to communicate with him. Benjamin has difficulty in relating to the world of his parents, from which he feels cut off by invisible barriers – as the words of Paul Simon's opening song, 'The Sound of Silence', suggest.

Benjamin belongs to a wealthy family in Los Angeles, affluent members of the world's richest society – financial insecurity is no longer a problem as it had been in earlier films about the difficulties of youthful characters. At his homecoming party after graduation, a family friend whispers one word of advice in his ear: 'Plastics'. Benjamin retires to his room, realizing that he is estranged from a world in which financial success is the only measure of value.

Benjamin's alienation from his culture throughout the film is symbolized by shots through glass, cutting him off from direct participation in others' experience. At the party, the guests are seen in wide-angle distortion through the eye-mask of Benjamin's new diving suit. Mrs Robinson's first approach to him is shown through a fish tank – she will be the predator in their relationship. Several times Benjamin's individual and nonconformist viewpoint is emphasized in subjective shots through the lenses of his sunglasses. When he finally runs off with Elaine, the audience sees the couple through the windows of the bus, creating a final barrier through which even their ultimate silence is unheard.

Although *The Graduate* brought the 30-year-old Dustin Hoffman to fame as a hero of youth culture, it did not establish him as a rebel in the Dean or Brando mould of the

Fifties. Benjamin graduated with honours and was the debating champion.

He is, above all, a nice guy who lives by his own standards of truth. He never really challenges the way things are; he just tries to remain personally genuine in a fundamentally hypocritical society. His uncertainty touches many chords in the audience: his difficulty in getting served at the bar, his fear of public embarrassment, his hesitancy and lack of social grace – problems every young adult has faced.

His naivety is at its height in his relationship with Mrs Robinson, Elaine's mother, who is magnificently portrayed as an alcoholic but infinitely seductive bitch by Anne Bancroft. He not unnaturally assumes that physical sex and emotional intimacy should go together. He therefore cannot understand Mrs Robinson's refusal to talk about herself and her interests even after they have made love. But Benjamin remains uncorrupted; he continues to call his mistress 'Mrs

Robinson', implicitly recognizing the distance between them in age, experience and outlook. He even explains to Mr Robinson, who is contemplating a divorce, that the affair meant no more to either of them than a gesture like shaking hands.

At the end of the film, Benjamin and Elaine remain the only two innocents. When he drags her off from the church, despite her just having married another man (whom she does not love), they get on a bus going . . . nowhere. The

aims of the rebellion have not yet been defined. But Benjamin has made his protest felt.

Mike Nichols, the film's director, has said:

'If there is anything I like in *The Graduate* it is the last three minutes of it – sitting on the bus, stunned and very well aware that it's not the end of anything. They don't know what the hell to say to each other . . . Many things are possible – it's not an end. Benjamin has many choices open to him.'

JOSEPH E. LEVINE PRESENTS A MIKE NICHOLS-LAWRENCE TURMAN PRODUCTION

This is Benjamin
He's a little worried about his future

THE GRADUAT

STARRING
ANNE BANCROFT AND **DUSTIN HOFFMAN · KATHARINE ROS**

SCREENPLAY BY
CALDER WILLINGHAM AND BUCK HENRY

SONGS BY
PAUL SIMON

PERFORMED BY
SIMON AND GARFUNKE

PRODUCED BY
LAWRENCE TURMAN

DIRECTED BY
MIKE NICHOLS

TECHNICOLOR® PANAVISION®

United Artists

Directed by Mike Nichols, 1967
Prod co: Avco Embassy. **prod:** Lawrence Turman. **sc:** Calder Willingham, Buck Henry, from a novel by Charles Webb. **photo** (Panavision, Technicolor): Robert Surtees. **ed:** Sam O'Steen. **art dir:** Richard Sylbert. **mus:** Dave Grusin. **songs:** Paul Simon (sung by Simon and Garfunkel). **cost:** Patricia Zipprodt. **sd:** Jack Solomon. **r/t:** 105 minutes. World premiere, Lincoln Art and Coronet Theatres, New York, 21 December 1967.
Cast: Anne Bancroft (*Mrs Robinson*), Dustin Hoffman (*Benjamin Braddock*), Katharine Ross (*Elaine Robinson*), Murray Hamilton (*Mr Robinson*), William Daniels (*Mr Braddock*), Elizabeth Wilson (*Mrs Braddock*), Buck Henry (*room clerk*), Brian Avery (*Carl Smith*), Walter Brooke (*Mr Maguire*), Norman Fell (*Mr McCleery*), Alice Ghostley (*Mrs Singleman*), Marion Lorne (*Miss de Witt*).

1

2

3

4

5

Benjamin returns home to Los Angeles after graduating from college in the east (1). At a cocktail party thrown by his parents to celebrate his homecoming, he is persuaded to show off his new diving suit. The guests all make a fuss of him but he rejects their unwanted advice and retires to his room. Mrs Robinson, the wife of his father's business partner, approaches him and talks him into driving her home (2).

When they reach her home, Mrs Robinson tries to seduce Benjamin but is prevented by the arrival of Mr Robinson (3). Their affair actually, if hesitatingly, gets started at a luxury hotel (4, 5). Benjamin is unable to communicate with his parents about his problems (6). When Mrs Robinson's daughter, Elaine, returns from college, Benjamin and Elaine are thrown together though Mrs Robinson warns him to stay away. On a

date, he tries to put Elaine off by taking her to a strip joint. She runs out, crying in disgust and shame; Benjamin apologizes, realizing that she is actually the only person he can talk to.

Mrs Robinson tries to break off the blossoming romance between them by telling Elaine that Benjamin tried to rape her. Disillusioned, Elaine returns to college in Berkeley but Benjamin follows her. Elaine believes Benjamin's account (7), realizing that her mother was lying, but it is too late. Mr Robinson arrives to take her off to her wedding with a wealthy student, Carl Smith. Benjamin pursues the couple and arrives at the church as the marriage service is concluding. He runs away with the bride, using the church cross as a weapon and barrier to prevent her parents from following (8). Elaine, still in her bridal gown, and Benjamin board a bus and ride away without speaking (9).

8

9

"John Wayne, American"

John Wayne's long, final illness in the spring and summer of 1979 unleashed a tidal wave of American emotion. As the media constantly reminded everyone, Wayne was the man who carried 'true grit' over from the movie screen into real life: no self-respecting American could fail to be moved by the sight of the Duke, ravaged by 'Big C' but still a vast and imposing presence, looming up before the TV cameras at the 1979 Academy Awards ceremony. It *was* an awesome occasion:

'Oscar and I have something in common,' he said that night. 'Oscar first came to the Hollywood scene in 1928. So did I. We're both a little weatherbeaten, but we're still here and plan to be around for a whole lot longer.'

Two months later he was dead, but even as the old man slipped away Maureen O'Hara and Elizabeth Taylor fought desperately to win him a Congressional Medal of Honour, the highest tribute that can be paid to an American. It was the least President Carter could do, and the American people were able to take part in the medal-wearing too with the mass-minting of duplicate gold awards bearing the simple legend 'John Wayne, American'.

Above all others Wayne was the film star whom America had chosen as its symbol of strength, bravery, manliness, patriotism and righteousness in the post-war years. The film journalist Alexander Walker has persuasively argued in his book *Stardom* that Wayne 'was the most complete example of a star who has taken his politics into films and his films into public image'.

A Republican at Republic

The image of Wayne as the ultimate American fighting for right grew up during World War II when he played the war-hero in Republic's *Flying Tigers* (1942) and *The Fighting Seabees* (1944), and in the wake of Hiroshima when American military might was most in need of justification. In *Back to Bataan, They Were*

Above: the Duke in jovial mood on set for The Cowboys (1972). *Right: James Stewart, John Ford and Wayne pose for a publicity shot during the filming of* The Man Who Shot Liberty Valance. *Right, background: Colonel Marlowe waves farewell to his beloved after escaping from the Rebels by blowing up a bridge in* The Horse Soldiers

Marion Michael Morrison, a name to be conjured with – yet known by all. It is curious that women don't really take to him while men idolize him, and both will always see him sitting squarely on the back of a horse with a six-gun at his hip. However, given that as John Wayne he remained a superstar for over four decades, there must have been more to him than that . . . or must there?

Above left: pioneers (Marguerite Churchill and Wayne) take to The Big Trail *(1930) in a realistic Western with 'grubby' actors. Above: Oliver Hardy and Wayne in* The Fighting Kentuckian *(1949), a tale of two men's fight to help French refugees settle in Alabama. Below: Sergeant Stryker (Wayne) leads an attack in* The Sands of Iwo Jima

Expendable (both 1945), the fiercely jingoistic *The Sands of Iwo Jima* (1949), and John Ford's cavalry trilogy – *Fort Apache* (1948), *She Wore a Yellow Ribbon* (1949) and *Rio Grande* (1950) – he played war leaders who were tough, courageous, compassionate and *American*. Meanwhile, back at the Hollywood front Wayne, a staunch Republican and President of the Motion Picture Alliance for the Preservation of American Ideals, was taking an active part in running Communists out of the film capital – and colleagues out of their livelihood.

The films that also involved Wayne on the production side are those which most cohesively unite his movie and public images. *Big Jim McLain* (1952), which he co-produced, is pro-McCarthyist propaganda with Wayne as a tough HUAC investigator pursuing 'pinkos'; in *The Alamo* (1960), his first film as director, he played Davy Crockett defending Texas against Santa Anna's Mexican army – a martyr for American freedom; *The Green Berets* (1968) was his second stab at direction and is a vituperative pro-Vietnam War film in which he plays a mercenary routing the Vietcong. As 'pro-American' propaganda this is strong, sometimes unpalatable stuff, and he even recorded an LP called 'Why I Love America' with Robert Mitchum. Now there is a hint of bathos in that title, as there is in the whole of Wayne's over-inflated image as the last American hero, and it would be feasible to suggest that Wayne was aware of it. His Republicanism and anti-Communism (he had read widely

Above left: ace Indian hunter Lt. Col. Kirby Yorke, who involves himself in the Apache wars to protect the settlers in Rio Grande. *Above: Townsend Harris, a USA envoy sent to hostile Japan to arrange a trade treaty in* The Barbarian and the Geisha *(1958)*

in Communist literature and in political science) were sincere, and he was a fervent supporter of Eisenhower, Goldwater and Nixon, but perhaps he knew too the power of talismans, bronze medals and movie images in the art of propaganda. Yet, strange as it may seem, in his greatest films Wayne's characters are not all that America would have them be.

South of the border . . .

If Wayne was and is a symbol of Americanism then, politically and socially, no other actor has done so much to undermine the self-righteous bluster of WASPish – White Anglo-Saxon Protestant – redneck values, both by espousing them and showing the neuroses nagging away at them. Wayne married three Spanish-Americans during his lifetime (so much for *The Alamo*) and eventually turned to Catholicism on his death-bed. If Ford, Hawks and the directors at Republic hadn't grabbed him for Westerns and war films in the late Forties and early Fifties, he might have been an effective star of *film noir*, so thoroughly ambiguous and troubled is his image when scrutinized. In fact Ford's *The Searchers* (1956) is a Western *film noir* with Wayne as a psychopath trapped in the alternatively light and dark landscape of his own mind. Even if Wayne *was* politically naive then surely he understood the dreadful frailty of his bloated, brow-beating characters and that the anger, insensitivity and spitefulness of Tom Dunson in *Red River* (1948), Sergeant Stryker in *The Sands of Iwo Jima* and Tom Doniphon in *The Man Who Shot Liberty Valance* (1962) showed the bully and the tyrant in the hero who defends his flag at all costs. These characters are tired, unhappy men, soured and warped by their own experiences and plunged into crises of conscience which they can only solve by blasting their way out.

For all their self-sufficiency and arrogant confidence Wayne's movie characters – his American heroes – are lonely, sulky, ill-tempered and desperate. In good moods they tend to be bluff and patronizing – Wayne's grin is cracked, his eyes narrowed under his brow with suspicion. In bad moments they are monstrous; recall the incident in *Red River* when Dunson bounds across the trail, draws and shoots the cocky gunslinger without stopping his relentless march and lays into his young foster-son Matt (Montgomery Clift), a fury of flailing fists and mad temper. 'I never knew that big sonovabitch could act,' Ford said to Hawks after seeing *Red River*. As old men or neurotics Wayne was especially effective and knew exactly what he was about, as did Ford – his patron and mentor – and in *The Searchers*, *The Horse Soldiers* (1959), a wearied view of the Civil War, and *The Man Who Shot Liberty Valance*, they share the knowledge that the American Dream has become an American nightmare.

No Janet for John

On other levels Wayne's characters are equally ill at ease. It is significant that in many of his films he is essentially womanless. In *Red River* he leaves his girl behind (intending to return) but she is killed by Indians; *She Wore a Yellow Ribbon* finds him as a mawkishly sentimental widower who confides in his wife's grave; in *Rio Grande* he is estranged from his wife because he burnt down her home in the Civil War; in *The Searchers* the woman he loves is married to his brother; *The Man Who Shot Liberty Valance* sees him lose his girl to the man who also usurps his heroism. The Wayne persona inevitably engenders sexual disharmony. For such an American hero Wayne frequently cut an impotent, asexual figure – so colossal that he swamps mere masculinity. He was certainly no Gable – after all, how many women find the Duke attractive? – and this is surely not the way the American male likes to view himself.

Of course there is an escape clause, for Wayne is seldom just a tyrant. After Dunson and Matt have fought themselves into the ground in *Red River*, Tess Millay (Joanne Dru) comes up to them: 'Whoever would have thought that you two could have killed each other?' she chides, and the loving father-son relationship is re-established. 'Come on Debbie, let's go home,' Ethan (Wayne) says to his niece instead of killing her as he had set out

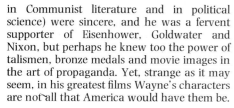

Filmography

1927 The Drop Kick (uncredited) (GB: Glitter); Mother Machree (ass. prop man; +extra). **'28** Four Sons (ass. prop man); Hangman's House (uncredited). **'29** Words and Music; Salute; Men Without Women. **'30** Born Reckless (ass. prop man); Rough Romance; Cheer Up and Smile; The Big Trail. **'31** Girls Demand Excitement; Three Girls Lost; Men Are Like That (GB: The Virtuous Wife); The Deceiver; Range Feud; Maker of Men. **'32** The Voice of Hollywood No 13 (short) (announcer only); Shadow of the Eagle (serial); Texas Cyclone; Two-Fisted Law; Lady and Gent; The Hurricane Express (serial); The Hollywood Handicap (short) (guest); Ride Him Cowboy (GB: The Hawk); The Big Stampede; Haunted Gold. **'33** The Telegraph Trail; The Three Musketeers (serial; re-edited into feature Desert Command/ Trouble in the Legion, 1946); Central Airport; Somewhere in Sonora; His Private Secretary; The Life of Jimmy Dolan (GB: The Kid's Last Fight); Baby Face; The Man from Monterey; Riders of Destiny; College Coach (GB: Football Coach); Sagebrush Trail. **'34** The Lucky Texan; West of the Divide; Blue Steel; The Man from Utah; Randy Rides Alone; The Star Packer; The Trail Beyond; The Lawless Frontier; 'Neath Arizona Skies. **'35** Texas Terror; Rainbow Valley; The Desert Trail; The Dawn Rider; Paradise Canyon; Westward Ho; The New Frontier; The Lawless Range. **'36** The Oregon Trail; The Lawless Nineties; King of the Pecos; The Lonely Trail; Winds of the Wasteland; The Sea Spoilers; Conflict. **'37** California Straight Ahead; I Cover the War; Idol of the Crowd; Adventure's End; Born to the West (reissued as Hell Town). **'38** Pals of the Saddle; Overland Stage Raiders; Santa Fe Stampede; Red River Range. **'39** Stagecoach; The Night Riders; Three Texas Steers (GB: Danger Rides the Range); Wyoming Outlaw; New Frontier; Allegheny Uprising (GB: The First Rebel). **'40** The Dark Command; Three Faces West; The Long Voyage Home; Seven Sinners (GB reissue title; Café of the Seven Sinners); Melody Ranch

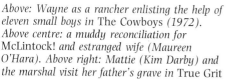

Above: Wayne as a rancher enlisting the help of eleven small boys in The Cowboys *(1972). Above centre: a muddy reconciliation for* McLintock! *and estranged wife (Maureen O'Hara). Above right: Mattie (Kim Darby) and the marshal visit her father's grave in* True Grit

to do in *The Searchers,* and it was Jean-Luc Godard who pinpointed the secret of Wayne's appeal when he wrote, 'How can I hate John Wayne upholding Goldwater and yet love him tenderly when abruptly he takes Natalie Wood into his arms in the last reel of *The Searchers?*' Elizabeth Taylor was near the mark too when she said in that Congressional Medal plea, 'He is as tough as an old nut and soft as a yellow ribbon'.

Wayne was capable of an extraordinary gentleness and chivalry and Ford was early to spot this when he cast him as Ringo, an outlaw who treats the whore Dallas (Claire Trevor) like a lady, in *Stagecoach* (1939). True, he was more accustomed to giving a girl a slap on the behind – most often Maureen O'Hara ('She's a big, lusty, wonderful gal . . . my kinda gal') who as the shrewish colleen of *The Quiet Man* (1952) warrants a playful smack and as the wife in *McLintock!* (1963) a thrashing with a shovel, but tenderness often undercuts his chauvinism. O'Hara seemed the only female

capable of bringing out the erotic in Wayne – caught bare-legged with him in a graveyard during the thunderstorm in *The Quiet Man* she charges the air between them with sexual electricity – despite his having made three films with Dietrich. In *Three Godfathers* (1948) and *The Alamo* Wayne also showed a familiarity with babies and toddlers, but those scenes are best forgotten. Tenderness and warmth are an acceptable part of the noble savage's make-up; allowed to be maudlin Wayne was embarrassing to watch.

Ford's *Stagecoach* had caught the right mixture of gentleness and toughness, and even gives a glimpse of the uncertainty in the Wayne hero. The opening shot of Ringo twirling his rifle over his arm saluted his arrival as a star, but in fact Wayne was already a well-known face, albeit in B pictures.

Shooting to stardom
He was born Marion Michael Morrison in Winterset, Iowa, in 1907, the son of a druggist who took the family West to Glendale, Los Angeles, when Marion was nine. In 1925 he won a football scholarship to the University of Southern California where the Western star Tom Mix saw him. Mix offered him a job shifting props at Fox and there Wayne met John Ford who employed him as a herder of

geese on the set of *Mother Machree* (1927). He appeared as an Irish peasant in Ford's *Hangman's House* (1928) and received his first screen credit as Duke Morrison for a bit-part in *Words and Music* (1929).

Then Raoul Walsh found him, changed his name to John Wayne and made him grow his hair long for the part of the wagon-train scout in the epic Western *The Big Trail* (1930). However, the film failed and despite a studio build-up, Wayne was consigned to B Westerns at Columbia, Mascot, Monogram (for whom he made a series as Singin' Sandy beginning with *Riders of Destiny* in 1933) and eventually Republic on Poverty Row. But he kept in with Ford and was finally bullied by him into a starring career that lasted for forty years.

By the Sixties Wayne had become an American institution, too formidable a presence for the good of his films except when working with Ford or Hawks. The long-awaited Oscar came for his portrayal of Rooster Cogburn, the one-eyed war-horse in *True Grit* (1969), but it was a tribute to Wayne's long career rather than to that particular performance. With his last film, *The Shootist* (1976), man and myth became inseparable: the movie begins with a sequence of clips from old John Wayne movies, a requiem for the character he is playing – an ex-gunfighter dying of cancer – and for himself.

The giant's shadow remains
As movie stars go John Wayne is pretty well indestructible, being the survivor of some two hundred films. Even the uncovering of the darker side of his image seems to inflate him all the more, as did the cancer he subdued for so long. 'I hope you die,' Martin Pawley (Jeffrey Hunter) shouts in rage at Ethan in *The Searchers*. 'That'll be the day,' Ethan grins back. Like Ethan, Wayne endures and is here to stay whether he is wanted or not; a dubious American hero but undoubtedly a remarkable screen presence.

(uncredited). '41 A Man Betrayed (GB: Citadel of Crime); Lady from Louisiana; The Shepherd of the Hills. '42 Lady for a Night; Reap the Wild Wind; The Spoilers; In Old California; Flying Tigers; Reunion in France (GB: Mademoiselle France); Pittsburgh. '43 A Lady Takes a Chance; In Old Oklahoma. '44 The Fighting Seabees; Tall in the Saddle. '45 Flame of the Barbary Coast; Back to Bataan; They Were Expendable; Dakota. '46 Without Reservations. '47 Angel and the Badman (+prod); Tycoon. '48 Red River; Fort Apache; Three Godfathers. '49 Wake of the Red Witch; The Fighting Kentuckian (+prod); She Wore a Yellow Ribbon; The Sands of Iwo Jima. '50 Rio Grande. '51 Operation Pacific; The Bullfighter and the Lady (prod. only); Flying Leathernecks; Jet Pilot. '52 The Quiet Man; Big Jim McLain (+co-exec. prod.). '53 Trouble Along the Way; Island in the Sky (+prod); Hondo (+co-exec. prod.). '54 The High and the Mighty (+exec. prod.). '55 The Sea Chase; Blood Alley (+exec. prod.). '56 The Con-

queror; The Searchers. '57 The Wings of Eagles; Legend of the Lost (+co-exec. prod.). '58 I Married a Woman (guest); The Barbarian and the Geisha. '59 Rio Bravo; The Horse Soldiers. '60 The Alamo (+dir; +prod). North to Alaska. '62 The Comancheros (+add. dir. uncredited); Hatari!; The Man Who Shot Liberty Valance; The Longest Day; How the West Was Won *ep* The Civil War. '63 Donovan's Reef; McLintock! (+exec. prod.). '64 Circus World (GB: The Magnificent Showman). '65 The Greatest Story Ever Told; In Harm's Way; The Sons of Katie Elder. '66 Cast a Giant Shadow (+co-exec. prod.). '67 El Dorado; The War Wagon (+co-exec. prod.). '68 The Green Berets (+co-dir; +exec. prod.); Hellfighters. '69 True Grit; The Undefeated. '70 Chisum; Rio Lobo. '71 Big Jake (+exec. prod.). '72 The Cowboys; Cancel My Reservation (guest). '73 The Train Robbers (+exec. prod); Cahill – United States Marshal (+exec. prod) (GB: Cahill). '74 McQ. '75 Brannigan (GB); Rooster Cogburn. '76 The Shootist.

A Shop on the High Street

Directed by Ján Kadár and Elmar Klos, 1965
Prod co: Československý Film. **sc:** Ladislav Grosman, Ján Kadár, Elmar Klos, based on a story by Grosman. **photo:** Vladimír Novotný. **art dir:** Karel Škvor. **mus:** Zdeněk Liška. **r/t:** 128 minutes. Released in Czechoslovakia as: *Obchod na korze*. Released in USA as *The Shop on Main Street*.
Cast: Ida Kamińska (*Rozálie Lautmannová*), Jozef Króner (*Tono Brtko*), Hana Slivková (*Evelina Brtková*), František Zvarík (*Markus Kolcocký*), Helena Zvaríková (*Rose Kolckocká*), Martin Holly (*Imro Kuchár*), Martin Gregor (*Katz, the barber*).

A Shop on the High Street, the first Czech feature film to win an Academy Award, was the seventh film collaboration of Ján Kadár (1918–79) and Elmar Klos (b.1910), who had been working together since 1952.

The story of this directorial tandem typifies the fate of talented, socialist-minded, engaged artists in Central Europe in the years following World War II. Klos had started his film career in the Thirties, establishing a studio to make publicity films for the BATA shoe empire, and had studied new techniques in Hollywood. During the war he proved himself a talented documentary director.

Kadár, a Hungarian-Slovak Jew, emerged from a Nazi labour camp in 1945 and two years later became an assistant in the new Bratislava film studios. Both he and Klos had been converted by their wartime experiences into dedicated communists. They came together as a creative team in Prague, where Kadár settled after political criticism of his first, independently directed feature, *Katka* (1951).

Separately or together, the two seemed destined to displease the authorities. Their first collaboration *Unos* (1953, *Kidnapped*) was intended as Cold War political propaganda, but was considered too realistic; nor was *Hudba z Marsu* (1955, Music From Mars), a musical comedy satirizing bureaucracy in high places, any more likely to please. They seemed on safer ground with a realistic, poetic and ostensibly non-political story of ordinary people, *Tam na konečné* (1958, The House at the Terminus), but were immediately in trouble again with *Tři přání* (1958, *Three Wishes*). The film's exposure of corruption and opportunism horrified the authorities; it was shelved and Kadár and Klos were banned from the studios for two years.

In 1963 they returned with what is probably their best film, *Smrt si říká Engelchen* (Death Is Called Engelchen), an unsparing contemplation of the horror of the war which at the same time discovered contemporary lessons in past history. In an atmosphere cautiously becoming more liberal they made *Obžalovaný* (1964, The Defendant), a socially critical fictional account of the trial of a group accused of 'economic' crimes; and then *A Shop on the High Street*. This is based on a story, *The Trap*, by Ladislav Grosman, which Kadár and Klos said:

'. . . aroused our interest because of its rather unusual treatment of the theme in relation to factual evidence and tragi-comedy, intensified through the humane approach of the author. The tragedy of the story rests on a single pair of characters and is a unique case of seeing fascism from within.

'*A Shop on the High Street* is one episode of a great tragedy. Basically it is a parable, though depicting realistic situations. Not even the most tragic scenes are deprived of a share of humour, but the audience knows it is a matter of life and death . . .'

Compared with the innovatory work from the new school of Czech directors that emerged in the Sixties, Kadár and Klos' film was conservative, even old-fashioned. In a perceptive review written at the time, Kenneth Tynan remarked that their 'self-denying respect for the script may well prevent them from ever becoming fashionable.'

A Shop on the High Street is for all that a considerable *tour de force*. With deftness and precision it balances with the brutal horror of the situation, a tone of intimate, everyday human comedy, exemplified in the misunderstandings of the exasperated Tono and the imperturbably uncomprehending old lady. From this balance emerges the point that the humankind that is capable of committing such monstrous deeds as are witnessed on the screen is individually composed of small, weak human beings. Tono is quite a pleasant, friendly, even well-meaning man, for whom fascism happens to offer a convenient economic way of life. Even his shrewish wife and fascist brother-in-law are the grotesque minor villains that are most frequently found in bucolic comedy.

Critics of the time, indeed, charged the film with taking things too lightly, by indulging in such whimsies as the coda. Behind the gentle exterior, though, lay a contemporary message, as the directors pointed out:

'The same thing could clearly take place anywhere, even today . . . We feel that no-one may be excluded from the society in which he lives, and no-one may be robbed of his rights as a human being. As soon as something like that can happen, anything can happen, thanks to the indifference of the bystanders. All that is needed is a little bit of cowardice, of fear.'

The message of the film was

clear enough for *A Shop on the High Street* to be unacceptable to the new regime that followed the Soviet invasion of Czechoslovakia in 1968. Kadár and Klos made one last film, *Hrst plná vody* (*Adrift*), released in 1969, but after the events of 1968 Klos was to be definitively banished from film-making. Kadár emigrated to North America and made three moderately successful films before his death: *The Angel Levine* (1970), *Lies My Father Told Me* (1975) and *Freedom Road* (1979). The first of these featured Ida Kamińska, the great star of the Warsaw Jewish Theatre and the actress who played Mrs Lautmannová in *A Shop on the High Street*. Ironically enough, Kamińska was herself driven away from her native Poland by the wave of anti-semitism that rose up during the years 1968–69.

A small town in wartime Slovakia in 1943. Tono Brtko, the impoverished local carpenter (1), and his wife find it hard to make ends meet, so Tono cheerfully accepts his fascist brother-in-law's offer (2) of a job as 'Aryan controller' (3) of a Jewish-owned button shop. The job does not provide the rewards Tono had hoped for: the shop has been losing money for years; the proprietor, Rozálie Lautmannová (4), is quite deaf, blissfully unaware of the true facts of the situation, and takes Tono for a voluntary assistant whom she pampers like a son (5). The local Jewish community, which has long supported the old lady, now extends its charity to Tono.

When the order to deport the Jews comes (6, 7), Mrs Lautmannová's name has been forgotten. The old lady has a momentary comprehension (8): she murmurs, out of painful old memories, the single word 'pogrom'. Tono is faced with a terrible dilemma – either he exposes her, or hides her and risks the consequences of concealing a Jew. In panic (9) he thrusts her down into a cellar and locks the door. He opens it again, when the danger has passed, only to find her dead. He hangs himself.

In a coda, the ghosts of Tono and Mrs Lautmannová drift through the town, dressed in the finery of her happy past (10).

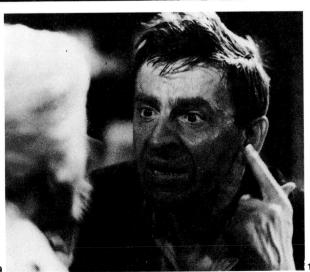

Poet of Malaise

Michelangelo Antonioni

Antonioni once named modesty as his greatest fault, but there are some who might laugh and call it obscurity instead. MGM, for instance, After the *coup* of *Blow-Up* (1966), they invited Antonioni to America and hired him to make what was supposed to be a prestigious blockbuster about student revolt – significant, violent, sexy and profitable. It proved to be a study of space and colour, with the incidental anger of the age dissolving into the ochre desert and the reverie of a perpetual explosion. No one got its point, or realized that the film was a rhapsody.

But, for Michelangelo Antonioni, the ending of *Zabriskie Point* (1970) was a heartfelt statement about the eclipse of love and human values. He had made the film he wanted, no matter how little he seemed to grasp the American language and movie idioms. *Zabriskie Point* is about a land marred by garish constructions and development plans. But its harsh and enigmatic purity is restored at the end by an act of cinematic will: the slow-motion disruption of all the ingredients of an advertiser's dream domestic interior. The disintegration of things attains a lyrical anguish in which the song subdues the pain without drifting into travesty. This world has already given up its soul, and so objects, space and the creep of time are all that remain.

Deserted spaces

Antonioni's career seems to show a drastic alteration in the middle Sixties. He had worked in Italy on a series of pained, psychological stories of love-affairs in which the dread of failure became more universal and somehow less circumstantial. Then he left his native country and began to travel – to England, to America, to China and to the several countries that comprise the existential scene shifts of *Professione: Reporter* (1975, *The Passenger*). .

But the change was less than it seemed. His movies have always been about the gaps between people and the relations between exterior and interior. *Blow-Up* has an odd insight into the real 'swinging' London, but it is much more fascinated by the way a photographer believes that his pictures have found truth at the far end of a magical park. Similarly, *The Passenger* is about the possibility of entering and leaving buildings – virtually the entire action can be expressed in those terms. Vagaries of place and time fade away as it

Above left and centre: The Passenger – *the glorious hotel standing alone in space, and Antonioni shooting part of the same film. Above right: in* Blow-Up *a promiscuous London fashion photographer, Thomas (David Hemmings, seen above with model Verushka), accidentally photographs a murder . . . but the evidence mysteriously disappears*

Below left: Cronaca di un Amore – *Paola and Guido (Lucia Bose and Massimo Girotti) have an adulterous affair, which the husband Enrico tries to have investigated. Enrico's death in a car-crash causes the lovers to panic, and Paola is left abandoned. Below:* La Notte – *a crisis in the marriage of Lidia (Jeanne Moreau) and Giovanni (Marcello Mastroianni as a novelist*

No other director seems as shy as Michelangelo Antonioni. He is unconvinced by society; his lovers look away from each other towards empty space. The director himself is so withdrawn, hesitant or difficult that he has released less than a handful of pictures in the course of the last fifteen years

works towards the sublime resolution in which the camera transcends one lethal room, wanders across a courtyard and then turns to look back at where it has been – like a spirit risen from the grave.

Passing strange

The Passenger is a spiritual film, and it reminds us of how in a 1957 interview, when asked what was the problem closest to his heart, Antonioni replied 'Can there exist a saint without God?' Religious authority never has a foothold in his films. Social institutions are regarded as prisons. But with his camera, Antonioni has tried to detect holiness, and

gradually he has taught audiences his own reverence for desolation.

His characters are wistful dreamers, torn between the search for satisfaction and encroaching decline, and sometimes unable to look at one another because of the pain attendant upon seeing and being seen. In the early Sixties, especially, he was treated as the studiously forlorn poet of pessimism and dismay, dissecting the wan and nervously restricted romanticism of actress Monica Vitti, who features in five of his works.

But that overlooks the real significance of detachment in Antonioni's films, and the way it has grown into something more like mystical

exhilaration. *The Passenger*, for instance, is his most resigned, calm and delighted film. It has found the world of space which people have done so much to confuse, and it has discovered beauty there. No other film-maker can invest place with such mystery and resonance, or make characters seem like pilgrims on a metaphysical threshold.

Profession: film-maker

Born in Ferrara, in 1912, Antonioni recalled it as 'a marvellous little city on the Paduan plain, antique and silent.' Already he had an intuition of the décor of his films; reality becoming an evocative model, like the deserted city in *L'Avventura* (1960, *The Adventure*).

The film's dilemma – the puzzle of a missing girl – begins to seem insoluble, but can be felt . . . like the scarred surface of the wall in *La Notte* (1961, *The Night*), when Lidia (Jeanne Moreau) pulls away a flake of rust, suggesting that the history of human time is being handled.

As a child, Antonioni played games that seem relevant to his films. He had a fascination for buildings, and he would draw plans, make façades and even construct three-dimensional models. He would add human figures to these ideal buildings, and begin to make up stories about what they were doing there. Thus the emblematic significance of an environment or

running out of ideas) leads them both to try to have affairs, but nothing comes of either dalliance. Below: in L'Eclisse Vittoria (Monica Vitti) ends a relationship with Ricardo and begins another with a young stockbroker Piero (Alain Delon), yet is unwilling to make it permanent. The film finishes with both of them failing to turn up at a pre-arranged rendez-vous.

Below right: Red Desert – Giuliana (Monica Vitti, in black) is a neurotic wife obsessed with her young son . . . until the arrival of Corrado, a visiting engineer. She tries to seduce him at a frustrated orgy (seen here), but only succeeds later when close to nervous breakdown after her son has pretended to be paralyzed as a kind of joke

real. *L'Avventura* has an ending that unduly wraps up the melodrama of sexual betrayal, but when it is just an expression of its central loss – the disappearance of Anna (Lea Massari) – then it is a model of abstract cinema.

L'Eclisse goes much further, and it is the most seriously overlooked of his films to date. Its long coda – of city sights and moments, the site of an appointment not kept, and of a street light coming on as an eclipse occurs – is a wondrous departure from the cold passion that existed briefly between Piero (Alain Delon) and Vittoria (Monica Vitti). It is as if a film-maker had managed to escape plot and character without denying humanism – and that is not far from Antonioni's total achievement.

Blow-Up never loses its beauty or its humour, never slackens its sense of the noble folly of preoccupation. More than most of Antonioni's pictures, it owes something to its source: the story by Julio Cortazar. Its people are photographs only, bewildered and hurt that they have no more substance. Nevertheless, the darkroom scenes and the reconstruction of the 'event' through pictures is a nostalgic tribute to narrative and suspense, just as Vanessa Redgrave gives an uncanny rendering of presence without explanation.

Antonioni's output had slowed down by the Seventies and Eighties; and to some, the slow, meandering *Identification of a Woman* (1982) may seem no more than a re-tread of earlier themes. But there is no denying the fine use of wide screen in the desert landscapes of *Zabriski Point*, or the purpose and social significance of *The Passenger* – so different, yet both of them elegies for a lost generation.

Above: in Zabriskie Point *Mark, a dissatisfied Californian student, steals a private plane; he meets Daria who also becomes a committed revolutionary. She vividly imagines blowing up an expensive villa in Death Valley. A desert love-in (here) symbolizes their attitude to bourgeois morality. Below:* The Passenger – *a famous TV documentary reporter (Jack Nicholson, here with Maria Schneider) assumes the identity of the dead man in his hotel room . . . which leads to trouble . . .*

a space: the lift-shaft in his first feature, *Cronaca di un Amore* (1950, Chronicle of a Love); the sense of fraud that hangs over the film-set in *La Signora Senza Camelie* (1953, Woman Without Camellias); the frontier of the beach in *Le Amiche* (1955, The Girl Friends); the grey wasteland of *Il Grido* (1957, The Cry) . . . and so on, to the tumult of the stock exchange in *L'Eclisse* (1962, The Eclipse), the cramped orgy room with boats looming up in the mist outside in *Deserto Rosso* (1964, Red Desert), the photographer's studio in *Blow-Up*. Finally, the African hotel, the London house, the Gaudi buildings and the impassive but glowingly sentient Hotel de la Gloria in *The Passenger*, a film in which Jack Nicholson learns that he can be still and let himself be carried along by the sweet flow of change, time and fiction.

Just as he was intensely fashionable in the late Fifties and early Sixties, so today Antonioni is not too far from neglect. The early films are not easy to see, and thus no one could easily appreciate the Renoir-like fluency of camera movement and spatial link in *Cronaca di un Amore*, *La Signora Senza Camelie* and *Le Amiche*. Perhaps love has wings so that it may fly away, but in *The Passenger* the images of flight suggest escape and transcendance more than loss, and in *Zabriskie Point* the stolen aircraft is like a mythological bird.

Reality eclipsed

The series of films that began with *L'Avventura* are sometimes perilously close to self-pity and intellectual pretension. *Red Desert* is a failure of nearly unbearable and uncommunicated distress, despite the first bold use of colour and the story of the island – the first imaginary location in an Antonioni film, and the clearest sign that none of the places has been merely

Filmography

1942 I Due Foscari (co-sc; +ass. dir. only); Un Pilota Ritorna (co-sc. only); Les Visiteurs du Soir (ass. dir. only) (FR) (USA: The Devil's Envoys). **'47** Caccia Tragica (co-sc. only) (GB: Tragic Pursuit); Gente del Po (doc. short) (+sc). **'48** N.U./Nettezza Urbana (doc. short) (+sc); Roma – Montevideo (doc. short) (+sc); Oltre l'Oblio (doc. short) (+sc). **'49** Bomarzo (doc. short) (+sc); L'Amorosa Menzogna (doc. short) (+sc); Superstizione (doc. short) (+sc); Ragazze in Bianco (doc. short) (+sc). **'50** Sette Canne, Un Vestito (doc. short) (+sc); La Villa dei Mostri (doc. short) (+sc); La Funivia del Faloria (doc. short) (+sc); Cronaca di un Amore (+co-sc; +ed). **'52** Lo Sceicco Bianco (co-sc. only) (USA/GB: The White Sheik). **'53** I Vinti (+co-sc) (IT-FR); La Signora Senza Camelie (+co-sc; +ed) (USA: Woman Without Camellias); Amore in Città *ep* Tentato Suicidio (+co-sc). **'55** Uomini in Più (doc) (prod. only); Le Amiche (+co-sc) (GB: The Girl Friends). **'57** Il Grido (+co-sc) (IT-USA) (GB: The Cry). **'58** La Tempesta (2nd unit dir. only, uncredited) (IT-YUG-FR) (GB: The Tempest). **'59** Nel Segno di Roma (co-dir. under pseudonym) (IT-FR-GER) (GB: Sign of the Gladiator). **'60** L'Avventura (+co-sc) (IT-FR) (USA/GB: The Adventure). **'61** La Notte (+co-sc) (IT-FR) (GB: The Night). **'62** L'Eclisse (+co-sc) (FR-IT) (USA/GB: The Eclipse). **'64** Deserto Rosso (+co-sc) (IT-FR) (USA/GB: Red Desert). **'65** I Tre Volti *ep* Il Provino; Michelangelo Antonioni (doc) (appearance as himself only). **'66** Blow-Up (+co-sc) (GB). **'70** Zabriskie Point (+co-sc) (USA). **'73** Chung Kuo/La Cina/China (doc) (+sc). **'75** Professione: Reporter (+co-sc) (IT-FR-SP) (USA/GB: The Passenger). **'80** Il Mistero di Oberwald (+co-sc: +co-ed). (USA/GB: The Oberwald Mystery). **'82** Identificatzione di una Donna (IT-FR) (USA/GB: Identification of a Woman).

Maestro

Charming, cool and sophisticated, or withdrawn, shy and very private? Every woman's idea of the ultimate Italian Romeo, or a reluctant Casanova? Which is the true Marcello Mastroianni?

Mastroianni

Marcello Mastroianni shot into the orbit of world fame in 1959. The rocket to launch him was director Federico Fellini's *La Dolce Vita* (The Sweet Life), even though by then Mastroianni was 35 and had appeared in over forty films. The man he plays in *La Dolce Vita* is immature rather than young; attractive to women without knowing how to make them happy; living in high society, without being rich.

Clearly it was this ability to project inadequacies that helped him to embody the disenchantment of the post-war generation so successfully. Casually elegant and suave, a snob-symbol rather than a sex-symbol, it was largely the publicity campaigns which built him up as the great Latin lover. In fact he has always been as popular with men as with women: men could identify with him. There are very few stars of this kind, but they shine longest: Humphrey Bogart, Steve McQueen or Clint Eastwood in the USA; Jean Gabin, Yves Montand and Jean-Louis Trintignant in France. But they are all tough action-men. Only Mastroianni has ever reached the top by appearing soft and passive, with the manners and bearing of an old-fashioned gentleman.

It is of course as misleading an image as only a consummate actor could project. The son of a small tradesman, Mastroianni has always been ambitious, as well as talented, and extremely hard-working, making three or four films a year; and in complete control of the considerable achievements of his career.

He was born in 1924 in Fontana Liri, near Frosinone, roughly halfway between Rome and Naples; but his family moved north to Turin during his childhood, and soon after to Rome, where he began training as a draughtsman. During World War II he was captured and sent to a German prison camp, from which he escaped, hiding in Venice until 1945, when he returned to Rome and found a job in the

accounts department of Eagle Lion Films, a Rank subsidiary. He spent most evenings at a drama club and was eventually noticed by the director Luchino Visconti who recruited him for his professional theatre company, and helped him to his first small part in the film, based on the novel by Victor Hugo, *I Miserabili* (1948, Les Misérables), directed by Riccardo Freda.

After a few more minor roles, he attracted attention in *Vita da Cani* (1950, *It's a Dog's Life*) and he was given increasingly important parts in a long series of unmemorable films, which established his popularity in Italy. He finally reached the festival circuit when Visconti cast him in *Le Notti Bianche* (1957, *White Nights*)

with Maria Schell and Jean Marais.

In 1959 Federico Fellini began to shoot *La Dolce Vita*, casting Mastroianni as the journalist Marcello, who hangs around with Rome's high society; more than an observer, but less than a catalyst. His boyish charm and obvious availability draw the attentions of beautiful women. But when the friend he admires as a clear-headed intellectual, kills himself and his two children, Marcello abandons journalism for the pursuit of pleasure but thereby only

The more mature Mastroianni (above), and as seen in an early film (below), I Soliti Ignoti (1958, Persons Unknown), with Vittorio Gassman (left) and Renato Rascel

burdens himself with a sense of futility as well as guilt.

Mastroianni then went on to appear in *Divorzio all'Italiana* (1961, *Divorce – Italian Style*), directed by Pietro Germi, which afforded him his first really good role, as the effete Sicilian nobleman who, in love with his teenage cousin, wants to rid himself of his wife. Most Italian comedies fail to travel but Germi's film contrived to caricature Italian stereotypes to everyone's liking.

A sharp contrast was called for from Mastroianni by the director Michelangelo Antonioni in *La Notte* (1961, *The Night*), in which Mastroianni plays a fashionable novelist, surrounded by lovely women, who fails to give, or even to understand, what they want of him. Unlike Fellini, Antonioni does not treat lack of emotion as a colourful neurosis which makes its victim more interesting; his images are bleak and distanced, showing his figures as cut off from each other and their own humanity. However, even in this negative role Mastroianni holds the balance against any other actor or actress.

Meanwhile, *Divorce – Italian Style* continued to win him acclaim, including the British Film Academy's Best Foreign Actor Award. Mastroianni became one of the most sought-after actors in Europe; in Italy, he ranked second only to Alberto Sordi. In 1962, he played in director Louis Malle's *Vie Privée* (*A Very Private Affair*) with Brigitte Bardot, and also in *Cronaca Familiare* (*Family Diary*) directed by Valerio Zurlini, before returning to Fellini for his second most famous role as the director-hero Luigi in *Otto e Mezzo* (1963, *8½*). As in so many of Fellini's films, dreams and memories come together with a present which is less real than either. Luigi is at a point of crisis; he has withdrawn to an out-of-season resort to re-write his script, but the people who claim his attention all turn up. The film's ending is a dream sequence which is also a resolution of his conflicts: he assumes the powers of a circus-master and brings everyone together in the ring for a grand finale. Throughout, Mastroianni hardly needs to act: he is there, while the others cavort around him.

The next major collaboration between Fellini and Mastroianni came twenty years after their first, in *La Città delle Donne* (1980, *City of Women*), which Mastroianni claims to be his hundredth film. Fellini's subject is the inability

Right: Mastroianni as a lonely man searching for love in White Nights *– meaning sleepless nights. Centre right: three of the friends intent on gorging themselves to death in* Blow Out, *played by Philippe Noiret (standing), Mastroianni and Michel Piccoli (right). Far right: in a more festive mood with Billie Whitelaw in* Leo the Last

of his generation to cope with even the first steps of female emancipation. Professor Snaporaz, played by Mastroianni, wants to have an affair with a beautiful woman he meets on a train: she leads him to a women's lib conference, which, like a nightmare, expands into a world run by women where he is totally bewildered by all that happens.

Mastroianni has repeatedly said that filming with other directors is work, but with Fellini it is a game. They are close friends: they share their attitudes and their sense of humour. But just as Fellini denies that his films are directly autobiographical, Mastroianni rejects the suggestion that he models any character he plays on Fellini. They both aim at creating the typical, sophisticated Italian of their generation. Their joint creation reflects centuries of male egotism which prevents such a man from formulating a dialogue with women, or even noticing that they are autonomous beings. In this way they have brought forth the anti-heroes of four shrill, flamboyant films, *La Dolce Vita*, *8½*, *Fellini's Roma* (1972) and *La Città delle Donne*, in which Mastroianni gives deliberately low-key performances, just being himself. But an actor's self is seldom as interesting as a complex part scripted by a good writer. To judge Mastroianni as an actor his work with other directors should also be looked at.

For example, in *Leo the Last* (1970), written and directed by John Boorman and made in London, Mastroianni uses his aristocratic manner and kindliness as an exiled prince who tries to found something like the Kingdom of Heaven in Bayswater. Boorman's film is as eccentric and unclassifiable as any of director Marco Ferreri's, and, while it failed at the box-office, it still contributes more to Mastroianni's standing than any number of routine comedies.

By this time Mastroianni's talents were divided equally between pot-boilers and serious acting in such masterpieces as Ferreri's *La Grande Bouffe* (1973, *Blow-Out*) in which he

plays the light-hearted playboy who joins his friends in eating themselves to death. In *Allonsanfán* (1974) under the joint direction of Paulo and Vittorio Taviani, he had to retain his patrician mannerisms and still lead a revolution; to become a traitor, and still hold the audience's sympathy. Many critics thought that he should have won the acting award at Cannes for playing the gentle, homosexual radio announcer in director-screenwriter Ettore Scola's *Una Giornata Particolare* (1977, *A Special Day*). Waiting for the police to arrest and deport him, he offers a tired, exploited but fervently fascist housewife, played well by Sophia Loren, her one and only genuine human contact.

The following year he turned in another heart-rending performance in Ferreri's *Ciao Maschio* (1978, *Bye Bye Monkey*) as an asthmatic, seedy professor in the desolate New York of the future. He was back in Cannes in 1980 in Scola's *La Terrazza* (1979, *The Terrace*) in which he plays a journalist whose ex-wife is more interested in her work than in his romantic attempts to woo her again. Like all the other fiftyish men in the film, he is

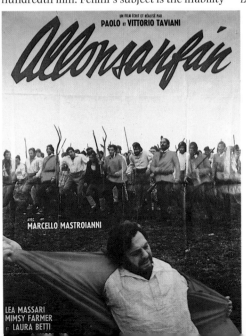

nonplussed by the change in women, by their wanting more from life than loving and being loved. Mastroianni manages to convey both nostalgia, and an intellectual capacity to respect, while regretting, the equal rights of women.

Sensibly, he has continued in the vein of playing middle-aged, almost elderly, character roles: as the aging dancer in *Ginger and Fred* (1985), the eager-to-please eccentric in *Macaroni* (1984), and the greying schoolteacher obsessed with a young girl in *The Beekeeper* (1986). It is a good man, as well as a good actor, that can grow old so gracefully.

Below far left: the poster for Allonsanfán. *Below left: Mastroianni, Vittorio Gassman and Ombretta Colli as members of a group of people who meet on* La Terrazza *during one hot Roman summer. Below: Mastroianni trapped in his nightmare world of female domination in* La Città delle Donne

Filmography
1948: I Miserabili (IT). '50 Vent'Anni (IT); Domenica d'Agosto (IT) (GB: A Sunday in August); Vita da Cani (IT) (GB: It's a Dog's Life); Cuori sul Mare (IT-FR). '51 Atto d'Accusa (IT) (GB: The Charge Is Murder); A Tale of Five Cities *ep* Passaporto per l'Oriente (GB); Contro la Legge (IT); Parigi è Sempre Parigi (IT-FR). '52 Le Ragazze di Piazza di Spagna (IT) (USA: Three Girls From Rome; GB: The Girls of the Spanish Steps); L'Eterna Catena (IT); Sensualità (IT) (GB: Enticement). '53 Gli Eroi della Domenica (IT); Febbre di Vivere (IT); Viale della Speranza (IT); Lulù (IT); Penne Nere (IT); Non è Mai Troppo Tardi (IT). '54 Tempi Nostri *ep* Il Pupo (IT-FR) (USA: The Anatomy of Love; GB: Slice of Life); Cronache di Poveri Amanti (IT); Tragico Ritorno (IT); La Valigia dei Sogni (IT); La Schiava del Peccato (IT); La Muta di Portici (IT); Casa Ricordi (IT-FR) (USA: House of Ricordi). '55 Giorni d'Amore (IT-FR); Peccato che Sia una Canaglia (IT) (GB: Too Bad She's Bad); Tam Tam Mayumbe (IT); La Bella Mugnaia (IT) (USA: The Miller's Beautiful Wife; GB: The Miller's Wife). '56 La Fortuna di Essere Donna (IT-FR) (GB: Lucky to be a Woman); Il Bigamo (IT-FR) (USA: A Plea for Passion; GB: The Bigamist); La Principessa della Canarie (IT). '57 Padri e Figli (IT-FR) (USA: A Tailor's Maid; GB: Like Father, Like Son); La Ragazza della Salina (IT-GER-YUG); Il Momento più Bello (IT-FR) (USA/GB: The Most Wonderful Moment); Le Notti Bianche (IT-FR) (USA/GB: White Nights); Il Medico e lo Stregone (IT-FR). '58 Un Ettaro di Cielo (IT) (GB: An Acre of Paradise); Racconti d'Estate (IT-FR) (USA: Love on the Riviera; GB: Girls for the Summer); I Soliti Ignoti (IT) (USA: Big Deal on Madonna Street; GB: Persons Unknown). '59 La Loi (FR-IT) (USA/GB: Where the Hot Wind Blows); Il Nemico di Mia Moglie (IT); Tutti Innamorati (IT); Amore e Guai (IT); La Dolce Vita (IT-FR). '60 Fernando I Re di Napoli (IT); Il Bell'Antonio (IT-FR); Adua e le Compagne (IT) (USA: Love à la Carte; GB: Hungry for Love). '61 La Notte (IT-FR) (GB: The Night); L'Assassino (IT-FR) (USA: Lady-Killer of Rome; GB: The Assassin); Fantasmi a Roma (IT) (GB: Phantom Lovers); Divorzio all'Italiana (IT) (USA/GB: Divorce – Italian Style). '62 Vie Privée (FR-IT) (USA/GB: A Very Private Affair); Cronaca Familiare (IT) (USA/GB: Family Diary). '63 Otto e Mezzo (IT-FR) (USA/GB: 8½); I Compagni (IT-FR) (USA/GB: The Organizer). '64 Ieri, Oggi e Domani (IT-FR) (USA/GB): Yesterday, Today and Tomorrow; Matrimonio all'Italiana (IT-FR) (USA/GB: Marriage Italian Style). '65 Casanova 70 (IT-FR); Oggi, Domani, Dopodomani (IT-FR); La Decima Vittima (IT-FR) (USA/GB: The Tenth Victim). '66 Io, Io, Io . . . e gli Altri (IT) (GB: Me, Me, Me . . . and the Others); Danger Grows Wild/The Poppy Is also a Flower (United Nations); Spara Forte, Più Forte, Non Capisco (IT) (USA: Shout Loud, Louder . . . I Don't Understand). '67 Lo Straniero (IT-FR) (USA: The Stranger; GB: The Outsider). '68 Questi Fantasmi (IT-FR) (USA: Ghosts, Italian Style); L'Uomo dai Palloncini (IT-FR) (USA: Break Up); La Moglie Bionda (IT-FR) (USA: Kiss the Other Sheik); Diamonds for Breakfast (GB); Amanti (IT-FR) (USA/GB: A Place for Lovers). '70 I Girasoli (IT-USSR) (USA/GB: Sunflower); Leo the Last (GB); Dramma della Gelosia, Tutti i Particolari in Cronaca (IT-SP) (USA: The Pizza Triangle; GB: Jealousy, Italian Style); La Moglie del Prete (IT-FR) (USA/GB: The Priest's Wife); Giuochi Particolari (IT-FR). '71 Scipione detto Anche l'Africano (IT); Ça N'Arrive Qu'aux Autres (FR-IT) (USA: It Only Happens to Others); Permette? Rocco Papaleo (IT). '72 Fellini's Roma (IT-FR); Correva l'Anno di Grazia 1870 . . . (IT); Liza/La Cagna (FR-IT); Che? (IT-FR-GER) (USA: Diary of Forbidden Dreams; GB: What?). '73 Mordì e Fuggì (IT); La Grande Bouffe (FR-IT) (USA/GB: Blow-Out); Rappresaglia (IT-FR) (GB: Massacre in Rome); L'Evénement le Plus Important Depuis que l'Homme a Marché sur la Lune (FR-IT) (USA/GB: The Slightly Pregnant Man); Salut l'Artiste (FR-IT) (USA: The Bit Player). '74 Touche Pas la Femme Blanche (FR-IT); Allonsanfán (IT); La Pupa del Gangster (IT-FR); C'Eravamo Tanti Amati (IT) (USA: We All Loved Each Other So Much). '75 Per le Antiche Scale (IT-FR) (USA/GB: Down the Ancient Staircase); Divina Creatura (IT) (USA: Divine Nymph). '76 La Donna della Domenica (IT-FR); Culastrisce, Nobile Veneziano (IT); Todo Modo (IT). '77 Signore e Signori, Buonanotte (IT); Una Giornata Particolare (IT-CAN) (USA/GB: A Special Day); Mogliamante (IT) (USA/GB: Wifemistress). '78 Doppio Delitto (IT-FR); Bye Bye Monkey/Ciao Maschio/Ciao, Male (IT-FR); Così Come Sei (IT) (USA: Stay as You Are). '79 Fatto di Sangue Fra Due Uomini (IT) (USA/GB: Blood Feud); L'Ingorgo (IT-FR-SP-GER); Giallo Napoletano (IT); La Terrazza (IT-FR). '80 La Città delle Donne (IT-FR); La Pelle; Fantasma D'Amore. '81 La Nuit de Varennes (FR-IT) GB: Revolution); Oltre la Porta (GB: Beyond the Door); '82 Gabriela (BRAZ); Storia di Piera (GB: The New World); Le Géneral de l'Armée Morte (FR-IT). '83 Enrico IV. '84 Le Due Vite di Mattia Pascal (USA/GB: The Two Lives of Mattia Pascal); '85 The Legend of the Holy Drinker; Maccheroni (GB: Macaroni); '85 Ginger e Fred (IT-FR-GER) (GB: Ginger and Fred); I Soliti Ignoti Vent'Anni Dopo (USA/GB: Big Deal on Madonna Street); '86 The Good Ship Ulysses; O Melissokomos (GR-FR) (USA/GB: The Beekeeper); Oci Ciornie (GB: Dark Eyes). L'Intervista; '87 Miss Arizona.

Films about people making films, films about their makers' personal problems and films full of intellectual references are three of the most irritating genres there are. $8\frac{1}{2}$ appears to be all three. Its exuberant tempo and striking imagery may carry one along, but it is just as likely to seem needlessly difficult and self-indulgent. Still, to treat it as a purely personal and intellectual film may be misleading.

$8\frac{1}{2}$ certainly does invite a personal reading. Its title refers to the number of films Fellini had directed up to then; Guido is, like Fellini, a film director of international repute; his marital difficulties seem obviously to refer to Fellini's own widely publicized problems. Moreover, the film is full of characteristic Fellini touches: clowns and tatty showbiz performers, big-breasted women and sexual grotesques, Marcello Mastroianni as hero, and a sweetly melancholic Nino Rota score.

Yet $8\frac{1}{2}$ can be taken as a metaphor of much wider significance. It recreates, with all the frustrations and vicissitudes, the experience of trying to come to terms with the world. Fellini's 'private' material stands for any person's individual experience as she or he confronts the world, trying to make sense of it.

If $8\frac{1}{2}$ is about making sense, it is also itself rather hard to make sense of. It seems to cry out for intellectual interpretation. Its complex structure, weaving between memories, dreams and waking life,

is made even more confusing by the welter of references to religion, ideas, the arts, the occult and so on. This allusive richness seems to be begging for a set of footnotes explaining each reference. Yet it is perfectly possible simply to treat each one as examples of different ways of making sense as they confront Guido.

Besides, in many ways $8\frac{1}{2}$ is a profoundly *un*intellectual film. There is, as elsewhere in Fellini, explicit anti-intellectualism in the figure of the critic Daumier. Played by the critic Jean Rougeul, he is cast, as is characteristic of Fellini, for his looks – a sharp-nosed, very unfleshy appearance, representing the carping anti-life stance that Fellini identifies as typical of intellectuals.

The ending of $8\frac{1}{2}$ too is a rejection of all kinds of intellectual or systematic attempts at making sense, and also of scouring one's past (as Guido has been doing) for clues to the present. When Guido meets Claudia, the screen goddess who is to play the ideal woman (here played by screen goddess Claudia Cardinale), he meets a pleasant, ordinary woman . . . not an ideal. It kills off an aspect of the film – how is he ever to find a woman to embody the ideal woman? – but he also learns from this that the real problem with his character (the character in the film, Guido himself) is that he does not know how to love. This is the clue to the final scene of the film where Guido, sitting in a car

listening to critic Daumier droning on, imagines gathering together everyone he has known and dancing round a circus ring with them. That will be the conclusion to the film, and it is also the conclusion to $8\frac{1}{2}$ – a simple celebration of the dance of life, a warm acceptance of other people.

However, the very last image is not this, but a small boy playing a melancholy tune on a flute. The boy is Guido as a child seen through Guido's memories. It was only in his imagination that he embraced

life simply; behind that he is still a confused small boy playing a sad little melody.

It is a difficult conclusion to come to terms with. Rhythmically it is hypnotic. Nowhere has Fellini more ravishingly combined music, the tempo of editing and the pace of both movement within the frame and movement of the camera, all orchestrated into a crescendo of affirmation with a coda of melancholy. For all this, $8\frac{1}{2}$ has set off a multitude of intellectual hares, and does offer itself as some kind of

Directed by Federico Fellini, 1963
Prod co: Cineriz. **prod:** Angelo Rizzoli. **sc:** Federico Fellini, Ennio Flaiano, Tullio Pinelli, Brunello Rondi. **photo:** Gianni Di Venanzo. **ed:** Leo Catozzo. **art dir:** Piero Gherardi. **mus:** Nino Rota. **prod man:** Nello Meniconi. **ass dir:** Guidarino Guidi. **r/t:** 138 minutes.
Cast: Marcello Mastroianni (*Guido Anselmi*), Claudia Cardinale (*Claudia*), Anouk Aimée (*Luisa Anselmi*), Sandra Milo (*Carla*), Rossella Falk (*Rossella*), Barbara Steele (*Gloria Morin*), Guido Alberti (*Pace, the producer*), Madeleine Lebeau (*actress*), Jean Rougeul (*Fabrizio Carini*), Caterina Boratto (*vision*), Annibale Ninchi (*Anselmi's father*), Giuditta Rissone (*Anselmi's mother*), Mario Pisu (*Mozzabotta*), Jacqueline Bonbon (*dancer*), Alberto Conochia (*production manager*), Ian Dallas (*mind-reader*), Edra Gale (*La Saraghina*), Tito Masini (*cardinal*), Cesarino Miceli Pardi (*production inspector*), Neil Robinson (*agent*), Mino Doro (*Claudia's agent*), Mario Tarchetti (*Claudia's press representative*), Eugene Walter (*American journalist*), Gilda Dahlberg (*his wife*), Annie Gorassini (*Pace's girlfriend*), Mary Indovino (*mind-reader's partner*), Mario Conocchia (*director*), Bruno Agostini (*production secretary*), John Stacy (*accountant*), Mark Herron (*Luisa's admirer*), Elisabetta Catalano (*Luisa's sister*), Alfredo De Lafeld (*cardinal's secretary*), Frazier Rippy (*lay secretary*), Maria Tedeschi (*college president*), Georgia Simmons (*nun*), Yvonne Casadei (*ageing soubrette*), Nadine Sanders (*air hostess*), Hazel Rogers (*negress*), Hedy Vessel (*dresser*), Rosella Como, Francesco Rigamonti, Matilde Calnam (*Luisa's friends*), Roberto Nicolosi (*doctor*), Riccardo Guglielmi, Marco Gemini (*Anselmi as a boy*).

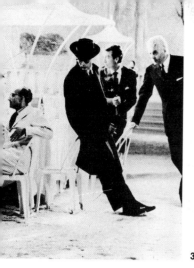

testament to both film-making and Fellini himself. In the face of this, there is something too ingratiating about the fantasy affirmation of life, something too maudlin about the little-boy-lost image. What Guido has supposedly learned from Claudia is the need to love, and the final images are supposedly an enactment of a new-found love. Nonetheless, as so often with the male-artist-in-crisis, familiar from mid-century art, it is not so much a declaration of love as a demand for it, and a demand for that most unconditional form of love that the small boy supposedly elicits from his mother. Musically, the ending feels like an affirmation; imagistically it looks like a plea. Ultimately, if $8\frac{1}{2}$ is to stand as a testament to creativity, it will depend on how the audience decides where its sympathies lie.

Guido, an internationally successful Italian film director, is trying to make his latest film (1). He already has some expensive sets and the rudiments of a story about a man who chases an ideal woman who rejects him. But he cannot get started.

He is overwhelmed by the clamour of his professional colleagues (2) and entangled in personal problems of his own making. These are exacerbated when his feather-brained mistress, Carla (3), and disconsolate wife, Luisa (4), both turn up where the film is being made.

Memories of childhood (5) and sexual fantasies assail him: a visit to a Cardinal; a vision of a harem (6); meeting his ideal – Claudia (7). Perhaps these ought to be the material for the film?

At a press conference he hides from reporters and his producer who want to know what film he is making, when he is saved by a band of clowns (8) and finally the whole cast of the film (9). He has various options – to commit suicide, to give up filming altogether, to make his peace with the world. . . .

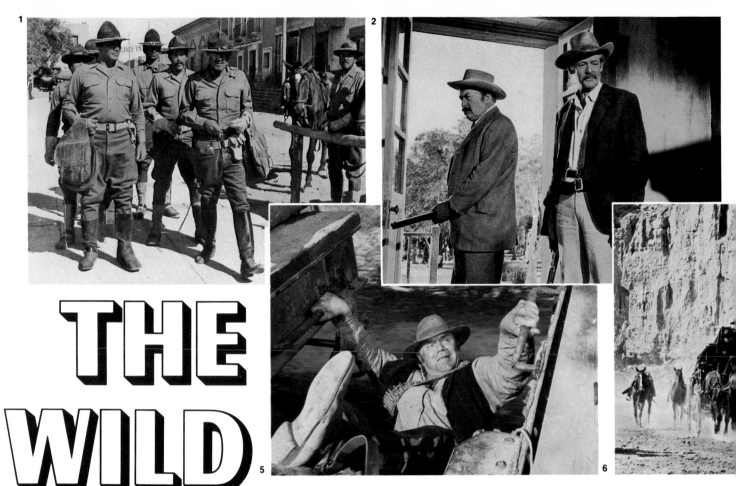

THE WILD BUNCH

The Wild Bunch is bracketed by two extraordinary set-pieces of chaotically lethal action. The film begins with the frantic shoot-up – slaughtering sundry innocent bystanders – that ensues from the Bishop gang's aborted raid on the Starbuck bank; and ends with the orgiastic ritual of destruction in which – hugely outnumbered – the gang's ultimate survivors go down fighting as they manage to take a horde of Mapache's troops to perdition with them. Never before had carnage been so graphically or operatically wrought upon the screen.

It is probably these that are the sequences which pin down the film in the popular memory. For all that its protagonists – ageing gunfighters stranded by the rising tide of modern life – are men out of their time, Peckinpah's movie coincided spectacularly (in all senses) with a given moment in film history. Although Arthur Penn's Bonnie and Clyde (1967) two years earlier had pointed the way to a treatment of death and injury both franker and more elaborate than had previously been deemed acceptable, it was

The Wild Bunch that fully embraced this development. 'I wanted to show,' said Peckinpah, 'what the hell it feels like to get shot.'

In some of Peckinpah's subsequent films his preoccupation with savagery may become sterile or even absurd, and the slow-motion effects which – following Penn's example – he put to such striking use in The Wild Bunch would later, in his own and other hands, become a cliché. But here the explicitness of the scenes of carnage completely unites with the implications of the material: the members of the Wild Bunch can only achieve a kind of meaning for themselves in obliteration by violent death.

At one level, of course, the movie offers a repudiation of the chivalric trappings of the Western genre: Peckinpah extends the conventions of the anti-Westerns of a decade earlier, such as Delmer Daves' Cowboy (1958). Unlike the hired guns of The Magnificent Seven (1960), Bishop and his followers do not sign up on the side of the oppressed Mexican peasantry, but

rather with their corrupt oppressors. Indeed, the desperadoes who comprise the Bunch, ready to shoot down perfunctorily one of their own wounded when he is unable to keep up with them, would surely in an earlier vintage have been treated as antagonists rather than the 'heroes'.

Finally, though, and not simply through the force of Lucien Ballard's magisterial wide-screen images of horsemen traversing daunting landscapes and engaging in exploits of derring-do (such as the dynamite nonchalantly touched-off with a lighted cigar in the train robbery), the vision which the film asserts is a romantic one. The plot crucially turns on the mutual dependence of Bishop and Thornton (played with marvellously haggard strength by Robert Ryan), and the former clearly accepts that Thornton's dilemma in becoming the 'Judas goat' of the railroad bosses stems from Bishop's own

earlier lapse in allowing his old comrade to be captured.

There is, too, an almost luxuriant romanticism about the Mexican villagers' ceremonial farewell to Bishop and his men, a sequence which is repeated by Peckinpah at the film's very end. And eventually – though too late – the Bunch themselves set aside their façade of cynical pragmatism in abandoning Angel to his fate, and commit themselves to an heroically suicidal gesture on his behalf: 'This time,' declares Pike Bishop, 'let's do it right'.

The Wild Bunch is not without flaws: there is too apparent a recourse to literary metaphor in the deployment of children for ironic effect, and in such details as the vultures which symbolize the degenerate bounty hunters. But the defects fade away to unimportance within the obvious grandeur of the overall design. This is a movie of true size.

Directed by Sam Peckinpah, 1969
Prod co: Warner Brothers/Seven Arts. **prod:** Phil Feldman. **assoc. prod:** Roy N. Sickner. **prod man:** William Faralla. **2nd unit dir:** Buzz Henry. **sc:** Walon Green, Sam Peckinpah, from a story by Walon Green, Roy N. Sickner. **photo** (Technicolor, Panavision 70): Lucien Ballard. **ed:** Louis Lombardo. **art dir:** Edward Carrere. **mus:** Jerry Fielding. **sd:** Robert J. Miller. **ass dir:** Cliff Coleman, Fred Gamon. **r/t:** 145 minutes.
Cast: William Holden (Pike Bishop), Ernest Borgnine (Dutch), Robert Ryan (Deke Thornton), Edmond O'Brien (Sykes), Warren Oates (Lyle Gorch), Jaime Sanchez (Angel), Ben Johnson (Hector Gorch), Emilio Fernandez (Mapache), Strother Martin (Coffer), L. Q. Jones (T. C.), Albert Dekker (Harrigan), Bo Hopkins (Crazy Lee), Bud Taylor (Wainscoat), Jorge Russek (Zamorra), Alfonso Arau (Herrera), Chano Urueta (Don José), Sonia Amelio (Teresa), Aurora Clavel (Aurora), Elsa Cardenas (Elsa).

The place is Texas, the year 1914. Disguised as soldiers, the Wild Bunch – an outlaw gang led by Pike Bishop and his sidekick Dutch – ride into Starbuck to rob the bank of a railroad payroll (1). But an ambush has been prepared by the rail bosses, who have had Pike's former comrade Deke Thornton released from a prison sentence to lead a band of bounty hunters against the Bunch (2).

The ambush goes wrong, and in a hail of crossfire many of the townspeople are killed. Most of the gang escape, and after picking up their veteran comrade Sykes, deemed too old for action, they head into Mexico. There they encounter the villainous warlord 'General' Mapache (3), who hires them to steal guns from an American army munitions train. When Angel, a patriotic Mexican who rides with the Bunch, finds his girl is living with Mapache, a bloodbath is narrowly averted (4). After resting-up at Angel's home village, the gang goes ahead with the train robbery (5).

Bishop realizes that Thornton will be onto the scheme, but succeeds in outwitting him. Once the train has been held up, Mapache attempts to double-cross the Bunch in a canyon (6), but he is forestalled and has to pay up. However, Mapache finds out that Angel has given some of the stolen guns to Mexican revolutionaries, and takes him prisoner (7).

Initially, the Bunch abandon Angel to his fate, but after seeing him tortured by Mapache, Pike, Dutch and the Gorch brothers (Sykes is left behind as look-out) enter Mapache's camp and demand Angel's release. In reply Mapache slits Angel's throat (8); Pike shoots Mapache dead (9), precipitating a bloody pitched battle between the Bunch and Mapache's troops, ending with no survivors (10). Later, Sykes appears on the scene with a group of revolutionaries; Thornton also arrives and decides to join them.

339

Pizza (or Pasta) Westerns

A new title for a famous movie menu. And the main ingredients? Clint Eastwood, a phantom of the plains swathed in the folds of his poncho; Lee Van Cleef, a grimacing black hawk – Zorro unmasked; a host of grubby villains with bandoliers over their shoulders; and the vision of director Sergio Leone, his cameras focused relentlessly on an echoing wasteland of blood and sand

The 'spaghetti' Western was never an accurate label. Spaghetti is all very well, a wholesome base for sauces, meats, clams, garlic and butter. But spaghetti is bland and monotonous to the eye, and the movies that bore the name were always startling visual events. The 'pizza' Western would have been closer, if you can imagine the lurid sunrise of bubbling cheese, the terracotta menace of pepperoni and the inevitable blood-bath of tomato paste. Pizzas are a sight to behold – if only they made them in CinemaScope shapes, they would be the perfect culinary equivalent for Sergio Leone's hallucinatory films. Except that most of them were actually shot in Spain. Perhaps the example really needed is paella – a desert background of saffron with the violent splashes of pimento, shrimp and chorizo.

These *are* edible films; they have so much ham in them. They are filled with stylized violence and cruelty; they are as serpentine with intrigue as they are loyal to the idea of destiny as the far, flat horizon. They know no other human impulses than greed, treachery, silent honour and the unswerving imperative of revenge, but they cannot be taken seriously. The Westerns made by Sergio Leone and Clint Eastwood are deliberate parodies, or fakes. They mark the end of the trustworthiness of the genre and the onset of a new riot of campness. It is as if the Western, and the American history it seems to represent, had been handed over to a director of television commercials for cheroots, serapes and hard liquor. The significance of the 'spaghetti' West-

ern is not just that non-Americans took over the genre, but that American audiences could no longer believe in their own greatest legend.

Early appetizers

There were uncompromising Westerns made in America in the Fifties, pictures that believed in the frontier, in the sheriff's essential role and in the epic dimension of heroism and landscape. *High Noon* (1952), *Shane* (1953) and the films of Anthony Mann are filled with genuine respect for physical space, small communities and a man's moral decision. But by the end of the decade, the Western was less convinced and far less solemn. Howard Hawks' *Rio Bravo* (1959) is a self-conscious reappraisal of the situation in *High Noon*, but it is also a game in which actors in cowboy hats and Western settings exchange the lines of a modern comedy. For Hawks, both *Red River* (1948) and *The Big Sky* (1952) had believed in the nineteenth century, in real space and problems to be overcome. *Rio Bravo* is a largely interior film in which the archetypal figures of John Wayne and Walter Brennan meet the unmistakably up-to-date Dean Martin, Ricky Nelson and Angie Dickinson. There are moments when the old situations are played straight, but *Rio Bravo*'s inner elegance and wit come from the sense of a stale ritual being jazzed up for 1959. Around the same time, old-timers like George Marshall and Raoul Walsh directed deflating comic Westerns, *The Sheepman* and *The Sheriff of Fractured Jaw* (both 1958). Newcomer Arthur Penn took the Billy the Kid saga, in *The*

Left-Handed Gun (1958), and gave it levels of psychological insight that would have terrified Robert Taylor, who played the outlaw in the 1941 version of *Billy the Kid*.

This is all relevant to the 'spaghetti' Western, for the parody could not occur before the myth of the West had been questioned. By 1960, with John F. Kennedy's manner suggesting the ultimate sheriff could be more like Cary Grant than John Wayne, America was suspicious of its own reliance on Western ethics as a basis for foreign policy. The new, ashamed awareness of Native Americans – so recently 'redskins' or 'hostiles' – was prompting a fresh study of frontier history. With *The Man Who Shot Liberty Valance* (1962) and *Cheyenne Autumn* (1964), even John Ford offered a sketchy apology for the wholesale dishonesty with which Hollywood had gilded the West. But on television, night after night, the same

Left: Rod Steiger (as the peasant bandit Juan), Sergio Leone and the crew of A Fistful of Dynamite. *Below: German poster of* For a Few Dollars More, *in which the two bounty hunters run down a drug-addicted killer*

lies were still being perpetrated in series like *Gunsmoke*, *Wells Fargo*, *Wagon Train* and *Rawhide*. Perhaps that was the final excess that made the Western seem sour and laid it open for satire.

Clint in the sun

Clint Eastwood was a veteran of *Rawhide*, but less than a star, when he went to Europe in 1964 to make *Per un Pugno di Dollari* (*A Fistful of Dollars*), a German-Spanish-Italian co-production, directed by Sergio Leone and shot in southern Spain. The headquarters of the Italian film industry, Cinecittà, had already tried to copy several American genres. But nothing matched the success of *A Fistful of Dollars*, a

rewrite the bad scripts and, since he and Leone had no language in common, Eastwood cut out a lot of his dialogue to avoid directing problems. His character, the Man With No Name, became a beautiful but nearly absurd icon of taciturnity. He was an angel of death, squinting into the sun, given weird grace by the serape, the cheroot and the wide-brimmed hat, and always glorified in Leone's audacious but equally mannered use of TechniScope.

Second and third courses

A Fistful of Dollars was so successful that it launched a trilogy. But whereas the first picture had been 96 minutes long, the others, *Per Qualche Dollari in Più* (1966, *For a Few Dollars More*) and *Il Buono, il Brutto, il Cattivo* (1967, *The Good, the Bad and the Ugly*), were 130 and 161 minutes. Leone slowed the pace, turning tension into a mocking treacle. The music of Ennio Morricone – like a rattlesnake in a drum-kit – added to the tongue-in-cheek menace. There was always a strong supporting cast: Gian Maria Volonté, in the first two; Lee Van Cleef in the last two. Van Cleef had been one of the gunmen in *High Noon*; Eli Wallach, who is in *The Good, the Bad and the Ugly*, had been the bandit chief in *The Magnificent Seven*.

Eastwood was established, and he would become one of the most commercially reliable stars of the Seventies as well as an adventurous director-producer. *Hang 'Em High* (1968), in which he starred soon after his return to America, is a spaghetti dish in the Hollywood style. Indeed it could be argued that the laconic, vengeful and supreme Harry Callahan, the cop Eastwood plays in *Dirty Harry* (1971) and its sequels, is cousin to the Man With No Name. In 1973 Eastwood directed and starred in *High Plains Drifter*, an absurdist Western that must have made Leone proud.

Leone himself made two more notable pictures. *C'Era una Volta il West* (1968, *Once Upon a Time in the West*) is his best film – his most extreme, formal and ridiculous arrangement of Western imagery, a feast of colour, space and Jacobean ritual. There is no Eastwood in it, but the film has Henry Fonda as a deliciously

phenomenon that seems to spring from the sardonic visual imagination of Leone and the hitherto unappreciated smouldering glamour in Eastwood's screen presence.

The film was a rip-off from the Akira Kurosawa film, *Yojimbo* (1961). But that was reasonable, for Kurosawa had often owned up to the way his seemingly authentic samurai films had been inspired by Westerns. Truly, the Western had become a kind of Esperanto; no wonder no-one trusted it. In 1960 John Sturges had made *The Magnificent Seven* as a tribute to Kurosawa's *Shichinin No Samurai* (1954, *Seven*

Samurai). The spectacular violence of that 'remake' and its Mexican settings influenced the films of Sam Peckinpah as well as the Italian Westerns. The seven, though, had been noblemen ready to die for their cause; Leone's invention was to make sleaziness and dishonesty the new norms. His pictures are full of unwashed, unshaved bandidos, the refugees from horror pictures. You know that they can't be trusted because their lip movements never fit what they are saying.

There was reason enough for Eastwood to say nothing. The actor was encouraged to

Above, left to right: 'vicious' Gian Maria Volonte, 'demonic' Henry Fonda – and the bounty. Right: the fathomless Man With No Name who cleans up a Mexican town in A Fistful of Dollars. Eastwood – 'Italian actors come from the Hellzapoppin' school of drama. To get my effect I stayed impassive, and I guess they thought I wasn't acting. All except Leone, who knew what I was doing.' Below: Colonel Mortimer (Van Cleef) lights a match on the hunchback (Klaus Kinski) in For a Few Dollars More; he wants to find out whether the gang is concocting a plot more important to them than avenging insults

wicked lead, along with Jason Robards Jr, Charles Bronson, Jack Elam, Woody Strode, Keenan Wynn and Claudia Cardinale, who has to take the leering abuse that is obligatory for voluptuous women in these films. *Giú la Testa* (1972, *A Fistful of Dynamite*) is remarkable for two ham-size performances: Rod Steiger as a Mexican outlaw; James Coburn as an IRA revolutionary.

The 'spaghetti' Western is not common now. Leone's films are few and far between, and Eastwood has moved further towards comedy. But its influence is total. There are so few Westerns made today because the genre has been revealed as not a true fable of rock, lead and dust, but a fabrication of pasta.

THE VIOLENT YEARS

Pain, fear, blood, violence, death – entertainment for the Sixties on screens that reflected the real world but added to it a dash of style

From *Psycho* and *Spartacus* (both 1960) to *The Wild Bunch* and *Easy Rider* (both 1969), the Sixties might be regarded as the period when screen violence gained a new aesthetic self-consciousness and something approaching academic respectability, at least in the public mind. To put it somewhat differently, the contemporary spectator of 1960, shocked by the brutal shower murder of Marion Crane (Janet Leigh) in *Psycho* as an event – without observing that it was a composite film effect created by several dozen rapidly cut shots – would have been much likelier to notice, in 1969, the use of slow motion in the depiction of several dozen violent deaths in *The Wild Bunch*.

The key film document of the decade, endlessly scrutinized and discussed, was not an entertainment feature at all, but the record of an amateur film-maker named Abe Zapruder of the assassination of John F. Kennedy in Dallas on November 22, 1963; the close analysis to which this short length of film was subjected was characteristic of a changing attitude towards the medium as a whole.

In the Sixties many established cultural, social and political values were radically thrown into question, at the same time that the media – including television and pop music as well as cinema – were becoming closely examined in their own right. (The late Marshall McLuhan's book *Understanding Media*, published in 1964, was widely regarded as a seminal text.) These two phenomena converged to create a different conception of what violence was, both as a method and as a subject.

Alfred Hitchcock, who always kept a close eye on fashion, might be considered as one barometer of that change. In *Psycho* and *The Birds* (1963) he approached the intricate problem of how to create the impression of violence in the spectator through technique and technology, from fast editing to detailed special effects. Yet by the time he made *Torn Curtain* (1966), a spy thriller, he was implicitly criticizing the technological fantasy engendered by such James Bond films as *Dr No* (1962), *From Russia With Love* (1963) and *Goldfinger* (1964), whereby a villain could be despatched virtually with the cool flick of a switch or push of a button. Hitchcock made this point by depicting the killing of a heavy as protracted, messy and extremely difficult – not the sort of thing that suave 007 normally had to contend with.

The unusually long-drawn-out deaths in *The Wild Bunch*, on the other hand, were defended by the director Sam Peckinpah as a cathartic strategy: 'to make violence so repulsive as to turn people against it,' was the way he expressed it in a trade journal. Other film-makers argued, quite simply, that a liberal display of violence was merely what their stories and their subject-matter demanded – most notably, in war films such as Samuel Fuller's *Merrill's Marauders* (1962), Robert Aldrich's *The Dirty Dozen* (1967) and John Wayne's *The Green Berets* (1968), and in such critiques of the genre as Jean-Luc Godard's *Les Carabiniers* (1963, *The Soldiers*) and Peter Watkins' television film *Culloden*

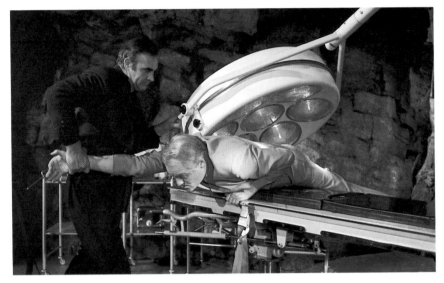

(shown by the BBC in 1964).

'Get up, you scum-sucking pig.' So the gunslinger played by Marlon Brando savagely challenged another tough character in *One Eyed Jacks* (1961). In the same year, gangs of juvenile delinquents fought each other in pitched battles ('rumbles') to the music of Leonard Bernstein in *West Side Story*, and a pool-hall hustler (Paul Newman) had his thumbs deliberately broken by rivals in *The Hustler*. But it would obviously be wrong to assign the Sixties any sort of monopoly in making violence look particularly glamorous, photogenic or graphic.

Yet the Sixties saw the introduction of the 'spaghetti' Western as well as the James Bond thriller; this suggests that the overall sense of violence possessing an aesthetic of its own was an increasingly international phenomenon, in which cultural cross-influences played a decisive part. This was no less true of the comic mishaps of Peter Sellers as Inspector Jacques Clouseau in *The Pink Panther* (1963) and *A Shot in the Dark* (1964) – both Hollywood comedies set on the Continent – and the violent, hallucinatory nightmares of European art

Above: James Bond (Sean Connery) getting the better of master criminal Blofeld (Charles Gray) in Diamonds Are Forever *(1971), Connery's last performance (until he returned as Bond in 1983) in the role that he had made his own in the Sixties. Below: a few of the lads have a friendly scrap in* Performance, *a complex British film combining the gangster genre with a way-out study of a reclusive pop star who has identity problems*

films as diverse as *Le Procès* (1962, *The Trial*), *Repulsion* (1965), *Blow-Up* (1966), *Weekend* (1967) and *Performance* (1970).

All these films highlighted the cross-breeding of American and European elements in a number of ways. 'Spaghetti' Westerns, for instance – spearheaded by a succession of hits starring Americans Clint Eastwood or Charles Bronson and directed by the Italian Sergio Leone, with music by the no less Italian Ennio Morricone – revitalized familiar American myths with Catholic symbolism, operatic intensity and a heavy emphasis on ritual, in films such as *Per un Pugno di Dollari* (1964, *A Fistful of Dollars*), *Per Qualche Dollaro in Più* (1966, *For a Few Dollars More*) and *C'Era una Volta il West* (1968, *Once Upon a Time in the West*). Later, this became intertwined with still other strains to produce even stranger mixtures: for instance, *El Topo* (1971, *The Mole*) was a gory Mexican surrealist variant of the 'spaghetti' Western with mystical, drug-culture overtones, and an early favourite in the midnight cult circuits.

Any thorough survey of international trends in stylizing violence would have to acknowledge the crucial role played by Japanese cinema – more specifically, by the team of director Akira Kurosawa and actor Toshiro Mifune, mainly in an inspired series of action films ranging from *Shichinin No Samurai* (1954, *Seven Samurai*) and *Kumonosu-Jo* (1957, *Throne Of Blood*) to *Yojimbo* (1961) and *Tsubaki Sanjuro* (1961, *Sanjuro*).

Violence was more sophisticated in some American films, but still remained harsh and controversial

Indeed, several commentators have claimed that the 'spaghetti' Western and all its derivatives can be seen growing directly out of *Yojimbo* – a film with plenty of American antecedents of its own. One American critic, Manny Farber, called it:

'. . . a bowdlerized version of Dashiell Hammett's novel *Red Harvest*, with a bossless vagabond who depopulates a town of rival leaders, outlaws and fake heroes.'

Another critic, Donald Richie, compared the town in the film to:

'. . . those God-forsaken places in the middle of nowhere remembered from the films of Ford, of Sturges, from *Bad Day at Black Rock* or *High Noon*.'

No less striking was the cross-fertilization in *Bonnie and Clyde* (1967) between *nouvelle vague* impulses (such as the mixture of moods and genres), Hollywood showmanship (in Arthur Penn's direction of Warren Beatty and Faye Dunaway) and perhaps just a dash of Kurosawa (in the slow-motion, balletic deaths, two years before *The Wild Bunch*). A grittier, black-and-white version of gangster lovers on the run followed in *The Honeymoon Killers* (1969) – interestingly enough, a favourite film of François Truffaut's – where the poetry had a more romantic tinge. Just prior to this, Truffaut had been paying his own homages to American-style violence in *Fahrenheit 451* (1966), his futuristic study of book-burning, and *La Mariée Etait en Noir* (1968, *The Bride Wore Black*), the tale of a widow's revenge on her husband's killers. And if the latter film smacked of Hitchcock even down to its emotive Bernard Herrmann score, English director John Boorman's exciting American thriller *Point Blank* (1967) drew upon the time-fragmented structures of *nouvelle vague* directors, particularly Alain Resnais. Here could also be detected a satirical offshoot of the equation of people with objects already noted in the Bond films; a violent gangster, played by Lee Marvin, in three separate scenes destructively attacks a car, a telephone and an empty bed.

A few real-life robberies of the period seemed to have been modelled closely after those in *Bonnie and Clyde*, once again raising the question of how seriously screen violence could affect public behaviour. To what degree should it be considered merely a reflection of already existing violence, as opposed to offering the spectator fresh inspirations and incentives? Recent studies of mass responses to violence, most of which have concentrated on television, have suggested that a great deal depends

TOO HOT...TOO BIG...FOR TV!

THE MANHUNT THEY HAD TO PUT ON
THE GIANT-SIZED MOVIE THEATRE SCREEN!

First full-length,
life-dimensioned
adventure of
"THE LINEUP"!

THE
LINEUP
starring
ELI WALLACH

(The sensation of "Baby Doll"
as the killer!)

ROBERT KEITH · WARNER ANDERSON
as LT. GUTHRIE

written by STIRLING SILLIPHANT · *based upon the CBS television series* "The Lineup" · *Original story by* LAWRENCE L. KLEE
Produced by JAIME DEL VALLE · *directed by* DON SIEGEL · A FRANK COOPER PRODUCTION · A COLUMBIA PICTURE

*Above far left: Ray Fernandez
(Tony Lo Bianco), an ageing
gigolo, and Martha Beck (Shirley
Stoler), a murderous nurse, in*
The Honeymoon Killers, *based
on a real-life couple executed in
1951. Above: Tony Curtis as* The
Boston Strangler *and one of his
victims. Above right: Eli Wallach
plays a ruthless psychopathic
killer in* The Lineup, *a spin-off
from a TV police series set in San
Francisco; the story concerns drug
smuggling. Right: Walker (Lee
Marvin) is aided by his sister-in-
law Chris (Angie Dickinson) in
recovering some money owed to
him in* Point Blank. *Below:
Charlie (Lee Marvin) and Lee (Clu
Gulager) are* The Killers *on a
mission of death in an institution
for the blind; but their curiosity
about their victim leads in turn to
their own deaths. Far left: Perry
Smith (Robert Blake) killed a
family of four* In Cold Blood *and
was hanged five years later. Left:
George Segal in a production shot
from* The St Valentine's Day
Massacre *(1967)*

on how the audience's identification is solicited,
and what sort of characters have been established
as role models. In the Sixties, the general use of the
gangster as identification figure gave way to a
similar use of the law enforcer. The critic Robert
Warshow had said in 1954:
'The two most successful creations of American
movies are the gangster and the Westerner: men
with guns.'
From this standpoint, there may be relatively
little difference between film-maker and novelist
Norman Mailer's playing successively a gangster in
Wild 90 and a policeman in *Beyond the Law* (both
1968), his first two independent features.
In fact, a closer look at the cinema's overall shift of
attention away from the criminal's viewpoint may
reveal a subtle subterranean continuity. The wolf
in sheep's clothing can be no less bloodthirsty than
the wolf without disguise, but his new social role
and costume might be enough to exonerate him in
part from guilt and society's censure. Thus, in 1963,
Underground film-maker Kenneth Anger could
explore the homo-erotic potential of Hell's Angels
bikers putting on their gear in *Scorpio Rising* – a sort
of striptease in reverse involving chain and leather
fetishes. And precisely ten years later, a fledgling
director, James William Guercio, could create a
comparably worshipful context while presenting
the detailed dressing-up of his own hero, a likeable
highway cop (Robert Blake), in *Electra Glide in Blue*
(1973).
In a recent study of crime movies, film historian
Carlos Clarens has noted that action director Don
Siegel shifted his own focus in mid-career from the
mad criminal in *Baby Face Nelson* (1957), *The Lineup*
(1958) and *The Killers* (1964) to the policeman in
Madigan, Coogan's Bluff (both 1968) and *Dirty Harry*
(1971). Hollywood's reluctance (with a very few
exceptions, such as *The Green Berets*) to deal directly
with the war in Vietnam during this period created
its own forms of displacement, whereby the emotional weight of the Vietnam experience became
transferred to domestic law-and-order thrillers like
Madigan or *Bullitt* (1968), which 'brought home'
the war only in the most oblique terms.
Meanwhile, as the political mood of the Sixties
became increasingly polarized, violence often came
to represent either society's aggression against the
young or youth's own reprisals, in such hits as *Wild
in the Streets, If. . . .* (both 1968), *Easy Rider* (1969)
and *Joe* (1970). At the same time, the legacy of an
equally violent past was being unearthed in certain
period films – the marathon dances in *They Shoot
Horses, Don't They?*, the oppression of the Paiute
Indians in *Tell Them Willie Boy Is Here* (both 1969).
Confronted by a more recent past of senseless
mass murders, *In Cold Blood, Targets* (both 1967)
and *The Boston Strangler* (1968) all tried to deal with
the missing motivations. *In Cold Blood*, adapted by
Richard Brooks from Truman Capote's non-fiction
account of the arbitrary murder of a family in
Kansas by two disaffected loners, added heavy doses
of Freudian flashback to the original material,
while *The Boston Strangler* focused in a quasi-
documentary manner on police procedure, using a
striking multi-image technique. *Targets* depicted a
character based on the real-life University of Texas
sniper and counterpointed his case with the story of
an ageing horror-film star (Boris Karloff), making
little attempt to explain the sniper's motives beyond
implied criticism of the gun laws and of the
boredom of American family life. Dryly pursuing
this two-part invention about contemporary
horror, the director Peter Bogdanovich followed the
lead of Truffaut by turning to Hitchcock for much of
his inspiration, as would other disciples in the
violent Seventies.

345

Clyde was the leader, Bonnie wrote poetry.

C.W. was a Myrna Loy fan who had a bluebird tattooed on his chest. Buck told corny jokes and carried a Kodak. Blanche was a preacher's daughter who kept her fingers in her ears during the gunfights. They played checkers and photographed each other incessantly. On Sunday nights they listened to Eddie Cantor on the radio. All in all, they killed 18 people.

They were the strangest damned gang you ever heard of.

WARREN BEATTY
FAYE DUNAWAY
BONNIE
and CLYDE x

MICHAEL J. POLLARD · GENE HACKMAN · ESTELLE PARSONS   DAVID NEWMAN and ROBERT BENTON · Charles Strouse · WARREN BEATTY · ARTHUR PENN   TECHNICOLOR® A WARNER BROS.—SEVEN ARTS RELEASE

The original script of *Bonnie and Clyde* passed through divers hands before the finished film opened in America to critical indignation and audience acclaim. David Newman and Robert Benton first submitted their script to Jean-Luc Godard and then François Truffaut, both of whom suggested improvements before turning it down. Then Warren Beatty bought the property and persuaded Warner Brothers (the studio responsible for the great gangster movies of the Thirties) to finance it with Beatty as star and producer and Arthur Penn as director. Robert Towne, who later wrote *Chinatown* (1974) and Beatty's *Shampoo* (1975), polished the final draft without taking screen credit. The result was one of the most popular and influential films ever made in America.

It is intriguing to speculate what Godard and Truffaut might have made of such an essentially American subject. There are echoes of *Bande à Part* (1964, *The Outsiders*) and *Pierrot le Fou* (1965, Pierrot the Fool) in Penn's approach to genre and his abrupt changes of mood but the connection with the French *nouvelle vague* is more general than specific: like the early films of the *nouvelle vague*, *Bonnie and Clyde* liberated a national cinema from aesthetic stagnation and, in so doing, captured the imagination of American youth who regarded the values of Hollywood as anachronistic and its genres as moribund. Not since Nicholas Ray's *Rebel Without a Cause* (1955) had young Americans seen their frustrations articulated quite so forcefully on the screen.

The film's vivid account of social banditry paralleled the growing counter-culture and Vietnam protest movement and was developed in many subsequent films – *Alice's Restaurant*, *Easy Rider*, *Butch Cassidy and the Sundance Kid* (all 1969), *Bad Company* (1971), *Badlands* (1973). The commercial success of *Bonnie and Clyde* was merchandized in the form of nostalgia for Thirties music and fashion and inevitably led to a rash of gangster movies. The film's graphic violence ricocheted into the Seventies and Eighties.

If the film's style was refreshingly contemporary, the subject was far from new. *Persons in Hiding* (1939) and *The Bonnie Parker Story* (1958) attempted to portray the squalid facts of the case whilst *You Only Live Once* (1937), *They Live By Night* (1948) and *Gun Crazy* (1949) were adapted from the same source material. In fact, Bonnie Parker and Clyde Barrow scarcely rated more than a footnote in the history books and their robberies, punctuated by a dozen murders, were little more than petty thefts. Clyde was thought to have been homosexual and Bonnie's husband was a gang member but their legend as romantic fugitives grew from their instinct for publicity. Bonnie's doggerel verse and their snapshots were published in newspapers and earned them the status of folk-heroes to the destitute farmers of the southern states.

The real Bonnie and Clyde would have loved Penn's film because it is their pathetic image of themselves that is evoked so arrestingly. It is essentially a film about those most fundamental American impulses – celebrity and material and sexual success. The film's heroes are located within the mythology of cinema: Bonnie sees Ginger Rogers sing 'We're in the Money' from *Gold-Diggers of 1933* (1933); Clyde consciously models himself on Al Capone; the farmers they meet on the road resemble the Joads in *The Grapes of Wrath* (1940). Indeed, the Barrow gang move across the derelict landscape like movie stars, travelling players in a script which contrives for them a vanglorious death and posthumous fame.

Snapshots of the real gang – grainy and unglamorous – are behind the credits which fade to blood red. From here Penn cuts to the glamorous features of Beatty and Faye Dunaway. The other gang members are photographed throughout in unflattering light (and Buck and Blanche are later facially disfigured) but Bonnie and Clyde are always beautiful. This romantic idealism of them is ambiguous – the film remains sufficiently detached for the audience to identify with them and the visceral pleasure derived from their exploits. Their naivety and conceit is disarming and the film's jauntiness is both amusing and seductive. But gradually the viewer's pleasure is undercut by sudden irruptions of appalling violence – a Keystone Cops getaway turns sour when a bank clerk has his face blown off. The film becomes preoccupied with death, foretold by Bonnie's poem which releases Clyde's sexuality and hastens his end. The slow-motion massacre turns the heroes into frenzied corpses. The ugly and humourless Texas Ranger, Hamer, lowers his smoking carbine and then stares directly into the camera, in silent and merciless admonishment of our own impulses.

Bonnie Parker is easily attracted by Clyde Barrow's reckless charm and when he nonchalantly robs a store she joins him (1) for a life of crime. After one of their hold-ups, they invite C. W. Moss, a car mechanic, to join them (2). The gang is completed by Buck, Clyde's ex-con brother, and his excitable wife, Blanche (3): they continue to rob banks.

The gang's exploits endear them to victims of the Depression but they narrowly avoid capture when the police surround their rented house (4, 5). Now wanted for murder, they are chased from state to state and humiliated by Sheriff Hamer who is humiliated when the trap he sets for them rebounds on himself.

2

3

5

6

8

9

Bonnie, though, senses the end is near and she visits her mother at a desolate rendezvous (6). Later the gang is ambushed (7), Buck is killed and Blanche, blinded, is taken prisoner. The others escape (8). C. W. takes Bonnie and Clyde to his father's house where they nurse their wounds (9). During this brief period of peace Bonnie has a poem published in a newspaper, and Clyde overcomes his impotence with Bonnie in a corn field.

Concerned for his son's safety, Mr Moss makes a deal with Hamer, and while driving in a quiet country lane (10 – production shot) Bonnie and Clyde die in a hail of bullets.

Directed by Arthur Penn, 1967
Prod co: Tatira/Hiller/Warner Bros. **prod:** Warren Beatty. **sc:** David Newman, Robert Benton. **photo** (Technicolor): Burnett Guffey. **ed:** Dede Allen. **art dir:** Dean Tavoularis, Raymond Paul. **mus:** Charles Strouse. **cost:** Theadora Van Runkle. **sd:** Francis E. Stahl. **r/t:** 111 minutes.
Cast: Warren Beatty (*Clyde Barrow*), Faye Dunaway (*Bonnie Parker*), Michael J. Pollard (*C. W. Moss*), Gene Hackman (*Buck Barrow*), Estelle Parsons (*Blanche*), Denver Pyle (*Frank Hamer*), Dub Taylor (*Ivan Moss*), Evans Evans (*Velma Davis*), Gene Wilder (*Eugene Grizzard*).

10

'If a famous old film with the same title had not already existed, I should have liked to call *La Battaglia di Algeri* The Birth of a Nation. This, in fact, is the sense of the story . . . because it tells of the pains and the lacerations which the birth of the Algerian nation brought to all its people.'

In his own words, Gillo Pontecorvo thus described his film of the rise of the nationalist movement in Algeria and its crushing defeat by the French five years before independence. It is both an overtly political film, following the struggle of the Algerian Liberation Front (FLN), as well as a profoundly human one in its account of the politicization of the rebel leader Ali La Pointe, as he moves from being a petty criminal to leader of the underground resistance and ultimately a martyr. The confusions, doubts and fears of the Algerians in their struggle for independence are believably conveyed, as is the violence and terrorism that accompanied the struggle.

Production of *Battle of Algiers* was an exciting political event in itself, since it used the Algerian people to recreate their own history. Four years after independence, with the full cooperation of the Algerian government, Pontecorvo returned to the site of the strongest FLN resistance – the Casbah – to use the actual locations for his film. He and his assistants spent two years collecting information from the accounts of over 10,000 eye-witnesses. The result is a highly atmospheric work, which captures the flavour of the Arab quarters of Algiers.

Its style is a documentary one, yet the film uses no newsreel footage to construct its events. It has been estimated that in making the film all 80,000 inhabitants of the Casbah took part in one form or another. Only a few professional actors were used; most of the players were people recruited from the streets and cafés because their faces fitted the character. One old man cried when his part was over – he was a thief and had to return to jail for 15 days. Indeed, Yacef Saadi, organizer of the Casbah resistance, who by 1966 had become the president of the Casbah Film company, and was one of the producers of *Battle of Algiers*, played himself in the film: 'I have substituted the camera for the

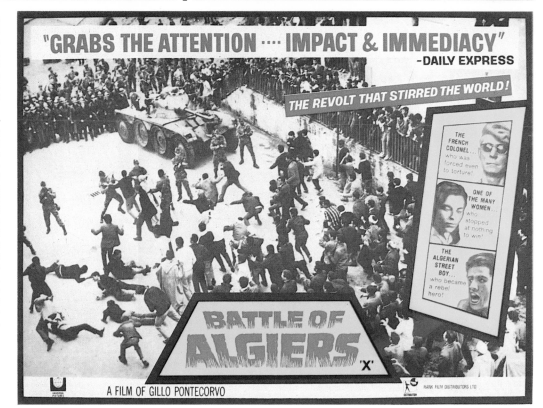

"GRABS THE ATTENTION .... IMPACT & IMMEDIACY"
—DAILY EXPRESS

THE REVOLT THAT STIRRED THE WORLD!

THE FRENCH COLONEL... who was forced even to torture!

ONE OF THE MANY WOMEN... who stopped at nothing to win!

THE ALGERIAN STREET BOY... who became a rebel hero!

BATTLE OF ALGIERS 'X'

A FILM OF GILLO PONTECORVO

RANK FILM DISTRIBUTORS LTD

machine-gun.'

Likewise, the production team was recruited on the spot. Pontecorvo only took a crew of nine with him from Italy. The rest was made up of local people with no previous experience of filming; this was the first feature film from independent Algeria. Marcello Gatti the cameraman virtually ran a training-school after each day's shooting, so that by the end of the film Algeria had a number of highly trained film technicians.

This central involvement of the Algerians in the production brings a vital authenticity to the historical events. The opposing forces are the French army, disciplined, trained and compact; and the FLN, disorganized and amateur in its fighting. The FLN argue that a terrorist campaign is needed to defeat the French, and thus organize themselves in a pyramidic structure. Each person knows only the contact that recruited him and the two or three people he has recruited. For them, the test of heroism is not the ability to inflict violence on others, but to

Directed by Gillo Pontecorvo, 1966

Prod co: Casbah Films (Algiers)/Igor Films (Rome). **prod:** Antonio Musu, Yacef Saadi. **prod man:** Sergio Merolle, Noureddine Branimi. **2nd unit dir:** Giuliano Montaldo. **sc:** Franco Solinas, from a story by Franco Solinas and Gillo Pontecorvo. **photo:** Marcello Gatti. **ed:** Mario Serandrei, Mario Morra. **art dir:** Sergio Canevari. **mus:** Ennio Morricone, Gillo Pontecorvo. **ass dir:** Fernando Morandi. **r/t:** 135 minutes. Italian title: *La Battaglia di Algeri*. **Cast:** Jean Martin (*Colonel Mathieu*), Yacef Saadi (*Saari Kader*), Brahim Haggiag (*Ali La Pointe*), Tommaso Neri (*Captain Dubois*), Fawzia El Kader (*Hahmal*), Michèle Kerbash (*Fathia*), Mohamed Ben Kassen (*Little Omar*).

withstand torture for as long as possible to save other lives and protect the network. Torture becomes the central strategy in the French campaign, since their prime need is to obtain information quickly to trace the network before it can be disbanded. The ambivalent attitude of the French forces is examined sympathetically in this film. Colonel Mathieu reluctantly recognizes that his only choice is to condone torture or accept defeat: 'Why are the Sartres always on the other side?' he wistfully asks.

Pontecorvo makes no moral judgment in the film, he portrays only the

necessary violence of the struggle while showing his wholehearted support for independence for the Algerian people. Violence, after all, was integral to both sides in the bloody struggle. The outcome is so powerful an indictment of the French occupation that it had to be withdrawn from Paris cinemas following threats of violence from right-wing organizations. Pontecorvo's declared aim was to make a film that came as close to the truth as possible, and in *The Battle of Algiers* – with the help of the Algerian people – he has undoubtedly produced a remarkable testament.

3

4

5

October 7, 1957. Ali La Pointe, a leader of the Algerian Liberation Army (FLN), is trapped in his house with three of his followers by Colonel Mathieu and his French paratroopers (1). He reminisces over the past three years.

1954. Ali La Pointe, a petty street criminal (2), is released from prison. After passing a test of loyalty to the FLN – shooting a policeman with a gun that he later discovers was not loaded – he is co-opted into the leadership.

November 1, 1954. The FLN begin to clear the town-centre's fortress-like Casbah of vice and crime. La Pointe kills a brothel-keeper; others methodically rid the area of prostitutes, drug-addicts, smugglers, spies and international outlaws. The Casbah becomes the fortified centre of resistance to the French.

November 2, 1954. European extremists, including prominent police officers, counter-attack by blowing-up sections of the Casbah (3). The FLN retaliate with a terrorist campaign of bombings in public places (4). Three Algerian women – disguised as French – smuggle bombs out of the Casbah in their baskets (5).

January 10, 1957. The French government sends in paratroopers, who receive a huge welcome from the European population (6). Colonel Mathieu swoops to make arrests and uses torture to extract confessions and information. A week's general strike is declared by the FLN to draw international attention to their struggle. Mathieu moves his men into the Casbah and escalates the assault. As the trap closes, the key leaders of the resistance are captured and die (7). Only La Pointe is left. Hunted at every turn (8), he tries to rebuild the now broken organization. One of his men is captured, and, under torture, discloses his whereabouts.

October 7, 1957. La Pointe's house, with him inside refusing to surrender (9), is blown-up in front of the crowded inhabitants of the Casbah. The movement has apparently been smashed.

December 1960. The entire Algerian population demonstrate with improvised FLN flags (10). The struggle continues.

July 5, 1962. Algeria achieves independence.

6

7

8

9

10

349

THIRD WORLD ON SCREEN

Conditions for film-making varied widely throughout the Third World; some countries had established industries while others had to start from scratch

Everywhere the Sixties were turbulent years. But the Third World, so-called because it comprised the areas outside the eastern and western power blocs, was making an unprecedented impact on the western capitalist world. Liberation struggles in Africa, Asia and Latin America had reached a decisive stage, gathering tremendous momentum, asserting a unity across three continents which was based on the ideal of self-determination and the ideology of anti-imperialism. The Cuban Revolution, the Algerian War of Independence, Africa and Vietnam – they were all exemplary situations, expressing the global scale of revolutionary consciousness within the oppressed Third World regions.

Third World cinema of the Sixties derived its impetus from these political developments. Its attitude towards cinema necessarily opposed the colonial film practices of the western countries, and was militantly political. Third World film-makers rejected the dominant values of escapist entertainment on the Hollywood model, and redefined the role of cinema as an integral part of the revolutionary process, a 'weapon' to be used against the dominant images of western cinema.

The antipathy towards the dominant Euro-American cinema was legitimate. The major film companies had monopolized film distribution and exhibition throughout the colonized regions, thereby preventing the emergence of any indigenous cinema industry that could effectively compete. Audiences in Third World countries were bombarded with third-rate films which invariably depicted non-European peoples in pernicious stereotypes. These negative associations, along with the films' idealized images of capitalist society, had a pervasive effect on the consciousness of the audience. Militantly political film-makers recognized the need to counteract these colonial pictures, and to construct alternative themes and images which would express a true identity and dignity. But different parts of the world had had different colonial experiences. Thus in Latin America the main target was American films; in North Africa it was the French and Egyptian film monopolies; and in black Africa the need was to destroy the Tarzan-type jungle mythology and the representation of Africans as 'savages'.

Of course nationalization was correctly seen by the newly formed Third World governments as the crucial factor in developing a national cinema, and therefore in evolving a new self-identity. But any moves in that direction were often met by opposition. When the Algerian government nationalized its film industry in 1964, for example, the major American companies, which controlled 40 per cent of the market, boycotted the country. Similar experiences occurred in other countries, as in Upper Volta in 1972.

Third World films vary widely, ranging from straightforward agit-prop newsreel and didactic documentaries to fictional narratives and films employing complex symbolism. These differences in

EL TIGRE SALTÓ Y MATÓ, PERO MORIRÁ... MORIRÁ...
documental cubano dirección: santiago alvarez

approach are to a large extent determined by the particular social, political, cultural and historical conditions in which individual film-makers work. But there are also stylistic differences based primarily on the film-maker's own aesthetic preoccupations.

The extent to which any of these differences

Above: El Tigre Saltó y Mató, Pero Morirá . . . Morirá *(1973, The Tiger Leaps and Kills, But It Will Die . . . Will Die) is a short Cuban documentary on the Chilean folksinger Victor Jara, killed by the ruling military junta*

AMULETO DE OGUM

um filme de NÉLSON PEREIRA DOS SANTOS

reinforced or undermined the political integrity of a political cinema was never very clear. Brazilian *Cinema Novo*, which included quite disparate film styles, got around the problem by emphasizing the importance of personal creative expression. Others, like the Chilean Miguel Littin, spoke in terms of adopting political 'strategies' in dealing with the question of politicized film practice, while the Chilean Aldo Francia insisted that: 'Films must also entertain.' The differences between varied postures did not pose a serious threat of disruption, since to be in some sense political was sufficient.

But at the same time there was a sense in which Latin American unity ran deeper than political alignments alone suggested. The majority of Latin American film-makers was uniformly concerned with theoretical questions, with notions of political engagement and with aesthetic methods. The terminology in which debates about political film were conducted was similar in the various countries. The films as well (in the way they manipulated imagery) reflected this sense of Latin American unity.

El Instituto Cubano del Arte e Industria Cinematográficos

presenta

presents

The situation on the African continent was completely the opposite. The colonial impact on the region had produced four or five sharp demarcations which deeply affected how the African world perceived and expressed political and cultural activity. The sub-regions included Egypt and the Middle East; North Africa, including Algeria, Morocco and Tunisia; the black French-speaking area; the black English-speaking countries; and the white-dominated South. These historically-produced divisions help to explain why Africa had been unable to create a forceful cinema. As for black Africa in particular, only the French-speaking countries had produced any film-makers of note.

In looking at the emergence of progressive film-making in the Third World, a useful distinction can be made between those countries which already had an established film industry, such as Brazil, Argentina and Egypt, and those that lacked an indigenous cinematic tradition and so had to start from scratch, as in Cuba and black Africa.

Interestingly, Cuba emerged as the country most influential in developing progressive film-making, influencing the Third World as a whole. In 1959, the new revolutionary government led by Fidel Castro set up the Cuban Institute of Cinematographic Art and Industry (ICAIC), only three months after overthrowing the Batista regime. The swiftness

of this action shows the importance that was given to cinema in the rebuilding of Cuban society. ICAIC produced several feature films as well as documentaries and weekly newsreels throughout the Sixties. The profoundly political and international outlook of progressive Cuban cinema is particularly evident in the documentaries of Santiago Alvarez and in Julio Garcia Espinosa's *Tercer Mundo, Tercera Guerra Mundial* (1970, Third World, Third World War), a documentary shot in North Vietnam and aimed specifically at a politically militant audience.

Politicized film-makers of the Third World were particularly concerned with the role of cinema in relation to the audience; they wanted to counteract the consumer-oriented model of the passive spectator established in Euro-American cinema. Octavio Getino and Fernando Solanas' widely acclaimed monumental film-essay *La Hora de los Hornos* (1968, Hour of the Furnaces) presents a Marxist historical analysis of neo-colonialism and oppression in Argentina in the form of 'chapters' and 'notes' – captioned divisions in the film – which form the basis for political discussions with the audience.

Adopting a progressive political perspective entailed raising questions about history, as in *Hour of the Furnaces*. In a different vein, Humberto Solás' *Lucia* (1968) powerfully dramatized three historical moments in the Cuban struggle for liberation, and highlighted the participation of Cuban women in each period. But very few films set out, as *Hour of the Furnaces* did, to activate a critical engagement with the historical process. Most political films were of an agit-prop kind, more concerned with agitation and propaganda than with analysis.

A significant number of Third World films during this period dealt with rural themes, since the politicized film-makers identified with the peasantry, which was the most oppressed class in the society. But there were marked differences in tone between Latin American films and films from Africa and the Middle East. In the Latin American films – with the notable exception of the Bolivian Jorge Sanjines' *Yawar Mallku* (1969, *Blood of the Condor*) – the image of rural life did not evoke a sense of social and cultural cohesion, at any level. The films tended to emphasize the grim and hopeless position of the peasant, often depicted as an isolated outsider, with a dependent family. This image of bleakness, with its undertones of violence, was brilliantly conveyed in the Brazilian Nelson Pereira Dos Santos' *Vidas Secas* (1963, *Barren Lives*) and the Chilean Miguel Littin's *El Chacal de Nahueltoro* (1970, *The Jackal of Nahueltoro*).

In the African context, Ousmane Sembene of Senegal worked the themes of exploitation and human despair somewhat differently. His protagonists were similar to the Latin American peasants only to the extent that they both represented non-urban types struggling to survive within a repressive environment, moving through their daily lives

Top left: O Amuleto de Ogum (1975, The Amulet of Ogum) is about a boy who is invulnerable to bullets. Top: the Brazilian bandit leader (Lorival Pariz) killed by Antonio-das-Mortes (1969, Antonio of the Dead).
Centre: The Money Order *shows how a poor man with two wives is ruined in Dakar by a money order sent from Paris. Above:* Cantata de Chile (1976, Cantata of Chile) *re-creates in a Cuban film the massacre of strikers by troops at Iquique in 1907*

351

Top: during the Battle of Algiers, *several Arab girls carry out bombs from the Casbah to plant in public places in the French quarter. Top right:* Lucia *(1968) shows the lives of three different Cuban girls called Lucia; in 1895 during the war of independence against Spain, in 1933 when the dictator Machado was overthrown, and in the Sixties during the literacy campaign. Above:* The Night of Counting the Years *culminates in the rescue of precious Egyptian mummies menaced by a tribe of tomb-robbers*

as isolated and vulnerable individuals. But the difference was that the Africans had a group identity or membership which they could ultimately fall back on. The peasants of the Latin American films did not have this; they occupied barren lands.

In Sembene's films, the main characters find themselves imprisoned in a deceptively attractive environment, the urban centre, and unable to return to their former lives in the village rural community. In *La Noire de . . .* (1966, *Black Girl*), the only film where he deals explicitly with colonial forms of relationships, the imprisonment is fatal. Sembene's preoccupation with the dichotomies between the rural and the urban, between tradition and change, was very much tied to the radical alterations which were occurring in African societies, and the effects these were having in the lives of ordinary people.

Egyptian films had been widely shown throughout the Arab world since the Thirties. These were mainly escapist comedies and cheap entertainment dramas. The revolution of 1952 led eventually to significant changes. In 1957, Nasser's government established the National Organization for the Cinema and, two years later, set up a film school. The Sixties saw the emergence of 'quality' films such as Youssef Chahine's *An-Nasr Salah Ad-Din* (1963, *Saladin*), which was Egypt's first epic film, and Hussein Kamal's *Al Mostahil* (1965, The Impossible) and *Al Boustagui* (1968, The Postman), while Shadi Abdelsalam's mysterious tale of mummy-robbers in the last century *El Mumia* (1970, *The Night of Counting the Years*) broke away completely from earlier conventions.

Another factor which contributed to the reorientation of Arab cinema was the Algerian Revolution. As in the Latin American experience, progressive cinema in Algeria was defined as an integral part of the Algerian cultural renaissance. The Provisional Government of the Algerian Republic set up a film committee in 1961 which became the Cinema Service. It made four films, including Chanderli and Lakhdar Hamina's *Djazaïrouna* (1961), a history of Algeria. Between 1962 and 1971, Algerian 'Cinema Moudjahid' (Arabic for 'freedom fighter') was almost exclusively concerned with anti-colonial war films. There was also an emphasis on big-budget co-productions during this period. For example, Casbah Films, a private production company founded in 1961 by Yacef Saadi, a liberation leader and principal organizer of the battle of Algiers, partly financed major films by European directors, such as Gillo Pontecorvo's *La Battaglia di Algeri* (1966, *Battle of Algiers*).

But Algerian film-makers did not limit their scope to the Algerian experience alone. Like the Cubans, they maintained close relations with other Third World struggles: for instance, Ahmed Rachedi's documentary compilation *L'Aube des Damnés* (1965, The Dawn of the Damned) presented a sharp critique of the European powers' multiple intervention in the African continent and the Third World generally. The concentration on war films during this period was officially encouraged, but young film-makers and audiences alike began to criticize the trend, attacking the films for not dealing with such crucial questions as the status of women in Algerian society, or the abuse of power. But it was not until the agrarian revolution of 1971, which forced a rethinking of political and cultural organization, that a new Algerian cinema emerged.

After the military defeat it suffered in 1967, the Palestinian resistance movement began to contribute to the changes in Arab cinema; but the development of a unified Palestinian cinema was initially hampered by the fact that each political organization had its own cinema service, propagandizing for its own aims. One organization, El Fatah, produced a number of shorts and medium-length films, as well as helping several foreign film producers, including the Italian Communist Party, The American 'Newsreel' group, the Tricontinental group and Jean-Luc Godard. But Palestinian cinema was still at an embryonic stage, and depended on the support of other sympathetic Arab film-makers.

Neither was African cinema an emerging force during this period. It consisted of only a handful of film-makers from French-speaking countries such as Senegal, Niger, Guinea and Chad – whose films were made in French. Only Ousmane Sembene achieved international recognition, with *Mandabi* (1968, *The Money Order*), his third film, but the first in which he used his own language, Wolof. This use of an indigenous African language in a major film represented a radical shift from conventional practice; it amounted to a way of saying that the film was made by an African for African audiences. A forceful African cinema would, however, steadily emerge during the Seventies.

THE GRIP OF TERROR

The roots of terror lie deep in the psyche, but psychological analysis of films can cast some fascinatingly vivid light into the primitive darkness

---

The 'terror' film is not easy to define, since it occupies an area bounded on the one side by the horror film and on the other by the thriller. The horror film relies heavily on the supernatural and the creation of monsters to create apprehension and anxiety in the audience, and the thriller requires intricate plots and mechanics for the provision of similar effects. The terror film exploits certain fundamental characteristics of the cinema to produce effects that are based much more explicitly in the manipulation of psychology and psychopathology. The cinema of terror is the cinema of madness, sadism and voyeurism located in human beings rather than in vampires or criminal conspiracies. Its true power lies in its premise that the agents of terror are apparently ordinary people. Hence the fascination of films that compel the audience to confront uncanny forces that are both repulsive and familiar.

In his famous essay on 'The Uncanny' in 1917, Freud seized on this combination of repulsion and familiarity to explain the potency of terror by suggesting that it represented the eruption into adult life of the most powerful and primitive infantile wishes and fantasies. These fantasies – of violent murder, torture and suchlike abominations – hold their sway on the adult mind because they strike profound resonances with aspects of the psyche that, although repressed from babyhood, live within everyone.

The very nature of the cinema itself is higly conducive to the invocation of these infantile fantasies. Like the infant, the audience is passively watching scenes over which it has no control. The physical size of the screen presents the audience with characters far larger than life. But above all the audience is gazing; just as the baby gazes at the spectacle of the world over which it has little control, so the audience is constantly entrapped by the lures of the world on the screen. Both the child and the audience are passive voyeurs captivated and seduced by a world on to which their identifications and fantasies are projected. The mechanisms of the cinema provide a most potent structure for the evocation of infantile terror.

A central feature of all films of terror is voyeurism. The Sixties started with two masterpieces of voyeuristic cinema, Hitchcock's *Psycho* and Michael Powell's *Peeping Tom* (both 1960). In *Psycho*, as in so many of Hitchcock's films, voyeurism is implicit from the start. The camera gradually moves in on and peers into a seedy hotel room where Marion Crane (Janet Leigh) lies half-undressed with Sam Loomis (John Gavin). But it is frustrated voyeurism that is exploited until the famous scene of the murder in the shower. Just as Norman Bates (Anthony Perkins) fails to get a full view of Marion's naked body as he spies on her in the motel, so the audience is also denied full voyeuristic satisfaction and obtains a sense of sadistic relief when she is killed. It is as if she is being punished for being tantalizing but inaccessible. Hitchcock here succeeds in putting the audience in exactly the same

psychological position as her killer, Norman Bates. This leads rapidly to identification with the murderer, though his guilt is as yet unknown to the audience on first viewing. As Bates anxiously watches Marion's car fail at first to become fully submerged in the swamp where he is hiding it, the audience prays that the car will be fully engulfed.

Peeping Tom was almost universally vilified when it was first released, since it was explicitly concerned with the voyeurism that underlies all films of terror. Its hero is a young man who derives sexual satisfaction from filming women as he murders them with the spiked end of his camera tripod. The entire film is a metaphor for the cinema of terror and the audience's relationship with the screen. Just as the hero is captivated and aroused by the cinematic murders he commits, so too is the audience. There is simply no escaping from the fact that a large part of the fascination of films of terror lies in the opportunity they give to re-experience primitive infantile desires. Powell made this quite

Top: Charlotte (Bette Davis) is tricked into shooting a scheming doctor with blanks as part of a plot to get her certified; later on, she does kill him and go mad in Hush . . . Hush, Sweet Charlotte. *Above: can the blind girl (Audrey Hepburn) get out of this tight spot in* Wait Until Dark *and kill the bad guy (Alan Arkin)? She can indeed*

anxieties about the supernatural are thus tamed in a way not dissimilar to what happens in *The Wizard of Oz* (1939). In Hiroshi Teshigahara's *Suna No Onna* (1964, *Woman of the Dunes*), an entomologist finds himself trapped in a hut at the bottom of a gigantic sandpit and is initially terrified and desperate. But trapped along with him is an attractive widow and the film proceeds to depict the ever-increasing erotic pleasures of their shared captivity. The hero's earlier helpless terrors have given way to an immersion in Oedipal bliss.

Not surprisingly the taming and mastery of neurosis is another common feature of the terror film. John Huston's *Freud* (1962), although not strictly a film of terror, ends with Freud's deciphering a terrifying dream about his mother and realizing that neurosis can be explained and overcome. In Hitchcock's *Marnie* (1964), one of the commonest of all neurotic complaints, a phobia, is finally cured. Marnie's phobia is based on a fear of blood and is cured at the emotion-releasing climax of the film in which Marnie relives the traumatic experience of killing a sailor to protect her mother. Although this dramatic cure may bear little relationship to actual psychiatric practice, it proves to the audience that the very neurosis masterfully exploited by Hitchcock throughout the film can be conquered.

Not all neurosis or psychosis can be tamed, and some films of terror operate by reasserting the

Childhood fears and passions can be aroused and also eased in the safety of the darkened cinema

power of infantile forces, refusing to reassure the audience that mastery over madness is possible. The ending of *The Birds* (1963) is scarcely encouraging for those with animal phobias, since the characters are allowed to escape from Bodega Bay only because of the inexplicable and uneasy truce established by their victorious persecutors. Even more strikingly, the journalist hero of Samuel Fuller's *Shock Corridor* (1963) ends driven into madness by the forces of the corrupt mental institution that he seeks to expose.

In many terror films infantile desires and fantasies are not expressed as neurosis or any formal kind of madness, but are rather represented by characters embodying the cruel and sadistic aspects of a child's emotional life. These murderous tendencies can be contained or vanquished in various ways. At the very crudest level, this can be accomplished by the villainous character's being caught, tamed or killed. The very fact that the villain gets his come-uppance must inevitably lead

Above: Michael Powell's Peeping Tom *was treated with critical contempt when it first appeared, despite its knowledgeable references to film-making and film criticism; now it is considered a masterpiece. Top: Harry (Peter Vaughan) in* Fanatic *attempts to kill his wife's boss, Mrs Trefoile – but she will turn the tables on him. Top left: in* Onibaba *a woman (Nobuko Otowa) finds that the stolen mask she uses to frighten her errant daughter-in-law has stuck to her face, rotting the flesh. Left: two mutually jealous Hollywood sisters destroy their own lives and each others' in Robert Aldrich's* What Ever Happened to Baby Jane?

overt, thereby incurring critical wrath; but *Peeping Tom* remains the most sophisticated film ever made about the psychological fascination of terror.

Films of terror do not operate solely in terms of the voyeuristic reliving of childish desires and fantasies, and the fantasies involved are not purely those of a murderous kind. Other forms of infantile anxiety can be exploited and then mastered. Such basic anxieties as fear of the dark, the unknown and things that go bump in the night may evoke infantile terrors which can then be written off when the evil is vanquished or the inexplicable is explained. Terence Young's *Wait Until Dark* (1967) presents the fears of the blind Susy Hendrix (Audrey Hepburn) as those of an infant terrorized by a bogey-man, Roat (Alan Arkin). The terror that pervades the film reaches its climax when the crazed Roat literally jumps out of a cupboard. But this terror is quickly dissipated as Susy kills her assailant and survives. Both she and the audience have, at least temporarily, mastered their fear of the dark.

Similar taming and mastery techniques operate in Kaneto Shindo's *Onibaba* (1965), one of a number of Japanese terror films that were distributed in the West during the Sixties. In *Onibaba*, a series of apparently demonic murders is shown to be the work of two women rather than of devils. Infantile

to a certain easing of the infantile fantasies and anxieties that have been engendered in the audience by the film.

Throughout the Sixties the British cinema produced a series of films featuring crazed, homicidal villains whose main function was to commit primitive acts of violence and then to be punished for them. For example, Hammer turned out *Maniac, Paranoiac* (both 1963) and *Fanatic* (1965), all using the standard trappings of ominous music, creaking floorboards and slowly turning doorknobs and all based on the premise that the beast could be tamed. Unfortunately the beasts in question were portrayed with little in the way of psychological interest or understanding to support them, and so the films merely provided a few predictable shocks.

A more interesting category of beast is that provided by early fantasies about bad parents or wicked siblings. It is such figures that are exploited in Robert Aldrich's Grand-Guignol Californian-gingerbread masterpieces *What Ever Happened to Baby Jane?* (1962) and *Hush . . . Hush, Sweet Charlotte* (1964). In *What Ever Happened to Baby Jane?*, Bette Davis as Baby Jane is the embodiment both of the feared bad mother who feeds the child dead rats instead of food and also of the resented villainous sibling who persecutes her crippled and disadvantaged sister, played by Joan Crawford. The major psychological pleasure produced by the film is the audience's infantile delight in seeing these archetypally terrifying beasts vanquished as Baby Jane receives her just deserts. The revenge of the wronged child is even more radically treated in *Village of the Damned* (1960) and in its sequel, *Children of the Damned* (1964). In both these films, all-powerful children terrify the adults surrounding them, and although they are finally defeated the

children act out, in the most graphic way, the infant's desire to turn the tables on malignant parental figures. This theme is further explored in Seth Holt's *The Nanny* (1965), a much underrated film in which Bette Davis once again portrays an archetypal bad mother-figure who gets her punishment at the hands of her charges. Even bad parents can be mastered.

Understanding, like Hitchcock, the infantile and neurotic roots of the film of terror, Roman Polanski is a talented exploiter of a potent neurosis, claustrophobia; the fear and horror that can be engendered by enclosed spaces, with anxieties to do

with being trapped or impinged upon, can be traced back to early infancy. The darkened cinema provides an excellent site in which to exploit these fears. Polanski combined his manipulation of claustrophobia with a profound loathing and contempt for mankind, and both features are prominent in his early Polish film *Nóz w Wodzie* (1962, *Knife in the Water*). It was with *Repulsion* (1965) that Polanski brought these elements together in his first terror film. In tracing the descent of Carol (Catherine Deneuve) into homicidal madness, Polanski not only extracts every ounce of claustrophobic terror from the flat in which the film is mostly set but he also infuses the scene with primitive Oedipal fears and resentments. As Carol overhears her sister in bed with a lover, Polanski strikingly evokes the terrors of the Primal Scene, Freud's term in describing the child's terror at the apparently violent implications of parental sexual intercourse. As Carol's paranoid psychosis begins to erupt, the audience is confronted with its own repressed memories of the first impingement of sexuality.

Another study of infants' fears was Blake Edwards' *Experiment in Terror* (1962), an extremely accomplished work in which Kelly Sherwood (Lee Remick) is pursued by a criminal while the FBI stands back helpless to intervene because he holds a hostage. Edwards puts the audience in the woman's place as she is threatened and harassed from a distance. The film brilliantly conveys Kelly's sense of infantile helplessness in a situation where quasi-parental intervention (from the FBI) cannot help her. The film's most chilling scene results from her having to hide herself amongst rows of mannequins as the killer tries to track her down – a scene so successful that a variant of it appeared in Michael Crichton's *Coma* (1978).

On the other hand, William Castle's *Homicidal* (1961) was a most crass attempt to capitalize on a

Above: cold-blooded radioactive children are secreted in the cliffs near Portland Bill in The Damned *(1962). Top: Harriet (Sheila Burrell) attacks an inquisitive detective to protect her insanely murderous nephew in* Paranoiac. *Left: schoolgirl Toby Sherwood (Stefanie Powers) is kidnapped as a hostage to force her sister to rob the bank where she works in* Experiment in Terror; *but the girl is rescued in time*

Above: Cathy (Constance Towers) fears that Johnny (Peter Breck), a journalist, is being driven mad by his undercover investigation of a murder in an asylum in Shock Corridor. *Top right: The Nanny (Bette Davis) is mysteriously involved in the drowning of a little girl, and it is no wonder that her other charge, ten-year-old Joey, is suspicious and resentful of her. Wendy Craig, who played the children's mother, was later herself to become a nanny in a British television series*

major hit. It was a transsexual version of *Psycho* with the fact of the villain's transsexuality not being revealed until the climax, with an accompanying pseudo-psychiatric explanation. Outrageously derivative on all counts, the film had a certain primitive charm. Towards the end of the Sixties Castle became considerably more artistically respectable and was the producer of Polanski's superior horror film *Rosemary's Baby* (1968).

If the content of the terror film is replete with infantile fantasies of a voyeuristic and sexual nature, the style and technique of terror is similarly related to sexuality. The most celebrated proponent of the theory of terror was Alfred Hitchcock, who repeatedly stressed the difference between suspense and shock. Shock is a cheap commodity. An unexpected and violent event provides an adrenalin spurt in the audience. There is no anticipation, no build-up – merely the cinematic equivalent of a violent assault.

Suspense is an altogether different matter. The audience is placed in a position of anticipation, of knowing that something frightening or dreadful will happen, and being denied only the knowledge of precisely when that event will occur. In *Psycho*, as the private detective Arbogast (Martin Balsam) enters the Bates' house, it is obvious that he will be attacked. Hitchcock sustains the suspense by slowing down the time of his entering the house and of his ascent of the staircase on which he will be murdered.

The dynamics of this situation are twofold. First, the audience is put in the position of the aggressor. The audience knows, just as the aggressor knows, that a violent act will be committed but the victim is unaware of this. The audience thus becomes implicated as an accomplice to the act, and so when

Arbogast's murder does occur the gratification of its voyeuristic sadism is enhanced. At the same time, the audience watching Arbogast ascend the staircase is afforded an opportunity to disavow the murder in advance. Viewers can voice or imagine a warning shout, such as: 'Don't go up those stairs!' or they can shut their eyes as if to disclaim what is already known to be coming. This double manoeuvre of suspense achieves what all neurotic symptoms achieve: the audience is permitted both

---

The desire to see the forbidden, the unknown or the feared, attracts audiences to films of suspense

---

to indulge its violent fantasies and simultaneously to protest its innocence.

There can be no doubt that the sexualized expression of primitive desires is in operation here. The whole mechanism of suspense is that of the progressive build-up of a tension that demands release. Suspense is the voyeuristic equivalent of foreplay in genital sexuality. Just as the intensity of genital sexual desire is increased by foreplay, so is the intensity of the voyeuristic satisfaction of terror increased by suspense.

The consequence of this aspect of suspense is that the audience is entrapped in a state of ever-increasing desire that will demand a resolution. As a stroke of promotional genius, Hitchcock refused to let anyone enter the cinema during the last reel of *Psycho*. But who in the audience could possibly leave, snared by the film's structure in undischarged sexual tension?

CAN'T STOP THE MUSICAL

When the musical seemed to be out on its feet, it was only gathering strength for a vigorous new burst of singing and dancing and all that jazz

There was a distinct break between the musicals of the Fifties and those of the Sixties. By the end of the Fifties, the producer Arthur Freed's unit at MGM, which had been a conveyor belt of classic musical dream-worlds, was breaking up fast. Stanley Donen and Gene Kelly had left, and were soon involved in mainly non-musical projects, for which there was more demand in a Hollywood with a growing sense of social awareness. In 1960, Vincente Minnelli made his last MGM musical *Bells Are Ringing*, which also represented the final demise of Freed's group.

While these signs may not have meant the death of the genre, they certainly provided evidence of a shift in sensibility, an adjustment to a more complex world. Paeans in praise of show business, for example, were being rendered somewhat anachronistic by such scorching visions of the world of entertainment as the depictions of Hollywood itself in *Sunset Boulevard* (1950), *The Bad and the Beautiful* (1952) and *The Big Knife* (1955). With Hollywood's broadening outlook, it was becoming harder to make a musical suffused with a sense of fantasy, of the dreamer triumphant over recalcitrant circumstances, and to render it convincing.

Even so, quite a few musicals of the 'hip' Sixties were made by old survivors from MGM, notably Vincente Minnelli, Charles Walters, George Sidney and Gene Kelly. Out of these, Walters, with *Jumbo* (1962) and *The Unsinkable Molly Brown* (1964), and Kelly, with *Hello, Dolly!* (1969), remained the most traditional, with nonetheless pleasing results. Sidney met the challenge of youthful material with a typical brash energy in *Bye, Bye Birdie* (1963) and *Viva Las Vegas* (1964), although his less 'swinging' *Half a Sixpence* (1967) was ultimately more inventive. It was Minnelli, though, who showed a real ability to adapt – the formal innovations of *On a Clear Day You Can See Forever* (1970) still seem fresh today.

If these directors were representative of a specialized approach to the genre, the Sixties and Seventies musical is really notable for its lack of emphasis on the need for specifically musical talent, in both directors and performers. This was owing partly to a drying-up of reserve musical talent from Broadway, which Hollywood had always relied upon, and partly to a new stress in the genre on such elements as characterization and narrative. Directors and stars were often strongly associated with more apparently realistic genres.

With regard to directors, the results were on the whole surprisingly satisfying. William Wyler, known mainly for prestigious dramas, showed great skill with *Funny Girl* (1968). To prove how easily two already adaptable directors picked up a feel for music, Francis Ford Coppola's *Finian's Rainbow* (1967) was particularly stylish, and Norman Jewison's *Fiddler on the Roof* (1971) was imaginatively conceived for the screen. More recently, Martin Scorsese, that Italian-American poet of New York street life, made the marvellous *New York, New York* (1977). Perhaps the most noteworthy in this strain of cross-over directors was

Robert Wise. Identified more with astringent thrillers, he left his mark upon the Sixties musical with such varied but ultimately satisfactory films as *West Side Story* (1961), *The Sound of Music* (1965) and *Star!* (1968). But on the debit side must be set the inept musical sense of Carol Reed in *Oliver!* (1968) and, still worse, of Richard Fleischer in the hamfisted *Dr Dolittle* (1967).

The pattern is the same for performers. In the theatre or on screen, directors and producers have become accustomed to casting dramatic stars in musicals. When the actor Jack Klugman complained to the lyric-writer Stephen Sondheim of his own poor vocal abilities for the Broadway show *Gypsy*, Sondheim simply replied: 'I don't want a musical star. I want a person I can believe in.'

Of course, there are stars of the two decades who have been connected specifically with film musicals. Julie Andrews is the most obvious. Petula Clark was delightful and underrated in *Finian's Rainbow* and *Goodbye Mr Chips* (1969). Liza Minnelli and Barbra Streisand are both outstanding talents. Nevertheless, Sondheim's 'believable' person is manifest on the screen in such offhand, casual

Below: the Irish leprechaun Og (Tommy Steele) tries to help Sharon McLonergan (Petula Clark) to dress up in Finian's Rainbow; *Sharon's father, Finian, has stolen a magic crock of gold and Og has followed him to America in search of the leprechauns' treasure*

musical performances as those of Rex Harrison in *My Fair Lady* (1964) or Clint Eastwood in *Paint Your Wagon* (1969). It is the approachability of this kind of star's musical manner (especially the sung-spoken style of the numbers, whether or not dubbed) that constitutes their attraction. The effect of the non-musical star depends upon the image brought over from roles in more realistic types of film. The musical has thus harnessed the iconographic significance of such stars as Natalie Wood in *West Side Story* and *Gypsy* (1962), Christopher Plummer in *The Sound of Music*, Richard Harris and Vanessa Redgrave in *Camelot* (1967), Peter O'Toole in *Goodbye Mr Chips*, Lee Marvin and Clint Eastwood in *Paint Your Wagon*, Cybill Shepherd and Burt Reynolds in *At Long Last Love* and James Caan in *Funny Lady* (both 1975).

Such stars and directors indicated a new emphasis upon the purely dramatic elements of the genre, a need to place the number in a more 'believable' world. Another manifestation of this spirit lay in the genre's growing self-consciousness and a broader social outlook. There was a tendency to deal more with everyday life and real problems, coming to the fore in the depiction of gang warfare and racial tension in *West Side Story*, office life in *How to Succeed in Business Without Really Trying* (1967), thinly-disguised prostitution in *Sweet Charity* (1969), the repression of the Jews in *Fiddler on the Roof*, the rise of Nazism in *Cabaret* (1972) and the harsh treatment of South African blacks in *Lost in the Stars* (1974). As if to clinch the point, the easy resolution, the genre's traditional concluding assertion of 'togetherness', was often eschewed in favour of such distinctly sombre endings as those of *Camelot*, *Goodbye Mr Chips*, *Sweet Charity*, *Paint Your Wagon*, *On a Clear Day You Can See Forever*, *Funny Lady* and *New York, New York*.

Similarly, there was a mocking, self-conscious tone. It is instantly recognizable in the acidic films of Bob Fosse – *Sweet Charity*, *Cabaret* and *All That Jazz* (1979) – where the numbers are explorations of various film-musical stylistic modes. It can be seen, too, in a whole variety of movies that play on the conventions of the genre: the iconography of the pop world and the media is examined in *A Hard Day's Night* (1964), *Phantom of the Paradise* (1974) and *Tommy* (1975); homage is paid to the tradition of the musical in *Let's Make Love* (1960), *At Long Last Love*, *Bugsy Malone* (1976) and *New York, New York*. There is even the unsophisticated camp nostalgia of *Grease* (1978), *Can't Stop the Music* and *Xanadu* (both 1980).

More than ever during the Sixties and Seventies, musicals have been based upon Broadway hit shows. During the same period, musicals were also generally becoming super-productions, of the type represented by *West Side Story*, *The Sound of Music* and *Funny Girl*. The reason was simple: the rivalry of television. The cinema's tactic was to present audio-visual spectacles unlike anything possible on the small screen, and often to recruit proven successes from the Broadway stage. It did not always work, of course; and when it failed, the financial repercussions could be as crippling as the slow paralysis caused by television. For instance, *Sweet Charity* made no profit for Universal, despite its fresh approach to previously successful material.

What is often complained of, regarding Broadway adaptations, is that the original is treated with too much reverence. But by the late Fifties, Hollywood was dealing with the type of musical drama originally pioneered by Rodgers and Hammerstein, which was too integrated to allow the free adaptations once made of original stage works. Further, while these films do follow the stage shows quite closely, the results need not be as slavish and uncinematic as they were in, for example, *Man of La Mancha* (1972) and *Mame* (1973). The long list of more memorable films includes *West Side Story*, *The Music Man* (1962), *My Fair Lady*, *The Sound of Music*, *Camelot*, *Finian's Rainbow*, *Sweet Charity*, *On a Clear Day You Can See Forever* and *Cabaret*.

Of original screen musicals, outstanding by any standards was the Gallic charm of Jacques Demy's romantic evocations of French provincial life in *Les Parapluies de Cherbourg* (1964, *The Umbrellas of Cherbourg*) and *Les Demoiselles de Rochefort* (1967, *The Young Girls of Rochefort*). Scorsese's *New York, New York* was an original film musical that explored the form with all the daring and inventiveness once shown by such Betty Comden and Adolph Green scripts as those for *Singin' in the Rain* (1952) and *The Band Wagon* (1953). It centred on the off-beat

romance and failed marriage of a jazz saxophonist and a dance-band vocalist. Then there were such pleasant diversions as Marilyn Monroe's penultimate movie *Let's Make Love*, *Robin and the Seven Hoods* (1964), *Thoroughly Modern Millie* (1967) and *Goodbye Mr Chips*. Yet, on the whole, the two decades have not matched the standard of the stream of screen originals once associated, in particular, with MGM.

One of the major developments in the genre during the period was its attempt to come to terms with youth and with post-Beatles popular music. In this the musical has generally taken a patronizing attitude to the energy and subversion of both youth themes and rock music.

Rock musicals themselves usually developed over-simplified youth themes, accompanied by middle-of-the-road music more appropriate to middle-aged audiences. *Godspell* and *Jesus Christ Superstar* (both 1973), for example, merely restated conventional religious values. *Hair* had initiated the Broadway youth-musical vogue in 1968; even then, its nude dancing could only ever have offended a truly Victorian sensibility. When the screen version finally appeared, a safe 11 years later in 1979, it was nothing but a pleasant reminder of an era long since gone, the hippie heyday. Only two screen originals, *Phantom of the Paradise*, a version of the Phantom-of-the-Opera story, and *Tommy*, based on The Who's very successful LP about a deaf, dumb and blind pinball player, came near to creating the anarchy, energy and imagination missing each week from *Top of the Pops* on British television.

Then, in 1977, came *Saturday Night Fever*. All at once, the dance musical was reinvented. The disco craze spread across Europe and the United States; and this film was followed by *Black Joy* (1977), *Thank God It's Friday* (1978), *The Music Machine* (1979), *Can't Stop the Music*, *Xanadu* and *Fame* (1980). All of them pushed the new dance style as the foremost element of the genre – no-one even sings in *Saturday Night Fever*. It was only in *Thank God It's Friday* and *Fame*, though, that the dancing reflected the true energy and invention of the actual disco floor. The exhilarating bursts of movement in these films made the mannered shuffling of *Saturday Night Fever* and the skate-bound plodding of *Xanadu* seem flat-footed.

The classic musical had never fully acknowledged the black origins of such elements as tap-dancing. At least the disco musical made a stab at identifying the cultural context of its subject. The excellent *Black Joy*, concerning immigrant life in London's Brixton, and *Thank God It's Friday*, an evening in the life of a Hollywood disco club, linked

the music with black artists, while the sheer skill and subversive eroticism of the solo dancing in *Fame* were inextricable from its black exponent, Gene Anthony Ray. The considerable gay influence upon disco was only limply noticed in the awful *Can't Stop the Music*, in which a pop group, the Village People, were 'normalized' by the presence of the central heterosexual couple.

Both *Saturday Night Fever* and *Xanadu* did identify disco as levelling out social inequalities. *Saturday Night Fever* splendidly utilized the dance floor as a place for stamping out problems, permitting control at least of this environment through skills that anyone could develop. *Xanadu* gave a sense of cultural harmony in its closing vision of disco as a meeting ground free from bias and prejudice.

Disco was seen by the film industry as a convenient and safe way of representing youth music and culture, and it accounted for the bulk of musicals in the late Seventies and early Eighties. But the British *Breaking Glass* (1980) explored, though only tentatively, the area of rock music's 'New Wave'.

In terms of directors, only Bob Fosse really specialized in the genre. Of the rest, both John Badham, who made *Saturday Night Fever*, and Alan Parker, of *Fame*, showed great potential, with a good feel for music, though a limited ability to provide convincing narrative contexts. All of Martin Scorsese's films were alive with music and movement; *New York, New York* explored the language of the film musical with all the cunning insight of Fosse but without the ego-flexing of the semi-autobiographical *All That Jazz*. *New York, New York* deserves recognition as one of the most entertaining and challenging musicals to appear since Freed's unit at MGM shuddered to a halt back in 1960.

Above: young people travel to Israel to re-enact the last days in the life of Jesus as a rock opera in Jesus Christ Superstar. *Below: the all-singing, all-dancing finale of* Grease *features, from left to right, Jeff Conaway as Kenickie, Olivia Newton-John as Sandy Olsson, John Travolta as her boyfriend Danny Zucco and Stockard Channing as Betty Rizzo, who decides to marry Kenickie*

THE LAST HEROES

Heroes were still heroic in the epic, the war film and the Western until doubt and cynicism began to creep in during the course of the Sixties

The Fifties saw the demise of the swashbuckling cycle which had been inaugurated at the end of World War II. Although many of these films had been produced on reduced budgets, some were able to match the lavishness of their pre-war counterparts by being filmed abroad, notably in Italy and Britain, where Hollywood production companies could utilize 'frozen' funds, cheap labour and ready-made castles. This cycle had also seen the return to swordfighting of many of the stars of pre-war swashbucklers. Errol Flynn, ageing and dissipated but still game, fenced and wooed his way through a series of modestly budgeted but engaging adventure films: *Against All Flags* (1952), *The Master of Ballantrae* (1953) and *The Dark Avenger* (1955); these were patterned on his Thirties' successes. Louis Hayward took over Flynn's old role of the pirate Captain Blood in *Fortunes of Captain Blood* (1950) and *Captain Pirate* (1952). Tyrone Power starred in a trio of rather stodgy epic-scale swashbucklers: *Captain From Castile* (1947), *Prince of Foxes* (1949) and *The Black Rose* (1950). Robert Taylor, now in dignified middle age, starred in three British-made chivalric romances from MGM: *Ivanhoe* (1952), *Knights of the Round Table* (1953) and *The Adventures of Quentin Durward* (1955).

But there were new, young adventurers arising to challenge the old stalwarts. In Hollywood, Universal-International and Columbia produced a stream of 'bread-and-butter' swashbucklers, economically made but generally done with verve and designed to showcase the riding, loving and fighting talents of their aspiring young actors. Universal's Tony Curtis, endearingly unabashed by his broad Brooklyn accent, performed with athletic grace and unflagging good humour in lively adventures both oriental, as in *The Prince Who Was a Thief* (1951) and *Son of Ali Baba* (1952), and occidental, as in *The Black Shield of Falworth* (1954) and *The Purple Mask* (1955). Columbia's John Derek, who combined the sensitive Italianate good looks of Tyrone Power with the fire and conviction of the young Errol Flynn, played the son of Robin Hood in *Rogues of Sherwood Forest* (1950), the first of a series of colourful swashbucklers. But for sheer style, no-one could beat Stewart Granger, whose virility, elegance and sardonic humour served him to good effect in such vintage swashbucklers as *Scaramouche* (1952), *Moonfleet* (1955) and *Lo Spadaccino di Siena* (1962, *Swordsman of Siena*) and in non-swashbuckling costume dramas such as *Young Bess* (1953) and *Beau Brummell* (1954), all for MGM.

Television inevitably spelled the decline of such films, for the small screen was crowded from the mid-Fifties onwards by a host of swashbuckling series, small-scale, black and white, often studio-bound, but well-acted, fast-moving and entertaining, typified by the long-running British *Adventures of Robin Hood*, starring former cinema swashbuckler Richard Greene. Hollywood turned instead to the epic in search of box-office crowd-pullers. Television could not recreate the glories of Babylon, Greece and Rome in wide screen format, in

colour and in stereophonic sound – even in the United States, colour TV sets were still quite rare at the end of the Fifties.

So D'Artagnan, Scaramouche and Captain Blood gave way to Alexander the Great, Ben-Hur and Cleopatra on the big screen. Vast budgets, armies of extras, teeming battle-scapes, huge reconstructions of ancient cities – these were now the order of the day. Cecil B. DeMille, who had definitely established the cinematic images of Cleopatra, Nero and the Crusaders in the Thirties, bowed out with *The Ten Commandments* (1956), which provided the new epic cycle with its greatest star, Charlton Heston. Heston went on to play the title roles in three of the greatest products of the cycle, *Ben-Hur* (1959), *El Cid* (1961) and *The War Lord* (1965). For a decade, the historical epic was to hold sway in the action and adventure field. The Bible, the classics and medieval legends were to be plundered for themes and stories.

Such films were generally derided by the critics, who enjoyed themselves enormously at the expense

Top: The War Lord *(Charlton Heston) of an 11th-century Normandy village rides in with, from left, his villainous brother (Guy Stockwell) and his faithful squire (Richard Boone), led by the village priest (Maurice Evans). The film's story of love and betrayal is set against a convincingly authentic background of druidic lore and ancient rural customs. Above: the Emperor of China (Robert Morley), seen here in an ornate oriental setting, schemes against Genghis Khan – but to little effect*

of troubled, over-budget productions such as *Cleopatra* (1963); they pounced gleefully on factual errors and comic miscastings like the hilarious appearances of Robert Morley as the Emperor of China and James Mason as his buck-toothed ambassador in *Genghis Khan* (1965). But they wilfully ignored the visual splendours, mythic power, imaginative strength and sheer physical energy of the best of the epics. These films did not set out to create an impression of 'everyday life in ancient times'. They dealt with gods and heroes, great deeds and great men, the stuff of myth and legend. At their best the epics were awesome tributes to Hollywood's film-making skill and entrepreneurial enterprise.

Kirk Douglas starred in and produced two of the best, *The Vikings* (1958) and *Spartacus* (1960). Richard Fleischer's *The Vikings*, with its screeching falcons, proud dragon-ships, wolf-pits and muscular celebration of fighting, feasting and savage retribution, was the cinema's definitive depiction of

The fall of the American epic was mighty in cost to the producers

the barbaric Norsemen of popular legend. Stanley Kubrik's *Spartacus* was a slave-revolt epic of immense intelligence, which made up for the miscasting in some parts (John Gavin, Tony Curtis) by the wealth of talent employed to flesh out the major roles – Charles Laughton, Laurence Olivier, Peter Ustinov and Kirk Douglas himself.

Charlton Heston distinguished himself in the two finest chivalric epics that the cinema has yet produced: Anthony Mann's *El Cid* and Franklin Schaffner's *The War Lord*. Intelligently scripted and majestically staged, both films gave memorable cinematic life to that misty borderland between cultures and between epochs when chivalry and paganism, violence and tenderness existed uneasily side by side. Much less well-known is J. Lee-Thompson's *Kings of the Sun* (1963), a sweeping, surging, often inspiring saga about the fate of the Mayan civilization in Central America, with Yul Brynner and George Chakiris giving outstanding performances.

But the epic cycle came to an end with *The Fall of the Roman Empire* (1964), the last film from the Samuel Bronston organization, telling the almost symbolic tale of the collapse of the Roman Empire in the face of tyranny and extravagance within and barbarian assault from without. Staged by Anthony Mann on a massive, imperial scale, it embraced pitched battles, chariot races, triumphal processions and court intrigue, and Mann elicited sensitive and thoughtful performances from Alec Guinness as the Emperor Marcus Aurelius and

James Mason as a Christian philosopher. But it was seriously flawed by a lacklustre, unhistorical hero (Stephen Boyd), whose climactic refusal to occupy the throne and save civilization must have caused El Cid, King Arthur, Alexander the Great and Julius Caesar to turn in their epic graves.

The British film industry also climbed aboard the epic bandwagon in this period, particularly with Clive Donner's *Alfred the Great* (1969) and Ken Hughes' *Cromwell* (1970), films as absorbing and thoughtful as they were sumptuous and expansive. Particularly fruitful as a subject, however, was the British Empire, which had provided Hollywood with a memorable cycle of adventure films in the Thirties. A new Imperial cycle produced at least three major works, all filmed on location and all depicting the gallantry of a handful of outnumbered but never down-hearted Britons fighting against overwhelming odds. J. Lee-Thompson's *North West Frontier* (1959) recreated a hazardous train trip across rebel-infested India in 1905. Led by Kenneth More, the Imperialists emerged triumphant and vindicated. Cy Endfield's *Zulu* (1963) was an awe-inspiring re-creation of the battle of Rorke's Drift in 1879 when 105 men of the South Wales Borderers held an isolated mission station against 4000 Zulus. Basil Dearden's *Khartoum* (1966) was an impressive, in-depth study of General Gordon, superbly played by Charlton Heston.

A much less sympathetic view of British Imperialism was taken in Tony Richardson's *Charge of the Light Brigade* (1968), which exposed the squalid slum conditions, brutal army discipline and official corruption and mismanagement of mid-Victorian Britain, as a prelude to the heroic blunder of Balaclava. It featured two hilarious performances, from John Gielgud as the monumentally vague Lord Raglan, who was never sure whether he was fighting the Russians or the French, and from Trevor Howard as the cholerically Blimpish libertine and snob, Lord Cardigan. Richard Williams' delightfully funny jingoistic cartoon inserts were in the style of *The Illustrated London News*. In David Lean's *Lawrence of Arabia* (1962) Peter O'Toole made an enormous impact as the white-robed mystic who leads the Arabs to victory against the Turks but fails to secure their independence from the scheming British.

The serious war films of the late Forties and Fifties, such as *Twelve O'Clock High* (1949), *Paths of Glory* (1957) and *Pork Chop Hill* (1959), with their 'war is hell' message, gave way in the Sixties to big-budget, all-action, all-star military spectaculars, of which the only possible message was 'war is fun'. The style continued until the end of the decade, after which the impact of Vietnam finally produced a clutch of films marked by bitterness and cynicism: *M*A*S*H*, *Catch-22* and *Too Late the Hero* (all three 1970). But typical of the big-budget blockbusters was J. Lee-Thompson's *The Guns of Navarone* (1961).

Top left: David Hemmings as Alfred the Great in a battle scene. Top: Michael Caine is also embattled as an officer engaged in hand-to-hand combat in Zulu. Centre: Kirk Douglas as a Viking who has just lost the sight of one eye in The Vikings, *a film dripping with spilt gore. Above: John Mills as Field-Marshal Sir Douglas Haig, who led the British forces in France during World War I, in* Oh! What a Lovely War, *which had a lengthy and star-filled cast list*

Above left: Lord Cardigan (Trevor Howard) has a spot of bother in Charge of the Light Brigade. *Above right: inside the German fortress a couple of American soldiers (Lee Marvin and Charles Bronson) are helped out of their German uniform disguises in* The Dirty Dozen, *a film which proved that villainous heroes could also be popular if most of them died heroically. Opposite page, top left: Burt Lancaster and Lee Marvin as a pair of professional adventurers and Claudia Cardinale as a runaway wife in* The Professionals, *set during the revolutionary period in Mexico (and top right) The Magnificent Seven are, from left to right, Yul Brynner, Steve McQueen, Horst Buchholz, Charles Bronson, Robert Vaughn, Brad Dexter and James Coburn.*
Far right: The Good, the Bad and the Ugly features Lee Van Cleef as the bad guy and Eli Wallach as the ugly one, who survives the concluding shoot-out rich but stranded

Right: the three-camera Cinerama was used to good effect in the Civil War episode of How the West Was Won, *directed by John Ford: a mother (Carroll Baker) says farewell to her elder son (George Peppard) as he sets off to fight on the Union side*

It was the first of a very profitable and popular series of films based on the works of Alistair MacLean. It bore all the MacLean hallmarks – preposterous plot, rudimentary characterization, all-star cast and non-stop action. In the same mould, *Where Eagles Dare, Ice Station Zebra* (both 1968) and many more, both war stories and adventure stories, followed in the Sixties and Seventies.

Genuine wartime episodes furnished the basis for other all-star spectaculars. Darryl F. Zanuck's production, *The Longest Day* (1962), re-created the D-Day landings, with John Wayne, Robert Mitchum and Henry Fonda leading the American forces and Richard Todd, Richard Burton and Kenneth More, the British. *Battle of the Bulge* (1965) restaged the last major German offensive of World War II, with Robert Shaw in good form as a ruthless blond Nazi tank commander. *Operation Crossbow* (1965) assembled yet more stars to play a host of cameo parts in the story of how Germany's V-2 rocket bases were identified and destroyed. The cycle did produce some impressive performances. George C. Scott deservedly won an Oscar for his virtuoso playing of the tempestuous General Patton in *Patton* (1970) and Laurence Olivier completely dominated another all-star epic, *Battle of Britain* (1969), with his quietly detached playing of Air Chief Marshal Sir Hugh Dowding. The major anti-war statement of the Sixties, Richard Attenborough's *Oh! What a Lovely War* (1969) was only intermittently successful in translating to the screen a concept that remained obstinately stage-bound.

Perhaps the key war film of the decade was Robert Aldrich's *The Dirty Dozen* (1967). It put to profitable use the idea of a bunch of assorted criminals recruited into the service of the Allies and employing their expertise at knifing, garrotting and dynamiting to knock out a vital Nazi target in France. With its virile anti-heroes cocking a snook at the Establishment while exercising their murderous talents, it proved enormously popular with the cinema's mainly youthful audiences. It inspired a whole series of imitations, including *Play Dirty* (1968) and *Kelly's Heroes* (1970), whose keynotes were violence, self-interest and increasing cynicism, which chimed well with the mood of the new generation.

As in epics and war films, so too in Westerns the rule was: size, scale, all-star action and no expense spared. The psychological Western of the Fifties was eclipsed by the likes of *How the West Was Won* (1962), a rambling chronicle of the expansion westwards of the United States, the first feature film in three-camera Cinerama. But the most trend-setting Western was John Sturges' *The Magnificent Seven* (1960). The group of outlaws (played by Yul Brynner, Steve McQueen, James Coburn, Charles Bronson, Robert Vaughn, Horst Buchholz and Brad Dexter) is hired to defend a Mexican village from bandits, but its members owe no allegiance to anyone or anything outside their group. This

central theme became a key idea in Sixties films. In Westerns, it led to no less than three sequels to *The Magnificent Seven* itself: *The Return of the Seven* (1966), *Guns of the Magnificent Seven* (1969) and *The Magnificent Seven Ride!* (1972); and to the reworking of the idea in *The Professionals* (1966), *The Wild Bunch* and, on a lighter level, the modish, whimsical *Butch Cassidy and the Sundance Kid* starring Paul Newman and Robert Redford (both 1969).

The theme was also transferred to the war film. Significantly, Steve McQueen, James Coburn and Charles Bronson all turned up in Sturges' *The Great Escape* (1963). *The Dirty Dozen* used a similar but more numerous group. In real life, the idea of the tough, all-male professional group, with no loyalty to anything outside itself, found expression in the Nixon gang, exposed and broken up after the Watergate break-in.

There were other important themes which, taken all together, suggested that the American Western might have reached the end of the trail. There was a group of Westerns about modern-day cowboys, living anachronisms in a changing world: *The Misfits* (1961), *Lonely Are the Brave* (1962) and *Hud* (1963). With many of the major Western stars getting old, the theme of the ageing cowboy became common and there were jokes about John Wayne's age in several of his later Westerns, though he turned his girth and his years to good use in his rumbustious performance as the one-eyed US marshal Rooster Cogburn in Henry Hathaway's *True Grit* (1969). Joel McCrea and Randolph Scott, veterans of scores of low-budget Westerns, retired from the screen after making unforgettable appearances in Sam Peckinpah's *Ride the High Country*

(1962). Echoes of that film's fierce elegiac pride can also be heard in *Will Penny* (1967) and *Monte Walsh* (1970).

Like the stars, the Western directors were growing older. The decade witnessed the retirement of three of the greatest. John Ford made his last masterpiece, *The Man Who Shot Liberty Valance* (1962), a moving, moody, meditative, wholly personal film, in which he decisively parted company with the tendencies of modern civilization. Then he got many of his old friends together for one last great trek, a flawed, all-star tribute to the fighting spirit of the Indians, *Cheyenne Autumn* (1964). Raoul Walsh bowed out with a characteristically brisk and vigorous cavalry Western, *A Distant Trumpet* (1964). Howard Hawks, having distilled the quintessence of his world-view into the ultimate

The autumnal Westerns gave way to a new kind of stylized violence

Hawksian statement of beliefs and values, *Rio Bravo* (1959), twice reworked it, as *El Dorado* (1967) and *Rio Lobo* (1970).

The decisive new development in the Sixties took place not in the United States but in Italy, where Clint Eastwood established his reputation as the new superstar in a trio of Italian-made Westerns of which the characterizing features were stylized violence and tough cynicism: *Per un Pugno di Dollari* (1964, *Fistful of Dollars*), *Per Qualche Dollaro in Più*

(1966, *For a Few Dollars More*) and *Il Buono, Il Brutto, Il Cattivo* (1967, *The Good, the Bad and the Ugly*). The success of these films brought Eastwood back to Hollywood to make a direct imitation of them, *Hang 'Em High* (1968). But it was Sam Peckinpah, whose *Ride the High Country* had said an eloquent farewell to the old Western, who now celebrated the triumph of the new ethic in his epochal *The Wild Bunch*. Violence had now arrived as big box-office.

In the early Sixties the American cinema was obsessed with size – epic themes, wide screens, three-hour running times, all-star casts. Genre spectaculars – *The Guns of Navarone* (1961), *El Cid* (1961), *How the West Was Won* (1962) – lured audiences away from their TV sets in huge numbers.

The Great Escape is a typical product of this inflationary period, scarcely justifying its length, but zestfully directed by John Sturges. The script – a watered-down version of Paul Brickhill's largely factual account – is an anthology of genre clichés established in many British prisoner-of-war camp dramas of the Fifties, except that here there is a formidable American presence.

The British films, such as *The Wooden Horse* (1950) and *The Colditz Story* (1955), consciously strove to create a microcosm of England behind barbed wire, where attitudes of class could maintain morale and discipline. The deprivations and dangers of incarceration were minimized to strengthen the point about British resilience and the known outcome of the war; eccentricity and xenophobia became patriotic attributes, and quips like 'See you at Simpson's' served to promote a nostalgia that was fast fading.

The Germans were rarely cast as loathsome villains, but tended to be characterized as 'goons' – incompetent and obsequious. But as the Cold War developed, with Germany divided and suddenly the frontline of Allied defence, war films began to make distinctions between ordinary soldiers and officers who merely acted under orders, and the sadistic and fanatical SS men.

The Great Escape simply spreads this judicious blend of political diplomacy and Allied fervour on an unusually broad canvas, using an extensive and superbly designed set built on location in Bavaria. As with *The Guns of Navarone*, it is essentially an adventure drama, only incidentally a war film, with sharply defined characters played by charismatic stars.

Significantly, the film kills off the entire British contingent (Richard Attenborough, Donald Pleasence, Gordon Jackson, David McCallum) whilst the more resourceful and independently-minded Americans (the more expensive actors) survive. The massacre of Attenborough and his countrymen is shown and then forgotten in the closing images that pay tribute to Steve McQueen's star presence.

The film is in some ways a reworking of *The Magnificent Seven* (1960), having an equally memorable thematic score by Elmer Bernstein, and starring three of the 'seven': McQueen, Charles Bronson (playing a Pole) and James Coburn (playing an Australian). The fourth American is the amiable James Garner, and as a star vehicle the film is brilliantly organized.

Garner plays a versatile scrounger, Hendley – a humanized version of William Holden's Sefton in

1

2

Stalag 17 (1953). He puts his illicit 'general store' to good use, applying the Americanized hard-sell to a timid and stupid German called Werner who is terrified of being sent to the Russian front. Hendley's growing loyalty to the blind and feeble Blythe marks him as the American with heart – a soft-skinned cynic. Bronson's Danny Velinski represents bulging muscles and a neurotic mind – the conscience of the audience. James Coburn's Sedgwick is an irresistible image of stoicism whose outlandish suitcase upsets the bureaucratic British-run escape routine, but does not prevent his peaceful and picturesque jaunt on a stolen bicycle to neutral Switzerland.

But most noteworthy is Steve McQueen as Hilts, the quizzical, independent tough-guy who dominates the film, playing off superbly against Attenborough's stiff-upper-lip Squadron Leader Bartlett. Attenborough arrives at the camp preceded by his reputation as a fearless fighter and staunch ally, but it

is the expectations aroused by Hilts that generate most tension. *The Great Escape* strongly confirmed McQueen's stardom, and it ingeniously cheats its audience by regularly sending him into solitary confinement, away from the action. And yet McQueen's constant tossing of a baseball in his cell increases the tension within both

himself and the audience. When the escape finally comes, the film indulges McQueen's love of speed by granting him a cathartic motorcycle chase across open fields. His final crash into a barbed wire barrier – possibly a foretaste of the Iron Curtain – sensibly prevents him from turning into some kind of comic-strip hero.

Directed by John Sturges, 1963

Prod co: Mirisch/Alpha. **prod:** John Sturges. **ass prod:** Robert E. Relyea. **sc:** James Clavell, W.R. Burnett, based on the book by Paul Brickhill. **photo** (De Luxe, Panavision): Daniel Fapp. **col:** De Luxe. **sp eff:** Paul Pollard. **ed:** Ferris Webster. **art dir:** Fernando Carrere. **cost:** Bert Henrikson. **mus:** Elmer Bernstein. **sd:** Harold Lewis. **ass dir:** Jack Reddish. **prod man:** Allen K. Wood. **r/t:** 173 minutes.
Cast: Steve McQueen (*Hilts*), James Garner (*Hendley*), Richard Attenborough (*Bartlett*), James Donald (*Ramsey*), Charles Bronson (*Danny Velinski*), Donald Pleasence (*Blythe*), James Coburn (*Sedgwick*), John Leyton (*Willie*), Gordon Jackson (*MacDonald*), David McCallum (*Ashley-Pitt*), Nigel Stock (*Cavendish*), William Russell (*Sorren*), Angus Lennie (*Ives*), Tom Adams (*Nimmo*), Robert Desmond (*Griffith*), Lawrence Montaigne (*Haynes*), Jud Taylor (*Goff*), Hannes Messemer (*Von Luger*), Robert Graf (*Werner*), Harry Riebauer (*Strachwitz*), Robert Freytag (*Posen*), Heinz Weiss (*Kramer*), Til Kiwe (*Frick*), Hans Reisser (*Kuhn*), George Mikell (*Dietrich*), Ulrich Beiger (*Preissen*), Karl Otto Alberty (*Steinbach*).

3

4

6

8

9

In 1942 Squadron Leader Bartlett arrives at Stalag Luft North, a top security German prisoner-of-war camp. He contacts Ramsay, the senior British officer, and proposes a mass breakout of 250 men. A nucleus of experts is assembled but an American –

Hilts – says he is breaking out next day (1). Testing a blind-spot between two watch-towers (2), Hilts is spotted and sent to the 'cooler' for solitary confinement, where he passes the time playing compulsively with a baseball.

Meanwhile, Bartlett's plan goes ahead and three tunnels – nicknamed Tom, Dick and Harry – are started. On his release Hilts volunteers to escape and be recaptured, after having memorized the surrounding countryside. Hilts has his day of freedom and is returned to the cooler. Another American, Hendley, scrounges special equipment from the Germans by bribing them with cigarettes and chocolate; Blythe forges identity papers; a Pole, Velinski, supervises the digging; others make civilian clothes and act as look-outs.

Hilts is released and starts an illicit distillery, and during impromptu Fourth of July

celebrations (3) the Germans discover Tom. Bartlett orders that all work be concentrated on Harry, and although Blythe begins to go blind, and Velinski suffers from claustrophobia (4), the tunnel is finally made ready. But because Harry is several yards short of the trees, the Germans discover the escape-in-progress (5) and only 76 men get away, travelling by train, plane, boat and on foot (6).

Hilts leads the Germans on a hair-raising motor-cycle chase, but crashes (7) and is arrested; Blythe is killed in a plane crash (8); Velinski and a few others manage to cross the border. Bartlett is recaptured after a chase in a village (9) and is summarily executed along with 50 others. As the Commandant leaves the camp in disgrace – some prisoners are returned – including Hendley and Hilts, the latter being thrown his baseball as he walks towards the cooler (10).

Born in 1925 in Cleveland, Ohio, Newman studied acting at the Yale University Drama School and at Lee Strasberg's Actors' Studio. After appearing in many live television dramas and on Broadway, he made his screen debut in *The Silver Chalice* (1955). After his second film, *Somebody Up There Likes Me* (1956), his stardom was assured, but Newman's major decade was really the Sixties when he created his four most memorable characters in *The Hustler* (1961), *Hud* (1963), *Cool Hand Luke* (1967) and *Butch Cassidy and the Sundance Kid* (1969), at the same time solidifying his clearly recognizable image.

This image was one of moody rebelliousness, rugged individualism, cool detachment and, above all, overpowering sex-appeal. Newman filled the vacuum created by the death of James Dean and decline of Marlon Brando. He ascended over others because he was best able to embody the alienation and restlessness of his era while possessing a traditional beauty that most of his contemporaries lacked. Paul Newman was simultaneously the perfect modern anti-hero and the link with a glamorous Hollywood that was rapidly fading into memory.

Dr Jekyll . . .

His screen persona and private personality have often been opposites. Like other Actors' Studio alumni, he considers himself a 'cerebral' actor and regards each role as an agonizing 'study session', yet he has played many spontaneous, uninhibited characters. He has also often portrayed supremely confident and charming types even though he is privately rather shy and insecure. Committed passionately to liberal and humanitarian causes, Newman has created a substantial gallery of men who are committed mainly to themselves, and although he has been married to one woman – actress Joanne Woodward – since 1958, his characters attack, insult and discard women, subordinating them entirely to male ambition.

Ambition is in fact a key aspect of the Newman image. Some of his characters are born on the wrong side of the tracks and pursue the American Dream of wealth and status, as in *The Young Philadelphians* (1959) and *Sweet Bird of Youth* (1962). Others are not necessarily interested in money – the goal may be winning a pool match in *The Hustler* or a motor race in *Winning* (1969), executing a mission such as helping Jewish refugees to enter Palestine in *Exodus* (1960), or excelling at music, the aim of Ram Bowen (Newman) in *Paris Blues* (1961) – but the means are similar. These men set aside considerations of love, family, humanity and morality, and push forward ruthlessly, alienating themselves from society in the process.

However, Newman's performances inspire identification with even his most arrogant and selfish characters' problems and obsessions. Many of his 'nasty' men at least have the

Right: Big Daddy (Burl Ives) learns he has cancer when his angry son (Newman) tells him during a confrontation in Cat on a Hot Tin Roof. *Centre right: ageing playboy Chance Wayne (Newman) and his lover (Shirley Knight) in* Sweet Bird of Youth. *Far right: private eye* Harper *closes in on his quarry aided by Fay Estabrook (Shelley Winters)*

Paul Newman

First, the eyes; dazzlingly bright blue and seeming – as one columnist put it – 'as if they have just finished taking a shower'. Then, the classic profile and sensual mouth, suggesting nothing less than a Greek statue or perhaps even Michelangelo's David. At the start, Paul Newman's success derived largely from his extraordinary looks and it took audiences – and critics – some time to discover the serious actor behind the façade

saving characteristic of recognizing their nastiness and turning it into charm; Newman's boyishness and sense of humour make them engaging. Of course this involvement is generated partly by his looks: he may characterize obnoxious, irresponsible, rough types, but his features usually suggest intelligence and sensitivity.

In addition, his portrayals of Brick in *Cat on a*.

Left: the famous features that have helped ensure Newman's continuing success. Below: in The Sting *he played an ingenious con-man out to trick a big-time gangster. Below right: as a pool shark in* The Hustler, *Newman scored one of his biggest hits*

Hot Tin Roof, Billy the Kid in *The Left-Handed Gun* (both 1958) and Luke in *Cool Hand Luke* evoke sympathy because of the extreme loneliness that their actions bring them. A remarkable number of his characters are also humanized by having to undergo severe physical punishment: he has his thumbs broken in *The Hustler*; his face smashed in *Sweet Bird of Youth*; is dragged by a horse in *The Life and Times of Judge Roy Bean* (1972); and is continually and mercilessly tortured in *Cool Hand Luke*. The extreme degradation and pain creates an atmosphere of vulnerability that facilitates audience identification.

Perhaps the most important reason for the appeal of Newman's heroes and anti-heroes is

that they seem to have embodied the general moods of their times. In key Fifties roles, playing characters like Rocky Graziano (*Somebody Up There Likes Me*) and Billy the Kid, he slipped into the Brando/Dean mould – the confused, inarticulate rebel who strikes out at the world without knowing why. Rocky's alienation from his uncaring father and Billy's general difficulty with father-figures struck another responsive chord at the time, allying them with Dean's characters as well as with other troubled youths in Fifties cinema.

Rebel with a cause
In the Sixties, Newman's image evolved into that of the relatively *intelligent* rebel, more in

Profile of a winner

control of himself and better able to define his cause. 'Fast' Eddie (*The Hustler*), Chance Wayne (*Sweet Bird of Youth*) and Hud Bannon (*Hud*) *can* describe what motivates them and although they are hardly set on improving society their very ability to articulate may have made them connect with youth during the Kennedy era.

Ironically, Newman's stated intentions in playing these ruthless opportunists was to have the audience condemn them. He hoped to show that men who have everything impressive to fellow Americans – attractiveness, charm, virility, an ability to seduce women and to feel equally comfortable drinking with the guys – often have 'the seed of corruption' in them, and succeed only at the cost of their souls. Yet they were vibrant, magnetic, and audiences were drawn to them.

The quintessence was Hud, the amoral modern Texan who could have been a prototype for J.R. Ewing (Larry Hagman) of the popular television series *Dallas*; arrogant, opportunistic, Machiavellian, incapable of warmth or affection, rotten to the core – and yet completely captivating. Newman pulled out all the stops, bringing to perfection his familiar characteristics: the cynical, aloof manner; the nasty, contemptuous voice; the sly, insinuating smile; the icy stare; the insolent sexiness. The ads proclaimed, 'Paul Newman *is* Hud'. Their assumption may have been inaccurate, but for audiences Newman and Hud were one.

'Cool' in the coolers

In the later Sixties, perhaps as a reflection of society's growing cynicism, most of Newman's films abandoned even the attempt to condemn their amoral protagonists. Harper, the slightly

Above: Newman as Luke Jackson in Cool Hand Luke, *the story of a convict's two years hard labour on a chain gang and his eventual death. Below: in* Hud *he plays an amoral rancher whose debauched way of life finally drives his young nephew (Brandon de Wilde) away from the ranch*

Above: Newman with Joanne Woodward on the set of Rachel, Rachel, *in which she plays a repressed schoolmistress. Below:* The Life and Times of Judge Roy Bean *starred Newman as the Judge and Roddy McDowall as Frank Gass but the beer-drinking bear stole the limelight*

Right: Newman and Woodward shooting a scene for WUSA *as they 'speed' along, the back-projected scenery lending it authenticity. Below right: in* The Verdict *(1982), the defence (James Mason) and the prosecution (Paul Newman) query a point of law in a malpractice suit*

worn, sardonic private eye in the 1966 movie of the same name, was a perfect embodiment of Sixties 'cool': anti-heroic and brutally exploitative, he is the master of flippancy, nastiness and the new art of the 'put on'. Now audiences were meant to regard the character as the hero, and they did, making Harper one of Newman's most popular roles.

Moviegoers also responded enthusiastically to *Cool Hand Luke*. Anti-establishment and anti-authority, Luke breaks the law not because of social deprivation – the excuse in most Thirties' films – but because it gives him something to do. The act of rebellion has become its own justification, making Luke an appropriate anti-hero for the late Sixties. Here Newman had returned to the silent rebel type, but unlike the Fifties rebel Luke chose to remain silent. He is neither confused nor directionless but is an intelligent individual who elects to separate himself from the rest of humanity. Yet, as opposed to 'Fast' Eddie and Hud, he has no definite goal and unintentionally becomes a martyr.

Coping with comedy

As Luke, Newman gave his most relaxed performance so far, but in *Butch Cassidy and the Sundance Kid* he is even looser and more casual. Butch, a ludicrous, failed opportunist and hopeless romantic, is a fascinating comic version of Newman's ambitious dreamers. In previous attempts at comedy – such as *Rally 'Round the Flag, Boys!* (1958) and *A New Kind of Love* (1963) – Newman was stiff and forced, but here he is spontaneous and appealing. This derives partly from the fact that Butch is an easy-going, naturally funny fellow instead of an exaggerated comic character, and partly from the pairing with Robert Redford, which creates an immensely attractive camaraderie that is rare in Newman's career. A huge success, the film had everything for contemporary audiences; hip cleverness, a casual attitude towards crime and violence, blundering anti-heroes instead of the traditional genre types, and good-natured but appropriately distanced relationships.

In the Seventies, Newman remained on the list of top box-office stars and two of his films, *The Sting* (1973) and *The Towering Inferno* (1974), far surpassed the grosses of *Butch Cassidy and the Sundance Kid*. Still, *The Sting*'s success may have been due more to the Newman/Redford partnership, or even to Redford's popularity alone, than to Newman's appeal, and *The Towering Inferno* did not seem to depend on the drawing power of its stars – the appeal of the disaster-movie being well established by then. Otherwise, Newman's only big hit since 1969 has been *Slap Shot* (1977), in which his late-career relaxation and sense of fun were strong contributions to his characterization of a hockey-coach.

His other Seventies work includes *The Drowning Pool* (1975) – a sequel to *Harper* that failed to recapture the original's magic – and several films in which Newman played such extremely unpleasant characters that audiences could not identify with them: a cynical, corrupt and thoroughly vicious opportunist in *WUSA* (1970); a stubborn reactionary in *Sometimes a Great Notion* (1971); and an exceedingly sadistic, violent man in *The Mackintosh Man* (1973).

His most challenging film in recent years has been *Buffalo Bill and the Indians . . . or Sitting Bull's History Lesson* (1976), a cynical exploration of show business in which Newman, adopting an ironic stance towards his character, seems to be exploring his own identity as a superstar. However, the film was so unremittingly bitter that it failed to find an audience.

New directions

During the late Sixties Newman decided to try his hand in another area and he has achieved some critical success as a director. *Rachel, Rachel* (1968) and *The Effect of Gamma Rays on Man-in-the-Moon Marigolds* (1972) are gentle, richly emotional and melancholy – yet never depressing – slices of ordinary people's lives. Both indicate a mature visual sensibility and feature excellent performances by Joanne Woodward who also appeared in the fourth film Newman directed, a television feature entitled *The Shadow Box* (1980). *Sometimes a Great Notion*, the story of the problems faced by a logging family, combined precise character portraits and vigorous outdoor adventure in the Howard Hawks mode. *The Glass Menagerie* (1987), a Tennessee Williams' adaptation, also stars Joanne Woodward. Like the other films he has directed, it is a sensitive and potent look at family life.

In 1986, Newman returned to the role that had previously made him famous. Martin Scorsese's *The Color of Money* cast him as fast Eddie Felson – The Hustler, 25 years on. Now it is young Vincent (Tom Cruise) who is the challenger and Eddie the coach – and history, as it is wont to do, repeats itself. Newman had been nominated three times previously for an Oscar; the honour that had hitherto evaded him finally came for this film.

Filmography

1955 The Silver Chalice. **'56** Somebody Up There Likes Me; The Rack. **'57** The Helen Morgan Story (GB: Both Ends of the Candle); Until They Sail. **'58** The Long Hot Summer; The Left-Handed Gun; Cat on a Hot Tin Roof; Rally 'Round the Flag, Boys! **'59** The Young Philadelphians (GB: The City Jungle). **'60** From the Terrace; Exodus. **'61** The Hustler; Paris Blues. **'62** Sweet Bird of Youth; Hemingway's Adventures of a Young Man/Adventures of a Young Man. **'63** Hud; A New Kind of Love; The Prize. **'64** What a Way to Go!; The Outrage. **'65** Lady L (USA-FR-IT). **'66** Harper (GB: The Moving Target); Torn Curtain. **'67** Hombre; Cool Hand Luke. **'68** The Secret War of Harry Frigg; Rachel, Rachel (dir; +prod. only). **'69** Winning (+co-exec. prod); Butch Cassidy and the Sundance Kid (+co-exec. prod). **'70** King . . . a Filmed Record: Montgomery to Memphis/Martin Luther King (doc) (co-narr. only); WUSA (+co-prod). **'71** They Might Be Giants (co-prod. only); Sometimes a Great Notion (+dir; +co-exec. prod) (GB: Never Give an Inch). **'72** Pocket Money (+co-exec. prod); The Effect of Gamma Rays on Man-in-the-Moon Marigolds (dir; +prod. only); The Life and Times of Judge Roy Bean (+co-exec. prod). **'73** The Mackintosh Man (GB); The Sting. **'74** The Towering Inferno. **'75** The Drowning Pool (+co-exec. prod). **'76** Silent Movie (guest); Buffalo Bill and the Indians . . . or Sitting Bull's History Lesson. **'77** Slap Shot. **'79** Quintet. **'80** When Time Ran Out . . .; Fort Apache, the Bronx. **'81** Absence of Malice. **'82** The Verdict. **'84** Harry and Son (+dir; +co-prod; +co-sc). **'86** The Color of Money. **'87** The Glass Menagerie (dir only).

Easy Rider

'A man went looking for America and couldn't find it anywhere' announced the posters that advertised *Easy Rider*. It was a fitting summation of the low-budget film which defied Hollywood traditions and, at the same time, grossed more money than many of the lavish productions of the same year. Although this was the first film either of them had directed, Dennis Hopper and Peter Fonda sold their product to Columbia for $355,000: it went on to take more than $20 million at the box-office.

With its spontaneity and sincerity and its roots firmly in Sixties culture, *Easy Rider* established a new trend in movies: the 'road' film. Hollywood was quick to catch on to the idea of films whose characters had no history and travelled for no apparent reason; the journey becoming a metaphor for life, and the adventures on the road an allegory of man's search for himself. It also fostered a new taste in motorcycles – the Harley-Davidson 'Chopper'.

Wyatt and Billy set off across America on their own personal odyssey looking for a way to lead their lives. On the journey they encounter bigotry and hatred from small-town communities who despise and fear their non-conformism.

and it is these who finally kill off the dreams that they do not understand. Although Wyatt and Billy also discover people attempting 'alternative life-styles' who are resisting this narrow-mindedness, there is always a question-mark over the future survival of these drop-out groups. The gentle hippy community who thank God for 'a place to stand' are living their own unreal dream. The rancher and his Mexican wife are hard-pushed to make ends meet. Even LSD turns sour when the trip is a bad one. Death comes to seem the only freedom. It is significant that, in the final scene, the solitary burning bike remains: Wyatt's spirit lives on.

The film's essential philosophy is controversial, if unspoken. Nonetheless, it is eloquently articulated through the pulsating rock soundtrack, the emphasis on dope-smoking as a common aspect of life, the loving shots of the rolling scenery as they ride across America, and the equation of motorbikes with freedom rather than with the hooliganism of *The Wild One* (1953) and its successors. It was, perhaps, the only film to portray the new culture from within that culture itself.

Easy Rider also works on a **5**

number of mythic and symbolic levels. Hopper had recently become engrossed in Thomism (a philosophical system based on the teachings of Thomas Aquinas) and indeed, it has been seen as the story of a modern prophet . . . from the difficulties of getting hotel rooms to the final violent 'crucifixion'. Another interpretation might suggest that Wyatt and Billy are the drop-out versions of their famous Western namesakes, reversing the traditional journey by travelling east on motorbikes rather than west on horses: a rejection of the old Hollywood and its myths and dreams. One further ironical aspect of this view is that Henry Fonda – Peter's father – once played Wyatt Earp in *My Darling Clementine* (1946). But there are no heroes in *Easy Rider*; identification is stimulated by the mood of the film rather than by characters who have no history and are therefore ideal subjects for mythical legend.

The filming process also rejected Hollywood traditions, as the crew themselves followed the same eastward journey, picking up their actors in the towns they passed through – often improvising action and dialogue. One dramatic scene in the diner, for instance, was done in this way: the locals were told that Hopper and Fonda were sexual

child-molesters, and the customers reacted appropriately vehemently. One actor not recruited *en route* was Jack Nicholson, who gained fame and an Oscar nomination for his portrayal of the liberal lawyer who drowns his uncertainties in alcohol.

In itself, *Easy Rider* is a work full of contradictions – including the fact that Hopper took time off from shooting to appear in *True Grit* (1969), a film with almost the opposite philosophy. Wyatt and Billy finance their journey from the proceeds of a cocaine sale, a hard drug which does not have the same idealistic connotations as marijuana. After their disappointment at the Mardi Gras, Wyatt acknowledges to Billy that 'we blew it'. There had to be another way to search for their freedom, one that was not betrayed from the start.

But despite its depressing message – that America has become so corrupt and bigoted that even those who try to find ways of escaping the system will be destroyed by it – the film is an exhilarating celebration of the alternatives that the Sixties offered. *Easy Rider* seems to say that if anyone blew it, it was America for not allowing a new and challenging, freer, more personal culture to exist.

Directed by Dennis Hopper and Peter Fonda, 1969
Prod co: Pando Company/Raybert Productions. **exec prod:** Bert Schneider. **prod:** Peter Fonda. **assoc prod:** William Hayward. **sc:** Peter Fonda, Dennis Hopper, Terry Southern. **photo** (Technicolor): Laszlo Kovacs. **sp eff:** Steve Karkus. **ed:** Donn Cambren. **art dir:** Jerry Kay. **songs:** 'The Pusher', 'Born to Be Wild' by Steppenwolf, 'I Wasn't Born to Follow' by The Byrds, 'The Weight' by The Band, 'If You Want to Be a Bird' by The Holy Modal Rounders, 'Don't Bogart Me' by Fraternity of Man, 'If Six Was Nine' by The Jimi Hendrix Experience, 'Let's Turkey Trot' by Little Eva, 'Kyrie Eleison' by The Electric Prunes, 'Flash, Bam, Pow' by The Electric Flag, 'It's Alright Ma (I'm Only Bleeding)', 'Ballad of Easy Rider' by Roger McGuinn. **sd:** Ryder Sound Service. **prod man/ass dir:** Paul Lewis. **r/t:** 95 minutes.
Cast: Peter Fonda (*Wyatt*), Dennis Hopper (*Billy*), Antonio Mendoza (*Jesus*), Phil Spector (*connection*), Mac Mashourian (*bodyguard*), Warren Finnerty (*rancher*), Tita Colorado (*rancher's wife*), Luke Askew (*stranger*), Luana Anders (*Lisa*), Sabrina Scharf (*Sarah*), Sandy Wyeth (*Joanne*), Robert Walker (*Jack*), Robert Ball, Carman Phillips, Ellie Walker, Michael Pataki (*mimes*), Jack Nicholson (*George Hanson*), George Fowler Jr (*prison guard*), Keith Green (*sheriff*), Hayward Robillard (*cat man*), Arnold Hess Jr (*deputy sheriff*), Buddy Causey Jr, Duffy LaFont, Blase M. Dawson, Paul Guedry Jr, Suzie Ramagos, Elida Ann Hebert, Rose LeBlance, Mary Kaye Hebert, Cynthia Grezaffi, Collette Purpera (*customers in café*) Toni Basil (*Mary*), Karen Marmer (*Karen*), Cathi Cozzi (*dancing girl*), Thea Salerno, Ann McLain, Beatriz Monteil, Marcia Bowman (*hookers*), David C. Billodeau, Johnny David (*men in pick-up truck*).

After the successful completion of a cocaine sale in California (1), Wyatt (known as Captain America) and Billy stash their money in Wyatt's fuel-tank and set off on their motorbikes across America (2) in order to reach New Orleans in time for Mardi Gras. Unable to get a hotel room because of their

long hair and general unkempt appearance, they sleep out in the open. A couple who are trying to make a living from their small ranch give them a meal. Continuing on the road, they pick up a hitch-hiker who takes them to a hippy community that he is heading for (3). The life-style

1

2

3

4

6

7

seems idyllic, but after a brief stay Wyatt and Billy move on.

When they arrive at a diner in a small town, they are insulted by the local rednecks as weirdo degenerates (4). They are arrested on some minor pretext by the local sheriff and thrown into jail where they meet George

Hanson, a liberal alcoholic lawyer (5). He gets them out and decides to join them on their trip to New Orleans. The next night, when the three of them are sharing a joint (6), their camp is attacked and George is clubbed to death by the sheriff he had antagonized.

Wyatt and Billy ride on (7). They

pick up two girls from the House of Blue Lights, the brothel that George dreamed of visiting, and go to the Mardi Gras, which seems plastic and dull. In a cemetery they all take LSD and share a bad trip (8).

Wyatt and Billy decide to carry on riding to Florida. On the road,

a jeep driver thinks he'll have a little fun with the two of them (9) and takes a pot shot at Billy, whom he accidentally shoots in the stomach (10). Wyatt rides off for help, but the driver returns and deliberately shoots him. In the closing image his bike lies burning on the tarmac.

9

10

1

2

6

Which side will you be on?

if....

ARTHUR LOWE · PETER JEFFREY · MONA WASHBOURNE · GEOFFREY CHATER · ANTHONY NICHOLLS

Introducing MALCOLM McDOWELL · RICHARD WARWICK · CHRISTINE NOONAN · DAVID WOOD · ROBERT SWANN

PARAMOUNT the cinema downstairs **FROM THURSDAY DECEMBER 19TH**
PICCADILLY CIRCUS Tel: 839.6494

Appearing when it did, at the end of a year of youthful dissidence and revolt, *If*.... has often seemed to be a film made purposely to reflect the revolutionary fervour of the late Sixties. The truth is quite different.

Sometime in 1966, I had a telephone call from a friend of mine, the director Seth Holt. Seth asked if I would be interested in the idea of directing a film with him as producer. He explained that John Howlett, a young writer with whom he had been working, had shown him a script about life in an English public school. John had written it with David Sherwin with whom he had shared horrific years at Tunbridge School. Seth had not felt competent to undertake such a subject as he had not been to public school himself.

I responded to the story, then entitled *Crusaders*, because I approved of its romantic and rebellious spirit, and because there was so much of my own experience that could relate directly to the subject; and not just my experience of school but my experience of society in the years that had followed. So from the beginning the making of *If*.... was a warmly and intimately personal experience.

I met John and David and liked them. As soon as they realized that I had no wish to 'tone down' their story, they were responsive to my ideas.

It was David who undertook the work of revising the script with me. He and I took *Crusaders* to pieces, invented some new characters,

new incidents and a new structure. We decided that we wanted to make a film in 'epic' style which would aim consciously at the dignity and importance of a general theme. I had early on started elaborating the idea of an apocalyptic finale, but as the script developed we were anxious from the beginning *not* to appear to be reflecting revolutionary student action in France or America. The only element of contemporary iconography to be seen in the film is a poster of Che Guevara: it had been pinned up on the wall by a boy at the school where we were shooting. I did not have the heart to take it down.

Seth Holt did not in the end produce the film. His own director's career suddenly reanimated itself — and anyway I do not think he really liked the direction in which David and I took the script. This was away from naturalism and towards a style which I would certainly claim to be realistic ('realism' implying a concern with essences rather than with surfaces) and poetic rather than 'fantastic'.

I am often asked how we managed to find the actors for *If*...., and particularly Malcolm McDowell. At first I thought that perhaps the script called for boys of exactly the age of the characters. But after some experiment, I realized that youth for the screen was a matter of temperament and character rather than of literal years. I remember vividly Malcolm's second audition on the stage of the Shaftesbury Theatre,

when he and Christine Noonan improvized with a marvellous, reckless intensity their love-hate scene in the Packhorse Café. They cast themselves in an instant.

Other key talents in *If*.... brought the blessing of familiarity. Arthur Lowe had given a fine performance in *This Sporting Life* (1963) and I had worked with Mary MacLeod, Graham Crowden and Jocelyn Herbert, the art director, at the Royal Court Theatre. Miroslav Ondříček, whom I had first met shooting for Miloš Forman when I visited Prague in the early Sixties, had been my cherished collaborator on *The White Bus* (1968).

It was hard to get the money to make *If*....; it has always been

hard to get money for any British film of originality and risk. Eventually Albert Finney and Michael Medwin, who had started their own production company, Memorial Enterprises Ltd, out of Albert's rewards for *Tom Jones* (1963), managed to impress Charles Bluhdorn, the idiosyncratic head of Paramount Pictures, and we secured his backing. It was generally imagined by everyone that our subject was 'too English' to appeal outside the British market. In the event, although the picture was enthusiastically received by the British critics, it did only averagely decent business in this country. It was abroad that it made its chief impact, in the United States, in Europe, and even behind

372

4

5

College House. Return. College reassembles for the Winter Term. The boys of College House inspect lists, find their places and unpack their things. New boys, like Jute and Biles, are 'scum'. Authority among the boys is represented by four prefects known as 'whips' (1) including the impeccable Rowntree and the puritanical Denson. Mick Travis, a senior boy, arrives wearing a scarf to hide the moustache grown in the holidays (2). He and his friends, Johnny and Wallace, have little respect for tradition. *College.* College settles down to a routine. Chapel. Learning.

Games. Jute is grilled until he is word-perfect in the obligatory slang. Mick covers his study walls with images of freedom and violence. Dreaming, he listens to primitive music on his record-player. Biles is hunted, captured (3) and strung upside-down in the lavatory.
Term time. Bobby Philips, Rowntree's attractive scum, serves tea to the whips. In his study, Johnny leafs through magazines while Wallace peers into the mirror for symptoms of decay and Mick writes notes for a philosophical credo. 'Violence and revolution are the only pure acts' (4).
Ritual and romance. Bobby is repelled by Denson's yearning for him. Enthralled, he watches Wallace perform on the horizontal bar in the gym; a friendship is formed. During a College match, when they should be 'cheering loudly', Mick and Johnny escape downtown, pinch a motor-bike, and ride off to adventure and excitement with the girl at the Packhorse Café (5) (a black-and-

white sequence).
Discipline. Mick, Johnny and Wallace are told by Rowntree that they have become a bad example to the House. They are beaten (6). *Resistance.* The pressures of authority mount. The three boys mingle blood in a ceremony of solidarity.
Forth to war. During a College Cadet Corps field exercise, Mick shoots and bayonets the chaplin. The Headmaster gives the rebels a last chance: the Privilege of Service. They discover a forgotten stack of ammunition while clearing out lumber from under the stage (7).
Crusaders. Speech Day. General Denson is addressing boys and parents when the hall goes up in smoke. The assembly pour out into the Quad (8), to be met by a hail of bullets. The rebels have installed themselves, with automatic weapons, on the roof. Bravely, the Headmaster steps forward. 'Trust me! . . .' he cries (9). The girl takes steady aim. The Establishment counter-attacks. Mick continues firing (10) . . .

7

8

Directed by Lindsay Anderson, 1968.
Prod co: Memorial Enterprises Ltd. **prod:** Michael Medwin, Lindsay Anderson. **sc:** David Sherwin, from a story by David Sherwin, John Howlett. **photo** Eastman Colour): Miroslav Ondřiček. **ass photo:** Chris Menges. **ed:** David Gladwell. **art dir:** Jocelyn Herbert. **mus:** Mark Wilkinson. **sd:** Christian Wangler. **ass dir:** John Stoneman. **r/t:** 111 minutes.
Cast: Malcolm McDowell (*Mick*), David Wood (*Johnny*), Richard Warwick (*Wallace*), Christine Noonan (*the girl*), Rupert Webster (*Bobby Phillips*), Robert Swann (*Rowntree*), Hugh Thomas (*Denson*), Michael Cadman (*Fortinbras*), Peter Sproule (*Barnes*), Peter Jeffrey (*Headmaster*), Anthony Nicholls (*General Denson*), Arthur Lowe (*Mr Kemp*), Mona Washbourne (*matron*), Mary MacLeod (*Mrs Kemp*), Geoffrey Chater (*Chaplain*), Ben Aris (*John Thomas*), Graham Crowden (*History teacher*), Charles Lloyd Pack (*classic master*), John Garrie (*music master*). Tommy Godfrey (*school porter*), Guy Ross (*Stephans*), Robin Askwith (*Keating*), Richard Everitt (*Pussy Graves*), Brian Pettifer (*Biles*), Michael Newport (*Brunning*), Charles Sturridge (*Markland*), Sean Bury (*Jute*).

it had its greatest impact and greatest effect. If only the British distributors could understand that it is not necessarily by 'international elements' in casting or in a script that a film can transcend the limitations of provincialism or parochialism. It is by the vitality of emotional impulse, the urgency and importance of what needs to be said. This is a truth which Americans seem to recognize, alas, much more readily than the English. But then, Americans are less scared and more stimulated by challenge.
LINDSAY ANDERSON

9

10

TRANSATLANTIC RAINBOWS

British films in the Sixties seemed to have found an American pot of gold to revive the industry but in the end it proved to be only Hollywood tinsel

The years 1958–63 witnessed the first stages of a profound social and cultural revolution in British life. It swept aside accepted traditions and conventions and it released all the pent-up energies and aspirations of youth, which found expression in a whole new world of music, fashion and sexual mores. Alongside the other developments came a renaissance in British film-making, often described as the 'New Wave'. A new and talented generation of film directors, many of them nurtured in the Free Cinema documentary movement, brought to the screen the frustrations, limitations and aspirations of working-class youth. Films such as *Room at the Top* (1959), *Saturday Night and Sunday Morning* (1960), *A Taste of Honey* (1961), *A Kind of Loving* and *The Loneliness of the Long-Distance Runner* (both 1962) were all accompanied by melancholy, dissonant jazz and were shot in black and white on genuine north-of-England locations; they explored this strange new world with sober realism and bleak compassion. In the main, these films were produced by small independent companies, raising money where and how they could – from National Film Finance Corporation loans, from deferred fees, from small American investments. Pre-eminent among them was Woodfall, founded by Tony Richardson and John Osborne and for a short time involving the Canadian financier Harry Saltzman. But alongside them were Joseph Janni's Vic Films, Bryanston – a consortium of 16 independent producers headed by Michael Balcon – and the enterprising Beaver Films of Bryan Forbes and Richard Attenborough.

Forbes and Attenborough perfectly exemplified the new method of film financing when they took no salary for producing *The Angry Silence* (1960), the controversial but highly praised film about the ostracism of a lone worker by strikers. Later they joined forces with Michael Relph and Basil Dearden, Jack Hawkins and Guy Green to form Allied Film-Makers, pooling their talents to produce a polished and popular 'caper' thriller, *The League of Gentlemen* (1960). Under this banner, Forbes and Attenborough went on to produce a series of sensitive, meticulously crafted off-beat dramas which

brought them deserved critical acclaim – *Whistle Down the Wind* (1961), *The L-Shaped Room* (1962) and *Seance on a Wet Afternoon* (1964).

But when Woodfall proposed a colour film of *Tom Jones*, Henry Fielding's classic eighteenth-century novel of a young man's growth to maturity, they were unable to raise the money from British backers and approached an American company, United Artists, for financial support. United Artists' decision to invest in the film and the enormous international success of *Tom Jones* (1963) were to change the face of British film-making. Bawdy, funny, uninhibited, *Tom Jones* celebrated a previous permissive age of gusto, gourmandizing and joyous free-living. It caught the mood of the moment. The Labour election victory in 1964 ended 13 years of Conservative rule with the promise of '100 days of dynamic action'. Censorship, prudery and convention were in retreat. Swinging London was born. It was a frenzied saturnalia, a cult of the new and the now, a world of colour supplements, pirate radio, glamorous television commercials, dolly birds, discos and boutiques, exciting music and freedom of thought and expression.

In the early Sixties United Artists also backed the desire of producers Harry Saltzman and Albert R. ('Cubby') Broccoli to bring Ian Fleming's chic spy

Above: Tony Richardson directing Charge of the Light Brigade, *a satirical look at the inefficiency and brutality of the Victorian military establishment. Below: in* What's New, Pussycat? *a sociable young man (Peter O'Toole) joins a suicidal American stripper (Paula Prentiss) in a routine at a fashionable Paris night-club. Below left: as* Isadora, *Vanessa Redgrave plays an American dancer who establishes a dancing school in the Soviet Union Opposite: echoing real life, Taylor plays a much-married millionairess in Joseph Losey's not-so-successful* Boom!

Above: in The Jokers *Michael Crawford* (centre) at a party as an alibi while 'borrowing' the crown jewels. Above right: *Michael Caine* as Alfie with two of his girlfriends, Annie (*Jane Asher*, left) and Gilda (*Julia Foster*). Below: *Lynn Redgrave* as a northern girl trying to succeed as a pop singer in Smashing Time (1967). Bottom: *Spike Milligan* and *Michael Hordern* as survivors of nuclear war in The Bed Sitting Room (1969)

thrillers to the cinema screen. The result was *Dr No* (1962). This film and its immediate follow-ups, *From Russia With Love* (1963) and *Goldfinger* (1964), all starring Sean Connery, created another cult hero – secret agent 007, James Bond, 'licensed to kill'. The films were an unbeatable blend of conspicuous consumption, brand-name snobbery, colour-supplement chic, comic-strip sex and violence, and technological gadgetry. Above all, the films were cool, stylish and knowing, and these were the prized characteristics of the Sixties.

The almost simultaneous success of Connery as James Bond and Albert Finney as Tom Jones with American and international audiences convinced American film companies that a bonanza awaited them in the United Kingdom. Britain had become the music and fashion centre of the world and, with the young, 'Britishness' was in. Overhead costs were lower in Britain than in the United States and there were reserves of acting, directing and technical talent to be tapped too. So American companies began to announce big British production programmes. Paramount, Columbia, Warner Brothers, Universal and the other major studios poured money into their British operations and were joined by leading American independents, including Joseph E. Levine's Embassy Films and Martin Ransohoff's Filmways. The independent British companies which had characterized the 'New Wave' were simply unable to compete.

By 1966, 75 per cent of British first-features were American-financed; in 1967 and 1968 that proportion had risen to 90 per cent. The last gasp of the native industry came with the sale of British Lion, the company which had released the bulk of the 'New Wave' films. Since the National Film Finance Corporation had a controlling interest in it, the government decided to sell off the company in 1964. After an unsavoury scramble by a variety of groups, a consortium headed by Michael Balcon acquired it, aiming to launch a viable programme of film-making independent of the American companies. But the lack of guaranteed circuit release, difficulties in raising capital and boardroom squabbles combined to defeat the venture and British Lion never became the projected 'third force' in British film-making.

The 'New Wave' had spent itself by 1964. Swinging London was now the theme, encouraged and financed by the Americans. Sober realism and earnest social comment gave way to fantasy, extravaganza and escapism; black-and-white photography and north country locations were superseded by colour photography and the lure of the

metropolis. Stars and directors who had made their names in 'New Wave' films forsook grim industrial landscapes and the pressures of working-class living. Tony Richardson and Albert Finney, the director and actor originally most associated with the 'New Wave', set the transition in motion with *Tom Jones*. Perhaps significantly Richardson, with the exception of the flawed *Charge of the Light Brigade* (1968), was never again to make a film of any consequence, critically, artistically or commercially. Karel Reisz, who had directed Finney in *Saturday Night and Sunday Morning*, went on to make *Morgan, a Suitable Case for Treatment* (1966), emphasizing fantasy in the story of a social and psychological misfit who identifies with a gorilla, and *Isadora* (1968), a lengthy and indulgent celebration of the American dancer Isadora Duncan, one of the dotty darlings of the Twenties, an earlier age of 'bright young things'.

Lindsay Anderson, whose *This Sporting Life* (1963) had been one of the crowning achievements of the 'New Wave', turned fantasy to good effect in his devastating *If* . . . . (1968), combining the dream of youthful revolt and sexual liberation with a comprehensive assault on the public-school system and the hierarchical society of which it was a microcosm. John Schlesinger, who had made his feature-film debut with the delicate and moving *A Kind of Loving* (1962), laid bare the essential hollowness of Swinging London in *Darling* . . . (1965), the story of a key icon of the age, the glamorous fashion model, played here by Julie Christie.

Just as Richardson, Reisz, Anderson and Schlesinger had been the characteristic directors of the 'New Wave', so the celebrants of the new style were Richard Lester, Clive Donner and Michael Winner. Lester's style, fragmented and breathtakingly fast-moving, was an amalgam of influences from television commercials, comic-strips and Goon Show surrealism. He was at his best in *A Hard Day's Night* (1964) and *The Knack* (1965), both of them photographed in black and white and set in highly stylized, dazzlingly designed decors. *A Hard Day's Night* enshrined the myth of the decade's greatest cult figures, the Beatles. *The Knack*, in which a simple young man played by Michael Crawford raced around trying to find out the secret of making out with girls, was an inextinguishable celebration of the London of Carnaby Street and the pirate radio station Radio Caroline.

Clive Donner's *Nothing But the Best* (1964) was the new era's equivalent to *Room at the Top*, redone as a black comedy in lavish colour. This time working-class aspirant Jimmy Brewster, played by

Alan Bates, jokily cons and murders his way to the top, in stark contrast to the earnest and painful ascent of Joe Lampton. *Here We Go Round the Mulberry Bush* (1968) took up the theme of *The Knack*, that of an inexperienced youth trying to lose his virginity. But this time the story was filmed in colour, set in Stevenage New Town and told with engaging humour, truthfulness and charm. Rather more in the Sixties mainstream was the frantic knockabout of Donner's *What's New, Pussycat?* (1965), in which actor/writer Woody Allen gave a first taste of his distinctive vision of the neurotic outlook and sexual hang-ups of modern urban man.

Michael Winner's films, particularly *You Must Be Joking* (1965), *The Jokers* and *I'll Never Forget What's-'is-Name* (both 1967) encapsulated the joky, cynical, remorselessly flip humour of the day. But perhaps most typical of the money-spinning American-backed British successes of the decade were Paramount's *Alfie* (1966), directed by Lewis Gilbert, charting the ruthless amatory progress of a cockney Casanova, and Columbia's *Georgy Girl* (1966), directed by Silvio Narizzano, a Cinderella story about the romantic misadventures of a lumpish provincial girl loose in London.

Amidst all the fun and frenzy a few films remained valiantly out of step with the mood of the times: Bryan Forbes' *The Whisperers* (1967) was a haunting study of loneliness and old age; and

Once again expensive productions for international markets failed too often at the box-office

Kenneth Loach's *Kes* (1969) was a moving and truthful account of a working-class lad's escape from his environment through his training of a kestrel.

Foreign directors produced some distinctive work in British studios. François Truffaut's *Fahrenheit 451* (1966), a science-fiction fantasy about a book-burning society of the future, was accounted one of the less successful efforts. But Antonioni's *Blow-Up* (1966) utilized the contemporary London scene and one of its key symbols, the fashion photographer, played by David Hemmings, for a characteristically opaque and multi-layered study of the relationship between illusion and reality. Roman Polanski, the Polish director, also found Britain a congenial setting for his own peculiar phantasmagoric visions of sexuality and instability, as expressed so powerfully in *Repulsion* (1965) and disturbingly in *Cul-de-Sac* (1966). Even Joseph Losey, the expatriate American long resident in Britain and the director

of a trio of films, scripted by the playwright Harold Pinter, which brilliantly and definitively laid bare the complexities of the British class system – *The Servant* (1963), *Accident* (1967) and *The Go-Between* (1971) – succumbed to the prevailing mood. On the one hand, he directed a brace of impenetrable baroque extravaganzas, *Boom!* and *Secret Ceremony* (both 1968), revelling in their decorative qualities at the expense of sense or meaning, and on the other, he turned out the comic-strip-inspired spy story *Modesty Blaise* (1966); it was in many ways the characteristic film of the period, a film for insiders, cultish and chic.

But it could not last. The bubble eventually and inevitably burst. Universal poured some £30 million into Britain in three years, 1967–69, producing a dozen films, few of which made any profit at all, and some of which were simply expensive fiascos. Despite the involvement of such directorial talents as Jack Gold, Joseph Losey, Peter Hall, Karel Reisz and even Charlie Chaplin, Universal produced failure after failure: *A Countess From Hong Kong* (1967), *Charlie Bubbles, Work Is a Four Letter Word* (both 1968), *Three Into Two Won't Go* (1969) and, to cap it all, the ludicrously titled *Can Hieronymus Merkin Ever Forget Mercy Humppe and Find True Happiness?* (1969), arguably the last word in self-indulgence. But more conventional film titles also failed at the box-office, including such hugely expensive British-made musicals as *Dr Dolittle* (1967), *Star!* (1968) and *Goodbye Mr Chips* (1969), and epics such as *Alfred the Great* (1969).

By 1969, almost all the Hollywood film companies were heavily in debt, the taste for 'Britishness' had passed and the films that were making money were such all-American works as *The Graduate* (1967) and *Butch Cassidy and the Sundance Kid* (1969). Their remedy was simple. They pulled out, virtually altogether and virtually all at once. By 1970 only Columbia had any sort of production programme in Britain at all. The British film industry collapsed. Symptomatic of its plight was the rapid dashing of the attempt to fill the vacuum when EMI took over Associated British Pictures in 1969, appointed Bryan Forbes as production chief and announced an ambitious production schedule. But the first three films released almost simultaneously failed and although *The Railway Children* (1970) and *Tales of Beatrix Potter* (1971) proved successful, Bryan Forbes had by then resigned and the experiment had been abandoned. With the Seventies, London stopped swinging, the butterfly culture of the Sixties flew away and, as economic recession, stagnation and unemployment loomed, there was a return to traditional values with the re-election of a Conservative government. The British film industry meanwhile lay flat on its back, where it was to lie for nearly a decade.

Top: Cyril Cusack as the Captain of the book-burning firemen in Fahrenheit 451. *Above: Edith Evans as an isolated old lady who hears voices whispering about her from the radio, the water-pipes and the walls in* The Whisperers. *Below: the Beatles inspired a feature-length cartoon,* Yellow Submarine *(1968). Below left: an Old Etonian (Denholm Elliott) selects an old school tie for an ambitious man (Alan Bates) in* Nothing But the Best

The last thing to trust in a Buñuel film is the story outline. The synopsis of *Belle de Jour* could be told in half-a-dozen ways, for the events that materialize on screen are always subject to the enigma of whether they are real or fantastic.

Early in the film, as Séverine and Pierre are riding in the landau, their good mood gives way to his frustration with her. He stops the landau and orders the coachmen to deal with her. They drag her through the undergrowth, hang her by the wrists from a tree and strip her to the waist. Pierre orders them to whip her, and then tells them to have their way with her. At this point Séverine wakes up in their bedroom and tells Pierre she was thinking of their life together.

It might be that the entire film is a dream – for surely it is the hope of all Surrealists that the whole of life might achieve the pregnant suspension of revery? The ending of *Belle de Jour* (the incapacitated husband and the passing of the empty landau) could be read as the passing fantasy in an ordinary, happy marriage – it would only be necessary to believe in such an alliance. Buñuel has never considered the possibility of total emotional happiness, and he sees sexuality as a form of pathology. He does not seek or believe in cure, and the sentimentality of the 'hospital' genre, where everyone is cured and made 'whole', is always replaced by an astringent humour and a reverence for fantasy.

Séverine is not a bitch or a victim. She is an obscure object of desire – supremely personified by the numbing beauty of Cathérine Deneuve in one of the outstanding examples of screen presence – and as such, Séverine's brimming sexual readiness is the perfect masquerade while Deneuve's impassivity is a touching rendering of inhibition.

Séverine cannot accept her sexuality in terms of love and marriage. She seeks abuse and humiliation, until the grotesque swagger of Marcel enters her life. She needs a way to tame the threat of marriage, and the eventual blankness of her husband is the one thing that can allow her security. Pierre becomes as still and obliging as all the antique furniture in her apartment and Séverine is left as a presiding nullity: like the meal that can never be eaten in *Le Charme Discret de la Bourgeoisie* (1972, *The Discreet Charm of the Bourgeoisie*).

Luis Buñuel was 67 when *Belle de Jour* was made. He said it would be his last film; he was weary, bored and unwell. With Jean-Claude Carrière, he adapted the Joseph Kessel novel for the Hakim Brothers' production company – it is their office in which Marcel pulls off a hold-up. By casting Catherine Deneuve, and showing her in various deliriously erotic situations – naked and in underwear – Buñuel effortlessly complied with and parodied the 'sexy art film'. *Belle de Jour* was the greatest commercial hit Buñuel had ever had: a perfect movie for wealthy women with free afternoons.

In all Buñuel's great work there is no distinction between humour, sexuality and terror, and he is unawed by the cruelty and loneliness of people. Buñuel denies tragedy or salvation; but he is devoted to the exquisite discrepancy between event and imagination. His shooting style is insolently effortless. Buñuel has the barest beauty in cinema: his sense of the single image is so intense that he can be contemptuous of expressiveness. The same attitude awaits the actors – everyone is cast in the way a director might cast television commercials. And yet, a tenderness prevails, so that no-one is ever patronized or exploited.

Above all, *Belle de Jour* is a warning against complacency. After seeing it, the potential in any staircase, any back-street, any refined woman is exposed. Buñuel enables the audience to see that photography cannot record the world because the world has no meaning. Film can only convey feeling and inwardness, and leaves no need for camera angles and expressive devices. It is a peephole into the soul – for anyone with the strength to look without experiencing either dismay or hysteria. *Belle de Jour* hovers between the deadness of life and the ecstasy of imagination.

Directed by Luis Buñuel, 1967
Prod co: Paris Film/Five Films (A Robert and Raymond Hakim production). **prod:** Henri Baum. **sc:** Luis Buñuel, Jean-Claude Carrière from the novel by Joseph Kessel. **photo:** Sacha Vierney. **ed:** Louisette Hautecoeur. **art dir:** Robert Clavel. **cost:** Hélène Nourry. **sd:** René Longuet. **ass dir:** Pierre Lary, Jacques Fraenkel. **r/t:** 100 minutes. Paris premiere, 24 May 1967
Cast: Catherine Deneuve (*Séverine Sevigny*), Jean Sorel (*Pierre Sevigny*), Geneviève Page (*Mme. Anaïs*), Michel Piccoli (*Henri Husson*), Francisco Rabal (*Hyppolite*), Macha Méril (*Renée*), Pierre Clementi (*Marcel*), Georges Marchal (*the duke*), Françoise Fabian (*Charlotte*), Maria Latour (*Mathilde*), Francis Blanche (*M. Adolphe*), François Maistre (*the teacher*), Bernard Fresson (*pock-marked man*), Muni (*Pallas*), Dominique Dandrieux (*Catherine*), Brigitte Parmentier (*Séverine as a child*), Iska Charvey (*Japanese client*).

Séverine is the young wife of Pierre, a successful surgeon. She is frigid in bed (1) but lusty in her dreams (2) and after Husson, an acquaintance, tells her that some other bourgeois wives are part-time prostitutes (3), Séverine makes her nervous way to a brothel (4) and begins to work for three hours every afternoon.

Her cool, blonde classiness is a great attraction, and Anaïs, the madam, prizes and schools her (5). Séverine yields to the humiliation and revels in it; she joins in the necrophiliac rites of a duke; enjoys the mysterious ways of a Japanese client (6); and finds satisfaction and love with Marcel, a young gangster (7). He is so enamoured of her that he follows her to her home and shoots Pierre down in the street, crippling him for life (8).

Séverine's afternoon activities remain a secret until Husson decides to tell Pierre what she has been doing. Pierre is crushed by the news and retreats into himself. Séverine is left watching over his helplessness (9), no longer troubled by her own sexual problems. The previously occupied landau – the perpetual dream image of her sexuality – passes the house, empty (10).

NEW MARTS FOR ART

Personal themes, motifs, obsessions, viewpoints became valuable assets for European directors as they made their mark with the world's expanding art-house audiences

Europe has traditionally been the centre for those sudden leaps forward in creative expression in the cinema that crystallize into movements. America generally absorbed the more obviously adaptable influences rather than allowing such movements to flower in its own ranks, as would happen in the Seventies. Hollywood has habitually tended to wait, watch the box-office success or otherwise of new styled European imports, and has then tried to enlist to its own ends the new stars and directors who have made a considerable mark.

But the Sixties was to see a new kind of development in the European cinema, something which would permeate production tendencies more gradually and become permanently rooted. The Sixties trend of personalized expression in the cinema was to infiltrate the upper levels of American production at least. It would also lead to the fuller acceptance of the European cinema in its own right and in its own languages during the decade and more especially during the Seventies in the expanding business of the art-house (or specialized) theatres to be found in the greater urban centres of the United States.

The new development in the European cinema .was the increased international reputation earned by the outstanding work of such established and new directors as Robert Bresson, Alain Resnais, François Truffaut, Claude Chabrol and Jean-Luc Godard in France, Federico Fellini, Michelangelo Antonioni and later Pier-Paolo Pasolini, Bernardo Bertolucci and Marco Bellocchio in Italy, Ingmar Bergman in Sweden and, more particularly with his work in Spain and France, the veteran Luis Buñuel. This highly personalized cinema was created by directors with the tenacity and integrity to stick to careers in film-making which were essentially self-made and which flourished on top of the mainstream, more purely commercial entertainment; its cumulative effect was to be the great contribution of the Sixties to modern cinema. But it could never have succeeded without the backing of an increasingly large, international public composed on the whole of the younger age-groups with the continuous, insistent support of a considerable number of informed critics and writers in the press and the specialized film journals.

What is meant by a personalized cinema? It must imply that a director feels himself to be in a sufficiently strong, or at least confident, position with his medium to allow his choice of subject to be determined by its relationship to his own private experience, observation and inspiration. Such choices stem from personal idiosyncrasies, personal instinctual needs, interacting with a complex, ancient and deeply rooted social structure. In much the same way as the serious novelist, the film-maker selects his subject-matter and style in accord with his own impulse to self-expression and his perception of the social world which he is portraying, pursuing his own themes and obsessions and working through his unresolved psychic tensions. This manner of working has generally been more

available to the European than to the American film-maker, because the cinema was accepted more whole-heartedly there as an art-form as well as a branch of the entertainment industry.

Europe is a continent comprising a variety of societies which, though distinctive, are all quite highly structured and rigid in their own national styles of living. The individual film-maker can take many rules and conventions for granted within the context of his own country.

Most European countries have either had a freer and more open system of production, distribution and exhibition (sometimes international) than in the United States or have been granted a measure of government subsidy – and sometimes both. This has allowed relatively low-budget experiment to take place, gradually building up a public for the new until it is adequate to cover costs and eventually become accepted. The many European film festivals also provide a market-place and forum in which new reputations can rapidly be made.

During the Sixties, European films on the higher levels of mainstream, international distribution established a wide public following. There was, for example, Bergman, most notably in demanding work that ranged from *Tystnaden* (1963, *The Silence*) to *Persona* (1966), each powerfully depicting a pair of contrasted women. Bergman's films were often, on his own admission, a form of personal therapy. He has rightly maintained that film is the art that, above all others, is responsive to portraying 'psychic states'. No film made up to its time was more complex in its demands on audiences than *Persona*, which entered into the ambivalent nature of a theatre actress's nervous breakdown occasioned by her deliberate withdrawal both from the tensions of private life and from her distress at the tortured

Top: Ingrid Thulin (left) as Ester in The Silence, *with Gunnel Lindblom as her younger sister Anna and Jörgen Lindström as Anna's ten-year-old son Johan; they are in a strange foreign city. Above: Balthazar the donkey is a childhood pet of Marie (Anne Wiazemsky) in Au Hasard, Balthazar and both are victimized by young thugs when Marie falls for their leader*

condition of the troubled world outside.

There was the very different case of Fellini, whose films became in the Sixties increasingly, and sometimes indulgently, an entertaining projection of some personal dilemma, as in *Otto e Mezzo* (1963, $8\frac{1}{2}$) – which is a study of a film director moving in and out of a condition of nervous exhaustion when the pressures become too great for him both in his career and in his private relationships. The following film *Giulietta degli Spiriti* (1965, *Juliet of the Spirits*), dedicated to Giulietta Masina, his wife and constant collaborator, reflected, at least in part, certain problems such as she might have faced in their marriage.

Godard, again to take a totally different personality of the Sixties, developed an entirely new, dialectical technique in film-making in order to make the screen a platform from which to debate or assert his personal position socially and politically; in the process, he became one of the most discussed and influential directors of the time. *A Bout de Souffle* (1960, *Breathless*) posited an existentialist

France and Italy dominated the field of personal cinema during the newly art-conscious Sixties

ethic of living for the moment; the hoodlum hero and his American girlfriend accept murder, theft and betrayal as the natural consequences of their values. Godard's later films of the decade were essentially works that confronted audiences with challenging social and political concepts involving them just as much as himself and his players, thus creating a new director-actor-audience form of combined relationship.

Bresson's obsessive melancholy darkened such poignant films as *Au Hasard, Balthazar* (1966, *Balthazar*) and *Mouchette* (1967); in these studies of the suffering of young girls, the downtrodden were trod even further down. The Sixties was the great decade of Antonioni's unique achievements, from *L'Avventura* (1960, *The Adventure*) to his American *Zabriskie Point* (1970). *L'Avventura* examined minutely the sudden and uncertain blossoming of a love affair in a couple searching for a missing girl, the man's fiancée. Avoiding any kind of conventional, dynamic theatricality, Antonioni's camera scrutinized the behaviour of people at the natural speed it would take them to resolve their personal dilemmas – the viewer was compelled to watch the nature of human indecision.

Eric Rohmer began in the Sixties a series of *Six Contes Moraux* (Six Moral Tales) which included *Ma Nuit Chez Maud* (1969, *My Night With Maud*) and *Le Genou de Claire*, (1970, *Claire's Knee*); these studies in conscience and repressed sexuality encouraged audiences to discover the details of the characters' reasoning rather than to observe their actions. Such extended, intimate contemplation was new to cinema, yet in time it came to command the respect of those audiences. Resnais' films revealed his deep interest in the way that responses to present experience are coloured by the traumas of the past, whether recollected or subconscious. He established himself in the Sixties as one of the more profound of modern film-makers, especially with *Hiroshima, Mon Amour* (1959, Hiroshima, My Love), *Muriel, ou le Temps d'un Retour* (1963, *Muriel*) and *La Guerre Est Finie* (1966, *The War Is Over*). Truffaut made personal, at times partially autobiographical films in the series about Antoine Doinel's growing up, including *Les Quatre Cents Coups* (1959, *The 400 Blows*), *Baisers Volés* (1968, *Stolen Kisses*) and *Domicile Conjugal* (1970, *Bed and Board*).

Buñuel was always the close observer of suffering rather than projecting any suffering he might himself have experienced during his difficult career; sardonic but never inhumane, he melted the ice-cap of bourgeois religious and sexual pretensions, daring to make a bold, personal challenge to his native country under Franco (or settle a personal vendetta) with *Viridiana* (1961), a critique of Spanish religious and moral values; and, in one of his

most startling films, to strip the archetypal sexual masks from a conventional, well-brought-up woman of the upper-middle class in *Belle de Jour* (1967). The socio-political, Marxist-influenced cinema represented by Pasolini's *Accattone* (1961) and *Il Vangelo Secondo Matteo* (1964, *The Gospel According to St Matthew*), Bellocchio's study of an inbred family *Pugni in Tasca* (1965, *Fists in the Pocket*) and Bertolucci's examination of the rise of Fascism *Il Conformista* (1970, *The Conformist*), established its roots during the Sixties. The period also saw the production in France of the highly personalized films of Louis Malle, Alain Jessua, Jacques Rivette and Agnès Varda.

In Britain, less inhibited, more openly proletarian subjects reached the screen with Karel Reisz's *Saturday Night and Sunday Morning* (1960), based on Alan Sillitoe's novel, and *Morgan, a Suitable Case for Treatment* (1966), from David Mercer's play; with Lindsay Anderson's *This Sporting Life* (1963), adapted from David Storey's novel; and with Tony Richardson's *Look Back in Anger* (1959), from John Osborne's play, and *A Taste of Honey* (1961), based on Shelagh Delaney's play. But these films were personalized cinema at one remove, since the subjects were more personal to the writers than to the directors themselves, as was so often the case in the British cinema of the Sixties.

In response to all this individualized work, critics began to adopt the word '*auteur*', in the sense of 'author of films', and apply it rather indiscriminately in order to discover personal veins, thematic predilections or technical quirks or twists in the work of directors in the more widely popular American genres of film-making. The European film had proved, however, that the personalized cinema was gradually moving into the forefront of critical attention. This trend was backed by the film festivals, the writings of the leading critics and commentators, the growing library of books about films, the increasing popularity of film studies in the

universities – particularly in North America – and the growth of the influence of the specialized cinemas and film societies. The more mature among the younger audiences turned their back on the banalities of television and made the highbrow cinema into a cult; the more markedly individual directors with artistic or socio-political interest, and those prepared to deal in depth with psychological and sexual subjects were particularly favoured. As the general film theatres and their audiences declined rapidly in numbers, the proportion of audiences remaining faithful to the art-house cinema, or newly discovering it as a lively, contemporary artform, rose – again bringing increased recognition to the work of the directors already discussed.

The effect in America of this maturation of the European cinema was to be only gradual. The strict bar against allowing financial backing for anything that seemed to suggest minority interests relaxed very rarely. American film-makers with a strongly individual flair – such as Stanley Kubrick, John Huston, Joseph Losey or John Cassavetes – worked in some instances abroad, notably in Britain. The rise of the independent producer and producer-director as the determining factor in superior American films led to a much greater variety of subject. Few American films of the period could be regarded as strictly personalized cinema in the sense that they fulfilled the inner needs of their makers, or projected their personal problems or exceptional personal experiences. Elia Kazan certainly made attempts at this when filming his own novels in *America, America* (1963) and *The Arrangement* (1969). But the more personalized cinema was to emerge in America during the Seventies, notably in the work of Woody Allen, whose first tentative comedy as writer, director and star was *Take the Money and Run* (1969), or in the post-Sixties work of such directors as Hal Ashby, Robert Altman, Paul Mazursky, Francis Ford Coppola and Martin Scorsese. ROGER MANVELL

Top left: the murder of Professor Quadri (Enzo Taroscio), a political activist, by Italian Fascist hirelings in France shortly before World War II – a climactic scene from The Conformist. *Top:* Viridiana *(Silvia Pinal), a few hours out of the convent where she is a novice, tries on her symbolic crown of thorns with a misplaced touch of innocent vanity. Above: Christine Doinel (Claude Jade) in* Bed and Board *makes herself up to resemble her husband's boring Japanese mistress Kyoko; the erring Antoine is eventually relieved to return to his wife*

Coppola Now

Above: Francis Ford Coppola – doing 'a Hitchcock' – as the director of a TV crew filming GIs in action in Apocalypse Now

'Francis Coppola likes to think of himself as a film-maker,' says Roger Corman. Coppola is a big boy now but his career is as diverse and sprawling as his films. In his search for creative autonomy – which began in the early Sixties when he was an employee on the Corman production line – he has woven a wide-angle saga of financial and technological overkill, setting himself up as a Hollywood godfather and producing several masterpieces along the way

Francis Ford Coppola's story to date has been an occasionally spectacular drama about making films – as opposed to directing them. His carefully nurtured public image is that of the artist struggling to change and control the means and conditions of production through which his work is realized. The parodoxes involved go beyond the usual, simple 'artist versus industry' opposition, climaxing perhaps in the grotesque notion of a weeping Coppola thanking his Zoetrope studio employees for agreeing to continue working on the musical *One From the Heart* (1981) without being paid.

The hustler

Coppola's aspirations to mogul status are hinted at when he describes how, as a child (he was born in Detroit, Michigan, in 1939), he made 'a little money' from showing the home movies his parents made. He would cut up the films and construct narratives with himself as

the hero, but was more interested in 'the exhibition end' and in technical matters. He was to become one of the new wave of young American film-makers in Hollywood in the Seventies and his career developed in archetypal 'movie brat' style. After obtaining a degree in theatre arts he moved on to the UCLA (University of California at Los Angeles) film school in 1960. Then he made some 'nudie' movies, won the Samuel Goldwyn Award for a screenplay (*Pilma, Pilma* – never filmed), and was picked up by producer-director Roger Corman. Work on several of Corman's pictures led to Coppola's first feature, *Dementia 13* (1963), shot in Ireland and using the cast and crew that had been assembled for Corman's *The Young Racers* (1963). Corman agreed to put up half the budget ($20,000) on the basis of Coppola describing a scene involving a lady, a lake, a drowned child and an axe murder. He then supposedly developed the storyline in

three-and-a-half days to contain these elements. Certainly individual images and scenes in the film are stronger than the actual plot. Perhaps most significant is Coppola's account of 'big disagreements' with Corman over the editing. This led to Coppola's quitting.

Next followed a spell as a writer with the Seven Arts company, a job obtained largely as a result of the Goldwyn award. Coppola's script for *Reflections in a Golden Eye* (1967) was not used, but his name appears on *This Property Is Condemned* (1966) – 'it was all very depressing' – and on *Paris Brûle-t-il?* (1966, *Is Paris Burning?*), of which he says, 'I could write a book about the troubles we had'. In 1964 he worked on *Patton*; it wasn't filmed until 1970 but, according to Coppola, 'the best scenes in the film, like the opening, are word-for-word from my script'. Coppola regards *You're a Big Boy Now* (1966), his next directorial credit after *Dementia 13*, as 'a con job' worked by himself and the producer Phil Feldman on Seven Arts. He wrote the script on Seven Arts time, but used his ownership of the book rights to get the director job. The film itself was very much a Sixties piece – a zany, Dick Lester-influenced fantasy about a young man trying to cope with women. Again, more interesting is Coppola's hustling attitude to the financing company:

'The way we worked was the way I work now, which is, I don't ask anybody if I can make a movie, I present them with the fact that I am going to make a movie, and if they're wise they'll get in on it.'

Already Coppola was setting his creative flair against the restrictive pressures of the film industry (the management and unions): 'You would never believe the thinking of some of those guys.'

His relationship with Warner Brothers-Seven Arts (the two companies had merged in 1967) was not improved during the making of *Finian's Rainbow* (1967), which was offered to Coppola while he was scripting *The Rain People* (1969). He wanted to film the musical (involving a dancing Irishman, a crock of gold, leprechauns, plus a very mild race issue that inspired Coppola to call the film 'a hot potato') on location, a desire almost totally thwarted by the studio. Veteran dance director Hermes Pan quit the film, Warners blew it up to 70mm (cutting off Fred Astaire's feet in the process) but Coppola considered the final product as having 'humanity and joy', though it was 'not a personal film of mine'.

Rain over America

Because Warners mistakenly believed that *Finian's Rainbow* would be a hit, they were prepared to back Coppola's next venture, the very 'personal' *The Rain People*. The film's narrative core – a pregnant woman (Shirley Knight) journeys across America and defines her maternal feelings through an encounter with a brain-damaged football player (Bruce Dern) – allowed Coppola a literal escape from the pressures of Hollywood as industry. He packed his tiny crew into a few vehicles and set off, armed with specially purchased lightweight equipment and prepared to improvise and edit *en route*. As an attempt at an early feminist movie, *The Rain People* was somewhat compromised by Coppola's fantasies about women:

'There's a kind of feminine, magical quality, dating back to the Virgin Mary or something I picked up in Catechism classes, that fascinates me.'

His paranoia about unions, arising this time from problems over the size of the crew, was meanwhile growing hand-in-hand with his image of himself as the isolated artist:

'They're [the unions] at my door every day . . . they feel I'm a sort of rat I guess. . . . How can I take a crew like that for a picture that's a personal statement. . . . Nobody wants to make it but me.'

All in all, Coppola's move in 1969 – along with George Lucas for whom he would later produce *American Graffiti* (1973) – to his own San Francisco studio, American Zoetrope, seems in retrospect an inevitable next step. The idea of independently producing low-budget features by young directors, exploiting technological developments and escaping not only the unions (more powerful in Los Angeles) but also what Coppola called 'the management breed . . . packages and deals' seemed fine. But Coppola's hustling streak backfired and Warner Brothers, whom he had persuaded to back Zoetrope, so intensely disliked its first feature, Lucas' *THX 1138* (1970), that they instantly withdrew their support. As a result, Zoetrope simply collapsed.

Day of the Godfather

At this point, the strands and oppositions within the Coppola story come together in the double-faced form of *The Godfather* (1972) and *The Conversation* (1974). He was seemingly chosen by Paramount to direct the former as much for his Italian blood as for any particular directorial aptitude for the task. But he was clear about the effects of its extraordinary commercial success: 'The Godfather made me very rich . . . Part of me really wants to take some control and own a piece of that film business.' Paramount offered as much when it set up the Directors Company to fund 'small' features directed by Coppola, Peter Bogdanovich and William Friedkin in conditions of relative autonomy. When the project folded, mainly because of the directors' commitments to other companies, Coppola had produced only one film for it. *The Conversation* is a combination of European 'art movie' and Hollywood thriller, and centres on a great performance by Gene Hackman as a paranoiac, alienated surveillance expert who becomes involved in a murder plot. The film was a critical success, but the formula whereby the commercial blockbuster – in this case *The Godfather* – subsidizes the 'personal project' is an unrealistically simplistic one. In this light *The Godfather, Part II* (1974) seems to occupy a gap – a film made by Coppola while he chose which path to take.

Despite statements since *The Godfather* like 'I don't want to make big commercial pictures', and his professed desire to make 'modest films about contemporary human situations', Coppola has plunged headlong into becoming the

Above: a cop (Robert Duvall) attempts to rape Natalie (Shirley Knight) in The Rain People. *Top: Petula Clark and Tommy Steele in the happier* Finian's Rainbow. *Top right: Mafia revenge – Woltz (John Marley) loses by a short head in* The Godfather. *Right: Harry Caul (Gene Hackman), all wired-up in* The Conversation. *Below right: Gregory Hines entertains the clientele of* The Cotton Club

last tycoon. In 1974 he purchased a theatre, a radio station and San Francisco's *City* magazine (from which he fired the entire staff). He also bought new production premises and a large share in a distribution company. Most important of all, Coppola resurrected *Apocalypse Now*, a project started by John Milius in 1969 which was originally intended for George Lucas. Shooting began in the Philippines in March 1976 with a budget of $12 million. This would eventually soar to $31.5 million. When the film finally appeared in 1979, critical responses to its vision of Vietnam as a psychedelic nightmare – filtered through Conrad's *Heart of Darkness*, Michael Herr's *Dispatches*, a *film noir*-style voice-over and the music of the Doors – were in a sense superfluous. More significant was the fact that Coppola had mortgaged his home to complete it and almost ruined his marriage, that a typhoon had wrecked the shooting, that it was entered as a 'work in progress' at Cannes, and that there were various different endings, and so on. Coppola himself played his part, informing the world that 'Apocalypse Now is not a movie. It is not *about* Vietnam, it is Vietnam'. So much for 'modest films'.

After the Apocalypse

Since *Apocalypse Now*, showmanship has turned into total brinkmanship. The list of Coppola's activities is bewildering. It ranges from the distribution of Godard's *Sauve Qui Peut (La Vie)* (1980, *Slow Motion*) and the financing of a new Godard feature, to the roadshow presentation of Abel Gance's *Napoléon* (1927); the financing of Wim Wenders' *Hammett* (1982) – suspended after 10 weeks' shooting; the rebirth of Zoetrope with the purchase of Hollywood General Studios; the hiring of Michael Powell as director in residence and Gene Kelly as house choreographer; a massive investment in new video technology. But the thin ice on which all this was happily skating became apparent when, after the problems with *Hammett* emerged, investors began to withdraw money from Coppola's own *One From the Heart* – and so he wept for his unpaid workers. Once again it was up to Paramount to dry his tears with a million-dollar investment to keep him afloat, at least temporarily.

After the musical fantasy, *One From the Heart*, he changed style with two intimate stories of youth growing up in mid-America. *The Outsiders* and *Rumble Fish* (both 1983) showed a new, gentler side of Coppola. *The Cotton Club* (1984), set in the world of gangs, boot-leggers and jazz marked a return to his former epic style, while *Peggy Sue Got Married* (1986) is a more whimsical portrayal of the Fifties. *Gardens of Stone* (1987), about soldiers training for Vietnam, is a personal, human story – and a continuation of Coppola's search for a new style.

Filmography

1960 Ayamonn the Terrible (short). **'62** The Magic Voyage of Sinbad (co-sc. only on re-ed. and dubbed version of USSR film: Sadko, 1952) (GB: Song of India); Tower of London (dial. dir. only). **'63** Battle Beyond the Sun (co-sc; +add. dir. under pseudonym on re-ed. and dubbed version of USSR film: Nebo Zobyot, 1959); The Young Racers (sd. only); The Terror (co-dir, uncredited; +assoc. prod); Dementia 13 (+co-sc) (USA-EIRE) (GB: The Haunted and the Hunted). **'66** This Property Is Condemned (co-sc. only); Paris Brûle-t-il? (co-sc. only) (FR) (USA/GB: Is Paris Burning?); You're a Big Boy Now (+sc). **'67** Finian's Rainbow. **'68** The Wild Racers (2nd unit dir. only). **'69** The Rain People (+sc). **'70** Patton (co-sc. only) (GB: Patton: Lust for Glory); THX 1138 (exec. prod. only). **'72** The People (orig. TV) (exec. prod. only); The Godfather (+co-sc). **'73** American Graffiti (co-prod. only). **'74** The Great Gatsby (sc. only); The Conversation (+co-prod; +sc); The Godfather, Part II (+prod; +co-sc). **'77** The Godfather (re-ed. version of The Godfather and The Godfather. Part II for TV with add. footage). **'79** Apocalypse Now (+prod; +co-sc; +co-mus; +act); The Black Stallion (exec. prod. only). **'81** The Escape Artist (exec. prod. only); One From the Heart (+co-sc). **'82** Hammett (exec. prod. only). **'83** The Outsiders (+exec. prod); Rumble Fish (+exec. prod; +co-sc); The Black Stallion Returns (exec. prod only); Koyaanisquatsi (exec. prod only). **'84** The Cotton Club (+co-sc). **'85** Mishima (exec. prod only). **'86** Peggy Sue Got Married. **'87** Tough Guys Don't Dance (exec. prod only); Gardens of Stone; Tucker (+co-prod). *1960–62: Coppola directed a number of 'nudie' shorts, including* The Peeper *and* Tonight for Sure (*intercut and re-released as:* The Wide Open Spaces); Come On Out; The Playgirls and the Bellboy/The Belt Girls and the Playboy.

In 1972 Paramount decided to make *The Godfather* the centrepiece of their new production strategy. The aim was to find one film a year that would be a really big box-office success, a success large enough to carry all the other productions. The right film would háve the benefit of both a large production and promotions budget, and it would be exhibited in such a way as to gain maximum impact – simultaneous, nationwide release backed by intense publicity. This impact would then be exploited by charging higher admission prices.

The choice of *The Godfather* proved .inspired. The film was an extravagant commercial success. Within days of its release it had recovered all initial outlay, and within weeks had become an extremely profitable enterprise. In commercial terms *The Godfather* became a landmark, an indication of what could be achieved by Paramount's scheme. It was also a landmark in less tangible ways. The director, Francis Ford Coppola, was seen as a representative of the new generation of Hollywood film-makers, and the success of the film, not only guaranteed his artistic future but also improved the prospects of his contemporaries.

Although it was directed by a 'new' film-maker, *The Godfather* is essentially a traditional film: the subject-matter – the world of ethnic crime – is familiar and has provided the basis for many previous films; the main thrust is a narrative one, though ranging widely in time and space; the story is told vividly and clearly; the stars are a mixture of established faces, such as Marlon Brando and Sterling Hayden, and promising newcomers – Al Pacino, James Caan and Diane Keaton.

In many ways what separates *The Godfather* from previous gangster films is the amount of money spent on it. This is not as cynical a comment as it sounds, for the money is translated into artistic values on the screen. It allows the narrative to develop in a leisurely way, giving the actors the opportunity to develop characterizations and allowing settings and costumes to have strong dramatic presence. Overall, the money enables the film to be turned into a substantial spectacle.

Of course, the availability of money does not guarantee its effective use; it is up to the film-maker to take advantage of the resources money brings within reach. Coppola's contribution to *The Godfather* is undoubtedly a crucial one. As a director, his talents incline towards the creation of spectacle, and like a director of musicals, he is able to choreograph the movement of large numbers of people; the opening wedding reception is a superb example in this respect. He is always conscious of the expressive use of colour; the contrast between the light golden tones of the Sicilian sequences and the dark, sombre ones of the interiors inhabited by the gangsters is striking. Coppola also seems particularly sensitive to the emotional physical presence of actors and actresses.

1

7

The Godfather is finely cast – Brando's considered authority, Al Pacino's controlled intensity, Robert Duvall's distanced influence, Diane Keaton's directness and vulnerability.

It has been said that *The Godfather* is a radical film. This is a difficult argument to sustain, for the point the film makes about the place of crime in American society (its intimate connections with the established representatives of law and politics, its control over legitimate enterprises, the analogies that can be made between the way crime and large corporations conduct their affairs) are all familiar ones, and hardly the marks of a radical view of American society. If anything, the film, with its admiration for a certain ideal of masculine purity based on honour, ruthlessness, the use of violence and the maintenance of the family, is reactionary in outlook.

The popular success of *The Godfather* is not easy to explain. The film's overall effect is rather cold and bleak and the ruthlessness of the central characters, their commitment to violence and repression of emotion make identification hard. A fictional world without moral basis, and characterized by bloody struggles, is not immediately attractive. However, some of the film's appeal can be explained. It has many of the pleasures of the nineteenth-century realist novel, providing an alternative social world that the reader or viewer can inhabit; it has a sense of the epic in its presentation of warring kingdoms whose rise and fall effect the lives not only of the chieftains, but also those of ordinary people.

But whatever *The Godfather's* appeal, it certainly doesn't sustain the view of many film producers and critics that the popular audience is looking for easy identifications and comfortable reassurances. The popular response is far more complicated than that.

Don Vito Corleone (1) – head of an Italian-American criminal 'family' and 'Godfather' to the Italian immigrants in New York – holds a lavish reception for his daughter's wedding (2), periodically returning to his office to settle any 'business' that crops up during the day.

The Don's power is illustrated when Johnny Fontane, a singing star he has backed (3), seeks his help in getting a part in a Hollywood movie. The Don asks the producer, Jack Woltz, to give Fontane the part. When friendly persuasion fails, Woltz finds the severed head of his favourite horse in bed with him. Fontane is given the part.

Another family, the Tattaglias, propose that the Don join in their drug-running trade. When he refuses, the Tattaglias shoot him down in the street (4). The Don survives, but his younger son Michael (5) takes revenge by killing a Tattaglia associate (6). He flees to Sicily (7) where he settles down and marries a local girl.

After two years news of his brother Sonny's death reaches Michael. His wife is then killed by a car bomb meant for him (8) and he returns to America. When the Don dies of a heart attack Michael becomes the leader of the 'family'.

A series of ruthless measures finally reinstates the Corleone family's position. A new Godfather has emerged in his father's image (9).

Directed by Francis Ford Coppola, 1972

Prod co: Alfran Productions. **prod:** Albert S. Ruddy. **assoc prod:** Gray Frederickson. **sc:** Mario Puzo, Francis Ford Coppola, from the novel by Mario Puzo. **photo** (Technicolor): Gordon Willis. **sp eff:** A. D. Flowers, Jow Lombardi, Sass Bedig. **ed:** William Reynolds, Peter Zinner, Marc Laub, Murray Solomon. **art dir:** Warren Clymer, Philip Smith. **cost:** Anna Hill Johnstone. **mus:** Nino Rota. **mus dir:** Carlo Savina. **sd:** Christopher Newman, Les Lazarowitz, Bud Grenzbach, Richard Portman. **ass dir:** Fred Gallo, Tony Brandt. **prod des:** Dean Tavoularis. **prod man:** Fred Caruso, Valerio De Paolis. **r/t:** 175 minutes.
Cast: Marlon Brando (*Don Vito Corleone*), Al Pacino (*Michael Corleone*), James Caan (*Sonny Corleone*), Richard Castellano (*Clemenza*), Robert Duvall (*Tom Hagen*), Sterling Hayden (*McCluskey*), John Marley (*Jack Woltz*), Richard Conte (*Barzini*), Diane Keaton (*Kay Adams*), Al Lettieri (*Sollozzo*), Abe Vigoda (*Tessio*), Talia Shire (*Connie Rizzi*), Gianni Russo (*Carlo Rizzi*), John Cazale (*Fredo Corleone*), Rudy Bond (*Cuneo*), Al Martino (*Johnny Fontane*), Morgana King (*Mama Corleone*), Lenny Montana (*Luca Brasi*), John Martino (*Paulie Gatto*), Salvatore Corsitto (*Bonasera*), Richard Bright (*Neri*), Alex Rocco (*Moe Greene*), Tony Giorgio (*Bruno Tattaglia*), Vito Scotti (*Nazorine*), Tere Livrano (*Theresa Hagen*), Victor Rendina (*Phillip Tattaglia*), Jeannie Linero (*Lucy Mancini*), Julie Gregg (*Sandra Corleone*), Ardell Sheridan (*Mrs Clemenza*), Simonetta Stefanelli (*Apollonia*), Angelo Infanti (*Fabrizio*), Corrado Gaipa (*Don Tommasino*), Franco Citti (*Calo*), Saro Urzi (*Vitelli*).

Scorsese, Scorsese

Peter Hayden's 1978 documentary about Martin Scorsese is appropriately entitled *Movies Are My Life*, for no other director of the new American cinema has quite so completely managed to merge the concerns of his personal life with older film genres which helped to form his consciousness of life and cinema. An Italian-American of the third generation, Scorsese was born in 1942 in Flushing, New York, but his parents moved to Little Italy in 1950, so that it was in the Italian, Catholic milieu of Manhattan that he grew up. His asthma prevented the more strenuous pastimes; as partial recompense his father took him to the movies at least twice a week, which inspired him to draw his own story-boards for imaginary films. He now says that when thinking back over his childhood, he often confuses events that really happened with events from Alice Faye vehicles or the films of John Ford and Samuel Fuller.

At 14 he decided he wanted to be a priest, but rock'n'roll, movies on 42nd Street and his gang pals on Lower East Side, New York, interested him more than the Church and took more of his time than his studies. Instead, in 1963, he enrolled in the English Department of New York University where he found himself more interested in cinema courses and was encouraged in his interest by Professor Haig Manoogian, to whom *Raging Bull* (1980) is dedicated. Among his fellow students and friends were Brian De Palma (through whom he met Robert De Niro), cameraman Michael Wadleigh (who later directed *Woodstock*, 1970) and Mardik Martin, who worked on several scripts with Scorsese.

A growing awareness of the French *nouvelle vague* from screenings at the New York Film Festival helped him to see the possibility of making personal films under almost amateur circumstances. At any rate, it is clear from his second 16mm short made at NYU – *It's Not Just You, Murray* (1965) – what sort of cinema was to be Scorsese's major influence: that film ends with a production number ('Love Is a Gazelle') in the manner of Busby Berkeley, a perfect example of popular American movies of the Thirties and Forties. That same film also indicated other central concerns which were to be developed in later films: *It's Not Just You, Murray* is a semi-fictionalized portrait of his uncle, set in Little Italy.

Dress rehearsals

In 1965 he attempted to make a 35mm feature – *Bring on the Dancing Girls* – a semi-autobiographical story. About a young man, raised in Little Italy as a Catholic, the film shows how a young girl brings confusion to his macho sense of 'angel or whore'. The $6000 Scorsese had borrowed for the film did not last

'People tell me that I am incapable of telling a story. I don't care. I have other things to say. And another way to say them.' For all his lack of concern with the commercialism of cinema, Martin Scorsese has nevertheless made pictures which have sold well. Starting out as a respected editor, he went on to exploit his Italian-American origins in the films he has directed. His success has certainly earned him a place in the vanguard of the new American cinema

long and he abandoned the project until 1967 when Haig Manoogian encouraged him to try it again, this time in an economically more realistic 16mm. The result was *I Call First* – released in 1968 under the title *Who's That Knocking at My Door?* – with Zina Bethune and Harvey Keitel. Seen now, the film has its own nervous intensity, a fine performance by Keitel, and striking black-and-white images, but seems something of a dress rehearsal for *Mean Streets* (1973) – itself already 'in the air' as a script.

After finishing *Who's That Knocking at My Door?* Scorsese made a 16mm short, *The Big Shave* (1967), which was a hit at the Experimental Film Festival in Knokke-le-Zoute,

Belgium. He stayed in Europe with cameraman Richard Coll and made publicity films for six months and co-wrote Pim de la Parra and Wim Verstappen's *Obsessions* (1969) in Holland. His reputation as an editor took him to Hollywood, and while editing and supervising post-production for François Reichenbach's *Medicine Ball Caravan* (1971), Scorsese met American International Pictures exploita-

Above: between feature films, Martin Scorsese hopes to make a series of documentary profiles. He himself appears in American Boy *(1978), the portrait of a friend. Below left:* Boxcar Bertha *– an outspoken, bloody drama about union activity*

tion producer Roger Corman who hired him to make an action film 'for the guys on 42nd Street'.

The producer expected something of a sequel to his own film *Bloody Mama* (1970). Instead, Scorsese's *Boxcar Bertha* (1972) is a strange meditation, with bursts of violence, on roving union organizers and other outcasts of the Depression. AIP was somewhat disconcerted and did not quite know what to do with the film, since Scorsese had doctored the screenplay to some extent. Nevertheless, *Boxcar Bertha* and its director had their supporters in the film industry and on the festival circuit, and they advised Scorsese to make a film to which he was more totally committed than this impersonal commercial exploitation work.

Italy isn't here any more

That film was *Mean Streets*, made for $550,000, which became a hit at both the New York Film Festival and in the 'Directors' Fortnight' at Cannes. The film is a portrait of a generation of Italian-Americans in the ghetto of Little Italy, caught between the Mafia and the Church. Harvey Keitel again plays a variation of Scorsese himself, attempting to free himself of his Catholic background and yet to 'save' those around him, particularly his best friend and his friend's epileptic sister . . . with catastrophic

results. Part of the film's excitement comes from the use of rock music, not only to underscore period but to comment on emotional states and point to how popular culture helps determine character.

For all its personal concerns, *Mean Streets* is very much a genre film, in a tradition that dates back at least as far as *Angels With Dirty Faces* (1938). Looked at from one angle, however, Scorsese has never made anything but genre films . . . but always with a difference. His next feature, *Alice Doesn't Live Here Any More* (1974) – the story of a widow's search for happiness on a trip across America in which she vacillates between the dream of a career and 'true love' – was in every way a woman's picture in the tradition of Sirk or Capra. It is probably the director's least personal film – Ellen Burstyn, who won an Oscar for her performance, had as much or more to say about the script as Scorsese or writer Robert Getchell. But Scorsese's own concerns are certainly not absent: the beginning in which an extract from an Alice Faye film is used to show how popular movies formed consciousness of identity, for example, or the unbalanced 'angel or whore' violence of the character played by Harvey Keitel, who is at one and the same time generous and loving with Alice, yet brutal to his own wife. *Alice*

Doesn't Live Here Any More showed that at least some of the problems found in Little Italy are also a part of Anglo-Saxon Protestant culture.

Street life

In 1976 New York City became not only the setting but a major character in *Taxi Driver*, the film which won the Golden Palm at Cannes and secured Scorsese's reputation as the most talented director of the new American cinema. While the script is by Paul Schrader, there are definite connections between *Taxi Driver* and *Mean Streets*. Here, however, the would-be 'saviour' becomes an exterminating angel, a killer praised and honoured for slaughtering a pimp. Ironically, though, it is praise for a paranoid murderer who could easily strike again. The film is a trip through hell with the 'real' city dissolving into an hallucination of odd colours and visual distortions – a hell from which there is no redemption.

Those who praise Scorsese for his 'realism' are missing the point, unless it is his emotional realism they have in mind. There is little difference finally between the way he uses the actual streets of New York in *Taxi Driver* and the purposely artificial sets of the city he uses in *New York, New York* (1977). What he had in mind was:

'A movie called *New York, New York* shot entirely in Los Angeles, which goes back to the old films I used to see as a kid, which reflected part of New York, but that was a fantasy of New York up on the screen. So, in the picture I tried to fuse whatever was a fantasy – the movies I grew up with as a kid – with the reality I experienced myself.'

In *New York, New York* Scorsese wants to take the viewer through the changes in the American consciousness from the open-ended,

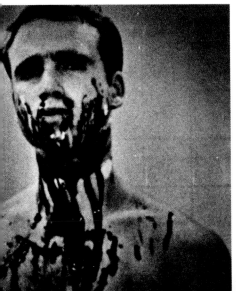

Left: Ellen Burstyn stars in Alice Doesn't Live Here Anymore, *a 'road' movie about a young widow and her son drifting in search of love and money. Bottom left: just after he graduated, Scorsese made the black comedy* The Big Shave – *a prize-winning short in which a minor accident turns into an arterial tragedy. Below: Jodie Foster as Iris and Robert De Niro as the* Taxi Driver

high-energy optimism following hard on the tail of World War II to the repressed disillusion of the Fifties. While he glories in the artificiality of the form – something akin to *The Glenn Miller Story* (1953) – he attempts to make the human relationships realistic, in part to determine whether those old forms can contain emotional realism without bursting open. He is only relatively successful, at least in the version of the film that was released – the original four-and-a-half hours were edited down to just over two. There is now an imbalance in the structure which loses sight of the character played by Robert De Niro in the second half, so that the emotional drive of the film is weakened.

The last round
The Last Waltz (1978), a documentary about the last performance by The Band, is a genre film – the 'concert' film with interviews. Aside from the fact that it was shot and edited with musical grace and energy, the film is easily the best of its type because it has a moving thesis which grows from the material rather than being imposed on it. Its theme is one that is shared in part by *New York, New York* – the portrait of the end of a musical and cultural era which, for all its excitement, is finally autumnal in tone.

Raging Bull is in the boxing-biography genre of the *Somebody Up There Likes Me* (1956) variety, but with a difference. Set more or less in the Italian milieu and again with something of the sexual angel-whore problem, of the love-hate relationship with the Anglo-Saxon blonde which is also in *Taxi Driver*, the film describes in one scene how Jake La Motta (the hero) is driven to a violent frenzy when he fears that his idealized, teenage wife might have been sleeping with his brother. But Scorsese has developed other favourite themes in new ways: redemption, love, friendship between men, the unconsidered act. Scorsese refuses to think of *Raging Bull* as a boxing film. *The King of Comedy* (1983) continued Scorsese's relationship with De Niro. In this film, De Niro plays Rupert Pupkin, a man convinced that he could be the greatest of stand-up comics. His arrogance impels him to kidnap a top TV host (Jerry Lewis) to get a spot on prime-time TV. Pupkin is a pathetic hero, and the film a cautionary tale of an obsessed nobody who deludes himself into believing he deserves to be a star.

His next film, *After Hours* (1985), is an original and episodic return to Scorsese's beloved mean streets. A black comedy of urban paranoia, it follows the idiosyncratic events of a night out that turns into a nightmare. His first film for four years, *After Hours*, starring Paul Hackett and Rosanna Arquette, is a stylish and quirky change of pace for Scorsese.

He continued his move into the more commercial side of cinema with *The Color of Money* (1986) which is effectively a remake of *The Hustler* (1961). Starring Paul Newman, again, as fast Eddie Felson 25 years older, and Tom Cruise as the contender, it is as sharp and pacy a study of pool and competition as the original.

Above: the Forties' musical drama New York, New York *follows the romance of singer Francine Evans (Liza Minnelli) and musician Jimmy Doyle (Robert De Niro)*

Below: De Niro in Raging Bull. *Bottom: 'Fast' Eddie Felson (Paul Newman) and the young challenger Vincent (Tom Cruise) take their cues for a battle of pool in* The Color of Money

Filmography
1964 What's a Nice Girl Like You Doing in a Place Like This? (short) (+sc). '65 It's Not Just You, Murray (short) (+co-sc; +act). '67 The Big Shave (short) (+sc). '68 Who's That Knocking at My Door? (+sc). '69 Obsessions (co-sc. only) (HOLL-GER). '70 Woodstock (doc) (ass. dir; +sup. ed); Street Scenes (doc) (prod. sup; +add. dir. only). '71 Medicine Ball Caravan (doc) (assoc. prod; +sup. ed. only (USA-FR) (GB: We Have Come for Your Daughters); Minnie and Moskowitz (ass. ed. only). '72 Elvis on Tour (doc) (montage sup. only); Unholy Rollers (sup. ed. only); Boxcar Bertha (+act). '73 Mean Streets (+co-sc; +act). '74 Italianamerican (doc. short) (+co-sc: + appearance as himself); Alice Doesn't Live Here Anymore. '76 Taxi Driver (+act); Cannonball (actor only) (GB: Carquake). '77 New York, New York. '78 The Last Waltz (doc) (+appearance as himself); Roger Corman; Hollywood's Wild Angel (doc. short) (appearance as himself only); American Boy (doc) (+appearance as himself); Movies Are My Life (doc) (appearance as himself only). '80 Raging Bull (+act); Il Pap'occhio (actor only) (IT). '83 The King of Comedy (act). '85 After Hours. '86 The Color of Money. '88 The Passion.

WUNDERKIND

Rainer Werner Fassbinder

If for each decade there is one country which shines in world cinema, for the Seventies it must have been West Germany. It is always difficult to say why this should be . . . what combination of social and economic forces with artistic tendencies . . . what totally unpredictable outbursts of individual talent. But even if one could suggest some tentative conclusions about the New German Cinema, it would be impossible to account for the appearance anywhere, at any time, of such an eccentric and many-faceted figure as the director Rainer Werner Fassbinder

Although in the eyes of posterity he may not prove to have been the most gifted of a generation which also includes Herzog, Wenders, Schlöndorff, Kluge and Straub, Rainer Werner Fassbinder undeniably made the biggest splash. It would have been difficult to guess at this from his obscure beginnings. When his first feature film *Liebe ist kälter als der Tod* (1969, *Love Is Colder Than Death*) was shown at the Berlin Film Festival in 1969, it left public and jurors alike nonplussed. Being a weird and pretentious combination of Maoist politics and static silences made it almost impossible to judge whether its maker actually had any talent which might possibly emerge once he had shed his two obsessive influences – Godard and Straub. But, it must also be admitted, the film had in full measure that ability to stick in the throat and irritate those who are normally peaceable to fury, and it was this which subsequently turned out to be one of Fassbinder's hallmarks.

Knowledgeable Germans said that this young man (23 at the time) had already done interesting work in the theatre as a writer, director, actor and general 'animator'. He was born in 1946 and was brought up largely by his mother after his parents' divorce. She had been a translator before becoming an actress, and she appeared as Lilo Pempeit in many of her son's films.

When he was 18 he entered a drama school where he met the first of his longtime associates, the actress Hanna Schygulla. In 1965 he made a ten-minute short – *Der Stadtstreicher* – the cast of which included another of his regular collaborators, Irm Hermann, and in 1967 he moved, with a group of friends, to a Munich fringe theatre called Action Theater, where he began directing productions and then writing his own texts. In 1968 the theatre was closed by the police, but Fassbinder and nine others (including Hanna Schygulla, Peer Raben, Kurt Raab and Irm Hermann) set up another group – Anti-Theater – also in Munich.

Sharp shooter

Thus, by the time Fassbinder began making feature films, he had not only experience, but, crucial to his methods of working, a sort of stock company of actors round him who were used to his ways, able to take his lightning changes of direction in their stride, and work as complete collaborators in the evolution of new works, whether on stage, screen or – later on – television. It was through them that Fassbinder's legendary productivity was possible: where other, more conventionally minded film-makers would labour for months to set up, cast and shoot a film, he could, and frequently did, knock one off in a matter of days.

Hence the alarming statistic that once Fassbinder had embarked on a career in films, he made in the first two years (1969–70) no fewer than *ten* features. Most of them had a wild, improvisatory quality which Fassbinder never wholly shook off, and indeed, when he tried to, he seemed to be in danger of

Top: favourite casting in his own films, Fassbinder as Eugen in Fear Eats the Soul. *Far left: Katrin Schaake and Ron Randell in the decadent melodrama* Whity. *Left: Wolfgang Schenck as Baron von Instetten and Hanna Schygulla as his young wife* Effi Briest

falling into the opposite trap of mandarin pretentiousness. The products of this period inclined towards Godard as the primary influence, both in their rough-and-ready shooting style and in their general commitment to a critique of bourgeois society.

A typical early Fassbinder film in these respects would be *Warum läuft Herr R. amok?* (1970, *Why Does Herr R. Run Amok?*), written and directed with Michael Fengler, in which an apparently happily married technical designer with a child, a lovely home and all the comforts of established middle-class life suddenly, for no stated reason, kills his wife, his son and a neighbour, then calmly goes to the office the next morning and there kills himself. What might have begun as a Marxist critique slips over into a refusal to comment that might be interpreted as Absurdist, anarchic or merely cool . . . according to taste.

Transatlantic meditations
Fassbinder's own cinematic passions have embraced many other things besides recent political cinema. He had a passion for the Western and for overheated Hollywood melodrama, particularly when directed by Douglas Sirk. He had also been known to approve of Rossellini's brand of neo-realism. Thus it should have come as no surprise to find him, amidst his tributes to Godard, suddenly veering towards Samuel Fuller in *Der amerikanische Soldat* (1970, *The American Soldier*). In the more than usually bizarre *Whity* (1971) he is to be found pastiching a whole range of American Westerns and steamy tales of the Old South, with the mulatto hero darkly brooding on vengeance against the white master-race, represented here by a bunch of sadists and dribbling half-wits.

In 1971 Fassbinder began on the series of films which were to make him an important international figure. These were interspersed from 1972 with films and series intended wholly or partly for television, some of which – *Acht Stunden sind kein Tag* (1972–73, Eight Hours Don't Make a Day) and *Berlin Alexanderplatz* (1980) – are very extensive. The first of the theatrical movies was *Der Händler der vier Jahreszeiten* (1972, *The Merchant of Four Seasons*), chronicling the economic rise and personal decline of a greengrocer in a sober style illuminated from time to time with flashes of bravura melodrama.

The second, *Die bitteren Tränen der Petra von Kant* (1972, *The Bitter Tears of Petra von Kant*), is a very literal but at the same time wholly cinematic transposition of a play by Fassbinder, who had continued throughout to work extensively in the theatre as well. It is the story of a spoilt fashion designer who has a brief lesbian affair, and in the course of a series of highly-charged meetings with her mother, her daughter, her best friend and most of the important people in her life, is finally deserted by them all and left alone.

The next to appear was *Angst essen Seele auf* (1974, *Fear Eats the Soul*) – an unexpectedly cheering view of a marriage between an elderly, widowed German char and a Moroccan immigrant worker younger than herself. For once, Fassbinder had told the subject in a minutely realistic manner which made it readily approachable by general audiences. With hindsight one may see that in the fourth, *Fontane Effi Briest* (1974, *Effi Briest*), a conspicuously well-upholstered adaptation of Theodor Fontane's famous turn-of-the-century novel about a dissatisfied wife and a fatal liaison, Fassbinder was already moving over, through a concern for surface polish and 'style', towards affectation and stuffiness.

Gloss or floss?
Finally, however, in *Faustrecht der Freiheit* (1975, *Fox*), the relatively sensational – or at any rate unfamiliar – subject-matter (homosexuality) helped to obscure this tendency for the moment. Though married briefly to the actress Ingrid Caven, Fassbinder had never sought to disguise his own homosexuality, and, in his episode of *Deutschland im Herbst* (1978, *Germany in Autumn*), he offered a scarifying picture of his own home life with a lover who later killed himself. In *Fox* he plays a rough, homosexual fairground-worker who wins a lottery, is taken up by supposedly grand homosexuals and then eventually cast aside by his elegant businessman-lover once his money has run out. The picture the film presents of a

Top left: in The Bitter Tears of Petra von Kant *self-pitying heroine (Margit Carstensen) is deserted by her lesbian lover and in isolation sinks into a serious breakdown. Top: Fassbinder himself stars as Fox, the naive homosexual doomed to lose his lover after being exploited and humiliated. Above: 'I don't throw bombs, I make films,' claims Fassbinder on the poster for* The Third Generation (1979), *a six-part comparison of the origins and forerunners of the new strain of German terrorists*

certain stratum of German society is quite appalling, though Fassbinder stoutly denied that the story was necessarily homosexual in its context. However its significance is read, it was seen as a gay movie by millions who had never seen such a thing before, and finally made Fassbinder a name outside the limited art-house circuit.

Its success seems to have had a slightly disorienting effect on Fassbinder, or perhaps

merely confirmed him in a direction he was already going. *Mutter Küsters Fahrt zum Himmel* (1975, *Mother Kuster's Trip to Heaven*) resumed the theme of *Fox* – the betrayal of the proletariat by the bourgeoisie – in another form, with the ruthless exploitation of a working-class heroine by perfidious middle-class politicos. But *Chinesisches Roulette* (1976, *Chinese Roulette*), *Satansbraten* (1976, *Satan's Brew*) and particularly *Despair* (1978), pursued an extravagant aestheticism to the exclusion of much else: *Chinese Roulette*, a melodramatic family tragedy exploring emotional sterility among the promiscuous rich, is at least foolish but fun. But *Despair*, though enlivened by a fine study in suppressed hysteria by Dirk Bogarde as a chocolate manufacturer slowly going mad, suffers from Fassbinder's relative insecurity directing in English. Neither is this helped by an excess of gloss applied to a film already overloaded with a subject from a Nabokov novel and an elaborately over-literate script by Tom Stoppard.

In einem Jahr mit 13 Monden (1978, *In the Year of Thirteen Moons*) managed the remarkable feat of making its weird subject – the last agonized days of a transsexual who cannot co-exist with either his/her male lover or ex-wife and teenage daughter – quite stodgy and dull.

Die Ehe der Maria Braun (1979, *The Marriage of Maria Braun*) whipped through thirty years of German history wrapped round the vaguely symbolic figure of a separated wife who uses sex to become a business tycoon, all for love of her absent husband. In *Lili Marleen* (1981) Hanna Schygulla sings the song about eighteen times for an ambiguous trip down memory lane in the good old bad old days. *Lola* (1981) combines elements from both films in the person of a cabaret singer who highlights provincial corruption in vamping a civic official and ends up owning the town brothel. *Die Sehnsucht der Veronika Voss* (1982, *Veronika Voss*) concerns a faded film star addicted to drugs and death. After these studies of women, Fassbinder returned to homosexual themes in his far from erotic *Querelle* (1982), adapted from a novel by Jean Genet, with a sailor (played by Brad Davis) as the vamp. He died in 1982 – aged only 36 – from a mixture of drink and drugs.

Top left: in Lili Marleen *Hanna Schygulla plays the singer. Top: bizarre adventures of a sham writer (Kurt Raab) in* Satan's Brew. *Above: in* The Marriage of Maria Braun *a wife (Hanna Schygulla) uses her beauty and brains to provide luxury for her husband's release after serving a sentence for a murder she had committed*

Filmography (including TV films)

1965 Der Stadtstreicher (short) (+sc; +act). **'66** Das kleine Chaos (short) (+sc; +act). **'67** Tony Freunde (actor only). **'68** Der Bräutigam, die Komödiantin und der Zuhalter (actor only) (USA/GB: The Bridegroom, the Comedienne and the Pimp). **'69** Fernes Jamaica (short) (actor only); Liebe ist kälter als der Tod (+sc; +ed; +co-des; +act) (GB: Love Is Colder Than Death); Alarm (actor only); Katzelmacher (+sc; +ed; +des; +act); Al Capone im deutschen Wald (actor only). **'70** Baal (actor only); Götter der Pest (+sc; +ed; +act) (USA/GB: Gods of the Plague); Das Kaffeehaus (video) (+sc); Warum läuft der Herr R. amok? (co-dir; +co-sc; +co-ed) (USA/GB: Why Does Herr R. Run Amok?); Frei bis zum nächsten Mal (actor only); Die Niklashauser Fahrt (co-dir; +co-sc; +co-ed; +act); Der amerikanische Soldat (+sc; +co-des; +lyr; +act) (USA/GB: The American Soldier). **'71** Rio das Mortes (+co-sc); Pioniere in Ingoldstadt (+sc); Mathias Kneissl (actor only); Whity (+co-sc; +co-ed; +act); Der plötzliche Reichtum der armen Leute von Kombach (actor only) (GB: The Sudden Fortune of the Poor People of Kombach); Warnung vor einer heiligen Nutte (+sc; +co-ed; +act) (GER-IT) (USA/GB: Beware of a Holy Whore). **'72** Der Händler der vier Jahreszeiten (+sc; +act) (USA/GB: The Merchant of Four Seasons); Die bitteren Tränen der Petra von Kant (+sc from his own play; +des) (USA/GB: The Bitter Tears of Petra von Kant); Acht Stunden sind kein Tag (5 parts) (+sc); Wildwechsel (+sc) (USA: Jail Bait; GB: Wild Game); Bremer Freiheit (video) (co-dir; +sc; +act). **'73** Super-Girl (actor only); Zärtlichkeit der Wölfe (prod; +act. only) (GB: Tenderness of the Wolves); Welt am Draht (2 parts) (+co-sc). **'74** Nora Helmer (video) (+sc); Angst essen Seele auf (+sc; +des; +act) (USA: Ali: Fear Eats the Soul; GB: Fear Eats the Soul); Martha (+sc); Fontane Effi Briest (+sc; +narrator) (USA/GB: Effi Briest); 1 Berlin-Harlem (actor only). **'75** Wie ein Vogel auf dem Draht (video) (+co-sc); Faustrecht der Freiheit (+co-sc; +act) (USA/GB: Fox/Fox and His Friends); Mutter Küsters Fahrt zum Himmel (+co-sc) (USA: Mother Kusters Goes to Heaven; GB: Mother Kuster's Trip to Heaven); Angst vor der Angst (+co-sc). **'76** Schatten der Engel (co-sc from his own play; +act. only) (SWIT-GER); Ich will doch nur, dass ihr mich liebt (+sc); Satansbraten (+sc) (USA/GB: Satan's Brew); Chinesisches Roulette (+sc) (GER-FR) (USA/GB: Chinese Roulette). **'77** Bolwieser (2 parts) (+sc); Frauen in New York. **'78** Deutschland im Herbst (ep only) (+sc; +act) (USA/GB: Germany in Autumn); Despair/Eine Reise in Lichts (GER-FR); In einem Jahr mit 13 Monden (+sc; +photo; +ed) (USA: In a Year of 13 Moons; GB: In the Year of Thirteen Moons). **'79** Bourbon Street Blues (short) (actor only); Die Ehe der Maria Braun (+co-sc; +act) (USA/GB: The Marriage of Maria Braun); Die dritte Generation (+sc; +photo) (USA/GB: The Third Generation). **'80** Berlin Alexanderplatz (13 parts) (+sc) (GER-IT). **'81** Lili Marleen (+co-sc; +act); Lola (+co-sc). **'82** Die Sehnsucht der Veronika Voss (+co-sc; +act) (GB: Veronika Voss); Querelle (+co-sc) (GER-FR); Theater in Trance (doc) (+comm); Der Bauer von Babylon (doc) (appearance as himself only) (GB: The Wizard of Babylon)

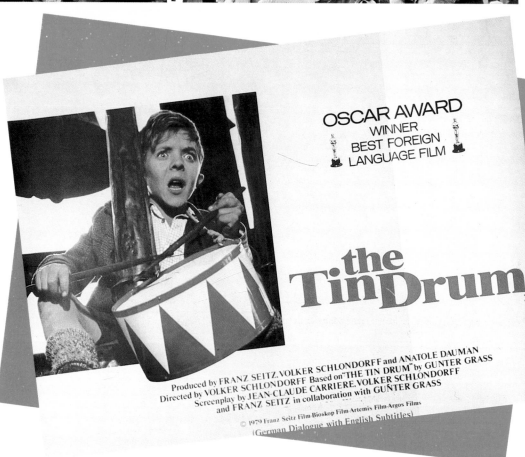

OSCAR AWARD
WINNER
BEST FOREIGN
LANGUAGE FILM

the TinDrum

X

Produced by FRANZ SEITZ, VOLKER SCHLONDORFF and ANATOLE DAUMAN
Directed by VOLKER SCHLONDORFF Based on "THE TIN DRUM" by GUNTER GRASS
Screenplay by JEAN-CLAUDE CARRIERE, VOLKER SCHLONDORFF
and FRANZ SEITZ in collaboration with GUNTER GRASS
© 1979 Franz Seitz Film-Bioskop Film-Artemis Film-Argos Films
(German Dialogue with English Subtitles)

The Tin Drum is probably the best-known novel in post-war German literature and the one that elevated its author, Günter Grass, to international fame. But Grass's reputation was established in the Sixties when there was hardly any German cinema to speak of. As the 'New German Cinema' began to emerge in the Seventies, Grass received numerous offers to adapt *The Tin Drum* for the screen; however, it was not until he was approached by the director Volker Schlöndorff and the producer Anatole Dauman that he felt satisfied enough to accept.

Volker Schlöndorff had been involved from the start with the movement towards a new German cinema, and among his early films *Der Junge Törless* (1966, *Young Törless*) testified to his understanding of the pre-Nazi period of German history. Furthermore, his historical drama *Der plötzliche Reichtum der armen Leute von Kombach* (1971, *The Sudden Fortune of the Poor People of Kombach*) showed the kind of insight into a peasant community that was to stand him in good stead for *The Tin Drum*.

Grass himself collaborated on the adaptation of his novel for the screen, but many new ideas emanated from Jean-Claude Carrière, a regular screenwriter for the director Luis Buñuel, who brought his own surrealistic perspective to the story. The central theme of both novel and film is the decision of the boy Oskar not to grow up – his refusal to accept 'adult' society in all its bizarre behaviour. And Schlöndorff frequently offers the audience Oskar's viewpoint (for instance much of the film is shot from knee-level), thus translating the world of 'grown-ups' into a bizarre pantomime of sexual and political exploitation that sometimes reaches grotesque proportions. He succeeds in creating an image of the world which is peopled with grotesque marionettes with overblown ambitions and inflated desires. In the same way, the touring circus act which Oskar joins during World War II offers a commentary on wartime events that is all the more telling for being 'distorted' or parodied by dwarfs.

In this context, the style of the film emerges as more mythological

than the easy blend of nostalgia and naturalism normally associated with films about this period. When Oskar disrupts a Nazi rally by beating his drum, the scene also functions on the level of fantasy. Similarly the compelling opening sequence in which the fugitive soldier hides beneath the woman's skirts conveys both the 'legend' of Oskar's parentage and the earthy realism appropriate to the location and period. Yet although *The Tin Drum* may look as if it is structured solely around a number of striking and potent images – most memorably the horse's head that is pulled out of the sea crawling with live eels – it is nonetheless an impressively coherent narrative, especially considering the daunting task of adapting a book of just under six hundred pages.

As for the performances, there can be no doubt that David Bennent's portrayal of Oskar is unique. Schlöndorff knew that the part could not be played by a dwarf if audiences were to achieve the vital sense of empathy and hostility towards the character. Moreover Grass was insistent that Oskar should not be seen as a dwarf but simply as a child who had ceased to grow. A child actor was the only solution and when Schlöndorff discovered that the actor Heinz Bennent, (with whom he had worked before) had a son of 12 whose facial features were years in advance of the rest of his body, the casting problem was solved. Ironically the arrested development that David Bennent genuinely suffers from rendered it impossible for him to play Oskar as a mature adult in

post-war Germany and Schlöndorff had to abandon his original plan of following the novel right through to its conclusion.

Apparently very satisfied with the film's successful transition from book to screen, Günter Grass has gone on to enjoy a revival in popularity, assisted by the fact that the film won the Best Foreign Film Oscar for 1979. The re-creation of Grass's native city of Danzig (now Gdansk) is a fine testament to Igor Luther's photography (making effective use of strong autumnal light in his exteriors) and to the art direction of Bernd Lepel. Visually the film is breathtaking and the occasional appearance of present-day features in the landscapes only serves to underline the contemporary relevance of the film's message.

Directed by Volker Schlöndorff, 1979.
Prod co: Franz Seitz Film/Bioskop-Film/GGB 14 KG/Hallelujah-Film/Artemis Film/Argos Film/in association with Jadran Film and Film Polski. **exec prod:** Anatole Dauman. **prod:** Franz Seitz. **sc:** Jean-Claude Carrière, Franz Seitz, Volker Schlöndorff, from the novel by Günter Grass. **photo** (Eastman Colour): Igor Luther. **ed:** Suzanne Baron. **prod des:** Nicos Perakis. **art dir:** Bernd Lepel. **mus:** Maurice Jarre. **ass dir:** Branco Lustig. Alexander von Richthofen, Wolfgang Kroke, Andrzej Reiter, Richard Malbequi. **r/t:** 142 minutes. German title: *Die Blechtrommel.* Released in USA and GB as *The Tin Drum.*
Cast: David Bennent (*Oskar*), Mario Adorf (*Alfred Matzerath*), Angela Winkler (*Agnes Matzerath*), Daniel Olbrychski (*Jan Bronski*), Katharina Thalbach (*Maria Matzerath*), Heinz Bennent (*Greff*), Andréa Ferreol (*Lina Greff*), Fritz Hakl (*Bebra*), Mariella Oliveri (*Roswitha Raguna*), Tina Engel (*Anna Koljaiczek as a young woman*), Berta Drews (*Anna Koljaiczek as an old woman*), Roland Teubner (*Joseph Koljaiczek*), Tadeusz Kunikowski (*Uncle Vinzenz*), Ernst Jacobi (*Gauleiter Lobsack*), Werner Rehm (*Scheffler, the baker*), Ilse Pagé (*Gretchen Scheffler*), Kate Jaenicke (*Mather Truczinski*), Helmuth Brasch (*Heilandt*), Wigand Witting (*Herbert Yruczinski*).

At the turn of the century in Poland, a peasant shelters a fugitive beneath her skirts and later gives birth to Agnes. After World War I, Agnes marries a Danzig grocer, Alfred Matzerath, but maintains her affair with her cousin Jan who may be the father of her son, Oskar.

At the age of three, Oskar resolves to stop growing. He becomes very attached to his toy drum (1), letting out a high-pitched scream capable of shattering glass if anyone tries to remove it.

In the city of Danzig, political upheaval is followed by the rise of the Fascist brownshirts (2). At a family outing (3) Alfred buys some eels that have been caught using a dead horse's head for bait, and later forces Agnes to eat them.

Agnes, pregnant by Alfred or Jan, loses the will to live and dies shortly afterwards. Oskar crawls for comfort beneath his grandmother's skirts (4). Alfred takes a young girl, Maria, to be his housekeeper and mistress, and then marries her (5).

Oskar leads Jan into the Polish post office which is under fire from the Germans (6). Jan is captured and executed. Through his friendship with a midget somnambulist, Roswitha (7), Oskar joins a circus which tours Europe performing for the Nazi top brass.

After the liberation, Oskar returns to Danzig where Alfred is shot as a collaborator. He resolves (8) to start growing again.

395

1

5

6

8

AGUIRRE, WRATH OF GOD

Aguirre, Wrath of God is Werner Herzog's archetypal tale of a voyage down a jungle river, the final destination of which is ultimate solitude, madness, and death. The film, which was the first to bring Herzog wide international acclaim, although his earlier features had not gone unremarked by some members of the critical community, was also an odyssey for its creators. The making of the film was an adventure at least as exciting as that shown on the screen.

The idea for the film was born when Herzog read, by chance, a dozen lines about Lope de Aguirre in a children's book. After reading what few historical documents still exist, Herzog wrote his scenario in only three days, inventing most of the narrative incidents and characters, although in some cases he used historical figures but gave them ficticious roles:

'Gonzalo Pizarro, the brother of the famous conquistador Francisco Pizarro, died six to eight years before my expedition in 1560. The monk Gaspar de Carvajal existed too, but his name is connected with

another very obscure expedition which had nothing to do with that of Aguirre . . . the rest of the script is pure invention . . . the language isn't realistic, it's more a hallucinatory language, unreal. It's like the ever-slowing movement in the film which becomes immobility.'

Filmed in Peru because Herzog wanted the authentic atmosphere of the jungle, the Amazon, and the presence of the Indians, *Aguirre, Wrath of God* took seven weeks to shoot – after nine months of pre-production organization. It was shot in more-or-less chronological order, partly because Herzog found the film crews' progress down the river directly related to the movement of the voyage in the film, and partly because as the numbers of crew and cast were reduced for the latter part of the film, so it became easier to move them deeper into the jungle.

The relatively low budget did not allow for much in the way of special effects and trickery, the use of which, in any case, Herzog would never have allowed:

'We took a lot of precautions, but

for me the making of a film must be physical. I put my entire body into the making of my films.'

So, the entire cast and crew found itself climbing up the face of a mountain, cutting through jungles and riding dangerous Amazonian rapids on native-built rafts. Even the accidents were written into the script: one night a storm raised the level of water and the violence of the river destroyed a number of rafts. That became part of the story.

Nor were the hazards of river and jungle the only things to be reckoned with. A good part of the exposed footage disappeared half way through the shooting in transit for European laboratories; there was no way it could have been re-filmed, even if there had been the money to do so. Herzog continued filming and the lost cans were later found at Mexico City airport.

The film was shot in English mainly because it was the only common language among the participants – who came from 16 different countries – but Herzog also knew that an English-language version was necessary for the international market. However, the little money that was allocated for post-synchronization left Peru with the man in charge of the process; both

absconded *en route*. This resulted in there being two versions, one in English and the other with a better-quality German soundtrack.

Then there was the 'Kinski affair'. Klaus Kinski, an actor of undoubted ability and owner of a bizarre and fascinating face, is well known for not being the easiest actor in the world to direct and control. Although he is perfect as Aguirre, sliding progressively into madness, he and the director began to have daily scenes of screamed

---

Directed by Werner Herzog, 1973
Prod co: Werner Herzog Filmproduktion with Hessischer Rundfunk. **prod:** Werner Herzog. **assoc prod:** Daniel Carino. **sc:** Werner Herzog. **photo (colour):** Thomas Mauch, Francisco Joan, Orlando Macchiavello. **sp eff:** Juvenal Herrera, Miguel Vazquez. **ed:** Beate Mainka-Jellinghaus. **mus:** Popol Vuh. **sd:** Herbert Prasch. **prod man:** Walter Saxer, Wolf Stipetić. **r/t:** 95 minutes. German title: *Aguirre, der Zorn Gottes*. Released in USA/GB as: *Aguirre, Wrath of God*.

Cast: Klaus Kinski (*Don Lope de Aguirre*), Cecilia Rivera (*Florès de Aguirre*), Ruy Guerra (*Don Pedro de Ursua*), Helena Rojo (*Inez de Atienza*), Del Negro (*Brother Gaspar de Carvajal*), Peter Berling (*Don Fernando de Guzman*), Daniel Ades (*Perucho*), Armando Polanah (*Armando*), Edward Roland (*Okello*), Daniel Farfan, Alejandro Chavez, Antonio Marquez, Julio Martinez, Alejandro Repullés, and the Indians of the Lauramarca Co-operative.

396

insults, ending finally in the two threatening to kill one another on the spot. Several years later, when Klaus Kinski signed to do two more films with Werner Herzog, he was reminded of the earlier film's problems:

'Yes, it is all true. We seriously would have killed each other. Still, that's a good film, and in this business, you know, one day you can scream ''Fuck you! I'm going to kill you!'' and mean it, and the next day hug and work well together.'

Still, whatever the problems in its making, from the first image of the almost mystic descent out of the cloud-misted heights to the final circling of the madman left alone on a raft with his 'kingdom' reduced to hundreds of monkeys, *Aguirre, Wrath of God* is one of the director's best films and all he intended it to be: an adventure film having the surface characteristics of the genre, but with something new inside, while at the same time being meant for a large public:

'It has the surface of an adventure film, but it is a very personal film. For me it is alive.'

I am the Wrath of God

In 1560 a thousand or more Spanish conquerors (including two women and a number of captured Indians) descend from the Andes into the virgin jungle (1) to look for El Dorado, the fabled land of gold. A fever decimates the army and their porters, and the commander Gonzalo Pizarro orders 40 men to explore the river by raft (2). If they fail to return after a week, they will be considered lost.

Don Lope de Aguirre is part of the group led by Don Pedro de Ursua. Early on in the expedition one of the four rafts is trapped in a whirlpool (3) and during the night the men on board are killed by Indians.

Aguirre organizes a revolt against Ursua (4) who is wounded by a gun-shot and nursed by his mistress Inez. Not yet sure of the loyalty of the soldiers, Aguirre proposes Don Fernando de Guzman as ruler of the New World, farcically dethroning Phillip II of Spain. However, Guzman refuses to allow Ursua to be executed.

The troupe begins to suffer from hunger, fever and hallucinations (5) – at one point they 'see' a full-masted ship hanging in the trees – and the jungle is ever more hostile, with daily Indian ambushes (6). They manage to capture one of the Indians, but when he rejects the Bible he is killed. Guzman is finally found dead and the way is clear for Aguirre's plan to found a new dynasty built on the offspring of his sexual union with his own daughter (7).

As the raft continues to drift (8), Ursua is taken into the jungle and hanged; Inez, who alone speaks out against Aguirre's plans, walks into the forest and disappears during an attack on an Indian village (9); and a grumbling soldier is decapitated. Aguirre rules supreme, but his subject soldiers soon perish. His daughter Florès, struck by an arrow, dies in his arms.

At one point Aguirre says 'I am the wrath of God', but the 'wrath of God' alone cannot prevent a horde of monkeys invading the raft as it slowly drifts – directionless – in the river's currents (10).

THEIR BRILLIANT CAREERS

'New Wave' Australian Film-makers

Considering the long period between 1940 and 1970 when locally produced feature films were so few and far between, the rebirth of home-grown cinema in Australia has been phenomenal. Helped by government funding, a number of talented young directors proved during the Seventies that there was a real possibility of making internationally successful, quality films . . . down under

In 1971 the Australian Government began to make available money to support a feature film industry, and a long cinematic drought was at last over. Perhaps it is not surprising that the initial films produced were almost all comedies . . . and broad 'ocker' comedies at that. Tim Burstall made *Stork* (1971), adapted from a play by David Williamson, whose ear for contemporary Australian vernacular had already earned him a secure place in the history of Australian theatre; now his racy dialogue and outrageous situations were able to keep cinema audiences laughing too. *Stork* is the story of a *ménage à quatre*, and its tall, gangling hero, Stork (Bruce Spence) is an endearing mixture of loud-mouthed extrovert and insecure virgin.

Burstall was the only one of the new directors of the Seventies who had, in fact, already made a feature film; as an energetic enthusiast he directed children's films and documentaries during the previous decade, and, in 1969, an extremely ambitious feature – *2000 Weeks*. This was a semi-autobiographical plea to people of talent to stay and work in Australia rather than flee to what at the time were seen

as the greater cultural attractions of Britain; the culture drain had reached epidemic proportions, and Burstall's film courageously dealt with the problem. Unfortunately, *2000 Weeks* was attacked by those very film critics who had all along been pressing for an indigenous movie industry. The attacks were certainly unjustified, for, though not a complete success, *2000 Weeks* was a breakthrough of considerable proportions.

Burstall rallied in the Seventies, and turned his back on the cultural credentials and aspirations of his past, preferring to make a series of commercial entertainments which proved popular at the box-office. He followed the success of *Stork* with the less ambitious *Alvin Purple* (1973), which merged 'ocker' comedy with soft-core sex inspired by Danish 'family porno' movies. The mixture proved a bonanza at the box-office, but the script (by Alan Hopgood) was weak and predictable. Two screenplays by David Williamson subsequently provided the basis of two of Burstall's best films – *Petersen* (1974) and *A Faithful Narrative of the Capture, Suffering and Miraculous Escape of Eliza Fraser* (1976). It was

Petersen, a comic drama set on a university campus, which made a star of Jack Thompson, perfectly cast as a labourer trying to improve his prospects with a belated education and becoming involved with the wife (Wendy Hughes) of his professor.

Less successful was *End Play* (1975), a somewhat predictable whodunnit scripted by Burstall himself, but he was back on form with *The Last of the Knucklemen* (1979), an excellent adaptation of a popular play by John Powers. Tim Burstall's style is punchy and sometimes unsubtle, and he has been accused of male chauvinism: after *Alvin Purple* he retaliated by sending up the women's movement in *Petersen*, which predictably attracted even more hostile criticism. He has an ambivalent love-hate attitude to his fellow film-makers, professing to scorn those who try to make 'personal' as opposed to avowedly commercial films, but he is generally respected as a battler who, after a serious early reverse, went on to prove he had his finger on the pulse of what the mass audience in Australia wanted to see.

Uniquely ocker
Meanwhile another 'ocker' hero – that stereotype uncouth, beer-drinking Australian male – had been created by Barry Humphries for the English anti-Establishment satirical magazine *Private Eye*. The immortal Barry McKenzie then emerged in two bawdy films by Bruce Beresford – *The Adventures of Barry McKenzie* (1972) and *Barry McKenzie Holds His Own* (1974) – both about the grotesque misadventures of a 'typical' Aussie in Pommyland. A film buff from his school-days, Beresford had made amateur films in Sydney before becoming film editor for the Nigerian Government's

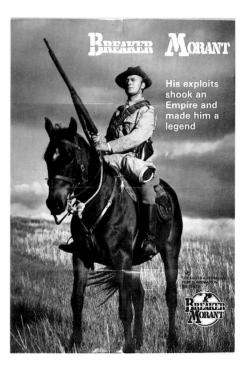

BREAKER MORANT

His exploits shook an Empire and made him a legend

Left: The Devil's Playground *explores the moralistic indoctrination of adolescent seminarians. Above: another side of repressed sexuality, in Bruce Beresford's butch, swaggering, broad comedy* Don's Party. *Above right: Beresford's* Breaker Morant; *historical subjects are still much favoured by 'New Wave' directors. Below right: the eerie* Picnic at Hanging Rock

directors set about remedying the omission. Michael Thornhill's *Between Wars* (1974) was a key early example: with a thoughtful screenplay by Frank Moorehouse, the film followed the career of an outspoken non-conformist (Corin Redgrave) from the end of World War I up to the outbreak of World War II.

The post-war theme would be taken up, with even more assurance, by Phillip Noyce in his remarkable debut film *Newsfront* (1978), which explores the career of another vociferous rebel – this time a newsreel cameraman (Bill Hunter) – between 1948 and 1956, as Australia became increasingly Americanized. *Newsfront*, with its witty script (by Bob Ellis) and skilful intercutting of vintage newsreel material, became one of the most popular films domestically, though its ingrained Australianism made it hard to export.

More and more nostalgia films came to be made, doubtless triggered by the enormous acclaim for Peter Weir's beautiful and haunting *Picnic at Hanging Rock* (1975), set on St Valentine's Day 1900, about some schoolgirls and a teacher who mysteriously and inexplicably disappear while exploring a monolithic rock in the Victorian countryside. This was one of the first quality films to win international recognition, and director of photography Russell Boyd won the 1977 British Film Academy Award for Best Photography for his visual contribution.

Peter Weir, who was to become one of the most impressive of the new film-makers in Australia, started his professional career in a humble capacity at a Sydney television station, and made his first films to entertain the station's staff at their annual Christmas party. His quirky sense of humour was much in evidence in his first feature – *The Cars That Ate Paris* (1974) – about the inhabitants of a small town who scavenge the cars they have deliberately caused to crash, but in his later films he tended to play down the humour in favour of a disturbing feeling that nature was somehow conspiring against mankind.

production unit and, in 1966, head of film production for the British Film Institute. He made the Barry McKenzie films largely because of his friendship with Barry Humphries, and the first of these was extremely successful. As a result, Beresford was able to direct the screen version of one of David Williamson's most popular plays, *Don's Party* (1976). Since then he has deliberately tried different genres, though *The Getting of Wisdom* (1977), set in a girls' boarding-school in 1900, was a long-cherished project. Certainly, it stands in complete contrast to his subsequent thriller *Money Movers* (1978). In 1980 Beresford produced two very successful films: the award-winning *Breaker Morant* and an amusing version of yet another Williamson play, *The Club*. Based on an incident during the Boer War, *Breaker Morant* – though very ambivalent towards its three 'heroes', accused by the British of atrocities against Boers – was widely praised for its acting and the tension of its court-room scenes.

Modest to a fault, Bruce Beresford is a quiet worker who deliberately tries to extend himself with each new film. He prefers a regular team of collaborators (Don McAlpine as director of photography, Bill Anderson as editor) and is highly respected as an economical, conscientious film-maker with an astringent sense of humour. Actors find working with Beresford particularly rewarding, and several have given their best performances in his films.

Back to the outback

For a time it seemed as though film-makers wanted to avoid contemporary subjects altogether, and more and more films were set in the past. Australian audiences had been denied seeing their history on film until now, and

Weir and Boyd collaborated again on *The Last Wave* (1977) in which water became a sinister force, firstly in the torrential rain that deluged the city of Sydney almost continuously through the film, and secondly in the vision of a giant tidal wave conjured up in the mind of the protagonist (Richard Chamberlain). Although *The Last Wave* was also a success in the United States, especially in California, Weir was only able to make a television feature – *The Plumber* (1979) – during the next three years. However, in 1981 he was able to realize his long-cherished ambition to make a film about the young Australians who took part in the Dardanelles campaign during World War I – a film called, simply, *Gallipoli*.

Weir is a master at creating cinematic tension, of making the ordinary seem extraordinary; he has deservedly become the most individualistic of the new Australian directors.

Digging up history

There have been two other splendid re-creations of turn-of-the-century Australia, for both of which Don McAlpine's photography has been widely praised: Beresford's *The Getting of Wisdom* and Gillian Armstrong's *My Brilliant Career* (1979). Both were adapted from autobiographical books by young women who had been forced to assume male pseudonyms so as to be able to have their work published in the first place. *My Brilliant Career* – the first theatrical feature made by a woman since the Thirties – was an enormous success all over the world with its sensitively told story of a feisty young woman who chooses a career in preference to a safe marriage; leading players Judy Davis and Sam Neill deserve particular mention.

Other period films traced Australian history in other areas. Ken Hannam's very underrated *Break of Day* (1976) was about life in a small town decimated by the loss of its menfolk as a result of World War I; it was set at the time of the first Anzac Day in 1920. Hannam, whose background was radio before he worked for the BBC directing television series, had started his feature film career with *Sunday Too Far Away* (1975), about the lives of sheep-shearers, and one of the best films of the Seventies. While those two were admirable, Hannam had less success with subsequent films – *Summerfield* (1977), a thriller, and *Dawn!* (1979), a biography of swimming champion Dawn Fraser.

Donald Crombie, who scored an immediate success with his first feature *Caddie* (1976), had worked at Film Australia on a series of accomplished documentaries. *Caddie*, with its luminous performance from Helen Morse, dealt with a family crisis, this time set in the Depression and written by a former barmaid who, as a single parent, had to struggle to bring up two children during that period. Some critics compared Crombie's sensitive direction with that of John Ford, a comparison further underlined in his second feature – *The Irishman* (1978) – about the impact of industrial changes on a small town (again set in the Twenties) and the resulting break-up of a family. A third feature, *Cathy's Child* (1979), about a Maltese woman's attempts to reclaim the baby kidnapped by her own husband, further underlined Crombie's concern with family situations, and confirmed his talent as a sensitive director of actresses.

Another director concerned mainly with social themes is Fred Schepisi, who entered the industry through newsreels, documentaries and commercials. His magnificent first film, *The Devil's Playground* (1976), is strongly autobiographical in its study of the repressive life of boys in a Catholic seminary in the Fifties. Schepisi also made one of the most important historical Australian films with *The Chant of Jimmie Blacksmith* (1978), an angry indictment of the mistreatment of the Aboriginal people. Though it was praised by all the critics, it apparently proved too threatening, for audiences stayed away wherever it was shown.

Out of the bush

Other film-makers emerged from different backgrounds and unexpected sources: Jim Sharman is a theatre director whose innovative stage productions of *Hair* and *Jesus Christ Superstar*, as well as *The Rocky Horror Show*, gained him an international reputation. In Australia he is also known for his excellent theatre productions of plays by Patrick White, and indeed his most satisfying film to date has been from a White script – *The Night The Prowler* (1978) – about an apparent rape in a bland environment and the degenerates lurking in self-satisfied suburbia. Sharman's most famous film, however, is *The Rocky Horror Picture Show*, which he made in 1975.

Contemporary themes have been dealt with in other interesting features: Michael Thornhill's *The FJ Holden* (1977) about the alienation of young people in Sydney's outer suburbs; John Duigan's treatment of a similar disenchantment in Melbourne, *Mouth to Mouth* (1978); Esben Storm's accomplished romantic drama *In Search of Anna* (1978) about a young man just out of prison; Steven Wallace's powerful *Stir!* (1980), based on the events leading up to a prison riot. And George Miller, who was a medical doctor before turning to film-making, made a violent thriller – *Mad Max* (1979) – which turned out to be very popular.

Above: in Newsfront *a cameraman (Bill Hunter) finds his assistant (Chris Haywood) drowned. Below: Richard Chamberlain in* The Last Wave. *Below Right:* The Picture Show Man *travels to outback towns with Freddy (John Ewart) and Larry (Harold Hopkins)*

It is encouraging to be able to say that, in general, films that have tried to be 'international' by importing foreign talent and adapting local themes to please some nebulous transatlantic audience have failed on every level. Overall, the most interesting aspect of the Australian revival of the Seventies is that so many films of quality were actually made. Considering the fact that there had been virtually no possibility of working in feature

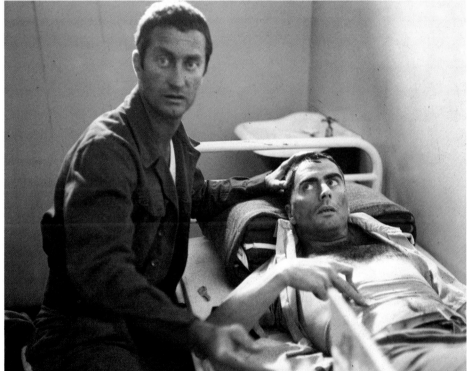

Top right: Sam Neill and Judy Davis in My Brilliant Career. *Right:* Stir! *– part of the trend towards social concern. Bottom right:* The Chant of Jimmie Blacksmith *– Gilda (Angela Punch) is married to an Aboriginal (Tommy Lewis) striving to join white society*

films for so many years, the standard of the work produced when the money *did* become available seems astonishingly high. Whether that quality can be sustained through the Eighties is very much a moot point, as tax incentive schemes – which look fine on paper – threaten to change the kind of film Australians can make. But, whatever the future, the Seventies proved to be an exhilarating decade for cinema down under.

1

2

3

The Aborigine
and the girl
30,000 years apart
...together

WALKABOUT
Just about the most different film you'll ever see

Filmed in its entirety in the Australian wilderness

20th Century Fox presents A MAX L. RAAB SI LITVINOFF PRODUCTION WALKABOUT starring JENNY AGUTTER · LUCIEN JOHN
DAVID GUMPILIL executive producer MAX L. RAAB produced by SI LITVINOFF directed and photographed by NICOLAS ROEG
screenplay by EDWARD BOND based on the novel by JAMES VANCE MARSHALL music by JOHN BARRY COLOR BY DE LUXE

Walkabout was to have been the first film directed by Nicolas Roeg, who had established himself by the mid-Sixties as one of Britain's leading cameramen for his work on such films as *The Caretaker* (1963), *Nothing But the Best, The Masque of the Red Death* (both 1964), *Fahrenheit 451* (1966) and *Far From the Madding Crowd* (1967). Roeg became fascinated by James Vance Marshall's novel, visited Australia to research settings and locations, and persuaded playwright Edward Bond to construct a screenplay. But the project then had to be shelved for lack of production support, and Roeg instead teamed up with Donald Cammell to make his joint directing debut with *Performance* (1970).

At first glance the two subjects could hardly look more different. *Performance*'s fetishistic study of a small-time London crook's metamorphosis in the claustrophobic home of a retired pop-star has little obvious connection with a trek through the Australian desert. But *Performance* too is about the fortuitous collision of opposites, their possible interaction and exchange, their final severance; and as it happens, the summary applies equally (with small variations) to Roeg's following films – *Don't Look Now* (1973), *The Man Who Fell to Earth* (1976) and *Bad Timing* (1980). It's all there in *Walkabout*, where the collision is both human (the white girl, the black Aborigine) and cultural (the city versus the outback); the interaction is a matter of both geographical and biological necessity (the girl is helpless in the aborigine's environment, as he would be in hers); and the severance is an inevitable consequence of two highly contrasted origins.

Roeg establishes the contrasts from the film's opening shots in which the bustling city is invaded by glimpses of desert, until, with a track from brick wall to open ground, he permits the wilderness to take over completely. At the end of *Walkabout* the pattern is reversed, with the invasion of the landscape by half-formed buildings, discarded equipment (the little boy actually sets an abandoned trolley in motion once more), and at last the city crowds themselves. As a result of Roeg's intercutting, city and desert appear symbiotic, each growing from the other; if the city-dwellers look disconcertingly like flowing sand, the wasteland, with its exotic wildlife, is also seen to have a teeming social structure, in which experience is the vital part of survival. Nature and civilization may be opposites, but they have the same roots, the same needs, and Roeg's examination of those needs reveals with each fresh illustration the special, even lethal, price that they demand.

The 'walkabout', explained in an opening title as an Aboriginal custom, is accordingly an education shared by the children of both cultures. For each, it provides the training for survival in a hostile environment. The Aborigine must learn how to find water, to kill lizards, to cook kangaroo meat. The girl, whom we first encounter in a classroom, must learn elocution, etiquette, and *haute cuisine*; education pursues her and her brother as they carry the radio on their journey, and ineffectual as its contribution may seem when there is no water, the measured tones of technology continue to echo across the outback long after the way home has become clear again and their brief benefactor has been left hanging from a tree. 'I can multiply 84 by 84', the six-year-old announces proudly to the smiling savage for

8

9

4

5

whom such skills are irrelevant; at the time, it seems incongruous, but it is the boy who lives and the Aborigine who dies.

Walkabout ends with the girl in her kitchen (as her mother was at the film's beginning). A voice speaks A. E. Housman's lines about 'the land of lost content . . . where I went and cannot come again' and we see a possibly remembered, possibly imagined bathing sequence with the girl, her brother and the Aborigine. Much enhanced by John Barry's soaring orchestration, this scene is a richly sentimental idyll, artificial enough to be subtly unconvincing. The viewer is invited, to recognize through it that while simplicity has many obvious attractions, and that nature specializes in simplicities, they are awesomely transient. The 'walkabout' provided the justification for the partnership and at the same time its limit; despite the many

erotic half-promises between boy and girl (and much of *Walkabout's* fascination comes from the delicacy with which it conveys their awareness of each other), they have no conceivable future together – which is why, having witnessed the gratuitous slaughter of wildlife by two white gunmen in a jeep, the Aborigine rises like a

skeleton from a landscape littered with bones to pay despairing homage to the female who has no further use for him. His time is past, even though Roeg's dislocated editing serves as a reminder that fragments of time, like bits and pieces of our upbringing, remain deeply embedded in the memories of us all.

Directed by Nicolas Roeg, 1971
Prod co: Max L. Raab – Si Litvinoff Films (Pty) Ltd (20th Century-Fox). **exec prod:** Max L. Raab. **prod:** Si Litvinoff. **assoc prod:** Anthony J. Hope. **sc:** Edward Bond, from the Novel by James Vance Marshall. **photo** (Eastman Colour): Nicolas Roeg. **sp photo:** Tony Richmond. **ed:** Anthony Gibbs, Alan Patillo. **prod des:** Brian Eatwell. **art dir:** Terry Gough. **mus:** John Barry. **add mus/songs:** 'Electronic Dance' by Billy Mitchell, 'Gasoline Alley' by Rod Stewart, 'Los Angeles' by Warren Marley, 'Hymnen' by Karl-Heinz Stockhausen. **sd rec:** Barry Brown. **sd re-rec:** Gerry Humphreys. **r/t:** 100 minutes. **Cast:** Jenny Agutter (*girl*), Lucien John (*brother*), David Gulpilil (*Aborigine*), John Meillon (*father*), Peter Carver (*no-hoper*), John Illingsworth (*husband*), Barry Donnelly (*Australian scientist*), Noelene Brown (*German scientist*), Carlo Manchini (*Italian scientist*).

A teenage girl and her brother are taken for a drive in the Australian bush by their father. As she lays out the picnic, the father suddenly produces a pistol (1) and starts shooting; when the children take cover, he shoots himself. Reassuring her brother that it is nothing serious, the girl leads him away into the desert (2). By nightfall they are completely lost.

Next day they find an oasis – but soon the water is gone and their situation looks desperate (3). Unexpectedly an Aborigine youth appears out of the desert (4); he is on his 'walkabout' – the six-month period in the wilderness which, by tribal custom, will establish his manhood. He takes them under his protection and guides them through the vast wasteland (5).

At last they reach an abandoned homestead (6) which seems a natural place for them to stay. But the Aborigine then takes the boy (7) and shows him a nearby highway that could lead the way back to civilization. Disturbed that he and the girl may shortly have to part company, the Aborigine paints himself and begins a dance of courtship (8); the girl retreats from him in terror (9), fearing violence of some kind. He continues the ritual for hours, past the point of exhaustion, and in the morning they find him dead (10). Seemingly unconcerned, they take the road back to safety, only to be greeted with hostility at the first town they reach (11).

Years later, the girl receives her husband home from the office. As he chatters of minor triumphs in his business affairs, she recalls a time when three children swam together in the sunlit waters of a far-distant lake.

7

0

11

Uphill racer
Robert Redford

Robert Redford, tall, blond and handsome, is the classic all-American screen hero and one of Hollywood's highest-paid stars. But at the peak of his acting profession, he seems to be forging a new and successful career for himself, this time in the field of direction

With his blond hair, blue eyes and clean-cut all-American appearance, Robert Redford seems to be perfectly cast as a star in the grand Hollywood tradition of the male romantic lead. Redford's emotional entanglements have usually been subsidiary to the main plot of his films: with the exceptions of Barbra Streisand, Jane Fonda and Meryl Streep, he has rarely played opposite actresses of equal calibre. Indeed, some would argue that his only screen affair has been with Paul Newman.

The films that work best are those in which there is a quiet questioning of the stereotyped American male, and which thereby gently subvert Redford's own pretty-boy image. He has attacked the notion of the attractive athletic winner – *Downhill Racer* (1969), *Little Fauss and Big Halsy* (1970). *The Electric Horseman* (1979) – commented on the heroic legends of the Hollywood West – *Butch Cassidy and the Sundance Kid, Tell Them Willie Boy Is Here* (both 1969), *Jeremiah Johnson* (1972) – and played the naive American caught up in somebody else's politics – *The Candidate* (1972), *The Way We Were* (1973), *Three Days of the Condor* (1975), *All the President's Men* (1976).

The cream on its way to the top
Redford's early life was not that of the well-to-do middle-class American that his appearance would seem to suggest. Born in 1937, the son of a milkman, Redford grew up in Santa Monica, California, in the shadow of the 'dream factory' itself. But he despised the movies, often shouting at the screen on visits to the cinema with his friends. Despite rebelling against the discipline of school, he won a baseball scholarship to the University of Colorado, but soon dropped out, believing there was more to life than sport. After hitch-hiking around various European capitals, painting, and 'loitering' in bars and cafés, he returned to America to study art at New York's Pratt Institute, and eventually found himself at the American Academy of Dramatic Arts. He had several minor roles on Broadway before the breakthrough came – the lead part in Neil Simon's domestic farce *Barefoot in the Park*. The play, directed by Mike Nichols, had rave reviews and Redford earned recognition for his comic ability. With a growing reputation on television, it was not surprising that he was soon much sought after by Hollywood.

Skimming the heights
However, his first film, *War Hunt* (1962), was a second-rate, low-budget venture about a psychotic private in Korea. It was not a great success for either its producers or Redford, but during the filming he met and struck up a long working relationship with the then actor Sydney Pollack – who later directed several of Redford's films. Redford's career continued with *Inside Daisy Clover* (1965), the film version of Gavin Lambert's novel about the machinations of Hollywood. He then went on to make a total flop, *Situation Hopeless, But Not Serious* (1965); turned in a highly praised performance as Bubber Reeves, the escaped convict whose presence brings out the mercenary tendencies of his home-town folk in *The Chase* (1966); starred with Natalie Wood in a Tennessee Williams' small-town melodrama, *This Property Is Condemned* (1966); and was sued by Paramount for walking out on the Western *Blue* (1968) (a wise decision on his part since the completed film, starring Terence Stamp, was not a success).

In 1967 he returned to Hollywood to fulfil an obligation to film *Barefoot in the Park*. Echoing his stage success, Redford's role as Paul Bratter, the straitlaced lawyer whose new wife (Jane Fonda) complains about his lack of spontaneity – he cannot even walk barefoot in the park – swept him to fame. Although Redford disliked Bratter's image he found a niche for himself as the fall-guy to his more active partner and he and Fonda made an

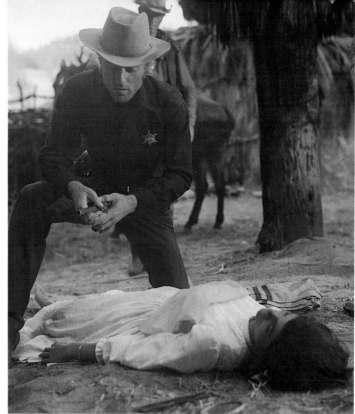

Opposite page: Redford with Gene Hackman, skiing champion and coach in Downhill Racer *(left), and with Natalie Wood and the director Sydney Pollack filming* This Property is Condemned *(right). Left: Michael J. Pollard and Redford as* Little Fauss and Big Halsy

Above left: Redford as Paul Bratter who drunkenly loses his inhibitions in Barefoot in the Park. *Above: Sheriff Cooper finds his quarry's fiancée (Katharine Ross) dead in* Tell Them Willie Boy Is Here. *Below: Jeremiah Johnson with Bear Claw (Will Geer)*

effervescent duo.

Redford was subsequently offered several major roles which he turned down – including the diffident Benjamin in *The Graduate* (1967). It was well worth the wait for 1969 was Redford's year – he had a critical success with *Tell Them Willie Boy Is Here*, made his long-cherished project *Downhill Racer*, and after Marlon Brando, Steve McQueen and Warren Beatty had all dropped out of the running he was offered what will probably remain his most memorable role, that of the Sundance Kid in *Butch Cassidy and the Sundance Kid*. The attractive vitality of the relationship between the two heroes, and their tongue-in-cheek humour, made the film a smash hit. Redford may not say much in the film, but his laconic, fast-shooting Sundance Kid complemented Newman's thoughtful Butch. The male cama-raderie and slick repartee encouraged the quick growth of buddy-buddy movies and four years later Newman and Redford were reunited on

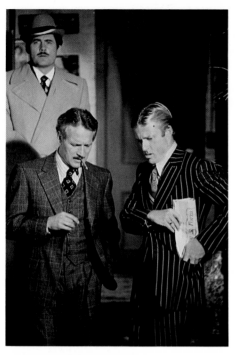

Far left: the partners in crime (Paul Newman and Robert Redford) act out their charade in front of the victim (Robert Shaw) in The Sting. Left: Robert Redford takes his place in court as assistant district attorney in Legal Eagles (1986). Below left: as Bob Woodward in All the President's Men

the screen in *The Sting* (1973). Once again under the direction of George Roy Hill, it is a witty story concerning a successful confidence trick on a racketeer. It was another hit.

How the West was

Butch Cassidy and the Sundance Kid made Redford a valuable property and enabled him to pick and choose his parts. Having deserted Hollywood for the mountains of Utah and a commitment to ecological preservation, many of his films comment on the values he left behind, with a recurrent theme being the false heroics of the Western. *Tell Them Willie Boy Is Here*, with Abraham Polonsky making a return to direction after years on the blacklist, tackles the treatment of the American Indians. Redford was originally offered the part of Willie Boy – the Paiute Indian who kills a chief while claiming his bride and finds himself hunted as a renegade – but, feeling that Indian roles should be played by Indians, he opted for the role of Sheriff Cope who learns to respect the Indian traditions. *Jeremiah Johnson*, a legendary story of a lone trapper who braves the elements to live his own life in the mountains, is another film that challenges Hollywood's heroic notions. Redford's Johnson is neither braver nor wiser than others: he is simply more determined to live free from interference. In a totally different setting, the wealthy Twenties as depicted by Scott Fitzgerald in *The Great Gatsby* (1974), Redford portrays another loner who rejects 'modern' society's materialism. However, the film failed because it was one of the few Redford films that indulged itself as a love story.

Redford has expressed his dislike of the born competitor who smiles as he clocks up the wins and the girls:

'What about the athlete who is a creep? We do tend to tolerate creeps if they win. They can behave any way so just forget that swell guy whom everyone loves and who came second.'

With 20,000 feet of unofficial footage from the Grenoble Winter Olympics, and after a two-year struggle, Redford was finally able to embody these views in *Downhill Racer* – a couple of seasons in the life of David Chappellet, a skier who is only admired so long as he keeps winning. That Redford's looks made it

Filmography
1962 War Hunt. **'65** Situation Hopeless, But Not Serious; Inside Daisy Clover. **'66** The Chase; This Property Is Condemned. **'67** Barefoot in the Park. **'69** Butch Cassidy and the Sundance Kid; Tell Them Willie Boy Is Here; Downhill Racer. **'70** The Making of Butch Cassidy and the Sundance Kid; Little Fauss and Big Halsy. **'72** The Hot Rock (GB: How to Steal a Diamond in Four Uneasy Lessons); Jeremiah Johnson; The Candidate (+ co-exec. prod). **'73** The Way We Were; The Sting. **'74** The Great Gatsby; Broken Treaty at Battle Mountain (doc) (narr. only). **'75** The Great Waldo Pepper; Three Days of the Condor. **'76** All the President's Men (+ co-exec. prod). **'77** A Bridge Too Far. **'79** The Electric Horseman. **'80** Brubaker; Ordinary People (dir. only). **'84** The Natural. **'85** Out of Africa. **'86** Legal Eagles. **'87** The Milagro Beanfield War (dir. only).

difficult to believe Chappellet is such a jerk emphasizes the very point the film is trying to make. *Little Fauss and Big Halsy* develops the same theme, this time on the motorcycle racetrack. The misguided admiration that Fauss (Michael J. Pollard) holds for his more confident fellow competitor Halsy (Redford) leads only to disillusionment. However, the most revealing image of the American athletic winner is in *The Electric Horseman*; the drunken, ex-rodeo champion rides out of town on the prize horse he has rescued from the breakfast-cereal company he publicizes. All that can be seen of him against the night is his illuminated outline – a visual indication of the hollowness of that kind of success.

A man for the people

Several of Redford's films have examined the manipulations and threats of modern politics: in *The Way We Were*, the McCarthy witch-hunt is the cause of the break-up of a young Hollywood couple's marriage when the wife Katie (Barbra Streisand) becomes involved in the campaign against the blacklist; *The Candidate* looks at competition in the electoral fight as a certain-to-loose well-intentioned contender (Redford) becomes seduced by the political arena; *Three Days of the Condor* is a spy thriller about a desk-worker for the CIA who, on returning to his office, finds all his colleagues shot dead, possibly by his own side; *Brubaker* (1980) investigates the clash of interests between a prison governor bent on reform and the corrupt local businessmen and politicians.

But undoubtedly Redford's major intervention into political film is *All the President's Men*. He had negotiated a film deal with Woodward and Bernstein even before the book of the Watergate cover-up investigation had been written. He then spent a long time researching the journalistic background by talking to the reporters and staff of the *Washington Post*. The resulting film – with Dustin Hoffman and Redford as the two intrepid reporters – is a strong indictment of power politics and the distortions which ensue.

Bridging the gap

Redford broke with tradition for two more romantic movies. In *Out of Africa* (1985), once again directed by Sidney Pollack, he played an Englishman gripped by the beauty of Africa and by the love of Karen Blixen (Meryl Streep). A beautifully photographed film, it reflects all of Redford's personal concerns with the environment and the freedom of the individual. Then in 1986 he added his lustre to the otherwise tepid *Legal Eagles*.

In 1981, he won his first Academy Award – not for acting, however, but for the direction of *Ordinary People* (1980), a highly emotional and perceptive study of family tensions based upon the guilt that the son Conrad (Timothy Hutton) feels over his brother's drowning. Starring Mary Tyler Moore and Donald Sutherland, the film was a commercial and a critical success and led to his second film as director – *The Milagro Beanfield War* (1987).

Left: Redford played a small role in A Bridge Too Far, *the story of the Allied defeat at Arnhem. Above right: an ex-rodeo rider decides to leave the bright lights behind in* The Electric Horseman. *Right: Redford discusses a scene from* Ordinary People *with Donald Sutherland*

THE LAST PICTURE SHOW

On its first appearance in 1971, *The Last Picture Show* had a potent effect on audiences everywhere. This evocative depiction of small-town life, recalled with such affection and loving detail, seemed like the kind of film that American cinema had well-nigh stopped producing for twenty years or more.

Reduced to a mere synopsis, the incidents depicted could easily appear no more than a slice of life from some Texan Peyton Place. But in Peter Bogdanovich's hands they unerringly convey the lost dreams, foolish aspirations and rivalries – the whole texture of life in a community in decline with not much of a remembered past and scant hope for a future. Chekhovian is the word which, without hyperbole, springs to mind.

All the film's adolescent sexual encounters bring their attendant disappointments and pain, but there is the wry implication that, with the passing years, nostalgia may well turn the pain into a treasured memory, so blur its edges that it can even be recalled with comfortable ruefulness as the one great chance that was missed. Thus it is that Sam the Lion, in the only long speech in the film, waxes lyrical to Sonny, as he fishes, about an idyllic moment from his youth when he and a girl

went swimming in the nude. The object of these reminiscences is by now a cynical fading beauty, alienated from her husband, capable of caustically advising her own daughter to do something about losing her virginity. She, too, clings to this long-ago attachment as her big moment: 'I guess if it wasn't for Sam, I'd just about have missed it, whatever it is,' she muses. The young folk, meanwhile, are amassing similar double-edged experiences to be nurtured and mellowed in memory's chest.

Bogdanovich's approach to his characters' shallow lives is never sentimental and often slyly humorous. Sitting in the tacky cinema, watching Minnelli's *Father of the Bride* (1950), Charlene removes her chewing-gum to kiss Sonny absently, fatuously absorbed in the never-never-land problems of Spencer Tracy coping with Elizabeth Taylor's coy pre-nuptial tantrums; later, in the last film to be shown before the cinema's closure (Hawks' *Red River*, 1948), John Wayne's herds making their impressive progress across the great prairies are a far cry indeed from the forlorn tumbleweed encroaching on this dying township where the only cattle seen are crowded in the back of a truck. The film clips

make their point as opiates, un-questioned grist to the fantasy mill which, with the demise of the old cinema, will now be supplied with coarser fodder by the new monster, television.

Already, in his first feature, *Targets* (1967), Bogdanovich had revealed an exceptional capacity for directing his actors and here he consolidates it. In the meticulously observed cramped interiors and grey exteriors (the whole film was shot in Archer City in north Texas) everyone finds his unobtrusive, unstarry place, superbly served by Robert Surtees' expressive black-and-white camerawork. For here is a film not so much shot in black and white but conceived in shades of those colours, best able to capture the period and the elegiac mood.

It seems perfectly natural that Ruth Popper should reward a spontaneous gesture of kindness from Sonny by inviting him into her kitchen for a drink; equally natural that the same neglected, middle-aged wife should entreat him to stay with her a little longer. A flutter of unrest clouds his face for a moment until the adolescent, himself in a state of emotional unrest, finds himself responding sympathetically to an older frustration he dimly apprehends. Their subsequent affair seems perfectly plotted and Ruth's transition from drabness to radiance and thence to shrill virulence when Jacy lures Sonny away from her is most movingly achieved by Cloris Leachman. All the relationships bear the same stamp of truth.

Bogdanovich's film is, in the Chekhovian sense, a comedy of empty lives where the characters occasionally go to ludicrous lengths to assert the fact that their existence is notable and their actions of importance. Jacy's bid for acceptance by the rich set is made by stripping naked on a diving board; she incites her mother's lover to rape her, and her elopement with Sonny, she hopes, will make her the talk of the town and provide her with a colourful *entrée* to her first year in college.

The Last Picture Show has about it that kind of purity of expression that only the very greatest directors – Donskoi, Ford, Mizoguchi, Satyajit Ray – are able to sustain consistently throughout their careers. Most achieve it only once. It is one of those films whose characters linger in the memory, and that is happily re-seen time and time again.

1

4

7

1951. In Anarene, a small, dust-laden, one-horse town in Texas (1), there are few distractions for the local youth apart from their sexual exploits and the weekly picture show. Sonny Crawford – having broken with his bovine, steady girlfriend Charlene, and though envious of his friend Duane (2), who seems to have found favour with the local belle Jacy – drifts into a liaison with Ruth (3), the neglected wife of the football coach.

Jacy has higher aspirations than Duane and leaves him at the local Christmas dance to attend a much smarter, nude swimming party where she attracts the attention of Bobby Sheen, a rich,

Directed by Peter Bogdanovich, 1971
Prod co: A BBS Production/Last Picture Show Productions for Columbia. exec prod: Bert Schneider. prod: Stephen J. Friedman. assoc prod: Harold Schneider. sc: Larry McMurtry, Peter Bogdanovich, based on the novel by Larry McMurtry. photo: Robert Surtees. ed: Donn Cambern. prod des: Polly Platt. art dir: Walter Scott Herndon. mus: 1951 recordings by Hank Williams, Bob Willis and His Texas Playboys, Eddy Arnold, Eddie Fisher, Phil Harris, Pee Wee King, Hank Snow, Tony Bennett, Lefty Frizzell, Frankie Laine, Johnnie Ray, Johnny Standley, Kay Starr, Hank Thompson, Webb Price, Jo Stafford. sd: Tom Overton. ass dir: Robert Rubin, William Morrison. prod man: Don Guest. r/t: 118 minutes. Premier, New York Film Festival 1971. Cast: Timothy Bottoms (*Sonny Crawford*), Jeff Bridges (*Duane Jackson*), Cybill Shepherd (*Jacy Farrow*), Ben Johnson (*Sam the Lion*), Cloris Leachman (*Ruth Popper*), Ellen Burstyn (*Lois Farrow*), Eileen Brennan (*Genevieve*), Clu Gulager (*Abilene*), Sam Bottoms (*Billy*), Sharon Taggart (*Charlene Duggs*), Randy Quaid (*Lester Marlow*), Joe Heathcock (*sheriff*), Bill Thurman (*Coach Popper*), Barc Doyle (*Joe Bob Blanton*), Jessie Lee Fulton (*Miss Mosey*), Gary Brockette (*Bobby Sheen*), Helena Humann (*Jimmie Sue*), Loyd Catlett (*Leroy*), Robert Glenn (*Gene Farrow*), John Hillerman (*teacher*), Janice O'Malley (*Mrs Clarg*), Floyd Mahaney (*Oklahoma patrolman*), Kimberley Hyde (*Annie-Annie Martin*), Noble Willingham (*Chester*), Marjory Jay (*Winnie Snips*), Joye Hash (*Mrs Jackson*), Pamela Keller (*Jackie Lee French*), Gordon Hurst (*Monroe*), Mike Hosford (*Johnny*), Faye Jordan (*nurse*), Charlie Seybert (*Andy Fanner*), Grover Lewis (*Mr Crawford*), Rebecca Ulrick (*Marlene*), Merrill Shepherd (*Agnes*), Buddy Wood (*Bud*), Kenny Wood (*Ken*), Leon Brown (*cowboy in café*), Bobby McGriff (*truck driver*), Jack Mueller (*oil pumper*), Robert Arnold (*Brother Blanton*), Frank Marshall (*Tommy Logan*), Otis Elmore (*first mechanic*), Charles Salmon (*roughneck driver*), George Gaulden (*cowboy*), Will Morris Hannis (*gas station man*), and the Leon Miller Band.

2

3

5

6

8

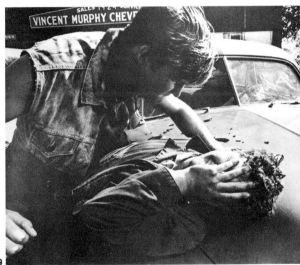

9

young playboy. To vent his frustration Duane, with Sonny, plays a cruel joke on Billy, a retarded boy, and is severely chastized by Sam the Lion (4), the cinema owner and Billy's protector. But Sam relents and on a fishing trip with Sonny reminisces (5) about how he once went swimming, naked, with a girl. Returning from a trip to Mexico with Duane, Sonny learns that Sam has suddenly died.

Sam's old flame was Lois Farrow, Jacy's mother, who now advises her daughter to lose her virginity (6). Jacy consents to go with Duane to a motel (7), mainly because Bobby Sheen has curtly told her he has no time for

virgins. It is an unsatisfactory session and Duane leaves town to enlist for Korea. Jacy learns of Bobby's imminent marriage and, out of pique, lures Sonny (8) away from Ruth. Duane returns and in the ensuing fight (9) Sonny's eye is badly hurt. Jacy is delighted to be the focal point of this row and coerces Sonny into eloping with her, making sure that her parents will find out in time and send her off to college.

Duane, due to leave for Korea, spends his last night in town with Sonny at the cinema's final show before it closes. Sonny sees Billy struck dead by a passing lorry and wretchedly returns to Ruth for consolation (10).

10

In the Sixties and Seventies Clint Eastwood seemed too good to be true. He transformed himself overnight from a smiling cowboy in a TV series into a deadly, inscrutable fantasy hero idolized by millions. Whatever he touched turned to gold, and so the biggest star in the world also became a highly successful director – and his popularity never diminishes

The Beguiler

There was an unexpected box-office lapse in the summer of 1980 – *Bronco Billy* didn't do very well. It should have been reliable business with Clint Eastwood's brushed leather face beneath a dashing white cowboy hat. He was surrounded by the people from previous hits. His deadpan reaction to mishap was funny, without destroying his authority. *Bronco Billy* had the air of a happy summer movie, as full of fights, laughs and male self-congratulation as *Every Which Way But Loose* (1978), the Eastwood Christmas film of two years before and a hit beyond anyone's wildest dreams. The latter was a departure: it was the first Eastwood film to try comedy action, as if to say, 'Look, this guy is 48, and he can't go around stomping on everyone for much longer'. It gave Clint an orang-utan to tuck under one arm, while the other retained its gentlemanly hold on Sondra Locke. The successful formula was repeated with *Any Which Way You Can* (1980), but *Bronco Billy* had been the first film to raise the possibility that Eastwood is not infallible.

The Man With No Failures
He has continued to enjoy unrivalled success at the box-office. Not every picture triumphed – one of the best, *The Beguiled* (1971), was too sardonic to please his following – but they all went about their business of entertaining large audiences. For more than two decades, Eastwood's films have been successful, even though critics such as Pauline Kael were alarmed by what they felt lay beneath the surface of such violent cop movies as *Dirty Harry* (1971). Eastwood himself was quiet, unstarry and inclined to stay at home at Carmel, California, rather than play the talk

shows. With an occassional sortie into local politics, he had gone from being actor to star to director and boss of his own company, Malpaso. That tight-knit operation took big profits from his popular pictures.

No-one has ever begrudged him this glory. He handles himself gracefully, especially because he has acted on the notion that turning out pleasant movies is not that difficult. His pictures are not expensive and they never strive after the difficult or the pretentious. Twenty years earlier he was a good-looking Californian kid with hair like James Dean's and swimming-pool blue eyes. He would look better as he matured, but if it hadn't been for the shyness of someone who had reached six foot by the age of 13, he might have carried showbiz on the strength of beauty alone. Not since Gary Cooper had an American male in pictures had it in his power to stop the breath

Above: death in the desert for adversaries of the Man With No Name – Eastwood in For a Few Dollars More *(and right). Below left: Clint learns to ballroom dance at the Universal talent school around 1955. His partner was Italian actress Gia Scala*

of men and women in the audience alike. No matter how tough the roles, the skin, the eyes and the very soft voice have hinted at a Malibu Apollo.

For a very few dollars . . .
He was born in San Francisco in 1930. The family was poor and Clint went from high school to manual labour, laying down the basis for that lean body. He was an army swimming instructor at Ford Ord, and then he started to study business at Los Angeles College. But physique and looks earned him offers from Universal – a starting contract at $75 a week. In 1955, he got a couple of walk-on parts in movies, including *Francis in the Navy*, starring Donald O'Connor and a talking mule.

Those were tough days. Clint looked too healthy and he spoke too clearly to fit the Brando style. He was in and out of work, taking acting classes by night and doing labouring jobs in the day. The body got harder, but he didn't put much faith in lessons or theory:

'The basic fundamental of learning acting is to know yourself, know what you can do. That's one big advantage of doing a series, if you can. You get to see yourself a lot, get to see what you can do wrong or right.'

His television series was *Rawhide*, and the role of Rowdy Yates was no more than an outline that a young actor could inhabit in front of the camera. Over two hundred episodes in seven seasons provided Eastwood with

that necessary view of himself. Now he is one of few screen stars with the instinctive assurance of knowing how a scene should be filmed. His face, his minimal reactions and his timing are a style such as Cooper and Bogart had possessed before him.

Even on *Rawhide* he was asking to direct some episodes. Eric Fleming, the lead star on the show, had no problems with Clint's ambitions. But CBS and the unions were very touchy and they restricted him to trailers. Still, it is a mark of Eastwood's love of movies that the urge to make them came early, apparently on a day when a stampede scene was being shot from a safe distance and Clint wondered why he couldn't carry a camera on horseback into the herd.

He could have been numbered with James Arness, Robert Horton or, indeed, Eric Fleming – stars in Western series who retired, got trapped in television, or in the case of Fleming, died in 1966 on the slide. Clint proved his initiative with what seemed an affront to Hollywood tradition. He went to Spain to make a Western for an Italian director. It was called *Per un Pugno di Dollari* (1964, *A Fistful of Dollars*) and he did it for $15,000: if the

Above: a budding director has a look for himself during the filming of Don Siegel's The Beguiled. *Right: Eastwood's directorial debut starred him as DJ Dave Garland who is plagued by the psychopathic woman (Jessica Walter) who asks him to* Play Misty for Me

'spaghetti' Western had proved cold and greasy the actor would have been thrown out in the garbage.

Leone and the language of death

However, the film was a huge, international hit that changed Eastwood's life and, in the Man With No Name, created a role model that still works in TV advertising. The film was made by Sergio Leone, whose English was as limited as Clint's Italian. But they got on well and understood that the image of a laconic but lethal man musing on a cheroot until blazing guns appeared from beneath his serape, could be sensational.

The costume was bought by Eastwood in America. He conceived the character, and he rewrote or cut many of his lines. *A Fistful of Dollars* and its sequels – *Per Qualche Dollaro in Più* (1966, *For a Few Dollars More*) and *Il*

Buono, il Brutto, il Cattivo (1967, *The Good, the Bad and the Ugly*) – were full of pregnant pauses just because of the language problem on set, but that only stimulated Leone's visual imagination and allowed Clint to become an awesome assassin, above words, a face always gazing into the sun so that the eyes seemed to be glints of some rare and impervious metal. A ruthless, implacable honour grew around the silence and the eyes that would not look away. The movies were like mescal dreams, poised wonderfully between suspense and absurdity.

In later years, Clint was often willing to have his super-hero outsmarted – by women, an elderly Indian and that orang-utan. But that's not new. Leone's films were very violent, and they played the action straight – if that's the way you wanted to read it. Yet the exaggerated compositions, the mannered acting and the feeling of time oozing out as slowly as ketchup all suggested a satiric attitude on the part of the director and his star.

The *Dollars* trilogy kept Clint occupied in the mid-Sixties. When he returned to America, he set about making this new kind of Western at home: *Hang 'Em High* (1968), *Two Mules for Sister Sara* (1970), *Joe Kidd* (1972) and *High Plains Drifter* (1973) are all in the same vein. The lesson that he had learned was that the outsider hero suited him – not just a nameless figure, but a man without known allegiances. In 1968, for the first time, he teamed up with Don Siegel, a director of

twenty years hard-earned experience and an expert story-teller with a predilection for toughness. Siegel had always found Hollywood stars squeamish when asked to be mean, but Clint was different:

'Eastwood has an absolute fixation as an anti-hero. It's his credo in life and in all the films that he's done so far . . . I've never worked with an actor who was less conscious of his good image.'

Coogan's Bluff – about an Arizona cop who comes on a manhunt to New York – isn't quite that heartless, but it did exploit the novelty of that handsome face snarling with hostility, of the Eastwood hero coolly laying any woman around. Siegel would be as important to Eastwood as Leone, but there were a few years of hesitation before the new partnership clicked. Eastwood was overshadowed by Richard Burton in Brian Hutton's *Where Eagles Dare* (1968) and by Lee Marvin in Joshua Logan's *Paint Your Wagon* (1969).

Play dirty for Siegel

The year in which he emerged as a Hollywood giant was 1971. For Siegel he acted in *The Beguiled*, about a fugitive in the American Civil War taken in by a household of women who take sweet vengeance on his complacent stud attitudes by amputating his injured leg. Then he directed his first film, *Play Misty for Me*, a slick thriller about a disc jockey who is haunted and nearly killed by a woman who

Above left: the calling of Coogan's Bluff? *Eastwood in his first role as a vicious cop for Don Siegel. Above: as Bronco Billy, a Wild West show proprietor with problems. Below: Philo (Eastwood) and Clyde, trucking partners in* Every Which Way But Loose

Above: Sergeant Highway (Eastwood) trains fighting marines but finds it more difficult than he expected in Heartbreak Ridge. Above right: as a cop forced to run The Gauntlet with a hooker (regular co-star Sondra Locke) – love blossoms, naturally. Clint directed both these films

phones up with the request of the title. In both these pictures Clint was making himself the victim of women, and surely that owed itself to the good humour of a happily married man lusted after by so many strangers.

Dirty Harry, though, was the major event of 1971, and the most controversial film he has ever made. Siegel's direction guaranteed its impact, but the subject went beyond mere entertainment. Dirty Harry Callahan is a San Francisco cop with an old-fashioned belief in the law and the will that must enforce it. The film is in two parts: first Harry tracks down a loathsome killer, a nasty mixture of spoiled kid

psychopath and glib hippy; but then bureaucracy and the technicalities of the law let the killer go free whereupon Harry makes a private war on him, eliminating him with prejudice and then tossing away his police badge in disgust.

Some people felt that the picture encouraged vigilante fascism, that it was urging less liberal law-and-order programmes (Eastwood had backed Nixon in 1968). But the picture is more the manifestation of a very independent, romantic morality that shows in the star's aversion to publicity, extravagance and institutions:

'We, as Americans, went to Nuremberg and convicted people who committed certain crimes because they didn't adhere to a higher morality; we convicted them on that basis – and they shouldn't have listened to the law of the land or their leaders at that time. They should have listened to the true morality.'

Softening the blows

It seems likely that he was affected by complaints about the violence in *Dirty Harry* and its successors, *Magnum Force* (1973), *The Enforcer* (1976) and *The Gauntlet* (1977). His antihero has mellowed to become a more relaxed, more amused and marginally less robust observer. That was the process of tolerance that worked so well in *The Outlaw Josey Wales* (1976), in which a righteous moral anger softens with time to become aware of foibles, frailty and humour. In many ways it is his most adventurous picture, a sign of the kindness he is often too shy or laid back to reveal.

Nor would anyone have expected *Breezy* (1973) from Eastwood. With William Holden and Kay Lenz, that was the story of a September-May romance, shamelessly sentimental but touching, solidly grounded and well acted. For Clint it was about a man who 'rediscovers life through the eyes of this young girl'. It was the first hint that he might be fearful of growing older, and it could have been a prelude to his own romantic interest in Sondra Locke. He resists confessions or the gossip press, but for some time he has worked with the younger, blonde actress who has not

really acted for anyone but Eastwood (though the failure of *Bronco Billy* apparently threatened their relationship).

Eastwood continues to direct and star in at least one big film a year, usually in his established Western genre, but occassionally making forays into other styles. *Firefox* (1982), for instance, took him to Eastern Europe to steal the blueprints for a new plane, while *Heartbreak Ridge* (1987) is set against the background of the Korean war. In 1985, the 'man with no name' returned as a preacher in *Pale Rider*, this time to defend the local community against the bad guys. Meanwhile, Eastwood took on that role himself and became, for a time, the Mayor of his local Californian town of Carmel.

Filmography
1955 Revenge of the Creature; Lady Godiva (GB: Lady Godiva of Coventry); Francis in the Navy; Tarantula; Never Say Goodbye. '56 Star in the Dust; The First Travelling Saleslady. '57 Escapade in Japan. '58 Lafayette Escadrille (GB: Hell Bent for Glory); Ambush at Cimarron Pass. '64 Per un Pugno di Dollari (IT-GER-SP) (USA/GB: A Fistful of Dollars). '66 Per Qualche Dollaro in Più (IT-GER-SP) (USA/GB: For a Few Dollars More). '67 Il Buono, il Brutto, il Cattivo (IT-GER-SP) (USA/GB: The Good, the Bad and the Ugly); Le Streghe *ep* Una Sera Come le Altre (IT-FR) (USA: The Witches *ep* A Night Like Any Other). '68 Hang 'Em High; Coogan's Bluff; Where Eagles Dare (GB). '69 Paint Your Wagon. '70 Gold Fever (doc. short) (appearance as himself); Two Mules for Sister Sara; Kelly's Heroes (USA-YUG). '71 The Beguiled; Play Misty for Me (+dir); Dirty Harry. '72 Joe Kidd. '73 High Plains Drifter (+dir); Breezy (dir. only); Magnum Force. '74 Thunderbolt and Lightfoot. '75 The Eiger Sanction (+dir). '76 The Outlaw Josey Wales (+dir); The Enforcer. '77 The Gauntlet (+dir). '78 Every Which Way But Loose. '79 Escape From Alcatraz. '80 Bronco Billy (+dir); Any Which Way You Can. '82 Firefox (+dir); Honkytonk Man (+dir; +prod). '83 Sudden Impact (+dir; +prod). '84 Tightrope (+prod); City Heat. '85 Pale Rider (+dir; +prod). '86 Heartbreak Ridge (+dir; +prod). '88 Bird (dir only); The Dead Pool (+dir; +prod).

Directed by Steven Spielberg, 1977
Prod co: Phillips/Columbia/EMI. **prod:** Julia Phillips, Michael Phillips. **assoc prod:** Clark Paylow. **sc:** Steven Spielberg. **photo** (Metrocolor, Panavision)**:** Vilmos Zsigmond, William A. Fraker, Douglas Slocombe. **col:** Robert M. McMillian. **add photo:** John Alonzo, Laszlo Kovacs, Steve Poster. **sp photo eff:** Richard Yuricich, Dave Stewart, Robert Hall, Don Jarel, Dennis Muren. **anim sup:** Robert Swarthe. **anim:** Harry Moreau, Carol Boardman, Eleanor Dahlen, Cy Didjurgis, Tom Koester, Bill Millar, Connie Morgan. **visual eff sup:** Steven Spielberg. **sp photo eff co-ord:** Larry Robinson. **project co-ord:** Mona Thal Benefiel. **eff unit project man:** Robert Shepherd. **video tech:** 'Fast' Eddie Mahler. **ed:** Michael Kahn. **art dir:** Dan Lomino. **design:** Joe Alves, Phil Abramson, Matthew Yuricich, George Jensen, Carlo Rambaldi. **sp mech eff:** Roy Arbogast, George Polkinghorne. **mech design:** Dom Trumbull, John Russell, Fries Engineering. **electronics design:** Jerry L. Jeffress, Alvah J. Miller, Peter Regla, Dan Slater. **models:** Gregory Jein, J. Richard Dow, Jor Van Kline, Michael McMillen, Kenneth Swenson, Robert Worthington. **mus/mus dir:** John Williams. **songs:** 'Chances Are' by Al Stillman, Robert Allen, sung by Johnny Mathis; 'When You Wish Upon a Star' by Leigh Harline, Ned Washington; 'The Square Song' by Joseph Raposo; 'Love Song of the Waterfall' by Bob Nolan, Bernard Barnes, Carl Winge, sung by Slim Whitman. **cost:** Jim Linn. **makeup:** Bob Westmoreland. **titles:** Dan Perri. **sd:** Gene Cantmessa, Buzz Knudson, Don MacDougall, Robert Glass. **Dolby sd sup:** Steve Katz. **sd eff:** Frank Warner, Richard Oswald, David Horton, Sam Gemette, Gary S. Gerlich, Chet Slomka, Neil Burrow. **tech adv:** Dr. J. Allen Hynek. **sp consultants:** Peter Anderson, Larry Albright, Richard Bennett, Ken Ebert, Paul Huston, David M. Jones, Kevin Kelly, Jim Lutes, George Randle, Jeff Shapiro, Rourke Engineering. **tech dialogue:** Colin Cantwell. **stunt co-ordinator:** Buddy Joe Hooker. **ass dir:** Chuck Myers, Jim Bloom. **r/t:** 135 minutes.
Cast: Richard Dreyfuss (*Roy Neary*), François Truffaut (*Claude Lacombe*), Teri Garr (*Ronnie Neary*), Melinda Dillon (*Jillian Guiler*), Bob Balaban (*David Laughlin*), J. Patrick McNamara (*project leader*), Warren Kemmerling (*Wild Bill*), Roberts Blossom (*farmer*), Philip Dodds (*Jean Claude*), Cary Guffey (*Barry Guiler*), Shawn Bishop (*Brad Neary*), Adrienne Campbell (*Silvia Neary*), Justin Dreyfuss (*Toby Neary*), Lance Henriksen (*Robert*), Merrill Connally (*team leader*), George DiCenzo (*Major Benchley*), Amy Douglass, Alexander Lockwood (*implantees*), Gene Dynarski (*Ike*), Mary Gafrey (*Mrs Harris*), Norman Bartold (*Ohio Tolls*), Josef Sommer (*Larry Butler*), Rev Michael J. Dyer (*himself*), Roger Ernest (*highway patrolman*), Carl Weathers (*military policeman*), F. J. O'Neil (*ARP project member*), Phil Dodds (*ARP musician*), Randy Hermann, Hal Barwood, Matthew Robbins (*returnees from Flight 19*), David Anderson, Richard L. Hawkins, Craig Shreeve, Bill Thurman (*air traffic controllers*), Roy E. Richards (*Air East pilot*), Gene Rader (*hawker*), Eumenio Blanco, Daniel Nunez, Chuy Franco, Luis Contreras (*federales*), James Keane, Dennis McMullen, Cy Young, Tom Howard (*radio telescope team*), Richard Stuart (*truck dispatcher*), Bob Westmoreland (*load dispatcher*), Matt Emery (*support leader*), Galen Thompson, John Dennis Johnston (*special forces*), John Ewing, Keith Atkinson, Robert Broyles, Kirk Raymond (*dirty tricks*).

Riding high on the success of *Jaws* (1975), Steven Spielberg began his ambitious project – initially entitled 'Watch the Skies' – with full studio backing. He constructed an enormous set in an airplane hangar in Mobile, Alabama, while shooting certain outdoor scenes in a section of Indiana desert land reminiscent of Jack Arnold's locations in *It Came From Outer Space* (1953) and *Tarantula* (1955). Over a year was spent shooting and re-shooting scenes on various other international locations with the help of some top cinematographers. These sequences jigsawed together for two versions, the first demanded by an impatient Columbia, released in 1977, and the second – Spielberg's authorized version – released three years later.

Although the *Special Edition* (1980) contains additional scenes, the overall effect of the two films is the same. Both are wonderful, brilliantly constructed science-fiction drama featuring complex special effects which are enhanced by Spielberg's single-minded, all-American, all-Hollywood vision. It is a mammoth spectacle, as gripping as Hitchcock, as magical as Disney's early animated features, and as humanely optimistic as the best of the Sixties television series *The Outer Limits* (1963–65).

The story is presented from three simultaneous viewpoints: that of the innocent child and his distraught mother, of an intrigued electrical engineer, and of a group of scientists led by François Truffaut playing in his first American movie. Everything revolves around five or six breathtaking set-pieces; the narrative intercuts between these 'close encounters', excitingly revealing the clues which lead to the moving climax when the extraterrestrials come to rest on Devil's Tower. Superbly edited throughout,

the film moves at an extraordinary pace, teasing the audience with constant references to the other beings as Lacombe and his UFO investigators discover the secret of the five musical tones – a signal continuously broadcast from outer space.

In the first sighting is encapsulated all the success of *Close Encounters of the Third Kind*: around the curve of the road come three multicoloured, gyrating shapes at incredible speed but slow enough to be in full view of witnesses and the audience. By shooting the special effects in 70mm and the rest in 35mm, which is then blown up to 70mm, the quality of the print is consistent so that the spacecraft look completely real. It is the immaculate special effects, integrated so perfectly with the heart-stopping narrative, which are the true stars of *Close Encounters*. The final sequence – the arrival of the mothership on Devil's Tower – is as startling as Cecil B. DeMille's parting of the waves in *The Ten Commandments* (1956). Anyone would find it difficult not to believe that this great citadel in the sky, twice as high as the mountain, really exists.

Unlike the swashbuckling heroics of that other high-budget, cosmic adventure movie *Star Wars* (1977, dir. George Lucas), the effectiveness of *Close Encounters* lies in our ability to believe that beyond the stars superior powers are benevolent and caring. In those closing moments the audience is allowed the kind of emotional participation not felt in cinemas since Judy Garland walked over the rainbow and Dumbo flew: perfect escapism for our troubled times.

CLOSE ENCOUNTER
OF THE FIRST KIND
Sighting of a UFO

CLOSE ENCOUNTER
OF THE SECOND KIND
Physical Evidence

CLOSE ENCOUNTER
OF THE THIRD KIND
Contact

WE ARE NOT ALONE

CLOSE ENCOUNTERS
OF THE THIRD KIND

A COLUMBIA·EMI Presentation

Lost on the road while trying to establish the cause of a massive power-cut, Roy Neary sees a set of bright lights approaching. Instead of passing straight by, the intense rays rise above his truck (1), and immediately there is a loss of all gravitational force in his cab.

In another part of the same black-out a young boy awakes to find the entire house in bizarre confusion; all the electrical appliances have switched themselves on. Amused and amazed, he runs into the night pursued by his fearful mother, and mysteriously appears at the edge of a hill-top road where Roy, Jillian and the boy witness three of the alien spacecraft.

Spurred on by newspaper and television reports, interested people turn up for these sightings (2). Meanwhile, a group of scientists led by Claude Lacombe has found evidence in other continents that a certain musical pattern can be linked with the aliens' efforts to communicate.

Jillian's son is invisibly kidnapped by the extra-terrestrials (3), and Roy alienates his own family by building a clay model of the visions he has seen of a flat mountain (4). As soon as he realizes, along with Jillian,

1

2

3

4

5

6

that the model in his living room
is the Devil's Tower in Wyoming
and that the aliens want them to
be there, he and Jillian race
across country.

On arrival they find everything
cordoned off by Lacombe (5) and
the military who have simulated a
nerve-gas scare. All the
unwelcome humans drawn there
are rounded-up for interrogation
(6), but Roy and Jillian escape.

An exciting chase culminates in
the discovery of a colossal
runway, a giant electronic board
covered with coloured strips, and
a powerful musical keyboard. All
their former paranoia is calmed
by this sight, and their weird
obsessions and premonitions now
seem crystal clear.

A fleet of dancing, whooshing,
neon-lit spaceships precede the
landing of the huge mothership.
Communication between the
scientists and the craft is initiated
by the playing of the five mystical
notes, and culminates in an extraterrestrial duet. Roy eventually
enters the mothership surrounded
by the aliens (7) — their embryonic
features clear and their intentions
obviously harmless. With sadness
Lacombe and his team watch the
friendly visitors leave (8). From a
vantage point, Jillian and her son
see the craft move off (9).

7

8

9

GALACTICA, DEMONICA

Chaos is come again in Seventies fantasies, whether in the gleaming
metallic future or in a disaster-prone, blood-smeared present

A major feature of Seventies cinema was the extraordinary popularity and creativity of its science-fiction and horror films. During the decade, these previously minor genres gained a new vigour and a firm standing at the box-office. *Jaws* (1975) and then *Star Wars* (1977) became the biggest commercial successes the industry had known, according to *Variety*'s 1979 listing.

The major screen manifestation of science fiction in the Sixties had been such impressive television shows as *Dr Who* (1963 onwards), *The Outer Limits* (1963–65) and *Star Trek* (1966–69), to which *Star Trek – The Motion Picture* (1979) was a late follow-up. In the cinema, the genre was not as prolific, although this decade saw the rise of the big-budget treatment of science fiction which was one of the characteristics of the Seventies strain. *The Time Machine* (1960), *Robinson Crusoe on Mars* (1964) and *Fantastic Voyage* (1966) all boasted impressive visuals, although the real precursor of the Seventies high-technology sheen was Stanley Kubrick's *2001: A Space Odyssey* (1968).

The superproduction aesthetic really arrived with George Lucas' *Star Wars* and *The Empire Strikes Back* (1980, produced by Lucas but directed by Irvin Kershner) and Steven Spielberg's *Close Encounters of the Third Kind* (1977) – ravishing audio-visual experiences which demonstrate the spectacle, power and excitement of high technology. Indeed, this auditory and visual clamour works against the faculty of analysis, in contrast to *2001* which uses its technology and effects to disorientate and alienate. Countering the ability to think clearly is perhaps a necessary strategy, since *Star Wars* and

The Empire Strikes Back ask the audience to accept the contradiction of a group of 'rebels' who wish to restore the old patriarchal order, and *Close Encounters of the Third Kind* forwards the proposition that lack of communication between the common man and the authorities can be resolved only by some sort of alien, quasi-divine intervention. It very much seems that, in the absence of actual communication with an alien culture, these films stand in as objects of awe and reverence.

Star Wars itself spawned a series of derivatives, which sometimes even included cute pet robots. The most obvious is *Battlestar Galactica* (1978), based upon the pilot episode of the television series about the survivors of a doomed planet in search of a new home; but this totally lacks the imagination of its model. *L'Umanoide* (1979, *The Humanoid*), a 'spaghetti' science-fiction film, also flatters by imitation but fails to impress. The only real contender is the underrated Disney production *The Black Hole* (1979). This is almost a remake of *20,000 Leagues Under the Sea* (1954) set in space, with Maximilian Schell playing the mad scientist intent on pushing his knowledge to the very limits.

Star Wars and *Close Encounters of the Third Kind* express a naive faith in space, almost as a new and exciting West to be opened up and explored, which is not necessarily shared by all science-fiction productions. *Alien* (1979) has similar production values, with stunning photography by Derek Vanlint and genuinely other-worldly designs by H. R. Giger, but it fascinatingly tries to combine the cool, abstract manner of Kubrick with the Fifties monster movie – having much the same story as *It! The*

Star Wars creates imaginary worlds populated by all manner of creatures, the product of a fruitful union between the fertile imagination of George Lucas and a popular tradition of fantastic stories in comic-books, paperbacks and movie serials

Above: when the Poseidon, *a luxury liner on its last voyage, capsizes in the Mediterranean, the passengers' New Year's Eve celebrations are greatly disrupted;* The Poseidon Adventure *was based on a popular novel by Paul Gallico. Top: the hero (Christopher Reeve) of* Superman, The Movie *flies effortlessly over the streets of New York, thanks to British special-effects artists. Top right: the world's tallest building goes up in flames, with the aid of two studios, 20th Century-Fox and Warners, and Irwin Allen, who also produced* The Poseidon Adventure

Terror From Beyond Space (1958). *Alien* is a menacing, brooding film, with fear and paranoia rife as a virtually indestructible life-form stalks the corridors of a spaceship eating its way through the crew one by one. The heroine stands up to this image of male sexual aggression, just as she withstands an attack from a male member of the crew, and comes through as the only survivor in a genre where men usually reign supreme.

Male fantasies are also the subject of two more super-productions, *Superman, The Movie* (1978) and *Flash Gordon* (1980). Both filter the original comic-strip images, and also those drawn from earlier films, through a knowing Seventies sensibility to achieve a finely balanced ironic distance from the material. *Superman, The Movie* is particularly successful because of its range of feelings, from the outrageously comic to a spectacular love scene in the skies over New York City. *Flash Gordon* celebrates the artifice of the original Buster Crabbe series, and along the way exposes the fallacy that only women, and never men, are supposed to be ornamental in films.

Loosely connected to the social-catastrophe element of science fiction (the havoc wrought by falling meteors, marauding monsters, dangerous chemical contamination or atomic blasts), and growing to fill the vacuum left by the passing of the spectacular epic, the disaster movie has claimed its share of the box-office in the Seventies. Very much in the manner of an epic for modern times, the disaster movie imagines the breakdown of social order and then dusts off old movie stars for their iconographic significance as heroic saviour figures. Generally the disasters take the form of attacks by one or several of the elements, as if to caution the audience that catastrophes are natural and not avoidable by political means.

At the conclusion of these films, all the marital and romantic problems that have been set out are resolved and old values are restored. The disaster movie may well be an older generation's way of rejecting life as it has developed in the allegedly 'cynical' Seventies and finding solace in the male screen heroism of Richard Harris in *Juggernaut*, Charlton Heston in *Airport 1975* and *Earthquake* (all three 1974), George C. Scott in *The Hindenburg* and Lorne Greene in *Tidal Wave* (both 1975), Rock Hudson in *Avalanche* (1978) and Sean Connery in *Meteor* (1979). But the genre cannot be too easily dismissed. *The Poseidon Adventure* (1972) depicts a world of order so dizzily inverted that the whole film takes place within a liner turned upside down. *The Towering Inferno* (1974), deservedly the most popular film of this type, holds together its various centres of interest with great skill and manages to make the consuming flames profoundly disturbing as they destroy an enormous new skyscraper.

For the variety of themes it tackles and the directorial talent it has attracted, the horror film is certainly one of the most interesting areas of Seventies cinema. As the critic Robin Wood has pointed out:

'It is a commonplace that the (ostensibly) celebratory family film disappeared from the American cinema in the Fifties. What happened was that its implicit content became displaced into the horror film. What is enacted symbolically in *Meet Me in St Louis* (1944) is "realized" in *Night of the Living Dead* (1968).'

In Vincente Minnelli's 1944 film, the child Tootie symbolically destroys her family through attacking a group of snowmen; in George Romero's later film, a daughter kills and then tries to eat her mother. One more late-Sixties film to suggest that the horror derives from within the family was Roman Polanski's *Rosemary's Baby* (1968), in which Rosemary (Mia Farrow) actually gives birth to the Antichrist.

With this trend proceeding into the Seventies, there developed some deeply disturbing visions of values in transition, of growing doubts about the sanctity of the nuclear family and its role in society. Children themselves, traditionally symbols of innocence, and young people are seen as monstrous progeny in *Dead of Night* (1972), *The Exorcist* (1973) and *Exorcist II: The Heretic* (1977), *It's Alive* (1974) and *It Lives Again* (1978), *The Omen* (1976) and *Damien – Omen II* (1978), *Carrie* (1976), *Martin* (1977), *The Fury* (1978) and *The Brood* (1979). The family itself is the collective monster in such films as *Frightmare* (1974) and *The Hills Have Eyes* (1977); and the home becomes the deadliest of traps in *Burnt Offerings* (1976) and *Full Circle* (1977). The overwhelming impression given by the best of these films is of a dark fantasy on the theme of Ken Loach's hard-hitting social drama *Family Life* (1971), in which her family and collusive authorities pressurize an independent-minded young woman into a mental home.

The new film-student generation of film-makers seems to have been particularly attracted to fantasy forms. The result has been innovation and exploration, but also a notable amount of homage to the cinematic past. Understandably, Hitchcock is the key influence, both in his identification mechanisms and in the various suspense techniques. The most stylistically self-conscious of the new directors are Brian De Palma, Steven Spielberg and John Carpenter. De Palma especially seems constantly to be remaking old Hitchcock films, heightening the Hitchcockian elements of style into delirious parody. The best of his films is probably *Sisters* (1972), derived from *Psycho* (1960), but his most ambitious project was the spectacular but misogynistic *Carrie*, in which a young girl's coming to

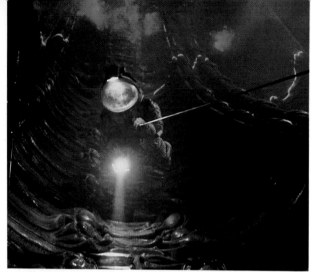

womanhood coincides with her development of destructive powers.

Spielberg began his career in features with small-scale but scary television movies: *Something Evil* (1971) is an assured Gothic horror tale with Sandy Dennis; and *Duel* (1971), with an excellent Richard Matheson screenplay, involves a motorist who finds himself menaced by an unseen but murderous truck-driver in a monstrous juggernaut. This is a simple, though terrifying, articulation of his favourite theme, the ordinary man in extraordinary circumstances. *Jaws* is on an altogether bigger scale, poised with great commercial acumen between straight thriller, monster movie and the disaster genre in its tale of a marauding shark. It

---

Children, sharks, ghosts, even truck-drivers could be a source of supernatural fear and menace in movies that touched on raw nerves

---

utilizes Hitchcockian detail, suspense and shock tactics with outstanding assurance; it is regrettable that the film's sexual undercurrents are so firmly directed against women.

John Carpenter is basically a frustrated old-time studio contract director. As if to stress the B-feature origins of cinematic science fiction, he dismantles the whole elaborate machinery of such space operas as *2001* in the glorious genre romp *Dark Star* (1974). In his hands, the genre has the intimacy and imagination of a good George Pal production, such as *The Time Machine*. Carpenter's two horror thrillers, *Assault on Precinct 13* (1976) and *Halloween* (1978), invoking respectively the worlds of Howard Hawks and Alfred Hitchcock, are among the most sheerly terrifying films ever made, turning the human attackers in each film into deeply disturbing monsters. *The Fog* (1980) is a straight horror picture, showing the return of a ghostly shipwrecked crew to wreak vengeance upon the descendants of their murderers. Embodiments of deep guilt, the ghouls stagger out of the luminous fog in a movie that itself summons up the ghost of the delicate, brooding intensity of Val Lewton's RKO horror productions in the Forties.

Carpenter is one of several newer directors whose movies have been made at a fraction of the cost of the average Seventies Hollywood product. His films still look quite polished, though, compared to the tacky, small-budget productions of such directors as David Cronenberg, Larry Cohen and George Romero. The least interesting of these three directors is Canadian David Cronenberg, whose *The Parasite Murders* (1975, released in Britain as

Shivers), *Rabid* (1977) and *The Brood* reveal beneath their squalid nastiness an immature attitude towards sexuality and a misogynistic tendency as pronounced as Brian De Palma's.

Larry Cohen and George Romero, on the other hand, make horror films which suggest progressive political attitudes. Cohen's *It's Alive* and *It Lives Again* manipulate images of the home with a creepy accuracy as they relate the stories of mutant babies on the rampage. *Demon* (1976) has been criticized as muddled on the level of sexual politics because of its treatment of the dual-sexed villain; but it ingeniously combines detective movie, science fiction and horror to attack the repressiveness of organized religion.

Romero's brand of political horror is demonstrated by such films as *The Crazies* (1973), about a small rural community fighting back in reaction to being accidentally contaminated with a germ-warfare bug, and *Dawn of the Dead* (1979, released in Britain as *Zombies*), a grim parody of consumerism involving a small group trapped within a huge hypermarket by hordes of flesh-eating zombies. The black sense of humour running through these films surfaces most distinctly in *Martin*, a vampire film that merely *refers* to the genre conventions as it concentrates upon the theme of sexual repression. Its use of a depressing contemporary suburban location to create atmosphere and its poetic conciseness in exploring Martin's pathological disturbance make it one of the finest films of the Seventies in any genre.

In science fiction of the Seventies, the director is by no means the only effective creator of such films

Top left: the dead captain (Joe Saunders) of a spacecraft is kept on ice for his brain's advice. Top: a space patrol explores the entrails of a strange planet and picks up from it a deadly Alien. *Centre:* Star Trek – The Motion Picture *deploys more elaborate technology than did the TV series. Above: publicity material for* Battlestar Galactica, *a TV spin-off starring Lorne Greene as Adama*

WESTWORLD

METRO-GOLDWYN-MAYER "WESTWORLD." YUL BRYNNER RICHARD BENJAMIN JAMES BROL...

10 SECONDS.
The Pain Begins.

15 SECONDS.
You Can't Breathe.

20 SECONDS.
You Explode.

SCANNERS

...Their thoughts can kill!

PIERRE DAVID and VICTOR SOLNICKI present DAVID CRONENBERG's SCANNERS starring JENNIFER O'NEILL STEPHEN LACK PATRICK McGOOHAN LAWRENCE DANE MICHAEL IRONSIDE produced by VICTOR SOLNICKI PIERRE DAVID executive producer CLAUDE HEROUX music by HOWARD SHORE written and directed by DAVID CRONENBERG A FILMPLAN INTERNATIONAL PRODUCTION AVCO EMBASSY PICTURES Release

heads, in a futuristic world that denies love or personal identity, reveal a really inventive use of cinema and the genre. Crichton, originally a medical doctor and a novelist, has singlemindedly pursued the theme of dehumanization by technology. He wrote the novels upon which are based the excellent *The Andromeda Strain* (1971) and *The Terminal Man* (1974), and he scripted and directed both *Westworld* (1973) and *Coma* (1978). *Westworld* remains his masterpiece, a highly inventive vision of an eerie adult Disney World which strips away male power fantasies through allowing his protagonists to indulge in re-enacting the myths of the West with robot figures.

Outside the USA and Canada, fantasy has been well represented, although on a smaller scale. From Italy, for example, Dario Argento came out with *Suspiria* (1977), a stylish horror film about demonism in a music college which plays on genre conventions and suspense mechanisms in a fasci-

---

Maybe filmgoers needed cinematic shocks to help them cope with real life in a disaster-prone decade

---

Above: two brothers fight a mental duel to the death as they struggle for control of each other's brain, with the fate of the world at stake, in David Cronenberg's Scanners *(1981). Top:* The Fog *comes to a Californian town, bringing with it the vengeful ghosts of sailors whose ship had been deliberately wrecked a century before. Top right: the robots of* Westworld *strike back when their control system goes wrong and they cease to be mere victims of holiday-makers pretending to be Western gunslingers*

as *Battlestar Galactica, Star Wars, Close Encounters of the Third Kind, Star Trek* and *Alien*. With new techniques in miniature photography, computer-linked cameras and automatic systems of mattes, special-effects teams led by such talented people as John Dykstra, Douglas Trumbull and Carlo Rambaldi provided the highly believable physical embodiment of the writers' visions. These manufactured dreams are heady indeed, and their formidable nature seems very much to be the implicit subject of *Star Wars, The Empire Strikes Back* and the last forty-five minutes of *Close Encounters of the Third Kind*. The former pair reduce the rich philosophical possibilities of science fiction to a galactic pinball game; and *Close Encounters of the Third Kind*, despite throwing up ideas on the urban nightmare, is ultimately dependent upon its thunderous conclusion, where the dumbstruck extras stand in for the audience's quasi-mystical experience in watching the film.

Two directors whose names have been especially linked with science fiction in the Seventies are George Lucas and Michael Crichton. Lucas, despite his later epics, will perhaps be most kindly remembered for his first feature *THX 1138* (1970). Its abstract images of white chambers and shaved

nating way. Roman Polanski's French movie *Le Locataire* (1976, *The Tenant*) is a horrific tale of loneliness and the bizarre illusions that can lurk beneath deadpan urban existence. Australian director Peter Weir's *The Cars That Ate Paris* (1974) is a consumer fantasy about a community that survives by crashing strangers' cars and then cannibalizing the wreckage.

The Russian Andrei Tarkovsky's coolly abstract and metaphysical *Solaris* (1972) portrays an alien planet's ability to manifest visitors' unconscious desires. There is an electric atmosphere generated by some images, but as the critic David Thomson has commented: 'An episode of *Star Trek* explored this theme with more wit and ingenuity, less sentimentality and a third the length.'

It was an error for Tarkovsky to have attempted to follow *2001*, a cinematic cul-de-sac, especially with a less dramatic use of decor and technology. Kubrick's film may have given fantasy a new respectability; but the way ahead paradoxically proved to be in the backward glance, sometimes with great self-consciousness, at the styles and iconography of an earlier Hollywood – yesterday's dreams and nightmares reassessed in the light of the troubled Seventies.

Riding Easy

For a star, Jack Nicholson has some surprisingly un-starlike qualities. He will take a minor role as soon as a starring one, merely for the challenge; he won't ask the salary he is worth if he knows the picture is of limited appeal; he will take parts out of a desire to work with a specific director or as a favour to a friend; and he dislikes publicity. Yet, it is just this sort of non-conformity that has made each of his performances to date so appealing

Jack Nicholson

No-one would dispute Jack Nicholson's right to stardom. He has two Oscars, the reputation for being hard to reach and is reluctant to give interviews – no matter that he might be bumped into at a neighbourhood restaurant or basketball game. As a box-office personality he has had several big hits that have pushed his salary very close to the top level.

Yet the casual, low-down mood of B pictures still hangs over him. He can be unshaven, shabby or downright unwholesome on screen – and he never comes near the monolithic glamour of Robert Redford or Clint Eastwood – but he is a most droll sexual rascal, as knowing as he is familiar and as likely to eat up a woman

Below: Jack Nicholson as the drifter in Rafelson's Five Easy Pieces, *seen here with two of the girls at the bowling-alley.*
Below right: with Bruce Dern as the brothers Staebler in The King of Marvin Gardens

as he could the camera. As a movie lover he goes all the way in terms of emotional commitment. He knows how absurd love is, but nothing deters him from its compulsion. Nicholson has never been tied down by the anxious self-esteem that limits Burt Reynolds. He is a very relaxed person and a truly romantic actor, always in search of extremes: death or ecstasy – the twin destinies of the B picture.

Other results of his low-budget background are that he believes in some pictures more than others; that he is rarely content to be a bankable star; and that the allegiances he formed in the Sixties still affect his choices of work. It is very difficult to think of a Nicholson film from the Seventies that is impersonal and unadventurous, and easy exploitation of his stardom doesn't move him much. He wants to shape his projects and be more deeply involved in things than is the case with most actors, and

the path he has taken is an example of how often the B-picture revival of the late Sixties was a breeding ground for people who were not just drug- or bike-crazy, but mad about movies too.

Born in New Jersey in 1937, Jack Nicholson had a difficult early life. His father was an alcoholic who left home before Jack was born, and his mother had to go into business to support the family. Never happy or occupied in high school, he drifted to Los Angeles in the late Fifties, one of the many who fancied being the next James Dean. He found a job in the cartoons department at MGM and took classes at the Jeff Corey acting school.

Sex and drugs and . . .

Over the next ten years Nicholson knocked around Hollywood, experimented with his life and did more hustling than most of his contemporaries. He married actress Sandra

Knight, had a daughter and divorced. He played around with motorbikes and drugs, and as far as work was concerned he was ready for whatever the low-budget director Roger Corman – or anyone else – could toss his way. His movies during this period included *The Cry-Baby Killer* (1958), *Too Soon to Love*, *The Little Shop of Horrors*, *Studs Lonigan* (all 1960), *The Trip*, *Hell's Angels on Wheels* (both 1967) and *Psych-Out* (1968).

The last two were directed by Richard Rush, who has finally received belated recognition for the stylish, camp existentialism of *The Stunt Man* (1980). Nicholson's work with Rush is a testament to his habit of working with odd, interesting people. Time and again he has found a special creative rapport with directors, and in the Sixties he managed this with both Monte Hellman and Bob Rafelson.

The ones that got away
Nicholson went to the Philippines with Hellman to make two back-to-back quickies – *Back Door to Hell* (1964) and *Flight to Fury* (1965). Those films are now only marginally harder to see than two intriguing, cryptic, sparse and beautiful Westerns they made together, *The Shooting* and *Ride in the Whirlwind* (both 1966).

Nicholson actually wrote the latter film, the clearest early sign of his ambition to be involved in the conception and creation of pictures. He has already directed twice – the excellent *Drive, He Said* (1971), about a college basketball star dodging military service, and *Goin' South* (1978), the story of a reforming outlaw – and while neither was a commercial success, it is probable that he will direct more as his looks match the raddled middle-age he tried out so thoroughly in *The Shining* (1980).

Raving with Rafelson
Bob Rafelson was a fellow-spirit, scornful of the old Hollywood. He and Nicholson have now worked together four times and are as close as, say, François Truffaut and Jean-Pierre Léaud. Rafelson was part inventor and owner of The Monkees, a pop group fashioned on the principle that any four kids with unkempt hair could be a rave for a year or so. With Nicholson as co-author, Rafelson made *Head* (1968), a surreal farce starring The Monkees, one of the best portraits of Sixties' lyrical anarchy. Thereafter, under Rafelson's direction, Nicholson did two diverse pieces of work that remain the best display of his acting versatility. In *Five Easy Pieces* (1970) he plays Bobby Dupea, a rough-

Nicholson as the lawyer who gives it all up for the life of a drifter in Easy Rider *(above, far left); as the boy who murders the men who beat him up in* The Cry-Baby Killer *(above left); and as the private eye hired by the mystery woman (Faye Dunaway) in* Chinatown *(above)*

neck oil-rigger who is actually a refugee from an earnest, musical family. The movie is a study of the thin line between liberty and irresponsibility, and it is a vital expression of Nicholson's equal interests in art and work and the life of outlaw sensuality.

Rafelson's *The King of Marvin Gardens* (1972) is a further exploration of the same theme. Nicholson and another old buddy, Bruce Dern, play the Staebler brothers. Nicholson depicts a lonely, introverted host on late-night radio: the artist as depressive, hoping to crystallize life's anguish, but despairing of his own happiness. Brother Dern is another kind of artist, a

Below left: Nicholson plays a sailor who decides to give a recruit a night to remember before being jailed for thieving in The Last Detail. *Below: looning around with the inmates in* One Flew Over the Cuckoo's Nest

Above: Nicholson displays that famous demonic leer as the dangerous but exciting lover of three bored suburban women in The Witches of Eastwick.
Below right: not a face to come home to – Nicholson as Jack Torrance in The Shining

relentlessly extrovert huckster who has crazy plans for a gambling kingdom in Hawaii. The balance of manic and depressive leads to a sharper tragedy than *Five Easy Pieces* offered, and *The King of Marvin Gardens* was too harsh for a big audience. It remains a masterpiece and the most deeply felt and self-effacing performance Nicholson has yet given.

However, those films were made in the wake of *Easy Rider* (1969) in which he had really made his mark. When Rip Torn refused to do the movie after a row with producer/star Peter Fonda and director/star Dennis Hopper, they cast Nicholson as the disillusioned young lawyer who tags along on the trip. It is probable that the enormous popularity of the movie owed much to Nicholson. He plays the sort of character a middle-class audience could identify with if it were to go along with the motorized vagrancy of the road.

Nicholson's new status allowed him to pick his parts more carefully in the Seventies. *On a Clear Day You Can See Forever* (1970) is the only unaccountable choice: a result of his financial need and a studio's forlorn attempt to reach the young audience. *Carnal Knowledge* (1971) came from a wish to work with the director Mike Nichols, and it was a highly profitable movie that established the actor as a model for many American sexual drives and disorders.

Flying high
Also in the Seventies, Nicholson was the figurehead of two unerringly commercial movies. *Chinatown* (1974), in which a Los Angeles private eye sets out on a seemingly simple case, was not a great risk, but it showed how fully Nicholson was the heir to Humphrey Bogart and John Garfield – an actor flawed with the dismay of *film noir*, however robust he may seem. *Chinatown* also enabled him to stand as a helpless victim of love and paranoia: though set in the Thirties, the film is utterly

modern in its politics. *One Flew Over the Cuckoo's Nest* (1975) was a more daring project, and Nicholson was probably the most negotiable element in the film. His raffish charm as MacMurphy, imprisoned in an insane asylum for rape, made the madman appealing; his anger moved audiences all over the world. The film was a triumph, despite MacMurphy's death. Significantly, Nicholson dies or fails on screen more often than any other star.

Despite these commercial departures, Nicholson's urge to experiment was not exhausted. Henry Jaglom's *A Safe Place* (1971) is a very personal, poetic film that was only made because of Nicholson's wish to help an old friend. *The Last Detail* (1973), in which Nicholson plays a naval officer escorting a prisoner to jail, is more middle-of-the-road, but *Professione: Reporter* (1975, *The Passenger*) was proof of Nicholson's undiminished appetite for challenge. Its director, Michelangelo An-

tonioni, is notoriously aloof from his actors, and the movie is patently esoteric, with all its emphasis on space, colour and identity. Yet Nicholson adapted very well to the fresh idiom, grasping the fatalism of the reporter who has a brief reprieve from stagnation when he takes on the identity of a dead man. It took Marlon Brando in *The Missouri Breaks* (1976) to make Nicholson look overawed, despite his brave attempt to stand up to the aggressively brilliant and versatile star. However, he did contribute to this very underrated picaresque Western, and seemed to learn from it for his own *Goin' South*.

Twinkle, twinkle, little star
In 1980 he gave one of his most daring performances as Jack Torrance in Stanley Kubrick's *The Shining*. The film and his playing received a mixed reception, some accusing Nicholson of over-acting. Yet *The Shining* was a comedy, not a horror movie, and no-one understood its dainty command of fantasy better than the actor. It remains the most bravura display of Nicholson's mastery of style and parody.

In the Eighties, Nicholson's persona has moved in a slightly new direction, concentrating on romance – but always with a Nicholson twist. He has starred opposite some of the most powerful women on the screen of the period – Jessica Lange (*The Postman Always Rings Twice*, 1981), Shirley Maclaine (*Terms of Endearment*, 1983 – for which he won his second Oscar), Kathleen Turner (*Prizzi's Honor*, 1985) and Meryl Streep (*Heartburn*, 1986). But his lovers are never straightforward and his romances never easy – there is always a twisted, almost psychotic, character waiting in the wings.

Prizzi's Honor, which cast him and Turner as two hit-men, trying to have an affair between assignments, makes the ultimate comment on Nicholson as a romantic hero. Violence and murder are inextricably intertwined in the Nicholson persona with sex, or even love, and it is this tension that makes his films ultimately so challenging. *The Witches of Eastwick* (1987) once again combines evil and lust in a comedy about a genteel back-water of the United States with Nicholson happily going over-the-top this time as yet another deranged lover.

Filmography
1958 The Cry-Baby Killer. '60 Too Soon to Love; Studs Lonigan; The Little Shop of Horrors; The Wild Ride. '62 The Broken Land. '63 The Raven; The Terror (+ add. dir, uncredited); Thunder Island (co-sc. only). '64 Ensign Pulver; Back Door to Hell (USA-PHIL). '65 Flight to Fury (+sc) (USA-PHIL). '66 The Shooting (+ co-prod); Ride in the Whirlwind (+ co-prod; + sc). '67 Hell's Angels on Wheels; The St. Valentine's Day Massacre; The Trip (sc. only). '68 Psych-Out; Head (+ co-prod; + co-sc). '69 Easy Rider (+ add. ed, uncredited). '70 Rebel Rousers; On a Clear Day You Can See Forever; Five Easy Pieces. '71 Drive, He Said (dir; +co-prod; + co-sc. only); Carnal Knowledge; A Safe Place. '72 The King of Marvin Gardens. '73 The Last Detail. '74 Chinatown. '75 Tommy (GB); Professione: Reporter (USA/GB: The Passenger) (SP-IT-FR); The Fortune; One Flew Over the Cuckoo's Nest. '76 The Missouri Breaks; The Last Tycoon. '78 Goin' South (+dir); '80 The Shining (GB). '81 The Postman Always Rings Twice. '82 The Border. '83 Terms of Endearment. '85 Prizzi's Honor. '86 Heartburn. '87 Ironweed; The Witches of Eastwick; Broadcast News.

The trouble with Harry...

. . . is that he tends to get into things over his head, into professional situations that viciously rebound on his private life. Harry Caul that is, or Harry Moseby, or indeed any of the middle-aged, menopausal males superbly portrayed on the American screen by Gene Hackman – one of the most relevant of modern superstars

For most moviegoers the first conscious encounter with Gene Hackman came with his portrayal of Buck Barrow, Clyde's elder brother in *Bonnie and Clyde* (1967), though he had previously played small roles in such films as *Lilith* (1964) and *Hawaii* (1966). But however impressive his performance as Buck Barrow was, it would have taken an act of clairvoyance to predict that Hackman would become a major box-office star of the Seventies, ranking as high as third in world popularity in 1972.

In appearance Hackman has always seemed middle-aged and his looks might best be described as 'everyday'. His face was never going to make his fortune in a business peopled by Newmans, Redfords and McQueens . . . or was it? Perhaps because Hollywood heroes of the Sixties were traditionally cast from the blue-eyed, blond-haired mould, a bulkier figure and more mature face like Hackman's would stand out from the crowd. Even so, under the old Hollywood star system, this ex-marine – 6ft. 2in. and weighing over 200lbs – would have found himself restricted to 'character' parts rather than top-lining roles such as 'Popeye' Doyle in William Friedkin's *The French Connection* (1971), the part that made him a star.

Because he arrived in Hollywood at the moment when the old studio system was breaking up, Hackman could see that casting was becoming more fluid, that 'types' mattered less than talent, and that a man who was heading for middle age – he was 37 when he appeared in *Bonnie and Clyde* – was not necessarily condemned to playing character parts.

Just an ordinary guy
At the outset his 'ordinary man' image enabled him to keep comfortably in work over the four years that separated *Bonnie and Clyde* from *The*

French Connection. Later Francis Ford Coppola was to say of his casting of Hackman in *The Conversation* (1974):

'Hackman was ideal for this role because of his utterly everyday appearance, the most important feature of the character.'

Hackman himself calls the films of this pre-stardom phase 'forgettable' but the period contains two performances of distinction by him – the ski-team trainer in Michael Ritchie's

Above: Hackman as a man whose impending marriage to his girl (Elizabeth Hubbard) is threatened by his cantankerous widowed dad in I Never Sang for My Father. *Top left: as Harry Moseby up to his neck trying to rescue a runaway girl (Melanie Griffith) who has just discovered the corpse of her lover in* Night Moves. *Top right: as a boorish Southern husband in* Lilith, *an asylum drama with Warren Beatty and Jessica Walter*

Above: Hackman in his Oscar-winning role of 'Popeye' Doyle, grimly intent on getting his man in The French Connection. *Right: as a priest saving souls from sea disaster in* The Poseidon Adventure, *with Pamela Sue Martin*

Downhill Racer (1969) and the middle-aged son who has to look after an elderly father (Melvyn Douglas) in *I Never Sang for My Father* (1970).

Eugene Hackman's own relations with his father were disrupted in his mid-teens when his parents were divorced; his mother brought him up in Danville, Illinois. The biographical detail at this point is almost identical to that supplied by the scriptwriter Alan Sharp for the character of Harry Moseby in Arthur Penn's *Night Moves* (1975), for many Hackman's finest screen performance. In 1946 Hackman lied about his age (which was 16) and got into the Marines. It was an experience that would serve him well physically in the business of being a star of action pictures like *The French Connection* and *French Connection II* (1975). After being discharged he took odd jobs and small parts in theatre and TV until he gradually carved himself a niche in Hollywood.

Hackman's method

On his approach to acting Hackman is quite candid. He told an interviewer in *Films in Review*:

'There's something of me in all the roles I play. It's finding this little something of you in the character and developing it. That's the art of acting.'

It may not be a profound definition perhaps, but it is a clear-headed and conscientious attitude to the business of creating a character as distinct from the mystification often indulged by actors talking of their craft. Hackman admits that he will think constantly about a new role for days but he does not 'become' the character. 'I live with him', he avers.

In the early Fifties when he was playing in summer stock and still ten years away from Hollywood, he used to watch Marlon Brando. In an interview in *Film Comment* he said:

'Really, I think I began in this profession because of Brando. I saw in Brando a kind of kinship, not because of his appearance, but because of something in his performance which made me think "I can do that". I'm sure that's why he has so many followers. People

see in Brando a kind of strength which can at the same time be an everyday approach to life.'

By 1978 Hackman had his name just beneath Brando's on the billing for *Superman, The Movie*.

To trace the run up to Hackman's 'arrival' with *The French Connection* is to discover a subtle alternating of sympathetic roles – for example, Buck Barrow and the stranded astronaut in *Marooned* (1969) – with downright unpleasant parts such as the gangleader in *Riot* (1968) and the corrupt cop in *Cisco Pike* (1971). Thus by the time he was cast in *The French Connection* his screen image, insofar as it existed in the mind of the moviegoer, was a decidedly ambiguous one. No-one could be sure whether 'Popeye' Doyle was a good guy or a bad guy. And that was the strength of his characterization.

Required to play a tough and streetwise cop on the trail of narcotics smugglers, Hackman served 'an apprenticeship' in Harlem with Eddie Egan, the real-life detective on whose exploits the source novel was based. 'It was scary as hell', Hackman told *Time* magazine. In the movie Hackman borrowed tricks from Egan such as shoving a suspect into a telephone booth to subdue him. He also did most of the hair-raising driving in *The French Connection* and constantly refused to have a double for action scenes. Asked what he thought of 'Popeye' Doyle's morality, Hackman made clear his broadly liberal politics:

'Most cops like the idea of a movie showing something of the reality they know, with a hero who is a very right-wing conservative – shit, let's be honest, Doyle is a fascist.'

Though the actor may choose to distance himself from the role, the sense of isolation that allowed Doyle to say 'Never trust a nigger. Never trust anyone' became a key feature of the Hackman screen persona. It was a stance that would alienate that persona further and consolidate the image of a loner that *The Conversation* and *Night Moves* would exploit to such advantage in the Hackman roles of Harry Caul and Harry Moseby respectively.

In the interim, however, there were three

films that variously extended the public's awareness of Hackman as a major star. *The Poseidon Adventure* (1972) saw him as a somewhat unothodox priest attempting to save people caught in the submerged ship but who insisted on helping 'winners not quitters'. In *Scarecrow* (1973) he played the egotistical tramp who dreams of running his own carwash. In *Zandy's Bride* (1974), opposite Liv Ullmann, he was a brutal, self-centred husband.

Private hell

The Conversation involves the lacing together of sounds and images from a conversation overheard by a professional eavesdropper who has picked up on a murder. The tables are turned in the course of the film and it is the 'bugger's' – Harry Caul's – privacy that is suddenly invaded, rendering him finally more paranoid than everyone else. The appearance of this movie at the time of Watergate was crucial to

Below left: 'Popeye' Doyle still pursuing a heroin czar in French Connection II. *Below: a glimpse of the public life of Secretary of Defense David Brice (Gene Hackman) in the thriller* No Way Out

Above left: in Zandy's Bride *Hackman is a Californian farmer who maltreats the wife (Liv Ullmann) he buys from a newspaper ad. Above right: 'Harry Caul' discusses* The Conversation *with Francis Ford Coppola*

more physical exertions as he raced a motor-boat along the Marseilles waterfront and simulated 'cold turkey' in an underworld cell. For a change of image Hackman accepted the role of Major Foster, an American in the French Foreign Legion, in *March or Die* (1977). He remained in uniform for a small role – earning himself a small fortune – in Joseph E. Levine's colossal *A Bridge Too Far* (1977).

Then Hackman found new strength as a character actor in a variety of roles, producing a comic villain in *Superman, The Movie* (1978) and its sequels, a hack journalist in Nicaragua in *Under Fire* (1983) and a drunken media man on his way down the ladder in Sidney Lumet's *Power* (1986).

But he has also developed his other persona as a sort of older and gentler 'Popeye' Doyle who now has to cope with the personal crises of middle age. In *Target* (1985), co-starring Matt Dillon, and *Twice in a Lifetime* (1986), with Ellen Burstyn and Ann-Margret, he has moved into family-based dramas – one dealing with his relationship with his son, the other with the problems that arise when a new love threatens his marriage. But it was back again to his more established drama for *No Way Out* (1987), a conspiratorial thriller with Hackman superb as a Secretary of Defense who has accidentally killed his mistress. Clearly he is still an all-round actor capable of a wide diversity of roles.

its success but the casting of the 44-year-old Hackman is also an essential factor. In his face and through his obsessive but outwardly normal behaviour, Hackman suggests the anxiety of the menopausal male who 'gets in over his head' and is bugged by his own technology. His portrayal of Harry Caul stands as a personification of the fear and loneliness at the heart of all the American conspirators in the mid-Seventies – not just Nixon's men but the CIA men and the big businessmen whose 'dirty tricks' were coming into the open.

To follow such a consummately low-key performance with that of the middle-aged private-eye in *Night Moves* was for Hackman a question of merging one 'Harry' into the next. In *Night Moves* Harry Moseby is hired to find the daughter of a movie mogul's widow. All around him things are collapsing, including his marriage, or becoming distorted – the missing-person job becomes a murder and larceny case – but Moseby appears to be

muddling through until he realizes that he is in over his head and that there is no way out of the twists and turns of the plot. Hackman's characterization is built on a series of shifts from tenderness to blind anger, clear-sightedness to confusion, suggesting that Moseby's ambivalence would have been well suited to the tense and uncertain world of Forties *film noir*.

Mainline connections

Around the time of *Night Moves* Hackman contributed a brilliant cameo to Mel Brooks' *Young Frankenstein* (1974) – he was a blind old man who welcomes the monster into his pathetic home only to spill boiling soup inadvertently into the creature's lap. *Bite the Bullet* (1975) saw him as a disillusioned cowboy entering an endurance horserace with his rival (James Coburn). *French Connection II*, directed by John Frankenheimer, had Hackman back as 'Popeye' Doyle, put through even

Filmography
1961 Mad Dog Coll. '64 Lilith. '66 Hawaii. '67 A Covenant With Death; First to Fight; Banning; Bonnie and Clyde. '68 The Split; Riot. '69 The Gypsy Moths; Downhill Racer; Marooned. '70 I Never Sang for My Father. '71 Doctors' Wives; Confrontation (short); The Hunting Party; The French Connection; Cisco Pike. '72 Prime Cut; The Poseidon Adventure. '73 Scarecrow. '74 The Conversation; Zandy's Bride; Young Franken-stein. '75 Night Moves; Bite the Bullet; French Connection II; Lucky Lady. '77 The Domino Principle (GB: The Domino Killings); A Look at Liv (doc) (appearance as himself only); A Bridge Too Far; March or Die. '78 Superman, The Movie; Formula 1, Febbre della Velocità/Speed Fever (doc) (appearance as himself only) (IT). '80 Superman II. '81 All Night Long. '83 Eureka (GB-USA); Under Fire; Uncommon Valor. '84 Misunderstood. '85 Target. '86 Power; Twice in a Lifetime; Hoosiers (GB: Best Shot). '87 Superman IV: Quest for Peace; No Way Out. '88 BAT – 21; Full Moon in Blue Water; Split Decisions.

Michael Cimino's HEAVEN'S GATE

KRIS KRISTOFFERSON in MICHAEL CIMINO'S 'HEAVEN'S GATE'
CO-STARRING CHRISTOPHER WALKEN · JOHN HURT · SAM WATERSTON · BRAD DOURIF
ISABELLE HUPPERT · JOSEPH COTTEN · JEFF BRIDGES
MUSIC BY DAVID MANSFIELD · DIRECTOR OF PHOTOGRAPHY VILMOS ZSIGMOND A.S.C. · PRODUCED BY JOANN CARELLI · WRITTEN AND DIRECTED BY MICHAEL CIMINO
DOLBY STEREO · TECHNICOLOR® · ORIGINAL MOTION PICTURE SOUNDTRACK ON LIBERTY RECORDS AND TAPES · United Artists A Transamerica Company

Directed by Michael Cimino, 1980

Prod co: United Artists. **exec prod:** Denis O'Dell, Charles Okun. **prod:** Joann Carelli. **sc:** Michael Cimino. **photo** (Technicolor): Vilmos Zsigmond. **sp eff:** Paul Stewart, Ken Pepiot, Stan Parks, Sam Price, Jim Camomile, Kevin Quimbell, Tom Burman, Tom Hoerber. **ed:** Tom Rolf, William Reynolds, Lisa Fruchtman, Gerald Greenberg. **art dir:** Tambi Larsen, Spencer Deverill, Maurice Fowler. **set dec:** Jim Berkey, Josie MacAvin. **cost:** Allen Highfill. **chor:** Eleanor Fazan. **mus:** David Mansfield, Joann Carelli. **add mus:** 'The Blue Danube' performed by The New York Philharmonic Orchestra conducted by Leonard Bernstein. **sd:** James J. Klinger, Richard W. Adams, Winston Ryder, Darin Knight. **ass dir:** Michael Grillo, Brian Cook. **prod man:** Charles Okun, Bob Grand, Peter Price. **r/t:** 148 mins.
Cast: Kris Kristofferson (*Averill*), Christopher Walken (*Champion*), John Hurt (*Irvine*), Sam Waterston (*Canton*), Brad Dourif (*Mr Eggleston*), Isabelle Huppert (*Ella*), Joseph Cotton (*The Reverend Doctor*), Jeff Bridges (*John H. Bridges*), Roseanne Vela (*beautiful girl*), Ronnie Hawkins (*Wolcott*), Geoffrey Lewis (*trapper*), Nicholas Woodeson (*small man*), Stefan Shcherby (*big man*), Waldemar Kalinowski (*photographer*), Terry Quinn (*Captain Minardi*), John Conley (*Morrison*), Margaret Benczak (*Mrs Eggleston*), James Knobeloch (*Kopestonsky*), Erika Petersen (*Mrs Kopestonsky*), Paul Koslo (*Major Lezak*), Robin Bartlett (*Mrs Lezak*), Tom Noonan (*Jake*), Marat Yusim (*Russian merchant*), Aivars Smits (*Mr Kovach*), Gordana Rashovich (*Mrs Kovach*), Neil Wilson (*Kovach's son*).

Heaven's Gate has become one of the most controversial movies of the last decade, earning comments ranging from 'the event we have been waiting for' to 'an unqualified disaster'. This lavish, epic Western, directed by Michael Cimino, relates the story of the Johnson County Wars – the attempted massacre in Wyoming in 1892 of immigrant small farmers by the wealthy Stock Grower's Association. But the film received such harsh criticism that it was withdrawn from cinemas to be re-edited after only a few days of showing.

The Johnson County War, as the original script was known, was written by Cimino nearly ten years before the film was made. It was only after the enormous financial and critical success of *The Deer Hunter* (1978) – the film that won Cimino an Oscar – that backing was forthcoming. Hollywood was delighted by the new generation of directors and their money-spinning ventures and were prepared to take risks believing it could bring in more profit. United Artists beat Warner Brothers in the race to back Cimino at an initial costing of $7.5 million. Rewriting increased the budget considerably but even the first version of the film cost over $36 million, making it one of the most expensive films ever made.

Cimino is wholeheartedly committed to visual authenticity and spared no costs in re-creating nineteenth-century America. He scoured the country looking for old-fashioned craftsmen. He brought in contemporary firearms and even transported an ancient locomotive miles across country, re-routing it to avoid the smaller, modern railway tunnels. To achieve the large and spectacular crowd scenes, he trained numerous extras to skate, waltz and handle firearms and horses. As a result the look of the film is sumptuous.

United Artists executives began to worry about the escalating costs and Cimino's inability to stick to a shooting schedule. But they believed that the finished product would be worth it and were as unprepared as Cimino for the critical onslaught that the original three-and-a-half hour film received. Pauline Kael wrote in *The New Yorker*:

'I thought it was easy to see what to cut. But when I tried afterward to think of what to *keep* my mind went blank.'

The critics argued that the film's narrative was too complicated to follow, that the extravagant set-pieces were pretentious and the heavy financial outlay purely self-indulgent. The re-edited version (75 minutes shorter) was, however, shown at the Cannes Film Festival and was favourably received by the European press. And it is in Europe that United Artists hope to rescue the film's reputation – and budget.

Finance was not the only problem to beset the production: fighting on the set and an animal lovers' boycott added to the difficulties. Even its factual reliability has been questioned. Some historians have suggested that only two people were killed in the war and that certainly Averill, Champion and Ella played very different roles in real life. Although obsessed with the visual authenticity of a film Cimino is no great stickler for historical accuracy: he defended the Russian-roulette scene in *The Deer Hunter* on the grounds that it was an excellent metaphor for the game of death that war forces men to play. Similarly the events and characters of *Heaven's Gate* represent the process through which a new ruling-class emerged in America after the confusion of the Civil War. The long opening sequence of the Harvard graduation ceremony, the pompous speeches and elaborate newly-found traditions, set the scene, playing an equivalent role to the wedding in *The Deer Hunter*. It locates the action that follows against the aspirations and ideals of America's wealthier families. Averill and Irvine, both representatives of their class, go West. Irvine reluctantly sides with the Association who have the implicit backing of the government but Averill betrays his origins, siding with the immigrant community.

Heaven's Gate is, in the end, a classic Western confrontation between heroes and villains, with the difference that the film is solidly on the side of the poor immigrant farmers. This bias caused the French magazine *Liberation* to call *Heaven's Gate* 'the first socialist Western'.

2

3

James Averill and Billy Irvine, two of the 1870 class of Harvard University (1), join in the dancing, drunkeness and rituals that attend the graduation ceremony.

Twenty years later Averill (2) returns to Casper, Wyoming (3) after a visit East, and is surprised to find the town crowded with poverty-stricken immigrants looking for work, and is worried to find Association members drawing clothes and arms on the Stock Grower's Association's account. Visiting the Association's club house he meets Irvine, who reveals the existence of a death-list consisting of the names of 125 small-holders and poor settlers in Johnson County that the wealthy cattle barons want to 'eliminate'.

Back in Sweetwater, the main town of Johnson County where he is the federal lawman, Averill delivers a birthday present of a pony and trap to Ella (4), the madam of the local brothel, with whom both Averill and Nathan D. Champion, the Association's local hired-gun, are in love.

After a roller-skating birthday party (5) at Heaven's Gate, Sweetwater's community centre, Averill tries to persuade Ella to leave the County for safety. The next day he publicly reveals the names on the death-list, among which Ella's name appears.

Champion asks Ella to marry him and she accepts. Averill accuses Champion of knowing about the death-list but Champion breaks his affiliation with the Association by killing one of the leaders.

The Association's hired gang of killers are converging on Sweetwater. Ella is nearly raped by members of the gang, but although Averill saves her he arrives too late to stop her girls from being brutally murdered. Champion (6) is also killed by Association men.

The citizens of Sweetwater panic and wildly attack the gang (7), killing many of them including Irvine (8). With Averill's help they organize their attack properly. They are winning when the Wyoming National Guard appear and arrest – or rescue – the remnants of the hired gang.

Rhode Island in 1900. Averill recalls his wedding day when the Association got in one last shot – the one that killed his bride, Ella.

6

8

Oshima's Empires

Nagisa Oshima – a one-man 'New Wave' at the start of his career – is now regarded as the father of a revolutionary young generation of Japanese film-makers. But in the West he is best known for the erotic *Ai No Corrida (Empire of the Senses)*

Nagisa Oshima has been called the least in-scrutable of Japanese directors. But as leader and chief theoretician of the 'New Wave' movement, which started in Japan at the same time as it did in France, he has also been thought both difficult and inaccessible. He is, however, a remarkable film-maker, known widely in the West mainly through *Ai No Corrida* (1976, *Empire of the Senses*), a treatise on physical sex, made for a French producer, that rivalled Bernardo Bertolucci's *Ultimo Tango a Parigi* (1972, *Last Tango in Paris*) for notoriety. To some, it was a strange movie for so radical and socially conscious a director, but to him, Sada and her lover are not crazed libertines; they are drop-outs from society at a time (in the Thirties) when Japanese imperia-lism was imposing a puritanical ethos upon the nation. 'Make love, not war' was at least a subsidiary text in the film.

Cruel story of youth

Oshima was born on March 31, 1932 in Kyoto. His father, the descendant of a samurai, was an accomplished amateur painter and poet who died when the boy was six, leaving a library which included a large number of Marxist and socialist texts. These Oshima read in the soli-tude of a lonely childhood, and by the time he left high-school he was ready to become a fully-fledged student activist as well as embryo writer and dramatist. Studying law at Kyoto University, he led a student group that got into trouble with the authorities: when the Em-peror visited the campus, the group held aloft placards imploring him not to allow himself to be deified because so many had died during the war in the name of his divinity.

When he graduated, he joined the Shochiku Film Company in 1954 as an assistant director,

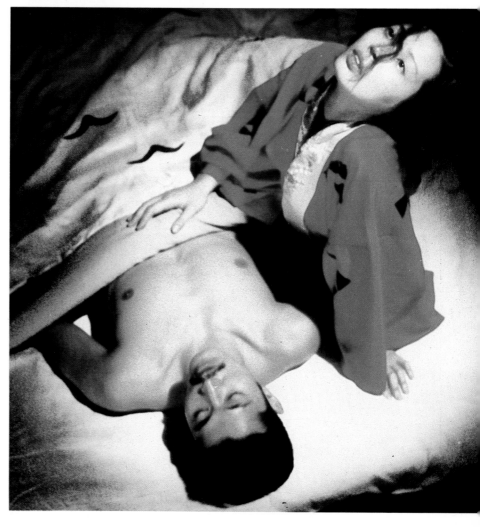

Left: Ai No Corrida, *the candidly erotic tale of the self-destructive passions of Kichi (Tatsuya Fuji) and his lover Sada (Eiko Matsuda).*
Above: revealing the sex problems of a young man, Diary of a Shinjuku Thief *has a deliberately documentary quality*

Above: in Ai No Borei, *a discharged soldier embarks on a torrid affair with a peasant woman. After killing her husband, they live together in constant fear, tormented by the ghost of the dead man*

despite his reputation as a 'red student' and the fact that there were over 2,000 applicants for only five jobs. Five rather desultory years later, he was entrusted with his first films as director: *Ai To Kibo No Machi* (1959, *A Town of Love and Hope*) and *Seishun Zankoku Monogatari* (1960, *Naked Youth*), two of the teenage *yakuza* (gangster) genre then popular. In 1960 he also made *Taiyo No Hakaba* (*The Sun's Burial*), a violent story about slum life in which a community of tramps, junkies and the un-employed sell their blood for food and clothing.

Each of these films contained obvious social

comment as well as the kind of excitements required of a commercial director, but his fourth film, also made that year, lost him his job. *Nihon No Yoru To Kiri* (1960, *Night and Fog in Japan*) was an attack on both the traditional Left and the muddled activists of the student movement, calling for real action from a new radicalism. When a socialist leader was as-sassinated a few days after the film's release, it was hastily withdrawn from circulation.

Oshima reacted by setting up his own production company and making *Shiiku* (1961, *The Catch*), in which a black American airman is imprisoned and eventually killed by villagers who are unaware that World War II has finally ended. It was an angry rejection of traditional moral values, suggesting that Japan's fierce nationalism and hatred of foreigners were responsible for the war. Only the village children are seen as a hopeful

portent – in the last sequence a young boy moves away from the communal fire and quietly builds one of his own.

The man who left Japan on film
His next features were all highly critical of Japanese society, and made in an easily-assimilated naturalist tradition that he finally began to eschew in 1967 with *Nihon Shunka-ko* (*A Treatise on Japanese Bawdy Songs*). In this extraordinary film, a band of students visiting Tokyo react to the alienation they feel by singing the songs and end up, in a fantasy scene, strangling a rich girl who has been the object of their erotic dreams.

In *Muri Shinju: Nihon No Natsu* (1967, *Japanese Summer: Double Suicide*) he again left realism behind with a story about a man who wants someone to kill him and a woman who wants a lover. The two meet, get involved, are mixed up in gang warfare and ultimately kill each other before the police can get them. Oshima's pessimism at this time seemed to know no bounds.

His first film to be shown extensively in the West was *Koshikei* (1968, *Death by Hanging*), based on the true story of a young Korean in Japan who raped and killed two girls and was hanged years later after he had confessed and reformed. In the film, the hanging fails and the hypocritical and mindless authorities force the Korean to go through a re-enactment of the crime before killing him. By now Oshima's films had become frankly revolutionary in

both form and content, and were influenced as much by Jean-Luc Godard as those of many other radical directors of the day all over the world. And again the West was to be startled by *Shinjuku Dorobo Nikki* (1969, *Diary of a Shinjuku Thief*), a fractured story full of life and vitality about the sex problems of a young student who steals books in Tokyo's version of Soho.

Tokyo Senso Sengo Hiwa (1970, *The Man Who Left His Will on Film*) developed from this anarchic superstructure, its protagonist being a young man who photographs student demonstrations in Tokyo, and tries to find within all his footage how a friend has disappeared. What he discovers, in fact, is that he himself has almost disappeared in the general worthlessness of his own life.

Empire of disillusion
But between these two films came a remarkable change of course, as if Oshima was trying to find some way of appealing to a wider audience. *Shonen* (1969, *Boy*) was a much more direct narrative, a moving story, again based on actual events, about a couple who wander across Japan, having trained their small son to run in front of passing cars and pretend to be injured so that they can claim compensation. Eventually they are cornered, but the boy – loyal to the last – cannot be made to confess. Using the child as a pathetic yet amazingly dignified emotional shuttlecock within a family of parasites, Oshima constructs an almost classical film which does not so much accuse the parents as blame a society that has produced such a perversion of the norm.

Gishiki (*The Ceremony*), made in 1971, was less obviously universal in appeal but perhaps Oshima's finest demonstration of the film-making art. The chronicle of a wealthy provincial family from the end of World War II to the present, it is punctuated by the marriages and funerals at which the family is drawn together. Dominated by an authoritarian grandfather, the older members show themselves to be both militaristic and feudal in their outlook, much

Right: the family saga The Ceremony *is a complex allegory of political degeneracy and a seeming attack on reactionary Japanese society, seen through the eyes of one son, suffering under an authoritarian grandfather*

to the disillusion of the younger elements. The film, formal in structure and stunning to look at, yields riches even to western eyes trying to decipher its many layers of meaning. By contrast *Natsu No Imoto* (1972, *Dear Summer Sister*) is virtually impenetrable without knowing that Okinawa – where it is set – was once part of the Japanese empire and also Japan's Ulster. Even then, this story of a Tokyo girl looking round the island for her long-lost brother and finding he is the tourist guide with whom she has had an affair, seems an allegory without a centre.

It scarcely prepared the world for *Ai No Corrida*, based on an incident during the Thirties when a Tokyo woman was found wandering the streets with her lover's severed penis in her hand. He had literally died of love, allowing himself to be strangled and mutilated in a final ecstasy of pleasure. It is all superbly filmed – an illustration of French writer Georges Bataille's thesis that equates the orgasm with *la petite mort*. But if the West was amazed and sometimes scandalized, in Japan the film was regarded as a blow for sexual equality, since, in their sexual encounters, the maidservant and the owner of the geisha house are shown as having become absolute equals, giving and taking what each wants. The woman on whom the film was based, incidentally, has long been a heroine of the women's movement in Japan, and Oshima underlined why.

After passion
In 1978, Oshima made another film in France for the same producer, and the fact that it was called *Ai No Borei* (*Empire of Passion*) suggested to some that he was trying to repeat that box-office triumph. In fact, the film was a ghostly thriller in which an adulterer is hounded by the police after plotting with a woman to kill

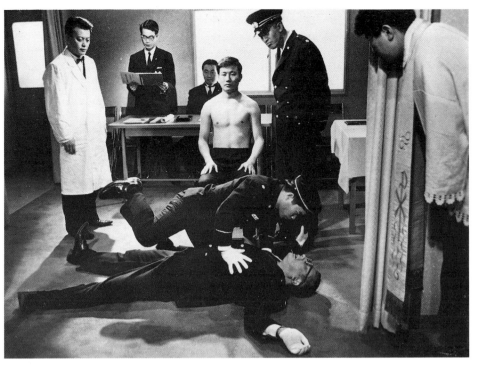

Far left: Yunbogi No Nikki (1965, Yunbogi's Diary) – a montage of still pictures, based on the life of a South Korean street boy and his struggle for survival. Left: a crisis for the police in Death by Hanging

her husband. There were social but hardly political implications, suggesting that Oshima, the 'activist samurai', might be beginning to lose his way. Yet, over all, he is undoubtedly as significant and skilful a director as most of the great Japanese film-makers of the generation before him. If he only occasionally evinces the universality of a Kurosawa or Ichikawa, his concerns are different and less reliant on commercial appeal.

Oshima clearly sees Japan developing blindly, its old values corrupted and its new ones worthless. Once a politicized director, he now says: 'No matter what political system we live under, people at the bottom stay there.' It is those people with whom he is most concerned, who await a revolution that never seems to come. In particular, the plight of the Japanese woman interests him greatly – for some time in the mid-Seventies he hosted a programme especially for them on Japanese television, with huge success.

Similar success greeted Oshima's first truly international piece *Merry Christmas, Mr Lawrence* (1983) a Japanese POW story, from a Laurens Van Der Post novella. The casting of pop giant David Bowie as one of the put-upon inmates may have helped, but there is no denying his directorial skill in presenting the erotica of the androgynous – as well as his concern, not for one nation only, but for all races. With this viewpoint, Oshima is bound to continue making fine films.

Filmography
1959 Tsukimiso (sc. only); Donto Ikooze (co-sc. only); Ai To Kibo No Machi (+sc) (USA/GB: A Town of Love and Hope). **'60** Seishun Zankoku Monogatari (+sc) (USA: Naked Youth); Taiyo No Hakaba (+co-sc) (USA/GB: The Sun's Burial); Nihon No Yoru To Kiri (+co-sc) (USA/GB: Night and Fog in Japan). **'61** Shiiku (USA/GB: The Catch). **'62** Amakusa Shiro Tokisada (+co-sc) (USA/GB: The Revolt). **'64** Chiisana Boken Ryoko (+co-sc) (USA/GB: A Child's First Adventure); Watashi Wa Bellett (+sc) (USA/GB: I Am Bellett). **'65** Etsuraku (+sc) (USA: The Pleasures of the Flesh); Yunbogi No Nikki (doc. short) (+prod; +sc; +comm) (GB: Yunbogi's Diary). **'66** Hakachu No Torima (USA/GB: Violence at Noon); Ninja Bugeicho (+co-prod; +co-sc) (USA/GB: Band of Ninja). **'67** Nihon Shunka-ko (+co-sc) (USA/GB: A Treatise on Japanese Bawdy Songs/Sing a Song of Sex); Muri Shinju: Nihon No Natsu (+co-sc) (USA/GB: Japanese Summer: Double Suicide). **'68** Koshikei (+co-prod; +co-sc; +narr) (USA/GB: Death by Hanging); Kaette Kita Yopparai (+co-sc) (USA/GB: Three Resurrected Drunkards). **'69** Yoiyami Semareba (short) (sc. only) (USA/GB: When the Evening Comes); Shinjuku Dorobo Nikki (+co-sc; +ed) (USA: Diary of a Shinjuku Burglar; GB: Diary of a Shinjuku Thief); Shonen (USA/GB: Boy). **'70** Tokyo Senso Sengo Hiwa (+co-sc) (USA/GB: The Man Who Left His Will on Film). **'71** Gishiki (+co-sc) (USA/GB: The Ceremony). **'72** Natsu No Imoto (+co-sc) (USA/GB: Dear Summer Sister). **'76** L'Empire des Sens/Ai No Corrida (+sc) (FR-JAP) (USA/GB: In the Realm of the Senses/Empire of the Senses). **'78** L'Empire de la Passion/Ai No Borei (+sc) (FR-JAP) (GB: Empire of Passion). **'83** Merry Christmas, Mr Lawrence (+co-sc) (JAP-GB). **'88** Max, Mon Amour.

AN AKIRA KUROSAWA FILM

Kagemusha

GEORGE LUCAS and FRANCIS FORD COPPOLA present
AN AKIRA KUROSAWA FILM A TOHO-KUROSAWA PRODUCTION

KAGEMUSHA (THE SHADOW WARRIOR) Starring TATSUYA NAKADAI TSUTOMU YAMAZAKI Co-starring KEN-ICHI HAGIWARA

Executive Producers AKIRA KUROSAWA TOMOYUKI TANAKA Directed by AKIRA KUROSAWA Written by AKIRA KUROSAWA MASATO IDE Music by SHINICHIRO IKEBE Assistant to Mr Kurosawa for International Version ALDIE BOCK

Costing some $6 million, Akira Kurosawa's breathtaking epic of sixteenth-century Japanese clans at war is the costliest Japanese film to be made to date. But Kurosawa – who has been highly regarded by the West since the Fifties, when films such as *Rashomon* (1950), *Shichinin no Samurai* (1954, *The Seven Samurai*) and *Kumonosu-Jo* (1957, *The Throne of Blood*) won international acclaim – found great difficulty financing this project. After the commercial failure of *Dodeska-Den* (1970), Kurosawa had to turn to the Soviet Union to secure backing for his subsequent *Dersu Uzala* (1975), which won an Oscar for Best Foreign Film. Despite this success, however, *Kagemusha* might never have been made if the Americans Francis Ford Coppola and George Lucas had not persuaded 20th Century-Fox to buy the international distribution rights in advance.

Loosely based on fact, *Kagemusha* is the story of the events leading up to the destruction of the Takeda clan at the Battle of Nagshino. Lord Shingen, the head of the Takeda clan, was known to have used a *kagemusha* (shadow-warrior) to take his place in battle

1

2

4

5

6

432

and so draw the enemy fire, and it is into the historical decline of the clan that Kurosawa introduces his fictional *kagemusha*: a thief saved from the gallows because of his resemblance to the lord.

Through a combination of political manoeuvering and the thief's emotional involvement in the process, Kurosawa examines the nature of power and its embodiment within the workings of the clan and in the fierce external struggle taking place against the enemy. When the thief presides over his first battle he apes the dead lord, sitting enthroned at the unwavering head of his troops – a supremely arrogant display of power that immobilizes the opposition. Later, after the impersonation has been publicly revealed and the thief ignominiously thrown out, the clan – leaderless and demoralized – is destroyed. It is the apparent rather than actual presence of Shingen that affects the outcome of the two battles – such is the illusory nature of power.

The second important issue raised by the film concerns the distinction between a noble and a common thief. The thief is uneducated, submissive and cowering;

Shingen is a proud man whose emblem emboldens him. With some extraordinary acting, Tatsuya Nakadai switches, in his dual role, from thief to lord without any change of costume or noticeable adaptation of mannerism – the thief, at times, becomes Shingen. Indeed, the *kagemusha* certainly comes to believe in the power of his impersonation, for seduced by his deception he dares to test the lord's own horse. However, animals are not so easily fooled as humans and the ruse is discovered.

Kagemusha recreates a beautiful and historic episode from life in a feudal clan. Using traditional Japanese costumes, paintings and poetry, a seductive counterpoint is created, as epitomized in the two opening sequences: the static yet rhythmical ceremony of the thief's presentation to the clan – a ceremony steeped in ritual and tradition; and the abrupt scene of a soldier clattering down cobbled steps amongst a sleeping army.

Kurosawa has both influenced and been influenced by American cinema. He acknowledges this by consciously taking the best of western films and incorporating their devices and techniques into the

traditions of Japan. The result is a film that is accessible to the west yet fundamentally Japanese in style and content. Its commercial success in Europe and America (as well as in Japan) is a vindication of Kurosawa's whole approach to film-making. The final battle-scene is the culmination of the contradictions that Kurosawa has set up. With brightly coloured flags indicat-

ing the varied functions of the army, the battle-lines are clearly drawn and impressively displayed. The clan's destruction is mapped out with awful logic, both from within (the loss of their leader) and without (the technological advancements in warfare). The final desecration, is perhaps one of the strongest indictments of war to be seen on the cinema screen

Directed by Akira Kurosawa, 1980
Prod co: Toho/Kurosawa Productions. **prod:** Akira Kurosawa, Tomoyuki Tanaka; (international version) Francis Ford Coppola, George Lucas. **assoc prod:** Teruyo Nogami. **sc:** Akira Kurosawa, Masato Ide. **sc sup:** Teruyo Nogami. **photo** (Eastman Colour): Takao Saito, Masaharu Ueda, Kauo Miyagawa, Asaichi Nakai. **ed:** Keisuke Iwatani. **ass dir:** Fumiaka Okada, Hideyuki Inoue, Takao Ohgawara, Takashi Koizumi. **art dir:** Yoshiro Muraki. **ass art dir:** Tsuneo Shimura, Akira Sakuragi, Katsumi Kobayashi. **set dec:** Hatsumi Yamamoto, Daisaburo Sasaki, Koichi Hamamura. **mus:** Shinichiro Ikebe, performed by the New Japan Philharmonic Orchestra conducted by Kotaro Sato. **cost:** Seiichiro Momosawa. **sd:** Fumio Yanuguchi. **prod man:** Toshiaki Hashimoto. **r/t:** 181 minutes.
Cast: Tatsuya Nakadai (*Shingen Takeda/the kagemusha*), Tsutomu Yamaaki (*Nobukado Takeda*), Kenichi Hagiwara (*Katsuyori Takeda*), Kohta Yui (*Takemaru Takeda*), Hideji Otaki (*Masakage Yamagata*), Hideo Murata (*Nobuhara Baba*), Takayuki Shiho (*Masatoyo Naito*), Shuhei Sugimi Sugimori (*Masanobu Kosaka*), Noboru Shimizu (*Masatoyo Hara*), Koji Shimizu (*Kasusuke Atobe*), Sen Yamamoto (*Nobushige Oyamada*), Mitsuko Baisho (*Oyunokata*), Kaori Momoi (*Otsuvanokata*), Kumeko Otowa (*Takemaru's nurse*), Tetsuo Yamashita (*Nagahide Niwa*).

3

It is 1573. The Takeda clan is in conflict with several rivals clans. After overcoming one of their enemies at Noda castle (1) a stray bullet wounds clan chief Shingen Takeda and, knowing that he is dying (2), he begs the clan to keep his death a secret in order to maintain Takeda supremacy. A thief – previously saved from execution in order to become Shingen's kagemusha (3) – takes his place with the connivance of the clan's hierarchy.

Rumours of Shingen's death eventually reach the Tokugawa clan, who attack and capture a Takeda stronghold. The kagemusha advises inaction, but Shingen's son Katsuyori leads his troops to war and two more strongholds are lost.

Incensed by the kagemusha's inactivity, Katsuyori then attacks

the Tokugawa fort. His troops are fighting a losing battle when the kagemusha arrives (4), and the latter's confident display of force manages to turn the tables and the Takeda defeat the Tokugawa. Encouraged by his success, the kagemusha attempts to mount Shingen's horse, but he is thrown and when the concubines realize that he lacks their leader's scars, the thief is expelled from the clan (5).

The Takeda go into battle once again (6). Leaderless, and finding themselves having to face recently introduced firearms, they are destroyed. From a lone vantage point (7) the kagemusha watches the battle. When he picks up the Takeda's standard he too is shot down and his body floats downriver past Shingen's last resting place.

7

ROBERT DE NIRO

ODD MAN OUT

'You talking to me? Well, who the hell else are you talking to? You talking to me? Well I'm the only one here.' Travis Bickle, the rabid urban avenger played by Robert De Niro in *Taxi Driver*, affirms his solitariness in front of a mirror. As the Seventies wore on it seemed De Niro himself was the only one 'here' – the one actor immediately identifiable with lost souls on the streets of New York, fall-guys of the Vietnam fall-out, and other victims of the age. The brilliance he brings to such roles makes him the most authentic movie-hero of his generation

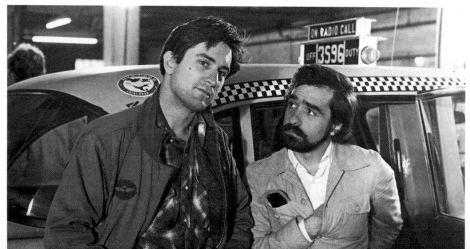

There is an agreeable symmetry to the fact that in *The Godfather, Part II* (1974) Robert De Niro played Vito Corleone, the young Sicilian who was to 'become' the old Mafia chief portrayed by Marlon Brando in *The Godfather* (1972). As Brando himself got older and his screen appearances rarer, it seemed for a long while that there was no-one to fill the void he was leaving: what other star was there possessed of such incredible sexual magnetism, who was at the same time a sensitive actor with a huge range, whose presence in even the most mediocre films lifted everything around him to a high level of intelligence and excitement?

Then in 1973 along came De Niro in *Bang the Drum Slowly* and, even more importantly, *Mean Streets*; it was not a 'new Brando' who had appeared, but an actor of the same class, and one who would obviously become, like Brando, a consummate *film* actor.

In 1973, however, De Niro – born on August 17, 1944 – was already 29 years old, and his career had begun much earlier:

Top: Travis Bickle preparing for his one-man war on New York's vice-peddlers in Martin Scorsese's Taxi Driver. *He gets a slug in the neck for his trouble but saves a child whore, kills a mafioso and becomes a hero. Back in his cab, though, he is still isolated in his madness; he remains, as Robert Philip Kolker says, 'his own passenger, threatening to take others for a ride.' Left: De Niro and Scorsese, a modern-day Wayne and Ford?*

Left: De Niro as film producer Monroe Stahr, looking remarkably like Irving G. Thalberg, in The Last Tycoon, with Ingrid Boulting as Kathleen. Above left: as Vito Corleone, hustling, in The Godfather, Part II. Above: as Alfredo Berlinghieri in Bertolucci's 1900

authenticity touched me, and I admire Walter Huston for his magic – remember The Treasure of the Sierra Madre (1948)? – and Jeanne Moreau because of something she emanates which always strikes me.'

In 1970 he played one of the gangster sons of Ma Barker (Shelley Winters) in Roger Corman's Bloody Mama, and the following year did three films – Ivan Passer's Born to Win, Noel Black's Jennifer on My Mind, James Goldstone's The Gang That Couldn't Shoot Straight – none of which won him fame and glory, but did get him noticed by other directors and producers.

'If I look back, I made a lot of films (independent or commercial, big and little) before I had any success, which was unforeseen. My luck was to be able to work and to learn; that's what an actor must never forget.'

His dying baseball player in John Hancock's Bang the Drum Slowly had audiences asking who he was and critics raving, and his Johnny Boy stole Martin Scorsese's Mean Streets (not an easy task when your co-star is the excellent Harvey Keitel), for which De Niro won the New York Film Critics Circle Award as Best Actor. The meeting with Martin Scorsese was particularly fortuitous:

'What matters to me is to work with a director who responds to me. That's been the case for a long time with Martin Scorsese. What's important in our work, which is very heavy and very slow, is a kind of complicity, solidarity, and at least a minimum of fun – which prevents migraines.'

Scorsese refers to De Niro as 'Mr Perfection', and credits the actor as a major contributor to each of the films, from improvising new dialogue to rearranging troublesome scenes so that they work: 'Our collaboration is a complete collaboration. We work together in total trust.'

The Italian job
From the almost crazy, self-destructive Johnny Boy, De Niro changed like a chameleon into Corleone, the Sicilian immigrant on his way to becoming the head of a Mafia family; the first role was all frenzy, the second a kind of elegant coolness. In Francis Ford Coppola's The Godfather, Part II, De Niro also worked extensively on his voice and intonation so that they

'I was born in Greenwich Village. I wanted to be an actor when I was 10, and then again when I was 16.' At 10, he attended New York's American Dramatic Workshop; at 16, he studied with Lee Strasberg and Stella Adler at the Actors' Studio.

'My parents were artists, and I thought they were Bohemian, and like all kids I wanted to rebel, so I decided to live a very conventional life. When it came time to make a real choice, however, I studied acting, which is what I always really wanted to do. My parents were very supportive; they were glad I hadn't become an insurance salesman.'

After working in semi-professional theatre outside New York City, he appeared Off-Broadway in a number of plays, including One Night Stands of a Noisy Passenger with Shelley Winters. In 1967, the director Brian De Palma, who had seen him on stage, hired De Niro to play a friend of the groom in The Wedding Party. They worked together again on the comedies Greetings (1968) and Hi, Mom! (1970). De Palma remembers:

'One day on Greetings, he came in to shoot a scene and I didn't recognize him. We had to put a label on him so that viewers would remember that it was the same character they had seen at the beginning. . . . He really lives his roles, and that changes him physically.'

Living an illusion
People who know him have remarked that De Niro 'isn't here' during the making of a film, and he is well known for his 'isolation' between takes.

'I can't cheat when I act. I know that the cinema is only an illusion, but not for me. The qualities of an actor must be those which Faulkner said were those of a writer: experience, observation, imagination. The preparation of a role, the experience of making a film, are hard. When you are 10, you dream of beauty, of glory, and you aren't aware of the reality: study and work. If one is really in a film, the rest of the world disappears. No obligations, no telephone, no everyday details, no bothers. Then when it is finished and you return to reality you have to lose all the weight of the character, and go back to other disciplines. You have time for yourself, and that can be a source of new problems.'

Aside from the major influences of his teachers – Lee Strasberg, Luther James and Stella Adler (who he says was the first to give him 'a total sense of the theatre and of a character') – he says that the actors who 'marked' him include Montgomery Clift, James Dean, Marlon Brando, Kim Stanley, Geraldine Page – and also Spencer Tracy:

'I know, he was more conventional, but his

matched exactly those of Marlon Brando's Corleone in *The Godfather*. De Niro won the 1974 Best Supporting Actor Oscar for his performance. Entirely different again, he played the alienated, paranoid Travis Bickle, dedicated to purifying New York and 'saving' the virtue of an adolescent whore through slaughter in Scorsese's *Taxi Driver* (1976). The film won the Golden Palm at the Cannes Film Festival and De Niro became a solid international star.

De Niro has said that he constantly finds it necessary to change directors and kinds of roles 'in order to escape from that vicious circle in which we all find ourselves at any given moment.' A complete change came with *1900* (1976), made in Italy by Bernardo Bertolucci and an international cast of stars all acting in their own languages (later to be dubbed into Italian). De Niro played a sympathetic Italian landowner at the turn of the century trying to come to terms with the idea of revolution and maintain his relationship with his longtime peasant friend.

Although Elia Kazan's *The Last Tycoon* (1976) was made ineffective by its trowelled-on period decor and absolute fidelity to F. Scott Fitzgerald's unfinished Hollywood novel, De Niro came through unscathed. His elegant performance in a role modelled on Irving G. Thalberg suggested – more than did the leaden script – that the character was a part of the old Hollywood, that he knew about and loved film, and that he had been caught up in a love affair he knew was finally an illusion more hopeless than the films he was making.

More directly and authentically connected to the old Hollywood, Scorsese's *New York, New York* (1977), with its re-creation of the New York of movies (as opposed to the 'real' New York) and of the Big Band era, gave De Niro a chance to improvise whole sequences of dialogue, to demonstrate that he has a fine comic talent, and to walk the razor's edge between the comic and the emotionally touching. Jimmy Doyle was also De Niro's first fully romantic role and suggested that if he had been a less talented and ambitious actor he might have had a full career as a conventional matinée idol.

In *The Deer Hunter* (1978), De Niro played a metal-worker whose hellish experiences in Vietnam make it impossible for him to return to a normal life until he comes to terms with what has happened to himself and his friends. The actor has high praise for Michael Cimino, the film's director:

'I responded to him. From the time I met him, he was full of his project, of his subject, and I could see he was ready and felt the film had to be made. We were open to one another, ready to meet anywhere and anytime to work together to the end. As with John Hancock (to say nothing of Martin Scorsese) I felt there was something fresh and something good there.'

Although the film was politically and aesthetically controversial (some praised its view of America healing itself while others criticized its verbosity), De Niro's sensitive portrayal of a man learning to understand himself was universally acclaimed.

Bring on the Bronx Bull

De Niro's work with Scorsese on *Raging Bull* (1980), the story of middleweight boxer Jake La Motta, again demonstrates the actor's incredible range and love of change. He played

La Motta as an inarticulate, instinctual animal. De Niro was fascinated by La Motta's 'destiny': 'He fought for everything and he lost everything.' The same passion for complete preparation that had made the actor learn the saxophone for *New York, New York*, here led him to take boxing lessons and gain 60lbs in four months for the scenes of La Motta in retirement. He also learned something about the inner character of the role:

'I don't like boxing. It's too primitive. But Jake is a more complex being than you think. Take his style: that way of uncovering his face to take blows and tire his opponents. In one way or another there has to be some feeling of guilt to deliberately look to get hit.'

De Niro's dedication earned him Best Actor Oscar for 1981. He continued his effective partnership with Scorsese in *The King of Comedy* (1983), this time playing a man who is convinced of his own talent as a stand-up comic. In De Niro's hands, Rupert Pupkin's arrogance and pathos made a studied comment on those who search after stardom.

By now, De Niro was established as the most capable actor of his generation but he could no longer continue to play out the conflicts of his times. He settled into middle-age with *Falling in Love* (1984), a gentle romance co-starring Meryl Streep, which marked a complete

Top left: in the Vietnam movie The Deer Hunter. *Top right: a guy, a suit and a sax – De Niro as Jimmy Doyle in* New York, New York. *Above: in* Angel Heart *(1987), De Niro has a cameo role as the devilish Lewis Cyphre who tempts a private eye down a bloody path*

change of pace.

Nevertheless, De Niro is still in demand whenever an epic picture is made which attempts to comment on the state of America. Sergio Leone's *Once Upon a Time in America* (1984) and Brian de Palma's *The Untouchables* both recruited him to add depth to historic investigations of America's past. He is an actor who will certainly survive the Eighties.

Filmography
'67 The Wedding Party. '68 Greetings. '70 Hi, Mom!; Bloody Mama. '71 Born to Win; Jennifer on My Mind; The Gang That Couldn't Shoot Straight. '73 Bang the Drum Slowly; Mean Streets. '74 The Godfather, Part II. '76 Taxi Driver; 1900/Novecento (IT); The Last Tycoon. '77 New York, New York. '78 The Deer Hunter. '80 Raging Bull. '81 True Confessions. '83 The King of Comedy. '84 Once Upon a Time in America; Falling in Love. '85 Brazil. '86 The Mission. '87 The Untouchables; Angel Heart. '88 Midnight Run.

NEWLY IN VIEW

Many smaller countries emerged from cinematic obscurity to make a new and exciting challenge for international attention in the Seventies

For a while at the beginning of the Seventies, it looked as if the cinema emerging from countries such as Switzerland, Canada and Algeria might become really competitive with the already established major cinemas of the world. It did not quite happen, for a variety of reasons, but it was certainly very exciting when it looked as if it might – when a Canadian crowd-pleaser, *The Apprenticeship of Duddy Kravitz* (1974), could win the Grand Prize at the Berlin Film Festival and an Algerian epic, *Ahdat Sanawouach El-Djamr* (1975, *Chronicle of the Years of Embers*), could take the Grand Prize at the Cannes Film Festival; when an actress from a Swiss film, Isabelle Huppert in *La Dentellière* (1977, *The Lacemaker*), could capture the British Film Academy Most Promising Newcomer of the Year Award and unknown directors from Spain, Iran, Belgium and Senegal could attract international attention and audiences.

At the beginning of the Seventies, the newly subsidized Canadian and Swiss cinemas were poised for international acclaim, the repressed Spanish cinema was about to emerge from the Franco era, the continent of Africa was waking up to the possibilities of film-making and from Belgium to Iran 'new waves' of film-makers were rolling forward. At the major international film festivals – Cannes, Berlin, Venice and London – where such developments are first noticed, it looked like the dawn of a new era as commercial distribution followed critical acclaim. The face of international cinema seemed to be changing.

By the early Eighties, the 'new waves' of the emergent cinemas of the Seventies had receded and the changes were rather less than had been hoped. Politics, economics and diminishing cinema audiences adversely affected many of these new cinemas. Some were nearly dead, like Iran's; others survived in a very different form, like Canada's.

Long a cultural dependent of the USA, Canada had no feature film-making of importance before the Sixties. The National Film Board was the basis of Canadian film culture and helped to spark off the *cinéma-vérité* movement in Canada that led to such films as *Pour la Suite du Monde* (1964, *The Moontrap*) by Michel Brault and Pierre Perrault and *Warrendale* (1967) by Allan King. The real launching for Canadian cinema came when the new Canadian Film Development Corporation began to finance feature films in 1968. First to win praise was the Quebec cinema and especially the films of Gilles Groulx, Claude Jutra, Gilles Carle, Denys Arcand and Jean-Pierre Lefebvre. These French-language film-makers had the advantage of not having to compete directly with the American cinema; to gain equal attention, the English-language film-makers had to become distinctively 'Canadian'.

Allan King developed an intimate documentary technique, having his biggest success with *A Married Couple* (1969). Robin Spry, after gaining acclaim for *Prologue* in 1969, created an acidic investigative style in such films as *One Man* (1977), about pollution, and *Drying Up the Streets* (1978), about drugs. Other film-makers utilized avant-garde techniques, the most influential being Michael Snow with *Wavelength* (1967), ⟷ (1969, also known as *Back and Forth*) and *La Région Centrale* (1971, *The Central Region*). David Cronenberg combined science fiction with anti-sexuality in *Stereo* (1969) and *Crimes of the Future* (1970), and then created a series of bizarre personalized horror films: *The Parasite Murders* (1975, released in Britain as *Shivers*), *Rabid* (1977), *The Brood* (1979) and *Scanners* (1981). His disturbing vision of the world has few parallels in the Canadian cinema.

The first English-language director to please both audiences and critics was Donald Shebib with *Goin' Down the Road* (1970), which had a nice, relaxed Canadian quality of its own. Unfortunately, none of his later films has had as much impact, though

Above left: in The Apprenticeship of Duddy Kravitz, *Duddy (Richard Dreyfuss) involves his Christian girlfriend Yvette (Micheline Lanctôt) in negotiating a land deal when the owners will not sell to a Jew; he finally gets the land but loses the girl. Above: hired gunman Jay Mallory (Donald Sutherland) is much concerned at* The Disappearance *of his estranged wife (Francine Racette) and follows her trail from Canada to England, only later discovering her connection with a murder plot*

Between Friends (1973) was widely shown. The greatest international success was Ted Kotcheff's screen version of Mordecai Richler's novel *The Apprenticeship of Duddy Kravitz*, a wryly comic tale of ambition in Montreal that became a box-office hit after winning the Grand Prize at Berlin. Kotcheff, who returned to Canada to make this film after a career in England, did not repeat this success in Canada but went on to Hollywood.

Many of the most successful Canadian directors, including Norman Jewison, Arthur Hiller, Sidney Furie and Daryl Duke, are not thought of as Canadian, though some returned from Hollywood when the international production era of the late Seventies provided an opportunity. The same was true of a Canadian-born star, Donald Sutherland, who came back for such 'Canadian' co-productions as *The Disappearance* and *Les Liens de Sang/ Blood Relatives* (both 1977). Even stars produced by the Canadian cinema itself, Geneviève Bujold, for example, eventually felt the necessity of moving on to Hollywood. The native Canadian industry was virtually swamped in the late Seventies by the trend to international film production, and not one genuinely Canadian English-language film was released in 1980.

The Swiss cinema that emerged in the Seventies was more impressive than its Canadian counterpart, despite a financial crunch at the end of the decade that partially crippled it. Swiss cinema hardly existed before the Sixties; its roots were in Fifties Britain – Alain Tanner and Claude Goretta were both associated with the Free Cinema movement and made the short *Nice Time* together in 1957. State finance and television money finally got the Swiss feature industry under way in the late Sixties and, as in Canada, it was the French-language film-makers who made the initial running, notably Alain Tanner with *La Salamandre* (1971, *The Salamander*), Michel Soutter with *Les Arpenteurs* (1972, The Surveyors) and Claude Goretta with *L'Invitation* (1973, *The Invitation*). All were founding members of the Group of 5 production company, which helped to make the Swiss cinema a viable international force. Tanner was interested in socio-political investigation, especially in *Le Retour d'Afrique* (1973, *Return from Africa*) and *Jonas: Qui Aura 25 Ans en l'An 2000* (1976, *Jonah Who Will Be 25 in the Year 2000*). Goretta was the explorer of human frailty, especially in his masterpiece *The Lacemaker*.

The Geneva-based French-language directors had a rather delicate Alpine-airy quality in their films, a stark contrast to the heavier work of the German-language directors who emerged from Zürich in the middle of the decade. Thomas Koerfer was the most intellectual, with such intensely Brechtian films as *Der Tod des Flohzirkusdirektors oder Ottacaro Weiss reformiert seine Firma* (1973, *The Death of the Director of the Flea Circus*), highly theatrical in style, and *Der Gehülfe* (1976, The Assistant). Daniel Schmid was more operatic and style-conscious, as he demonstrated in *La Paloma* (1974) and *Schatten der Engel* (1976, Shadows of Angels). Rolf Lyssy put Swiss society under a critical microscope in *Konfrontation* (1975, *Konfrontation: Assassination in Davos*) and *Die Schweizermacher* (1978, *The Swissmakers*).

The biggest disappointment of the Seventies was the new Spanish cinema. At the beginning of the decade, a group of young film-makers headed by Carlos Saura seemed certain to give birth to a major new cinema as Franco's hold on Spain weakened. Good films were produced and new directors did appear but the new freedom did not lead to the expected breakthrough.

Spanish cinema has a long tradition, but Luis

Left: The Woman in a Twilight Garden *is divided between a collaborator husband and a lover in the Resistance. Far left: Theodor Angelopoulos (right) directs his* O Megalèxandros, *set in 1900. Above far left: Des Morts (1978, Of the Dead) is a bloodsoaked Belgian documentary on death and funeral rites around the world. Top far left: a supermarket cashier (Miou-Miou) is jailed for undercharging in* Jonah Who Will Be 25 in the Year 2000. *Centre top:* Piccadilly Circus *is where people search for a* Nice Time *on a Saturday night. Top right: the Spanish* Camada Negra *(1977, Black Brood) is an outspoken political film about a group of right-wing terrorists masquerading as a choir and was made soon after Franco's death. Above: a little girl (Ana Torrent) believes she has befriended Frankenstein's monster in* The Spirit of the Beehive

Buñuel was the only important director to come out of pre-World War II Spain. The modern Spanish cinema, after the disaster of the Civil War, grew up in the Fifties with Luis Berlanga's *Bienvenido, Mr Marshall* (1953, *Welcome, Mr Marshall*) and Juan Bardem's *Muerte de un Ciclista* (1955, *Death of a Cyclist*). The combination of Italian director Marco Ferreri and Spanish writer Rafael Azcona brought a Buñuelesque feeling back to Spanish cinema through grotesque films such as *El Cochecito* (1959, *The Wheelchair*). Buñuel himself returned to make *Viridiana* (1961) in Spain – it was banned as soon as it was finished. The obsessions of Carlos Saura became central to Spanish cinema in such films as *La Caza* (1966, *The Hunt*), *Peppermint Frappé* (1967), *Cría Cuervos* (1976, *Raise Ravens*) and *Deprisa, Deprisa* (1981, *Quickly, Quickly*).

The best Spanish film of the Seventies was Victor Erice's *El Espiritu de la Colmena* (1973, *The Spirit of the Beehive*); few other films were able to reflect the psychological state of Spain with such accuracy and effectiveness. Two of the finest talents to develop during the Seventies were José Luis Borau with *Furtivos* (1975, *Poachers*) and Jaime Camino with *Las Largas Vacaciones del 36* (1976, *The Long Holidays of 1936*). Pilar Miró's *El Crimen de Cuenca* (1980, The Cuenca Crime) depicted the Civil Guard as being less than angelic; it was totally banned in Spain and a military court ordered all copies destroyed. The death of Franco had not changed Spain as much as had been hoped.

Belgium, like Canada and Switzerland, is a country divided along linguistic lines, and this makes its already small population almost too fractional to support a native film industry. In effect, there was none until the Sixties. Top talents, such as director Jacques Feyder and writer Charles Spaak, emigrated to France; and it was left to the documentarists, notably Henri Storck, to keep Belgium's film reputation alive. Belgium's breakthrough year was 1967, when André Delvaux' *De Man Die Zijn Haar Kort Liet Knippen* (1966, *The Man Who Had His Hair Cut Short*) won the British Film Institute's Sutherland Trophy as the most original and imaginative film of the year, and Jerzy Skolimowski's *Le Départ* (1967, The Departure) won the Grand Prize at Berlin.

Harry Kümel made an outstanding debut in 1968 with the Dutch co-production *Monsieur Hawarden*, a baroque fantasy of ideas. A similar approach worked less well in such later films as *Malpertuis: Histoire d'une Maison Maudite* (1972, *Malpertuis*) and *Het Verloren Paradijs* (1977, The Lost Paradise). André Delvaux had more success with his later films, working in both French and Flemish. His finest achievement was an epitome of poetic ambiguity, *Rendez-vous à Bray* (1971, *Rendezvous at Bray*); but he has continued to excel in such films as *Belle* (1973) and *Une Femme Entre Chien et Loup* (1979, *Woman in a Twilight Garden*).

The second wave of Belgian directors emerged from the avant-garde in the early Seventies, led by the highly original Chantal Akerman, whose *Jeanne Dielman, 23 Quai du Commerce, 1080 Bruxelles* (1975) was a deliberately paced but powerful piece of intensely feminist cinema, over three-and-a-half hours long. Her later films, including *Les Rendez-vous d'Anna* (1978, Anna's Rendezvous), increased her reputation. Jean-Jacques Andrien made a strong impact in 1975 with his hallucinatory *Le Fils d'Amr Est Mort* (Amr's Son Is Dead). One of Akerman's associates, Samy Szlingerbaum, became a director himself in 1980 with the sensitive Yiddish-language *Bruxelles – Transit* (Brussels – Transit).

The Netherlands has always had close links with Belgium in film production because of the language

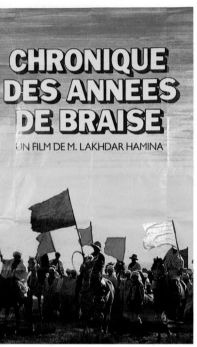

Above: Chronicle of the Years of Embers *shows the part played by one family from 1939 to 1954 in the events leading up to the Algerian struggle for independence from France. Top:* To Proxenio tis Annas *(1972, Anna's Engagemaent) is a touching Greek tale of a maid (Anna Vaguena) whose engagement to an eligible young man (Stavros Kalarogiou) is arranged and then broken off. Top right:* The Herd *won the British Film Institute Award in 1979 as the most original and imaginative film shown at the National Film Theatre*

situation – Flemish and Dutch are very similar. These co-productions have sometimes been of key importance – for example, the documentary *Borinage* (1933) and Fons Rademakers' commercial success *Mira* (1971) – and they can call on governmental sources in each country for funds, which is some compensation for the problems caused by the two languages.

Greece was another country with remarkable achievements during the Seventies, mostly through the work of one man. The country has a film production history going back to 1912, though its industry did not effectively get started until after World War II. It began to get international attention in the Fifties, especially the work of Michael Cacoyannis, including *Kyriakatiko Xypnima* (1954, *Windfall in Athens*), *Stella* (1955) and *Electra* (1962), probably the best screen adaptation of Greek tragedy, with fine camerawork by Walter Lassally, excellent music by Mikis Theodorakis and a superb central performance by Irene Papas. Cacoyannis had his biggest commercial success with *Zorba the Greek* (1964). The other major hit was American Jules Dassin's *Pote Tin Kyriaki* (1959, *Never on Sunday*), which made Melina Mercouri into an international star and helped to erase the HUAC blacklist stain from Dassin's film career.

Strict controls of content affected the young Greek film-makers in the Seventies as commercial production began to drop and audiences slipped away to television. The major film-maker who emerged was Theodor Angelopoulos, whose *Anaparastassis* (1970, Reconstruction) was a critical hit at the 1971 Berlin Festival. Angelopoulos seemed to have borrowed stylistically from Miklós Jancsó for his second, more overtly political film *Meres Tou 36* (1972, Days of 36); but the borrowings were fully absorbed in his third film and masterpiece *O Thiassos* (1975, *The Travelling Players*), perhaps the greatest film in the history of Greek cinema. His more recent films, also long and epic in style, are *I Kinigui* (1977, The Hunters) and *O Megalèxandros* (1980, Alexander the Great), mixing history and myth with political and cinematic awareness in long, continuous shots.

Greece's neighbour, Turkey, produced nearly two hundred films in 1979, but is mainly known around the world for the work of Yilmaz Güney, who began as a star actor and went on to writing and directing, taking his popular audience with him. His criticisms of injustice aroused the animosity of officialdom and he was imprisoned on

political grounds. Later, he received a 19-year sentence for shooting a judge and had to make films from prison, directed on his behalf by his associate Zeki Ökten. *Sürü* (1979, *The Herd*) and *Düsman* (1980, The Enemy) were made in this way.

The development of the continent of Africa as a film-making centre in the Seventies was capped by the Cannes prize won by Algeria in 1975 for Mohammed Lakhdar Hamina's *Chronicle of the Years of Embers* and reinforced by the festivals of African films in Tunisia and Upper Volta. Actually the African cinema was split into two segments, divided by geography and other characteristics. North Africa is as much part of Arabic as of African cinema, as can be seen by the festival set up in Carthage with strong participation from Egypt, Tunisia, Algeria and Morocco. The other African countries, although divided linguistically by their backgrounds as French or English colonies, united to create the Black African Festival in Ougadougou.

Film festivals were show-cases and useful markets for small nations

These festivals became meeting grounds for the exchange of ideas and co-operation.

In North Africa, the obvious leader in the Seventies should have been Egypt, the 'Hollywood of the Nile', with a long-established film industry producing over fifty features a year. In fact, Egypt failed signally to give a lead; Algeria and, in black Africa, Senegal set the pace. But Egypt's top directors, Youssef Chahine and Salah Abu Seif, already established by their earlier work, continued to develop in the Seventies, often in co-productions with other North African countries. The best-known film of the period was Shadi Abdelsalam's *El Mumia* (1970, *The Night of Counting the Years*), but this director made no further films in the Seventies, a reflection on the state of the Egyptian industry.

Algeria, on the other hand, full of revolutionary fervour, became inspired around the time of Italian Gillo Pontecorvo's magnificent co-production *La Battaglia di Algeri* (1966, *Battle of Algiers*). Ahmed Rachedi directed *L'Aube des Damnés* (1965, The Dawn of the Damned) and this was followed in 1967 by Mohammed Lakhdar Hamina's small masterpiece *Le Vent des Aurès* (Wind From the Aurès). Hamina's Cannes prize winner was not at all the

only notable Algerian film of the Seventies.

Tunisia, with slightly less fervour, also produced interesting films, including the Grand Prize winner of the 1980 Carthage Film Festival, *Aziza*, Abdellatif Ben Ammar's fine study of a young girl. Ben Ammar's earlier films, *Une Si Simple Histoire* (1970, A Very Simple Story) and *Sejnane* (1974) were also worthwhile, as was Ridha Bahi's attack on speculative tourist development, *Soleil des Hyènes* (1977, Hyena's Sun) and Naceur Ktari's slick *Assqufara* (1976, The Ambassadors). Morocco, like Tunisia, did not really develop a film industry but still turned out some valuable films, including Ahmed El Maanouni's *Alyam Alyam* (1978, Oh the Days) and Ben Barka Souhel's *Mille et une Mains* (1974, Thousand and One Hands). Unfortunately the best films were not always popular in their own countries.

The films of black Africa were made from a genuinely new viewpoint. Black African cinema began in Senegal where the first all-African film, *Afrique sur Seine* (1955, Africa on Seine), was made in French by Paulin Vieyra. The first film made in a black African language, Wolof, was Ousmane Sembene's fine *Mandabi* (1968, The Money Order). Sembene has become the leader of African cinema, not only for his inspiration but because of the quality of his films. His *Emitaï* (1972) and *Ceddo* (1977, Outsiders) can bear comparison with the best cinema of any other country. Other directors have made films in Senegal and in such countries as Nigeria, Mauritania, the Ivory Coast and Niger. African cinema showed considerable promise as it moved into the Eighties.

Regrettably the same cannot be said of the brilliant cinema that developed in Iran in the Seventies. By 1980, it was virtually dead, with most of its major directors living outside the country and film production practically at a standstill, compared with an output of over a hundred films a year in the late Sixties. This was a real loss, in quality as well as quantity, since the Iranian cinema had produced four directors of international stature during the Seventies. The first to be noticed was Daryush Mehrjui, whose *Gav* (1968, The Cow) attracted attention at the film festivals of Venice and London in 1971. The attention paid to *The Cow* soon changed the face of Iranian cinema; by 1973, when Mehrjui helped to found the New Film Group, the Iranian cinema was a creative force of originality and strength. Mehrjui himself had commercial as well as critical success with *Postchi* (1972, The

Postman); but he ran into enormous censorship problems from the medical establishment over *Dayereh Mina* (1975, The Cycle).

Bahram Beyzai attracted attention at the first Teheran International Film Festival in 1972 with *Ragbar* (Downpour) and then made a terrific impression with the mysterious *Gharibeh-va-meh* (1974, The Stranger and the Fog). His *Tcherikeh Tara* (1980, The Ballad of Tara) was the last major film to come out of the new Iranian cinema of the Seventies, shot partially before and finished after the revolution. The third major director was Bahman Farmanara, whose *Shazdeh Ehtejab* (Prince Ehtejab) won the Grand Prize at the 1974 Teheran Festival and whose ambitious *Saiehaieh Bolan de Bad* (*Tall Shadows of the Wind*) came out in 1979.

Farmanara and Beyzai both had strong elements of mysticism in their work; the fourth major Iranian director appeared, at least on the surface, to be a pessimistic realist. Sohrab Shahid Saless, one of the most important directors to appear anywhere in the world during the Seventies, began his career with the bleak but beautiful *Yek Ettefaghe Sadeh* (1973, A Simple Event), about a poor child, and *Tabiate Bijan* (1974, Still Life), about an old couple. He then went to Germany to make a study in alienation, *In der Fremde* (1975, Far From Home), and became a filmmaker in exile, creating a unique, quiet style of desperation that expressed Seventies *angst* in the way that Ingmar Bergman's films had depicted Fifties anguish. Saless has continued to work in Germany and to make outstanding films, including the startling *Ordnung* (1980, All in Order), a reflection on the meaning of madness.

Finally, the Philippines, the second biggest film-producing country in the world (251 features in 1971), has come into the limelight of world cinema after long being neglected, despite its prizes gained at Asian festivals. By a quirky chance, the first director from the Philippines to attract attention in Europe was the naive, self-taught Kidlat Tahimik, whose *Mababangong Bangungot* (1977, The Perfumed Nightmare) appeared like a work of primitive art at that year's Berlin Film Festival and won the Critics' Prize. However, the first director from the Philippines who seemed able to achieve international stature was Lino Brocka. His *Insiang* was shown at Cannes in 1978, to be followed by *Jaguar* in 1980. In 1981, his earlier film *Maynila, Sa Mga Kuko Ng Liwanag* (1975, Manila: In the Claws of Darkness) became the first Filipino film to get commercial distribution in Britain.

Top: Youssef Chahine's Askndrie . . . Lie? (1979, Alexandria . . . Why?) is an Egyptian–Algerian co-production set in the British-occupied port city during World War II; the main character is a young man (Mohsen Mohiedini) who wants to go to California to train as an actor and does so after the war. Above: a poor man (Mamadou Guye) and his wives (Ynousse N'Diaye and Issa Niang) are only further impoverished by The Money Order sent to him by his nephew

Passions, Politics &

Pasolini's cinema refuses easy, conventional critical definitions and consequently has been frequently misunderstood. Lacking – indeed rejecting – the superficial stylistic and thematic continuities so beloved of the critical consensus, its contradictions have been vaguely dubbed as Christian-Marxist. However, this does isolate an aspect of Pasolini's cinema: namely, that it is particularly deeply embedded in Italian cultural and political life with all its conflicting traits and elements, the most important of which is the opposition between the two commanding ideologies of Catholicism and Communism.

Born in 1922 in Bologna, northern Italy, Pier-Paolo Pasolini came from a social background for which there is no real English equivalent:

'My origins are fairly typical of petit-bourgeois Italian society. I am a product of the Unity of Italy. My father belonged to an old noble family from the Romagna, while my mother comes from a Friulan peasant family which subsequently became petit bourgeois.'

He admitted 'an excessive, almost monstrous love' for his mother, and that he lived 'in a state of permanent, even violent tension' with his father – a Fascist supporter, tyrannical and overbearing. Pasolini grew up with a dislike of institutionalized religion (his father was a non-believer who made the family go to church for social reasons) and was not a practising Catholic; however, he also admired his mother's 'poetic and natural' sense of religion and admitted in himself a tendency towards mysticism: 'I see everything in the world, objects as well as people and nature, with a certain veneration.'

Poet and peasant
At seventeen Pasolini began to write poetry in the Friulan dialect. Significantly, Friuli was not only his mother's native area, it also represented a regionalism of which his father – as both a Fascist and an inhabitant of central Italy – strongly disapproved. But Pasolini's interest in peasant dialects does not simply relate to his family, it also attests to a somewhat backward-looking, romantic, idealized

It was a cruel irony that Pier-Paolo Pasolini's death – in brutal and mysterious circumstances – should resemble a legend worthy of one of his own films. His early work had been about delinquency, and contained searching political allegory, and although often condemned as obscene, his poetic interpretations of classical stories could be said to have created myths for the modern world

vision of the peasantry as a source of 'true, natural values' which is as prevalent in his cinematic as his literary works. This early penchant for obscure dialect poetry was also connected with the current vogue for literary aestheticism – the idea that the language of poetry is absolute and sufficient unto itself. This cultivation of form for its own sake returns in Pasolini's cinema, representing a vigorous and stimulating attack on outworn forms of naturalism such as neo-realism, as well as a tendency towards extreme impenetrability.

Pasolini's favourite authors were deemed degenerate by the Fascists, and so, fuelled by hatred for his father, Pasolini developed a visceral anti-Fascism and turned towards Marxism. After the war, his Marxist leanings were reinforced at the University of Bologna, and he actually joined the Communist Party briefly in 1947–8. However, as he admits, his Marxism was emotional, aesthetic and cultural rather than directly political, and was strongly linked to his attachment to the (largely Catholic) peasantry. Indeed, Pasolini displayed only the sketchiest awareness of the works of Marx and Lenin, and none of his films could be said to adopt a rigorous, coherent and thoroughgoing Marxist point of view.

Cinema Roma
In 1950 Pasolini came to Rome, both the political capital of Italy and the home of Cinecittà, and thus an ideal place for someone interested in both film and politics. Here he became a scriptwriter, working mainly on would-be artistic low-life films – the last dying gasps of neo-realism – though he also had a hand in Fellini's *Le Notti di Cabiria* (1957, *Nights of Cabiria*) and Bertolucci's *La Commare Secca* (1962, *The Grim Reaper*).

Pasolini's work on Roman underworld films fitted perfectly with his interest in the Roman sub-proletariat, that was for him the urban equivalent of the Friulan peasantry. His earliest novels and films are set in this sector of society rather than among the organized, industrial proletariat. His first film *Accattone* (1961) is the chronicle of a small-time hustler, which, for all its employment of seemingly neo-realist devices (fragmentary narrative, non-professional actors, seedy locations, etc.), is significant precisely for its departures from the genre.

Though the film may be set among the sub-proletariat, it is not *about* them as a class and does nothing to elucidate their social condition. In this respect Pasolini's use of dialect here is less 'realistic' than a hermetic formal device which, as in his poetry, draws attention to the sounds of the words themselves. Similarly, the film's fractured structure, in which many shots appear to fulfil no clear narrative function, is less a 'realist' feature than the filmic equivalent of poetic language: metaphorical, connotative and largely self-referential.

Accattone, like so much of Pasolini's work, operates not on the level of the psychological and the social, but on that of fable and myth. His second film – *Mamma Roma* (1962) – is the story of an ex-prostitute who tries unsuccessfully to give her son a 'respectable' bourgeois background. It introduces another key Pasolini theme, and one that is exposed more fully in *Teorema* (1968, *Theorem*): the unacceptable face of the modern bourgeois and petit-bourgeois worlds.

Of Marx and myth
With *Il Vangelo Secondo Matteo* (1964, *The Gospel According to St Matthew*) Pasolini

Pasolini

Top far left: Franco Citti as Accattone, the young pimp operating in Rome's delinquent quarters. Top left: Judas (Otello Sestili) gives the kiss by which Jesus (Enrique Irazoqui) is betrayed in The Gospel According to St Matthew. *Above: freely reworking Sophocles,* Oedipus Rex *overflowed with grandeur*

took an already much mythologized subject. Clearly influenced by Rossellini's *Francesco, Giullare di Dio* (1950, *Flowers of St Francis*), Pasolini almost reverses the trajectory of *Accattone* by moving from the mythical and sacred to the everyday. Generally read as an attempt to pull Christianity back to its popular, primitive roots, it was largely this film which earned him the 'Christian-Marxist' tag. However, it could also be argued that the representation of the various 'modern' accretions to the Gospel demonstrates that the Bible possesses no one fixed meaning, but various different meanings which have come to it over centuries of social usage. Ultimately the film expresses a belief in the virtues of the people independent of social classes, while its view of history is too cloudy

and romanticized to be considered properly materialist. In line with Pasolini's reverence for what he calls the sacred, the miracles are allowed to retain their sense of mystery.

Coinciding with the upsurge in left-wing political activity in the late Sixties, Pasolini retreated increasingly into the creation of a largely mythical universe, with films such as *Edipo Re* (1967, *Oedipus Rex*), *Teorema*, *Porcile* (1969, *Pigsty*) and *Medea* (1970). It was hardly surprising that he should be attracted by the Oedipus legend, not only in *Oedipus Rex* but throughout many of his films in which its presence (though not always immediately obvious) acts as a structure of images and ideas informing the whole. *Oedipus Rex* is framed by a contemporary prologue and epilogue, set in

the Friulan countryside and Bologna respectively. The main action occurs not in an historically specific ancient Greece, but in a seemingly timeless pre-historical North Africa, a world of primitive drives and desires. This is presented as deliberately strange and distanced, like someone else's dream, affording the spectator no possibility of involvement and identification.

Before the Fall
Like many Pasolinian figures Oedipus inhabits

Above left: the convent gardener in one of The Decameron *tales has to fertilize more than his flowers. Above: Pasolini's pessimistic and bestial comparison of destructive societies*

Filmography

1955 La Donna del Fiume (co-sc. only) (IT-FR) (USA/GB: Woman of the River). **'56** Il Prigioniero della Montagna (co-sc. only). **'57** Le Notti di Cabiria (co-sc. only) (IT-FR) (USA: Nights of Cabiria; GB: Cabiria). **'58** Marisa la Civetta (co-sc only (IT-SP); Giovani Mariti (co-sc. only) (IT-FR). **'59** La Notte Brava (co-sc. only) (IT-FR) (GB: Night Heat); Morte di un Amico (co-sc. only) (GB: Death of a Friend). **'60** Il Bell'Antonio (co-sc. only) (IT-FR); La Lunga Notte del '43 (co-sc. only); Il Carro Armato dell'Otto Settembre (co-sc. only); La Giornata Balorda (co-sc. only) (IT-FR) (USA: From a Roman Balcony; GB: A Day of Sin); Il Gobbo (actor only) (IT-FR) (GB: The Hunchback of Rome). **'61** La Ragazza in Vetrina (co-sc. only) (IT-FR) (GB: The Woman in the Window); Accattone (+sc). **'62** La Canta delle Marane (short) (co-sc. only); Mamma Roma (+sc); La Commare Secca (co-sc. only) (GB: The Grim Reaper). **'63** RoGoPaG/Laviamoci il Cervello ep La Ricotta (+sc) (IT-FR); La Rabbia (first part of doc. compilation only; +sc). **'64** Comizi d'Amore (doc) (+comm; +appearance as interviewer); Il Vangelo Secondo Matteo (+sc) (IT-FR) (USA/GB: The Gospel According to St Matthew). **'65** Sopraluoghi in Palestina (+comm; +co-narr). **'66** Uccellacci e Uccellini (+sc) (USA: Hawks and Sparrows). **'67** Le Streghe ep La Terra Vista dalla Luna (+sc) (IT-FR) (USA: The Witches); Edipo Re (+sc; +mus. sup; +act) (USA/GB: Oedipus Rex); Requiescant (actor only) (IT-GER). **'68** Capriccio all'Italiana ep Che Cosa Sono le Nuvole? (+sc); Teorema (+sc) (USA/GB: Theorem); Appunti per un Film sull'India (+sc). **'69** Amore e Rabbia/Vangelo '70 ep Il Fiore di Campo (+sc) (IT-FR) (USA/GB: Love and Anger); Porcile (+co-sc) (IT-FR) (USA/GB: Pigsty). **'70** Medea (+sc) (IT-FR-GER); Ostia (co-sc. only); Appunti per un'Orestiade Africana (+sc) (IT-FR) (GB: Notes for an African Oresteia). **'71** Il Decameron (+sc; +act) (IT-FR-GER) (USA/GB: The Decameron). **'72** Dodici Dicembre (anonymous co-dir); I Racconti di Canterbury (+sc; +act) (IT-FR) (USA/GB: The Canterbury Tales). **'73** Storie Scellerate (co-sc. only) (IT-FR) (GB: Bawdy Tales). **'74** Il Fiore delle Mille e Una Notte (+sc) (IT-FR) (USA/GB: Arabian Nights). **'75** Salò o le Centoventi Giornate di Sodoma (+sc) (IT-FR) (USA/GB: Salo or the 120 Days of Sodom).

a pre-moral world, obeying only his basic drives before eventually being forced to enter into knowledge, to understand the significance of his acts and to realize that certain desires are taboo. But by then it is too late and retribution inevitably follows, making many of Pasolini's films akin to pagan versions of the myth of the Fall, set in the realms of the universal and the mythic as opposed to the personal and the psychological. Indeed, his trilogy of tales – *Il Decameron* (1971, *The Decameron*), *I Racconti di Canterbury* (1972, *The Canterbury Tales*), *Il Fiore delle Mille e Una Notte* (1974, *Arabian Nights*) – celebrates a pre-lapsarian world, the invocation of an almost magical past in which innocence is still possible. *Arabian Nights* in particular is a paean to guiltless sexuality, to the naked human body and to frank sexual

desire; a film in which, unusually, the male heterosexual vision does not dominate, and male and female beauty and desire are treated in an unconventionally equal manner.

After the relative innocence of the trilogy Pasolini plunged back into the horrors of a twentieth century in the grip of Fascism with *Salò o le Centoventi Giornate di Sodoma* (1975, *Salo or the 120 Days of Sodom*). Transposing the Marquis de Sade's eighteenth-century erotic tales to a castle in northern Italy during

the last days of Mussolini, Pasolini presents an increasingly extreme series of orgies and tortures in order to demonstrate that sex is no longer a means of liberation but simply one more tool of oppression. The point may be debatable, but not the horrifying cruelty and pessimism of this uncannily valedictory work.

Pasolini was battered to death by a teenage youth shortly after completing *Salo* on November 2, 1975, in circumstances that still remain clouded and controversial.

Top: The Canterbury Tales, *part of the trilogy of medieval subjects which borrowed from the more erotic stories in Boccaccio and Chaucer. Right: a grotesque pan-sexual travesty of the marriage sacrament in* Salo – *declared obscene, blasphemous and anti-establishment in the Italian courts, but a virulent attack on fascism*

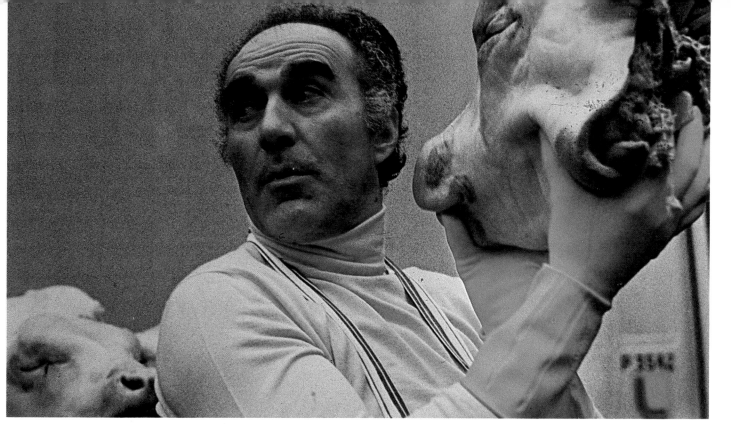

Michel Piccoli
Bourgeois or bizarre?

For several decades a leading man and character actor on both stage and screen, Michel Piccoli lends all his roles – off-beat or conventional – a welcome degree of elegance and sardonic humour

There is a certain irony, that Michel Piccoli would probably relish, in the fact that the films for which he is best known and most valued in England and America are those for which he was most reviled in France.

Born in Paris in 1925, Piccoli was on the stage for ten years before taking to the movies

Above: gluttony comes to a head in Blow-Out. *Below left: the film within a film, screenwriter (Piccoli), director (Fritz Lang), producer (Jack Palance) and assistant director (Jean-Luc Godard) as they appear in* Contempt

in the mid-Forties. In a working career spanning forty-odd years he has made something like three films a year. Yet, due to the vagaries of film distribution, the dozen or so that have been seen outside France are mostly those he made during the late Sixties and early Seventies.

This was, of course, the time of *les événements* of 1968, when everyone in Paris – even actors – nailed their colours to the mast. Piccoli's French audiences were surprised and then outraged at the sight of the man who had previously encapsulated all that they revered in suave, slightly foreign charm (he had played Don Juan in a long-running television serial) suddenly appearing in Luis Buñuel's surreal scourges of the bourgeoisie, financing and starring in the anarchic *Themroc* (1973), or eating himself to death in *La Grande Bouffe* (1973, *Blow-Out*).

Contemplating contempt

In fact, the signs of his breaking out of the 'reasonable' mould had been there long before: witness his work for Jean-Luc Godard in *Le Mépris* (1963, *Contempt*) in which he plays a writer paid to do a re-hash of 'The Odyssey' for a megalomaniac producer. The only advice Godard gave him has since become famous: 'Your character is like a character from *Marienbad* who wants to play in *Rio Bravo*', and it is some measure of Piccoli's capabilities that not only does he embody that minimal direction perfectly, he also suggests an abrasiveness and hurt quite at odds with his recognized 'image' of that time.

Piccoli can certainly appear to be as withdrawn and insulated as the nameless participants in Resnais' *L'Année Dernière à Marienbad* (1961, *Last Year in Marienbad*), but it

445

clearly does not spring from any emotional indifference. As *Contempt* demonstrated, his awareness of the social pressures bearing down on him, the prostitution of his talents and his wife's contempt for him are almost too strong to allow his character any impassioned response. Yet it was Piccoli's urbanity that continued to appeal to his countrymen. *Les Choses de la Vie* (1970, *The Things of Life*) is a typical example of the middle-of-the-road commercial ventures in which Piccoli involved himself too often to enable his homeground audience to appreciate his more outlandish talents. *The Things of Life* gave him the role of another comfortable, suave womanizer, yet there are still moments that he made his own: a finicky taste in shirts – they had to be a certain shade of blue, a certain cut of collar – betrayed an appealing fastidiousness, a quality that film critic David Thomson pinned down with 'There is a marvellous note of the gloomy connoisseur in Piccoli'. It markedly resurfaces, albeit in different mood, in *Blow Out*

when he expands at length on the wonders of rubber gloves!

Indeed, *Blow Out* might be regarded as the pivot of his career, the moment when he finally alienated his French audience and appeared to the rest of the world as 'himself': scabrous but charming, immersed in – but subtly distanced from – the outrages of his surroundings. A man who could regard with perfect equanimity both the surreal fetishism of those rubber gloves and the proposition of eating himself to death.

Having their cake and eating it

Blow Out is in many ways a mirror image of Buñuel's *El Angel Exterminador* (1962, *The Exterminating Angel*), where a party of house guests find themselves locked in a room without anything to eat. In *Blow Out* the director Marco Ferreri inverts Buñuel's world into a crueller version in which four men willingly withdraw from everyday life and commit group suicide in an orgy of gluttony. Whether continuing his ballet practice, flexing himself sedately at the wall bars or finally exploding on the verandah, Piccoli continues to convey the same slightly removed intellectuality that is perfectly suited to Ferreri's brand of Surrealism. By keeping his sceptical distance he also invites the audience to view the bizarre nature of ordinary objects or the cruelty of human appetites.

It is this quality that so enhances Ferreri's earlier *Dillinger è Morto* (1969, *Dillinger Is Dead*). Cinematically, the film achieves a tranquil perfection in terms of formal composition, but it is Piccoli's quiet concentration that makes it one of the most purely reflective films ever made. He roams the house, alone and silent; whether caressing the images that a projector throws on a wall, making a salad or dismantling an old revolver, he judges to perfection the distance between the spiritual needs of humans and the oppressive weight of the world of objects.

Similarly, the achievement of a man taking

Below left: Renée (Jane Fonda) falls in love with the son of her husband (Piccoli) in La Curée *(1966, The Game Is Over). Above: LeCoeur (Piccoli) presides over the ladies of Le Moulin Bleu in* Lady L *(1965)*

apart his life and striking out for freedom reaches a peak of anarchic enthusiasm in *Themroc*, a film financed by Piccoli and in which he unusually appears as a fully paid-up member of the working class. Throwing over his oppressive family and job, he reverts to a state of nature – knocking down the walls of his flat, sleeping with his sister and eating policemen. The cry of anger from this modern caveman revealed a rare side to Piccoli; a sheer physicality rarely glimpsed since.

Semi-detached

Given his usual air of detachment, it is perhaps strange that he has not worked more with Claude Chabrol, the most sardonic observer of the French bourgeoisie. His role in *Les Noces Rouges* (1973, *Red Wedding*) personified the small-town urges of the petit bourgeois, but the best-remembered sequence – his seduction of Stéphane Audran in the local museum – has distinct overtones of Surrealism.

It is the sort of touch that Buñuel has made his own and which certainly underlines Piccoli's presence in both *Le Charme Discret de la Bourgeoisie* (1972, *The Discreet Charm of the Bourgeoisie*) and *Le Fantôme de la Liberté* (1974, *The Phantom of Liberty*). Indeed, Buñuel's famous three-quarter-length shots seem ideally suited to capture Piccoli's talents: the imposing physical presence, broad chest, thick neck and leonine head can all be contained in the frame. The emotional intimacy of the close-up is rarely demanded, and the characters' ironic detachment underlines the bizarre aspects of any surrounding world.

Below left: Rada Rassimov in Grandeur Nature *(1974, Life Size). Above: a scene from* Themroc.

Filmography

1945 Sortilèges (GB: The Sorcerer). **'49** Le Point de Jour; Le Parfum de la Dame en Noir. **'50** Sans Laisser d'Adresse; Terreur en Oklahoma (short) (GB: Terror of Oklahoma). **'51** Chicago Digest (short). **'52** Torticola contre Frankensberg (short); Saint Tropez, Devoir de Vacances (short). **'54** Destinées *ep* Jeanne d'Arc (FT-IT) (USA: Daughters of Destiny; GB: Love, Soldiers and Women). **'55** Interdit de Séjour (GB: The Price of Love); French Cancan (FR-IT) (USA: Only the French Can); Tout Chante Autour de Moi; Les Mauvaises Rencontres; Ernst Thälmann, Führer seine Klasse (E.GER). **'56** Marie Antoinette (FR-IT) (GB: Shadow of the Guillotine); La Mort en ce Jardin (FR-MEX) (USA: Gina; GB: Evil Eden). **'57** Les Sorcières de Salem (FR-E.GER) (GB: The Witches of Salem); Nathalie (FR-IT) (USA/GB: The Foxiest Girl in Paris). **'58** Rafles sur la Ville (GB: Trap for a Killer); Tabarin (FR-IT). **'59** La Bête a l'Affût. **'60** La Dragée Haute; Le Bal des Espions. **'61** Le Vergini di Roma (IT-FR-YUG) (USA/GB: Amazons of Rome); Le Rendez-vous de Nöel (short); Fumée, Histoire et Fantaisie (short); Le Rendez-vous (FT-IT); La Chevelure (short). **'62** Climats (GB: Climates of Love). **'63** Le Doulos; Le Jour et l'Heure (FR-IT) (USA: The Day and the Hour); Le Mépris (FR-IT) (USA/GB: Contempt). **'64** Le Journal d'un Femme de Chambre (FR-IT) (USA/GB: The Diary of a Chambermaid); Paparazzi (doc. short) (as himself). **'65** La Chance et l'Amour (FR-IT); De l'Amour (FR-IT) (GB: All About Loving); Le Coup de Grâce; Masquerade (GB); Marie Soleil; Lady L (FR-IT); Compartiment Tueurs (USA/GB: The Sleeping Car Murders); Café Tabac (short). **'66** La Guerre Est Finie (GB: The War Is Over); La Curée (FT-IT) (USA/GB: The Game Is Over); Les Ruses du Diable; Les Créatures (FR-SWED); Paris Brûle-t-il? (USA/GB: Is Paris Burning?); La Voleuse (FR-GER). **'67** Les Demoiselles de Rochefort (USA/GB: The Young Girls of Rochefort); Un Homme de Trop (FR-IT) (USA: Shock Troops); Belle de Jour (FR-IT); Mon Amour, Mon Amour (GB: My Love, My Love). **'68** Benjamin, ou les Mémoires d'un Puceau (GB: Benjamin, or the Diary of an Innocent Young Man); Diabolik (IT-FR) (USA/GB: Danger: Diabolik); La Chamade (FR-IT) (GB: Heartbeat); La Prisonnière (FR-IT) (GB: Woman in Chains). **'69** Dillinger è Morto (IT) (GB: Dillinger Is Dead); La Voie Lactée (FT-IT) (USA/GB: The Milky Way); Topaz (USA); L'Invitée (FR-IT). **'70** Les Choses de la Vie (USA/GB: The Things of Life); L'Invasion (FR-IT). **'71** Max et les Ferrailleurs; La Poudre d'Escampette (USA: Touch and Go); La Décade Prodigieuse (USA/GB: Ten Days' Wonder). **'72** Liza/La Cagna (FR-IT); L'Udienza (IT); Le Charme Discret de la Bourgeoisie (FR-SP-IT) (USA/GB: The Discreet Charm of the Bourgeoisie); L'Attentat (FR-IT-GER) (USA: The French Conspiracy; GB: Plot); César et Rosalie (narr. only) (FR/IT/GER) (USA/GB: César and Rosalie). **'73** La Femme en Bleu (FR-IT); Themroc; Les Noces Rouges (USA: Wedding in Blood; GB: Red Wedding); La Grande Bouffe (FR-IT) (USA/GB: Blow-Out); Le Far-West (BELG-FR). **'74** Touche pas à la Femme Blanche; Le Trio Infernal (FR-GER-IT) (GB: The Infernal Trio); Grandeur Nature (FR-SP-IT) (USA: Love Doll; GB: Life Size); Le Fantôme de la Liberté (USA/GB: The Phantom of Liberty); Vincent, François, Paul et les Autres (USA: Vincent, François, Paul and the Others). **'75** La Faille (FR-GER-IT); Léoner (FR-SP-IT); 7 Morts sur Ordonnance (FR-SP-GER). **'76** L'Ultima Donna (IT-FR) (USA/GB: The Last Woman); F. Comme Fairbanks; Mado (FR-GER-IT); Todo Modo (IT). **'77** René la Canne (FR-IT); Des Enfants Gâtés (USA: Spoiled Children); L'Imprécateur; La Part du Feu. **'78** L'Etat Sauvage; Strauberg ist da (GER); La Petite Fille en Velours Bleu; Le Sucre. **'79** Giallo Napoletano (IT); Le Divorcement; Le Mors aux Dents. **'80** Salto nel Vuoto (IT-FR); Der Preis für Uberleben (GER); Atlantic City USA (CAN-FR) (USA/GB: Atlantic City). **'81** La Fille Prodigue; Une Etrange Affaire; Espion, Lève-Toi. **'82** La Passante du Sans-Souci (FR-GER); Passion (FR-IT); Le Prix du Danger; Oltre la Porta (IT); Une Chambre en Ville; Que les Gros Salaires Lèvent le Doigt! Le General de l'Armée Morte (+ prod; + co-sc) (FR-IT). **'83** Viva la Vie. **'84** Le Matelot 512; La Diagonale du Fou (SWITZ) (USA/GB: Dangerous Moves); Adieu Bonaparte. **'85** Peril à la Demeure (USA/GB: Death in a French Garden); Partir Revenir; **'86** Mauvais Sang; Le Paltoquet; Mon Beau-Frère a Tué Ma Soeur. **'87** La Rumba. **'88** Y'A Bon les Blancs (USA/GB: Um, Good De White Folks).

GHSTBUSTERS

With its high-tech thrills undercut by flippant humour, *Ghostbusters* charmed its American audience to the tune of $212 million on its 1984 summer release. The key to its style lies with a group of writers and actors who have come to dominate Hollywood mainstream comedy in the Eighties.

Its roots lie in the anti-Vietnam, taboo-breaking Sixties when *National Lampoon* magazine emerged with its mix of foul-mouthed humour and literary parody. America's rock generation responded to its scatalogical irreverence. In the Seventies, director/producer Ivan Reitman successfully produced radio and stage shows under the *Lampoon* banner using such talent as John Belushi, Chevy Chase, Dan Aykroyd, Bill Murray, Gildna Radner and Harold Ramis. All were to appear in television's equivalent, *Saturday Night Live*, which attracted a cult late-night following of 20 million people.

Hollywood reached this audience with *National Lampoon's Animal House* (1978) (produced by Reitman and co-written by Harold Ramis) which made John Belushi's gross anti-hero a star and $80 million at the box-office. Its audience responded to the flaunting of authority and the basic desire to have a good time. Institutions were systematically sent up in *Caddyshack* (1980 — the exclusive club), *Stripes* (1982 – the army) and *National Lampoon's Vacation* (1984 – the family).

The financial success of these films gave Reitman little trouble in securing a $30-million film budget from Columbia, the biggest yet for a comedy. *Ghostbusters* is very much in the spirit of previous *Lampoon*-inspired films. While comedy antecedents like *The Cat and the Canary* (1939) and *The Ghost Breakers* (1940) with Bob Hope maintained an atmosphere of menace, *Ghostbusters* doesn't care but delights in the ghostly mayhem wreacked in Manhattan; the first spook is caught only after much destruction of an exclusive hotel.

We are never meant to believe in the film's heroes as scientists. Bill Murray's Venkman is first seen ingratiating himself with a female student by falsifying her telepathic capabilities. He is out to have fun and, by implication, so are we. By the time New York is engulfed by supernatural phenomena, these 'scientists', cigarettes drooping from their mouths, act like hard-boiled crimefighters of the Fifties, cleaning up the city with a world weary air.

Bill Murray is a key to the film's success. His laid-back cynicism

wonderfully undermines the abnormal events surrounding him. (It is a subversive attitude for a special-effects film of a genre that wants its audience to marvel at its expensive and spectacular sequences.) Murray appears slightly detached from the action. His one-liners seem pitched towards the audience rather than the characters. 'I think we better split up,' he suggests while tracking a ghost, 'we can do more damage that way.' Reitman's previous work with Murray pays off in his intelligent use of the actor. Murray works best when reacting to, rather than initiating, a situation; his attempt to play a 'straight' role carrying the dramatic weight in John Byrum's adaptation of Somerset Maugham's *The Razor's Edge* (1984, given to Murray in exchange for his role in *Ghostbusters*) was less than

satisfactory. Exposition is left to Dan Aykroyd.

Aykroyd had established a television partnership with John Belushi in the Seventies taking their creations, *The Blues Brothers* (1980), on to film in 1980. His original script for *Ghostbusters* was envisaged as another vehicle for them both, implying a more raucous approach to the plot. Although Belushi's death ended the partnership, Aykroyd still works best in comedy teams – Eddie Murphy (*Trading Places*, 1983), Chevy Chase (*Spies Like Us*, 1985) and Tom Hanks (*Dragnet*, 1987). He is a marvellously laconic comic feed rather than a solo turn, making Murray's lion's share of the best lines all the more appropriate.

The film's climatic battle takes place in a studio-bound apartment-block setting that contrasts with the

real New York location scenes that precede it. Its artificiality gives the action even more of a cartoon air. By now the film is blatantly urging its audience to join in. Ray Parker Jr's title song has the built-in refrain 'Ghostbusters' which encourages audience participation. Cheering crowds chant the title as the phanton fighters arrive to do battle. The end credits roll over a similar scene of adulation as the victors return.

While attempting lighter comedy in the romantic thriller *Legal Eagles* (1986), with Debra Winger and Robert Redford, even there Reitman could not resist large-scale car chases and pyrotechnics. In *Ghostbusters* his orchestration of action and intelligent use of the leading actors magically adds up to a film that is sheer lunacy from beginning to end.

6

Returning from investigating an apparition in the New York Public Library, university parapsychologists Venkman, Stantz and Spengler (1) discover funding for their department has been discontinued. Undaunted they buy a disused fire station and set up in private practice as 'ghostbusters'.

Venkman is immediately attracted to their first client, Dana Barrett, whose flat is experiencing poltergeist disturbances. More interested in sex, he loses the case but is later called with his partners to investigate disruptions at a smart hotel. They eventually capture a glutinous green ghost. Success and an escalation of supernatural activity leads to fame and over-work.

Venkman's persistence finally gets him a date with Dana who has now become possessed as 'The Gate Keeper' for an ancient spirit (2). Her health-obsessed neighbour Louis is chased by a large hell-hound (3) before being 'taken over' as 'The Key Master'.

Meanwhile, an environmental-protection officer arrests the scientists and shuts down their spectral holding-tank, unleashing a variety of ghouls and ghosts throughout the city.

All are drawn to Dana's apartment block. Research reveals it was built originally by worshippers of a demonic, Sumerian demi-god, Gozer. A desperate mayor releases the ghostbusters to prevent 'a disaster of biblical proportions'. Dana and Louis metamorphose into hell-hounds as Gozer first confronts its adversaries in the form of a woman (4). Selecting the mode of the city's destruction from a stray thought by Stantz, Gozer becomes a Staypuft Marshmallow Man (5) to flatten the city. Eliminating this threat with their nuclear-powered ionization rays, the ghostbusters can only destroy Gozer by taking the death-defying step of crossing their laser streams (6). However, Dana and Louis become human again and the city is saved to much cheering.

Directed by Ivan Reitman, 1984

Prod co: Columbia-Delphi. **prod:** Ivan Reitman. **sc:** Dan Ackroyd, Harold Ramis. **photo** (Metrocolor/Panavision): Laszlo Kovacs, (New York) Herb Wagreitch. **ed:** Sheldon Kahn, David Blewitt. **prod dir:** John De Cuir. **art dir:** John De Cuir Jr, (New York) John Moore. **cost:** Theoni V. Aldredge. **mus:** Elmer Bernstein. **song:** Ray Parker Jr. **sd:** Richard Beggs, Tom McCarthy Jr. **ass dir:** Gary Daigler, Katterli Frauenfelder, (New York) Peter Giuliano, John Pepper, Bill Eustace. **sp eff:** Richard Edlund (sup), John Bruno (art dir), Conrad Buff (ed). **stunt co-ord:** Bill Couch. **r/t** 105 mins.
Cast: Bill Murray (Doctor Peter Venkman), Dan Aykroyd (Doctor Raymond Stantz), Sigourney Weaver (Dana Barrett), Harold Ramis (Doctor Egon Spengler), Rick Moranis (Louis Tully), Annie Potts (Janine Melnitz), William Atherton (Walter Peck), Ernie Hudson (Winston Zeddmore), David Jovan (Gozer), Michael Ensign (Hotel Manager), Alice Drummond (Librarian), David Margulies (Mayor).

MOCK SCHLOCK HORROR

The career of John Landis

John Landis quickly established himself as one of America's foremost comedy directors, his zany humour proving irresistably popular with youthful audiences

As with so many young film-makers working today, it was a film featuring the special effects of Ray Harryhausen that started John Landis on his career; when the eight-year-old Landis returned from seeing *The Seventh Voyage of Sinbad* (1958) his future was decided.

Born in Chicago in 1950, John Landis was the third child of Marshall and Shirley Landis. When he was four months old the family moved to the Westwood section of Los Angeles where his love for movies was to begin.

Once his mind was made up about his career, Landis attempted to 'get into movies'. Disappointment followed disappointment until he managed to find himself a job as mail boy with 20th Century-Fox. This immediately put the young enthusiast into contact with professional writers and directors, one such being Andrew Marton, perhaps best known for his second-unit work on several big action films.

In 1969 Marton went off to Yugoslavia to work on *Kelly's Heroes* (1970). Landis withdrew his savings from the bank, bought an airplane ticket to London and from there made his way to the location of *Kelly's Heroes*, where he was able to secure a job as a 'gopher' ('gopher this, gopher that'). As the lengthy production progressed Landis assumed greater responsibilities; by the end of shooting he was a production assistant. Meanwhile, Landis also became friends with Clint Eastwood's stand-in,

Jim O'Rourke. Following the completion of *Kelly's Heroes* the pair remained in Europe to work on several Italian-made Westerns, including *Valdez Is Coming* (1971). Landis, who had never previously done stunt work, found himself falling off horses and coaching non-English-speaking actors.

High-speed hits

After being involved in nearly seventy such films, Landis and O'Rourke returned to Hollywood. However, American film production was going through a slump and they were unable to find work. It was during this period that Landis saw the British-made monster movie *Trog* (1970). The film so outraged and amused him that he set about writing his own monster-movie spoof *Schlock!* (1973).

With money raised from relatives and

friends, Landis and O'Rourke managed to produce the film in just 13 days. As well as directing it Landis had a starring role as the title monster: the Schlock suit was designed by his long-time friend, special-effects makeup artist Rick Baker. *Schlock!* became a late-night drive-in classic in America, and in 1973 won the Grand Prix at the 14th Annual Science Fiction Film Festival in Trieste. In 1975 the film went on to win the award for the Best Comedy Sequences at the Chamrousse Comedy Film Festival in France, where Landis picked up the Best Actor award.

It was while promoting *Schlock!* on the Johnny Carson television chat-show that Landis was spotted by David Zucker, co-creator of the popular Kentucky Fried Theatre. Zucker introduced Landis to his partners Jim Abrahams and Jerry Zucker. After a year's work together this foursome, along with producer Robert K. Weiss, had made a four-sketch, ten-minute pilot film. Following its successful screening in west Los Angeles, Kim Jorgensen, owner of the Parallax cinema chain, offered to find backing for a feature-film version.

Kentucky Fried Movie (1977), made on a small budget of $600,000, was completed in 23 days. The film proved to be a surprise hit and brought Landis to the attention of Sean Daniel,

Left: Landis and victims of An American Werewolf in London. *Above: certainly no Roman he – John Belushi at a fraternity 'do' in* National Lampoon's Animal House. *Above right:* The Blues Brothers – *Dan Ackroyd (left) and Belushi with Ray Charles (centre). Below: A film that lived up to its advertising. Below right:* Three Amigos – *Chevy Chase, Steve Martin, Martin Short*

a Universal production executive. Daniel referred Landis to producers Marty Simmons and Ivan Reitman who were preparing a film, *National Lampoon's Animal House* (1978), based on the American college-humour magazine National Lampoon. After a couple of months with the scriptwriters, Landis took a crew on location to Oregon. The hugely successful comedy completed shooting in 36 days, with Landis averaging the extraordinary number of 30 camera set-ups a day.

Banishing the blues

With *National Lampoon's Animal House* quickly becoming one of the biggest money-spinners in Universal's history – and its star John Belushi equally quickly becoming a national institution through his performances (both live and recorded) with his soul music group the Blues Brothers – it was only natural that Universal should team Landis and Belushi for a film based on the Blues Brothers. With $27 million at his disposal John Landis turned *The Blues Brothers* (1980) into a surreal musical comedy, full of spectacular car chases and musical showcases for artists such as Cab Calloway, Ray Charles and Aretha Franklin.

Unfortunately for *The Blues Brothers*, two other big-budget Hollywood films by young directors began to attract publicity of a negative type at the time of its production. Both Steven Spielberg's *1941* (1979) – in which Landis actually has a small part – and Michael Cimino's *Heaven's Gate* (1980) were running well over budget and schedule, and to the general press it seemed natural to lump *The Blues Brothers* into the same category. In fact *The Blues Brothers* came in slightly under

budget and on time and inaccurate reports that the film was a mammoth 'financial disaster' still annoy Landis.

With *National Lampoon's Animal House* and *The Blues Brothers* to his credit, Landis was able to realize his long-cherished project *An American Werewolf in London* (1981) through his own British-based production company Lycanthrope Films Limited. The script was initially turned down by dozens of producers who felt this particularly off-beat mix of comedy and horror was untenable. However, Landis went on to create a blend of ghoulish humour that was highly successful.

Landis' career was troubled by the accidental death of actor Vic Morrow during the filming of *Twilight Zone: The Movie* (1983), which resulted in prolonged court action. He continued making wild comic capers, with new stars such as Chevy Chase, Dan Aykroyd and Eddie Murphy, which took him into high finance, *Trading Places* (1983), espionage, *Spies Like Us* (1985), smuggling, *Into the Night* (1985) and Hollywood and Westerns, *Three Amigos* (1986).

Filmography
1970 Kelly's Heroes (uncredited prod. ass. only). '73 Schlock! (+ sc; + act). '77 Kentucky Fried Movie. '78 National Lampoon's Animal House. '79 1941 (actor only). '80 The Blues Brothers (+ co-sc; + act). '81 An American Werewolf in London (+ sc). '83 Twilight Zone: The Movie (ep dir); Trading Places. '85 Spies Like Us; Into the Night (+ act). '86 Three Amigos. '87 Amazon Women on the Moon; Quest.

This film is totally out of control!

FRESH... FRANTIC... FUNNY...
REFRESHINGLY REBELLIOUS... RIBALD... LAVISH...
RUDE... HILARIOUS... ZANY... BRILLIANT...

MERYL STREEP

Hollywood royalty

Hollywood has always had its own aristocracy, and in the Eighties the Queen of the lot was Meryl Streep

Without doubt Meryl Streep is the front-ranking screen actress of the Eighties. She is certainly its highest-paid. In 1987 she was (successfully) demanding $4 million a movie. Jane Fonda and Glenn Close grumbled that she was getting all the best parts. Cher, her co-star in *Silkwood* (1983), called her 'an acting machine in the same sense that a shark is a killing machine. That's what she was born to be'. Robert Benton, who directed Streep in *Kramer vs Kramer* (1979), declared. 'There's nothing she can't do. Like De Niro she has no limits. I've watched Meryl over the years, and she's so staggeringly different in *Kramer* from the way she is in *The Deer Hunter*, and try as I might, I can't figure out why. She has an immense backbone of technique, but you never catch her using it.' De Niro himself called Streep 'a pure actress', his favourite.

She has worked opposite Redford, Nichol-son, Woody Allen, Alan Alda and Dustin Hoffman, and they all have nothing but praise for her. Hoffman's adulation, however, was tempered with ambiguity: 'We fought over scenes to the point where we were really angry with each other. I mean, you're in the ring with Sugar Ray Leonard. But I had to respect her', he said. 'Nobody today is doing what she's doing. *Nobody.*'

In an era where box-office takings equals

Two very different Karen's for Meryl Streep: in Out of Africa *(above), she plays the Danish writer Karen Blixen, in love with the tranquil beauty of Africa; while in* Silkwood *(below), she portrays Karen Silkwood, a lively worker in a plutonium processing plant. She received Oscar nominations for both roles*

futurism, androids and Vietnam, Meryl Streep has hung on to the best women's parts with her canines. She ploughs as much energy into obtaining her roles as she puts into performing them. The director Alan J. Pakula had decided on an unknown actress to play the part of Sophie Zawistowska in his film version of William Styron's best-selling novel *Sophie's Choice* (1982). Streep procured a pirated copy of the script 'through nefarious means' and fell in love with it. Her agent contacted Pakula, but he said he wasn't interested. The part was cast. She then pestered Pakula for an interview personally until, at last, he conceded to a meeting. She arrived at his home, glowered at the photographs of the 'unknown actress' plastered over the walls, and then went to work on him. 'I threw myself on the ground,' Streep admitted, '"Please, God, let me do it", I begged.' She got the role and won an Oscar for it.

She was equally determined to play the part of Karen Blixen in *Out of Africa* (1985). The director, Sydney Pollack, didn't think her sexy enough – he wasn't even interested in an interview. Again, Streep pestered her way into a submission from the film-maker. And she made him believe she was sexy enough. She got the role and the film won six Oscars. She was nominated for the sixth time.

What Pollack forgot was that a good actress can *play* sexy – and that a great one can *become* sexy. Mike Nicholls, who directed Streep in *Silkwood* (1983) and *Heartburn* (1986) averred, 'Meryl is actually *great* – there is no other performer I would say this of'. 'Meryl' will also point out that she was voted 'Best Looking' at high school. But her younger brother indicates that she 'was pretty ghastly'. She *was* an ugly duckling: spectacles, puppy-fat and a propensity for bossiness made her an unbearable adolescent. But the glasses were replaced by contact lenses, the flesh was toned up and the bossy streak was carefully disguised – Meryl Streep was going to continue to get her own way.

It is a fact of life that whenever an actor becomes entirely too successful – Streisand, Hoffman, Pacino – they become difficult. That is their perfectionism coming out. But when a performer works as hard as Meryl Streep does, and produces such outstanding results, then they deserve their own perfectionism.

Streep *becomes* her characters. She talks to them, she waters them and she expects to be treated in character when she is at work. On the set of *Ironweed* (1987), in which she played a Depression-era drunk, director Hector Babenco ended up grabbing her by the shoulders, pushing her in place and grunting at her, as she failed to respond to intellectual direction. Once again, she had become the part.

Streep is, however, as fiercely domestic as she is unstintingly professional. The mother of three children, she has served her term of cooking, washing, ironing, shopping and doubling up as child-chauffeur. Although a multi-millionairess, she prefers to keep in touch with her own reality, not to stint as wife and mother. After all, how is an actress expected to impersonate *people* if closeted in an ivory tower? But Streep does resent the invasion of her privacy, and strives to live in relative solitude on a multi-million-dollar estate with her husband, sculptor Don Gummer, and a full-time nanny. The rest of the time she's in exotic climes making movies.

Her own background is modestly ordinary. She was born Mary Louise Streep on June 22, 1949, in suburban New Jersey. Her father was a pharmaceutical executive, her mother a commercial artist. The family – Mr and Mrs, two sons and Meryl – lived a comfortable middle-class existence and periodically treated themselves to ball games, museums, ballet and the theatre.

At 12, Mary Louise took singing lessons and began to think of performance as a career. Her first characterization, she claims, was as a 'blonde homecoming queen' when she joined class at Bernards High School, minus her glasses and with peroxided hair. 'I was your perfect *Seventeen* magazine knockout', she glowed. She was the perfect Miss America. She was also a cheerleader and starred in all the high school musicals: *The Music Man, Li'l Abner, Oklahoma*.

At Vassar College Mary Louise dropped the Sandra Dee look and opted for Stanislavsky. Her *Miss Julie* was a landmark at the college and carried her into an honours programme with Dartmouth and then on to Yale on a three-year scholarship. In between, the actress dabbled with a rep company playing Shaw and Chekhov for $48 a week.

The Yale School of Drama, enabling her to play 15 roles a year, was an intense programme. 'I was constantly throwing up, on my way to an ulcer', she said. Her Fine Arts degree from Yale propelled her to New York, where she talked herself into an audition for Pinero's *Trelawny of the Wells* which, naturally, she got. The producer was Joe Papp and he subsequently cast her as Isabella in *Measure for Measure* at the Shakespeare in the Park. Also in

Above: Streep and Robert De Niro in Michael Cimino's The Deer Hunter – *sharing their last few hours of idyllic friendship at a wedding before the young men go off to war. Below: mother and son in* Kramer vs Kramer – *Streep with Justin Henry*

the cast was John Cazale, best known as Fredo in the *Godfather* films, and the couple fell in love. For two years they lived together, at a time when Streep's career was on the ascent and Cazale's health on the wane.

Streep made her film debut in Fred Zinnemann's *Julia* (1976), as the aristocratic friend of Jane Fonda, and then landed the female 'lead' in a TV film, *The Deadliest Season* (1977), a tough hockey drama. She was offered a small part in Michael Cimino's *The Deer Hunter* (1978) – as Christopher Walken's girlfriend – and accepted it because Cazale had a leading role. Robert De Niro was the above-title star, as Michael, who was also in love with Streep's character. 'They needed a girl between two guys and I was it', the actress explained. 'But I was ecstatic to be in it because of John.' Cimino thought the part too small and suggested Streep write her own lines to bolster it up a bit. She did, and won her first Oscar nomination. Sadly, it was Cazale's last film.

While he was dying of bone cancer in New York, Streep had to honour her contract to play the wife of a concentration-camp victim in *Holocaust*, a mini-series filming in Austria. The experience was harrowing – both the grimness of the role and her enforced separation from the dying man she loved. After *Holocaust* was completed, she stayed by Cazale's side until his death in March, 1978.

Streep buried her sorrow in work and, freshly armed with an Emmy award for *Holocaust*, was in demand. She took the role of seductress in *The Seduction of Joe Tynan* (1979), a Southern lawyer who sets her sights on

In 1982, for her role of the emotionally tormented Polish immigrant in *Sophie's Choice*, Streep won her second Academy Award. At the podium on Oscar night she was so nervous that she dropped her speech, but managed to inform her audience, 'No matter how much you try to imagine what this is like – it's just so incredibly thrilling, right down to your toes'.

The following year she was nominated for *Silkwood*, the true story of Karen Silkwood, a factory worker contaminated by plutonium and of her fight to expose the leak. For *Out of Africa* Streep was nominated a sixth time, for her part as the strong-willed Danish authoress who falls for an English adventurer (Redford) in the bush. In keeping with the quality of all of the actress's work, the picture accumulated six Oscars, including a statuette for best film.

Babenco's *Ironweed*, based on the novel by William Kennedy, was less well-received, accused of self-indulgence and unremitting grimness, but Streep was superb – tragic, detached, subtly graceful. Playing brilliantly off her friend Jack Nicholson ('a master, the Mick Jagger of the movies'), she was nominated a seventh time. In the history of Hollywood, no other actress has been so honoured in so short a period. Long live the Queen.

Filmography
1976: Julia. '77 The Deadliest Season (TV). '78 The Deer Hunter. '79 Manhattan; The Seduction of Joe Tynan; Kramer vs Kramer. '81 The French Lieutenant's Woman. '82 Still of the Night; Sophie's Choice. '83 Silkwood. '84 Falling in Love. '85 Plenty; Out of Africa. '86 Heartburn. '87 Ironweed. '88 Azaria (aka Evil Angels).

Above: for Sophie's Choice, *playing opposite Kevin Kline, Streep mastered a Polish accent. Below right: in* The French Lieutenant's Woman *her accent was immaculately English*

married Senator Alan Alda, and gets him; she was Woody Allen's lesbian ex-wife in *Manhattan*; and, in her last supporting role, was the estranged wife of Dustin Hoffman in *Kramer vs Kramer*. Each film, released within nine months of each other, was showered with critical praise. In each film, Meryl Streep was edging closer towards stardom.

The Oscar for *Kramer vs Kramer* brought it. 'Holy mackerel!' she cried on Oscar night, thanking Hoffman and Robert Benton in her acceptance speech. Later that night she left her prize behind in the lavatory, explaining, 'It shows how nervous I really was'.

In spite of Streep's habitual appearance at the Oscar ceremony, the actress has never lost her awe of the occasion. Her annual election for Best Actress has almost become an in-joke. After her nomination for *The Deer Hunter* and win for *Kramer*, she was nominated for her next performance, Sara Woodruff, in *The French Lieutenant's Woman* (1981). The Los Angeles Herald-Examiner raved over her portrayal: 'We can believe this woman is all things – crazy, visionary, pure, despoiled – because Streep has incorporated all the possibilities into her performance.' Streep was less confident of her version of the mysterious beauty: 'I couldn't help wishing that I was more beautiful', she told *Time* magazine, 'I really wished I was the kind of actress who could have just stood there and said it all.'

Woody Allen

Woody Allen's first films were broad satires. In his later work he has opted for an increasingly baleful – and autobiographical – view of the world, one where love and sex become more and more impossible and death emerges as the biggest single fact of life. He directs movies in which he plays pained misfits possessed of a lacerating, self-deprecating wit and surrounded by hopelessly neurotic women. No other film-maker so readily associated with comedy has presented such a despondent and pessimistic vision of relationships and adult behaviour in modern bourgeois America

Films about love and other neuroses

In his nightclub act, Woody Allen tells about once being offered a fortune to make some vodka advertisements and not knowing whether to accept or not. 'I needed the money,' he laments, 'but I feel that drinking intoxicating beverages is immoral.' Wracked by indecision, he seeks trustworthy advice – from his psychiatrist, his bank manager, finally his rabbi. 'Don't do it!' cries God's spokesman. 'Vodka is evil! Refuse the money!' He does, and immediately feels a better man for it. Later, he sees one of the ads he has righteously turned down. It shows Senta Berger in a skimpy bikini reclining on a sun-drenched beach holding a cool vodka and tonic. Her lips are provocatively parted, her eyes smoulder with desire for the man beside her. The man is Allen's rabbi.

There, in angstful and Talmudic miniature, is the key to Woody Allen's vision and popular appeal as a film-maker. Critics have called his work undisciplined, confused, emotionally self-indulgent, psychologically and artistically dishonest. But audiences composed largely of the educated middle and upper classes have nevertheless come more and more to identify with the nerve-wracking little fables he builds upon his view of the world, and to agree, wryly, that modern urban life really is plagued by the treachery, false counsel, neurotic insecurity and pandemic philistinism he portrays.

Since 1966, when *What's Up, Tiger Lily?* was released, Allen has made or starred in approximately one film a year – and while none has been a box-office smash all have earned money, nearly all go on being shown and re-shown in big-city cinemas around the world, and many are already considered comedy classics.

Born Allen Stewart Konigsberg in New York in 1935, he dropped out of university and began to write for television and top American comedians before working as a dramatist and stand-up comic himself. Allen's early films are, in fact, more like nightclub routines than proper movies – gags strung together around a theme with no serious attempt at organic cinematic composition. *What's Up, Tiger Lily?* is really the old game of putting funny captions to familiar pictures – in this case an English soundtrack to a Japanese samurai thriller – producing verbal pyrotechnics like, 'Heathen Pig! Saracen Dog! Spanish Fly!' *Take the Money and Run* (1969), in which Allen plays Virgil Stockwell, an underprivileged *schlemiel* chasing the American Dream (or Nightmare) who tries cello first, then bank robbery, and ends up getting life, is an episodic documentary send-up of 'committed' sociological problem films complete with voice-over, psychoanalytic asides and comments from Jewish parents

Above: Woody as Isaac Davis who, having just been told by the girl he has deserted to 'have a little faith in people', confides in his tape-recorder in Manhattan

disguised in funny noses. *Bananas* (1971) stars Allen as Manhattan drop-out Fielding Mellish in a banana-republic revolution and is a topical bistro act – with palm trees – satirizing television ads, radical politics and New York culture snobbery.

Sex and the single sheep

Everything You Always Wanted to Know About Sex, But Were Afraid to Ask (1972) is a series of revue sketches built loosely around the title of Dr David Reuben's pop sexology best-seller. Leaning hard on one-liners, innuendo, and a lot of ridiculous libidinal props, it is especially notable for one finely directed sequence featuring Gene Wilder as an hysterical psychiatrist who falls in love with a sheep, loses all, and ends up on Skid Row swigging Woolite. *Play It Again, Sam*, made by Herbert Ross in 1972 from Allen's Broadway play, is the story of a romantic creep-hero possessed by the spirit of Humphrey Bogart. The film is important for Allen's first clearly defined performance as the 'little man' victimized by his own fears and self-loathing – the now familiar

455

Allen persona – and for introducing Diane Keaton as his leading lady (she co-starred in four of his next six films). *Sleeper* (1973), Allen's fourth directorial outing and the first with a tight enough script to begin looking like a proper movie, is a parody of a science-fiction thriller taking a backwards look at Sixties and Seventies mid-cult American absurdities.

Love and Death (1975), a fondly observed parody of *War and Peace* and perhaps the best conceived of Allen's comedies, is his tribute to the classical literature that seems to play so important a role in his own vision of himself. Dealing with the themes of the title that will become steadily more important in his later films (at times insufferably so), the film ends with a hallmark sequence (reminiscent of the vodka joke) in which Allen, as Boris Grushenko, condemned to death for attempting to assassinate Napoleon (of *course* he failed), is solemnly promised by an angel that God means to spare his life – following which he is promptly and hitchlessly executed. Martin Ritt's *The Front* (1976) is the first film starring Allen to abandon a specifically funny format, and it serves as a bridge to the films that follow. An exposé of the McCarthyist persecution of film and television writers in the Fifties, it features Allen as Howard Prince, small-time hustler and pontificating 'front' for the scripts of blacklisted writers, who eventually finds some principles in himself, takes a stand against the Red-baiters and wins back the girl he loves as a reward.

Panic in New York

Beginning with *Annie Hall* in 1977, Allen abruptly shifted tone in his films, dropped the earlier improbable formats, became nearly autobiographical, and began using humour as a counterpart to stories he deliberately intended as small, poignant tragedies of New York city life. The old worries still persist in the films that follow – the philistines still hedge him in, eliciting more wounded stares and painful, self-annihilating jokes – but new, more profound worries appear, too: a gnawing, almost panic-stricken doubt about the value of his own celebrity, and attached to that doubt, as if by handcuffs, the harrowing question of women and their power to save or destroy him. In *Annie Hall*, *Manhattan* (1979) and *Stardust Memories* (1980), the dominant issue is the hero's failure to sustain a relationship with a woman, each time caused by his obsessive insecurity about his creative in-

tegrity and the real value of his work. In *Annie Hall*, Allen's insecurity takes the form of Pygmalion-playing. Alvy Singer, successful New York Jewish comedian and all-in masochist, already 16 years in analysis, meets Annie (Diane Keaton), mixed-up Midwestern WASP, decides he's in love, and immediately starts trying to turn her into somebody she isn't – somebody as bright, culturally-hip, guilt-ridden and insecure as he is – so he won't have to risk something 'permanent' is the apparent underlying psychology. Eventually, of course, it works. Annie discovers life with Alvy isn't fun anymore, leaves him and goes out to Hollywood – the ultimate betrayal – where, as Allen not altogether inaccurately observes, 'the only cultural advantage is that you can make a right turn on a red light'. They remain friends, but Annie has failed her test, and Alvy can safely retreat back to the lonely land of the misunderstood – where, presumably, he feels most comfortable.

Interiors (1978), Allen's first 'serious' film as director, is consecrated to this same brand of gratuitous suffering in such unbalanced excess that it comes dangerously close to self-parody. Publicly proclaiming *Interiors* as his first 'important' film, Allen democratically divides his private insecurities this time among several characters (but doesn't appear himself). The performances are uniformly good. The film *looks* superb, and was obviously planned with great care. But because it was made in self-conscious imitation of the films of Ingmar

Top left: as Fielding Mellish, a famous revolutionary in drag in Bananas. *Above: Woody Allen meets Leo Tolstoy – a scene from* Love and Death. *Below: as the bookmaker who operates as* The Front *for blacklisted TV writers and finally decides to defy HUAC*

Bergman (one of Allen's heroes and an unparalleled master of controlled mood), the script's excesses stand out against the carefully modulated background like something meant deliberately to shock, embarrass and ultimately be laughed at. It is arguable that if Allen had been less preoccupied with Bergman's style he might have made a better film of *Interiors* – except that, free of Bergman's influence, he almost certainly would not have made the film at all. For if there is one thing Allen has always stood against, it is pre-

456

temporarily defected mistress, who does not. Eventually Isaac opts for Mary, occasioning a moving scene in which he must convince the tearful Tracy that she is wasting her life with a man twice her age and should go to London where a place in an acting school has been offered her. Tracy, heartbroken, agrees to leave him. Isaac only realizes Tracy was right for him all along when Mary announces she is leaving, too. But whether the realization grows from Isaac's actually having learned something about himself, or merely from panic at being suddenly left with no woman at all, is never properly explored.

Stardust Memories – a dream-like time-wandering, film-within-a-film imitation of Fellini's *Otto e Mezzo* (1963, $8\frac{1}{2}$) – is another creative *crise-de-coeur*, this time delivered by Sandy Bates (Allen), enormously popular maker of insignificant comedy movies, who,

Above right: fruit of the future? Woody in Sleeper. *Below: a rare moment of warmth between Renata (Diane Keaton) and Joey (Marybeth Hurt) in* Interiors. *Below right: Sandy greets his French mistress (Marie-Christine Barrault) in* Stardust Memories

tentiousness in art, and *Interiors*' greatest single failing is that it is pretentious.

With *Manhattan*, Allen returned to New York realism and the proven path blazed by *Annie Hall* (winner of the 1977 Oscars for Best Picture, Best Director, Best Script and Best Actress). This time Allen is Isaac Davis, a successful television-comedy writer in mid-life crisis who, having lost his wife to another woman, is trying two new women: 17-year-old Tracy (Mariel Hemingway), who loves him, and Mary (Diane Keaton), his best friend's

suffocated by his sycophantic fans and undeserved celebrity, longs to rid himself of 'upbeat endings' and do something meaningful with his life before it's too late. Death fills his dreams and visions, and there is a persuasive desperation about the character, lacking in the previous films, that makes his need for a woman's love more convincing. Now there are three, a universal triumvirate, who represent for Allen the three possible roads to salvation. Dorie (Charlotte Rampling), a neurotic actress plagued by jealousy and her own creative uncertainties, embodies the contemporary woman, Allen's female counterpart, and offers passion, excitement, intelligence and an immediate understanding of his own dilemma. Daisy (Jessica Harper), a young musician Sandy meets at the resort hotel where he is attending a retrospective festival of his own films (which he despises), symbolizes inno-

cence, a fresh start, and like Tracy in *Manhattan*, unconsidered allegiance. Isobel (Marie-Christine Barrault), a Frenchwoman with two children who has recently left her husband, represents wisdom, maturity, patience, home, stability. All three relationships fail, but the failures seem right in this film, consistent with the figure Sandy knows he has become: a player of old love scenes, still hopeful but running short of illusions and, apparently, time.

After this bleak exercise, Allen turned unexpectedly to light pastiche with *A Midsummer Night's Sex Comedy* (1982), an almost frivolous, six-handed chamber piece (in the style of Ingmar Bergman's *Smiles of a Summer Night* (1955). Here, Allen, as Andrew Hobbs, plays a frustrated husband and would-be lover trying to solve life's sweet mystery during a country weekend spent with two other equally befuddled couples. Ultimately, Hobbs fails to win his idealized love (Mia Farrow in her first Allen film), but at least Allen permits a happy resolution to the marital dilemma, and in so doing offers a first glimpse of some important changes to come in his next films.

Enter Mia Farrow
Did Mia Farrow's entry into Allen's life actually inspire a new vision or merely coincide with creative and personal shifts of attitude already underway? The fact remains that from *Sex Comedy* onwards Allen's films become progressively more humanistic and mature, much less neurotically defensive, far more confidently crafted, and very much more trusting of women. In *Zelig* (1983), we meet a lovable, schizoid *nebische* (Zelig/Allen) who, unable to match his own uncertain personality to the baffling facts of life in jazz-age America and pre-Hitler Germany, keeps finding himself being transformed, chameleon-like, into replicas of the more dominant figures around him. The film is notable for its economy and visual innovation plus a new willingness on Allen's part to sacrifice disruptive, set-piece gags for the sake of a cohesive story. But the real novelty lies in a resolution which not only sees Zelig cured of schizophrenia by his psychiatrist (Mia Farrow again), but actually allows him to triumph in winning her love!

The old themes – sexual confusion, injustice, neurotic guilt – are again at issue in Allen's next film, *Broadway Danny Rose* (1984), but this time all the shoes are on other feet. Danny Rose (Allen), the world's worst personal manager, overcomes multiple adversity – a collection of hopelessly unbookable club acts, threats from the Mafia, betrayal by his one and only successful client – because he knows who he is, knows what's ethically right, and sticks to both with the tenacity of somebody who might

almost be called a hero. This time it's his girlfriend, Tina Vitale (played brilliantly by Mia Farrow), who suffers neurotic insecurity, mistrusts love and has to be saved. Historically, the film goes back to Allen's nightclub days on Broadway, and in that sense it completes a circle begun with the earliest comedies. But it also introduces a new theme that is little short of revolutionary for Allen: the idea that guilt is *normal*, even *human*; that it is not something repellent for a psychiatrist to cure him of but a quality of spirit that actually helps him feel concern for others.

That concern becomes central to Allen's next film, *The Purple Rose of Cairo* (1985), a touching and visually pyrotechnic evocation of America in the Depression years which stars Mia Farrow as Cecelia, a penniless, downtrodden café waitress who escapes each day to the local picture palace in order to loose herself in the celluloid magic of the same Thirties movies that had so strongly influenced Allen when he was a boy. For Cecelia, however, that magic takes on an extraordinary new dimension when one day the handsome hero of the romance she is watching suddenly steps through the screen, descends to her seat in the darkened auditorium and declares his love. On the surface, *Purple Rose* is merely a dream comedy about the saving role of cinema in Thirties America. Deep down, though, it marks Allen's first really honest confrontation with the complex identity crises that had so overburdened his earlier work with unresolved *angst*. In this sense the film may fairly be described as signalling Allen's definitive breakthrough from prodigality into genuine maturity as an artist.

The two films that follow, *Hannah and Her Sisters* (1986) and *Radio Days* (1987), both deal with aspects of intimate family life; and both, in their candour, humanity and readiness to use humour as an expression of affection as well as irony, seem clearly to confirm that breakthrough. *Hannah*, which many feel is Allen's greatest film to date, may be likened to a two-year-long game of martial musical chairs in which three sisters (played by Farrow, Dianne Wiest and Barbara Hershey) first fall out of romantic equilibrium and then back into it again, taking their husbands, lovers and parents on a brilliantly observed New York City 'buggyride' in the process. The film may also be likened to his unhappy *Interiors* – both are undeniably Bergmanesque family sagas – but there all comparison ends; so determinedly, in fact, that it almost seems Allen made *Hannah* in order deliberately to lay *Interiors'* ghost for good. Ghosts of another kind, childhood ghosts, permeate the unashamedly nostalgic *Radio Days*, an episodic excursion through Allen's own boyhood and youth in Brooklyn with continuity provided by Tommy Dorsey, Glen Miller, Fred Allen, Bing Crosby and the rest of that splendid company of pre-TV entertainers who nightly entered America's living rooms through the magical medium of the radio speaker. *Radio Days* is charming, untraumatic, far less demanding than *Hannah*. But it is beautifully directed and conceived, and the powerful sense of a now fully mature, master craftsman at work promises even greater achievements for the future.

Filmography
1965 What's New, Pussycat? (sc; + act. only). **'66** What's Up, Tiger Lily? (add. dir; + assoc. prod; + co-sc; + act, on re-ed. and dubbed version of Japanese film: Kizino Kizi, 1964). **'67** Casino Royale (actor only) (GB). **'69** Take the Money and Run (+ co-sc; + act); Don't Drink the Waer (orig. play only). **'71** Bananas (+ co-sc; + act). **'72** Play It Again, Sam (sc. from own play; + act. only); Everything You Always Wanted to Know About Sex, But Were Afraid to Ask (+ sc; + act). **'73** Sleeper (+ co-sc; + act; + mus). **'75** Love and Death (+ sc; + act). **'76** The Front (actor only). **'77** Annie Hall (+ co-sc; + act). **'78** Woody Allen: An American Comedy (doc) (apearance as himself; + narr. only); Interiors (+ sc). **'79** Manhattan (+ co-sc; + act). **'80** Stardust Memories (+ sc; + act); To Woody Allen, From Europe With Love (doc) (appearance as himself only). **'82** A Midsummer Night's Sex Comedy (+ sc; + act). **'83** Zelig (+ sc; + act). **'84** Broadway Danny Rose (+ sc; + act); The Purple Rose of Cairo (+ sc). **'86** Hannah and Her Sisters (+ sc; + act). **'87** Radio days (+ sc; + act); September.

Above: in Broadway Danny Rose, *Woody Allen takes a characteristically episodic and nostalgic look at vaudeville. Below: Mia Farrow and Dianne Wiest play two of the sisters of* Hannah and Her Sisters, *a personal and comic analysis of the problems Jewish men face in forming stable relationships*

007

In 1962, when *Dr No* was released, the cinema saw the birth of a potent and powerful hero who has delighted and entertained audiences around the world ever since

James Bond has become a symbol of the times who carries on, through film after film, his own unique and stylish adventures regardless of three changes of actor. The Bond films are one of the most successful series of all time – there have been a staggering 1.75 billion paid admissions to see them at the cinema and, with television showings and video releases, it is estimated that over half the world's population has seen a Bond movie at one time or another.

From book to film
It all started rather modestly when producers Harry Saltzman and Albert R. Broccoli teamed up to make a low-budget movie – $90,000 – from a parochial British thriller with a little-known star. *Dr No* is a fast, action-packed thriller which pits the wits of James Bond (Sean Connery) against the evil, metal-handed Dr No (Joseph Wiseman), taking Bond to Crab Key off the coast of Jamaica to locate No's headquarters. It was a very modern adventure, for its time, both in its pacing and style and in its settings, the highlight of which is a nuclear reactor.

Dr No repaid its backers, United Artists, from the British release alone (which took a record-breaking £700,000) in a success that surprised everybody. Two years and two films later, it was clear that Bond was here to stay. Sean Connery, as 007, was world famous and Ian Fleming was reported to be on President Kennedy's favourite reading list.

Goldfinger (1964), the third film in the series, is considered by many to be the highpoint of the early Bond films. The villainous Goldfinger (played by Gert Frobe, whose shock of ginger hair made him quite a cuddly opponent) is out to make a massive killing on the gold market, by detonating a nuclear bomb inside Fort Knox and contaminating a large chunk of the gold supply. This film is memorable for Ken Adam's glittering interior of Fort Knox which provides the background for the final fight between Bond and Goldfinger's taciturn henchman, Oddjob (Harold Sakata).

All the elements that audiences have come to know and love are in place in *Goldfinger*: the fast-moving action-packed story which barely pauses for breath; the evil villain with his indomitable henchmen bent on world destruction; the exotic locations which, over the years, have taken Bond around the world; the unlikely gadgets supplied by the ever-ready, patient Q; the enemy's lethal high-tech weaponry countered by Bond's quick thinking; the beautiful girls who surround him at every turn; the inevitable, exciting car chase (in later films ski and boat chases were added); the explosive ending where the villain's headquarters are

Licensed to Kill

Above: the familiar logo that introduces a James Bond film is usually accompanied by Monty Norman's evocatively menacing musical theme. Below: James Bond (Sean Connery) encounters Honey (Ursula Andress) on the beach at Crab Key in Dr No

destroyed; the racy music including the memorable 'James Bond theme' and the popular title-song sung by a chart-topping performer. *Goldfinger* created the blueprint and Sean Connery, relaxed and slightly sneering, mocked his way through it all.

Forging a new Bond
Connery stayed for a further three films (with an interlude in which Australian actor, George Lazenby, played Bond in the not-so-successful *On Her Majesty's Secret Service*, 1969). Connery injects a rather callous humour into the series which largely consists of throwing in witty one-liners, delivered in a dead-pan manner immediately after some vicious act. It had the effect of mitigating the violence, and putting the films in the family entertainment category. By the time he left the Bond films, Connery was indelibly linked with the role of 007 and many

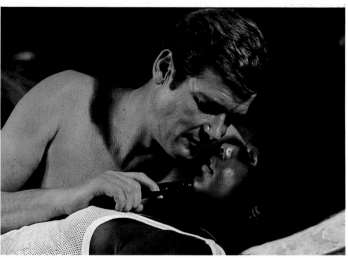

thought he could never be replaced.

But then came Roger Moore, known to TV viewers as *The Saint*. Where Connery had a brutal charm, Moore had a more sophisticated ease which propelled the series into a tongue-in-cheek mould. With Moore, 007 and his exploits could never quite be taken seriously – he himself was always laughing at them. In the Seventies, that was no bad thing and the Bond movies remained successful, drawing on a younger, more cinematically aware audience. Starting with *Live and Let Die* (1973), Moore played in seven Bond films, carrying on the tradition in his own inimitable fashion.

Live and Let Die took Bond back to Jamaica on the trail of Dr Kananga, otherwise known as Mr Big (played by Yaphet Kotto), who has fingers in every crooked pie from Harlem to voodoo. the highlights of the film are its stunts – an escape in a hang-glider (not so trendy at that time), a chase in a London bus which has its roof knocked off going under a low bridge, and a spectacular speedboat chase across the Louisiana Bayou country in which boats speed around the twists and turns of the river, jump across the roads that traverse it and crash into each other at an alarming rate.

In his later Bond films, Moore started to get more serious. *For Your Eyes Only* (1981) returns to the original Bond film style; it is a taut thriller located in the complex milieu of the Greek underworld where nobody is ever sure exactly who is on whose side. It also contains some of the best underwater fight scenes in the series. *Octopussy* (1983) was mainly shot against the exotic backdrop of India. Its convoluted plot involves jewels smuggled from the Kremlin archive and an attempt by a lone Soviet General to start World War III. Maud Adams plays the title role as the wealthy jewel thief who is supported by an all-woman army. The final scene where the girls, who are all acrobats and circus performers, storm the villain's headquarters is a tense and extremely amusing showdown.

By *A View to a Kill* in 1985, Moore was getting too long in the tooth to continue as a dashing secret service agent, and he was all but outplayed by the villains, Christopher Walken and Grace Jones. In *The Living Daylights* (1987), Timothy Dalton took over the lead. A soft-spoken, Welsh-born actor, Dalton is a more romantic Eighties Bond – a gentler hero than any of his predecessors. *The Living Day-*

lights opens with an SAS exercise in Gibraltar, which includes a breath-taking car chase around the rock's peak, and ends up amongst the Afghan rebels – a highly topical plot-line.

Rogue Bonds

Saltzman and Broccoli bought the rights to all the Fleming titles except *Casino Royale*, which was later made into a spoof spy adventure with several Bonds including Woody Allen, David Niven and Peter Sellers. But there has been another Bond outside of the series. *Never Say Never Again*, brought Connery back to the role of 007 in 1983. The story behind its making is a complex one. Before Saltzman and Broccoli were involved with Bond, Fleming had written *Thunderball*, his ninth novel. Kevin McClory of Xanadu Productions and Jack Whittingham collaborated with Fleming on a screenplay entitled *Longitude 78 West*. Plans for a film fell through and *Thunderball* was published based on that story. Fleming did not, however, acknowledge the story's source and McClory went to court to claim his due. The lengthy battle ended when McClory won the screen rights to the novel and he joined forces with Broccoli and Saltzman for *Thunderball*. McClory also won the rights to the character of Blofeld, the rarely-seen villain with the white cat who features in many of the early Bonds, and when he sold his interests, *Never Say Never Again* was able to be made.

But it is the 15 films of the series that are the essential Bond. These films have constantly kept abreast of the times, transforming Fleming's sometimes dated hero into a modern man, coping with high-tech and space-age adventure. Its women too, have changed, from the beautiful but precious girls of the early Bonds to their more active and competent heirs in tune with the aspirations of modern women. Fleming's cold-war villains, SMERSH, the Soviet Secret Service agency, were replaced by SPECTRE, a freelance organization whose initials stand for the Special Executive for Coun-

Top left: the poster from Goldfinger, *the film that set the Bond style. Above: Roger Moore's first appearance as 007 was in* Live and Let Die. *Left: the spectacular set of the villain's headquarters in* The Man With the Golden Gun

terintelligence, Terrorism, Revenge and Extortion – and in the later films, Bond has even teamed up with the Soviets to preserve world peace. It is an approach that has helped keep the series up-to-the-moment with contemporary attitudes.

Gadgets, gimmicks and girls

There have been imitations, on the large and small screen, but none have had the same universal appeal – or those classic, unforgettable scenes and images: the moment when Honey (Ursula Andress) emerges from the sea in *Dr No* wearing only a very skimpy white bikini; the evil Rosa Klebb (Lotte Lenya) with her poisoned spiked toecaps in *From Russia With Love*; the menacing *Goldfinger* and his taciturn henchman, Oddjob (Harold Sakata); the tiny helicopter, Little Nellie, who flies into action in *You Only Live Twice*; the first spectacular ski chase in *On Her Majesty's Secret Service*;

the amazing car jump with its 360° roll in *The Man With the Golden Gun*; the titanic struggles between Bond and the indestructible Jaws (Richard Kiel) in *The Spy Who Loved Me* and *Moonraker*; Grace Jones as the deadly May Day in *A View to a Kill* and the dramatic fight in the back of the plane in *The Living Daylights*.

The plots of the Bond films have now become so familiar that they are effectively predictable. There is something comfortably reassuring about the formula and part of the fascination of a new Bond film is watching how, once again, the film-makers give the same old elements new twists and turns. The smallest changes bring groans and protest from fans – for instance, Lois Maxwell who, as Miss Moneypenny, quietly flirted her way through all the Bond films was replaced by Caroline Bliss in *The Living Daylights*; fortunately the gruffly lovable Q (Desmond Llewelyn) remains to nag Bond into shape.

Whatever the changes – there have been five Bond directors (Terence Young, Guy Hamilton, Lewis Gilbert, Peter Hunt and, most recently, John Glen), numerous scripwriters (with Richard Maibaum responsible for most of the screenplays) and a whole host of production designers, cameramen and editors – the Bond phenomenon continues. But the most serious hurdle has yet to be jumped. There are only a couple of Fleming titles left and while others, including Kingsley Amis, have written Bond books, it remains to be seen what happens when the titles run out. The evidence to date, however, suggests that no matter what the problem, James Bond is likely to go into newer and bigger adventures for some time to come.

Top left: Grace Jones makes an unusually muscular Bond girl in From a View to a Kill. *Top: Timothy Dalton, the fourth actor to take on the mantle of 007, makes his first Bond appearance in* The Living Daylights. *Left: in* Octopussy, *Bond (Moore) pits his wits against a jewel thief (Louis Jourdan). Above:* Octopussy *was Moore's sixth Bond film*

harrison **ford**

As Han Solo and Indiana Jones, Harrison Ford has the distinction of appearing in five out of the ten most successful films of all time

In the Star Wars and Indiana Jones adventures, Ford plays a brawny, glamorous hunk, with a gentle and endearing sense of humour that allows the action not to be taken too seriously – and, quite obviously, audiences love it. Changing his style more recently, by moving into straighter roles and more dramatic films, he has been nominated for an Oscar (for his role in Peter Weir's *Witness*, 1985) and is now establishing himself as an actor of note. But when he first swash-buckled his way onto the screen in *Star Wars* in 1977, he seemed to materialize out of nowhere.

Paging Mr Jones
In fact, Ford had already had a promising career in television. He was one of those actors who had settled into a comfortable, if not very satisfactory, niche, playing guest-star parts in TV series such as *Gunsmoke* and *The Virginian*. He likes to cite his first film role, as a bell-boy in a 1968 James Coburn film. His part consisted of the memorable line 'paging Mr Jones'. He left this challenging world to concentrate on his other talent – carpentry. He had small parts in George Lucas' *American Graffiti* (1973) and Francis Ford Coppola's *The Conversation* (1974), but basically suported himself with odd wood-working jobs before the big break came along.

In the Star Wars series, Ford had the meaty adult role, playing alongside the softer Luke Skywalker (Mark Hamill) and Princess Lea

(Carrie Fisher). While the other two have a youthful innocence about them which compliments the mystic overtones of the plot, Ford is the tough, macho one of the trio. He is the cynical space pilot whose predatory instincts for survival mask the inevitable heart of gold. He is the full-grown male designed to attract the older audiences, without which the series would be little more than a children's adventure story.

Yet, despite the succes of *Star Wars* and its two sequels, *The Empire Strikes Back* (1980) and *The Return of the Jedi* (1983), Ford did not

wish to continue with the series. Rumoured to have coveted a grand death scene in the most recent episode, he had to content himself with winning the Princess' love – and remaining alive. The future of the series, which was originally conceived as three separate trilogies, now seems in doubt.

Jones strikes again
His next venture proved that Ford had an enviable problem: every film he appeared in seemed to spawn sequels faster than *Rocky*. As Indiana Jones in *Raiders of the Lost Ark* (1981) and *Indiana Jones and the Temple of Doom* (1984), Ford tracked down antiques in far-flung places with a delightful tongue-in-cheek charm that was equally at home with fossils or tarantulas. After the roaring success of *Raiders* (it even overtook *Star Wars* at the box-office). Ford was worried about type-casting and landing himself in another long-running series. Nevertheless, he reported for work, brown felt hat in hand, and the sequel also hit the charts. Indiana Jones is a very modern hero, epitomized by the classic comic scene in the casbah where, faced with a man whirling a lethal sword around, he shrugs his shoulders, pulls out his gun and shoots the would-be assassin. The dynamic duo of Steven Speilberg and George Lucas who made *Raiders* are still planning a third film and, of course, it wouldn't be Indiana Jones without Ford.

Ford played another space-age hero in Ridley Scott's *Blade Runner* (1982), a lavishly-designed futuristic adventure which cast Ford

Above: Harrison Ford's most challenging role to date is in The Mosquito Coast. *Left: he is seen here in a scene from* Indiana Jones and the Temple of Doom *with Kate Capshaw*

Above: Blade Runner *was yet another fantasy adventure film for Ford. Above right:* Hanover Street *(1979) was released just before he became a big star. Right: in* Witness, *he plays a police captain whose assignment takes him into the closed Amish community*

as Rick Deckard, a cool android detective. *Blade Runner* itself was a disappointment – it's Marlowe-style commentary only pointed up its lack of originality and sparkle. But Ford, who had his hair cropped short for the part, out-shone the spectacular backgrounds and convinced both critics and audiences that he could actually act, not just indulge in – however enjoyable – mindless heroics. *Blade Runner* was only a partial move away from Solo and Jones; it was still a comic-strip adventure, with Ford playing the dynamic hero who saves the world against all odds. But it was a step in the right direction.

Star witness

His next role was the more complete change that he was looking for. In *Witness* (1985), he plays a police captain, John Book, whose murder investigation takes him outside Philadelphia into the closed community of the Amish. The Amish limit contact with the outside world and their strictures prohibit most modern appliances – including cameras, radios, telephones and automobiles. Parachuted into a society in which there is no crime, the hard-bitten city cop has to learn a new way of life – one that eventually leads him into a romantic entanglement with a young Amish woman, played by Kelly McGillis.

Director Peter Weir observes all this with a freshness that never even approaches sentimentality. It is a remarkable film, in which Ford gives a remarkable performance, combining toughness and tenderness in just the right amounts. The scene where he and McGillis dance to music from a forbidden radio in her father's outhouse is, without a word being spoken, one of the most moving, romantic moments of contemporary films.

Judging by the general standard of acting in *Witness*, which was unusually high. it was undoubtedly Weir who helped Ford to find the performance which won him an Oscar nomi-

nation and it was therefore no surprise to find that Ford's next film was also directed by Weir. *The Mosquito Coast* (1986), based on the novel by Paul Theroux, is a story of the madness and decline of modern civilization. It is an epic theme, and one which gave Ford his most challenging role to date. In it he plays Allie Fox, a brilliant, opinionated inventor who pits his wits against nature and only starts to crack up when his world turns against him. It is a study of obsession – of Fox's dreams of harnessing power to build a life unencumbered with fast food and pollution. With glasses and a peaked cap, Ford rose to the occasion and portrays a character who, in the end, does not evince even a spark of sympathy in his dealings with his wife (Helen Mirren), his son (River Phoenix) – or his dream. It was a role that certainly broadened Ford's horizons – and choices – as an actor.

With a reputation for shunning the limelight (Weir commented during the filming of *Witness* that Ford 'has no interest in his star image at all'), Ford rarely gives interviews or seeks publicity, preferring to live his personal life quietly. He even boasts of his ability to change

his appearance enough to be unrecognizable when he walks around the streets. Born in Chicago in 1942, the son of an advertising executive, he dropped out of college and married at the age of 21. He has two children, aged 17 and 14 by his first marriage. He now spends several months a year in Wyoming where he is actively involved in conservation and lives with his second wife, Melissa Mathison. Her claim to fame is that she scripted *E.T. – the ExtraTerrestrial* – the only movie in recent years to outgross a Ford film.

Filmography
'66 Dead Heat on a Merry-Go-Round. '67 Journey to Shiloh; A Time for Killing (GB: The Long Ride Home); Luv. '70 Zabriski Point; Getting Straight. '73 American Graffiti. '74 The Conversation. '77 Star Wars; Heroes. '78 Force Ten From Navarone. '79 Hanover Street; Apocalypse Now; The Frisco Kid. '80 The Empire Strikes Back. '81 Raiders of the Lost Ark. '82 Blade Runner. '83 Return of the Jedi. '84 Indiana Jones and the Temple of Doom. '85 Witness. '86 The Mosquito Coast. '88 Frantic.

WOMEN IN MIND

In the old days of the Hollywood studio system, actresses had set images dictated by their studio heads who would mastermind their careers. Films were a Garbo, a Hepburn, a West or a Monroe vehicle. Today's top actresses are a different breed of star operating in a highly competitive climate

An Eighties actress can no longer rely on a single persona, but must constantly adapt her image. Faye Dunaway, who has spent 20 years occupying the higher echelons of her profession, was recently deglamorized for Barbet Shroeder's *Barfly* (1987). She optimistically commented in an interview at that time: 'In the past they insisted on stars having set images, and being those images. Now it is easier. We are not contracted to studios. We are the masters of our own destinies. We haven't such power over our fans, but we have much more over our careers. It's a game of course. But it's a different one, and most of us like it better. We can control the work we do, and sometimes initiate it.'

Marilyn Monroe, the cinema's ultimate sex symbol and one of the last actresses under the old studio system, signalled the future in 1954 with the launch of her own production company, in an attempt to avoid the manufactured parts that had made her famous. Jane Fonda's championing for career independence is a yardstick for others to aspire to. And it took a Barbra Streisand to get cherished project *Yentl* (1983) off the ground – although her juggling act as director, producer, writer and star bombed with the critics and the cinema-going public alike.

This move to control their own careers can be seen as a direct result of the scarcity of decent parts for actresses in the Eighties. In the new Hollywood of packages and deals, with studio executives liaising with powerful agents, actresses can either sit around waiting for a career to continue gaining momentum, or attempt to launch their own projects. In the search for another *Top Gun* (1986), aimed like a missile at the movies' new adolescent audience, the financiers behind films constantly crave a fresh female face to accompany the latest male teenage idol. The results can be depressing, giving aspiring actresses little more to do than drape themselves around their male co-star and look pretty.

Indeed, it is surprising that many younger actresses, without the superstar status to carry a film, have been able to show their talent at all. The rising tide of ladies, such as Rosanna Arquette, Daryl Hannah, Jamie Lee Curtis, Molly Ringwald, Ally Sheedy, Demi Moore, Meg Tilly and Mary Elizabeth Mastrantonio need to flow very carefully. . . .

With such a demand for roles, the fact that one actress, acting-perfectionist Meryl Streep, has first refusal on most scripts – only excluding overtly glamorous characters – must also be disheartening. But parts by default (and in the long shadow of Streep) are better than no parts at all.

Both actors and actresses experience the rollercoaster pressure of being in and out of favour with the public. It is a rare talent who will achieve that stratosphere of superstardom occupied by Barbra Streisand, Jane Fonda and to a lesser extent Goldie Hawn, Sally Field and Diane Keaton. A whole roll-call of actresses, nursing trunks full of Oscars and rave reviews, rest by the wayside waiting to rekindle their former glories.

Jill Clayburgh (*An Unmarried Woman*, 1978) seems unlikely to recapture her Seventies success, despite a good performance with Barbara Hershey in Andrei Konchalovsky's *Shy People* (1987). Whoopi Goldberg, discovered by Steven Spielberg for his adaptation of Alice Walker's *The Color Purple* (1985), followed with obvious misses *Jumpin' Jack Flash* (1986), *Burglar* (1987) and *The Telephone* (1987), and it is unlikely that her latest film, *Fatal Beauty*

Above: in the highly successful Top Gun, *Kelly McGillis plays an astrophysicist who falls for one of her trainees (Tom Cruise). Left: in* The Morning After, *Jane Fonda still looks glamorous despite playing a lush who is working through a mid-life crisis*

(1988), will reinstate her. Nor is an Oscar win a guarantee of continued stardom as Sissy Spacek has experienced after the success of *The Coal Miner's Daughter* (1980). For some inexplicable reason she fell from box-office favour, although her performances in both *Missing* (1982) and *The River* (1984) were acting of a high standard.

Even acting whirlwind Debra Winger (most recently in *Black Widow*, 1987, and *Betrayed*, 1988), who was once described by Pauline Kael as 'a major reason to go on seeing movies in the Eighties', seems to have nearly outstayed her welcome; although this is probably due more to her notorious temperament than her thespian ability.

Women's careers seem particularly fragile. As director John Badham has said: 'If you're a talented woman and very beautiful . . . you will be burned out within four or five years when the next beautiful talented girl comes along who is kinda fresh. You know, "Ho, hum, We're tired of Teri Garr now, let's move on to Kathleen Turner."'

Five actresses, all currently 'hot', to use a favourite Hollywood expression, reflect the pressures to keep one step ahead of becoming yesterdays news. Each brings unique qualities that enable them to strike a chord in audiences and thereby keep their names in the forefront, perfectly positioned to capture the eye of those that count, the film-makers. Each gives a clue as to the qualities necessary to succeed, whilst retaining the essential individuality of the independent Eighties actress.

Presently combining smouldering sexuality and glamour with a talent for vibrant comedy is Kathleen Turner. Arguably *the* sex symbol of the decade, Turner has swiftly established herself with a string of different parts in some big box-office hits, after a sensational debut in *Body Heat* (1981), Lawrence Kasdan's modern *film noir* that recalls *Double Indemnity* (1944). Turner plays a seductress who uses a besotted lover (William Hurt) to clear her path to a rich, single future. Turner superbly emulated the *femmes fatales* of the Forties – Stanwyck, Crawford, Davis and Tierney – then beautifully parodied the very same creature in the Steve Martin comedy *The Man with Two Brains* (1982) as his adulterous wife.

Disproving co-star and producer Michael Douglas' initial fear that the lead in the slapstick adventure *Romancing the Stone* (1984) would de-glamorize her, Turner established herself as a bankable property with a rare ability to be both desirable and funny at the same time. In *Romancing the Stone* (and in its sequel, *The Jewel of the Nile*, 1986), she subtly developed the growing confidence of romantic novelist Joan Wilder caught in an adventure more suitable for her next book.

Crimes of Passion (1984) showed her willingness to take chances. As part-time hooker China Blue, she struggled to give resonance to the dual roles of career woman by day, dominatrix by night. The end result, directed by Ken Russell, was uneven, teetering on the edge of puerile fantasy. An appearance in the macho-dominated *A Breed Apart* (1984) with Rutger Hauer is best forgotten.

Holding her own with scene-stealing Jack Nicholson in one of John Huston's last and best, *Prizzi's Honor* (1985), her hit woman to his hit man recalled *Body Heat* and a type of woman that could become a Turner trademark – supercool and in total control.

Above: Kathleen Turner inherits the mantle of the femme fatale *in* Body Heat, *starring opposite William Hurt. Below: Rosanna Arquette began to make her name as a delightfully kookie actress in* Baby It's You *(1984). Bottom: seductive Kim Basinger was still only playing supporting roles when she appeared in* The Natural *with Robert Redford and Glenn Close*

Next, stepping in for Debra Winger, Turner grabbed the opportunity to play dissatisfied 42-year-old Peggy Sue who finds herself back in her Fifties high-school days as an 18-year-old in *Peggy Sue Got Married* (1986). Again her air of vulnerability and confidence was well used and earned her a best-actress Oscar nomination and put her indisputably in the leading-actress bracket.

Turner's twin appeal – pin-up looks and the ability to convey the sultry and amusing – look set to keep her career on the ascendancy. American critic Richard Schikel has heralded her as 'the movies' first authentically mysterious female presence since Garbo was hiding in plain sight.' And, most important, her choice of roles has proved astute. Her next three films continue the mixed formula that has made her a success: *The Accidental Tourist* (1988), which reunited her with Lawrence Kasdan and William Hurt from *Body Heat*; *Julia and Julia* (1988) with pop-star turned actor Sting; and *Switching Channels* (1988), a remake of *The Front Page*.

Another actress who has brought sexuality to the screen is Jessica Lange. In *The Postman Always Rings Twice* (1981) she is the embodiment of repression as a bored housewife tempted by a hobo (Jack Nicholson) working for her fat older husband. If one thing singled out Bob Rafelson's remake of James Cain's novel, it was the frantic and explicit passion conveyed by Nicholson and Lange. To the surprise of many, the film did not mark a notable debut, but the re-emergence of an actress most critics (Pauline Kael aside) had tagged as just another good-looking blonde.

Lange – model and occasional acting student – was picked by Dino De Laurentiis in 1976 as

However, it was her fifth film, *Frances* (1982), the story of tragic Hollywood victim and Forties actress Frances Farmer, that really heralded a new fully fledged star. Lange tackled Farmer head on, recreating an unconventional character with great understanding. Contrasting with the dramatic intensity of *Frances*, Lange plays a dizzy soap star in the commercial winner *Tootsie* (1982) with Dustin Hoffman. She was nominated by the Academy for both films, losing out in the best actress stakes to Meryl Streep (*Sophie's Choice*), but picking up an Oscar for best supporting actress in *Tootsie*. The stigma of her disastrous debut was irrevocably history.

An on and off the screen partnership with playwright and actor Sam Shepard resulted in *Country* (1984), which highlights the plight of the American farming community in near documentatary form. The couples' next venture, *Far North* (1988) has Lange playing an up-town girl who returns from the big lights to help her troubled family. This gentle comedy marks Shepard's directorial debut.

Another biographical film, *Sweet Dreams* (1985), about the strained life of country singer Patsy Cline, consolidated her growing reputation. For *Country* and *Sweet Dreams* she again received Oscar nominations. Acting showcase *Crimes of the Heart* (1986) had its moments with Lange sharing centre stage with Diane Keaton and Sissy Spacek as three unusual sisters, but failed to transfer to the screen the wit of Beth Henley's Broadway success.

Like Turner she can hop from serious drama and complex character studies to comedy. But her strength is in tackling real people, helped by an ability to provide a forceful presence through movement and gesture. She plans to adapt Jayne Anne Phillip's novel *Machine Dreams* for her own production company Prairie Films, and has a strong role in Taylor Hackford's *Everybody's All American*, which charts a relationship from the Fifties to the Eighties.

Most film actresses first hone their skills through theatrical backgrounds or television experience. The Cher of the Eighties is a phenomenon. With no formal training she has established herself as an actress in demand, shedding the glitzy skins of two former careers that have kept her in the public spotlight since the Sixties. Her latest films *Suspect* (1987) and *Moonstruck* (1987) are a revelation.

Above: Kelly McGillis gives a stunning performance as the Amish widow who falls for the police captain (Harrison Ford) in Peter Weir's Witness. *Left: Kathleen Turner looks remarkably young playing a teenager in* Peggy Sue Got Married. *Below left: Turner, again, in* Body Heat, *the film which established her as a seductive* femme fatale. *Below: in films like* Mask, *Cher has successfully moved from singing to a second career in acting*

the new Fay Wray in his remake of *King Kong* and lodged firmly in the grasp of the great ape. *King Kong*'s dismal flop nearly axed her career; as the most visible target of the film she was out of work for three years.

She resurfaced as the Angel of Death, little more than a technical device, in Bob Fosse's satirical musical *All That Jazz* (1979). A lightweight comedy *How to Beat the High Cost of Living* (1980) did little to forward her apparently terminal career. *Postman* halted the slide into obscurity and proved a turning point in her fortunes.

Cher, whose full name is Cherlin Lapiere Sarkisian, admits that she always wanted to be an actress. However, she first emerged with partner-then-husband in the Sixties duo Sonny and Cher. And in the Seventies she was a television celebrity with *The Sonny and Cher Comedy Hour*. After the collapse of her marriage she pursued a solo singing career whilst seeking out her break into movies.

Cher had appeared in William Friedkin's *Good Times* (1967) and *Chastity* (1969), but it was in Robert Altman's interpretation of the Broadway play *Come Back to the Five and Dime, Jimmy Dean, Jimmy Dean* (1982) that she raised eyebrows. Next, once again adding far more than curiosity value to a film, she gave excellent support as the lesbian friend of Karen Silkwood (Meryl Streep) in *Silkwood* (1983), directed by Mike Nichols. She earned a best supporting actress Oscar nomination and led Streep to describe her as 'an instinctive actress with rare honesty'.

In a film that was surrounded by on-set intrigue and squabbles, Cher again proved that her natural ability perfectly captured strong forthright and essentially off-beat women. Peter Bogdanovich's *Mask* (1985) saw her as the biker mother of a physically deformed boy, and again her performance was acclaimed. However, a two-year gap followed, with no roles that tempted her. She held out for the right script, as she had done when first trying to break into the movie business. *The Witches of Eastwick* (1987) offered three roles for actresses (her co-stars were Susan Sarandon and Michelle Pfeiffer) in an adaptation of John Updike's novel. Unfortunately the witches lost out to some irrelevant special effects and an over-blown devil of a role for Jack Nicholson.

She moved on to Peter Yates' *Suspect*, an intelligent thriller concerning a public attorney led to illegalities by a juror (Dennis Quaid) in the quest to clear a Vietnam veteran accused of murder. Next came the effervescent Norman Jewison comedy *Moonstruck* (for which she won the Best Actress Oscar), with Cher falling for her fiance's one-handed brother (Nicolas Cage). Not content with waiting for another chance at a big part, she is currently hoping to develop her own projects including *Rain or Shine* and *Forever Sad Heart*.

An actress with an impeccable background is Glenn Close, co-star of monster-hit *Fatal Attraction* (1987). An established Broadway

Glenn Close as the seductress of Fatal Attraction *(top) with co-star Michael Douglas and earlier in* The Big Chill *(above centre).*

Above: Jack Nicholson with Cher, Susan Sarandon and Michelle Pfeiffer in The Witches of Eastwick. *Left: Kim Basinger in* No Mercy.

fixture, she is an example of the growing breed of actors and actresses who attempt to balance a theatre and film career. Laden with Emmy and Tony awards for her stage and television work, she has also picked up three Academy Award nominations for best supporting actress: *The World According to Garp* (1982), *The Natural* (1984) and *The Big Chill* (1983).

Close's skill as an actress has never been in doubt. The parts she has undertaken have all been sensitively played. However, for most of her films she has, in her own words, only had 'basically the same *type* of woman – motherly, strong and serene' to tackle. All that changed in a *volte face* of astonishing proportions with Adrian Lyne's box-office winner *Fatal Attraction*, co-starring Michael Douglas (another actor who has recently successfully gone against type) and Anne Archer. As glamorous Alex Forest, possibly the supreme anti-heroine of the decade, she gave an Oscar-winning performance of frightening excellence, meticulously detailing the frizzy-haired seductress's decline into an obsessive psychopath.

Close is now in the position of repeating the range that had previously been confined to the stage. Notable parts include circus impressario P.T. Barnum's sexy wife in *Barnum* (1986), and opposite Jeremy Irons in Tom Stoppard's *The Real Thing* (1987), directed by Mike Nichols. The often androgynous cinema image of Glenn Close has been turned on its head, and future parts for *the* latest bankable actress will hopefully be equal to the talents of one of the most interesting and talented female faces in American movies.

Kim Basinger, by contrast, is an ex-model who has been elevated to the coveted status of movie star without actually appearing in a film that has genuinely achieved *both* critical and public acclaim. The offers she continues to receive show, however, that glamour still can hold sway in an environment where actresses' are eager to strip away the gloss (Farrah Fawcett's near-rape victim in *Extremities*, 1986, being an obvious example).

After adorning the covers of fashion magazines in the late Sixties and Seventies, her first leading acting opportunity came through tele-

vision with *Portrait of a Centrefold* (1978), only a slight departure from her former career, and *From Here to Eternity* (1980). Her feature debut came soon after in *Hard Country* (1981), a spin-off from *Urban Cowboy* (1980), in which she played a wife struggling within a faltering marriage. James Bond beckoned Basinger for *Never Say Never Again* (1983), featuring a relaunched and rehatched Sean Connery. She had little to do but angle her razor-sharp cheekbones and lend attractive support to the heroics and high jinks. And in Blake Edward's *The Man Who Loved Women* (1983) she again played a sexpot, and this time delivered several amusing lines.

Robert Altman's *Fool for Love* (1985) offered Basinger more to hang her acting abilities on. Yet the film (adapted from co-star Sam Shepard' off-Broadway play), while giving her moments of brilliance, did not find enough room for her to develop a plausible character amidst the vocal histrionics. The setting, a motel on the edge of a desert, contributed to the claustrophobic feel. Shepard is reported to have recommended her on the grounds that 'I don't think she'll try to act too much'.

Adrian Lyne's controversial but empty *Nine$\frac{1}{2}$ Weeks* (1986) placed her opposite rising star Mickey Rourke. Basinger gave a spirited display, depicting a woman's painful, reluctant and ultimately degrading sexual awakening. The actress in Basinger, despite considerable manipulation by her director, found it ultimately rewarding: 'I knew it would stretch my emotions. As an actress it was the greatest thing that ever happened to me.'

No Mercy (1986), a vigilante cop movie with Richard Gere, did little for Basinger's thespian accomplishments. Blake Edward's *Blind Date* (1987) allowed her another stab at comedy, playing a brunette (not her usual blonde) disaster area called Nadia, whose *raison d'être* was to create comic situations from which

Top left: Cher continues to establish herself as an actress of note in Moonstruck *with Nicholas Cage. Top: in* Tootsie, *Jessica Lange played opposite a very different kind of woman – Dustin Hoffman in drag. Above: Kim Basinger tries her hand at comedy with Jeff Bridges in* Nadine

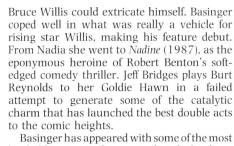

Left: Jessica Lange as Frances, *the tragic film star. Below left: Glenn Close and Jeff Bridges in the tense courtroom drama* Jagged Edge *(1985). Bottom left: Meryl Streep and Cher formed a dynamic partnership in* Silkwood. *Bottom: Kathleen Turner as China Blue in* Crimes of Passion

more discrimination in her choice of roles.

All the above leading actresses are approaching their forties. For those beyond fifty the cinema is a wasteland for leading roles. Only Jane Fonda has been able to continue to play female leads, although mature actresses like Anne Bancroft made the transition to more subtle parts and character acting. That said, there is still a place for women in the movies. Indeed, a spate of films have seen men regulated to the sidelines: Bette Midler and Shelley Long in women-buddy movie *Outrageous Fortune* (1987); Sissy Spacek, Diane Keaton and Jessica Lange in *Crimes of the Heart* (1987); Susan Sarandon, Michelle Pfeiffer and Cher in *The Witches of Eastwick* (1987); Theresa Russell and Debra Winger in *Black Widow* (1987). Yet Hollywood still has a long way to go before it catches up with the truer and more incisive commentary seen on television with series like *Cagney and Lacey* and *The Golden Girls*.

The chance to remain at the top end of the pile is harder than ever for the Eighties' star actress. They may have the control the movie queens and sex sirens of yesterday lacked and, in some cases, yearned for. Streisand, who returned with *Nuts* (1987) after a five year absence from films, remarks: 'Women in the movies are just learning to stretch after all these years. It's about time.' But actresses can spend more time searching for good parts than performing them. And that exclusive quality, stardom, can depend on box-office success to keep the offers flowing.

If one conclusion can be drawn from the career of a leading actress in the Eighties, it is the paramount need to diversify. As Kathleen Turner commented: 'I believe that through versatility you can establish a staying power, a durability – that's an exclusive quality in Hollywood today.'

Bruce Willis could extricate himself. Basinger coped well in what was really a vehicle for rising star Willis, making his feature debut. From Nadia she went to *Nadine* (1987), as the eponymous heroine of Robert Benton's soft-edged comedy thriller. Jeff Bridges plays Burt Reynolds to her Goldie Hawn in a failed attempt to generate some of the catalytic charm that has launched the best double acts to the comic heights.

Basinger has appeared with some of the most bankable actors in the movies, but she has been unlucky enough to pick films that have not taken off. Nevertheless, her striking appearance, and a growing ability to tackle lightweight comedy, may allow her to exercise

BATTLE SCARS

The Vietnam war, and its close political ally Cambodia, created a blot on the US record too big to erase. On the level of popular culture, at least, it has been something rarely tackled and best pushed to the back of the mind. Like the recurring pain of an old war wound, however, it has refused to go away

Hollywood's first real confrontation with the subject of the Vietnam war was delayed as long as the late Seventies, if one discounts John Wayne's gung-ho *The Green Berets* (1968). *Go Tell the Spartans* and *The Boys in Company C* (both 1977) were both of interest, though the former is conveniently set back in 1964, before the main operation was launched, and the latter is more a satire on military inefficiency. Bigger box-office draws were *The Deer Hunter* (1978) and *Apocalypse Now* (1979), inflated epics which fudged the issues with metaphors and star turns.

It could be said that the Vietnam movie was dragged screaming into the Eighties by one man. Having volunteered himself in 1967, and served in Vietnam for 15 months, Oliver Stone brought an uncompromising and liberal sensibilty to bear – first upon South American strife in *Salvador* and then on Vietnam in *Platoon* (both 1986).

Prior to his foray into the field, the Eighties had given Vietnam and Cambodia short shrift. Robert Altman's *Streamers* (1983), set in a US army barracks at the dawn of America's involvement in Vietnam, settled for a confused scenario of sexual and racial relationships. More popular were the MIA adventures, *Uncommon Valour* (1983), *Missing in Action* (1984) and the infamous *Rambo: First Blood Part II* (1985). In all these films, the plea not to forget the vets was overridden by a flurry of macho heroics. Only the British production *The Killing Fields* (1984) displayed intelligence, even though in overall feel it harked back to the epic posturing of *The Deer Hunter* and *Apocalypse Now*.

Platoon, apart from being the first movie to concentrate wholly on the Vietnam combat zone, brought to the genre the harrowing, gut-level style of such classic Hollywood directors as Robert Adrich and Samuel Fuller. The sheer physical hell of jungle life and warfare can almost be touched and smelled. Beside this, the movie also strips away any feeling of glory, firstly through the hero/narrator's gradual loss of his initial idealism, and secondly through the grim depiction of the kind of body-building, beer-can-chewing, gook-bashing masculine aggression which war feeds on. There is, admittedly, an easily definable 'good guy' and 'bad guy', and the Vietnamese do remain shadowy figures outside the drama's parameter, but the film's strengths overcome its weaknesses.

The success of *Platoon* opened the floodgates, if rather inauspiciously, with *The Hanoi Hilton* and *Hamburger Hill* (both 1987). The latter is a film which makes a great display of surface realism in portraying the horror of Vietnam's

The Cinema of Guilt

Hill 937, but in all other respects it returns us to the territory of *The Green Berets*. Equally dire is *The Hanoi Hilton*, a hamfisted attempt to cover the plight of the US POWs in North Vietnam's Hao Lo prison.

Stanley Kubrick's contribution to the Vietnam movie is characteristically eccentric. An essentially broken-backed beast, the first half of *Full Metal Jacket* (1987) is an oddly hermetic barrack-room drama of the dehumanizing techniques of military drill. If this section's study of escalating madness is reminiscent of *The Shining* (1980), the second half, set in the area of combat, flies off in all directions between a superior *Hamburger Hill* and an even more doped-out *Apocalypse Now*. And speaking of the latter film, its creator, Francis Coppola, returned again to the genre with *Gardens of Stone* (1987), this time to tackle the subject from the homefront. By the standards of *Platoon*, the approach is less political than liberal-humanist, but Coppola's film does break new ground by rejecting the manic stereotypes of the genre and focusses instead on the confused, totally human figure of 'Nam vet drill sergeant Clell Hazard (James Caan).

While the Eighties' Vietnam military dramas break exciting new ground, those films portraying the return of the vet do not really match earlier examples of the type, such as *Taxi Driver* (1976) and *Coming Home* (1978). At the bottom of the heap lies *The Exterminator* (1980) and *Exterminator II* (1984). whose 'Nam vet antihero goes haywire with a blowtorch when a gang paralyse his friend. Not much better is *First Blood* (1982), with Sylvester Stallone as an ex-Green Beret who leads smalltown cops on a merry dance through booby-trapped forests after being wrongly arrested. *Taxi Driver* had already covered the same ground as both these films, and to far more penetrating effect in its portrayal of unhinged moral outrage.

There is still more anger in the vet-turned-cop crime thrillers *Year of the Dragon* (1985) and *Lethal Weapon* (1987). In the first, a prematurely-aged Mickey Rourke is a little too heroized as a racist, out-of-order NYC cop. In the second, a finely-tuned action film, Mel Gibson plays a near-suicidal vet hunting down a criminal circle of ex-Vietnam mercenaries.

More seriously, *Birdy* (1984) and *Cease Fire* (1985) deal with vets whose sanity is fragmented by haunting visions of Vietnam battlefields. In *Birdy*, the scenario of William Wharton's novel has been rather artificially updated from World War II to Vietnam. *Cease Fire*, which could have been a more effective domestic melodrama, suffers from a strained theatricality and a wooden performance from Don Johnson. One of the best Vietnam civilian dramas of the Eighties is *Purple Haze* (1982), set in the summer of 1968. In this sensitive movie, which follows a young man's expulsion from college, the threatening spectre of the war is felt as powerfully as the fly-infested jungles of *Platoon*.

Waste, guilt, anger and madness are themes explored from various angles by the Eighties Vietnam movie, and in *Platoon* it was done with a new realism and sense of political perspective. In fact, *Platoon* dealt with guilt in the political arena while, for instance, *Fatal Attraction* (1987) dealt with it on a domestic scale, in the realm of personal relationships. These two popular films may seem strange bedfellows, but together they appear to signal the twilight of the carefree, yuppy-dominated Eighties.

Two different reactions to the Vietnam war – madness in Alan Parker's Birdy *(opposite page left) and resignation in Oliver Stone's* Platoon *(opposite page below). Two excursions into Vietnam – Gene Hackman in* Uncommon Valour *(top left) and Sylvester Stallone in* Rambo: First Blood Part II *(centre left). Bottom left: Chuck McQuary starred in* Purple Haze. *Above: James Caan plays an officer training recruits for war in Coppola's* Gardens of Stone. *Below: death and destruction as depicted by Stanley Kubrick in* Full Metal Jacket. *Bottom: Robert Altman's* Streamers *took place entirely in the barrack room*

GÉRARD DEPARDIEU

Left: Truffaut's romantic melodrama Le Dernier Métro *cast Depardieu opposite Catherine Deneuve. Above: in* Loulou, *he was teamed with Isabelle Huppert. Below: a detail from the poster of* Le Retour de Martin Guerre *(1982) with Natalie Baye*

Gérard Depardieu is without question the most important male star to have emerged in French cinema since the Seventies. Distinctive and commanding rather than conventionally handsome in appearance, he has a ruggedness which clearly marks him as the successor to Jean-Paul Belmondo and Jean Gabin

Whereas in previous decades on the French screen, performers like Charles Boyer and Alain Delon represented an alternative, matinee-idol image of Gallic masculinity, Depardieu in the present day stands in unchallenged eminence.

Since making his first film appearance in 1970, Depardieu has assuredly not gone short of employment. But while he has played a wide variety of roles in seemingly countless movies – good, bad and indifferent – those through which his screen presence has developed tend to have in common a quality of impulsiveness and unpredictability. To say the least, he is an actor who physically and otherwise asserts himself in front of the camera.

The key to this assertiveness may arguably lie in his own past. Born in 1948, he had a poverty-stricken upbringing as one of the six children of an industrial labourer, a reality from which he sought to escape by sneaking into the local cinema through the side door. He ran away from home at the age of 13 and for several years lived on his wits on the fringes of society.

Having made the breakthrough to professional acting, he appeared in numerous supporting roles and by 1974 was attracting real attention. This was the year in which he played a secondary part in *Stavisky* – significantly, one of the last movies to use Belmondo as a romantic lead – and in *Les Valseuses* played the leading role of an amorally drifting young petty crook: it was in the spirit of jagged, even threatening, sensuality projected by this film that Depardieu's movie personality seemed to crystallize.

He achieved wider fame when he was cast as the peasant son in Bernardo Bertolucci's epic *Novecento* (1976); this was of course a costume role, but its proletarian quality contrived to maintain the link with the actor's image of contemporary idiosyncrasy. Indeed, it seems appropriate that when, many years later, he would be cast in ostensibly conventional heroic guise in the Foreign Legion romance *Fort Saganne* (1984), the character he played would prove to be haunted by the memory of his peasant origins.

At any rate, the film which clinched his star status was *Loulou* (1980), and his role in it, echoing that in *Les Valseuses*, was again that of an opportunistic, sexually aggressive layabout, with whom a middle-class girl (Isabelle Huppert) enters into a fraught relationship. Within this tough-guy stance, however, could be glimpsed a hint of soulfulness, and it was this quality, with its suggestions of vulnerability, that was brought to the fore in two films directed by François Truffaut. In *Le Dernier Métro* (1980) he was cast as an actor in a wartime theatre troupe who is taken under the

cop of *Police* (1985), in which his ambiguous brand of magnetism is deployed at full pitch. More bizarrely, in the farce *Tenue de Soirée* (1986), he appears at the climax in full transvestite regalia, and since then he has featured to strongly sympathetic effect as the hunchbacked hero-victim of the rural melodrama *Jean de Florette* (1986), a film which met with huge success at the French box-office.

Depardieu is a contradictory figure: despite the instinctive-seeming tenor of his playing, he professes to dislike improvisation; and despite his very 'modern' quality, he voices a preference for acting in period costume. What is not surprising, however, is the discovery that he likes working in a hurry. And as he moves into his forties, there seems to be few enough signs of his needing to slow up.

Filmography

1970 Le Beatnik et le Minet (short); A Christmas Carol (unfinished). **'71** Le Crie du Cormoran, le Soir Au-dessus des Jonques; Nathalie Grainger; Le Viager; Le Tueur. **'72** Un Peu de Soleil Dans l'Eau Froide; La Scoumoune (GB: Scoundrel; USA: The Jinx); Au Rendez-vous de la Mort Joyeuse; L'Affaire Dominici; Deux Hommes Dans la Ville. **'73** Rude Journée Pour la Reine; Les Gaspards (USA: The Holes); Les Valseuses (USA: Going Places; GB: Making It); Stavisky. . . . La Femme du Gange (GB: The Woman of the Ganges). **'74** Vincent, François, Paul . . . et les Autres (USA: Vincent, Francois, Paul and the Others). **'75** Pas si Méchant que ça (USA/GB: This Wonderful Crook); 7 Morts sur Ordonnance (GB: 7 Deaths on Prescription) (FR-SP-GER); Je T'aime, Moi Non Plus (GB: I Love You, I Don't); Maîtresse; 1900 (IT); La Dernière Femme/L'Ultima Donna (IT-FR) (USA/GB: The Last Woman). **'76** Barocco; René la Canne; Baxter – Vera Baxter. **'77** Le Camion (GB: The Lorry); Die Linkschandige Frau (GB: The Left-Handed Woman); Dites-lui que J'Aime (GB: This Sweet Sickness); Préparez Vos Mouchoirs (USA/GB: Get Out Your Mouchoirs); Violenta (SWITZ); La Nuit Tous les Chants Sont Gris. **'78** Bye Bye Monkey/Ciao Macshio/Ciao, Male (IT-FR); Le Sucre; Les Chiens (GB: The Dogs); Le Grand Embouteillage (FR-IT). **'79** Loulou; Rosy la Bourrasque (FR-IT). Buffet Froid; Mon Oncle d'Amérique (GB: My American Uncle). **'80** Je Vous Aime; Le Dernier Métro (USA/GB: The Last Metro); Inspecteur la Bauvre. **'81** La Femme d'à Côté (GB.USA: The Woman Next Door); La Chèvre (GB: The Goat); Le Grand Frère; Le Choix des Armes (USA: Choice of Arms; GB: Choice of Weapons); Trois Hommes à Abbatre. **'82** L'Africain; Danton; Le Retour de Martin Guerre (USA/GB: The Return of Martin Guerre). **'83** La Lune Dans le Carniveau (USA/GB: The Moon in the Gutter); Les Compères (GB: Father's Day); **'84** Fort Saganne; Le Tartuffe (+dir); Rive Droite, Rive Gauche; **'85** Une Femme ou Deux (USA/GB: A Woman or Two); Paris Moliers. **'86** Jean de Florette; Police; Tenue de Soirée; Rue de Départ; Les Fugitifs (USA/GB: The Fugitives); **'87** Sous le Soleil de Satan (USA/GB: Under the Sun of Saturn); Camille Claudel; Funny Place for an Encounter; L'Oeil du Cheval (GB: The Horse's Eye); Cyrano de Bergerac.

---

protective wing of Catherine Deneuve. In *La Femme d' à Côté* (1981), in the business-suited guise of a provincial engineer, he seems to have been more rigorously stripped of romantic trappings, but only on the surface, for the film turns into a tale of *amour fou* between Depardieu and his neighbour's wife (Fanny Ardant). Truffaut utilizes the actor's air of estrangement to lend credence to the curious events of the film.

It was the title role in Andrez Wajda's *Danton* (1982) that gave Depardieu his next major part, one that strikingly capitalized on the actor's expansive sensuality, heightened by contrast with the frigid remoteness captured in

Wojciech Pszonick's portrayal of Robespierre.

While Depardieu continued to appear in commercial pictures as bland as *Les Compères* (1984), he could hardly be accused of resting on his laurels. He ventured into film direction with a carefully mounted version of Molière's *Le Tartuffe* (1984), playing once again the leading role he had taken on stage with the Theatre National de Strasbourg. He even appeared in a stage show with the rock star Barbara; he claimed to enjoy the experience, but said he would not wish to sing on the screen.

Probably his most memorable film role since Danton has been the aggressive plainclothes

Continental Drift

If one theme can be said to be common to the European cinema of the Eighties, it is that of voyaging and exploration, both cultural and geographical, though what has prompted these journeyings may well be far more the hard reality of shrinking audiences – and thus dwindling film figures – than any prevailing spirit of the times

For some film-makers, of course, the motive for moving base is more precise. The prime example is that of Andrei Tarkovsky, unquestionably the pre-eminent Soviet director of his generation, who in 1983 opted for life in the West, subsequently making *Nostalghia* (1983) in Italy and *The Sacrifice* (1986) in Sweden. Appropriately enough, both films treat themes of exile and alienation, though in the case of the latter these are only an element in wider preoccupations about religious faith and nuclear apocalypse, and tragically the director was himself to die within only a few months of *The Sacrifice* being completed.

Sometimes, the reasons for travel are more practical and parochial. Ingmar Bergman, by whose work *The Sacrifice* was clearly influenced, returned to Sweden to make the magisterial family chronicle *Fanny and Alexander* (1983) – which he claimed would be his farewell to the cinema – but had earlier made such films as *The Serpent's Egg* (1978) and *From the Life of the Marionettes* (1981) in West Germany, whence he had transposed himself for tax reasons.

The past few years have, alas, seen the withering of West Germany's own new cinema, which contributed so importantly to the film scene of the Seventies. The prolific Rainer Werner Fassbinder died violently in 1982, leaving as his last work *Querelle* (1982), a strange, unsatisfactory adaptation from a tale by the French writer Jean Genet.

The eclectic Werner Herzog, who had ventured into Transylvanian myth with his visually stunning version of the Dracula tale, *Nosferatu* (1979), next made a return visit to the jungles of South America to film *Fitzcarraldo* (1982), with the same star, Klaus Kinski. This time, partnered by Claudia Cardinale, he was at the centre of a bizarre story of a visionary adventurer's scheme to build an opera house in the middle of nowhere, in a work which, combining daunting spec-

Above: Klaus Kinski is the eccentric explorer of Herzog's Fitzcarraldo *while below: his daughter, Nastassja stars in* Paris, Texas

tacle with metaphysical provocation, is by any reckoning one of the decade's key movies. After this, Herzog journeyed forth again, this time to Australia to make *Where the Green Ants Dream* (1984), a comparatively minor film but one with its own charge of poetry in its address to Aboriginal beliefs.

Wim Wenders has, by contrast, been primarily active in the USA, whether attempting with the ingenious *Hammett* (1982) a homage to the Hollywood private-eye genre, or ploughing a more offbeat furrow with *Paris, Texas* (1984), with its powerful evocation of existential angst in the wide-open spaces of the southwest, as well as showcasing a remarkable performance by Nastassja Kinski (daughter of Klaus), an actress who has emerged as one of the most important new faces of the past several years.

Premature death also claimed one of the French cinema's key creative artists, François Truffaut, who died in 1983. The movies of Truffaut's last few years are perhaps unlikely to be ranked among his best achievements. But *Le Dernier Métro* (1980) was an expansive romantic melodrama (ironically, rather in the 'well made' manner against which Truffaut's early work was seen as being in reaction), while his final picture, *Vivement Dimanche!* (1983), was an appealing lightweight thriller, filmed in monochrome as if in tribute to the movies Truffaut had grown up watching.

The other key figure in the *nouvelle vague* of French film-makers a generation before was, of course, Jean-Luc Godard who, having been in self-imposed exile from commercial production for most of the Seventies, returned to something like mainstream work in the Eighties. With Godard, however, any such terms are strictly relative, and while a film such as *Sauve Qui Peut* (1980) boasted star names (Isabelle Huppert, Nathalie Baye) and a plot of sorts, it remained resolutely – not to say taxingly – experimental in spirit. Of Godard's other movies, which even included a nominal adaptation of *King Lear* (1987), the most satisfying was *Prénom Carmen* (1983), telling a free version of the Carmen story in jaggedly scatological contemporary terms, and featuring the director himself in a self-caricaturing role as a prematurely senile film-maker.

The nearest equivalent to a latterday

Top: Fanny Ardant and Jean-Louis Trintignant star in Vivement Dimanche! *François Truffaut's last film before his death in 1983. Above: Jean-Jacques Beneix's* Diva *is a quirky look at modern life which became something of a cult movie particularly among young audiences. Right: of the three versions of* Carmen *made in the Eighties, Francesco Rosi's was the only operatic one, starring Placido Domingo and Julia Migenes*

nouvelle vague was represented by movies such as *Diva* (1981), directed by Jean-Jacques Beneix, and *Subway* (1985), by Luc Besson – chic, fantasticated thrillers, displaying both a repertoire of technical bravura and a fascination with the more bizarre aspects of contemporary popular culture. In rather the same vein was Leos Carax's *Mauvais Sang* (1986), whose flights of philosophical fancy betray a more overt debt to early Godard.

Carmen has been a heroine much on view in recent cinema. The leading Spanish director, Carlos Saura, has lately devoted himself in the main to dance films, and his *Carmen* (1983), featuring Antonio Gades and Laura del Sol, is a

Above: Rosi's Chronicle of a Death Foretold *told the story of an enigmatic and wealthy stranger (Rupert Everett) who came to the village of Carthagena in Colombia looking for a bride (Ornella Muti). Right: Bertolucci's* The Last Emperor *followed the life of Pu Yi, seen here aged 15 played by Wu Tao, the last dynastic ruler of China, from his childhood to his old age after the revolution*

perhaps over-ingenious modern-dress flamenco version of the story, which nonetheless claimed many admirers. Apart from the rather special case of Saura's work, the most striking Spanish movie of the past decade was surely Victor Erice's hallucinatory *El Sur* (1983). This was the director's first film since *Spirit of the Beehive* (1973), but the long wait was more than justified by the new film's qualities of formal rigour and power of feeling in retelling another story of a quest for personal and cultural identity.

The Italian cinema also had its *Carmen* (1984), and this time an operatic one, with the original Bizet score thrillingly filmed by Francesco Rosi, utilizing real locations to enhance the melodrama in properly cinematic terms. Where this excursion into Spanish lore showed Rosi in top form, his next project was further flung but less successful. This was *Chronicle of a Death Foretold* (1987), filmed in South America with an international cast including Rupert Everett and Ornella Muti, and uneasy in its exoticism despite having an analytical plot structure reminiscent of some of the director's best earlier work.

Ermanno Olmi, who together with Rosi has been a chief exponent of extending the Italian realist tradition, made in *The Tree of Wooden Clogs* (1978) a poetic, unsentimental evocation of peasant life in northern Italy at the turn of the century. But Paolo and Vittorio Taviani, whose *Night of San Lorenzo* (1982) was a plangent story of wartime Italian experience, seemed less at home with a more fanciful foray into the early twentieth century; *Good Morning Babylon* (1986) was largely set (though not filmed) in America, albeit that it had a promising idea in following the fortunes of Italian

workmen employed to construct the sets of D.W. Griffith's epic *Intolerance* (1916).

Bernardo Bertolucci, the most flamboyant talent to emerge in the Italian cinema during the 1960s, appeared rather at a loss after the over-reaching epic *Novecento* (1976), about coming to terms with smaller-scale undertakings. Neither *La Luna* (1979) nor *Tragedy of a Ridiculous Man* (1981), particularly the latter with its attempt to address such contemporary issues as terrorism in balanced terms, suggested a director altogether clear of his bearings; and it seems significant that Bertolucci should have triumphantly returned, with *The Last Emperor* (1987), a US–Italian co-production partly filmed in China, to a blockbuster-sized and operatically heightened view of public events – which was awarded nine Oscars, including Best Picture and Best Director.

But what tends to distinguish Italian cinema is that its comparative veterans have continued to be active. Michelangelo Antonioni, no mean globetrotter himself over the past two decades, returned to homeground to make *The Oberwald Mystery* (1981). In content this marked an unexpected withdrawal to *fin-de-siècle* romanticism, being an adaptation of Cocteau's *The Eagle Has Two Heads*, but in form it adventurously embraced video techniques. Moreover, Antonioni's subsequent movie, *Identification of a Woman* (1982), was not only

vividly contemporary but treated eroticism with a frankness which lent a new value to a potentially debased currency, and into the bargain returned to the main theme – the divorce between society and sentiment – of the director's influential films of the early Sixties.

And then there is Federico Fellini. It may have seemed that in such a film as *And the Ship Sails On* (1983), with its stylized vision of Europe before World War I, the director was retreating, however elaborately, into a pseudo-allegorical world, and that his 'committed' days were over. But *Ginger and Fred* (1986), with its elderly, but still game, music-hall characters lovingly portrayed by two of Italy's now legendary stars, Marcello Mastroianni and Guiletta Masina, offered an impression of contemporary Rome and its admass culture, which still managed to rage against the dying of the Variety lights.

Not only that, but in *Intervista* (1987), made to celebrate the 50th anniversary of the Cinecitta studios, Fellini contrives to combine within one entertainment both an ironic tilt at television and a surrealistic celebration of his first contacts with the topsy-turvy milieu of movie-making. By journeying with such off-handedly casual expertise into his own and his medium's past, Fellini offers encouragement as to how the medium will continue to confront past, present . . . and even future.

JOHN CARPENTER'S
States of Siege

The films of John Carpenter can be seen as a series of portrayals of escalating crises leading to disaster, a cheerful illustration of the consequences of high-gloss technology. In Carpenter's world, the comfort of the conventional household is always being undermined by something seethingly untameable in the cellar, preparing to exact a violent revenge in return for past neglects

It seems an essential part of boyhood that cellars should be converted into chambers of horror, that monsters should be modelled from all available materials, that the authenticity of ghosts, dinosaurs and vampires should be urgently explored, and that all films about aliens should be analysed at length. Among the many such boyhoods of this century still continuing with undimmed enthusiasm into maturer years are those of Ray Bradbury,

George Lucas, Robert Bloch, Ray Harryhausen and Forrest J Ackerman. Aiming to outshine them all is the fizzing whiz-kid, John Carpenter.

Little horror
At five, he was watching *It Came from Outer Space*, as soon as it was released in 1953, in 3-D:
'I deserted my mother and dashed up the aisle in terror. But by the time I had reached the lobby I was in love with movies.'
At eight, he saw *Forbidden Planet* (1956):
'I still haven't gotten over it. Not a single, dry, computer-punched image in the bloated *2001* could start that kind of spine tingle.'
At eleven, chilling photographs testify to the fact that he was wrapping himself in sheets in the basement, masquerading as The Mummy to scare visiting friends. By the time he was fourteen, he had created four 8mm epics: *Revenge of the Colossal Beasts, Gorgo vs Godzilla, Terror From Space, Sorcerers From Outer Space*.

Left: the kidnapper's go-between (Frank Doubleday) in Escape From New York. *Below: preserved Commander Powell (Joe Saunders) gives 'telepathic' advice in* Dark Star

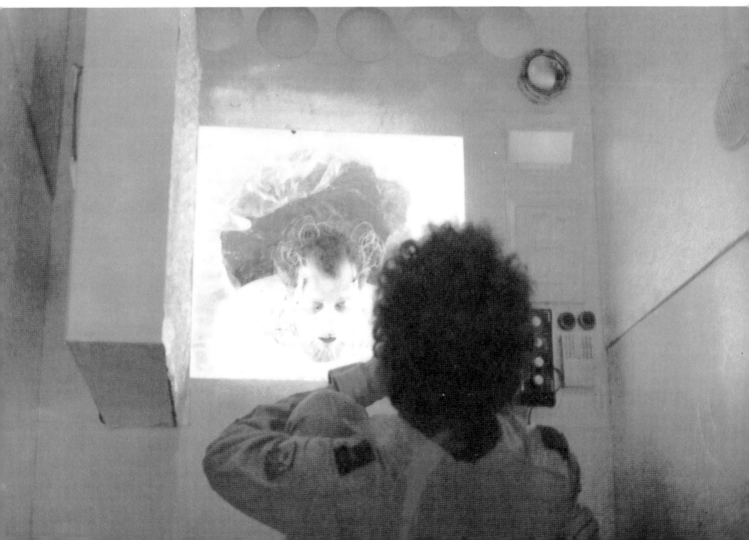

By fifteen, Carpenter had formed his own company, Emerald Productions, equipped with projectors, still cameras, professional lighting and a rear-projection screen, and had made what he termed his 'first really promising film', *Warrior and the Demon*. It starred an animated insectoid of uncertain origin tearing down a palace. By sixteen, he had created *Gorgon the Space Monster*, with a battery of special effects involving robots, spaceships and laser-beams. In the following year, he published his own magazine, *Fantastic Films Illustrated*, handpainting the covers of the first issue in watercolours and commissioning articles on such matters as 'Muscles and Mythology' and 'A Psychiatrist Considers UFOs'.

Since there seemed nothing else to do with him, the movie-mad teenager was packed off by his parents to study film at the University of Southern California. It was home from home: 'A marvellous experience. I took every production class they had. I learned everything I could about the camera, about sound, about editing.'

He worked on a whole batch of student projects, around fifteen of them, and in 1970 came up with a co-written, co-directed Academy Award Winner for Best Live Action Short ('I never understood why') called *The Resurrection of Bronco Billy*. Carpenter also edited, and composed the music. Not surprisingly, the film was about a youth who sees the world in movie terms, casting himself in the role of Western Hero in an attempt to transcend his uncongenial city environment. Later in the same year Carpenter was at work on *Dark Star*, and there was no looking back.

The story of the making of *Dark Star* has often been told, not least because the co-writer, special-effects man, and funniest member of the cast was fellow-student Dan O'Bannon, later to find fame as the creator of *Alien* (1979). Scraping together $6,000 of their own, Carpenter and O'Bannon slowly constructed a 45-minute 16mm film, creating 16 sets in their California homes, in a boiler room, and occasionally on a genuine soundstage:

'From the beginning I wanted the picture to have a certain look, something best described as RKO Radio Pictures circa 1950. . . . It took me three-and-a-half years, with a cast and crew of incredibly talented people. The making of the picture is a saga of pain and blood and love. It took on a life of its own after the second year and became a sort of Frankenstein monster that demanded strength and perseverance to give it birth.'

A dark horse out of the blue

With the help of additional funds from a Canadian distributor, and then from the independent producer Jack Harris (who had also been instrumental in getting a number of other careers off the ground) the birth of *Dark Star* finally took place in 1974. It was an immediate flop and a long-term hit, now recognized as a brilliant precursor to the *Star Wars* (1977) era. It was both outrageously funny and technically enthralling, for all that its space equipment had been cobbled together from heating insulation, vacuum-cleaner parts, cake tins, and industrial packaging:

'I still can't believe we did it all, including the blow-up to 35mm, for a grand total of $60,000. That's what it costs a major studio to sneeze. You have to be abnormally motivated to make a feature film on that money . . .'

The 'Dark Star' is a spacecraft conveying four men on an interminable mission to find and destroy any planets that are likely to cause a supernova by developing unstable orbits and crashing into the nearest sun. The quest renders the crew and their equipment equally unstable; the bombs that they carry for demolishing planets have some degree of intelligence and one of them keeps threatening to end it all by exploding prematurely. There is a rebellious alien bouncing around the ship, a talking computer sweetly announcing an ever-growing list of calamities, and the former captain, dead but preserved in cold storage, insisting on discussing irrelevant issues by means of electrodes planted in his brain.

The starting-point for *Dark Star* was Ray Bradbury's short story of an exploding spaceship, *Kaleidoscope*, in which the characters are flung their separate ways into space and maintain a precarious radio contact until the end.

While *Dark Star* was being prepared for release, Carpenter wrote *The Eyes of Laura Mars*, in which a sophisticated young woman finds herself psychically linked with the activities of a homicidal maniac. Gradually she

Above: John Carpenter and Jamie Lee Curtis (daughter of Janet Leigh and Tony Curtis) break during the making of The Fog. *Right: Carpenter turns his hand to a spoof adventure with* Big Trouble in Little China *in which Jack Burton (Kurt Russell) tries to rescue these two glamorous ladies from an evil magician*

realizes that the trail of killings is heading in her direction. The project was snapped up as a Barbra Streisand vehicle (although it ultimately starred Faye Dunaway), underwent all kinds of translations, and was finally unrecognizable on its release in 1978. Other Carpenter scripts – *Blood River* and *Black Moon Rising* – also went off on their own (abortive) careers without him. Then came a $200,000 offer out of the blue, and, since tiny budgets were of no concern to the maker of *Dark Star*, the result was *Assault on Precinct 13*, (1976), whipped up on a shooting schedule of 24 days.

Eyes West

Assault on Precinct 13 is the terrifying account of the siege of a police station, terrifying because the attack is silent, insane, and unstoppable, and because the defenders have as little chance of survival as those of the Alamo.

Carpenter pays obvious homage to Howard Hawks in the story (one clue, for instance, is provided by the dripping of blood), in his manner of filming (the two men share a love of the wide screen), and in his pseudonymous credit as editor (John T. Chance, the name of the John Wayne character in *Rio Bravo*, 1959). The central character is called Ethan, as was John Wayne in Ford's *The Searchers* (1956). All these factors make the film a special pleasure for movie-buffs. Another less elevated inspiration was George Romero's *Night of the Living*

Dead (1968). The remorseless encircling of the police station in *Assault on Precinct 13* by killers who appear unconcerned about being blown to bits so long as, eventually, their compatriots get inside, is a clear restaging of Romero's fantasy, even to the final encounter when, rather aimlessly waving clubs at the cornered survivors, the assailants are conveniently roasted alive.

The rescue leaves one in little doubt about its unlikelihood, but of course the whole point of the exercise, as with *Rio Bravo*, is that courage and concerted action will be the salvation of

Below left: The Fog followed on the heels of Carpenter's successful halloween horror. Below centre: Snake (Kurt Russell. right). is given the task of rescuing the kidnapped President from New York – now a giant prison containing three million criminals – in Escape From New York. Bottom: Assault on Precinct 13 (left) – the siege of a Los Angeles police station by a ghetto gang – proved an unexpected success; Halloween (right) was much better received as a result. Below right: Halloween's ghost. Below: another version of the Elvis story

the situation that makes it credible – the abrupt street murders that spark off the siege (the little girl being shot through her ice-cream is a shattering brutality), the pursuit by the demented father. the sudden first death on the steps of the police station, and the eerie ballet of leaping paper and shattering furniture as the building is hit by a silent hail of bullets. Unlike any of his later films, *Assault on Precinct 13* carries a stunning conviction; it comes altogether too close for comfort.

However. despite the strengths of the film. Carpenter's career seemed to falter: *Assault on Precinct 13* was a box-office failure in the States, and he turned back to scriptwriting; *Escape from New York* (1981) went to Fox; *Prey* was bought by Warners who also took on Carpenter as producer but cancelled after spending $500,000 on sets; and *High Rise* was renamed *Someone Is Watching Me*, when it was produced for NBC television in 1978. With elements of Hitchcock's *Vertigo* (1958) and *Rear Window* (1954), it is the story of a voyeuristic killer with designs on Lauren Hutton. Made with satisfying efficiency, it was while filming that Carpenter met Adrienne Barbeau, who later became his wife. Gratify-

ingly. as he had made it for television, he was given his Union card and his agent was offered other scripts, among them *Elvis* (1979): 'I'm a tremendous rock'n'roll fan – I saw the title and said "Yes". Elvis' music had done a lot for me, and I wanted to pay some of that back.' The film was good if unremarkable, quickly and respectfully made with a fine impersonation by Kurt Russell (who once appeared in an Elvis movie) as the doomed singer. Strangely, it fits the Carpenter pattern of stories about outcasts, isolated communities, and attack from all sides.

But the turning point came a little earlier, in December 1977. when *Assault on Precinct 13* turned into the hit of the London Film Festival. The producer-distributor who had been trying to get the film moving in the States was so delighted with the British reaction that he offered Carpenter a new concept, not at first sight a particularly suitable selection, called 'The Babysitter Murders'. Naturally the budget was minimal – $400,000 – and naturally this was no problem. The film became *Halloween* (1978), and a new era began for horror movies.

The most distinctive element in *Halloween* is its camerawork, which, as well as using Hitchcockian subjectivity in its assaults on one

cowering victim after another (the opening sequence places the audience inside the killer's mask and the knife in its hands), sets a rhythm of placidly disquieting elegance as it glides among the wide suburban avenues of Haddonfield. Whatever is felt about the story – which becomes more and more implausible – there is no denying the rising tension with which Carpenter prepares the audience for shock after shock, or the disturbing contrast achieved between the peaceful family homes. all glowing lights and persuasive furnishings, and the bloodletting that bursts loose inside them. For Carpenter, the ghouls of Halloween lurk within everyone, indestructible and unavoidable, eternal plague-carriers to a sick society.

Music to chill to
With *The Fog* (1980), the ghouls are on the prowl again, as drowned sailors return to terrorize the Californian coastal village that caused their deaths exactly 100 years earlier. With many members of his stock company (Tom Atkins, Charles Cyphers, Nancy Loomis, John Strobel) augmenting a stronger star cast of Janet Leigh. her now-famous daughter (thanks to *Halloween*) Jamie Lee Curtis, Hal Holbrook and, in the leading role, Adrienne Barbeau, Carpenter clearly intended to enjoy himself with this one, adding – almost gratuitously – some Romero-influenced chills and gore, and a wealth of special effects. Music, as with *Halloween*, is a dominating aspect; constructed by Carpenter it is credited to the Bowling Green Philharmonic Orchestra (his home town is Bowling Green, Kentucky). The obsessively repeated piano phrases over thudding bass tones insinuate themselves into the audience's consciousness like a ritualistic chant, growing irresistibly to the crescendo when the anticipated threat can no longer be avoided – and then, after all, permitting it to leap out from a deadly silence.

The Eighties saw Carpenter's energy unchecked. *Escape From New York* is the ultimate siege film: the whole of New York has become a maximum security jail in which the President is being held hostage by the inmates. *The Thing* (1982) is a chilling story of an alien buried in the Antarctic ice. *Christine* (1983) is another, more obvious, horror based on a Stephen King novel. *Starman* (1984) tells of a visitor from outer space who leaves a 'starchild' behind him. Carpenter's most surprising film of the period is *Big Trouble in Little China* (1986), starring Carpenter regular Kurt Russell. It is an action comedy which combines kung fu, ghosts and monsters into a side-splitting – and highly colourful – spoof adventure.

the home team. Once the shock has worn off – and it is not a film to leave the audience unscathed – it is evident that where Carpenter cannot yet match up to Hawks is in the subtlety of his characterizations. His cast is excellent – impressive for being a collection of unknowns – yet they remain, even after several viewings, curiously anonymous; some wisecracks, plenty of memorable images, but nothing to compare with John Wayne and Angie Dickinson.

It is the *situation*, not the people, that carries the film. And it is Carpenter's development of

Filmography
1970 The Resurrection of Bronco Billy (short) (co-dir; +co-sc; +ed; +mus). '74 Dark Star (+prod; +co-sc; +mus). '76 Assault on Precinct 13 (+sc; +ed. under pseudonym; +mus). '78 Someone Is Watching Me (orig. TV) (sc. only); Halloween (+co-sc; +mus); The Eyes of Laura Mars (co-sc. only). '79 Elvis (orig. TV) (GB: Elvis – The Movie). '80 The Fog (+co-sc; +mus). '81 Escape From New York (+co-sc; +mus); Halloween II (co-prod only). '82 The Thing; Halloween III (co-prod+mus only). '83 Christine (+mus). '84 Starman. '86 Black Moon Rising; Big Trouble in Little China. '87 Prince of Darkness.

Ad Lib

From successful commercials to commercial success. In 1982 Colin Welland, with Oscar in hand, warned Hollywood that 'The British are coming!' But he never expected the fighting force to emerge from TV commercials

In a bar in North Carolina, a college student asked an English film critic if there were any film directors in England. The critic pointed out that the two box-office blockbusters showing at the local mall, *Beverly Hills Cop II* and *Fatal Attraction*, were both made by British film-makers. After voicing his surprise at this, the student continued: 'Yes, but has England produced any household-name directors?' What did the student consider household? 'You know, Hitchcock or Spielberg'. Preserving his patience, and suppressing a smile, the critic informed the student that Hitchcock was, in fact, English.

They have been creeping up on us, and from all directions. Richard Attenborough, winner of an Academy Award for his direction of *Gandhi* (1982), was an actor. David Leland, who introduced us to Emily Lloyd in *Wish You Were Here* (1987), was an actor. Playwright and screenwriter John Boorman and Michael Winner started as film critics (both at the age of 17), as did Lindsay Anderson, who co-edited the controversial *Sequence* magazine in the late Forties. Michael Apted and John Irvin emerged from television; while Irvin's cameraman on *Hamburger Hill* (1987) became a director overnight when he replaced Russell Mulcahy on *Rambo III* (1988). Nicolas Roeg, arguably Britain's most iconoclastic film-maker, also started as cameraman, winning high acclaim for his lighting of *The Masque of the Red Death* (1964) and *Far From the Madding Crowd* (1967). But the five English film-makers who have had the biggest impact on Hollywood in terms of box-office turn-over, Oscar nominations and the securing of major stars, surfaced from another medium entirely: the television commercial.

The most controversial of this quintet is Alan Parker, a short, chubby, scabrous Cockney,

Above: Eddie Murphy in Beverly Hills Cop II. *The second of the popular series was directed by Tony Scott. Right: Emily Lloyd shot to instant fame as the star of David Leyland's directoral debut* Wish You Were Here, *a nostaligic look at the Fifties*

with an outspoken manner and a knack for directing children. After a career in advertising he directed *The Evacuees* (1971) for the BBC, a bewitching evocation of wartime childhood, for which he won an International Emmy and a British Academy Award. He made his large-screen debut with *Bugsy Malone* (1977), directing an entire cast of children as gangsters (complete with false moustaches), in a musical homage to the crime thriller of the Twenties and Thirties. Custard pies provided the artillery and a 13-year-old Jodie Foster the sex appeal. For the British cinema of the Seventies, steeped in a burgeoning realism, the concept of *Bugsy Malone* was outlandish, not to say foolhardy.

But the film worked, it was a sensation at the Cannes Film Festival and an enormous public success. It also accrued eight British Academy Awards and Parker was awash with offers to direct other musicals.

He bit typecasting in the bud by coming up with a ferocious prison drama, *Midnight Express* (1978), the true story of drug smuggler Billy Hays and of his brutal imprisonment in a Turkish prison. Amnesty International was up in arms, the Turkish embassy in London sent out angry letters of protest to local reviewers and Parker was fast becoming a household name, at least, in London and Ankara. Still, the public liked the film, it broke box-office records in Britain and, in the USA, was Oscar-nominated for best picture, director, screenplay, music, editing and supporting actor (the always-wonderful John Hurt).

Publicly badmouthing the British film industry for its reticence to finance local product, Parker accepted an offer to make an American musical and came up with *Fame* (1980). Set in New York's High School of the Performing Arts, *Fame* was a powerful and moving look at the emotional exposure of drama school; it won two Oscars for music, and propagated a long-running cult TV series.

Next came *Shoot the Moon* (1981), a harrowing examination of a bad marriage, with Albert Finney and Diane Keaton chewing the furniture; and then another musical, a brilliant realization of the Pink Floyd album *The Wall* (1982), a cinematic masterpiece of rock and image that sent British educationalists into paroxysms of rage. *Birdy* (1984) was a quirky, whimsical story of a boy who dreams of flying, with a whiplash in its tail aimed at the Vietnam war; and then there was more controversy over *Angel Heart* (1987), a mesmerizing tale of voodoo and satanism, with Robert De Niro as the devil. The Motion Picture Association of America slapped an 'X' certificate on the film, immediately denying it exhibition in about 800 theatres. Parker fought back and wrestled for a halfway solution – the excision of ten seconds' worth of Mickey Rourke's rear. In Britain, the film was released uncut.

Above left: child actress Jodie Foster is one of the stars of Bugsy Malone, *the film which established Alan Parker in the United States of America. His next,* Fame *(centre), about aspiring teenage performers, did even better at the box-office and spun-off a long-running and popular TV series. His most recent release,* Angel Heart *(right) stars Mickey Rourke as a seedy detective whose life takes a diabolical turn. Below: Parker, seen here on the set of* Angel Heart, *is now one of Hollywood's most highly regarded directors*

Parker is emotionally divided about his occupation of Hollywood. He loves England, but cannot tolerate the pussyfooting of its moneymen, and yet he's shocked by the censorship in America. His standing in Hollywood is considerable, although the respect afforded him is mingled with more than a little fear.

Ridley Scott, a small, ginger-haired man from the North-East of England, emerged at about the same time. A graduate of the Royal College of Art (in a graphic design and advertising department), he became a star director of commercials, spearheaded by a homely, nostalgic campaign for Hovis, the wholemeal loaf.

Vignettes for Benson and Hedges cigarettes, Chanel perfume, Levis, Pepsi and Apple computers accumulated a number of awards, while Scott's first feature, *The Duellists* (1977), was voted best film at Cannes. From the novella by Joseph Conrad, the story centred on a long-running feud between two Napoleonic swordsmen, played by Keith Carradine and Harvey Keitel. Like *Bugsy Malone*, it was produced by David Puttnam and unanimously praised for its photography.

In common with Alan Parker, Scott was determined to avoid being typecast and leapt from the romance of Conrad to the horror of outer space. The posters screamed, 'In space no one can hear you scream' and *Alien* (1979) became a box-office phenomenon, sold to an eager public with the finesse of a high-concept commercial. The poster for *Alien* featured a giant egg in space, about to explode, hovering over an ominous latticework. It didn't mean anything – as Scott will be the first to admit – but it caught the eye, sold the film and word of mouth did the rest.

Blade Runner (1982), starring Harrison Ford as android-hunter, was less successful, but had an admiring following – and was a triumph of production design. *Legend* (1985) really was a dud by anybody's standards, a long-held dream of Scott's to create the ultimate fable of good and evil on an elephantine budget. Tom Cruise, with long, lank hair, played Jack O' The Green, and looked decidedly ill-at-ease, while Tim Curry stole the acting honours as an outrageously camp Prince of Darkness. Again, the film was visually breath-taking, and for some that was enough – enough to allow Scott financing for what some say is his best film, *Someone To Watch Over Me* (1987). Tom Berenger starred as a happily-married cop in love with a murder witness (Mimi Rogers, Mrs Tom Cruise) and the trade paper *Variety* noted that 'Scott consistently commands attention with his trademark visual style'; another critic attested to its 'style, substance *and* entertainment content'. Love him or hate him, Scott takes films out of the screenplay and lodges them in the memory.

Above: a scene from Ridley Scott's science-fiction fantasy Alien. *Right: he also directed the romantic thriller* Someone to Watch Over Me *(1988) starring Tom Berenson. Left: David Bowie and Catherine Deneuve in* The Hunger. *Below: Harrison Ford starred in Scott's* Blade Runner, *a futuristic adventure whose lavish sets reflected its budget*

Hugh Hudson, a grey-haired, no-nonsense Old Etonian, had a long and distinguished career in commercials before the mighty hand of Puttnam hauled him out of the recesses of anonymity. Hudson chose *Chariots of Fire* (1981) for his debut feature, a stirring tale of two British runners sprinting to glory in the 1924 Olympics. Against the odds, and *Reds* in particular, *Chariots of Fire* won the Oscar for the best film, script, music and costumes and prompted its scenarist, Colin Welland, to cry to a packed audience on Oscar night: 'The British are coming!'.

And so they came. Hudson himself directed a successful and highly aesthetic Tarzan adventure, *Greystoke; The Legend of Tarzan, Lord of the Apes* (1984), starring Christopher Lambert as Tarzan and Sir Ralph Richardson as the grandfather; and snared Al Pacino, Donald Sutherland and Nastassja Kinski to star in *Revolution* (1985), his epic version of the events in America in and around 1776; it was an impressive if somewhat improbable study of American history. In 1988 he began work on his first truly American film, filmed in San Antonio with Donald Sutherland top-billed.

Adrian Lyne began his career in the mailroom of London's J. Walter Thompson Advertising Agency, and made his very first feature film (for David Puttnam, naturally) in America. *Foxes* (1980), starring Jodie Foster and Scott Baio (both from *Bugsy Malone*), was a likeable and involving tale of the teenage microcosm in the San Fernando Valley, but little prepared the world for Lyne's next film, *Flashdance* (1983), which established Jennifer Beals as a star and spawned a best-selling soundtrack. *Nine½ Weeks* (1986) was not so successful, but its battles with the censor and the candid performances of its stars, Mickey Rourke and Kim Basinger, generated some healthy controversy. However, Lyne was stung by the critical battering he received and swore off directing – until the screenplay for *Fatal Attraction* (1987) landed on his desk. The story of the infidelity of a successful New York Attorney (and of the hair-raising consequences) pushed the film through the box-office roof and lassoed half a dozen Oscar nominations, including those for best film and director. *Fatal Attraction*, and its theme of adultery, became *the* talk at cocktail parties and the film soon ranked as the third-highest-grossing movie ever directed by an Englishman.

The two *most* successful, *Beverly Hills Cop II* (1987) and *Top Gun* (1986), were both realized by Tony Scott, younger brother of Ridley. Winner of virtually every major award in advertising, and a co-partner with Ridley in a commercial production company, Tony Scott cut his directorial teeth on *The Hunger* (1983), a stylistic vampire fantasy starring Catherine Deneuve and David Bowie.

On a rafting trip down the Colorado river with producers Don Simpson and Jerry Bruckheimer, Scott first heard of *Top Gun*. The visual imagery of *The Hunger* suited the designer style of the new film, and Simpson and Bruckheimer, who had made a healthy profit on Adrian Lyne's good-looking *Flashdance*, were again seeking the 'look' of a slick, efficient commercial. Scott gave them the visual panache they wanted, added Tom Cruise (from his brother's recently-completed *Legend*) and sat pretty while *Top Gun* raked in a domestic net of $80 million. In real terms, that is more money than either *Rambo* or *Gone With the Wind* made. And Scott's *Beverly Hills Cop II*, also for Simpson and Bruckheimer, netted even more than that. Tony Scott, to date, is the hottest director working in Hollywood.

With the emergence of the multi-stylistic music video, the 'look' in Hollywood has become increasingly important. And Britain, with its reputation for high-quality commercials, was a utopian breeding ground for the perfect Eighties' film-maker. The movies of Parker, Hudson, Lyne and the Scott brothers share one essential ingredient: a visual, almost 'painterly' flair that, in the early Eighties, was virtually non-existent in Hollywood.

Top right: Hugh Hudson's Chariots of Fire *put British films of the Eighties on the map. Centre right: Adrian Lyne was the director of* Fatal Attraction – *the smash hit of 1987, and nominated for all the major Oscars. Right: Tony Scott's* Top Gun, *starring Tom Cruise as would-be ace naval pilot and would-be ace stud, found less favour in the Oscar stakes but was the runaway box-office hit of 1986.*

The Killing Fields

Directed by Roland Joffé, 1984
Prod co: Goldcrest Films and Television. **prod:** David Puttnam. **sc:** Bruce Robinson. **photo** (Eastman Color)**:** Chris Menges. **ed:** Jim Clark. **art dir:** Roger Murray Leach, Steve Spence. **prod des:** Roy Walker. **cost:** Judy Moorcroft. **mus:** Mike Oldfield, Paul McCartney, Puccini. **sd:** Clive Winter. **ass dir:** Bill Westley, Sompol Sungkawess, Gerry Toomey, David Barron, David Brown, Buranee Rachjaibun, Charles Hubbard, Alan Goluboff, Howard Rothschild. **sp eff sup:** Fred Cramer. **stunt cord:** Terry Forrestal. **r/t:** 142 mins.
Cast: Sam Waterson (Sydney Schanberg), Doctor Haing S. Ngor (Dith Pran), John Malkovich (Al Rockoff), Julian Sands (Jon Swain), Craig T. Nelson (Military Attaché), Spalding Gray (US Consul), Bill Paterson (Dr MacEntire), Athol Fugard (Doctor Sundesval), Graham Kennedy (Dougal), Katherine Kragum Chey (Ser Moeun, Pran's Wife), Monirak Sisowath (Phat), Ira Wheeler (Ambassador Wade), Patrick Malahide (Morgan), Nell Campbell (Beth).

At a production cost of $15 million, *The Killing Fields* was British producer David Puttnam's most ambitious film to date. He had been inspired by a piece in *Time* magazine telling of the reunion between journalist Sydney Schanberg and his former Cambodian aide Dith Pran after a four-year separation. Male friendship in adversity is a common theme in Puttnam productions – *Midnight Express* (1978), *Chariots of Fire* (1981) and *The Mission* (1986). It suggests a pervading influence at work in all his projects.

The Killing Fields clearly establishes an emotional rather than political setting in its opening moments as an idyllic landscape is filled with helicopters and napalm. A voice-over from Schanberg immediately follows, focussing on his relationship with Dith Pran. Structurally, this keeps unclear the origins of the conflict in Cambodia and the Khmer Rouge. The film demands a humane engagement with events rather than an analysis of them.

For a film featuring journalists, the process of news gathering in the field is secondary, making Pran's decision to stay while his family is evacuated more to do with friendship than journalistic pride. The reporters of *Under Fire* (1983) and *Salvador* (1986) are actively involved in the events surrounding them. In *The Killing Fields* they seem rather helpless. Their only major scene together is in the confines of the French Embassy as the Khmer Rouge decide their fate. (An episode in Chantal's opium parlour, the journalists' favourite meeting place in Phnom Penh, was cut from the final version.) The film is more concerned with people than journalism.

This is stressed as scene after scene tries to reconcile the vast with the intimate, though without the allegorical excesses of *Apocalypse Now*. A scene of crowds welcoming the Khmer Rouge into Phnom Penh is followed by a visit to an ill-equipped hospital full of bloody bodies. In violent conflict, attention

is concentrated on innocent victims (a screaming child covering its ears during a bombing; a corpse entwined with a bike). Wider political consequences are expressed by telling individual details: Kissinger's picture in a shredder heralding the American embassy's evacuation; the Khmer Rouge smashing a picture of Brezhnev.

The film's most affecting moment comes during Pran's escape to Thailand. Crossing the killing fields themselves, where the Khmer Rouge executed three million of Cambodia's seven million inhabitants, we witness one man's struggle amidst a landscape strewn with human bones and skulls: an individual's suffering expressing that of millions.

The remarkable stoicism of Pran under Kampuchean rule is movingly portrayed by the simplicity and directness of Dr. Haing S. Ngor's performance. A non-professional actor, Ngor was working as an advisor for an Indo-Chinese employment scheme in Los Angeles when he heard about casting for the film. He lost his whole family to the Khmer Rouge but managed to escape to Thailand in 1979. Knowing that Ngor had lived through the events being re-created on screen intensifies its emotional impact.

5

To its immense credit, in a British film of startling passion, there is only one melodramatic moment, when John Lennon's 'Imagine' plays as Schanberg and Pran are reunited in Thailand at the film's conclusion. As an anthem of universal harmony it seems naive and inappropriate for what has gone before. Yet the film offers no easy resolution. The final images are of dissolute refugees and a feeling of continued suffering. The abiding strength of The Killing Fields lies in its humanity.

8

6

9

7

Ironically, this but highlights the inadequate development of the relationship between Schanberg and Pran. While the latter's ordeal dominates the second half of the film, only Schanberg's guilt is felt as the emotional link with Pran while he searches for him from America.

Yet the truth of the underlying story is clearly reflected in the credibilty of the film. It is also a testimony to the commitment of its makers and to Puttnam's guiding hand. His initial investors had wanted a star package (Dustin Hoffman, Sidney Lumet and Paddy Chayevsky as star, director and writer respectively) but Puttnam re-

fused. Casting a self-effacing star such as Sam Watertson ensured that Pran's character was not overwhelmed. Former actor Bruce Robinson had been on Puttnam's payroll since 1975, working on various unproduced projects before being given the task of adapting Schanberg's story. Roland Joffé was an untried cinema director, but had already established a reputation for his television work. Both Robinson and Joffé had strong left-wing sympathies, with Puttnam toning down the script's originally explicit anti-American stance. What Puttnam utilized to great effect was their intense humanist concern.

Cambodia. August 1973: New York Times foreign correspondent Sydney Schanberg (1) arrives in Phnom Penh. Helped by his aide and translator Dith Pran, they smuggle themselves into a city destroyed by an American bomber (2) – apparently as a result of a computer error.

March 1975: The fighting has escalated as the Khmer Rouge advance towards Phnom Penh. Dith Pran's family is airlifted with the American evacuation of the city (3). Schanberg and colleagues Jon Swain and Al Rockoff are taken prisoner by the new militia (4) and held captive until Pran pleads successfully for their release (5). Taking refuge in the French embassy, a desperate attempt to fake a British passport for Pran fails, forcing him to stay while remaining foreign nationals are expelled.

Back in America, Schanberg tries to trace Pran but without success. Now a slave labourer for the new regime (6), Pran realizes his best defence is silence as the new rulers eradicate Cambodia's

past to create Kampuchea in Year Zero. Escaping from his work detail (7), a long trek leads Pran to become the servant of Phat, a Khmer Rouge village leader. Schanberg wins a Journalist of the Year award, and condemns American foreign policy in South East Asia in his acceptance speech. Al Rockoff accuses him of deliberately allowing Pran to remain behind in Cambodia at the time of the airlift, despite the known dangers, for his own ends.

Kampuchea is now at war with Vietnam. Phat discovers Pran's former identity when he is caught listening to an English radio broadcast (8). However, Phat is now more worried about the new regime's policies and in-fighting, and entrusts his young son to Pran before he himself is killed by a rival faction. Pran begins a long journey to Thailand (9) but the boy is killed by a land mine on the way. News reaches a thankful Schanberg of his friend's safe arrival in Thailand. Schanberg and Pran are eventually reunited in a refugee camp in 1979.

THE BRAT PACK

Practically every member of the so-called Brat Pack has denied his association with it. But the fact remains that he (or she) has little say in the matter. The label is purely journalistic; it was invented by the media. So if the press wish to brand a young actor a member of the Brat Pack, then a member he is

The basis for the denial, surely, is that 'brat' is not an entirely flattering term. And no self-respecting artiste would wish to be part of a 'pack'. Nevertheless, the allusion is something of a backhanded compliment. On the whole, the films of the Brat Pack are good films or, at the very least, contain a high standard of acting.

Before the advent of *The Outsiders* (1983), adolescent performance was limited to such dross as *Friday the 13th* (1980) and *Porky's* (1981). Francis Coppola, a serious film-maker by anybody's standards, recognized the market for serious teenage films and exploited it accordingly. He had lost a great deal of money on *Apocalypse Now* (1979) and *One From the Heart* (1981), and needed a quick hit. Back in 1972 when he directed *The Godfather*, he employed inexpensive actors. At $50,000 Marlon Brando was the most costly, while such unknowns as Al Pacino, James Caan, Robert Duvall and Diane Keaton worked for peanuts. Later, thanks to the phenomenal success of *The Godfather*, Coppola could no longer afford these same actors. With *The Outsiders*, the story of troubled youth in 1960's Oklahoma, the director hoped to repeat *The Godfather* formula. Based on the cult, best-selling novel by S.E. Hinton, *The Outsiders* was a *Gone With the Wind* version of *Rebel Without a Cause*, and starred a host of teenage actors as a motley crew of down-market misfits. The film was variously attacked for its violence and sentimentality, but the performances were invariably praised. The Great Public took to it, and *The Outsiders* was a hit. Today, Coppola would, once again, be unable to afford his cast.

As Ponyboy Curtis, C. Thomas Howell had the central role of the sensitive outcast on the run from a neighbourhood gang calling themselves the 'socs' (pronounced 'soaches', alluding to their social superiority). Howell exhibited little merit in the role – besides his boyish good looks – and went on to appear in some dubious material: *Tank*, *Grandview USA*.

Above: Francis Coppola's The Outsiders *was the film that started the Brat Pack Phenomenon. The Brats (left to right) are: Emilio Estevez (Two-Bit), Rob Lowe (Sodapop), C. Thomas Howell (Ponyboy), Matt Dillon (Dallas), Ralph Macchio (Johnny), Patrick Swayze (Darrel) and Tom Cruise (Steve). Below: Matt Dillon in* The Flamingo Kid

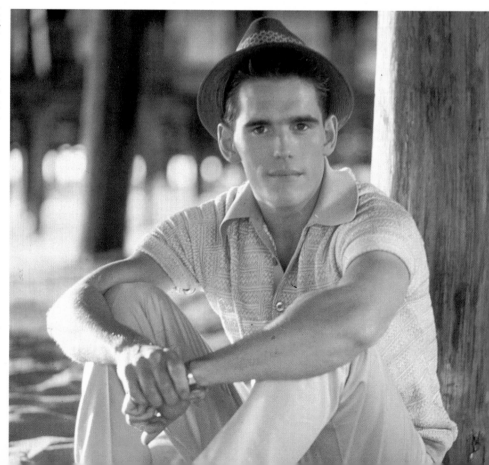

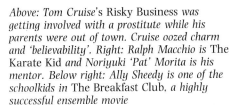

Red Dawn (all 1984) and Secret Admirer (1985). In Robert Harmon's taut, chilling thriller The Hitcher (1986), he provided the emotional, human core of the movie and finally proved that he was an actor to be taken seriously. In the periodically amusing Soul Man he played a law student (disguised as a negro in order to win a minority scholarship) and found himself with a hit. After that, Howell landed the title role in Franco Zeffirelli's prestigious Young Toscanini (1988), opposite Elizabeth Taylor.

Second-billed in The Outsiders was Matt Dillon, already a veteran of seven movies (he made his debut in Jonathan Kaplan's Over the Edge, 1979). Dillon's dark good looks and Brandoesque mumble had already secured him a sizeable following, and Rumble Fish (1983), Coppola's follow-up to The Outsiders, cemented his stardom. Rumble Fish was another Brat Pack product of note (a further look at alienated youth from the pages of S.E. Hinton), which spawned its own roster of young stars: Mickey Rourke, Vincent Spano, Nicolas Cage, Christopher Penn. Meanwhile, Dillon glowed in the charming, nostalgic The Flamingo Kid (1984), and then all but committed professional suicide with a series of badly misjudged vehicles – Rebel, Native Son (both 1986) and The Big Town (1987). Inexplicably, his cult standing appears to remain undamaged.

Third down the cast list of The Outsiders was Ralph Macchio, an intelligent, deceptively young-looking actor who started his professional life as a singer and dancer. The 'prettiest' member of the Brat Pack, Macchio fought against his looks and showed his mettle in a powerful TV film, The Three Wishes of Billy Grier (1984), in which he played a boy suffering from a rare ageing disease. Born in 1961, Macchio is still saddled with playing teenagers in the late Eighties. He won more good reviews in 1986 on stage in Cuba and His Teddy Bear, opposite Robert De Niro, at the Public Theatre in New York, but is still best known as The Karate Kid (1984), a film which raked in over $100 million at the American box-office. Top-

Above: Tom Cruise's Risky Business was getting involved with a prostitute while his parents were out of town. Cruise oozed charm and 'believability'. Right: Ralph Macchio is The Karate Kid and Noriyuki 'Pat' Morita is his mentor. Below right: Ally Sheedy is one of the schoolkids in The Breakfast Club, a highly successful ensemble movie

ping that, the inevitable sequel became the second highest-grossing film of 1986.

The most popular film of 1986 was Top Gun, starring Tom Cruise. This, and the sensational box-office returns of Risky Business (1983) and The Color of Money (1986) crowned Tom Cruise the box-office King of the Brat Pack. For all the media coverage of the likes of Sean Penn and Matt Dillon, their takings so far have never equalled their fame. Until Tom Cruise, all the publicity in the world couldn't turn the Brats into serious popular icons – Clint Eastwood, Burt Reynolds, Sylvester Stallone and their peer group were still the reigning gods of Hollywood. And yet the majority of moviegoers were between the ages of 14 and 25 at a time (1986) when Stallone was 40, Reynolds was 51 and Eastwood 56. But the times were a-changing.

The phenomenal business of 48 HRS (1982), Trading Places (1983), Beverly Hills Cop (1984) and The Golden Child (1986) nudged Eddie Murphy into the top box-office spot. In 1986 he was 25; but at 21 he had already been flaunting his Midas touch. Although young, Murphy was not a brother of the Brat Pack, partly because of his insular popularity. Cigar-chewing tycoons paid him millions (he received close to $16 million for Quest, 1988) to star, hog and saturate their movies. The true Brat Pack emerged from ensemble pictures, like The Outsiders and Rumble Fish, and later The Breakfast Club (1985), St Elmo's Fire and River's Edge (1986).

Michael J. Fox, the same age as Eddie Murphy, also showed enormous box-office strength with such successes as *Back to the Future* (the top-grossing film of 1985) and *The Secret of My Success* (1987) but, again, was not a member of the Brat Pack. Like Murphy, Fox is an alumnus of television, and took his popularity from the small screen to the large.

If we are dealing with semantics here, then the operative word is 'pack'. Howell, Dillon, Macchio and Cruise graduated to film stardom as a 'pack'. Sean Penn, although more famous for his brattish public behaviour and marriage to Madonna, carved his name as an actor in Amy Heckerling's *Fast Times at Ridgemont High* (1982), an ensemble comedy that also featured Nicolas Cage, Judge Reinhold, Eric Stoltz and Anthony Edwards.

But Coppola's *The Outsiders* is *the* seminal Brat Pack picture, the film that inspired one American journalist to originally coin the phrase – a pun on the original 'Rat Pack' that comprised Frank Sinatra, Dean Martin, Sammy Davis Jr and Peter Lawford.

Tom Cruise's role in *The Outsiders* was small (he was eighth billed), but the film showered enough kudos on him for him to land the lead in Paul Brickman's *Risky Business*, a zany comedy with an electric soundtrack. Commercially, this was far more successful and catapulted the actor into another hit, *All the Right Moves* (1983), an amiable high-school caper. *Legend* (1985), a fairy tale from Ridley Scott, was a mistake, although Cruise found it 'stunning and gorgeous and poetic'. It dive-bombed

Above right: Eddie Murphy, seen here with Dan Aykroyd and Jamie Lee Curtis on the set of Trading Places, *might be young but he is not technically a brat. Below: Patrick Swayze is best known for his he-man image. Right: Rob Lowe in* Oxford Blues – *having to stretch himself to succeed both with his rowing team and with his titled charmer*

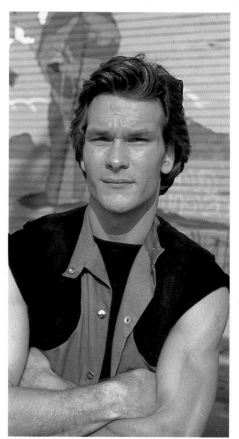

downbeat crime caper, that made him the youngest writer-director-star in Hollywood history. Unfortunately, *Wisdom* was not a success, but Estevez bounced back (as star) in the hugely popular *Stakeout* (1987), an enjoyable comedy-thriller with Richard Dreyfuss.

For his next film, Emilio Estevez returned to the safe world of the ensemble piece. *Young Guns* (1988), directed by Chris Cain, starred Estevez as Billy the Kid, with Charlie Sheen and Kiefer Sutherland in support. Interestingly, Sheen and Sutherland heralded an entirely new generation of Brat Packers. Sheen, the son of Martin Sheen and brother of Emilio, and Sutherland, the son of Donald Sutherland, were very much the leading lights of this fresh crop of stars. In *Platoon* (1986), Charlie Sheen starred alongside such raw recruits as Kevin Dillon, brother of Matt, and Francesco Quinn, son of Anthony. In *The Wraith* (1986), he was supported by Nick Cassavetes, son of John, and Griffin O'Neal, son of Ryan.

Now that the likes of Estevez and Dillon are playing responsible grown-up adults, the siblings are taking over. By 1988 Paul Dillon, Renée Estevez, Chad Lowe, Christopher Penn, Matthew Penn, Ramon Sheen and Don Swayze were all making movies.

at the box-office. Public favour returned with *Top Gun*, an aviation spectacular complete with stunning stunts, Kelly McGillis and a top-selling soundtrack. Cruise's performance, however, left a lot to the imagination, but he made up for it in Martin Scorsese's *The Color of Money* – as a dynamic pool hotshot, all bravado and empty-headedness. Paul Newman won an Oscar as the boy's coach, but Cruise gave as good as he got. After that, Tom Cruise found it hard to keep his name out of the papers.

Another media darling was Rob Lowe, who played Sodapop Curtis, Howell's older brother, in *The Outsiders*. Lowe's good looks got in the way of good reviews, while journalists concentrated on his love life (that seemed to equal Warren Beatty's). Some crass movies didn't help. However, *About Last Night . . .* (1986) was a hit, and his daring role of a mentally retarded hick in *Square Dance* (1987) won him a Golden Globe nomination.

Patrick Swayze was the last of Coppola's Curtis brothers, and the actor's career seemed to be similarly saddled with bad movies. The critics had great fun shredding *Grandview USA*, *Red Dawn* and *Youngblood* (1986), but were stopped in their tracks by *Dirty Dancing* (1987), a modest, 1963-set romance that grew into an enormous box-office phenomenon, grossing over $100 million worldwide. Swayze was nominated for a Golden Globe as best actor and, almost overnight, found himself a beefcake hero of teenage magazines.

Emilio Estevez's part in *The Outsiders* was small, almost forgettable, but he was an honoured member; he received poster billing (seventh) and his face adorned the artwork. He was, therefore, a *bona fide* 'Outsider' and, furthermore, the son of actor Martin Sheen (though preferring to use his family's real Spanish name). He had the perfect credentials to become a star. In 1984 he was the lead in an overnight cult hit, *Repo Man*, in which he plays a naive, punk, automobile repossessor. That,

alone, qualified Estevez as a success story, but his participation in two more 'seminal' Brat Pack pictures made him the Leader of the Pack.

Film-maker John Hughes, like Coppola, had been taking the teenage market seriously, albeit in a lighter vein. His first film as director, *Sixteen Candles* (1984), a spot-on comedy of adolescent angst, was an enormous success and had transformed Molly Ringwald and Anthony Michael Hall into stars. Hughes, Ringwald and Hall reteamed for an ensemble, classroom comedy-drama, *The Breakfast Club*, with Estevez, Judd Nelson and Ally Shedy also in the cast. This was an even bigger hit and established the ensemble teen pic as a box-office catch. The Brat Pack, now official, were swapping films and co-stars like dancing partners, and box-office returns showed that the public was enjoying the game.

Estevez next co-starred in Joel Schumacher's *St Elmo's Fire*, alongside old friends Rob Lowe, Judd Nelson and Ally Sheedy. Newcomers to the class included Andrew McCarthy, Mare Winningham and Demi Moore, the last-named becoming Estevez's fiancée (she later married Bruce Willis). And so it went on. Ally Sheedy and Rob Lowe teamed up for *Oxford Blues* (1984); Lowe and Demi Moore were paired for *About Last Night . . .*; Moore and Estevez co-starred in *Wisdom* (1986) . . . .

Estevez, besides becoming a regular ensemble actor, has evolved into an auteur film-maker. After *The Outsiders* and *Rumble Fish*, and earlier *Tex* (1982), with Dillon and Estevez), the writer S.E. Hinton had become all the rage, and Estevez optioned the rights to her novel *That Was Then . . . This Is Now*. 'I thought I'd hire a writer to adapt it,' he said, 'but I had some time on my hands, so I wrote a draft.' The draft turned into a screenplay and then (in 1985) into a film, directed by Christopher Cain and starring Estevez in his best role to date as a quick-tempered layabout. A year later he wrote, starred in and directed *Wisdom*, a

MICKEY

ROURKE
From rebel to anti-star

A former boxer and product of the Miami streets, Mickey Rourke still prefers the company of Hell's Angels to Hollywood starlets, yet, through films as diverse as *Rumble Fish* and *Barfly*, he has become one of the most sought-after actors of his generation

In an age of anti-stars, Mickey Rourke has emerged as a super-anti-star; the genuine article. In the late Eighties he became a media obsession in spite of the lack of a hit movie, a famous girlfriend or a flair for ostentation. Indeed, Mickey Rourke flaunts his now-legendary appearance of stubbled chin, greasy hair and rumpled clothes with a carefree nonchalance. While others among Hollywood's heroes promote an air of street-wisdom – and punch out a photographer or two – Rourke smiles benevolently, chainsmoking a packet of Marlboros. He can't escape the glare of his own publicity, but he takes it on the chin, like a man with a reserve of machismo to spare.

Although the star holds a fascination for the public (and the paparazzi), Rourke's films have to make do with cult status. He turned down the leads in *Beverly Hills Cop* (1984) and *Top Gun* (1986) and has opted to work with directors he admires. He isn't interested in commercial success, yet he commands over a million dollars a picture. In spite of a reputation to be difficult to work with, film-makers are queueing up for his services. Mickey Rourke is, in short, an anomaly.

Of Irish-Scottish descent, he was born Philip Rourke in New York in 1950. His parents divorced when he was seven and he moved with his mother to Florida, where he grew up in Miami's treacherous Liberty City district, sharing a bedroom with six brothers. At school he studied poorly and hung out with gangs who did drugs and little else. His aspiration was to be a boxer, but after only four fights (which he won) self-discipline deserted him. A friend asked him to appear in a college production of French writer Jean Genet's *Deathwatch*; he did, and liked it. At the time he knew little about acting and had barely heard of Steve McQueen or Clint Eastwood.

Deciding on acting for a career, Rourke borrowed several hundred dollars from his sister and moved to New York – and almost starved. He joined the Actor's Studio and took any job he could find – as cinema usher, towel boy in a massage parlour, night manager of a brothel . . . New York was a bad, lonely experience and Rourke, at the age of 24, tried his luck in Hollywood. At first, California was no better (he took the job of a bouncer at a transvestite club), until, after 78 auditions, he landed the part of a psychopath in a TV movie. The film, *City in Fear* (1979), was not that bad, and marked David Janssen's final appearance (as a world-weary columnist), and Rourke's first (as a killer-on-the-loose).

The actor made his big-screen debut in Steven Spielberg's *1941*, lost amongst that film's many wasted cameos, and returned to television for a good role in *Act of Love* (1980), with Ron Howard. In Michael Cimino's underrated, ill-fated *Heaven's Gate* he played henchman to Christopher Walken, and shortly after his appearance was shot to smithereens. In Lawrence Kasdan's *Body Heat* (1981) he had a bigger part and made an indelible impression. As an explosives expert he was so quiet, yet so intense, that he upstaged the film's star, William Hurt. It was a small, even an insignificant role, but it lingered in the memory thanks to Rourke's subtle delineation. Unlike so many of his contemporaries who exhibited a frenetic vigour, Rourke conveyed everything through a charismatic stillness, a lowering of the voice, a thoughtful stare.

In Barry Levinson's *Diner* (1982), Rourke got poster billing for the first time and found himself in a sleeper hit. He wasn't pleased with the film (at the least, he's ambivalent), but the critics and public loved it. As the velvet-voiced, womanizing hairdresser, Boogie – complete with dark shirts and slicked-back hair – Rourke ambled off with the picture, an ensemble piece at that.

Next came a small part in Nicolas Roeg's *Eureka*, in which he was sixth-billed ('I'd rather do a small part on a Roeg film than a big one in a Hollywood meatball movie', he said). This was followed by his role as the Motorcycle Boy in Francis Coppola's cult *Rumble Fish* (1983), a huge success in Europe, less so in America. Once again Rourke displayed a knowing calm, a slow, meditated confidence that mocked the high-octane energy of the younger kids around him (Matt Dillon, Vincent Spano, Nicolas

Cage). Filmed in black-and-white, and with a strong score from The Police's Stewart Copeland, *Rumble Fish* is the sort of self-conscious, stylized film that creates myths. Soon every fashion magazine worth its weight in gloss was featuring Dillon and Rourke on their covers, proclaiming Rourke in particular as an icon for our times.

The Pope of Greenwich Village (1984) was less well received, but solidified Rourke's reputation as a smooth-talking, street-smart hustler. In Adrian Lyne's *Nine½ Weeks* (1985) he stepped up-market to play a Wall Street banker, albeit with a bizarre taste for the unnatural in sex. An erotically-charged love story (between Rourke and Kim Basinger), the film caused a considerable stir as the *Last Tango* of its era. However, Rourke didn't think it went far enough. 'I wanted to go *all the way* with it', he told Playboy magazine. 'I wanted to show every ****ing emotion that was going on with me and Kim'. Even in its mild form, it shocked a growingly conservative world.

Hailed as a new Brando and James Dean for the early Eighties, Rourke was ageing so fast that soon critics were comparing him to Bogart. In Cimino's *Year of the Dragon* (1985) he played a forty-ish, white-haired, jaded detective waging a one-man war on Chinatown. An atmospheric, steel-fisted thriller, *Year of the Dragon* was dismantled by the critics in a ritual attack on the director of *Heaven's Gate*. Rourke is proud of the film, and of his performance, and has violently defended both. After the film's critical and financial flogging, however, Rourke went into semi-retirement, spending time with his wife, actress Debra Feuer, and hanging out with his omnipresent entourage of Hell's Angels.

The English film-maker Alan Parker enticed him back to work with the role of Harry Angel, a seedy, down-at-heel private eye who makes a pact with the Devil (Robert De Niro). Set in 1955 in New York and New Orleans, Parker's *Angel Heart* (1987) opened up a fresh can of worms when the American censor dumped an X certificate on it. The offending scene showed a naked Rourke making love to a young black girl (Lisa Bonet) under a torrent of blood. After the expedient excision of a few seconds, *Angel Heart* was eventually released – to public indifference.

More controversy surrounded Rourke's next

Opposite: a portrait of Mickey Rourke as seen in The Pope of Greenwich Village. *Above left: in Coppola's* Rumble Fish, *he is The Motorcycle Boy. Above: Faye Dunaway stars opposite Rourke in* Barfly. *Below: the young buddies in* Diner *are played by Rourke, Kevin Bacon, Daniel Stern and Paul Reiser. Bottom: in the highly erotic* Nine½ Weeks, *Rourke's co-star is the sensual Kim Basinger*

picture, *A Prayer For the Dying* (in which he was a disillusioned IRA hitman), when the director – Mike Hodges – disowned it after the film had been re-edited. Then the director of *Barfly* (1987), Barbet Schroeder, offered to cut his fingers off if Cannon Films failed to supply the promised capital which, in the event, they did. Rourke played an alcoholic down-and-out poet, based loosely on the life of the film's scriptwriter Charles Bukowski, and was extraordinary in a rhetorical, larger-than-life performance. However, it was Faye Dunaway, as Rourke's drinking partner and bedmate, who stole the reviews.

In *Homeboy* (1984), based on his own screenplay, Rourke played a small-time pugilist, a hero of the actor's adolescent boxing days. Michael Seresin, lighting cameraman on *Angel Heart*, directed, and Christopher Walken and Debra Feuer co-starred. The project was the realization of a long-held dream.

Whatever Rourke chooses to do in the future, it is unlikely to be obvious. He complains, 'I've watched actors I've admired over the years sell out. That's the worst crime of all'. Ironically, Rourke was in two of the most expensive flops of all time – *1941* and *Heaven's Gate* – and went on to star in a series of noncommercial ventures, few of which ever saw their money back. Yet film-makers still flock to his side, and good film-makers at that. And that is the mark of a truly remarkable actor.

Filmography
1979 City in Fear (aka Panic on Page One) (TV); 1941. '80 Act of Love (TV); Heaven's Gate; Fade to Black. '81 Body Heat. '82 Diner; Eureka. '83 RumbleFish; Rape and Marriage; The Rideout Case (TV). '84 The Pope of Greenwich Village. '85 Nine½ Weeks; Year of the Dragon. '87 Angel Heart; A Prayer For the Dying; Barfly. '88 Homeboy (+ sc).

MUSCLING IN

The predominant style of the Eighties screen hero – as exemplified by Sylvester Stallone's wide shoulders and small head – fought at home and abroad not just to protect number one, but to uphold 'freedom' (Uncle Sam and the flag) in the face of its destruction by the scum of the earth

In the face of a number of 'copycat' sniper killers the press has used *Rambo* (1985) as a stick to beat the cinema industry with. In a sense, however, the Eighties invented Rambo. This decade has seen a marked growth in the more chilling, paranoid leisure activities of survival courses, adventure games and war games. 'Rambo-style' sharp-shooters have drawn attention to the armoury of weapons being amassed by civilians. A little more inocently, perhaps, there is also the ever-growing popularity for unarmed combat courses, especially amongst young males. Are we rehearsing for the aftermath of Armageddon, worried at what we see as the rising tide of crime, or upset at what is perceived as society's growing Libertarianism?

In its turn, Eighties cinema has laid stress on muscles and weapons – whether it is Sylvester Stallone flexing his pectorals in the jungles of Cambodia (*Rambo*) or Sigourney Weaver sporting a repeat-action rifle so huge she needs a harness to hold it (*Aliens*, 1986). There is also a sense that many of these people are not simply fighting for themselves, but are hero-saviours stemming the tides of dark unreason which threaten to swamp Western civilization. Whether it is sword and sorcery, thrillers or science fiction, there is now a lot more at stake in the battle's outcome, and there is little or no opportunity to take something as trivial as romance on board.

The prevailing male image of Eighties cinema has been set by Stallone, as it was by Clint Eastwood in the Seventies. This is not simply because of the popularity of his films, or because of their outspoken 'fight back' message. It is due to the sheer complexity of his image. Stallone originates from the Hell's Kitchen area of New York City, and his forceful rise to fame fits in with the USA's image of its freedom of opportunity as well as echoing the heroic triumph of his characters from the wrong side of the track. His persona is deliberately that of a beefy, battling working-class guy, refusing to become society's underdog, and waving the American flag with pride.

The contradictions of this image, which are endless, are at the very heart of his appeal. He is an iron-pumping man's man, but with a love of kids, and soft, spaniel eyes, which endear him to female audiences (particularly the Rocky films – 1976, 1979, 1982, 1985 – and *Over the Top*, 1987). He comes from the mean streets himself, but nonetheless is out to erase the 'scum' and 'vermin' from the sidewalk (*Cobra*, 1986). He is a rebellious loner, always cutting his way through the red tape of officialdom, and yet in the last analysis he is the most militantly loyal of citizens (*First Blood*, 1982, and *Rambo*). The image is thus balanced out to appeal to a wide range of contemporary responses.

The most influential hero-saviour figure next to Stallone is Mel Gibson's Mad Max. In *Mad Max* (1979), *Mad Max 2* (1981) and *Mad Max Beyond Thunderdome* (1985), Gibson is a man with a mission, as well as possessing the muscle and guile to carry it out. Compared to the punk eccentricity of Max's character, however, Stallone's heroes have a straight-arrow

Above left: Dolph Lundgren suitably attired for saving the galaxy in Masters of the Universe.
Left: Sylvester Stallone looks his most dangerous in Rambo

openness. Max is more of a prickly loner, driven on by a spirit of vengeance, only reluctantly defending post-holocaust civilization against the crazies. In Gibson's steel-cold eyes can be seen the glint of insanity, brought even further to the surface in his traumatized 'Nam vet character in *Lethal Weapon* (1987).

Chuck Norris is another warrior holding darkness at bay, staunchly fighting all political adversaries of the American way. It was Middle Eastern hijackers in *Delta Force* (1986), communist guerillas in *Missing in Action* (1984) and nothing less than Russian terrorists in *Invasion USA* (1985). Chuck, though, has none of Max's madness nor Stallone's contradictions, and it is likely that the memory of his paranoid films will outlive that of their star.

Far more flamboyant fun can be found in the company of such comic-strip heroes as Arnold Schwarzenegger, Dolph Lundgren, Harison Ford and Christopher Reeve. Lundgren, the least of these, is also the most (six foot six, and 240 pounds), a blond Siegfried clone saving the galaxy as the redoubtable He-Man in *Masters of the Universe* (1987). He is, however, more ham than beefcake, and it is the mighty-thewed Schwarzenegger to whom one turns for a string of inventive vehicles and the wit to inject them with a rather camp send-up of macho. In both *Commando* (1985) and *Raw Deal* (1986), he plays retired special agents breaking up criminal operations, and both contain parodies of the style in which Rambo fetishistically straps on layer after layer of weapons. Similarly, in *Conan the Barbarian* (1982) and *Conan the Destroyer* (1984), Arnie takes time between sword blows to puncture the pomposity of Robert E. Howard's superman with some dry, Bond-style one-liners. The same mode of presentation continues with *Predator* (1987), in which *Alien* (1979) is crossed with *Commando*.

A distinct and quite 'preppy' style of superhero comes with Harrison Ford and Christopher Reeve. Both Indiana Jones and Superman are alter egos for rather shy, bungling, bespectacled figures who, for most of their lives, languish respectively in a museum and a newspaper office. Even the real-life images of the two stars are behind this revisionist concept of the superhero, as both are also quite strongly identified with more 'serious' actorly endeavours (such as Ford's *Mosquito Coast*, 1986, and Reeve's *The Bostonians*, 1984). Nonetheless, the duo made their names from their square jaws and huge shoulders, shown to best advantage in sweaty, torn shirts

or designer blue-and-red tights. They helped revive the spirit of kids' Saturday morning shows, with a light, tongue-in-cheek apporoach, in such popular series as *Raiders of the Lost Ark* (1981), *Indiana Jones and the Temple of Doom* (1984) and the four Superman movies (1978, 1980, 1983, 1987).

On the subject of heroic bulk, one cannot ignore the fact that changing representations of women's roles have resulted in some action-picture heroines the like of which have not been seen since Raquel Welch hung up her guns in the mid-Seventies. The dauntingly statuesque Brigitte Nielsen (*Red Sonja*, 1985) and Grace Jones (*Conan the Barbarian*, 1984) each swirled a mean sword. The threatening quality of beauty wedded to an amazonian physique resulted, however, in both women being cast next as villainesses who come to sticky ends. Nielsen was the baddie in *Beverly*

Top: Christopher Reeve displays his flying skills as Superman. *Above: Grace Jones flexs her muscles in* Conan the Destroyer. *Right: in* Blade Runner, *Rutger Hauer is a powerful android, loose on Earth, who is being tracked down by Harrison Ford*

Top left: Nick Nolte plays a small town marshall in Walter Hill's Extreme Prejudice. *Top right: Hill also directed* Streets of Fire, *a gang movie starring Michael Paré. Above: Mel Gibson and Danny Glover make a formidable duo in Richard Donner's violent cop thriller* Lethal Weapon. *Right: Harrison Ford plays Indiana Jones, the ultimate tongue-in-cheek hero of the adventure epic* Raiders of the Lost Ark

Hills Cop II (1987) and Jones was on the wrong side in both *A View to a Kill* (1985) and *Vamp* (1986). The most interesting Eighties female action heroine is Sigourney Weaver, an actress whose intelligence and classiness give Flight Officer Ripley believable stamina and bravery, without recourse to Nielsen and Jones' rippling biceps. In *Alien* and *Aliens*, it took a woman to show the real nature of back-against-the-wall heroism, without any uncomfortable intimations of 'might is right'.

The Eighties also presented images of heroism and toughness through a range of younger and newer faces. In the main, the characters played by many of the Brat Pack and other fresh talent are lean and hungry tough guys who hail from the mean streets, often Brando-style loners who find romance impossible, perfunctory or tragic. Actors like Eddie Murphy, Sean Penn, Matt Dillon, Emilio Estevez, Tom Cruise, Rob Lowe, Charlie Sheen, Patrick Swayze, Michael Paré, Matthew Modine and Ralph Macchio are slighter in build than the man-mountains, or even the woman-mountains, and their characters have no messianic aura. They are closer in spirit to the rebel tough guys of the Fifties and Sixties – figures such as James Dean, Jack Nicholson, Peter Fonda, Steve McQueen, Jon Voight and, of course, Brando. Only the diminutive Ralph Macchio, who rose to fame in the teen melodrama *The Outsiders* (1983), and went on to kick-punch opponents of law and order into shape in *The Karate Kid* (1984) and *The Karate Kid, Part II* (1986), comes near to the pumped-up heroism of Rocky. The message, however, is gentler: when your back's against the wall, turn your opponent's might against them. The secret is in knowing yourself.

The younger set are involved mainly in crime or gambling scams. Sean Penn, stockily-built troublemaker on and off screen, is entangled with drugs and selling secrets in *The Falcon and the Snowman* (1985), avenges a rival while riddled with bullets at the end of *At Close Range* (1986) and is a poor man's Indiana Jones in *Shanghai Surprise* (1986). Martin Sheen's offspring Emilio Estevez and Charlie Sheen both feature as gun-toting, fresh-faced criminals, respectively, in *The Boys Next Door* (1985) and *Wisdom* (1986). Afterwards, Charlie goes to Vietnam in *Platoon* (1986). In *Streets of Fire* (1984), Michael Paré plays a reluctant gang leader in a Brando T-shirt, finally settling with his rival in a confrontation with sledgehammers. Less heavy, Matt Dillon and Tom Cruise challenged the big guys with dice and cues respectively in *The Big Town* (1987) and *The Colour of Money* (1986). Tom then climbed higher as the eccentric, risk-taking student pilot and stud in *Top Gun* (1986). In fact, the kids are all in trouble, taking on the world in a do-or-die bid for glory.

With the more mature tough guys who loom large in the Eighties, but do not pose as our hero-saviours, it is difficult to define trends. Perhaps the most typically Eighties in spirit are Rutger Hauer and Micky Rourke. In the face of the hero-saviours' moral muscle, and the romantic rebellion of adolescence, these two offer us a cynical, burnt-out, horror-tinged image of manhood in a state of dilemma. Rather like Mel Gibson, both these men combine a rugged handsomeness with the threat of cold, heavy-lidded eyes. Hauer was a beautiful but deadly android in *Blade Runner* (1982), a smiling bogeyman with a knife in *The Hitcher*

(1986) and a medieval rape-and-pillage artist in *Flesh and Blood* (1985). Rourke, after flirting briefly as a Brat Packer in *Diner* (1984) and *Rumble Fish* (1983), has played characters older than himself, specializing in violent men and gloomy dramas. In *Year of the Dragon* (1985) he is a half-crazed 'Nam vet NYC cop, in *Prayer for the Dying* (1988) he plays an IRA hitman, and for *Barfly* (1987) he sinks to skid row as a pugilistic drunken bum.

If Hauer and Rourke have chosen the loneliest and least glorious style of machismo, then Kevin Costner and Dennis Quaid have modelled their images on the attractive charm, wit and cheeky nonchalance of more established stars such as Burt Reynolds and Robert Redford. Costner first gallops heroically on to the screen as a hired gun in *Silverado* (1985), and his charisma and athleticism help him nail Al Capone in *The Untouchables* (1987) and uncover corruption in the corridors of power in *No Way Out* (1987). Quaid also brushes with the criminal element in *The Big Easy* (1987), but his laid-back, affable nature and natural bent for light comedy have shot him to stardom as the madcap commander of a miniaturized sub in *Innerspace* (1987).

Above: Mel Gibson as Mad Max roams the deserted streets of the post-apocalyptic world of Mad Max Beyond Thunderdome. *Below left: Kevin Costner plays Eliot Ness, the dedicated* treasury man on the trail of Al Capone in The Untouchables. *Below right: Sigourney Weaver takes an uncharacteristically macho role for a woman as an astronaut confronting the* Alien

If traditionalism is the key to stars like Costner and Quaid, then it must also be admitted that few established male action stars have shifted with grace into the Eighties. In *Tough Guys* (1986), veteran heavies Burt Lancaster and Kirk Douglas prove the point in an embarrassing rearguard action to try and out-stud and out-shoot the new guys on the block. Only old faithful Clint Eastwood has continued to assert his presence. *Sudden Impact* (1983) may have been a very tired fourth Dirty Harry movie, and *City Heat* (1984) overplayed the joke of sending up old macho images, but the remainder of Clint's Eighties output comes under the 'fascinating if flawed' category. *Tightrope* (1984) sees him as a bitter single parent whom the story increasingly identifies with the sex murderer he pursues. Similarly, the enjoyable but muddled *Heartbreak Ridge* (1986) has Eastwood, as the drill sergeant, reading women's magazines throughout, in an attempt to readjust the balance of his personality. It is this willingness of Eastwood to question his image 'every which way' which keeps even his duller movies buoyant.

Although the presiding male image of the Eighties is that of Stallone – musclebound and militant, strongly nationalistic while anti-authoritarian, unromantic while loving kids – the challenge of this statement has been taken up by a whole variety of narratives and stars, to temper, develop or undermine it. The Indiana Jones movies interpret it as comic-strip wish-fulfillment; Mel Gibson asserts the barely suppressed hysteria; Schwarzenegger reduces it to fetishism and camp; the Brat Pack strips it of all of its messianic associations; Sigourney Weaver's Ripley re-establishes heroism as a state that has less to do with bellicose displays of strength than the application of stamina and intelligence. Then again, no overview of the Eighties action star should ignore a figure like Mickey Rourke, bravely focussing on the dark underside of heroism. There may be an allegory for the decade in his movie *Angel Heart* (1987), in which a personable detective hunts down a satanic killer, only to discover that he himself is the monster of the story.

495

'CROCODILE' DUNDEE

Directed by Peter Faiman, 1986
Prod co: Rimfire Films, for 20th Century-Fox. **prod:** John Cornell. **sc:** Paul Hogan, Ken Shadie, John Cornell. **photo:** Russell Boyd. **ed:** David Stiven. **cost:** Norma Moriceau. **sd:** (Australia) Martin O'Neill, (New York) Gretchen Rau. **ass dir:** Mark Turnbull. **r/t:** 98 mins.
Cast: Paul Hogan (Michael J. 'Crocodile' Dundee), Linda Kozlowski (Sue Charlton), John Meillon (Walter Reilly), David Gulpilil (Neville Bell), Mark Blum (Richard Mason), Michael Lombard (Sam Charlton), Irving Metzman (Doorman).

Behind the success of 'Crocodile' Dundee the phenomenon, lies the figure of 'Hoges'. The actual movie is no more than a rather amiable, broken-backed romp, a jumble of the kind of set-pieces that made Paul Hogan's TV show an international success. One is forced to enquire, for example, why Dundee is something of a poseur in the outback section (he pretends to Sue that he can tell the time by the sun, or that he shaves with a hunting knife), but when he reaches New York transfigures into a genuine hero. Are we to conclude that even a loud-mouthed, outback ocker can teach decadent, Northern-hemisphere city-slickers a trick or two?

The real appeal of the movie, and its organizing principle, is Hoges, a persona of Paul Hogan, the 'Darling of Down-Under'. Hogan's career began in 1972 at the age of 30, when he burst onto Aussie TV's 'New Faces' as the irreverent ocker in singlet, shorts and footy-boots. Before that, among other things, he had sat at the top of the Sydney Harbour Bridge driving home rivets. Later, he met John Cornell – now his partner, manager, co-producer and friend – a man who soon had Hoges fronting his own show, with director Peter Faiman at the helm. 'The Paul Hogan Show' reached viewers in 26 countries, and the Hogan/Cornell/Faiman partnership was forged.

2

1

3

like an American film. As a result, most of the movie is set in the States, to place Hoges' likeable, easy-going, rough-but-honest appeal against the sophisticated sin-bin of the Big Apple. To Americans, Hoges is all their yesterdays, with a pre-Fifties innocent assurance about what the world is. He is a latterday John Wayne, the drawl replaced by a twang, who comes out of the wasteland to re-establish basic values. For this reason, Hoges has never appealed as much to pommy audiences, whose culture is quite separate from that of big continents such as Australia and North America. The English respond more to the acidic, decadent satire of Barry Humphries' Dame Edna – someone Hogan considers a national embarrassment.

Before 'Crocodile' Dundee, Hogan had taken a quite credible stab at a straighter role in the hugely successful Australian TV mini-series Anzacs. The result, however, was a little like Clint Eastwood singing – it was intriguing to know it was possible, but was really only a novelty. The climax of Hogan's career so far has been the character of Dundee, fuelled as it is by the ever-present persona of Hoges. It is here that Hogan perfected the balance between wholesomeness, irreverance, gauchiere, self-assurance, tongue-in-cheek, and lazy, blue-eyed charm. The formula was so right that the appeal was global. The ocker has charisma. And the secret of this success is the way Hogan has never lost touch with the man who sat up in the rigging of the Sydney Harbour Bridge.

Perhaps, then, we should be talking about Hoges the phenomenon rather than 'Crocodile' Dundee? It is not simply that any sequel would be unthinkable without the man, but that the movie's loose, episodic structure relies upon Hogan's personality to weld it together and give it direction. Even the flat, misjudged romantic ending becomes forgivable for the spectacle of Dundee walking on the shoulders of commuters to reach Sue at the other end of the subway platform. Even a situation as dull and frustrating as New York commuter-jams at rush-hour is comically surmountable for Hoges.

Sue Charlton, a New York reporter, is sent on an assignment to the Australian outback town of Walkabout Creek to interview the legendary trapper Michael J. 'Crocodile' Dundee (1). He meets her and offers to show her the remote spot where he was supposedly bitten by a giant crocodile, having dragged himself back to tell the tale. In the bush (2), they meet various of his friends, including kangaroo hunters and the Aborigine Neville. They come across snakes, he rescues her from a real crocodile attack, and they take a swim in Lake Echo. Partly for the publicity, and partly from the growing feelings between them, Sue asks Dundee to accompany her to New York (3), at the magazine's expense. He is given a luxury suite in an expensive hotel, though

he sleeps on the floor and hangs up a washing line (4). On his first night on the town, he meets and slugs Sue's pretentions fiancé, then is driven to a bar where his outfit (leather, with croc's teeth in the band of an ubra hat) renders him the object of curiosity for a black street hustler, a transvestite, and two prostitutes, whose pimp he also slugs. He is next invited to Sue's parents' house for her 'welcome home' party (5), where he is upset to hear her fiancé, Richard, officially announce his engagement to Sue. He leaves the party drunk and returns to the hotel. Sue tries to phone and explain that it is him, not Richard, that she cares for. Eventually, she arrives and pursues him to a subway station (6), where they are reconciled on the platform.

Another factor leading up to the phenomenon of the movie was a whole series of TV commercials, in which Hoges was always selling more than a product – he was selling Australia. The British ads for that famous brand of amber nectar ('Strewth, he's got no strides on!') and the US ones for the Australian Tourist Commission ('I'll put another shrimp on the barbie'), became the most successful TV ads campaign ever. Even without the follow-up effect of 'Crocodile' Dundee, Hoges' appearances on TV resulted in a 40 per cent rise in requests for Australian visas from North America.

As Hogan himself points out: 'Crocodile' Dundee has not been promoted as an Australian film because Australian films tend to end up on the art circuit and are regarded as foreign films. Paramount wanted 'Crocodile' Dundee to look and feel

MEL GIBSON

The heart-throb from Down Under

With the emergence of the new Australian cinema, many stars were created, but none bigger than Mel Gibson, the most popular star to surface from the Antipodes since Errol Flynn

As pure, unadulterated sex appeal goes, Mel Gibson was the hottest new star of the Eighties. The enormity of his following is daunting – especially to Mel Gibson. And when the actor took his clothes off in *Lethal Weapon* (1987), he guaranteed an international hit. To date, it is his most successful film.

'I know I'm a fantasy figure to a lot of people', he once said, 'but, for most, that's as far as it goes. I'm romantic – but I wouldn't expect every woman to tear her clothes off when she meets me.'

Many would, though. But Gibson's appeal isn't merely limited to hysterical females, but to a large audience of men as well, from bankers to bikers. As an actor he is minimalist, unsmiling, undemonstrative – not unlike Clint Eastwood in terms of emotional underkill. Yet he emanates an authority, a virility, that belies his boyish good looks. His sexiness is of the unconscious kind, which is the sexiest of all. Girls want to mother him, men want to fight alongside him. He's not a machine, but is somehow indestructible. He's entirely human, but carries an air of Roman divinity. Sigourney Weaver, Gibson's co-star from *The Year of Living Dangerously*, described him as 'the most gorgeous man I've met'. Others have declared him as the 'sexiest man alive' and, reverting to hyperbole, 'the most gorgeous man in the Universe'. The quotes are genuine.

Gibson himself, a happily married man and father of four, is surprised by his enormous, magazine-staple-bending appeal, preferring to spend his time on his 600-acre farm in the Australian outback. His dream is to sire 12 children and stay put. Hollywood is a tempting Holy Grail, however, and though content to be a cattle farmer most of the time, Gibson does periodically traverse the Pacific to make a hit movie.

He was born in upstate New York in January, 1956, one of 11 children to an American railway engineer. When he was 12, he and his family emigrated to Australia where, history relates, his father augmented their income by winning a series of TV quiz shows. Gibson Jr settled into his Antipodean lifestyle badly, unhappy at school and provided with the uncaring monicker of 'Yank'. He became an inveterate brawler, was ruthlessly bullied, and retreated behind a barrier of solitude.

'When I was growing up,' he said, 'I thought about being an actor. It was really a sort of

Left: Martin Riggs (Mel Gibson) is a Lethal Weapon, *trained to kill the criminals of the Los Angeles streets*

romantic thing. I'd go to the movies and see Humphrey Bogart and say to myself, "He's great, I wish I was Humphrey Bogart". But I never took it that seriously. I never really thought that it would happen.'

After (thankfully) graduating from high school, he attempted an assortment of low-paying jobs, and it was then that his sister put his name down for the National Institute of Dramatic Art in Sydney. In spite of hundreds of aspiring actors who applied annually to the school, Gibson won a place, and was soon a favoured leading light at the Institute. One co-student was none other than Judy Davis (*My Brilliant Career, A Passage to India*), who played Juliet to his Romeo.

Such was his flourishing talent and good looks, that in his second year Gibson was spotted by a casting director and given a sizeable supporting role (as a layabout) in a surfing picture, *Summer City* (1977). Luckily for him, the film was not successful, and enabled him to make his first mistakes in virtual privacy. Shortly afterwards he was cast in another low-budget film, this time in the title role – in George Miller's *Mad Max* (1978).

In spite of Gibson feeling 'intensely uncomfortable, unhappy and uncertain' during filming, the director was impressed with his new star. 'He has screen presence and a wide range of abilities,' Miller enthused, 'but more than that he seems to be deeply obsessed with the craft of acting.'

In the film, Gibson played a futuristic cop on the trail of a gang of vicious motorcyclists who murdered his wife and child. The violence was over-the-top, but the stunts were so spectacular and the atmosphere so unnerving that the film, *pro rata*, became the most profitable ever made. At a cost of $300,000 it reaped in nearly $100 million worldwide. Gibson was an overnight star in practically every quarter of the world – bar the USA. The American distributors dubbed over the Australian accents and all but threw the film away.

His next picture *Tim* (1979), was an altogether happier experience. Again he had the title role, a mentally-retarded youth involved with an older woman, played by Piper Laurie. Gibson took his part extremely seriously, visited mental institutions and observed his own seven-year-old nephew. Laurie was most impressed. 'It's incredible', she said, 'when you realize it's only Mel's second (*sic*) feature film. It's not an easy role, yet he brings a warmth and presence you could only expect from an actor who has been around for a long time.' Gibson's efforts were rewarded when he walked off with that year's best actor award bestowed by the Australian Film Institute, the highest honour of Australian cinema.

A year later he became inexplicably involved in a trite action-drama, *Attack Force Z*, an experience he regretted from the word go. He was unhappy making it, and 'didn't like it' when it was belatedly released.

Gallipoli (1981) was another matter. Directed by Peter Weir, the film traces the events leading up to the massacre of Anzac troops on the Turkish peninsula in World War II. Arguably one of the finest war films ever made, it was a huge success Down Under and did excellent art-house business in the USA. Along with the Australian film industry, Mel Gibson was beginning to make himself felt on the American market. Again, he won the AFI award for best actor.

Above: Mad Max, *the first of the Australian series set in a post-apocalyptic nightmarish world, established Gibson internationally. Left: Peter Weir's story of the massacre at* Gallipoli *cast Gibson as a young soldier caught up in events beyond his control. Below: in* The Year of Living Dangerously *he played opposite Sigourney Weaver in a drama of war-torn Indonesia*

The real turning point came with George Miller's sequel to *Mad Max*, christened *The Road Warrior* in the States and, more prosaically, *Mad Max 2* elsewhere. The film was an enormous success at the box-office. Indeed, the sequel was far superior to the first film and saw Max as a lone crusader, protecting a desert-bound, oil-producing community from the savage attacks of a bizarre army of freaks. The picture's sartorial imagination fuelled the world's fashion industry, and the car stunts set new standards for celluloid death-defiance. Max himself became a cult hero.

Although Gibson still felt uncomfortable in the role ('I found it difficult to contain the

Left: Gibson followed in the footsteps of Clark Gable and Marlon Brando as Fletcher Christian in The Bounty. *Above: with Sissy Spacek in* The River, *a gripping story of the problems of mid-West farmers. Right: he starred with Diane Keaton in the highly romantic movie* Mrs Soffel

character', he said; 'the dialogue I had – all 14 lines or so – was hard to say with a straight face'), he admired the new film. 'It goes one better than the first. You can see George Miller has really been studying his craft.'

Mad Max 2 is Australia's biggest international hit to date, so successful that MGM was prepared to finance half the budget of Mel Gibson's next project, *The Year of Living Dangerously* (1982), directed by Peter Weir. The star played an Aussie reporter caught in the Communist uprising of 1965 Indonesia, trapped between his love for a British Embassy official (Sigourney Weaver) and his duty to 'the story'. It was a gripping, atmospheric drama and Gibson mixed charisma with sweat in another outstanding performance.

He was now a certified star in America and soon the Hollywood paycheques were beckoning. Most budding stars would have capitalized on the chance, but Gibson wanted to continue to prove himself as an actor. 'Being labelled a "star" by the media isn't necessarily a choice you make yourself', he noted. 'Your concern is to continue trying to do good work.' Turning his back on Los Angeles, he turned to the theatre and starred in a highly acclaimed revival of *Death of a Salesman*, with Warren Mitchell.

In 1984 it was time for his first wholly American film. In the steps of Errol Flynn, Clark Gable and Marlon Brando, he played Fletcher Christian in Dino De Laurentiis' long-awaited version of the mutiny on *The Bounty* (1984), opposite Anthony Hopkins' Captain Bligh. Although American-financed, the film was directed by fellow-Antipodean Roger Donaldson and boasted a sterling supporting cast of British players: not least Laurence Olivier, Edward Fox, Daniel Day Lewis, Bernard Hill and Liam Neeson. Gibson battled manfully with his English vowels but for once was lost amongst the competition.

Two more American films followed in quick succession: Mark Rydell's involving rural drama *The River*, with Sissy Spacek; and Gillian Armstrong's *Mrs Soffel*, with Diane Keaton. In the former Gibson played a Tennessee farmer struggling to keep his land and was quite convincing as a Southerner after hours of reading William Faulkner and Eudora Welty

out loud. Ironically, the erstwhile 'Yank' was now struggling to hide his Australian accent.

In *Mrs Soffel* he portrayed another American, a condemned murderer who is sprung from prison by the scripture-spouting wife of the prison warden, and with whom he falls in love. Although both films were more successful in America than the original *Mad Max*, neither echoed the international triumph of Gibson's earlier work.

Inevitably, the actor returned to Australia to star in *Mad Max Beyond Thunderdome* (1985), in this instance with script approval. Then, he said: 'At last there's a chance to give the character three dimensions, a shape, some kind of humanity'. Equally inevitable was the film's media hype and American box-office success, helped, no doubt, by Tina Turner's star turn as villainess, a fantastic creature with silver hair and mind-boggling decolletage. Two

hit songs from the film, 'We Don't Need Another Hero' and 'One of the Living', both sung by La Turner, aided the film's exposure. Mel Gibson was back on top.

Another two years passed before he cemented his superstardom in the title role of *Lethal Weapon* (1987). Title role? Exactly, Gibson starred as Martin Riggs, registered as a 'lethal weapon' with the Los Angeles Police Department. Directed by Richard Donner, the film was a first-class, near-perfect crime thriller and showcased Gibson's best performance in a Hollywood film to date. He looked totally at home as the American psychopathic cop who kills first and asks questions afterwards. Trained in a variety of deadly martial arts, Riggs is equally at ease behind a well-aimed kick or a mega-bore automatic. He is a perfect killing machine. Physically in peak condition, Gibson exhibited an animal agility as Riggs that made Mad Max look like RoboCop.

Unlike so many video quickies, *Lethal Weapon* stood out as a human drama as well. Riggs is on the edge because he has just lost his wife and is ready to erupt until he befriends fellow-cop Roger Murtagh (Danny Glover), a stable, middle-aged family man. It is this central relationship that makes the film doubly engaging and ensured its critical success, which in turn turned it into the fifth highest-grossing film of 1987.

Next, Gibson was signed to star in Robert Towne's *Tequila Sunrise*, opposite Michelle Pfeiffer, a picture originally written for Warren Beaty in 1981. Mel Gibson is now in the market for the best roles Hollywood can offer. He may be a resident Australian, but he has also 'made it' as a Yank in Tinseltown.

Left: after several American films, Gibson returned to Australia for Mad Max Beyond Thunderdome

---

Filmography
1977 Summer City. '78 Mad Max. '79 Tim. '80 Attack Force Z (former The Z Men). '81 Gallipoli; Mads Max 2 (US: The Road Warrior). '82 The Year of Living Dangerously. '84 The Bounty; The River; Mrs Soffel. '85 Mad Max Beyond Thunderdome. '87 Lethal Weapon.

INDEX

M

N

Acknowledgements

Many of the illustrations come from stills issued to publicize films made or distributed by the following companies: ABC, ABC Circle Films, Action Films, Aldrich and Associates, Allied Artists, Alpha, American International Pictures, Andrea Films, Kenneth Anger, Anglo Amalgamated, Anouchka Films, The Archers, Artcraft, Artfilm, Artists Associés, Avco Embassy, BBS Studio Barrandov, Barbican Films, Barker Films, Georges de Beauregard, Biograph Co., British and Commercial Gas Association, British International Pictures, British Lion, British Transport Films, Samuel Bronston, Luis Buñuel/Salvador Dali, Butterfly, Les Films du Carosse, CBS, Central Office of Information, Československský Film, Ceylon Tea Board, Chadwick Pictures, Champion, Charles Chaplin Corporation, Charles Chaplin Productions, Cine-Alliance/Gray Films, Cinégraphic/GPC, Cinema Centre, Cineriz, Cinés, Citel, Clarendon Pictures, Cocinor, Columbia, Comicque Film Corporation, Compton-Cameo, Constantin Film, Copacabana, Cosmograph, Crown Film Unit, Les Films du Cyclope, Daiei, Dansk Kulturfilm, Dear Films, Decla/Bioscop, Dino de Laurentiis, Cecil B. de Mille, Vittorio de Sica, © Walt Disney Productions, Stanley Donen, Drew Associates, Stephen Dwoskin, Eagle Lion, Ealing Films, L'Ecran Francaise, Edison Company, Elton Corporation, EMI, Empire Marketing Board, EPI-Club de L'Ecran, Epoch, Eon, Essanay, Euro International, Excelsa-Film, FRD, FR 3, Factory Films, Douglas Fairbanks Productions, Famous Artists, Famous Players/Lasky, Federiz/Francoriz, Feature Productions, Filmways, Filmverlag der Autoren, First Artists, First National, Folly Films, Fox Film Corporation, Francinex, Franco-London Films, GB Instructional Films, GPO Film Unit, Gainsborough Pictures, Gas Light and Coke Company, Gaumont, Gaumont British, Samuel Goldwyn, Goldwyn Company, Goskino, Grand National, Felix Greene/San Francisco Chronicle, Greenwich Films, D. W. Griffith, Robert and Raymond Hakim, Hammer, Howard Hawks Productions, Hepworth, Hillbilly, Hoche Productions, Homeland, Howard Hughes, Hungaro Films, ICAIC, IPC Films, Thomas Ince, Inspiration Pictures, Itala Film, Janus Films, Kairos Film, Buster Keaton Productions, Keystone, Kindai, Stanley Kramer, Leacock-Pennebaker, Leguan Films, Lenfilm, Lion's Gate, Lira Film, Harold Lloyd Corporation, London Films, Lucasfilm, Lumière Brothers, Lux Films, MCA, MGM, Mafilm, Maran Film, Les Films Marceau, Marianne Productions, Marianne Mirisch, Markische Film, Memorial Films, Metro Pictures, Mezhrabpomfilm, Mirisch Corporation, Monogram, Mosfilm, Mutual, National Film Board of Canada, Nero Film, New Era, Vicomte de Noailles, Nordisk Tonefilm, Nouvelles Éditions Francaises, ORTF/Son et Lumiere/RAI, Orion, Societe des Films Osso, PAA, Films Marcel Pagnol, Palomar, Pan-Film der Dafu-Film-Verleit, Panaria, Pathé, Pathé Cinema, André Paulvé, Pax, PEA/PPA, Pickford Corporation, Pioneer Pictures, Films de la Pleiade, Film Polski, Carlo Ponti, Carlo Ponti Productions, Prana Film, Otto Preminger, Prometheus, Produzione Europee Associates, RKO, Rafran, Rafran/San Marco, Rank, Rank Films, Rastar, Realisation d'Art Cinematographique, Regent, Lotte Reiniger, Remus, Eige Renmei, Films Jean Renoir, Republique, Révillon Frères, Leni Riefenstahl, Rizzoli Film, Hal Roach, Rome/Paris Films, Rusconi, Sandrews, Satyajit Ray Productions, Sedif, BP Schulberg, David O. Selznick, Selznick International, Larry Semon Productions, Mack Sennett, Seven Arts, Sevzapkino, Shamley, Shamley/Alfred Hitchcock, Shin kankaku-ha, Shintoho, Shochiku, Sigma, Simcap, Film SOFAR, Silver Films, George Albert Smith, Société du Film d'Art, Société Generale de Films, Solar, Sovkino, Specta Films, Robert Stigwood, Stoll, Svensk Filmindustri, Svenska Biograph, Svensk Filminspelning, Tango Films, Elizabeth Taylor-Mead, Terra Films, Thames Television, Titanus, Tobis, Tobis-Klangfilm, Toho, Tonfilm, Tokyo Eiga, Transatlantic Pictures, Triangle, Twentieth Century Fox, Two Cities, UGC/CICC, UFA, UPA, Ukrainfilm, Unifrance, United Artists, Universal, Universal International, Universal Prod ENIE-Franco London Films, Vic Films, Vides, King Vidor, Vitagraph, Viva International, Volkdeutsche Gmbh, VUFKU, Vostok Kino, Hal B. Wallis, Walturdow, Walter Wanger, Warner Bros, Westi, Wolper Films, Woodfall, World Film Services, Richard Zanuck.

In addition we would like to thank: Lindsay Anderson, Arts Council, Artificial Eye, Atmosphere, Australian Film Commission (London), Martin Auty, Keith Bartlett, BBC, Claude Beylie, Bison Archives, Bowerhouse Model Associates, Annette Brown, Cactus Films, Kingsley Canham, Ugo Casiraghi, Leo Castelli Gallery New York (collection of Mr and Mrs Burton), Československský Filmovy Ústav Filmovy Archiv, Cinema Bookshop, Cine Images, Cinegate Ltd., Frank Conner, Contemporary Films, Donald Cooper, Peter Cowie, Culver Pictures Inc., Susan D'Arcy, Arnold Desser, Deutsches Kinemathek, Walt Disney Productions, Downton Advertising Ltd., Stephen Dwoskin, Greg Edwards Archive, Phil Edwards, D. Elley, Ed Emshwiller, Filmexport, Joel Finler Collection, John Fleming, Institut Francais, Peter Gidal, Denis Gifford, Thomas Gilcrease Institute, Ronald Grant Archive, K. G. Hall, Bernard Happe, Harris Films, Sally Hibbin, David Hine, Robert Hunt Picture Library, Archivio IGDA, Imperial War Museum, India House, Japan Film Library Council, Derek Jarman, David King Collection, Robert Kingston Films, Ray Kirkpatrick, Ian Knight, Kobal Collection, Kodak Museum, Leevers-Rich, Liberty Cinema, Mainline Pix, Raymond Mander and Joe Mitcheson Theatre Collection, Dan Miller, Museum of Modern Art Film Stills Archive, National Film Archive/Nederlands, National Film Theatre, National Film Board of Canada, Other Cinema, D. A. Pennebaker, Popperfoto, Firoze Rangoonwalla, Rex Features, David Robinson Collection, Steve Roe, Barry Salt, Samuelson Film Services, Saturday Evening Post, Scorcese Archive, Stiftung Deutsche Kinemathek, Swedish Film Institute, Talisman Books, Tate Gallery, Thames Television, John Topham Picture Library, Adrian Turner, UPI, United States Brewers Association, Tise Vahimagi, Vinten Ltd., M. Wanamaker, Graham Webb, Bob Willoughby, Wisconsin Center For Film And Theatre Research, Ken Wlaschin.